Ireland

a travel survival kit

John Murray
Sean Sheehan
Tony Wheeler

Ireland – a travel survival kit

1st edition

Published by
    Lonely Planet Publications
    Head Office: PO Box 617, Hawthorn, Vic 3122, Australia
    Branches: PO Box 2001A, Berkeley, CA 94702, USA
                     12 Barley Mow Passage, Chiswick, London W4 4PH, UK

Printed by
    Colorcraft Ltd, Hong Kong

Photographs by
    John Murray (JM)
    Sean Sheehan (SS)
    Tony Wheeler (TW)
    Front cover: Enjoying a pint, Allihies, County Cork (JM)

Published
    January 1994

National Library of Australia Cataloguing in Publication Data

Murray, John.
    Ireland: a travel survival kit.

    Includes index.
    ISBN 0 86442 194 X.

    1. Ireland – Guide-books. I. Sheehan, Sean. II. Wheeler, Tony. III Title. (series: Lonely Planet travel survival kit).

914.1704824

text & maps © Lonely Planet 1994
photos © photographers as indicated 1994
climate charts compiled from information supplied by Patrick J Tyson, © Patrick J Tyson, 1994

John Murray

A native Irishman, John Murray graduated in marine zoology from Trinity College Dublin in 1986. He headed off to the South Pacific and Australia working as a scuba instructor and underwater archaeologist. Flat broke, he earned a ticket home with an article for the Qantas inflight magazine – his first journalistic venture. Now based in Ireland, he works as an adventure-film-maker, TV reporter and photo-journalist. His career has taken him to North and South America, Africa and Asia; most recently he made a film of the first successful Irish ascent of Mt Everest.

Sean Sheehan

Sean Sheehan was born and brought up in Hackney, London, went to university in Wales and then Oxford in England, and now lives in Ireland. Ten years of teaching in Newcastle and London drove him to South-East Asia where he lived for six years. During that time, alongside acquiring a thirst for travel, he wrote a non-Lonely-Planet guide to Malaysia and Singapore, edited school editions of Shakespeare, ran a computer column for a British publication and worked for a Japanese magazine. He is now growing his own (potatoes, that is) in the west of Ireland and getting high on the unpolluted air.

Tony Wheeler

Tony wrote the chapter on Dublin and made a large contribution to the Belfast chapter. He was born in England but grew up in Pakistan, the Bahamas and the USA. He returned to England to do a degree in engineering at Warwick University, worked as an automotive design engineer, returned to university to complete an MBA in London, then dropped out on the Asian overland trail with his wife Maureen. Eventually settling down in Australia, they've been travelling, writing and publishing guidebooks ever since, having set up Lonely Planet Publications in the mid-1970s. Travel for the Wheelers is considerably enlivened by their daughter Tashi and their son Kieran.

From the Authors

John Murray John would like to thank Finuala for her endless patience, Ronan Murray for his sterling assistance and his father Gerry for looking after the DIY and garden during the writing of this epic.

Tony Wheeler Thanks to the Irish Tourist Board (particularly Gordon Stepto at their Australian office) and the Northern Ireland Tourist Board (particularly Jim Paul in London), to Terry & Gillian Dixon in Belfast, to Sean Sheehan for an amusing night at Kilcrohane and to the many interesting and helpful people I met all over the island.

From the Publisher

This book was edited by Caroline Williamson, with much help from Vyvyan Cayley and Tom Smallman, and from Simone Calderwood and Tony Wheeler on the proofing. The maps were drawn by Chris Love, who also did the layout. The cover design was by Margaret Jung, and Matt King drew most of the illustrations. Thanks to Michelle Stamp for design support.

Warning & Request

Things change – prices go up, schedules change, good places go bad and bad places go bankrupt – nothing stays the same. So if you find things better or worse, recently opened or long since closed, please write and tell us and help make the next edition better.

Your letters will be used to help update future editions and, where possible, important changes will also be included in a Stop Press section in reprints.

We greatly appreciate all information that is sent to us by travellers. Back at Lonely Planet we employ a hard-working readers' letters team to sort through the many letters we receive. The best ones will be rewarded with a free copy of the next edition or another Lonely Planet guide if you prefer. We give away lots of books, but, unfortunately, not every letter/postcard receives one.

Contents

Map Legend

BOUNDARIES

— · — · — · — .... International Boundary
— · · — · · — .... Internal Boundary
+·+·+·+·+·+·+·+ .... National Park or Reserve

SYMBOLS

◉ NATIONAL .... National Capital
● PROVINCIAL .... Provincial or State Capital
● Major .... Major Town
● Minor .... Minor Town
■ .... Places to Stay
▼ .... Places to Eat
⊠ .... Post Office
✈ .... Airport
ℹ .... Tourist Information
◉ .... Bus Station or Terminal
P .... Parking
66 .... Highway Route Number
☾ ✝ ⊞ ☪ ...... Mosque, Church, Cathedral
∴ .... Temple or Ruin
♒ .... Pub
✚ .... Hospital
✳ .... Lookout
⟁ .... Lighthouse
⚠ .... Camping Area
⊓ .... Picnic Area
⌂ .... Hut or Chalet
▲ .... Mountain or Hill
⊢■⊣ .... Railway Station
═══ .... Road Bridge
⊢■⊣ .... Railway Bridge
⌢⌢⌢ .... Escarpment or Cliff
⌣ .... Pass
⊓⊔⊓⊔ .... Ancient or Historic Wall

ROUTES

.... Motorway
.... Major Road or Highway
...... Unsealed Major Road
.... Sealed Road
..... Unsealed Road or Track
.... City Street
.... Railway
.... Subway
.... Walking Track
.... Ferry Route

HYDROGRAPHIC FEATURES

.... River or Creek
.... Canal
.... Intermittent Stream
.... Lake, Intermittent Lake
.... Coast Line
.... Spring
.... Waterfall

.... Salt Lake or Reef

.... Glacier

OTHER FEATURES

Park, Garden or National Park

.... Built Up Area

... Market or Pedestrian Mall

.... Plaza or Town Square

.... Cemetery

Note: not all symbols displayed above appear in this book

Introduction

Ireland is one of Western Europe's most lightly populated, least industrialised and, in a word, least 'spoilt' countries. It also has one of the longest and most tragic histories in Europe.

That long history is easy to trace, from Stone Age passage tombs and ring forts, through ancient monasteries and castles, down to the great houses and splendid Georgian architecture of the 18th and 19th centuries. The tragic side is equally easy to unearth. The destruction wrought by the Vikings from the end of the 8th century AD onwards is still visible in the ruins of once-great monasteries. The country's history since the arrival of the English in the 12th century is punctuated with rebellion and repression. Oliver Cromwell's visit in 1649-50 is still remembered with horror; and the Irish population has still not recovered from the mass starvation and emigration resulting from the potato famine in the mid-19th century. The 20th century has been no less turbulent, and the Troubles continue in Northern Ireland today.

Travellers could be forgiven for forgetting this sad history, however, faced with the peaceful green landscape of the centre, with its lakes and mountains, or the magnificent cliffs of the wild Atlantic coast, and the off-shore islands which have been inhabited for millennia. Many traces of traditional culture survive in these remote western areas, and there are still communities in which Irish is the first language.

The narrow medieval streets of cities such as Dublin, Cork and Galway can still be found – a traffic planner's nightmare. Dublin

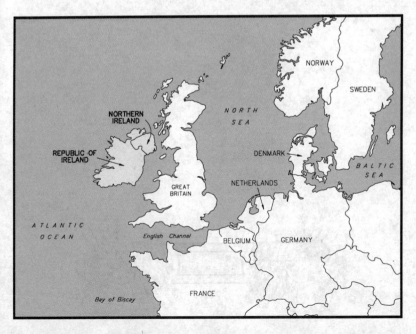

11

was at its architectural peak in the 18th century, and many of those fine buildings have lasted for over 200 years almost unchanged. But these are not museum cities: they are friendly places with wonderful pubs, live music, good theatres and – when it's not raining – cheerful street life. In the North, Belfast and Derry are also remarkably welcoming places, in spite of the continuing military conflict. It's worth emphasising that they are probably safer for visitors than most other European cities!

When the distinction between Ireland the island and Ireland the state needs to be made in this book, the state is referred to as the Republic of Ireland. Northern Ireland is always referred to as such. You may hear Ireland (the state) referred to as Eire, the Republic, Southern Ireland, the Free State or simply 'the South'. Northern Ireland may be dubbed Ulster, 'the six counties' or 'the North'. Prior to the division of Ireland, the old province of Ulster actually comprised nine counties. Six of these went into Northern Ireland and the other three into the Republic of Ireland.

Facts about the Country

HISTORY
First Settlers

Ireland was probably first settled by humans about 10,000 years ago, at the end of the last Ice Age. This is relatively late in European prehistory, as Palaeolithic or Old Stone Age people were living in southern England 400,000 years ago and in Wales 250,000 years ago.

With the low sea levels of the last Ice Age, there were land or ice bridges between Ireland and Britain and between Britain and mainland Europe. But conditions in Ireland would have been hostile until the glaciers receded, between 12,000 and 10,000 years ago, and prey animals such as deer and boar would have been scarce. These increased in numbers as the weather improved. Around 12,000 years ago, the Irish giant elk flourished, and there were probably no humans around to hunt it.

As the ice caps melted, there was an enormous rise in the sea level, and about 9000 years ago Ireland was cut off from Britain. It was around this time that the first humans seem to have reached Ireland, possibly across the land bridge or in small hide-covered boats. These people were Middle Stone Age (Mesolithic) hunter-gatherers. They would have lived in small family or tribal groups collecting fruit and nuts and hunting any animals they could tackle. Their lifestyle would have been similar to that of the Australian Aborigines or the Kalahari bushmen. The traces of these first Irish men and women are faint: a few scattered rubbish dumps or middens, containing shells and the bones of small animals. Their weapons and tools included flint axes and slivers of flint called microliths, which were used as blades set in a bone or wooden handle. They hunted boar, kept dogs and had a fondness for eels and salmon. The richest concentration of these early sites are in northern Ireland, including one at Mt Sandel near Coleraine, and date from around 8000 to 6000 BC.

First Farmers

While the first settlers were busy discovering Ireland, the greatest revolution in human history had already taken place in the fertile crescent of the Middle East. It was another 2000 or 3000 years before farming reached Ireland, around 4000 BC. Farming marked the arrival of New Stone Age or Neolithic times, and archaeologists cannot be certain whether a new wave of farmers colonised Ireland or whether the concept of farming filtered through with just a few immigrants.

A settlement from this era was discovered near Lough Gur in County Limerick, the traces of pottery, wooden houses and implements indicating a much more prosperous and settled way of life than before. Near Ballycastle in north Mayo, a remarkable complex of intact stone field walls dating from these times has been discovered hidden under a vast blanket of bog. Also around this time was born one of the first Irish exports. Tievebulliagh Mountain near Cushendall in County Antrim has an outcrop of remarkably hard stone called porcellanite, and it formed the basis of a thriving stone-axe industry. Tievebulliagh stone axes have been found as far away as the south of England.

From about 3000 BC, these farmers built the extraordinary passage graves at Newgrange, Knowth and Dowth in the Boyne Valley. Over 1000 megalithic tombs survive from the Neolithic period, and two large Neolithic settlements have been discovered in the Six Mile Water Valley in County Antrim.

The Bronze Age

The next great human revolution was the ability to work metal and track down the tin and copper ores which could be amalgamated to produce bronze. This heralded the Bronze Age, which in Ireland is characterised by a reduction in the scale and number of stone tombs but produced a wonderful legacy of gold and bronze metalwork.

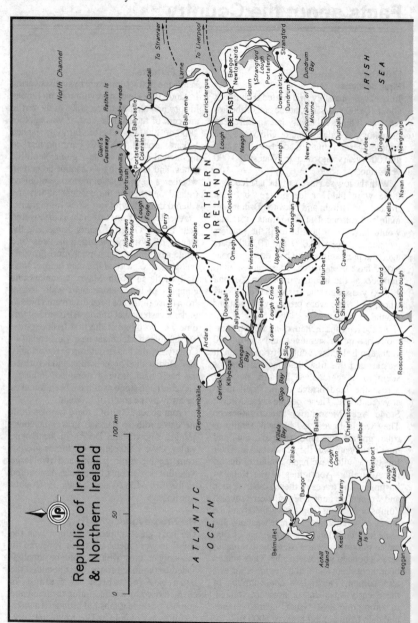

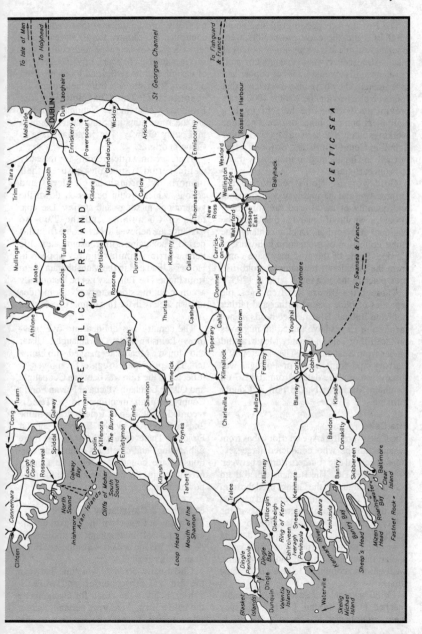

The Bronze Age started in Ireland about 2500 BC, and the early prospectors were amazingly astute at tracking down sources of metal. Almost everywhere that modern geologists have discovered traces of copper and other metals, they have also discovered that someone else had got there some 4000 years previously, without the help of modern equipment and mapping. Bronze Age mine workings can still be seen on Mt Gabriel near Schull in County Cork, and St Kevin's Bed or Cave in Glendalough is thought by many to be an early mine.

Gold-working flourished during the Bronze Age, and the quality of craftsmanship and quantity of metal used say something about the wealth of Ireland at this time. The National Museum in Dublin contains the finest collection of prehistoric goldwork in Europe. Some of the gold may have come from the Wicklow Mountains. A gold rush took place in the area much later, in 1795.

Through the Bronze and Iron Ages, the tentacles of trade spread farther and farther out from Ireland. Blue faience beads manufactured in Egypt have turned up in graves on the Hill of Tara in County Meath, as did amber from Scandinavia. The skeleton of a Barbary ape from Spain or Portugal was discovered in a site dating from 200 BC on Eamhain Macha or Navan Fort in County Armagh.

The Celts

The Celts were Iron Age warrior tribes from eastern Europe who conquered large sections of central and southern Europe between 800 and 300 BC. The Romans called them 'Galli' or Gauls and the Greeks used the term 'Keltoi' or Celts. Both societies had cause to fear the Celts, who plundered Rome in the 4th century AD and were described by contemporary scholars as fierce and dashing warriors. The use of iron was by now widespread throughout Europe, although bronze weapons also continued to be used for some time.

Celtic warriors and adventurers probably reached Ireland around 300 BC, and they were certainly well ensconced by 100 BC. In relatively small numbers, they moved in, controlled the country for 1000 years, and left a legacy of language and culture that survives today. They had a distinctive style of design, and its swirls and loops are seen on many Irish artefacts from the 2nd and 1st centuries BC. Good examples are the Broighter Collar in the National Museum and the Turoe Standing Stone near Loughrea in County Galway. The Irish language is Celtic in origin.

There are no written records for the early Celtic period. Chieftains ensured their immortality through heroic deeds and actions, which would be passed down the generations in songs and stories. The epic tales of Cúchulainn and the Táin Bó Cuailnge are believed to have come from this period. Cúchulainn is the consummate Celtic hero warrior; similar figures appear in Homer's Iliad and in the Mahabharata poem from India. The Táin may not be historically accurate but the stories may give some idea of Irish society in the first couple of centuries AD.

The country was divided into five provinces: Leinster, Meath, Connaught, Ulster and Munster. Meath later merged with Leinster. The principal struggle for power as reflected in the Táin was between Connaught and Ulster. Eamhain Macha or Navan Fort in County Armagh, mentioned in the Táin, is recorded in the map of Ireland drawn in the 2nd century AD by the Egyptian scholar Ptolemy. There were perhaps 100 or more minor kings and chieftains controlling sections of the country, and Tara in County Meath became the base for some of the most powerful leaders.

St Patrick & Christianity

The westward march of the Roman empire came to a halt in England. As the empire declined, Ireland became an outpost of European civilisation.

Christianity arrived sometime between the 3rd and 5th centuries, and while St Patrick is given the credit for evangelising the native Irish, there were certainly earlier missionaries. Some scholars dispute that there was a St Patrick at all, and claim the stories about him are really about these early clerics, or later inventions. However the evidence suggests that there was a St Patrick who lived in the 5th century, and that at the age of 16 he was kidnapped from Britain by Irish pirates. During six years in Ireland as a slave tending sheep, Patrick found religion. After escaping back to Britain, he was instructed to return to Ireland by powerful visions. Patrick first went to Europe to train as a cleric, and from around 432 AD spent the rest of his life converting the Irish to Christianity. His base was Armagh in County Down, probably chosen because of the symbolic pagan significance of nearby Eamhain Macha.

Much of our knowledge of Patrick comes from his own writings. St Patrick's 'Confession' is a copy of one such account from the 9th-century 'Book of Armagh' held in Trinity College, Dublin.

As Europe sank into the Dark Ages, Ireland in the 7th and 8th centuries became a 'land of saints and scholars', with thriving monasteries where monks illuminated manuscripts, including the world-famous 'Book of Kells'. Outstanding among the monasteries were Clonmacnois in County Offaly and Glendalough in County Wicklow. Monks such as Colmcille and Columbanus founded monasteries abroad. But at the end of the 8th century, slim powerful boats appeared off the north and east coasts of Ireland, ushering in a new and more turbulent period of Irish history.

The Vikings

In 795 AD, a fleet of Viking longships sailed down the west coast of Scotland, raiding St Colmcille's monastery on Iona before turning their attentions to the east coast of Ireland. They came ashore either at Rathlin Island off the Antrim coast or Lambay Island near Dublin. Irish weapons and soldiers were no match for the superbly armed and ferocious Norsemen.

In passing, it must be said that the local Irish clans were just as fond of raiding the monasteries as the Vikings were. Monasteries were places of wealth and power, and were often caught up in intertribal squabbles. But the increasingly frequent Viking raids burned into the consciousness of Irish monks, and into their accounts of these times. Round towers were built to act as lookout posts and places of refuge in the event of an attack.

It wasn't long before the Vikings started to settle in Ireland and form alliances with native families and chieftains. They established many settlements which bear Viking names today including Wicklow, Waterford and Wexford. They founded Dublin, which in the 10th century was a small Viking kingdom.

The struggles continued between the Vikings and the native Irish, who learned many lessons in the art of warfare. The most decisive defeat for Viking ambitions was at the Battle of Clontarf in 1014, by Irish forces led by Brian Ború, who was aided in the fight by other Vikings from Waterford and Limerick. The elderly Brian Ború was killed by retreating Vikings.

However, large numbers of Vikings settled in Ireland, marrying with the native Irish, converting to Christianity and joining in the struggle against the next wave of invaders – the Normans.

The Norman Conquest

In 1066 the Normans under William the Conqueror invaded and conquered Britain. They were former Vikings themselves, who had settled in northern France 150 years previously, came to terms with the French king, and adopted the local language, religion and military technology. They made no immediate effort to get involved in Ireland, but this could only be a matter of time. When they did come over, they were, ironically, responding to an invitation by an Irish chief.

The king of Leinster, Dermot MacMurrough, and the king of Connaught, Tiernan O'Rourke, were arch rivals. Their relationship was not improved by MacMurrough's kidnapping of O'Rourke's wife in 1152 (it appears she went willingly). O'Rourke defeated MacMurrough, who fled abroad in 1166 to search for foreign allies. After arguing his case in France, MacMurrough got a hearing from the astute Henry II of England, who was too busy to get involved himself but encouraged MacMurrough to seek help elsewhere among his subjects.

MacMurrough went to Wales, where he met Richard de Clare, Earl of Pembroke, better known as Strongbow, who agreed to muster an army and return to Ireland with MacMurrough. In return he demanded MacMurrough's daughter in marriage and the inheritance of the kingship of Leinster once MacMurrough was dead. Mac-Murrough agreed, and the stage was set for 800 years of English involvement in Ireland.

In May 1169, the first Norman forces arrived in Bannow Bay, County Wexford. MacMurrough joined them, and they took Wexford Town and Dublin with ease. The next group of Normans arrived in Bannow Bay in 1170, led by his lieutenant Raymond le Gros, and defeated a considerably larger Irish and Viking army on Baginbun Head.

In August 1170, Strongbow himself arrived, and with le Gros took Waterford after a fierce battle. A few days later MacMurrough arrived and handed over his daughter Aoife to Strongbow. After MacMurrough's death the following year, Strongbow set about consolidating his new position as king of Leinster.

Meanwhile in England, Henry II was watching events in Ireland with growing unease. Technically Strongbow was one of Henry's subjects, but his independence of mind and action was worrying.

In 1171, Henry II sailed from England with a huge naval force, landed at Waterford and declared the place a royal city. He took a semblance of control, but the new Norman lords still did pretty much as they pleased.

Just as the Vikings first settled and were then absorbed so were the new Anglo-Norman intruders. Barons like De Courcy and De Lacy set up power bases very similar to native Irish kingdoms, outside the control of the English king. Over the centuries English control gradually retreated to an area around Dublin known as 'the Pale'. Hence the expression 'beyond the Pale' for an area beyond control.

Henry VIII

In the 16th century, Henry VIII moved to reinforce English control over his unruly neighbour. He was particularly worried that France or Spain might use Ireland as a base from which to attack England. The principal power brokers in Ireland were the Anglo-Norman Fitzgeralds, earls of Kildare. Henry sought to bring about their downfall.

In 1534, Garret Óg, the reigning earl, was meeting with Henry in London. The story goes that his 27-year-old son Silken Thomas heard rumours that his father had been executed. Silken Thomas gathered his father's forces and attacked Dublin and the English garrisons. In London Garret Óg was however very much alive and well, and Henry packed off a large army to Ireland which easily crushed Silken Thomas's rebellion. The Fitzgeralds may have been trying to prove they were still a force to be reckoned with in Ireland.

Thomas and his followers surrendered, but they were subsequently executed in what became known as the 'pardon of Maynooth'. This pattern of retribution was to become familiar in following centuries. The Fitzgerald estates were divided among English settlers, and an English viceroy was appointed.

Meanwhile Henry was involved in a separate battle – with the pope, over the difficult matter of his divorce from Catherine of Aragon. In 1532 he broke with the Catholic Church. With the downfall of the earls of Kildare in 1535, Henry was also able to launch an assault on the property of the Catholic Church in Ireland. The wealthy Irish monasteries were dissolved – at considerable profit to the crown – over the next few years. In 1541 Henry ensured that the Irish Parliament declared him king of Ireland.

Elizabeth I

Under Elizabeth I, the English consolidated their power in Ireland. The forests of Ireland were proving invaluable as a source of wood for shipbuilding, and oak was turned into charcoal for smelting ores. Strategically, too, Ireland was important as a possible back door for an invasion from England's enemies in mainland Europe.

English jurisdiction was established in Connaught and Munster despite a number of rebellions by the local ruling families. The success of Elizabeth's policies was borne out when survivors of the 1588 Spanish Armada were washed up on the west coast of Ireland and were mostly massacred by the local sheriffs and their forces.

The thorn in Elizabeth's side was Ulster, the last outpost of the Irish chiefs. Hugh O'Neill, Earl of Tyrone, was the prime mover in the last serious assault on English power in Ireland. O'Neill had been educated in London, and Elizabeth believed that he would be loyal. A story is told of O'Neill ordering lead from England to reroof his castle; in reality the lead was for bullets. From 1594, O'Neill moved into open conflict with the English and proved a courageous and crafty foe. The English forces stepped up their campaign against him but met with little success until 1601.

In September 1601, a Spanish force landed in Ireland to join O'Neill. Unfortunately, the Spanish disembarked at Kinsale in County Cork, almost 480 km (300 miles) from O'Neill's territory. O'Neill was forced to march south to join them, and after an exhausting journey ended up fighting the Battle of Kinsale near Cork in unfamiliar country. The Irish were defeated by the English forces under Lord Mountjoy, while the Spanish army was pinned down in Kinsale.

Kinsale was the end for O'Neill and for Ulster. Although O'Neill and his forces made it back to Ulster, their power was broken, and 15 months later in 1603 he surrendered and signed the Treaty of Mellifont, handing over power and authority to the English crown. O'Neill was allowed to stay on in Ulster on condition that he pledge allegiance to the crown, which he did. But after a couple of frustrating years of subjugation and harass-

Hugh O'Neill, Earl of Tyrone

ment, O'Neill and 90 other Ulster chiefs boarded a ship in Lough Swilly to leave Ireland for ever. This was the 'Flight of the Earls', and it left Ulster leaderless and open to English rule.

With the native chiefs gone, a 'plantation' got under way – an organised and ambitious expropriation of land which sowed the seeds for the division of Ulster that we see today. Huge swathes of land were confiscated from the Irish and large numbers of new settlers came from Scotland and England. They brought a new way of life and a different religion. Unlike most previous invaders, they didn't intermarry with the native Irish, and kept their culture and their religion very much to themselves. And so living among these new landowners was an impoverished and very angry population of native Irish Catholics.

Cromwell

In 1641, worried by developments in England and Ireland, the Irish and Old English Catholics took up arms. What happened subsequently is a matter of debate: certainly a considerable number of the new settlers were killed, but modern historians have revised the likely number of deaths down to perhaps 2000, from earlier widely exaggerated estimates; and many Catholics were also killed, in revenge. Stories of the 1641 atrocities have been used in anti-Catholic propaganda ever since.

The English Civil War kept most of the English busy at home for most of the 1640s. The Irish and Old English Catholics in Ireland supported the side of the Catholic Charles I, and after his execution, the victorious Oliver Cromwell, leader of the parliamentarians, decided to come over to Ireland and sort them out. He arrived in 1649, and rampaged through the country, leaving a trail of death behind him and shipping many of the defeated as slaves to the Caribbean. Others were dispossessed and exiled to the harsh and infertile lands in the west of Ireland, 'to hell or to Connaught'. Two million hectares of land were confiscated – more than a quarter of the country – and handed over to Cromwell's supporters. Cromwell's tour of Ireland has never been forgotten.

The Battle of the Boyne

The 1660 Restoration saw Charles II on the English throne. He kept his Catholic sympathies firmly in check. In 1685 his brother James succeeded him. James II's more open Catholicism raised English ire, and he was forced to flee the country at the beginning of 1689, intending to raise an army in Ireland and regain his throne from the Protestant William of Orange.

In late 1688, with rumours spreading among Irish Protestants that Irish Catholics were about to rise in support of James II, the Protestant citizens of Derry heard that a Catholic regiment was to be stationed in their city. After furious debate among the local worthies, 13 apprentice boys purloined the keys to the city and slammed the gates in the face of James's soldiers.

In March 1689 James II himself arrived from France at Kinsale, and marched north to Dublin, where the Irish parliament recognised him as king and began to organise the return of expropriated land to Catholic landowners. The siege of Derry began in earnest in April, and ended after

mass starvation with the arrival of William's ships in July. The Protestant slogan 'No Surrender!' dates from the siege, which acquired mythical status among Irish Protestants over the following centuries.

William of Orange himself made his landfall in 1690 at Carrickfergus, just north of Belfast, with an army of up to 36,000 men, and the Battle of the Boyne took place on 12 July. It was fought between Irish Catholics (led by James II who was a Scot) and English Protestants (led by William of Orange who was a Dutchman). To make things more complicated, James was William's uncle and his father-in-law. James II's principal supporter was Louis XIV of France, and fear of growing French power led both the Catholic king of Spain and the pope himself to back William and the Protestant side!

William's victory was a turning point, and is commemorated to this day by northern Protestants as a pivotal victory over 'popes and popery'. The final surrender of the Irish came in 1691, when the Catholic leader Patrick Sarsfield signed the Treaty of Limerick.

Penal Times

The Treaty of Limerick contained quite generous terms of surrender for the Catholics, but these were largely ignored, and replaced by a harsh regime of penal laws a few years later. They were passed by a Protestant gentry anxious to consolidate their powers and worried that Louis XIV of France might attempt an invasion of Ireland. Also known as a 'popery code', these laws forbade Catholics from buying land, bringing their children up in their own religion, and from entering the army, navy or legal profession. All Irish culture, music and education was banned. There were also lesser restrictions imposed on Presbyterians and other nonconformists.

The Catholics organised open-air masses at secret locations usually marked by a 'mass rock', and illegal outdoor schools known as 'hedge schools' continued to teach the Irish language and culture. Among the educated classes, many Catholics converted to Protestantism to preserve their careers and wealth.

After 1715, strict enforcement of the penal laws eased off, although many of the restrictions to do with employment and public office still held. A significant majority of the Catholic population were now tenants living in wretched conditions. By the mid-18th century, Catholics held less than 15% of the land in Ireland, and by 1778 barely 5%. Many middle-class Catholics went into trade.

The 18th Century

Meanwhile Dublin thrived, ranking as Europe's fifth-largest city. The Irish ruling class were members of the established Protestant Episcopalian Church, and were descendants of Cromwellian soldiers, Norman nobles and Elizabethan settlers. They formed a new and prosperous upper class known as the Protestant Ascendancy. There was a Protestant-only parliament, but laws still had to be approved by the British crown and parliament.

A strong 'patriot' party developed under the leadership of Henry Grattan and Henry Flood. When the American War of Independence broke out, Britain was in a difficult position. The majority of her forces had to be withdrawn from Ireland to fight in the colonies, leaving security in Ireland largely at the hands of Protestant 'volunteer' forces under the control of the landowners and merchant classes. To avoid further clashes with the increasingly independent Irish parliament, the British government in 1782 allowed the Irish what it considered to be complete freedom of legislation. The new Irish governing body was known as Grattan's parliament. However, London still controlled much of what went on in Ireland through royal patronage and favours.

To achieve prosperity in Ireland, Grattan had espoused improved conditions and rights for Catholics. Henry Flood and the majority of other Protestant members were not as sympathetic, and in the life of the parliament – nearly 20 years – little progress was made.

The French Revolution

In the late 18th century, revolution was in the air, with the American War of Independence and – much more shocking to Britain – the French Revolution of 1789. No longer could the aristocracy and entrenched politicians be complacent about the poverty-stricken masses. In Ireland, an organisation known as the United Irishmen had been formed, and its most prominent leader was a young Dublin Protestant and republican, Theobald Wolfe Tone.

The United Irishmen had been founded by Belfast Presbyterians and started out with high ideals of bringing together men of all creeds to reform and reduce England's power in Ireland. Their attempts at gaining power through straightforward politics were fruitless, and when war broke out between England and France the United Irishmen found they were no longer being tolerated by the establishment. They reformed themselves as an underground organisation committed to bring about change by any means, violent or otherwise. Tone was keen to enlist the help of the French, who fresh from their European victories were easily persuaded.

In 1796, a French invasion fleet approached Bantry Bay in County Cork. On shore the local militia were ill-equipped to repel them. On board one of the French ships was Wolfe Tone, decked out in a French uniform and itching to get into action. However, a strong offshore wind repelled every attempt by the fleet to get up the bay to a safe landing spot. A few attempted to drop anchor but as the wind strengthened into a full gale, the ships were forced to head for the open Atlantic and back to France. A disappointed Wolfe Tone went back with them.

In Ireland, the government woke up to the the serious threat posed by the United Irishmen and similar groups. A nationwide campaign got underway to hunt them out and it proved extremely effective. Meanwhile another group of United Irishmen led by Lord Edward Fitzgerald tried to mount a rebellion, which also failed because of informers and poor communications between the rebels. After uncovering this attempted rebellion, the government and army really got stuck into the population in search of arms and rebels. Floggings and indiscriminate torture sent a wave of panic through the country and sparked off the only really serious fighting of the year, which became known as the 1798 Rising. Wexford, a county not noted for its rebellious tendencies, saw the fiercest fighting, with Father John Murphy leading the resistance. After a number of minor victories the rebels were finally and decisively defeated at Vinegar Hill near Enniscorthy.

Meanwhile the French had been planning another invasion, and a few months after Vinegar Hill a small fleet landed in County Mayo and achieved some minor successes but was soon defeated. Wolfe Tone himself arrived later in the year with another French fleet which was defeated at sea. Wolfe Tone was captured and brought to Dublin where he committed suicide in his prison cell. It was the end for the United Irishmen and ironically led to the demise of the independent Irish parliament.

The Protestant gentry, alarmed at the level of unrest, was much inclined to cuddle back up to the security of Great Britain. In 1801, the Act of Union came into being. Many of the wealthier Irish Catholics supported the Act; the English prime minister William Pitt had promised to remove the last of the penal laws, most of which had been repealed by 1793. The Irish parliament voted itself out of existence, and around 100 of the MPs moved to the House of Commons in London.

As if to remind them of the rebellious nature of the country, a tiny and completely ineffectual rebellion was staged in Dublin in 1803, led by a former United Irishman, Robert Emmet. Less than 100 men took part and Emmet was caught, tried and executed. He gave a famous speech from the dock which included the oft-quoted words: 'Let no man write my epitaph...When my country takes her place among the nations of the earth, then and not till then let my epitaph be written'.

The Great Liberator

While Emmet was swinging from the gallows, a 28-year-old Kerry man called Daniel O'Connell (1775-1847) was set on a course that would make him one of Ireland's greatest leaders. The O'Connell family were from Caherdaniel in County Kerry and had made their money from smuggling. Remarkably, the family managed to hang onto their house and lands through penal times.

In 1823, O'Connell founded the Catholic Association which soon became a vehicle for peaceful mass protest and action. In an 1826 general election, the Association first showed its muscle by backing Protestant candidates in favour of Catholic emancipation. The high point was in the election of 1828 when O'Connell himself stood for a seat in County Clare, even though being a Catholic he could not take the seat. O'Connell won easily, putting the British parliament in a quandary. If they didn't allow O'Connell to take his seat, there might be a popular uprising. Many in the House of Commons favoured emancipation, and the combination of circumstances led them to pass the 1829 Act of Catholic Emancipation allowing Catholics the right to be elected as MPs.

Although William Pitt had promised to repeal the last of the penal laws after the Act of Union, it hadn't happened. The remaining laws had denied Catholics the right to sit in parliament and take important offices. Emancipation was the removal of these last few hurdles.

After this great victory, O'Connell settled down to the business of securing further reforms. Ten years later he turned his attentions to re-establishing an Irish parliament. Now that Catholics could become MPs, such a body would be very different to the old Protestant-dominated Irish parliaments.

In 1843 the campaign really took off, with O'Connell working alongside the young Thomas Davis. His 'monster meetings' attracted up to half a million supporters, and took place all over Ireland. O'Connell exploited the threat that such gatherings represented to the establishment, but he baulked at the idea of a genuinely radical confrontation with the British. His bluff was called when a monster meeting at Clontarf was prohibited and O'Connell called it off.

He was arrested in 1844 but went out of his way to avoid any kind of violent clash. 'Be you, therefore, perfectly quiet', he told a meeting in Dublin. After serving a short spell in prison, O'Connell returned to Derrynane. He quarrelled with the Young Ireland movement and never again posed a threat to the British. He died four years later in 1847, as his country was being devoured by famine.

The Great Famine

Ireland suffered its greatest tragedy in the years 1845-49. The potato was the staple food of a rapidly growing but desperately poor population. From 1800 to 1840 the population had rocketed from four to eight million, but between 1845 and 1849 a succession of almost complete failures of the potato crop resulted in mass starvation, emigration and death.

During this time, there were excellent harvests of other crops such as wheat, but these were too expensive for the poor. While millions of its citizens were starving, Ireland continued to export food. Some landlords did their best for their tenants, but many others ignored the situation from their homes in England.

Two or three million Irish people died or emigrated as a result of the famine, and emigration continued to reduce the population during the next 100 years. Huge numbers of Irish settlers who found their way to the USA carried with them a lasting bitterness. Irish-American wealth would later find its way back to Ireland to finance the independence struggle, and such money continues to come in support of the IRA (Irish Republican Army).

Parnell & the Land League

In spite of the bitterness aroused by the famine, there was hardly any challenge to Britain's control of Ireland for quite some time. The abortive Fenian rising in March 1867 had its most publicised action in Man-

chester when 30 Irishmen attempted to free two of their leaders. In so doing they killed an English policeman, either by accident or design. Three of them were executed and became known in nationalist circles as the 'Manchester Martyrs'.

In the 1870s and 1880s a man called Charles Stewart Parnell (1849-91) appeared on the political scene. The son of a Protestant landowner from Avondale in County Wicklow, he had much in common with other members of the Anglo-Irish ascendancy. But there were differences. Parnell's mother was American, and her father had fought the English in America. Parnell's family supported the principle of Irish independence from England.

Charles was a boisterous young man, educated in England, and he attended Cambridge before becoming an MP for County Meath. He quickly became noticed in the House of Commons as a passionate and difficult member who asked all the wrong questions.

In 1879 Ireland appeared to be facing another famine as potato crops were failing once again and evictions were becoming widespread. Cheap corn from America had pushed grain prices through the floor and with it the earnings of the tenants who paid their rent from grain they grew on their plots. A Fenian called Michael Davitt began to organise the tenants, and early on found a sympathetic ear in the unlikely person of Parnell. This odd pair were the brains behind the Land League, which initiated widespread agitation for reduced rents and improved working conditions. The conflict heated up and there was violence on both sides. Parnell instigated the strategy known as 'boycotting' against tenants, agents and landlords who went against the Land League's aims and were thus treated as lepers by the local population. Charles Boycott was a land agent in County Mayo and one of the first people the new strategy was used against.

The 'land war', as it became known, lasted from 1879 to 1882 and was a momentous period. For the first time, tenants were defying their landlords en masse. An election in 1880 brought William Gladstone to power in England. In the face of the situation in Ireland, he introduced his Land Act of 1881, which improved life immeasurably for tenants, creating fair rents and the possibility of tenants owning their land.

A crisis threatened in 1882 when two of the crown's leading figures in Ireland were murdered in Phoenix Park, Dublin. However, reform had been achieved, and Parnell now turned his attentions to achieving a limited form of autonomy for Ireland called Home Rule. Parnell had an extraordinary ally in William Gladstone, who in 1886 became Prime Minister for the third time and was dependent on Parnell for crucial support in parliament. But Gladstone and Parnell were defeated partly as a result of defections from Gladstone's own party.

But the end was drawing near for Parnell. For 10 years he had been having an affair with Kitty O'Shea, who was married to a member of his own party. When the relationship was exposed in 1890, Parnell refused to resign as party leader, and the party split. Parnell was deposed as leader and the Catholic Church in Ireland turned against him. The 'Uncrowned King of Ireland' was no longer welcome. Parnell's health deteriorated rapidly and he died less than a year later.

Home Rule Beckons

Gladstone was elected as prime minister for the fourth time in 1892 and this time managed to get his 'Home Rule for Ireland' bill through the House of Commons but it was thrown out by the House of Lords. The Protestant community, most numerous in the north-east, were becoming more and more alarmed at Gladstone's support for Home Rule, which might threaten their status and privileges.

By now eastern Ulster was quite a prosperous place. It had been spared the worst effects of the famine, and heavy industrialisation meant the Protestant ruling class was doing nicely.

While Gladstone had failed for the time being, the Ulster Unionists were now acutely

aware that Home Rule could surface again, and they were determined to resist it, at least as far as Ulster was concerned. A Protestant vigilante brigade was formed, called the Ulster Volunteer Force (UVF), and it held a series of mass paramilitary rallies. The Unionists were led by Sir Edward Carson and in 1911 their worst nightmare seemed ready to unfold.

In Britain a new Liberal government under Prime Minister Asquith had removed the House of Lords' power to veto bills, and began to put another Home Rule for Ireland bill through Parliament – the political price being demanded for the support of the Irish Home Rule MPs. The bill was put through in 1912 against strident Unionist and conservative English opposition, which mounted in ferocity.

As the UVF grew in strength, a republican group called the Irish Volunteers, led by the academic Eoin MacNeill, was set up in the south to defend Home Rule for the whole of Ireland. They lacked the weapons and organisation of the UVF, however, which succeeded in large-scale gun-running in 1914. There was widespread support for the UVF among officers of the British Army.

Despite opposition, the Home Rule Act was passed, but suspended at the outbreak of WW I in August 1914. The question of Ulster was left up in the air. Many Irish nationalists believed that Home Rule would come after the war and that by helping out they could influence British opinion in their favour. John Redmond, the leader of the Irish Home Rule party, actively encouraged people to join the British forces to fight Germany.

The Gaelic Revival

While all of these attempts at Home Rule were being shunted about, something of a revolution was taking place in Irish arts, literature and identity. The Anglo-Irish literary revival was one aspect of this, championed by the young William Butler Yeats. The poet had a coterie of literary friends such as Lady Gregory, Douglas Hyde, John Millington Synge and George Russell. They unearthed many of the Celtic tales of Cúchulainn, and wrote with fresh enthusiasm about a romantic Ireland of epic battles and warrior queens. For a country that had suffered centuries of invasion and deprivation, these images presented a much more attractive version of history. Yeats and his friends were decidedly upper-crust themselves, and pursued the new literature and poetry primarily through the English language, aiming at the educated classes. A national theatre was born in Dublin from their efforts, and it later became the Abbey Theatre.

At the same time people like Douglas Hyde and Eoin MacNeill were doing their best to ensure the survival of the Irish language and the more everyday Irish customs and culture. They formed the Gaelic League in 1893 which among other aims, pushed for the teaching of Irish in schools. The League stressed the importance of the Irish language and culture to the Irish identity. In the 1890s it was primarily a cultural outfit and only assumed a nationalistic aura later on.

There were many other forces at work. The Gaelic Athletic Association was by now a thriving and strongly politicised organisation. A small pressure group called Sinn Féin was set up, with Arthur Griffith proposing that all the Irish MPs should abandon the House of Commons in London and set up a parliament in Dublin (a similar strategy to that employed by Hungary in gaining its independence from Austria). Another group, the Fenians, also called the Irish Republican Brotherhood (IRB) believed in independence through violence if necessary. Socialism was rumbling away in Dublin amongst the hungry tenement dwellers who had to put up with some of the worst urban housing conditions in Europe.

It must be said however that the majority of Dubliners were probably much more concerned with WW I, and while some might have believed independence from Britain was a nice idea, their passions went no further than that.

The Easter Rising

Many Irishmen with nationalist sympathies went off to the battlefields of Europe believing their sacrifice would ensure that England stood by its promise of Home Rule for Ireland. The Home Rule Act had been passed just before the war broke out and would in theory be put into action once the war was over. However a minority of nationalists in Ireland were not so trusting of England's resolve. The Irish Volunteers split into two groups, those who supported Redmond and a more radical group who abhorred this approach and believed in a more revolutionary course of action.

Two small groups – a section of the Irish Volunteers under Patrick Pearse and the Irish Citizens' Army led by James Connolly – staged a rebellion that took the country by surprise. On Easter Monday 1916, they marched into Dublin and took over a number of key positions in the city. Their headquarters was the GPO on O'Connell St, and from its steps Pearse read out to nonplussed passers-by a declaration that Ireland was now a republic and that his band were the provisional government. Less than a week of fighting ensued before the rebels surrendered in the face of superior British forces and firepower. The rebels were not popular, and as they were marched to jail they had to be protected from angry Dubliners.

The leader of the Irish Volunteers was Eoin MacNeill, and the rising had been planned by Pearse and others without his knowledge. When he discovered the plans at the last minute, MacNeill attempted to call the rebellion off, resulting in very few turning up on the day. The Germans were also supposed to arrive in U-boats and this didn't happen.

So what might have been a real threat to British authority fizzled out completely. Many have said that Pearse knew they didn't stand a chance but was preoccupied with a blood sacrifice, a noble gesture by a few brave souls that would galvanise the nation. Whether he believed this or not, a blood sacrifice was on the way.

The Easter Rising would probably have had little impact on the Irish situation, had the British not made martyrs out of the leaders of the rebellion. Fifteen were executed. Pearse was shot three days after the surrender, and nine days later James Connolly was the last to die, shot in a chair because he could not stand on a gangrenous ankle. Many others were sentenced to death and reprieved. The deaths provoked a sea change in public attitudes to the Republicans, whose support climbed from then on.

In the 1918 general election, the republicans stood under the banner of Sinn Féin and won a large majority of the Irish seats. Ignoring London's Parliament, where technically they were supposed to sit, the newly elected Sinn Féin deputies – many of them veterans of the 1916 Rising – declared Ireland independent and formed the first Dáil Éireann, which sat in Dublin's Mansion House under the leadership of Eamon de Valera. While the Irish had declared independence, the British had by no means conceded it, and a confrontation was imminent.

The Anglo-Irish War

The day the Dáil convened in Dublin in January 1919, two policemen were shot dead in County Tipperary. This was the beginning of the bitter Anglo-Irish war, which lasted from 1919 to the middle of 1921. This was the period when Michael Collins came to the fore, a charismatic and ruthless leader who masterminded the campaign of violence against the British while at the same time serving as minister for finance in the new Dáil.

The war quickly became entrenched and bloody. On the Irish side was the Irish Republican Army (the IRA), and on the other a coalition of regular British Army soldiers and two groups of quasi military status who rapidly gained a vicious reputation: the Auxiliaries and the Black & Tans. The IRA formed 'flying columns', small groups of armed volunteers formed to ambush British forces, and on home ground, they operated successfully. A truce was eventually agreed in July 1921.

After months of negotiations in London, the Irish delegation signed the Anglo-Irish Treaty on 6 December 1921, which gave 26 counties of Ireland independence and allowed six largely Protestant Ulster counties the option of opting out. If they did (a foregone conclusion), a Border Commission would then decide on the final frontiers between north and south. This treaty might have sounded like the answer to all of Ireland's problems. In fact it had quite the opposite effect.

The Civil War

The negotiations on the Treaty had been largely carried on the Irish side by Michael Collins and Arthur Griffith. Both men knew that many Dáil members would not accept the loss of the north, or the fact that the British king would still be head of the new Irish Free State. All Irish MPs would still have to swear an oath of allegiance to the crown. Under pressure from Britain's Lloyd George and after a spell of exhausting negotiations, they signed the Treaty without checking with de Valera in Dublin.

Collins regarded the issue of the monarchy and the oath of allegiance as largely symbolic, and he hoped that the northeastern six counties would not be a viable entity and would eventually become part of the Free State. During the treaty negotiations he had been encouraged to think that the Border Commission would decrease the size of that part of Ireland remaining outside the Free State. He hoped that he could convince the rest of his comrades. But he knew the risks and declared, 'I have signed my death warrant.'

In the end Collins couldn't persuade his colleagues to accept the Treaty. De Valera was furious, and it wasn't long before a bitter civil war broke out between comrades who a year previously had fought alongside each other.

Ireland since Partition

For the history of Ireland since partition, see the introductions to the Republic of Ireland and Northern Ireland.

GEOGRAPHY

Ireland is divided into 32 counties. The

Republic of Ireland consists of 26 counties, and Northern Ireland of six. The northernmost point in the South is actually farther north than anywhere in the North! To confuse things further the island is traditionally divided into four provinces: Leinster, Ulster, Connaught and Munster. Northern Ireland is often loosely referred to as Ulster, but three of the Republic of Ireland's counties – Donegal, Cavan and Monaghan – were also in the old province of Ulster, which with the six counties of Northern Ireland makes a total of nine.

The area of the island of Ireland is 84,404 sq km: 14,139 sq km in the north and 70,265 sq km in the south. It stretches about 500 km north to south and 300 km east to west, and the convoluted coastline extends for 5630 km.

Landscape

It can be as little as 50 km from the heart of one of Ireland's major cities through the midland plains to an isolated sweep of mountains and bogland.

The island is saucer-shaped. Most of the higher ground is close to the coast, while the central regions or midlands are largely flat. Almost the entire western seaboard from Cork to Donegal is a continuous bulwark of cliffs, hills and mountains with few safe anchorages. The only significant breaches in the chain are the Shannon estuary and Galway Bay.

The western mountain ranges are not particularly high but they are often beautiful. The highest mountains are in the south-west; Carrantuohill in Kerry's Magillicuddy Reeks is the tallest of the lot – at only 1041 metres (3414 feet). The highest in Leinster is Lugnaquilla in the Wicklow Mountains at 926 metres (3039 feet).

The Shannon is the longest river in Ireland or Great Britain. It runs for 259 km (161 miles) from its source in Cavan's Cuilcagh Mountains down through the midlands before emptying into the wide Shannon estuary west of Limerick City. Lough Neagh in Northern Ireland is the island's largest lake, covering 383 sq km.

The midlands of Ireland lie above Carboniferous limestone deposited between 300 and 400 million years ago. On the surface, the flat landscape is mostly rich farmland or raised bogs, huge swathes of brown peat rapidly disappearing under the machines of the Irish Peat Board, Bord Na Mona.

As you travel west from the midlands, the soil becomes poorer and the fields smaller, and stone walls more numerous. The Cromwellian cry 'to hell or to Connaught' was not without foundation, as the land west of the Shannon cannot compare with that of fertile counties like Meath and Tipperary. On the western seaboard, small farmers struggle to make a living by raising sheep, potatoes and some cattle. Before the famine, the pressure on land was enormous; eight million people had to be fed and they farmed in the most inaccessible places. Up the hillsides above today's fields, you may see the faint regular lines of pre-famine potato ridges called 'lazy beds'.

Ice Ages

The last Ice Age had a huge impact on the Irish landscape. It lasted from 100,000 to just over 10,000 years ago, and most of the country was glaciated. Characteristic U-shaped valleys were carved out by glaciers, as were the small deep-set corrie lakes high on the mountainsides. Most of the baked sedimentary rocks covering the Wicklow Mountains were stripped away exposing the underlying granite. In County Clare limestone appeared when a layer of waterproof shale and sandstone was removed.

Many of Ireland's mountains and hills have a round, smooth profile, formed by the abrasive effect of moving ice. The ice also deposited soil in its wake, leaving a layer of boulder clay on many parts of the country. Drumlins are small round hills of boulder clay that were dropped and shaped by the passing ice, and there is a large belt of them across the country from County Cavan to Clew Bay in County Mayo. The result is the characteristic 'basket of eggs' topography.

Often pieces of rock were picked up and dropped a long way from their source, and so you find granite 'glacial erratics' as they are called on the limestone desert of Clare's Burren region. Here the ice polished the limestone to mirror smoothness, and in some places you can see deep scratches on the surface of the stone, engraved by harder stones embedded in the moving ice.

CLIMATE

Ireland is farther north than either Newfoundland or Vancouver yet the climate is exceedingly mild with a mean annual temperature of around 10°C (50°F). The temperature only drops below freezing intermittently during the winter and snow is scarce – perhaps one or two brief flurries every year. The coldest months of the year are January and February, when daily temperatures range from 5°C (41°F) to 8°C (47°F) with 7°C (45°F) the average. During the summer, temperatures during the day are a comfortable 15°C (59°F) to 20°C (68°F). During the warmest months of July and August the average is 16°C (61°F). A hot summer's day in Ireland is 22 to 24°C although it has reached 30°C for a few days in recent years and everyone is talking about it. There are about 18 hours of daylight

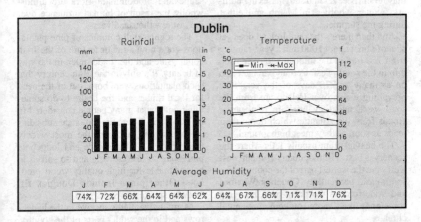

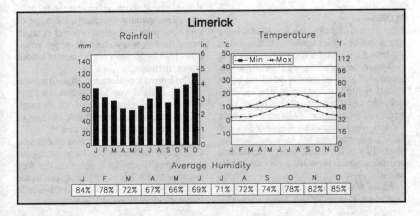

during July and August, and it's only truly dark after about 11 pm.

The reason Ireland has such a mild climate is the moderating effect of the Atlantic Ocean and particularly the Gulf Stream. This is an enormous current which moves clockwise around the Atlantic bringing warm water up to western Europe from the Caribbean. Often the Gulf Stream brings Caribbean sealife with it, and turtles and triggerfish are commonly washed up on the west coast of Ireland.

One thing you can be sure about Irish weather is how little you can be sure of. It may be shirtsleeves and sunglasses in February, winter woollies in March and either during the summer.

And then there's the rain. Ireland does get a lot of rain – about 1000 mm a year, ranging from 750 mm in the midlands to over 1300 mm in the south-west. Certain parts get rain on as many as 270 days of the year. The prevailing winds over Ireland are from the south-west, and they bring in rainbearing clouds from the Atlantic which dump their loads as soon as they meet high ground.

The heaviest rain usually falls where the scenery is best. The mountains of south-west Kerry are the wettest part of the country. The south-east, particularly Counties Wexford and Waterford, is the driest area, enjoying something like a more southern continental climate.

FLORA

After the end of the last Ice Age 10,000 years ago, a shrubby flora similar to that found in modern Arctic tundra took hold. This was eventually replaced by oak forest, which established itself on most of the island. In the upland regions and on more exposed hillsides, the oak was mixed with or replaced by birch and pine. In the lower regions where the soil was richer there was also elm and alder. Underneath the oak trees were smaller plants like holly, hazel, ferns, mosses and brambles, which provided a rich habitat for animals.

About 6000 years ago, the first farmers cleared small areas for their crops, the begin-

ning of a long process of deforestation. Substantial tracts of natural oakwood survived until the mid-16th century AD. The next 200 years saw the country being stripped of its oak for ship timbers, charcoal, tanning and barrels. So extensive was the clearance that by the mid-18th century almost all of the country's timber was being imported, right down to the staves for barrels.

Today almost no genuine native oak forest survives. There are remnants in the Killarney National Park and in south Wicklow near Shillelagh, and smaller fragments near Tullamore and Abbeyleix. The Irish landscape and predominant flora are almost wholly the result of human influence over the last few thousand years.

The regular dull columns of pine plantations are a now a major feature of the Irish countryside and don't add much in the way of beauty. It's only in the 20th century that such plantations were born, out of the need for local timber and the desire to do something with what many people considered to be wasteland. There are still state subsidies for plantations, although the most widely used species – sitka spruce and lodgepole pine – are so fast growing and so soft as to be unsuitable for high quality wood products. Other pines include Douglas fir, Norway spruce and Scots pine.

Many native plants survive in the hedgerows and in the wilder parts of the country. Because intensive agriculture has only arrived comparatively recently, the range of surviving plant and animal species is much larger than in many other European countries. Irish hedgerows are a blaze of colour in summertime.

The Burren limestone region in Clare was covered in light woodland before the early settlers arrived. However many of the original plants live on, a remarkable mixture of Mediterranean and alpine species.

The bogs of Ireland are home to a unique flora adapted to wet, acidic and nutrient-poor conditions. Sphagnum moss is the key bogplant and is joined by plants such as the sundew, which uses its long hairs covered in sweet sticky stuff to catch insects.

Bogs

Raised bogs are formed when sphagnum moss gains a foothold in a low-lying waterlogged area. The moss accumulates as it dies, retaining a lot of water, and the bog starts to form. The centres of these bogs are higher than the edges, hence the term 'raised bog'. These are mostly found in flat areas such as the midlands; the most famous example in Ireland is the Great Bog of Allen, which once covered as much as 100,000 hectares.

The bogs found covering hills and valleys are known as blanket bogs, and they develop on acid soil in a very wet climate, which usually means 240 days of rain a year or more. There are good examples of blanket bogs still surviving in Wicklow, Sligo, Antrim and the Slieve Bloom Mountains.

The bogs of the midlands have been worked by the Irish Peat Board (Bord Na Mona) since 1932. A whole range of enormous machines does the job. At the present rate of destruction most of Ireland's bogs have just a few years to go, wiping out 10,000 years of accumulation.

In many areas, bogs are prevented from draining off into the Shannon by *eskers*, long glacial ridges which are the remains of the banks of long-gone meltwater rivers that ran underneath glaciers. 'Esker' is one of the few Irish words to enter the English language. The best known of these eskers is the Esker Riada, which translates as the Kings' Road; this great esker ran across much of the country and was used as the principal highway between Leinster and Connaught. You can still see parts of it today near the main road to Dublin. The Clonmacnois monastery sits on this esker, in the north-west corner of County Offaly.

Bog conservation is a recent phenomenon, as bogs have always been seen either as large tracts of potential fuel or as useless and dangerous ground. On top of this they were closely tied to the stereotype of the bog Irishman, so no-one had much affection for them. Now that these great raised bogs have almost been obliterated, there is an urgent need to conserve some (many would say all) of what's left. Bogs are home to their own unique family of plants and insects.

Due to the acidity and lack of oxygen in the peat, fragile organic artefacts are occasionally preserved, which would have disintegrated long ago in any other environment. The countless relics, some of them 5000 years old, include Iron Age wooden highways, preserved bodies and wooden wheels and buckets. Among more recent items are 300-year-old packets of cheese and butter. ∎

FAUNA

The most common native mammals of any size are foxes and badgers and while there are plenty about you are unlikely to see any on a casual visit. Smaller mammals include rabbits introduced by the Normans for food, hares, hedgehogs, red and grey squirrels, shrews and bats. Red deer roam the hillsides in many of the wilder parts of the country, particularly the Wicklow Mountains, and in the Killarney National Park, which holds the country's only herd of native red deer. Sika deer and other red deer have been introduced from abroad.

Less common in Ireland are the elusive otters, stoats and pine martens which are usually found in remote areas such as the Burren in County Clare or Connemara in County Galway. Sea mammals include grey and common seals which are found all around the coastline and can often be seen if you keep quiet and know where to look. There are substantial colonies of grey seals living on uninhabited islands off County Mayo and around the shores of Strangford Lough in Northern Ireland.

Dolphins often swim close to land, particularly in the bays and inlets off the west coast, and for many years Dingle Harbour has had a famous resident bottle-nosed dolphin called Fungie. There are whales in the sea off Ireland, but they tend to be so dispersed and stay so far out to sea that they are rarely sighted.

Ireland is home to a wide range of birds. Some, such as brent, barnacle and Greenland white-fronted geese, are seasonal visitors, escaping from the Arctic cold and overwintering in Ireland in places like the Wexford Slobs and Dublin's North Bull Island. Also found during the winter are teal, redshanks and curlews.

The coastlines are home to a huge variety of seabirds, and most of them breed in the late spring and early summer, the best time to view them. Little Skellig out in the Atlantic off County Kerry is the second largest gannet colony in the world, with some 25,000 pairs breeding annually on the rock.

Birds of prey include hen harriers, sparrow hawks and the odd buzzard. The magnificent peregrine falcon has made something of a recovery in recent years and can be found nesting on cliffs in Wicklow and elsewhere.

One of Ireland's rarer native birds is the corncrake, which used to be common in grasslands and meadows, but has been slowly disappearing. Corncrakes can still be found in some remote and undisturbed areas, such as low-lying flooded grasslands of the Shannon Callows and parts of County Donegal. Choughs – unusual crows with bright red feet and beaks – can be seen in the west, particularly along coastlines with extensive sand-dune complexes.

The spotted Kerry slug is found as the name suggests in Kerry. So are natterjack toads, Ireland's only species of toad, which live in sandy areas behind Inch Strand and near Castlegregory on the north side of the Dingle Peninsula.

POPULATION

The total population of Ireland is about five million: 3.5 million in the South, 1.5 million in the North. This figure is actually lower than it was 150 years ago. Prior to the potato famines between 1845 and 1849 the population was around eight million. Death and emigration reduced the population to around six million, and emigration continued at a high level for the next 100 years. It was not until the 1960s that Ireland's population finally began to increase again.

Dublin is the island's largest city and capital of the Republic with up to 1.5 million people living within commuting distance of the city centre. In order of size the Republic's next largest cities are Cork with 175,000, Limerick with 76,500 and Galway with 47,100. Belfast is the principal settlement in Northern Ireland with 300,000 people in 1988.

PEOPLE

If you can make generalisations about a people, the Irish are a fair-skinned, dark-haired race with quite a number of red-haired and freckled members thrown in for good measure. On the whole they are very friendly and accommodating towards foreigners. They are not particularly outgoing. Introductions and conversations are usually low key until some mutual respect is established. If you want to get on with people, don't crash into a B&B or a country pub and make lots of noise. Go quietly, say hello and let conversation arise naturally.

There are few of the class distinctions so prevalent in England, and while advertising and marketing people will divide the population into wealth and class brackets, the boundaries of these are quite fluid. Movement between social classes is common and more to do with personal wealth than birth or background. There are the vestiges of an upper class made up of the descendants of the Protestant landed gentry, but their status and their houses are being taken over by the new business elite.

Genetically, the Irish are remarkably homogenous. There has been little movement of population into the country from elsewhere. Scholars suggest that modern Irish people are mainly descendants of the tribes that were living in Ireland before St Patrick. Invaders such as the Vikings, Normans and British have added to this gene pool, but their characteristics have been diluted through the whole population.

Even the Catholics and Protestants of Northern Ireland are more closely related than they might imagine. Settlers from Scotland and England have produced a distinctive Protestant culture which has remained separate to this day. But scholars suggest that Catholics and Protestants are genetically almost identical.

RELIGION

The Republic of Ireland is 95% Roman Catholic and 5% Protestant. For years the breakdown in the North was given as 70% Protestant and 30% Catholic, but recent figures suggest it is more like 60% Protestant and 40% Catholic.

Most Irish Protestants are members of the Church of Ireland, an offshoot of the Church of England and the Presbyterian Church.

The Catholic Church used to be cited in the Constitution as having a special position in the Republic but that reference was dropped in 1972. It does still wield considerable influence in the South, and large numbers of the population attend mass every Sunday; it's part of the weekly routine and the social circuit.

The Catholic Church has always taken a strong line on abortion, contraception and divorce, which are forbidden by law, and has opposed attempts to change the present conservative regime on these matters. The Church is treated with a curious mixture of respect and derision by various sections of the community.

Oddly enough, the primates of both the Roman Catholic Church and the Church of Ireland sit in Armagh, the traditional base of St Patrick, which is in Northern Ireland. The country's religious history clearly overrides its current divisions.

CULTURE & ARTS
Sport

Ireland has a couple of native games with a large and enthusiastic following.

Gaelic football is a fast and exciting spectacle. The ball used is round like a soccer ball, but the players can kick, handle and run with the ball as in rugby. They can pass it in any direction but only by kicking or punching. The goalposts are similar to rugby posts, and a goal, worth three points, is scored by putting the ball below the bar, while a single point is awarded when the ball goes over the bar. Gaelic football is popular all over the country, and Northern Ireland has done well in recent All-Ireland competitions.

Hurling is Ireland's most characteristic sport. It's a ball-and-stick game something like hockey, but much faster and more physical. Visitors are often taken aback by the crash of players wielding what look like ferocious clubs, but injuries are surprisingly infrequent. The goalposts and scoring method are the same as Gaelic football, but the leather ball or *sliotar* is the size of a baseball. A player can pick the ball up on his stick and run with it for a certain distance. Players can handle the ball briefly and pass it by palming it. The players' broad wooden sticks are called hurleys.

Hurling has an ancient history and is mentioned in many old Irish tales. Cúchulainn was a legendary exponent of the game. Today hurling is played on a standard field, but in the old days the game might have been played across country between two towns or villages, the only aim being to get the ball to a certain spot or goal.

Both Gaelic football and hurling are played nationwide by a network of town and country clubs and under the auspices of the Gaelic Athletic Association, the GAA. The most important competitions are played at county level, and the county winners out of each of the four provinces come together in the autumn for the All-Ireland finals, the climax of Ireland's sporting year. Both finals are played in September at Dublin's Croke Park in front of huge crowds.

Handball is another Irish sport with ancient origins and is also governed by the GAA.

Soccer and rugby union enjoy considerable support all over the country, particularly around Dublin, and soccer is very popular in Northern Ireland.

The international rugby team consists of members from the North and the Republic and has a tremendous following. The highlights of the rugby year are the international matches played against England, Scotland, Wales and France between January and March. Home matches are played at Lansdowne Road in Dublin.

The North and the Republic field separate soccer teams and both have a good record in international competitions. The Republic's team got to the last stages of the 1990 World Cup in Italy; the country went berserk and the game's profile went through the roof. Many of the home players from North and South play professional soccer in Britain, and various British club teams have strong followings in Ireland.

Athletics is also popular, and the Republic usually has a few international athletes, particularly in middle and long-distance events. Boxing has traditionally had a strong working-class following, and Irish boxers are often the only Olympic medal winners or world champions the island produces. Barry McGuigan, Michael Carruth and Wayne MacCullough are some recent heroes.

Music

Irish music, with traditional instruments like the flute, the *bodhrán-a* goatskin drum, the fiddle and the *uileann* pipes, is the Irish art visitors are most likely to encounter. Almost every town and village in Ireland seems to have a pub renowned for its traditional music. If you find yourself in a music pub and most drinkers are quietly listening to the players, you are expected to do the same. Also clapping, unless everybody is doing it, is not really acceptable as it interferes with the music.

Dublin music pubs are keen on claiming they were the birthplace for this or that act. The Gresham on O'Connell St claim the Chieftains started out there in the early 1960s. They're the best known exponents of traditional Irish music and have made numerous albums, including the popular *Irish Heartbeat* with Van Morrison, composed a number of film soundtracks; various members of the band have played with some of the biggest international names in rock and roll.

The Irish are equally keen on country and western, and more recently rock music. After the two big rock music countries – the USA and the UK – Ireland vies with Australia as the next largest centre for rock music. Van Morrison, the Belfast Cowboy, was lead singer with the 1960s band Them, whose anthem *Gloria* was a Beatles-era classic. 'Van the Man' moved on to a solo career in the USA, and his *Astral Weeks* is regularly listed by critics as one of the seminal records of the 1960s. Although he has never generated a mass following, Van Morrison certainly has some faithful fans, and he's kept them happy with a stream of expertly crafted records.

In the 1970s and 1980s a number of Irish acts made it on the international scene, including Phil Lynott and Thin Lizzy, Bob Geldof and the Boomtown Rats, Chris de Burgh, the Pogues and the Hothouse Flowers.

Sinéad O'Connor worked her way through a number of Irish bands, meanwhile making ends meet serving tables at Dublin's popular Bad Ass Cafe before releasing *The Lion & the Cobra* in 1987 when she was 19. 'I Do Not Want What I Haven't Got' propelled her to megastardom

Dublin band U2 did time on the Irish pub circuit in the late 1970s and early 1980s. From the late 1980s on, albums like *Unforgettable Fire*, *Joshua Tree* and *Rattle & Hum* were all major international sellers, and in late 1991 *Achtung Baby* was hailed as one of the year's best rock records. *Zooropa*, released in 1993, is their most recent album. Today U2 are Ireland's best-known musical export and one of the most popular bands in the world.

Cinema

Dublin and Ireland have made numerous movie appearances, most recently in *The Commitments*, by the English director Alan Parker, a wonderful, bright and energetic 1991 hit about a north Dublin soul band. *The Commitments* accurately records north Dublin's scruffy atmosphere although Dublin audiences (well, north Dublin ones at least) were somewhat amused by some of the geographical jumps around the city which the characters managed to make! The British film *The Long Good Friday* starring Bob Hoskins is perhaps the most interesting commercial film to feature the IRA.

The 1992 Tom Cruise and Nicole Kidman vehicle *Far & Away* provided some picturesque views of the west coast region, and Dublin's Temple Bar district stood in for late

19th-century Boston! You might still see the alternative name painted on the popular Norseman pub in Temple Bar.

Neil Jordan is one of the most talented writers and directors working today, and has been building up an impressive body of work. Jordan's films include *Mona Lisa* starring Bob Hoskins, *Cal* starring Stephen Rea, *The Company of Wolves*, *The Miracle* and the recent multi-Oscar-nominated *The Crying Game* – Jordan won an Oscar for the script.

While Jordan has been working away, other Irish film-makers have also been making the headlines. Noel Pearson and Jim Sheridan's *My Left Foot* won Oscars for Daniel Day-Lewis and Brenda Fricker with the true story of Dublin writer Christy Brown, who was crippled with cerebral palsy. Sheridan and Pearson went on to make *The Field* with Richard Harris, filmed around Leenane in County Galway.

Hear My Song about the Irish tenor Joseph Locke was a surprise success, as was *Into the West*, a delightful story of two children and a mythical white horse.

At the time of writing, David Putnam is working on a film called *War of the Buttons* in Skibbereen, County Cork.

Many films have featured Dublin. *My Left Foot* is a wonderful movie (and *Down all the Days*, the book it came from, was a wonderful book) and managed to make some interesting peregrinations around Dublin including visits to John Mulligan's, the pub reputed to pull the best Guinness in Ireland. John Huston's superb final film was *The Dead*, released in 1987 and based on a story from James Joyce's *Dubliners*. Joseph Strick attempted the seemingly impossible task of putting *Ulysses* on screen in 1967. The film was promptly banned in Ireland.

The 1970 David Lean epic *Ryan's Daughter* with Sarah Miles, Robert Mitchum, Trevor Howard and John Mills was filmed on the Dingle Peninsula in County Kerry and the place and the film have been inextricably linked ever since. The Dingle Peninsula has simply become 'Ryan's Daughter country'.

Hollywood came to Ireland earlier on in 1952 when John Ford filmed John Wayne as the *The Quiet Man*, wooing Maureen O'Hara in Cong, County Sligo. You can take Quiet Man tours in Cong today.

Ireland has also been a pure and straightforward backdrop, Youghal in County Cork was Captain Ahab's port in John Huston's 1956 *Moby Dick*. The Irish countryside was used for the WW I aerial epic *The Blue Max* (1966), and *Educating Rita* used Trinity College as its quintessentially English university! An Irish documentary which many visitors see while in Ireland is *Man of Aran*, a 1934 account of the hard life on those barren and storm-swept islands off Galway. The Troubles in the North have spawned a number of films, including the 1982 *Angel* and 1984 *Cal*. The IRA made an earlier appearance in the 1947 film *Odd Man Out*.

Irish actors like Liam Neeson, Patrick Bergin and Gabriel Byrne pursue successful careers, following in the footsteps of Richard Harris, Peter O'Toole and Maureen O'Hara.

Cinema & Ireland by Kevin Rockett, Luke Gibbons and John Hill (Croom Helm, England, 1988) tells the complete story of films and Ireland.

Literature

Of all the arts the Irish have probably had the greatest impact on literature, see the Books & Maps section in the Facts for the Visitor chapter for more on the Irish way with words.

Architecture

Ireland is packed with prehistoric graves, ruined monasteries, crumbling fortresses and many other solid reminders of its long and often dramatic history. The buildings used in the country over the last few thousand years fall into a number of groups and you are likely to come across examples of some or all of them on your travels.

The simplest structures are standing stones and stone circles which in Ireland date from the Stone or Bronze Ages and were erected all the way up to Christian times.

The earliest settlers built houses of wood and reeds of which nothing survives except the faint traces of post-holes. The principal surviving structures from Stone Age times are the graves and monuments the people built for their dead, usually grouped under the heading of megalithic tombs, or 'great stone' tombs.

Megalithic Tombs Among the most easily recognisable megalithic tombs are dolmens, massive three-legged structures rather like giant stone stools, in which a number of bodies were interred before the whole structure was covered in earth. Most are 4000 to 5000 years old. Usually the earth eroded away leaving the standing stones. There are good examples at Poulnabrone in Clare, Proleek near Dundalk, and at Browne's Hill near Carlow; the cap stone at Browne's Hill weighs more than 100 tonnes. Dolmens are the best known type of chambered tomb or gallery graves; similar but more complex are wedge tombs, cist graves and court cairns.

Passage graves such as Newgrange and Knowth in Meath are huge mounds with entrances through narrow stone-walled passages leading to burial chambers. They are surrounded by stone circles of unknown significance. Some passage graves were made from piles of stones erected near or on hill tops, sometimes called cairns. Good examples are on the Slieve Na Calliaghe hills in Meath and Seefin in County Wicklow.

Ogham Stones These are peculiarly Irish standing stones. They date from the 4th to 7th centuries AD, and are marked on the edge with groups of straight lines – an early form of Irish script. They usually mark graves and are inscribed with the name of the deceased. The majority are found in Counties Cork, Kerry and Waterford, and many have been moved; you may find them incorporated in walls, buildings or gateposts.

Forts Ring forts, 'fairy rings' and raths are all one and the same. The Irish names for forts – *dún*, *rath*, *caiseal/cashel* and *caher* – have ended up in the names of countless towns, villages and townlands. The Irish countryside is peppered with the remains of

over 30,000. The earliest known examples date from the Bronze Age, and ring forts have been built and used for many thousands of years since. Some were lived in as late as the 17th century. Wooden and other types of houses were built within the forts' protective confines.

The most common type was the ring fort, with circular earth and stone banks topped by a wooden palisade fence to keep intruders out and surrounded on the outside by a moat-like ditch. Ring forts are found everywhere and were the basic family or tribal enclosure in Ireland for thousands of years. They may have protected anything from one family to the entire court of a tribal chieftain. Ring forts may have up to three earthen ramparts surrounding them; Mooghaun Fort near Dromoland Castle in County Clare is a particularly fine example. Outside Clonakilty in County Cork, Lisnagun ring fort has been reconstructed to give some idea of its original appearance.

Some forts were constructed entirely of stone; Staigue Fort in Kerry and Cathair Dhún Iorais on Clare's Black Head are fine examples. Promontory forts were built on headlands or on cliff edges, which gave natural protection on one side. The Iron Age fort of Dún Aengus on the Aran Islands is a superb example.

The Normans used many ring forts to their advantage by building inside them. A characteristic Norman fort is the motte and bailey, a small flat topped hill surrounded by earthen banks at the base for further protection. These were largely military in purpose, built to protect and secure the Normans' newly conquered territory.

Crannógs Crannógs are artificial islands found in many Irish lakes and are the equivalent of a ring fort on water. Many of them were built completely by humans: wooden piles were driven into the lake floor and the structure built up with wood, stone, earth and anything else the builders could lay their hands on. After the island had been built, the occupants built wooden fences and a house to live in. Craggaunowen Archaeological

Centre in Clare has a reconstructed example, and the lake near Fair Head in County Antrim has an easily spotted original.

The midland lakes have many crannógs, which today are usually overgrown with little betraying their artificial origins, except perhaps the too-perfect circular outline. Sometimes they were built in bogs, or the original lake has since become a bog; and many are now hidden below the water level. Estimates put the number in Ireland at over 250. Crannnógs date back to the Bronze Age and like the ring forts were used by humans right up to the 16th and 17th centuries. Often there was a secret causeway leading out to the crannóg, just under the surface of the water, and it twisted and turned so that ignorant intruders would have difficulty using it.

Monasteries & Churches The vast majority of early monasteries were built of perishable materials particularly wood. Sometimes the central church or chapel was stone and these are often the only structures that survive. The early stone churches were often very simple, some roofed with timber like Teampall Benen on the Aran Islands or built completely of stone like Gallarus Oratory on the Dingle Peninsula. Early hermitages include the small beehive huts and buildings on the summit of Skellig Michael off County Kerry.

As the monasteries grew in size and stature so too did the architecture. The 'cathedrals' at Glendalough and Clonmacnois are good examples, although they are still tiny when compared with modern cathedrals.

Round towers have become symbols of Ireland, and these tall stone needle-like structures were built largely as lookout posts and refuges in the event of Viking attacks. The earliest round towers were built in the late 9th or early 10th centuries.

That other great Irish symbol, the Celtic cross, comes from these Christian times. Some suggest that the circle imposed on the arms of the cross represents pagan sun worship being incorporated into the new faith. They developed from simple crosses with rough designs to complex works decorated with high-relief scenes, usually of Biblical characters and tales.

Ireland's early church architecture developed in isolation, as Europe was experiencing the Dark Ages. However, foreign influences began to take effect in the 11th and 12th centuries, and the Cistercians, a European order of monks, established their first Irish monastery at Mellifont, County Louth, in 1141. The strict and formal layout of these new establishments was radically different to the simple and relatively random layout of the traditional Irish monastery as exemplified by nearby Monasterboice, Glendalough in Wicklow and Clonmacnois in Offaly. Cormac's Chapel on the Rock of Cashel shows strong foreign influence, and elements of European Romanesque design became common in Irish monasteries and buildings. Elaborately carved doorways are common, with human and animal heads intricately interwoven into the stone patterns.

With the Normans came the Gothic style of architecture: tall vaulted windows and soaring V-shaped arches were incorporated in the churches and cathedrals of this period.

Castles & Mansions The Normans first built temporary motte-and-bailey forts – raised and flattened mounds with a keep on top and a walled enclosure or bailey surrounding them. Once they had established themselves, however, they built more permanent stone castles. The great castle at Trim, County Meath, is the best example. Castles and cathedrals were built in Dublin and the other large towns.

Many of the castles you see today are the tall thin tower houses built between the 14th and 17th centuries for local landlords or chieftains. They are often inside a protective wall called a *bawn*. The earliest forms of these are simple small keeps with few embellishments, while the later forms became more like large fortified stone houses with sophisticated features, bigger windows, and less emphasis on security.

From the 17th century on, as the established landowning families became wealthier and felt more secure, they built great mansions, particularly in the less rebellious parts of the country around counties Kildare, Meath, Dublin and Wicklow. Castletown House near Celbridge, Russborough House near Blessington and Carton House in Maynooth are good examples.

In Georgian times, Dublin became one of the architectural glories of Europe, with simple and beautifully built Georgian terraces of red brick, with delicate glass fanlights over elegant doorways. Dublin's Georgian heritage has suffered badly but you can still see fine examples around Merrion and Fitzwilliam Squares.

The traditional Irish thatched cottage, built to suit the elements and the landscape, is becoming rare.

LANGUAGE

English is spoken throughout Ireland, but there are still parts of western Ireland known as *gaeltacht* areas where Irish is the native language. Irish is a Celtic language probably first introduced to Ireland by the Celts in the last few centuries BC. Irish is similar to Scottish Gaelic, and has much in common with Welsh and Breton.

Officially the Republic of Ireland is bilingual, and many official documents and roadsigns are printed in both English and Irish. The reality however is a little more complex. Irish is compulsory in both primary and secondary schools, and most colleges and universities require prospective students to pass the subject in their school-leaving exams. Despite this, few of the population are conversant in Irish. Many complain that it's a waste of time studying a difficult language that is not in everyday use.

For many centuries Irish was looked down upon as the language of the poor, and strenuous efforts were made by the English to wipe it out. Social advancement meant giving up Irish. Today it still carries a stigma, and most of today's hip youngsters would consider speaking Irish to be uncool.

Irish is badly taught in schools, with far too much emphasis on the complex grammar

and far too little emphasis on speaking the language. Most Irish school leavers would be hard pressed to hold a simple conversation in Irish despite having just completed 13 years of daily classes in the subject.

However, Irish continues to survive and attitudes are changing, albeit slowly. There is an Irish-language radio station, Radio Na Gaeltachta, broadcast from Connemara, and RTE, the Irish national broadcasting station, has daily news bulletins and programmes in Irish. An increasing number of people derive intense satisfaction from speaking and keeping alive an ancient aspect of Ireland's culture.

Most native speakers are concentrated in the gaeltacht regions in Kerry, Galway, Mayo, the Aran Islands, Donegal and Ring, County Waterford.

Some useful words in Irish include *fáilte* – welcome, *gardaí* – police, *fir* – man, *mna* – women, *an lar* – town centre.

Greetings & Civilities

Hello.
  Dia Dhuit. literally 'God be with you' (dee-a-gwit)
Goodbye.
  Slán Agat. (slawn aguth)
Good night.
  Oiche mhaith. (eeheh woh)
Welcome.
  Céad mhíle fáilte. ie a hundred thousand welcomes. (kade meela fawlta)
Thank you.
  Go raibh maith aguth. (goh rev moh aguth)
Thank you very much.
  Gur a mhíle maith agat. (gur a mila moh agut)
  Go raibh mile maith agat. (goh rev meela moh aguth)
Please.
  Le do thoil. (le do hull)
Excuse me.
  Gabh mo leiscéil. (gawv mo lesh scale)
How are you?
  Conas a tá tú? (kunas a thaw two)
I am fine.
  Táim go maith. (thawm gohmoh)

What is your name?
Cad is anim duit ? (cod is anim dit)
John Murray is my name.
John Murray is anim dom.
(J M iss anim dumb)
another/one more
ceann eile (keown ella)
good, fine, OK
go maith (go moh)
nice
go deas (goh dass)
yes
tá/sea (thaw/shah)
no/it is not
níl/ní hea (knee hah)

Questions & Comments

What time is it?
Cén tam é? (kane towm ay)
Why?
Cén fáth? (kane faw)
What is this?
Cad é seo? (kod ay shawh)
What is that?
Cad é sin? (kod ay shin)
How much/how many?
Cé mhéid? (kay vaid)
expensive – very dear
ana dhaor (ana gare)
where is...?
cá bhfuil...? (kaw will)
which way?
cén slí? (kane shlee)
I don't understand.
Ní thuigim. (knee higgim)
this/that
é seo/é sin (ay shoh/ay shin)
big/small
mór/beag (moor/beeugh)
open/closed
oscailte/dúnta (uskulta/doonta)
slowly/quickly
go mall/go tapaidh
(guh mowl/guh top-igg)

Travelling & Places

I would like to go to...
Ba mhaith liom dul go dtí... (baw woh lum dull go dee)

I would like to buy...
Ba mhaith liom cheannach... (bah woh lumb kyarok)
ticket
ticéid (tickaid)
boat/ship
bád/long (bawd/lung)
car/bus
gluaisteáin/bus (glooshtawn/bus)
here/there
anseo/ansin (anshuh/onshin)
stop/go
stad/ar aghaidh (stod/err eyeg)
town square
lár an baile (lawr an vollyeh)
street/road
sráid/bóthar (sroyed/bowher)
town/city
baile/cathair (bollyeh/kawher)
bank/shop
an banc/siopa (an bonk/shuppa)
post office
oifig an poist (if-ig on pwist)

Hotels & Accommodation

one night
oíche amháin (eeheh a woin)
one person
aon duine (ayn dinnah)
bed/room
leaba/seomra (lyabah/showmra)
toilet
leithreas (lehrass)

Time

today/tomorrow
inniu/amárach (innyuv/amawrok)
hour/minute
huair/noiméid (oor/nomade)
week/month
seachtain/mí (shocktin/mee)
What time is it?
Cén tam é (kane towm ay)
7 o' clock
seacht a chlog (shocked ah klug)

Monday
dé luan (day loon)
Tuesday
dé máirt (day mawrt)

Wednesday
dé céadaoin (day kaydeen)
Thursday
déardaoin (daredeen)
Friday
dé haoine (day heena)
Saturday
dé sathairn (day saheren)
Sunday
dé domhnaigh (day downick)

Numbers

half	*leath* (lah)
1	*aon* (ayn)
2	*dó* (doe)

3	*trí* (three)
4	*cathar* (kahirr)
5	*cúig* (koo-ig)
6	*sé* (shay)
7	*seacht* (shocked)
8	*ocht* (ukth)
9	*naoi* (nay)
10	*deich* (jeh)
11	*aon deag* (ayen deeuct)
12	*dó deag* (doe dayugg)

And so on...

100	*céid* (kade)
1000	*míle* (meal-ah)

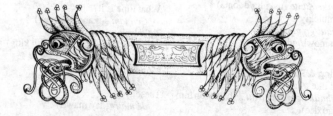

Facts for the Visitor

VISAS & EMBASSIES

For citizens of most Western countries no visa is required to visit Ireland. UK nationals born in Great Britain or Northern Ireland do not require a passport, but you may be asked for some form of identification. Visas are required from Indians, Pakistanis, non-UK passport Hong Kongers and citizens of some African states.

Irish diplomatic offices overseas include:

Australia
    20 Arkana St, Yarralumla, Canberra, ACT 2600 (☎ 06-273 3022)
Canada
    170 Metcalfe St, Ottawa, Ontario K2P 1P3 (☎ 416-745 8624)
Denmark
    Ostbanegade 21, ITH, DK-2100 Copenhagen (☎ 423 233)
France
    12 Ave Foch, 75116 Paris (☎ 45 00 20 87)
Germany
    Godesberger Allee 119, 5300 Bonn 2 (☎ 37 69 37, 38 & 39)
Italy
    Largo del Nazareno 3, 00187 Rome (☎ 678 25 41, 42, 43, 44 & 45)
Japan
    Kowa Building No 25, 8-7 Sanbancho, Chiyoda-ku, Tokyo (☎ 263 06 95)
Netherlands
    9 Dr Kuperstraat, 2514 BA The Hague (☎ 363 0993 194)
Portugal
    Rua Da Imprensa (a Estrela) 1-4, 1200 Lisbon (☎ 396 1569)
Spain
    Claudio Coello 73, 1st floor, Madrid 1 (☎ 576 3500)
Sweden
    Ostermalmsgatan 97 (IV), 114 59 Stockholm (☎ 661 80 05, 74 09 & 32 41)
Switzerland
    Eigerstrasse 71, Berne 3007 (☎ 46 23 53 & 54)
UK
    17 Grosvenor Place, London SW1X 7HR (☎ 071-235 2171)
USA
    2234 Massachusetts Ave NW, Washington, DC 20008 (☎ 202-462 3939)

In addition there are consulates in the USA in Boston, Chicago, New York and San Francisco.

Foreign Embassies in Ireland

See the Dublin and Belfast sections for diplomatic offices in those cities.

CUSTOMS

The usual tobacco, alcohol and perfume regulations apply to duty-free imports. Dublin and Shannon airports place great emphasis on their competitive duty-free shopping.

Customs regulations within the European Community (EC) changed radically in 1993. There is now no customs inspection apart from those concerned with drugs and national security, and the traditional limits on the amount of alcohol and tobacco that can be taken from one country and another have gone. The quotas on duty-free goods purchased at the airport duty-free shops have however remained the same. So while you can bring vast quantities of cheap wine from France to Ireland, for example, wine purchased on board a ferry from Britain or at an airport remain subject to the normal restrictions.

MONEY
Currency

In Ireland the Irish pound or punt (IR£) is used, and like the British pound sterling it's divided into 100 pence (p). Irish banknotes come in denominations of IR£100, IR£50, IR£20, IR£10 and IR£5. Coins come in the form of IR£1, 50p, 20p, 10p, 5p, 2p and 1p. The best exchange rates are obtained at banks, usually open 10 am to 12.30 pm and 1.30 to 3 pm Monday to Friday. In larger towns and cities, more and more banks are staying open at lunch time. In Dublin they stay open until 5 pm on Thursdays. The custom of closing for lunch may soon be stopped. *Bureaux de change* and other exchange facilities are usually open longer hours but the rate and/or commission will be worse. Building societies often handle foreign exchange and are open longer hours than the banks.

The British pound sterling (£) is used in Northern Ireland and comes in the same banknote and coin denominations as the Irish punt. In Northern Ireland banks are open 10 am to 3.30 pm weekdays and most stay open until 5 pm on Thursdays. Don't confuse Northern Irish pounds (issued by the Bank of Ireland or Allied Irish Banks) with Republic of Ireland pounds (issued by the Central Bank of Ireland). 'Sterling' or 'Belfast' are giveaway words on the Northern Irish notes. The Northern Irish pound sterling is worth the same as the British variety but the notes are not however very readily accepted in Britain.

If you've not obtained some currency in advance there are unofficial money-changers near the border between north and south, often at petrol stations.

Most major currencies and brands of travellers' cheques are readily accepted in Ireland but carrying them in pounds sterling has the advantage that in Northern Ireland or Britain you can change them without exchange loss or commission. Eurocheques can be cashed in Ireland.

Exchange Rates

A$1	=	IR£0.49	=	£0.46
C$1	=	IR£0.56	=	£0.52
NZ$1	=	IR£0.40	=	£38
US$1	=	IR£0.73	=	£0.68
IR£1	=		=	£0.93

Currency Regulations

You can bring in to the Republic as much currency as you wish but on departure you are not allowed to take out more than IR£150 in Irish notes and no notes larger than IR£20. Foreign currency in excess of IR£1200 may be taken out of the country only if you brought it in with you. There are no limits on the import and subsequent export of travellers' cheques or letters of credit.

Credit Cards

Major credit cards – particularly Visa, MasterCard and Access – are widely accepted and you can obtain cash advances on your card from a bank and from some cash machines (ATMs), north and south. The Allied Irish Bank (AIB) cash machines are particularly useful.

Costs

Costs vary around the country but a hostel bed will cost IR£5 to IR£10 a night. If you're not staying in a hostel your costs increase dramatically by having to eat out. A meal at lunch time costs IR£3 to IR£5 and in the evening this can easily double. A cheap B&B will cost about IR£12 to IR£20 per person while a more luxurious B&B or guesthouse with attached bathroom would be anything from about IR£15 to as much as IR£40. Dinner in a reasonable restaurant with a glass of wine or a beer will cost from IR£8 to IR£15.

Assuming you stay at a hostel, eat a light pub lunch and cook your own meal in the evening, you could get by on IR£15 a day. In practice you usually spend more.

Many places to stay have different high and low season prices. Some places may have not just a high season but a peak high season price. Entry prices are usually lower for children or students than for adults.

At busy times of the year, B&Bs may add a few pounds on to their price. Watch out for the awful practice of charging an extra 50p or IR£1 for a bath. A pint of Guinness is at least IR£1.60 and the Irish rounds system – you take your turn in buying drinks for the assembled company – is a good way of spending a remarkable amount of money in a remarkably short space of time.

Car hire is extremely expensive, and petrol costs over IR£2.50 (US$4) a gallon.

Sightseeing Discounts

Many parks, monuments and gardens in the Republic of Ireland are operated by the Office of Public Works. From any of these sites for IR£10 (children IR£4) you can get a Heritage Card giving you unlimited access to all these sites for one year – worthwhile if you're planning a serious onslaught on Ireland's plentiful supply of castles, monasteries and other sites. In Northern Ireland the National Trust has a similar deal but it's less useful for most visitors as there are fewer sites. If, however, you are also visiting Britain then National Trust membership (£24, under-23 £11, family £44) is well worth while.

x NATIONAL TRUST

Tipping
Fancy hotels and restaurants usually add a 10% or 12% service charge and no additional tip is required. Simpler places usually do not add service; if you decide to tip, just round up the bill or add at most 10%. Taxi drivers do not have to be tipped, and 10% is fine. Porters should get 50p per bag. Tipping in bars is not expected, but the distinction between pubs and restaurants is blurred by bars becoming more like restaurants at lunch time.

Consumer Taxes
Value Added Tax (VAT) applies to most goods and services in Ireland. Visitors can claim back the VAT on large purchases which are subsequently exported outside the European Community. If you buy something from a Cashback Store you will be given a Cashback Voucher which can be refunded at Dublin or Cork airports, or can be stamped at ferry ports and mailed back for refund.

WHEN TO GO
In July and August the crowds will be greatest and the costs the highest. In the quieter winter months, however, you may get miserable weather and many tourist facilities will be shut. Visiting Ireland in June or September has a number of attractions: the weather can be better than any other time of the year, and it's less crowded, but everything is open.

WHAT TO BRING
A raincoat or an umbrella is a necessity. Walkers should be well prepared if they are crossing exposed country. Dress is usually casual, and you are unlikely to come across many coat-and-tie-type regulations. Bring some warm clothes, as even during good summer weather it gets chilly in the evenings.

Bear in mind the strict regulations about birth control in Ireland. Condoms are not always easily available in rural areas, though they are becoming available in pharmacies and pub vending machines in the cities.

LAUNDRETTES
Most hostels have cheap laundry facilities. Irish self-service laundrettes almost all offer a service wash; for IR£3 to IR£4 they'll wash, dry and neatly fold your dirty washing.

SUGGESTED ITINERARIES
Depending on the length of your stay, you might want to see and do the following things:

Two days:
Visit Dublin and perhaps a couple of places nearby – Powerscourt and Glendalough to the south, or Newgrange, Mellifont and Monasterboice to the north.
One week:
Visit Dublin, Newgrange, Mellifont, Monasterboice, the Burren and Kilkenny.
Two weeks:
As above, plus the Ring of Kerry, Killarney and Cork.
One month:
With your own car you could cover all the main attractions around the coast but you'd be moving quite fast. This would be more difficult to achieve within a month on public transport.

Two months:

You'd have time to explore Ireland thoroughly with a car or motorcycle, reasonably thoroughly with a bicycle. You could do some walking as well.

TOURIST OFFICES

The Irish Tourist Board, or Bord Fáilte, and the Northern Ireland Tourist Board operate separate tourist offices but produce some joint brochures and publications.

Local Tourist Offices

Dublin has Bord Fáilte, Dublin Tourism and Northern Ireland Tourist Board offices. Belfast has Northern Ireland and Bord Fáilte offices. Elsewhere in Ireland and Northern Ireland there is a tourist office in almost every town big enough to have half a dozen pubs, (it doesn't take much population to justify half a dozen pubs in Ireland). These offices are friendly, helpful and well informed and will find you a place to stay and book it for a flat IR£1 charge (£1 in the North), a useful service in the busy summer months. Opening hours are usually 9 am to 6 pm Monday to Friday and 9 am to 1 pm on Saturday but the hours are often extended in summer.

Overseas Representatives

Some of the offices of the Bord Fáilte include:

Australia
5th floor, 36 Carrington St, Sydney, NSW 2000 (☎ 02-299 6177)

Belgium
Avenue de Beaulieu 25, 1160 Bruxelles (☎ 02-673 9940)

Canada
160 Bloor St East, Suite 934, Toronto, Ontario M4W 1B9 (☎ 416-929 2777)

Denmark
Box 104, 1004 Kobenhavn K (☎ 033-15 8045)

France
33 Rue de Miromesnil, 75008 Paris (☎ 1-47 42 03 36)

Germany
Untermainanlage 7, W 6000 Frankfurt Main 1 (☎ 069-23 64 92)

Italy
Via S Maria Segreta 6, 20123 Milano (☎ 02-8690541)

Netherlands
Leidsestraat 32, 1017 PB Amsterdam (☎ 020-22 31 01)

New Zealand
Dingwall Building, 87 Queen St, Auckland 1 (PO Box 279, ☎ 09-379 3708)

Northern Ireland
53 Castle St, Belfast BT1 1GH (☎ 071-493 3201)

Sweden
Box 5292, 102 46 Stockholm (☎ 08-662 8510)

UK
150 New Bond St, London W1Y 0AQ (☎ 071-493 3201)

USA
757 Third Ave, New York, NY 10017 (☎ 212-418 0800)

Tourist information for Northern Ireland is handled by the British Tourist Board, although you may also find offices of the Northern Ireland Tourist Board in some locations:

Canada
111 Avenue Rd, Suite 450, Toronto, Ontario M5R 3J8 (☎ 416-925 6368)

UK
11 Berkeley St, London W1X 5AD (☎ 071-493 0601)

USA
Suite 500, 276 5th Ave, New York, NY 10001 (☎ 212- 686 6250)

USEFUL ORGANISATIONS

The Union of Students in Ireland Travel (USIT) is the Irish youth and student travel association. Their London office is at London Student Travel (☎ 071-730 3402),

52 Grosvenor Gardens, London SW1W OAG. In the USA they can be found at the New York International AYH Hostel (☎ 212-663 5435), 895 Amsterdam Ave (at 103rd St), New York, NY 10025. USIT issue ISIC (International Student Identity Card) cards, and also organise cheap fares to Ireland for students.

For IR£7 full-time students can have a Travelsave Stamp affixed to their ISIC card. This gives a 50% discount on Irish Rail and Bus Éireann services. Enquire at the USIT offices in London or New York, or in Dublin (☎ 679 8833) at 19 Aston Quay. They have offices in most major cities in Ireland, including Belfast, Waterford, Cork and Galway.

BUSINESS HOURS & HOLIDAYS
Business Hours
Offices are open 9 am to 5 pm Monday to Friday, shops a little later. On Thursdays and/or Fridays shops stay open later. Many are also open on Saturdays or Sundays. In winter, tourist attractions are often open shorter hours, fewer days per week or may be shut completely.

Outside the cities, shops and businesses often close for one afternoon in the week. It varies from region to region. In small towns most shops are also likely to close for an hour at lunch time.

Pub Hours
In the Republic pubs are open, Monday to Saturday, from 10.30 am to 11.30 pm between June and September. For the rest of the year closing time is 11 pm. In Dublin, pubs close for a 'holy hour' which may be one or more hours in the afternoon. On Sunday the opening hours are 12.30 to 2 pm and 4 to 11 pm. The only days when pubs are definitely closed are Christmas Day and Good Friday.

In the North pubs open from 11.30 am to 11 pm, Monday to Saturday. On Sunday the hours are 12.30 to 2 pm and 7 to 10 pm but pubs in Protestant areas often stay closed all day.

Public Holidays
Public holidays in the Republic of Ireland (IR), Northern Ireland (NI) or both are:

New Year – 1 January
St Patrick's Day (IR) – 17 March
Good Friday
Easter Monday
May Holiday (IR) – 1 May
May Holiday (NI) – first Monday in May
June Holiday (IR) – first Monday in June
The 12th (NI) – 12 July (next day if 12 July is a Sunday)
August Holiday (IR) – first Monday in August
August Holiday (NI) – last Monday in August
October Holiday (IR) – last Monday in October
Christmas Day – 25 December
St Stephen's Day/Boxing Day – 26 December

The St Patrick's Day and St Stephen's Day/Boxing Day holidays are taken on the following Monday should they fall on a weekend.

In Northern Ireland the main thing to remember is that many tourist attractions are closed on Sunday mornings, rarely opening until around 2 pm, well after church finishing time.

Festivals & Events
January There are regular horse races at a number of tracks throughout the country, including Leopardstown in County Dublin and Naas in County Kildare. The international rugby season usually begins in January.

February In Dublin the International Film Festival begins at the end of the month and international rugby between Ireland and England takes place at Lansdown Park in Dublin, usually in the middle of the month. In Belfast there's a music festival.

March New Yorkers may well be disappointed at the celebrations for St Patrick's Day on 17 March. Dublin has a parade and smaller celebrations take place in the other cities but none of it compares with the razzmatazz in New York. It's a national holiday so shops and businesses close and the day passes off unostentatiously in the countryside, apart from the traditional wearing of a shamrock leaf in one's lapel.

In Dublin, March also sees the World Irish Dancing Championship take place.

April Two major sporting events: the Irish Grand National at Fairyhouse, County Meath, and the final of the Gaelic football league competition in Dublin.

May At the Royal Dublin Society showgrounds, the Spring Show features agricultural and farming pursuits. At Ennis in County Clare, the Fleadh Nua is a festival of traditional music and dance, while Cork has its own International Choral & Folk Dance Festival. At Bantry, in the same county, there's a Mussel Festival. In Belfast there's a marathon.

June In Dublin, 16 June is Bloomsday when Leopold Bloom's Joycean journey around the city is reenacted and various readings and dramatisations take place around the city. More bookish events can be found in Listowel in County Cork with its Writers' Week literary festival. Some 48 km (30 miles) from the capital the Irish Derby takes place at the Curragh. Up in Donegal, at Rathmullen, an international fishing festival takes place.

From June to the middle of August pilgrims leave from Pettigo in County Donegal for the boat trip to Lough Derg and the penitential Stations of the Cross. Across the border in Belleek there's a small Fiddle Stone festival while in Belfast there's a Jazz & Blues Festival.

July In the North July is the marching month and every Orangeman in the country hits the streets on the 'Glorious 12th', to celebrate the Protestant victory at the Battle of the Boyne. Because of the possibility of violence at this time the military presence leading up to the 12th is very heavy and security is extremely tight.

Fishing events get under way in Athlone and in Mayo, while on the last Sunday of the month there's a mass pilgrimage to the top

of Croagh Patrick. The Galway Arts Festival begins in late July.

August The second week sees the annual Dublin Horse Show at the Royal Dublin Society showgrounds, Ireland's answer to Wimbledon and Ascot when it comes to showing off one's social status. Horseracing takes place in Tralee in County Kerry, and for the last week of the month Tralee has the Rose of Tralee Festival. In the same county at Killorglin the ancient Puck Fair heralds unrestricted drinking for days and nights. Kilkenny has an Arts Week and Clifden in County Galway has the Connemara Pony Show.

In Ballycastle in County Antrim the Oul' Lammas Fair occurs over the last weekend of the month and attracts holidaymakers as well as enterprising traders.

The August Bank Holiday weekend (the first Monday in August and the Saturday and Sunday that precede it) is the time for Ireland's major annual rock festival known as Féile, at Thurles in County Tipperary.

September The All-Ireland Hurling and Football finals both take place in September. In Lisdoonvarna, County Clare, the Matchmaking Festival gets down to business. Cork has its Film Festival, Sligo its Arts Week, Waterford an International Festival of Light Opera and Dublin a Theatre Festival. Belfast has its own Folk Festival.

October An International Jazz Festival takes over the city of Cork, with special boat trains bringing audiences from Britain and elsewhere. The Dublin Theatre Festival takes place over two weeks in October. On the last Monday of the month Dublin has its marathon, while Ballinasloe in County Galway hosts the country's biggest cattle and horse fair. Kinsale in County Cork is home to Ireland's gourmet festival.

November In Wexford the Opera Festival is a prestigious event attracting audiences and participants from all parts of the world. In the

North the Belfast Festival takes place at Queen's University.

December Christmas is a quiet affair in the countryside though on 26 December the ancient practice of Wren Boys is reenacted, when groups of children dress up and expect money at the door after singing a few desultory hymns.

POST & TELECOMMUNICATIONS
Postal Services
Post offices in the South are open 8 am to 5.30 or 6 pm Monday to Saturday, smaller offices closing for lunch. Postcards cost 28p to EC countries, 38p outside Europe, while aerograms cost 45p. An air-mail letter to the US or Australia costs 52p. All mail to Britain and Europe goes by air so there is no need to use air-mail envelopes or stickers.

Post office hours in the North are from 9 am to 5.30 pm Monday to Friday and 9 am to 1 pm on Saturday. Postal rates are as in Britain – 22p for letters by 1st-class mail, 17p 2nd-class, and 37p for letters and postcards to the USA and Australia.

Mail to both the North and the Republic can be addressed to poste restante at post offices but is officially only held for two weeks. Writing 'hold for collection' on the envelope may have some effect.

Over 95% of letters within the country are delivered the next working day. To North America it's about 10 days, the UK and rest of Europe between three and five days and Australia between a week and 10 days.

Telephone
Old-fashioned pay phones where you rolled coins down ramps and pressed buttons mysteriously labelled A and B are disappearing; these days phones are modern electronic wonders, north or south. Telecom Éireann has spent over IR£1 billion on the system since 1984, acquiring one of the most up-to-date digital systems in the world, with 60% digital exchanges versus 40% in the UK. Phone cards, which save fishing for coins and give you a small discount, are worth having. International calls can be dialled directly from pay phones.

Calls from Ireland To call a UK number (except for Northern Ireland) from the South dial 0044 plus the area code (minus the 0) plus the number. Thus an 071 number in London would start 0044-71. To call elsewhere overseas dial 00 then the international code for that country (1 for the USA or Canada, 44 for Britain, 61 for Australia, 64 for New Zealand, 65 for Singapore, 852 for Hong Kong, etc) then the area code (dropping any leading 0) and then the number. The one variation is that to call Northern Ireland from Ireland you dial 08 and then the Northern Irish area code *without* dropping the leading 0. The international operator for enquiries or for making reverse charge calls is 114, or 10 for help with calls within Ireland and to Britain.

Calls from Northern Ireland From Northern Ireland dial 010 for international access followed by the country code. Dial 155 for the British Telecom international operator.

Call Costs In the South the standard rate for a five-minute local call is 20p. When making a long-distance phone call from a hotel room bear in mind that the cost will be at least doubled.

The cost of a three-minute direct-dialled international call from Ireland varies according to the time of day. Reduced rates are available after 6 pm and before 8 am; between midnight and 8 am and between 2 and 8 pm to Australia. Charges are approximately:

UK	IR£0.97–£1.05
France & Germany	IR£1.48–£IR1.83
North America	IR£2.52–IR£3.36
Australia	IR£5.16

Direct Home Calls Rather than placing reverse charge calls through the operator in Ireland you can dial direct to your home country operator and then reverse charges or charge the call to a local phone credit card.

To use the direct home service dial the following codes followed by the area code and number you want. Your home country operator will then come on the line before the call goes through:

Australia	1 800 5500 61 + number
New Zealand	1 800 5500 64 + number
USA – AT&T	1 800 5500 00 + number
USA – MCI	1 800 5510 01 + number
USA – Sprint	1 800 5520 01 + number

Pay Phones & Phonecards Callcards are available in 10, 20, 50 and 100 unit versions in the Republic of Ireland. Each unit gives you one local phone call. Cardphones are very useful for making international calls since you do not have to carry a sack of coins to the phonebox. Note that you cannot make international calls via the operator from a cardphone.

Fax & Telegrams
Faxes can be sent from post offices or other specialist offices. Phone the operator on 196 in the South to send international telegrams.

TIME
Ireland is on GMT (Greenwich Mean Time) or UTC, the same as London. Without making allowances for daylight-saving time changes, when it is noon in Dublin or London it is 8 pm in Singapore, 10 pm in Sydney or Melbourne, 7 am in New York and 3 am in Los Angeles or San Francisco.

Also as in Britain, clocks are advanced by one hour from mid-March to the end of October. During the summer months it stays light until very late at night, particularly on the west coast where you could still just about read by natural light at 11 pm. In the middle of November it is dark from 5 pm to 8 am.

ELECTRICITY
Electricity is 220 volts AC, 50 cycles, and plugs are usually flat three-pin, as in Britain. Apart from shavers, if you have a round two-pin plug bring with you a plastic converter that plugs into the three-pin plug.

Many bathrooms have a two-pin 110-120 volt AC source for shavers which is useful if you have any 110 volt gadgets.

WEIGHTS & MEASURES
As in Britain progress towards metrication in Ireland is slow and piecemeal. Food in shops is priced and weighed in metric; beer in pubs is still served in pints.

BOOKS & BOOKSHOPS
English may be an adopted language but the Irish truly have a way with it! A glance in almost any bookshop in Ireland will reveal huge Irish-interest sections: fiction, history, current events, and numerous local and regional guidebooks. Many larger cities have more than one good bookshop, Waterstone's and Eason's being familiar names, and many small towns will also have a small but well-stocked bookshop. Most, if not all, of the books below should be available in bookshops and libraries across Ireland. They are all paperback unless stated otherwise.

History & Politics
The three volumes that make up *The Green Flag* by Robert Kee (Penguin, London, 1989) offer a useful introduction although the emphasis is more on narrative than analysis. The focus of interest in Kee's books is the 19th and 20th centuries. For an introduction to earlier times try *The Course of Irish History* by Moody and Martin (Mercier Press, Cork, 1987) which has been reprinted many times.

A Concise History of Ireland by Máire & Conor Cruise O'Brien (Thames & Hudson, London, revised 1985) is a readable and comprehensively illustrated short history of Ireland. *Ireland – A History* by Robert Kee (Abacus, London, 1980) covers similar ground in a similar format in a book developed from a BBC/RTE TV series.

The classic study of the 1845-49 famine when some two million Irish emigrated to America or perished through lack of food is *The Great Hunger* by Cecil Woodham Smith (Hamilton, London, 1985). Liam O'Flaherty used the catastrophe as the basis for his novel *Famine* (Wolfhound Press, Dublin, 1988).

The Begrudger's Guide to Irish Politics by Breandán O'hEithir (Poolbeg Books, Dublin, 1986) is a semi-humorous account of the contemporary political scene.

The North

The problem with books about Northern Ireland's recent confused history is that they're in constant need of updating. Currently the most up-to-date book is also the most serious and far-reaching attempt to get to grips with Ulster's story. *A History of Ulster* (Blackstaff Press, Belfast, 1992) by Jonathan Bardon is a phone directory of a book which not only goes right back to prehistoric Ulster but also ticks off the Troubles, bomb blast by bomb blast, right up to 1992. Surprisingly it's not just thorough, it's also readable.

German academic Sabine Wichert, a Belfast resident since the early '70s, manages to bring an outsider's inside view to the the question in *Northern Ireland since 1945* (Longman, Harlow, 1991). Patrick Buckland's *A History of Northern Ireland* (Gill & Macmillan, Dublin, 1981) is concise but somewhat out of date. *The Troubles*, edited by Taylor Downing (Thames Mac-Donald, London, 1980) was written to accompany a TV series on the conflict but also suffers from being over 10 years old. J Bowyer-Bell's *The Troubles – A Generation of Violence* (Gill & MacMillan, Dublin, 1993) is a much more recent account. Gerry Adams, the President of Sinn Féin, gives his account of the Troubles in *The Politics of Irish Freedom* (Brandon Books, Dingle, 1986).

The Dispossessed (Picador, London, 1992) investigates the background and reality of poverty in Britain through the 1980s. Writer Robert Wilson and photographer Donovan Wylie are both Belfast born and the book concentrates on the story in London, Glasgow and Belfast.

Paisley by Ed Moloney and Andy Pollack (Poolbeg Books, Dublin, 1986) is a compelling account by two Irish journalists of the rise to power of the charismatic leader of the Democratic Unionist Party (not the Unionist Party) and the Free Presbyterian Church of Ulster (not the Presbyterian Church). If nothing else read the introduction with its astonishing Paisley speech.

Despatches from Belfast by Davic McKittrick (Blackstaff Press, Belfast, 1989), the Irish correspondent for the UK newspaper the *Independent* covers 1985-9 with well-informed articles from a liberal point of view.

Literature & Fiction

If you took all the Irish writers off the university reading lists for English Literature the degree courses could probably be shortened by a year! Jonathan Swift (1667-1745), William Congreve (1670-1729), George Farquhar (1678-1707), Laurence Sterne (1713-68), Oliver Goldsmith (1728-74), Sheridan (1751-1816), Oscar Wilde (1854-1900), George Bernard Shaw (1856-1950), W B Yeats (1856-1939), John Millington Synge (1871-1909), Sean O'Casey (1880-1964) and James Joyce (1882-1941) are just some of the more famous names born before 1900. A list for the 20th century would be just as prestigious.

Literary Dublin – a History by Herbert A Kenny (Gill & Macmillan, Dublin, 2nd edition 1991) traces the history of Dublin's rich literary culture.

James Joyce left Ireland as a young man for a life of exile, and although he was contemptuous of his country ('the pig that eats her own farrow'), his fiction is rooted in Irish life and culture. *Dubliners* (published in 1914 after 10 years of censorship tangles) is a collection of remarkable short stories, especially the final story *The Dead*, which John Huston turned into an equally memorable film. *Portrait of the Artist as a Young Man* (published in serial form from 1914) is a semi-autobiographical tale of a young man coming to realise his artistic vocation.

Ulysses (first published 1922) has such topographical realism that it has produced a spate of Dublin guides based on the events in the novel. See the Dublin chapter for suggestions of *Ulysses* walking guides. Although much has changed in 90 years there is still enough left to sustain a steady flow of Joyce admirers, bent on retracing the events of Bloomsday – 16 June 1904.

The poetry of W B Yeats ranks high in the literary canon. His *Love Poems*, edited by Norman Jeffares (Gill & Macmillan, Dublin, 1988) is probably the most accessible for anyone new to his writing.

Oliver St John Gogarty (1878-1957) carried a lifelong resentment over his appearance as Buck Mulligan in *Ulysses* but it didn't prevent him from presenting his views of Dublin in *As I Was Going Down Sackville Street* (published 1937) and other volumes of his memoirs. He was also a renowned wit.

A very funny post-Joyce novelist is Flann O'Brien, real name Brian O'Nuallain and second pseudonym Myles na Gopaleen, whose novels include *The Third Policeman*, *At Swim-Two-Birds* and *The Dalkey Archive* (Penguin, London).

The Informer (published 1925) by Liam O'Flaherty (1896-1984) was the classic book about the divided sympathies which plagued Ireland throughout its struggle for independence and the ensuing civil war. Edna O'Brien is a more recent novelist; her *The Country Girls* (1960) enjoyed the accolade of being banned.

Dublin schoolteacher Roddy Doyle made a big name for himself with his comic descriptions of north Dublin life; he won the Booker prize in 1993 with his *Paddy Clarke Ha Ha Ha*. Earlier, *The Commitments* was made into an internationally successful film. *The Snapper* and *The Van* (Penguin) also trace the trials and tribulations of the Rabbitt family.

Christy Brown's marvellous *Down all the Days* summed up Dublin's back street energy in a slightly earlier era with equal abandon. J P Donleavy's *The Ginger Man* was another high-energy excursion around Dublin, this time from the Trinity College perspective. It received the church's seal of approval by lingering on the Irish banned list for many years.

Dermot Bolger's *The Journey Home* (1990) would certainly have been banned in the old days, for this is modern Dublin at its darkest: political corruption, drugs, violence, unemployment and a pervading sense of hopelessness. John McGahern is another name amongst modern Irish writers, with titles like *The Barracks* (1963) and *Amongst Women* (1990) to his credit. Aidan Carl Mathews' work includes the novel *Muesli at Midnight*.

For a taste of modern Irish poetry try *Contemporary Irish Poetry* edited by Fallon and Mahon (Penguin, London, 1990). Seamus Heaney is there of course, and so are a host of other poets from both the North and the Republic. *A Rage for Order* edited by Frank Ormsby (Blackstaff Press, Belfast, 1992) is a vibrant collection of the poetry of the Northern Ireland crisis.

Tom Paulin writes memorable poetry about the North; try *The Strange Museum*. Other notable contemporary poets are Eavan Boland, Paul Muldoon and Derek Mahon.

A New Book of Dubliners edited by Ben Forkner (Methuen Paperbacks, London, 1988) is a fine collection of Dublin-related short stories, stretching from James Joyce through to stories from the 1980s and including works by Liam O'Flaherty, Samuel Beckett, Oliver St John Gogarty, Flann O'Brien, Sean O'Faolain, Benedict Kiely and others.

The Irish way with words applies just as strongly north of the border as south – in fact it's astonishing how many good writers a place as small as Northern Ireland manages to turn out. The Troubles feature in much of their writing.

Bernard MacLaverty's *Cal* (Penguin, London, 1983) traces a life where the choices are miserable and the consequences terrible and inevitable. *Cal* and McLaverty's other novel, *Lamb*, were both made into films. Those no-win political situations are also seen in Brian Moore's *Lies of Silence* (Vintage, London, 1990), which was shortlisted for the Booker Prize. Moore is a prolific writer; not all his books are about Ireland.

In Glenn Patterson's amusing first novel *Fat Lad* (Minerva, London, 1992) the political situation is a backdrop to a story which captures the feel of life in Belfast today. And the title? It's an Ulster children's mnemonic for learning the names of the six counties: Fermanagah-Armagh-Tyrone FAT Londonderry....

Robert McLiam Wilson's first novel was the award-winning *Ripley Bogle* (Picador, London, 1989) which follows 'the prince of the Pavements... the Parkbench King', a West Belfast tramp, through London, with flashbacks to his youth. The follow-up was *Manfred's Pain* (Picador, London, 1992).

Recently republished, after 20 years out of print, *Call My Brother Back* (Poolbeg Books, Dublin, 1939) by Michael McLaverty recounts growing up on Rathlin Island and the Falls Rd in the 1920s; much of the feel of his Belfast survives to this day. More recently, Jennifer Johnston's *The Old Jest* (Penguin, London, 1979) also goes back to Ireland between the wars, though here the protagonist is an Anglo-Irish girl growing up in the South at a time when change is about to sweep through the country, with a sense that the Anglo-Irish ascendancy is in its final days.

Visitors' & Residents' Accounts

To understand the Anglo-Irish read David Thomson's *Woodbrook* (Vintage Books, London, 1990). As a young man Thomson came to the north-west to act as tutor to an Anglo-Irish family and his book charts his gradual awakening to the reality around him.

The nature of life in the north has attracted writers to the region and compelled residents to write about it. *Titanic Town* (Mandarin, London, 1992) is subtitled *Memoirs of a Belfast Girlhood*, and Mary Costello manages to make growing up in the tough Andersonstown area of West Belfast funny and sad in equal measures. From Sinn Féin president Gerry Adams, *The Street* (Brandon Books, Dingle, 1992) is a collection of stories dealing with life in West Belfast where he grew up.

The Crack – A Belfast Year (Grafton, London, 1987) by Sally Belfrage is a reporter's accounts from a series of visits to Belfast in the 1980s.

In the mid-1970s Irish travel writer Dervla Murphy jumped on her faithful bicycle Roz, the same one she took to India in the 1960s, and rode off to explore Northern Ireland. The result was *A Place Apart* (Penguin, London, 1978), but so much has changed in the nearly 20 years since that visit that the book is rather dated.

More recently, American travel writer Paul Theroux included Northern Ireland on his round Britain itinerary for *Kingdom by the Sea* (Penguin, London, 1983). Travelling round most of Britain made the famously sour Theroux even more dyspeptic than usual but, surprisingly, he warmed towards the Ulster people. It's no surprise at all that P J O'Rourke gave Belfast a chapter in his book *Holidays in Hell* (Picador, London, 1988). Like many other visitors O'Rourke found Belfast altogether too tame for its reputation. Where are the appalling slums?

For cycling visitors Eric Newby's *Round Ireland in Low Gear* is another Newby classic of travel masochism complete with lousy weather, steep hills, high winds and predatory trucks.

Guidebooks

The *Irish Cycling Guide* by Brendan Walsh (Gill & Macmillan, Dublin, 1992) is a set of suggested tours with details of distances and types of road. Martin Ryle's book *By Bicycle in Ireland* has details of 22 routes.

The best local walking guides are the *New Irish Walk Guides* series from Gill & Macmillan (Dublin). They cover large areas, and at around IR£6 represent good value if you intend to do a lot of walking and climbing.

Irish High Crosses by Richardson & Scarry (Mercier Press, Cork, 1990) is an illustrated inventory and survey of some of the most typically Irish of all the monuments that stud the landscape. Much more recent, and unlikely to last nearly as long, are the colourful and often transient murals of the North reveal the opposing ideologies of the Republicans and the Loyalists; *Drawing

Support is a collection photographed by Bill Rolston (Beyond the Pale Publications, Belfast, 1992).

Tracing your Ancestors
The Irish Roots Guide by Tony McCarthy (Lilliput Press, Dublin, 1991) serves as a useful introduction. Other recent publications include *Tracing Your Irish Roots* by Christine Kinealy (Blackstaff Press, Belfast, 1990) and *Tracing Your Irish Ancestors: A Comprehensive Guide* by John Grenham (Gill & Macmillan, Dublin, 1992). All these publications, and other items of genealogical concern, may be obtained from the Genealogy Bookshop, 3 Nassau St, Dublin 2.

MAPS
There are numerous good quality maps of Ireland. The Michelin Map of Ireland No 405 (1:1,000,000) has most of the scenic roads very accurately highlighted in green. The four maps – North, South, East and West – that make up the Ordnance Survey Holiday Map series are useful if you want something more detailed than a whole Ireland map. Their scale is 1:250,000.

For greater detail the Ordnance Survey covers the whole island in 25 sheets with a 1:126,720 scale (half an inch to one mile). This series, however, is being replaced by a new series of 89 maps with a 1:50,000 scale (two cm to one km). The new maps are a pleasure to use and it always worth checking to see if the area you want is available in the new series.

Special maps for the Kerry Way and the Dingle Way are available from tourist offices, and at a pinch they will suffice. For the Ulster Way section maps are available from the Sports Council for Northern Ireland (House of Sport, Upper Malone Rd, Belfast BT9 5LA).

Tim Robinson of Folding Landscapes, Roundstone, County Galway, produces superbly detailed maps of the Burren, the Aran Islands and Connemara and has a detailed map as part of the hill walking guide guide to Connemara by Joss Lynam.

NEWS LETTER
Belfast Telegraph
Irish Independent
THE IRISH TIMES

MEDIA
Newspapers & Magazines
The Irish Republic has six national daily newspapers and five national Sunday newspapers. The daily *Irish Times* is a bastion of liberal opinion and good journalism and is often mentioned as being up there with the world's best newspapers. The *Irish Press* was founded by Eamon de Valera and for a long time was Republican in orientation and supportive of the Fianna Fáil party, although it has been less so in recent years. The biggest seller is the *Irish Independent* which tends to be lighter in content than the others, with more features and gossip. The *Cork Examiner* has a good journalistic reputation and the *Star* is the country's daily tabloid.

On the Sunday front, the *Sunday Tribune* has a liberal approach and claims to be good at investigating and breaking stories. The *Sunday Independent* and *Sunday Press* mirror their daily equivalents, and the biggest seller is the *Sunday World* with plenty of titillation. The *Sunday Business Post* concentrates on financial matters.

In the North you will find the *Belfast Telegraph* and the tabloid and staunchly Protestant *News Letter*. British papers and magazines are readily available in both the North and the South. They sell at a slightly higher price in the South than in Britain but still undercut the Irish newspapers.

Radio & TV
The Republic of Ireland has two state-controlled TV channels and three radio stations. The state-controlled TV channels are RTE 1 and Network 2. British BBC and indepen-

dent TV programmes can be picked up in many parts of the country and offer a welcome substitute for the often dreary Irish programming. In its defence, RTE isn't that bad by international standards. It may appear parochial but local topics are always of limited interest to outsiders.

A programme worth watching is *The Late Late Show*, the longest-running chat show in the world, hosted on Friday nights during the winter by Gay Byrne, Ireland's top media personality. The show has a good mix of celebrities and current affairs, and is often an interesting window into Irish life. Current affairs programmes such as *Tuesday File* and *Prime Time* are also worth a look. Watch out for Gaelic football and hurling matches on at weekends. Many hotels and pubs have satellite TV from the European Astra satellite.

Irish radio, AM or FM, varies in quality. Many of the morning programmes consist of phone-ins. RTE Radio One (88-90 FM or 567/729 MW) has a good mix of documentaries, music and talk shows. Broadcasters like Gay Byrne, Pat Kenny and Marion Finucane may give an insight into the country's foibles. RTE's 2FM (92-93 FM or 612/1278 MW) is the national pop music station and does what pop stations do. Mind you, it is a good forum for upcoming Irish rock talent and is where U2 got their first airing. The *Gerry Ryan Show* in the morning is worth listening to. Radio na Gaeltachta (92.5-96 FM or 540/828/963 MW) is the national Irish-language service.

Since recent broadcasting legislation, a host of regional radio stations have taken off, offering good local services. The best of them are LM FM in Counties Louth and Meath broadcasting on 95.8 FM, Radio Kerry on 97.6 FM and Clare FM on 96.4 FM. In Dublin 98 FM and FM 104 stations offer an unending diet of classic international rock and pop tunes. As with TV it is possible to tune into British BBC radio and independent channels, though the further west you go the weaker the signal.

In Northern Ireland, there are two TV stations – BBC NI and Ulster TV, which mix their own programming with input from their parent companies in the UK – BBC and ITV respectively.

Censorship

For many years books and films in Ireland suffered under an absurdly restrictive censorship code. The Censorship of Publications Act of 1929 became more farcical and silly as time went on. At one time Ireland was in the peculiar position of providing taxation advantages to encourage authors to live and work in the country and at the same time banning whatever they wrote. Even between 1960 and 1965, when censorship was definitely on the wane, nearly 2000 books were banned. Films banned in the 1960s included *Ulysses, Paddy* and *Of Human Bondage*, all of them made in Ireland!

The censors seem to have become much more liberal of late although Madonna's recent opus *Sex* was banned in Ireland – after it had completely sold out! *Basic Instinct*, the controversial 1992 Michael Douglas/Sharon Stone sex and death saga, was shown uncut in Ireland while even in the USA it had to have at least one cut.

HEALTH

Apart from cholesterol, Ireland poses no serious threats to health. The Catholic distaste for contraception does not prevent condoms being sold through pharmacies, if the pharmacist isn't personally opposed! Condoms are also available from vending machines in some pubs and nightclubs. The pill is only available on prescription.

Citizens of EC countries are eligible for medical care; other visitors should have medical insurance or be prepared to pay. The Eastern Health Board Dublin Area (☎ 71 9222) at 138 Thomas St, Dublin 8 has a Choice of Doctor Scheme which can advise you on a suitable doctor from 9 am to 5 pm, Monday to Friday. Your hotel or your embassy can also suggest a doctor.

WOMEN TRAVELLERS

Although women are in some ways second-class citizens in Ireland they're also

---

The Debate on Abortion

Over the last decade Ireland has been doing its best to tie itself into knots over the thorny issue of abortion.

Prior to 1983, therapeutic abortions were legal, and doctors could use their discretion as to whether or not a pregnancy was 'life-threatening' for the woman. Abortion for any other reason, including severe malformation or pregnancy due to rape, was and still is not permitted.

In 1983 the law was tightened and incorporated into the constitution, but in such woolly terms that things went on much as before, with one remarkable exception: women could no longer be given any information about seeking abortions abroad. English phone books were duly taken out of libraries, and women's magazines were impounded at the airports.

While the trips to Liverpool abortion clinics continued unabated, Ireland held the moral high ground of protecting the unborn child at any cost – until 1992, when parents whose 14-year-old daughter had allegedly been raped by her friend's father took her to England for an abortion. They contacted the Garda to ask if tissue from the foetus could be collected and used in the prosecution of the alleged rapist. They were then issued with an injunction ordering them to bring the girl back, foetus intact, or face prosecution. All hell broke loose. The matter went to the Supreme Court, which fudged the issue by saying that the girl could travel to the UK for an abortion since she was suicidal.

Anti-abortion campaigners demanded that the High Court prevent women leaving the country to seek abortions abroad. The prospect opened up of pregnancy tests at airports. Others interpreted the High Court ruling to mean that abortion was now legal in Ireland if the woman was suicidal.

A referendum took place on the matter in 1992, on the same day as the general election. The right to travel abroad for an abortion was supported by a clear majority. The option of making abortion available to all women in Ireland was not offered.

As Mary Carney TD pointed out on a TV discussion programme, while abortion is illegal in Ireland, an Irish woman is more likely to have an abortion than a woman in the Netherlands, where abortion is freely available. ∎

---

generally treated respectfully. In many ways Ireland is one of the safest and least harassing countries for women, with the obvious exception of the big towns and cities. Nevertheless the usual care should be taken; see the warning on hitch-hiking in the Getting Around chapter.

DANGERS & ANNOYANCES

Ireland is probably safer than most countries in Europe but the usual precautions should be observed. Dublin has its fair share of pickpockets and sneak thieves waiting to relieve the unwary of unwatched bags. See the Dublin chapter for more details on precautions in that city.

If you're travelling by car do not leave valuables on view inside when the car is parked. Dublin is particularly notorious for car break ins and foreign-registered cars and rent-a-cars are prime targets. Cyclists should always lock their bicycles securely and be cautious about leaving bags on the bike, particularly in larger towns or more touristy locations.

The police in the Republic are called by their Irish name of Garda Siochana, or just garda for one policeperson and gardaí (gardee) for more than one. In Northern Ireland the police are called the Royal Ulster Constabulary (RUC) and ☎ 999 is the emergency number in both the North and the South. After dialling ☎ 999 you should specify whether you want the police (gardaí), fire, ambulance or boat or coastal rescue.

Obviously there is a certain amount of danger in Northern Ireland but not to such an extent that should deter you from visiting the place. If you confine yourself to the Antrim coast you may well never see the British Army, but in Derry or South Armagh, on the other hand, it is impossible to escape their presence. Tourists will be treated with courtesy by the security forces, but you can expect to be asked for some form of identification at roadblocks and in other encounters. An English accent can be a help or a hindrance, depending on who you're dealing with.

Most Irish people have little experience of those with different coloured skin, and some prejudice – and curiosity – is inevitable, but it is most unlikely to reach the level of personal hostility that is so common in parts of Britain.

Gay life is simply not acknowledged in most parts of Ireland, although in 1993 it was decriminalised in the Republic for consenting adults over the age of 17. In Dublin and Cork there are openly gay communities, but in rural areas there's a conspiracy of silence and repression.

FILM & PHOTOGRAPHY

Ireland has enough spectacular seascapes, ancient ruins, picturesque villages and interesting faces to keep any photographer happy. But almost always it is the mood that makes the shot and Ireland is noted for its rapidly changing and unusual light. In bright sunlight, west coast beaches can look like the tropics, and then a couple of hours and a few clouds later, Arctic Norway. Try and be imaginative with monuments and Celtic crosses, get the sun behind or at the side of your subject, use fill flash, get low with a wide-angle lens and put some plants or other points of interest in the foreground.

The best times for pictures are early morning and late evening when the sunlight is low and warm. If you are keen and using slide film, the slower the film the better, eg Fuji Velvia 50 ASA or Ektachrome 64 or 100 ASA. Irish light can be very dull, so to capture the sombre atmosphere you may need faster film, eg 200 or 400 ASA, and a small tripod will be useful. In good weather a polariser is terrific for cutting out haze and giving punchy primary green fields and blue skies with cotton-puff clouds. A plastic bag is handy to stop your camera getting wet.

Film & Processing

There are plenty of camera shops in the cities and bigger towns but in smaller towns and villages it is the chemists or pharmacies that stock film and arrange for processing. They will usually have Fuji or Kodak print film. Slide film is usually Fujichrome or Ektachrome, but don't depend on them having any in stock. Kodachrome is becoming increasingly scarce and has to be sent to France for processing. Chemists and many of the smaller camera shops are expensive so stock up beforehand.

In Dublin you can buy very reasonably priced film at LSL Photolabs (☎ 01-781078) at 25 Lennox St, Dublin 8, or at Quirke Lynch (☎ 01-964666) 41 Lower Rathmines Rd. Most towns and cities have good quality one-hour processing shops. Developing and printing a 24-exposure print film typically costs around IR£7 for one-hour service or IR£4 to IR£5 for slower turnaround. Slide processing costs about IR£5 a roll and takes a few days, though Quirke Lynch and the Film Bank (☎ 01-606082) at 102 Lower Baggot St have a same-day service.

Photographing People

You can't generalise about how Irish people will react to having their photographs taken. As always being courteous and having a chat beforehand will make things a lot easier for the photographer.

WORK

With unemployment reaching 20% in the South and well over 10% in the North this is not a good country for casual employment, although there is a great deal of seasonal work in the tourist industry. Ireland is a member of the EC (European Community) so citizens of any other EC country can work in Ireland.

If you have an Irish parent or grandparent, it is fairly easy to obtain Irish citizenship without necessarily renouncing your own nationality, and this opens the door to employment throughout the EC. Obtaining citizenship is not an overnight procedure, so enquire about the process at an Irish embassy or consulate in your own country.

ACTIVITIES

Ireland is a great place for doing things and

the Tourist Board puts out a wide selection of Information Sheets covering everything from surfing (great surf along the west coast) to scuba diving, with hang-gliding, bird-watching, fishing, ancestor tracing, horse riding, cycling, sailing and canoeing along the way.

Walking

Walking is particularly popular although you must come prepared for wet weather. The Tourist Board have free information sheets on popular long-distance walks like the Wicklow Way, Kerry Way and others, but if you are planning more than one day's walking it is worth investing in one of the route maps available. The Wicklow Way is 132 km (83 miles) long and was the first long-distance path to be properly established with route maps and trail markers.

County Kerry has two major walks: the Kerry Way is the longest, taking up to nine days in all but it easy to start and end anywhere along the way. The Dingle Way is shorter and less demanding. The Ulster Way is rightly considered a strenuous walk and attracts more experienced hikers. See the guidebook section under Books & Bookshops for details of walking guides.

Cycling

See the Bicycles section under Getting Around for details on bicycle touring in Ireland, the Tours section under Getting There & Away for details of cycling tours and the Books & Bookshop section for cycling literature.

Fishing

The Republic of Ireland is renowned for its fishing and many visitors come to Ireland for no other reason. On private stretches of rivers a permit is usually required and the average price is IR£10 a day. In addition a state national licence is required for salmon and sea trout fishing. This costs IR£25 annually or IR£10 for three weeks and can be purchased from a local tackle shop or direct from the Central Fisheries Board (☎ 01-379206), Balngowan House, Mobhi Boreen,

Glasnevin, Dublin 9. The Board also sells an inexpensive *Angling in Ireland* brochure that sets out what can be caught and where. It is not necessary to have any licence for brown trout, rainbow trout or coarse fish (coarse fishing refers to freshwater species other than the salmon and trout family). However, a system of certificates is being introduced for trout and coarse fishing and the latest details on this are best obtained from a local tackle shop.

In the North a rod licence is required and this is obtainable from the Foyle Fisheries Commission (☎ 0504-42100), 8 Victoria Rd, Derry BT47 2AB, for the Foyle area and the Fisheries Conservancy Board (☎ 0762-334666), 1 Mahon Rd, Portadown, Craigavon, County Armagh, for all other regions (£10 for 15 days). In addition a permit is required from the owner and this is usually the Department of Agriculture, Fisheries Division (☎ 0232-63939), Stormont, Belfast BT4 3PW who charge £3.50 a day or £10 for 15 days.

Golf

There are about 200 golf courses ranging from illustrious and expensive ones at Killarney and Portmarnock near Dublin to more modest places like the one at Castletownbere on the Beara Peninsula. In County Cork green fees average about IR£8 but the top-notch places will charge more than three times this. Women, incidentally, can play but are not usually allowed to become full members of most golf clubs in the South. The North has over 50 golf courses and fees are about the same as in the South.

Scuba Diving

Ireland has some of the best scuba diving in Europe, almost entirely off the west coast. Popular diving centres include Lavelle's on Valentia Island, County Kerry; Kilkee Diving Centre, County Clare; Clare Island Diving Centre based at O'Grady's Hotel on Clare Island, County Mayo; and Scubadive West based at Glassilaun Beach near Letterfrack in County Galway.

Oceantec Diving ((☎ 01-280 1083) in Dun Laoghaire, County Dublin, is a five-star PADI centre with a dive shop and school. They can arrange dive vacations on the west coast.

HIGHLIGHTS
Scenery, Beaches & Coastline
The scenery is one of Ireland's major attractions, whether it's those soft green fields, awesome cliffs tumbling into a ferocious Atlantic or rocky and barren areas in the far west. Highlights include the beautiful scenery around the Ring of Kerry and the Dingle Peninsula, the barren stretches of the Burren, the rocky Aran Islands and the beautiful lakeland areas south and north.

Favourite stretches of Ireland's 3200 km (2000 miles) of coastline include the wildly beautiful Cliffs of Moher, the Connemara and Donegal coasts and the wonderful Antrim Coast Road of Northern Ireland. There are some fine beaches (and marginally warmer water) around the south-east coast, and some great surfing around the west and north-west coasts.

The EC Blue Flag flies over the cleanest and safest beaches of Ireland. If the beach is not a Blue Flag one it is best to enquire locally before venturing out for a swim.

Museums, Castles & Houses
Trinity College Library with the ancient 'Book of Kells' is on every visitor's must-see list, but Dublin also has the fine National Museum and National Gallery. Belfast has an excellent museum and the extensive Ulster Folk Museum just outside the city.

Ireland is littered with castles and forts of various types and in various stages of ruination. The Stone Age forts on the Aran Islands are of particular interest but there are other ancient ring forts all over Ireland. Castles are numerous and prime examples are Dublin Castle, Charles Fort at Kinsale and Kilkenny Castle, not forgetting Blarney Castle with its famous Stone!

The Anglo-Irish aristocracy left a selection of fine stately homes, many of them now open to the public like Castletown House, Malahide House, Westport House, Bantry House and Mount Stewart, and the beautiful gardens at Powerscourt.

Religious Sites
Stone rings, portal tombs or dolmens and passage graves are reminders of an earlier pre-Christian Ireland. The massive passage grave at Newgrange is the most impressive relic of that time. Early Christian churches, many well over 1000 years old, are scattered throughout Ireland, and ruined monastic sites, many of them with round towers, are also numerous. Glendalough, Mellifont Abbey, Grey Abbey, Inch Abbey and Jerpoint Abbey are particularly interesting monastic sites. The rock-top complex at Cashel is one of Ireland's major tourist attractions, and the beehive huts built by monks on Skellig Michael, off the coast of Kerry, are well worth visiting.

Islands
'Like whales, like castles, like sleeping giants – the islands of Ireland are ranged along the horizon in a host of mysterious shapes.' So goes the tourist board brochure – but, yes, there are all sorts and shapes of islands, inhabited and uninhabited, some of them easily accessible and others requiring the private hire of a boat.

The Aran Islands in County Galway and Achill Island in County Mayo are the most touristy, but it is not difficult to find more isolated ones. The Skelligs have already been mentioned, and their wildlife is fascinating. The Blaskets, off the Dingle Peninsula in County Kerry, are glorious on a fine day and are worth seeing now, before the houses that were inhabited up until 1953 are restored and become part of yet another interpretative centre. Tory Island, off the Donegal coast, is a wild place and is the surprising home of a group of local artists. County Cork has a number of accessible islands, of which Clear Island is famous for its birdlife and scenery and nearby Sherkin Island has sandy and safe beaches.

ACCOMMODATION

The Bord Fáilte's annual *Guest Accommodation* book costs IR£4 and has an awesome list of B&Bs, hotels, camp sites and other accommodation. It far from exhausts the possibilities, however, as there are also a great many places which are not 'tourist-office approved'. This does not necessarily mean they are in any way inferior to the approved places. The Northern Ireland Tourist Board publishes its own *Where to Stay* book (£2.95) which covers the same ground.

If you're travelling on a tight budget, the numerous hostels offer the cheapest accommodation to be found and are also great centres for meeting fellow travellers and exchanging information. In summer they can be heavily booked but so is everything else. Bord Fáilte offices will book accommodation for a fee of IR£1 in their locality, IR£2 in another town. All this really involves is phoning a place on their list; but in high summer, when it may take numerous phone calls to find a free room, that can be a pound well spent. The Northern Ireland Tourist Board provides a similar service.

Camping

Camp sites are not as common as on the continent but there are still plenty of them around Ireland. Some hostels also have camping space and usually offer the use of the kitchen and shower facilities, which often makes them better value than the main camp sites. At commercial sites, costs are typically IR£3 to IR£7 for a tent and many have coin-operated showers. Many sites have different rates depending on the type of tent you have (a two-person tent as opposed to a family tent being the usual distinction) and whether you arrive by bike or car.

Free camping is generally possible as long as you ask permission from the farmer. Around the touristy parts of Kerry and Cork, farmers have wised up to asking for a pound or two, but it should never be too difficult to find one who will let you camp for nothing.

Hostels

An Óige, the Irish Youth Hostel Association, has nearly 50 hostels scattered round the country and there are another half dozen in Northern Ireland. Youth hostels are open to members of the International Youth Hostel Association, members of An Óige (annual membership IR£7.50) or to any overseas visitor for an additional nightly charge of IR£1.25. Pay the additional charge six times (total IR£7.50) and you become an International Youth Hostel Federation member. To use a hostel you must have or rent a sheet sleeping bag. Nightly costs vary with the time of year but in July-August are usually IR£4.50 to IR£5.90 except for the more expensive Dublin hostel. Rates are cheaper if you're under 18. Prices quoted are all high season and for those over 18.

Over the last few years An Óige hostels have changed a lot for the better. They now operate a fax-a-bed-ahead facility that books accommodation in advance. Bookings can be made by credit card at many of the larger hostels and some hostels have family and smaller rooms. And these days you can take a car to a youth hostel. Membership enquiries should go to An Óige (☎ 01-304555; fax 01-305808), 61 Mountjoy St South, Dublin 7, or to the Youth Hostel Association of Northern Ireland (☎ 0232-324733; fax 0232-439699), 56 Bradbury Place, Belfast.

Nowhere else in Europe have independent hostels popped up like they have in Ireland. Independent Hostel Owners is a co-operative group who put out a booklet listing nearly 100 hostels all over Ireland. This is available for 40p from the Information Office at Dooey Hostel, Glencolumbkille, County Donegal (☎ 073-30130) or from bookshops.

There are no membership requirements and no curfew. Another 20 or so are members of the Irish Budget Hostels group which carries the additional cachet of being Bord Fáilte approved. There are still more independent hostels which are members of neither group. Independent hostels are usually a bit cheaper than the An Óige ones. They emphasise their easy-going ambience and lack of rules, and competition from the independents has forced the official hostels to rethink their rule books in recent years.

B&Bs

If you're not staying in hostels you are probably staying in a B&B. It sometimes seems every other house in Ireland is a B&B and you'll stumble upon them in the most unusual and remote locations.

The typical cost is IR£10 to IR£14 a night, and you rarely pay less or more than that, except in the big towns where some luxurious B&Bs can cost IR£25 or more a night. They usually do not have private bathrooms but where they do the cost is just a pound or two higher. At some places costs are higher for a single room. Most B&Bs are very small, just two to four rooms, so in summer they can quickly fill up. With so many to try there's bound to be someone with a spare room, however.

Breakfast at a B&B is almost inevitably cereal followed by 'a fry', which means fried eggs, bacon and sausages. A week of B&B breakfasts exceeds every known international guideline for cholesterol intake, but if you decline fried food you're left with cereal and toast. If your bloodstream can take the pressure, you'll have eaten enough food to last you till dinnertime, but it's a shame more places don't offer alternatives like fruit or the delicious variety of Irish breads and scones, which are widely available. In Northern Ireland you may meet the awesome 'Ulster Fry', which adds fried bread, blood sausage, tomatoes and assorted other fried foods to the basic version.

Hotels

Hotels are hotels, although in Ireland payment for a night's stay usually includes breakfast. It is possible to negotiate better deals than the published rates, especially out of season. Ask if any discounts are given and try to think of a reason why you in particular merit one. Out of the main holiday season hotels often have special deals for certain days of the week, but this is usually quite flexible and can often be extended to whatever days you want.

Other Possibilities

Guesthouses are often just like larger and more expensive B&Bs, but sometimes they are more like small hotels with a restaurant, lounge room and telephone and TV in the rooms. Farmhouse accommodation usually means it's a B&B on a farm; they are sometimes excellent value and you may get a chance to see how the farm works. Country houses are rural B&Bs, usually costing a little more and in a rather grander than usual house.

Self-catering accommodation is often on a weekly basis and usually means an apartment or house where you look after yourself. The rates vary from from one region and season to another. A smart cottage around Kinsale in August could be around IR£400 a week, sleeping six people, while the equivalent in Longford in April could be less than IR£70.

FOOD

It's frequently said that Irish cooking doesn't match up to the ingredients and traditional Irish cooking tends to imitate English – ie cook it until it's dead, dead, dead. Fortunately the Irish seem to be doing a better job than the English in kicking that habit and you can generally eat quite well. Of course if you want meat or fish cooked until it's dried and shrivelled and vegetables turned to mush, there are plenty of places that can still perform the feat.

Irish meals are usually meat-based. Beef, lamb and pork chops are the old reliables. A really traditional meal is bacon and cabbage, a delicious combination it makes too, and should be tried at least once.

The curious Irish aversion to seafood probably has, like so many other Irish curiosities, a religious connection. Ireland has always been a meat-eating country but it's also been a strictly, even bizarrely, Catholic one. Until very recently the Catholic Friday fasting restrictions were strictly adhered to, so fish became something you were forced to have on Friday and, like long-suffering schoolchildren, if you're forced to eat it you don't like it. As a result Ireland is an island with a remarkably small fishing industry, and fish is still in the process of finding a place on the Irish dining table. Try it – the trout and salmon are delicious.

Fast food is well established, from traditional fish & chips to more recent arrivals like burgers, pizzas, kebabs and tacos. Pubs are often good places to eat, particularly at lunch time when a bowl of the soup of the day (usually vegetable) and some good bread can make a fine and economical meal.

There are some superb vegetarian places and *The Vegetarian Guide to Ireland* (East Community Co-Op, Main St, Scariff, County Clare) costs IR£1.50 and lists about 50 vegetarian restaurants and B&Bs. Most of them are mentioned in this book and frequently they turn out to be run by British or other European people who have settled in Ireland. Hotels and restaurants often feature a vegetarian dish on their menus but you'll soon tire of unimaginative vegetable lasagne. At the more expensive restaurants it is always a good idea to inform them in advance that you want a vegetarian meal. If you are vegetarian then staying at a B&B can be a bad deal. The best excuse for the high prices charged by most B&Bs is the huge breakfast they serve. The vegetarian alternative will usually be just cornflakes and toast, but the charge will be the same. See the B&B section for information on the famous Irish breakfast.

Irish bread has a wonderful reputation and indeed it can be very good, but unfortunately there's a tendency to fall back on the infamous white-sliced bread, *pan* in Irish. B&Bs are often guilty of this crime. Do try some soda bread, made from flour and buttermilk.

Irish scones are a delight; tea and scones is a great snack at any time of day. Even pubs will often offer tea and scones.

It is common for Irish people to eat their main meal of the day at lunch time, and every town will have at least one hotel or restaurant, offering special three-course meals for around IR£5 or less. A similar meal in the evening will be at least double the cost.

There are several specialist food and restaurant guides to Ireland. Bord Fáilte has its own publication of recommended restaurants but the restaurants concerned simply pay for their entry and submit their own writeup. The Northern Ireland Tourist Board has its own *Where to Eat* book for £1.95 and covers everything from the very expensive to the local Chinese takeaway.

Traditional foods include:

Bacon & Cabbage
: a stew consisting simply of its two named ingredients: bacon and cabbage

Barm Brack
: an Irish cake-like bread

Boxtys
: rather like a filled pancake

Dublin Coddle
: a semi-thick stew made with sausages, bacon, onions and potatoes

Guinness Cake
: a popular fruitcake flavoured with Guinness beer

Irish Stew
: this quintessential Irish dish is a stew of mutton, potatoes and onions, flavoured with parsley and thyme and simmered slowly

Soda Bread
: Belfast is probably the place in Ireland for bread at its best, but soda bread in particular, white or brown, is found throughout the country

DRINKS

In Ireland a drink means a beer – either lager or stout. Stout usually means Guinness, the famous black beer of Dublin, although in Cork it can mean a Murphy's or a Beamish. If you don't develop a taste for stout (and you should at least try) a wide variety of lager beers are available including Irish Harp or Smithwicks and many locally brewed 'imports' like Budweiser, Fosters or Heinekin. Simply asking for a Guinness or a Harp will get you a pint (570 ml, IR£1.55 to IR£2

Whiskey & Beer

Apart from imbibing large quantities of alcoholic refreshments, the Irish have also been responsible for some important developments in the field. They were pioneers in the development of distilling whiskey (distilled three times and spelt with an 'e' as opposed to the twice-distilled Scotch whisky). The Irish adopted the dark British beer known as porter (since it was particularly popular with the porters who worked around Covent Garden market in London). Promoted by the Guinness family, it soon gained an enduring stranglehold on the Irish taste for beer. In neighbouring Britain, Foster's and other modern lager beers have taken a slice of the market from the traditional British bitter, but in Ireland Guinness still reigns unchallenged.

In an Irish pub, talk is just as important an ingredient as the beer though the talk will often turn to the perfect Guinness. Proximity to the St James's Gate Brewery is one requirement for perfection, for although a Guinness in Kuala Lumpur can still be a fine thing, Guinness is at its best in Ireland. The perfect Guinness also requires expertise in its 'pulling'. If you want a perfect pint you do not simply hold the glass under the tap and slosh it in. The angle at which the glass is held, the point at which the pouring is halted, the time that then passes while the beer settles and the head subsides and the precision with which the final top-up is completed, are all crucial in ensuring satisfaction. ∎

in a pub). If you want a half pint (80p to IR£1) ask for a 'glass' or a 'half'. Children are allowed in pubs until 7 or 8 pm at night and in smaller towns this restriction is treated with customary Irish flexibility.

Irish coffee is something you will see marketed in touristy hotels and restaurants. Sometimes the impression is given that the drink is traditional. Nothing could be further from the truth; it's a modern phenomenon and was considered a bit of a novelty when served to the first trans-Atlantic passengers arriving at Shannon. It's a mixture of coffee and whiskey served in a heated glass and topped with cream.

When ordering a whiskey Irish people never ask for a Scotch (though Scottish whisky is available); they use the brand name of an Irish whiskey instead: Paddy's, Powers, Bushmills or whatever. It may seem dear but the Irish measure is generous, by law.

Nonalcoholic drinks in pubs and hotels are restricted to the predictable brand-named fizzy ones, and to judge by the prices they charge you might think they were deliberately discouraging customers from drinking them. Coffee is available in nearly all pubs, from 40p to 70p usually, but don't expect a smile if you order one at 10.30 pm on a busy night.

ENTERTAINMENT

A Guinness to go with the pub music is the most popular form of entertainment in Ireland. If it's suggested that you visit a particular pub for its 'good crack', don't think you've just found the local dope dealer. 'Crack' is Irish for a good time – convivial company, sparkling conversation and rousing music.

A 'medieval banquet' finds its way on to many tourist itineraries, with the one at Bunratty Castle in County Clare probably being the best known. They tend to be expensive and the food is often disappointing. During the summer local festivals and concerts are a common event and it is always worth calling in at the local tourist office to check on what's available and coming up.

Theatre is popular, especially in the summer when a number of touring groups travel around the country. Dublin, particularly, is renowned for its excellent theatres and there is always a broad range of plays and shows on. Most famous is the Abbey Theatre, founded by W B Yeats, Lady Gregory and other writers and artists behind the Anglo-Irish literary revival. The Gate Theatre is a much smaller company but has been putting on a remarkable variety of new and unusual work in recent years. The Gaiety and Olympia Theatres are beautifully preserved old showhouses which host a mix of plays, pantomimes and shows.

THINGS TO BUY
Clothing

All over the country, but especially in County Galway, it is possible to purchase Aran sweaters. The name derives from the islands where they were first made by the women as working garments for their husbands. Handknitted ones, not unnaturally, are going to cost a lot more than machine-made ones. County Donegal is famous for its tweeds and there are a couple of good stores in Donegal Town with a large selection. It can be purchased in lengths or finished as jackets, skirts or caps. Tweed is also produced in County Wicklow and County Dublin. Handwoven shawls and woollen blankets make lovely presents.

Irish linen is of high quality and comes in the form of everything from blouses to handkerchiefs. The Irish produce some high quality outdoor activities gear – they have plenty of experience with wet weather. Irish lace is another fine product, at its best in Limerick, or Carrickmacross in County Monaghan.

Crystal

Waterford crystal is world famous and is obtainable all over Ireland, although the company has recently reduced its workforce in Waterford and has moved some business overseas. Smaller manufacturers of crystal produce fine work and at prices that are far more attractive. In the North, Tyrone Crystal is based outside Dungannon and the factory can be toured free of charge, with no obligation to purchase from the showroom.

Pottery

All over the country there are small potteries turning out unusual and very attractive work. The village of Belleek in Country Fermanagh straddles the Northern Ireland border with Donegal and produces delicate bone china. In the South the area around Dingle in County Kerry has superb pottery. Enniscorthy in County Wexford, and Kilkenny and Thomastown in County Kilkenny, also stand out in this regard. Generally, throughout west Cork and Kerry there are countless small workshops that open in the summer with their stocks of pottery and other craftwork.

Food & Drink

Irish whiskey is not just spelt differently; it also has its own distinctive taste. The big names are Paddy, Jameson, Powers and Bushmills, and they are not always readily available in other parts of the world. Two Irish liqueurs are very well established: Irish Mist and Bailey's Irish Cream.

Over the last few years some excellent hand-made cheeses have become available and are worth considering as a gift to take home. Two from west Cork are particularly worth mentioning: Gubbeen is a soft cheese from Schull while Mileens is more spicy. Tipperary has its own Cashel Blue and Cooleeny cheeses.

Other Items

Other possibilities include jewellery, especially claddagh rings, enamel work and baskets woven of willow or rush. Connemara marble is a natural green stone found in the west of Ireland and is often cunningly fashioned into Celtic designs.

Getting There & Away

AIR

Dublin is Ireland's major international airport, although all flights to or from North America have to operate via Shannon. Aer Lingus is the Irish national airline with international connections to other countries in Europe and to the USA. Ryanair is the next largest Irish airline, with routes to Europe and the USA.

There are charter flights between Belfast and overseas centres, but most Belfast connections are to England and Scotland.

Students should contact USIT, the Irish student and youth travel organisation, for cheap air fares to Ireland – see under Useful Organisations in the Facts for the Visitor chapter.

✽ Aer Lingus

RYANAIR

To/From the UK

Aer Lingus is the main operator between the UK and the Republic of Ireland. British Airways only flies to Belfast in Northern Ireland; they do not fly to Dublin or anywhere else in the South. Dublin is linked by a variety of airlines to several cities in the UK.

The Republic of Ireland There are flights between Dublin and all the major London airports. Aer Lingus and British Midland fly from Heathrow, Aer Lingus fly from Gatwick, Ryanair fly from Luton and Stansted; Connections are generally frequent; in the summer Aer Lingus may have 15 Heathrow-Dublin services daily and British Midland another seven or eight.

The regular one-way economy fare from London to Dublin is £70, but advance purchase fares are available offering round-trip tickets for as low as £60 to £70. These should be booked well in advance as seats are often limited.

Heathrow can be reached by airport bus or by the underground. There are regular train services to Gatwick from Victoria Station, and there are also regular trains between Stansted and Liverpool St Station.

UK addresses and London phone numbers are:

Aer Lingus (☎ 081 899 4747), 228 Regent St, London W1
British Airways (☎ 081-897 4000), travel shops throughout London and Britain
British Midland (☎ 071-589 5599), PO Box 60, Donington Hall, Castle Donington, Derby DE7 2SB
Ryanair (☎ 071-435 7101), 235-37 Finchley Rd, London NW3 6LS

Other places in the British Isles with flights to Dublin are:

Birmingham:	Aer Lingus, British Midland
Blackpool:	Manx
Bristol:	Aer Lingus
Cardiff:	Manx
East Midlands:	Aer Lingus
Edinburgh:	Aer Lingus
Glasgow:	Aer Lingus
Isle of Man:	Manx
Jersey:	Manx, Aer Lingus
Leeds/Bradford:	Aer Lingus
Liverpool:	Manx, Ryanair
Luton:	Ryanair
Manchester:	Aer Lingus
Newcastle:	Aer Lingus, Gill Air

Fares between Manchester and Dublin are similar to London-Dublin fares but other connections can be much more expensive.

Other cities in Ireland with air connections from the UK include Cork, Shannon and Galway.

Northern Ireland Belfast has a regular British Airways shuttle service from London Heathrow. Costs on the shuttle range from as low as £63 for a one-way standby or £117 for an advance purchase return to as high as £102 for a regular one-way. There's a £76.50 student/youth fare. British Midland Airways offer similar fares, but Britannia Airways (Belfast International) and Manx Airways (Belfast City) fly from Luton to Belfast for just £45. Luton Airport is only 45 minutes north of London. There are also connections between Belfast and other centres including flights to and from the convenient Belfast city airport.

Belfast has two airports: Belfast International Airport at Aldergrove is 30 km north of the city, while Belfast City Airport is virtually in the city centre.

To/From North America

There are no direct flights to Ireland from Canada, and all flights from the USA must put down in Shannon on their way to Dublin. Because competition on flights to London is so much fiercer it will generally be cheaper to fly to London first. From Ireland to the USA, Virgin Airlines via London is often the cheapest option.

Aer Lingus connect Dublin (and Shannon) with New York and Boston. Their New York office (☎ 212-557 1110 and 1-800-223 6537) is at 122 East 42nd St, New York. In Canada they can be contacted in Montreal (☎ 514-866 6565) and Toronto (☎ 416-362 6565) although they do not actually fly to Canada. The only other North American operator with direct connections to Ireland is Delta Airlines, who operate Atlanta-Shannon-Dublin, linking into their huge US network.

During the summer high season the round trip between New York and Dublin with Aer Lingus costs US$750 midweek or US$780 at weekends. Usually there are advance purchase fares offered early in the year which allows you to fly from New York to Dublin for around US$600 return. In the low season, discount return fares from New York to London will be in the US$350-450 range, in the high season US$550-650. From the west coast fares to London will cost from around US$150 more. Check the Sunday travel sections of papers like the *New York Times, Los Angeles Times, Chicago Tribune* or *San Francisco Chronicle-Examiner* for the latest fares. The *Toronto Globe & Mail*, the *Toronto Star* or the *Vancouver Province* will have similar details from Canada. Offices of Council Travel or STA in the USA or Travel CUTS are good sources of reliable discounted tickets.

To/From Australia & New Zealand

Excursion or Apex fares from Australia or New Zealand to Britain can have a return flight to Dublin tagged on at no extra cost. Return fares from Australia vary from

---

Shannon Airport

Shannon Airport is a topic of considerable controversy in Ireland. In the early days of trans-Atlantic aviation, flying between the US and Europe was impossible without a refuelling stop, so Shannon thrived as the first airport on the eastern side of the Atlantic. In the jet age Shannon is simply an anachronism, and the only flights that *have* to stop in Shannon are Aeroflot's Moscow-Havana services. At some point in Irish history, however, it was decided that all flights between Ireland and North America must – by law – put down in Shannon. Since it's only about 200 km from Shannon to Dublin, this is clearly uneconomic, and Aer Lingus loses millions every year on this unnecessary stop. Apart from Delta, all the US and Canadian operators have simply opted not to fly to Ireland at all.

A furious argument rages over whether airlines should be allowed to fly directly to Dublin, but so far local interests (and politicians) have sustained the Shannon stopover remains obligatory. This may soon change. Aer Lingus has been losing money by the container-load for some years, and the government has finally decided the time to face reality has arrived. Dramatic staff cuts are one suggestions; cutting out the Shannon stopover is another. ∎

Landscapes

Pubs

around A$1600 (low season) to A$2500 (high season) but there are often short-term special deals available. STA and Flight Centres International are good sources of reliable discounted tickets in Australia or New Zealand. The cheapest fares from New Zealand will probably take the eastbound route via the USA but a Round-the-World ticket may well be cheaper than a return. Air Lingus have an office in Sydney at Level 5, 34-36 Carrington St, Sydney 2000 (☎ 02-299 6211).

To/From Europe

Dublin is connected with major centres in Europe. From Paris, fares to Dublin range from 755 to 915 FF one-way, 1205 to 1730 FF return. Other places in Europe with connections to Dublin are:

Amsterdam, Netherlands:	Aer Lingus
Barcelona, Spain:	Iberia
Brussels, Belgium:	Aer Lingus, Sabena
Cologne, Germany:	Lufthansa
Copenhagen, Denmark:	Aer Lingus, SAS
Dusseldorf, Germany:	Aer Lingus
Frankfurt, Germany:	Aer Lingus, Lufthansa
Lisbon, Portugal:	TAP
Madrid, Spain:	Aer Lingus, Iberia
Malaga, Spain:	Viva Air
Milan, Italy:	Aer Lingus, Alitalia
Moscow, Russia:	Aeroflot
Munich, Germany:	Lufthansa, Ryanair
Paris, France:	Aer Lingus, Air France
Rome, Italy:	Aer Lingus, Alitalia
Zurich, Switzerland:	Aer Lingus

SEA

There is a great variety of services from France and Britain to Ireland using modern car ferries. There are often special deals, return fares and other money-savers worth investigating.

Want to travel free? On some routes the cost for a car includes up to four or five passengers at no additional cost. If you can hitch a ride in a less than full car, it costs the driver nothing extra.

To/From the UK

The Britrail Seapass is an extension of a normal Britrail Pass and permits a return sea crossing to Ireland on top of unlimited use of British Rail services. This pass can only be purchased outside the UK. The Inter-Rail pass gives a reduction on services from Holyhead or Fishguard in Wales to Dun Laoghaire or Rosslare in Ireland. B&I ferries offer a 50% discount to travellers with a Travelsave stamp in their ISIC card (see Facts for the Visitor).

There are services from eight ports in England, Scotland and Wales (and from the Isle of Man) to six ports in Ireland. The shipping lines are as follows:

Stena Sealink (☎ 0233-647022), Charter House, Ashford, Kent TN24 8EZ, for services from Holyhead, Fishguard and Stranraer.
Isle of Man Steam Packet (☎ 0624-661661), Imperial Buildings, Douglas, Isle of Man, for services from Douglas.
B&I Line (☎ 071-499 5744), 150 New Bond St, London W1Y 0AQ, for services from Holyhead and Pembroke.
Swansea Cork Ferries (☎ 0792-456116), Ferryport, Kings Dock, Swansea SA1 BRU, for services from Swansea.
Belfast Ferries (☎ 051-922 6234), Brocklebank Dock, Bootle, Merseyside L20 1DB, for services from Liverpool.
Norse Irish Ferries (☎ 051-944 1010) for services from Liverpool to Belfast.
P&O (☎ 05812-276) for services from Cairnryan to Larne.
SeaCat (☎ 081-554 7061) for services from Stranraer to Belfast by catamaran.

There are some interesting possibilities for those who are also touring the UK. Figures quoted are one-way fares for a single adult, for two adults with a car and for four adults with a car.

Swansea to Cork The 10-hour crossing costs £26/179/179 at peak times but it operates only from March to November.

Fishguard & Pembroke to Rosslare This popular short crossing takes 3½ hours (Fishguard) or 4½ hours (Pembroke) and costs as much as £23/180/180 on peak season weekends; at other times of year the cost can drop as low as £17/75/75.

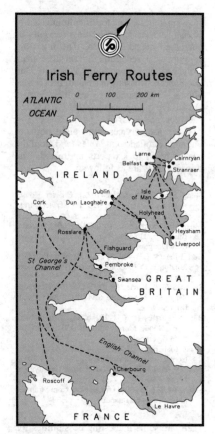

Irish Ferry Routes

ATLANTIC OCEAN

0   100   200 km

Larne
Cairnryan
Belfast
Stranraer

I R E L A N D

Dublin
Isle of Man
Dun Laoghaire
Cork
Holyhead
Rosslare
Heysham
Liverpool
Fishguard
St George's Channel
Pembroke
Swansea   G R E A T
B R I T A I N
English Channel
Cherbourg
Roscoff
Le Havre

F R A N C E

and driver, £30 for each additional passenger, including dinner, breakfast and cabin accommodation. There are also the Isle of Man Steam Packet services from Liverpool and Heysham via Douglas (Isle of Man). A small car costs £69 in the peak season, passengers cost £36 each.

Stranraer to Belfast The glamorous new SeaCat service uses an Australian-made high-speed catamaran to race across in just 1½ hours at a cost of £19/126/141 at peak times.

Stranraer & Cairnryan to Larne There are as many as 15 sailings daily on this route which takes about 2½ hours and costs £18/132/132 at peak times, down to as low as £16/100/100 at other times.

To/From France
Le Havre to Rosslare takes 21 hours and costs FF595/2000/3190. Cherbourg to Rosslare is slightly faster at 17 hours but the cost is the same. In summer there are ferries from Le Havre to Cork taking 22 hours, again at the same fare. A new service between Cherbourg and Cork is being introduced in 1993. These services are all operated by Irish Ferries and can be used by Eurail pass holders. In France contact Transports et Voyages (☎ 1-42 66 90 90), 8 Rue Auber, 75009 Paris. Inter-Rail passes also give reductions on these routes.

There are also Roscoff to Cork services in summer, taking 14 hours at a cost of F465/1800/2730. The operator is Brittany Ferries.

ROAD & SEA
Bus Éireann and National Express operate Supabus services direct from London and other UK centres to Dublin, Belfast and other cities. For details in London contact the Coach Travel Centre (☎ 071-730 0202) or the Irish Tourist Board (☎ 071-493 3201). Slattery's (☎ 071-4821604/485-1438) is an Irish bus company with routes from London, Liverpool, Manchester and north Wales to Dublin, Galway, Tralee, Ennis and Listowel.

Holyhead to Dublin & Dun Laoghaire The crossing takes 3½ hours and costs £23/180/180 at peak season, down to £17/94/94 in the off season. In mid-1993 Stena Sealink introduced their Sea Lynx car ferry service between Holyhead and Dublin. Using Australian high-speed catamarans like the Northern Ireland SeaCats, the crossing takes less than two hours.

Liverpool & Heysham to Belfast The Norse Irish overnight service is not heavily promoted but it's easy to get to Liverpool from London. The trip costs £100 for a car

London to Dublin takes about 13 hours and costs £42 one-way or £60 return during the summer and Christmas peak periods.

Citylinking/Ulsterbus (☎ 071-636 9373), Victoria Coach Station, 164 Buckingham Palace Rd, London SW1W 0SH, operates services between London, Birmingham, Manchester, Stranraer and Belfast daily. The one-way London to Belfast fare is £38 (students £28) and the trip takes 13 hours.

LEAVING IRELAND

There is no airport departure tax from Dublin or Belfast.

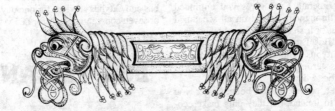

Getting Around

On the map, travelling around Ireland looks very simple. The distances are short and there's a network of roads and railways. In practice there are a few problems. In Ireland from A to B is never a straight line and there are always a great many intriguing diversions to make. Public transport is often expensive (particularly train services), infrequent or both. Plus public transport simply does not reach many interesting places. Having your own transport can be a major advantage.

DISCOUNT DEALS

Eurail passes are valid for bus and train travel in the Republic of Ireland but not in Northern Ireland.

Inter-Rail passes offer free train travel within the Republic of Ireland but only give a 34% reduction in Northern Ireland.

For IR£7 full-time students can have a Travelsave Stamp affixed to their ISIC card. This gives a 50% discount on Irish Rail and Bus Éireann services. See under Useful Organisations in the Facts for the Visitor chapter.

There is a variety of unlimited travel tickets for buses and trains, in the North and south. Rambler Tickets are available for bus-only or train-only travel in the Republic of Ireland. They cost IR£26 (three days), IR£60 (eight days) or IR£90 (15 days). A bus-and-rail version costs IR£78 (eight days) or IR£115 (15 days). Children under 16 pay half fare, and your bicycle can come along for the ride for an additional IR£22.

An Emerald Card gives you unlimited travel throughout Ireland on all scheduled services of Irish Rail, Northern Ireland Railways, Bus Éireann, Dublinbus, Ulsterbus and Citybus. The card costs IR£105 (or pounds sterling equivalent) for eight days or £180 for 15 days.

These passes can be bought after you arrive in Ireland, but they only make eco-

nomic sense if you're planning to travel around Ireland at the speed of light.

AIR

Ireland is too small for flying to be necessary, but there are flights between Dublin and Cork, Galway, Knock, Shannon, Sligo, Waterford and other centres. Most journeys within Ireland take between 30 and 40 minutes. The two main companies operating within the country, as well as handling international flights, are Aer Lingus and Ryanair. Aer Lingus have offices in Dublin, Cork, Belfast, Limerick and Shannon. Ryanair's head office is in Dublin, with ticket offices at Dublin, Cork, Shannon, Waterford, Galway, Knock and Kerry airports.

One useful air service is the short flight across to the Aran Islands. See the Galway chapter for details.

BUS

Bus Éireann is the Republic's bus line, with services all over the South and to the North. Fares are not much more than one-third the regular railway fares, and special deals are often available such as cheaper midweek return tickets. Bear in mind that the winter bus schedule is often drastically reduced and many routes simply disappear after September. The national timetable only costs 50p, but it doesn't include the fares. Details of unlimited-travel Rambler Tickets are given in the Discount Deals section.

Ulsterbus is the service in the North. An Ulsterbus Freedom of Northern Ireland Ticket gives you unlimited travel on Ulsterbus and Citybus services for one day for £9 or seven consecutive days for £25.

Private buses sometimes compete with Bus Éireann, and sometimes run where the national buses are irregular or absent. The larger ones will usually carry bikes free but always check in advance. Some of the private companies are properly licensed and all passengers are insured, but if this is going to worry you then ask beforehand.

Sample bus fares and travelling times are:

Dublin–Cork
  IR£12, 4 hours 40 minutes
Dublin–Limerick
  IR£10, 3 hours
Cork–Limerick
  IR£9, 2 hours
Killarney–Cork
  IR£8, 2 hours
Derry–Belfast
  £5.30, 1 hour 40 minutes
Derry–Cork
  £17, 11 hours
Derry–Galway
  £14, 6 hours 30 minutes
Limerick–Killarney
  IR£11, 2 hours 25 minutes
Limerick–Rosslare
  IR–13, 4 hours
Limerick–Donegal
  IR£16, 6 hours
Galway–Limerick
  IR£9.30, 2 hours 25 minutes

Local country buses can work out quite expensive, and services are usually infrequent. From Bantry in south-west Cork, for example, there is only one bus a week running the 16-mile journey to the last village on the Sheeps Head Peninsula, and the half-hour journey costs over IR£6. The private buses in County Donegal are a notable exception: Feda O'Donnell buses, for example, charge IR£4 for any journey within the county.

TRAIN

Iarnród Éireann, the Irish railway system, operates trains on routes which fan out from Dublin. Distances are short in Ireland; the longest trip you can make by train from Dublin is just over four hours to Tralee. Regular fares from Dublin include Belfast IR£13.50, Cork IR£31.50 and Galway IR£24. As with buses, special fares are often available and a midweek return ticket is often not much more than the single fare. Travelling by train on a single ticket is expensive, and it's worth considering how to use a return ticket. First-class tickets cost IR£4 to IR£7 more than the standard fare for a single journey. Ordinary seats can be reserved for IR£1. If you're under 26 you can get a Faircard for IR£8 which gives you a 50% discount on regular fares.

Northern Ireland Railways has three routes from Belfast, one of them linking with the system in the South.

CAR & MOTORBIKE

As in the UK driving is on the left. Safety belts must be worn by the driver and front-seat passengers. Motorcyclists and their passengers must wear helmets. Minor roads may sometimes be potholed and will often be very narrow but the traffic is rarely heavy except as you go through popular tourist towns.

Speed limits in the North and South are generally the same as in Britain: 70 mph (112 kph) on motorways, 60 mph (96 kph) on other roads and 30 mph (48 kph) or as signposted in towns. These limits tend to be treated with some disdain in the South.

The Irish can't seem to make up their minds on metrication. In the Republic speed limits are in miles per hour, distance signs appear in km and miles, and most car speed-

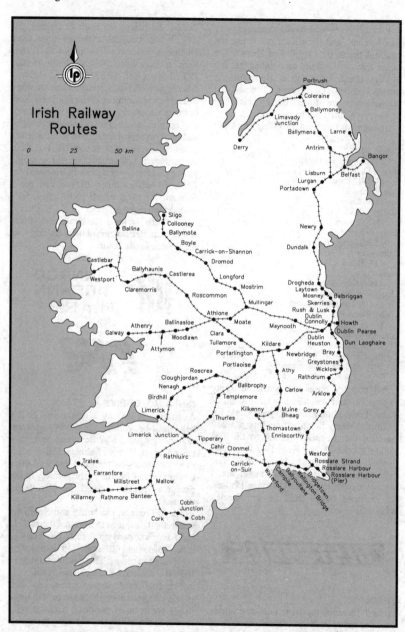

Irish Railway Routes

0   25   50 km

ometers are still imperial rather than metric. There used to be a useful distinction between the green signposts that gave distances in km as opposed to the older white signs that used miles, but now there are new white signs using km as well! In the North, speed limits and other laws are as in Britain.

There are parking meters in Dublin and a handful of other cities but usually parking is regulated by disk parking (you have a disk which rotates to display the time you park your car) or 'pay and display' tickets. It is often loosely enforced in the South. Never leave valuables unattended in your car in Dublin, and see the Dublin chapter for further car parking warnings.

In the North, beware of Control Zones where your car absolutely must not be left unattended – you may come back to find that it's been blown up. Double yellow lines by the roadside mean no parking at any time, and single yellow lines warn of restrictions. Red, white and blue kerbstones mean you're in a Protestant area; green, white and orange mean it's Catholic!

Petrol is 15% cheaper in the North. Unleaded petrol is available throughout the North and South. The Automobile Association (AA) have offices in Belfast (☎ 0232-328924), (Dublin ☎ 01-779481) and Cork (☎ 021-276922). The AA breakdown number in the Republic is ☎ 1800-667788; in the North ☎ 0800-887766.

Rental

Car rental in Ireland is expensive and in high season it's wise to book ahead. Off season some companies simply discount all rates by about 25%, and there are often special deals. Some smaller companies make an extra daily charge if you go across the border, North or South.

Typical weekly high-season rental rates with insurance and unlimited distance in the Republic of Ireland are IR£225 for a small car (Ford Fiesta), IR£260 for a medium-sized car (Ford Escort) and IR£320 for a larger car (Ford Sierra). In the North similar cars would cost about 10% less.

Avis, Budget, Hertz, Thrifty and the major local operators, Murray's Europcar and Dan Dooley, are the big rental companies. There are many smaller and local operators.

BICYCLE

Many visitors explore Ireland by bicycle. Although distances are relatively short, the most interesting areas can be hilly and the weather is often wet. Despite these drawbacks it's a great place for bicycle touring and facilities are good.

You can either bring your bike with you or rent in Ireland. Typical rental costs are IR£7 to IR£10 a day or IR£30 to IR£35 a week. Bags and other equipment can also be rented. Rent-a-Bike has eight offices around the country and offers one-way rentals between its outlets for an extra IR£5. The head office of Rent-a-Bike (☎ 01-725399) is at 58 Lower Gardiner St, Dublin 1. Raleigh's Rent-a-Bike have agencies throughout the country, North and South. Contact them at Raleigh Ireland (☎ 01-626 1333), Raleigh House, Kylemore Rd, Dublin 10. There are also many local independent outlets.

Bicycles can be transported by bus on some routes for IR£4. By train the cost is typically IR£6.

There are numerous tourist office publications on cycling plus a number of books and guides on the subject. See the Books & Bookshops section. See the Tours section for details of cycling tours around Ireland.

HITCHING

While we don't recommend hitching – it's never entirely safe in any country, and the local maniac may not carry an identifying badge – hitching in Ireland is generally easy. The major exceptions are in heavily touristed areas where the competition from other hitchers is severe and the cars are usually full to the brim with families. There are usually large numbers of Irish hitch-hikers on the road.

The usual hitching rules apply. Carry cardboard and a marker pen so you can make a sign showing where you're going. Try to look like a visitor and put your backpack out on view, ideally with a flag on it. Making yourself an obvious tourist is especially important in the North.

Women hitching alone should be extremely careful – if in doubt, don't. Many local women hitch alone without serious problems, but a tourist is likely to be more at risk. *Sea Legs: Hitch-hiking the Coast of Ireland Alone* by Rosita Boland (New Island Books) tells the tale of an Irishwoman's solo (yes, the Irish are always doing things against the rules) exploration of Ireland by thumb.

BOAT

There are many boat services to outlying islands and across rivers. Some of the river services make interesting little short cuts, particularly for cyclists. Cruises on the Shannon and on the old canals are popular and there are a variety of trips on lakes and loughs.

If you ask at the tourist offices you will not always get the full information on boats because they won't recommend, or sometimes even mention, operators who don't fulfil all their regulations. The various boats to the Skellig Islands, for instance, do not exist as far as official tourist literature is concerned, and if you ask about visiting Skellig Michael you will be directed to the Skellig Experience boat trip which doesn't actually land on the island. Details of unofficial boat trips are given under the relevant sections.

LOCAL TRANSPORT

There are comprehensive local bus networks in Dublin, Belfast and some other larger towns. The DART (Dublin Area Rapid Transport) line in Dublin and the service from Belfast to Bangor are the only local railway lines. Taxis in Ireland tend to be expensive, but in Belfast and Derry there are share-taxi services operating rather like buses.

TOURS
General Tours

In the US there are a number of companies offering whirlwind coach tours of Ireland. American Express Vacations (☎ 800-241 1700) have 10 and 12-day packages and can be contacted at Box 5014, Atlanta, GA 30302. Similar deals can be found with TWA Getaway Vacations at 28 South 6th St, Philadelphia, PA 19106. From the UK CIE Tours International (☎ 071-629 0564) at Ireland House, 150-151 New Bond St, London, WIY 9FE do a one-week tour plus a 10-day tour that includes the North. More expensive tours are operated by Abercrombie & Kent (☎ 800-323 7308), and include accommodation in castles and country houses.

Cycling Tours

Irish Cycling Safaris (☎ 01-978440), 7 Dartry Park, Dublin 6, organise tours for groups of cyclists in the south-west, the south-east and Connemara, with bikes, guides, a van that carries luggage, and B&B accommodation.

Walking Tours

Irish Wilderness Experience (☎ 064-329992), 50 Woodlawn Park, Killarney, offers hiking tours in the south-west. British Coastal Trails (☎ 619 1211), 150 Carob Way, Coronado, CA 92118, USA, include Ireland in their brochure of walking tours. For details of hiking tours in the North along the Ulster Way contact the Ulster Rambling Federation (☎ 02656-63360), 5 Rowan Rd, Ballymoney, County Antrim.

Republic
of
Ireland

The Republic of Ireland

HISTORY

The Irish Free State, as it was known until 1949, was established after the signing in December 1921 of the Anglo-Irish Treaty, between the British government and an Irish delegation led by Michael Collins. Eamon de Valera had been elected president of the new republic in August, and he remained in Dublin during negotiations. He was not consulted before signing, and he was outraged when the delegates returned with what he and many other republicans regarded as a betrayal of the IRA's principles.

The Treaty was ratified in the *Dáil* – the Irish parliament – in January 1922, and in June the country's first general election resulted in victory for the pro-Treaty forces. Fighting broke out two weeks later.

Amazingly, the Civil War was primarily about the oath of allegiance to the crown, rather than the exclusion of the six counties from the Irish Free State. Of the 400 or more pages of Dáil records on the Treaty debate, only seven deal with the issue of Ulster. The rest focus on the oath and the crown.

Collins was ambushed and shot dead in Cork by anti-Treaty forces, and de Valera was imprisoned by the new Free State government, under its new prime minister William Cosgrave, which went so far as to execute 77 of its former comrades. The Civil War ground to an exhausted halt in 1923.

After boycotting the Dáil for a number of years, de Valera founded a new party called Fianna Fáil (Warriors of Ireland) which won nearly half the seats in the 1927 election. De Valera and the other new TDs managed within weeks to persuade themselves to go through the formality of taking the oath which had been the cause of so much bloodshed. Fianna Fáil won a majority in the 1932 election, and remained in power for 16 years. De Valera introduced a new constitution in 1937 doing away with the oath and claiming sovereignty over the six counties of the North. In 1938 the UK renounced its right to use certain Irish ports for military purposes, which it had been granted under the Treaty. The South was therefore able to remain neutral in WW II.

In 1948 Fianna Fáil lost the general election to Fine Gael – the direct descendants of the first Free State government – in coalition with the new republican Clann an Poblachta. The new government declared the Free State to be a republic at last. Ireland left the British Commonwealth in 1949.

GOVERNMENT

The Republic has a parliamentary system of government loosely based on the British model. The lower house is known as the Dáil (pronounced 'doyle') and the prime minister is the *taoiseach* (pronounced 'teashock'). The Dáil has 166 elected members and sits in Leinster House on Dublin's Kildare St. MPs are known as TDs (*teachta Dála*).

The principal political parties are Fianna Fáil and Fine Gael, although the Labour Party has been making great strides in recent years and currently forms part of the government in coalition with Fianna Fáil. The upper house is the Senate or *Seanad* and senators are nominated by the taoiseach or elected by university graduates and councillors from around the country. The Senate's functions are limited; senators debate on and pass legislation framed in the Dáil, but many critics claim it is merely a happy hunting ground for failed TDs.

The constitutional head of state is the president, who is elected by popular vote for a seven-year term, but has little real power. The popular current incumbent, Mary Robinson, has however wielded considerable informal influence on the government's social policies, contributing to a shift in attitudes away from the traditionally conservative positions on issues such as divorce and abortion.

The Republic's electoral system is proportional representation, a complex but fair system where voters mark the electoral candidates in order of preference. As first-preference votes are counted and candidates are elected, the voters' second and third choices are passed on to the various other candidates.

Founded by Eamon de Valera and other notables, Fianna Fáil have been the driving force in Irish politics since the early years of the state. Fianna Fáil have almost always won the greatest number of seats in general elections, and have usually been either in government or barely out of it. Fianna Fáil has always been a catch-all party, claiming to be the voice of the rural populace, urban workers and business community in turn with no apparent difficulty. Many of Ireland's most notable leaders have come from the party's ranks, including Eamon de Valera, Sean Lemass, Jack Lynch, and more recently the colourful and wily Charlie Haughey. The current party leader and taoiseach is Albert Reynolds. Fianna Fáil has in the past usually taken an extremely conservative line on social matters, particularly when it came to divorce, abortion and contraception.

Fine Gael's image has been clean cut, worthy, middle-class and university-educated.

Labour have been on the fringes of power for most of their existence but have shared in various coalition governments with Fine Gael. Recently the Labour Party has moved to occupy the middle ground and attracts support from all classes of voters. The party now sits in government with Fianna Fáil.

A few years ago there was a split in Fianna Fáil and the result was the formation of the small Progressive Democrat party led by Dessie O'Malley, which went into coalition with Fianna Fáil to form a government not long afterwards. The only other party of consequence is the left-wing Democratic Left.

Coalition has been a feature of most recent governments in the Republic, as the once mighty Fianna Fáil has found itself less and less able to muster the parliamentary majorities it used to command.

ECONOMY
While the Republic of Ireland is often regarded as a basically agricultural country, there has been much light industrial investment since the 1970s, and the majority of people today work in manufacturing or service industries. Big-spending governments in the 1970s and 1980s left a huge national debt which the present government is still having to cope with. However, since 1987 spending has been brought under control, and the debt is now at a sustainable level.

Many of the Republic's key economic indicators would suggest that the economy is in good shape. Exports continue to reach record levels and completely outstrip imports. In 1992 the Republic had a trade surplus of $3.5 billion; the UK was the main trading partner followed by the EC and the USA. The trade surplus for the Republic as a percentage of GDP is the largest in the developed world, a not inconsiderable achievement. It also means that Ireland's small open economy is heavily dependent on the state of the world economy. Inflation is currently low, running at around 3%; and GDP grew at an average of 5% for the last six years. This was among the highest growth rates in the world at a time when many of the world's richest countries were suffering. Over the last 10 years the Republic has to some extent reduced its massive dependence on the UK economy. The Republic's economy has largely managed to avoid the economic downturn currently being endured by that of the UK.

The Irish government has encouraged educational concentration on computers and software, and Irish firms have made imaginative use of new openings in the field. A computer user on the east coast of the USA, making an early morning phone call to a California software support system, may actually find themselves talking to a software specialist in ireland. It's cheaper to bounce calls back over the Atlantic than to have people on call in Silicon Valley in the wee hours of the morning.

But despite what seems like a lot of good

news, the Republic still has enormous economic problems, principally unemployment. Over 300,000 people are unemployed, representing a massive 20% of the workforce. This situation and the incredible costs of social welfare and unemployment payments are a problem that looks set to continue for some time yet.

To make matters worse, emigration to the UK and the USA has ceased to be an effective safety valve, as these countries' economies have also been going through tough times. Ireland's unemployment problems almost certainly cannot be solved domestically and are dependent on an international recovery, especially in the UK. Taxes are high in the Republic, and petrol, drink, tobacco, cars and luxury items are particularly expensive. Tourism is enormously important, and Ireland now attracts visitors from all over Western Europe as well as from the English-speaking nations.

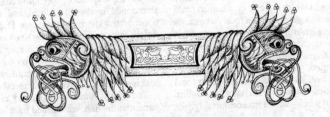

Dublin

Ireland's capital and its largest and most cosmopolitan city, Dublin is a city of great contrasts. Prosperous Georgian squares can quickly give way to areas where any sign of elegance has long since faded into decay. There's little modern architecture of any note. Dublin is a curious and colourful place, an easy city to like and a fine introduction to Ireland.

Since Ireland finally achieved independence in 1921, Dublin has had a new role as the capital of the country. It's still one of the smallest European Community (EC) capitals, and it's a quiet and slow-moving place. However, it's also a place with soul. The city's literary history seems to bump against you at every corner and the pubs are open to all comers. An evening with a succession of pints of Guinness, that noble black brew, is as much a part of the Dublin experience as the Georgian streets and the fine old buildings.

It's not only the pubs which are easily accessible. Dublin is a city on a human scale so it's easy to get around on foot. Accommodation is plentiful and varied, ranging from cheap and cheerful backpacker hostels to elegant five-star hotels. The food is surprisingly varied, with dishes from every corner of the world as well as down-to-earth local specialities such as Irish stew or Dublin coddle. It's a city which fits comfortably, like

a warm old coat; it may not always be fashionable, but it's always a pleasure to put on.

HISTORY

Dublin officially celebrated its millennium in 1988 but there were settlements here long before 988 AD. The first early Celtic habitation was on the banks of the River Liffey, and the city's Irish name, Baile Átha Cliath, 'the Town of the Hurdle Ford', comes from an ancient river crossing that can still be pinpointed today. St Patrick's Cathedral is said to be built on the site of a well used by Ireland's patron saint for early conversions in the 5th century.

It was not until the Vikings turned up that Dublin became a permanent fixture. By the 9th century, raids from the north had become a fact of Irish life, but some of the fierce Danes chose to stay rather than simply rape, pillage and depart. They intermarried with the Irish and established a vigorous trading port at the point where the River Poddle joined the Liffey in a black pool, in Irish a *dubh linn*. Today there's little trace of the Poddle, which has been channelled underground and flows under St Patrick's Cathedral to dribble into the Liffey by the Capel St (or Grattan) Bridge.

Norman and then early English Dublin was still centred around the black pool which gave the city its name. The boom years came with the 18th century, the period of the Protestant Ascendancy when for a time London was the only larger city in the British Isles. As the city expanded, the nouveaux riches abandoned medieval Dublin and moved north across the river to a new Dublin of stately squares surrounded by fine Georgian mansions. The planning of this magnificent Georgian Dublin was assisted by the establishment in 1757 of the Commission for Making Wide & Convenient Streets!

The city's slums soon spread north in pursuit of the rich, who turned back south to new homes on Merrion Square, Fitzwilliam Square and St Stephen's Green. When James Fitzgerald, the Earl of Kildare, commenced construction in 1745 of Leinster House, his magnificent mansion south of the Liffey, he was mocked for this foolish move away from the centre and into the wilds. 'Where I go society will follow,' he confidently predicted and he was soon proved right. Today Leinster House is used as the Irish Parliament building and it is right in the centre of modern Dublin.

The Georgian boom years of the 18th century were followed by more trouble and unrest, and the Act of Union in 1800, ending the separate Irish Parliament, spelt the end of Dublin's century of dramatic growth. Dublin entered the 20th century a downtrodden and dispirited place.

The Easter Rising of 1916 caused considerable damage to parts of central Dublin, particularly along O'Connell St where the GPO was gutted. The struggle between British forces and the IRA led to more damage to Dublin including the burning of the Custom House in 1921. A year later Ireland was independent but had tumbled into the Civil War which inflicted still more damage on the city, including the burning of the Four Courts in 1922 and a further bout of destruction for O'Connell St.

Peace finally came to Ireland but Dublin was exhausted – a shadow of its Georgian self. Today however Ireland's decline has bottomed out and Ireland's new role in the European Community holds prospects of better times to come. The city's expansion has continued south to Ballsbridge, Dun Laoghaire and beyond.

ORIENTATION

Greater Dublin sprawls around the arc of Dublin Bay, bounded to the north by the hills at Howth and to the south by the Dalkey headland.

North of the River Liffey the important streets for visitors are O'Connell St, the major shopping thoroughfare, and Gardiner St, with many B&Bs. Many of the hostels are located in this area. The main bus station or Busáras and one of the two main railway stations are near the southern end of Gardiner St, which becomes very run down as it continues north. Immediately south of the river is the intriguing old Temple Bar area and the expanse of Trinity College. Nassau St along the southern edge of the campus and pedestrianised Grafton St are the main shopping streets south of the river.

The post codes for central Dublin are Dublin 1 immediately north of the river and Dublin 2 immediately south. The posh Ballsbridge area south-east of the centre is Dublin 4.

Finding Addresses

Finding addresses in Dublin can be complicated by the tendency for street names to change every few blocks and for streets to be subdivided into upper and lower or north and south parts. It doesn't seem to matter if you put the definer in front of or behind the name – thus you can have Lower Baggot St or Baggot St Lower, South Anne St or Anne St South. Street numbering often runs up one side of a street and down the other, rather than a more logical system of having odd numbers on one side and even on the other.

INFORMATION
Tourist Information

The Dublin Tourism and Bord Fáilte offices offer more or less identical services. If you arrive by air or sea, you will find tourist offices at the airport (☎ 844 5387) and on the waterfront at Dun Laoghaire (☎ 280 6984).

In the city the Dublin Tourism office (☎ 874 7733) is at 14 O'Connell St Upper. This office is open from 8.30 am to 8 pm Monday to Saturday and 10.30 am to 2 pm on Sunday in the summer months, but it can get very crowded, with long queues for accommodation bookings and information. The head office of the Irish Tourist Board (☎ 676 5871) at Baggot St Bridge has an information desk and though it is less conveniently located – well to the south of the city

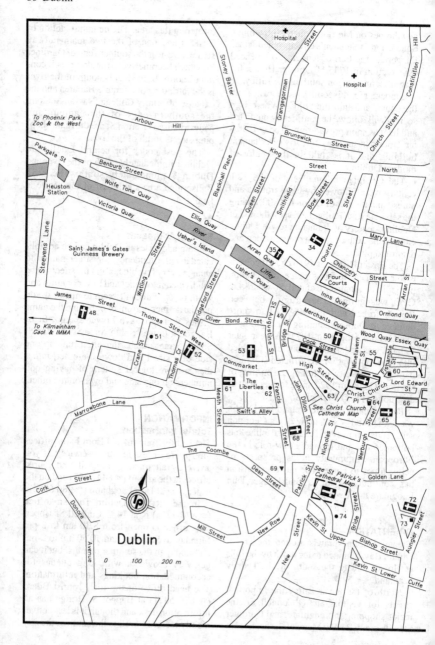

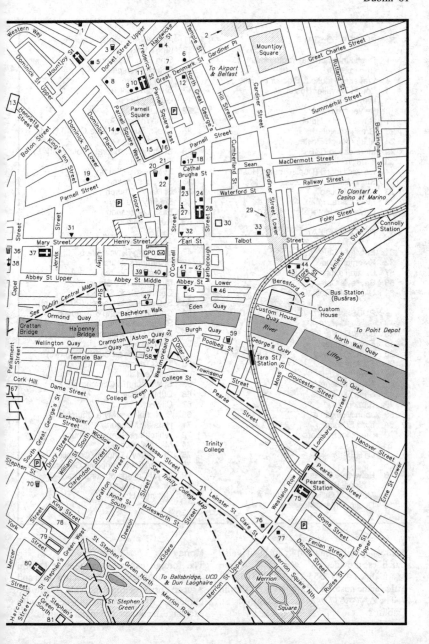

centre, beyond St Stephen's Green – it is also much less crowded.

An Óige (☎ 30 4555, fax 30 5888) has its office at the hostel at 61 Mountjoy St, Dublin 7. The AA (☎ 677 9481) is at 23 Suffolk St, Dublin 2.

Money
The foreign exchange counter at Dublin Airport is in the baggage collection area and is open for most flight arrivals. There are numerous banks around the centre with exchange facilities. American Express and

Thomas Cook are across the road from the Bank of Ireland and the Trinity College entrance.

Post & Telephone

Dublin's famed GPO is on O'Connell St, north of the river, and is open 8 am to 8 pm Monday to Saturday, 10.30 am to 6 pm Sunday and holidays. For stamp collectors there's a Philatelic Office in Henry St Arcade near the GPO. South of the river there's a handy post office on Anne St South, just off Grafton St, which is well patronised by foreign visitors and used to dealing with their curious requests.

By the end of 1994 all Dublin telephone numbers will have been converted to seven digits. Where possible, we have given the new phone numbers in this book. If you have difficulties with a six-digit number, it may have already been converted.

Books & Bookshops

Dublin is the only city in the world which can boast three winners of the Nobel Prize for Literature – George Bernard Shaw in 1925, W B Yeats in 1938 and Samuel Beckett in 1969. The Irish pride in this literary track record is exemplified in the Dublin Writers' Museum on Parnell Square.

James Joyce is, of course, the most Dublin-oriented of Irish writers, and serious Joyce groupies can make their own Bloomsday tour of the city with a number of books which follow the wanderings of *Ulysses'* characters in minute detail. *Joyce's Dublin – A Walking Guide to Ulysses* by Jack McCarthy (Wolfhound Press, Dublin, 1988) traces the events chapter by chapter with very clear maps. *The Ulysses Guide – Tours through Joyce's Dublin* by Robert Nicholson (Mandarin Paperbacks, London, 1988) concentrates on certain areas and follows the events of the various related chapters. Again there are clear and easy-to-follow maps.

Dublin has also featured prominently in more recent books by authors ranging from J P Donleavy's *The Ginger Man* to Roddy Doyle's *The Commitments*. Stephen Conlin's *Dublin – One Thousand Years* (The

O'Brien Press, Dublin, 1988) is an evocative collection of watercolour views recreating Dublin over the centuries. The Irish bookshop chain Eason publishes a series of slim booklets on areas of Irish interest, including several on Dublin.

Directly opposite Trinity College at 27/29 Nassau St is Fred Hanna's (☎ 677 1255) excellent bookshop. Round the corner at 57 Dawson St is the large and well-stocked Hodges Figgis (☎ 677 4754). Facing it across the road at 7 Dawson St is Waterstone's (☎ 679 1415), which also carries a wide range of books. At 24 Grafton St, the Dublin Bookshop (☎ 677 5568) has a particularly good selection of books of Irish interest. North of the Liffey, Eason (☎ 873 3811), at 40 O'Connell St near the post office, has a wide range of books and one of the biggest selections of magazines in Ireland.

A number of bookshops cater to special interests. Forbidden Planet (☎ 671 0688) at 36 Dawson St, Dublin 2, is a wonderful science fiction and comic book specialist. The Sinn Féin Bookshop is at 44 Parnell Square West, Dublin 1. An Siopha Leabhar on Harcourt St, just off St Stephen's Green, has books in Irish. The IMMA at the Royal Hospital Kilmainham and the National Gallery on Merrion Square both have bookshops offering a good range of art books. There's a bookshop in the Dublin Writers' Museum on Parnell Square North, Dublin 1. The Library Book Shop at Trinity College has a wide selection of Irish interest books, including, of course, various titles on 'The Book of Kells'.

George Webb (☎ 677 7489) at 5 Crampton Quay, Dublin 1, has old books of Irish interest. So do Green's Bookshop (☎ 676 2554) at 16 Clare St, Dublin 2, and Cathach Books (☎ 671 8676) at 10 Duke St, Dublin 2.

Films

Dublin has made numerous movie appearances, recently in *The Commitments*, a bright and energetic 1991 hit about a north Dublin soul band. The film neatly captures north Dublin's scruffy atmosphere. The movie *My*

Left Foot was as wonderful as the book it came from, *Down all the Days*. It also managed to make some interesting peregrinations around Dublin, including visits to John Mulligan's, the pub reputed to pull the best Guinness in Ireland. Renowned director John Huston's final film, *The Dead*, released in 1987, was based on a James Joyce story from *Dubliners*.

Medical Services

The Eastern Health Board Dublin Area (☎ 671 9222) at 138 Thomas St, Dublin 8, has a Choice of Doctor Scheme which can advise you on a suitable doctor from 9 am to 5 pm Monday to Friday.

Dangers & Annoyances

Dublin has its fair share of pickpockets and sneak thieves waiting to relieve the unwary of unwatched bags. If you have a car, do not leave valuables inside the car when it is parked. Dublin is notorious for car break-ins, and foreign-registered cars and rental cars are a particular target. Cyclists should always lock their bicycles securely and remove anything removable. Certain areas of Dublin are not safe at night and visitors should avoid run-down, deserted-looking and poorly lit areas. Campers should resist the temptation to put up their tents in Phoenix Park.

Phone ☎ 999 (free call) for police, ambulance or fire brigade. Other useful numbers include:

Poisons Information Centre
Beaumont Hospital, Beaumont Rd, Dublin 9 (☎ 37 9964, 37 9966)
Rape Crisis Centre
70 Leeson St Lower, Dublin 2 (☎ 661 4911, 661 4564)
Drugs Advisory & Treatment Centre
30/31 Pearse St, Dublin 2 (☎ 677 1122)

Laundry

Convenient laundries in north Dublin include the Laundry Shop at 191 Parnell St, Dublin 1, off Parnell Square, and the Laundrette at 110 Dorset St Lower near the An Óige Hostel. South of the centre and just north of the Grand Canal is Powders Laundrette at 42A Richmond St South, Dublin 2. If you're staying north-east of the centre at Clontarf there's the Clothes Line at 53 Clontarf Rd.

Embassies & Consulates

You will find embassies of the following countries in Dublin. For citizens of New Zealand and Singapore, the closest embassies are in London.

Australia
6th floor, Fitzwilton House, Wilton Terrace, Dublin 2 (☎ 676 1517)
Canada
65/68 St Stephen's Green, Dublin 2 (☎ 478 1988)
Denmark
121 St Stephen's Green, Dublin 2 (☎ 475 6404)
France
36 Ailesbury Rd, Dublin 4 (☎ 269 4777)
Germany
31 Trimleston Ave, Booterstown (☎ 269 3011)
Italy
63 Northumberland Rd, Dublin 4 (☎ 660 1744)
Japan
22 Ailesbury Rd, Dublin 4 (☎ 269 4244)
Netherlands
160 Merrion Rd, Dublin 4 (☎ 269 3444)
New Zealand
(in London) New Zealand House, Haymarket, London SW1 4QT (☎ 071-930 8422)
Norway
Hainault House, 69 St Stephen's Green, Dublin 2 (☎ 478 3133)
Portugal
Knocksinna House, Foxrock (☎ 289 4416)
Singapore
(in London) 2 Wilton Crescent, London SW1X 8HG (☎ 071-235 8315)
Spain
17A Merlyn Park, Dublin 4 (☎ 269 1640)
Sweden
Sun Alliance House, Dawson St, Dublin 2 (☎ 671 5822)
Switzerland
Ailesbury Rd, Dublin 4 (☎ 671 5822)
UK
33 Merrion Rd, Dublin 4 (☎ 269 5211)
USA
42 Elgin Rd, Dublin 4 (☎ 668 8777)

CULTURAL & SPORTING EVENTS

Highlights of the Dublin year include the following events:

March – The St Patrick's Day Parade with an international marching band competition and up to a quarter of a million spectators.

May – At the Royal Dublin Society Showground, the Spring Show with agricultural and farming pursuits.

The Irish Football Association Cup Final.

August – The Dublin Horse Show at the Royal Dublin Society Showground.

September – The All Ireland Hurling Final.

October – The Dublin Theatre Festival.

ALONG THE LIFFEY

The Liffey comes down to Dublin from the Wicklow Hills, passing the open expanse of Phoenix Park and flowing under 14 city bridges (one of which is pedestrian and one a railway) before reaching Dublin Harbour and Dublin Bay. As the crow flies it's only about 20 km from its source to the sea, but the Liffey contrives to twist and turn for over 100 km along its route and changes remarkably in that distance. Even well into the city, around Phoenix Park, the Liffey is still a rural-looking stream, and if you're waiting for a train at Heuston Station you can wander over to the river and watch the fish in the remarkably clear water below.

The city doesn't make much of its river. The best views are to be had from O'Connell Bridge or, just upstream, from the pedestrian Ha'penny Bridge of 1816 which leads to the colourful Temple Bar area. There have been bridges over the Liffey for nearly 800 years; the oldest currently standing is the Liam Mellows Bridge which was originally built at Queen's Bridge in 1768. It's still popularly known as the Queen St Bridge, for the simple reason that Queen St runs down to it.

The River Poddle originally joined at the Liffey near the Grattan Bridge, better known as the Capel St Bridge. The bridge crosses the river from Capel St and the road runs straight up to Dublin Castle. The black pool or *dubh linn* at this point gave the city its name, but today the miserable Poddle runs its final five km in an underground channel and trickles into the Liffey through a grating on the south side of the river just downstream from the bridge.

The Liffey does more than divide Dublin into northern and southern halves – there's a psychological break between north and south also. The movie *The Commitments* played upon this division, with run-down north Dublin as the place with 'soul'.

Although Liffey water was once a vital constituent in Guinness, you may be relieved to hear that this is no longer the case.

Dublin Harbour

In medieval times the River Liffey spread out into a broad estuary as it flowed into the bay. That estuary has long since been reclaimed (Trinity College has stood on it for 400 years) and the Liffey is embanked as far as the sea.

Dublin Harbour first came into existence in 1714, when the Liffey embankments were built. North Wall Quay was then built, and later a five-km breakwater known as the South Wall was added, followed by the North and South Bull Walls. The South Wall starts at Ringsend, where Cromwell first set foot in Ireland in 1649. From here it runs out to the Pigeon House Fort, built from 1748 and now used as a power station, and from there continues a further two km out to the 1762 Poolbeg Lighthouse at the end of the breakwater. It's a pleasant, though surprisingly long, stroll out to the lighthouse.

Custom House

James Gandon was 18th-century Dublin's pre-eminent architect; the Custom House, the Four Courts building farther up the river, the King's Inns and some elements of the parliament building (now the Bank of Ireland) are among his masterpieces.

The Custom House, his first great building, was constructed between 1781 and 1791 just past Eden Quay, in spite of vociferous local opposition.

In 1921, during the independence struggle, the Custom House was set alight and completely gutted in a fire that burned for five days. The interior was later extensively redesigned, and a further major renovation took place between 1986 and 1988.

The building stretches for 114 metres along the Liffey and the best complete view is obtained from across the river, though a close-up inspection of its many fine details is also worthwhile. The building is topped by a copper dome with four clocks and, above that, a five-metre-high statue of Hope.

Four Courts

On Inns Quay beside the river the extensive Four Courts with its 130-metre-long façade was another of James Gandon's masterpieces. Construction of the building, which began in 1786 and soon engulfed the Public Offices (built a short time before at the western end of the same site), continued through to 1802. By then it included a Corinthian-columned central block connected to flanking wings with enclosed quadrangles. The ensemble is topped by a diverse collection of statuary.

There are fine views over the city from the upper rotunda of the central building. The original four courts – Exchequer, Common Pleas, King's Bench and Chancery – branched off this circular central building. The 1224 Dominican Convent of St Saviour formerly stood on the site but was replaced first by the King's Inns and then by the present building. The last parliament of James II was held here in 1689.

The Four Courts played a brief role in the 1916 Easter Rising, without suffering any damage, but the events of 1922 were not so kind. When anti-Treaty republicans seized the building and refused to leave, the building was shelled from across the river; as the occupiers retreated, the building was set on fire and a great many irreplaceable early records were burnt. This event sparked off the Civil War. The building was not restored until 1932.

SOUTH OF THE LIFFEY

South Dublin has the fanciest shops, almost all the restaurants of note and a majority of the hotels, as well as most of the reminders of Dublin's early history and the finest Georgian squares and houses.

Trinity College

Ireland's premier university was founded by

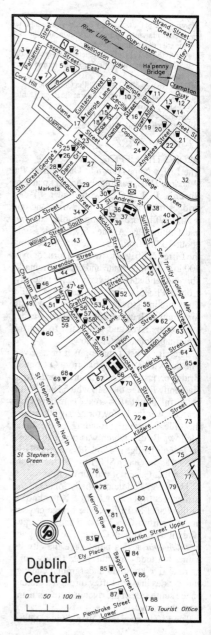

Dublin
Central

0   50   100 m

■ PLACES TO STAY

1	Clarence Hotel
24	Bloom's Hotel
28	Central Hotel
44	Westbury Hotel
71	Buswell's Hotel
76	Shelbourne Hotel

▼ PLACES TO EAT

3	Poco Loco
4	Pizza on the Corner
7	Les Frères Jacques
11	Cellary Café
12	Omar Khayyam
13	Elephant & Castle
14	Gallagher's Boxty House
15	Fat Freddy's Pizza Parlour
16	Bad Ass Café
17	La Mezza Luna
18	Well Fed Café
19	Rock Garden Café
23	Broker's Restaurant
26	Bewley's Café
29	Trattoria Pasta Pasta
30	QV2
34	Munchies
36	Trocadero Restaurant
39	Cornucopia
45	Judge Roy Bean
48	Bewley's Oriental Café
49	Pasta Fresca
56	Eddie Rocket's Diner
57	Independent Pizza Company
61	Subs n Salad
69	La Stampa
70	Polo One
81	Galligan's Café
86	Miller's Pizza Kitchen
88	Georgian Fare

🍺 PUBS

2	Garage Bar
6	Bad Bob's
9	Norseman
10	Temple Bar
20	Auld Dubliner
21	Oliver St John Gogarty
25	Dame Tavern
27	Stag's Head
33	Old Stand
35	International Bar
38	O'Neill's
46	Neary's
47	Bruxelles
51	McDaid's
52	Bailey
54	Davy Byrne's
58	John Kehoe's
83	O'Donoghue's
84	Doheny & Nesbitt's
85	Baggot Inn
87	James Toner's

OTHER

5	Project Arts Centre
8	Olympia Theatre
22	Stock Exchange
31	Post Office
32	Bank of Ireland
37	St Andrew's Church (Protestant)
40	Thomas Cook
41	American Express
42	Civic Museum
43	Powerscourt Shopping Centre
50	Gaiety Theatre
53	Dublin Bookshop
55	Hodges Figgis Bookshop
59	Post Office
60	Aer Lingus
62	Waterstone's Bookshop
63	Fred Hanna's Bookshop
64	Northern Ireland Tourist Board
65	Kilkenny Shop
66	St Ann's Church
67	Mansion House
68	Forbidden Planet
72	Bram Stoker's House
73	National Library
74	National Museum
75	Leinster House
77	National Gallery
78	Huguenot Cemetery
79	Natural History Museum
80	Government Buildings
82	Irish Ferries

Queen Elizabeth I in 1592 on land that had been confiscated from a monastery. By providing an alternative to education on the Continent, the queen hoped that the students would avoid being 'infected with popery'. The college is right in the centre of Dublin though at the time of its foundation it was outside the city walls. Archbishop Ussher, whose scientific feats included the precise dating of the act of creation to 4004 BC, was one of the college's founders.

Officially, the university's name is the University of Dublin, but Trinity College happens to be the institution's sole college. Until 1793 Trinity College remained completely Protestant apart from one short break. Even when the Protestants allowed Catholics in, the Catholic Church forbade it, a restriction which was not completely lifted until 1970. To this day Trinity College is still something of a centre of British and Protestant influence even though the majority of its 7000 students are Catholic. Women were first admitted to the college in 1903, earlier than at most British universities.

During the summer months walking tours depart regularly from the main gate on College Green, Monday to Saturday from 9.30 am to 4.30 pm, Sunday from noon to 4 pm. The IR£3.50 cost of the walking tour is good value since it includes the fee to see 'The Book of Kells' (see that section).

Main Entrance From College Green (the street in front of the college), the 'Front Gate' or Regent House entrance to the college's grounds was built in 1752-59 and is guarded by statues of the poet Oliver Goldsmith (1730-74) and the orator Edmund Burke (1729-97).

Around the Campanile The open area reached from Regent House is divided into Front Square, Parliament Square and Library Square. The area is dominated by the 30-metre Campanile, designed by Edward Lanyon and erected in 1852-53 on what was believed to be the centre of the monastery that preceded the college. To the left of the Campanile is a statue of George Salmon, the College Provost from 1886 to 1904, who fought bitterly to keep women out of the college. He carried out his threat to permit them 'over his dead body' by promptly dropping dead when the worst came to pass.

Chapel & Dining Hall Clockwise around the Front Square from the entrance gate, the first building is the chapel, built from 1798 by the architect Sir William Chambers (1723-96) and since 1972 open to all denominations. It's noted for its extremely fine plasterwork by Michael Stapleton, its Ionic columns and its painted, not stained, glass windows. The main one is dedicated to Archbishop Ussher, the college's founder, who so precisely dated the act of creation.

Next to the chapel is the dining hall, originally designed in 1743 by Richard Castle but dismantled only 15 years later because of severe problems caused by inadequate foundations. The replacement was completed in 1761 and may have retained elements of the original design. It was extensively restored after a fire in 1984. The popular Buttery Restaurant is found here.

Graduates' Memorial Building & the Rubrics The 1892 Graduates' Memorial Building forms the north side of Library Square. Behind it are the tennis courts in the open area known as Botany Bay. The popular legend behind this name is that the unruly students housed around the square were suitable candidates for the British penal colony at Botany Bay (Sydney) in Australia. At the east side of Library Square, the red-brick Rubrics Building dates from around 1690, making it the oldest building in the college. It was extensively altered in an 1894 restoration and then underwent major structural modifications in the 1970s.

Old Library To the south of the square is the Old Library, which was built in a rather severe style by Thomas Burgh between 1712 and 1732. The Library's 65-metre Long Room contains numerous unique ancient texts and 'The Book of Kells' is displayed in the Library Colonnades.

Despite Ireland's independence, the Library Act of 1801 still entitles Trinity College Library, along with three libraries in Britain, to a free copy of every book published in the UK. Housing this bounty requires nearly another km of shelving every year and the collection amounts to around three million books. Of course these cannot

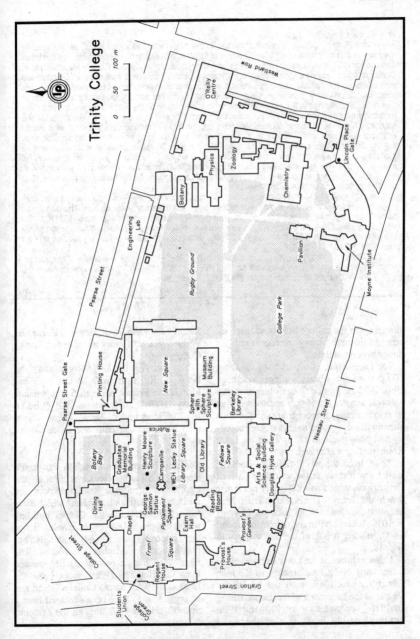

Trinity College

The Book of Kells

For visitors, Trinity College's prime attraction is the magnificent 'Book of Kells', an illuminated manuscript dating from around 800 AD – one of the oldest books in the world. Although the book was brought to the college for safekeeping from the monastery at Kells in County Meath in 1654, it undoubtedly predates the monastery itself. It was probably produced by monks at St Columcille's monastery on the remote island of Iona, off the coast of Scotland. When repeated Viking raids made their monastery untenable, the monks moved to the temporarily greater safety of Kells in Ireland in 806, bringing their masterpiece with them. In 1007 the book was stolen and then rediscovered three months later, buried in the ground. Some time before the dissolution of the monastery, the metal shrine or *cumdach* was lost, possibly taken by looting Vikings who would not have valued the text itself. About 30 of the beginning and ending folios have also disappeared.

'The Book of Kells' contains the four gospels of the New Testament, written in Latin, as well as prefaces, summaries and other text. If it were merely words, 'The Book of Kells' would simply be a very old book – it's the extensive and amazingly complex illustrations which make it so wonderful. The superbly decorated opening initials are only part of the story, for the book also has numerous smaller illustrations between the lines.

The 680-page (340-folio) book was rebound in four calfskin volumes in 1953. Two volumes are usually on display, one showing an illuminated page and the other showing text. The pages are turned over regularly but you can acquire your own reproduction copy for a mere US$18,000. If that's too steep, the library bookshop has various lesser books, including *The Book of Kells* (paperback, Thames & Hudson, London, 1980) with some attractive colour plates and text for less than IR£10.

'The Book of Kells' is usually on display in the East Pavilion of the library Colonnades, underneath the actual library. As well as 'The Book of Kells', the 807 'Book of Armagh' and the 675 'Book of Durrow' are on display in the East Pavilion. ■

all be kept at the college library, so there are now additional library storage facilities dotted around Dublin.

The Long Room is mainly used for about 200,000 of the library's oldest volumes. Until 1892 the ground floor Colonnades was an open arcade, but it was enclosed at that time to increase the storage area. A previous attempt to increase the room's storage capacity had been made in 1853, when the Long Room ceiling was raised.

Apart from the world-famous 'Book of Kells', on display is the so-called harp of Brian Ború, which was definitely not in use when the army of this early Irish hero defeated the Danes at the Battle of Clontarf in 1014. It does, however, date from around 1400, making it one of the oldest harps in Ireland.

Other exhibits in the Long Room include a rare copy of the Proclamation of the Irish Republic, which was read out by Patrick Pearse at the beginning of the Easter Rising in 1916. The collection of 18th and 19th-century marble busts around the walls features Jonathan Swift, Edmund Burke and Wolfe Tone, all former members of Trinity College.

You can visit the Long Room and 'The Book of Kells' from 9.30 am to 5 pm Monday to Friday, noon to 5 pm Sunday. Entry is IR£2.50 (students and children IR£2, children under 12 free). There's a very busy book and souvenir shop in the Colonnades.

Reading Room, Exam Hall & Provost's House Continuing clockwise around the Campanile there's the Reading Room and the Public Theatre or Exam Hall, which dates from 1779-91. Like the Chapel building which it faces and closely resembles, it was the work of William Chambers and also has plasterwork by Michael Stapleton. The Exam Hall has an oak chandelier rescued from the Houses of Parliament (now the Bank of Ireland) across College Green and an organ said to have been salvaged from a Spanish ship in 1702, though the evidence indicates otherwise.

St John the Eagle, Book of Kells

Behind the Exam Hall is the 1760 Provost's House, a particularly fine Georgian house where the provost or college head still resides. The house and its adjacent garden are not open to the public.

Berkeley Library To one side of the Old Library is Paul Koralek's 1967 Berkeley Library. This solid square brutalist-style building has been hailed as the best example of modern architecture in Ireland, though it has to be admitted the competition is not great. It's fronted by Arnaldo Pomodoro's 1982-83 sculpture *Sphere with Sphere*.

George Berkeley was born in Kilkenny in 1685, studied at Trinity when he was only 15 years old and went on to a distinguished career in many fields but particularly in philosophy. His influence spread to the new English colonies in North America where, among other things, he helped to found the University of Pennsylvania. Berkeley in California, and its namesake university, are named after him.

Arts & Social Science Building & Douglas Hyde Gallery South of the old library is the 1978 Arts & Social Science Building, which backs on to Nassau St and forms the alternative main entrance to the college. Like the Berkeley Library it was designed by Paul Koralek; it also houses the Douglas Hyde Gallery of Modern Art (☎ 70 2116). Fellows Square is surrounded on three sides by the two library buildings and the Arts & Social Science Building.

The Dublin Experience After 'The Book of Kells' the college's other big tourist attraction is the Dublin Experience, a 45-minute audiovisual introduction to the city. Shows take place in the Old Library every hour from 10 am to 5 pm daily from late May to the beginning of October. Entry is IR£2.75 (students or children IR£2.25). Combined tickets to 'The Book of Kells' and the Dublin Experience are available.

Around New Square Behind the Rubrics Building, at the eastern end of Library Square, is New Square. The highly ornate 1853-57 Museum Building has the skeletons of two enormous giant Irish elk just inside the entrance and the Geological Museum upstairs.

The 1734 Printing House, designed by Richard Castle to resemble a Doric temple and now used for the integrated circuits fabrication laboratory of the engineering department, is at the north-west corner of New Square.

At the eastern end of the college grounds are the rugby ground and College Park, where cricket games are often played. There are a number of science buildings at the eastern end of the grounds. The Lincoln Place Gate at this end is usually open and makes a good entrance or exit from the college, especially if you are on a bicycle.

Bank of Ireland
The imposing Bank of Ireland building (☎ 677 6801), on College Green directly opposite Trinity College, was originally built in 1729 to house the Irish Parliament. When

the parliament voted itself out of existence by the Act of Union in 1800, it became a building without a role. It was sold with instructions that the interior be altered to prevent it from being used as a debating chamber in the future. Consequently, the large central House of Commons was remodelled but the smaller chamber of the House of Lords survived. After independence the Irish government chose to make Leinster House the new parliamentary building and ignored the possibility of restoring this fine building to its original use.

The building involved a string of architects over a long period of time yet somehow manages to avoid looking like a hotchpotch of styles. Edward Lovett Pearce designed the original central part of the building which was constructed between 1729 and 1739, and the east front was designed by James Gandon in 1785. Other architects involved in its construction were Robert Park and Francis Johnston, who converted it from a parliament building to a bank after it was sold in 1803.

Inside, the banking mall occupies what was once the House of Commons but offers little hint of its former role. The Irish House of Lords is much more interesting with its Irish oak woodwork and late 18th-century Waterford crystal chandelier. The tapestries date from the 1730s and depict the Siege of Derry in 1689 and the Battle of the Boyne in 1690, the two great Protestant victories over Catholic Ireland.

The building can be visited during banking hours, Monday to Friday from 10 am to 3 pm, on Thursday to 5 pm. Guided tours take place on Tuesdays at 10.30 am, 11.30 am and 1.45 pm. The building's alternative role as a tourist attraction is not pushed very hard. You'll probably have to ask somebody if you want to find your way to the House of Lords.

Around the Bank of Ireland

The area between the Bank and Trinity College, today a constant tangle of traffic and pedestrians, was once a green swathe and is still known as College Green.

The traffic island where College Green, Westmoreland St and College St meet houses public toilets (no longer in use) and a statue of the poet and composer Thomas Moore (1779-1852), renowned for James Joyce's comment in *Ulysses* that standing atop a public urinal was not a bad place for the man who penned the poem 'The Meeting of the Waters'. At the other end of College St, where it meets Pearse St, another traffic island is topped by a 1986 sculpture known as *Steyne*. It's a copy of the *steyne*, the Viking word for stone, erected on the riverbank in the 9th century to stop ships from grounding, and not removed until 1720.

Temple Bar

West of College Green and the Bank of Ireland, the maze of streets that make up Temple Bar are sandwiched between Dame St and the river. It's one of the oldest areas of Dublin and now has numerous restaurants, pubs and trendy shops.

Dame St, which forms the southern boundary of the Temple Bar area, links new Dublin (centred around Trinity College and Grafton St) and old (stretching from Dublin Castle to encompass the two cathedrals). Along its route Dame St changes name to become Cork Hill, Lord Edward St and Christ Church Place.

Temple Bar Information For information specifically on Temple Bar, the Temple Bar information centre (☎ 671 5717) on Eustace St publishes a *Temple Bar Guide*. The notice board in the Resource Centre/Well Fed Café on Crow St offers a useful collection of local goings-on. Morrigan Books' *Heritage Guide to Temple Bar* has an interesting map and description of the area.

Temple Bar History This stretch of prime riverside land was the property of Augustinian friars from 1282 until Henry VIII made his big land grab in 1537 with the dissolution of the monasteries. Temple Lane was known as Hogges Lane at that time and gave access to the friars' house. During its monastic era the Temple Bar area was marshy land that had only recently been reclaimed from the river. Much of the area was outside the city walls and the River Poddle flowed through it, connecting the black pool with the Liffey.

The land was named after a former owner, Sir William Temple (1554-1628). The term 'bar' referred to a riverside walkway.

The narrow lanes and alleys of Temple Bar started to take form in the early 18th century when this was a disreputable area of pubs and brothels. Through the 19th century it developed a commercial character with many small craft and trade businesses, but in the first half of the 20th century it went into decline, along with most of central Dublin.

In the 1960s it was decided to demolish the whole area to build a major bus station, but these plans took a long, long time to develop and meanwhile the area became a thriving countercultural centre. In the 1980s the bus station plan was abandoned and Temple Bar was encouraged to develop as a centre for restaurants, shops and entertainment. Plans for the future include public squares, apartments, a student housing centre, a Viking museum on the riverside and a second pedestrian bridge over the Liffey.

Exploring Temple Bar The western boundary of Temple Bar is formed by Fishamble St, which is the oldest street in Dublin, dating back to Viking times. Christ Church Cathedral, originally dating from 1170, stands beside Fishamble St. There was an even earlier Viking church on this site.

In 1742 Handel conducted the first performance of his *Messiah* in the Dublin Music Hall, which stood at that time behind what is now the Kinlay House Refectory. The Music Hall, which had opened a year earlier in 1741, was designed by Richard Castle; the only reminder of it today is the entrance and the original door, which stand to the left of Kennan's engineering works.

Parliament St, which runs straight up from the river to the City Hall and Dublin Castle, has Read's Cutlers at No 4. This is the oldest shop in Dublin, having operated under the same name since 1760. At the bottom of the street, beside the river, the Sunlight Chambers has a beautiful frieze around the buildings. Sunlight was a brand of soap manufactured by the Lever Brothers, who were responsible for the turn-of-the-century building. The frieze shows the Lever Brothers' view of the world and soap: men make clothes dirty, women wash them!

Eustace St is particularly interesting, with the popular Norseman pub at the river end and the 1715 Presbyterian Meeting House. The Dublin branch of the United Irishmen, who set themselves up to campaign for parliamentary reform and equality for Catholics, was first convened in 1791 in the Eagle Tavern, now the Friends Meeting House.

Merchant's Arch leads to the Ha'penny Bridge. If you cross to the north side of the Liffey, pause to look at the statue of two stout Dublin matrons sitting on a park bench with their shopping bags. In typically irreverent Dublin fashion the sculpture has been dubbed 'the hags with the bags'. The Stock Exchange lives on Anglesea St, in a building dating from 1878. The Bank of Ireland also occupies a corner of Temple Bar.

Dublin Castle

Dublin Castle (☎ 679 3713) is more palace than castle. It was originally built on the orders of King John in 1204 and enjoyed a relatively quiet history despite a siege by Silken Thomas Fitzgerald in 1534; a fire which destroyed much of the castle in 1684; and the events of the 1916 Easter Rising. It was so lightly defended in 1916 that it would probably have fallen had the insurrectionists only realised they faced such lightweight opposition. The castle was used as the official residence of the British viceroys of Ireland, until the Viceregal Lodge was built in Phoenix Park. Earlier it had been used as a prison; Red Hugh O'Donnell, one of the last of the great Gaelic leaders, escaped from the Record Tower in 1591, was recaptured, and escaped again in 1592.

Only the Record Tower, built between 1202 and 1258, remains intact from the original Norman castle. Parts of the castle's foundations remain, and a visit to the excavations is by far the most interesting part of the castle tour. The castle moats, now completely covered by more modern developments, were once filled by the River Poddle.

The castle tops Cork Hill, behind the City Hall on Dame St, and tours are held from 10 am to 12.15 pm and 2 to 5 pm Monday to Friday, afternoons only on weekends. The tour costs IR£1 (children 50p).

Castle Tour The main Upper Yard of the castle with the entrance underneath the Throne Room is reached either directly from Cork Hill or via the Lower Yard. Starting from the main entrance, the castle tour takes you round the state chambers, which were developed during Dublin's British heyday but are still used for official state occasions. The sequence of rooms the tour takes you through may vary. From the entrance you ascend the stairs to the Battle-Axe Landing, where the viceroy's guards once stood, armed with battle-axes.

To the left is a series of drawing rooms, formerly used as visitors' bedrooms. The castle gardens, visible from the windows of these rooms, end in a high wall said to have been built for Queen Victoria's visit to block out the distressing sight of the slums on Stephen St. James Connolly was detained in the first of these rooms after the siege of the GPO in 1916. From here he was taken to Kilmainham Jail to face a firing squad, still unable to stand because of a bullet wound to his ankle.

From the long State Corridor you enter the State Drawing Room, which suffered serious damage in a fire in 1941. It has been restored with furniture and paintings dating from 1740. From there you enter the ornate Throne Room, which was built in 1740.

The long Portrait Gallery, at one time divided into a series of smaller rooms, has portraits of some of the British viceroys. It ends at an anteroom from which you enter George's Hall, tacked on in 1911 for King George V's visit to Ireland. From these rooms you return through the anteroom to the blue Wedgwood Room (yes, the whole room does look like Wedgwood china), which in turn leads to the Bermingham Tower, originally dating from 1411 but rebuilt in 1775-77. The tower was used as a prison on a number of occasions, particularly during the independence struggle from 1918 to 1920. Leaving the tower you pass through the 25-metre-long St Patrick's Hall with its painted ceiling. The Knights of St Patrick, an order created in 1783, were invested here and their standards are displayed around the walls. Now Irish presidents are inaugurated here and it is used for receptions. Note the huge painting on the ceiling.

St Patrick's Hall ends back on the Battle-Axe Landing but the tour now takes you down to the Undercroft where remnants of the earlier Viking fort, the 13th-century Powder Tower and the city wall can be seen. This excavation of the original moat is now well below street level.

Bedford Tower & Genealogical Office Other points of interest in the castle include the Bedford Tower and the 1552 Genealogical Office, directly across the Upper Yard from the main entrance. In 1907 the collection known as the Irish Crown Jewels was stolen from this tower and never recovered.

The entranceway to the castle yard beside the Bedford Tower is topped by a figure of justice which has always been a subject of mirth. She faces the castle and has her back to the city – seen as a sure indicator of how much justice the average Irish citizen could expect from the English. And the scales of justice had a distinct tendency to fill with rain and tilt in one direction or the other, rather than assuming the approved level position. Eventually a hole was drilled in the bottom of each pan so the rainwater could drain out.

Royal Chapel In the Lower Yard is the Church of the Holy Trinity, previously known as the Royal Chapel, which was built in Gothic style by Francis Johnston in 1807-14. Decorating the exterior are over 90 heads of various Irish personages and assorted saints carved out of Tullamore limestone.

Record Tower Towering over the chapel is the Record Tower, which was used as a storage facility for official records from 1579 until they were transferred to the Record Office in the Four Courts building in the early 19th century. When the Four Courts was burnt out at the start of the Civil War in 1922, almost all these priceless records were destroyed. Although the tower was rebuilt in 1813 it retains much of its original appearance, including the massive five-metre thick walls.

City Hall & Municipal Buildings

Fronting Dublin Castle on Lord Edward St, the City Hall was built by Thomas Cooley in 1769-79 as the Royal Exchange and later became the offices of the Dublin Corporation.

The City Hall was built on the site of the Lucas Coffee House and an Eagle Tavern in which Dublin's infamous Hell Fire Club was established in 1735. Parliament St (1762), which leads up from the river to the front of City Hall, was the first of Dublin's wide boulevards to be laid out by the Wide Streets Commission.

The 1781 Municipal Buildings, immediately west of the City Hall, were built by Thomas Ivory (1720-86), who was also responsible for the Genealogical Office in Dublin Castle.

Christ Church Cathedral

Christ Church Cathedral (Church of the Holy Trinity) (☎ 677 8099) is on Christ Church Place, just south of the river and west of the city centre and the Temple Bar district. Dublin's original Viking settlement stood between the cathedral and the river. This was also the centre of medieval Dublin, with Dublin Castle nearby and the Tholsel or town hall (demolished in 1809) and the original Four Courts (demolished in 1796) both beside the cathedral. Nearby on Back Lane is the only remaining guildhall in Dublin. The 1706 Tailor's Hall was due for demolition in the 1960s but survived to become the office of An Taisce, the Irish National Trust.

The cathedral was originally built in wood by the Danes in 1038. It was subsequently rebuilt in stone from around 1170, by Richard de Clare, Earl of Pembroke (better known as Strongbow). The archbishop of Dublin, Laurence (Lorcan in Irish) O'Toole, was later to become St Laurence, the patron

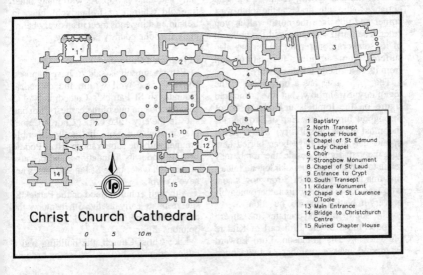

1 Baptistry
2 North Transept
3 Chapter House
4 Chapel of St Edmund
5 Lady Chapel
6 Choir
7 Strongbow Monument
8 Chapel of St Laud
9 Entrance to Crypt
10 South Transept
11 Kildare Monument
12 Chapel of St Laurence O'Toole
13 Main Entrance
14 Bridge to Christchurch Centre
15 Ruined Chapter House

Christ Church Cathedral

0   5   10 m

saint of Dublin. Strongbow died in 1176 and Laurence O'Toole in 1180, before the church was complete. Nor was their cathedral destined to have a long life: the foundations were essentially a peat bog and the south wall collapsed in 1562. It was soon rebuilt, but the central tower was also a replacement for two earlier steeples which had burnt down. Most of what you see from the outside dates from a major restoration between 1871 and 1878 by the architect G E Street. Above ground level the north wall, the transepts and the western part of the choir are almost all that remain from the original. Even the flying buttresses to the north wall date from the 19th-century restoration.

Through much of its history Christ Church vied for supremacy with nearby St Patrick's Cathedral, but like its neighbour it fell on hard times in the 18th and 19th centuries and was virtually derelict when the major restoration took place. Earlier, the nave had been used as a market and the crypt had housed taverns. Today, of course, both these Church of Ireland cathedrals are outsiders in a Catholic nation.

From the south-east entrance to the churchyard you walk by the ruins of the chapter house, dating from 1230. The entrance to the cathedral is at the south-west corner and you face the north wall as you enter. The north wall survived the collapse of its southern counterpart, but it has also suffered from subsiding foundations and from its eastern end it leans visibly.

The south aisle has a monument to the legendary Strongbow, but the armoured figure on the tomb is unlikely to be of Strongbow himself (the Earl of Drogheda is the most likely possibility). His internal organs may indeed have been buried here and the half-figure beside the tomb may relate to that burial. A popular legend relates that this half-figure is of Strongbow's son, who was cut in two by his father when his bravery in battle came into question.

The south transept contains the superb Baroque tomb of the 19th earl of Kildare (died 1734). His grandson, Lord Edward Fitzgerald, was a member of the United Irishmen and died in the abortive 1798 rebellion. The entrance to the Chapel of St Laurence is off the south transept and contains two effigies, one of them reputed to be that of either Strongbow's wife or sister. Laurence O'Toole's embalmed heart was placed in the Chapel of St Laud.

At the east end of the cathedral is the Lady Chapel or Chapel of the Blessed Virgin Mary. Also at the east end is the Chapel of St Edmund and the chapter house, the latter closed to visitors. Parts of the choir, in the centre of the church, and the north transept are original, but the baptistry was added at the time of the 1875 restoration.

An entrance by the south transept descends to the unusually large arched crypt which dates back to the original Danish church of 1000 years ago. Curiosities in the crypt include 1670 stocks that once stood in the cathedral yard. A glass display case houses a mummified cat which, until it was vandalised in 1992, used to chase a mummified mouse. From the main entrance a bridge, part of the 1871-78 restoration, leads to the Christchurch Centre, which was also added at that time.

The cathedral is open from 10 am to 5 pm daily and entry is 50p. As with many other fine old Church of Ireland churches in Ireland, making ends meet in an overwhelmingly Catholic country is not easy.

St Patrick's Cathedral
St Patrick himself is said to have baptised converts at a well within the cathedral grounds, so St Patrick's Cathedral (☎ 475 4817) stands on one of the earliest Christian sites in the city. Like Christ Church Cathedral it was built on distinctly unstable ground, with the subterranean River Poddle flowing under its foundations, and because of the high water table St Patrick's does not have a crypt.

Although a church stood on the Patrick St site from as early as the 5th century, the present building dates from 1190 or 1225 – opinions differ.

Like Christ Church, the building had a rather dramatic history. A storm brought

Top: River Liffey, Dublin (JM)
ttom: Leinster House, Dublin (JM)

Top: Drogheda, County Meath (JM)
Bottom: Mellifont Abbey, County Louth (TW)

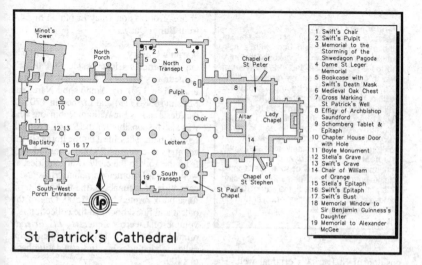

St Patrick's Cathedral

1 Swift's Chair
2 Swift's Pulpit
3 Memorial to the Storming of the Shwedagon Pagoda
4 Dame St Leger Memorial
5 Bookcase with Swift's Death Mask
6 Medieval Oak Chest
7 Cross Marking St Patrick's Well
8 Effigy of Archbishop Saundford
9 Schomberg Tablet & Epitaph
10 Chapter House Door with Hole
11 Boyle Monument
12 Stella's Grave
13 Swift's Grave
14 Chair of William of Orange
15 Stella's Epitaph
16 Swift's Epitaph
17 Swift's Bust
18 Memorial Window to Sir Benjamin Guinness's Daughter
19 Memorial to Alexander McGee

down the spire in 1316 and soon after the building was badly damaged in a fire. An even more disastrous fire followed in 1362 which required the addition of Archbishop Minot's west tower in 1370. For some reason it was constructed at a slight angle to the rest of the cathedral. In 1560 one of the first clocks in Dublin was added to the 43-metre tower, and a 31-metre spire in 1749. Cromwell, during his 1649 visit to Ireland, converted St Patrick's to a stable for his army's horses, an indignity to which he subjected numerous other Irish churches. Jonathan Swift was the dean of the cathedral from 1713 to 1745. Prior to its mid-19th-century restoration the cathedral became a ruin, with a collapsed roof and individual chapels walled off as separate churches.

Its current form dates mainly from some rather overenthusiastic restoration in 1864 which included the addition of the flying buttresses. St Patrick's Park, the expanse of green beside the cathedral, was a crowded slum until it was cleared and its residents evicted in the early years of this century.

On entering the cathedral from the southwest porch you come almost immediately to the graves of Swift and Esther Johnson or Stella, Swift's long-term companion. On the wall are Swift's own Latin epitaphs to the two of them, and a bust of him.

The huge Boyle Monument was erected in 1632 by Richard Boyle, the Earl of Cork, and is decorated with numerous painted figures of members of his family. It briefly stood beside the altar until, in 1633, the lord deputy of Ireland, Thomas Wentworth, the future earl of Strafford, complained that worshippers were unable to pray without 'crouching to an Earl of Cork and his lady... or to those sea nymphs his daughters, with coronets upon their heads, their hair dishevelled, down upon their shoulders'. This broadside was enough to have it shifted, but although Wentworth won this round of his bitter conflict with the earl of Cork, the latter had the final say when he contributed to the process of Wentworth's impeachment and execution. The figure in the centre on the bottom level is of the earl's five-year-old son, Robert Boyle (1627-91), the future scientist. His contributions to physics include Boyle's Law, which relates the pressure and volume of gases.

In the north-west corner of the church is a cross on a stone slab, which once marked the position of St Patrick's original well. The south transept was formerly a separate chapter house.

During the cathedral's decay in the 18th and 19th centuries the north transept was virtually a separate church. It now contains memorials to the Royal Irish Regiments.

The Swift corner in the north transept features Swift's pulpit, his chair and a book-filled glass cabinet containing his death mask.

The Guinness family were noted contributors to the cathedral's restoration and a monument to Sir Benjamin Guinness's daughter stands in the Chapel of St Stephen beneath a window bearing the words 'I was thirsty and ye gave me drink'! The chapel also has a chair used by William of Orange at a service in the cathedral after his victory at the Boyne.

The cathedral is open from 9 am to 6 pm Monday to Friday, 9 am to 5 pm Saturday (to 4 pm November to April), and 8.30 to 9 am and 10 am to 4.30 pm Sunday. Entry is 90p (children 30p). The cathedral's choir school dates back to 1432 and the choir took part in the first performance of Handel's *Messiah* in 1742. You can hear the choir every day except Wednesdays in July and August. You can get to the cathedral on bus No 50, 50A or 56A from Aston Quay or No 54 or 54A from Burgh Quay.

Marsh's Library

On St Patrick's Close beside St Patrick's Cathedral is Marsh's Library (☎ 54 3511), founded in 1701 by Archbishop Narcissus Marsh (1638-1713) and opened in 1707. It was designed by Sir William Robinson, who was also responsible for the Royal Hospital, Kilmainham. The oldest public library in the country, it contains 25,000 books dating from the 16th to the early 18th centuries, as well as maps, numerous manuscripts and a collection of incunabula, the technical term for a book printed before 1500. One of the oldest and finest books in the collection is a volume of Cicero's *Letters to his Friends* printed in Milan in 1472. The manuscript collection includes one in Latin dating back to 1400.

The three alcoves where scholars were once locked in to peruse rare volumes have remained virtually unchanged for three centuries. A bindery to repair and restore rare old books operates from the library. The library, hardly surprisingly, makes an appearance in Joyce's *Ulysses*.

Marsh's Library is open Monday and Wednesday to Friday from 10 am to 12.45 pm and 2 to 5 pm, Saturday from 10.30 am to 12.45 pm. An entry donation of IR£1 is requested. You can reach the library by taking bus No 50, 50A or 56A from Aston Quay or No 54 or 54A from Burgh Quay.

St Werburgh's Church

Hidden away on Werburgh St, just south of Christ Church Cathedral and tucked away beside Dublin Castle, St Werburgh's stands on ancient foundations. Its early history, however, is unknown. It was rebuilt in 1662, in 1715, and again in 1759 (with some elegance) after a fire in 1754. It is linked with the Fitzgerald family; Lord Edward Fitzgerald, who joined the United Irishmen and was a leader of the 1798 rebellion, is interred in the vault. In what was an unfortunately frequent theme of Irish uprisings, compatriots gave him away and his death resulted from the wounds he received while being captured. Major Henry Sirr, his captor, is buried in the graveyard. A Baroque tower was added to the church in 1768, but was demolished in 1810 when Dublin Castle authorities, concerned about its use as a lookout over the castle, had it declared unsafe.

Despite its long history, fine design and interesting interior, the church is not in use today. A note at the front directs you to a house round the corner if you want to have a look inside. If you can't raise anybody there, you could try phoning (☎ 478 3710). Werburgh St was also the location of Dublin's first theatre and Jonathan Swift was born just off the street in Hoey's Court in 1667.

St Audoen's Churches

Lucky St Audoen has two churches to his name, both just west of Christ Church Cathedral. The Church of Ireland church is the older and smaller building, and indeed is the only surviving medieval parish church in the city. Its tower and door date from the 12th century, the aisle from the 15th century and various other bits and pieces from early times, but the church today is mainly a 19th-century restoration. The tower's bells include the three oldest bells in Ireland, all dating from 1423.

The church is entered via an arch beside Cook St, to the north of the church. Part of the old city wall, this arch was built in 1240 and is the only surviving reminder of the city gates. Parts of an even earlier Viking church of St Colmcille may be included in the later constructions.

Joined onto the older Protestant St Audoen's is the newer and larger Catholic St Audoen's, which was completed in 1846. The dome was replaced in 1884 after it collapsed, and the front with its imposing Corinthian columns was added in 1899.

The Flame on the Hill is an audiovisual display on Ireland before the arrival of the Vikings which is presented in the new St Audoen's. It is shown Monday to Friday at 11.30 am, 2, 3 and 4 pm and costs IR£1.50 (children and students IR£1).

The National Museum

The National Museum (☎ 661 8811) on Kildare St east of St Stephen's Green was completed in 1890 to a design by Sir Thomas Newenham Deane. The star attraction is the Treasury, which has two superb collections and an accompanying audiovisual display.

One of the collections is of Bronze and Iron Age gold objects, including a magnificent gold collar and a delicate little gold model of a galley, both from the Broighter Hoard (1st century BC), the Gleninsheen Gorget – another collar – from about the 8th century BC, and other hoards discovered by railway workers, ploughmen and peat cutters – rarely by archaeologists.

The other Treasury collection is from medieval times. Outstanding among the objects on display are the 8th-century silver Ardagh Chalice, the 12th-century Cross of Cong, which once enshrined a supposed fragment of the True Cross, and the beautiful 8th-century Tara Brooch, made of gold, enamel and amber.

Other exhibits focus on the 1916 Easter Rising and the independence struggle between 1900 and 1921. Numerous interesting displays relate to this important period of modern Irish history. There are also displays on Irish decorative arts, ceramics, musical instruments and Japanese decorative arts. Dublin 1000 tells the story of Dublin's Viking era, with exhibits from the excavations at Wood Quay – the area between Christ Church Cathedral and the river, where, despite protests, the Dublin City Council decided to plonk its headquarters. Frequent short-term exhibitions are also held.

The museum is open Tuesday to Saturday from 10 am to 5 pm and Sunday 2 to 5 pm. Entry is free but guided tours are available for IR£1.

The National Gallery

Opened in 1864, the National Gallery on Merrion Square is particularly strong, of course, in Irish art but also has high-quality collections of every major school of European painting.

On the lawn in front of the gallery is a statue of the Irish railway magnate William Dargan, who organised the 1853 Dublin Industrial Exhibition at this spot; the profits from the exhibition were used to found the gallery. The gallery entrance is guarded by a statue of George Bernard Shaw, who was a major benefactor of the gallery. The proceeds from *My Fair Lady* certainly helped the gallery's acquisition programme.

The gallery has three wings: the original Dargan Wing, the Milltown Rooms and the Modern Wing. The Dargan Wing's ground floor has the imposing Shaw Room, lined with full-length portraits and illuminated by a series of spectacular Waterford crystal chandeliers. Upstairs the series of rooms is dedicated to the Italian early and high Renaissance, 16th-century north Italian art and 17th and 18th-century Italian art. Fra Angelico, Titian and Tintoretto are among the artists represented here.

The central Milltown Rooms were added in 1899-1903 to house the art collection of Russborough House which was presented to the gallery in 1902. The ground floor displays the gallery's fine Irish collection plus a smaller British collection, with works by Reynolds, Hogarth, Gainsborough, Landseer and Turner. One of the highlights is the room at the back of the gallery displaying works by Jack B Yeats (1871-1957), the younger brother of W B Yeats. Other rooms relate to specific periods and styles of Irish art, including one room of works by Irish artists painting in France.

Upstairs are works from Germany, the Netherlands and Spain. There are rooms of works by Rembrandt and his circle and by Spanish artists of Seville. The Spanish collection features works by El Greco, Goya and Picasso.

The Modern Wing was added in 1964-68 but at the time of writing is closed for major redevelopment. The gallery also has an art reference library, a lecture theatre, a good bookshop and an excellent and deservedly popular restaurant. The gallery hours are from 10 am to 6 pm Monday to Saturday (to 9 pm Thursday), and 2 to 5 pm on Sunday.

Entry is free and there are guided tours at 3 pm on Saturday and at 2.30, 3.15 and 4 pm on Sunday.

Leinster House – The Dáil

Both the lower house (Dáil) and the upper house (Seanad) of Ireland's parliament, the Oireachtas na hÉireann, meet in Leinster House on Kildare St. The entrance to Leinster House from Kildare St is flanked by the National Library and the National Museum. Originally built as Kildare House in 1745-48 for the earl of Kildare, the name of the building was changed when he also assumed the title of duke of Leinster in 1766. One of the members of the Fitzgerald family who held the titles was Lord Edward Fitzgerald, who died of wounds he received in the abortive 1798 rebellion.

Leinster House's Kildare St frontage was designed to look like a town house, whereas the Merrion Square frontage was made to look like a country house. Richard Castle, the house's architect, later built the Rotunda Hospital in north Dublin to a similar design. The lawn in front of the Merrion Square country-house frontage was the site for railway pioneer William Dargan's 1853 Dublin Industrial Exhibition, which in turn led to the creation of the National Gallery. There's a statue of him at the National Gallery end of the lawn. At the other end of the lawn is a statue of Prince Albert, Queen Victoria's consort. Queen Victoria herself was commemorated in massive form on the Kildare St side from 1908 until the statue was removed in 1948. The obelisk in front of the building is dedicated to Arthur Griffith, Michael Collins and Kevin O'Higgins, architects of independent Ireland.

The Dublin Society, later named the Royal Dublin Society, bought the building in 1814 but moved out in stages between 1922 and 1925, when the first government of independent Ireland decided to establish their parliament there.

The Seanad or Senate meets in the north-wing saloon, while the Dáil meets in a less interesting room that was originally a lecture theatre added to the original building in

1897. When parliament is sitting (usually between November and May) you can arrange a visit; ask at the Kildare St entrance.

Government Buildings

On Merrion St Upper, on the south side of the Natural History Museum, the domed Government Buildings were opened in 1911, in a rather heavy-handed Edwardian interpretation of the Georgian style. On Saturdays 40-minute tours are conducted from 10.30 am to 12.45 pm and 1.30 to 4.45 pm. You get to see the Taoiseach's office, the ceremonial staircase and the cabinet room. Tickets are available on the day from the National Gallery ticket office.

Across the road at No 24 is Mornington House, a Georgian mansion thought to be the birthplace of the Duke of Wellington, who was somewhat ashamed of his Irish origins. It's possible that his actual birthplace was Trim in County Meath. The mansion is now occupied by a government department.

The National Library

Flanking the Kildare St entrance to Leinster House is the National Library, which was built in 1884-90, at the same time and to a similar design as the National Museum by Sir Thomas Newenham Deane and his son Sir Thomas Manly Deane. Leinster House, the library and museum were all part of the Royal Dublin Society (formed in 1731), which aimed to improve conditions for poor people and to promote the arts and sciences. The library's extensive collection has many valuable early manuscripts, first editions, maps and other items. Temporary displays are often held in the entrance area and the library's reading room featured in *Ulysses*. The library is open Monday to Thursday from 10 am to 9 pm, Friday 10 am to 5 pm and Saturday 10 am to 1 pm.

Heraldic Museum & Genealogical Office

On the corner of Kildare and Nassau Sts, the former home of the Kildare St Club is shared by the Heraldic Museum and Genealogical Office and the Alliance Française. It's a popular destination for visitors intent on tracing their Irish roots. The Kildare St Club was an important right-wing institution during Dublin's Anglo-Irish heyday. Note the whimsical though rather worn stone carvings of animals that decorate the building's windows.

The Heraldic Museum's displays follow the story of heraldry in Ireland and Europe. It's open Monday to Friday from 10 am to 12.30 pm and 2.30 to 4.30 pm.

Natural History Museum

Just as the National Library and the National Museum flank the entrance to Leinster House on the Kildare St side, the National Gallery and Natural History Museum perform the same function on the Merrion St Upper/ Merrion Square side.

The Natural History Museum (☎ 661 8811) has scarcely changed since 1857 when Scottish explorer Dr David Livingstone delivered the opening lecture. It's known as the Dead Zoo, but despite that disheartening appellation it's well worth a visit, for its collection is huge and surprisingly well kept. That moth-eaten look which afflicts neglected collections of stuffed animals has been kept well at bay and children in particular are likely to find it fascinating.

The collection of skeletons, stuffed animals and the like covers the full range of Irish fauna and includes three skeletons of the Irish giant elk, which became extinct about 10,000 years ago.

The museum hours are 10 am to 5 pm Tuesday to Saturday, 2 to 5 pm on Sunday. Entry is free.

Grafton St

Grafton St was the major traffic artery of south Dublin until it was turned into a pedestrian precinct in 1982. It's now Dublin's fanciest and most colourful shopping centre with plenty of street life and the city's most entertaining buskers. The street is equally lively after dark as some of Dublin's most interesting pubs are clustered around it.

Apart from fine shops, such as the Switzers (opened in 1838) and Brown Thomas (opened in 1848) department stores,

Grafton St also features Bewley's Oriental Café. This branch of the chain has an upstairs museum relating to the company's history.

Back from Grafton St on William St South is the elegantly converted Powerscourt Townhouse shopping centre. Built between 1771 and 1774, this grand house has a balconied courtyard, and, following its conversion in 1981, now shelters three levels of modern shops and restaurants. The Powerscourt family's principal residence was Powerscourt House in County Wicklow and this city mansion was soon sold for commercial use. It survived that period in remarkably good condition and in its new incarnation it forms a convenient link from Grafton St to the South City Market on South Great George's St. The building features plasterwork by Michael Stapleton, who also worked on Belvedere House in north Dublin.

Dublin Civic Museum

The Dublin Civic Museum (☎ 667 9426) is at 58 William St South, just a stone's throw from Grafton St. Its displays relate to the history of the city, with exhibits ranging from artefacts from Viking Dublin to a model of a Howth tram and the head from the Lord Nelson statue on O'Connell St which was toppled by the IRA in 1966.

The museum is open Tuesday to Saturday from 10 am to 6 pm, Sunday 11 am to 2 pm, and entry is free.

Mansion House

Mansion House on Dawson St was built in 1710 by Joshua Dawson, after whom the street is named. Only five years later the house was bought as a residence for the Lord Mayor of Dublin. The building's original brick Queen Anne style has all but disappeared behind a stucco façade tacked on in the Victorian era. The building was the site for the 1919 Declaration of Independence but it is generally not open to the public. Next door is the **Royal Irish Academy**, also generally not open to visitors.

St Stephen's Green

On warm summer days the nine hectares of St Stephen's Green provide a popular lunchtime escape for city office workers. The Green was originally an expanse of open common land where public whippings and hangings took place. The Green was enclosed by a fence in 1664 when Dublin Corporation sold off the surrounding land for buildings. A stone wall replaced the fence in 1669 and trees and gravel paths soon followed within. By the end of that century restrictions were already in force prohibiting buildings of less than two storeys or those constructed of mud and wattle. At the same time Grafton St, the main route to the Green from what was then central Dublin, was upgraded from a 'foule and out of repaire' laneway to a crown causeway.

The fine Georgian buildings around the square date mainly from Dublin's mid to late 18th-century Georgian prime. At that time the north side was known as the Beaux' Walk and it is still one of Dublin society's most esteemed meeting places. Further improvements were made in 1753, with seats being put in place, but in 1814 railings and locked gates were added and an annual fee of one guinea was charged to use the Green. This private use continued until 1877 when Sir Arthur Edward Guinness, later Lord Ardilaun, pushed an act through parliament which once again made the Green a public place. The gardens and ponds of the central park date from 1880 and were financed by the wealthy brewer.

Across the road from the west side of the Green are the 1863 **Unitarian Church** and the **Royal College of Surgeons**, the latter with one of the finest façades around St Stephen's Green. It was built in 1806 and extended in 1825-27 to the design of William Murray. Forty years later Murray's son, William G Murray, designed the Royal College of Physicians building on Kildare St. In the 1916 Rising, the Royal College of Surgeons was occupied by the colourful Countess Markievicz (1868-1927), an Irish nationalist married to a Polish count. The countess would have handled modern media with aplomb; her first question upon taking the college was the whereabouts of the scalpels, implying they would be useful in hand-to-hand combat with British troops. The columns still bear bullet marks.

At one time the main entrance to the Green was on this side but now it is through the **Fusiliers' Arch** at the north-west corner of the Green from Grafton St. Modelled on the Arch of Titus in Rome, the arch commemorates the 212 soldiers of the Royal Dublin Fusiliers who died in the Boer War (1899-1902).

A path from the arch passes by the duck pond while around the fountain in the centre of the Green are a number of statues, including a bust of Countess Markievicz. The centre of the park also has a garden for the blind, complete with signs in Braille and plants which can be handled.

On the eastern side of the Green there's a children's play park and to the south is a fine old **bandstand**, erected for Queen Victoria's jubilee in 1887. Concerts often take place here in the summer.

Just inside the Green at the south-east corner, near Leeson St, is a statue of the Three Fates, presented to Dublin in 1956 by West Germany in gratitude for Irish aid immediately after WW II. The north-west corner, opposite the Shelbourne Hotel and Merrion Row, is marked by the Wolfe Tone Monument to the leader of the abortive 1796 invasion. The vertical slabs which serve as a backdrop for Wolfe Tone's statue have been dubbed 'Tonehenge'. Just inside the park at this entrance is a memorial to the victims of the potato famines.

Notable buildings around the Green include the imposing old 1867 **Shelbourne Hotel** on the north side, with statues of Nubian princesses and their ankle-fettered slave girls decorating the front. Just beyond the Shelbourne is a small **Huguenot cemetery** dating from 1693, when many French Huguenots fled here from persecution under Louis XIV.

Grafton St runs from the north-west corner of the Green, while Merrion Row, with its popular pubs, runs from the north-east. At the south-east is Leeson St, the nightclub centre of Dublin. The Hotel

Conrad, Dublin's Hilton Hotel, is just off the square from this corner on Earlsfort Terrace, as is the National Concert Hall.

Harcourt St, from the south-west corner, was laid out in 1775. Well-known names associated with the street include Edward Carson, who was born at No 4 in 1854. As the architect of Northern Irish 'unionism' he is an easy scapegoat for many of the problems caused by Ireland's division. Bram Stoker, author of *Dracula*, lived at No 16 and George Bernard Shaw at No 61. For 99 years from 1859 to 1958 the Dublin-Bray railway line used to terminate at Harcourt St Station, which was once at the bottom of this road.

At No 80/81 on the south side of the Green is **Iveagh House**, where the Guinness family was once domiciled; today the Department of Foreign Affairs lives there. Designed by Richard Castle in 1730, this was his first project in Dublin. He went on to create many more buildings, including Leinster House and the Rotunda Hospital.

At No 85/86 on the south side of the Green is **Newman House**, which is now part of University College Dublin. These buildings have some of the finest plasterwork in the city. No 85 was built between 1736 and 1738 by Richard Castle for Hugh Montgomery MP. The particularly fine plasterwork was by the Swiss stuccodores Paul and Philip Francini (also known as Paolo and Filippo Lafranchi) and can be best appreciated in the wonderfully detailed Apollo Room on the ground floor.

Richard Chapel Whaley MP had taken possession of No 85 in 1765 but decided to display his wealth by constructing a much grander home next door at No 86. Whaley's son Buck contrived to become an MP while still a teenager and also one of the more notorious members of Dublin's Hell Fire Club. He was also a noted gambler, once walking all the way to Jerusalem to win a bet.

The Catholic University of Ireland, predecessor of University College Dublin, acquired the building in 1865. Some of the plasterwork was a little too detailed for strict Catholic tastes, however, so cover-ups were prescribed. On the ceiling of the upstairs

Saloon the previously naked figure of Juno was clad in what can best be described as a furry swimsuit.

The Catholic University named Newman House after its first rector, John Henry Newman. Gerard Manley Hopkins, professor of classics at the college from 1884 until his death in 1889, lived upstairs at No 86. It was not until some time after his death that his innovative if rather depressive poetry was published. His room is now preserved as it was during his residence. Among former students of the college are James Joyce, Patrick Pearse, leader of the 1916 Easter Rising, and Eamon de Valera.

The restoration of Newman House is a relatively recent project and will continue for some time. The house is open June to September from 10 am to 4.30 pm Tuesday to Friday, Saturday 2 to 4.30 pm and Sunday 11 am to 2 pm. At other times of the year phone (☎ 475 1752 or 475 7255) for information. The IR£1 (concessions 75p) entry includes a video about the building and a good guided tour.

Next to Newman House is the **Catholic University Church** or Newman Chapel, built in 1854-56 with a colourful neo-Byzantine interior that attracted a great deal of criticism at the time. Today this is one of the most fashionable churches in Dublin for weddings.

Merrion Square

Merrion Square, with its well-kept central park and elegant Georgian buildings, dates back to 1762 and has the National Gallery on its west side. Around this square you can find some of the best Georgian Dublin entrances – there are fine doors and fanlights, ornate door knockers and more than a few foot scrapers where gentlemen would remove mud from their shoes before venturing indoors. Oscar Wilde's parents, the surgeon Sir William Wilde and the poet Lady Wilde, who wrote under the pseudonym Speranza, lived at 1 Merrion Square North. Oscar was born in 1854 at the now near-derelict 21 Westland Row, just north of the square.

W B Yeats (1865-1939) lived first at 52 Merrion Square East and later, in 1922-28, at 82 Merrion Square South. George (Æ) Russell (1867-1935), the 'poet, mystic, painter and co-operator', worked at No 84. Daniel O'Connell (1775-1847) was a resident of No 58 in his later years. The Austrian Erwin Schrödinger (1887-1961), co-winner of the 1933 Nobel Prize for physics, lived at No 65 between 1940 and 1956. Dublin seems to attract the writers of horror stories: Joseph Sheridan Le Fanu (1814-73), who penned the vampire classic *Carmilla*, was a former resident of No 70. The UK Embassy was at 39 Merrion Square East until it was burnt out in 1972 in protest against Bloody Sunday in Derry, Northern Ireland.

Damage to fine Dublin buildings has not always been the prerogative of vandals, terrorists or protesters. Merrion Square East once continued into Fitzwilliam St Lower in the longest unbroken series of Georgian houses anywhere in Europe. In 1961 the Electricity Supply Board knocked down 26 of them to build an office block. The Architectural Association, however, does live in a real Georgian house. It's at 8 Merrion Square North, a few doors down from the Wilde residence. The house at No 12 is open to the public on Saturday and Sunday afternoons from noon to 4 pm.

The Leinster Lawn at the western end of the square has the 1791 **Rutland Fountain** and an 18-metre obelisk honouring the founders of independent Ireland. Merrion Square has not always been merely graceful and affluent, however. During the 1845-51 potato famines, soup kitchens were set up in the gardens, which were crowded with starving rural refugees.

At the south-east corner of Merrion Square the Electricity Supply Board, having demolished most of Fitzwilliam St Lower to construct a new office block, had the decency to preserve one of the fine old Georgian houses at **No 29 Fitzwilliam St Lower**. It has been restored to give a good impression of genteel home life in Dublin between 1790 and 1820.

The house is open from 10 am to 5 pm Tuesday to Saturday and 2 to 5 pm on

Sunday. Entry is free and includes an audio-visual display on the house's history followed by a guided tour.

Merrion St Upper & Ely Place

Merrion St Upper was built around 1770, and runs south from Merrion Square towards St Stephen's Green. The Duke of Wellington was probably born at the now rather run-down 24 Merrion St Upper. On the other side of Baggot St, Merrion St becomes Ely (pronounced 'e-lie') Place.

John Philpot Curran (1750-1817), a great advocate of Irish liberty, once lived at No 4, as did the novelist George Moore (1852-1933). The house at No 6 was the residence of the earl of Clare. Better known as Black Jack Fitzgibbon (1749-1802), he was a bitter opponent of Irish political aspirations, and in 1794 a mob attempted to storm the house. Ely House at No 8 is one of the best examples of a Georgian mansion in the city. The plasterwork is by Michael Stapleton and the staircase which illustrates the Labours of Hercules is one of the finest in the city. At one time the surgeon Sir Thornley Stoker (whose brother Bram Stoker wrote *Dracula)* lived here. Oliver St John Gogarty (1878-1957) lived for a time at No 25, but the art gallery of the Royal Hibernian Academy now occupies that position.

Fitzwilliam Square

South of Merrion Square and east of St Stephen's Green, the original and well-kept Fitzwilliam Square is a centre for the Dublin medical profession. Built between 1791 and 1825, it was the smallest and the last of Dublin's great Georgian squares. It is also the only square where the central garden is still the private domain of residents of the square. William Dargan, the railway pioneer and founder of the National Gallery, lived at No 2, and Jack B Yeats lived at No 18.

Other South Dublin Churches

St Andrew's Church The Protestant St Andrew's Church is on St Andrew's St near Trinity College, the Bank of Ireland and Grafton St. Designed by Charles Lanyon, the Gothic-style church was built in 1860-73 on the site of an ancient nunnery. Across the street, on the corner of Church Lane and Suffolk St, there once stood a huge Viking ceremonial mound or *thingmote*. It was levelled in 1661 and used to raise the level of Nassau St, which had previously been subject to flooding.

There is also a Catholic St Andrew's Church behind Trinity College on Westland Row, beside Pearse Station.

Whitefriars Carmelite Church Next to the popular Avalon House backpackers hostel on Aungier St, the Carmelite Church stands on the former site of the Whitefriars Carmelite monastery. The monastery was founded in 1278 but, like other monasteries, was suppressed by Henry VIII in 1537 and all its lands and wealth were seized by the crown. Eventually the Carmelites returned to their former church and re-established it, dedicating the new building in 1827.

In the north-east corner of the church the 16th-century Flemish oak statue of the Virgin and Child escaped destruction during the Reformation; it probably once belonged to St Mary's Abbey in north Dublin. The church's altar contains the remains of St Valentine, of St Valentine's Day fame. The relics were donated to the church in 1836 by the pope.

St Ann's Church St Ann's on Dawson St near Mansion House was built in 1720 but is now lost behind an 1868 neo-Romanesque façade. There's a fine view of it looking down Anne St South from Grafton St, and it is noted for its lunch-time recitals.

St Stephen's Church Built in 1825 in Greek Revival style, St Stephen's, complete with cupola, is at the far end of Mount St Upper from Merrion Square. Because of its appearance, it has been nicknamed the 'Pepper Canister Church'.

South Dublin Theatres

Dublin's famous **Abbey Theatre** is north of the Liffey, but the city's first theatre opened in 1637 on Werburgh St, near Dublin Castle and the two cathedrals. It was closed by the Puritans only four years later, but another theatre, Smock Alley Playhouse or Theatre Royal, opened in 1661 and continued for over a century. Today theatres south of the Liffey include the Gaiety on King St South, just off Grafton St. Built in 1871, this is Dublin's oldest theatre and now hosts a variety of performances.

The 1892 **Olympia Theatre** on Dame St in Temple Bar is the city's largest and second-oldest theatre and is a venue for popular performances. It was previously known as the Palace Theatre and Dan Lowry's Music Hall. Also south of the Liffey is the **Tivoli Theatre** on Francis St in the Liberties. A number of other Dublin theatres are listed under Other Theatres in the Other Sights section.

NORTH OF THE LIFFEY

Though south Dublin has the lion's share of the city's tourist attractions, there are still many reasons to head across the Liffey, starting with Dublin's grandest avenue.

O'Connell St

O'Connell St is the major thoroughfare of north Dublin and probably the most important and imposing street in the whole city, even though its earlier glory has gone. It started life in the early 18th century as Drogheda St, named after Viscount Henry Moore, the earl of Drogheda. There are still a Henry St, a Moore St and an Earl St nearby. The earl even managed to squeeze in an Of Lane! At that time Capel St, farther to the west, was the main traffic route and Drogheda St, lacking a bridge to connect it with south Dublin, was of little importance.

In the 1740s Luke Gardiner, later Viscount Mountjoy, widened the street to 45 metres to turn it into an elongated promenade bearing his name. However, it was the completion of the Carlisle Bridge across the Liffey in 1794 which quickly made it the city's most important street. In 1880 the Carlisle Bridge was replaced by the much wider O'Connell Bridge which stands today.

Gardiner's Mall soon became Sackville St, but it was renamed again in 1924 after Daniel O'Connell, the Irish nationalist leader whose 1854 bronze statue surveys the avenue from the river end. The bullet marks are a legacy of the Easter Rising in 1916 and the Civil War in 1922.

The street's most famous monument was a victim of explosive redesign. In 1815 O'Connell St was graced with a Doric column topped by a statue of Nelson, the English captain who defeated the French at Trafalgar. It predated his column in Trafalgar Square (London) by 32 years, but in 1966, in an unofficial celebration of the 50th anniversary of the 1916 Rising, this symbol of British imperialism was damaged by an explosion and subsequently demolished. Nelson's demise put an end to the quip that the main street of the capital city of this most piously Catholic of countries had statues honouring three noted adulterers: O'Connell at the bottom of the street, Parnell at the top and Nelson in the middle.

The site of Nelson's demolished column is halfway up the street, between Henry and Earl Sts, opposite the GPO. Nearby, a figure of James Joyce lounges nonchalantly at the top of pedestrianised Earl St North. Just beyond the former site of the column is a fountain figure of Anna Livia, Joyce's spirit of the Liffey – a 1988 addition to the streetscape. It was almost immediately dubbed the Floozie in the Jacuzzi.

The tourist office and the Gresham Hotel are on the right before the figure of Father Theobald Mathew (1790-1856), the 'apostle of temperance', a hopeless role in Ireland. This quixotic task, however, also resulted in a Liffey bridge bearing his name. The top of the street is completed by the imposing statue of Charles Stewart Parnell (1846-91), Home Rule advocate and victim of Irish morality.

O'Connell St has certainly had its share of drama; its high-speed redevelopment began during the 1916 Rising when the GPO building became the starting point for, and main centre of, the abortive revolt. Only six years later in 1922 the unfortunate avenue suffered another bout of destruction when it became the scene of a Civil War clash that burnt down most of the eastern side of the street.

Poor O'Connell St was to suffer even more damage in the 1960s and 1970s when Dublin went through a period of rampant development under extremely lax government controls. Developers seemed to have open slather to tear anything down and sling anything up so long as there was a quid in it and the fast-food and cheap-office-block atmosphere today is a reminder of that era.

Close to O'Connell St is an energetic and colourful open-air market area just to the west on Moore St. The Abbey Theatre and the Catholic St Mary's Pro-Cathedral are to the east. At the top of O'Connell St is Parnell Square.

General Post Office

The GPO building on O'Connell St is an important landmark physically and historically. The building, designed by Francis Johnston and opened in 1818, was the focus for the 1916 Easter Rising when Patrick Pearse, James Connolly and the other leaders read their proclamation from the front steps. In the subsequent siege the building was completely burnt out. The façade with its Ionic portico is still pockmarked from the 1916 clash and from further damage wrought at the start of the Civil War in 1922. The GPO was not reopened until 1929. Its central role in the history of independent Ireland has made it a prime site for everything from official parades to protest rallies.

Abbey Theatre

Opened in 1904, the Abbey Theatre (☎ 878 7222) is just north of the Liffey on the corner of Marlborough St and Abbey St Lower. The Irish National Theatre Society soon made a name not only for playwrights like J M Synge and Sean O'Casey but also for Irish acting ability and theatrical presentation. The 1907 premiere of J M Synge's *The Playboy of the Western World* brought a storm of protest from theatregoers, and Sean O'Casey's *The Plough & the Stars* prompted a similar reaction in 1926. On the latter occa-sion W B Yeats himself came on stage after the performance to tick the audience off!

The original theatre burnt down in 1951. It took 15 years to come up with a replacement and the dull building fails to live up to its famous name or the company's continuing reputation. The smaller Peacock Theatre at the same location presents new and experimental works.

St Mary's Pro-Cathedral

On the corner of Marlborough and Cathedral Sts, just east of O'Connell St, is Dublin's most important Catholic church, built between 1816 and 1825. The Pro-Cathedral was originally intended to be built on O'Connell St, but fears that such a prominent position would provoke anti-Catholic feeling among the English led to its site being comparatively hidden. Unfortunately, the cramped Marlborough St location makes it all but impossible to stand back far enough to admire the front with its six Doric columns, modelled after the Temple of Theseus in Athens.

The 1814 competition for the church's design was won by John Sweetman, a former owner of Sweetman's Brewery. Who organised the competition? Why William Sweetman, John Sweetman's brother. And did John Sweetman design it himself? Well, possibly not. He was living in Paris at the time and may have bought the plans from a French architect who designed the remarkably similar Notre Dame de Lorette in Paris.

Tyrone House

On Marlborough St, opposite the Pro-Cathedral, the sombre Tyrone House, built in 1740-41, is now occupied by the Department of Education. It was designed by Richard Castle and features plasterwork by the Francini brothers. On the lawn is a marble *Pietà* (statue of the Virgin Mary cradling the dead body of Jesus Christ) sculpted in 1930 and given to Ireland by the Italian government in 1948 in thanks for Irish assistance immediately after the war. This area was once a busy red light district known as

Monto and featured in Joyce's *Ulysses* as Nighttown.

Parnell Square

The principal squares of north Dublin are impoverished relations of the great squares south of the Liffey. Parnell Square's north side was built on lands acquired in the mid-18th century by Dr Bartholomew Mosse and was originally named Palace Row. The terrace was laid out in 1755 and Lord Charlemont bought the land for his home at No 22 in 1762. Charlemont's home was designed by Sir William Chambers, who also designed Lord Charlemont's extraordinary Casino at Marino to the north-east of the city centre. Today the building is home to the Municipal Gallery of Modern Art. The street was completed in 1769 and the gardens were renamed Rutland Square in 1786, before acquiring their current name.

In 1966 the northern slice of the square was turned into a Garden of Remembrance for the 50th anniversary of the 1916 Rising. Its centrepiece is a sculpture by Oisin Kelly depicting the myth of the Children of Lir, who were transformed into swans for 900 years. The square also contains the Gate Theatre, the Ambassador Cinema and the Rotunda Hospital.

There are some fine, though generally rather run-down, Georgian houses on the east side of the square. Oliver St John Gogarty, immortalised as Buck Mulligan in Joyce's *Ulysses*, was born at No 5 in 1878. On the other side of the square, at 44 Parnell Square West, you can find the Sinn Féin Bookshop.

Dr Bartholomew Mosse, who originally acquired the land on which Parnell Square is built, opened the **Rotunda Hospital** in 1757. This was the first maternity hospital in the British Isles, built at a time when Dublin's burgeoning urban population suffered horrific levels of infant mortality. The hospital shares its basic design with Leinster House because Richard Castle reused the floorplan as an economy measure.

To his Leinster House design Castle added a three-storey tower which Mosse had intended to use as a lookout to raise funds for the hospital's operation. The Rotunda Assembly Hall, now occupied by the Ambassador Cinema, was built as an adjunct to the hospital as another fundraiser. At one time an adjacent pleasure garden was another money-raising venture. Over the main entrance of the hospital is the Rotunda Chapel, built in 1758 with superb coloured plasterwork by Bartholomew Cramillion.

The Rotunda Hospital still functions as a maternity hospital. The Patrick Conway pub opposite the hospital dates from 1745 and has been hosting expectant fathers since the day the hospital opened.

At the top end of O'Connell St, in the south-east corner of Parnell Square, is the **Gate Theatre**, opened in 1929 by Micheál MacLiammóir and Hilton Edwards. MacLiammóir continued to act at his theatre until 1975, when he retired at the age of 76 after making his 1384th performance of the one-man show *The Importance of Being Oscar* (Oscar being Oscar Wilde, of course). The Gate Theatre was also the stage for Orson Welles's first professional appearance. The building dates from 1784-86 when it was built as part of the Rotunda complex of the Rotunda Maternity Hospital.

The **Municipal Gallery of Modern Art** or Hugh Lane Gallery (☎ 874 1903) at 22 Parnell Square North has a fine collection of work by the French Impressionists and of 20th-century Irish art.

The gallery was founded in 1908 and moved to its present location in Charlemont House, formerly the Earl of Charlemont's town house, in 1933. The gallery was established by wealthy Sir Hugh Lane, who died in the 1915 sinking of the *Lusitania*, which was torpedoed off the southern coast of Ireland by a German U-boat. The Lane Bequest Pictures, which formed the nucleus of the gallery, were the subject of a dispute over Lane's will between the gallery and the National Gallery in London. A settlement was finally reached in 1959 which split the collection.

The gallery includes a shop and the Gallery Restaurant. The gallery is open

Tuesday to Friday from 9.30 am to 6 pm, Saturday 9.30 am to 5 pm, Sunday 11 am to 5 pm. Entry is free.

The **Dublin Writers' Museum** (☎ 872 2077) at 18 Parnell Square North is next to the Hugh Lane Gallery. It celebrates the city's long and continuing history as a literary centre. The one big omission is material about more recent writers. One could almost believe that the spark faded after WW II, which is far from the truth.

The museum also has a bookshop and the Chapter One restaurant. Next door at No 19 the Irish Writers' Centre provides a meeting and working place for contemporary writers.

Entry is IR£2.25 (students IR£1.50, children 70p) and it's open from 10 am to 5 pm Tuesday to Saturday, 1 to 5 pm Sunday. In July and August it's also open 10 am to 5 pm on Monday. From October to March it only opens Friday, Saturday and Sunday.

The soaring spire of the **Abbey Presbyterian Church** at the corner of Frederick St and Parnell Square North, overlooking Parnell Square, is a convenient landmark. Dating from 1864 the church was financed by the Scottish grocery and brewery magnate Alex Findlater and is often referred to as Findlater's Church.

National Wax Museum

Every city worth its tourist traps has a wax museum. Dublin's National Wax Museum (☎ 872 6340) is on Granby Row, just north of Parnell Square. Along with the usual fantasy and fairy-tale offerings, the inevitable Chamber of Horrors and a rock music 'megastars' area, there are also figures of Irish heroes like Wolfe Tone, Robert Emmet and Charles Parnell, the leaders of the 1916 Rising, and the Taoiseachs (prime ministers). The museum is open Monday to Saturday from 10 am to 5.30 pm, Sunday 1 to 5.30 pm. Entry is IR£2.50 (children IR£1.50).

Great Denmark St

From the north-east corner of Parnell Square, Great Denmark St runs eastwards to Mountjoy Square, passing by the 1775 Belvedere House which has been used since 1841 as the Jesuit **Belvedere College**. James Joyce was a student there between 1893 and 1898 and describes it in *A Portrait of the Artist as a Young Man*. The building is renowned for its magnificent plasterwork by the master stuccodore Michael Stapleton and for its fireplaces by the Venetian artisan Bossi.

Mountjoy Square

Built between 1792 and 1818, Mountjoy Square was a fashionable and affluent centre at the height of the Protestant Ascendancy, but today it's just a run-down symbol of north Dublin's urban decay. Viscount Mountjoy, after whom the square was named, was that energetic developer Luke Gardiner, who briefly gave his name to Gardiner Mall before it became Sackville St and then O'Connell St. The square was in fact named after him twice, as it started life as Gardiner Square.

Legends relate that this was where Brian Ború pitched his tent at the Battle of Clontarf in 1014. Residents of the square have included Sean O'Casey, who set his play *The Shadow of a Gunman* here, though he referred to it as Hilljoy Square. As a child James Joyce lived just off the square at 14 Fitzgibbon St.

St Francis Xavier Church

Built in 1829-32 on Gardiner St Upper, the Catholic St Francis Xavier Church has a superb Italian altar and coffered ceiling. It was originally intended that the church be built on Great Charles St, behind Mountjoy Square.

St George's Church

St George's Church is on Hardwicke Place off Temple St, but was originally intended to be built in Mountjoy Square. It was built by Francis Johnston from 1802 in Greek Ionic style and has a 60-metre-high steeple modelled after that of St Martin-in-the-Fields in London. The church's bells were added in 1836 and originally hung in a bell tower in Francis Johnston's own back garden in nearby Eccles St. Not surprisingly, neighbours complained about the noise and

Johnston eventually willed them to the church. This was one of Johnston's finest works and the Duke of Wellington was married here, but the church is no longer in use.

St Mary's Abbey

Despite the intriguing history of St Mary's Abbey, there is little to see, the opening hours are very restricted and even finding the abbey is rather difficult. It is just west of Capel St in Meetinghouse Lane, which runs off a street named Mary's Abbey. When the abbey was founded in 1139 this was a rural location, far from the temptations of city life to the south of the Liffey. In 1147, soon after its foundation by the Benedictine monks, it was taken over by the Cistercians. Until its suppression in the mid-16th century this was the most important monastery within English-controlled Ireland. St Mary's property was confiscated by Henry VIII in 1537; it turned out to be the most valuable in all of Ireland, at a total of £537. Mellifont Abbey to the north of Dublin came in second at £352 but no other monastery in the whole country was worth over £100.

The abbey was virtually derelict when the next century rolled around, although at that time Dublin had not started its sprawl north of the river. Records indicate that in 1676 stones from the abbey were used to construct the Essex Bridge and it was not until comparatively recently that the remaining fragments were rediscovered.

The chapter house, where the monks used to gather after morning mass, is the only surviving part of the abbey, which in its prime encompassed land stretching as far east as Ballybough. The floor level in the abbey is two metres below street level – a clear indication of the changes wrought over eight centuries. Exhibits in the abbey tell of the destruction of the Reformation in 1540 and the story of the statue from St Mary's which is now in the Whitefriars Carmelite Church on Aungier St in south Dublin.

The abbey is only open from mid-June to September and even then only on Wednes-days from noon to 6 pm. Entry is IR£1 for adults, 40p for students or children.

St Mary's Church

In Mary St, between Capel and O'Connell Sts, St Mary's was designed in 1697 by Sir William Robinson, who was also responsible for the Royal Hospital Kilmainham. The church was completed in 1702 and a roll call of famous Dubliners were baptised there. It was in this church that John Wesley, the founder of Methodism, preached for the first time in Ireland in 1747. Nevertheless, like so many other fine old Dublin churches, it is no longer in use. Irish patriot Wolfe Tone was born on the adjacent Wolfe Tone St.

St Michan's Church

Named after a Danish saint, St Michan's Church on Church St Lower, near the Four Courts, dates from its Danish foundation in 1095, though there's barely a trace of that original church to be seen. The battlement tower dates from the 15th century but otherwise it was rebuilt in the late 17th century and considerably restored in the early 19th century and again after suffering damage in the Civil War.

The church contains the organ which, it is claimed, Handel played for the first-ever performance of his *Messiah*, but the main attraction is the mummified human remains in the subterranean crypts. With more than a little Irish blarney your guide will insist that the vault's special atmosphere accounts for their perfect preservation. In fact they're as dried, shrivelled and crumbling as you might expect after the odd few centuries.

Tours are conducted regularly from 10 am to 12.45 pm and 2 to 4.45 pm Monday to Friday, and on Saturday mornings only. The cost is IR£1.20 (children 50p).

Irish Whiskey Corner

Just north of St Michan's Church, the Irish Whiskey Corner (☎ 872 5566) is in an old warehouse on Bow St, Dublin 7, and the admission charge of IR£2 includes entry to the museum, a short film and a sample of Irish whiskey.

King's Inns & Henrietta St

North of the river on Constitution Hill and Henrietta St is King's Inns, home for the Dublin legal fraternity. This classical building is another James Gandon creation though it suffered many delays between its design in 1795 and its final completion in 1817. Along the way a number of other architects lent a hand, including Francis Johnston, who added the cupola. The building is normally open only to members of the Inns.

Henrietta St, leading up to the south side of the building, was Dublin's first Georgian street and has buildings dating from 1720 but is unfortunately now in a state of extreme disrepair. These early Georgian mansions were large and varied in style and for a time Henrietta St rejoiced in the name Primate's Hill, as the archbishop of Armagh and other high church officials lived there. Luke Gardiner, who was responsible for so much of the early development of Georgian north Dublin, lived at 10 Henrietta St.

OTHER SIGHTS

There's still much more to see in Dublin. To the west are the Guinness Brewery in the colourful Liberties area, Kilmainham Jail and Phoenix Park. To the north and north-east are the Royal Canal, Prospect Cemetery, the Botanic Gardens, the Casino at Marino and Clontarf. To the south and south-east are the Grand Canal, Ballsbridge, the Royal Dublin Showground and the Chester Beatty Library.

St Catherine's Church

Westward from St Audoen's Church, towards that more recent Dublin shrine, the Guinness Brewery, is St Catherine's Church, whose huge front faces on to Thomas St. The church was built on the site of St Thomas Abbey, which King Henry II built in honour of Thomas à Becket, the Archbishop of Canterbury, after having him killed. The church was completed in 1769 and after narrowly escaping redevelopment in the 1960s is now used as a community centre. After being hanged, the corpse of patriot Robert Emmet was put to the further indignity of being beheaded outside the church in 1803.

Guinness Brewery

Moving west past St Audoen's churches, Thomas St metamorphoses into James's St in the area of Dublin known as the Liberties. Along James's St stretches the historic St James's Gate Guinness Brewery (☎ 53 6700, ext 5155). From its foundation by Arthur Guinness in 1759, on the site of the earlier Rainsford Brewery, the operation has expanded down to the Liffey and across both sides of the street. It covers 26 hectares and for a time was the largest brewery in the world. The oldest parts of the site are south of James's St; at one time there was a gate spanning the street.

In the Guinness Hop Store on Crane St, visitors can watch a Guinness audiovisual display and inspect an extensive Guinness museum. It is not a tour of the brewery, but your entry fee includes a glass of the black stuff.

In its early years Guinness was only one of dozens of Dublin breweries but it outgrew and outlasted all of them. At one time a Grand Canal tributary was cut into the brewery to enable special Guinness barges to carry consignments out onto the Irish canal system or to the Dublin port. When the brewery extensions reached the Liffey in 1872, the fleet of Guinness barges became a

familiar sight. There was also a Guinness railway on the site, complete with a spiral tunnel. Guinness still operates its own ships to convey the vital fluid to the British market. Over 50% of all the beer consumed in Ireland is brewed here.

The Guinness family became noted philanthropists. Sir Benjamin Lee Guinness, grandson of the brewery founder, restored St Patrick's Cathedral. Sir Benjamin's son, Lord Ardilaun, opened St Stephen's Green to the public and converted it into a park, and his brother Lord Iveagh helped to build a wing of the Rotunda Hospital.

Hours are 10 am to 4.30 pm (last audiovisual display at 3.30 pm) Monday to Friday. Entry is IR£2 (children 50p). To get there take bus No 21A, 78 or 78A from Fleet St. The upper floors of the building house temporary art exhibits.

IMMA & Royal Hospital Kilmainham

The IMMA or Irish Museum of Modern Art (☎ 671 8666) at the old Royal Hospital Kilmainham is close to Kilmainham Jail. The gallery only opened in 1991 and the exhibits are somewhat dwarfed by their expansive surroundings. There are also regular temporary exhibits.

The Royal Hospital Kilmainham was built in 1680-87 but not as a hospital. It was in fact a home for retired soldiers and continued to fill that role until after Irish independence. It preceded the similar Chelsea Hospital in London and inmates were often referred to as 'Chelsea Pensioners' although there was no connection. At the time of its construction it was one of the finest buildings in Ireland and there was considerable muttering that it was altogether too good a place for its residents. The building was designed by William Robinson, whose work included Marsh's Library.

Kilmainham Gate was designed by Francis Johnston in 1812 and originally stood, as the Richmond Tower, at Watling St Bridge near the Guinness Brewery. It was moved to its current position opposite the jail in 1846 as it obstructed the increasingly heavy traffic to the new Kingsbridge

Railway Station, now known as Heuston Station.

The museum's excellent restaurant is hidden away in the basement at the back of the building. The IMMA is open from 10 am to 5.30 pm Tuesday to Saturday and noon to 5.30 pm on Sunday. Entry is free and there are guided tours on Sunday. You can get there on bus No 24, 79 or 90 from Aston Quay outside the Virgin Megastore.

Kilmainham Jail

Built in 1792-95, the threatening old Kilmainham Jail (☎ 53 5984) on Inchicore Rd played a key role in Ireland's struggle for independence and was the site of the executions that followed the 1916 Easter Rising. During each act of Ireland's long and painful path to independence from neighbouring England, at least one part of the performance took place at the jail. The uprisings of 1799, 1803, 1848, 1867 and 1916 all ended with the leaders being confined in Kilmainham. Robert Emmet, Thomas Francis Meagher, Charles Stewart Parnell and the 1916 Easter Rising leaders were all visitors, but it was the executions in 1916 which most deeply etched the jail's name into the Irish consciousness. Of the 16 executions that took place between 3 and 12 May after the Rising, 14 were conducted here. As a finale prisoners from the Civil War struggles were held here from 1922, before its final closure in 1924.

A visit starts with an excellent audiovisual introduction followed by a tour. Incongruously sitting outside in the yard is the *Asgard*, the ship which successfully ran the British blockade to deliver arms to nationalist forces in 1914. The tour finishes in the gloomy yard where the 1916 executions took place. You almost expect to see the gates swing back and a wounded James Connolly brought in to face the firing squad.

Opening hours are 11 am to 6 pm daily from July to September, and 1 to 4 pm Monday to Friday and 1 to 6 pm on Sunday from October to May. Phone ☎ 53 5984 for further details. Entry is IR£1.50 (children 60p) and you can get there by bus No 23, 51, 51A, 78 or 79 from the city centre.

Phoenix Park

The 700-plus hectares of Phoenix Park makes it one of the world's largest city parks, dwarfing Central Park in New York (a mere 337 hectares) and all the London parks – Hampstead Heath is only 324 hectares. There are gardens and lakes, a host of sporting facilities, the second-oldest public zoo in Europe, various government offices, the Garda (police) Headquarters, the residences of the US ambassador and the Irish president, and even a herd of deer.

The land was originally confiscated from the Kilmainham priory of St John to create a royal deer park. It was turned into a park by Lord Ormonde in 1671 but was not opened to the public until 1747 by Lord Chesterfield. The name Phoenix is actually a corruption of the Irish words for clear water, *fionn uisce*. The park played a crucial role in Irish history, as Lord Cavendish, the British Chief Secretary for Ireland, and his assistant were murdered here in 1882 by an Irish nationalist secret society called the National Invincibles. Lord Cavendish's home is now Deerfield, the US ambassador's residence, and the murder took place outside **Áras an Uachtaráin**, from 1782 until 1922 the viceroy's residence, now occupied by the Irish president. It was built in 1751 and enlarged in 1782 and again in 1816. From 1922 until the final ties with the British crown were cut in 1937 it was the home of Ireland's governor-general.

Near the Parkgate St entrance to the park is the 63-metre-high **Wellington Monument** obelisk. It took from 1817 to 1861 to be built, mainly because the Duke of Wellington fell out of public favour during its construction. Nearby are the People's Garden, dating from 1864, the bandstand in the Hollow and the Dublin Zoo. Main Rd separates the Hollow and the zoo from the Phoenix Park Cricket Club of 1830 and from Citadel Pond, usually referred to as the Dog Pond.

Established in 1830, **Dublin Zoo** (☎ 677 1425) is one of the oldest in the world. It's mainly of interest to children – there's even a pets' corner. The lion-breeding programme dates back to 1857 and produced the lion that roars at the start of MGM films. Entry is IR£4.20 (children IR£1.80) and it's open from 9.30 am to 6 pm Monday to Saturday, and from 11 am on Sunday. The 12-hectare zoo is in the south-east corner of extensive Phoenix Park and can be reached by bus No 10 from O'Connell St or No 25 or 26 bus from Abbey St Middle.

Behind the zoo, on the edge of the park, the Garda Síochána Headquarters (police headquarters) has a small **police museum**.

Main Rd runs right through the park past the Irish President's residence on the right. In the centre of the park the **Phoenix Monument**, erected by Lord Chesterfield in 1747, looks very unphoenix-like and is often referred to as the Eagle Monument. The southern part of the park is given over to a large number of football and hurling fields, and, though they occupy about 80 hectares (200 acres), the area is known as the Fifteen Acres.

White's Gate, the park exit from its north-west side, leads to Castleknock College and Castleknock Castle. Near White's Gate and Quarry Pond at the north-west end of the park are the offices of the Ordnance Survey, the government mapping department. South of this building is the attractive rural-looking Furry Glen and Glen Pond corner of the park.

Looping back towards the Parkgate entrance, you'll see **Magazine Fort**, which stands on Thomas' Hill. The fort took from 1734 to 1801 to build and never served any discernible purpose although it was a target for the 1916 Easter Rising.

The Royal Canal

Constructed from 1790, by which time the older Grand Canal was already past its prime, the Royal Canal, which encircles Dublin to the north, was a commercial failure, but its story is certainly colourful. It was founded by Long John Binns, a Grand Canal director who quit the board because of a supposed insult over his occupation as a shoemaker. He established the Royal Canal principally for revenge but it never made money and actually became known as the Shoemaker's Canal. In 1840 the canal was sold to a railway company and tracks still run alongside much of the canal's route through the city.

The Royal Canal towpath makes a relaxing walk through the heart of the city. You can join it beside Newcomen Bridge at Strand Rd North, just north of Connolly Station, and follow it to the suburb of Clonsilla and beyond, over 10 km away. The walk is particularly pleasant beyond Binns Bridge in Drumcondra. At the top of Blessington St, near the Dublin Youth Hostel, a large pond which was used when the canal also supplied drinking water to the city, now attracts waterbirds.

Prospect Cemetery

Prospect or Glasnevin Cemetery, the largest in Ireland, was established in 1832 as a cemetery for Roman Catholics, who faced opposition when they conducted burials in the city's Protestant cemeteries. Many of the cemetery's monuments and memorials have staunchly patriotic overtones with numerous high crosses, shamrocks, harps and other Irish symbols. The cemetery's most imposing memorial is the colossal monument to Cardinal McCabe (1837-1921), the Archbishop of Dublin and Primate of Ireland.

A modern replica of a round tower acts as a handy landmark for locating the tomb of Daniel O'Connell, who died in 1847 and was reinterred here in 1869, when the tower was completed. Charles Stewart Parnell's tomb is topped with a huge granite rock. Other notable people buried here include Sir Roger Casement, who was executed for treason by the British in 1916 and whose remains were not returned to Ireland until 1964; the republican leader Michael Collins who died in the Civil War; the docker and trade unionist Jim Larkin, a prime force in the 1913 general strike; and the poet Gerard Manley Hopkins.

The most interesting parts of the cemetery are at the south-eastern Prospect Square end. The cemetery watchtowers were once used to keep watch for body snatchers. *Ulysses* pauses at the cemetery and there are a number of clues for Joyce enthusiasts to track down.

National Botanic Gardens

Founded in 1795, the National Botanic Gardens, directly north of the centre on Botanic Rd in Glasnevin, were used as a garden before that time, but only the Yew Walk, also known as Addison's Walk, has trees dating back to the first half of the 18th century. Unfortunately, much of the gardens are like a rather dull garden allotment – you start to wonder where the potato beds are.

The gardens cover 19 hectares and are flanked to the north by the River Tolka. The series of curvilinear glasshouses date from 1843-69 and were created by Richard Turner who was also responsible for the glasshouse at the Belfast Botanic Gardens and the Palm House in London's Kew Gardens. Dublin's gardens also have a palm house, built in 1884. Among the pioneering botanical work conducted here was the first attempt to raise orchids from seed, back in 1844. Pampas grass and the giant lily were first grown in Europe in these gardens.

The gardens are open Monday to Saturday from 9 am to 6 pm in summer and 10 am to 4.30 pm in winter, Sundays 11 am to 6 pm in summer and 11 am to 4.30 pm in winter. The conservatories have shorter opening hours. Entry is free. You can get there on bus No 13 or 19 from O'Connell St or No 34 or 34A from Abbey St Middle.

The Casino at Marino

The Marino Casino on Malahide Rd in Marino, just north-east of the centre, is not a casino at all. This curious structure was built as a pleasure house for the earl of Charlemont in the grounds of Marino House in the mid-18th century. Although Marino House itself was demolished in the 1920s the Casino survives as a wonderful folly.

Externally the building, with its 12 Tuscan columns forming a temple-like façade and its huge entrance doorway, creates the expectation that inside it will be a simple single open space. But inside it's an extravagant convoluted maze: the flights of fancy include chimneys for the central heating which are disguised as roof urns, downpipes hidden in columns, carved draperies, ornate fireplaces,

The Earl & the Casino

The somewhat eccentric James Caulfield (1728-99), later to become the Earl of Charlemont, set out on a European grand tour at the age of 18 in 1746. The visit was to last nine years, including a four-year spell in Italy, and he returned to Ireland with a huge art collection and a burning ambition to bring Italian style to the estate he acquired in 1756. He commissioned Sir William Chambers to design the casino, a process which started in the late 1750s, continued into the 1770s, and never really came to a conclusion, in part because Lord Charlemont frittered away his fortune.

When Lord Charlemont married, the Casino became a garden retreat rather than a bachelor's quarters. It's said that a visit from Charlemont's mother-in-law would send him scuttling down a 400-metre-long underground tunnel that joined the main house to the casino. Another building would have housed the art and antiquities he had acquired during his European tour, so it's perhaps fitting that his town house on Parnell Square, also designed by Sir William Chambers, is now the Municipal Gallery of Modern Art.

Despite his wealth Charlemont was a comparatively liberal and free-thinking aristocrat. He never fenced in his demesne and allowed the public to use it as an open park.

He was not the only local eccentric; in 1792 a painter named Folliot took a dislike to the lord and built Marino Crescent at the bottom of Malahide Rd purely to block his view of the sea. Bram Stoker (1847-1912), author of *Dracula*, was born at 15 Marino Crescent.

After Charlemont's death his estate, crippled by his debts, collapsed. The art collection was dispersed. ∎

---

beautiful parquet floors constructed of rare woods and a spacious wine cellar. A variety of statuary adorns the outside but it's the amusing fakes which are most enjoyable. The towering front door is a sham, and a much smaller panel opens to reveal the secret interior. Similarly, the windows have blacked-out panels to hide the fact that the interior is a complex of rooms, not a single chamber.

In 1870 the town house was sold to the government. The Marino estate followed in 1881 and the by then decrepit Casino in 1930. Serious restoration is continuing and although the Casino grounds are only a tiny fragment of the Marino estate, trees and planting will help to hide the surrounding houses.

The Marino Casino is open daily from 9.30 am to 6.30 pm from mid-June to September. At other times of the year ring the Casino (☎ 33 1618) or the Office of Public Works (☎ 661 3111, ext 2386) for details of opening hours. You can visit the building only on a guided tour; entry is IR£1 (children 40p). The Casino is just off Malahide Rd, north of the junction with Howth Rd in Clontarf. Bus No 20A, 20B, 27, 27A, 27B, 32A, 42 or 42B will take you there from the centre.

Clontarf & North Bull Island

Clontarf, a bayside suburb five km north-east of the centre, has popular cheaper B&Bs. The name was originally *cluain tarbh*, the bull's meadow, and it was here in 1014 that Brian Ború defeated the Danes at the Battle of Clontarf. The Irish hero was killed by fleeing Danes who found the old man in his tent, and his son and grandson died in the battle. The Normans later erected a castle here which was handed on to the Knights Templar in 1179, rebuilt in 1835 and later converted into a hotel.

The North Bull Wall, extending from Clontarf about a km into Dublin Bay, was built in 1820 at the suggestion of Captain William Bligh of HMS *Bounty* mutiny fame, in order to stop the harbour from silting up. The marshes and dunes of North Bull Island are home to the Royal Dublin and St Anne's golf courses. Many birds migrate here from the Arctic in winter, and at times the bird population can reach 40,000. There's an interpretive centre reached by the northern causeway to the island.

The Grand Canal

Built to connect Dublin with the River Shannon, the Grand Canal makes a graceful six-km loop around south Dublin. At its eastern end the canal forms a harbour connected with the Liffey at Ringsend. True Dubliners, it is said, are born within the confines of the Grand and Royal Canals.

For more information on the canal, look for the book *The Grand Canal* by Conaghan, Gleeson & Maddock (Office of Public Works.

Although Parliament proposed the canal in 1715 work did not commence until 1756. Construction was so slow that in 1775 a visitor commented that 'it bids fair for being completed in three or four centuries'. Nevertheless, in 1779 the first cargo barges started to operate to Sallins, about 35 km west of Dublin. Passenger services commenced a year later, when the terminus of the canal was the James's St Harbour, near the Guinness Brewery. By 1796 it was the longest canal in Britain or Ireland. It extended for 550 km, of which about 250 km was along the Rivers Shannon and Barrow.

Railways started to spread across Ireland from the mid-19th century and the canal went into decline. WW II provided a temporary respite, but the private canal company folded in 1950 and the last barge carried a cargo of Guinness from Dublin in 1960.

The canal fell into disrepair and in the early 1970s the St James's St Harbour and the stretch of canal back from there to the Circular Line were filled in. Recently the canal has enjoyed a modest revival as a tourist attraction. Despite the very limited number of boats that now ply the canal, all the locks are in working order.

The Grand Canal enters the Liffey at **Ringsend**, through locks that were built in 1796. The large **Grand Canal Dock**, flanked by Hanover and Charlotte quays, is now used by windsurfers.

At the north-west corner of the dock is **Misery Hill**, once the site for the public execution of criminals. It was once the practice to bring the corpses of those already hung at Gallows Hill, near Baggot St Upper, to this spot, to be strung up for public display for anything from six to 12 months.

Just upstream from the Grand Canal Dock

is the new **Waterways visitors' centre**, built by the Public Works Department as an exhibition and interpretation centre on the construction and operation of Irish canals and waterways.

A memorial to the events of the 1916 Rising can be seen on the **Mount St Bridge**. A little farther along, Baggot St crosses the canal on the 1791 **Macartney Bridge**. The main office of Bord Fáilte is on the north side of the canal, and Bridge House and Parson's Bookshop are on the south side.

This lovely stretch of the canal with its grassy, tree-lined banks was a favourite haunt of the poet Patrick Kavanagh. Among his compositions is the hauntingly beautiful *On Raglan Road*, a popular song which Van Morrison fans can find on the album *Irish Heartbeat* with the Chieftains. Another Kavanagh poem requested that he be commemorated by 'a canal bank seat for passers-by' and Kavanagh's friends obliged with a seat beside the lock on the south side of the canal. A little farther along on the north side you can sit down by Kavanagh himself, cast in bronze, comfortably lounging on a bench and watching his beloved canal.

The next stretch of the canal has some fine pubs, such as the *Barge* and the *Portobello*, both right by the canal. The Portobello is a fine old-fashioned place with music on weekend evenings and Sunday mornings. The *Lower Deck* on Richmond St and *An Béal Bocht* (The Poor Mouth) on Charlemont St are also near the canal. You could also pause for a meal at the *Locks Restaurant*. The Institute of Education Business College by the Portobello was built in 1807 as Portobello House; as the Grand Canal Hotel, it was the Dublin terminus for passenger traffic on the canal. The artist Jack B Yeats lived here for seven years until his death in 1957.

Farther west from here the **Circular Line** is not so interesting and is better appreciated by bicycle rather than on foot. The spur running off the Circular Line alongside Grand Canal Bank to the old St James's St Harbour has been filled in and is now a park and bicycle path.

Ballsbridge & Donnybrook

Just south-east of central Dublin, the suburb of Ballsbridge was principally laid out between 1830 and 1860 and many of the streets have British names with a distinctly military flavour. Many embassies, including the US Embassy, are located in Ballsbridge. It also has some middle-bracket B&Bs and several upper-bracket hotels. If you're not staying in Ballsbridge, the main reasons for a visit are the Royal Dublin Showground, the Chester Beatty Library and the Lansdowne Rd rugby stadium.

Adjoining Ballsbridge to the south is Donnybrook, at one time a village on the banks of the River Dodder. For centuries it was famous for the Donnybrook Fair which was first held in 1204. By the 19th century it had become a 15-day event centred around horse dealing, which was such a scene of drunkenness and sexual debauchery that the increasingly sedate residents of Donnybrook had it banned in 1855.

Royal Dublin Society Showground On Merrion Rd in Ballsbridge, south of the centre, the Royal Dublin Society Showground is used for various exhibitions through the year. The society was founded in 1731 and had its headquarters in a number of well-known Dublin buildings, including, from 1814 to 1925, Leinster House. The society was involved in the foundation of the National Museum, Library, Gallery and Botanic Gardens. The two most important annual events at the showground are the May Spring Show and the August Dublin Horse Show. The Spring Show is dedicated to farming and agricultural pursuits, while the Horse Show includes an international showjumping contest and attracts the horsey set from all over Ireland and Britain.

Tickets can be booked in advance for the Spring or Horse shows by contacting the Ticket Office (☎ 668 0645), Royal Dublin Society, PO Box 121, Ballsbridge, Dublin 4.

Chester Beatty Library & Gallery of Oriental Art This library and gallery (☎ 669 2386) houses the collection of the mining engineer Sir Alfred Chester Beatty (1875-1968). It includes over 20,000 manuscripts, numerous rare books, miniature paintings, clay tablets, costumes and other objects, predominantly from the Middle and Far East.

The gallery includes a reference library and a bookshop, but unfortunately only a tiny fraction of the total can be shown at any one time.

The gallery is south of the centre at 20 Shrewsbury Rd, Dublin 4. This is just beyond Ballsbridge en route to Dun Laoghaire. Bus No 5, 6, 6A, 7A or 8 from Eden Quay, No 46 or 46A from College St or No 10 from O'Connell St will take you there. Alternatively, take the DART to Sandymount Station, Sydney Parade. Opening hours are 10 am to 5 pm Tuesday to Friday, 2 to 5 pm on Saturday. Entry is free and there are guided tours on Wednesday and Saturday at 2.30 pm.

Pearse Museum

Patrick (or Padráig in the Irish he worked so hard to promote) Pearse was a leader of the 1916 Rising and one of the first to be executed by firing squad at Kilmainham Jail. St Enda's, the school he established with his brother Willie to further his ideas of Irish language and culture, is now a museum (☎ 93 4208) and memorial to the brothers.

The Pearse Museum is at the junction of Grange Rd and Taylor's Lane in Rathfarnham, south-west of the city centre. It's open every day from 10 am to 12.30 pm and from 2 pm to 4.30 pm (February, November), to 5.30 pm (March, April, September, October), to 6 pm (May to August) and to 3.30 pm (December, January). Entry is free and you can get there on a No 16 bus from the city centre.

Marlay Park

This park area south of the centre at Rathfarnham in Dublin 16 has numerous attractions, including a model railway with rides for children on Saturday afternoons. The park is the northern starting point for the Wicklow Way walking track.

Other Museums

Apart from the museums described in the north and south Dublin sections, there are a number of other smaller museums or museums of specialist interest.

George Bernard Shaw House (☎ 872 2077) at 33 Synge St, Dublin 2, is open from 10 am to 5 pm Monday to Saturday, 2 to 6 pm Sunday and holidays, May to September. Entry is IR£1.75 (students IR£1.40, children 90p).

The **Irish Traditional Music Archive** (☎ 661 9699), at 63 Merrion Square South, collects, preserves and organises traditional Irish music. It's open to the public by appointment.

The **Geological Survey of Ireland** (☎ 660 9511) at Haddington Rd, Dublin 4, has exhibits on the geology and mineral resources of Ireland. It's open Monday to Friday from 2.30 to 4.30 pm.

The **Irish Jewish Museum** (☎ 53 4754) at 3/4 Walworth Rd, off Victoria St, Portobello, Dublin 8, is housed in what was once a synagogue and relates the history of Ireland's Jewish community. It's open Sunday, Tuesday and Thursday from 11 am to 3.30 pm.

The **Museum of Childhood** (☎ 97 3223) is at The Palms, 20 Palmerston Park, Rathmines, Dublin 6, south of the centre. Its main display is a collection of dolls, some of them nearly 300 years old. The museum is open Sunday from 2 to 5.30 pm and may be open longer hours during the summer months. Entry is IR£1 (children 75p).

The **Irish Architectural Archive & Architecture Centre** at 73 Merrion Square South, Dublin 2, traces Dublin's architectural history from 1560 to the current day. The archive is housed in a fine 1793 town house. The Royal Institute of the Architects of Ireland has its headquarters across the square at 8 Merrion Square North, and exhibitions and displays are also held there.

The **Plunkett Museum of Irish Education** (☎ 97 0033) is at the Church of Ireland College of Education, Rathmines Rd Upper, Dublin 6, and is open on Wednesday from 2.30 to 5 pm.

Other Galleries

Apart from the National Gallery and the IMMA south of the river and the Hugh Lane Municipal Gallery of Modern Art north of the river, there are also a great many private galleries, arts centres and corporate exhibition areas.

The **Douglas Hyde Gallery** (☎ 70 2116) is in the Arts Building in Trinity College, and the entrance is on Nassau St. The **City Arts Centre** (☎ 677 0643) at 23/25 Moss St has changing exhibitions in its Gallery 1 and Gallery 2. The galleries are open Monday to Saturday from 11 am to 5 pm and entry is free.

In the **Bank of Ireland** building on Baggot St Lower, just past Fitzwilliam St towards the tourist office and Ballsbridge, there are usually changing displays of contemporary Irish art.

SPORTS & ACTIVITIES

Dublin offers plenty of sporting opportunities for both spectators and participants.

The All Ireland Hurling Final takes place on the first Sunday in September at Dublin's

Hurling

Croke Park and attracts a crowd of 60,000 to 80,000 spectators.

The All Ireland Football Final takes place at Dublin's Croke Park on the third Sunday in September.

The Irish love of horse racing can be observed at Leopardstown and Phoenix Park, Dublin's two central racecourses. Horses of less exalted breeds can be found at the horse-trading market behind the Four Courts building in central Dublin on the first Sunday of each month.

Beaches & Swimming

Dublin is hardly the sort of place to work on your suntan and even a hot Irish summer day is unlikely to raise the water temperature much above freezing. However, there are some pleasant beaches and many Joyce fans feel compelled to take a dip in the Forty Foot Pool at Dun Laoghaire. Sandy beaches near the centre include Dollymount (six km), Sutton (11 km), Portmarnock (11 km), Malahide (11 km), Claremount (14 km) and Donabate (21 km). Although the beach at Sandymount is nothing special, it is only five km from central Dublin. There are outdoor public pools at Blackrock, Clontarf and Dun Laoghaire.

Scuba Diving

The Irish Underwater Council (☎ 872 7011) is on the 2nd floor, 5/7 O'Connell St Upper, Dublin 1. They publish the quarterly magazine *Subsea*. Oceantec (☎ 280 1083) is a dive shop in Dun Laoghaire that organises local dives. See the Dun Laoghaire section for more information.

Sailing & Windsurfing

Howth and Dun Laoghaire are the major sailing centres in the Dublin area, but you can also go sailing at Clontarf, Kilbarrack, Malahide, Rush, Skerries, Sutton and Swords. See the Dun Laoghaire section for details of the sailing clubs there. The Irish Sailing Association (☎ 280 0239) is at 3 Park Rd, Dun Laoghaire.

Dinghy sailing courses are offered by the Irish National Sailing School (☎ 280 6654), 115 George's St Lower, Dun Laoghaire, and by the Fingall Sailing School (☎ 845 1979) Upper Strand, Broadmeadow Estuary, Malahide.

Windsurfing enthusiasts can head to the Surfdock Centre (☎ 668 3945) at the Grand Canal Dock, Dock Rd South, Ringsend, Dublin 4. Surfdock runs windsurfing courses here costing from IR£25 for a three-hour 'taster' session to IR£50-80 for longer courses. You can also rent sailboards from IR£6 an hour.

Fishing

Fishing tackle shops in Dublin can supply permits, equipment, bait and advice. Check the classified phone directory under Fishing Gear & Tackle. Sea fishing is popular at Howth, Dun Laoghaire and Greystones. The River Liffey has salmon fishing (only fair) and trout fishing (good). Brown trout are found between Celbridge and Millicent Bridge, near Clane, 20 km from the centre. The Dublin Trout Anglers' Association has fishing rights along parts of this stretch of the Liffey and on the River Tolka.

Gliding & Hang-Gliding

Phone ☎ 31 4551 for information on hang-gliding from the Sugar Loaf in County Wicklow. Contact the Dublin Gliding Club (☎ 282 0759, 298 3994) for information on gliding.

PLACES TO STAY

Dublin has a wide range of accommodation possibilities, but in summer finding a bed can be difficult in anything from the cheapest hostel to the most expensive five-star hotel. If you can plan well ahead and book your room, it will make life easier, but the alternative is to head straight for one of the tourist offices at the airport, by the harbour in Dun Laoghaire or in Dublin itself and ask them to book you a room. For a flat fee of IR£1 plus a 10% deposit on the cost of the first night, they will find you somewhere to stay, and will do so efficiently and with a smile. Sometimes this will require a great deal of phoning around so it can be a pound well spent.

Accommodation in central Dublin can be neatly divided into areas north and south of the River Liffey. The south side is generally neater, tidier and more expensive than the north side. Prices drop as you move away from the centre. The seaside suburbs of Dun Laoghaire and Howth are also within easy commuting distance of central Dublin on the convenient DART rail service.

Camping

There's no convenient central camping ground in Dublin. *Do not* try to camp in Phoenix Park – a German cyclist camping there was murdered in 1991. The *Shankill Caravan & Camping Park* (☎ 282 0011) is 16 km south of the centre on the N11 Wexford Rd. A site for two costs IR£5 in summer. You can get there on bus No 45 or 46 from Eden Quay. Other sites are *Donabate* near Swords and *Cromlech* just beyond Dun Laoghaire.

Hostels

Since there are no conveniently central camp sites in Dublin, shoestring travellers usually head for one of Dublin's numerous hostels. One is operated by An Óige, the national youth hostel association, whereas the others are independently run. Hostels offer the cheapest accommodation and are also great centres for meeting other travellers and exchanging information. In summer (late June to late September) they can be heavily booked but then so is everything else.

North of the Liffey The *Dublin International Youth Hostel* (☎ 30 1766) on Mountjoy St is a big and well-equipped hostel in a restored and converted old building. From Dublin Airport, bus No 41A will drop you off in Dorset St Upper, a few minutes' walk from the hostel. It's a longer walk from the bus and railway stations but it's well signposted. The hostel is in the run-down northern area of the city centre, though not in the worst part of it. The nightly cost is IR£9 and there's an overflow hostel for the height of the summer crush.

Just round the corner from the An Óige hostel is the middle-sized *Young Traveller Hostel* (☎ 30 5000) on St Mary's Place, just off Dorset St Upper. All the rooms accommodate four people and have a shower and washbasin but there are no kitchen facilities. The nightly cost is IR£8.50 including breakfast.

Cardijin House Hostel (☎ 878 8484), subtitled 'Goin' My Way', is a smaller, older hostel at 15 Talbot St, east of O'Connell St. The nightly cost is IR£6 plus 50p for a shower. The *Marlborough Hostel* (☎ 878 8484) is at 81/82 Marlborough St, right behind the Dublin Tourism office and next to the Pro-Cathedral. It has dorms accommodating four to 10 people and the nightly cost is IR£7.50 per person irrespective of the dorm size. Double rooms cost IR£11 per person.

The big *Dublin Tourist Hostel* (☎ 36 3877), better known as *Isaac's*, is at 2/5 Frenchman's Lane, a stone's throw from the Busáras or Connolly Railway Station, and not far from the popular restaurants and pubs on either side of the Liffey. In some rooms traffic noise is the penalty for the central location. This very well equipped hostel is in a converted 18th-century wine warehouse. It costs IR£5.50 to IR£6.25 for dorms, IR£11.25 each for doubles or IR£15.25 for singles. The restaurant is good value.

South of the Liffey South of the Liffey, *Kinlay House* (☎ 679 6644) is also very centrally located but, again, some rooms can suffer from traffic noise. It's right beside Christ Church Cathedral at 2/12 Lord Edward St. Kinlay House is big and well equipped and costs from IR£8.50 per person for four-bed dorms, IR£10.50 to IR£13 for the better rooms (some with bathrooms) and IR£17 for a single. A continental breakfast is included.

Avalon House (☎ 475 0001) at 55 Aungier St is nicely positioned just west of St Stephen's Green. It's in an old building that was comprehensively renovated and opened in 1992. It is very well equipped and some of the cleverly designed rooms have mezzanine levels, which are great for families. The basic nightly cost is IR£7 including a continental breakfast. A bed in a room with attached bathroom costs IR£11 in the four-bed rooms, IR£12.50 in the two-bed rooms. The largest dorms accommodate eight. To get there take bus No 16, 16A, 19 or 22 right to the door or No 11, 13 or 46A to nearby St Stephen's Green. From the Dun Laoghaire ferry terminal you can take a No 46A bus to St Stephen's Green or the DART to Pearse Station.

Student Accommodation

In the summer months you can stay at Trinity College or University College Dublin (UCD). Trinity College sometimes has accommodation on campus in the city, but it's expensive at IR£25 per person. At *Trinity Hall* (☎ 97 1772), Dartry Rd, Rathmines, rates are IR£14 to IR£17 for singles or IR£12 to IR£15 if you share a twin. If you're under 25 and have a student card, the price may drop. There are some family rooms where children aged under 10 can stay for free with two adults. To get there, take bus No 14/14A from D'Olier St beside the O'Connell Bridge.

UCD Village (☎ 269 7696) is six km south of the centre, en route to Dun Laoghaire. Accommodation here is in apartments, with three single rooms sharing a bathroom and a kitchen/meals/living area. It's very modern and well appointed but a little far out and, at IR£16.50 (IR£96 a week), rather expensive. For a family a three-room apartment at IR£48 could be good value. If you have a car, the ease of parking may compensate for the distance; if you don't, bus No 10 departs every 10 minutes from O'Connell St/St Stephen's Green and goes direct to the campus. After 5 pm on Saturday and all day Sunday you have to switch to a No 46A from Fleet St near Trinity College and ask for the Montrose Hotel stop. Either way the fare is 95p.

B&Bs

B&Bs, the backbone of cheap accommodation in Ireland, are well represented in Dublin and typically cost IR£15 to IR£20 per person per night. The cheaper B&Bs usually do not have private bathrooms, but where they do the cost is often just a pound or two more. Dublin also has some more luxuriously equipped B&Bs costing from IR£25 per person, but this category is usually monopolised by the boutique hotels and guesthouses. At some places the per person costs are higher for a single room.

If you arrive when accommodation is tight and you don't like the location offered, the best advice is to take it and at the same time try to book something more conveniently located for subsequent nights. Booking just one or two days ahead can often provide a much better choice.

If you want something cheap but close to the city, Gardiner St Upper and Lower in Dublin 1 on the north side of the Liffey is the place to look. It's a rather grotty and run-down area, but it is cheap.

If you're willing to travel farther out, you can find a better price and quality combination north of the centre at Clontarf or in the seaside suburbs of Dun Laoghaire or Howth. The Ballsbridge embassy zone, just south of the centre, offers convenience and quality but you pay more for the combination. Other suburbs to try are Sandymount (immediately east of Ballsbridge) and Drumcondra (north of the centre en route to the airport).

Gardiner St There is a large collection of places on Gardiner St Lower, near the bus and railway stations, and another group on Gardiner St Upper, farther north near Mountjoy Square. The B&Bs are respectable if rather basic.

O'Brien's Hotel (☎ 874 5203) at 38/39 Gardiner St Lower is a more expensive place with singles from IR£22 to IR£26 and doubles from IR£40 to IR£50. There are 22 rooms in this large and rather plain place, but only a handful with attached bathrooms. At 75 Gardiner St Lower is the *Maple Guest House* (☎ 874 0225, 874 5239) which has singles/doubles for IR£27.50/40 or IR£37.50/60 with attached bathroom.

The extremely plain *Harvey's Guesthouse* (☎ 874 8384) at 11 Gardiner St Upper and

Stella Maris (☎ 874 0835) next door at No 13 are near Mountjoy Square. Singles are IR£16, doubles IR£28 to IR£32. There are several more B&Bs in the next few buildings, such as *Flynn's B&B* (☎ 874 1702) at No 15, *Carmel House* (☎ 874 1639) at No 16 and *Fatima House* (☎ 874 5410) at No 17. Just off Gardiner St Upper from Mountjoy Square at 3/4 Gardiner Place is the *Dergvale Hotel* (☎ 874 4753, 874 3361). Regular rooms are slightly more expensive, and singles/doubles with attached bathroom cost IR£26/44.

Hardwicke St is only a short walk from these Gardiner St Upper places and has a number of popular B&Bs, such as *Waverley House* (☎ 874 6132) at No 4 or *Sinclair House* (☎ 874 6132) next door at No 3. At these places singles cost IR£16 to IR£20 and doubles IR£28 to IR£32.

Clontarf There are numerous places along Clontarf Rd, about five km from the centre. One of these is the friendly *Ferryview* (☎ 33 5893) at No 96. Farther along there's the slightly more expensive *White House* (☎ 33 3196) at No 125, *San Vista* (☎ 33 9582) at No 237, *Bayview* (☎ 33 9870) at No 265, *Sea-Front* (☎ 33 6118) at No 278 and *Sea Breeze* (☎ 33 2787) at No 312. These Clontarf Rd B&Bs typically cost IR£14 to IR£20 for singles, IR£25 to IR£35 for doubles. Bus No 30 from Abbey St will get you there for 95p.

Ballsbridge & Donnybrook Ballsbridge is not only the embassy quarter and the site for a number of upper bracket hotels but is also the locale for a number of better quality B&Bs, such as *Morehampton Townhouse* (☎ 660 2106, fax 660 2566) at 46 Morehampton Rd, Donnybrook, directly opposite the Sachs Hotel. Singles/doubles are IR£33/50. All rooms are centrally heated and have bathrooms and the excellent breakfast proves that there can be more to life than just bacon and eggs.

Mrs O'Donoghue's (☎ 668 1105) convivial but signless place at 41 Northumberland Rd costs IR£24/40. Despite its imposing

Victorian presence there are only eight rooms in this fine and very traditional B&B.

Mid-Range Guesthouses & Hotels

The line dividing B&Bs, guesthouses or cheaper hotels is often a hazy one. Places in this middle-range bracket usually cost from IR£25 to IR£50 per night per person. Some of the small, centrally located, boutique-style hotels in this category are among the most enjoyable places to stay in Dublin.

These middle-range places are a big jump up from the cheaper B&Bs in facilities and price but still cost a lot less than Dublin's expensive hotels. Breakfast is usually provided (it usually isn't in the top-notch hotels) and it's very good (unlike that offered by some base-level B&Bs). Many of these hotels offer fruit, a choice of cereals, croissants, scones and other morning delights. And bacon and eggs as well, of course – this is Ireland.

North of the Liffey – Dublin 1

Just north of the Liffey at 35/36 Abbey St Lower is *Wynn's Hotel* (☎ 874 6131, fax 677 7487). This older hotel is only a few steps away from the Abbey Theatre. It has 63 rooms, all with attached bathroom, which cost IR£45/72 for singles/ doubles. Right by the river the *Ormond Hotel* (☎ 872 1811, fax 872 1909), Ormond Quay Upper, Dublin 1, has 55 rooms with attached bathroom for IR£50/76. A plaque outside notes its role in *Ulysses*.

Farther from the river is *Barry's Hotel* (☎ 874 6943, fax 874 6508) at 1/2 Great Denmark St, just off Parnell Square. It's only a few minutes' walk from O'Connell St but it's on the edge of the better part of north Dublin, before the decline sets in. The hotel's 30 recently refurbished rooms cost IR£29.75/59.50 with attached bathroom.

Across the road is the *Belvedere Hotel* (☎ 872 8522, 874 1413) opposite Belvedere College, which James Joyce attended as a boy. The 40 rooms, all with attached bathroom, cost IR£30/60 for singles/doubles.

South of the Liffey – Dublin 2

The *Fitzwilliam* (☎ 660 0448, fax 676 7488) at

41 Fitzwilliam St Upper, Dublin 2, is very centrally located, right on the corner of Baggot St Lower. Despite this location it's surprisingly quiet at night. There are 12 rooms in this recently renovated small hotel, all of which have en suite bathroom, costing IR£41/72 for singles/doubles at the height of the summer season.

Even more central is *Georgian House* (☎ 661 8832, fax 661 8834) at 20/21 Baggot St Lower, equally close to St Stephen's Green or Merrion Square. Once again this is a fine old Georgian building in excellent condition. Its 34 rooms all have attached bathrooms and cost IR£45/72 in summer. The breakfast is excellent and at night the restaurant is noted for its seafood. There's also a car park.

Also close to St Stephen's Green is the *Harcourt Hotel* (☎ 478 3677, fax 75 2013) at 60 Harcourt St. Set in a magnificent Georgian building, this hotel has 22 rooms which cost IR£35/60 or IR£55/100 for the rooms with attached bathroom. George Bernard Shaw lived here from 1874 to 1876. Closer to the Green at 21/25 Harcourt St is the *Russell Court Hotel* (☎ 478 4991, fax 478 1576) with 21 rooms, all with attached bathroom and costing IR£57/82 a night.

Another place off St Stephen's Green is *Leeson Court* (☎ 676 3380, fax 661 8273) at 26/27 Leeson St Lower, at the start of Dublin's nightclub block. The 20 rooms have attached bathrooms and cost IR£55-60 for singles and IR£76-88 for doubles.

At 6/8 Wellington Quay, overlooking the River Liffey and backing on to the fascinating Temple Bar area, is the *Clarence Hotel* (☎ 677 6178, fax 677 7487), a larger old hotel. There are 67 rooms, all en suite, with nightly costs of IR£45/72. The hotel was bought by the band U2 in late 1992.

Elsewhere in Dublin *Ariel House* (☎ 668 5512, fax 668 5845) is at 52 Lansdowne Rd, Dublin 4, two km south-east of the centre in the Ballsbridge area. It's conveniently close to Lansdowne Rd Station and near the big Berkeley Court Hotel. There are 27 rooms,

all en suite, and the nightly cost is IR£50/100 for singles/doubles, but breakfast is extra.

Continue down Lansdowne Rd and it changes names to Herbert Rd, where you will find the *Mt Herbert* (☎ 668 4321, fax 660 7077) at 7 Herbert Rd, Dublin 4, about three km from the centre. This larger hotel was once the Dublin residence of an English lord. There are 135 rooms, most of them en suite, which cost IR£53/57, but breakfast is extra.

The *Ashling Hotel* (☎ 677 2324) is on Parkgate St, Dublin 8, 2.5 km from the centre and directly across the river from Heuston Station. This well-equipped hotel has 56 rooms costing IR£48.50/70 for singles/doubles.

Expensive Hotels
Above IR£50 per person or IR£100 for a double is Dublin's top bracket. Hotels in this price range are divided into two categories: the city's best hotels, most of them categorised as A* hotels by the Irish Tourist Board and all of them costing well over IR£100 for a double; and the other expensive hotels, which fall just below the top bracket in standards and price but are still somewhat more expensive than the middle range.

Almost-but-not-quite Top Bracket At the top end of O'Connell St in north Dublin, farther up from the Gresham Hotel, is the *Royal Dublin Hotel* (☎ 873 3666, fax 873 3120). It has 117 rooms at IR£81/108 for singles/doubles.

The nicely situated new *Bloom's Hotel* (☎ 671 5622 & 671 5508, fax 671 5997) is on Anglesea St, right behind the Bank of Ireland in the colourful Temple Bar district. The hotel has 86 rooms costing IR£90/110 for singles/doubles. Just south of Dame St is the *Central Hotel* (☎ 679 7302, fax 679 7303) at 1/5 Exchequer St, which has 68 rooms at IR£95/140 without breakfast. It has recently been comprehensively renovated and though the rooms are rather small it's very well located.

Close to the National Museum, *Buswells* (☎ 676 4013 & 661 3888, fax 676 2090) is on Molesworth St and has singles/doubles for IR£57/90 without breakfast. The small *Longfield's* (☎ 676 1367, fax 676 1542) is at 9/10 Fitzwilliam St Lower, between Merrion and Fitzwilliam squares, and has 26 rooms at IR£85/99 for singles/doubles.

Stephen's Hall (☎ 661 0585, fax 661 0606) is just a stone's throw from the south-east corner of St Stephen's Green at 14/17 Leeson St Lower. The 37 rooms, all with attached bathroom, cost IR£90/130, including breakfast.

In Donnybrook, just beyond Ballsbridge, is the *Sachs Hotel* (☎ 668 0995, fax 668 6147) at 19/29 Morehampton Rd, Dublin 4. This is about three km south-east of the centre. This small but elegant and expensive place has 20 rooms, all en suite, costing IR£82/124.

The Top Bracket Dublin has seven hotels which have the Irish Tourist Board's A* rating. Even a single room at these hotels can cost IR£100 or more, though most guests will have probably booked through an agency or as part of a package and obtained some sort of discount from the rack (published) rates.

The city's best known hotel is the elegant *Shelbourne*, strategically placed overlooking St Stephen's Green and indubitably the best address to meet at in Dublin. Despite the prices the rooms are a little cramped, but afternoon tea at the Shelbourne is something all Dublin visitors should experience, regardless of whether they stay there.

The *Conrad* is run, of course, by the Hilton group and is just south of St Stephen's Green. This popular business hotel is one of Dublin's newest. Also close to St Stephen's Green, the modern *Westbury* is in a small lane just off Grafton St, the pedestrianised main shopping street of south Dublin. Rooms on the upper floors offer views of the Dublin hills. The *Mont Clare* is a classic old hotel on elegant Merrion Square. The newest top-bracket hotel in Dublin is the *Davenport Hotel*, which opened in mid-1993 opposite the Mont Clare on Westland Row. *Berkeley Court*, south-east of the centre in Ballsbridge

in a quiet and relaxed location, offers spacious rooms. Ireland's largest hotel, the modern *Burlington* is also south of the centre, just beyond the Grand Canal. In the same general area is *Jury's Hotel & Towers*, a large, modern hotel. In the summer months the Irish Cabaret here is a popular attraction.

The long-established *Gresham* is on imposing O'Connell St Upper.

Berkeley Court Hotel A*
    Lansdowne Rd, Dublin 4; two km from the centre, 195 rooms, swimming pool, IR£140/156 (☎ 660 1711, fax 661 7238)
Burlington Hotel A*
    Leeson St Upper, Dublin 4; two km from the centre, 451 rooms, IR£92/135 (☎ 660 5222, fax 660 8496)
Conrad Hotel A*
    Earlsfort Terrace, Dublin 2; 190 rooms, IR£135/160 (☎ 676 5555, fax 676 5076)
Davenport Hotel
    Westland Row, Dublin 2; 90 rooms, IR£110/140 (☎ 661 6799, fax 661 9555),
Gresham Hotel A*
    O'Connell St Upper, Dublin 1; 191 rooms, IR£110/140 (☎ 874 6881, fax 878 7175)
Jury's Hotel & Towers A*
    Ballsbridge, Dublin 4; 2.5 km from the centre, 384 rooms, swimming pool, IR£101/119 (☎ 660 5000, fax 660 5540)
Mont Clare Hotel A
    Merrion Square, Dublin 2; 74 rooms, IR£150 (☎ 661 6799, fax 661 5663)
Shelbourne Hotel A*
    St Stephen's Green, Dublin 2; 142 rooms, IR£150 for singles, from IR£180 for doubles (☎ 676 6471, fax 661 6006)
Westbury Hotel A*
    off Grafton St, Dublin 2; 195 rooms, IR£140/156 (☎ 679 1122, fax 679 7078)

Airport Hotels There are several hotels near Dublin Airport, including the large *Forte Crest Hotel* (☎ 844 4211, fax 842 5874), off the N1 motorway beside the airport. It has 188 rooms costing IR£110/140 for singles/doubles.

PLACES TO EAT

Restaurants are divided into four popular zones. The trendy Temple Bar enclave and Dame St along its southern boundary are packed with restaurants of all types. There are also numerous restaurants on both sides of busy Grafton St and along Merrion Row and Baggot St.

North of the Liffey

Dining possibilities north of the Liffey essentially consist of fast food, cheap eats or chains. Which is not to say that you'll eat badly here, just that the choice of restaurants is much better to the south.

Fast Food & Cafés O'Connell St is the fast-food centre of Dublin. At No 34 there's an *Abrakebabra*, at No 9 there's a *Burger King*, at Nos 14 and 52 there are branches of *La Pizza* and at No 62 there's a *McDonald's*.

Isaac's and the *Dublin International Youth Hostel* (see Hostels in the Places to Stay section) both have good cafeteria-style facilities. At 1/2 O'Connell St the *Kylemore Café* is a big, fast-food place which is also good for a cup of tea or coffee any time of day. At 5/7 O'Connell St there's the *International Food Court* with a variety of counters, including *Beshoff's* for fish & chips.

There's a *Bewley's Café* north of the Liffey at 40 Mary St.

If you're around the Corporation Fruit Market, between Chancery St and Mary's Lane, pop in to *Paddy's Place* (☎ 873 5130) where the food is as staunchly Irish as the name. It's open from 7.30 am to 3 pm Monday to Friday so you can go there for an early breakfast or a filling lunch-time Irish stew or Dublin coddle.

Restaurants Restaurant possibilities north of the Liffey are distinctly limited, but *Chapter One* (☎ 873 2266, 873 2281) at the Dublin Writers' Museum on the north side of Parnell Square is worth a look even though the food is resolutely conservative. They serve lunch and dinner and feature a menu for patrons of the Gate Theatre, on the other side of the square.

Closer to the river at 101 Talbot St (off O'Connell St to the east and just north of the Abbey Theatre) is *101 Talbot St* (☎ 874 5011), open for lunch Monday to Saturday, dinner Tuesday to Saturday. This is a brave attempt to bring good food north of the river. The prices are reasonable and the food moderately adventurous and very well prepared.

Temple Bar

The old, interesting and rapidly revitalising Temple Bar area is Dublin's most concentrated restaurant area. It's bounded by the river to the north, Westmoreland St to the east and Christ Church Cathedral to the west. The southern boundary is Dame St and its extension, Lord Edward St, but for convenience's sake restaurants on both the northern and southern side of Dame St are listed in this section.

Fast Food & Cafés *Abrakebabra* has a branch at the O'Connell Bridge end of Westmoreland St. Ireland's most famous purveyor of fish & chips is *Beshoff's* (☎ 677 8026) at 14 Westmoreland St, also just south of O'Connell Bridge. There's now a restaurant area with waiter service upstairs.

Backpackers staying at *Kinlay House* at the Christ Church Cathedral end of Lord Edward St (see Hostels in the Places to Stay section) will find good cafeteria-style facilities there. The *Well Fed Café* (☎ 677 2234) at 6 Crow St is a big and busy alternative-style place with large portions of food. It's a great place for lunch or a snack and caters particularly well to vegetarians. It's open from 10.30 am to around 8.30 pm Monday to Friday, only to 4.30 pm on Saturday.

Cellary (☎ 671 0362), at 1 Fownes St just off Wellington Quay, offers 'veg and demi-veg' food! That seems to mean vegetarian but not strictly so. Either way their soup of the day and a bread roll make a tasty lunch. There's a restaurant section upstairs which opens on Thursday to Saturday evenings.

Café Carolina (☎ 671 4005) at 66 Dame St offers dishes of the shepherd's pie, lasagne or chicken curry variety.

Italian Restaurants Temple Bar has all sorts of restaurants but the Irish passion for pasta and pizza comes through loud and clear – Italian food is definitely the number-one option.

The very popular *Bad Ass Café* (☎ 671 2596) at 9/11 Crown Alley is a cheerful and bright warehouse-style place just south of Ha'penny Bridge. It offers pretty good pizzas from IR£3 to IR£7 in a very convivial studentish atmosphere. One of its claims to fame is that Sinéad O'Connor once worked here as a waitress. A couple of doors down is *Paddy Garibaldi's* (☎ 671 7288) at 15/16 Crown Alley. Here it's that popular variation (locally at least) on Italian food – Irish-Italian – with burgers and steaks to complement the pizza and pasta.

A couple of blocks over at 20 Temple Lane is *Fat Freddy's* (☎ 679 6769), an equally popular pizzeria although the prices are a bit higher at around IR£5 to IR£9. *Pizzeria Italia* (☎ 677 8528) at 23 Temple Bar is another simple pizzeria offering classic pizzas at standard prices. It's open from Tuesday to Saturday.

You can also find pizza at the fancier *Pizza on the Corner* (☎ 671 9308) at 38/40 Parliament St on the corner of Dame St. This spacious and bright restaurant has pizzas at IR£3.25 to IR£5.25 and a wide international selection of beers at IR£1.50 and IR£2. At 71 Dame St, right beside the Olympia Theatre, *Da Lorenzo* is a basic Italian restaurant offering pasta dishes from IR£5 to IR£8 and pizzas from IR£4 to IR£7.

La Mezza Luna (☎ 671 2840) is also on Dame St but the entrance is round the corner in Temple Lane. This slightly more up-market restaurant is enormously popular, and you may have to book a table or be prepared to wait. The pasta dishes are great value at IR£4 to IR£6. It's open Monday to Thursday from 12.30 to 11 pm, Friday and Saturday 12.30 to 11.30 pm and Sunday 4 to 10.30 pm.

Restaurants Despite the plethora of trattorias, ristorantes and pizzerias, there's more to Temple Bar than pizza and pasta. The *Rock Garden Café* (☎ 679 9114) (see the Discos & Nightclubs section under Entertainment) is done up in what could be called techno-sleaze style. You can get a very respectable burger or Mexican dish for IR£6 to IR£9 and

get into the show cheaply. It's at 3A Crown Alley, directly across from the Bad Ass Café.

Burgers are a speciality at the popular and bustling *Elephant & Castle* (☎ 679 3121) at 18 Temple Bar but the menu also extends to curries, and vegetarian and pasta dishes and encompasses a wide range of international influences. It's also open until reasonably late every night of the week. Right next door at 20/21 Temple Bar is the equally popular *Gallagher's Boxty House* (☎ 677 2762). A boxty is rather like a stuffed pancake and tastes like an extremely bland Indian *masala dosa*. Real Irish food is not something that's widely available in Dublin so it's worth trying. On the corner of Wellington Quay and Asdills Row is *Omar Khayyam* (☎ 677 5758), a popular and very good Middle Eastern restaurant offering all the usual Lebanese-style dishes. Count on paying around IR£15 a head. You can remain in the Arab world at *Le Restaurant Casablanca* (☎ 679 9996) at 22 Temple Bar. Here the food is Moroccan and includes such North African specialities as tahini and couscous. The Casablanca is open every day.

Poco Loco (☎ 679 1950) at 32 Parliament St offers very straightforward Tex-Mex interpretations of Mexican food but they do have Corona beer (cerveza if you wish!) and their combination plates are great value at IR£5 to IR£8. It's open weekdays for lunch and every day for dinner.

Dame St's international mix of restaurants includes Chinese possibilities like *Fan's Cantonese Restaurant* (☎ 679 4263, 679 4273) at No 60. *Les Frères Jacques* (☎ 679 4555) at No 74 is one of Temple Bar's fancier places with set meals for IR£20. The food is as French as the name would indicate, the mood is slightly serious, and the bill can make quite a dent in your credit card limit. It's open Monday to Friday for lunch, Monday to Saturday for dinner.

Turn off Dame St into Crow St where you'll find *Tante Zoé's* (☎ 679 4407) at No 1. It's open Monday to Saturday for lunch, Monday to Sunday for dinner and is yet more proof of how cosmopolitan Dublin dining can be, since Cajun and Creole food is the speciality. The next lane again is Fownes St Upper, where your taste buds can continue their travels to Portugal at the *Little Lisbon* (☎ 671 1274). It's open every day, and Australians will feel right at home here as it has a BYO licence, allowing you to bring your own wine.

The *Broker's Restaurant* (☎ 679 3534) at 25 Dame St serves up truly traditional Irish fare – you can even have Irish stew – and three-course meals for around IR£8. *Nico's* (☎ 677 3062) at 53 Dame St also offers conservative food, except that here it's Italian, though strongly under the Irish influence. It's solidly popular and open for dinner Monday to Saturday, and also for lunch on weekdays.

Around Grafton St

Pedestrianised Grafton St is the No 1 shopping street in south Dublin and notably deficient in restaurants and pubs. The streets to the east and west of Grafton St are more promising. Dame St restaurants are all covered in the Temple Bar section.

Fast Food & Cafés Grafton St is the fast-food centre south of the Liffey with a *McDonald's* at No 9, a *Burger King* at No 39 and *La Pizza* just round the corner at 1 St Stephen's Green North. *Captain America* (☎ 671 5266), at 44 Grafton St at the St Stephen's Green, has burgers until midnight every night of the week.

Round the corner from Dublin Castle at 2 Werburgh St is *Leo Burdock's* (☎ 54 0366), next to the Lord Edward Pub. It is frequently claimed to dole out the best fish & chips in Ireland. You can eat them down the road in the park beside St Patrick's Cathedral. It's open in the evenings from Wednesday to Saturday and on Monday.

The Grafton St area has office workers, Trinity College students and tourists to feed and there are plenty of cafés and restaurants to keep them happy at lunch time. Backpackers staying at *Avalon House* on Aungier St (see Hostels in the Places to Stay section) will find good cafeteria-style facilities there.

Bewley's is a huge cafeteria-style place that offers good-quality food, including breakfast, lunch-time sandwiches (IR£1.50 to IR£3) and complete meals (IR£2.50 to IR£3.50). Bewley's is equally good for a quick cup of tea or coffee and actually offers a choice of teas, a very pleasant surprise in a country where tea is usually made strictly to the British recipe – white and sweet.

There are three branches of Bewley's cafés around the centre. The 78 Grafton St branch is the Bewley's flagship, with the company's interesting little museum upstairs. It's open from 7.30 am to 10 pm Monday to Wednesday, to 1 am Thursday and to 2 am Friday and Saturday. On Sunday it's open from 9.30 am to 7 pm. The branch at 11/12 Westmoreland St is open from 7.30 am to 7 pm Monday to Saturday and 10 am to 6 pm Sunday. There's also a branch at 13 South Great George's St.

Subs n Salads is on Anne St South just off Grafton St and turns out filling sandwiches, baps (an Irish version of a bread roll) and rolls for IR£1.20 to IR£2, snappily and with a smile. Eat there or even better, if it's a sunny day, have a park picnic in nearby St Stephen's Green. At 6 Anne St South is the *Coffee Inn* (☎ 677 0107) with good coffee, outdoor tables (weather permitting) and late opening hours every night of the week. There are pizzas and pasta dishes to go with the coffee.

Munchies on the corner of Exchequer St and William St South, just west of Grafton St, claims to produce the best sandwiches in Ireland. For IR£1.70 (sandwiches) or IR£1.90 (baps) you can check if it's true. There are other branches of Munchies around Dublin. A little closer to Grafton St at 19 Wicklow St is *Cornucopia* (☎ 677 7583), a popular wholefood café turning out all sorts of goodies for those trying to escape the Irish cholesterol habit. It's open for lunch Monday to Saturday and until 8 pm on weekday evenings, 9 pm on Thursdays. Head the other way along Exchequer St to the new *Wed Wose Café* at No 18.

The Powerscourt Townhouse shopping centre, in its wonderfully restored old building between William St South and Clarendon

St, has many eating places and makes a great place for lunch. They include *Blazing Salads II* (☎ 671 9552), a very popular vegetarian restaurant on the top level with a variety of salads for 60p each. It's open Monday to Saturday from 9.30 am to 6 pm. In the open central area is *Mary Rose*, a good place for lunch or a coffee. *O'Brien's* is a popular sandwich place with a daily lunch-time soup and sandwich special for IR£2.95. There are other branches at 54 Mary St and in the St Stephen's Green shopping centre.

The large *Kilkenny Kitchen* (☎ 677 7066) is on the 1st floor of the Kilkenny Shop at 6 Nassau St. The generally excellent food is served cafeteria-style and at times the queues can be discouragingly long. At peak times there's a simpler food counter which can be faster. The Kilkenny Kitchen is open Monday to Saturday from 9 am to 5 pm, and to 8 pm on Thursday.

The *Coffee Bean* (☎ 679 7140) is at 4 Nassau St, also opposite Trinity College. It's popular with college students, and from the upstairs room you can gaze across the college grounds. The food comes in healthy quantities, in healthy style (plenty of vegetarian dishes) and with lots of salads. Within Trinity College is the basement *Buttery Café*, which is OK if you like everything with chips.

Fitzer's slick outlets are a great place for lunch or early evening meals on weekdays. There's a Fitzer's (☎ 677 1155) at 52 Dawson St, towards the Trinity College and Nassau St end. The best Fitzer's however is in the National Gallery, and is covered in the Merrion Row, Baggot St & Beyond section.

Restaurants St Andrew's St, just west of Grafton St's northern end, is packed with good restaurant possibilities. The excellent *Trocadero* (☎ 677 5545, 679 9772) at 3 St Andrew's St offers no culinary surprises and that is exactly why it is so popular. Simple food, straightforward preparation, large serves and late opening hours are the selling points. The Troc, as it's locally known, is open past midnight every night except Sunday, when it closes just a little earlier.

Across the road, *QV-2* (☎ 677 3363, 677 2246) at 14/15 St Andrew's St manages to look more expensive than it is. There are good pasta dishes for IR£5.50 to IR£6.50 and main courses for IR£8 to IR£12, but vegetables cost extra. It offers good, mildly adventurous food, pleasant surroundings and a dessert called Eton Mess (IR£1.95) which should not be missed. It's open every day for lunch and dinner until after midnight.

Still on St Andrew's St the *Cedar Tree* (☎ 677 2121) at No 11A is a Lebanese restaurant with a good selection of vegetarian dishes. Or turn the corner to *La Taverna* (☎ 677 3665) at 33 Wicklow St. It's open Monday to Saturday for lunch and every day for dinner and combines sunny Greek food with an equally sunny atmosphere. At 12A Wicklow St the *Imperial Chinese Restaurant* (☎ 677 2580) is open every day but is notable for its lunch-time dim sums.

Pasta Fresca (☎ 679 2402) is at 3/4 Chatham St, just off Grafton St's southern end. This modern, cheerful restaurant proves once again that the Irish really like their Italian food. It has very authentic pasta dishes for IR£6.50 to IR£8.50 and is open from breakfast time until reasonably late Tuesday to Saturday, but on Monday it closes at 7 pm. Just off Chatham St, *Pizza Stop* (☎ 679 6712) at 6 Chatham Lane is a very popular pizzeria with pizzas for IR£4 to IR£7. Alternatively, at 27 Exchequer St, a bit to the north, there's the popular *Trattoria Pasta Pasta* (☎ 679 2565) with pasta dishes for around IR£7.

There are several pubs with good food close to Grafton St. The *Stag's Head* (☎ 679 3701) is on Dame Court, and, apart from being an extremely popular drinking spot during the summer months (see the Entertainment section), it also turns out simple, well-prepared and very economical meals. At 37 Exchequer St on the corner of St Andrew's St is the *Old Stand*, another very popular place for pub food with meals at about IR£5.

Davy Byrne's at 21 Duke St has been famous for its food ever since Leopold Bloom dropped in for a sandwich. It's now a rather swish watering hole but you can still eat there. Directly across the road the *Bailey* (☎ 677 3055) at 2 Duke St also has a restaurant serving traditional Irish food like Irish stew or Dublin coddle. Farther west the *Lord Edward Seafood Restaurant* (☎ 54 2420) is in the Lord Edward Pub at 23 Christ Church Place opposite Christ Church Cathedral and has pub-style seafood. It's open Tuesday to Friday for lunch and Thursday to Saturday for dinner.

Head to Mexico at *Judge Roy Bean's* (☎ 679 7539) at 45/47 Nassau St on the corner of Grafton St for popular tacos and an equally popular bar. *Eddie Rocket's* (☎ 679 7340) at 7 Anne St South is a 1950s-style American diner ready to dish out anything from breakfast at 7.30 am to an excellent late-night burger from IR£2.85. Friday and Saturday nights it's open right through to 4 am. Next door is the trendy, popular *Independent Pizza Company* (☎ 679 5266) at 8 Anne St South. These are pizzas prepared with some pizzazz.

Restaurant Mahler (☎ 679 7117) is in the Powerscourt Townhouse shopping centre on William St South but its entrance is actually on the street. The speciality is food presented simply but stylishly. It's open Monday to Saturday for lunch and morning or afternoon coffee. On Friday and Saturday it's also open for dinner, and during the summer tourist season it's open on the other weekdays as well. The *Periwinkle Seafood Bar* (☎ 679 4203) is also in the Powerscourt Townhouse shopping centre and serves economically priced seafood lunches with the accent on shellfish.

Regular visitors to India may remember Rajdoot as a popular brand of Indian motorcycle; those in search of Indian food in Dublin can scoot down to *Rajdoot Tandoori* (☎ 679 4274, 679 4280) for superb north Indian tandoori dishes. It's at 26/28 Clarendon St in the Westbury Centre, behind the Westbury Hotel. Nearby, and with similarly Mogul-style Indian cuisine, is the *Shalimar* (☎ 671 0738) at 17 South Great George's St. They offer a wide variety of delectable Indian breads.

La Stampa (☎ 677 8611) at 35 Dawson St is Dublin's up-market Italian restaurant with a large and very attractive Georgian dining area; when it's buzzing this is one of the nicest places to eat in the city. It's open from lunch time until late every day and main courses are in the IR£8 to IR£12 range, including vegetables.

The very stylish *Polo One* (☎ 676 3362) is at 5/6 Molesworth Place, a smaller lane off Molesworth St, tucked in behind St Ann's Church which fronts on to Dawson St. The food is that modern international style which combines European flavours with a hint of California. There are set menus at IR£15 for lunch or IR£22 for dinner and the wines are pricey but the food tastes just as good as it looks.

Finally, on Stephen St Lower, behind the big St Stephen's Green shopping centre, the recently opened *Break for the Border* is a very big and busy restaurant, bar and entertainment complex serving Tex-Mex food until late. Look for the Western horse and rider statue out front.

Merrion Row, Baggot St & Beyond

Merrion Row, leading out south-east from St Stephen's Green, and its extension, Baggot St, is a busy boulevard for middle to upper bracket guesthouses, popular pubs and an eclectic selection of restaurants.

Fast Food & Cafés Merrion Square, connected to Merrion Row by Merrion St, has a restaurant well worth a detour, particularly at lunch time. The National Gallery *Fitzer's* (☎ 668 6481) is right inside the gallery (entry is free). The artistic interlude as you walk through makes a pleasant introduction to this slightly pricey but very popular restaurant. It has the same opening hours as the gallery (Thursdays until 8.30 pm) and has meals for IR£4.25 to IR£5.25, as well as salads, sandwiches and wine. There's a *Fitzer's Take-Out* (☎ 660 0644) at 24 Baggot St Upper.

Starting from the Shelbourne Hotel on St Stephen's Green, *Galligan's Café* (☎ 676 5955) at 6 Merrion Row is a great place for breakfast from 7.30 am weekdays or from

9 am on Saturday and for lunch or afternoon snacks. Farther along, *Georgian Fare* (☎ 676 7736) at 14 Baggot St Lower has good sandwiches, while *Miller's Pizza Kitchen* (☎ 676 6098) at 9/10 Baggot St Lower is firmly in pastaland.

On the other side of the street *Istanbul Kebabs*, also labelled *Bosphorus Kebabs*, is a popular place for late-night cheap eats. It's right next to the Baggot Inn on Baggot St Lower.

Restaurants There's quite an international collection of restaurants among the colourful Baggot St pubs, one of which is *Eureka* (☎ 676 2868) at 142 Baggot St Lower. This authentically Greek restaurant is open Monday to Thursday for lunch, every day for dinner. A bit farther along is *Ayumi-ya* (☎ 662 0233, 662 0223), in the basement at 132 Baggot St Lower, a very Westernised Japanese steakhouse offering good-value set meals comprising a starter, soup, main course, dessert and tea or coffee from IR£10 to IR£13. There are no surprises here but the food is good. There's a second branch of Ayumi-ya in the suburb of Blackrock and this is a more formal place serving more traditional Japanese food.

The *Ante Room* (☎ 660 4716), 20 Baggot St Lower, located underneath the popular Georgian House guesthouse, is a seafood specialist with main courses for IR£8 to IR£14.50 and traditional Irish music on most nights.

Restaurant Patrick Guilbaud (☎ 676 4192) has a reputation as Dublin's best place for French food in the modern idiom and the restaurant itself is equally modern. Don't come here unless your credit card is in A1 condition. The smooth décor and service is backed up by delicious food. There's nothing overpoweringly fancy about anything, it's just good food, beautifully prepared and elegantly presented. There's a set menu for IR£25 but with drinks and service you should count on at least IR£40 per person. Patrick Guilbaud is at 46 James's Place, just off Baggot St Lower beyond Fitzwilliam St.

It's open for lunch and dinner Monday to Saturday.

You can slide backwards in time by continuing along Baggot St, across the Grand Canal and on to Pembroke Rd where you will find *Le Coq Hardi* (☎ 668 4130) at No 35. This is the older counterpart of Patrick Guilbaud with heavier, more traditional French dishes and a superb wine list. The bill is likely to be a little heavier as well. It's open for lunch Monday to Friday and for dinner Monday to Saturday.

Also out from the centre is the *Lobster Pot Restaurant* (☎ 668 0025) at 9 Ballsbridge Terrace, Dublin 4. It's a staunchly old-fashioned place offering substantial and solid dishes in an equally substantial atmosphere. As the name indicates, seafood is the speciality. Prices are fairly high. Close by at 15/17 Ballsbridge Terrace is *Kites Chinese Restaurant* (☎ 660 7415, 660 5978), where Chinese food with style is the story and the prices are moderate to high – this is not a cheapie.

Back towards the centre at 74 Leeson St Lower, in the heart of Dublin's nightclub strip, is the *Hungry Wolf* (☎ 676 3951), open for lunch or dinner but especially noteworthy for being open until very late at night with food to satisfy the Leeson St nightclubbers.

If you're after real Irish food then *Oisin's* (☎ 475 3433) at 31 Camden St Upper is the place to go. Camden St is to the south-west of St Stephen's Green, a block over from Harcourt St. The menu offers all the traditional Irish dishes, including Irish stew and Dublin coddle, and it's done well but is also expensive. Oisin's is open for dinner Tuesday to Sunday.

The *Old Dublin* restaurant (☎ 01-542085) at 90 Francis St makes an interesting departure from the standard Irish menu, specialising in Russian and Scandinavian food. It costs around IR£20 a head but it's worth the splash.

Finally, west of the city centre, the IMMA (Irish Museum of Modern Arts) at the Royal Hospital Kilmainham has an excellent café in the basement. If you're planning a visit to the museum, it's well worth including a lunch stop in your itinerary.

ENTERTAINMENT

Dublin has theatres, cinemas, nightclubs and concert halls, but just as in every village throughout the emerald isle, the pubs are the real centres of activity. Dublin has hundreds of pubs and they're great for anything from a contemplative pint of Guinness to a rowdy night out with the latest Irish rock band. For what's on info get the fortnightly magazine *In Dublin* or the giveaway *Dublin Event Guide*.

A Pub Crawl

See the Tours section for information on the excellent and highly recommended Literary Pub Crawl, which on summer nights makes a fine introduction to some of Dublin's pubs and to Ireland's literary history. Pubs must close at night by 11.30 pm, or by 11 pm in winter.

A visit to the city should properly include a walking tour of some of the best of the old pubs. A traditional Irish pub has *snugs*, partitioned-off tables where you can meet with friends in privacy. Some snugs will even have their own little serving hatches, so drinks can be passed in discreetly should the drinkers not want to be seen ordering 'just the one'.

Even in medieval times the city was well supplied with drinking establishments and in the late 17th century a count revealed that one in every five houses in the city was involved in selling alcohol. A century later another survey counted 52 public houses along Thomas St in the Liberties. There may not be quite so many today but Dublin still has a huge selection of pubs, so there's no possibility of being unable to find a Guinness should you develop a terrible thirst.

A Dublin pub crawl should start at the *Brazen Head* on Bridge St just south of the Liffey beyond Christ Church Cathedral. This is Dublin's oldest pub, though its history is uncertain. Its own sign proclaims that it was founded in 1198, but the earliest reference to it is in 1613 and licensing laws did not come into effect until 1635. Others claim that it was founded in 1666 or 1688, but the present building is thought to date from 1754. The sunken level of the entrance courtyard is a clear indicator of how much street levels have altered since its construction. In the 1790s it was the headquarters of the United Irishmen, who, it would appear, had a tendency to talk too much after a few drinks, leading to numerous arrests being made here. At that time Robert Emmet was a regular visitor. Not surprisingly, James Joyce mentioned it in *Ulysses* with a recommendation for the food: 'you get a decent enough do in the Brazen Head'.

From the Brazen Head walk eastward along the Liffey to the trendy Temple Bar district and dive into those narrow lanes for a drink at popular pubs like the *Norseman* and the *Temple Bar*. On summer evenings young visitors to Dublin congregate for a nightly street party that stretches along Temple Bar from one pub to the other. Next door to the Clarence Hotel on Essex St East, the *Garage Bar* is owned by the rock band U2 and has an appropriately garage-like décor complete with a porcupine car.

On Fleet St in Temple Bar, the *Palace*, with its tiled floor and mirrors, is frequently pointed out as a perfect example of an old Dublin pub. It's popular with journalists from the nearby *Irish Times*. On the corner of Temple Bar and Anglesea St is the *Auld Dubliner*, and on the opposite corner, at the junction of Fleet and Anglesea Sts, is the recently restored and renovated *Oliver St John Gogarty*.

From Temple Bar cross Dame St, itself well supplied with drinking establishments, to the intersection of Dame Court and Dame Lane, where *Dame Tavern* and the *Stag's Head* face each other from opposite corners. Here, too, a street party takes place between the pubs on summer evenings. The *Stag's Head* was built in 1770, then remodelled in 1895 and is sufficiently picturesque to have featured in a postage stamp series on Irish pubs.

Continue down Dame Lane past the *Banker's* to *O'Neill's* on Suffolk St. It's only a stone's throw from Trinity College, so this fine old traditional pub has long been a student haunt. A block over on Exchequer St is the *Old Stand*, furnished in Victorian style and renowned for its sporting connections and fine pub food. On the other corner, on Wicklow St, the *International Bar* has entertainment almost every night, including a Comedy Cellar on Wednesdays.

Emerge on to Grafton St, which, despite being Dublin's premier shopping street, is completely publess. Fear not – there are numerous interesting establishments just off the street, including two on Duke St where the *Bailey* and *Davy Byrne's* face each other across the street. *Davy Byrne's* was Bloom's 'moral pub' in *Ulysses* and he stopped there for a Gorgonzola cheese sandwich with mustard washed down with a glass of Burgundy. It also featured in *Dubliners*, but after a recent glossy refurbishment it has become something of a yuppie hang-out and Joyce would hardly recognise it. The door from 7 Eccles St in north Dublin, the Bloom home in *Ulysses*, was salvaged when the building was demolished in 1982 and can now be seen in the *Bailey*.

On Harry St, also off Grafton St, you'll find *McDaid's*, once the 'local' of writer Brendan Behan, now a bit of a tourist trap. Across the road from it is the *Bruxelles*. On Anne St South there's *John Kehoe's* with its old snugs, where patrons can still savour their Guinness in privacy. Chatham St features *Neary's*, a showy Victorian era pub with a particularly fine frontage, popular with actors from the nearby Gaiety Theatre.

From the end of Grafton St turn along the north side of St Stephen's Green, the 'Beaux Walk', and continue on past the Shelbourne Hotel to Merrion Row for a drink at *O'Donoghue's*. In the evening you'll probably have music to accompany your pint as this is one of Dublin's most famous music pubs. The folk group the Dubliners started out here. On summer evenings a young and international crowd spills out into the courtyard beside the pub.

Merrion Row changes name to become Baggot St Lower and facing each other across the street are two very traditional old pubs – *James Toner's* and *Doheny & Nesbitt's*. Toner's, with its stone floor, is almost a country pub in the heart of the city and the shelves and drawers are reminders that it once doubled as a grocery store. Doheny & Nesbitt's is equipped with antique snugs and is a favourite place for political gossip among politicians and journalists; Leinster House is only a short stroll away. *Baggot Inn*, close to Toner's, is a popular pub for rock music. If you continue farther along Baggot St you'll come to *Larry Murphy's* and the *Henry Grattan*.

Backtrack a few steps to Merrion St Upper and walk north past Merrion Square to *Kenny's* on Lincoln Place, which is tucked in behind Trinity College and has long been a Trinity student haunt. It's well known for its spontaneous traditional music sessions. Continue round the edge of Trinity College towards the river where you'll come to *John Mulligan's* on Poolbeg St, another pub that has scarcely changed over the years. It featured as the local pub in the film *My Left Foot* and is popular with journalists from the nearby newspaper offices. Mulligan's was established in 1782 and has long been reputed to have the best Guinness in Ireland as well as a wonderfully varied crowd of 'regulars'.

South of the centre there are some interesting pubs along the Grand Canal (see the Grand Canal section) and the traditional *An Béal Bocht* on Charlemont St.

Brendan Behan

No thorough pub crawl should be restricted to pubs south of the Liffey, so head north to try *Slattery's* at 129 Capel St, on the corner of Mary's Lane, and *Sean O'Casey's* at 105 Marlborough St, on the corner of Abbey St Lower. Both are busy music pubs where you'll often find traditional Irish music downstairs and loud rock upstairs. Other north Dublin pubs to sample are the *Oval* on Abbey St Middle, another journalists' hang-out, and *Abbey Mooney's* on Abbey St Lower.

Head farther north to the *Patrick Conway* on Parnell St. It has been in operation since 1745, and new fathers have been stopping in here for a celebratory pint from the day the Rotunda Maternity Hospital opened across the road in 1757. *Joxer Daly's* at 103/104 Dorset St Upper is a Victorian-style pub, which is conveniently close to the Young Traveller and An Óige hostels.

Pub Entertainment

There's considerable overlap between music styles at the various Dublin pubs – some specialise solely in one type of music, others switch from night to night. Others may have one band on upstairs and another, of an entirely different style, downstairs.

Rock Music Various pubs specialise in rock music, and some of them charge an entry fee. The *Rock Garden Café* in Temple Bar (see the Discos & Nightclubs section) has rock bands on every night, often with an early and a late show. *McGonagle's* on Anne St South is another possibility. *Whelan's*, the *Purty Loft* and the *Baggot Inn* are other places which hold rock sessions almost every night. Other pubs which often have rock music are *An Béal Bocht*, *Fibber McGee's*, the *Grattan*, the *International* and *Larry O'Rourke's*. During the summer months the *Olympia Theatre* has 'Midnight at the Olympia' performances on Friday and Saturday nights.

Traditional & Folk Music Traditional Irish music and folk music also have big followings in Dublin pubs. Some of these entertainment pubs may switch from rock

one night to folk the next to Irish traditional the night after. They include *An Béal Bocht*, the *Auld Dubliner*, *Boss Croker's*, the *Brazen Head*, *Larry O'Rourke's*, *O'Donoghue's*, the *Purty Loft*, *Sir Arthur Conan Doyle's*, *Slattery's* and the *Wexford Inn*.

Country Music Along with all the other popular music forms in Ireland, there's a real passion for country music. It's especially popular at *Bad Bob's* in Temple Bar (see the Discos & Nightclubs section). Pubs where country music is popular include *Barry's Hotel*, the *Lower Deck* and the *Purty Loft*.

Jazz & Blues Jazz and blues are also played at several pubs, including the *Barge*, *Boss Croker's*, the *Grattan*, *Harcourt Hotel*, *McDaid's*, *Hotel Pierre* and *Slattery's*. *Sach's Hotel* and *Jury's Hotel* also have jazz sessions on Sundays.

Comedy Given the international fame of the Irish joke, it's surprising that there aren't more comedy venues in Dublin. Several pubs have comedy acts from time to time, such as the *Waterfront* and the *Purty Loft*. The *International Bar* has a regular Wednesday night Comedy Cellar – which takes place upstairs, of course.

Venues The phone numbers and locations of the music and entertainment pubs mentioned here are as follows:

An Béal Bocht
    58 Charlemont St, Dublin 2 (☎ 475 5614)
The Auld Dubliner
    17 Anglesea St, Dublin 2 (☎ 677 0527)
Bad Bob's Backstage Bar
    East Essex St, Dublin 2 (☎ 677 5482)
The Baggot Inn
    143 Baggot St, Dublin 2 (☎ 676 1430)
The Barge Inn
    42 Charlemont St, Dublin 2 (☎ 475 0005)
Barry's Hotel
    Great Denmark St, Dublin 1 (☎ 874 6943)
Boss Croker's
    39 Arran Quay, Dublin 7 (☎ 872 2400)
The Brazen Head
    Bridge St, Dublin 8 (☎ 677 9549)

Fibber Magee's
    Gate Hotel, Parnell St, Dublin 2 (☎ 874 5253)
The Grattan
    165 Capel St, Dublin 1 (☎ 873 3049)
The Harcourt Hotel
    60 Harcourt St, Dublin 2 (☎ 778 3677)
The International Bar
    23 Wicklow St, Dublin 2 (☎ 677 9250)
Jury's Hotel
    Ballsbridge, Dublin 4 (☎ 660 5000)
Larry O'Rourke's
    72 Dorset St Upper, Dublin 1 (☎ 30 6693)
The Lower Deck
    Portobello Harbour, Dublin 8 (☎ 475 1423)
McDaid's
    3 Harry St, Dublin 2 (☎ 679 4395)
McGonagle's
    Anne St South, Dublin 2 (☎ 677 4402)
The Night Train (O'Dwyer's Pub)
    8 Mount St Lower, Dublin 2 (☎ 676 1717)
O'Donoghue's
    15 Merrion Row, Dublin 2 (☎ 661 4303)
Hotel Pierre
    Seafront, Dun Laoghaire (☎ 280 0291)
The Purty Loft
    Old Dunleary Rd, Dun Laoghaire (☎ 280 1257)
The Rock Garden
    3A Crown Alley, Dublin 2 (☎ 679 9114)
Sach's Hotel
    19/29 Morehampton Rd, Dublin 4 (☎ 668 0995)
Sir Arthur Conan Doyle
    160 Phibsborough Rd, Dublin 7 (☎ 30 1441)
Slattery's
    129 Capel St, Dublin 1 (☎ 872 7971)
The Waterfront
    Sir John Rogerson's Quay, Dublin 2 (☎ 677 8466)
The Wexford Inn
    16 Wexford St, Dublin 2 (☎ 478 0391)
Whelan's
    25 Wexford St, Dublin 2 (☎ 478 0766)

Irish Entertainment

There are several places in Dublin where tourists can go for an evening of Irish entertainment comprising Irish songs, Irish dancing and probably a few Irish jokes thrown in along the way.

Jury's Irish Cabaret (☎ 660 5000) at Jury's Hotel, Ballsbridge, Dublin 4, features 2½ hours of Irish music, song and dance. This has been a tourist favourite for 30 years. You can either come for dinner and the show from 7.15 pm (IR£29.50) or just for the show from 8 pm (IR£17.50, including two drinks).

It operates nightly except Mondays from the beginning of May to mid-October.

Similar performances are put on at the *Burlington Hotel* (☎ 660 5222) at Leeson St, Dublin 4. The two-hour performances take place nightly from 8 pm May to October. Dinner starts an hour earlier and the cost for dinner and the show is IR£27.90. The *Clontarf Castle* (☎ 33 2321, 33 2271) at Castle Ave, Clontarf, Dublin 3, also has shows from 7.30 pm Monday to Saturday.

Cinema

Dublin's restaurants are overwhelmingly south of the river, pubs are more evenly spread between north and south, but city cinemas are more heavily concentrated on the north side.

The multiscreen first-run cinemas are the four-screen *Adelphi* (☎ 873 1161, 98 Abbey St Middle, Dublin 1); the four-screen *Carlton* (☎ 873 1609, 52 O'Connell St Upper, Dublin 1); and the five-screen *Savoy* (☎ 874 8487, O'Connell St Upper, Dublin 1). The three-screen *Screen* at College St (☎ 671 4988 & 872 3922, College St, Dublin 2) is south of river and is more art house, less big release. Ditto for the *Light House* (☎ 873 0438, Abbey St Middle, Dublin 1). The *Irish Film Centre* (☎ 679 5744) has two screens at 6 Eustace St in Temple Bar.

Entry prices are generally between IR£3 and IR£5, though there may be reduced prices for afternoon shows. Late-night shows take place from time to time, particularly at the Carlton and Savoy on Saturday nights.

Theatre

Dublin's theatre scene is small but busy. See the Theatre section for more information about the histories of some of Dublin's best known theatres. Theatre bookings can usually be made by quoting a credit card number over the phone and the tickets can then be collected just before the performance.

The famous *Abbey Theatre* (☎ 878 7222) is on Abbey St Lower, Dublin 1, near the river. This is Ireland's national theatre and it puts on new Irish works as well as a steady series of revivals of classic Irish works by W B Yeats, J M Synge, Sean O'Casey, Brendan Behan, Samuel Beckett and others. The smaller *Peacock Theatre* is part of the same complex.

Also north of the Liffey is the *Gate Theatre* (☎ 874 4045) on the south-east corner of Parnell Square, right at the top of O'Connell St. It specialises in international classics and older Irish works with a touch of comedy by playwrights such as Oscar Wilde, George Bernard Shaw and Oliver Goldsmith. It was built between 1784 and 1786 as part of the Rotunda building but did not become the Gate Theatre until 1929.

The *Olympia Theatre* (☎ 677 8962) is on Dame St, and often has rock concerts as well as plays. The *Gaiety Theatre* (☎ 677 1717) on King St South opened in 1871 and puts on modern plays and TV shows. Over in the Liberties the *Tivoli Theatre* (☎ 54 4472) is on Francis St, Dublin 8, directly opposite the Iveagh Market.

Experimental and less commercial performances take place at the *City Arts Centre* (☎ 677 0643) at 23/25 Moss St, Dublin 2, and at the *Project Arts Centre* (☎ 671 2321), 39 Essex St East, Temple Bar, Dublin 1. Several pubs host theatrical performances. These include *An Béal Bocht* (☎ 475 5614), 58 Charlemont St, Dublin 2, and the *International Bar* (☎ 677 9250), 23 Wicklow St, Dublin 2. Puppet performances are put on at the *Lambert Puppet Theatre & Museum* (☎ 280 0974) in Clifton Lane, Monkstown.

Theatrical performances also take place at:

Andrew's Lane Theatre
    9/17 St Andrew's Lane (☎ 679 5720)
Focus Theatre
    6 Pembroke Place, Dublin 2 (☎ 676 3071, 689 2000)
New Eblana Theatre
    Busáras, Dublin 1 (☎ 679 8404)
Players' Theatre Trinity
    College, Dublin 2 (☎ 677 2941, ext 1239)
Riverbank Theatre
    Merchant's Quay, Dublin 2 (☎ 677 3370)

Concerts

Classical concerts are performed at the *National Concert Hall* (☎ 671 1888) on Earlsfort Terrace, Dublin 2, just south of St Stephen's Green. There are often lunch-time concerts with entry prices of around IR£3 to IR£4. Classical performances may also take place at the Bank of Ireland Arts Centre on Foster Place, at the Hugh Lane Gallery on Parnell Square or at the Royal Dublin Showground Concert Hall.

Big rock concerts are held at the *Point Depot* at East Link Bridge, North Wall Quay, by the river. The building was originally constructed as a railway terminus in 1878. The Lansdowne Rd stadium, a mecca for rugby enthusiasts, is also used for big rock performances. Smaller performances often take place at the pleasantly tatty *Olympia Theatre* (☎ 677 8962) in Dame St, Temple Bar.

Bookings can be made either directly at the concert venue or through HMV at 18 Henry St, Dublin 1 (☎ 873 2899), and 65 Grafton St, Dublin 2 (☎ 79 5332). Golden Discs (☎ 677 1025 for concert bookings) also handles concert bookings through its outlets, which are at Grafton Arcade, 8 Earl St North, St Stephen's Green shopping centre and St Anne's Lane.

Discos & Nightclubs

Leeson St Lower, to the south-east of St Stephen's Green, is the nightclub quarter of Dublin, with a whole string of clubs along this one busy block. They're easily pin-pointed by the black-suited bouncers lined up outside, but which clubs are currently in changes from one year (or even one month) to another. It's probably best just to follow the crowds – if it looks busy it's likely to be good. Leeson St clubs usually stay open until around 4 am and there are no admission charges, but the price of drinks certainly makes up for that; count on paying at least IR£15 for a bottle of very basic wine.

Other popular venues usually do have an entry charge. *Lillie's Bordello*, whose entrance is in an alley off Grafton St at the Trinity College end, is usually open to 2 am.

In Temple Bar the *Rock Garden Café* on Crown Alley also operates until around 2 am, with a rock band every night. Entry prices depend on the act and the day but are usually around IR£6 to IR£8. Eating in the restaurant section will give you a reduction on the entry charge. Also in Temple Bar is *Bad Bob's* on East Essex St where again there's music every night, except that here it's usually country music rather than rock. Entry is in the IR£6 to IR£8 bracket. Still in Temple Bar, *Club M* at Bloom's Hotel is very popular.

McGonagle's on Anne St South typically charges IR£4 to IR£6. *Break for the Border* on Stephen St Lower is a huge new entertainment complex combining a bar with a Tex-Mex restaurant.

Buskers

Dublin is well set up for free entertainment in the form of buskers, but contributions are always gratefully accepted. The best of the city's plentiful supply work busy Grafton St, where they are occasionally hassled by shopkeepers (for blocking access to their concerns) and by the police but are mainly left to get on with it. At the Trinity College end of Grafton St you'll usually trip over pavement artists, busily chalking their pictures around the statue of Molly Malone. Farther along the street you're likely to meet crooning folk singers, raucous rock bands, classical string quartets and oddities like the saw doctor who produces surprisingly tuneful noises from a bowed saw and sells cassettes of his recordings.

GETTING THERE & AWAY

The USIT (Union of Students in Ireland Travel) Travel Office (☎ 679 8833) in Dublin is at 19 Aston Quay, right by the river and O'Connell Bridge.

Air

Dublin is Ireland's major international airport gateway with flights from all over Europe. Flights from North America have to come via Shannon. See the Getting There & Away chapter for details on flights and fares.

There is no airport departure tax from Dublin.

Airline offices in Dublin include:

Aer Lingus (☎ 37 7777 for UK enquiries, 37 7747 for elsewhere)
 42 Grafton St, Dublin 2
 41 O'Connell St Upper, Dublin 1
 12 George's St Upper, Dun Laoghaire
Aeroflot
 Dublin Airport (☎ 842 5400)
Air France
 29/30 Dawson St, Dublin 2 (☎ 677 8899)
Alitalia
 60/63 Dawson St, Dublin 2 (☎ 677 5171)
Birmingham European Airways (☎ 021-27 2211)
British Midland
 Nutley, Merrion Rd, Dublin 4 (☎ 283 8833)
Delta Airlines
 24 Merrion Square, Dublin 2 (☎ 676 8080)
Iberia Airlines
 54 Dawson St, Dublin 2 (☎ 677 9486)
Lufthansa
 Grattan House, Mount St Lower, Dublin 2 (☎ 676 1595)
Manx Airlines
 Dublin Airport (☎ 84 23555)
Ryanair
 3 Dawson St, Dublin 2 (☎ 677 4422)
Sabena World Airlines
 7 Dawson St, Dublin 2 (☎ 671 6677)
SAS
 Dublin Airport (☎ 842 1922)
TAP Air Portugal
 54 Dawson St, Dublin 2 (☎ 679 8844)
Viva Air
 54 Dawson St, Dublin 2 (☎ 677 9846)

Note that British Airways does not fly to Dublin. For British Airways enquiries call ☎ 1-800 62 6747.

Ferry

There are two direct services from Holyhead on the north-west tip of Wales – one to Dublin, and the other to Dun Laoghaire, the port on the southern side of Dublin Bay. See the Getting There & Away chapter for details.

Bus & Ferry

There are coaches direct from London and other UK centres to Dublin – see the Getting There & Away chapter for details.

Bus

Standard one-way fares from Dublin include Belfast IR£10, Cork IR£11 or Galway IR£9. These fares are much cheaper than the regular railway fares, return fares are usually only a little more expensive than one-way, and special deals are often available. Busáras, Bus Éireann's central bus station, is just north of the Custom House and the River Liffey. Phone ☎ 30 2222 for information.

Buses to Belfast in Northern Ireland depart from the Busáras three times a day Monday to Saturday, and twice on Sunday. Services from the Glengall St Bus Station in Belfast operate with the same frequency. The trip takes about three hours and costs IR£9.50 one way or IR£12 for a return within one month.

Train

Trains fan out from Dublin. Connolly Station (☎ 36 3333), just north of the Liffey and the city centre, is the station for Belfast, Derry, Sligo, Wexford and other points to the north. Heuston Station (☎ 36 5421), just south of the Liffey and well west of the centre, is the station for Cork, Galway, Killarney, Limerick, Waterford and other points to the west, south and south-west.

The longest trip you can make by train from Dublin is about three hours to Galway or Killarney. Fares are high: examples of regular fares from Dublin are Belfast IR£14, Cork IR£31.50, or Galway IR£24. As with buses, special fares are often available. A same-day return to Belfast can cost as little as IR£13, a pound less than a one-way ticket! First-class tickets cost about IR£4 to IR£7 over the standard fare for a single journey. The Iarnród Éireann Travel Centre (☎ 36 6222) is at 35 Abbey St Lower.

GETTING AROUND
To/From Dublin Airport

Dublin Airport (☎ 37 9900) has an exchange counter in the baggage arrivals area, a bank that keeps regular banking hours, a post office (closed for lunch, Saturday afternoons and all day Sunday), a tourist information office that also books accommodation, shops, restaurants, bars, a hairdresser, a nursery, a church and car-hire counters. The airport is 10 km north of the centre and can be reached from the city by bus or taxi.

Airport Bus Services The Express Airport Coast operates to/from the central bus station (Busáras) near the river in central Dublin and less frequently to/from Heuston Station for IR£2.50 (children IR£1.25). It takes about half an hour. Timetables are available at the airport or in the city. Monday to Saturday city to airport services go about every 20 to 30 minutes from 7.30 am to 10.40 pm. On Sunday they operate less frequently from 7.55 am to 10.20 pm. Monday to Saturday airport to city services operate from 8.10 am to 11.15 pm. On Sunday they run from 7.30 am to 10.55 pm. The demand for seats can sometimes exceed the capacity of the bus, in which case it's worth getting a group together and sharing a taxi.

The alternative service is the slower 41A bus, which makes a number of useful stops on the way, terminates across the river on Eden Quay and costs IR£1.10. It can take up to one hour but it has longer operating hours and runs more frequently than the express bus.

There are direct buses between the airport and Belfast.

Airport Taxi Services Taxis are subject to all sorts of additional charges for baggage, extra passengers and 'unsocial hours'. However, a taxi usually costs IR£10 or less between the airport and the centre, so between four people it's unlikely to be more expensive than the bus. There's a supplementary charge of 80p from the airport to the city, but this charge does not apply from the city to the airport. Make sure the meter is switched on, as some Dublin airport taxi drivers can be as unscrupulous as their brethren anywhere else in the world.

To/From the Ferry Terminals

Buses go to the Busáras from the Dublin Ferryport terminal (☎ 874 3293) after all B&I ferry arrivals from Holyhead. For the

10 am ferry departure from Dublin, buses leave the Busáras at 9 am. For the 9.45 pm departure, buses depart from the Busáras at 8.15 and 9 pm and from Heuston Station at 8.15 pm.

To travel between the Dun Laoghaire Ferryport (☎ 80 1905) and Dublin, take a No 46A bus to St Stephen's Green or the DART (see the Train section) to Pearse Station (for south Dublin) or Connolly Station (for north Dublin).

To/From Connolly & Heuston Stations
The 90 Rail Link Bus runs between the two stations up to four times an hour at peak periods and costs a flat 60p. Connolly Station is a short walk north of the Busáras.

Bus
The Dublin Bus company (Bus Átha Cliath) has an information office (☎ 873 4222) at 59 O'Connell St, directly opposite the tourist office. Buses cost from 55p up to a maximum of IR£1.10 for one to three stages. Ten-ride tickets are available at a small discount. One-day passes cost IR£2.80 for the bus, or IR£4 for bus and rail. Other passes include a one-week bus pass for IR£10.50, or a bus and rail pass for IR£14 (plus IR£2 for an ID photo). Late-night buses run from the College St-Westmoreland St-D'Olier St triangle until 3 am on Friday and Saturday night.

The bus station or Busáras is just north of the river, behind the Custom House and has a left-luggage facility (IR£1.10, backpacks IR£1.60).

Train
The DART (Dublin Area Rapid Transport) provides quick rail access to the coast as far north as Howth and as far south as Bray. Pearse Station is convenient for central Dublin south of the Liffey and Connolly Station for north of the Liffey. Monday to Saturday there are services every 10 to 20 minutes, sometimes even more frequently, from around 6.30 am to midnight. Services are less frequent on Sunday. It takes about 30 minutes from Dublin to Bray at one extreme or Howth at the other. Dublin-Dun

Laoghaire only takes about 15 to 20 minutes. There are also Suburban Rail services north as far as Dundalk, inland to Mullingar and south past Bray to Arklow.

A one-way DART ticket from Dublin costs IR£1 to Dun Laoghaire or Howth, IR£1.20 to Bray. Within the DART region, a one-day unlimited-travel ticket costs IR£3 for an adult, IR£1.50 for a child or IR£4.50 for a family. A ticket combining DART and Dublin Bus services costs IR£4, IR£2 and IR£5.50 respectively, but this ticket cannot be used during Monday to Friday peak hours (7 to 9.45 am, 4.30 to 6.30 pm). A weekly DART and bus ticket costs IR£14 but requires an ID photo. A Dublin Explorer ticket allows you four days DART and bus travel for IR£10 but cannot be used until after 9.45 am Monday to Friday.

Bicycles cannot be taken on DART services but they can be taken on the less frequent suburban train services, either in the guards' van or in a special compartment at the opposite end of the train from the engine. There is a IR£2 charge for transporting a bicycle up to 56 km.

There are left-luggage facilities at both Heuston and Connolly railway stations (IR£1, backpacks IR£2 at Connolly).

Taxi
Taxis in Dublin are expensive with an IR£1.80 flagfall and the usual rapid increase thereafter. In addition there are a number of extra charges – 40p for each extra passenger, 40p for each piece of luggage, IR£1.20 for telephone bookings and 40p for unsocial hours, which means 8 pm to 8 am and all day Sunday. Public holidays are even more unsocial and require a higher supplement.

Taxis can be hailed on the street and are found at taxi ranks around the city, including on O'Connell St in north Dublin, College Green in front of Trinity College and St Stephen's Green at the end of Grafton St. There are numerous taxi companies that will dispatch taxis by radio. Try All Sevens Taxi (☎ 677 7777), City Cabs (☎ 872 7272) or National Radio Cabs (☎ 677 2222). Phone the Garda Carriage Office on ☎ 873 2222, ext 395/406 for any complaints about taxis.

Car & Motorcycle

As in most big cities, having a car in Dublin is as much a millstone as a convenience, though it can be useful for day trips outside the city limits.

There are parking meters around central Dublin and a selection of open and sheltered car parks. You don't have to go far from the centre to find free roadside parking, especially in north Dublin. However, the police warn visitors that it's safer to park in a supervised car park, since cars are often broken into even in broad daylight close to major tourist attractions. Rental cars and cars with foreign number plates, which may contain valuable personal effects, are a prime target.

Car Rental

See the Getting Around chapter for information on car rental. Murrays/Europcar, Avis, Budget and Hertz have desks at the airport, but numerous other operators are based close to the airport and will deliver cars for airport collection. Typical weekly high-season rental rates with insurance and unlimited mileage are IR£280 for a small car (Ford Fiesta), IR£325 for a middle-size car (Ford Escort) and IR£375 for a larger car (Ford Sierra). Insurance will add another IR£60 a week. There are many smaller local operators with lower prices.

Some of the main rental companies in Dublin are:

Argus Rent-a-Car
    59 Terenure Rd East, Dublin 6 (☎ 90 4444)
Avis Rent-a-Car
    108 Leeson St Upper, Dublin 2 (☎ 677 6971)
Budget Rent-a-Car
    Dublin Airport, Dublin 9 (☎ 842 0793)
Dan Dooley Car & Van Rentals
    42/43 Westland Row, Dublin 2 (☎ 677 2723)
Hertz Rent-a-Car
    149 Leeson St Upper, Dublin 2 (☎ 676 7476)
Murrays/Europcar Car Rental
    Baggot St Bridge, Dublin 4 (☎ 668 1777)
Payless Car Rental
    Dublin Airport, Dublin 9 (☎ 840 7920)

Practical Car Rental
    19 Nassau St, Dublin 2 (☎ 671 5540)
Thrifty Rent-a-Car
    14 Duke St, Dublin 2 (☎ 679 9420)
Windsor Car Rentals
    Rialto, Dublin 8 (☎ 54 0800)

Bicycle

Dublin is a good place to get around by bicycle, as it is small enough and flat enough to make bike travel a breeze. Many visitors explore farther afield by bicycle, a popular activity in Ireland despite the often less-than-encouraging weather.

All the hostels seem to offer secure bicycle parking areas but if you're going to have a bike stolen anywhere in Ireland, Dublin is where it would happen. Lock your bike up well. Surprisingly, considering how popular bicycles are in Dublin, there's a real scarcity of suitable bicycle parking facilities. Grafton St and Temple Bar are virtually devoid of places to lock a bike. Elsewhere, there are signs on many suitable stretches of railing announcing that bikes must not be parked there.

Bicycle Rental You can either bring your bike with you or rent in Dublin, where typical rental costs are IR£7 to IR£10 a day or IR£35 a week.

Rent-a-Bike has eight offices around the country and offers one-way rentals between its outlets for an extra IR£5. The head office of Rent-a-Bike (☎ 872 5399, 872 5931) is at 58 Gardiner St Lower, Dublin 1. It's just round the corner from Isaac's Hostel and a stone's throw from the Busáras. They don't offer daily rentals but you can extend a weekly rental by the day.

Raleigh Rent-a-Bike agencies can be found all over Ireland, north and south of the border. Contact them at Raleigh Ireland (☎ 626 1333), Raleigh House, Kylemore Rd, Dublin 10. Raleigh agencies in Dublin include:

Joe Daly
    Main St Lower, Dundrum, Dublin 14 (☎ 298 1485)

Little Sport
> 3 Merville Ave, Fairview, Dublin 3 (☎ 33 2405, fax 36 6792)

C Harding
> 30 Bachelor's Walk, Dublin 1 (☎ 873 2455, fax 873 3622)

T Hollingsworth
> 54 Templeogue Rd, Templeogue, Dublin 6W (☎ 90 5094, 92 0026)

Hollingsworth Bikes
> 1 Drummartin Rd, Stillorgan, Dublin 14 (☎ 296 0255)

McDonald's Cycles
> 38 Wexford St, Dublin 2 (☎ 475 2586)

The Cycle Centre
> Unit 7, Old Bawn Shopping Centre, Firhouse Rd, Tallaght, Dublin 24 (☎ 51 8771)

Ray's Bike Shop
> 2 Milltown Centre, Milltown, Dublin 6 (☎ 283 0355)

Mike's Bikes
> Unit 6, St George's Mall, Dun Laoghaire Shopping Centre (☎ 280 0417)

The C Harding outlet on Bachelor's Walk is very conveniently located only a few steps off O'Connell St and right by the river. Daily, three-day and weekly rates are offered.

TOURS

Many Dublin tours operate only during the summer months but at that time you can take bus tours, walking tours and bicycle tours. You can book these tours directly with the operators or through your hotel front desk, at the various city tourist offices or with a travel agent or American Express.

Bus Tours

Gray Line has tours around Dublin and farther afield but only in the summer. Reservations can be made through Dublin Tourism (☎ 874 4466, 878 7981, 661 2325 & 661 9666), 14 O'Connell St Upper. Different morning and afternoon tours are available, each costing IR£13, including any admission charges, and lasting 2¾ hours. The two tours can be combined for IR£25. There is a variety of half-day tours out of Dublin to Newgrange, Malahide Castle, Powerscourt Gardens or Newbridge House, each costing IR£13. Day-long tours out of Dublin cost IR£25 and include tours to Glendalough and

the Wicklow Mountains, to the Boyne Valley and various combinations of the half-day tours.

Gray Line also has nightlife tours to the Jury's Irish Cabaret (IR£17.50 with two drinks or IR£29.50 with dinner) or to Doyle's Irish Cabaret (IR£17.50 with two drinks or IR£27.90 with dinner). See the Irish Entertainment section under Entertainment for more details.

Dublin Bus (☎ 872 0000) tours can be booked at their office at 59 O'Connell St Upper or directly across the road at the Bus Éireann counter in the Dublin Tourism office (☎ 874 4467), 14 O'Connell St Upper. The three-hour tour uses an open-top double-decker bus as long as the weather permits and operates three times daily in summer and twice daily for much of the rest of the year. From mid-January to early March, however, it only operates on Tuesday, Friday and Saturday, and from mid-December to mid-January it does not operate at all. The tour costs IR£7 (children IR£3.50).

Dublin Bus tours out of the city operate daily during the summer months, take 2¾ hours and also cost IR£7 (children IR£3.50). The North Coast Tour does a loop via Howth, Malahide, the Casino at Marino and the Botanic Gardens. The South Coast Tour goes via Dun Laoghaire, Bray and Greystones and then returns through the mountains via Enniskerry. An evening visit to the Irish Culture & Music Centre at Monkstown lasts 3½ hours and operates on Tuesday, Wednesday and Thursday in summer. The cost is IR£10 (children IR£6), including the live show.

Dublin Bus also operates a hop-on hop-off Heritage Trail bus which does a city tour six times daily from mid-April to late September. There are three additional daily circuits during the peak summer months. The IR£5 (children IR£2.50) ticket lets you travel all day, getting on or off at the 10 stops.

You can book Bus Éireann tours directly at the Busáras (☎ 36 6111), or through the Bus Éireann desks at the Dublin Bus office (59 O'Connell St Upper) or Dublin Tourism office (14 O'Connell St). During the summer months they operate a Monday to Saturday city tour which takes 3¾ hours and costs IR£9 (children IR£4.50), including entry to the 'Book of Kells' exhibit.

Bus Éireann also has several day tours outside Dublin. Tours to Glendalough and Wicklow are conducted daily from June to mid-September, and daily except Friday for a couple of additional months. The cost is IR£12 (children IR£6). A full-day tour to the Boyne Valley and Newgrange operates on Sunday, Tuesday and Thursday from mid-May to late September and also costs IR£12 (children IR£6). A Sunday tour to Powerscourt is held from early-May to mid-September and costs IR£10 (children IR£5). In the summer months there are also day tours farther afield to places such as Kilkenny, the River Shannon, Waterford and Lough Erne.

Walking Tours

During summer there are various walking tours which are a great way to explore this very walkable city. A Trinity College walking tour departs frequently from Front Square just inside the college and costs IR£3.50 (concessions IR£3), including entry to the 'Book of Kells' exhibit. See the Trinity College section for more details.

Tour Guides Ireland (☎ 679 4291) operates 1½ to two-hour walks for IR£4; that price permits an adult to bring two children as well. The tours start from Bewley's Café on Grafton St or from the Dublin Writers' Museum on Parnell Square, and explore medieval Dublin, 18th-century Dublin, literary Dublin or Dublin's north side, or simply entail an early evening stroll around central Dublin.

Historical Walking Tours (☎ 84 50241) are conducted by Trinity College history graduates, take two hours and depart from the front gates of Trinity College. The walks take place several times daily and in the evening on weekends.

The Dublin Literary Pub Crawl (☎ 54 0228) operates five days a week, starting at 7.30 pm from the Bailey on Duke St, just off Grafton St. The walk is great fun and costs IR£5 (student stand-by IR£4), though Guinness consumption can quickly add a few pounds to that figure. The two actors who lead the tour put on a theatrical performance appropriate to the various places and pubs along the way. The particular pubs chosen vary from night to night but could include Mulligan's on Poolbeg St, the Palace Bar on Fleet St, the Stag's Head on Dame St, Davy Byrne's on Duke St, McDaid's on Barry St, Neary's on Chatham St, the Norseman on Eustace St, the Long Hall on George's St or O'Neill's on Suffolk St.

Bicycle Tours

City Cycle Tours (☎ 671 5606, 671 5610), at 1A Temple Lane, Temple Bar, operates three daily Dublin bicycle tours Monday to Saturday, and one on Sunday. The cost is IR£10 (students or YHA members IR£8.50), including use of a bicycle and crash helmet and any admission charges. Participants have to be at least 14 years of age.

Tour Guides

Bord Fáilte approved guides can be contacted via the tourist board. The recommended fees for a full-day approved guide in Dublin are approximately IR£50 in English, rather more in a foreign language.

Around Dublin

Although the centre of Dublin is set back from the bay, there are a number of seaside suburbs around the curve of Dublin Bay. Dun Laoghaire to the south and Howth to the north are historic ports and popular day trips from the city. Connected to central Dublin by the convenient DART rail service, they also make interesting alternatives to staying right in the city. Malahide with its castle, the imposing Anglo-Irish mansion of Newbridge House, and the village of Swords are other Dublin area attractions.

DUN LAOGHAIRE

Dun Laoghaire (pronounced 'dun leary'),

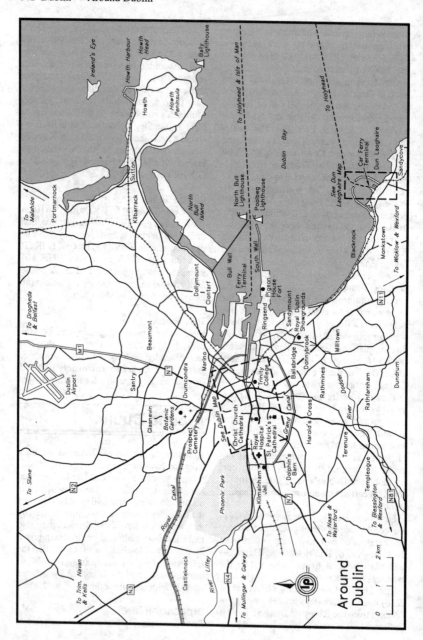

Around
Dublin

only 13 km south of central Dublin, is both a busy harbour with ferry connections to Britain and a popular resort. From 1821, when King George IV departed from here after a visit to Ireland, until Irish independence in 1922, the port was known as Kingstown. There are many B&Bs in Dun Laoghaire, they're a bit cheaper than in central Dublin and the fast and frequent DART rail connections make it easy to stay out here.

History

There was a coastal settlement at the site of Dun Laoghaire over 1000 years ago, but it was little more than a small fishing village until 1767, when the first pier was constructed. Dun Laoghaire grew more rapidly after that time and the Sandycove Martello Tower was erected in the early 19th century, as there was great fear of an invasion from Napoleonic France.

Construction of the harbour was proposed in 1815 to provide a refuge for ships unable to reach the safety of Dublin Harbour in inclement weather. Originally, a single pier was proposed, but engineer John Rennie proposed to build two massive piers enclosing a huge 100-hectare (250-acre) artificial harbour. Work commenced in 1817 and by 1823 the workforce comprised 1000 men. However, despite huge expenditure the harbour was not completed until 1842, Carlisle Pier was not added until 1859 and parts of the West Pier stonework have never been finished. The total cost approached one million pounds, an astronomical figure in the mid-19th century.

Shipping services commenced to/from Liverpool and Holyhead, and the completion of a rail link to Dublin in 1834 made this a state-of-the-art transport centre. The line from Dublin was the first railway anywhere in Ireland. It's only just over 100 km from Dun Laoghaire to Holyhead in Wales and a ferry service has operated across the Irish Sea on this route since the mid-19th century.

The first mail steamers took nearly six hours to make the crossing, but by 1860 the crossing time was reduced to less than four

hours and on one occasion in 1887 the paddle steamer the *Ireland* made the crossing in less than three hours. Car ferries were introduced in the early 1960s. During WW I the RMS *Leinster* was torpedoed by a German U-boat 25 km from Dun Laoghaire and over 500 lives were lost.

Orientation & Information

The tourist office (☎ 280 6984) is on St Michael's Wharf, near the Dun Laoghaire ferry terminal. Pembrey's Bookshop at 78 George's St Lower, almost at the junction with Marine Rd, has a good selection of books. Across the road there's a branch of Eason, the newsagent and bookshop chain. The Star Laundrette is at 47 George's St Upper.

George's St Upper and Lower, which runs parallel to the coast, is the main shopping street through Dun Laoghaire. The huge harbour is sheltered by the encircling arms of the East and West Piers. Sandycove with the James Joyce Museum and the Forty Foot Pool is about a km east of central Dun Laoghaire.

The Harbour

The 1290-metre East and 1548-metre West piers, each ending in a lighthouse from the 1850s, have always been popular walking sites (especially the East Pier), bird-watching and fishing (particularly from the end of the West Pier). You can also ride a bicycle out along the piers (bottom level only). In the last century the practice of 'scorching' – riding out along the pier at breakneck speed – became so prevalent that bicycles were banned for some time.

The East Pier has an 1890s bandstand and a memorial to Captain Boyd and the crew of the Dun Laoghaire lifeboat who were drowned in a rescue attempt. Near the end of the pier is the 1852 anemometer, one of the first of these wind-speed measuring devices to be installed anywhere in the world. The East Pier ends at the East Pier Battery with a lighthouse and a gun saluting station, which is useful when visiting VIPs arrive by sea.

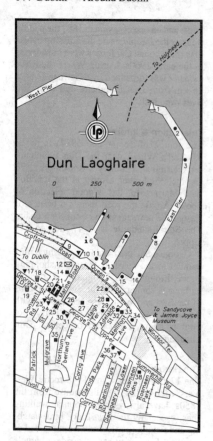

The harbour has long been a popular yachting centre and the Royal Irish Yacht Club's building, dating from around 1850, was the first purpose-built yacht club in Ireland. The Royal St George Yacht Club's building dates from 1863 and that of the National Yacht Club from 1876. The world's first one-design sailing boat class started life at Dun Laoghaire with a dinghy design known as the *Water Wag*. A variety of specifically Dublin Bay one-design classes still race here, as do Mirrors and other popular small sailing boats.

Carlisle Pier, opened in 1859, is also known as the Mailboat Pier and was modified to handle drive on/drive off car ferries in 1970. St Michael's Pier, also known as the Car Ferry Pier, was added in 1969. Over on the West Pier side of the harbour are two anchored lightships which have now been replaced by automatic buoys.

National Maritime Museum

The National Maritime Museum is housed in the Mariner's Church in Adelaide St, built in 1837 'for the benefit of sailors in men-of-war, merchant ships, fishing boats and yachts'. The window in the chancel is a replica of the Five Sisters window at York Minster in England. The museum is open May to September from 2 to 5.30 pm Tuesday to Sunday; entry is IR£1.20 (children 60p).

Exhibits include a French ship's longboat captured at Bantry in 1796 from Wolfe Tone's abortive invasion. The huge clockwork-driven Great Baily Light Optic came from the Baily Lighthouse on Howth Peninsula. It operated from 1902 until 1972, when it was replaced with an electrically powered lens.

There's a model of the *Great Eastern* (1858), the early steam-powered vessel built by English engineer Isambard Kingdom Brunel, which proved a commercial failure as a passenger ship but successfully laid the first transatlantic telegraph cable between Ireland and North America. There are various items from the German submarine U19 which landed Sir Roger Casement in Kerry in 1916 (see the Sandycove section). These were donated 50 years after the event by the U-boat's captain, Raimund Weisbach.

Around the Town

Nothing remains of the *dún* or fort that gave Dun Laoghaire its name, as it was totally destroyed during the construction of the railway line. The railway line from Dun Laoghaire towards Dalkey was built along the route of an earlier line known as the Metals. This line was used to bring stone for the harbour construction from the quarries at Dalkey Hill. By means of a pulley system, the laden trucks trundling down to the harbour pulled the empty ones back up to the quarry.

On the waterfront is a curious monument to King George IV to commemorate his visit in 1821. It consists of an obelisk balanced on four stone balls, one of which is missing as a result of an IRA bomb attack. On the other side of the coast road is the *Christ the King* sculpture, which was created in Paris in 1926, bought in 1949 and then put in storage until 1978 because the religious authorities decided they didn't like it.

Sandycove

Only a km south of Dun Laoghaire is Sandycove, with a pretty little beach and the Martello Tower that houses the James Joyce Museum. Sir Roger Casement, who attempted to organise a German-backed Irish opposition force during WW I, was born here in 1864. He was captured after being landed in County Kerry from a German U-boat and executed by the British as a traitor in 1916.

James Joyce Museum South of Dun Laoghaire in Sandycove is the Martello Tower where the action commences in James Joyce's epic novel *Ulysses*. It now houses a James Joyce Museum with photographs, letters, documents, various editions of Joyce's work and two death masks of Joyce on display. The museum was opened in 1962 by Sylvia Beach, the Paris-based publisher who first dared to put *Ulysses* into print.

A string of Martello towers were built around the coast of Ireland between 1804 and 1815 in case of invasion by Napoleon's forces. The granite tower stands 12 metres high with walls 2.5 metres thick and was copied from a tower at Cape Mortella in Corsica. Originally, the entrance to the tower led straight into what is now the 'upstairs'. Other tower sites included Dalkey Island, Killiney and Bray, all to the south of Dun Laoghaire, and to the north, Howth and Ireland's Eye, the island off Howth.

There are fine views from the tower. To the south-east you can see Dalkey Island with its signal tower and Killiney Hill with its obelisk. Howth Head is visible on the northern side of Dublin Bay. Right next to the tower is the house of architect Michael Scott, who owned the tower from 1950 until it was turned into a museum. There's another

---

Holiday in Sandycove

In 1904 Oliver St John Gogarty – the 'stately, plump' Buck Mulligan of *Ulysses* – rented the Martello Tower from the army for the princely sum of £8 a year and Joyce stayed there briefly. The stay was actually less than a week, as another guest, Samuel Chenevix Trench (who appears in *Ulysses* as the Englishman Haines), had a nightmare one night and dealt with it by drawing his revolver and taking a shot at the fireplace. Gogarty took the gun from him, yelled 'Leave him to me' and fired at the saucepans on the shelf above Joyce's bed. Relations between Gogarty and Joyce had been uneasy after Joyce had accused him of snobbery in a poem, so Joyce took this incident as a hint that his presence was not welcome and left the next morning. He was soon to leave Ireland as well, eloping to the Continent with Nora Barnacle in 1904. Trench's aim did not improve, as just five years later he shot himself, fatally, in the head. ∎

Martello Tower not far to the south near Bullock Harbour.

The tower is open May to September from 10 am to 1 pm and 2 to 5 pm Monday to Friday, 10 am to 5 pm Saturdays and 2 to 6 pm Sundays. In April and October it's still open weekdays but not on weekends. Entry is IR£1.75 (students IR£1.40, children 90p). At other times of the year the tower is only open on weekdays and then only to groups for a flat fee of IR£40. Contact Patsy O'Connell at Dublin Tourism (☎ 280 8571) for more details.

You can get to the tower by a 30-minute walk along the seafront from Dun Laoghaire Harbour, a 15-minute walk from Sandycove DART Station or a five-minute walk from Sandycove Ave West, which is served by bus No 8.

The Forty Foot Pool Just below the Martello Tower is the Forty Foot Pool, an open-air sea water bathing pool that probably took its name from the army regiment, the Fortieth Foot, which was stationed at the tower until it was disbanded in 1904. At the close of the first chapter of *Ulysses*, Buck

Mulligan heads off to the Forty Foot Pool for a morning swim. A morning wake-up here is still a Dun Laoghaire tradition, winter or summer. In fact a winter dip is not that much braver than a summer one since the water temperature only varies by about 5°C, winter or summer. Basically, it's always bloody cold.

When it was recently suggested that in these enlightened times a public stretch of water like this should be open to both sexes, the 'forty foot gentlemen' put up strong opposition. They eventually compromised with the ruling that a 'togs must be worn' sign would now apply after 9 am. Prior to that time nudity prevails and swimmers are still predominantly 'forty foot gentlemen', and the odd brave woman.

Activities

A series of walks in the Dun Laoghaire area make up the signposted Dun Laoghaire Way. The *Heritage Map of Dun Laoghaire* includes a map and notes on the seven separate walks.

Scuba divers head for the waters around Dalkey Island. Oceantec (☎ 280 1083, fax 284 3885) is a dive shop at 10/11 Marine Terrace in Dun Laoghaire. They rent diving equipment at IR£17.50 for half a day; a local dive costs IR£27.50.

Places to Stay

B&Bs Rosmeen Gardens is packed with B&Bs. To get there, walk south along George's St, the main shopping street; Rosmeen Gardens is the first street after Glenageary Rd Lower, directly opposite People's Park. *Mrs Callanan* (☎ 280 6083) is at No 1, *Rathoe* (☎ 280 8070) is at No 12, *Rosmeen House* (☎ 280 7613) is at No 13, *Mrs McGloughlin* (☎ 280 4333) is at No 27, *Annesgrove* (☎ 280 9801) is at No 28 and *Mrs Dunne* (☎ 280 3360) is at No 30. Prices here are IR£16 to IR£18 for singles, IR£28 to IR£35 for doubles.

There are also some B&Bs on Northumberland Ave, like *Innisfree* (☎ 280 5598) at No 31. Close to the harbour is *Bayside* (☎ 280 4660) at Seafront, 5 Haddington Terrace, which is slightly more expensive with singles for IR£20, doubles from IR£30. Others can be found on Mellifont and Corrig avenues.

Hotels Dun Laoghaire has a number of attractively situated seaside hotels. The port's premier hotel is the A-rated *Royal Marine Hotel* (☎ 280 1911, fax 280 1089) on Marine Rd, only two minutes' walk from the Dun Laoghaire car ferry terminal. There are 104 rooms, all with attached bathroom, costing IR£100/120 for singles/doubles.

Also pleasantly located on Royal Marine Rd is the small *Port View Hotel* (☎ 280 1663, fax 280 0447). About half of the 20 rooms have en suite facilities and these better rooms cost IR£29.50/49 for singles/doubles. The larger *Hotel Pierre* (☎ 280 0291, fax 284 3332), is also close to the waterfront at 3 Victoria Terrace. There are 36 rooms, almost all of them with en suite facilities at IR£29/50. Close by on Haddington Terrace is the *Kingston Hotel* (☎ 280 1810, fax 280 1237) with 24 rooms, all with attached bathroom, costing IR£32/55.

Places to Eat
Fast Food Branches of *McDonald's, La Pizza* and *Abrakebabra* can all be found on George's St. Just off George's St on Patrick St is the *Ritz Café* for traditional fish & chips.

Restaurants *Outlaws* (☎ 284 2817) at 62 George's St Upper offers steak, burgers and other 'Wild West' fare. *Café Society* (☎ 280 1100) at 19 George's St Upper has a standard menu offering dishes like steaks or chicken Kiev. *Darby O'Gill* on George's St Upper, on the corner of Northumberland Ave, offers a very similar menu but with a little Irish flavour.

Dilshad Tandoori Restaurant (☎ 284 4604) on Convent Rd has a standard Indian menu; the tandoori dishes have a good reputation. Alternatively, there's the *Krishna Indian Restaurant* (☎ 280 1855) on the 1st floor at 47 George's St.

Near the harbour *Restaurant Na Mara* (☎ 280 6787) is in what used to be the

railway station and offers more expensive food with the emphasis on seafood. *Trudi's* (☎ 280 5318) at 107 George's St Lower is another fancier restaurant offering excellent and slightly adventurous food. Count on paying around IR£20 to IR£25 per person, including drinks. It's open in the evening from Tuesday to Saturday.

On Marine Parade, between Dun Laoghaire and Sandycove, is *La Vie en Rose* (☎ 280 9873), which serves old-fashioned but high-quality French cuisine. Prices are also rather high. It's open Tuesday to Friday for lunch, Monday to Saturday for dinner.

Entertainment
Popular pubs include *Cooney's* at 88 George's St Lower and *Dunphy's*, right across the road at No 41. Farther out along George's St is *Smyth's*, with its very original interior. The *Hotel Pierre* is noted for its jazz performances, and the *Purty Loft* on the Old Dunleary Rd often has traditional Irish music or rock.

Getting There & Away
See the introductory Getting There & Away chapter for details of the ferries between Dun Laoghaire and Holyhead in the UK.

Bus No 7, 7A or 8 or the DART rail service will take you from Dublin to Dun Laoghaire. It only takes 15 to 20 minutes to cover the 12 km by DART with a one-way fare of IR£1.

DALKEY
South of Sandycove is Dalkey, which has the remains of a number of old castles. **Bulloch Castle** overlooking Bullock Harbour was built by St Mary's Abbey in Dublin in the 12th century. On Castle St in Dalkey are two castles – the **Goat Castle** and **Archibold's Castle**. On the same street is the ancient **St Begnet's Church**, dating from the 9th century.

Dalkey Quarry is now a popular site for rock climbers, and originally provided most of the stone for the gigantic piers at Dun Laoghaire Harbour.

Dalkey has several holy wells, including **St Begnet's Holy Well** on Dalkey Island which is reputed to cure rheumatism. The island has an area of nine hectares and lies just a few hundred metres offshore. The waters around the island are popular with local scuba divers. A number of rocky swimming pools are also to be found along the coast at Dalkey.

HOWTH

The bulbous Howth Peninsula delineates the northern end of Dublin Bay. Howth town is only 15 km from central Dublin and is easily reached by DART train or by simply following the Clontarf Rd out around the north bay shoreline. En route you pass Clontarf, site of the pivotal clash between Celtic and Viking forces at the Battle of Clontarf in 1014. Farther along is North Bull Island, a wildlife sanctuary where many migratory birds pause in winter. Howth is a popular excursion from Dublin and has developed as a residential suburb (see Map 16 at the back of this book).

History

Howth's name (which rhymes with 'both') has Viking origins, and comes from the Danish word *hoved* or head. Howth Harbour dates from 1807-09 and was the main Dublin harbour for the packet boats from England. The Howth Rd was built to ensure rapid transfer of incoming mail and dispatches from the harbour to the city. The replacement of sailing packets with steam packets in 1818 reduced the transit time from Holyhead to seven hours, but Howth's period of importance was short because by 1813 the harbour was already showing signs of silting up. It was superseded by Dun Laoghaire in 1833. Howth's most famous arrival was King George IV, who visited Ireland in 1821 and is chiefly remembered because he staggered off the boat in a highly inebriated state. He did manage to leave his footprint at the point where he stepped ashore on the West Pier.

In 1914 Robert Erskine Childers' yacht *Asgard* brought a cargo of 900 rifles in to the port to arm the nationalists. During the Civil War Childers was court-martialled by his former comrades and executed by firing squad for illegal possession of a revolver.

The *Asgard* is now on display at Kilmainham Jail. Howth's popularity as a seaside escape from Dublin made the Howth electric trams famous, but they were withdrawn in the late 1950s.

Howth Town

Howth is a pretty little town built on steep streets running down to the waterfront. Although the harbour's role as a shipping port has long gone, Howth is now a major fishing centre and yachting harbour.

St Mary's Abbey stands in ruins near the centre and was originally founded in 1042, supposedly by the Viking King Sitric, who also founded the original church on the site of Christ Church Cathedral in Dublin. It was amalgamated with the monastery on Ireland's Eye in 1235. Some parts of the ruins date from that time but most of it was built in the 15th and 16th centuries. The tomb of Christopher St Lawrence (Lord Howth), in the south-east corner, dates from around 1470. There are instructions on the gate about where to obtain the key to the abbey.

Howth Castle & Desmesne

Howth Castle's demesne was acquired by the Norman noble Sir Almeric Tristram in 1177 and has remained in the family ever since, though the unbroken chain of male succession finally came to an end in 1909. The family name was changed to St Lawrence when Sir Almeric won a battle at, so he believed, St Lawrence's behest.

Originally built in 1564, the St Lawrence family's Howth Castle has been much restored and rebuilt over the years, most recently in 1910 by the British architect Sir Edwin Lutyens. A legend relates that in 1575 Grace O'Malley, the 'Queen' of western Ireland, dropped by the castle on her way back from a visit to England's Queen Elizabeth I. When the family claimed they were busy having dinner and refused her entry, she kidnapped the son and only returned him when Lord Howth promised that in future his doors would always be open at meal times. As a result, so it is claimed, for many years the castle extended an open invitation to hungry passers-by. Despite Grace O'Malley's actions, the castle is no longer open, but the gardens can be visited in spring and summer and there's a popular golf course beyond the castle.

The castle gardens are noted for their rhododendrons, which bloom in May and June, for their azaleas and for a long stretch of 10-metre-high beech hedges which were planted back in 1710. The castle grounds also have the ruins of 16th-century **Corr Castle** and an ancient dolmen known as **Aideen's Grave**. It is said that Aideen died of a broken heart after her husband was killed at the Battle of Gavra near Tara in 184 AD, but that's probably mere legend as the dolmen is thought to be much older.

The castle is only a short walk from the centre of Howth.

Transport Museum

The National Transport Museum has a variety of exhibits, including double-decker buses, fire engines and trams. A Hill of Howth tram which operated from 1901 to 1959 is in the process of being restored. In June, July and August the museum is open Monday to Friday from 10 am to 6 pm. Throughout the year it is open Saturday and Sunday from 2 to 6 pm in summer, 2 to 5 pm in winter. Entry is IR£1 (children 50p). You can reach the museum by entering the castle gates and turning right just before the castle.

Around the Peninsula

The 171-metre Summit offers views across Dublin Bay to the Wicklow Hills. From the Summit you can walk to the top of the Ben of Howth, which has a cairn said to mark a 2000-year-old Celtic royal grave. The 1814 Baily Lighthouse at the south-east corner is on the site of an old stone fort or 'bailey' and can be reached by a dramatic clifftop walk. There was an earlier hilltop beacon here in 1670.

Ireland's Eye

Only a short distance offshore from Howth is Ireland's Eye, a rocky sea-bird sanctuary with the ruins of a 6th-century monastery.

There's a **Martello Tower** at the north-west end of the island, where boats from Howth land, while the east end plummets into the sea in a spectacularly sheer rock face. As well as the sea birds wheeling overhead, you can see young birds on the ground during the nesting season. Seals can also be spotted around the island.

Boats (☎ 31 4200 for information) shuttle out to the island from the East Pier of Howth Harbour during the summer, most frequently on weekend afternoons. The cost is IR£3 (children IR£1.50) return. Don't wear shorts if you're planning to visit the monastery ruins, as they are surrounded by a thicket of stinging nettles. And do take your garbage away with you – far too many island visitors don't.

Farther north from Ireland's Eye is **Lambay Island**, a more remote and even more important sea-bird sanctuary.

Places to Stay

There are several B&Bs along Thormanby and Nashville Rds with typical overnight costs of IR£14 to IR£16 per person. *Gleann-na-Smol* (☎ 32 2936) is on Nashville Rd, *Morven* (☎ 32 2164) is farther along on Nashville Park, while *Hazelwood* (☎ 39 1391) and *Highfield* (☎ 32 3936) are both on Thormanby Rd.

The *St Lawrence Hotel* (☎ 32 2643) on Harbour Rd, directly overlooking the harbour, has 12 rooms, all with attached bathroom. Singles/doubles cost IR£26/52 including breakfast. On the Dublin side of Howth village there are good views of Ireland's Eye from the *Howth Lodge Hotel* (☎ 39 0288) where rooms with attached bathroom cost IR£44.50/59 for singles/doubles. By the golf course in the grounds of Howth Castle is the larger *Deer Park Hotel* (☎ 32 2624), charging IR£37/58.

Places to Eat

If you want to buy food and prepare it yourself, Howth has fine seafood, and you can buy it, fresh from the trawler, at the string of seafood shops along the West Pier.

The *Pizza Place* (☎ 32 2255) at 12 West

Pier has reasonably priced pizzas and pasta dishes along with a great selection of Italian ice creams. Other economical alternatives include Howth's plentiful supply of pubs, like the *Pier House* (☎ 32 4510) on the East Pier. The *Abbey Tavern* (☎ 39 0307) by St Mary's Abbey has traditional Irish entertainment in the evenings. The *St Lawrence Hotel* (☎ 32 2643) by the harbour has a carvery restaurant that is open daily.

King Sitric (☎ 32 5235) at the East Pier is well known for its fine seafood and is open for lunch and dinner Monday to Saturday. Main dinner courses cost IR£16 to IR£18 or you can have a set dinner menu for IR£22.

Entertainment

Howth's pubs are noted for their jazz performances. You can try the *Cock Tavern*, the *Royal Howth Hotel*, the *Waterside Inn*, the *Pier House*, the *Abbey Tavern* and others – they're all likely to have something on and are all in the centre.

Getting There & Away

The easiest and quickest way to get to Howth from Dublin is by the DART, which will whisk you out there in just over 20 minutes for a fare of IR£1.

SWORDS

The village of Swords is 16 km north of Dublin and five km west of Malahide. The Archbishop of Dublin built a fortified palace here in the 12th century, but the castellated walls date from the 15th century and numerous other modifications were made over the centuries. The windows to the right of the main entrance date from around 1250.

Swords also had an ancient monastery but today only its 23-metre-high round tower remains and that was rebuilt several times between 1400 and 1700. It stands in the grounds of the Church of Ireland. The body of Brian Ború was kept overnight in the monastery after his death in 1014 at the Battle of Clontarf, when his forces defeated the Vikings.

Buses from Dublin depart every half-hour or so and take less than an hour.

MALAHIDE

Malahide, on the coast beyond Howth, has virtually been swallowed by Dublin's northward expansion. The well-kept 101 hectares of the Malahide Demesne, which contains Malahide Castle, is the town's principal attraction. The Talbot Botanic Gardens are next to the castle and the extensive Fry Model Railway is in the castle grounds.

Malahide Castle

Despite the vicissitudes of Irish history, the Talbot family managed to keep Malahide Castle (☎ 45 2655, 45 2337) under their control from 1185 to 1976 apart from a short interlude while Cromwell was around (1649-60). The castle is the usual hotchpotch of additions and renovations; and the oldest part of it is a three-storey 12th-century tower house. The façade is flanked by circular towers which were tacked on in 1765.

The castle is packed with furniture and paintings, and Puck, the family ghost, is still in residence. The 16th-century oak room with its decorative carvings is a high point, along with the medieval Great Hall with family portraits and a minstrel gallery.

The castle's opening hours vary through the year. All year it's open Monday to Friday from 10 am to 12.45 pm and 2 to 5 pm. From November to March it's also open on weekends and holidays from 2 to 5 pm. From April to October weekend hours are extended: Saturdays 11 am to 6 pm and Sundays and holiday 2 to 6 pm. Entry is IR£2.50 (students IR£1.90, children IR£1.25). A family ticket for two adults and up to four children costs IR£7. Combined tickets are sold for the castle and railway.

The parkland around the castle is open daily from 10 am to 5 pm in the middle of winter and to 9 pm at the height of summer.

Fry Model Railway

Ireland's biggest model railway covers 240 sq metres and in O-gauge (track width of 32 mm) authentically displays much of Dublin and Ireland's rail and public transport system, including the DART line and Irish Sea ferry services. There's also a separate

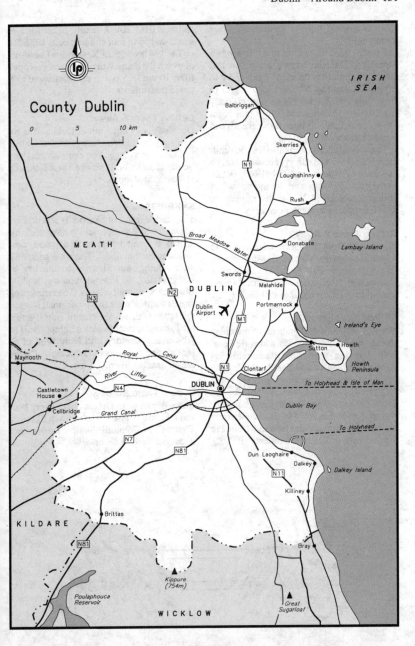

room exhibiting railway models and other memorabilia.

From April to September it's open Monday to Thursday from 10 am to 1 pm and 2 to 5 pm, Saturday 11 am to 1 pm and 2 to 6 pm, Sunday and holidays 2 to 6 pm. In June, July and August it's also open Friday from 10 am to 1 pm and 2 to 5 pm. From October to March it's open on weekends and holidays from 2 to 5 pm.

Entry is IR£2.10 (students IR$1.50, children IR£1.15). You can get combined castle and railway tickets for IR£4 (IR£3, IR£2). Family tickets for two adults and up to four children cost IR£6.25 for the railway or IR£10 for the railway and castle.

Getting There & Away
Bus No 42 from Talbot St takes about 45 minutes to get to Malahide. Alternatively, take a Drogheda train to the Malahide town station, only 10 minutes' walk from the park. Malahide is 13 km north of Dublin.

NEWBRIDGE HOUSE
North of Malahide at Donabate is Newbridge House (☎ 43 6534, 43 6535), a historic Georgian mansion with fine plasterwork by Robert West and a traditional farm. It's open April to October from 10 am to 1 pm and 2 to 5 pm Tuesday to Friday, 11 am to 6 pm Saturdays, 2 to 6 pm Sundays and holidays. During November an March it's open only on Saturday, Sunday and holidays from 2 to 5 pm. Entry is IR£2.20 (students IR£1.80,

children IR£1.20). A family ticket for two adults and up to four children costs IR£6.50.

The 144 hectares of Newbridge Demesne, of which the house is the centrepiece, is open from 10 am to 5 pm in midwinter and to 9 pm in midsummer.

Getting There & Away
Donabate is 19 km north of Dublin. Bus No 33B runs from Eden Quay in central Dublin to Donabate village. You can also get there on the suburban rail service from Connolly or Pearse St stations.

SKERRIES
The seaside resort of Skerries is 30 km north of Dublin. St Patrick is said to have made his arrival in Ireland here at Red Island, now joined to the mainland. There's a good cliff walk south from Skerries to the bay of Loughshinny. At low tide you can walk to **Shenick's**, a small island off Skerries. **Colt** and **St Patrick's** are two other small islands, the latter with an old church ruin. Farther offshore is **Rockabill** with a lighthouse. The 7th-century **Oratory and Holy Well of St Moibhi** and the ruins of **Baldongan Castle** are all near the town.

Getting There & Away
Buses depart from Dublin about every hour and take just over an hour to reach Skerries. Trains from Connolly Station are less frequent but slightly faster.

County Wicklow

Not all of Ireland's impressive landscapes are in the west of the country. Barely 16 km (10 miles) south of Dublin, you can drive for an hour through wild and desolate scenery, without seeing more than a handful of houses or people.

The most beautiful parts of County Wicklow are within a broad north-south swathe running down the centre of the mountains, beginning at Glencree and ending somewhere around Avoca. At Glendalough are some of the best preserved early Christian remains in the country.

County Wicklow's rolling granite hills are the source of Dublin's River Liffey. Southern Wicklow was one of the last outposts of the Gaelic Irish: using remote valleys like Glenmalure and the Glen of Imaal as hideouts, families like the O'Tooles and the O'Byrnes would grasp any opportunity to harry and attack the English.

Such was the crown's concern that they built an access road to the bandits from Dublin through the heart of the mountains. Today, thanks to their efforts, the Military Rd takes you through the finest Wicklow scenery.

In northern Wicklow, the Anglo-Irish gentry felt close enough to the safety of Dublin to build magnificent mansions at Russborough near Blessington and Powerscourt near Enniskerry. Unfortunately the latter was destroyed by fire in 1974, though the exquisite formal gardens are still one of the county's biggest draws.

The county's highways and main towns, many of them dormitories for Dublin, lie along the relatively narrow coastal strip south to Wexford. It's a pleasant trip south and there are some fine beaches along the way, especially at Brittas Bay, the first of a chain stretching from here to County Waterford.

The Wicklow Mountains

From Killakee, just north-west of Glencree, you can turn your back on the sprawl of Dublin and travel for 30 km (18 miles) on the Military Rd across vast sweeps of heather-clad moors, bogs and mountains embedded with small corrie lakes.

The Wicklow Mountains are a vast granite intrusion or batholith, an upwelling of hot igneous rock which consolidated some 400 million years ago. The heat baked the overlying clays and sedimentary rocks producing shiny mica schists which can be seen across the county but particularly in the rivers and streams around Glenmalure. These soft metamorphosed rocks have weathered away over the millennia, exposing the granite, but significant traces remain, particularly on top of Lugnaquilla (926 metres, 3039 feet), where a cap of schist remains.

The mountains were rounded and shaped during the Ice Ages, producing the smooth profiles you see today. While flattening the peaks, the ice also created deep valleys such as Glenmacnass, Glenmalure and Glendalough. Corrie lakes such as Lough Bray Upper & Lower were gouged out by ice at the head of glaciers.

Beginning on Dublin's southern fringes, the narrow Military Rd winds down to the remotest parts of Wicklow. The best place to

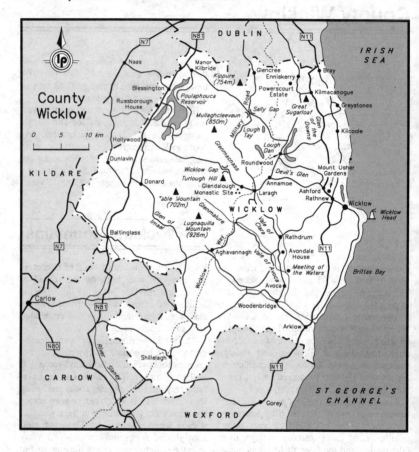

join it is at Glencree via Enniskerry, from which it runs south through the Sally Gap, Glenmacnass, Laragh, Glendalough and on to Glenmalure and Aghavannagh.

The road was built in the first years of the 19th century by the British to get access to the Wicklow rebels, including Michael Dwyer, who were holed up in the southern half of the county, particularly around Glenmalure. Barracks were built at Glencree, Glenmalure and Aghavannagh. The road was a considerable feat of engineering, travelling across open bog and barren mountainscapes for 50 km (32 miles).

Enniskerry is a good starting point, and on the trip south, there's a diversion east at the Sally Gap to have a look at Lough Tay, Lough Dan and the Luggala Estate. Farther south you pass the great waterfall at Glenmacnass before dropping down into Laragh with the magnificent valley and monastic ruins of Glendalough nearby. But don't stop here. Continue south over and up the valley of Glenmalure, and if you are fit enough climb Lugnaquilla, Wicklow's highest peak.

There are two principal passes over the mountains from east to west: the Sally Gap at the northern end and the Wicklow Gap farther south, over which you can head west from Glendalough.

The western flanks of the mountains are not as attractive as the centre or the east. The Glen of Imaal, north-west of Aghavannagh, is one of the most remote and scenic spots on the west side.

There are An Óige youth hostels at Glencree, the Devil's Glen, Blessington, Knockree near Enniskerry, Glendalough, Glenmalure and Aghavannagh.

ENNISKERRY

Enniskerry owes its origin to the adjoining Powerscourt Estate. The landlord built this elegant, picturesque little village to accompany his impressive manor, the entrance to which is just south of the village square. Set round a small triangle, the rows of cottages ooze quiet charm. A number of pleasant little cafés have sprung up recently and are great places to unwind after a foray into the mountains, for which Enniskerry is an excellent base.

Heading west up the hill takes you through some lovely scenery into Glencree and the hamlet of the same name 10 km (six miles) up at the head of the valley, which leads to the Military Rd.

Enniskerry has so far escaped the blight of modern urban development, though this may change as Dublin expands and the Powerscourt Estate is developed. Don't miss the small detour to Powerscourt Waterfall & Gardens. Unfortunately the mansion was gutted by fire in 1974.

Places to Stay

B&Bs *Cherbury* (☎ 01-282 8679) overlooks the valley. It's in Monastery one km from Enniskerry on the Glencree road. Rooms with bathroom cost IR£19/28 for singles/doubles. In the village is *Corner House* (☎ 01-286 0149) costing IR£18/26 for singles/doubles.

Hotels The attractive *Enniscree Lodge House* (☎ 01-286 3542) is up on the right as you head from Enniskerry up into Glencree,

and has wonderful views. Inside it's cosy with open fires, a snug little bar, and good food. B&B runs from IR£32.50 to IR£37.50 and they are closed from October to mid-February.

The *Powerscourt Arms* (☎ 828903) is right in Enniskerry village facing the square. It has the potential to be a terrific little country hotel but is currently run of the mill, though reasonably priced. B&B costs IR£15.

Places to Eat

There are a couple of lovely little cafés cum restaurants in Enniskerry. Up the hill past the post office is the *Harvest Home*, a small deli, bread shop and restaurant which is open all day with main courses in the IR£3 to IR£5 range. *Poppies* on the square is similar, and also sells home-made bread and jams.

For more luxurious surroundings, you have a couple of choices on the road west leading to Glencree. The first is *Curtlestown House Restaurant* (☎ 01-282 5803), an up-market restaurant in a farmhouse about five km (three miles) along. It's fairly expensive, with a set menu at IR£17.95, but the food is delicious. They are open for dinner and lunch only on Sundays. *Enniscree Lodge House* (☎ 01-286 3542) further up the same road also serves excellent food. Dinner will cost you IR£20 or more.

Getting There & Away

Enniskerry is just three km (1½ miles) west of the N11, the main Dublin to Wicklow, Arklow and Wexford road, and you can catch express buses in Busáras, Dublin, which will drop you at the turnoff for Enniskerry. Local bus No 44 goes to Enniskerry from Hawkins St in Dublin, or you can take the DART train to Bray and get bus No 85 from the station.

POWERSCOURT ESTATE

This 64-sq-km estate near Enniskerry is a big tourist attraction; its formal gardens have fine views over the surrounding countryside. The main entrance to the house and estate is 500 metres south of the square in Enniskerry. Driving past the entrance, you go around the edge of the estate and eventually towards the famous Powerscourt waterfall.

The layout of the present estate dates from the 17th and 18th centuries and the 20-hectare formal gardens were laid out in the 19th century, with the magnificent natural backdrop of the Great Sugarloaf to the east. There are five garden terraces extending for over 500 metres down to Triton Lake. The Italian Gardens took 100 men 12 years to complete.

The wilder parts of the estate were the setting for films such as John Boorman's *Excalibur* and *Barry Lyndon*, and Laurence Olivier's 1943 *Henry V*.

Powerscourt House (1731) is by Richard Castle, who also designed Dublin's Leinster House and Russborough House in Blessington. Today it is owned by the Slazenger family.

A disastrous fire gutted the interior in 1974 just before the house was due to be opened to the public. As part of a tourist development package for Enniskerry, a consortium has applied to restore the shell and convert it into a luxury hotel. Part of the package involves extensive housebuilding on the estate which may in future detract from its beauty.

Powerscourt Estate (☎ 01-286 7676) is open March to October, 9.30 am to 5.30 pm daily, admission is IR£2 (students IR£1) and guided tours are available. There is a teashop and garden centre. A full-length ramble takes just over an hour or there are shorter routes taking in just the highlights.

A longer walk of six km (four miles) carries you out to a separate part of the estate and a lovely ramble down a track to the **Powerscourt Waterfall**, at 130 metres (400 feet) the highest in Britain or Ireland. It's most impressive after heavy rain.

You can also get to the falls by road, following the signs from the estate entrance. The waterfall is open all year round, 9.30 am to 7 pm or dusk in winter, and admission is 70p. The road to the waterfall continues along the southern slopes of Glencree and joins up with the Military Rd which goes south to the Sally Gap.

GLENCREE

Just south of the border with Dublin is Glencree, a small leafy hamlet set into the side of the valley of the same name. The valley opens east giving a magnificent view down to the Sugarloaf Mountain and the sea. The valley floor is home to the Glencree Oak Project, an ambitious plan to reforest part of Glencree with native oak vegetation which once covered most of the country.

The village has a tiny shop and a hostel, but – remarkably – not one pub. The village is also home to a German cemetery, dedicated to German servicemen who died in Ireland during WW I and WW II, mostly after shipwrecks or plane crashes. The cemetery is a poignant and peaceful place. Just south of the village, the former military barracks are now a sort of retreat house and reconciliation centre.

The Military Rd leads on south meeting the Sally Gap, one of the two main east-west routes over the Wicklow Mountains.

Places to Stay

Hostels The stone *An Óige* hostel (☎ 01-864037) is right in the middle of the village just up from the German cemetery. It has 40 beds costing IR£3.50 low season and IR£4.50 from June to September.

The *Knockree* An Óige hostel (☎ 01-2864036) is seven km (four miles) south-west of Enniskerry, at the base of Knockree Mountain. It is right by the Wicklow Way in a converted farm. It's open all year round and charges IR£3.50 a night low season or IR£4.50 from June to September.

SALLY GAP

The Sally Gap is one of the two main passes across the Wicklow Mountains from east to west. From the turn-off on the lower road between Roundwood and Kilmacanogue just north of Roundwood, the narrow road passes above the dark waters of Lough Dan and Lough Tay and the Luggala Estate. It then heads up to the Sally Gap crossroads where it cuts across the Military Rd and heads for Blessington (23 km), following the young River Liffey, still only a stream. Just north of the Sally Gap crossroads is Kippure Mountain with its TV transmitter. The surrounding bogs have dark lines cut into them by turfcutters.

LOUGH TAY & LOUGH DAN

Lough Tay lies like a spilt pint of Guinness at the bottom of a spectacular gash in the mountains five km (three miles) east of the Sally Gap crossroads and about the same distance from Roundwood off to the southeast. Lough Tay's beauty starred in John Boorman's film *Excalibur* and Boorman himself lives in the area. The lake is part of Luggala, an estate owned by Garech de Brun, a member of the Guinness family and an Irish music enthusiast. At the north end of Lough Tay above a creamy brown beach sits Luggala House, overlooked by some spectacular cliffs on the far side of the valley. These are popular with rockclimbers.

Luggala Estate covers almost all of the valley, as far down as Lough Dan, which nestles among lower hills to the south. The road to the Sally Gap skirts the top of the valley on the eastern side and is crossed by the Wicklow Way walking trail which continues south past Lough Dan.

There are some magnificent walks around the valley. A convenient starting point for any of the walks is just before the road dips over the southern edge of the valley and down towards Roundwood. Here, a small private road heads down into the valley and you are allowed to walk or cycle (but not drive) down this. Down the road you pass the private entrance to Luggala House and a small estate cottage with a sign indicating the distance to Lough Dan as '2 Irish Miles'.

The first and easiest option is to walk all the way down to Lough Dan to the south, which from the top of the road is about four km (2.5 miles) each way. There is a lovely view of the cliffs and Lough Tay from among the trees at the valley floor. If you look carefully along the way, you can make out the traces of the old potato furrows (lazy beds) on the hills, dating from famine times,

and there are also ruined cottages. This is part of the Wicklow Way.

Another option is to walk round Lough Tay. As before, follow the private road to the valley floor but then head north-west up the mountain to the cliffs overlooking the lake. This mountain is called Fancy. You can continue north from there, meet the road to the Sally Gap and then return to your starting point.

ROUNDWOOD

Roundwood is widely touted as the highest village in Ireland, though it's hardly Mont Blanc. The village is pleasant but nondescript: essentially one long main street which leads south to Glendalough and southern Wicklow. In the village there are turnoffs for Ashford to the east and the south shore of Lough Dan to the west. Unfortunately, almost the entire southern shoreline of Lough Dan is private property and you cannot get down to the lake on this side.

Roundwood has some nice pubs which are usually packed with tired walkers on weekend afternoons. There are shops, a post office and a thriving country market held every Sunday afternoon from March to December in the small hall on the Main St.

North-west of the village you will find some of the best scenery in the county on the road to the Sally Gap, with a tremendous panorama over Lough Tay and the Luggala Estate. From up here you can walk down to Lough Dan through the estate.

Places to Eat

The *Roundwood Inn* (☎ 01-281 8107) is a popular pub and restaurant at the north end of Main St. They do excellent snacks and the restaurant is good but expensive. They are open for dinner from 7.30 pm except Monday and for lunch only on Sunday.

Getting There & Away

The Dublin to Glendalough bus (see under Glendalough) passes through Roundwood.

GLENMACNASS

The most desolate section of the Military Rd

runs between the Sally Gap crossroads and Laragh through wild bogland. Along the way you may catch glimpses of Lough Dan off to the east, and until you reach the top of Glenmacnass Valley not a single building breaks the sense of isolation.

The highest mountain to the west is Mullaghacleevaun (848 metres, 2788 feet), and the River Glenmacnass flows south and tumbles over the edge of the mountain plateau into Glenmacnass in a great foaming cascade. The drop marks a boundary between granite and metamorphosed schist.

There is a car park near the top. Be careful when walking on rocks near the falls, as a number of people have slipped to their deaths. There are fine walks in the area up Mullaghacleevaun or the hills to the east of the waterfall car park.

THE WICKLOW GAP

The Wicklow Gap is the second major pass over the mountains and its eastern end begins just to the north of Glendalough (see the following section). The road climbs through some lovely scenery north-west up along the Glendassan Valley, passing the remains of some old lead and zinc workings before meeting a side road which leads south and up Turlough Hill, the site of Ireland's only pumped storage power station.

A lake was created on the summit and a tunnel was bored down through the hill to the other lake at its base. The water is pumped to the top reservoir at times of low electricity demand and sent down through the turbines in the tunnel at times of high demand. You can walk up the hill to have a look over the top lake and tours are available upon request from the Electricity Supply Board (☎ 0404-45113), with one week's notice.

GLENDALOUGH

Glendalough, the 'glen of the two lakes' is a magical place, an ancient monastic settlement tucked beside two dark lakes overshadowed by the sheer walls of a deep valley. It's one of the most picturesque settings in the Wicklow Mountains or for that matter in Ireland.

It's barely an hour from Dublin and is consequently busy, well established on the coach tour circuit. Try and get there early or late in the evening or out of season.

History

Glendalough's past and present status is thanks to St Kevin, an early Christian bishop who established a monastery here in the 5th century. Kevin was a member of the royal house of Leinster and his name is derived from Ceomghan, meaning the 'fair one' or 'well featured'. He is said to have lived from 498 to about 619 AD, reaching the remarkable age of 120.

From rough beginnings as a hermitage on the south side of the Upper Lake, only accessible by boat, this little monastery began to attract followers. In time it became a monastic city catering to thousands of students and teachers. During the Dark Ages, Glendalough was one of the places that gave Ireland its reputation as the island of saints and scholars.

The main sections of the monastery are thought to have been a few hundred metres west of the round tower, and it must have spread over a considerable area. Most of the present stone buildings date from between the 10th and 12th centuries. A famous son of Glendalough was St Laurence O'Toole who studied here and became Abbot of Glendalough in 1117 and Archbishop of Dublin in 1161.

Glendalough's remote location was still within reach of the Vikings, who sacked the monastery at least four times between 775 and 1071. The final blow came in 1398, when English forces from Dublin almost completely destroyed it. Efforts were made to rebuild, and some life lingered on here as late as the 17th century, when under renewed repression the monastery finally died, over 1100 years after its foundation.

Geography

Glendalough Valley was carved out by a series of glaciers, the last one retreating around 12,000 years ago. There was once one long deep lake which was later divided

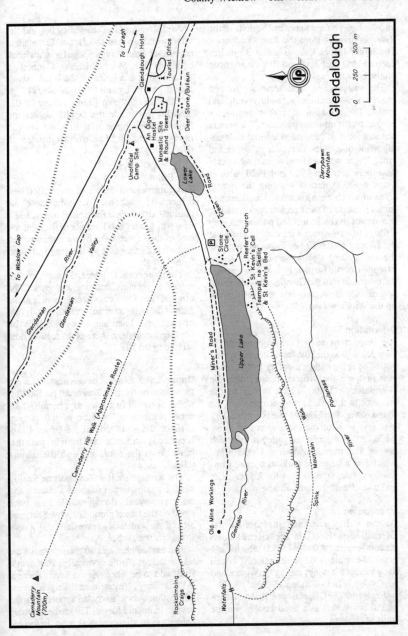

Glendalough

0   250   500 m

To Laragh

Glendalough Hotel

Tourist Office

An Óige Hostel

Deer Stone/Bullaun

Monastic Site & Round Tower

Unofficial Camp Site

Lower Lake

Green Road

Stone Circle

Reefert Church

St Kevin's Cell

Teampall na Skellig & St Kevin's Bed

St Kevin's Bed

Derrybawn Mountain

Glendassan River

Glendassan Valley

To Wicklow Gap

Miner's Road

Upper Lake

Camaderry Hill Walk (Approximate Route)

Old Mine Workings

Glenealo River

Waterfalls

Rockclimbing Crags

Spink Mountain

Poulanass River

Poulanass Walk

Camaderry Mountain (700m)

into the two you see today by the delta of the River Poulanass from the southern slopes. The larger Upper Lake is about 35 metres deep and has deep layers of fine silt and ooze on the bottom.

The surrounding mountains are formed mostly of 400-million-year-old granite and schist, the remains of earlier sediments cooked by the upwelling granite. The granite has a number of mineral veins in it containing white quartz and ores of lead, silver and zinc. There were extensive mining operations here between 1800 and 1920, with as many as 2000 miners working the mines, some of which were known as Van Diemen's mines because of their remote location. The remains of the buildings and poisonous grey tailings from the mines are clearly visible at the far end of the Upper Lake and high on the surrounding slopes. Some of the shafts extended north for nearly two km through the mountain into the Glendassan Valley, and you can see the remains there while driving up the Wicklow Gap.

Orientation

It's important to get your bearings in Glendalough as the ruins and sites are spread out all over the valley. Coming from Laragh you first see the visitors' centre, then the Glendalough Hotel which is beside the entrance to the main group of ruins and the round tower. The Lower Lake is a small dark lake just west of the main group of ruins, while farther west up the valley is the much bigger and more impressive Upper Lake which has a large car park with more ruins nearby. Make sure to visit the Upper Lake and take one of the surrounding walks.

Information

At the valley entrance just before the Glendalough Hotel is the Glendalough visitors' centre (☎ 0404-45325) which has a good 20-minute video presentation. It's open daily except Mondays during the winter, and admission is IR£1 (students 70p).

Exploring the Glendalough Valley (Office of Public Works) is a good booklet on the trails in the area.

At the west end of the valley beyond the mine workings and the Upper Lake are a couple of large crags, popular with rock climbers. The Mountaineering Council of Ireland publish a guide to the routes available from Joss Lynam (☎ 01-2884672).

The Calliaghstown Riding Centre (☎ 01-589236) just inside the Dublin border run Ireland's only horse trail ride, 40 km (25 miles) over the Wicklow Mountains to Glendalough.

The Ruins

The principal remains are of seven churches, a monastic gatehouse (the only one of its kind in existence), a fine round tower, and a monastic graveyard. The bulk of the ruins are east of the Lower Lake by the round tower, and some farther east by the approach road from Laragh.

The more scenic Upper Lake has a smaller group of remains near the car park. The original site of St Kevin's settlement is at the base of the cliffs towering over the south side of the Upper Lake and accessible only by boat; unfortunately, there is no regular boat service to the site.

Upper Lake Sites The earliest sites are thought to be those at **Teampall na Skellig**, where St Kevin first lived as a hermit. It's a small platform at the base of the vertical cliffs on the south side of the Upper Lake. It's directly across the lake from the path that leads down the north shore to the mining village.

The terraced shelf at Teampall na Skellig has the reconstructed ruins of a church and early graveyard. Rough wattle huts once stood on the raised ground nearby. Scattered around are some early graveslabs and simple stone crosses.

Just east of here and 10 metres above the lake waters is a little cave called **St Kevin's Bed**, said to be where Kevin lived. There is a local story – more than likely a recent fabrication – about a woman appearing in the cave to tempt old Kevin. The earliest human habitation in the cave was long before St

Kevin's era. It may have been the burial chamber of a Bronze Age chief or perhaps even a prehistoric mine, as there is evidence that people lived in the valley for many thousands of years before the monks arrived.

In the green area just south of the car park is a large **stone circle**, thought to be the remains of an early Christian caher or stone fort.

Follow the lakeshore path south-west of the car park and in a quiet leafy clearing you will find the considerable remains of **Reefert Church** above the tiny River Poulanass. This is a small, plain 10th-century Romanesque-style nave-and-chancel church with some reassembled arches and walls. Traditionally, Reefert ('king's burial place') was the burial site of the chiefs of the local O'Toole family, and they probably built the church on the site of an earlier one. The surrounding graveyard has a number of rough stone crosses and slabs, most made of shiny mica schist.

If you follow the lake path to the west, you will find, at the top of a rise overlooking the lake among trees, the scant remains of **St Kevin's Cell**, a small bee-hive hut.

Lower Lake Sites While the Upper Lake has the best scenery, the most fascinating buildings lie in the lower part of the valley east of the Lower Lake.

Just round the bend from the hotel is the stone arch of the monastery **gatehouse**, the only surviving example of a monastic entranceway in the country. There used to be another storey and a containing wall. Just inside the entrance is a large slab with an incised cross.

Inside the entrance is a graveyard which is still used; the gravestones span many centuries. The 10th-century **round tower** is 33 metres (110 feet) tall and 16 metres (50 feet) in circumference at the base. The upper storeys and conical roof were reconstructed in 1876. Near the tower to the south-east is the **Cathedral of St Peter & St Paul**, the main body or nave of which dates from the 10th century. The chancel and sacristy date from the 12th century. Inside are some good carvings and early gravestones.

At the centre of the graveyard to the south of the round tower is the **Priest's House**. This odd little building dates from 1170 AD and has been heavily reconstructed. It may have been the location of shrines of St Kevin. Later during penal times it became a burial site for local priests – hence the name. The 10th-century **St Mary's Church** is 140 metres south-west of the round tower. It probably stood originally outside the walls of the monastery and belonged to nuns of the valley's convent. It has a lovely western doorway.

A little to the east are the scant remains of **St Kieran's Church**, the smallest of Glendalough's churches, which commemorates St Kieran, the founder of Clonmacnois Monastery in County Offaly.

Glendalough's trademark is **St Kevin's Church or Kitchen** at the southern fringes of the enclosure. This little church, with miniature round-tower-like belfry, protruding sacristy and steep stone roof, is a little masterpiece in stone. How it got its name as a kitchen is unknown as there is no indication that it was anything other than a church. The oldest parts of the building and the belfry date from the 11th century and the structure has been remodelled since. But it is still a classic early Irish church. It was used by Catholics up to 1850 and now stores carvings and slabs that are not on public display.

On crossing the river just south of these two churches, at the junction with the green road, is the **Deer Stone** in the middle of a group of rocks. Legend has it that when St Kevin needed some milk for two orphaned babies, a doe stood here waiting to be milked. The stone is what is known as a *bullaun*, and you find them around monastic sites. They were grinding stones for medicines or food. Many are thought to be prehistoric and were widely regarded as having supernatural properties. Women who bathed their faces with the water from the hollow would be beautiful forever. The early churchmen brought them into their monasteries, perhaps hoping to inherit some of the stones' powers.

The road east leads to the **Saviour's Church** with its detailed carvings, and west is a nice woodland trail leading up the valley past the Lower Lake to the Upper Lake.

Glendalough Walks

Numerous fine walks fan out from Glendalough. The first, easiest and most popular option is the gentle but delightful walk along the north shore of the Upper Lake to the lead and zinc mine workings which date from 1800. It's about 30 minutes' walk to the mines. The best route is along the lake shore rather than on the road which runs 30 metres in from the shore. You can continue on up the head of the valley if you wish. Just to the north overlooking the mine workings are fine crags popular with rock climbers.

Alternatively you can go up Spink Mountain, the steep ridge with vertical cliffs running along the south flanks of the Upper Lake. You can go part of the way and turn back, or complete a circuit of the Upper Lake by following the top of the cliff, eventually coming down by the mine workings and back along the north shore. The circuit takes about three hours.

The third option is a hike up Camaderry, a mountain hidden behind the hills that flank the northern side of the valley. It starts on the road just 50 metres back towards Glendalough from the entrance to the Upper Lake car park. Head straight up the steep hill to the north and you come out on open mountains with sweeping views in all directions. You can then continue up Camaderry to the north-west or just follow the ridge west looking over the Upper Lake. To the top of Camaderry and back takes about four hours.

If you are intending to go on a serious hike, make sure you take all the usual precautions, have the right equipment and most importantly tell someone where you are going and when you should be back. For Mountain Rescue, ring ☎ 999. For more detailed information on walking in the area, check *Hill Walker's Wicklow* or *New Irish Walk Guides, East & South East* both by David Herman. For walking partners check at the hostels or go on an organised walk with Tiglin Adventure Centre (☎ 0404-40169).

Places to Stay

Camping It is difficult to camp anywhere near the ruins or the lakes, but you could try the Glendassan Valley close by. To get there go round the corner from the hotel past the monastery entrance and then head west past the little stone cottage and along the road towards the lower lake. Take the first turn right, which will take you round a corner and into the next valley and you should easily be able to find a good spot.

Another lovely spot where people pitch tents is way up at the head of the Upper Lake near the old mine workings. Alternatively the independent *Old Mill Hostel* (see the following section) will let you pitch a tent for IR£2.50 a night and has the advantage of washing and cooking facilities.

Hostels Glendalough's superior *An Óige Youth Hostel* (☎ 0404-45143/45342) is about 300 metres west of the round tower. It has good facilities and is open year round. Low season, they charge IR£3.80 a night and IR£5.50 a night from June to September.

The independent *Old Mill Hostel* (☎ 0404-45156) is housed in farm buildings about four km (three miles) from Glendalough. It's one km south of Laragh on the road to Rathdrum. They charge IR£5 a night for a bed in dorms or IR£6.60 in double rooms. There is a craft centre nearby.

B&Bs Most B&Bs are in or around Laragh, the village three km east of Glendalough, or on the road down into Glendalough itself. *Elizabeth Kenny* (☎ 0404-45236) is next door to the shop cum post office in Laragh. Farther down towards Glendalough opposite Trinity Church is *Valeview* (☎ 0404-45292). Both charge IR£12.

Laragh Trekking Centre (☎ 0404-45282) charges IR£18/28. The house is in Glenmacnass: turn north at the shop cum petrol station in Laragh on the Dublin side of the bridge, and keep going for almost four km (two miles). Five km (three miles) north-east of Glendalough in Annamoe on the main road to Roundwood is *Carmel's* (☎ 0404-45297), which costs IR£15/24 for singles/doubles. They are open March to October.

Hotel The *Glendalough Hotel* (☎ 0404-45135) has one of the best locations in the country. The main older block is right next to the monastic ruins and the river runs underneath the dining room. However, except for the bar, the hotel has a tired feel. B&B runs from IR£25 to IR£34.

Country House *Derrybawn House* (☎ 0404-45134) stands in wooded grounds just south of Laragh on the road to Rathdrum. B&B costs from IR£18 to IR£22.50. They are open all year round.

Places to Eat

About the best place for anything substantial is the *Wicklow Heather Restaurant* (☎ 0404-45157), opposite the post office in Laragh, which does good helpings at reasonable prices. There's a headless chef mannequin outside the gate. A set lunch will cost you from IR£4 to IR£6 depending on your main course and they're open for dinner until 9 pm.

During the summer, a little cottage up a lane opposite the Glendalough Hotel does delicious scones, ginger cake and tea or coffee. You can't miss their sign.

The *Glendalough Hotel* (☎ 0404-45135) has a straightforward restaurant and serves food in the bar.

Getting There & Away

All year round, a private bus service runs to Glendalough from outside the College of Surgeons off St Stephen's Green in Dublin, at 11.30 am and 6 pm daily. For further details contact St Kevin's Coach Service (☎ 01-281 8119).

GLENMALURE

Deep in the mountains, near the southern end of the Military Rd, is Glenmalure, a sombre and majestic blind valley overlooked on its western side by Wicklow's highest peak, Lugnaquilla, and flanked farther up by classic scree slopes of loose boulders. After coming over the mountains into Glenmalure you turn north at Drumgoff bridge and it's about six km (3.5 miles) up Glenmalure to a car park where trails lead off in various directions.

The upper slopes of the hills around Glenmalure have a cap of mica schist, a shiny flat rock which sparkles in the streams. This is the baked remains of the sedimentary rock that used to cover the area before the upwelling of hot granite which formed the Wicklow Mountains some 400 million years ago.

For a long time, Glenmalure was a stronghold of resistance against the English. Various clans, particularly the O'Byrnes, made forays up into the Pale, harassing and harrying the crown's forces and loyal subjects. The most famous clan leader was Fiach MacHugh O'Byrne. In Glenmalure in August 1580 he defeated an army of 1000 English soldiers led by the Lord Deputy, Lord Grey de Wilton; over 800 men died in the battle. English control in Ireland was set back for decades. Fiach was captured in 1597 and his head was impaled on the gates of Dublin Castle.

Near Drumgoff is a memorial – Dwyer's or Cullen's Rock, which commemorates both the Glenmalure battle and another rebel who holed up here, Michael Dwyer. Men were hanged from the rock during the 1798 Rising.

Michael Dwyer, a 1798 leader born in the nearby Glen of Imaal, successfully sustained the struggle against the English for five years from this remote outpost before being captured in 1803 and deported to Australia, where he died in 1825. For more details, see the Glen of Imaal in the West Wicklow section of this chapter. There are some ruined barracks at the foot of the valley.

Walks

The options are to climb Lugnaquilla; to head up the blind valley east of the car park, the lovely Fraughan Rock Glen; or to go straight up Glenmalure passing the small seasonal An Óige hostel. The head of Glenmalure and parts of the neighbouring

Glen of Imaal are military land, well posted with warning signs. Heading farther north-east, the trail takes you over the hills to Glendalough, while going north-west brings you into the Glen of Imaal.

Places to Stay

About one km up from the car park in Glenmalure is the small *An Óige* youth hostel. It has no phone or electricity, and opens only in July and August and occasional Saturdays. There is another much bigger *An Óige* hostel (☎ 0402-36102/36366) 14 km (eight miles) west in Aghavannagh, housed in the barracks It was once used as a shooting lodge by Charles Stewart Parnell. They charge IR£3.50 low season and IR£4.50 high season. Both these hostels make good bases for climbing Lugnaquilla.

THE WICKLOW WAY

The Wicklow Way was the first trail set up in the country, opening in 1981. It is also the longest at 132 km (83 miles), so long that it neither starts nor finishes within County Wicklow itself. From its beginnings in Marley Park, Rathfarnham, in south Dublin, the trail leaves the city behind and enters a mountain wilderness. Forest walks, sheep paths, bog roads and mountain passes connect up to provide one of the most spectacular walks you could wish for. The walk passes Glencree, Powerscourt, Djouce Mountain, Luggala, Lough Dan, Glenmacnass, Glendalough, Glenmalure and Aghavannagh before heading into Carlow.

To get to the start of the walk from Dublin city, take bus No 47, 48A or 48B from Hawkins St or join it later at Glencree by getting bus No 44 to Enniskerry or the DART train to Bray and bus No 85 to Enniskerry. There are many possible detours: up Glenmacnass to the waterfall, down to the shores of Lough Dan, up to the summit of Lugnaquilla – all well worth the effort.

For the entire trail allow eight to 10 days, plus time for diversions. It's easy to pick up sections, and many of the other routes described in this chapter are part of the Wicklow Way. There are An Óige hostels at Glencree, Knockree, Glendalough, Glenmalure and Aghavannagh.

Some sections are desolate and the weather can change quickly. Good hiking boots, outdoor gear and emergency supplies are essential. For more details on the route pick up the Bord Fáilte Information Sheet No 26B from a tourist office. *The Complete Wicklow Way* by J B Malone or *The Wicklow Way, from Marlay to Glenmalure* by Michael Fewer are good guides to the trail.

West Wicklow

The western slopes of the Wicklow Mountains were less deeply glaciated, and the landscape is not spectacular. From the Sally Gap crossroads to Kilbride, however, you pass the upper reaches of the River Liffey and some lovely wild scenery. It's also a picturesque trip over the Wicklow Gap from Glendalough.

The most interesting features of West Wicklow are the Poulaphouca or Blessington Reservoir, Russborough House nearby, and farther south the Piper's Stones near Donard and the lovely Glen of Imaal.

BLESSINGTON

Blessington is 35 km (22 miles) from Dublin and its wide, pleasant main street is lined on both sides by solid 17th and 18th-century town houses. It used to be an important stop on the stage-coach run between Dublin, Carlow, Waterford and Kilkenny, and from 1888 to 1932 a tram ran from here to Terenure in Dublin.

The village is near the shores of Poulaphouca, a reservoir created in 1940 to drive the turbines of the local Electricity Supply Board (ESB) power station to the east of the town and also to supply Dublin with water.

Blessington owes its origins to an archbishop of Dublin, Michael Boyle, who designed the village in the 1670s. Boyle's manor, Downshire House, was destroyed by fire in 1760, but the village soon acquired Russborough House. The village was all but destroyed by rebels in 1798. Blessington is only 13 km (eight miles) from Naas in County Kildare.

Information

There is a seasonal tourist office (☎ 045-65092) in the town open during July and August.

Places to Stay & Eat

Hostels The An Óige *Baltyboys Hostel* (☎ 045-67266) is on the peninsula opposite Russborough House. It is open from March to November and is five km (three miles) from Blessington. Go along the road to Poulaphouca and turn east at Burgage Cross heading for Valleymount. In the low season they charge IR£3.50 and high season (June to September) IR£4.50. There is brown trout angling on the reservoir.

B&Bs The *Heathers* (☎ 045-64554) is in Poulaphouca overlooking the reservoir some six km (four miles) along the Baltinglass road from Blessington and only three km (two miles) from Russborough House. B&B is IR£18/24 for singles/doubles. Also in Poulaphouca is the *Conifers* (☎ 045-64298), open all year round and charging IR£17/24.

Hotels The *Downshire House Hotel* (☎ 045-65199) is on Main St in Blessington. It has quite a good restaurant and charges IR£32 for B&B.

Country Houses The early 19th-century *Manor* (☎ 01-582105) has 18 hectares of gardens with views over the Wicklow Hills. It's about 10 km (six miles) north-west of Blessington, just south of Manor Kilbride. B&B is a hefty IR£37 to IR£40. They are open April to October. The rambling *Rathsallagh House* (☎ 045-53112) is 20 km (12 miles) south of Blessington in Dunlavin. The excellent dinner will cost you about IR£25 per person and B&B is from IR£44 to IR£55.

Getting There & Away

Blessington is serviced by suburban bus No 65 from Dublin and express bus No 58 going to and from Waterford two or three times a day.

RUSSBOROUGH HOUSE

Just five km (three miles) south-west of Blessington is one of the finest houses in Ireland, built for the Leesons, major players in Ireland's 18th-century brewing industry.

Russborough House (☎ 045-65239), a magnificent Palladian villa, was built between 1740 and 1751. It was designed by Richard Castle, at the height of his fame and ability, with the help of another architect, Francis Bindon from County Clare. The front facade is enormous. The granite central building is flanked on each side by two long and elegant wings connected to the main block by curving, pillared colonnades. This 275-metre frontage is further extended by granite walls and baroque gates, and topped off with urns and heraldic lions. The interior has many impressive state rooms and remarkable plasterwork by the Francini brothers, Paul and Philip, whose work can also be seen in Celbridge's Castletown House in County Kildare.

Joseph Leeson filled the house with works of art, furniture and other treasures. The house stayed in the family until 1931. In 1952 it was sold again, to Sir Alfred Beit, nephew of another Sir Alfred Beit, co-founder of de Beers. The older Sir Alfred had used his diamond wealth to purchase important works of art. The nephew inherited the lot, and paintings by Velasquez, Vermeer, Goya and Rubens now fit comfortably into their grand surroundings. Lovers of antique silver, furniture and porcelain will have a field day. Unfortunately art thieves have also had a couple of good days, and the house has had two major burglaries in the last 20 years.

The house was closed to the public until 1976, when Sir Alfred set up the Beit Foundation, making the house a centre for the arts. The house is open every day from 10.30 am to 5.30 pm from June to August. In April, May, September and October it is open on

Sundays and bank holidays only. Admission is IR£2.50 or IR£1.50 for students, for the main tour of the house including all the important paintings. An additional tour of the bedrooms upstairs containing more silver and furniture costs IR£1.

ATHGREANY PIPER'S STONES
Not far south of Blessington on the minor road between Hollywood and Donard are the Athgreany Piper's Stones, a prehistoric stone circle of 14 large lumps of granite in verdant surroundings. Another single boulder sits outside the circle. Many stones and stone rings throughout the country are called piper's stones or circles because they are said to be people turned to stone for dancing on or near pagan ground. The circles are said to be the dancers and the odd stone outside is the piper.

GLEN OF IMAAL
Seven km (four miles) south-east of Donard, the Glen of Imaal is about the only scenery of real consequence on the western flanks of the Wicklow Mountains. And a lovely place it is too. The glen is named after Mal, a brother of the 2nd-century king of Ireland Cathal Mór, and is nine km long by six km wide. The north-eastern slopes of the glen are mostly cordoned off by the army for use as a firing range and for manoeuvres. Keep an eye out for red danger signs.

The area's most famous son was Michael Dwyer, who led rebel forces during the 1798 Rising and held out for many years in the hills and glens around here. On the south-east side of the glen at Dernamuck is a small whitewashed thatched cottage, where Dwyer and three friends were surrounded by 100 English soldiers. One of his companions, Samuel McAllister, ran out the front, drawing fire and meeting his death, while Dwyer escaped into the night. Dwyer was eventually deported to Australia and jailed on Norfolk Island, but he became chief constable of Liverpool near Sydney before he died in 1825. The cottage is now a small folk museum.

Donard is a tiny hamlet in the glen about eight km (five miles) south-east of Dunlavin. *Ballinclea An Óige Hostel* (☎ 045-54657) is three km south of Donard on the road to Knockanarrigan and 13 km from Glenmalure. It charges IR£3.50 low season and IR£4.50 from June to September.

BALTINGLASS
In the far west of Wicklow, 27 km (17 miles) south-west of Blessington, is Baltinglass on the banks of the River Slaney. This small town grew up around the **Abbey of Vallis Salutis**, which was founded in 1148 by Dermot MacMurrough for the Cistercians, as a satellite to Mellifont Monastery in County Louth. It was MacMurrough, as king of Leinster, who 'invited' the Anglo-Normans to Ireland, an offer they gratefully accepted. The rest, as they say, is history. Some locals suggest MacMurrough was laid to rest here in 1171, though he is more than likely buried near his base in Ferns, County Wexford. Records suggest that the parliament of Ireland met for three days in the abbey in 1397.

The abbey ruins lie 350 metres north of the town centre and consist of a long nave with a number of simple Gothic arches and the barest remnants of a cloister. The eastern section of the structure was used as a Protestant church long after the dissolution of the monasteries in 1541. A Gothic-style bell tower was added in 1815.

A stiff climb to the summit of Baltinglass Hill to the north-east brings you to **Rathcoran**, a large hill fort and a Bronze Age cairn which contains a number of passage graves.

The Coast: Bray to Wicklow

The N11 from Dublin to Wexford skirts Bray inland and runs on down through Wicklow, keeping a few km in from the sea. South of Kilmacanogue you see the Great Sugarloaf Mountain to the west and pass through a great glacial rift, the Glen of the Downs, carved out by floodwaters from an Ice Age lake, with its slopes covered in native oak and beech. There is a forest walk up to a ruined teahouse on top of the ridge to the east.

If you are travelling farther south, the coastal route is best, through Greystones, Kilcoole and then some lovely country lanes down to Rathnew before you rejoin the main road again. Worth seeing in the region of Wicklow Town are the Mount Usher Gardens near Ashford and the fine beaches of Brittas Bay which stretch on south into County Wexford. The inland road from Arklow up into the mountains through Woodenbridge and Avoca is pleasant, but not as grand as the mountains farther north.

BRAY

Bray is a big dormitory town on the coast just south of Dublin. In Victorian times it was the Brighton of Ireland, a bustling seaside resort with a long straight promenade, fronted by a beach and backed by hotels and lodging houses, all nicely overshadowed by Bray Head to the south. There even used to be a cable car from the prom up to the summit.

The waterfront is now home to B&Bs, cheap hotels and amusement arcades. The promenade, a wonderful construction, is badly in need of an expensive overhaul. The heart of Bray is its main street, lined with chain stores, other shops and pubs.

The locals are doing something to improve the look of the town. The Tudor-style town hall at the top of Main St has been refurbished with a restaurant, art gallery, museum and heritage centre (☎ 01-286 0987). The other major development has been a small aquarium on the promenade.

There is a fine six-km (four-mile) cliff walk around Bray Head to Greystones from the south end of the promenade. Bray Head has many old smuggling caves and rail tunnels including one which is 1.5 km long, the second longest in Ireland, built by the engineer Isambard Kingdom Brunel in 1856. The inland rail route was an easier and more

obvious choice but the local earl didn't want the railway through his land.

There is a seasonal tourist office (☎ 01-286 7128) in the town hall at the top of Main St. The main post office is off the south end of Main St on Quinsboro Rd. The Bray Bookshop on the Main St is excellent and has opened a branch on Grafton St in Dublin. They have maps and walking guides to Wicklow.

Things to Buy

The biggest and best local craft shop is a bit out of town. Avoca Handweavers (☎ 01-286 7466) in Kilmacanogue on the N11 has a huge array of hand-made crafts and garments. Weavers will answer questions while working away on their looms making tweed. A café serves snacks and lunches. If coming from Bray, turn right up by the town hall and continue for three km (two miles) and turn left for one km when you come to the N11 dual carriageway.

They have a shop and mill (☎ 0402-5105) in the village of Avoca in south Wicklow where most of the cloth is woven, but the branch near Bray is more accessible.

Golf

There are some 18-hole golf courses nearby. Woodbrook (☎ 01-282 1838) is a championship links just north of town, and Bray Golf Club (☎ 01-286 2092) is nearby. Inland is Old Conna Golf Club (☎ 01-282 6055).

Getting There & Away

Train Plunkett Railway Station (☎ 01-363333) is 500 metres east of Main St just off the seafront. There are DART electric train services into Dublin (Pearse, Tara and Connolly stations) and north to Howth every five minutes at peak times and every 20 or 30 minutes at quiet times.

Bray Station is also on the mainline to Wexford and Rosslare Harbour, and there are four diesel trains daily in each direction and two on Sundays. They stop at Greystones, Wicklow and Arklow.

Bus Bus Éireann (☎ 01-366111) double-decker bus Nos 45 and 84 run every 45 minutes or so between Dublin and Bray. A good place to catch them in Dublin is outside Trinity College on Nassau St. Both go past Bray Railway Station and bus Nos 84 and 84A run on to Greystones. Bus No 85 runs from Bray Station to Enniskerry.

Getting Around
Taxi Bray Cabs (☎ 01-286 1111) are at 39 Quinsboro Rd and Bray Taxis (☎ 01-282 9826) are at 5 Main St.

Bikes E R Harris (☎ 01-286 3357), 87 Greenpark Rd or 78 Main St (☎ 01-286 7995), are official Raleigh dealers, with bikes for IR£7 a day or IR£30 a week plus deposit.

GREYSTONES TO WICKLOW
Greystones, eight km (five miles) south of Bray, was once a charming fishing village, and the seafront around the little harbour is idyllic, with a broad bay and beach sweeping around to Bray Head. In summer, the bay is dotted with dinghies and windsurfers. The countryside around the town is now being overrun with housing developments.

Kilcoole, three km south of Greystones, is noteworthy only as the setting for Ireland's leading TV soap opera, *Glenroe*, broadcast on Sunday nights.

Continuing south from Kilcoole the road joins the N11 at Rathnew and runs on to Ashford and the **Mount Usher Gardens** (☎ 0404-40116). This lovely eight-hectare garden is informally laid out around the River Vartry and has rare plants from around the world. Admission is IR£2 (students IR£1.20). There is a seasonal tourist office (☎ 0404-40150) in Ashford during the summer.

The **Tiglin Adventure Centre** (☎ 0404-40169), six km (four miles) west of Ashford off the Roundwood road, runs courses in many different sports and organises treks throughout the mountains. East of the centre and three km from Ashford is the **Devil's Glen**, a deep and lovely wooded glen with a fine walking trail along its length.

WICKLOW TOWN
Wicklow Town is a fairly ordinary country town boasting a fine big harbour which hosts the start of the biennial Round Ireland yacht race. The sweep of beach and bay to the north and the bulge of Wicklow Head to the south are the locale's best features. It is 27 km (17 miles) south of Bray.

The name Wicklow comes from 'Vykinglo', a Viking word variously interpreted as lookout, signal point or Viking meadow. The ruined Black Castle on the coast at the south end of town and some narrow streets are about all that remains of Wicklow's Viking and Anglo-Norman past.

The few remaining fragments of the Black Castle are on the shore at the south end of town, with pleasant views up and down the coast. The castle was built by the Fitzgeralds from Wales in 1178 after they were granted lands in the area. At the time they were under attack from the Wicklow O'Byrne and O'Toole clans. The castle used to be linked to the mainland by a drawbridge, and rumour has it that an escape tunnel ran from the sea cave underneath up into the town. At low tide you can swim or snorkel into the cave.

The tourist office (☎ 0404-67904) in Market Square is open all year round.

AROUND WICKLOW TOWN
Starting just 16 km (10 miles) south of Wicklow is a string of fine beaches: Silver Strand, Brittas Bay and Maheramore. With high dunes, safe shallow bathing and white powdery sand, the beaches attract droves of people from Dublin in good weather. Caravan parks lie behind the dunes. Even at busy times there is plenty of room.

South Wicklow

RATHDRUM
Rathdrum is a quiet country hamlet to the south of Glendalough and the Vale of Clara, the pleasant valley leading north to Laragh. Twisting roads lead down to a stone bridge

over the Avonmore River which joins with the Avonbeg at the 'meeting of the waters' farther south in Avoca. There is not much to this peaceful village, just a few old houses and shops although in the late 19th century it could have claimed to be the unofficial capital of Wicklow, as it had considerable industry and a poorhouse.

In the 18th and 19th centuries, Rathdrum had a healthy flannel industry. In 1861 the railway and the fine aqueduct were built.

The wealthy Whaley family once resided in Whaley Abbey nearby. These characters were considered eccentric even by the standards of the 18th-century upper class. Richard Whaley was known as 'Burn Chapel' Whaley for his efforts as a priesthunter. His son was Buck Whaley (1766-1800), a notorious rake and gambler. Once he accepted a wager to walk to Jerusalem and play handball against the Wailing Wall, winning £15,000 in the process.

Avondale House

In 1846 the great Irish politician Charles Stewart Parnell was born in Avondale House (☎ 0404-46111), almost three km south of Rathdrum. The house dates from 1779 and has a small museum dedicated to Parnell which is open from May to October. The rest of the building is home to the Irish Forestry Service which looks after the estate. Its 209 hectares of woodland are open to the public all year round and there is an arboretum and nature walks.

Places to Stay & Eat

Most of the good B&Bs near Rathdrum are in Corballis, along the road south to Avoca and Arklow.

Beechlawn (☎ 0404-46474) is 500 metres from Rathdrum on the road to Avoca and Arklow, and costs IR£16/24 for singles/doubles, or IR£26 with bathroom. The *Hawthorns* (☎ 0404-46217) is also in Corballis, one km from Rathdrum. B&B is IR£16/24, or IR£28 with bathroom. A little farther along the same road is *St Bridget's* (☎ 0404-46477). B&B is IR£17/24.

THE VALE OF AVOCA

The Avonbeg and Avonmore rivers come together to form the River Avoca at the 'meeting of the waters', a lovely spot made famous by the poem of the same name by Thomas Moore (1779-1852):

There is not in this wide world a valley so sweet
As that vale in whose bosom the bright waters meet;
Oh! the last rays of feeling and life must depart,
Ere the bloom of that valley shall fade from my heart.

The Vale of Avoca meanders through a gentle and darkly wooded valley, charming but not awe-inspiring.

For several hundred years, there were active copper mines in the area which left a section of badly scarred landscape northwest of Avoca village. They also polluted the River Avoca, once famous for its salmon. The last mine closed in 1982.

The village of Avoca has some nice country pubs beside a bridge over the river. Nearby is Avoca Handweavers (☎ 0402-35105) selling tweeds and garments of their own making and other Irish products. They have a good café which is open during the day.

Five km (three miles) north-east in Cronebane is the 'mottie stone' near the meeting of the waters. This is described variously as the halfway point between Dublin and Wexford, some sort of Stone Age ritual site, or a hurling stone of the legendary Celtic warrior, Fionn MacCumhaill.

Places to Stay

Camping There are two well-equipped camp sites near the village of Redcross, about seven km (four miles) from Avoca on the R754 country road. *Johnson's* (☎ 0404-48133) is just north of Redcross and charges IR£4.50 per tent and 30p per person, while the *River Valley Park* (☎ 0404-41647) is just south of the village and charges IR£5 per tent and 50p per person.

B&Bs The Georgian *Riverview House* (☎ 0402-35181) is highly recommended. The *Arbours* (☎ 0402-35294) is in an old farmhouse and has great breakfasts. Both cost IR£16/24 for singles/doubles.

Ashdene (☎ 0402-35327) is two km outside Avoca in Knockanree Lower. B&B is IR£12 to IR£18 single, IR£24 for doubles. It's open Easter to October. *Greenhill's* (☎ 0402-35197) is also in Knockanree Lower. B&B is IR£17/24.

ARKLOW

Besides Bray, Arklow is probably County Wicklow's busiest town. The name in Irish is Inbhear Mór meaning 'great estuary'. It's a thriving commercial shopping centre with some light industry, notably a pottery and a large fertiliser plant north of the town (which has scaled down its operations but still frequently releases some questionable white smoke). You could use Arklow as a base to explore farther into the Wicklow hills, but it is not a particularly attractive place in its own right.

From humble origins as a minor fishing village, Arklow became one of the busiest ports in the country and a well-known boat-building centre. A famous shipyard, Tyrrells, continues the tradition and Sir Francis Chichester's *Gypsy Moth* and the Irish training vessel the *Asgard II* were built here. In 1841 the port had as many as 80 schooners working out of the harbour. It exported ores from the Avoca mines, and during WW I munitions and explosives from a local factory. A small maritime museum traces the town's sea-going past.

During the 1798 Rising, Arklow saw some of the fiercest fighting when some 20,000 of the rebels led by Father Michael Murphy tried to storm the town and were defeated by the better equipped and trained British Army. Murphy and 700 men died in the battle, and a monument to them sits near the Catholic church today.

Nearby attractions include the Brittas Bay beaches to the north and the Vale of Avoca to the east. There are some reasonable walks along the shore either side of the town.

Places to Eat

During the summer, the *Riverview Café* down by the river is good for snacks. The best two pubs in town for food and entertainment are *Kitty's* and *Christie's*, both on Main St. Kitty's food is excellent and so is the atmosphere. Upstairs, there is music (usually rock) a few times a week. Christie's also has good food and a nice and reasonably cheap conservatory restaurant out the back.

Getting There & Away

Bus Éireann has regular buses from Busáras, Dublin to Arklow via Wicklow Town. There are trains from Dublin (Connolly or Pearse St stations) four times daily and twice on Sundays (☎ 01-735555 for recorded information).

Counties Wexford & Waterford

County Wexford

County Wexford takes up the south-east corner of Ireland and many visitors arrive at Rosslare Harbour on the ferries from Wales and France. Most of them speed through Wexford en route to Dublin, Kilkenny or the west coast, and while Wexford hasn't a huge amount to divert them, there are a few spots worth looking over.

Geographically, the county is almost entirely flat, except near its western borders with Carlow and Kilkenny where the Blackstairs Mountains rise to 796 metres (2610 feet) at their highest point, Mt Leinster. There are some pleasant routes through these little-explored hills, particularly west from Enniscorthy and over the Sculleoge Gap. Good flat land and a healthy annual dose of sunshine favour tillage crops like oats and wheat which struggle under damper conditions elsewhere.

Wexford Town itself is pleasant enough, but retains few traces of its Viking past. To its north, a string of fine beaches runs along the coast towards County Wicklow. In the centre, Enniscorthy is an attractive hilly town on the banks of the River Slaney. Farther west, the River Barrow runs right by New Ross, which is a good base to explore the lovely upper reaches of the river.

On the south coast is the fishing village of Kilmore Quay and farther west is the flat and lonely Hook Peninsula, where you will find one of the oldest lighthouses in the world.

WEXFORD TOWN

Wexford vies with Waterford City for the position of principal settlement in the south-east. It was once a thriving port, but over the centuries the slow-moving River Slaney has deposited so much silt and mud in the estuary as to make the channel almost unusable. Now most commercial sea traffic goes through Waterford and all passenger traffic through Rosslare Harbour, 20 km (12 miles) to the south-east.

A settlement called Menapia appeared on Ptolemy's map of Ireland in the 2nd century AD, where Wexford sits today. The Vikings arrived in the region around 850 AD, attracted by its handy location near the mouth of the River Slaney. The Viking name Waesfjord means 'harbour of mud flats' or 'sandy harbour'. The Normans captured the town just after their first landings in 1169, and traces of their fort can still be seen in the grounds of the Irish National Heritage Park north of town at Ferrycarrig.

Cromwell included Wexford in his 1649 Irish tour. Three-quarters of the 2000 inhabitants were put to the sword, including all of the town's Franciscan friars – the standard treatment for towns that refused to surrender. After Wexford, surrender became increasingly popular.

During the 1798 Rising, Wexford was once again in the thick of the action. Enniscorthy to the north saw heavier fighting, but the rebels under their leader Bagenal Harvey made a determined stand in Wexford Town before they were defeated.

Wexford is an attractive town, particularly the approach from the east with the bridge, the quays and the church spires reflected in the broad still waters of the Slaney estuary. The town itself centres on the long water-

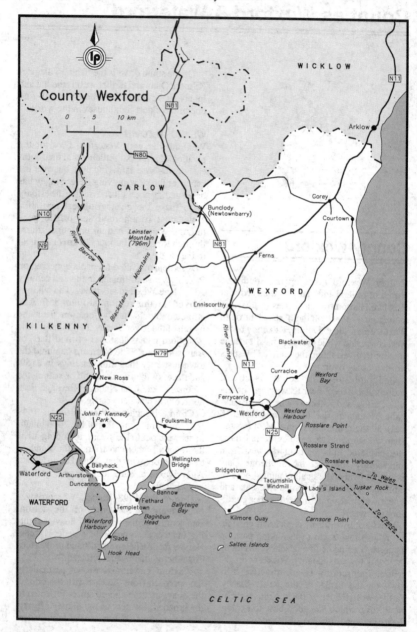

County Wexford

0 5 10 km

front quays and Main St which runs behind them. There are still a few boats but little effort has been made to use the waterfront to advantage.

Little remains of the Viking influence. Among the few traces are pieces of the old town walls near the Rowe St Church and the Westgate, and the narrowness of many of the streets. Today, they are packed with pubs, shops and restaurants. The city is renowned for its opera festival.

Orientation

From the bridge at the north end of town, the quays run south-east along the waterfront, first as Commercial Quay, becoming Custom House Quay, through the small kink called the Crescent and on for a short time as Paul Quay before turning inland. They are all roughly parallel to the Main Sts which run a block inland. To the north is Selskar St, which runs south as North Main St and then South Main St. Most of the banks, shops and commercial areas are along the Main Sts.

Information

The tourist office (☎ 053-23111) is on the waterfront at Crescent Quay. It's open May to September 9 am to 6 pm, Monday to Saturday, and Sundays in July and August between 10 am and 5 pm. The rest of the year it's open 9 am to 5.15 pm, Monday to Friday. Pick up the *Visitors' Guide* and the *Welcome to Wexford* booklet. The bookshop called the Book Centre is on North Main St.

The main post office is on Anne St and is open every day except Sunday from 9 am to 5.30 pm. My Beautiful Laundrette (☎ 053-24317) is on St Peter's Square and is open six days a week. Disc parking is in operation in the town and discs can be bought in most newsagents.

The Quays & Main St

The quays are of little interest except as a place for an evening stroll. North and South Main Sts are busier and more interesting. From Selskar St to South Main St is the main shopping thoroughfare; it's a pleasant area to wander round.

The Crescent

Besides the Chamber of Commerce building and the tourist office, the Crescent is home to a statue of Commodore John Barry, a local seaman born in 1745, who emigrated to America and founded the US navy during the American Revolution. The US Navy presented the statue to Wexford in 1956 and it has been visited by such notables as presidents Eisenhower and Kennedy.

The Bull Ring

Between Commercial Quay and North Main St is the Bull Ring, at one time a centre for bull-baiting and other medieval entertainments but also the site of Cromwell's long-remembered massacre. There's no reminder of that bloody event today and the Bull Ring is merely the intersection of a number of streets. The *Lone Pikeman* statue by Oliver Sheppard commemorates the participants in the 1798 Fenian rebellion.

The town market is right beside the Bull Ring and there is usually a market here on Fridays and Saturday mornings.

The Westgate

Some stretches of the town walls remain, including a fine section by the Cornmarket. There is only one survivor of the original six town gates: the Westgate, at the north end of town in from the bridge. The Westgate dates from 1300, was built as a toll gate and is now the focus for Wexford's reconstruction of its Viking past. Part of the wall encloses Selskar Abbey just to the south and it can be scaled from inside the abbey grounds.

The Westgate Centre (☎ 053-42611) beside the gate has an audio-visual display on the history of Wexford. Admission is IR£1, and it's open 10 am to 9 pm, April to September, and to 6 pm at other times.

Selskar Abbey

Selskar Abbey's dilapidated state is a result of Cromwell's visit in 1649. It is claimed that Henry II spent the 40 days of Lent in 1172 in the abbey as penance for murdering Thomas à Becket two years earlier, but in fact the abbey was not built until 20 years later.

Strongbow's sister Bascilla is supposed to have married one of his brave lieutenants, Raymond le Gros, in the abbey.

The present red sandstone structure dates from 1190 and was founded by Alexander de la Roche after a crusade to the Holy Land. In the abbey grounds a newly cut gravestone to a Mrs McGee (erected by an interested local historian) states that she was 'A woman perfect in every office of life' and that one of her sons was Thomas D'Arcy McGee 'a founding father of Canada, who was assasinated in Ottowa on April 7th 1868'.

For the key to the abbey grounds, ask at Mr Murphy's house, 9 Selskar Court, just south of the abbey.

Other Sights

South of the Bull Ring on Main St is **St Iberius' Church** of 1760. Near the corner of King and Barrack Sts is a plaque marking the centre of **St Doologue's Parish**, said by locals to be the smallest parish in the world at just two hectares in size. Above Kelly's Pub on South Main St is the birthplace of William Cody Sr, who was the father of Buffalo Bill Cody, the famous American frontiersman. Robert McClure, who discovered the North-West Passage, was born above White's Hotel on the corner of George and North Main Sts.

Organised Tours

Guided tours are provided free during the summer by the Wexford Historical Society every evening at 8 pm from Talbot and White's hotels. For more information contact the tourist office.

The Wexford Opera Festival

This is an excuse for Wexford folk to shake out their cocktail dresses and dinner jackets and prepare for a huge influx of cultured visitors. The festival is held over 17 days every October. It began in 1951 and has grown to be the premier opera event in the country, presenting many rarely performed operas and shows to packed audiences.

During the festival, the town is transformed, with street theatre, poetry readings and exhibitions every day. Pub music is at its peak, with blues, jazz and traditional Irish groups.

Tickets for the principal operas are hard to come by and pricey. Booking is essential and should be done at least three months in advance. You can write to the Wexford Opera Festival at Theatre Royal, High St, Wexford, Ireland, or phone the festival office (☎ 053-22240) or the box office (☎ 053-22144).

Places to Stay

Camping The *Ferrybank Camping & Caravan Park* (☎ 053-44378) is right across the river from the town centre, off the Dublin road. The park has good facilities and is open from Easter to mid-September. A tent costs IR£4 for one person, IR£5 for two or IR£6 for three.

O'Gorman's Camping & Caravan Park (☎ 053-37221) is just south of Curracloe village and is open from April until the end of September. They have reasonable facilities and charge IR£5 (low season IR£4).

B&Bs Most B&Bs in or around Wexford are IR£13 a night or more. Half a km from the centre on St John's Rd, *Kilderry* (☎ 053-23848) has three rooms (one with own bathroom) at IR£13 or IR£14 with bath. *Westgate House* (☎ 053-22167) near the railway station has 12 rooms from IR£13 to IR£16 with own bathroom. *Chez Nous* (☎ 053-24104) is on the New-Line road, 1.5 km (one mile) from the town centre; go to the south end of South Main St and head straight up King St to Bishops Water. They have four rooms with own bathroom at IR£13, and they are open April to November. The *St George Guesthouse* (☎ 053-22691) at the top of Georges St charges IR£13 to IR£16 with own bathroom. On John St, *St Aidan's Mews* (☎ 053-22691) has rooms from IR£13 to IR£17.

Ardruadh (☎ 053-23194) is on Spawell Rd at the north end of town beyond the Westgate, and costs IR£15 for B&B. *Heritage View* (☎ 053-45168) is 3.5 km (two miles) north of town, overlooking the

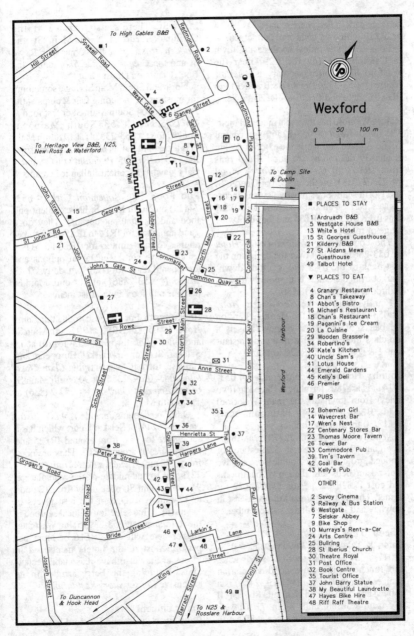

Wexford

0   50   100 m

■ PLACES TO STAY

1 Ardruadh B&B
5 Westgate House B&B
13 White's Hotel
15 St Georges Guesthouse
21 Kilderry B&B
27 St Aidans Mews Guesthouse
49 Talbot Hotel

▼ PLACES TO EAT

4 Granary Restaurant
8 Chan's Takeaway
11 Abbot's Bistro
16 Michael's Restaurant
18 Chan's Restaurant
19 Paganini's Ice Cream
20 La Cuisine
29 Wooden Brasserie
34 Robertino's
36 Kate's Kitchen
40 Uncle Sam's
44 Emerald Gardens
45 Kelly's Deli
46 Premier

▼ PUBS

12 Bohemian Girl
14 Wavecrest Bar
17 Wren's Nest
22 Centenary Stores Bar
23 Thomas Moore Tavern
26 Tower Bar
33 Commodore Pub
39 Tim's Tavern
42 Goal Bar
43 Kelly's Pub

OTHER

2 Savoy Cinema
3 Railway & Bus Station
6 Westgate
7 Selskar Abbey
9 Bike Shop
10 Murrays's Rent-a-Car
24 Arts Centre
25 Bullring
28 St Iberius' Church
30 Theatre Royal
31 Post Office
32 Book Centre
35 Tourist Office
37 John Barry Statue
38 My Beautiful Laundrette
47 Hayes Bike Hire
48 Riff Raff Theatre

heritage park in Ferrycarrig, and costs IR£14 or IR£16 with own bathroom per person.

Four km (three miles) north-east of town in Castlebridge (on the L29) near the Wexford Slobs bird sanctuary is *Aherlow House* (☎ 053-23249) with B&B at IR£13 to IR£16 double and IR£17 to IR£20 single.

Hotels Wexford has the usual modern hotels. The *Talbot Hotel* (☎ 053-22566) is a central Grade A place and while the exterior design is ghastly the rooms are good. B&B runs from IR£37.50 to IR£55. *White's Hotel* (☎ 053-22311), on the corner of George St and North Main St, is mostly new but incorporates part of an old coaching inn. B&B runs from IR£25 to IR£35 and they do a wide range of food.

The comfortable *Wexford Lodge Hotel* (☎ 053-23611) is just over the bridge on the east bank of the river and is a little down-market from the others with rooms with own bathroom at IR£28 to IR£30.

Finally there is the *Ferrycarrig Hotel* (☎ 053-22999) beside the Heritage Park on the banks of the River Slaney. This is a top-class modern hotel with a good restaurant. B&B runs from IR£30 to IR£50.

Country Houses *Clonard House* (☎ 053-23141) is a 1780s farmhouse three km (two miles) from town off the main Waterford road. B&B with own bathroom costs IR£18/30 for singles/doubles.

Newbay House (☎ 053-22779) is an 1820s Georgian country house in 12 hectares of wooded grounds. The double rooms have four poster beds and their own bathrooms and cost IR£28 per person plus IR£22 for dinner. The house is three km north-east in Newbay and is open March to November.

Places to Eat

Cafés & Takeaways *Kelly's Deli* (☎ 053-22011) at 80 South Main St do sandwiches and lunches with some good vegetarian choices. *Kate's Kitchen* (☎ 053-22456) is a coffee shop cum deli on Henrietta St open all day from 7.30 am until 8 pm. *La Cuisine* (☎ 053-24986) is a similar place at 80 North

Main St. There's also *Joanne's* at the Cornmarket end of North Main St, the *Wooden Brasserie* on the corner with Rowe St and the *Chapter Coffee Shop* under the Book Centre on North Main St.

North and South Main Sts have something for most tastes, including fish & chips at the *Premier* at 104 South Main St or fast food at *Uncle Sam's* at 53 South Main St. *Robertino's* (☎ 053-23334) at 19 South Main St is a pleasant Italian place with pizzas from IR£3.85 to IR£4.95. *Paganini's* on Commercial Quay has excellent Italian ice cream.

Pub Food The *Bohemian Girl* (☎ 053-24419) on North Main St has excellent pub food and a restaurant upstairs. They do a good hot lunch for IR£4 to IR£5 and a three-course tourist dinner for IR£8.95. They usually have some vegetarian options and are open 11 am to 11.30 pm daily. *Tim's Tavern* (☎ 053-23861) at 51 South Main St has fine pub food and tourist menus.

Restaurants For Chinese food, the *Lotus House* (☎ 053-24273) is at 70 South Main St and *Chan's Takeaway* (☎ 053-46110) at 15 Selskar St. For up-market European and Chinese food, it's worth trying *Chan's Restaurant* (☎ 053-22356) at 90 North Main St or the *Emerald Gardens* (☎ 053-24836) at 117 South Main St.

Other restaurants include *Abbot's Bistro* (☎ 053-46244) at Selskar Court which has a set dinner for two from around IR£25 and other dishes at around IR£7. They are open from 5.30 pm. *Michael's Restaurant* (☎ 053-22196) is a good middle-of-the-road place at 94 North Main St, open daily from 12 noon to 12 midnight. One of the best places in town with a fine selection of local seafood is the *Granary* (☎ 053-23935) at Westgate. Dinner here will cost IR£16 or more per person. Most of the hotels mentioned in Places to Stay also have reasonable restaurants, including the Ferrycarrig with its expensive *Conservatory Restaurant*.

Entertainment

Pubs Even for Ireland Wexford has a lot of

pubs, many of them strung along North and South Main Sts where you'll find *Tim's Tavern*, the *Commodore* and the *Bohemian Girl*. The *Goal Bar* (☎ 053-43731) on South Main St has a beer garden and regular music sessions.

On Cornmarket, towards the abbey ruins, is the atmospheric old *Thomas Moore Tavern*. Music often features at the *Wren's Nest* and the *Tower Bar* on the quay. For the 22 to 30 age group the pub to go to is the *Centenary Stores* just off North Main St. The *Wavecrest Bar* on Commercial Quay has Irish music almost every night during the summer.

Cinema & Theatre Wexford has a number of theatres and there is almost always a show on somewhere. The *Riff Raff Theatre* (☎ 053-22141) is in Larkin's Lane off South Main St, the *Theatre Royal* (☎ 053-22144) is in High St, and the *Arts Centre* (☎ 053-23764) is in the Cornmarket and caters for exhibitions, displays, theatre, dance and music performances.

There is a new *Savoy* three-screen cineplex near the railway station.

Getting There & Away
Continue south from the quays for Rosslare and Rosslare Harbour. For Duncannon or Hook Head, turn west either at the Crescent along Harpers Lane or from Paul Quay along King St.

Note the short cut between Wexford and Waterford by taking the Ballyhack to Passage East ferry and avoiding the longer route via New Ross. Cyclists in particular will find this easier.

Train O'Hanrahan Railway Station (☎ 053-22522) is on the north end of town in Redmond Place near the waterfront. Wexford is on the Dublin to Rosslare Harbour line and is serviced by three trains daily in each direction. The train offers a lovely view of the town as it passes along the quays. There are also three trains daily (only two on Sundays) to Rosslare Harbour taking 30 minutes.

Bus The Wexford office of Bus Éireann (☎ 053-22522) is at the railway station on Redmond Place at the north end of the quays past the main bridge over the river. It's open from 8.30 am to 6 pm. There are five daily buses to Dublin and also services to Waterford and Rosslare Harbour.

The Ardcavan Coach Company (☎ 053-22561) operates between Dublin and Rosslare Harbour daily. Their Wexford stop is at Crescent Quay by the tourist office.

Bus Éireann have limited local services to Gorey via Courtown, Carne and Kilmore Quay. During July and August, they run tours of the surrounding areas.

Getting Around
The Bike Shop (☎ 053-22514) at 9 Selskar St and Hayes (☎ 053-22462) at 108 South Main St both have bikes for IR£7 a day or IR£30 a week. Murrays Rent-a-Car (☎ 053-22122) has an office on Redmond Place up towards the railway station.

For taxis call Wexford Taxi Services (☎ 053-41608) or Andrews Taxi Service (☎ 053-45933).

AROUND WEXFORD TOWN
Irish National Heritage Park
Four km north of Wexford, beside the Dublin to Rosslare N11 road at Ferrycarrig, is the Irish National Heritage Park (☎ 053-22211/41733). This is an outdoor theme park, which attempts to condense and package a country's entire history in one place. It's quite interesting and the tour, included in the entry price, is good.

From the entrance you visit recreations of dwelling places, graves and fortifications used in Ireland over many thousands of years. There is a Mesolithic camp site, a Neolithic farmstead, a dolmen, a cyst burial tomb, a stone circle, a rath or ring fort, a monastery, a crannóg or lake settlement, a Viking shipyard, a motte and bailey, a Norman castle and a couple of other smaller displays. A replica Viking longship sits at anchor in the River Slaney just out from the park.

The park has some drawbacks: a major

road and a railway line run through it; the Norman castle is concrete painted white; and there would be a lovely view of the River Slaney and Ferrycarrig Tower but for a large green wire fence in the way.

Entry is IR£3.50 (children IR£1.50). Opening hours are 10 am to 7 pm from March to October with last admissions at 5 pm.

Johnstown Castle
The former home of the Fitzgerald and Esmonde families is a splendid 19th-century Gothic-style castellated house overlooking a small lake and surrounded by 20 hectares of well-kept thickly wooded gardens. The castle and its outbuildings now hold an agricultural research centre, the headquarters of the Irish Environmental Protection Agency and an agricultural museum.

The castle interior is off limits, but the grounds and the museum (☎ 053-42888) are open to the public. There is an admission charge of IR£1.50 and the gardens are open every day 9 am to 5 pm, while the museum is open 9 am to 5 pm Monday to Friday, 2 pm to 5 pm on weekends. Times vary in winter. The castle is seven km (four miles) south-west of Wexford on the way to Murntown.

The Wexford Wildfowl Reserve
Four to five km north-east of Wexford town are the North Slobs, a swathe of low-lying land reclaimed from the sea, which is still held back by a long retaining wall. The slobs are home to half the world's population of Greenland white-fronted geese in winter, some 10,000 birds. It's a great sight on winter evenings to go out to the sea wall and watch the V-shaped formations of geese fly overhead out into the darkness of the bay, where they pass the night on sandbanks and islands.

Wintertime is also good for brent geese from Arctic Canada, and throughout the year you will see mallard, pochard, godwits, mute and bewick swans, redshank, terns, coot, oystercatchers and many more species.

The Wexford Wildfowl Reserve (☎ 053-23129) was set up here to protect the many different species and provide them with feeding grounds. It has shelters, a meeting room and an observation tower.

To get to the Slobs and the nature reserve go out of Wexford on the Dublin road, over the bridge and north for 3.5 km (two miles) until you see a signpost for the reserve pointing to the right.

The Raven
This nature reserve near Curracloe is a lovely spot. A long walk through forest brings you out on dunes where you may see Greenland white-fronted geese and various waders. To get there take the Dublin road out of town, follow the signposts for Curracloe Beach and watch out for signs for the Raven off to the right.

Curracloe
Curracloe is one of a string of magnificent beaches that line the coast north of Wexford Town and into Wicklow. The beach is over 11 km (seven miles) long. Extensive dunes behind the beach provide some shelter, and you can pitch a tent here if you are discreet. Curracloe Beach is 15 km (nine miles) north-east of Wexford off the Dublin road. There is a camp site nearby.

ROSSLARE HARBOUR
At the south-east tip of the country, Rosslare Harbour is 20 km (12 miles) from Wexford Town and has busy ferry connections to Wales and France. The harbour surrounds are not particularly pretty but there are plenty of places to stay if you have to wait for your boat.

Information
There are two tourist offices. The one in the ferry terminal building (☎ 053-33622) is open year round while the one by the main Wexford road in Kilrane (☎ 053-32232) is open April to September.

Places to Stay
Camping Official camp sites are found in Rosslare itself but you could camp on the beach or in a field nearby.

Hostel There is an *An Óige Hostel* (☎ 053-33399) just up the hill from the ferry terminal on Goulding St. This big hostel has 85 beds and costs IR£5 October to May and IR£6.50 June to September. The hostel opens early or late for ferry arrivals and departures and will also accept advance credit-card bookings.

B&Bs One of the cheapest places around is *Glenville* (☎ 053-33142) on St Patrick's Rd near the harbour, at IR£14/24 for singles/doubles. *Laurel Lodge* (☎ 053-33291) is a km from the ferries. The rooms cost IR£16/26 with own bathroom. In town, overlooking the harbour, the big *Ailsa Lodge* (☎ 053-33230) has rooms with bathrooms from IR£12 to IR£15.

Quite a number of the local B&Bs are in Kilrane, a km inland on the Wexford road. *Kilrane House* (☎ 053-33135) is a 19th-century house with open fires and rooms at IR£14.50/26 for singles/doubles with own bathroom, and IR£18 to IR£20 single. *Blantyre* (☎ 053-33536) is 200 metres off the Wexford road and has rooms at IR£16/26.

Hotels Rosslare Harbour has plenty of modern hotels. The *Hotel Rosslare* (☎ 053-33110) sits on top of the cliff overlooking the ferry port and has plenty of facilities and excellent bar food. B&B costs from IR£23 to IR£38. The *Tuskar House Hotel* (☎ 053-33363) is barely 250 metres from the ferry terminal and has 20 bedrooms with their own bathrooms at IR£23 to IR£29 per person for B&B.

Places to Eat
Rosslare Harbour's hotel bars and restaurants are fine for the short time you are likely to be there. At *Hotel Rosslare* (☎ 053-33110) an excellent lunch costs IR£6 to IR£10 and they usually have some vegetarian choices. The attractive *Portholes Bar* offers good bar food, specialising in seafood, with main courses from around IR£4.

Getting There & Away
Ferry Three ferry companies operate to and from Rosslare Harbour and there is a convenient train and bus station.

Sealink (☎ 053-33115) have a day and a night connection to Fishguard in Wales from where there are rail connections to London. Except on Monday B&I Line (☎ 053-33311) also have a day and a night connection to Pembroke in Wales. Depending on the season, Irish Ferries (☎ 053-33158) have one to four sailings a week to and from Le Havre and Cherbourg in France. Sailing time is around 24 hours.

Train Trains (☎ 053-33114) operate from the ferry terminal and there are three services daily (two on Sundays) to Dublin via Wexford. There are two services daily to Waterford.

Bus There are at least three daily buses to Wexford and Dublin, and a single daily service to Galway via Kilkenny in July and August.

Car Rental Budget (☎ 053-33318), Hertz (☎ 053-33238) and Murrays (☎ 053-32181) have car hire desks in the terminal.

ROSSLARE STRAND
Rosslare Strand is about eight km (five miles) north of Rosslare Harbour and 15 km (nine miles) south of Wexford Town. The long golden beaches attract huge crowds in summer and there are also good walks north to Rosslare Point and an excellent 18-hole golf course (☎ 053-32203) nearby. The long shallow bay is ideal for windsurfing, and boards, wetsuits and tuition are available from Leo Lambert (☎ 053-32101).

Places to Stay
Camping The *Burrow Camping & Caravan Park* (☎ 053-32256) is just south of the village and has excellent facilities including showers, a laundrette, cooking facilities and tennis courts. They are open March to November and charge a hefty IR£8 per tent or IR£5 if you are hiking or cycling. The nearby *Rosslare Holiday Park* (☎ 053-32427) has similar facilities but is cheaper,

charging IR£5.50 per tent high season or IR£4.50 low season. Hikers and cyclists pay IR£2 per person and it is open May to September.

B&Bs *Decca House* (☎ 053-32410) is one km from Rosslare Strand, and the five rooms cost IR£16/26, or slightly more with bathroom. *Grahmorack* (☎ 053-32295) is 3.5 km (two miles) inland. Go to Tagoat on the main road to the harbour and turn south; the house is signposted and is one km down the road. There are four rooms costing IR£13 per person.

Hotels *Kelly's Strand Hotel* (☎ 053-32114) has every sports and leisure facility in the book and is popular with families. The restaurant is good, with a full dinner for around IR£18 and lunch for IR£7 to IR£10. B&B runs from IR£38 to IR£41. Cheaper places include the *Burrow Park Hotel* (☎ 053-32190) near the centre of the village at IR£16 to IR£21 for B&B.

Getting There & Away

The trains on the main line between Dublin, Wexford and Rosslare Harbour stop at Rosslare Strand. Bus services are limited. A single daily bus from Wexford at 6 pm to Rosslare Harbour stops at Rosslare Strand.

SOUTH OF ROSSLARE HARBOUR

Nine km (six miles) south of Rosslare Harbour is **Carnsore Point**, where Ireland's first nuclear power station was to be built. Thankfully, vociferous opposition – and the cost – killed the project. Carnsore Point was noted as the country's south-easternmost point in the map drawn by Ptolemy in the 2nd century AD. Offshore to the east is Tuskar Rock Lighthouse.

Carne has a fine beach, and the *Carne Beach Camping & Caravan Park* (☎ 053-31131), near the point, is open May to September and costs IR£7 per tent or IR£3 for hikers and cyclists. You could also camp along the beach somewhere. There is excellent pub food and seafood in the *Lobster Pot* (☎ 053-31110) bar and restaurant in Carne.

Turning west brings you to **Tacumshin**, where in 1840 Nicholas Moran built the Tacumshin Windmill, one of Ireland's few thatched windmills. The key can be picked up from the little shop where you park; there may be a charge. Just to the east is **Lady's Island**, the site of an early Augustinian priory and still a centre of devotion. Both Tacumshin and Lady's Island have small brackish lakes which are home to many migrating and breeding birds through the year. Lady's Island is best from autumn to spring, and you may see brent geese, shell duck, redshank, godwits, mute swan, teal and various terns.

Bridgetown is 12 km (eight miles) south-west of Wexford Town on the way to lovely Kilmore Quay. This was the first area in Ireland to be colonised by the Anglo-Normans. To the west, en route to Hook Head, the Irish chapter of Hell's Angels meet at **Wellington Bridge** over the June bank holiday weekend! **Hook Head** is well worth a detour and you can save yourself a circuitous trip north by taking a ferry from Ballyhack across to Passage East in Waterford (see Passage East). There is no public transport to this area.

Forth, Bargy & Yola

Faint remnants of a dialect called *yola* still survive in the south-east of Wexford, which is sometimes called 'Forth & Bargy'. Yola stood for 'ye olde language' and was a mixture of old French, English, Irish, Welsh and Flemish. Examples of the language would be to *curk*, meaning to sit on your thighs or a *chi o' whate* meaning a small amount of straw, to be *hachee* is to be bad-tempered and a *stouk* is a truculent woman. ■

KILMORE QUAY

Peaceful Kilmore Quay is a small fishing village on the east side of Ballyteige Bay, noted for its lobster and deep-sea fishing.

The village's Seafood Festival in the second week of July includes all types of seafood tastings, music and dancing.

Lining the attractive main street up from the harbour are a number of whitewashed thatched cottages. The harbour is the jumping-off point for the Saltee Islands, which are clearly visible out to sea. In the harbour the Guillemot Lightship houses a small maritime museum, open during the summer. To the north-west a good sandy beach stretches towards Cullenstown. ·

Places to Stay & Eat

Killtuck Hostel (☎ 053-29883) is a good place to stay, two km from Kilmore Quay on the main Wexford road. It charges IR£5 a night in dorms or IR£7 for private rooms, and also has a low-priced café.

Coral House (☎ 053-29640) is in Grange, Kilmore two km (1.5 miles) along the R739 road, and B&B costs IR£18/26 for singles/doubles. Another local B&B is *Sarshill House* (☎ 053-29604) with B&B for IR£13.

Food and drink possibilities include the *Wooden House Restaurant & Bar*, the *Silver Fox Restaurant* or the *Hotel Saltees* (☎ 053-29601), which has a good-value tourist menu and B&B from IR£23 to IR£26.

Getting There & Away

Public transport to Kilmore Quay is very limited. On Wednesdays and Saturdays only there are two buses leaving Wexford Town at 10 am and 3.30 pm, returning at 10.35 am and 4.10 pm (4.35 pm on Saturday). Every Friday there is a private bus from Kilmore Quay to Wexford. For details, ask at the post office.

SALTEE ISLANDS

The Saltee Islands are four km (2.5 miles) offshore from Kilmore Quay and have some of the oldest rocks in Europe, dating back 2000 million years or more.

Once the haunt of privateers and smugglers, the Saltees are one of Ireland's most important bird sanctuaries and home to over 375 recorded species, principally gannets,

guillemots, cormorants, kittiwakes, puffins and Manx shearwaters. The best time to visit is in the spring and early summer nesting season, as once the chicks can fly, the birds leave, and by early August it's very quiet.

The Saltees – nicknamed the 'graveyard of a thousand ships' – were touched by the 1798 Rising, for it was here that two of the Wexford rebel leaders, Bagenal Harvey and Dr John Colclough, were found hiding before they were brought to Wexford, hanged and beheaded. The Saltees were bought in 1943 by Michael Neale who then crowned himself Prince Michael, the 'First Prince of the Saltees'. He even erected a throne and obelisk in his own honour on the Great Saltee. Luckily you don't need his royal consent to venture onto the islands, just the name of someone who can get you there – try the tourist office in Wexford or local boatmen like Willie Bates (☎ 053-29644) or Tom O'Brien (☎ 053-29727). Fares are IR£6 to IR£10 return – bargain with the boatmen. The trip should take about 45 minutes. For more on the islands read *The Saltees, Islands of Birds & Legends* by Richard Roche and Oscar Merne, published by O'Brien Press.

THE HOOK PENINSULA

The south-west of the county is dominated by the long tapering finger of Hook Peninsula, terminating at Hook Head. Cromwell's statement that Waterford Town would fall 'by Hook or by Crook', referred to the two possible landing points from which to take the area: here or at Crooke in County Waterford. In good weather, it's a fine journey out to the lighthouse at the tip of the head and back along the west side to Duncannon. On the west side is a car ferry to Passage East in County Waterford saving a detour to the north via New Ross (see the Passage East section).

On the way out to Hook, **Tintern Abbey** is a 12th-century Cistercian abbey in a lovely rural setting. Currently being restored, it was founded by William Marshall, Earl of Pembroke after he nearly perished at sea. Continuing south towards the head, Fethard-on-Sea is the largest village in the area.

Just south of Fethard is **Baginbun Head** near Bannow Bay, where the Anglo-Normans made their first landings in Ireland in May 1169. Joining forces with the far larger army of Dermot MacMurrough, they captured Wexford in the same year. Ramparts were built to fortify the headland at Baginbun, until more Normans arrived in 1170 under Raymond Le Gros. Shortly after he landed, 3000 Irish-Norse soldiers set out from Waterford City and attacked Baginbun, outnumbering the defenders seven to one.

Le Gros stampeded a herd of cattle onto them and then taught them a lesson in organised warfare. Seventy of Waterford's citizens and soldiers were captured, had their legs broken and were thrown over the cliffs to their death. So it was to be that:

At the creek of Baginbun,
Ireland was lost and won.

After the Norman leader Strongbow had landed at Passage East with another 1200 men, the Normans gathered their forces and in August 1170 marched on to Waterford City. This was the beginning of 800 years of English involvement in Ireland.

Today at Baginbun, a small road leads down to a battered memorial overlooking Baginbun Beach and the headland out to the right. If you look carefully at the headland, you can make out the overgrown earthen ramparts built by the Normans when they first arrived. The stone **Martello Tower** dates from the early 1800s. Bannow Bay to the east, the first landing area of the Normans, is the site of a lost town – Norman or Viking – which was swamped by sand and the sea in the 1600s.

The journey out to **Hook Head** is lovely, the land extremely flat with few houses interrupting the open space. About two km from the head, turning left at a T-junction brings you down to the odd little village of **Slade** with an imposing ruined castle dominating the harbour. There are usually a couple of boats moored here but otherwise it is a quiet and sleepy place.

Farther south, Hook Head itself is crowned by Europe's, and possibly the world's, oldest **lighthouse**. It's said that monks lit a beacon on the head from the 5th century and that the first Viking invaders were so happy to have a guiding light that they left the monks alone. In the 12th century a more solid beacon was erected by the Norman Raymond le Gros, and 800 years later that is largely the structure you see today. Tours of the lighthouse can be made by arrangement (☎ 051-97178).

There are lovely walks both sides of the head, a haunting and beautiful place in the evening. Be careful of the numerous blowholes on the west side of the peninsula. The rocks around the lighthouse are carboniferous limestone, rich in fossil remains. If you search carefully, you may find 350-million-year-old shells and tiny disc-like pieces of crinoids, a type of starfish. Hook Head is also a good vantage point for bird-watching, and over 200 species have been recorded passing through the area.

The village of **Duncannon** is a small resort with a lovely beach and a nice view over Waterford Harbour. On the west of the village is Duncannon Fort, one of many structures built on this site since pre-Norman times.

Four km to the north of Duncannon is **Ballyhack** where there is a year-round ferry to Passage East in County Waterford – see the Getting There & Away section. Ballyhack also has a 14th-century **Knights Templar castle** overlooking the estuary.

Dunbrody Abbey is a beautiful ruin on the west side of Hook Head near the village of Campile and about nine km (six miles) north of Duncannon. It was built around 1170 AD by the English Cistercian monks of Buildwas in Shropshire, England. Various buttresses and supports had to be added later, to keep it upright. Most of the structure is still there and it is a fine sight among the fields. **Dunbrody Castle** nearby is owned by Lord Patrick Belfast and has been recently opened to the public.

Scuba Diving

Hook Head is popular with divers; the best

spots are out from the little inlet under the lighthouse or from the rocks at the south-west corner of the head. The underwater scenery is pleasant, with lots of little caves, crevasses and gullies. The depths are no more than 15 metres. If it's too rough try Churchtown, about one km back from the point just before the road goes inland by the ruined church. Follow the path west to some gullies and coves. Otherwise try the rocks south of Slade harbour. Tanks can be filled at the Naomh Seosamh Hotel in Fethard and in summer there are often local dive groups here.

Places to Stay

Fethard-on-Sea has most of the area's accommodation, but there are a few places on the west side of the peninsula around Duncannon and Ballyhack.

Camping The *Fethard Camping & Caravan Park* (☎ 051-97123) is at the north end of town while the *Ocean Island Caravan Park* (☎ 051-97202) is about a km farther north. Both charge around IR£5 per tent or caravan and are open Easter to September. The best bet of all is to stock up and head a farther 12 km (seven miles) out to Hook Head where there is lovely camping along the shore. There is a shop and small petrol station about five km (three miles) from the headland for replenishing supplies.

The *Duncannon Caravan & Camping Park* (☎ 051-89193) is open March to November and charges IR£5.50 per tent or IR£4.50 if you are hiking or cycling. You are just as well off camping by the beach, in a field or better still heading for Hook Head.

Hostel The only hostel in the region is the Arthurstown *An Óige Hostel* (☎ 051-89186), one km from Ballyhack on the west side of the peninsula. The hostel has 30 beds and is open March to September inclusive. Bed charges are IR£5.50.

B&Bs In Fethard the *Hotel Naomh Seosamh* (☎ 051-97129) on the main street is popular and good fun at weekends; it costs IR£17 to

IR£19 and has a diving compressor. *Bore a Trae House* (☎ 051-97102), three km from Fethard on the way to the head in Temple-town, is a good B&B costing IR£13.

Beverely House (☎ 051-62158), north of Fethard in Saltmills, costs IR£14. *Weston House* (☎ 051-89241), in Ramsgrange along the Wellington Bridge road from Arthurs-town, costs IR£14 to IR£15.

Places to Eat

Fethard's hotels and pubs are the principal eating spots on the peninsula but nowhere stands out. Restaurants are almost non-existent but on the west side of the peninsula, Ballyhack is home to the *Neptune Bar & Seafood Restaurant* (☎ 051-89284) a terrific little place serving simple but delicious seafood.

Hopetown House in Foulksmills has the *Cellar Restaurant* (☎ 051-63771), with dinner from IR£15 or a midweek special from IR£13.50. The *Moorings Seafood Bar & Restaurant* (☎ 051-89242) in Duncannon has good seafood, with a four-course dinner costing from IR£12, while the *Templar's Inn* in Templetown (☎ 051-97162) also specialises in seafood and has main courses from IR£8 to IR£10. The *King's Bay Inn* (☎ 051-89173) in Arthurstown offers main courses from IR£5 to IR£10.

Getting There & Away

Particularly if you're travelling by bike, it's worth taking the 10-minute crossing between Wexford and Waterford on the Ballyhack to Passage East ferry. For details on fares and times see under Passage East, County Waterford. Bus services are virtually non-existent, although on Mondays and Thursdays a bus on a run from Wexford to Waterford will drop you in Fethard. It leaves Wexford at 2.50 pm.

NEW ROSS

New Ross, 34 km (21 miles) west of Wexford Town, is a sizeable settlement astride the River Barrow. New Ross is not an especially pretty town, with large oil storage tanks and old warehouses looming over the river banks. The east bank is better than the west, with some small, steep, narrow streets and St Mary's Church.

New Ross was the scene of fierce fighting during the 1798 Rising when a group of rebels under Bagenal Harvey tried to take the town. They were repelled by the defending garrison leaving 3000 people dead and much of the town in ruins.

Information
A tourist office (☎ 051-21857) operates from the refurbished grain store building on the quay during July and August. The post office is on Charles St, just off the quay. The John F Kennedy Trust (☎ 051-25239) is based in the same old grain store building on the quay as the tourist office. It has a genealogical database for people wishing to trace their ancestors from the region.

St Mary's Church
St Mary's Church is a roofless ruin on Church Lane and was founded by William and Isabella in the 13th century. Inside is a rough slab with some barely decipherable words, 'Isabel...Laegn' which can be translated roughly as 'Isabel of Leinster'. She died around 1220 and was buried in England so this may be some sort of memorial to her. The key to the church is available from the caretaker across the road.

Places to Eat
Katie Pat's (☎ 051-22404) on the quay is good for cheap sandwiches and lunches from IR£2.50 for a hamburger. It also has a restaurant upstairs and serves dinner from 5 pm to 9 pm, with main courses in the IR£5 to IR£11 range. Across the road from Katie Pat's is *John V's Pub*, which does a good lunch in the bar. It has a restaurant upstairs with a good selection of seafood. *Sweeney's Deli* (☎ 051-21963) just up the hill from the bridge serves sandwiches and snacks during the day and also has a restaurant upstairs with good seafood and dinner from IR£15. For a more formal meal try the hotel restaurants or the *Galley Cruising Restaurant* (☎ 051-21723) on the quay.

Getting There & Away
Bus Éireann (☎ 053-22522) have a twice-daily service to Dublin from outside the Mariners Bar, on the quay. They also have services to Wexford, Waterford and the odd bus down towards Hook Head.

Getting Around
You can hire bikes from Edward Prendergast (☎ 051-21600) at Abbey House, The Quay. Boland's Car Rental (☎ 051-21213) are along the Waterford road while Budget Rent-a-Car (☎ 051-21550) are based at Shannon Motors. Taxis are available from Paddy Donovan (☎ 051-21937) or Jack Dunphy (☎ 051-21341). Dinghies are available from New Ross Boating Club on the opposite bank from the Galley Restaurant mooring.

AROUND NEW ROSS
Five km (three miles) south of New Ross, **Dunganstown** was the birthplace of Patrick Kennedy, grandfather of John F Kennedy. Patrick left Ireland for the USA in 1858 and JFK visited the town during his presidency. The original Kennedy house is no longer there but there is a small cottage belonging to the Ryan family who are direct descendants, and a small plaque marks the spot.

A couple of km to the south, the **John F Kennedy Park & Arboretum** (☎ 051-88171) covers 252 hectares of woodlands and gardens with more than 4500 species of trees and shrubs. The park was opened in 1968 in memory of the late US president, and was funded by some prominent Irish-Americans. There are a couple of km of pleasant shaded walks with rest spots.

Slieve Coillte hill, opposite the park entrance, offers a splendid view of the surrounding countryside and out to the Saltee Islands. You can drive or walk to the top and it's not necessary to pay the IR£1 park entry fee just to go up the hill. A map of the park costs 50p.

GOREY
The small market town of Gorey is 20 km (12 miles) south of Arklow, on the main Dublin to Wexford road and below the foot-

hills of the Wicklow Mountains. There is a street market on Saturdays.

During the 1798 Rising, Gorey was attacked by a group of rebels trying to reach the coast road to Dublin. They camped on Gorey Hill just south-west of the town and there is a small memorial to their efforts at one end of Main St. There is a good ramble out to Tara Hill seven km (four miles) north-east of town. The Church of Ireland parish church has some fine stained glass by Michael Healy from around 1904.

The tourist office (☎ 055-21248) on Lower Main St is open July to August only, 10 am to 6 pm Monday to Saturday.

COURTOWN

Seven km (four miles) south-east of Gorey along the L31 is the small seaside resort of Courtown at the mouth of the River Ounavarra. The beach to the north of the village is popular with Irish holidaymakers and there are also the usual amusements, takeaways and seaside guesthouses. The Bayview Hotel dominates the village beachfront. This area has the lowest rainfall in Ireland.

Places to Stay
Camping *Courtown Caravan & Camping Park* (☎ 055-25280) is well signposted just inland from Courtown. They charge IR£8 per tent or IR£5.50 if you are hiking or cycling, and have excellent facilities. Otherwise you could find a quiet spot among the dunes and pitch your tent for free.

B&Bs *Riverchapel House* (☎ 055-25120), one km from the harbour, is open March to October and costs IR£12. *Seamount House* (☎ 055-25128) is in the village and costs for IR£18/30 for singles/doubles.

Places to Eat
Good restaurants include the *Bosun's Chair* in Ardmine, two km south of Courtown along the coast (☎ 055-25198) and the *Cowhouse Bistro* (☎ 055-25219) at Tomsilla Farm, outside of town on the main road to Gorey.

FERNS
Ferns is 17 km (11 miles) south-west of Gorey. Most traffic whizzes on south, bound for Wexford and Rosslare Harbour, but this sleepy little village was for several hundred years, up to the 13th century, the administrative capital of Leinster and also an important diocese in the province. It was the base for the MacMurroughs, the kings of Leinster, and in particular for Dermot MacMurrough, the king who brought the Normans to Ireland and died here in 1171.

Ferns Castle
The remains of the castle at the north-west end of the village are thought to be on the site of Dermot MacMurrough's previous castle and they date from around 1220 AD. There are a couple of intact walls, a surviving part of the moat, and one complete tower which can be climbed with a superb view from the top. To the left of the door at the top is a murder hole through which oil or arrows could be dropped on attackers below. The castle was largely destroyed and most of the population of the town put to death in 1649 by Parliamentarians under Sir Charles Coote.

Other Sights
Other antiquities include fragments of the 13th-century **Cathedral of St Aidan** (now part of the modern Church of Ireland cathedral) with a graveyard and the remains of a high cross said to mark the grave of Dermot MacMurrough. Father Redmond, who is buried in the graveyard, is said to have saved the life of a young student in France, one Napoleon Bonaparte. Outside the graveyard is **St Moling's Well**, and there are also some remains of an **Augustinian monastery**, founded by Dermot MacMurrough in the 1150s.

Places to Stay
B&B The friendly *Clone House* (☎ 054-66113) is a 350-year-old farmhouse three km (two miles) from Ferns on the Enniscorthy road, with four bedrooms, three with own bathroom, for IR£13 to IR£15.

Country House North-west of Ferns near Bunclody, the lovely 18th-century *Clohamon House* (☎ 054-77253) has an 80-hectare estate including a working farm, and they have salmon fishing on a private stretch of the River Slaney. B&B is expensive at IR£35 to IR£40 and dinner is IR£20. Open March to November, the house has five rooms, with massive four-poster beds; reservations are essential. It has an internationally renowned Connemara pony stud farm.

Places to Eat
The *Celtic Arms* (☎ 054-66490) at the south end of Main St has lunches or dinner, and there is a takeaway at the Dublin end of the town.

Getting There & Away
Bus Éireann buses on the main Dublin to Wexford route stop in Ferns. There are at least five daily buses in both directions; contact Wexford bus station (☎ 053-22522) for details.

MT LEINSTER
Bunclody, on the border with County Carlow 16 km (10 miles) to the west of Ferns, is a good base from which to climb Mt Leinster, at 796 metres (2610 feet) the highest mountain in the Blackstairs. If you want to drive to the top, take the Borris road out of Ferns for eight km, turn left at the sign for the Mt Leinster Scenic Rd, and continue to the radio mast at the top. The last few km are on narrow, exposed roads with steep fall-offs, so drive slowly and watch out for sheep. Mt Leinster also has one of the best locations for hang-gliding in the country.

ENNISCORTHY
Enniscorthy is an attractive hilly town on the steep banks of the River Slaney in the heart of County Wexford, 20 km (12 miles) north-west of Wexford Town. It was the site of some of the fiercest fighting of the 1798 Rising and has a good local museum.

During the first and second weeks in July, Enniscorthy holds its annual Strawberry Fair. Near the town you can find numerous potteries including Hillview and Carley's Bridge potteries, both on the road to New Ross; Badger's Hill Pottery, farther along the same road; and Kiltrea Bridge Pottery, north-west of the town.

Information
The tourist office (☎ 054-34699/35926) in the town centre is open July and August only. Brochures and books can be found in the Wexford County Museum when the office is closed. The Book Shop is on Court St the main post office is at the bottom of Castle Hill on Abbey Square. Hilltop Cleaners are on Duffry Hill while Four Hour Service Dry Cleaners is in Rafter Mall.

Enniscorthy Castle & Wexford County Museum
Enniscorthy's impressive Norman castle dates from 1205 and was a private residence until 1951. It is the town's major attraction: a fine stout building with drum towers at the three corners. The poet Edmund Spenser lived here for a time and it is said locally that he was given the castle as a present by Queen Elizabeth I for the many flattering things he said about her in his great work *The Faerie Queene*.

It was the site of a fierce battle in 1649, and during the 1798 Rising the rebels took control of the town and used the castle as a prison. Today it houses the Wexford County Museum (☎ 054-35926) which includes

---

The 1798 Rising
In the Market Square there is a memorial by Oliver Sheppard to commemorate Father John Murphy and his band of rebels who stormed the town in May 1798. One faction marched under the banner MWS, for 'Murder Without Sin'. It was on Vinegar Hill, to the east of the town, that the last major battle of the rising took place, when on 9 June a force of 20,000 troops led by generals Lake and Johnson almost completely surrounded the rebels, who held out against huge odds for 30 days. The windmill on the hill, now ruined, was the rebel command post. ■

many different displays covering particularly the 1798 and 1916 risings as well as a collection of pottery, military memorabilia and policemen's hats and patches from around the world.

The castle and museum are open weekdays in summer from 10 am to 6 pm (closed for lunch) and from 2 to 6 pm on Sundays. In winter it just opens 2 to 6 pm. Admission is IR£1.50.

Activities
Enniscorthy has a reasonable 18-hole golf course; for more information contact Enniscorthy Golf Club (☎ 054-33191). Contact Boro Hill Equestrian Centre (☎ 054-44117) for horse riding.

Places to Stay
B&Bs *Murphy's* (☎ 054-33522) at 9 Main St costs around IR£14. *Woodville House* (☎ 054-47810), with comfortable rooms for IR£13 to IR£14, is six km (four miles) south on the Ballyhogue road, a minor road along the west side of the River Slaney. It is open from April to October.

In Ballycarney, *Oakville House* (☎ 054-88626) overlooks the Slaney Valley. The gardens are particularly nice, and B&B is IR£16 single or IR£24 to IR£26 double. The house is nine km (six miles) away signposted off the N80 road to Bunclody.

Hotels The comfortable *Murphy Flood's Hotel* (☎ 054-33413) is conveniently located on Main St just up from Market Square. B&B costs from IR£25 to IR£27.

Country House *Ballinkeele House* (☎ 053-38105) is a lovely old mansion dating from 1840 on a 160-hectare farm, 10 km southeast from Enniscorthy in Ballymurn. They have four elegant rooms for IR£26 to IR£28 B&B. They are open April to November and dinner is IR£15.

Places to Eat
There is a variety of small restaurants and bistros in the low and moderate price ranges. The *Antique Tavern* on Slaney St has good

and affordable lunches. The *Concord* on Rafter St and *Waffle's Bistro* on Castle Hill have lunches under IR£5. The *Coffee Shop* is on Court St. The *Royal Palace* Chinese restaurant (☎ 054-34000) is at 24 Rafter St.

Murphy Flood's Hotel also has a restaurant with dinner at around IR£15 a head, or you could try the *Tavern* in Templeshannon, on the east bank of the river.

Getting There & Away
Train Enniscorthy is on the Dublin to Rosslare Harbour line with three trains daily, two on Sundays in each direction. The station (☎ 054-33488) is on the east bank of the river

Bus The Bus Éireann bus stop is on the riverfront just down from the Antique Tavern, and is serviced by four daily buses (three on Sundays) to Dublin, as well as services to Rosslare Harbour and Wexford Town.

County Waterford

Wedged in the south-east corner of Ireland, County Waterford combines low farmland and sandy coastlines rather like those of Wexford with the more rugged landscape typical of much of County Cork.

WATERFORD CITY
Like Kilkenny, Waterford has a medieval feel, with narrow alleyways leading off many of the larger streets. Reginald's Tower houses the city museum and marks the Viking heart of the city. The area around the tower is one of the most attractive in the city, and later Georgian times also left a legacy of fine houses and commercial buildings, particularly around the Mall, George St and O'Connell St.

Waterford, however, is first and foremost a commercial city and port. The estuary is deep enough to allow large modern ships right up to the city's quays. The port has been

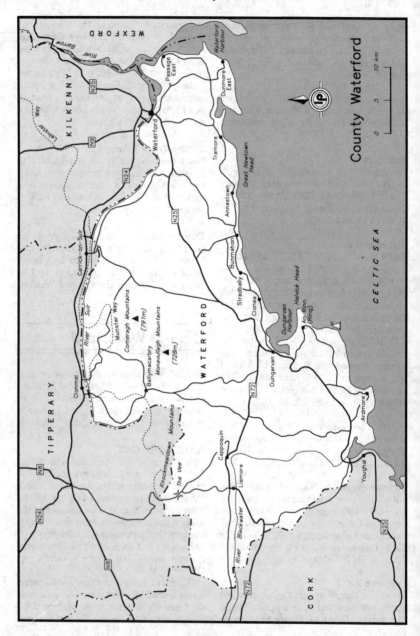

County Waterford

used since earliest times and is still one of the busiest in Ireland.

Waterford crystal is made here: the hand-blown cut glass is one of Ireland's most famous exports.

History

Waterford City's origins go back to the 8th century, when a group of Vikings settled at a convenient riverside site called Port Lairge which they renamed Vadrafjord. Recent archaeological excavations suggest a date of 915 AD for the city's foundation. The deep inlet with access upriver to the heart of south-east Ireland was an ideal highway for their sturdy longships. The Norse established an independent fortified city which became a booming trading post.

Waterford's strategic importance ensured that its fortunes were closely linked to those of the country as a whole (see the History section in Facts about the Country). In 1170 an Irish/Viking army sallied forth from the city to do battle with the newly arrived Anglo-Normans and was roundly defeated: 70 prominent citizens were thrown off Baginbun Head to their deaths. Later that year the city was besieged by Strongbow, who overcame a desperate defence.

Henry II of England turned up in Waterford in October 1171, rather concerned about Strongbow's new assertiveness. He declared the place a royal city, which it remained for almost 500 years.

In 1210 King John extended the original Viking city walls and Waterford became the most powerful city in Ireland, and an important trading centre. In the 15th century, Waterford City twice resisted the forces of two pretenders to the English crown, Lambert Simnel and Perkin Warbeck. This earned it the motto from a grateful Henry VII, *Urbs intacta manet Waterfordia*, the 'unconquered city'.

In 1649 the town defied Cromwell for eight days before he withdrew. In 1650, Cromwell's forces returned and the city held out for over two months, finally surrendering to his son-in-law Ireton on honourable terms. Although the city thus escaped the custom-ary slaughter, a great deal of damage was done and the city's population subsequently declined as Catholics were either exiled to the west of the country, 'to Hell or to Connaught', or shipped as slaves to the Caribbean.

Orientation

Waterford lies on the tidal reach of the River Suir 16 km (10 miles) inland. The main shopping street runs directly back from the River Suir, beginning as Barronstrand St and changing names as it runs south to become Broad St, Michael St and John St before intersecting with Parnell St, which runs north-east back up to the river, becoming the Mall on the way. Most of the sights and shopping areas lie within this triangle.

There are several attractive tiny malls like George's Court and Broad St Mall which you could easily walk straight past. Reginald's Tower at the top of the Mall and the Clocktower at the top of Barronstrand St are good landmarks. The railway station is across the river.

Information

The friendly tourist office (☎ 051-75788) is near the river at 41 Merchant's Quay. It's open 9 am to 7 pm weekdays in the high season and for a shorter time at the weekends, and 9 am to 5.15 pm from November to March.

There are a couple of good bookshops: the Book Centre on Michael St and the Gladstone Bookshop on Gladstone St. *Selected Walks through Old Waterford* is a handy walking-tour guide to the city, available in bookshops or at Reginald's Tower.

The Washed Ashore Laundrette is right in the centre at 36 Merchant's Quay and D's Wash Away is farther out at 109 Barrack St. The post office is on Parade Quay upriver from Reginald's Tower.

City Walls

Waterford's city walls were originally built by the Vikings around 1000 AD, and then extended by King John two centuries later. After those of Derry, these are the best sur-

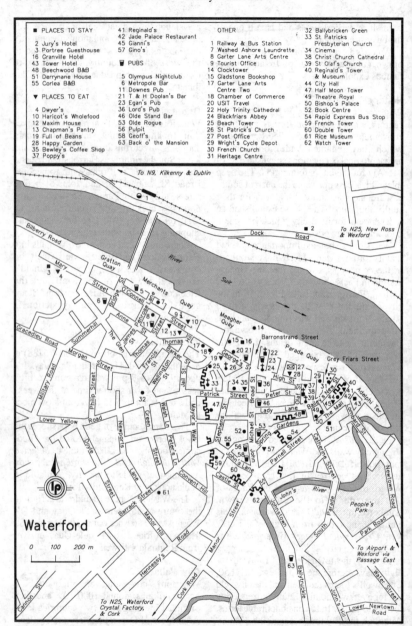

■ PLACES TO STAY
2 Jury's Hotel
3 Portree Guesthouse
16 Granville Hotel
43 Tower Hotel
48 Beechwood B&B
51 Derrynane House
55 Corlea B&B

▼ PLACES TO EAT
4 Dwyer's
10 Haricot's Wholefood
12 Maxim House
13 Chapman's Pantry
19 Full of Beans
28 Happy Garden
35 Bewley's Coffee Shop
37 Poppy's

41 Reginald's
42 Jade Palace Restaurant
45 Gianni's
57 Gino's

♥ PUBS
5 Olympus Nightclub
6 Metropole Bar
11 Downes Pub
21 T & H Doolan's Bar
23 Egan's Pub
36 Lord's Pub
46 Olde Stand Bar
53 Olde Rogue
56 Pulpit
58 Geoff's
63 Back o' the Mansion

OTHER
1 Railway & Bus Station
7 Washed Ashore Laundrette
8 Garter Lane Arts Centre
9 Tourist Office
14 Clocktower
15 Gladstone Bookshop
17 Garter Lane Arts
Centre Two
18 Chamber of Commerce
20 USIT Travel
22 Holy Trinity Cathedral
24 Blackfriars Abbey
25 Beach Tower
26 St Patrick's Church
27 Post Office
29 Wright's Cycle Depot
30 French Church
31 Heritage Centre

32 Ballybricken Green
33 St Patricks
Presbyterian Church
34 Cinema
38 Christ Church Cathedral
39 St Olaf's Church
40 Reginald's Tower
& Museum
44 City Hall
47 Half Moon Tower
49 Theatre Royal
50 Bishop's Palace
52 Book Centre
54 Rapid Express Bus Stop
59 French Tower
60 Double Tower
61 Rice Museum
62 Watch Tower

Waterford

0   100   200 m

viving city walls in Ireland. Near the Theatre Royal in the Palace Garden are some remnants which stretch out near the houses in Spring Garden Alley. A number of towers also remain, including one on Patrick St, another near Railway Square (the Watch Tower), the French Tower at one end of Castle St and Reginald's Tower on the Mall.

Reginald's Tower

The most handsome and historically interesting remnant of the city walls is Reginald's Tower, which was built by the Normans in the 12th century. It stands on the site of the original wooden tower built by the Viking Reginald the Dane in 1003 AD and looks rather like a great stone barrel. The tower is strategically situated by the river and was the key fortification in the city walls. The original wooden Viking tower was the last stronghold to fall when the Normans overcame the Vikings. The present tower is 25 metres high (78 feet) and the walls three to four metres thick.

Within days of the Norman takeover in 1170, the victor, Strongbow, cemented his military success with a diplomatic marriage to Dermot MacMurrough's daughter Aoife – in the upper room of the tower, according to legend. In fact, the wedding took place in Christ Church Cathedral and the feast was held in the tower. There is a fine painting of the wedding in the National Art Gallery in Dublin. Many of Waterford's English royal visitors stayed here in this 'safe house', including Richard II, Henry II and James II, who took a last look at Ireland from the tower before departing to exile in France.

Over the years the tower has been many things, including a mint, an ammunition depot and a police station. It now houses the Waterford Civic Museum (☎ 051-71227) which is open Monday to Saturday. The entrance fee is 75p or IR£1 for a ticket that includes entrance to the heritage centre.

The museum contains an impressive collection of city charters, granting all sorts of honours and rights to the place. There is a brass plaque known as the Nail which once stood in Waterford's Customs House and was the site for payments to be made, the origin of the term 'cash on the nail'.

There are also some artefacts connected to one of Waterford's most famous sons, Thomas Francis Meagher (1823-67). Born in the Granville Hotel, this Young Ireland leader was captured in Derrynane House (now a B&B) for his part in the 1848 Rising and was shipped to a penal colony in Australia. From there he escaped to America where he was the captain of the 'Fighting 69th' Irish Brigade in Fort Sumter and Fredricksburg in the American Civil War. Meagher later became Governor of Montana and died in 1867 while spending the night on a Missouri paddle steamer. He went for a walk on deck, tripped on a coil of rope and fell overboard. His body was never recovered.

The roof of Reginald's Tower is closed off and in any case only affords a view north onto the docks. The steps are of varying heights to hinder a quick ascent by attackers. Right behind the tower is Reginald's restaurant and pub which incorporates a section of the old city wall inside the building. The two arches in this wall were sallyports, from which boats could 'sally forth' on to the inlet which used to flow right by the wall.

The Mall

The Mall is a spacious 18th-century street running back from the riverside. It was built on reclaimed land which until 1735 was a tidal inlet running alongside the city wall. The **City Hall** was built in 1788 by local architect John Roberts and a remarkable Waterford-glass chandelier hangs in the council's meeting room. There is a replica of this in Philadelphia's Independence Hall in the USA. The hall was completely renovated in 1992 and there is a fine Waterford coat of arms out front. The **Theatre Royal** nearby is the finest intact 18th-century theatre in the country.

Beyond the City Hall is the **Bishop's Palace**, begun in 1741 and for which a stretch of city wall had to be demolished. One of the finest townhouses in Ireland, it was designed by Richard Castle or Cassels who was also responsible for Powerscourt House, Westport House and Dublin's Leinster House and Rotunda Hospital. It is now used as the city engineering offices.

As the Mall runs south-west away from the river, the name changes to Parnell St and then Manor St where it is flanked by two good stretches of Anglo-Norman wall. On the east side of the road is **Watch Tower** while Castle St runs west by **Double Tower** and **French Tower**.

Christ Church Cathedral
Behind the City Hall is Christ Church Cathedral in Cathedral Square. It was designed by John Roberts and building began between 1770 and 1773 and went on for 20 years.

A Viking church was first built on the site around 1050, and was enlarged, extended and rebuilt numerous times in the following centuries. It suffered at the hands of Cromwell's troops and was eventually demolished to make way for the present building. During demolition, a remarkable collection of 15th-century Italian priest vestments were uncovered, which are now on display in the Heritage Centre.

The tomb of James Rice, who died in 1469, is well worth a look. It was moved here from a chapel which Rice founded in the earlier Viking church. His body is depicted in a state of decay with worms and frogs crawling out of it, and his right hand has been broken off at the wrist. Rice was Lord Mayor of Waterford on seven occasions.

The building also houses some John Wesley bibles. The cathedral is Church of Ireland and closes at 4 pm.

With the Georgian corporation offices and engineering offices nearby tastefully restored, Cathedral Square provides a pleasant, quiet area in which to sit and relax.

The French Church
The extensive ruins of the French Church, also known as 'Grey Friars' are on Grey Friars St. The church was built in 1240 by Franciscan monks and later Henry III laid on honours and riches. The building was used as a hospital after the 16th century and the suppression of the monasteries by Henry VIII. One of the hospital's last leading doctors was T F Meagher's father, Thomas Meagher Senior, Mayor of Waterford.

The name of the church comes from the French Huguenot refugees who used it in the 17th and 18th centuries, after which it fell into ruins. Among the memorial stones inside is one to the architect John Roberts. You can pick up the key to the church from across the road.

Heritage Centre
Next to the ruins of the French Church on Grey Friars St is the small heritage centre (☎ 051-71277) with displays of local Viking artefacts, including jewellery, pottery and leatherwork. It also houses the vestments found during the building of Christ Church Cathedral. Entry is 75p or IR£1 including entrance to Reginald's Tower. It is open from April to October inclusive between 10 am and 8 pm on Mondays to Fridays and between 10 am and 5 pm on Saturdays. From November to March admission can be gained by contacting the City Hall (☎ 051-73501). Waterford Corporation have produced an excellent leaflet covering the various digs that have taken place in the city.

Other Buildings
The ruins of the Dominican **Blackfriars Abbey** on Arundel Square date from 1226 and possess an intact square tower. The monks were disbanded in 1541.

Nearby on Barronstrand St is the Catholic **Holy Trinity Cathedral**, built between 1792 and 1796 by John Roberts who also designed the Protestant Christ Church Cathedral and was himself a Protestant. The exterior is – perhaps deliberately – plain but the interior is sumptuous with a fine carved pulpit, painted pillars with Corinthian capitals and Waterford-crystal chandeliers. It's a surprising contrast to the austere interior of Roberts' Christ Church Cathedral.

Edmund Ignatius Rice, founder of the Christian Brothers, established his first school at Mt Sion in Waterford. On Barrack St there's a **Rice Museum** at the school site.

Round Tower, Glendalough, County Wicklow (JM)

Top: Pub, County Wexford (TW)
Left: Hook Lighthouse, County Wexford (JM)
Right: Root Crusher, County Wexford (JM)

At **Ballybricken Green** bull baiting took place from the 15th to 18th century. Nearby is the old city wall's **Half Moon Tower** by Patrick St. **St Patrick's Church** on Jenkins' Lane is an 18th-century Catholic chapel which managed to survive the savage suppression of Catholicism at that time. At the top of Jenkins' Lane is the **Beach Tower**, another remnant of the old city wall.

On Olaf St, **St Olaf's Hall** is named after a favourite Viking saint and was founded by the Norse king, Sitric, around 870 AD during Waterford's earliest years. After falling into ruins it was almost totally rebuilt in 1734 and remains much as you see it today.

The **Chamber of Commerce** building on Great George's St was originally built as a town house by John Roberts and has a magnificent staircase.

Waterford Crystal

The first Waterford glass factory was established at the west end of the riverside quays in 1783. This first phase of the business closed in 1851 due to punitive taxes imposed on the raw materials by the English government. It was not revived until 1947 and it took almost five years before production was up and running. Today, highly skilled workers continue the tradition and produce remarkable work that is sold all over the world. The glass is a heavy lead (over 30%) crystal made up of three basic ingredients: red lead, silica sand and potash.

Tours of the Waterford Crystal plant, two km out of town on the Cork road, are free. Officially you're supposed to book in advance (☎ 051-73311) but in practice you can generally just turn up. If you do want to book, then it can be done direct or through the tourist office. The glass blowers and cutters (all men) take about five years to learn their trade. About 80% of the output is exported to the USA.

The full tours take about 40 minutes and operate Monday to Friday for a cost of IR£2. There are about six full tours daily between 10.15 am and 3.15 pm after which you can part with your money in the Crystal Gallery if you so wish. There are also mini-tours every half hour during the day and at weekends in the summer months, from 11 am to 5 pm. Buses run to the factory from the clocktower on the quays.

The last few years have been difficult for the company as demand has been falling while at the same time there has been increased competition from other brands. There have been threats to move production overseas which would be a huge blow to local employment, the skilled workforce and the prestige of the city.

Aeromobilia Museum

Waterford Airport has a small museum (☎ 051-72367) with a collection of aircraft including some exhibits housed inside an old Douglas DC-6. It's open June to August from 10.30 am to 5 pm daily and the rest of the year from 2.30 to 5.30 pm on Sundays.

Walking Tours

Jack Burtchaell (☎ 051-73711) runs guided walking tours from the Granville Hotel twice daily. The cost is IR£3.

Golf

Waterford has an 18-hole golf course; for more information contact Waterford Golf Club (☎ 051-76748). There is another fine 18-hole course beside Waterford Castle (☎ 051-71633).

Cruises

The Galley Cruising Restaurant (☎ 053-21723) operates out of Waterford and New Ross during June, July and August. There is a two-hour cruise including afternoon tea which leaves from Meagher Quay at 3 pm and costs IR£5.

Alternatively Viking Cruises (☎ 051-72800) operate two-hour trips down to the Passage East/Ballyhack area for IR£5. They have sailings three times daily at 1.30 pm, 4 pm and 8 pm, April to September. Departure is just across from Reginald's Tower and bookings can also be made through the tourist office.

Festivals

Waterford has a Light Opera Festival in September/October. Although not as famous as Wexford's Opera Festival, it has cheaper and more easily accessible shows. Booking is still advisable. Much of the city takes part with pub singing competitions and late bar extensions. Contact the Theatre Royal, The Mall, Waterford (☎ 051-74402) or Maurice Cummins, Secretary, Waterford Opera Festival (☎ 051-32001).

Places to Stay

Camping The nearest camp sites are at Tramore.

Hostels There is a private hostel in Waterford, but women who have stayed there have reported problems.

B&Bs *Beechwood* (☎ 051-76677) is central at 7 Cathedral Square and has three rooms at IR£12 per person. The friendly *Portree Guesthouse* (☎ 051-74574) on Mary St costs IR£11 to IR£14. Another reasonable place is *Rice House* (☎ 051-71606) at 35 Barrack St, costing IR£13 to IR£16. The Mall and its extension Parnell St are good places to look and you could try *Derrynane House* (☎ 051-75179) at 19 The Mall, with rooms at IR£13. A good new place is *Corlea* (☎ 051-75764) at 2 New St, which does B&B for IR£12 to IR£13.

Shalom (☎ 051-72681) is four km (2.5 miles) along the Cork road and costs IR£13 or IR£14 with own bathroom. *Knockboy House* (☎ 051-73484) is almost five km (three miles) from Waterford on the Dunmore East road, set back from the road, near the River Suir; you can recognise it by the glass conservatory. They charge IR£13 or IR£15 with own bathroom. In Cheekpoint, a small fishing village five km (three miles) east of the city, is the *Three Rivers Guesthouse* (☎ 051-82520) overlooking the estuary. Rooms have their own bathrooms and cost from IR£17 to IR£20.

Hotels *Granville Hotel* (☎ 051-55111) is a lovely old building and top-class hotel on Meagher Quay in the city. B&B runs from IR£36.50 to IR£46.50. For a bedside view of Reginald's Tower there is the *Tower Hotel & Leisure Centre* (☎ 051-75801) at the north end of the Mall, which has an indoor pool, jacuzzi, sauna and gymnasium. B&B in good hotel rooms is IR£38 to IR£48.

On the other side of the river there's *Jury's Hotel* (☎ 051-32111), part of the well-known chain. They have much the same facilities and charge IR£50 for B&B.

If you hanker for luxury, try the beautiful *Waterford Castle* (☎ 051-78203) on an island three km downstream of the city. It has splendid old-world rooms and restaurants. B&B runs from IR£51 to IR£100.

Country Houses It's well worth pushing on to *Blenheim House* (☎ 051-74115), three km (two miles) out on the Passage East road, signposted to the left. This is a stately Georgian house dating from 1763, in two hectares of garden. It only costs IR£15 for B&B with own bathroom.

Another delightful place is *Prendiville's Guesthouse & Restaurant* (☎ 051-78851) in a restored stone lodge one km out on the Cork road. B&B runs from IR£18 to IR£22.

Places to Eat

Cafés & Snacks *Chapman's Pantry* (☎ 051-74938) is a terrific little coffee shop cum restaurant behind the deli of the same name on Meagher Quay next to the Granville Hotel. It's open all day from 8 am to 6 pm and the deli downstairs is good too. At 11 O'Connell St, *Haricot's Wholefood* has main courses like vegetable bake from IR£3.75 to IR£5. Their brown-bread ice cream is a must. They're open Monday to Friday from 10 am to 8 pm, Saturday to 5.45 pm. *Full of Beans* is a wholefood shop at 9 Georges Court.

Bewley's, the coffee-house chain, has an outlet here in the Broad St mall. There is a good snack place in the *Garter Lane Arts Centre* (☎ 051-55038) at 50 O'Connell St.

Pub Food *T & H Doolan* on Great George's St is good for lunches as is *Egan's* on Barronstrand St. At 5 Michael St, the *Olde*

Stand (☎ 051-79488) is a Victorian pub serving good bar food downstairs and a wide range of seafood and steaks upstairs.

McAlpin's Suir Inn (☎ 051-828182), in Cheekpoint five km from Waterford, is a well-known place and the crowds at weekends are testament to the quality of their seafood. They do food in the evenings only from around 6.30 to 9.30 pm, Tuesday to Saturday.

Restaurants Once again the Chinese and the Italians dominate the foreign invasion. *Gino's* on Applemarket just off Michael St and *Gianni's* on the Mall do good pizzas. For Chinese meals and takeaways, there is *Maxim House* (☎ 051-75820) on O'Connell St or the *Happy Garden* on Arundel Square. For upmarket Chinese the *Jade Palace* (☎ 051-55611) on the Mall is said to be one of the best (and most expensive) Chinese restaurants in Ireland.

The middle-of-the-road *Reginald's* bar and restaurant (☎ 051-55087) is behind Reginald's Tower. The popular *Strongbow's* at 124 Parade Quaydoes chicken, steak and fish. *Poppy's* (☎ 051-70008) at 18 High St is bright and cheerful with vegetarian specials.

One of the best, if not the best place in town is *Dwyer's* (☎ 051-77478) at 5 Mary St in an old barracks near the bridge. The food is sophisticated but comes in generous helpings. They have a good special dinner rate of IR£12 between 6 and 7.30 pm; later on a full dinner is in the IR£18 range. The other good place in town is *Prendiville's Restaurant* (☎ 051-78851) in a Gothic lodge out on the main Cork road. The excellent food and dinner will cost IR£18 or more.

If you are feeling ostentatious you could make your way the five km (three miles) east to Ballinakill and *Waterford Castle* (☎ 051-78203) a top-class castle hotel. The restaurant here is very good, and dinner will cost at least IR£30 a head.

Entertainment

Pubs There are lots of pubs, many featuring music. The venerable *T & H Doolan* on Great George's St incorporates a remnant of the 1000-year-old city wall. Sinead O'Connor played here in the early days of her career. A good place for local rock bands is the *Back o' the Mansion* club on the top of John St.

Geoff's and the *Pulpit*, located where John St becomes Michael St, both attract a young and lively drinking crowd. The Pulpit has a nightclub upstairs, the *Preacher's*. Across the road from those two is the *Olde Rogue* while back towards the river is *Lord's*, just off Broad St. *Egan's*, on Barronstrand St, has the odd karaoke night and a fully-fledged nightclub upstairs called *Snags*. Other popular pubs include the *Metropole* on the corner of Bridge and Mary Sts with the Metroland Ballroom next to it. *Reginald's* near the tower has a nightclub and occasional jazz sessions. There is also the *Olympus* nightclub in the Tower Bar. The main student bar in town is *Downes* pub on Thomas St off O'Connell St.

Cinema & Arts Centres The five-screen cinema is just off Broad St on Patrick St. The *Garter Lane* (☎ 051-55038) and *Garter Lane Two* arts centres are both on O'Connell St and have craft fairs, exhibitions, poetry readings and works from their theatre company, the Red Kettle Theatre Group. They're open Tuesday to Saturday.

Getting There & Away

USIT Travel (☎ 051-72601) are at 36-37 George's St. If you are heading to or from Wexford see Passage East for information on the useful short cut using the ferry service there.

Air Waterford Airport (☎ 051-75589) is six km (four miles) south of the city and has flights to Dublin, Manchester, Stansted and London with Manx Air (☎ 1-800-626627) and Ryanair (☎ 051-75580/75589).

Train From Plunkett Railway Station (☎ 051-73401) on the north side of the river, there are regular train connections to Dublin,

Kilkenny, Limerick, Wexford and Rosslare Harbour.

Bus The Bus Éireann intercity station (☎ 051-73401) is based at Plunkett Railway Station just over the bridge on the north side of the river. There are plenty of buses daily to Dublin, Cork, Limerick and just about everywhere you may want to go. For bus times and fares ring ☎ 051-79000. Rapid Express Club (☎ 051-72149) on Michael St have connections to Dublin and Tramore.

Suirway Bus Company (☎ 051-82209) provides the most comprehensive local service to outlying towns and villages. Most depart from outside the tourist office on Meagher Quay.

Getting Around

The tourist office has desks for Budget (☎ 051-21670) and South East Rent-a-Car (☎ 051-21550). Wright's Cycle Depot (☎ 051-74411) on Henrietta St is a Raleigh Rent-a-Bike outlet. Taxis are operated by BBC Cabs (☎ 051-79080) and there is a taxi rank at Plunkett Station.

PASSAGE EAST

Heading east from Waterford City on the coast road, your first port of call will probably be Passage East, 12 km (eight miles) away, with its little harbour and thatched cottages at the foot of low hills. The Ballyhack to Passage East ferry is a useful short cut between Waterford and Wexford.

Passage East has seen a lot of traffic in its time. Strongbow landed here in 1170 with 1200 men before his march on Waterford City. A year later Henry II arrived with 4000 men, while King James left Ireland from here in 1690 after his defeat at the Battle of the Boyne.

Just south of the village is **Crooke** of Cromwell's phrase 'by hook or by crook'. Near Crooke are the remains of the Geneva Barracks. Built in the 18th century as part of a settlement for Swiss refugees, the buildings were turned into barracks after the plan fell through. It was here that a young rebel of the

1798 Rising came to confess his sins. The priest turned out to be an army officer disguised in a cassock, arresting the lad and subsequently hanging him. The story has been immortalised in the song *Croppy Boy*.

Places to Eat

Chives (☎ 051-82646) is a handy little seafood restaurant in Passage East with dinner served from 7 to 10 pm. Main courses are around IR£6.50.

Getting There & Away

If you are heading to or from Wexford, there is a car ferry across the estuary from Passage East to Ballyhack in County Wexford. This can save you an hour's drive via New Ross to the north. The ferry company (☎ 051-82488) is on Barrack St in Passage East and the ferry operates a continuous service from 7.20 am to 10 pm from April to September and 7.20 am to 8 pm the rest of the year. On Sundays first sailings are at 9.30 am. Crossing time is 10 minutes and the cost for a car is IR£3.50 one way, IR£5.50 return, for pedestrians 80p one way and IR£1 return, or cyclists IR£1 one way and IR£1.50 return. The Suirway bus company (☎ 051-82209) has two buses daily from Waterford to Passage East.

DUNMORE EAST

Dunmore East is a busy little fishing village on a coastline of low red sandstone cliffs and discreet coves. The most popular beaches are Counsellor's Beach, facing south among the cliffs, and Lawlor's Beach, right in the village. Dunmore East has plenty of neat thatched cottages, many of them summer homes. The attractive stone harbour is overlooked by the unusual Doric lighthouse built in 1823, and is thronged with boats during the summer when there is a nightly fish market. There is a good view of Hook Head lighthouse across the water in Wexford. The noisy birds nesting in the cliffs above the harbour are kittiwakes. There's a good sailing club.

Places to Stay

Camping *Dunmore East Caravan & Camping Park* (☎ 051-83174) is just south of the village and open from Easter until the end of September. They have good facilities and charge IR£5 per tent.

B&Bs *Church Villa* (☎ 051-83390) is one of a row of old cottages in the town opposite the Protestant Church and near the Ship Restaurant. Its cosy rooms, most with showers, cost IR£13. *Dunmore Lodge* (☎ 051-83454) is an old country lodge within a few minutes' walk of the village. It costs IR£15 and is open March to November.

Foxmount Farm (☎ 051-74308) is a 17th-century country house on its own farm with good rooms at IR£19/30 for singles/doubles. Dinner is IR£12, served at 7 pm. It's open March to November. The house is six km (three miles) from Dunmore East.

Hotels The *Candlelight Inn* (☎ 051-83215) is a hotel and restaurant overlooking the estuary. It costs from IR£25 to IR£30 with bathroom.

The *Haven Hotel* (☎ 051-83150) is a Victorian mansion in extensive grounds overlooking the sea. B&B runs from IR£30 to IR£35. The *Ocean Hotel* (☎ 051-83136) in town runs from IR£20 to IR£30.

Places to Eat

The *Candlelight Inn* has a good restaurant, with dinners from around IR£14. The *Ship Inn & Restaurant* (☎ 051-83144) is on a corner overlooking Dunmore Bay. The food, both in the bar and restaurant, is good, particularly the seafood, and there are vegetarian options. It's open daily during the summer season for lunch from 12.30 pm and for dinner from 7 to 10 pm.

The *Strand Inn* (☎ 051-83174) is near the harbour and the food can be imaginative, with vegetarian choices. A full dinner will cost you around IR£14, but the bar food is more than adequate. They are open for lunch between 12.30 and 2.30 pm and for dinner from 7 to 10 pm.

For regular pub food try any of the hotels or the *Anchor Bar* which is also worth trying for music.

Getting There & Away

There are four daily buses in summer and three in winter between Waterford city tourist office and Dunmore East. Contact the Suirway bus company (☎ 051-82209) for details.

TRAMORE

Tramore is 10 km (seven miles) south of Waterford and the busiest of Waterford's seaside resorts. An enormous five-km (three-mile) beach is backed with 30-metre-high dunes at the east end.

Tramore is a fairly tacky resort, with amusements, a boating lake, bumper cars and lines of fast-food outlets down by the promenade. There are regular race meetings during the summer with the principal gathering in mid-August.

Great Newtown Head is plainly visible to the south-west with its standing pillars and the **Iron Man**, a huge painted iron figure of an 18th-century sailor in white breeches and blue jacket with his arm pointing seaward to warn approaching ships. The pillars and the corresponding pair on Brownstown Head opposite, were erected by Lloyds of London in 1816; 360 lives had been lost in a shipping disaster when a boat mistook Tramore Bay for Waterford Harbour and was wrecked on the shore.

Eight km (five miles) north of Tramore and signposted off the L26 are the two **dolmens** of Knockeen and Gaulstown.

Information

The tourist office (☎ 051-81572) on the square is open June to August, Monday to Saturday, 10 am to 6 pm.

Celtworld

Apart from the beach, Tramore's big visitor attraction is Celtworld, in an ultra-modern hall by the amusement arcade, where visitors are 'brought back through the centuries to the arrival of ancient tribes to Ireland'. The IR£3.95 admission pays for a mildly interesting half-hour audiovisual presentation of battles, heroes, sorcerers and monsters based on the work of Jim Fitzpatrick, Ireland's leading exponent of a colourful Celtic artistic style. An expensive (IR£18,000) facsimile of 'The Book of Kells' is also on display. Celtworld is open 10 am to 11 pm in the summer and to 5 pm at other times.

Golf
There is an 18-hole golf course (☎ 051-86170) on the outskirts of town.

Places to Stay
Camping There are three caravan and camp sites near Tramore. The one with the best facilities is *Newtown Cove Caravan & Camping Site* (☎ 058-81979) on the road to Great Newtown Head and Dungarvan. It's open May to September, and costs IR£7 for a tent or caravan or IR£3 per person for hikers and cyclists. Other sites are *Atlantic View Caravan & Camping* (☎ 051-81610) on the seafront, which charges IR£6, and *Fitzmaurice's Caravan & Camping* (☎ 051-81968), near Atlantic View on the inland side of the road, with similar facilities and charging IR£7.

B&Bs *Oban House* (☎ 051-81537) at the north-east end of town at 1 Eastlands, Pond Rd, overlooks the bay and costs IR£18/26. *Venezia* (☎ 051-81412) is in a cul-de-sac off Church Grove Rd and costs IR£14 with bathroom. *Cliff House* (☎ 051-81497) on Cliff Rd overlooks the bay and costs IR£13.

Mountain View (☎ 051-96107) is in Fennor, seven km (four miles) west of Tramore on the Dungarvan road. It's one of the few thatched cottage B&Bs in the country and costs IR£17/26. It's open April to November.

Getting There & Away
Bus Éireann (☎ 051-73401) has more than 15 buses daily between Waterford City and Tramore.

TRAMORE TO DUNGARVAN
The road between Tramore and Dungarvan,

41 km (26 miles) to the west along the coast, is punctuated with numerous small villages set in tidy coves. The route is surprisingly scenic with plenty of places to stop and enjoy the views. **Annestown**, **Bunmahon** and the picturesque **Stradbally** come in quick succession along a winding road. Eight km (five miles) to the west of Stradbally is the popular Blue Flag beach at **Clonea**, with the recently opened *Clonea Strand Hotel* (☎ 058-42416) and its 10-pin bowling alley and Turkish baths. There is a surfing beach farther west in **Ballinacourty**.

The *Cove Bar* in Stradbally has reasonable pub food or there is *Ye Olde Bank Restaurant* five km (three miles) from Stradbally in Kilmacthomas.

DUNGARVAN
Dungarvan is a small port and market town which grew up in the shelter of an Anglo-Norman castle. Old records suggest that in the 3rd century AD, a tribe called the Decies or Deise settled around here and the surrounding area now bears their name.

Today the fairly modern but nondescript town is the administrative centre for Waterford County and has a lovely setting at the foot of forested hills on the wide bay where the River Colligan meets the sea. Until the river was bridged in the last century the shallow crossing was known as 'Dungarvan's Prospects'; women had to raise their skirts to wade across and the sight was famous among local men.

Abbeyside (the north-east part of town) was the birthplace of Ernest Walton, whose work on nuclear fission won the Nobel Prize for physics in 1951. The town park is named after him.

Dungarvan is 48 km (30 miles) from Waterford City and makes a convenient base from which to explore west Waterford and the Monavullagh, Comeragh and Knockmealdown mountains to the north.

Orientation & Information
The town's central shopping area is centred around the neatly laid out Grattan Square on the south side of the river. Greater

Dungarvan consists of Dungarvan town itself and Abbeyside over the bridge in the north-east part of town.

The tourist office (☎ 058-41741) in the town centre is open from 16 June to 4 September.

Things to See & Do

King John's Castle (1185), a Norman construction by the quays, is not in great condition but is being restored. The **Old Market House** has a small heritage museum (admission free). As you drive out of Dungarvan to the west, you'll pass a **monument** to the greyhound Master McGrath which won the Waterloo Cup three times in the 1860s.

For information on fishing and deep-sea boating trips contact Cormac Walsh (☎ 058-43514). Dungarvan has a nine-hole golf course; contact Dungarvan Golf Club (☎ 058-41605). There are also two 18-hole golf courses, Knocknagranagh (☎ 058-41605) and the West Waterford Golf Club (☎ 058-43216) just outside of town.

Places to Stay

B&Bs The friendly *Abbey House* (☎ 058-41669) on Friarswalk, Abbeyside is near the church and costs IR£13 to IR£15. The *Fáilte Guesthouse* (☎ 058-43216) overlooks the sea from the Youghal road and costs IR£17/30 for singles/doubles with bathroom.

The *Old Rectory* (☎ 058-41394) is just out of town on the Waterford road with rooms, two with own bathroom, at IR£14 per person. Almost eight km (five miles) west of Dungarvan on the N25 Youghal road, *Seaview* (☎ 058-41583) has sweeping views over Dungarvan and the sea and rooms, some with bathroom, cost IR£13 per person, IR£14 with bath.

Nine km (six miles) from Dungarvan on the coastal route to Tramore, *Park House* (☎ 051-93185) in Stradbally is a mid-19th-century farmhouse and rooms (only one with bathroom) are IR£13 per person or IR£14 with bath. Dinner costs around IR£12.

Hotels *Lawlor's Hotel* (☎ 058-41122) on T F Meagher St is just off Grattan Square. B&B is IR£20 to IR£30 with bathroom. The *Park Hotel* (☎ 058-42899), north-west of the town centre and well signposted, has well-equipped rooms at IR£27 to IR£29 B&B. They also have a health and fitness centre.

Places to Eat

Dining possibilities are limited but the *Ormond Café* in Grattan Square does good snacks during the day. *An Bialann* in the square does snacks all day, and *Hayes Hot Bread* on Main St has good coffee, buns and pastries. The *Mill* restaurant and wine bar has good inexpensive pizzas. For pub food *Downey's* on Main St is one of the better places. For a more formal dinner try one of the hotels, especially the *Park* which has a reasonable restaurant. For straightforward Chinese dinners and takeaways try *Jumbo's* on the causeway.

Entertainment

An Gabha is a new pub on Main St which attracts a young crowd. The *Buttery Bar* in Lawlor's Hotel is one of the trendiest places in town. Downey's in Main St and the *Moorings* on the quay have a good atmosphere at weekends. The *Anchor* on the quay has local bands and traditional Irish music. For a genuine Irish-music scene head out to Helvick on the Ring peninsula and the pub *Tigh an Cheoil* or to *Seanchaí*, a few km out on the Cork road.

Getting There & Away

Bus Éireann services run to Dublin, Waterford, Killarney and Cork from the stop on Davitt's Quay.

Getting Around

Murphy's Toys & Cycles (☎ 058-41376) is the Raleigh bike dealer on Main St and has bikes for IR£7 a day or IR£30 a week.

AN RINN (RING)

An Rinn or Ring, 12 km (seven miles) to the south of Dungarvan on Helvick Head, is a gaeltacht – Irish speaking area, with its own special heritage and culture – one of the most famous in Ireland. Many an Irish teenager has studied the language in Ring College (☎ 058-46104) on the Helvick Head road. The school runs ceilís most nights during the summer and there are also evening seisúns (sessions) of traditional music and dance in the bar *Tigh an Cheoil* (☎ 058-46209) in an old cottage in Baile Na nGall on the way to Helvick Head. On the road to Youghal, the *Seanchaí* pub is beside the road in the middle of nowhere and they also have frequent music sessions. *Mooney's* pub (☎ 058-46204) in Ring has excellent sessions every night during the summer.

There is no real town or village out here; the community is spread all over the peninsula. Most of the signposts are in Irish so you're better off just wandering around and not aiming at anywhere in particular except perhaps Ring College and Helvick Harbour.

Aisling B&B (☎ 058-46134) is six km (four miles) from Dungarvan at Gurtnadiha and charges IR£9 for B&B. It is closed from 24 July to 14 August. Failoeán (☎ 058-46127) overlooks the pier at Helvick Head and charges IR£11 for B&B. *Helvick View* (☎ 058-46297) near Helvick Head is the only other B&B around. All households speak Irish and English.

ARDMORE

South of Helvick Head the coast road veers inland and 23 km (14 miles) later brings you back to the sea at Ardmore. A popular seaside resort with a Blue Flag beach, Ardmore has a main street of pretty, pastel-coloured buildings. Unfortunately, an ugly sprawl of caravan parks spoils the coastal view to the east. However, don't let this put you off: the town is a nice little place and the beach is lovely.

It is claimed locally that St Declan set up shop here between 350 and 420 AD, well before St Patrick turned up from Britain to convert the heathens. The name comes from *Ard Mór* or 'great hill'. There is a walk being developed at present which traces an old

pilgrimage way from Ardmore to the Rock of Cashel in Tipperary.

Information

There is a locally run tourist office (☎ 024-94444) just off Main St beside the amusement arcade. It's open May to September, seven days a week.

St Declan's Church & Oratory

Above the town on the site of St Declan's original monastery stand the ruins of St Declan's Church and a fine slender round tower. The 30-metre (97-foot) tower dates from the 12th century, relatively late. Each of its four storeys is marked on the exterior wall by a ring of projecting stones.

The outer west gable wall of the 13th-century church has some stone carvings retrieved from an older 9th-century church and placed here. They show the Archangel Michael weighing souls, the Adoration of the Magi and a clear depiction of the Judgement of Solomon. Inside the church are two Ogham stones.

The little building in the compound is the 8th-century St Declan's Oratory or Beannachán, which predates the tower and cathedral. It was restored in the 18th century and is traditionally said to be the resting place of St Declan. The depression in the floor is due to worshippers removing earth from the grave site – it was supposed to protect from disease.

St Declan's Well

Overlooking the sea, St Declan's Well is beyond the Cliff House Hotel to the south of the town. Pilgrims once washed in this holy well. Beside it are the ruins of the Dysert Church. There's a fine cliff walk leading from the well. At the south end of the beach is **St Declan's Stone**, said to have arrived on the waves from Wales following St Declan. Crawling under it on St Declan's day (24 July) is said to be a cure for rheumatism as well as bringing spiritual benefits.

The ruin on the headland south of the village looks promising, but it's only an 1860s coastguard station.

Places to Stay & Eat

B&Bs *Byron Lodge* (☎ 024-94157) is a 150-year-old house on the edge of town, with rooms at IR£14 to IR£15 and a good dinner if it's available. It's open April to October. To get there find the thatched cottage on the main street in Lismore and turn up the road beside it passing through a crossroads. Byron Lodge is up on your right. *Paddy Mac's* pub on Main St offers good pub snacks and lunches, with dinner on Sunday only. Beside the pub is the small *Beachcombers Restaurant* which serves snacks, soups and spaghetti for IR£4 to IR£5. Across the road is the *Cup & Saucer Restaurant* for middle-of-the-road quiche, jacket potatoes and fish & chips.

Newtown View House (☎ 024-94143) is a guesthouse and restaurant in Grange, about five km inland from Ardmore and signposted off the main Dungarvan to Youghal N25 road. This family farm has rooms with own bathroom for IR£29 for two. The dinners will keep you going for days.

Hotels The *Cliff House* (☎ 024-94106) is a big, white building on the low cliffs overlooking the bay. Rooms cost IR£25 to IR£31. In the village the *Round Tower Hotel* (☎ 024-94494) costs IR£20 B&B.

Getting There & Away

The bus stop is at O'Reilly's pub on Main St. There are three buses daily to Cork, all year round. During July and August there are three daily buses to Dungarvan and two during the rest of the year. All are Bus Éireann services.

NORTH COUNTY WATERFORD

Some of the most scenic parts of County Waterford are in the north of the county around **Ballymacarbry** and into the **Nire Valley** which runs through the heart of the rugged Comeragh Mountains. This area is just below Clonmel in County Tipperary.

While not as rugged as the west of Ireland, the mountain scenery has a beauty of its own. Most of the hills are of red sandstone from the Devonian period, some 370 million years

ago. They form the easternmost extension of a great mass of this rock which underlies most of the scenery of Cork and Kerry.

The lovely wooded valleys and heathery mountains are good for hill walking and pony trekking. Melody's Pony Trekking (☎ 052-36147) in Ballymacarbry have horses for half or full-day outings and are open Easter to October. The Nire Valley area forms part of the Munster Way walking trail from Carrick-on-Suir; for information contact any local tourist office.

Touraneena heritage centre (☎ 058-47353), 15 km (nine miles) from Dungarvan on the R672, has displays of bread and butter-making, home-curing bacon and a working forge showing Irish country life of old. It's open 10 am to 8 pm all year round.

Places to Stay & Eat

Hanora's Country Cottage (☎ 052-36134) in the Nire Valley costs IR£17/26 with own bathroom. Their tearoom cum restaurant does excellent snacks and lunches. From the main Dungarvan to Clonmel road, drive to Ballymacarbry and turn east off the T27 to Nire Church.

Nire Valley Farmhouse (☎ 052-36149) is just north-west of Ballymacarbry and does B&B at IR£12 to IR£14. Farther north on the same road is *Clonanav Farm* (☎ 052-36141), Ballymacarbry, Nire Valley, charging IR£18 for B&B with own bathroom and IR£12 for dinner. They are open from mid-March to mid-October. Anglers are well looked after.

Getting There & Away

There is a single bus service to and from Dungarvan on Tuesdays and to Clonmel on Fridays. Contact Waterford bus station (☎ 051-73401) for details.

WEST COUNTY WATERFORD

The small market town of **Cappoquin** is overlooked by the Knockmealdown Mountains. The River Blackwater takes an abrupt turn southwards near the town and the Blackwater Valley to the west is picturesque. There is excellent coarse and game fishing locally and Glenshelane Park, just outside the town, has some lovely forest walks and picnic spots. Salmon-fishing permits are available from the Toby Jug Guesthouse (☎ 058-54317). The Blackwater Valley is also where traces of the earliest Irish peoples have been found, mesolithic microliths or small stone blades from 9000 years ago.

Cappoquin is 17 km (11 miles) west of Dungarvan and is of little note except for **Mt Melleray Cistercian Abbey** (☎ 058-54404) just to the north of town. The abbey was founded in 1832 by a group of Irish monks who had been expelled from a monastery near Melleray in Brittany, France. A fully functioning monastery, Mt Melleray is open to male and female visitors for quiet reflection or those who just wish to see something of the monks' daily routine. They have a guesthouse and don't charge for a bed, but it would be bad manners not to make a contribution.

From Cappoquin you should not miss the detour up into the Knockmealdowns along the **Vee Scenic Drive** on the Clogheen road. At the summit is the magnificent **Vee Gap** with outstanding views south over Waterford and north over Tipperary. The return drive down to Lismore is almost as good.

Places to Stay
Aglish House (☎ 024-96191) is a beautiful stone farmhouse in Aglish, just south from Cappoquin on the minor road by the River Blackwater, which charges IR£18/30 for singles/doubles and IR£12 for dinner. *Coolhilla* (☎ 058-54054) is in Ballyhane, three km from Cappoquin, open all year round, and costing IR£16/27 with own bathroom.

Getting There & Away
There are two daily buses (one on Sunday) on a route between Waterford, Dungarvan, Cappoquin and Lismore.

LISMORE
Lismore is a small town, beautifully situated on the River Blackwater at the foot of the Knockmealdown Mountains. The river rolls on south to Youghal and the sea. The fertile Blackwater Valley is where some of the earliest traces of the Stone Age inhabitants of Ireland have been found.

Lismore was the location of a great monastic university first founded by St Cartach or Carthage in the 7th century. In the 8th century, with St Colman at the helm, the monastery became a huge centre of learning. From the 10th century on, it was sacked many times by the Vikings but hung on as the religious capital of Deise (Deices).

Viking

Information
Lismore has a seasonal tourist office (☎ 058-54975) in the heritage centre, in the old courthouse in the town centre. It's open from Easter to the end of October between 10 am and 5.30 pm weekdays, and between 2 pm and 5.30 pm at the weekends. You'll also find a bureau de change there.

St Carthage's Cathedral
Up to the 17th century, the remains of eight churches were still to be found locally but

today little remains of its former greatness. The striking cathedral (1633) sits among peaceful gardens. Inside are some noteworthy tombs including a MacGrath family crypt dating from 1557 as well as the small chapel of St Colmcille.

Lismore Castle

From the Cappoquin road there are fine glimpses of the majestic Lismore Castle overlooking the river. In the 12th century Henry II came through the area and chose this site for a castle, which was eventually erected by Prince John, Lord of Ireland, in 1185. The castle was the local bishop's residence until 1589, when it was presented to Sir Walter Raleigh along with some 200 sq km (20,000 hectares) of the surrounding countryside.

Raleigh, a famous soldier and favourite of Queen Elizabeth I, later sold it to the Earl of Cork, Richard Boyle. His 14th child, Robert Boyle (1627-91), was born here and is credited with being the first methodical modern scientist. Boyle's Law is the principle that the pressure of a gas varies with its volume at a constant temperature, and it was a discovery fundamental to modern physics. Boyle also dabbled in alchemy and established that air has weight. He was deeply interested in religion and had the Old Testament printed in Irish, Welsh, Malay and Turkish.

Lismore Castle passed to the Duke of Devonshire in 1753 and his descendants still own it today. The present castle mostly dates from the 19th century, but does incorporate small sections of the earlier buildings. It was during the rebuilding that the 15th-century 'Book of Lismore' and the Lismore Crozier (now in the National Museum, Dublin) were discovered. The book documents the lives of a number of Irish saints but also holds an account of the voyages of Marco Polo. A more recent occupant of the castle was Adele Astaire, sister of Fred Astaire.

The castle is closed to day trippers but can be rented by the week by seriously rich groups. It costs between IR£7200 for four to IR£15,000 for 12 people. The Castle

Gardens (☎ 058-54424) are open from May to September, admission is IR£2.

Lismore Interpretive Centre

The Lismore interpretive centre (☎ 058-54975) is in the old courthouse in the town centre. This is an audiovisual presentation of local history and attractions, legends, follies and walks along the River Blackwater. It's open June to October and there are shows every half hour with a small admission charge of IR£2.

Golf

Contact Lismore Golf Club (☎ 058-54026) for information on the nine-hole course.

Places to Stay

Camping There is no official camp site nearby but you could try fields out of town or near the castle.

Hostel *Lismore An Óige Hostel* (☎ 058-54390) is a basic hostel in Glengarra, six km (four miles) from Lismore. To get there go north out of Lismore heading for the Vee Gap and watch out for the signpost to the hostel to the left. They have 36 beds and charge IR£4.50 in the high season. It's closed from October to March. The hostel is near one end of the Munster Way walking trail.

B&Bs *Beechcroft* (☎ 058-54273) on Deerpark Rd, about one km from the town centre, costs IR£11 to IR£13. *Ballyrafter House* (☎ 058-54002) is one km north of town. They are open Easter to October and charge IR£24 per person. The excellent dinner is around IR£18.

Hotels *Lismore Hotel* (☎ 058-54219) is a straightforward hotel charging IR£29/48 for B&B, IR£10 less in the low season.

Places to Eat

The cosy *Celtic Kitchen Café* across from the Heritage Centre on Main St has good snacks during the day; it also serves dinner. *Roche's Café* on East Main St above the Roche's supermarket does middle-of-the-road lunches and dinners from IR£5 to IR£10. *Rose's West End* pub on West St offers soup and toasted sandwiches.

Getting There & Away

The bus stop is at Rose's West End pub on West St. There are two buses daily (one on Sunday) on the Waterford City, Dungarvan, Cappoquin, Lismore route, in the morning and evening. There are more than 10 buses daily between Lismore and Dungarvan. For details contact Waterford bus station (☎ 051-73401).

THE MUNSTER WAY

This walking trail covers some 60 km (38 miles) between the Vee Gap near Lismore and Carrick-on-Suir in County Tipperary. The southern section of the walk goes through the Knockmealdown Mountains, including the picturesque sweep of scenery around the Vee Gap. Lismore An Óige Hostel is a handy starting point.

East of the Vee Gap the Munster Way crosses a path which marks the ancient roadway Rían Bó Phádraig or 'the track of St Patrick's cow'. This was a highway and pilgrimage route connecting Lismore with Ardfinnan and Cashel. Nearby is a modern memorial to Liam Lynch who was killed during the Irish Civil War in 1922-23. The route continues on forest trails passing through Newcastle. It heads north then turns east and north again as it heads for Tipperary. In Clonmel, it runs on a towpath besides the River Suir and heads east through Kilsheelan to Carrick-on-Suir. The route is clearly laid out with black markers bearing yellow arrows.

There is more information about the Munster Way on the detailed Bord Fáilte Information Sheet No 26J. For more details on the Tipperary part of the walk, see the chapter on Counties Limerick & Tipperary.

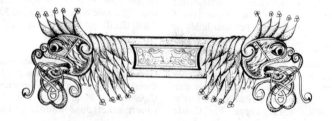

County Cork

County Cork has everything which makes Ireland so attractive. The northern part of the county is renowned for fishing while the main tourist trail heads down to Kinsale, the gourmet capital of Ireland, and west through the historic towns of Clonakilty and Skibbereen to the peninsulas jutting out into the Atlantic. These underpopulated extremities of land are rich in history and nature and offer wonderful scenery to accompany the excellent walking and cycling possibilities. Highlights of the county include kissing the Blarney stone and a boat trip out to Skellig Rock off the Iveragh Peninsula.

The Coast of West Cork (Appletree Press, Belfast, 1991) was first published in 1977, but it keeps its appeal and makes a useful companion for the historically-minded visitor to the south-west.

Cork City

The Irish Republic's second largest city is a surprisingly appealing place, where it's easy to find a day or two drifting away. By day the city centre is buzzing and at night there's a very lively pub scene. A number of historical attractions in the area have been developed over the last couple of years.

HISTORY
The town dates back to the 7th century and survived Cromwell's visit but fell to King William in 1690. In the 18th century it was an important commercial centre with a major butter market that shipped its produce across the world. A century later the potato famine turned Cork into a sorry place, where disillusioned and dispossessed Irish folk said farewell to their homeland. The port of Cobh remained a departure point for Irish emigrants right up to the 1960s.

Cork played a key role in Ireland's independence struggle. Thomas MacCurtain, a mayor of the city, was killed by the Black & Tans in 1920. His successor, Terence MacSwiney, died in Brixton Prison in London after 75 days on hunger strike. The Black & Tans were at their most unpleasant in Cork and much of the town was burnt down during their reign of terror. As a finale, Cork was also a centre for the civil war that followed independence, and Irish leader Michael Collins was ambushed and killed outside Cork. Today Cork is noted for its rivalry with Dublin. It has always been a pugnacious town with fiercely proud residents. Enquire at the tourist office about the new heritage centre, focusing on the city's history, which is soon to open in Blackrock to the north-east of the city.

ORIENTATION
The town centre is an island between two channels of the Lee River. Oliver Plunkett St and the curve of St Patrick's St are the main central roads. The railway station and several hostels are north of the river, and MacCurtain St is the main thoroughfare here. The Shandon area, rising on a hill to the north of the river, is an interesting older area to wander around.

INFORMATION
The tourist office (☎ 021-273251), on Grand Parade near the western end of Oliver

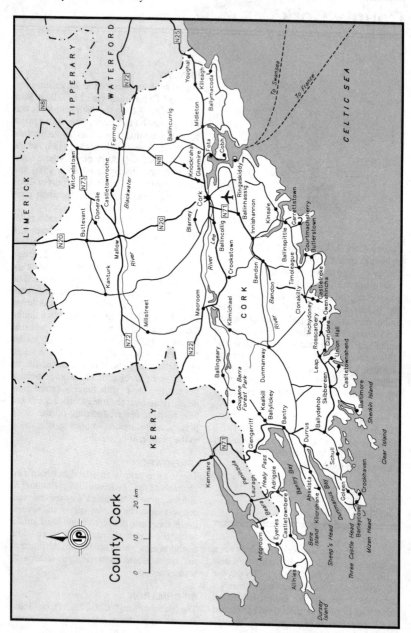

County Cork

Plunkett St, opens from 9 am to 7 pm and from 2 to 5 pm on Sundays in July and August, and from 9 am to 6 pm six days a week in June. In winter it closes at 5.30 pm and for an hour at lunch. The office organises official, free walking tours in summer, each Tuesday and Thursday at 7.30 pm. There are also walking tours of the university at 2.30 pm, Monday to Friday, which start at the main gates on Western Rd and cost IR£2 (children 75p). Cars can be rented from the tourist office. The South Quay Co-op on Sullivan's Quay has a useful notice board.

Cycle tours are handled by Rothar (☎ 021-274143) to Blarney and Cobh for IR£15 and East Cork for IR£20, departing from St Finbarr's at 10 am (Sunday 11 am).

Bookshops

Waterstone's big bookshop runs between St Patrick's and Paul Sts. Eason on St Patrick's St has a wide, general stock. In the Paul St area there are a number of smaller book-shops: Connolly's, next to the shopping centre in Paul St, has a second-hand selection, the Mercier Press have their shop in French Church St, and the Collins Bookshop in Carey's Lane is also good. The Shelf is a useful second-hand bookshop on George's Quay.

Laundry

There's a laundrette at 14 MacCurtain St across from the big Isaacs Hostel or you could try the College Laundrette on Western Rd opposite the gates of the University College of Cork.

Camping Equipment

The Tent Shop in Rutland St off South Terrace (☎ 021-965582) hires out equip-ment, while the Scout Shop near Isaac's on MacCurtain St sells cheaper equipment but doesn't hire it out. Around the corner from Isaac's, in York St, Tents & Leisure sells and hires out tents.

Parking

Parking coupons, obtainable at newsagents, should be displayed inside the car window and are needed to park virtually anywhere in the city centre. Alternatively, use the big car park behind the Merchant Quay shopping centre, or park for free in the Shandon area.

WALKING TOURS
South & West

This tour begins not far from the tourist office and ends at the Cork Public Museum, from where it is a short walk back to the town centre. On Grand Parade between Oliver Plunkett St and Washington St, is the small Bishop Lucey Park on the Washington St side. To one side of the arched entrance to the park there is an alleyway. At its end on the right an old church now houses the Cork Archive Centre. Past the church is the **Triskel Arts Centre** (☎ 021-272022) – an important venue for films, theatre and the like.

Going to the left down South Main St, the Tudor-style Beamish & Crawford brewery is not easily missed. Opposite, Snotty Joe's pub is on the corner of Tuckey St. Go down Tuckey St where, at the end on the left, a bollard bears testimony to the days when Grand Parade was an open canal and boats moored by the quayside. Turn to the right and follow Grand Parade past the 18th-century bow-fronted houses, passing on your left an ornate nationalist monument. As you con-tinue around to the South Mall there is a smaller monument on the right, just past the public toilets, to the victims of the Hiroshima and Nagasaki atomic bombs.

Down South Mall the **Imperial Hotel** comes into view on the left. The hotel, dating back to 1816, was where Michael Collins, commander-in-chief of the army of the Irish Free State, slept the night before setting out for a journey that would end in ambush and death on 22 August 1922. On the night he arrived at the Imperial the two sentries in the lobby were asleep and Collins literally knocked their heads together out of irritation.

At the end of South Mall the **City Hall** looms across the river. In 1963 President John F Kennedy visited Ireland and gave an address from the steps of City Hall. He had returned as a conquering hero to the land his great-grandfather had left, and the crowd in Cork was the biggest ever to gather in the city.

From the bridge at low tide, cormorants can be seen diving for fish. Across the bridge four pubs come into view on Union Quay, all music venues. Union Quay leads on to George's Quay with **Holy Trinity Church** on the right across the river. On the other side of the road is a colourful display mounted on the wall outside Fitzpatrick's second-hand shop; unfortunately what is on display inside is nowhere near as interesting.

The next bridge on the right is the single-arched **Parliament Bridge** that was built in 1806 to commemorate the Act of Union which six years earlier had seen the end of the Irish parliament and the dispatch of its members to Westminster in London. The next bridge is the **South Gate Bridge** of 1713, which marks the site of the medieval entrance to the city. Bishop St and **St Finbarr's Cathedral** are straight on.

From the cathedral it is a short walk west to **University College Cork** where, in the corridor of the quadrangle building that faces Western Rd, there is a collection of Ogham stones. They are in the corridor of the north wing, which is the one with a tower, directly behind you as you face the main entrance to the Boole Library.

If you face the front of the Boole Library and walk to the left, the Department of Plant Science comes into view; behind this building is the Honan Chapel. This small chapel was built in 1915 and is well worth a visit. The stained-glass windows and modernistic use of Celtic designs are intriguing.

Go back to the quadrangle and follow the pathway through the north wing by the tower. Follow the road down to the main gate. As you come out at the main gates the **Cork Public Museum** is close by, on the other side of the road and to the left behind Western Rd in Fitzgerald Park. After visiting the museum, head back to the city along

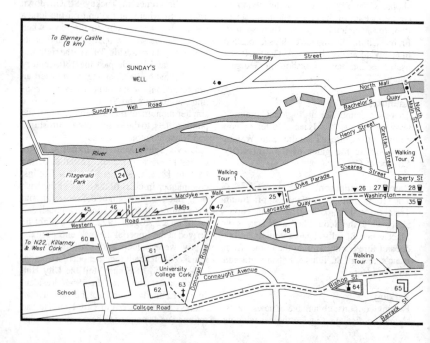

Mardyke Walk, turning right in Mardyke St at the corner with Clifford's restaurant and then left before the hospital onto Western Rd, which becomes first Lancaster Quay and then Washington St, before reaching Grand Parade.

North

This circular tour begins and ends at the corner of St Patrick's St and Grand Parade, outside the Queen's Old Castle shopping centre (named after a guard tower on the medieval city walls).

From the shopping centre follow the bend of St Patrick's St (the street was built over a branch of the river). On the left a sign points to the Pugin Church of Peter & Paul. The street ends at St Patrick's Bridge with St Patrick's Quay on the other side to the right. The quayside was once crowded with foreign ships loading up with salted butter, but these days there's only the occasional vessel to be seen.

Cross the three-arched bridge and turn to the left along Camden Place with its late 18th-century Georgian houses. Follow the road round to the right, and then take Dominick St to the left. Once the commercial heart of Cork, this area is now run down, despite the expensive Shandon Craft Centre in what was once the Cork Butter Exchange. The round building nearby, the Firkin Crane building, housed the weighing scales for the butter-casks (firkins). There are plans to open this building to the public. At the corner with Church St there is no mistaking St Ann's Church with the famous Shandon Steeple.

Head down Church St and turn left into Shandon St which heads down to the North Gate Bridge. Across the bridge is the beginning of North Main St, looking decidedly shabby. Towards the end of North Main St, on the left, is the back of the Queens Old Castle shopping centre. Walk through the centre to get back to your starting point.

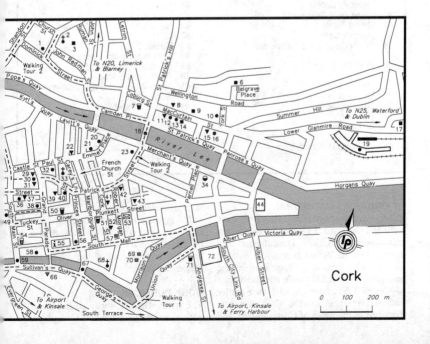

Cork

■ PLACES TO STAY

3   Kinlay House Shandon Hostel
6   Sheila's Cork Tourist Hostel
9   Isaac's Hostel
14 Metropole Hotel
17 Cork International Tourist Hostel
45 Campus House Hostel
46 An Óige Hostel
48 Jury's Hotel
57 Imperial Hotel
60 Castlewhite Apartments
69 Morrisons Island Hotel
70 Moore's Hotel

▼ PLACES TO EAT

8   O'Briens Café
11 Figgerty's Café
15 Luciano's Pizzeria
22 Bully's Restaurant
25 Clifford's Restaurant
26 O'Keeffe's Restaurant
29 Floury Hands Café
31 Other Place
37 O'Briens Café
39 Oyster Tavern
41 Bewley's Café
42 China Gold Restaurant
43 Gino's Pizzeria
52 Halpin's Café
66 South Quay Co-op Restaurant

🍺 PUBS

7   Hoddle & Stile
27 Grasshopper
28 Washington Inn
35 Reardens
50 de Lacy House
51 An Bodhrán Pub
54 An Spailpín Fánach Pub

71 Lobby, Charlie's, An Phoenix & Donkey's Ears Pubs

OTHER

1   Shandon Craft Centre/Cork Butter Market
2   St Ann's Shandon Church
4   Cork City Gaol
5   North Gate Bridge
10 Tents & Leisure
12 Everyman Palace Theatre
13 Laundrette
16 Scout Shop
18 St Patrick's Bridge
19 Kent Railway Station
20 Cork Opera House
21 Crawford Art Gallery
23 Eason Bookshop
24 Cork Public Museum
30 Queens Old Castle Shopping Centre
32 Waterstone's Bookshop
33 Church of St Peter & St Paul
34 Bus Station
36 Triskel Arts Centre
38 Bishop Lucey Park
40 USIT Travel Office
44 Customs House
47 College Laundrette
49 Beamish & Crawford Brewery
53 GPO
55 Tourist Office
56 Cork to Swansea Ferry
58 Nationalist Monument
59 South Gate Bridge
61 North Wing of University College
62 Boole Library
63 Honan Chapel
64 St Finbarr's Cathedral
65 Elizabeth Fort
67 Parliament Bridge
68 Holy Trinity Church
72 City Hall

ST FINBARR'S CATHEDRAL

The foundations for this imposing Protestant cathedral were laid in 1865 and construction was completed in 1879. The cathedral was designed by the Victorian architect William Burges, who was also responsible for the restoration of Cardiff Castle and the design of Castell Coch near Cardiff. Two earlier cathedrals stood on the site; one was damaged in the siege of Cork in 1690, and its replacement, built from 1735, was superseded by the present construction. Tours of the cathedral are sometimes available (☎ 021-963387/964742). Nearby are the fragmentary remains of the 17th-century Elizabeth Fort.

CORK PUBLIC MUSEUM

The ground floor is mostly given over to the nationalist struggle, in which Cork played an important role, while the 1st floor has displays on ancient metallurgy and fossils.

The museum is in Fitzgerald Park behind Western Rd. The bus stops at the main gates of the university; and on the other side of the road there is a brown sign pointing the way to the left. Entry is free and it's open Monday to Friday from 11 am to 1 pm and 2.15 to 5 pm, to 6 pm in summer, closed on Saturday but open Sunday afternoon from 3 to 5 pm.

ST ANN'S CHURCH, SHANDON

Open from 10 am to 4 pm, the church tower has two walls faced with limestone and two with sandstone. The weathervane in the shape of a salmon was chosen because, it seems, the monks of the city reserved for themselves the right to fish salmon in the river. There is a charge of IR£1.50 for viewing the church, climbing the tower and ringing its famous bells. They even provide the music sheets so you can chime out 'Waltzing Matilda' or other favourites. It costs IR£1 to just view the church interior and its small collection of 17th-century books that includes the letters of John Donne.

CORK CITY GAOL

Furnished cells, exhibits and audiovisual displays tell the story of this 19th-century prison. Open from 9.30 am, the last tour is at 7 pm and costs IR£2.75 (children IR£1.50, students IR£2). There's a shop and refreshment area, also. The gaol is on Sunday's Well Rd, west of the city. Enquire at the tourist office about a bus service departing for the gaol from outside the tourist office; it costs IR£1 return.

FESTIVALS

The Cork International Jazz Festival takes place in late October and there's an International Film Festival in September. Tickets for both can sell out quickly, and programmes are available from the Cork Opera House, Emmett Place (☎ 021-270022). A Choral Festival takes place towards the end of May and the International Folk Dance Festival in September in Cobh. The Cork Youth Arts Festival takes place at the end of June; details are available from the Triskel Arts Centre.

PLACES TO STAY
Camping

The *Cork City Caravan & Camping Park* (☎ 021-961866) is on Togher Rd quite close to the centre. It is signposted from the Wilton/city hospital roundabout on the main road to West Cork, and bus No 14 from the centre stops outside. The site is conveniently close both to the Wilton shopping centre and the city. *Bienvenue Caravan & Camping Park* (☎ 021-312711) is on a slip road opposite the entrance to Cork Airport on the R600.

Hostels

The competition between hostels in Cork is fierce. At 48 MacCurtain St, quite close to the centre, *Isaac's* (☎ 021-500011) is a new place in a fine old building. A bed costs IR£5.50 in the big dorms, IR£7.50 in the smaller four to six-bed dorms, IR£13.50 in private doubles, and IR£18.50 for a single. A light breakfast is included except for the cheapest beds. There's a good cafeteria, kitchen facilities and bicycle hire, but the dorms are closed from 11 am to 5 pm.

Also new and almost as central is *Kinlay House Shandon* (☎ 021-508966) at Bob & Joan Walk in the old Shandon district just north of the river, immediately behind St Ann's Church, Shandon. Dorm beds in rooms for four cost IR£7, twin rooms are IR£10.50 each or singles are IR£15, all including a light breakfast. It's a friendly and well-run place.

Beyond Isaac's, towards the railway station and back from MacCurtain St on Belgrave Place, Wellington Rd is *Sheila's Cork Tourist Hostel* (☎ 021-505562) which is neat, clean, tidy and very well equipped. There's even a sauna! Dorm beds are IR£5.50, shared rooms IR£7 each and singles IR£8. They rent bicycles.

The *Cork International Tourist Hostel* (☎ 021-509089) at 100 Lower Glanmire Rd is just beyond the railway station and is small, friendly and engagingly scruffy. The nightly cost is IR£4.50.

On the other side of the centre is the *An Óige Hostel* (☎ 021-543289) at 1/2 Western Rd. It's a big, well-organised hostel and costs IR£5.90 per night. The rooms are shut between 10 am and 5 pm, although there is access to the sitting room and a small kitchen. There are bikes for rent at IR£7 a day. Take bus No 8 two km out of the centre. *Campus House* (☎ 021-343531) is beyond the An Óige Hostel at 3 Woodland View, Western Rd. It's small but tidy and costs IR£5.

Finally in summer you can stay at *Castlewhite Apartments* (☎ 021-276871, ext 2867), the student accommodation for University College Cork on Western Rd. Rooms range from singles at IR£15 to six-bedroom apartments at IR£71, each with its own kitchen/dining area, and they are less expensive if rented for a week.

B&Bs

Lower Glanmire Rd beyond the railway station is lined with economical B&Bs. *Tivoli House* (☎ 021-506605) at No 143 is one of the cheapest. Others include *Kent House* (☎ 021-504260) at No 47, *Oakland* (☎ 021-500578) at No 51 and *Tara House* (☎ 021-500294) at No 52. Singles are IR£14 to IR£20, doubles IR£25 to IR£35. Tivoli is the area further east with more places, including the 20-bed *Lotamore House* (☎ 021-822344) at I£25/44.

On the opposite side of town, along Western Rd to West Cork, there are plenty of B&Bs like *St Kilda's* (☎ 021-273095), a big blue house with its own car park out the front, close to the gates of the university. A few doors along are *Antoine House* (☎ 021-273494) and *Killarney House* (☎ 021-270290). Prices range from IR£16/40. Least expensive is *St Anthonys* (☎ 021-541345) at IR£13 per person, a little further west at Victoria Cross where the road branches off for Blarney. If coming into Cork from the west, all these places are on the left after the roundabout at Cork hospital.

Hotels

The biggest in the city is *Jury's* (☎ 021-276622) on the stretch of road between Washington St and Western Rd known as Lancaster Quay. Singles/doubles are IR£83/98, excluding breakfast, and there's a small outdoor swimming pool. The *Imperial* (☎ 021-274040) is more centrally located in South Mall but doesn't have a car park. Rooms cost IR£75/110. Across from the South Mall in Morrison's Quay is the *Morrisons Island* (☎ 021-275858), with rooms at IR£70/98 excluding breakfast, and *Moore's Hotel* (☎ 021- 271291) where rooms cost from IR£40/60. Both these hotels face the river.

The *Metropole* (☎ 021-508122) on Mac-Curtain St, with rooms from IR£75/110, was originally a temperance hotel, a rare institution in Ireland. Its magnificent facade has lasted well.

Good value, especially for families, is the *Forte Travelodge* (☎ 021-310722), near the airport at the Kinsale Rd roundabout, where a room for up to three adults and a child is IR£32. Breakfast is not included but there's a Little Chef restaurant attached.

PLACES TO EAT
Cafés & Takeaways

There are numerous places around Oliver Plunkett St and the pedestrian-only streets connecting it with St Patrick's St, including several fast-food places. *Bewley's* on Cork St is a popular café, an offshoot of Bewley's in Dublin. *Halpin's* at 14/15 Cork St is similar in style with deli and restaurant. Good sandwiches cost from IR£1.25.

Try *O'Briens* for tea, scones, sandwiches and good home-made ice cream. There's one on Washington St, near the tourist office and town centre, and one at 39 MacCurtain St near Isaac's and other hostels. Also in MacCurtain St *Figgerty's* is OK for an economical breakfast or lunch.

Floury Hands on Grand Parade in the centre also does good sandwiches and coffee. The *Crawford Gallery Restaurant* in Emmet Place offers very good food at reasonable prices.

Between St Patrick's St and the pedestrian area of Paul St are several narrow lanes, too small to show on the map, with good places for a sandwich or meal. Try the *Ginger Bread House* or *Thyme Out* on French Church St for lunch or a coffee or tea. The café at the *Triskel Arts Centre* is also worth a visit.

The *Other Place*, a gay meeting place, has an inexpensive café. It is obscurely located at the end of an alleyway that begins on Grand Parade between the Queen's Old Castle centre and the corner with Washington St. Finally if you're out at the museum try the pleasant little *Tea Room* which has good-value sandwiches and meals for IR£3.

Restaurants

In the pedestrian area between St Patrick's and Paul Sts, *Bully's* at 40 Paul St is a reasonably priced restaurant with pizza and pasta; French Church St has the *Huguenot Bistro*, a fancier place with interesting main courses at IR£5 to IR£6; and a block away in Carey's Lane there's *Café Mexicana* and *Paddy Garibaldi's* (yes it's Irish-Italian).

Gino's at 7 Winthrop St off Oliver Plunkett and *Luciano's* on MacCurtain St are two good pizzerias.

For vegetarians, the *South Quay Co-Op*, upstairs at 24 Sullivan's Quay, has imaginative starters at IR£1.75 to IR£2.50, main courses at IR£5.50 to IR£7. In the Queen's Old Castle centre the *Naturalle* has a variety of meals from IR£3.

The *Oyster Tavern* is in Market Lane, an alleyway near Burger King on St Patrick's St. A set dinner is IR£22.50, lunch is IR£10 and bar food is available. There are a few fancy Chinese restaurants on St Patrick's St: *China Gold* is typical, with a set meal for two at IR£27.

Isaac's hostel has a good restaurant with meals around IR£6, mixing continental food with traditional Irish cuisine to produce dishes like Provençal bean stew with Clonakilty black pudding.

Jury's Hotel on Western Rd has good restaurants: the *Glandore* is open from 7 am to 11 pm and costs around IR£15 per head, while the *Fastnet* is open evenings only at IR£22 per head. A good meal in *Clouds* at the Imperial Hotel could be enjoyed for

around IR£16. The *Riverview* at the Metropole has an evening special at IR£10, a set dinner at about IR£17.50 and an à la carte menu. It also does high tea all day long at around IR£5 to IR£8.

There are a few restaurants offering fine dining and alternatives to the traditional Irish menu. *Clifford's* (☎ 021-275333) on Dyke Parade across from Jury's has a reputation for dishes in the style of nouvelle cuisine, while *O'Keeffe's* (☎ 021-275645), nearby at 23 Washington St, is a small and cosy place open for dinner only. Two others are in the suburbs: *Arbutus Lodge* (☎ 021-501237) is west of town in Montenotte while *Lovetts* (☎ 021-294909) is south in Douglas. Reservations are necessary and you can expect to pay at least IR£25 per person.

ENTERTAINMENT
Pubs

Cork's rivalry with Dublin even extends to drink. A pint of Murphy's is the stout of choice here, or a Beamish, which is often cheaper. On Union Quay from the corner of Anglesea St, the *Lobby*, *Charlie's*, *An Phoenix* and the *Donkey's Ears* are all side by side, and virtually every night one or other will have music.

Farther along on George's Quay, *Mojo's* is popular with bikers. On Oliver Plunkett St, *de Lacy House* at No 74 and *An Bodhrán* at No 42 regularly feature Irish music, as does the *An Spailpín Fánach* on South Main St. This pub, which the tourist board pub guide calls 'probably the oldest pub in Ireland', has a little loft bar which is easily missed. Just around the corner in Tuckey St, the *Shelter* has live bands.

The *South Quay Co-Op* on Sullivans's Quay has live music on Thursday evenings. Up the hill from here, at 48 Barrack St, the artier *Nancy Spain's* has music. The *Hoddle & Stile* has folk music and is in Coburg St, just across St Patrick's Bridge. In Washington St there is a cluster of popular student pubs with music; two of them are either side of the imposing Court Building – the *Washington Inn* and *The Grasshopper* – while *Reardens* pub is on the other side of the road.

More sedate music is played in the bars at the Imperial and Metropole hotels.

Theatres & Galleries

Cork prides itself on its cultural pursuits. The mainstream theatre is the *Cork Opera House* (☎ 021-276357) in Emmet Place, but the *Triskel Arts Centre* (☎ 021-272022) is more adventurous. The centre is off South Main St and its notice board will advertise all artistic events in the city. The *Everyman Palace* (☎ 501673) is also in MacCurtain St. The *Crawford Art Gallery*, in Emmet Place, is worth a visit and has no admission charge. Enquire at the tourist office about evenings of traditional dance and song held at the Firkin Crane building in Shandon.

GETTING THERE & AWAY

USIT (☎ 021-270900) is hidden away at 10/11 Market Parade, an arcade off St Patrick's St near the Grand Parade junction.

Air

Cork Airport has direct flights to Dublin, Manchester, London, Paris, Rennes and Amsterdam. Other overseas flights go via Dublin. For flight information call ☎ 021-311000 or contact the Aer Lingus office at 38 Patrick St (☎ 021-274331). The airport is north-west of the city and takes about 20 minutes to reach by car.

Ferry

There are ferry connections with the UK and France. The Cork to Swansea ferry has an office at 52 South Mall (☎ 021-271166), and an office at the ferry terminal (☎ 021-378036) which is open for arrivals and departures only. The return fare in July for a car and passengers ranges from IR£250 (mid-week) to IR£360 (weekend). Before the end of May, fares range from IR£160 to IR£180. The single passenger fare without a car ranges from IR£18 before 25 May to IR£26 in August. The ferry operates during the summer months only.

Brittany Ferries (☎ 021-504888) has an office next to the tourist office; the service to Roscoff only operates during the summer months. Irish Ferries (☎ 021-504333) has an office at 9 Bridge St and operates services to Le Havre and Cherbourg.

The ferry terminal is at Ringaskiddy, about 15 minutes by car from the city centre.

Train

The Kent Railway Station (☎ 021-504888) is across the river on Lower Glanmire Rd. There is a regular train connection to Dublin and Limerick; sometimes it is necessary to change trains at Mallow.

Bus

The bus station (☎ 021-506066/508188) is on the corner of Merchant's Quay and Parnell Place on the central island. You can get to almost anywhere in Ireland from Cork and there are direct services to Dublin, Limerick and Killarney.

Hitching

Lower Glanmire Rd, beyond the railway station, is not only lined with cheap B&Bs, it's also often lined with hitchhikers, heading out of town to Dublin.

GETTING AROUND
To/From the Airport

A bus operates regularly between the airport and the bus station, all week.

Bicycle Rental

A number of the hostels rent bicycles at around IR£7 a day, or try Carroll Cycles (☎ 021-508923) at Dillon's Cross.

Two places handle the Raleigh Rent-a-Bike scheme: Cycle Scene (☎ 021-301183) at 396 Blarney St, and the Cycle Repair Centre (☎ 021-276255) at 6/7 Kyle St. If you hire a bike in Limerick at Emerald's Cycles you can drop it off at the Cycle Repair Centre, and vice versa.

Around Cork

BLARNEY CASTLE

Even the most untouristy visitor will probably feel compelled to kiss the Blarney Stone and get the gift of the gab or, as an 18th-century French consul put it, 'gain the privilege of telling lies for seven years'. It was Queen Elizabeth I who invented the word, due to her exasperation with Lord Blarney's ability to talk endlessly without ever actually agreeing to her demands. Bending over backwards to kiss the sacred rock requires a head for heights. The castle itself, a tower house, dates from 1446 and is built on solid limestone.

The castle is open Monday to Saturday from 9 am to 6.30 or 7 pm, or to sundown. Sundays it's open 9.30 am to 5.30 pm or sundown. Entry is IR£3 (students IR£1.50, children IR£1). Your enjoyment of a visit to Blarney will probably be in inverse relation to the number of coach tours there at the time. Getting there at opening time is one way of beating the crowds.

The adjacent **Blarney House** is open 12 noon to 5.30 pm from Monday to Saturday, from June to September. It is a late 19th-century baronial house full of Victorian trappings and chandeliers made of Waterford glass. Entry is IR£2.50 (IR£1.50, IR£1).

The **Blarney Woollen Mills** is a giant tourist shop in Blarney village selling everything from quality garments to tacky green telephones in the shape of Ireland accompanied by a 'no blarney' guarantee.

Places to Stay

Accommodation is not in short supply and the tourist office (☎ 021-381624), which has a left luggage room, will make bookings.

Hostel A couple of km outside of Blarney on the road to Killarney there is an unaffiliated hostel (☎ 021-385580).

B&Bs Blarney has a host of B&Bs, most of them only open from April or May to October or November. Three exceptions are *Elmgrove House* (☎ 021-385136) on Shournagh Rd, *Mrs Callaghan* (☎ 021-385035) on Station Rd and *Knockawn Wood* (☎ 021-870284) at Curraleigh, six km (four

miles) outside the village. These three are open all year.

Hotels There are two big hotels: the *Blarney Park* (☎ 021-385281) and *Christy's* (☎ 021-385011), both costing around IR£80 for a double. The Blarney Park has a leisure centre with a pool and a slide and a supervised children's room. Both the pool and the babysitting service are free of charge.

Places to Eat

The village of Blarney has a number of restaurants and pubs serving food. The *Blarney Stone Restaurant* has food starting at IR£2.50 and *Mackey's* next door serves meals for IR£8. Bar food at the *Muskerry Arms* opposite is reasonably priced at around IR£3 and at night the pub has a steak and seafood restaurant.

Entertainment

Blair's Inn is six km (four miles) outside of Blarney at Cloghroe but it is worth the trip on a Sunday or Monday when traditional ballad sessions take place. In town itself the *Muskerry Arms* usually has some kind of live music every night of the summer.

Getting There & Away

Buses run regularly from the Cork bus station and there are also private services from some of the hostels.

BALLINCOLLIG

The village of Ballincollig is eight km (five miles) west of Cork on the main road to Killarney and has recently opened its Royal Gunpowder Mills. Throughout the 19th century this was one of the largest gunpowder manufacturing plants in Europe. Open from 10 am to 7 pm, admission is IR£2 (children IR£1). There's a regular city bus service to the village from the bus station in Cork.

COBH

Cobh (pronounced 'cove') was for many years the port of Cork, and has always had a strong connection with Atlantic crossings.

The very first crossing of the Atlantic by a steamship was made from Cobh by the *Sirius* in 1838. The *Titanic* made its last stop here before its fateful Atlantic crossing and it was near Cobh that the *Lusitania* was sunk in 1915. On a more cheerful note, Cobh was home to the world's first yacht club. The Royal Cork Yacht Club was founded here in 1720, but now operates from Crosshaven on the other side of Cork Harbour.

Cobh is actually on Great Island which fills much of Cork Harbour and is joined to the mainland by a causeway. In the British era it was known as Queenstown, because it was the place where Queen Victoria arrived in 1849, on her first visit to Ireland. Today it's a picturesque little port with few reminders of its unhappy history.

Information

Cobh Tourism (☎ 021-811391) is based at Westbourne House, not far from the station.

St Colman's Cathedral

Cobh is dominated by the massive but comparatively recent St Colman's Cathedral. Construction of the French-Gothic-style cathedral commenced in 1868 but it was not completed until 1915. The Irish communities in Australia and the USA contributed a large part of the construction cost. The cathedral is noted for its 47-bell carillon, the largest in Ireland. The biggest bell weighs in at 3440 kg. St Colman (522-604) is the patron saint of the local diocese of Cloyne.

Lusitania Monument

There's a *Lusitania* monument, depicting two sailors on either side of an angel, by the waterfront of the port. A km north of the town in Clonmel's churchyard there is a communal grave for the bodies retrieved from the sinking.

Cobh Museum

The Cobh Museum has a maritime emphasis and is open 3 to 6 pm on Sundays year round and on Wednesday as well from May to September.

Cobh Heritage Centre

The Cobh heritage centre has displays on the mass emigrations following the famine, the era of the great liners and the tragedies of the *Titanic* and *Lusitania*. The heritage centre is at Cobh's old railway station and admission is IR£3.50 (children IR£2.50). Opening hours are 10 am to 6 pm, and there is a craft and coffee shop.

Festivals

Cobh has an International Folk Dance Festival in July, the Cobh People's Regatta in August and the International Sea Angling Festival in September.

Places to Stay

Cobh's best B&B is *Westbourne House* (☎ 021-811391) which costs IR£10 and is on the left if you're walking up from the station. If that is full ask their advice or try *Mrs O'Rourke* (☎ 021-812450) at Bellavista in Bishop's Rd, with singles/doubles from IR£18/28.

The *Commodore* (☎ 021-811277) is the premier hotel and features a heated indoor pool. Singles/doubles cost from IR£32/56 in summer.

Places to Eat

There are only a few places serving food. *Jim's Place* on West Beach is typical with meals from IR£3. The *Commodore Hotel* has a set lunch for IR£8, bar meals from IR£3.50 and dinner for IR£17. *Lumberjacks* in Pearse Square is a takeaway but also has seats. *Clippers* is down by the station.

Entertainment

Pub music is never far away in the summer. The *Commodore Hotel* has music on Saturday nights, and other bars like the *Well House* or the *Rotunda* are worth checking out. The oldest bar in town, *Mansworth's* on Middleton St near the cathedral, has traditional ballad sessions and 1960s music every night of the week in July and August.

For sailing activities contact Eddie English (☎ 021-811237) on East Beach. The local riding school (☎ 021-811908) has pony trekking and Marine Transport (☎ 021-811485) handle harbour cruises.

Getting There & Away
Cobh is 24 km (15 miles) from Cork, off the main N25 Cork to Rosslare road. There is a regular train service and the last bus for Cork leaves at 10.10 pm from outside the post office.

FOTA WILDLIFE PARK
Unique in Ireland, the Fota Wildlife Park (☎ 021-812678) is ideal for children of all ages. Giraffes, ostriches, monkeys, kangaroos and penguins wander freely, and lemurs invade the coffee shop. Cheetahs, who can run at nearly 100 km/h, don't have the room to do that here but they are bred and exported to countries like India where they originally came from. Ostriches are also bred. This is not a safari park so cars are left outside and visitors walk around to view the animals. Admission is IR£3 (students IR£2.60, children IR£1.60). The car park is another IR£1.50. It's open from April to October, 10 am to 5 pm, from 11 am on Sundays.

Fota House
Fota House (☎ 021-812555) is in the grounds of the park and is famous for its collection of landscape paintings. The house was closed after a ceiling collapsed but may have reopened by the time you read this. There will be separate admission charges.

Getting There & Away
The park is 16 km (10 miles) from Cork, and the Cork to Cobh train stops at the park.

MIDLETON
The Jameson heritage centre whiskey distillery is the only reason to go to Midleton but this alone makes it a worthwhile trip. Whiskey has been distilled here since the early 19th century, and original works were opened to the public after a new distillery was opened in 1975.

Guided tours start with a film show and then a walkabout that covers the whole process, from the storeroom where local farmers had their barley weighed and deposited, to the malting process and on to the milling powered by a superb waterwheel. The original stills remain in position, including the largest one in the world. You will also discover the crucial differences between Irish whiskey and Scotch whisky. This is one of the better heritage places in Ireland for a visitor to get a real sense of the working lives of the people. The tour includes a tipple in the bar, and snacks are available.

Admission is IR£3.50 (children IR£1.50) and tours are available in French and German.

Places to Stay
The *Jasmine Villa Caravan & Camping Park* (☎ 021-883234) is six km (four miles) from Midleton in the direction of Cork. It is situated off the main Cork to Waterford road and signposted on the dual carriageway.

Getting There & Away
A number of buses from Cork stop at Midleton.

YOUGHAL
Youghal (pronounced 'yawl') is an interesting little town near the border with County Waterford and close to Ardmore, another pleasant coastal resort. In 1588 its mayor was Sir Walter Raleigh and tradition has it that he planted the first potatoes here after bringing them back from the New World.

Orientation & Information
Youghal consists of little more than one north-south main street, appropriately called Main St and carrying one-way traffic for most of its length. If you come through Youghal in the wrong direction (bound from Waterford to Cork) you could easily miss the lot.

The old Clock Gate at the south end of Main St is Youghal's major landmark and nearby is the tourist office (☎ 024-92390) in Market House. From October to April phone ☎ 024-92374 to enquire about walking tours. The tourist office also has a *Tourist Trail* booklet to lead you around the town.

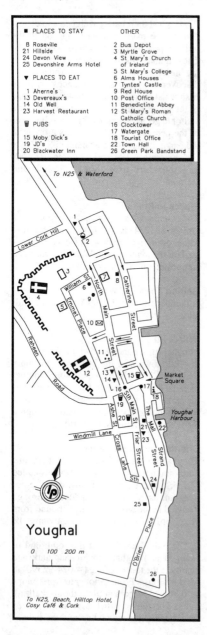

■ PLACES TO STAY	OTHER
B Roseville	2 Bus Depot
21 Hillside	3 Myrtle Grove
24 Devon View	4 St Mary's Church
25 Devonshire Arms Hotel	of Ireland
	5 St Mary's College
▼ PLACES TO EAT	6 Alms Houses
	7 Tyntes' Castle
1 Aherne's	9 Red House
13 Devereaux's	10 Post Office
14 Old Well	11 Benedictine Abbey
23 Harvest Restaurant	12 St Mary's Roman
	Catholic Church
☗ PUBS	16 Clocktower
	17 Watergate
15 Moby Dick's	18 Tourist Office
19 JD's	22 Town Hall
20 Blackwater Inn	26 Green Park Bandstand

To N25 & Waterford

Lower Cork Hill

William St

North Main St

Catherine Street

Emmet Place

Rahen Road

Market Square

Youghal Harbour

5th Main St

The Mall

Ashe St

Windmill Lane

Cross Lane

Friar Street

Strand Street

5th

O'Brien Place

Youghal

0   100   200 m

To N25, Beach, Hilltop Hotel,
Cosy Café & Cork

Youghal's safe beaches stretch away south of town.

Clocktower

Youghal's landmark is the curious clocktower which actually bridges Main St. This was originally the site of the Iron Gate, a key part of the town's fortifications, but it was replaced by the present building, a combination of clocktower and jail, in 1777. The countryside around Youghal was a hotbed of rural unrest and the new jail soon proved too small. First of all the jailer's quarters were moved elsewhere and then an additional storey was added to the building. Horrific events took place here with prisoners routinely tortured, flogged or even hung from the tower's windows. Steps lead uphill from the clocktower to Town Wall Rd/Raheen Rd which runs outside the city walls.

Benedictine Abbey

All that now remains of this 14th-century abbey is one gable wall with a Gothic doorway that is easily missed, set into the street with houses either side. Open the door and walk down the narrow passageway which contains the original piscina, a perforated stone basin used for carrying away the water used in rinsing the chalice during a Mass.

Red House & Alms Houses

Continue farther up Main St to Red House which was built in 1706 by a Dutchman and takes its name from its red brickwork. It displays characteristics of Dutch architecture, like the cornerstones positioned under the triangular gable, and a roof in which each face has two slopes, the lower one being steeper than the upper one.

A few doors farther up the street are the Alms Houses, built in 1610 by Richard Boyle, the local lord, to house ex-soldiers.

Tyntes' Castle

Across the road from the Alms Houses is Tyntes' Castle which dates from the 15th century. It was originally in a defensive riverfront position but the silting up and changing course of the River Blackwater has left it high and dry. About 100 years after it was built the castle was confiscated from its original owners and taken over by Sir Robert Tyntes. Today the building is sadly decaying.

Myrtle Grove

Scholars dispute whether Sir Walter Raleigh ever lived at Myrtle Grove but that claim, nevertheless is the house's chief claim to fame. It was built in the mid-17th century for the warden of nearby St Mary's College. Tours of the house (☎ 024-92274 for information) may take place on Tuesday, Thursday and Saturday at 2.30 and 4 pm for IR£2 (children IR£1.50).

St Mary's Church of Ireland

Just uphill from Myrtle Grove is St Mary's Church of Ireland or St Mary's Collegiate Church. A Danish church is said to have stood here in the 11th century, but after its destruction in a storm the present church was built in 1220 incorporating elements of the earlier church. Over the centuries there have been various additions and alterations to the church, not always aesthetically pleasing, but it remains one of the oldest churches in Ireland still in use. Richard Boyle's monument shows himself, his wife and all 16 of his children; those shown lying down died as infants. There is another noted Boyle monument in St Patrick's Cathedral in Dublin. The church also has a 14th-century eight-sided baptismal font and many interesting gravestones, some with Norman-French inscriptions.

Town Walls

St Mary's churchyard is bounded by a fine stretch of the old town wall, and by walking up behind the church you can walk along the wall and see one of the remaining turrets. Unless you do a bit of scrambling you'll have to come back the same way. Town Wall Rd running alongside the wall offers a good view of this solid construction and you can continue around the outside of the wall and then take the road and steps down to the clocktower.

The walls date back at least to the 15th century although they were strengthened in the following century. They are among the best preserved medieval walls in Ireland.

Organised Tours

From May to September walking tours (adults IR£2, students IR£1) are booked from the office. They operate Monday to Saturday at 11 am, 3 and 7.30 pm (Sunday 3 pm only) and can be booked at the tourist office.

Enquire also at the tourist office about river cruises, which depart at 3 pm and cost IR£3 (children IR£1.50). There are also harbour trips (☎ 024-92820) departing from the jetty in Market Square and costing IR£2.

Places to Stay

Camping The *Summerfield Caravan & Camping Park* (☎ 024-93537) is just over one km west of Youghal off the main Cork road. Pitching a tent for a night costs from IR£4.50 plus 50p per adult, and IR£2.75 for cyclists. The *Sonas* camp site (☎ 024-98132) is about 15 km (10 miles) to the south. To get there, take the road off the N25 (west of town) to the village of Ballymacoda, then head west through the village. A small tent here is charged only IR£1, or IR£2 for cyclists.

B&Bs The least expensive accommodation is at *Hillside* (☎ 024-92468), in town on the one-way road leading to Cork. A single bed is IR£5, with continental breakfast IR£7.50 and with the usual eggs & bacon breakfast IR£9. However, this place was up for sale at the time of writing.

Devon View (☎ 024-92298) is at the Cork end of town, almost opposite the Devonshire Arms. Nearby is *Lee House* (☎ 024-92292) at 24 Friar St and both places have doubles for IR£26. Coming into town from Waterford, *Roseville* (☎ 024-92571) is in new Catherine St near the beginning of the one-way street. Singles/doubles here are IR£16/26.

Hotels The only hotel in town is the

Devonshire Arms (☎ 024-92827) with singles/doubles from IR£30/59. The *Hilltop Hotel* (☎ 024-92911) is out of town in the Cork direction and is less expensive with singles/doubles for IR£25/40.

Places to Eat

The best general menu is to be found at the *Old Well* in the middle of town. The *Cosy Café*, just out of town at the Cork end, is another good-value place serving a four-course meal for IR£4. The *Harvest Restaurant* on Friar St serves Chinese food.

The *Shamrock Restaurant* serves typical Irish dishes for between IR£3 and IR£8. The *Devonshire Arms* has a bar menu in the IR£3 to IR£8 range, lunch for IR£9 and dinner IR£18.50. The stylish *Devereaux's* has main courses from IR£6 and quick meals for IR£2.

Aherne's (☎ 024-92424), at the Waterford end of town, is an award-winning restaurant/pub famous for its seafood fresh from Youghal Bay or the nearby River Blackwater estuary. Dinner is IR£18.50, lunch IR£11 and reasonably priced bar food is available throughout the day.

Entertainment

The *Blackwater Inn* and *JD's* on Main St usually have music. *Moby Dick's* is near the tourist office and has a ballad session every Tuesday night. The pub is renowned for being John Huston's port of call during the filming of *Moby Dick* in Youghal in 1954 and the memorabilia on the walls commemorate the fact. The holiday weekend at the end of August is the occasion for Youghal's busking (street music) festival and the pubs will be particularly lively at that time.

Getting There & Away

The Tralee to Rosslare bus stops in Youghal connecting the town with Killarney, Cork and Waterford. The Cork to Waterford bus also stops in Youghal.

Getting Around

Bikes can be hired from *Troy's* (☎ 024-92509) at 7/8 South Main St, an agent for the Raleigh Rent-a-Bike scheme.

West Cork

KINSALE

If the Walt Disney team set out to produce a picture-perfect Irish village, they'd end up with Kinsale minus the traffic jams. It is easily reached from Cork by taking the route south to the airport. Partly on account of heavy promotion by Bord Faílte, it attracts more and more visitors each year. An added attraction is its undisputed claim as the gourmet capital of Ireland.

History

As early as the 13th century Kinsale was in the hands of the Anglo-Normans.

In September 1601, a Spanish fleet anchored at Kinsale and was besieged by the English. The Irish army marched the length of the country to attack the English, but were defeated in battle outside Kinsale on Christmas Eve. For the Catholics of Kinsale, the immediate consequence was that they were banned from the town completely, and it was another 100 years before they were allowed to return. Historians now give 1601 as the beginning of the end of Gaelic Ireland.

After 1601 the town developed apace as a ship-building port. In the early 18th century Alexander Selkirk left Kinsale Harbour on a voyage that was to leave him stranded on a desert island for years, providing Daniel Defoe with the idea for *Robinson Crusoe*. Nowadays, the town's nautical tradition is maintained by yacht owners and deep-sea anglers.

Information

The tourist office (☎ 021-774026) is in the centre of town close to where the buses stop. A *Town Trail* booklet guides the visitor to local places of interest, and various tourist-oriented activities start from outside the office.

Museum

There's a small museum in the old courthouse building where the enquiry into the

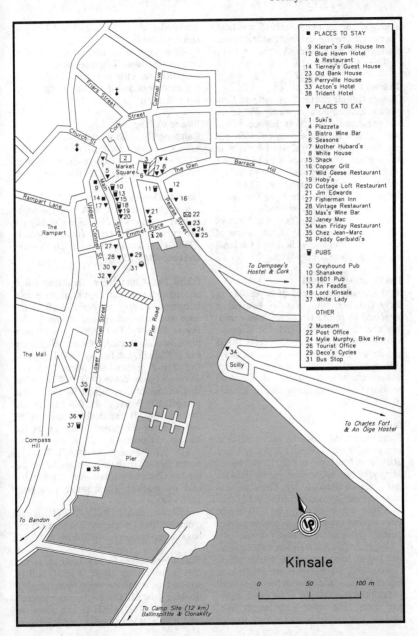

To Dempsey's
Hostel & Cork

To Charles Fort
& An Óige Hostel

To Bandon

To Camp Site (12 km)
Ballinspittle & Clonakilty

Kinsale

0   50   100 m

sinking of the *Lusitania* in 1915 was held. The most interesting exhibits inside are those dealing with the disaster. Admission is 40p (children 10p).

Charles Fort

Outside Kinsale are the huge ruins of 17th-century Charles Fort, reputedly one of the best preserved star forts in Europe. It was built in the wake of the events of 1601 and remained in use until 1922 when it was burnt down by anti-Treaty forces of the IRA. Entry is IR£1 (children and students 40p) and it's open 9 am to 6.30 pm in summer. The rest of the year it's open 9 am to 5 pm Tuesday to Saturday and 2 to 5 pm on Sunday.

The fort is three km (two miles) east of town and is signposted in the centre of Kinsale. You can also walk there by following the signposted Scilly Walk.

The Gourmet Festival

Held annually at the end of September or early October, this four-day festival is organised by the 12 restaurants that constitute the Good Food Circle of Kinsale. Membership for the four days costs IR£65 and includes entry to various events and a 10% discount in the restaurants. One-day tickets are also available; details and booking from Peter Barry, Scilly, Kinsale (☎ 021-774026).

Tours

Cycle tours leave from the tourist office at around 9.30 am, 1.30 and 5 pm and cost IR£4.50 for four hours or IR£3 for two hours. Bring your own bike or hire one for IR£4 for half a day or IR£6 all day. There are also horse and carriage tours costing IR£3 (children 50p), which take you on a 20-minute jaunt around town with an amusing commentary provided by the chatty driver.

One of the two privately run walking tours also begins from outside the tourist office. Costing IR£2.50, the tours are available in French, German and Spanish five times a day – check the window poster for exact departure times. The other walk begins from outside the museum every day except Wednesday, at 11.45 am, 2.45 and 7.30 pm, and costs IR£1.

Water tours are available from an office opposite the Super Valu supermarket and cost from IR£1 for a trip to James Fort, IR£5 for a harbour tour and IR£10 for a trip up the River Bandon.

Places to Stay

Camping The official camp site is *Garrettstown House Holiday Park* (☎ 021-778156/775286) which is 12 km (eight miles) from town near the village of Ballinspittle.

Hostels *Dempsey's Hostel* (☎ 021-772124) is a couple of minutes' walk from the centre of town and costs IR£4 a night plus 50p for showers. The *An Óige Hostel* (☎ 021-772309) is at Summercove near Charles Fort and costs IR£5.50.

B&Bs The tourist office has a useful free accommodation list detailing price and amenities at every registered B&B in the town and surrounding area. *Kieran's Folk House Inn* (☎ 021-772382) is a friendly place centrally located in Guardwell, the top end of Main St, and has very good rooms at IR£25 per person. On Main St itself, *Tierney's Guest House* (☎ 021-772205) has singles/doubles from IR£20/30. Next to the post office in Pearse St the *Old Bank House* (☎ 021-774075) has doubles from IR£50 and is under the same ownership as the Vintage restaurant.

The *Scilly House Inn* (☎ 021-772413), across the road from the Spaniard pub on the road to Charles Fort, is a very comfortable and up-market guesthouse charging IR£65/80.

Millwater House (☎ 021-772505) is just over a km from town on the Bandon road and has singles/doubles for IR£20/28.

Hotels First choice for sea views and amenities is the *Trident Hotel* (☎ 021-772301), situated near the harbour, with singles/doubles from IR£60/58 in the summer. *Acton's* (☎ 021-772135) is just down the road a little nearer to town, and has rooms for about the same price. On Pearse St the *Blue Haven* (☎ 021-772209), famous for its restaurant, has 10 bedrooms from IR£49/74. At the other end of the street is the far less expensive but faded *Perryville House* (☎ 021-772731). The huge rooms are ideal for families and cost IR£40.

Places to Eat

The competition between restaurants is fierce. If your credit card won't stretch to a meal at one of the dozen or so 'Good Food Circle' restaurants, you can still eat well at many more mundane establishments. In summer, reservations are often advisable.

Places to Eat – bottom end The *Copper Grill*, just down from the Blue Haven in Pearse St, does breakfast for IR£3, has a children's menu and meals are around IR£4. The *Wild Geese Restaurant* on Main St does a similarly priced breakfast, and main dishes cost between IR£3 and IR£7. The *Shack*, just across the road, serves a tasty lasagne for IR£4 and children's meals are IR£3. And if you want to escape from seafood try *Suki's* Asian cuisine on Guardwell, where meals will cost you less than IR£10; it has a takeaway service as well. A good place for sandwiches and inexpensive meals is *Mother Hubbard's* at the corner of Pearse St. Tucked away down Lower O'Connell St is *Paddy Garibaldi's* (which has a restaurant in Cork also), serving pizzas and burgers for under IR£5.

There is more than one upmarket place serving affordable food at lunch time and *Seasons* near Market Square is worth checking out. *Max's Wine Bar* (☎ 021-772443) in Main St has a tourist menu before 8 pm, at IR£12; fish & chips are IR£6.75 and a vegetarian meal is IR£6.50. The atmosphere inside is old-world and relaxing. *Janey Mac* on Main St is another wine bar, serving food like stuffed pitta bread for IR£4.

In the centre of Kinsale the *White House* pub (☎ 021-772125) is the oldest in town and the small restaurant is behind the bar. It's rather a functional place but the food is excellent and lunch at under IR£5 is good

value. The evening bar menu has similar prices and a three-course dinner between 6 and 7.30 pm is IR£12. Other pubs worth a look for a drink and a bite to eat are the *1601* in Pearse St and the old-style *Greyhound* near Market Square.

Another of the Good Food Circle restaurants that is moderately priced is *Jim Edwards'* (☎ 021-772541), probably the best place for a steak in town. The *Fisherman Inn* serves dinner for less than IR£10, while *Hoby's* is a small, unpretentious place serving a three-course dinner for IR£12.50.

Places to Eat – top end The comfortable *Blue Haven* (☎ 021-772209) pub and restaurant on Pearse St is deservedly popular. Dinner is between IR£15 and IR£20, mainly seafood and specialising in lobster. A large selection of bar food is always available, including a vegetarian special for IR£8.50. The *Vintage Restaurant* (☎ 021-772502) on Main St is another favourite with gourmets. Dinner is IR£25, with main courses around IR£16.

For about IR£15 dinner can be had at the *Cottage Loft* (☎ 021-772803) on Main St. An evening meal at the *Bistro Wine Bar* (☎ 021-774193) on Guardwell is a couple of pounds dearer, but for a light lunch try their oysters at IR£4.

Man Friday (☎ 021-772260) is different, if only because it isn't rubbing shoulders with other prestigious restaurants. It is located at Scilly, a short and pleasant walk in the direction of Fort Charles. The walk is worth it for the good food and generous portions. Back in town two of the hotels have restaurants belonging to the Good Food Circle: the *Captain's Table* at Acton's and the *Savannah* at the Trident. The latest addition to the Circle is *Chez Jean-Marc* on Lower O'Connell St, where you can have Parisian cuisine with original overtones for around IR£25.

Entertainment

Kinsale has a lively pub scene in the summer and music is never difficult to find. The *1601* on Pearse St is always crowded, as is *An*

Feadós on Main St and *The Shanakee* around the corner. Just across the road, *Kieran's Folk House Inn* also has a popular bar. Out at Scilly, the *Spaniard* is a cosy pub with character. Nightclubs in town include the *White Lady*, near the Trident hotel on Lower O'Connell St and popular with younger people. The *Bacchus Brasserie*, attached to Kieran's Folk House Inn, attracts an older crowd.

Getting There & Away
Buses connect Kinsale with Cork three or four times a day. The bus stop is at the Esso garage near the tourist office.

Getting Around
Bikes, including a few children's ones, can be hired from Mylie Murphy (☎ 021-772703) in Pearse St. There is also *Deco's Cycles* (☎ 021-77884) in Main St. Taxis (☎ 021-772642) can be hired locally.

KINSALE TO CLONAKILTY
Following the quays west out of Kinsale the main R600 road passes through Ballinspittle and Timoleague before joining the main road from Bandon to reach Clonakilty. In Timoleague a detour is possible by going south to Courtmacsherry and continuing on to Clonakilty by way of a small coastal road that goes through Butlerstown.

Ballinspittle
If you've been to Knock in Mayo you'll appreciate knowing that this village narrowly avoided a similar fate. In the summer of 1985 a grotto outside of town with a statue of the Virgin Mary began to attract worshippers after it was reported that the statue had moved. Thousands, and then tens of thousands, of people reported seeing the same phenomenon and Ballinspittle was on the map. There were similar reports in other parts of the country but the whole thing came to a sudden end. The grotto is by the side of the main road before entering Ballinspittle from the direction of Kinsale.

Timoleague Friary
The friary was probably founded in the 13th century but the buildings date from various periods with alterations still being made in the early 17th century. In 1642 the place was vandalised by the English and all the stained glass was smashed, but the remains are still one of the best preserved Franciscan friaries in Ireland.

The friary is clearly visible from the road approaching Timoleague from Kinsale. The entrance is around the back.

Timoleague Castle Gardens
A moss-covered base is all that remains of the 13th-century castle that once stood here. However, the gardens are attractive and worth visiting. The palm trees in the two gardens are a startling reminder of the mild climate, and there is a superb *Callistemon linearis* (bottlebrush) tree. Admission is IR£1.50 (children IR£1) from 11 am to 5.30 pm. Follow the signs from the centre of Timoleague village or from the friary.

Places to Stay
Camping *Sexton's* camp site (☎ 023-46347) is signposted off the main road outside of Timoleague on the main road to Clonakilty.

Hostel Outside Timoleague on the right side of the road to Clonakilty, *Lettercollum House* (☎ 023-46251) was once a convent but is now a hostel and restaurant. There are three doubles and three family rooms at IR£8 per person (children IR£4) and dorm beds for IR£5.

B&Bs *Travara Lodge* (☎ 023-46493) in Courtmacsherry is an interesting Georgian house that also opens a restaurant at night. Singles/doubles are from IR£13/26. Taking the coastal scenic road from Courtmacsherry brings you to Butlerstown and *Sea Court* (☎ 023-40151), another Georgian house, with four bedrooms at IR£35 each.

Hotel The *Courtmacsherry* (☎ 023-46198) has seen better days but it remains a comfort-

Top: Cape Clear, County Cork (TW)
Left: Cobh, County Cork (TW)
Right: Blarney Castle, County Cork (TW)

Top: Dingle Peninsula, County Kerry (JM)
Bottom: Sneem, Ring of Kerry, County Kerry (TW)

able and friendly place with singles/doubles from IR£22/44. There's a self-catering wing and a riding stable attached.

Places to Eat
On the road from Kinsale to Timoleague, the *Pink Elephant* (☎ 023-49608) bar and restaurant cannot easily be missed. Good bar food is available all day, the restaurant opens around 5 pm for high tea and dinner between 7 and 9.30 pm. Prices are reasonable and, compared to some of the Kinsale places, very good value. Also signposted off the main road but on the other side of Timoleague, Lettercollum House has an interesting restaurant that serves easily the best food in the area. Meat and vegetarian à la carte dinners are available around the IR£10 mark, and a vegetarian set dinner is IR£7.50. In Timoleague village, *Dillon's* pub serves excellent bar food. Dinner at the restaurant in *Traverna Lodge* B&B is IR£12 and mostly features local seafood.

Getting There & Away
The only bus service leaves Cork at 5.45 pm for Timoleague and departs from there, outside Pat Joe's pub, at 8 am bound for Cork.

CLONAKILTY
This small town was founded early in the 17th century by the first Earl of Cork who settled it with 100 English families and planned it to be a Protestant town from which Catholics would be excluded. The plan was a failure: Clonakilty is now very Irish and very Catholic – witness the Presbyterian chapel that has been turned into a post office.

From the mid-18th until the mid-19th century the town was a centre for producing linen, employing over 10,000 people. The bakery by the public water pump was once a linen hall, and where the fire station now stands there was a linen market. The town library has been wonderfully converted from a corn mill, which was driven by the nearby river.

Today Clonakilty is well geared to the tourist market and there are a number of places to visit in the vicinity.

Orientation & Information
The tourist office (☎ 023-33226) is in Asna St but only opens during July and August, between 10 am and 6 pm Monday to Saturday, closing for lunch from 1 to 2 pm. Just three km (two miles) south of town is Inchydoney, one of the best beaches in Cork, but there is a dangerous riptide, and when lifeguards are on duty a red warning flag indicates danger.

West Cork Regional Museum
The museum is the best in Cork with much material relating to the industrial and social history of the area. It is particularly interesting for its exhibits on the nationalist struggle in the first two decades of this century. It is open from May to October, Monday to Saturday, 10.30 am to 5.30 pm and 2.30 to 5.30 pm on Sunday. Admission is IR£1 (50p for students and children free).

Horse Riding
The Rosscarbery Riding Centre (☎ 023-48232) is a farm that organises horse trekking at IR£10 per person for 90 minutes.

The farm is 11 km (seven miles) west of Clonakilty on the N71 and is signposted opposite the turn-off for Owinhincha Beach. The Henry Ford Homestead (☎ 023-39117) and the Burgatia Riding Centre (☎ 023-48232) offer a similar service.

Fishing
Deep-sea fishing and shore angling is possible at Ring. For details of boats for hire contact P Houlihan at Blackbird's pub in Connolly St. There is also Fin's Tackle Shop (☎ 023-34377) just off Emmet Square and advice could be sought here as well. For details about fishing on the nearby Argideen river ring ☎ 023-46199.

Festivals
A 10-day festival is held at the beginning of July. Contact the tourist office for details of events; you may also like to ask about a new

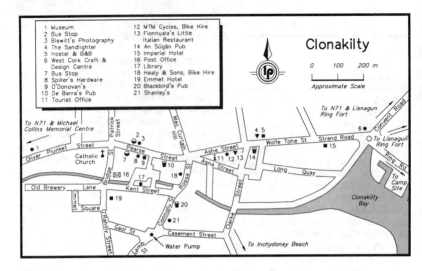

Model Village and an Animal Village which will shortly open.

Places to Stay
Camping *Desert House Caravan & Camping Park* (☎ 023-33331) is within walking distance of town on the road to Ring and overlooking the river.

Hostel At 5 Strand Rd, next to the Sandlighter restaurant, *Pauline Lowney* (☎ 023-33157) has beds for IR£5.

B&Bs There are places to be found on the N71 on both sides of Clonakilty. Within walking distance there is *Desert House* (☎ 023-33331), which is also the camp site, on the road to Ring.

Two km (three miles) along the Inchydoney road, *Youghals House* (☎ 023-33349) has singles/doubles for IR£14/24. Going 15 km (nine miles) west from Clonakilty the 17th-century house attached to *Castle Salem* (☎ 023-48381) does B&B for IR£11, plus evening meal for IR£17.50, or IR£100 for a week including evening meal. Ask for the bed that William Penn (founder of Pennsylvania) slept in.

Hotels The least expensive is the *Emmet* (☎ 023-33394), facing the lovely Emmet Square, with singles/doubles from IR£14/28. Next is the *Imperial* (☎ 023-34185), at the end of Strand Rd, at IR£16/32 while the dearest is *O'Donovan's* (☎ 023-33250) in the middle of town on Pearse St. There is also a hotel at the beach, the *Inchydoney* (☎ 023-33143), with doubles for IR£34.

Places to Eat
The *Sandlighter* on Wolfe Tone St has set meals and à la carte from IR£10 to IR£20, with bar food costing from IR£5 to IR£15. Dinner at the *Emmet* hotel will cost you IR£10, at the *Imperial* IR£13 and IR£16 at *O'Donovan's*. The last of these is also the best place for a snack or coffee during the day, although it does attract the crowds with its IR£4 lunches. *Fionnuala's Little Italian Restaurant* has pizzas from IR£6, is open seven days a week and has live music on Wednesday and Saturday nights and during the Sunday brunch period. Pub food is not difficult to find and *An Súgán* boasts a national bar food award which it has won three years running.

Entertainment

Clonakilty has a lively pub scene, especially in July during the festival period. *An Súgán* on Wolfe Tone St and *De Barra's* on Pearse St are crowded at weekends. Other places to try are *Blackbird's* or *Shanley's* in Connolly St. The popular *O'Donovan's* hotel has regular music from 9.30 pm on Monday, Wednesday, Friday and Saturday and old-time dancing on Sunday evenings during July and August. The *Emmet* hotel also has musical nights, often attracting well-known bands, and a weekend disco.

Things to Buy

The West Cork Craft & Design Centre is above the Super Valu supermarket at the east end of town. It has guaranteed, but pricey, West Cork crafts and gifts: pottery, candles, kites, jewellery and knitware.

Black pudding, made from the blood of pigs and a common ingredient in the full Irish breakfast, is found throughout Ireland but Clonakilty black pudding is particularly renowned. As such it features on menus in some of the most expensive restaurants in the county, and quite often the source is Twomey's Butchers at 16 Pearse St. The shop has a reputation for making the best black pudding in Cork.

Getting There & Away

From Monday to Saturday the Cork to Killarney bus stops in Clonakilty. It leaves at 10.25 am from outside Spiller's hardware shop in Pearse St, reaching Killarney just after 2 pm. The bus for Cork leaves at 7.10 am and 7.20 pm from outside Blewitt's photography shop, opposite the Bank of Ireland on Pearse St, reaching Cork in 80 minutes. The single fare is IR£5.90.

Getting Around

Bicycles can be hired from MTM Cycles (☎ 023-33584) in Ashe St or Healy & Sons in Rossa St.

AROUND CLONAKILTY
Cycling Tour

This is a short tour that leads to Castlefreke, just east of Rosscarbery. Take the N71 west, and after five km (three miles) take the left turn signposted for Rosscarbery, Long Strand, Red Strand and Rathbarry. Continue along this road until reaching a junction that points to Rosscarbery six km (four miles) and Owenahincha two km (1.2 miles). There is a lodge on the right side of the road, the original entrance to the Castlefreke Estate. Follow the road up by the lodge for 600 metres into a car park and ignore the old sign warning against trespassers. The pathway leads to the remains of a castle that was built in 1790 by the Freke family. The story goes that when the last of the line emigrated to Kenya, he stood at the bottom of the stairs and shot out the eyes in a portrait of an early ancestor, before walking out of the house.

The tour can be extended by following the main road down to Inchydoney Beach and then back up to the N71. From there it is a short distance to the causeway at Rosscarbery. A left turn on the other side of the causeway leads to Coppinger's Court and Dromberg Stone Circle. To reach Coppinger's Court follow the road for 1.5 km (one mile), ignoring the small turning on the left, and 200 metres after a sign for Vicky's Frames turn left. Cross a bridge and turn right at the T-junction. Coppinger's Court, a four-storey fortified house of the 17th century, is in a field on the right. The tall Elizabethan chimneys are well preserved.

The road returns to the main road taken from Rosscarbery and turning left leads to a sign on the left for Dromberg stone circle.

The main road carries on to Glandore, which has a small beach, and a bridge over the estuary leads to Union Hall.

Lisnagun Ring Fort

There are over 30,000 ring forts scattered across Ireland, but this is the only one that has been reconstructed in order to give some impression of how they were used. Excavation began in 1987 and the result is a successful restoration of a 10th-century defended farmstead, complete with souterrain and a central hut that was thatched

Michael Collins

As a young man Collins left Ireland to work as a civil servant in London but returned in 1916, at the age of 26, and took part in the Easter Rising. The experience convinced him that continued armed struggle was the only way to secure independence, and he rose to fame as the leader and organiser of a new type of urban and rural guerilla warfare.

Michael Collins inspired tremendous respect among the Irish and fear among the British who had offered a high reward for his capture. He became a living legend, not least for the ease with which he evaded arrest at checkpoints.

Collins managed to place infiltrators in various parts of the British civil and military presence in Ireland. On one memorable occasion he was conducted into the headquarters of the Dublin detective force by a double agent, and spent the night reading secret reports. His 'flying columns' and assassination squads were very successful and helped to drive the British to the negotiating table in 1921.

He did not want to travel to Downing St and negotiate terms and asked that de Valera take his place. De Valera refused, and in London Collins signed a treaty which left the six counties of the North still under British rule. He felt at the time that this was the best deal that could be secured, mainly because he knew military resistance was at breaking point. He prophetically declared, 'I have signed my own death warrant'.

On his return to Ireland, civil war broke out with de Valera heading the anti-Treaty group. Collins was killed in an ambush near Macroom in Cork, five days short of his 31st birthday. ■

by someone who spent a month working on it for free in return for his food.

The fort is open daily from 1 to 6 pm; admission is IR£1.50 (children 50p).

There is a sign to the fort on the N71 outside of town on the Bandon road or, from Clonakilty itself, take a turning at the Fax Bridge roundabout at the end of Strand Rd. The turning is the one between the road to Bandon and the road to Ring, but it is only signposted for a local B&B and not the fort. Follow the road for about three km (two miles) and there is a sign to the right for the fort.

West Cork Heritage Centre

This new centre has opened in the town of Bandon, 20 km (13 miles) to the north-east of Clonakilty and situated on a river of the same name. This was a major Protestant settlement in the 17th century, infamous for excluding Catholics. It bore a notice on the city walls declaring:

Jew, Turk or atheist
May enter here, but not a papist.

Under which, apparently, was scrawled:

Whoever wrote this wrote it well
For the same is written in the gates of Hell.

The Centre has various exhibits relating to local life through the ages, the most successful being the recreated country shop and bar. Admission is IR£2 and it's open from April to October, Monday to Saturday from 10 am to 6 pm, and on Sunday from 2 to 6 pm.

Michael Collins Memorial Centre

The centre is a memorial to Michael Collins, who was born here in 1890. The actual old house where he was born and lived for about 10 years is still standing and has been repaired. His family then built a new house where Collins lived until he emigrated to London in 1906. Very little of this home remains for it was burnt down by the Black & Tans in 1921. Despite the meagre remains, the place manages to create an aura of respect for a man who would be heartbroken to see the results of the treaty he signed in 1921.

The Memorial Centre is signposted on the N71, five km (three miles) west of Clonakilty.

Castle Salem

The most surprising aspect of this 15th-century castle is the entrance. In the 17th century a house was built onto one of the three-metre-thick castle walls, and at the top of the house's carpeted staircase an ordinary-looking door opens onto the 1st floor of the castle. There is not that much to see and the castle is slowly crumbling away.

The castle was originally called Benduff Castle. Cromwell confiscated it, and gave it to an English soldier, Major Apollo Morris, who later became a Quaker. He renamed it Shalom, Hebrew for peace, which turned into Salem. An old Quaker churchyard is behind the wall on the right immediately after entering the grounds, and it is said that William Penn visited Morris in the house.

Castle Salem is signposted on the N71, 15 km (nine miles) west of Clonakilty. Entry is IR£2 (children IR£1).

ROSSCARBERY TO SKIBBEREEN

The main N71 road from Rosscarbery to Skibbereen goes via Leap, but far more interesting is a longer route that begins by turning left at the end of the causeway at Rosscarbery. This travels nearer to the sea and takes in a number of interesting places.

Rosscarbery

This small town, where O'Donovan Rossa, founder of the Fenian Movement, was born in 1831, has a 12th-century Romanesque church with an elaborately carved doorway. The town is at the head of a landlocked inlet of Rosscarbery Bay. Turn right, if coming from Clonakilty, at the end of the causeway. The shallow estuary here is wonderful for watching wading birds.

Drombeg Stone Circle

There are scores of stone circles in West Cork but this one, nine metres (30 feet) in diameter and dating to around 100 BC, is one of the best. On the west side is a horizontal stone faced by two stones on the east that are larger than the others in the ring. The axis of these two stones with the recumbent one opposite is aligned to the midwinter sunset.

Nearby is a cooking place with a stone trough where hot stones can bring water to the boil in 15 minutes and keep it hot for hours afterwards.

Travelling from Clonakilty the N71 crosses a causeway at Rosscarbery; at the other end a road is signposted off to the left for Drombeg, Coppinger's Court and B&Bs. Along this road another sign points to the left which leads to the site.

Glandore

This little fishing village becomes sentient in the summer when well-off boating folk arrive. It would dismay William Thompson (1785-1833) who owned land here and established a commune as a model of his socialist philosophy. Marx refers to him in *Das Kapital*.

Union Hall

Disappointingly there is no union hall in this small village. It was named after the Act of Union in 1801, which abolished the separate Irish parliament. The equally unfortunate Irish name, Brean Traigh, means 'foul beach'. Jonathan Swift came here in 1723 to grieve over the death of his friend Vanessa. Outside Union Hall on the road to Castletownshend is the small **Ceim Hill Museum** (☎ 028-36280) run by a local farmer. Exhibits range from Stone Age and Iron Age artefacts to more recent documents. Admission is IR£2 (children IR£1) and it's open from 10 am to 7 pm.

Places to Stay

Rosscarbery At *Mrs Horrigan's* (☎ 023-48161) in the Post Office House, B&B is a modest IR£10.50. The *Carbery Arms* (☎ 023-48101) is in the large town square and has singles/doubles for IR£12/30.

Glandore The *Meadow Camping Park* (☎ 028-33280) is just outside the village on the road to Rosscarbery. Pitches are IR£3 and IR£4 plus IR£1 per adult (IR£3 for cyclists). One km from Glandore, *Mrs Mehigan* (☎ 028-33233) does B&B on her Kilfinnan farm, charging from IR£15 to IR£25. Across the estuary bridge in Union Hall, *Mr O'Mahony* (no telephone) at Maulicurrane does B&B for IR£10. The *Marine Hotel* (☎ 028-33366) attracts anglers.

Near Leap *Mont Bretia* (☎ 028-33663) distinguishes itself in a number of ways. The rate is a reasonable IR£11.50, a four-course wholefood evening meal is IR£10, or IR£5 for the main dish only; patrons can bring their own drink. Free tea and coffee are available all day, and the use of mountain bikes is also free. It is near Adrigole but they will collect guests from Skibbereen or Leap.

By road from Clonakility, take a right turn signposted for Drinagh off the main road, eight km (five miles) from Leap and just a couple of km (one mile) before Skibbereen. After five km (three miles) look for the Adrigole creamery and take the second left at the fork just past it. The place is up on the left.

Places to Eat
In Rosscarbery's large square there is a pleasant teashop, *Roisin's*, and *Calnan's* pub just off the square serves inexpensive bar food all day. *Glandore's Marine Hotel* serves bar food at lunch and in the evening. In Castletownsend *Mary Ann's* is an old pub serving local seafood in the bar at lunch time and early evening. The pub's restaurant (☎ 028-36146) opens in the evening.

Getting There & Away
There is no bus service to Glandore or Union Hall, but the Clonakilty to Goleen bus stops in Rosscarbery.

SKIBBEREEN
The market town of Skibbereen should really twin with a town in Algeria, for this west Cork market town owes its existence to the Algerian raiding party which raided nearby Baltimore in 1631. The frightened English settlers moved west and established two settlements which grew into Skibbereen. For a long time the town was associated with its Protestant founders, but during the famine years Skibbereen became known for the sufferings of the local Catholic peasantry. The repercussions were long-lasting: nearly half

the area's population emigrated in the first half of the 20th century. Today the town prospers from the weekly market and a steady influx of tourists on the west Cork trail.

Orientation & Information
The town's landmark is the statue dedicated to the heroes of the many Irish rebellions against the British. It stands at the junction of three roads and close to the post office. The road that goes past with the post office on the left leads south to Lough Hyne and Baltimore. The main shopping street, Main Rd, leads to a junction with Ilen St which heads west to Ballydehob and Bantry. North Rd heads towards the main Cork roads and houses the tourist office (☎ 028-21766), which has a good selection of maps and books on sale.

There is a laundrette on Main St opposite the Eldon Hotel, and another one behind the Busy Bee fast-food joint on Ilen St near the West Cork Hotel, that stays open until 9 pm. There are two small bookshops along North St, one of them selling second-hand books.

Things to See & Do
The weekly **market**, every Tuesday and Wednesday, is worth a visit if only to try and make sense of the machine-gun patter of the auctioneer. Along North Rd, next to the town's church, is the **West Cork Arts Centre**, open from 12.30 pm each day and worth checking out to see what's on. Art exhibitions are hosted regularly and in summer there is often something theatrical or musical in the area. The notice board outside lists useful information regarding local events as does the very pleasant library on the opposite side of the road. A few miles out of town, signposted on the road to Baltimore, **Tragumna**, consisting of a pub and a knitwear shop, meets the ocean, and bathing is possible here in fine weather.

Places to Stay
Hostel The *Russagh Mill Hostel* (☎ 028-22451) recently opened. It's about one mile from town on the road to Castletownshend,

on the left next to a stone-built corn mill, and charges IR£5 a night.

B&Bs The road to Baltimore is lined with places. In town *Windmill House* (☎ 028-21606) is a guesthouse with singles/doubles from IR£18/32, while *Illenside* (☎ 028-21605) at 18 Bridge St has rooms for IR£12/23.

Hotels The *West Cork Hotel* (☎ 028-21277), opposite the river on Ilen St, is the best at IR£50 a night for two. On Main Rd the *Eldon Hotel* (☎ 028-21300) has a quiet charm and singles/doubles here start at IR£16.50/35.

Places to Eat

The *Eldon Hotel* on Bridge St has a good bar menu and meals from IR£3 are available until 9 pm. The enterprising *Sables Restaurant* and wine bar is also on Bridge St and serves lunch for IR£4.24, dinner for IR£16.50 and IR£10 for a tourist menu dinner. Sables is closed on Sunday.

In Bridge St (the continuation of Main St in the direction of Schull), *Annie May's* pub has above average bar food in the IR£2 to IR£10 price range. For coffee and snacks, try *Ann O'Donovan's* next door, or the *Stove*, at the post office end of Main St, which also serves breakfast all day. *Field's Coffee Shop* is popular with local shoppers.

Definitely the most exotic menu is to be found at the *Backroom*, down past the tourist office in North St. Indonesian and Asian favourites like nasi goreng for IR£6.50 and daging rendang for IR£8.50 cost a lot more in Skibbereen than Yogyakarta but where else in the west of Cork will you find them? Further down North St, the *Windmill Tavern* has a wide-ranging menu in the IR£3 to IR£12 range. Further down the road again, by the Arts Centre, the *Ivanhoe Wine Bar* does a four-course lunch for IR£5.

Island Cottage (☎ 028-38102) is on Hare Island in Roaring Water Bay. You have to make a reservation and arrange transport, which adds IR£3 per person to the cost of the IR£14 set dinner. It's good value and good fun.

Entertainment

Sean Og's bar in Market St, near the square, has music most weekend nights, as does *Kearney's Well* in North St. *Annie May's* has some interesting musical evenings and the *West Cork Hotel* has a Wednesday cabaret from 4 pm, costing IR£3 per person.

Also worth a visit is the *Stag's Head* at Caheragh on the road to Drimoleague. In the past, when dance halls were unheard of, music and dance sessions were held on a specially surfaced area outside of pubs. The Stag's Head has recreated such a venue and there are regular Sunday afternoon dancing sessions.

Getting There & Away

Bus Éireann information is available from O'Cahalales bar next to the Eldon Hotel on Main St. Buses run daily to Cork, Baltimore, Schull, Drimoleague and Killarney, but as the schedules change during the summer and at weekends it is best to check. The bus stop is opposite the Eldon Hotel.

Getting Around

Bicycles can be hired from Roycroft & Son (☎ 028-21235, 21810 after hours) in Ilen St.

LOUGH HYNE

Lough Hyne is a saltwater lake connected to the sea by a narrow channel, and this area is now a nature reserve, with seldom-used small roads. Baltimore could be reached from here. Nearby is **Knockomagh Wood**, an attractive mixture of deciduous and evergreen trees on the right of the road approaching the lough.

Lough Hyne is six km due south of Skibbereen, and well signposted. Take the road that goes out of town keeping the post office on the left.

BALTIMORE

Situated 13 km (eight miles) down the River Ilen from Skibbereen, Baltimore has a population of around 200. During the summer months this doubles, with an influx of sailing folk and visitors to Sherkin and Clear Islands. Back in 1631 Baltimore was sacked by Algerian pirates who took over 100 people, mostly English settlers, back to Algeria as slaves.

Information

There is a small tourist office at the harbour (☎ 028-20441) which is open from 9.30 am to 5.30 pm, Monday to Saturday, closed between 12.30 and 1.30 pm for lunch. Accommodation on Clear and Sherkin Islands can be arranged through this office.

Sea Angling

There are a number of operators offering boats for chartered fishing trips. Contact the Baltimore Sea Angling Association (☎ 028-20145) for booking and information. The Algiers Inn (☎ 028-20352) also organises sea angling trips, and shorter journeys for mackerel and pollack fishing.

Places to Stay

Rolf's Hostel (☎ 028-20289) has 40 beds costing IR£4.50. Camping is possible, although at IR£3.50 per person this works out expensive for a group or family. The guesthouse *Algiers Inn* (☎ 028-20145) is open all year with beds from IR£13. There are a few B&Bs, *Corner House* (☎ 028-20143) being centrally located, with doubles from IR£26 but singles a steep IR£22 and IR£26.

Places to Eat

There is a string of restaurants overlooking the harbour. *Harbour Restaurant* has meals for IR£5 to IR£10 and serves breakfast and children's meals. *Chez Youen*, a few doors down, does French-style seafood, with lunch for IR£11.50 and dinner from IR£21 to IR£32. The *Pride of Baltimore*, above the Declan McCarthy pub, has a minimum order of IR£6 per head and a set dinner for IR£10.50.

For light meals try the inexpensive *Lifeboat Restaurant*, open from 9 am to 6 pm. It also manages the post office and a bureau de change. The *Customs House* is a quieter place with a seafood set dinner for IR£15; lunch is IR£8.

Getting There & Away

Buses from Skibbereen travel to Baltimore and back. Check the schedule at the tourist information office in Skibbereen or the information point on the Baltimore pier. Being only 13 km (nine miles) away, it is easily cycled from Skibbereen, and hitching is possible.

CLEAR ISLAND

The boat from Baltimore takes 45 minutes to cover the 11-km (seven-mile) journey to this island and it's a stunning trip on a clear day, retracing the route through the harbour that the Algerians took when they launched their attack on the village of Baltimore.

Clear Island is the most southerly point of Ireland apart from the Fastnet Rock which lies six km (four miles) to the south-west. It has about 150 Irish-speaking inhabitants, one shop and three pubs. It is a place for country walks and birdwatching; the island is probably the best place in Europe for watching the Manx shearwater and other seabirds.

Orientation & Information

The island is five km (three miles) long and just over 1.5 km (one mile) wide at its broadest. It narrows in the middle where the north and south harbours are divided by an isthmus. There is a tourist information post beyond the pier, open from 4 to 6 pm every day in July and August, but if it's closed the useful IR£2 *Walkers' Guide* is available in the nearby coffee shop.

Walking Tour

This is a circular route that takes from one to three hours.

After arriving in North Harbour, turn left at the end of the pier and take the road up the hill, ignoring the path that goes left at the coffee shop with a signpost to the heritage centre. At the shop junction go left across the isthmus; South Harbour soon comes into view. Wild flowers abound on the island; along this stretch of road the hairy birdsfoot trefoil (a yellow pea flower, lying close to the ground and with distinctive hairy leaves) can be found – it only occurs in one other spot in Ireland.

The road leads to the hostel. Turn left just before you reach it and follow the road up past the school and post office. As you go uphill, the island's two wind generators come into view on the right. They provided all the island's needs until the increase in summer visitors. However, to avoid the relatively small expenditure needed to upgrade the system, the windmills will be removed and underground cables laid from Sherkin Island. Meanwhile, the government is spending more than the money needed to upgrade Clear Island's generators on a similar wind-energy system on Inishvickillaun, the small Kerry island owned by the former Taoiseach, Charles Haughey.

At the T-junction, turn left and head towards the eastern end of the island. There are a couple of turnings on the left that lead down to the sea but there are no beaches to speak of. The lovely sandy beaches in the distance are on Sherkin Island.

Returning to the T-junction, rather than turn left continue straight on to the **heritage centre**. In the summer it is open from 3.30 to 5.30 pm, entry is IR£1 (children 50p), and it contains exhibits on the history and culture of the island. There are fine views looking north across the water to the Mizen Head Peninsula. From the centre it is a short distance downhill to the shop and pubs.

Birdwatching

The Bird Observatory is a white-fronted two-storey building by the harbour. Turn right at the end of the pier and it's 100 metres along. If you have not booked in to stay here it is still worth calling in and asking about any birdwatching trips that might be planned. Clear Island is famous for its movements of large seabirds, especially in July and August when Manx shearwaters, gannets, fulmars and kittiwakes regularly fly past the south of the island. The guillemot is the only notable seabird that breeds on the island; the others live on the westerly Kerry rocks and fly past the island heading for the Celtic and Irish seas. In the evening they

return and the sight is equally amazing; in summer up to 35,000 shearwaters can fly past in an hour, just above the surface of the water.

The best place to view the seabirds is at Blananarragaun, the south-west tip of the island. To reach it from the pier, head up to the shop and turn right, following the sign for the camp site. When the road comes to an end just go due south to the end of the spur of land.

The Bird Observatory has a useful library of books but the one to read up beforehand is *The Natural History of Cape Clear Island* edited by Sharrock (London, 1973). The book is no longer in print so only libraries will have copies.

Places to Stay

The camp site (☎ 028-31149) costs IR£2 per person (children IR£1.50) and is signposted from the shop. It is open from 1 June to the end of September.

The *An Óige Hostel* (☎ 028-39144) costs IR£5.50, is open all year and is a short walk from the pier. The *Bird Observatory* (no telephone) has limited hostel accommodation for IR£5 which can be booked through Kieran Grace (☎ 01-785444), 84 Dorney Court, Shankill, County Dublin. There is no harm in just turning up and seeing if a bed is available. It's most likely to be full at the beginning of October.

B&B is available at *Cluain Mara* (☎ 028-39153) for IR£15, evening meal IR£10, and is available all year. The house is up behind the last of the three pubs and is signposted. Another possibility is *Harbour View* (☎ 028-39102). New self-catering cottages are about to become available; ring the Cluain Mara for details.

Places to Eat

There is no restaurant on the island so bring your own food. There is one shop near the pier but its stock is limited. The café serves light meals. There are three pubs within staggering distance of each other and at night drinking-up time is generous.

Getting There & Away

The boat office (☎ 028-39119) and the tourist office in Baltimore have boat timetables.

From Baltimore the return cost is IR£7 (children IR£3.50, IR£16 family ticket for two adults and two children). There is no extra charge for bikes. From Schull (☎ 028-28138) the return cost is IR£6 (children IR£2 and bikes IR£1). Boats leave from the pier in Schull during July and August at 10 am, 2.30 and 4.30 pm, and sometimes there's a service in May also.

SHERKIN ISLAND

People tend to visit this small island – it's five km (three miles) long and about the same wide – for two reasons: the beaches and the two pubs. There are three sandy areas: Trabawn, Cow and Silver strands, all on the far side of the island and reached by road from the pier. All three are safe for swimming and suitable for children. In late August each year a regatta is held and the pubs stay open even longer than usual. The best place for general information is the post office (☎ 028-20181), which is beside the road running across the island from the pier to the beaches.

Places to Stay & Eat

Camping is free; ask permission from the farmer first.

B&Bs on the island includes *Garrison House* (☎ 028-20185), *Island House* (☎ 028-20314), *Cuina* (☎ 028-20384), the *Jolly Roger Tavern* (☎ 028-20379) and *Buggy's* (☎ 028-20384). These all charge about IR£15 per person, with the exception of Buggy's which is IR£12 (IR£8 for children).

The two pubs, at Garrison House and the Jolly Roger, both serve bar food. The Jolly Roger is the older of the two and near the remains of the old O'Driscoll Castle; to get there turn right just before the post office.

Getting There & Away

There is a regular boat service from Baltimore (☎ 028-20125) and the journey takes less than 10 minutes. The boat service runs seven times a day, starting at 10.30 am; the last boat leaves Sherkin at 8.45 pm. The fare is IR£3 return.

The Mizen Head Peninsula

From Skibbereen the road winds west to Ballydehob. Expatriates from Britain and north European countries are scattered across west Cork, and while Kinsale attracts the well-heeled, others such as the less economically advantaged, or blow-ins as they are semi-affectionately called, have discovered the land around Ballydehob. From the town the road goes west to Schull, with Mt Gabriel in view most of the time, easily identified by the two tracking spheres perched on the summit. They are part of an air-and-sea monitoring system, and some years ago the IRA tried to bomb the installation claiming it was part of NATO (Ireland is not a member of NATO). Around 1500 BC the lower slopes of the mountain were extensively mined for copper. The mountain's summit can be reached by road.

From the top of Mt Gabriel and most high ground on the peninsula, there are views of the Fastnet Lighthouse on a rock 11 km (seven miles) off the coast. The first lighthouse was built there in 1854 and was replaced in 1906 by a sturdier one which is now fully automated.

The next stop west is Goleen, a small village passed through on the way to Crookhaven, Barleycove and Three Castle Head. The end of the peninsula offers history, nature and the best beach in west Cork.

Returning from Mizen Head you can take a coastal road that keeps Dunmanus Bay on the left for most of the way to Durrus. At Durrus one road leads on to Bantry and the other goes out west to the Sheep's Head Peninsula.

BALLYDEHOB

The name of this picturesque village comes from the Irish Beal Atha an dha Chab, meaning 'the ford at the mouth of two rivers'. Coming into the village from the east, look out for the old 12-arched tramway viaduct.

Places to Stay

There is a small but cosy camp site (☎ 028-37232) about 200 metres from the village on the road to Durrus. Charges are IR£2.50 per person (IR£1 for children). B&B in Ballydehob is available at the *Ballydehob Inn* (☎ 028-37139) from IR£16/32 for singles/doubles. On the road to Schull, *Lynwood* (☎ 028-37124) has rooms for IR£18/28.

Places to Eat

The *Ballydehob Inn*, on the corner of the road to Durrus, serves bar food and has a restaurant. *Duggan's* is in the centre of the village opposite the garage and is the least expensive place for light meals and takeaways. *Annie's*, a few doors down, does lunch for IR£7.50, and dinner for IR£20. The menu is seafood and steaks. A similar menu, but better prepared food, can be found at the *Teach Dearg Restaurant* (☎ 028-37282) to the north-east of Ballydehob at Scarteenakilleen, reached by turning right off the road to Bantry.

Getting There & Away

The twice-daily bus between Clonakilty and Schull stops in Ballydehob.

SCHULL

A small village at the foot of Mt Gabriel (401 metres or 1339 feet), Schull in summer is as touristy as anywhere on the Ring of Kerry. In winter the craft and antique shops are mostly closed. For the best view of its harbour and Fastnet Rock, take the road from Ballydehob to Durrus and Goleen, and turn off for Schull after five km (three miles).

Information

Tourist information is available, in the summer only, from a small office in a car park opposite the Spar supermarket in the main street. It opens from 2 to 6 pm, and on Sunday from noon to 2 pm. Also during the summer a boat for Clear Island leaves from the pier.

Mizen Books and Fuschia Books are both on the main street.

The Planetarium

The only planetarium in the Republic (☎ 028-28552) has an eight-metre dome and a video and slide show. From 23 June to 29 August it is open from 11 am to 8 pm (closed from 1 to 2 pm and all day Monday and Sunday) with star shows on Tuesday, Thursday and Saturday at 7 pm. Admission is IR£2.50 (children IR£1.50).

At the Goleen end of the village there is a sign pointing the way to the left to the planetarium.

Places to Stay

B&Bs The two best B&Bs are at opposite ends of the village. Coming in from Ballydehob a sign on the left points the way to *White Castle Cottage* (☎ 028-28528), overlooking Roaring Water Bay and the ruins of a castle. Singles/doubles range from IR£16 to IR£26. More expensive is *Corthna Lodge Country House* (☎ 028-28517), a short distance out of the village and signposted at the Goleen end; its rooms are IR£22/36.

Hotels In Schull the *East End Hotel* (☎ 028-28101) in Main St has singles/doubles ranging from IR£20 to IR£35. *Colla House* (☎ 028-28105) is similarly priced.

Self-Catering Self-catering accommodation is popular around Schull and most of the places are usually booked in advance. Cottages at Colla pier, just outside the village, and another cluster of cottages overlooking the harbour can be booked through *O'Keeffe* at 48 Main St (☎ 028-28122). In July and August the price for a four-bedroom cottage rockets to IR£495 a week; in May it's IR£220, and June IR£330. Holiday homes that sleep four can be booked through *Veron-*

ica Desmond of Gurteenroe, Bantry, Cork (☎ 027-50525) for IR£230 in July and August, IR£90 in May.

Places to Eat

The *Courtyard* in Main St is a bar and restaurant down an alley beside a wholefood shop of the same name with a coffee bar at the back. The coffee bar serves light meals that includes a vegetarian choice, the bar has tasty seafood and the restaurant has a meat and seafood menu. Prices are reasonable. To sample some of the locally baked bread with coffee try *Adele's*, also in Main St. The largest bar menu is to be found at the *Bunratty Inn* at the Goleen end of the village. *Andy's* on Main St serves fish & chips, burgers and the like.

There are two cheese-making farms near Schull; their produce features on village menus, and you can also visit them and buy cheese wholesale. Contact either *Gubbeen House* (☎ 028-28231) or *West Cork Natural Cheeses* (☎ 028-28593) to check they are open and receive directions.

Getting There & Away

Twice a day a bus leaves Clonakilty, at 10.25 am and 7.05 pm, for Schull via Skibbereen and Ballydehob. The bus leaves Schull at 8.05 am and 5.30 pm from near the AIB bank at the Goleen end of the village.

Getting Around

Bicycles can be hired from the Cotter's Yard craft shop (☎ 028-28165), for IR£8 per 24 hours. Boats can sometimes be hired from Schull Watersport Centre (☎ 028-28554).

WEST OF SCHULL TO MIZEN HEAD

The road west from Schull leads to the small village of Goleen. The surrounding area is, in the words of the local TD in danger of declining into a land of 'briars, bullocks and bachelors'. From Goleen one road runs out to Mizen Head and the other to Crookhaven.

Crookhaven

The village is built on the far side of a spur of land that runs eastwards enclosing a harbour. The road from Goleen comes down to the north side of the harbour, passing the remains of a once-thriving stone quarry. Crookhaven was once very important as the most westerly harbour along the coast. Mail from America was collected here and the place was a busy port for sailing and fishing ships from all over the world.

Today the village still attracts a few sailing people and there are a couple of B&Bs, pubs and seafood restaurants.

Barleycove

This is west Cork's most splendid beach, and because a smaller beach nearer the camp site attracts holidaymakers, Barleycove itself is never crowded. It's a great place for children, with long stretches of sand and a safe sandy area where a stream flows down to the sea.

Mizen Head

A lighthouse stands on an island of rock connected to the mainland by a bridge. Visitors are not allowed on the bridge but there are tremendous views all around. Follow the main path beyond the car-park area and pass beneath the concrete arch on the right. Just a little farther on, a path goes up to the right by rough steps, which lead to the top of the cliff and more spectacular views. Head for the old signal house but keep to the left of it and avoid the cliff edge. A path makes its way around a huge cleft and eventually comes to a sheep fence. The fence can be climbed and the open heath crossed to Three Castle Head. The whole journey to Three Castle Head would take at least an hour and should only be undertaken on a fine dry day when visibility is clear.

Three Castle Head

A prime reason for making the journey to Three Castle Head is to visit the 13th-century castle at the end of the headland. Once a stronghold of the O'Mahoneys, it is mentioned in the 'Annals of Innisfallen' as having been built in 1217. Today it stands a lonely ruin by the side of a supposedly haunted lake, with a sheer drop to the sea behind it.

Leaving the car park of the Barley Cove Beach Hotel, do not turn left for Mizen Head but go right and then left at the first T-junction. This quickly leads to another junction with a sign pointing left to the Ocean View B&B. Go right instead, follow the road to its end, and climb the farm gate on the right. Ask permission to visit the castle from the house, and check on which path to take.

Places to Stay

Camping There is a camping and caravan site (☎ 028-35302) at Barleycove, open from May to September, which is popular and expensive (IR£6 and IR£5 for tents, plus IR£1 per person).

B&Bs In Goleen *Mrs Hill* (☎ 028-35225) has rooms available from the end of March to late October. Crookhaven has *Marconi House*, on the right when entering the village, where Marconi erected a radio mast in 1902, and *Galley Cove* (☎ 028-35137) half a km outside the village, to your left when approaching it. The closest accommodation to Mizen Head is at the *Barley Cove Beach Hotel* (☎ 028-35234). B&B during the summer is IR£78 for a double, more at weekends, and there are self-catering units that range from IR£75 a week in winter to IR£365 during the summer. Along the road from the hotel to Three Castles Head there are a couple of farms offering B&B in summer.

Self-Catering There's plenty of self-catering accommodation on the peninsula. At Crookhaven some of the old coastguard cottages can be rented from *O'Keeffe's* (☎ 028-28122) at 48 Main St, Schull.

Places to Eat

In Goleen the *Heron's Cove Restaurant* is open from noon for seafood and steaks. Lunch is IR£7.50, dinner IR£12. Crookhaven has a couple of pubs serving food, such as the *Welcome Inn* which does a three-course meal for IR£12.50 and the *Crookhaven Inn* with a bar menu until 8 pm, mostly featuring seafood open sandwiches

from IR£1.70 to IR£5.50. *Marconi House* also has a restaurant and, on the left just before entering the village, *Journey's End* restaurant offers seafood lunches and dinner from IR£12 (IR£16 for lobster). At the *Barley Cove Beach Hotel* there is a restaurant, bar food and afternoon tea. Lunch in the restaurant is around IR£9 while dinner is IR£17.50.

The best place for food is the *Altar Restaurant* (☎ 028-35254), on the left side of the road between Schull and Goleen and just before the right turn off to Durrus.

Getting There & Away

The Clonakilty to Goleen bus leaves Clonakilty at 7.05 pm and stops in Rosscarbery, Leap, Skibbereen, Ballydehob and Schull. It can be flagged down anywhere along the road. There is no bus to Crookhaven or west of Goleen.

BANTRY

Bantry narrowly missed fame in the late 18th century, thanks to the storms that prevented a massive French landing. A local Englishman, Richard White, was rewarded with a peerage for his efforts in trying to alert the military in Cork. His grand home is open to the public and this, along with an exhibition devoted to the events of 1796, is now the main attraction of the town.

Before Irish independence, Bantry Bay was a major anchorage for the British navy, and after WW II Spanish trawlers were regular visitors to the town. The deep waters of the bay were also exploited by Gulf Oil who built an oil terminal on Whiddy Island and brought an unexpected prosperity to the town. The island comes close to Bantry Harbour and can be seen from the Cork road when entering the town. In 1979 a fire broke out at the terminal and 51 lives were lost. Although Gulf Oil still have an interest in the island, huge oil tankers are no longer a familiar sight in Bantry Bay.

Orientation & Information

The two main roads into Bantry both lead to the large town square, now mostly given over to a free car park, but once the location of an important cattle market on the first Friday of each month. A fair of sorts is still held on that day, and some of the region's many expatriates, known as 'hippies' or 'blow-ins' to the locals, are to be found selling their wares.

During summer the tourist office (☎ 027-50229) is open on the south side of the square. On the north side are the headquarters of Earthwatch (☎ 027-50968), Ireland's main ecological campaigning group. The square also houses a laundrette.

Museum

There is a small museum just behind the fire station (from May to September, Tuesday and Thursday, 10.30 am to 1 pm, Wednesday and Friday 3 to 5.30 pm). It houses a modest local history collection.

Bantry House

Bantry House is superbly situated overlooking the bay. Parts of the house date back to the mid-18th century but the fine north front overlooking the sea was added in 1840. The gardens are beautifully kept and the house is noted for its French and Flemish tapestries and the eclectic collection assembled by the 2nd Earl of Bantry during his overseas peregrinations between 1820 and 1850. Entry is IR£2.50 (students IR£1.50, children free with family) and it's open 9 am to 6 pm daily, to 8 pm during the summer. The old kitchen, with range intact, is now a tearoom and craft shop. The grounds can be viewed free.

French Armada Exhibition Centre

In the grounds of the house is a French Armada exhibition (IR£2.50, students IR£1.50, children IR£1) recounting the sorry saga of the attempted French landing of 1796. The exhibit centres around the scuttled French frigate *La Surveillante*, which it is hoped will eventually be raised from Bantry Bay.

On the main Bantry to Cork road, about three km (two miles) outside town and almost opposite Barry's garage, there is an anchor from one of the French ships, found by a trawler in 1964.

Kilnaruane Pillar Stone

This pillar stone may once have formed part of a High Cross as it bears characteristic carved scenes from the Bible, such as Saints Paul and Anthony in the desert which is on one of the south-west panels. Coming out of Bantry it is signposted on the left immediately after the Westlodge Hotel. The stone is in a field 500 metres along on the right.

Cruises

Whiddy Island can be reached by a boat (☎ 027-50494) which leaves from the pier every hour on the hour during the summer, from 10 am onwards; the last boat on the return journey departs from Whiddy at 11.30 pm, and the journey costs IR£4 return. On the island the *Bank House* pub and restaurant (☎ 027-51739) serves bar food and meals, mostly seafood. A four-course dinner costs around IR£20.

Festivals

In the second week of May Bantry holds a Mussel Fair – mussels are usually distributed around the pubs.

A regatta takes place in August.

Places to Stay

Camping The nearest camp site is *Eagle Point* (☎ 027-50630), six km (four miles) from town on the road to Glengarriff.

Hostel The *Bantry Independent Hostel* (☎ 027-51050) is off the Glengarriff Rd at Bishop Lucy Place; take the fork by the Key Properties office and continue uphill almost to the top. The nightly cost is IR£5 and boat trips are organised from here in a local fishing boat.

B&Bs Top of the range is *Bantry House* (☎ 027-50047, fax 027-51417) where a room for two is IR£95. There are plenty of ordinary B&Bs around including a number around the central square, out along the

Glengarriff Rd and at the top end of town, just beyond the oddly shaped library building. *Shangri-La* (☎ 027-50244), on the Glengarriff road, has a good reputation but fills up quickly. In town *Vickery's Inn* (☎ 02750006) has singles/doubles from IR£14/28.

Green Lodge (☎ 027-66146) is a vegetarian B&B costing IR£24 for two, and it's a little way out of town near Ballylickey. To get there, take the road to Glengarriff and you'll see a sign pointing the way where the road turns off to Macroom.

Hotels The *Bantry Bay Hotel* (☎ 027-50062) is near the square and has singles/doubles for IR£30/50. Bantry's other hotel is the *Westlodge* (☎ 027-50360), a charmless building a couple of km (one mile) outside of town on the road to Cork. Singles/doubles here start are IR£43/67 and it has its own indoor swimming pool.

Self-Catering There are eight holiday homes on Whiddy Island available for weekly or weekend bookings. Contact the Bank House restaurant (☎ 027-51739) on the island for details.

Places to Eat
The expensive and highly acclaimed *O'Connor's* is right next to the tourist office. At the other end of Bridge St, *Ó Síocháin* has a standard café-style menu with main courses around IR£5. Opposite the supermarket, *Vickery's Inn*, once the coaching inn, does a three-course lunch for IR£6, specials for IR£3.50, and dinner for IR£12; the food is unadventurous but filling. *Peter's* is a steak house with meals from IR£6.

A number of pubs serve bar lunches. The popular *Vickery's Inn* is comfortable and costs around IR£4. The only vegetarian place in town is *5A* in Barrack St but it closes at 5.30 pm. *Nicholson's* is a new place on the other side of the road and offers the best array of sandwiches and snacks in Bantry.

Larchwood House Restaurant (☎ 027-66181) is outside town but worth the journey for the five-course dinner costing around IR£22. The chef and proprietor has a proper respect for vegetables. To get there turn right at the sign about three km (two miles) out on the road to Glengarriff.

Also off the road to Glengarriff, signposted where a right turn leads to Macroom, the *Tra Amici* (☎ 027-50235) is an elegant Italian restaurant. It's open from 7.30 to 9.30 pm and meals cost around IR£20.

Entertainment
The *Wolfe Tone Tavern* near the square has musical evenings and *James Crowley* nearby is another reliable venue throughout the summer. The *Bantry Bay Hotel* is also worth a look and the *Anchor Tavern*, even without music, is an interesting old pub.

Getting There & Away
During summer only there is an express bus service between Cork and Killarney that stops in Bantry. It leaves for Glengarriff, Kenmare and Killarney at noon and departs for Skibbereen, Clonakilty and Cork at 6.10 pm. Throughout the year there are three buses a day between Cork and Bantry.

The private Berehaven bus travels between Castletownbere and Bantry via Glengarriff. The first bus leaves Bantry at 11.25 on Monday, 3.45 pm on Tuesday, Friday and Saturday.

Getting Around
Bicycles can be hired from Carrowell (☎ 027-50278), on the right side of the Glengarriff road behind a small minimarket. From the top of Barrack St it is less than a km away. The daily rate is IR£5 to IR£6 and longer rentals could be negotiated.

GOUGANE BARRA FOREST PARK
There is a green island in lone Gougane Barra
Where Allua of song rushes forth as an arrow,
In deep vallied Desmond – a thousand wild fountains
Come down to that lake from their home in the mountains.
J J Callanan, 18th-century Cork poet

This is the most picturesque part of inland Cork. The source of the River Lee is a mountain lake, fed by numerous streams. St

Finbar, the founder of Cork, came here in the 6th century and established a monastery. He had a hermitage on the island in the lake, which is now approached by a short causeway. There is a small modern chapel on the island.

A road runs through the park in a loop and a number of meandering paths that lead off it. There is a signboard map in the park, and it is worth heading for Bealick's summit for the fine views. Take the road to Glengarriff from Bantry and after five km (three miles) turn right at the bridge, signposted for Macroom. There is a signposted turning to the left for Gougane Barra about 28 km (18 miles) before Macroom.

Places to Stay & Eat

Near the main park entrance is the *Gougane Barra Hotel* (☎ 026-47069), with singles/doubles for IR£35/64. Bar food is available and there is a café next door as well as a gift shop.

Carrying on along the road to Macroom, you come to Ballingeary and the *Tig Barra* hostel (☎ 026-47016). It is about three km (two miles) from the turn-off to Gougane Barra to the left of the main road. Camping is available for IR£2.50.

B&B is available from *O'Mahoney* (☎ 026-47023) at Cois Laoi Farmhouse. As the name of the farm might suggest, people around Ballingeary speak Irish.

Sheep's Head Peninsula

This is the least visited of Cork's three peninsulas although it has a charm all of its own. There are no substantial antiquities, but a loop road runs close to the sea for most of the way and there are wonderful seascapes to appreciate and country walks where other visitors will be few and far between.

The second turning on the right after leaving Bantry for Cork is the beginning of the **Goat's Path Scenic Route**, which approaches the peninsula from the northern side. The southern part of the loop road

begins farther along the main road, just past the Esso garage.

WALKING TOURS

The start of a walk to the top of **Seefin** (334 metres, 1136 feet) is at the top of the Goat's Path. Across the road from here rests a forlorn imitation of Michelangelo's *Pietà*, erected by an American with local family roots. While there is no obvious path it is not difficult to aim for the summit and reach it in less than 45 minutes. There are fine views from the top, and not many people go there.

A good two to three-hour walk could also be enjoyed by taking an overgrown road that begins 50 metres to the right of the *Pietà* statue. It is utterly remote until it joins a surfaced road that heads out farther west along the peninsula and eventually crosses over to the southern side from where the main road leads back to Kilcrohane. A left turn at the village church would return you to the start of the walk at the top of the Goat's Path.

PLACES TO STAY

Just west of Ahakista a sign points the way to *Hillcrest* B&B (☎ 027-67045) with singles/doubles from IR£18.50/27. There are other B&Bs dotted along the road and the rates are almost identical so it's just a matter of picking one that takes your fancy.

In the village of Kilcrohane, the *Dunmahon* (☎ 027-67092) has doubles for IR£28, and the *Bay View* pub (☎ 027-67068) has a few rooms. Five km (three miles) west of Kilcrohane, *Farmhouse B&B* (☎ 027-67136) lives up to its name: a genuine working farmhouse with great views of the sea.

The *Dunbeacon Campsite* (☎ 027-61246) is about five km (three miles) from Durrus on the road to Goleen. The charges are IR£1 per adult plus IR£1 for a car. Children under 10 are not charged.

PLACES TO EAT
Durrus

Cronin's is a pub with bar food and a small bistro next door. Opposite the post office, where the road to Kilcrohane begins, there is a small café. Just outside Durrus, on the road to Goleen, *Blair's Cove* (☎ 027-61127) is reputed to serve wonderful seafood and meat dishes. Dinner is in the IR£30 price range.

Ahakista & Kilcrohane

Arundel's pub in Ahakista serves soup and sandwiches, and has a pleasant garden at the back in which to eat them. *Shiro Japanese Dinner House* (☎ 027-67030) is opposite the pub and charges outrageous prices for dinner at its two tables. Sandwiches and soup are served in Kilcrohane's two pubs, and dinner at the *Dunmahon* is IR£10.

GETTING THERE & AWAY

There is no public transport apart from two Saturday buses that depart from Bantry at 10 am and 2.30 pm for Durrus and Kilcrohane.

Beara Peninsula

The appeal of the Beara Peninsula lies in its startling natural beauty, best experienced by climbing the hills and cycling the roads. It's a lot bigger and much wilder than its neighbouring peninsula to the south. While the Mizen Head and Sheep's Head peninsulas are lush and green, reminiscent of the Ireland imagined by long-departed emigrants, the Beara is desolate, a harsh and rocky landscape which had to be fought for survival. As well as the usual smattering of B&B places there are some interesting hostels and camp sites. A quick visit could easily extend itself into a longer stay.

It's wonderful walking country, and the Beara Way is a new long-distance walk, 215 km (133 miles) long, linking Glengarriff with Kenmare via Castletownbere, Bere Island, Dursey Island and the north side of the peninsula. Much of the route is along green roads and should be fully signposted for 1994. Contact the tourist office at Kenmare or Castletownbere for maps and details.

ORIENTATION & INFORMATION

There are no tourist offices on the peninsula so any enquiries should be made to those at Glengarriff or Kenmare, which head the southern and northern bays respectively. Kenmare and a small part of the peninsula to the west of the town are in Kerry and therefore covered in that chapter.

A trip round the coastal roads is 137 km (85 miles). You could drive it in one day, but little would be achieved except a lot of gear changes. The spectacular Healy Pass joins Adrigole with Lauragh in Kerry. Castletownbere is well placed as a base for exploring the peninsula.

GLENGARRIFF

This village's fame is due to its proximity to Garnish Island and its location on the main West Cork to Killarney road. The village itself is strung out along the main road with the Eccles Hotel at one end. At the other end, the roads to Kenmare and the Beara Peninsula divide. Its sheltered position at the head of Bantry Bay, together with the influence of the Gulf Stream, give it a particularly mild climate, and the local flora are lush and sometimes exotic.

During the second half of the 19th century Glengarriff became a popular retreat for prosperous Victorians. They would sail from England to Ireland then take the train to Bantry from where a paddle steamer chugged over to Glengarriff. By 1850 the road to Kenmare had been blasted through the mountains and the link with Killarney was established.

A major attraction is the Italianate garden on Garnish island.

Information

During July and August tourist information (☎ 027-63084) is available from the small portacabin in the car park outside the Eccles Hotel. It opens from 9.30 am to 5 pm (closed between 1 and 2 pm). Local walk leaflets are available.

Fees for fishing rights on the river are payable at the Maple Leaf pub (IR£5 a day, IR£10 a week).

Spotted Slug

Garnish Island
This small island (15 hectares, 37 acres) was turned into an Italianate garden in the early years of the 20th century. It was designed by Harold Peto, who brought in exotic plants never before seen in Ireland, and they continue to flourish, providing a blaze of colour in a landscape usually dominated by greens and browns. There is a walkway on the island to the Martello Tower.

Boats leave from the seafront in the village (☎ 027-63081) and from the Blue Pool just a little way west on the Castletownbere road (☎ 027-63170; IR£4 for adults and IR£2 for children). The gardens on the island (☎ 027-63040) have a separate entrance charge of IR£1.50.

Glengarriff Woods
The woods were part of the estate of the White family of Bantry House in the 18th century. Oak and pine were planted, and after the government took over in the 1950s the range of trees was expanded. The thick cover of trees maintains humid conditions that allow a profusion of ferns and mosses to flourish. At the beginning of the walk look out especially for very small white flowers on red stems rising from rosettes of leaves: kidney saxifrage, rare elsewhere.

The woodlands and bogs also provide a home for the Kerry slug (*Geomalacus maculosus*), only found here and in parts of Kerry and the Iberian Peninsula. Coffee-coloured with cream spots, it has been described as the aristocrat of slugs.

Leave Glengarriff in the direction of Kenmare; the entrance to the woods is about one km (half a mile) along on the left.

Places to Stay
Camping *Dowling's Caravan & Camping Park* (☎ 027-63154) is two km (one mile) west of Glengarriff on the road to Castletownbere. It has its own licensed bar and music in the summer. Close by is *O'Shea's Caravan & Camping Park* (☎ 027-63140). Both charge IR£6 for a tent but O'Shea's fee for cyclists, at IR£5, is IR£2 less than Dowling's.

Hostels The German-run *Tooreen Hostel* (☎ 027-63075) is four km (2.5 miles) out on the Kenmare road and they will collect you from the village. Bikes can be hired here.

B&Bs On the seafront, *Mrs Guerin* (☎ 027-63079) has three beds for IR£13 each. *Island View House* (☎ 027-63081) has beds from IR£13 to IR£15.

Hotels *Eccles Hotel* (☎ 027-63003) is the grand old hotel of Glengarriff, boasting literary guests that have included Thackeray, Yeats and Shaw. Facing the sea on the main road at the Bantry end of the village, it offers rooms for two with breakfast at IR£56. The other hotel is *Connolly's Golf Links* (☎ 027-63009) with doubles from IR£36.

Places to Eat
Lunch and dinner at *Eccles* are IR£9 and IR£16.50 respectively, and afternoon tea is pleasant amid the faded elegance of the foyer.

Johnny Barry's on Main St is a seafood restaurant, and there's music just across the road in the *Maple Leaf* lounge. Coffee shops are not hard to find.

Getting There & Away
The bus stop is opposite Johnny Barry's Restaurant. The Cork to Killarney bus leaves for Kenmare and Killarney at 12.25 pm and for Bantry, Clonakilty and Cork at 5.30 pm. This is a summer-only service, from 8 June to 26 September. All year there is an express

service between Cork and Glengarriff that travels inland via Dunmanway.

The private Berehaven bus departs for Bantry at 7.45 am and 5.20 pm on Monday, 11.20 am Tuesday, Friday and Saturday, and 8.15 am on Thursday (travelling on to Cork on Thursday). It leaves for Castletownbere at 11.55 am and 8.50 pm on Monday, 4.15 pm on Tuesday, Friday and Saturday, and 8.25 pm on Thursday.

CASTLETOWNBERE

Castletownbere developed out of the mining industry at Allihies, and it is the main town on the peninsula.

Tourist information (☎ 027-70344) is available during the summer from a garden shed squeezed in next to the fire station in the town square. It's open from 11 am to 5 pm, Monday to Saturday, closing between 1 and 2 pm.

There is a good supermarket, a post office with a limited bureau de change, a laundrette and a string of pubs, some with music at night. There are also fishing boats for hire (☎ 027-75062).

A sign to the west of the town points to a **stone circle** which is 1.5 km (one mile) along the road on the right-hand side.

Places to Stay

There are half a dozen B&Bs, including *Mrs S Murphy* (☎ 027-70099) along West End, and *Mrs Harrington* (☎ 027-70252) on the road to Glengarriff.

Places to Eat

The *Old Cottage Restaurant*, just before entering town from the Glengarriff side, and *Jack Patrick's* in town both do lunch and dinner. There is also the *Old Bank Seafood Restaurant* and on the way out to Dursey the *Hole in the Wall* pub has sandwiches and snacks. The *Berehaven Inn* has a set lunch for under IR£5.

Stephanie's is a new restaurant on the main street at the west end of town, serving local seafood. Dinner is around IR£25 per person. *Niki's*, on the right when you enter the town from the east, has its home inside an old pharmacy and has seafood dinners for around IR£10. It also does reasonable lunches and breakfasts.

Getting Around

Bikes can be hired from *Dudley Cycles* (☎ 027-70293). Heading out of town to the west, turn right at the signpost for the stone circle; Dudley is a few hundred metres up the road.

BERE ISLAND

The island was once the base for the British navy. At the outbreak of WW II, Winston Churchill wanted to continue using it, and a deal for the return of the six northern counties was discussed. However it was not to be.

Today there is little reason to visit the island and this is reflected in the fact that tourist accommodation is limited to one B&B, *Mrs O'Sullivan* (☎ 027-75011) at Harbour View. It would make sense to ring in advance.

A ferry service for **Bere Island** runs from Castletownbere quay; IR£12 return for a car including driver, IR£3 for an adult, IR£1.50 for children. During July and August there are five boats a day, from 10.30 am to 6 pm.

DUNBOY CASTLE & PUXLEY CASTLE

Little now remains of Dunboy Castle, the fortress of the O'Sullivans, who ruled supreme for three centuries before succumbing to the English with cannon and 4000 men in 1602. It's signposted after Castletownbere.

Nearby the roofless remains of Puxley Castle bear testimony to the vast wealth generated by the copper mined on the estate of the Puxley family. It was built in the 19th century, and although it was burnt down during the War of Independence, enough of it remains to show the extravagance of its style.

ALLIHIES COPPER MINES

Copper was discovered in 1810 and mining started two years later. It brought wealth to the Puxley family who owned the land but low wages and dangerous, unhealthy work conditions for the workforce, which at one time numbered 1300 men, women and children. Experienced miners from Cornwall were brought into the area, and the ruins of their stone cottages remain. As late as the 1930s, over 30,000 tonnes of pure copper were being exported but by 1962 the last mine was closed.

Walking Tour

The mines are just north of the village of Allihies, 19 km (12 miles) west of Castletownbere, and signs point the way to the remains of an untidy quarry. An old road leads up to the ruins of a chimney stack, from where the road can be followed further up, passing an old reservoir on the right. Mine shafts are scattered around the place but they are fenced off and the main chimney stack can be approached in relative safety. The track eventually leads to Eyeries and can be followed for as long as you wish. Half an hour's walk leads to a point with a view of Coulagh Bay and Kenmare Bay beyond. You can climb the hills by cutting over the moor to the right, but it is best to consult one of the local walking guides such as *West Cork Walks* by Kevin Corcoran (O'Brien Press, Dublin).

DURSEY ISLAND

At the end of the peninsula the island of Dursey is only 250 metres away, and a cable car connects the 20 or so inhabitants and their cattle with the mainland. Three hundred people sought refuge here in 1602, when Dunboy Castle was under siege by the English; they were slaughtered and thrown into the sea.

The best time to go across is between 9 and 11 am; confirm your return time with the cable-car operator. Note that cattle get precedence over humans in the queue for the ride! Normally the service resumes between 2.30 and 5 pm. The charge is IR£1, increasing to IR£1.50 in July and August.

While there is no tourist accommodation available on the island it is easy to find somewhere to camp. There are some great walks around the island and the signal tower is an obvious destination. Bikes are not allowed on the cable car.

SUGARLOAF MOUNTAIN

After leaving Glengarriff for Castletownbere there is a turning on the right after eight km (five miles). It is half a km after a disused school on the right of the road, opposite a blue sign in the middle of nowhere announcing that this is a Community Alert Area. After turning right, follow the road for 1.5 km (one mile), leaving your bicycle or car near the single two-storey house with pine trees behind it or near the bungalow just past it.

Sugarloaf Mountain is best approached by walking up behind the houses and crossing an old road. A steady approach up the side of the mountain would reach the triangulation point at the summit (440 metres, 1440 feet) in about an hour. From the top there are excellent views: the Caha Mountains to the north, Hungry Hill to the west, Garnish Island to the east and Bantry Bay spread out to the south. On the way up, around the old road, it is not difficult to spot the great butterwort, an insectivorous plant, in May and June.

HUNGRY HILL

Hungry Hill is the highest point on the peninsula at 686 metres. A sign points to one route to the top, seven km (4.5 miles) west of Adrigole. A longer but more comfortable ascent begins by ignoring this sign, carrying along the road, and turning right just past a church on the right side of the road. This road goes north until blocked by a wire sheep gate. A vehicle could be left just before this or taken past for another km or more. The overgrown road eventually stops near some lakes and from here, keeping the lakes to the left, you head up the east ridge and climb the summit from the north side. A quicker descent can be made by following the stream down the south-west side to some farmhouses and a road that connects with the one where you began. The whole journey will take at least five hours but the rockscapes are fabulous and the views of West Cork from the stone circle at the top are tremendous.

Less arduous would be a walk to the end of the road and a picnic by the lakes.

Daphne du Maurier's novel *Hungry Hill* is based on the Puxley family, who owned the copper-rich land at the end of the peninsula.

PLACES TO STAY

For accommodation in Glengarriff and Castletownbere, see under those towns.

Camping

The *Adrigole Hostel* on the Castletownbere side of Adrigole village also has camping space. Before Castletownbere the *Wheel Inn Holiday Centre* (☎ 027-7009) is pleasantly situated with views of Bere Island; at a flat rate of IR£5 a pitch this is good value for a group.

The *Beara Hostel*, on the other side of town, has camping for IR£3.50 per person and it also possible to camp in the scenic grounds of *Puxley Castle*. Enquiries should be made at the house on the right after passing the main gate. At Allihies the *Riding Centre* (☎ 027-70340) rents camping space.

Hostels

The *Adrigole* private hostel (☎ 027-60132), IR£5 per person, is between Adrigole and Castletownbere. About three km (two miles) west of Castletownbere, just past the sign for Dunboy, the *Beara Hostel* (☎ 027-70184) is also on the main road. The *Garranes Hostel* (☎ 027-73147) is between Castletownbere and Allihies, superbly located on the Bantry Bay side a couple of km off the road (hard work if you're pushing a loaded bike). Next door is a Buddhist retreat centre. At Allihies there is an *An Óige Hostel* (☎ 027-73014).

In the village a new hostel is *Bonnie Braes* (☎ 027-73107), with mountain bikes for hire. Halfway along the 20 km (12 miles) route between Allihies and Eyeries there is the new *Sycamore Hostel* (no telephone), which may or may not be there in a year's time. All these hostels charge IR£5 per person.

B&Bs

Most places are to be found along the L61/R572 just after Glengarriff, and there are a few around Adrigole some 24 km (15 miles) west. Allihies has a couple, the one approved by the tourist board being *Mrs O'Sullivan* (☎ 027-73019) at Glenera. Just by the cable car point for Dursey Island, the coffee shop, *Windy Point House* (☎ 027-73017), does B&B.

On the L62/R571 there are two at Eyeries, *Mrs Coghlan Mason* (☎ 027-74178) and *Mrs O'Sullivan* (☎ 027-74058), and one four km (two miles) east of Ardgroom, just across the Kerry border.

PLACES TO EAT

Places to eat in Glengarriff and Castletownbere are listed under those towns.

In Allihies there's the homely *Atlantic Seafood Restaurant*, and *O'Neil's* pub which does bar food. Out at the cable-car point for Dursey, *Windy Point House* has sandwiches and snacks at reasonable prices, and there is a café and craft shop on the approach to Eyeries from Allihies.

GETTING THERE & AWAY

A local bus leaves Bantry at 3.45 pm on Tuesday, Friday and Saturday, stopping in Glengarriff and then Castletownbere. On Monday its departure times are 11.25 am and 8.20 pm. On Thursday the service originates in Cork, from where it departs at 6 pm, reaching Bantry at 7.45 and Glengarriff at 8.25 pm. These local buses depart from Castletownbere at 10.30 am on Tuesday, Friday and Saturday, 7 am and 4.30 pm on Monday, and 7.30 am on Thursday (bound for Bantry and Cork).

GETTING AROUND

Due to the limited bus service a bicycle or car is needed to see all of Beara. The Super Valu supermarket in Castletownbere has a few bicycles for hire, and so does the *Bonnie Braes* hostel in Allihies.

North Cork

The chief reason for visiting north Cork is for the fishing and the golf. There is a small but distinguished number of country houses open to the public for evening meals and short stays, often with fine gardens. North Cork is not the budget traveller's territory: permission for a day's fishing on the Blackwater could cost IR£30, and a night for two in a country house with dinner could easily approach IR£200. There are no hostels or official camp sites, but B&B places are never far away and the towns all have affordable places for meals.

FERMOY

This small town has around 5000 people and a pub for roughly every 200 of them, if anything a little below par for Ireland. Fishing is *the* attraction, and the town hosts a Fishing Festival in the week that straddles May and June, in an attempt to lure visitors from England during their Bank Holiday weekend and then Irish anglers the week after for their Bank Holiday weekend.

Information

The tourist office (☎ 025-31811) is in the same shop as a travel agent in the main square. It is open all year from 9 am to 6 pm. The 18-hole golf club (☎ 025-31472) is 1.5 km (one mile) out of town on the road to Cork.

Fishing

In Fermoy fishing enquiries should be made to Jack O'Sullivan (☎ 025-31110) at 4 Patrick St, just two doors down from the tourist office, in a men's clothes store of the same name.

MALLOW

Twice the size of Fermoy, Mallow is a prosperous town in the Blackwater Valley that caters for fishing, golfing and horse racing. It's well provided with restaurants and pubs.

In the 19th century visitors to the town's spa christened it the 'Bath of Ireland'. The tourist office (☎ 022-42222) is on Bridge St near the castle. It is open 9.30 am to 5.30 pm, from May to September.

AROUND MALLOW

About 13 km (eight miles) north-east of Mallow, **Doneraile Forest Park** is a large 18th-century park with herds of deer, open without charge from 11 am to 7 pm or sundown in winter. The nearby town of the same name was once owned by the English poet Edmund Spenser, and the slight remains of **Kilcolman Castle**, where he wrote part of the *Faerie Queene*, are five km (three miles) to the north. The first recorded steeplechase in 1752 ended in Doneraile after heading off from the steeple of a church in nearby Buttervant. Halfway between Mallow and Fermoy on the N72 near the town of Castletownroche **Annes Grove Gardens** (☎ 022-26145) is a small, formal 18th-century garden.

From Mallow to Killarney, a distance of 49 km (30 miles), the landscape is nondescript; the only worthwhile detour would be to the 17th-century **Kanturk Castle**. It is said that the mortar was mixed with the blood of the builders who were forced to work on it. The English however objected to such a massive mansion being built by an Irish chief, and did not allow the roof to be installed. The roofless remains are very well preserved.

Kanturk Town has a golf course (☎ 029-50534), fishing possibilities (☎ 029-50257) and a small museum that opens on Sundays in the summer.

Camping (☎ 029-50257) is possible in the town park, and near the Bank of Ireland the café serves meals till 2 or 3 am.

Inland Cork

The most popular route from Cork is to Kinsale and then the coastal road through Clonakilty and Skibbereen. From

Skibbereen the Mizen Head Peninsula is close by and the main road heads north to Bantry.

An alternative route from Cork to Bantry is inland via Macroom, and the road from Macroom to Bantry has its own scenic attractions, most notably at Gougane Barra. The quickest route between Killarney and Cork is also via Macroom.

There is one other inland route to Bantry which takes the main road to Bandon and Dunmanway. This is actually the quickest way to reach Bantry and the Beara Peninsula from Cork but it is the least interesting. The road is a good one for driving but has no other attraction and the towns along the way are not the sort to detain visitors.

MICHAEL COLLINS AMBUSH SITE

Michael Collins, commander-in-chief of the army of the new Provisional Government that had just won independence from Britain, left Macroom on the morning of 22 August 1922, on a quick tour of West Cork. He was recognised by anti-Treaty forces, who were holding a secret meeting in the area. In the evening they ambushed his car and Collins was shot dead. It seems that Collins ignored his companions' advice to drive on after the first shots were fired, choosing instead to make a fight of it.

The site of the ambush is marked by a stone memorial with an inscription in Irish. Each year, on the anniversary of the killing, a commemorative service is held by the roadside.

About 200 metres past the memorial there is another stone inscribed with the words: 'On this road too died 17 terrorist officers of the British forces on 28/11/20.'

The site is about 10 km (six miles) from Macroom on the road to Dunmanway.

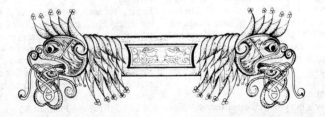

County Kerry

While the town of Killarney bursts at the seams during the summer months and the Ring of Kerry has queues of tour coaches, the rest of the county is big enough for visitors to find some solitude. The tourist hype does little to detract from the wild splendour of the landscape. There are countless opportunities for walks and bike rides where your only companions will be the birds soaring above. Especially beautiful is the Dingle Peninsula; an interesting local guide to the area is *The Dingle Peninsula* (Brandon Books) by Stephen MacDonagh.

Killarney & Around

KILLARNEY

By the time you reach Killarney you will have seen plenty of heavily touristed Irish towns but this is the Numero Uno. There is more registered accommodation here than anywhere else outside the capital. On the other hand there are lots of easy escapes if you want to explore the delights of Kerry and avoid the excesses, and on the whole Killarney is still more a tourist town than a tourist trap.

Information

Killarney's busy but efficient tourist office (☎ 064-31633) is in the town hall right in the centre of town and is open from 9.15 am to 5.30 pm from Monday to Saturday. Tracks & Trails (☎ 064-35277) at 53 High St provide valuable information on mountaineering, fishing and other outdoor pursuits. The Four Seasons Laundrette is in the Innisfallen arcade, just a few doors down Main St from the tourist office. Another laundrette lurks behind the Spar supermarket at the Plunkett St end of College St. The Killarney Bookshop is at 32 Main St.

St Mary's Cathedral

Built in 1842-55, this church was designed by Pugin. During the famine years the building was used to house the destitute. It's cruciform with a square tower and a spire that reaches 87 metres (285 feet). It's in Cathedral Place at the far end of New St.

National Museum of Irish Transport

This interesting collection of old cars, bicycles and assorted odds and ends includes an 1844 Meteor Stanley Tricycle found in a shop's 'unsold stock' in 1961! It also has a 1910 Wolseley that belonged to the Gore-Booth family and was used by Countess Markievicz and W B Yeats.

The museum is in East Avenue Rd. It's open from April to October, 10 am to 8 pm daily, and until 6 pm during the rest of the year. Entry is IR£2.50 (children IR£1).

Fishing

Fishing for trout and salmon is possible in the Rivers Flesk and Laune as well as in the lakes themselves. There are also many small lakes with brown and rainbow trout around the southern side of Killarney towards Kenmare, but there is no coarse fishing in the region. Permits, licences, equipment and information are available from O'Neill's (☎ 064-31970) at 6 Plunkett St.

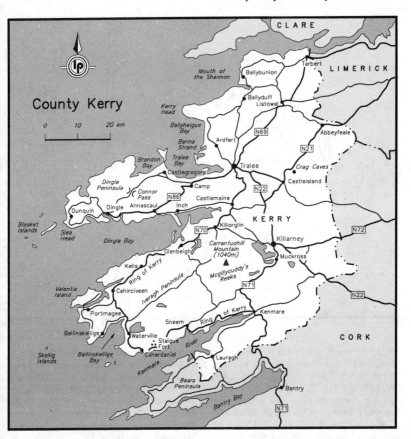

County Kerry

0   10   20 km

Organised Tours

Walking tours, including night walks, are organised by Tracks & Trails (see the Information section).

There are 11 daily watercoach cruises on Lough Leane, leaving from Ross Castle between 10.30 am and 5.45 pm. Bookings can be made through the tourist office or direct from the two companies: Destination Killarney (☎ 064-32638) at Scotts Gardens or Killarney Watercoach Cruises (☎ 064-31068) at 3 High St.

Phone ☎ 064-31068 for information on Gap of Dunloe tours: by car to Kate Kearney's, then saddle pony or trap through the Gap, finishing with a boat trip back to Killarney. Be warned: the Gap is the busiest tourist spot in the area.

Horse-riding trips are organised by O'Sullivan's (☎ 064-31686) of Ballydowney on an hourly basis or for longer three and six-day rides.

Places to Stay

Camping The *Fossa Caravan & Camping Park* (☎ 064-31497) is 5.6 km (3.5 miles) west of town on the road to Killorglin. A tent is IR£3.50 per night plus IR£2.50 per person,

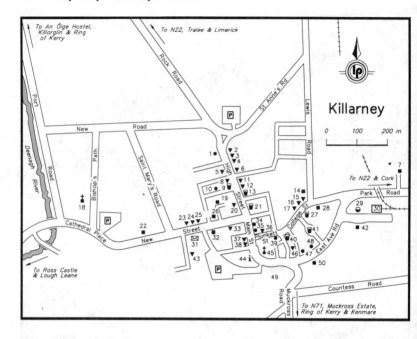

IR£3.50 for a cyclist or hiker. Almost next door, with similiar rates but fewer facilities, is the *Beech Grove Caravan & Camping Park* (☎ 064-31727), across from the Hotel Europe. Nearer to town and with similiar rates is *Fleming's Whitebridge Caravan & Camping Park* (☎ 064-31590). It's 1.6 km (one mile) out along the N22 road to Cork. Further along this road and less expensive is *White Villa Farm Caravan and Camping Park* (☎ 064-32456).

The only Killarney hostel offering camping space is the *Donash Lodge* (☎ 066-64554).

Hostels Killarney has plenty of hostels. The small but popular *Súgán* (☎ 064-33104) is right in the centre on Lewis Rd, by the junction with College St, and costs IR£5. At night the kitchen serves a public restaurant, and residents cannot cook for themselves but can get cheap meals.

The *Four Winds* (☎ 064-33094) is also conveniently central at 43 New St and also costs IR£5. In the same street *Neptune's Killarney Town Hostel* (☎ 064-35255) is a big new place with 100 beds and a kitchen and laundry. Dorms cost from IR£6.50 per person, and there are some private rooms and family rooms with own bathroom. A free bus meets buses and trains.

A little out of town is the *Bunrower House Hostel* (☎ 064-33914), under the same ownership as the Súgán. Heading for Kenmare, take a right turn at the Esso garage on the road signposted for Ross Castle. It's a 20-minute walk and there's regular free transport between the two hostels. It costs IR£5 and has a laundry.

The large An Óige *Killarney International Hostel* (☎ 064-31240) is two km west of the centre at Aghadoe House and costs IR£5.90. A hostel bus meets trains from Dublin and Cork. The *Fossa Holiday Hostel* (☎ 064-31497) is slightly farther out and has some hostel accommodation near its camp site.

■ PLACES TO STAY

7   Belleville Farm House Hostel
14   Súgán Hostel & Restaurant
19   Neptune's Hostel
22   Four Winds Hostel
26   Belvedere
28   Arbutus Hotel
32   Eviston House
42   Great Southern Hotel
50   Killarney Park Hotel

▼ PLACES TO EAT

2   Bricín Restaurant
3   Gaby's Restaurant
4   Foley's Restaurant
5   Sceilig Restaurant
6   Crock of Gold Restaurant
8   Burgerland
11   Allegro Restaurant
12   Dugg's Café
15   Picasso Restaurant
16   Cronin's Restaurant
17   Fáilte Restaurant
20   Sheila's Restaurant
23   Grunt's Café
24   Busy B's
25   Den Joe's
33   Caragh Café
36   Allegro Fast Food

37   Stella's Restaurant
38   Flesk Restaurant
43   An Taelann Restaurant
46   Kiwi's Retreat

◻ PUBS

9   Courtney's Pub
13   O'Connor's Pub
21   Laurels Pub
27   Buckley's Bar
40   Kiely's Pub
41   Scott's Gardens

OTHER

1   Tracks & Trails
10   O'Sullivan's Bike Hire
18   St Mary's Cathedral
29   Bus Station
30   Railway Station
31   Post Office
34   Killarney Bookshop
35   O'Neill's Fishing Tackle & Bike Hire
39   Laundrette
44   Tourist Office & Town Hall
45   St Mary's Church
47   Destination Killarney, Lake Tours
48   National Museum of Irish Transport
49   Jaunting Cars

The *Park Hostel* (☎ 064-32119) is about a km from the railway and bus station on the road to Cork and costs IR£5 a night. Also just off Park Rd, the road to Cork, the *Belleville Farm House Hostel* (☎ 064-31482) is on the edge of town but within walking distance of the centre, costing IR£5, or IR£6 for two people to camp in the adjacent field.

Two new hostels have recently opened near Killarney and both have a free pick-up service from town. *Peacock Farm Hostel* (☎ 064-33557) is in Gortdromakiery, Muckross and charges IR£5 a night. To get there, take a left turn on to the Lough Guitane road, just after the jaunting car entrance at Muckross House. *Donash Lodge* (☎ 066-64554) is at Longfields, Firies North, about 15 km (10 miles) in the direction of Tralee on the N22; it charges IR£4 per night. If you take the Tralee bus or train to Farranfore, the hostel will pick you up by arrangement in advance. Both these hostels have one double room.

B&Bs Killarney has an awesome number of B&Bs, but finding a room can be difficult in the high season. As usual the answer is to let the tourist office do the looking. Muckross Rd is particularly dense with B&Bs. Expect to pay up to IR£40 a double in some of the guesthouses, like *Kathleen's Country House* (☎ 064-32810) three km (1.8 miles) out of town on the road to Tralee. The average price of a regular B&B is IR£30.

Hotels Places costing from IR£50 and more for a double include *Eviston House* (☎ 064-31640) and the *Belvedere* (☎ 064-31133), both in New St. Also centrally located is the *Arbutus* (☎ 064-31307) on College St, recently modernised and with a friendly atmosphere. Strung out along Muckross there's *Whitegates* (☎ 064-31164), the *Lake* (☎ 064-31035) and *Randles Court* (☎ 064-35205).

Moving up into the IR£100-plus range there's the *Killarney Ryan* (☎ 064-31555) on the Cork road or the *Great Southern* (☎ 064-31262), built in the 19th century opposite the railway station, for the convenience of Victorian travellers. A modern hotel which is just as posh and plush is the *Killarney Park* (☎ 064-35555) in Kenmare Place. Along Muckross Rd there's the *Gleneagle* (☎ 064-31870), with a holiday atmosphere that attracts younger folk, or *Muckross Park* (☎ 064-31938) four km (2.4 miles) from town and next to a very popular pub. Nearer to town on the same road there's the sedate *Cahernane* (☎ 064-31895), built in 1877 as a home for the earl of Pembroke.

Out at Fossa on the road to Killorglin, the *Hotel Europe* (☎ 064-31900) boasts an Olympic-size swimming pool, while near the Gap of Dunloe the *Dunloe Castle* (☎ 064-44111) is a modern building in its own grounds complete with a ruined castle.

Places to Eat
Cafés & Takeaways
Fast-food places include *Burgerland* in the High St and *Allegro Fast Food* in Plunkett St. There is also *Den Joe's* in New St. The *Bricín* in High St has vegetarian meals but their cheaper food is only available at lunch time. For lunch-time sandwiches try *Grunts Café* on New St, *Dugg's Café* on High St or the *Killarney Bakery* across the road.

Mid-Range Restaurants
At the following places a meal will cost IR£5 to IR£10, although some are cheaper at lunch time: on College St *Picasso* and *Cronin's*, and in High St the *Allegro* and *Crock of Gold*.

Near the tourist office on Main St, *Stella's* is a straightforward place of the '& chips' variety. Just round the corner on New St, the *Caragh Café* is similar. Farther down High St from the tourist office, *Sceilig* has a more upmarket menu with pizza, pasta and spe-

cials at around IR£4 to IR£5, other dishes at IR£6 to IR£10. A few doors down is the similarly priced *Sheila's*.

The *Súgán* hostel opens its restaurant during the evenings and vegetarian meals make up 90% of the imaginative menu. It's closed on Mondays. The vegetarian *An Taelann* is tucked away down Bridewell Lane, off New St just past the post office.

Among the hotel restaurants, the *Colleen Bawn* in the Eviston House Hotel has a decent tourist dinner for IR£9. (Go downstairs to the Danny Mann lounge, to see a wall display on the origin of the restaurant's name.) The hotel also has *Café Chinos*, a jazzy-looking place serving pizzas and burgers.

Expensive Restaurants
In this category an evening meal for two will cost at least IR£20. In College St try the *Fáilte* and a few doors down the *Monte Carlo* Chinese restaurant which is cheaper at lunch time. At the top end of High St is *Foley's*. *Bricín* next door has a bookshop downstairs and a restaurant above with some vegetarian dishes. Nearby, *Gaby's* is a seafood place, as is the *Flesk* restaurant, down the road in Main St.

At the main junction of New, High and Main Sts, the *Laurels* pub and restaurant is a very popular place. *Kiwi's Retreat* (closed Sundays) is situated in the lane that joins East Avenue Rd with College St, and you can bring your own wine with you.

Entertainment
Killarney has lots of pubs and many have music although it's often highly tourist-oriented. Top of the list in that department would have to be the *Laurels* on Main St; their music pub is back behind the main pub, reached by the side alley. It's extremely touristy, with a nightly show in summer from 9.30 to 11 pm and an entry charge of IR£2.50. 'And this is for all the Canadians in the audience' (or Germans, Scots, Australians, you name it) – but it's good-humoured and done well.

More expensive musical entertainment can be had at the *Great Southern Hotel*

(☎ 064-35392) for IR£7.50. The *Killarney Manor Banquet* (☎ 064-31551) hosts a dinner and musical entertainment experience for IR£25, open from April to October; a reservation is best made, as coach parties often fill the place. *Scott's Gardens* on College St also has music most nights.

Other pubs where there's a good chance of music include *Buckley's Bar* in the Arbutus Hotel on College St. *O'Connor's* on High St is popular with young people who spill out into the side alley on summer nights. *Courtney's*, across the road on High St, has authentic Irish music. Other pubs to try include *Charlie Foley's* on New St and *Kiely's Bar*, the *Jug O'Punch*, the *Dunloe Lodge* and the *Tatler Jack Bar*, all on College St.

The *Danny Mann Lounge* in the Eviston House Hotel usually has a band and sometimes a display of Irish dancing. The hotel also has a disco, *Scoundrels*, with a IR£4 admission charge but there are frequent free nights for women who turn up before 11 pm.

Late-night revellers have the *Busy B's* on New St, with a IR£2 admission charge after midnight.

Getting There & Away

Train Travelling by train to Cork involves changing at Mallow, but there is a direct route to Dublin via Limerick. Phone ☎ 064-31067 for details.

Bus Bus Éireann (☎ 064-34777) operate from the railway station, with regular links to Tralee, Cork, Galway, Limerick, Shannon, Westport, Waterford and Rosslare. The Ring of Kerry has its own service in the summer, departing Killarney at 8.45 am and 1.25 pm (no early bus on Sunday) for Killorglin, Caherciveen, Waterville, Caherdaniel, Sneem and back to Killarney.

A new tourist bus operates between Tralee and Killarney (7 to 30 August only), and for IR£6.50 return includes free entry to either Kerry the Kingdom museum in Tralee or the National Museum of Irish Transport in Killarney, whichever is your destination.

There are five buses a day and three on Sunday.

Getting Around

Bicycles are the ideal way to explore the Killarney area as the sights are scattered, many of them only accessible by bike or on foot, and in summer the traffic jams can be horrendous. A number of places hire bikes at around IR£5 a day. There's O'Sullivan (☎ 064-31282) in Pawn Office Lane off High St, and the Laurels pub has its own bike hire (☎ 064-32578) in Old Market Lane that runs alongside the pub. The hire includes a map, panniers and repair kit, and there are good deals for group or weekly hire. O'Neill's (☎ 064-31970) on Plunkett St has children's bikes and will deliver free to your accommodation. Some of the hostels have their own bike-hire service.

If you're not on two wheels Killarney's traditional transport is the horse-drawn jaunting car, complete with a driver known as a *jarvey*. The pick-up point is on East Avenue Rd just past the tourist office but they also congregate in the N71 car park opposite Muckross House and at the Gap of Dunloe.

AROUND KILLARNEY
Knockreer

You can walk to the Knockreer Estate, just beyond the cathedral to the west of town. There's fine scenery around Lough Leane (the Lower Lake), the restored Ross Castle and Inisfallen Island on the lake with its ancient monastery ruins. Knockreer House is open during the summer, and has exhibitions on the wildlife and history of the area.

Muckross House & Gardens

Once you escape the suburbs to the south, you can dive into the extensive grounds of the Muckross Estate. Muckross Abbey was founded in 1448 and put to the torch by Cromwell's troops in 1652. The tombs of the abbey's founder, various Kerry chieftains, and several noted Irish poets are to be found in the choir.

Muckross House (☎ 064-31440) has

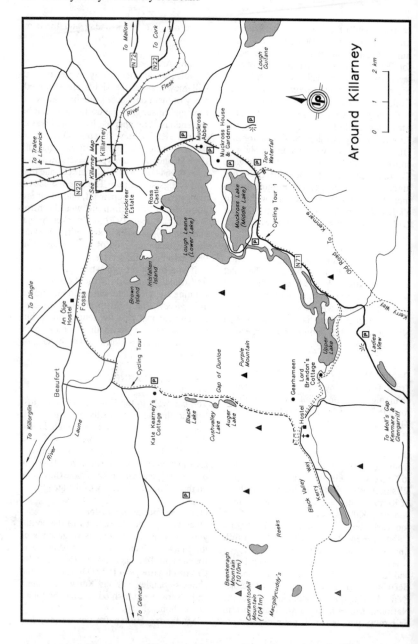

Around Killarney

museum exhibits as well as period furnished rooms. It's open daily from 9 am to 7 pm in summer, and till 5.30 pm in winter. Entry is IR£2 (children IR£1). Next to the house a new exhibition, dealing with life in Kerry in the 1930s, is about to open. Continuing east you come to the Meeting of the Waters, Torc Waterfall and finally the road climbs up to Ladies' View which takes its name from Queen Victoria's ladies-in-waiting, who liked it.

The house is six km (four miles) from town and vehicle access is about one km (half a mile) beyond the Muckross Park Hotel on the N71 Kenmare road. There is a car park about a mile before this on the N71, and directly opposite is an entrance for pedestrians and cyclists. During the summer there is a tourist bus operating from town to the house.

Ross Castle

Ross Castle dates back to the 14th century when it was a residence of the O'Donoghues, and it was the last place in Munster to succumb to Cromwell's forces under the command of Ludlow. According to a prophecy, the castle would only be captured from the water. In 1652 Ludlow had floating batteries brought up river from Castlemaine, then transported overland before launching them on to the lake. Seeing the prophecy about to be fulfilled, the defenders reportedly surrendered promptly. Ross Castle has been undergoing restoration work for some years now.

From Killarney, turn right opposite the Esso garage at the beginning of the Kenmare road, just past the roundabout. The castle is at the bottom of the road near the car park.

Inisfallen Island

The first monastery on the island is said to have been founded by St Finian the Leper in the 7th century. The island's fame dates from the early 13th century when the 'Annals of Inisfallen' were written here. The Annals, now resident at Oxford University, remain a vital source of information for early Irish history. Nothing is now left of the original

monastery, but there is a 12th-century oratory with a carved Romanesque doorway and a ruined priory nearby.

From Ross Castle, boats can be hired for rowing on Lough Leane at IR£3 an hour for up to three people or IR£12 for the whole day. The journey to Inisfallen island, which can be seen from the departure point, takes at least 20 minutes. Bunrower House Hostel has its own boat which is free to residents.

Gap of Dunloe

This is Killarney tourism at its worst. Every day throughout the summer, cars and buses disgorge countless visitors at Kate Kearney's cottage who then proceed to take a pony-and-trap ride through the Gap of Dunloe. The one-hour trip costs IR£10 per person (family IR£25). A two-hour trip is IR£15 per head. You could also walk through the narrow gorge to the Black Valley Hostel at the other end, but don't do this in summer if you want to be alone.

At the turn of this century some 20 men were garrisoned in a Royal Irish Constabulary barracks on the Gap to safeguard the passage of tourists who were arriving on tours established by Thomas Cook & Company in London. Only the ruins of the barracks remain, for the burgeoning crowds of tourists are now welcomed into the county with open arms by a local population grateful for the income.

Cycling Tours

The first of two return trips from Killarney is via the Gap of Dunloe and Black Valley Hostel. The route is marked on the Around Killarney map.

This is an adventurous 30-km ride that covers a variety of terrains: smoothly surfaced roads, small country lanes, rough tracks, bogland, wood, uphill and down through the dramatic ice-carved Gap of Dunloe. Make a day of it and bring a picnic.

Leave Killarney on Port Rd heading for Killorglin and the Ring of Kerry. After passing through the village of Fossa it is one km (0.6 miles) to the first signpost left to the Gap of Dunloe. Turn left here and continue down this small road for 2.6 km (1.6 miles), until a T-junction is reached. Turn right at the junction and follow the sign pointing to the left for the Gap – the other road leads up to the Dunloe Castle Hotel and Beaufort.

Head for Kate Kearney's Cottage, and from there cycle to the head of the Gap, at 242 metres (794 feet). The view from the top is glorious and only good brakes are needed to facilitate the speedy descent into the Gearhameen Valley. At the bottom do not turn right, which is marked as a cul-de-sac. Turn to the left instead and pass by a church on the right, and the Black Valley Hostel which is almost immediately after it.

About two km (1.2 miles) past the hostel there is a Y-junction. Take the left side, signposted for Gearhameen, Hillcrest B&B and Brandon's Cottage. After 100 metres there is another Y-junction; this time bear right, following the signpost to Brandon's Cottage (not left to the B&B).

Follow the Kerry Way signs across the bridge that leads to Brandon's Cottage on the left. Drink and light food is available here. Keeping Brandon's Cottage on the left, continue on and bear left at the pathway further down. Less than 100 metres along here, by the side of a clogged stream cut into the bog, there is an iron and wooden gate. Go through the gate and turn right immediately, leaving the path that goes along the stream.

After 150 metres cross a small bridge and follow the path that cuts its way through the bog and furze. The Upper Lake comes into view on the left. Once on the path in the woods of Derrycunnihy look for a walking sign that is signposted to Derrycunnihy. This path will bring you out on to the N71 where a left turn on the main road takes you on a comfortable ride back down into Killarney.

The second trip is via Lake Acoose and Moll's Gap. It's a return trip of about 80 km (50 miles), and its route is marked out on the Ring of Kerry map. This tour could be done in one day, or you may choose to spend a night at Glencar at the Climber's Inn or a nearby B&B (see the Kerry Way section).

Follow the route given for the previous cycle tour, until you reach the junction point-

ing to the Gap of Dunloe and the Dunloe Castle Hotel. Turn left for the Gap of Dunloe but after less than 1.2 km (one mile) turn right – it is signposted west to Glencar. For the next 16 km (10 miles) the road continues through a series of crossroads – where you always go straight ahead – and then one T-junction where you turn left for Lake Acoose. Where there are signposts always follow the directions to Glencar.

Just at the end of the lake, set below Beenkeragh and Carrantuohill mountains, the road turns to the right, heading for Glencar, and 3.2 km (two miles) further along you'll find the Climber's Inn on the right. It is about another 1.6 km (one mile) to Bealalaw Bridge but just before reaching it turn left and then, almost immediately, turn to the right. After another 2.4 km (1.5 mile) turn right again – following the road straight on here will eventually bring you to a dead end, so you will need to return to the junction if you missed the turning.

After turning right, as just directed, follow the rising road that leads through the Bellaghbeama Gap and then down to a T-junction. From Glencar this is a distance of about 16 km (10 miles). At the T-junction turn left and continue to the east, climbing along the R568 for 10 km (6 miles), until reaching Moll's Gap. The hard work is now over and it's an easy 22 km (14 miles) back down to Killarney.

THE KERRY WAY

The Kerry Way is 215 km (135 miles) long, making it the longest marked footpath in the republic. The walk starts and ends in Killarney and stays inland for the first three days, winding through the spectacular Macgillycuddy's Reeks and past 1041-metre (3404-foot) Carrantuohill, the highest mountain in Ireland, before moving around the coast through Cahirciveen, Waterville, Caherdaniel, Sneem and Kenmare. It is undoubtedly the best way of seeing the Iveragh Peninsula, rock by rock. Generally well marked, the route does not require any special skills and can be walked by any reasonably fit person. A compass helps but is not essential. Rainwear and waterproof boots are. One of the glories of this walk is that except at the hostels you are unlikely to come across anyone, least of all tourists.

If you are short of time, you could spend three days walking to Glenbeigh from where a bus or hitch could return you to Killarney. This takes in the spectacular Black Valley section and each day's walk is relatively short. There is hostel accommodation for the two nights, first at the Black Valley and then Glencar. Details follow for the first three days of the Kerry Way.

Maps

The tourist board has its own map guide for IR£2 which divides the entire Kerry Way into 12 sections, but far more useful is the new 1:50,000 Ordnance Survey map No 78, entitled *The Reeks*. The Kerry Way is clearly marked and there are some general notes on the different sections. *New Irish Walk Guides: Southwest* (Gill & Macmillan) also covers the entire Way with maps and detailed notes.

Supplies

Bringing food is essential, but on the first day snacks and coffee are available at Lord Brandon's Cottage. From there it is 2.5 km (1.5 miles) to the Black Valley Hostel where the hostel shop has a few supplies. During the second day there is nowhere selling or serving food apart from a small shop at the Climber's Inn pub. The third day's walking passes a small shop about halfway along the route, but that's it until you reach Glenbeigh.

Killarney to Black Valley

The starting point is the entrance of the Killarney National Park at Muckross. The lakeside road leads to the Torc Waterfall. The total distance of 22 km (14 miles) can be shortened by starting the walk at the Torc Waterfall, cutting out the roadside walk and making the journey to the Black Valley easily manageable in one day.

To get to the Torc Waterfall early in the morning, you would need to hitch or drive.

There's a car park in front of the tourist information point.

After the Torc Waterfall, the path goes left crossing a stone bridge and joins a green road. Turn left here and carry on for a few metres, ignoring a sign that points to a turning on the right. Carry straight on keeping the river on your left. This path, the old Kenmare road, travels across bogland and eventually meets a surfaced road with a sign left for Kenmare. Turn to the right instead, signposted for the Black Valley, until you reach the main N71 road by the side of an old church. A few metres past the church, on the road to Kenmare, the Way sign takes you into the wood on the right. The path leads to Lord Brandon's Cottage and then a short leg takes you to the An Óige *Black Valley Hostel* (☎ 064-34712). You should plan to arrive at the hostel at around 5.30 pm because it is very closed before then and very full afterwards. It's best to book in advance. The hostel has 50 beds and costs IR£5.50 a night in the high season.

Black Valley to Glencar

This 20-km (12-mile) leg is one of the best on the Way. After leaving the hostel, disregard the unsurfaced road going off to the right, which leads to the Gap of Dunloe and back to Killarney. Follow the way ahead to the west that is signposted as a cul-de-sac. It leads through a wood and past houses and rough ground to a small forest of pine trees. Crossing a stile the path goes past a farmhouse and through a gate onto a surfaced road which soon becomes a green road. Keep a careful eye on the tiny signs along this stretch because it is easy to get lost here.

From here on the path is marked by cairns as you ascend to the summit separating the Black Valley from the Bridia Valley, where you can practise your yodelling. The descent leads to a surfaced road which could be used to reach Glencar if weather makes the right turn to the Lack Rd seem unsuitable. Weather permitting, though, you can turn right at the Way sign on the surfaced road and walk uphill. There are more wonderful views from the summit of the Lack Rd pass. You carry on down to the surfaced road (the one you could have stayed on if the weather is misty), where a left turn leads to Glencar and a well-earned rest at the rather dilapidated *Climber's Inn* (☎ 066-60101). The owner is friendly and accommodating and a bed costs IR£4. The owners of a nearby B&B (☎ 066-60162) will pick you up from the Climber's Inn. Alternatively, you can stop walking earlier, after descending from the Black Valley and before ascending the Lack Rd pass, at the *Mountain Lodge* (☎ 066-60173), which does B&B.

Glencar to Glenbeigh

The first and final stages of this day's walk are the most interesting. The middle part is mainly through planted forests, but the approach to Glenbeigh has exhilarating views.

Leaving the Climber's Inn, the Way is marked down a short lane that emerges on a surfaced road. Turn right and at the main junction cross the bridge to the left. Almost immediately the walking sign points to the right, along the river. The path leads through planted forests and comes out on a surfaced road that goes past a shop to a Y-junction. Leave the main road and go left uphill.

There are two routes down to Glenbeigh. To take the shorter route look for a fading walking sign and turn to the left through a gate. This leads through the Windy Gap at the top of which Glenbeigh and the Dingle Peninsula come into view. It's an easy walk down the other side and along a quiet road into the town.

The other route involves staying on the green road and offers magnificent views of Carragh Lake. Towards the end, though, walking along a surfaced road is necessary. For accommodation possibilities see the Glenbeigh section later.

The Ring of Kerry

The Ring of Kerry, the 179-km circuit of the Iveragh Peninsula, is one of Ireland's premier tourist attractions. Although it can be 'done' in a day by car or bus, or three days by bicycle, the more time you take the more you'll enjoy it. Getting off the beaten tourist track is also worthwhile, the Ballaghbeama Pass cuts across the peninsula's central highlands with some spectacular views and remarkably little traffic. Anticlockwise is the 'right' way to tackle the ring but in the high season it's probably worth doing it in the 'wrong' direction in order to avoid the tourist buses all shuffling round in the same direction from Killarney.

GETTING AROUND

The Ring of Kerry bus leaves Killarney in summer at 8.45 am and 1.25 pm (no early bus on Sunday), and stops at Killorglin, Caherciveen, Waterville, Caherdaniel and Sneem before returning to Killarney. For details of other buses in the area ring ☎ 064-34777.

KILLORGLIN

The first town on the Ring, travelling anticlockwise from Killarney, is Killorglin, famed for its annual Puck Fair Festival.

Information

A new Visitor's Information Centre should be open by the time you read this. It is to be situated in Market St in the centre of town.

The Puck Fair Festival

This is a rumbustious three-day celebration that takes place annually during the second weekend in August. The name of the festival derives from the custom of installing a billy goat (a puck), horns festooned in ribbons, on a pedestal in the town centre and leaving it there while everyone takes advantage of the special licensing hours. Pubs stay open till 3 am, although it often seems that they simply serve for three days nonstop. Accommodation is hard to come by if you haven't booked in advance.

Places to Stay

Camping Just under two km (one mile) from the bridge in Kilorglin, on the road to

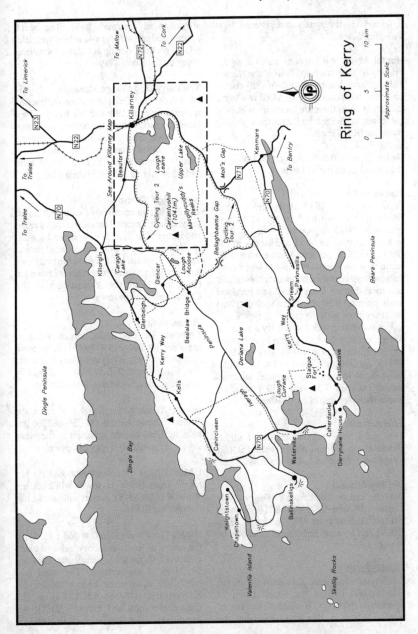

Ring of Kerry

Killarney, is the small unregistered *West Camping Site*.

Hostel About two km (one mile) from the bridge, on the road to Tralee, the *Laune Valley Farm* hostel (☎ 066-61488) comes complete with satellite TV. A bed in a dorm is IR£5.50, plus there are six rooms with own bathroom at IR£6 a bed, and three double rooms at IR£14 each.

B&Bs There is the usual string of B&Bs on the roads in and out of town.

Places to Eat
Food for under IR£5 is available from *Bunkers*, a combined pub/restaurant/ takeaway. *Nick's Restaurant* (☎ 066-61219) in Main St does seafood and steaks in the IR£12 to IR£20 bracket. A more interesting menu is at *Bianconi* (☎ 066-61146), a cosy pub and restaurant next door, with seafood and meat dinners from IR£12 and bar food available until 9.30 pm. There is also a pizza bar that closes with the pub.

For something more sedate try a relaxing dinner, country-house style and surrounded by antiques, at *Caragh Lodge* (☎ 066-69115) for IR£24. A stroll by the lake and a drink in the lounge precede dinner which is served between 7.30 and 8.30 pm; afterwards there are drinks by the fireside.

Entertainment
Two pubs have regular music at night. *Bianconi* has a piano player while the *Old Forge* has traditional ballad sessions.

Getting Around
Bicycles can be hired from *O'Shea's Cycle Centre* (☎ 066-61919/61180) in Lower Bridge St. Bikes are IR£5 a day, weekly IR£30, and helmets and panniers can also be rented.

GLENBEIGH
Continuing west from Killorglin for 10 km (six miles) brings the small town of Glenbeigh into view. Nestled at the floor of Seefin Mountain, this small town has the attraction of a superb Blue Flag beach (unpolluted and safe for swimming with lifeguards on duty during the day), as well as being on the Kerry Way.

The Kerry Bog Village Museum
Next to the Red Fox pub this new attraction recreates an early 19th-century Kerry village through a series of replica houses: turfcutter, blacksmith, dairy, hen house, labourer's cottage and a thatcher. The museum is outside Glenbeigh on the road to Killorglin and admission is IR£2 (children IR£1).

Rossbeigh Strand
The five km (three miles) of sand look across to the Dingle Peninsula and even with a camp site in the vicinity it is easy to find a quiet spot. Swimming is safe and the mud flats at the eastern spit of land is good birdwatching territory. To get there, bear right for three km (two miles) at the Y-junction at the Caherciveen end of town.

Places to Stay
Camping The *Glenross Caravan & Camping Park* (☎ 066-31590/68451) is in town next to the Glenbeigh Hotel. The other camp site, *Falvey's* (☎ 066-68238), is down by Rossbeigh Beach and overlooks the sea.

Hostel At the Killorglin end of town the *Hillside House Hostel* (☎ 066-68228) has beds for IR£4 but the manager of the place says it is for sale so it may disappear.

B&Bs *Village House* (☎ 066-68128) has rooms from IR£26 in town, while *Ocean Wave* (☎ 066-68249), a short walk away, has doubles for IR£35.

Hotels The *Towers Hotel* (☎ 066-68212), in the centre of town, is a cosy, relaxed place well used to families. Singles/doubles are IR£38/56 in the summer. The other two hotels are at opposite ends of town: the *Falcon Inn* (☎ 066-68215) is at the Cahirciveen end and charges IR£20 per person, while the *Glenbeigh* (☎ 066-68333) is by the side of the road to Killarney; the rate here is IR£20 and IR£25 per person.

Places to Eat

The *Glendale* has dishes between IR£4 and IR£8. Opposite the Towers Hotel, *Bini's* is open till 10 pm, with meals around IR£5. The *Red Fox Inn* serves pub lunches and dinners. On the beach the *Ross Inn* has pub food.

The three hotels all have restaurants. The fresh seafood at the *Glenbeigh* is excellent, the atmosphere a little quieter than the others and a set dinner costs IR£15. Set dinners are IR£18 at the *Towers* and IR£12.50 at the *Falcon Inn*.

Entertainment

The *Towers* and *Glenbeigh* hotels have music in their bars and the *Red Fox Inn* usually has something happening from Wednesday to Sunday. The *Ross Inn* has bands, and local shops will have posters for events there.

KELLS

Between Glenbeigh and Caherciveen, near Kells, the route of the old Great Southern & Western Railway can be clearly seen on the hillside, with its tunnels and retaining walls. The small beach near Kells is three km (two miles) off the road, but it doesn't look very clean. On the main road there is the Caitin Beatear's pub/heritage centre.

Places to Stay

The *Kells Bay Caravan & Camping Park* (☎ 066-77647) is 1.5 km (one mile) off the road and signposted. *Mrs Golden* (☎ 066-77601) at the post office does B&B for IR£13.50 or there is *Seaview* (☎ 066-77610) down by the beach.

Places to Eat

Caitin Beatear's is a pub and restaurant and the thatched roof is a magnet for coach parties. Irish stew and seafood feature on the menu and musical sessions are held regularly throughout the summer. It doubles as a small heritage centre with wall displays, farm machinery, and a neolithic standing stone not far away.

CAHIRCIVEEN

As late as 1815, there were only five houses in Cahirciveen. Daniel O'Connell, whose name is indissolubly linked with the early 19th-century campaign for the Catholics' right to vote, came from near here. The ruins of his home can still be seen on the left of the new bridge entering town from the Kells end. There are prehistoric sites in the area.

Information

The tourist office (☎ 066-21288) is in the old Protestant church at the Waterville end of town. It has a little craft and coffee shop as well. The White Strand, about five km (three miles) away, is safe for swimming. Coming from the Waterville end of town turn left at the junction of Bridge and Church Sts and go over the bridge, passing the site of a yet-to-be-opened heritage centre.

Places to Stay

Camping *Mannix Point Caravan & Camping Park* (☎ 066-72806), a 15-minute walk from the town, is well run and charges a flat rate of IR£2.75 per person (children IR£1.20), including showers. As with the hostel, boat operators for the Skelligs will pick up passengers from the camp site.

Camping is also possible at the hostel, at IR£3 per person, including showers and use of kitchen.

Hostel The *Sive Hostel* (☎ 066-72717) is at the east end of the long main street. Beds are IR£5, there are some private rooms, and trips to the Skelligs can be arranged from here.

B&Bs In Newmarket St *O'Driscoll's Town House* (☎ 066-72531) has rooms, as well as being a pub and restaurant. At the east end of town, *Riverdale House* (☎ 066-72316) has singles/doubles for IR£14/28. *Mount Rivers* (☎ 066-72509) costs from IR£15/24 and is an attractive old house on the road east to Killarney.

Hotel The only hotel here is the *Ringside Rest* (☎ 066-72543) on Valentia Rd, which offers singles/doubles for IR£20/35.

Places to Eat

Meals at *Grudles* are the best value at around IR£5. The *Old School House* (☎ 066-72426) has a reputation for first-class seafood, at around IR£20 a head. The seafood at the *Ringside Rest Hotel* restaurant is OK, though the place lacks charm.

Food can be taken away from the *Red Rose Restaurant* in Church St opposite the O'Connell Memorial Church, and *Kevy's* in Main St.

Entertainment

The *Sceilig Rock Bar* is good for traditional music, every night of the week. There is also the *Harp* which sometimes has discos. The *Shebeen* is more touristy. The *Anchor Bar* doesn't have music but there's a good atmosphere. If you don't like any of these, then there's almost 50 more to visit!

Getting Around

Bicycles can be hired from Casey's (☎ 066-72474) on the main street.

VALENTIA ISLAND

Valentia is 11 km long and three wide (seven miles by two), but it doesn't feel like an island, especially if you come by road. In the summer it's a popular resort and scuba-diving centre.

The main town is Knightstown, three km (two miles) from the Ring of Kerry road and accessible by ferry. It is named after the Knight of Kerry who once owned it. Most visitors reach the island by the long bridge from Portmagee, turning right at the other end for the road to Chapeltown and then Knightstown. See the following Skellig Island section for information about the Skellig Experience Centre on Valentia Island.

Heritage Centre

The main item of interest here is the history of the Valentia-US cable. The island was chosen as the site for the first transatlantic telegraph cable, and when the connection was made in 1858, the town of Cahirciveen was in direct contact with New York, but not with Dublin! It worked for 27 days before it failed, but went back into action some years later. The telegraph station was in operation until 1966.

The centre is open from May to September, from 11 am to 6 pm, and is situated in an old school on the road from Knightstown to the quarry.

The Quarry

In the 19th century the quarrying of slate was an important activity, with boats from the nearby harbour carrying away the roofing slates and flagstones. If you ever wondered what Charing Cross railway station in London and San Salvador station in El Salvador have in common, the answer is that they were both roofed with slate from Valentia. A disused quarry tunnel has been converted into a tasteless religious grotto, but despite this the place retains a sense of history.

Beginish & Church Islands

These two small islands are both in the harbour. The beach on Beginish is excellent and swimming is safe here. Church Island, to the east, has the remains of an 8th-century oratory and some beehive huts. Enquire at the Royal & Pier Hostel about boat trips to the islands.

Angling & Diving

For sea angling trips contact Dan McCrohan (☎ 066-76142) at Knightstown. For diving there are two reliable centres: Des Lavelle (☎ 066-76124) and the Valentia Hyperbaric Diving Centre (☎ 066- 76225).

Places to Stay

Hostels There are two hostels on Valentia Island. The *Ring Lyne Hostel* (☎ 066-76103) is at Chapeltown, halfway between the bridge and Knightstown. The *Royal Pier Hostel* (☎ 066-76144), down by the harbour, has beds for IR£5 and IR£6.50. You can book here for trips to the Skelligs.

The *An Óige Hostel* (☎ 066-76141) at Knightstown occupies three of the former coastguard station cottages.

B&Bs Before Knightstown, *Glenreen Heights* (☎ 066-76241) has singles/doubles for IR£18/28. In Knightstown by the harbour, the Victorian building that is now home to the *Royal & Pier Hostel* also does B&B for IR£15 a head. Also on the waterfront, *Lavelle's* (☎ 066-76124), once part of the original transatlantic telegraph station, is now a diving centre, with rooms for two at IR£29, singles IR£16.

Places to Eat
At the western end of Knightstown the *Islander Café* is OK but the *Gallery Kitchen* is more inviting, being a restaurant, wine bar and sculpture gallery. Meals are available to non-residents at the *Ring Lyne*, which has a bar and restaurant; three-course meals at IR£6.50, IR£8.25 or IR£12 are served till 10 pm. The *Royal Pier Hostel* also has a restaurant and an evening meal is IR£8. At Chapeltown, *Curran's petrol station* has a coffee shop doing light meals and snacks.

For pub food, *Boston's* serves very good home-cooked dishes. Two of the pubs at Portmagee, the *Bridge Bar* and the *Fisherman's Bar*, are also worth trying.

Entertainment
In Chapeltown the *Ring Lyne* has musical sessions after 9.30 pm, most evenings of the week. In Knightstown, *Boston's Bar* comes alive on Friday and Sunday. In Portmagee the *Bridge Bar* is worth checking out and sometimes has free set-dancing lessons.

Getting There & Away
The Maurice O'Neill bridge at Portmagee leads to Valentia Island. For pedestrians and cyclists there is a ferry from Reenard to Knightstown that takes 15 minutes.

Getting Around
There are no buses on the island but bikes

can be hired from Curran's (☎ 066-76297) at Chapeltown.

THE SKELLIG ISLANDS
I tell you the thing does not belong to any world that you and I have lived and worked in: it is part of our dream world.
George Bernard Shaw, 1910.

A boat trip to the Skellig Islands is one of the highlights of Ireland, and Shaw's comment still holds good. The 217-metre (712-foot) jagged rock of Skellig Michael, the larger of the two, looks like the last place on earth that anyone would try to land, let alone establish a community. Yet early Christian monks survived here from the 7th until the 12th or 13th century. They were influenced by the Egyptian Coptic Church founded by St Anthony in the deserts of Egypt and Libya, and their desire for solitude led them to this remote, most westerly corner of Europe.

After the introduction of the Gregorian calendar in 1582, Skellig became a popular spot for weddings. Marriages were forbidden during Lent, but since Skellig operated by a different calendar, a quick trip over to the islands allowed those unable to wait for Easter to tie the knot. In time these annual pilgrimages became an excuse for other jollifications, and crates of alcohol were hauled over to facilitate the merrymaking. There is even a record of the police being called to the island.

The Monastery
The monastic buildings are perched on a saddle in the rock, some 150 metres (500 feet) above sea level. The oratories and beehive cells vary in size, the largest cell having a floor space of 4.5 by 3.6 metres (15 by 12 feet), and they're all astounding. The projecting stones on the outside have more than one possible explanation: steps to reach the top and release chimney stones, or maybe holding places for turf that covered the exterior. There are interior rows of stones in some of the cells, and the guides who live on the rock during the summer will provide a possible explanation for these as well.

Very little is known about the life of the monastery, but there are records of a Viking raid in 812 and again in 823. Monks were killed or taken away but the community recovered and carried on.

Bird Life

From the boat look out for the diminutive storm petrel, a black bird that darts around over the water like a swallow, and the large fulmar with a wingspan of 107 cm (42 inches). Kittiwakes – seagulls with black-tipped wings – are easy to see and hear around the covered walkway just after stepping off the boat. They spend the winter at sea but thousands come to Skellig Michael to breed between March and August.

On the rock itself the delightful puffins with their multicoloured beaks and waddling steps are all around. The puffin lays one egg in May at the end of a burrow and the parent bird will be seen guarding its nest, with as much dignity as it can manage.

The boat trip should take you past the Small Skellig where some 20,000 pairs of gannets breed. Check beforehand if the boat will pause to look for basking seals. The visitors' centre at the Skellig Experience has a good display on the birdlife, worth visiting in advance.

The Skellig Experience Centre

This visitor centre (☎ 064-31633) – a new Bord Fáilte venture – is well worth a visit and has interesting exhibitions on the life and times of the monks, the history of the lighthouses on Skellig Michael, and the wildlife. A 15-minute audiovisual show deals with the monastery.

The boat trip does not actually land on Skellig Michael. It does get close, however, and there are good opportunities for photography; the onboard commentary is good too. The centre and boat have access for the disabled.

Admission to the centre only is IR£3 (students IR£2.70, children IR£1.50) while the cruise and centre is IR£15 (students IR£13.50, children IR£8.50). The Skellig Experience visitors' centre is on the left just

before the bridge from Portmagee to Valentia.

Getting There & Away

Joe Roddy (☎ 066-74268) operates from Ballinskelligs which, given the name, may well be the monks' original departure point. He has two boats: a fast launch that gets there in 35 minutes and a slower one that takes about an hour. He is also very knowledgeable on the history and ornithology of the rocks and will gladly dispense information. His boats usually go at 10 am and 3.30 pm but ring to confirm.

Other boats from Ballinskelligs are Sean Feehan (☎ 066-79182) and J B Walsh (☎ 066-79147).

Brendan O'Keefe (☎ 066-77103) operates from Portmagee and can be contacted at the Fisherman's Bar pub in Portmagee. Also departing from Portmagee is Murphy's (☎ 066-77156) and Casey's (☎ 066-77125). The latter's main booking office is in Cahirciveen (☎ 066-72437/72069).

On Valentia, Lavelle's (☎ 066-76124) or the Royal & Pier Hostel (☎ 066-76144) do trips. Near Caherdaniel, Sean O'Shea (☎ 066-75129) also runs a trip.

The standard fare for most of the operators is IR£15 but you may be able to negotiate reductions for students or children.

WATERVILLE

This popular resort is situated on a narrow bit of land between Ballinskelligs Bay and Lough Currane. Charlie Chaplin was probably the town's most famous visitor, and photographs of him here can be seen in the Butler Arms pub.

Fishing

There are lots of angling possibilities around Waterville. Lough Currane is a free fishing lake for sea trout while the Inny River is a breeding ground for wild salmon and trout. Sea angling takes in mackerel, pollack and shark. For information ask at O'Sullivan's, a tackle shop between the hostel and Silver Sands on the main street, or enquire at the Lobster Bar (☎ 066-74183).

SKELLIG RING

The Skellig Ring is a scenic route that leaves the main road to Cahirciveen after Waterville. It begins with a turn to the left, clearly signposted, and goes down to an unmarked junction: the short road to the left goes to Ballinskelligs Bay, the road straight on goes to the departure point for the Skelligs, and a right turn eventually leads to Portmagee. It makes an interesting cycling route, but there are lots of small unmarked roads and it's easy to take a wrong turning.

Ballinskelligs Monastery

The exact relationship between this monastery and the one on Skellig Michael is not clear. It was probably founded after the monks left Skellig in the 12th or 13th century. The sea is gradually wearing away at the ruins and it's the sort of place that children like to explore. Take the road down to Ballinskelligs Bay and walk to the remains from there.

Ballinskelligs Bay

At the western end of this Blue Flag beach are the last remnants of a castle, a 16th-century stronghold of the McCarthys.

Places to Stay

The *An Óige Hostel* (☎ 066-79229) is reached by turning right at the small junction after passing the Sigerson Arms on the Skellig Ring. Its beds cost IR£5.50 a night. The *Sigerson Arms* (☎ 066-79104) has half a dozen beds for IR£16 and, overlooking the bay near the hostel, *Sea View* (☎ 066-79317) has a few rooms for a little less.

Places to Eat

After leaving Waterville but before reaching the beach the *Sigerson Arms* is passed on the left. This pub is about the only place where food can be found.

CAHERDANIEL
Derrynane National Historic Park

The coastal area around Caherdaniel was once the centre of large-scale smuggling with France and Spain, a source of wealth for the O'Connells. They owned Derrynane House and the surrounding parkland, evading official restrictions on the purchase of land by Catholics with the help of a co-operative Protestant.

The house is open to the public and is largely furnished with items relating to Daniel O'Connell, the campaigner for Catholic emancipation. The dining room is full of early 19th-century furniture and silver given to O'Connell by grateful Catholics. The drawing room is renowned for its table, which was carved over a period of four years by two men. The adjoining parkland includes a sandy beach and Abbey Island, which can usually be reached on foot across the sand. A little way to the east of the house is an Ogham stone.

The park is open from May to September, Monday to Saturday, from 9 am to 6 pm. Between October and April the hours are 1 to 5 pm. Admission is IR£1 (children 40p).

STAIGUE FORT

This 2000-year-old fort is one of the finest dry-stone buildings in Ireland. The five-metre (18-foot) circular wall is up to four metres (13 feet) thick and surrounded by a large bank and ditch. It is similar in style to the Grianan of Aileach in County Donegal but has not been restored to the same degree.

The exact age of the fort is not known but it probably dates from the 3rd or 4th century AD. It cannot be seen from the sea, although it has sweeping views down to the coast. It may have been a communal place of refuge, or a royal residence as the sophisticated staircases incorporated into the walls suggest. The answer is lost in time, but the fort remains an astonishing testimony to the skill of its builders.

It's about three km off the main road, reached by a country lane which narrows as it climbs to the site. In summer the road and car-park area are the scene of absurd traffic jams! There's an honesty box by the gate asking for 50p, children free.

SNEEM

Visitors have differing reactions to the oddly

named town of Sneem (pronounced 'shneem', derived from the Irish *snaidhm*, meaning 'knot' or 'twist', from the snaky river.) It's quaint to some, while to others, who never see the place in winter, it seems to have sold out completely to tourism.

Information
The Homestead Gift Shop (☎ 064-45179) in New St, has tourist information seven days a week and sells a local walking guide.

Ask about local fishing at the Homestead Gift Shop. There's shore fishing at a number of spots, and Lough Fadda, six km (four miles) out of town by the Kenmare road, is stocked with rainbow trout. Hussey's sports shop does licences.

Museum
The small museum (☎ 064-45182), housed in the old courthouse, looks like a cluttered antique shop inside. The curator, Tim Reilly, may talk about the exhibits. A newspaper cutting shows that Charles de Gaulle stayed in Sneem in 1969 – perhaps recovering from the ferment of 1968.

The museum is open seven days a week during the summer, from 10 am to 5.30 pm (closed 1 to 2 pm), and admission is 50p.

Places to Stay
Camping There is a small *camp site* (☎ 064-45181) in town. Turn down past the bridge, near the church. Campers can fish in the river nearby. The *Willow Hill Farm Hostel* has tent sites at £2 per person.

Hostel Six km (four miles) from town just off the Kenmare road, *Willow Hill Farm Hostel* (☎ 064-45378) has beds for IR£5.

B&Bs *Woodvale House* (☎ 064-45181) is next to the camp site in town and is owned by the same family. Doubles are IR£27. *Derry East Farmhouse* (☎ 064-45193) is out of town on the road to Waterville and has singles/doubles from IR£17/26, and an evening meal for IR£11.50.

Hotel The *Great Southern* (☎ 064-45122) is

a few km along the Kenmare road, and costs from IR£100 for a double. The guest list includes Charles de Gaulle, Princess Grace of Monaco and Bernard Shaw (who wrote most of *St Joan* here).

Places to Eat
The *Village Kitchen* in the main street does tasty home-made dishes. Other places nearby do snacks. *Riverain*, near the village green, has a tourist menu for IR£10.50. *Stone House* starts at about IR£5; lobster goes for IR£17. The *Sacre Coeur Restaurant* has fish in the IR£5 to IR£10 range.

The *Pygmalion Restaurant* at the Great Southern is the most prestigious place on the Ring of Kerry. Lunch is IR£14 and dinner IR£21, plus a 13% service charge.

Getting Around
Burns Bike Hire (☎ 064-45140) in town is open all week. Bikes are IR£5 a day and IR£30 a week. The hostel also hires bikes.

KENMARE
This pastel-painted little town is a good alternative to Killarney as a base in the Ring of Kerry area. It's touristy but not as big as Killarney. Henry, Main and Shelbourne Sts make a neat triangle defining the town centre. Henry St is dedicated to tourism, with almost every place a pub, a restaurant or a B&B. An ancient stone circle is signposted from the park end of Main St, beyond the Henry St junction.

Information
The new tourist office (☎ 064-41233), next to the new heritage centre near the town square, is open from 9.30 am to 7 pm, Monday to Saturday, throughout the summer. The Kenmare Bookshop is on Shelbourne St near the Main St corner.

Places to Stay
Camping The *Ring of Kerry Caravan & Camping Park* (☎ 064-41366) is four km (2.5 miles) west of town on the Sneem road. A tent site is IR£6.50 or IR£3.50 for a cyclist.

Hostels *Kenmare Private Hostel* (☎ 064-41260) is on Main St. The *Fáilte Hostel* (☎ 064-41083) is at the junction of Henry and Shelbourne Sts. There's also a house about a km out of town, just past the Sneem turnoff, that is labelled *Private Hostel*. It's open in summer and has tent sites. Seven km (four miles) beyond Kenmare on the road to Killarney, behind a Catholic church, the *Bonane Hostel* (☎ 064-41098) has beds at IR£5 and breakfast for IR£3. Camping costs IR£3 per head, without the use of the kitchen.

B&Bs *O'Shea's* (☎ 064-41453) in Henry St has doubles for IR£24, and there are plenty more places on the road out to Killarney.

Hotels Two of Ireland's most expensive hotels compete for business in Kenmare: the *Park* (☎ 064-41200) and the *Sheen Falls Lodge* (☎ 064-41600). The Park is older, but Sheen Falls is next to the old Kenmare cemetery, with the remains of a 7th-century church and a walk down to the sea. A double at either will set you back over IR£200. The *Kenmare Bay* (☎ 064-41300), less than a km out of town on the road to Sneem, is cheap by comparison at a mere IR£64.

The *Lansdowne Arms* (☎ 064-41386) in William St has doubles from IR£52. *Dromquinna Manor* (☎ 064-41657) is five km (three miles) out of town on the Sneem road, by the sea, with doubles from IR£70.

Places to Eat
Cafés & Fast Food Try the simple *Clifford Café* on Main St with its outdoor patio, or the fancier *Mickey Ned's* or the *Dunboy Café* on Henry St. The *Swiss Bell* is a seafood restaurant, opposite the Kenmare Bay Hotel on the road to Sneem.

Foley's on Henry St does a pub lunch for IR£3.50 and dinner for around IR£5. *Le Brasserie* opposite does lunch for IR£3.50. The comfortable *Horseshoe* on Main St has meals for under £5.

Restaurants Places in town include the *Purple Heather Bistro* on Henry St and *An Leath Pingin* on Main St. The *Park* and *Sheen Falls Lodge* both have French-style restaurants. They both serve IR£17 lunches and IR£35 dinners. *Long Lake* (☎ 064-45100), 18 km (11 miles) from town on the road to Sneem, is equally exclusive, with a five-course dinner for IR£30. All three restaurants require reservations.

Things to Buy
Quills Woollen Market has a large store in the centre of town.

Getting Around
Finnigan's (☎ 064-41083) at the Fáilte Hostel has bikes for IR£5 to IR£7 a day. In June and July a cycling club (☎ 064-41333) organises tours – IR£2.50 to nonmembers.

The Beara Peninsula

Most of this peninsula is in County Cork, but a small part in the north-east is in Kerry.

CYCLING & WALKING TOURS
About one km (half a mile) west of Lauragh on the R572 there is a road off to the left marked for Glanmore Lake. Take the first turning to the right along this road and follow it until it comes to an end by a couple of farms, the first of which has a stone circle in its back yard. Although the road ends, a pathway continues across the stream and into the valley until it ends by the remains of some stone dwellings. This is a pleasant and undemanding walk which takes less than an hour from the stone circle.

A more exhilarating walk is to head up behind the house with the stone circle, crossing a sheep fence and keeping to the right of the stream. A stiff climb leads to a hanging valley with mountains on both sides. Avoid the one on the left and head right to climb the shorter summit of Cummeennahillan (361 metres, 1183 feet). From here you can walk along the ridge of the mountain and down through holly woods and invasive rhododendrons through another farm to the Glanmore Lake road. The longer trek takes at least a couple of hours, but a wander around the top of Cummeennahillan offers tremendous views from the top and a fine descent along the hanging valley.

DERREEN GARDENS

The gardens are now over a century old and were planted by the fifth Lord Lansdowne. An abundance of plants thrives here, including many imported from warmer climates. The gardens are open from April to September from 11 am to 6 pm and admission is IR£2.50. They are just west of Lauragh, which can be reached from Kenmare or from Adrigole in the south, via the Healy Pass.

PLACES TO STAY
Camping
The *Creveen Lodge Caravan & Camping Park* (☎ 064-83131) is 1.5 km (one mile) south-east of Lauragh on the Healy Pass road and is open from Easter to the end of September.

Hostel
The An Óige *Glanmore Lake Hostel* (☎ 064-83181), five km (three miles) from Lauragh, is open from April to September.

B&Bs
Hillside is distinctively located 13 km (eight miles) from Lauragh on the Healy Pass road. Otherwise there is the usual smattering of places on the road out from Kenmare.

Tralee & North Kerry

The north Kerry landscape is mediocre at best and many travellers rush through the area on the way to Clare via the ferry at Tarbert. However, there are some places of historical interest and the coastal strip is popular with Irish holidaymakers.

TRALEE
The town has some tourist attractions but may not detain you for long. The Dingle Peninsula is the major reason for coming here. The Rose of Tralee festival is a beauty contest, and most of the B&B places increase their prices by IR£3 or IR£4 for its duration, helping to create a seedy commercialism that lingers on after the crowds have departed.

The town has a long history of rebellion. In the 16th century the last ruling earl of the Desmonds was captured south of the town and executed. His head was sent to Elizabeth I, who had it exposed on London Bridge. The Desmond property was given to Sir Edward Denny. The Desmond castle once stood at the junction of Denny St and the Mall .

Tralee has a strong Republican tradition, and until quite recently there was a Sinn Fein office in the town.

Information
The tourist office (☎ 066-21288), open all year, is situated at the side of the Ashe Memorial Hall. The building is named after Thomas Ashe, a Kerryman who in 1916 led the largest Easter Rising action outside of Dublin. He died the following year from medical neglect after being forcibly fed while on hunger strike in prison.

Kerry the Kingdom
Upstairs in the Ashe Memorial Hall is a museum that gives a compact history of Ireland, with a Kerry bias of course. Downstairs the Medieval Experience recreates the 15th-century walled town of Tralee and visitors are shunted around in little buggies with a voice-over commentary. Children enjoy it.

The exhibition is open from 9.30 am to 6 pm during July and August, and from 3 to 5 pm the rest of the year including Sunday. Admission is IR£2.50 (children IR£1.50).

Steam Railway
Between 1891 and 1953 a narrow-gauge railway connected Tralee with Dingle. The first short leg of the journey, from Tralee to Blennerville, has been reopened. The train leaves Ballyard on the hour and the fare is IR£2.50 (children IR£1.50, students IR£2). Outside April to September ring ☎ 066-28888 for details of special trips.

Blennerville Windmill

This is the largest working mill in Ireland or Britain. It was built around 1800 by the local landlord, and fell into disuse by 1880 before being restored to its present grandeur. A short video tells the story of its history and there are guided tours.

There is also an exhibition about the thousands of emigrants who boarded the coffin ships for a new life in the USA. There are craft shops and a cafeteria.

The windmill is open from 10 am to 6 pm (8 pm in August), 1 to 6 pm on Sunday, from March to early November. Admission is IR£2.50 (children IR£1.50 and students IR£2). To get there, take the main road west to Dingle for just over one km. It is difficult to miss.

Siamsa Tíre

This is the National Folk Theatre of Ireland (pronounced 'shee-am-sah-tee-reh') whose performances, in song, dance and mime, recreate aspects of Gaelic culture. The shows are folksy at best. Events take place at the company theatre (☎ 066-23055), close to the tourist office, at 8.30 pm throughout the summer. Admission is IR£6 and a family ticket IR£20.

Getting There & Away

Train There is a regular train between Dublin and Tralee. The railway station (☎ 066-23522) is walking distance from town.

Bus An expressway bus connects Dublin and Tralee, via Limerick and Listowel. There is also a bus to Rosslare via Killarney, Cork and Waterford. Other services run to Clifden, Ennis, Kenmare, Shannon, Westport and Derry, and locally to Dingle and Dunquin.

Getting Around

Bikes can be hired from Tralee Gas & Bicycle Supplies (☎ 066-22018) in Strand St or E Caball (☎ 066-22231) in Ashe St. At the end of Castle St, O'Halloran also has bikes for rent.

AROUND TRALEE

The obvious attraction outside Tralee is the Dingle Peninsula but north Kerry has its own modest appeal and the ecclesiastical buildings at Ardfert are well worth a visit.

Ardfert Cathedral, Churches & Priory

Most of the present church dates back to the 13th century but the Romanesque doorway is 12th century. The architecture is English, but St Brendan the Navigator was educated in Ardfert and founded a monastery here. Set into one of the interior walls is an effigy popularly said to be of the saint. The cathedral is on the road to Ballyheigue from Tralee, which passes through Ardfert.

Turning right in front of the cathedral and going down the road for less than one km brings you to the remains of a **Franciscan Friary**, dating from the 13th century but with 15th-century cloisters.

Banna Strand

This eight-km (five-mile) stretch of sandy beach will always be better known for its history than for its recreational qualities. Sir Roger Casement (1864-1916) landed here on 21 April 1916 from a German submarine. He was planning to bring in rifles for the Easter Rising but was arrested as soon as he landed. He was tried for treason and executed in London but many years later his body was returned to Ireland. Approaching the beach there is a sign pointing left to the Casement memorial. It is one km (half a mile) down to the left, past the caravan park.

The beach itself is safe for swimming, as is the smaller but equally sandy beach at Ballyheigue to the north.

Crag Caves

One of Ireland's more recent tourist attractions, the caves were discovered in 1983 when problems with water pollution led to a search for the source of the local river. The entrance to the caves had been known for years but they had never been explored.

The caves are open from March to November, 10 am to 6 pm (closing at 7 pm in July and August), with guided tours for

IR£3 (children IR£2, family IR£8). Coffee and snacks are available.

From Tralee or Killarney look for the sign on the right of the N21 after Castleisland. Coming from Limerick on the N21 the turning is on the left at the top of the hill approaching Castleisland.

Places to Stay

Camping You can camp for free on the sand dunes at Banna, and there are public toilets, but no showers, at the main entrance to the beach. There are a couple of caravan parks stretched along the beach that attract Irish holidaymakers. A little farther north at Ballyheigue there is another safe beach, and camping is possible at *Casey's Caravan & Camping Park* (☎ 066-33195). For IR£3 camping is also possible at the *Breakers Hostel*.

Hostel The *Breakers* (☎ 066-33242) is an IHO hostel on Cliff Rd at Ballyheigue. Beds are IR£4 and private rooms are available.

Hotel The *Banna Beach Hotel* (☎ 066-34103) is open from May to September. Doubles cost IR£36 and there are self-catering units.

Places to Eat

In Ardfert *O'Sullivan's* pub does bar food. After Ardfert but before Banna the *Bayside Bistro* is open till 8 pm and does the usual meat and fish dishes, including takeaway service. Dinner at the *Banna Beach Hotel* is around IR£12 and bar food is available throughout the day.

Getting There & Away

There is a bus between Tralee and Ballybunion that stops near Banna and in Ardfert.

RATTOO ROUND TOWER & MUSEUM

The only complete round tower in Kerry is in fine condition with six floors. The top windows face the four points of the compass which indicates that this was an important monastic site in the 9th and 10th centuries.

Nothing else remains from that era. To the east are the ruins of a 15th-century church.

The tower is visible from the main road before entering the small town of Ballyduff. The turning left is signposted.

Just outside Ballyduff, there is a small museum at Knappogue (☎ 066-31000), dedicated to the history of North Kerry.

BALLYBUNION

In June 1834 a longstanding feud between two Ballybunion families culminated in a massive brawl on the beach, involving over 3000 combatants. During the summer the beach is still crowded, but only with Irish holidaymakers who have made Ballybunion a popular seaside resort. Apart from the usual seaside attractions there is little to see except the ruins of Ballybunion Castle that overlook the beach. Tourist information is available from a small cubicle, on the left as you enter the Ambassador Golf Hotel.

LISTOWEL

Listowel's only real attraction is the annual Writers' Week although there are some places of interest in the vicinity. Tourist information is available from the Arts Centre (☎ 068-22590) in the middle of the market square, from June to September. McGuire's in Church St is the only bookshop in town.

Writers' Week

John B Keane is probably the most famous writer associated with Listowel, especially since the filming of *The Field*. He owns a pub in the town and usually features in Writers' Week. Brian McMahon, a short story writer, is another literary talent from the town.

The literary festival, which is the main reason for visiting Listowel, takes place each May – details from Writers' Week, PO Box 147, Listowel, County Kerry. Many of the events take place in the St John's Arts Centre (☎ 068-22566) in the square.

Getting There & Away

Situated on the Shannon estuary, the town is just south of the car ferry that crosses to County Clare. The ferry leaves either every hour or every half-hour according to demand.

AROUND LISTOWEL
Carrigafoyle Castle
The location of this castle is very attractive, perched above the Shannon estuary. It was probably built at the end of the 15th century by the O'Connors, who ruled most of northern Kerry. It was besieged by the English in 1580, later retaken by O'Connor but fell again to the English under George Carew in 1600, during the suppression of O'Neill's rebellion, and was finally destroyed by Cromwell's forces in 1649. Climb the spiral staircase to the 29-metre (80-foot) top for a good view of the estuary.

The castle is 1.5 km (one mile) west of the village of Ballylongford, which can be reached from Listowel, Ballybunion or Tarbert.

Lislaughtin Abbey
This Franciscan friary was also founded by the O'Connors in the late 15th century. When the castle was attacked in 1580, this friary was also raided and three elderly friars were murdered in front of the altar. In the National Museum in Dublin there is a processional cross from this abbey, known as the Ballylongford Cross.

Take the small road to Saleen from the village of Ballylongford and the ruins of the abbey come into view.

The Dingle Peninsula

Less touristy and just as beautiful as the Ring of Kerry, the Dingle Peninsula is the Ireland of *Ryan's Daughter*, with an extraordinary number of ring forts, high crosses and other ancient monuments. Dingle is the main town. Ferries run from Dunquin to the bleak Blasket Islands, off the tip of the peninsula.

A handy local walking guide for the area west of Dingle is *The Dingle Peninsula* by Maurice Sheehy (only available locally).

TRALEE TO DINGLE VIA CONNOR PASS
There are two routes from Tralee to Dingle, though they both follow the same road out of Tralee past the windmill. Near the village of

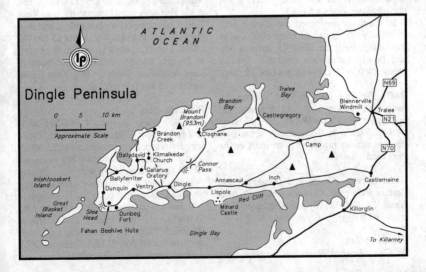

Camp a right fork heads off to the Connor Pass, while the main road via Annascaul brings you to Dingle more quickly. The Connor Pass route is more beautiful, and goes past the Castlegregory Peninsula, which divides Brandon and Tralee bays.

Connor Pass

This pass, sometimes spelt with a single 'n', is the highest in Ireland at 456 metres (1496 feet), and has impressive views of Dingle harbour and Mt Brandon to the north.

Places to Stay

Camping There are three camp sites near Castlegregory. The *Anchor Camping & Caravan Park* (☎ 066-39157) is close to the beach: 19 km (12 miles) from Tralee, three km (two miles) before Castlegregory, and signposted on the main road. *Seaside Caravan & Camping Park* (☎ 066-30161) is also on the beach, but the coin-operated hot taps put people off. The *Green Acres Caravan & Camping Park* (☎ 066-39158) is close to Crutch's Country House Hotel.

Hostels The *Connor Pass Hostel* (☎ 066-39179) is by the road at Stradbally, close to Castlegregory, and the proprietor runs the pub opposite. Beds are IR£5.

In Castlegregory itself the *Euro-Hostel* (☎ 066-39133) is part of Fitzgerald's bar in the village. Beds are IR£4.50, showers 50p and family rooms are available. *Lynch's Hostel* (☎ 066-39128) charges similiar rates.

B&Bs *Griffin's* (☎ 066-39147) is on the main road one km from Castlegregory, and beds cost IR£13 to IR£15. *Mrs Ferriter* (☎ 066-39263) at Beenoskee, Cappatigue, charges similar rates and is on the Connor Pass road.

Hotel Between Tralee and Dingle on the Connor Pass road, *Crutch's Country House Hotel* (☎ 066-38118) has singles/doubles from IR£40/60.

Places to Eat

In Castlegregory *Barry's* is a pizza and burger place. The *Fermoyle Restaurant* at Crutch's Country House Hotel serves dinner for IR£18 and bar food is also available here.

Getting Around

In Castlegregory there are two shops that hire bikes during the summer: Lynch's and Finn's. They are both in the small village.

TRALEE TO DINGLE VIA ANNASCAUL

For drivers this route has little to recommend it other than being faster than the Connor Pass route. By bicycle it is less demanding. On foot the journey constitutes the first three days of the Dingle Way.

The Dingle Way

This is a 178-km (112-mile) circular route that continues past Dingle to Dunquin and returns to Tralee via Castlegregory. There is a Bord Fáilte map guide for the walk; for more detail try *New Irish Walk Guides: Southwest*. The first three days to Dingle are not difficult, and are partly along quiet roads.

The first day, from Tralee to Camp, is the least interesting and you could take the bus to Camp and start from there. From Camp to Annascaul is 17 km (10.5 miles) and from Annascaul to Dingle 19 km (12 miles). You could also walk from Camp to the Bog View Hostel, about eight km (five miles), and then the next day on to Lispole, about 15 km (10 miles). From Lispole it is nine km (six miles) to Dingle. There is a lovely excursion to Lake Annascaul. From the Bog View Hostel this is a 15-km (10-mile) return trip.

Places to Stay

The *Bog View Hostel* (☎ 066-58125) is halfway between Tralee and Dingle. It is a friendly place, and the rates are IR£5.50 for a bed, IR£6 for a bed in a two-bed room and IR£14 for a private room with a double bed.

If you want to unwind with the help of a Shiatsu massage that costs IR£15 an hour.

A few km past the Bog View on the road to Dingle is the *Fuschia Lodge Hostel* (☎ 066-57150). The hostel near Lispole is the *Seacrest* (☎ 066-51390). Beds are IR£5, double rooms are IR£13 and showers cost

50p. The Seacrest is just over one km from the village and has a free pick-up service.

Places to Eat

Vegetarian meals are available for IR£5 at the *Bog View Hostel*, though you'd better check if you're not actually staying there.

In Annascaul the *Anchor Restaurant* has dishes at IR£10. *Brackluin House* in the village also does evening meals. The *South Pole* bar commemorates Tom Crean, a villager, who went to the South Pole with Scott.

CASTLEMAINE TO DINGLE

Travelling from Killarney to Dingle the quickest route is by way of Killorglin and Castlemaine. At Castlemaine a road heads west to Dingle, soon meeting the coast and passing Inch on the way to joining the main Tralee road to Dingle. Apart from the odd pub or two there is little provision for food so bring your own.

Minard Castle

This 15th-century castle has been in a dangerous condition since its destruction by Cromwellian forces in the 17th century. Children should not be left unsupervised.

The castle is signposted on the left after leaving Inch on the way to Dingle; it is three km (two miles) from the main road.

Places to Stay

Hostels About 16 km (10 miles) from Castlemaine, just before Inch, the *Inch Hostel* (☎ 066-58181) is a friendly place with beds for IR£5 and private rooms for IR£11. There are a couple of bikes for hire.

B&Bs At the Castlemaine end of Inch, *Waterside* (☎ 066-58129) has ocean views from some rooms. A double is IR£26, or IR£27 with own bathroom.

On the other side of Inch *Red Cliff* (☎ 066-57136) was once owned by Dr Eamonn Casey, Bishop of Galway, who used it for a liaison. The mother of his son went public in 1992, and journalists turned up in force. See the section on Bishop Casey in the Galway chapter.

Entertainment

Foley's pub in Inch has music in summer. The main attraction locally is the six-km (four-mile) sand spit that runs into Dingle Bay – a location for the film of *The Playboy of the Western World*. The sand dunes were once home to Iron Age settlements.

DINGLE

The attractive little port of Dingle makes a good base for exploration of the Dingle Peninsula, and has a famous resident dolphin.

Information

The tourist office (☎ 066-51188 and 51241) is in the centre of town and opens from April to October. There is a bureau de change at the Craft Village on The Wood. There is a laundrette at the end of Green Lane, the lane opposite the church in Green St.

Fungie the Dolphin

Dolphins are not usually a common sight in Dingle Bay, but in the winter of 1983 the crews of fishing boats began to notice a solitary bottlenosed dolphin that followed their vessels, jumped about in the water and on more than one occasion leapt over their boats. He came to be known as Fungie, the nickname of a local fisherman, and is now an international celebrity.

During the summer, boats (☎ 066-51619) leave the pier regularly for a one-hour trip that takes you out to the dolphin. The cost is IR£5 (children, IR£2.50) and while there's no charge if the dolphin isn't around, he usually turns up. A boat also leaves each morning at 8 am for those who want to swim with Fungie; the trip lasts two hours and the cost is IR£10 (children IR£5).

It's just as easy to watch Fungie from the shore. From Dingle take the road to Tralee and turn right down a lane about 1.5 km (one mile) from the Shell garage. The turning is easy to miss so look for a set of whitish gateposts beside the lane. About 100 metres further on are the whitish gateposts and the lane going down to the left. At the bottom of the lane is a tiny parking space and if you walk along the sea wall towards the old tower

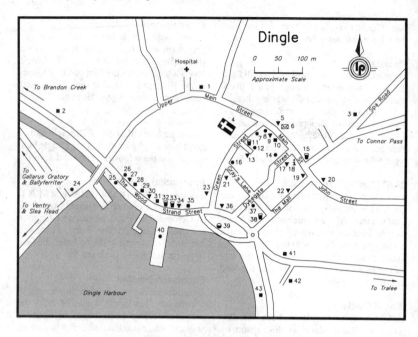

you will come to the mouth of the harbour. If you're in a car, remember when parking that this land is owned by someone who needs access to his fields.

Wetsuits can be hired from Flannery's (☎ 066-51163), in a two-storey house near the pier, or from Seventh Wave (☎ 066-51548), just across the bridge on the road out west. Seventh Wave have children's suits as well and a small display relating to Fungie. The cost is around IR£12 for the whole day. The Ballintaggart Hostel also has wetsuits for hire, mainly for residents.

Fishing

Enquire at the tourist office for details of sea fishing trips or contact the boatman himself (☎ 066-51163). Tuna and shark fishing trips can be made with Sea Ventures (☎ 066-51552) at Milltown.

Places to Stay

Camping Three of the hostels provide for campers: at the *Seacrest*, furthest out of town near Lispole it's IR£2.50 while *Westlodge/Westgate* and *Ballintaggart* charge IR£2.

Hostels In town, *Lovett's* (☎ 066-51903) is a small family house with beds for IR£5. It's down the road opposite the garage, less than 100 metres from the town roundabout, on the way to Tralee. Near the Craft Village on The Wood, *Westlodge/Westgate Hostel* (☎ 066-51476) is far larger with 30 beds at IR£4 a night, and a stove that encourages a campfire atmosphere at night.

The *Marina Hostel* is a new place near the pier with no phone as yet. There are 20 beds for IR£5 and private rooms for IR£14 (IR£10 in the winter). Close to town is the *Rainbow Hostel* (no phone), with a free pick-up from the bus stop and beds for IR£5, (IR£25 for the week) and family rooms at IR£15. Unlike some hostels, the kitchen here is big enough to handle a crowd.

Along the road to Tralee is the *Ballintagg-*

■ PLACES TO STAY

1 Boland's B&B
2 Rainbow Hostel
3 Hillgrove Hotel
10 Benner's Hotel
28 Westlodge/Westgate Hostel
29 Marina Hostel
31 Marina Inn
35 Murphy's Pub/B&B
41 Alpine House
42 Lovett's Hostel
43 Skellig Hotel

▼ PLACES TO EAT

5 Islandman
9 Lord Baker's
13 Café Ceol
17 An Café Liteártha
19 Old Smokehouse
20 Doyles Restaurant
21 Beginish
22 Shamrock
23 Fenton's
27 Sméara Dubha
30 Singing Salmon

34 Asgard
36 Forge Restaurant

🍺 PUBS

11 Dick Mack's
15 Small Bridge Bar
32 Máire de Barra Pub
33 Star Bar
38 O'Flaherty's

OTHER

4 St Mary's Church
6 Post Office
7 Bike Hire
8 Bike Hire
12 Laundrette
14 Bike Hire
16 Lisbeth Mulcahy Shop
18 Tourist Office
24 Seventh Wave
25 Brian De Staic Jewellery
26 Craft Village
37 Bike Hire
39 Bus Stop
40 Pier & Dolphin Boats' Departure Point

art Hostel (☎ 066-51454). It has a free shuttle service to and from town, bike hire, a bureau de change, pony trekking and a resident ghost, and charges IR£5 a night.

B&Bs *Alpine House* (☎ 066-51250) is a guesthouse on the road to Tralee, just east of the roundabout with doubles for IR£31. The rooms are bigger than most, and the sea views are terrific. In town *Boland's* (☎ 066-51426) has beds from IR£14. The comfortable *Doyle's Townhouse* (☎ 066-51174 at the bottom of John St costs from IR£28 per person. A couple of pubs down by the pier have gone into B&B; the *Marina Inn* offers B&B for IR£10 or just a bed for IR£6. *Murphy's* (☎ 066-51450) has rooms with separate bathroom for IR£24, plus tea and coffee making facilities. Along this road there is a host of unregistered B&Bs and the Mall has quite a few as well.

Hotels *Benner's* (☎ 066-51638) on Main St

is attractively and comfortably furnished, with singles/doubles from IR£36/64. With higher prices and about four times the number of rooms is the *Skellig Hotel* (☎ 066-51144). A 10-minute walk from town southeast of the roundabout brings this idiosyncratic, some would say charmless, building into view. The strange-looking foyer area is supposed to represent clocháns, the beehive huts found in the area. Singles/doubles here are from IR£62/104. The normal-looking *Hillgrove* (☎ 066-51131) is on Spa Rd, within walking distance of town. Doubles here are IR£50.

Places to Eat

Dingle has some good restaurants, and while many are expensive there are also a number of places offering cheap meals. Cheap here means paying around IR£5, while expensive means a bill in the IR£50-plus region for two.

Cafés & Takeaways *An Café Liteártha* is a

bookshop with a small inexpensive café at the back serving drinks and sandwiches. The *Weaver's Café* is part of the Craft Village and does pricey vegetarian salads for IR£4.

At *Café Ceol*, at the end of the lane opposite the church in Green St, dinner is served upstairs while the café is below. Pleasant surroundings match congenial prices, between IR£2 and IR£5, and vegetarians are well catered for. Another unpretentious place is the *Old Smokehouse* at the corner of the Mall and Main St. Pizza, lasagne and the like are all around IR£4.

Restaurants Farther down the Mall, the *Shamrock Restaurant* is squarely aimed at budget-minded travellers and families. Farther down again, near the roundabout, *Greany's Restaurant* does lunch for IR£6.50, dinner for IR£9. The *Forge Restaurant* nearby has meals in the IR£5 to IR£10 range.

Lord Baker's in Main St is a seafood restaurant offering lunch for IR£4.50 and a choice of dinners at IR£12 to IR£16. Facing the pier, the *Singing Salmon Restaurant* has pizzas for IR£5, or double that for steaks and seafood. The *Asgard*, farther along, is open seven days a week for lunch and dinner. The tourist menu is IR£8 and there are vegetarian dishes for IR£5. *Fenton's Restaurant* in Green St has a set dinner for IR£12, but the imaginative seafood lunch menu is only about IR£5.

Pubs are usually the best place for a meal below IR£5. The pub strip is along by the pier and the *Máire debarra* pub has lunches for IR£4 and afternoon specials like sausage & chips for IR£2. The *Star Bar* next door does toasted sandwiches for IR£1.30 and meals for around IR£5. *Benner's Hotel* has a very comfortable bar and lunch is IR£4.50.

The *Beginish Restaurant* (☎ 066-51588) in Green St can be relied on for a good seafood meal. The set dinner is IR£16 (IR£13.50 if you skip the starter or dessert), the portions are generous and the place has a genteel air. Vegetarians are catered for if you book in advance and the wine list is impressive.

Doyle's Seafood Bar (☎ 066-51174) at the bottom of John St is excellent. They do dinner only, and most main courses are in the IR£10 to IR£13 range.

Sméara Dubha is a vegetarian restaurant, operating from a bungalow next to the Westlodge/Westgate Hostel, which is only open during the summer. It's expensive for vegetarian food, but below IR£10 a head.

The *Islandman Restaurant* on Main St is upmarket from Café Liteártha, but also boasts a bookish atmosphere. A salmon steak is IR£10.50, set dinner IR£9 and the vegetarian stuffed pitta bread IR£7.

Entertainment

Many of the pubs have live music, and three in particular are worth checking out: *O'Flaherty's* near the roundabout, *Murphy's* down by the pier and the *Small Bridge Bar*, at the end of Main St by the bridge. In Green St, *Dick Mack's* is an old-style pub with the shop counter on one side and the drinking counter opposite. Musical evenings are sometimes held at *Café Ceol* off Green St.

Things to Buy

At the Craft Village on The Wood there are a number of workshops specialising in leatherware and garments. If you want your name inscribed in Ogham script on a piece of jewellery go to Brian de Staic. They also have an outlet in Green St.

In Green St, Lisbeth Mulcahy sells pottery and woven garments like scarves – expensive but nice. Her husband has his own workshop west of Dingle near Ballyferriter (see that section).

Getting There & Away

Buses stop outside the car park at the back of the Super Valu store. The bus leaves Tralee at 1.45 pm Monday to Friday, at 4.15 pm Monday to Saturday, with an extra evening bus on Friday at 8.10 pm. In summer the extra evening bus leaves Monday to Saturday.

From Dingle the bus to Tralee leaves at 7.25 and 10.30 am, and on Sunday at 2 pm.

Getting Around

There are several bike-rental places. Dingle Bike Hire is a few doors down from the Super Valu car park and the bus stop, while Moriarty (☎ 066-51316) on Main St does the Raleigh Rent-a-Bike scheme. Around the corner in Green St there is another bike-rental place, and in Dykegate St two more, one at each end.

WEST OF DINGLE

The area west of Dingle has the greatest concentration of ancient sites in Kerry if not the whole of Ireland, and to do them justice you should use one of the local specialist guides, on sale in the An Café Liteártha, the Islandman bookshops or the tourist office. The sites listed here are among the most interesting and easiest to find.

The land west of Dingle has other attractions. It is a genuine Irish-speaking area. The landscape is dramatic, except when it's hidden in mist, and there are striking views of the Blasket Islands from Slea Head. The sandy beach nearby, Coumenole, is lovely to walk along but like most of those in the area it is treacherous for swimming.

Tourism came late to Dingle but the area is handling it well, avoiding the tackiness of Killarney. In 1971, David Lean made the film *Ryan's Daughter* here. Much of it was shot near Dunquin, and the ruins of the film's schoolhouse can still be found. Film buffs should enquire at Kruger's pub in Dunquin.

A new **heritage centre** is about to open in Dunquin, the focus of which will be the culture of the Blasket Islands.

Orientation

If you cross the bridge west of Dingle and turn north just after Seventh Wave, you come to a Y-junction after five km (three miles). To the right are Kilmalkedar Church (two km) and Brandon Creek; from here you could return to Dingle on a circular route. If you turn left at the Y-junction, you come to Gallarus Oratory and the Riasc site, from which you can reach Ballyferriter and Dunquin, for boats to the Blasket Islands.

The road continues down the coast and back to Dingle, via Ventry.

Kilmalkedar Church

This 12th-century Romanesque church was once part of a complex of religious buildings. The characteristic Romanesque doorway has a tympanum with a head on one side and a mythical beast on the other. The church has an Ogham stone and an alphabet stone. About 50 metres away is a two-storey building known as St Brendan's House, believed to have been the residence of the medieval clergy. The road connecting these two ruins is the beginning of the Saint's Rd, the traditional approach to Mt Brandon.

Brandon Creek

St Brendan set off from this inlet in the 5th century and sailed to America, according to the information board. As Tim Severin proved, voyagers could indeed have done this journey hundreds of years before Columbus. The fishing boats add to the creek's atmosphere, and on a warm day the water is inviting.

Carry on along the road that you turned off to reach the church. After a few km turn right at the junction that points to An Dooneen B&B and carry on for nearly two km (1.5 miles) until reaching the tiny village of Bothar Bui where the IHO hostel is. Carry straight on to the next junction and turn left for Brandon Creek which is about one km (half a mile) along this road. A right turn at this junction returns to Dingle.

Gallarus Oratory

Simple but stunning, this superb dry-stone oratory is reason enough for visiting the Dingle Peninsula. It is in perfect condition, apart from a slight sagging in the roof, and has withstood the assault of the elements for some 1200 years. The interior and exterior walls may have been plastered, as some sign of mortar remains. Shaped like an upturned boat, it has a doorway on the west side and a small round-headed window on the east side. Inside the doorway are two projecting stones with holes which once supported the door.

Gallarus Oratory

Bear left at the Y-junction (see Orientation), and after two km (1.5 miles) turn left at the sign. The oratory is half a km down the road on the left.

Riasc Monastic Settlement

The remains of this 5th or 6th-century monastic settlement are impressive. Excavations have revealed, among other finds, the foundations of an oratory first built with wood and later stone, a kiln for drying corn and a cemetery. Most interesting is a pillar with beautiful Celtic designs.

A sign points the way from the Y-junction (see Orientation). Follow the road for four km (2.5 miles) and just before a T-junction there is a rotting sign to the site which is pointing back the way you came. Follow instead the sign for the Reask View B&B and the site is half a km up this road.

Ballyferriter

This small village is named after Piaras Ferriter, a poet and soldier who emerged as a local leader in the 1641 rebellion and was the last Kerry commander to submit to Cromwell's army. Near the village are the Three Sisters hills, Smerwick Harbour and the remains of **Dun An Oir Fort**. During the 1580 rebellion in Munster, the fort was held by an international brigade of Italians, Spaniards and Basques. On 17 November, English troops under Lord Grey attacked the fort and the people inside surrendered. 'Then putt I in certeyn bandes who streight fell to

execution. There were 600 slayne', said the poet Edmund Spenser, who was secretary to Lord Grey.

To reach Ballyferriter go north on the R559 road towards the Gallarus Oratory. At the Y-junction four km (2.4 miles) from Dingle take the left fork. After another three km (1.8 miles) take a left turn at a T-junction just after an iron bridge. After about 300 metres turn right at a brown sign for the An Oíge hostel and the Golf Links Hotel. Ballyferriter is one km further along that road.

To get to Dun An Oir, head out of Ballyferriter in a westerly direction. After one km (0.6 mile) turn right at a brown sign to Smerwick Harbour. After a further 1.5 km (0.9 mile), take the right fork at a Y-junction. After 2.6 km (1.6 miles), turn right at the T-junction and after roughly 300 metres you'll see a signpost to the fort, indicating a poorly-surfaced road.

Social, cultural and historical aspects of life on the Dingle Peninsula and the Blasket Islands are the concern of the **Ballyferriter heritage centre** (☎ 066-56100). It is open over Easter and from June to the end of September, seven days a week, from 10 am to 6 pm. Admission is IR£1 (children and students 50p).

Louis Mulcahy Pottery

This is not the only pottery shop on the peninsula but it is certainly one of the most interesting. Visitors can see the potters at work and the two floors of the shop display a variety of pieces, costing from IR£5 to IR£500. Tea sets, bowls, lamps, vases, platters – if it can be fashioned from clay you are likely to see it here. Purchases can be mailed overseas from the shop (☎ 066-56229). The workshop is on the road just after Ballyferriter and before Dunquin.

Dunbeg Fort & Beehive Huts

This promontory fort has a sheer drop to the Atlantic and four outer walls of stone. Inside are the remains of a house and a beehive hut as well as an underground passage. The fort is eight km (five miles) from Dunquin.

From Dunbeg Fort to Slea Head there are many beehive huts, forts and church sites. The **Fahan** huts are accessible from more than one place and you will see signs pointing the way from the road. There is usually a 50p admission charge.

Mt Brandon

At 953 metres (3127 feet) Mt Brandon is the second-highest mountain in Ireland. There are two main routes up: a gradual one from the west and a more exciting one from the east. You should give yourself at least five hours for the climb. Gill & Macmillan's *New Irish Walk Guides: Southwest* by Sean O'Suilleabhain has details of both routes. The book is available in both bookshops in Dingle.

If you want to climb the mountain, with or without a guidebook do make sure there is no danger of a mist descending, as the top is frequently shrouded in cloud. If you do get caught, you may need a compass to make your way down. Travelling along the road from Dingle to Brandon Creek you will see two signs pointing the way. The traditional way up the mountain is by way of the Saint's Rd that starts at Kilmakedar Church. The eastern, more demanding, approach starts just beyond the village of Cloghane which is signposted on the left after leaving Dingle and descending the Connor Pass.

The ruins of St Brendan's Oratory mark the summit. The legend is that the navigator saint climbed the mountain with his seafaring monks before they set out in their curraghs for the journey to Greenland and America.

There is a shower available at the An Bothar pub for 50p (see B&Bs in the following section).

Places to Stay

Camping The most westerly camp site in Europe is *Campaill Theach an Aragail* (Oratory House Camp) (☎ 066-55143) near Gallarus Oratory. A family tent costs IR£6 a night, cyclists IR£4.50 each. Free camping is possible near Ferriter's Cove (see Ballyferriter) but there are no facilities.

Hostels *Tigh an Phoist Hostel* (☎ 066-55109) is at Bothar Bui village, attached to a shop, with beds for IR£5.50. On Tuesday and Friday the Dingle to Ballydavid bus goes close. By road follow the directions for Brandon Creek above.

An Cat Dubh (☎ 066-56286), (Black Cat Hostel), is at Ballyferriter, just past the Granville Hotel on the road to Dunquin. The rate is IR£5, including showers.

There is an An Oíge Hostel (☎ 066-56145) at Dunquin which is perfect for visiting Great Blasket Island, being close to the ferry departure point. It charges IR£5.90 a night.

B&Bs Dunquin has *Kruger's* (☎ 066-56127) and is as close as possible to the Blasket Islands. From the pub it is a short walk to the ferry. The place is still in the Kruger family, and the story of a male member of the family is recounted on one of the pub's walls, along with photographs relating to two films made in the locality, *Ryan's Daughter* with Robert Mitchum and Sarah Miles and *Far & Away* with Tom Cruise and Nicole Kidman. A bed is IR£13.

Ballyferriter has a few B&Bs. At Wine Strand *Cul Dorcha* (☎ 066-56286) is a short walk from the bus stop. *Reask View House* (☎ 066-56126) has five beds for IR£13.

An Bothar (☎ 066-55342) is a friendly pub doing B&B and is ideally located if you want to climb Mt Brandon. To get there, go to the Tigh an Phoist Hostel and carry on until a junction. The road to the left goes to Brandon Creek. Turn right instead; the B&B is half a km along the road to Dingle. From Dingle a more direct route would be to turn right before the bridge over the river. If you take this route you will meet two other B&Bs before An Bothar. *Sheehy's* (☎ 066-51453) is within walking distance of Dingle while *Murphy's* (☎ 066-51745) is a couple of km farther along the road. Both charge IR£13 for a bed.

Hotels The two hotels west of Dingle are both in Ballyferriter. *Ostan Dun An Oir* (☎ 066-56133) is reached by taking the first right turn after the An Cat Dubh Hostel on the road from Ballyferriter to Dunquin. Singles/doubles are IR£38/60 and there's an outdoor heated swimming pool.

The *Granville* (☎ 066-56116) is just before the An Cat Dubh Hostel. Singles/doubles here are from IR£20/30.

Self-Catering If you want to spend a week exploring the Dingle Peninsula, there are two groups of self-catering cottages. *Dingle Wine Strand Cottages* (☎ 061-53582) have 22 cottages near Ballyferriter. Summer rates are in the IR£300 to IR£400 a week bracket, but they do sleep eight. The postal address is Geraldville, North Circular Rd, Limerick.

Ventry Holiday Cottages (☎ 066-51588) sleep six and are a little less expensive. The postal address is Mr Moore, Green St, Dingle.

Places to Eat

Ballyferriter is the best place for a meal. The *Gallery Restaurant* is part of the *Teach Pheig* pub and the three-course meal for IR£5 is available day or night. Vegetarian meals are prepared on request. The nearby *Ostan Dun an Oir Hotel* also does food.

On the road from Dunquin to Slea Head the *Pottery Café* does meals and snacks and *An Bracan Feasa*, over 13 km (eight miles) from Dunquin, is a self-service restaurant by the side of the road.

In the Mt Brandon area, bar food is available at the *An Bothar* pub, and near the Riasc monastic site the *Tig Ohric* pub does sandwiches.

Getting There & Away

There is a regular bus service from Dingle to Dunquin, via Ventry, Slea Head and Ballyferriter. During the summer there is also a bus service between Killarney and Dunquin, via Inch and Dingle. The bus leaves Killarney weekdays only at 10.20 am and reaches Dunquin at 1.05 pm. It leaves

from the hostel at Dunquin at 2.55 pm for the return journey.

THE BLASKET ISLANDS

There are four big islands and three smaller ones. Great Blasket is the largest and the most visited. It is six km by 1.2 km (four miles by 0.75 miles), and is mountainous enough for strenuous walks including a good one detailed in Kevin Corcoran's *Kerry Walks*. There are the remains of an old church and the views are wonderful.

The last islanders left for the mainland in 1953 but lyrical stories of their lives survive. Three books in particular are currently in print and easily available in Dingle. The best is the English translation of Thomas O Crohan's *The Islandman*; the other two are Maurice O'Sullivan's *Twenty Years A-Growing* and translation of Peig Sayers' *Peig*.

For some time the government has been trying to buy up the empty property lots on the Great Blasket, and compulsory purchase orders have now been processed for the most part. There are plans to renovate some of the dilapidated homes on the island and to build a pier which will allow larger boats to ferry visitors across.

Places to Stay

There is one small *hostel* which opens during the summer, but camping is free. If the hostel is full, the *An Oíge* hostel on the mainland is within walking distance of the ferry point.

Getting There & Away

Boats (☎ 066-56188) operate throughout the summer, weather permitting, costing IR£8 return. On Monday and Thursday the first bus for Dunquin leaves Dingle at 8.50 am and this will still give you half an hour before the first boat leaves around 10 am. In the summer there is a daily bus leaving Dingle at 12.30 pm, 10.30 am on Sunday. The last boat from Great Blasket leaves around 3 pm.

Counties Limerick & Tipperary

County Limerick

In the past County Limerick has suffered from a bad tourist press but there are good reasons for not skipping the small county that contains the third largest town in the Republic. Apart from the historical interest and amenities of Limerick City itself, there are fascinating historic and prehistoric sites to the south of the city that make ideal excursions by bicycle. The nearby town of Adare is one of the prettiest in Ireland, in dramatic contrast with the proletarian Limerick City.

LIMERICK CITY

Limerick is an instantly recognisable name and one of the larger cities in Ireland. Until recently it has also been one of the dullest cities in the country, but an imaginative new interpretative centre in King John's Castle, together with the many sites around the city, is turning Limerick into a place of interest in its own right, rather than just a convenient crossroads.

History

History has weighed heavily on the city of Limerick since the Vikings first arrived in the 10th century. The Vikings and the native Irish fought over the town until Brian Boru's forces defeated the Norsemen at the Battle of Clontarf in 1014, preparing the way for a final attack on the town by the Irish.

After the arrival of the Normans in Ireland, King John paid a visit in 1210 to celebrate the completion of his castle, work on which had started 10 years earlier.

In 1690, Limerick acquired heroic status in the on-going saga of the English occupation of Ireland. After the Battle of the Boyne, the defeated Jacobite forces withdrew west behind the famously strong walls of Limerick. Surrender seemed only a matter of time, but the Irish Jacobite leader Patrick Sarsfield slipped out with 600 men and launched a surprise attack on the English supply train. Cannons, mortars and 200 wagons of ammunition were destroyed. Sarsfield and his followers returned undetected to Limerick.

Months of bombardment followed and eventually Sarsfield sued for peace with dignity. The terms of the Treaty of Limerick were agreed and Sarsfield and about 12,000 soldiers, many with their wives and children, were allowed to leave the city and set sail for France. The treaty also guaranteed religious freedom for Irish Catholics, but the English later reneged on it, and enforced fierce anti-Catholic legislation. Decades of unrest followed, and this act of betrayal came to symbolise the injustice of British rule.

In 1919 a general strike took place in the city to protest against British military rule. A Strike Committee took charge of running essential services, and for one week the city of Limerick operated outside all legal structures. The Strike Committee even issued its own banknotes. It became known as the Limerick Soviet.

Orientation & Information

The tourist office (☎ 061-317522), with a bureau de change, is in a new building at Arthur's Quay near the river. It is open from 9 am to 6.30 pm, seven days a week in July

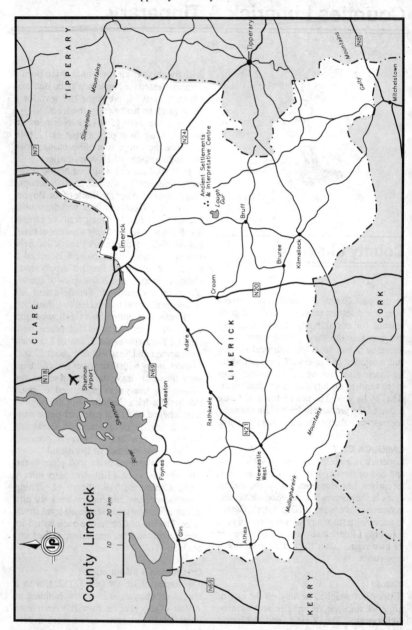

and August (9.30 am to 5.30 pm on Saturday and Sunday). The rest of the year it is open from 9.30 am to 5.30 pm, Monday to Saturday.

The necessary parking discs can be purchased here. Otherwise use the large car park attached to the adjacent Arthur's Quay shopping centre. The tourist office is also home to a Bus Éireann desk and Limerick City Tours (☎ 061-301587) who conduct a two-hour walking tour that begins at 11 am and 2.30 pm, Monday to Friday, from June to August. It costs IR£3.50 (children IR£1, students IR£2.50).

The main street through town changes names from Patrick St to O'Connell St to O'Connell Ave, as it runs south.

Laundrettes can be found in Cecil St, Ellen St and Broad St. One of the city's better second-hand bookshops, O'Brien's Bookshop, is next to the Savoy Centre in Bedford Row. There's a branch of the Eason bookshop chain on O'Connell St.

St Mary's Cathedral

This is the oldest building in the city, founded in 1172 by Donal Mor O'Brien, King of Munster. The Romanesque west doorway survives from this period, with the chancel and chapels added in the 15th century. There are grand tombs, memorial stones and splendid black oak misericords – seats for choristers, carved with pictures of animals and other figures, dating from around 1489.

Between June and September at 9.15 pm there is a *son et lumière* show on the history of the city and church; admission is IR£2.50 (children and students IR£1.50). After restoration, it will be possible to climb to the belfry and view the city (IR£1).

The graveyard outside has many 18th-century tombstones.

King John's Castle

The castle was built on the site of an earlier fortification at the beginning of the 13th century, to administer and guard the rich Shannon region. The new cannon technology necessitated stronger walls and defences

than ever before, and the castle became the most formidable bastion of English power in the west of Ireland.

Two floors of the interpretative centre set forth the tragic and heroic story of Limerick. In the courtyard there are replicas of three classic machines of early castle warfare: two catapults – a mangonel and a trebuchet, the latter capable of hurling a 200-kg missile – and a battering ram.

Underneath the castle there are some fascinating archaeological excavations showing the development of the castle and attempts by the besiegers to tunnel beneath the walls.

The audiovisual show is disappointing but there are plans to move the more interesting animated display of the signing of the Treaty, presently in the town hall, into the castle.

The castle is open seven days a week between May and October from 9.30 am to 5.30 pm. Admission is IR£3 (children and students IR£1.50).

Across the river from the castle the **Treaty Stone** marks the spot on the riverbank where the Treaty of Limerick was signed. The subsequent English sellout rankles in Limerick to this day.

City Museum

The museum occupies two three-storey houses, dating back to 1751, in the corner of John's Square, near St John's Cathedral. There's an extensive collection on the history of the city over the last two centuries, but surprisingly little on the Limerick Soviet, banknotes issued by the strikers being the main exhibit.

It's open from Tuesday to Saturday, 10 am to 1 pm and 2 to 5 pm, entrance free.

Hunt Museum

Situated at the time of writing in Limerick University, this museum (☎ 061-333644) will eventually relocate, probably in 1994, to the Granary House in Michael St. Although hard to find at present, it is worth looking for, as it contains probably the finest collection of Bronze Age, Celtic and medieval treasures outside Dublin. It is not a big museum and

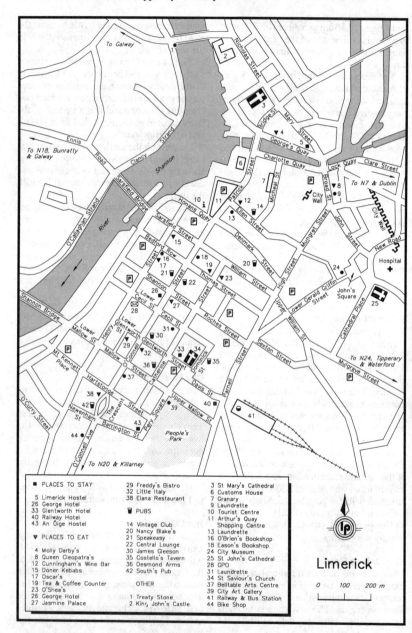

PLACES TO STAY	29 Freddy's Bistro	3 St Mary's Cathedral
	32 Little Italy	6 Customs House
5 Limerick Hostel	38 Elana Restaurant	7 Granary
26 George Hotel		9 Laundrette
33 Glentworth Hotel	PUBS	10 Tourist Centre
40 Railway Hotel		11 Arthur's Quay
43 An Óige Hostel	14 Vintage Club	Shopping Centre
	20 Nancy Blake's	13 Laundrette
PLACES TO EAT	21 Speakeasy	16 O'Brien's Bookshop
	22 Central Lounge	18 Eason's Bookshop
4 Molly Darby's	30 James Gleeson	24 City Museum
8 Queen Cleopatra's	35 Costello's Tavern	25 St John's Cathedral
12 Cunningham's Wine Bar	36 Desmond Arms	28 GPO
17 Oscar's	42 South's Pub	31 Laundrette
19 Tea & Coffee Counter		34 St Saviour's Church
23 O'Shea's	OTHER	37 Belltable Arts Centre
26 George Hotel		39 City Art Gallery
27 Jasmine Palace	1 Treaty Stone	41 Railway & Bus Station
	2 King John's Castle	44 Bike Shop

Limerick

0   100   200 m

there's an explanatory leaflet that lists and describes all the contents. One of the major attractions is a superb Bronze Age shield. The only other one of the kind in Ireland is in the National Museum in Dublin.

While the museum is still housed at the university, take the N7 Dublin road and look for the sign on the left to the university, at the traffic lights. If you miss it, the next junction has a sign for the actual museum; the road leads to an unmarked roundabout and the university is to the left. Ask for directions in the university foyer or follow signs to the Charles Bianconi building and take the lift to the 3rd floor. It is open from 9.30 am to 5.30 pm, seven days a week, from May to September. Admission is IR£1.60 (children 90p).

Limerick City Art Gallery

The permanent collection includes work by artists such as Jack B Yeats and Sean Keating. It is open all year from 10 am to 1 pm and from 2 to 6 pm Monday to Friday, and from 10 am to 1 pm only on Saturday. There is no charge for admission. The gallery is in a corner of People's Park, not far from the An Óige hostel.

St Saviour's Dominican Church

This 19th-century church contains a statue of Our Lady that was given to the Dominicans of the city in 1640 by a rich Limerick citizen. He wanted to do something to atone for the fact that his uncle had sentenced a man to death for allowing a priest to say mass in his house. The church is open from 7.30 am to 8.15 pm from Monday to Saturday, 7.30 am to 2.45 pm on Sunday.

Places to Stay

Camping The *Shannon Cottage Caravan & Camping Park* (☎ 061-377118) is about 12 km (eight miles) from Limerick, reached by turning left at Birdhill – the signpost is easily missed – on the N7 road to Dublin. After Birdhill follow the signs to O'Brien's bridge and turn sharp right after crossing the bridge. Small/family tents costs IR£6/7 and IR£3 for a hiker or cyclist. Curraghchase Caravan &

Camping Park (☎ 061-396349) is 25 km (16 miles) from Limerick; turn off the N21 at Adare from where it is signposted. From June to the end of August tents are IR£3 a night plus IR£2 per person (children IR£1). Hikers and cyclists pay a flat rate of IR£3 per person. The charge includes entry to the Curraghchase Forest Park.

Hostels The *An Óige Hostel* (☎ 061-31462) is at 1 Pery Square, a short walk across People's Park from the bus and railway station. A bed costs IR£5.90. The large independent *Limerick Hostel* (☎ 061-45222) is at Barrington's House on George's Quay and costs IR£4.90 in rooms for two to four. Single rooms go for IR£6.50. Both hostels are strict, and the latter is not as friendly as most independent hostels.

B&Bs *Alexandra* (☎ 061-318472) at 6 Alexandra Terrace, O'Connell Ave, the Cork road, is handily close to the centre and has singles/doubles from IR£16/26. Otherwise the Ennis Rd (N18) running out of Limerick to Ennis and Galway is lined with B&Bs for several km, including *Clifton House* (☎ 061-451166) just one km out with singles/doubles from IR£17/26. One km further on, *Parkview* (☎ 061-451505) has rooms for IR£18/28. Further out again, just next to the Ryan hotel, *Mrs Gavin* (☎ 061-453690) has three doubles for IR£24, sharing washroom facilities.

Hotels Many of the big hotels are strung out along the Ennis Rd (N18). *Jurys* (☎ 061-327777) is half a km from town with singles/doubles from IR£68/84. *Greenhills* (☎ 061-453033) has rooms from IR£44/64 and unlike Jurys the rate includes breakfast. The two other big hotels on the Ennis Rd are the *Limerick Inn* (☎ 061-326666), five km from town, with rooms from IR£75/88, and *Limerick Ryan* (☎ 061-453922) with rooms from IR£44. Neither of these two include brekafast in their room rates. The *Two Mile Inn* (☎ 061-53122), which is four km from Limerick, does include breakfast and has singles/doubles from IR£46/64. Just one km from town, *Woodfield House* (☎ 061-453022) has singles/doubles from IR£ 35/56.

Castletroy Park (☎ 061-33556) is three km from town on the Dublin Rd and singles/doubles there start at IR£81.50/106. The *George* (☎ 061-414566) is centrally located on O'Connell St. It's a comfortable hostelry with singles/doubles for IR£35/50, excluding breakfast, and an overnight garage. The *Glentworth* (☎ 061-413822), in the street of the same name, has rooms for IR£33/50. The least expensive hotel is the *Railway* (☎ 061-413653) on Parnell St across from the station, with rooms for IR£22/42.

Places to Eat

Cafés & Takeaways For cheap eats try the modern *Sails Restaurant* in the equally modern Arthur's Quay shopping centre across from the tourist office. Nearby *Doner Kebabs* on Henry St is open until commendably late at night. *Luigi's* features 15 varieties of burger and is conveniently located across from the railway station on Parnell St. Under the renovated Granary on Michael St by Charlotte Quay is *Doc's Bar* with average lunch-time pub food in a pleasant location. Decent coffee is brewed at the *Tea & Coffee Counter* in Thomas St, off O'Connell St. Residents at the independent hostel will find *Queen Cleopatra's*, just across the road and over the bridge, handy for inexpensive breakfasts between 9 am and 1 pm.

Restaurants For vegetarians, *O'Shea's* restaurant in Little Catherine St usually has something on the menu. They do an Irish breakfast for IR£1.50, and regular dishes for around IR£3. Vegetarian meals are also available at *Freddy's Bistro*, tucked away down Theatre Lane that runs between Lower Mallow and Lower Glentworth Sts; it's open on Sunday. *Oscar's* restaurant, part of the Savoy Centre cinema complex accessible from Henry St or Bedford Row, always has non-meat dishes for under IR£5.

If you're looking for a more expensive

dinner, the excellent and trendy *Cunningham's Wine Bar* at 3 Ellen St is open Monday to Saturday and does some imaginative pasta dishes. Dishes are cheaper, at IR£5, between 5.30 and 8 pm. Pizzas cost from IR£4 to IR£7. On George's Quay, just up from Limerick Hostel, there is *Molly Darby's* pizzeria with dishes from IR£5 to IR£8 and outdoor tables. The alfresco mood can be maintained at the *Locke Bar* next door. Another Italian place is *Little Italy* at the bottom end of O'Connell St with dishes between IR£5 and IR£10.

The *Elana* Greek restaurant, at the bottom of O'Connell St next to the Jesuit church, costs at least IR£10 for a meal, but they do have a happy hour between 5 and 7 pm when prices are reduced.

The *Jasmine Palace* (☎ 061-42484) is probably the best Chinese place in town, and conveniently located in the mall on O'Connell St. A Cantonese meal for two would be about IR£30.

The *George Hotel* has a set dinner for IR£15 and less expensive à la carte. Between 3 and 5.30 pm there is a budget menu with dishes for around IR£3.

Entertainment

The music scene shifts by the night but there's often something on at the popular *Nancy Blake's* on Upper Denmark St or the *Speakeasy* on O'Connell St. Just up from Cunningham's on Ellen St, the *Vintage Club* has traditional music on Wednesday and Friday nights.

Other possibilities include the busy *Central Lounge* on Thomas St, *Costello's Tavern* on Dominick St and *South's Pub* at 4 Quinlan St (the short section joining O'Connell Ave and O'Connell St). In Glentworth St near the corner with O'Connell St there is the *James Gleeson* pub and in the next block on Catherine St the *Desmond Arms* boasts an Irish karaoke night.

The *Belltable Arts Centre* (☎ 061-319866) is a regular venue for the travelling theatre companies that tour Ireland in the summer.

Getting There & Away

Air If you fly to Ireland from the USA you'll arrive first in Shannon Airport (☎ 061-61666), just over the border in County Clare; all flights from North America are required to stop there en route to Dublin, although this is likely to change in the near future.

Train There are services to all the main towns served by rail. Enquire for details at the tourist office or the station itself (☎ 061-418666).

Bus Bus Éireann services operate from the bus and railway station (☎ 061-418855), a short walk south of the centre. There are regular connections to Dublin, Cork, Galway, Killarney, Rosslare, Donegal, Sligo, Derry and most other centres. There is a Bus Éireann desk in the tourist office.

Getting Around

Buses run regularly connecting Shannon Airport with the Limerick bus and railway station for IR£3.20. There are also bus services from Shannon to Dublin.

As Limerick is quite a small city with a lot of one-way streets, there are only bus services out to the suburbs and not around the city centre itself. A walk across town, from the cathedral to the railway station, takes about 15 minutes.

Taxis are easy to arrange: try Economy (☎ 061-411422) or Treaty (☎ 061-415566). Car hire is also available through Treaty at 29 Thomas St (☎ 061-416512. Other car hire agencies are Thrifty at 4 The Crescent (☎ 061-453049), Windsor (☎ 061-327850) and Cara (☎ 061-455811), both of which are on the Ennis Rd.

Bicycles can be hired at Emerald Cycles (☎ 061- 16983), 1 Patrick St and returned in Dublin, Cork or Galway. The rate is IR£7 a day, IR£30 a week and IR£6 extra if returning outside of Limerick. Bikes can also be hired at the Bike Shop (☎ 061-315900) on O'Connell Ave and from the An Oíge hostel.

AROUND LIMERICK CITY

There are three places south of Limerick that could be taken in on a day's tour, by car or bike. The road that leads to Lough Gur, the R512, continues on to the historic town of Kilmallock and from here it is a short journey to the village of Bruree, former home of Eamon de Valera. From Bruree a country road leads across to the village of Bruff where the R512 can be rejoined for the journey back to Limerick. Apart from pubs in Bruree and more pubs and an ice-cream parlour in Kilmallock there is little to recommend in the way of food. Picnic spots, however, are not difficult to find. The best B&B along the way is *Deebert House* (☎ 063-98106) in Kilmallock, with singles/doubles from IR£16/26.

Lough Gur

Gathered around a small horseshoe-shaped lake south of Limerick are a number of Stone Age remains. Coming from the city, the first is a 4000-year-old **stone circle** by the side of the road. With its 113 stones it's one of the largest in Ireland. One km farther along the road a left turn goes up towards Lough Gur; 100 metres past a church there is a **wedge tomb** on the other side of the road.

Another two km (1.2 miles) along is the **interpretative centre** (☎ 061-85186), with a half-hour slide and video presentation on the prehistoric remains. There is also a small **museum** with neolithic artefacts and a replica of the Lough Gur shield that is now in the National Museum in Dublin. The 700 BC shield is 72 cm in diameter with six raised bosses designed to weaken the impact of an enemy's sword. The charge for the museum and presentation is IR£1.70 (children 90p, family IR£4.05), and the centre's open from 10 am to 6 pm from early May to the end of September.

The area around the lake can be explored on foot, and there are burial mounds, standing stones, ancient enclosures and other remains dotted around. There is a festival held here around the summer solstice (21 June); check with the tourist office or the interpretative centre for details.

Take the N24 road to Waterford south from Limerick. There is a sign to Lough Gur indicating a right turn at the roundabout outside town. After 18 km (11 miles) there is parking space on the left for the stone circle.

Kilmallock

Kilmallock was once the third largest town in Ireland, after Dublin and Kilkenny. It developed around an abbey founded in the 7th century by St Mocheallóg, hence the name – Cill (church) of Mocheallóg. From the 14th to the 17th centuries it was the seat of the earls of Desmond.

On the way into town from the Limerick road, the first place to see is the four-storeyed **King's Castle**, a 15th-century tower house with the street pavement running through it. On the other side of the road a lane leads down to a tiny **museum** that houses a small local collection and a model of the town in 1597. The museum is open from 1.30 to 5.30 pm on Monday to Friday, 2 to 5 pm on Saturday and Sunday and costs IR£1 to enter (children 50p). At other times the curator,

Tommy Bohan, may be contacted in Lord Edward St, through the gates just before the Bank of Ireland and upstairs.

Beyond the museum and across the River Lubagh is the 13th-century **Dominican Priory** with an attractive 13th-century east window, and a tower and south window added in the 15th century. Kilmallock surrendered to Cromwell's forces in the 1640s and the priory was sacked and partly destroyed.

Back on to King's Castle and a little farther on, to the right, is a **medieval stone mansion**, just one of the 30 or so that once housed the prosperous merchants and landowners of the town. Going back to the main street and continuing up Sarsfield St there is a turning on the left that goes down to the **Collegiate Church** which includes a round tower which may have belonged to an earlier monastery on the site. The fine door in the south wall of the north transept dates back to the 13th-century origins of the church, while

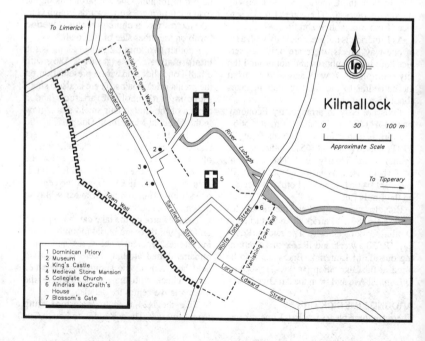

1 Dominican Priory
2 Museum
3 King's Castle
4 Medieval Stone Mansion
5 Collegiate Church
6 Aindrias MacCraith's House
7 Blossom's Gate

Eamon de Valera

As a young teacher of mathematics, de Valera attended a meeting in 1911, which was organised to protest at the visit to Ireland of the British monarchy. He found himself listening to the idea of an independent Irish republic and was quick to join the new Irish Volunteers. During the 1916 uprising he commanded an outpost on a main road, and ambushed British reinforcements travelling into Dublin, securing the greatest military success of the rebellion.

Like the other leaders he was sentenced to death for his role in the uprising but his US citizenship helped secure him a life sentence instead. In June 1917 he was included in an amnesty and was elected Sinn Féin MP for East Clare. He was president of Sinn Féin during 1917-26. In 1918 he was imprisoned, but escaped in 1919, with the aid of a duplicate key, from Lincoln Prison in England.

When the IRA split in 1921 over the Anglo-Irish Treaty, de Valera led the anti-Treaty forces in a bitter civil war. After the war he continued to be elected, this time for the Irish Parliament, but refused to swear the contentious oath of allegiance to the British king. Eventually he managed to enter parliament, skirting the oath by claiming his motive in entering parliament was to ensure its abolition. He formed a new party, Fianna Fáil, and established a government in 1932. Its new constitution abolished the oath and included a claim of sovereignty over the six counties of the north. That claim is still part of the constitution.

De Valera's idyllic vision of self-sufficient rural communities has since been ridiculed. He is probably held in less regard now than at any time earlier in the 20th century. ∎

---

the impressively carved door on the south side of the nave is 15th century.

Continuing back up Sarsfield St and turning right at the next junction leads to **Blossom's Gate**, the only surviving gate of the original medieval town wall, traces of which can be seen in the vicinity. Going back to the junction and carrying on down Wolfe Tone St leads to a 15th-century house on the right where the Irish poet Aindrias Mac Craith died in 1795.

Kilmallock is on the R512 that leads to Lough Gur from Limerick.

Bruree

Eamon de Valera was born in New York in 1882, to an Irish mother and Spanish father. His father died when he was two years old, and his mother sent the young Eamon to Ireland in 1885 with his uncle. As a child he lived in a small cottage in Bruree and attended a Christian Brothers school in the nearby town of Charleville. The cottage where he spent his formative years is open to the public, but there's precious little in it. At the Kilmallock end of the village there is a sign pointing to the cottage and it is just over one km (0.7 mile) from this sign. Look for a parking space on the left next to a small slate-roofed cottage. The key to the house is available from the next house 200 metres farther up the road on the right-hand side.

The museum at the other end of Bruree contains a variety of items associated with him. It also has a local collection of folk objects. It is open from 9 am to 4.30 pm, Tuesday to Friday, 2.30 to 5 pm on Saturday and Sunday, IR£2 (children 50p).

The village can be reached off the N20 road connecting Limerick and Cork; it is 32 km (20 miles) from Limerick, twice as far from Cork. If coming from Kilmallock there is a small direct road to Bruree.

FOYNES

If you're heading west from Limerick, pause at Foynes to visit the interesting little **Flying Boat Museum**, a reminder of Foynes's brief role as the eastern terminus of the first transatlantic airline service. There's a sister museum to Foynes at La Guardia Airport in New York, the US terminus of the pioneering pre-WW II flying-boat operations.

Entry is IR£2 (children IR£1), open from 10 am to 6 pm seven days a week from April to the end of October.

ADARE

This attractive village south-west of Limerick is tourist Ireland at its most sanitised and manicured. Charming thatched cottages and antique shops abound. The comely layout of the village was created by the third Earl of Dunraven in the first half of the 19th century. Coach tours make an obligatory stop in Adare and its cultivated prettiness means high prices for food and accommodation.

Information

The tourist office (☎ 061-396255) is on the main street and open from mid-April to the end of October from 9 am to 6 pm (7 pm in July & August), closing at 1 pm on Sunday.

Adare Friary

The ruins of a Franciscan friary founded by the Earl of Kildare in the 15th century, and restored in 1875, stand in the middle of the Adare Manor golf course beside the river Maigue. Permission to enter should be obtained from the club house. The church has a well-preserved sedilia (set of seats for priests in the south wall of the chancel) and windows.

Desmond Castle

Dating back to the early 13th century the castle was partly rebuilt in the following century and besieged by English forces in 1580. When Cromwell's army took possession in the 17th century, this castle had already lost its strategic importance. Restoration work is currently in progress and the castle is best viewed from the bridge on the main road at the north end of the village.

Adare Manor

The Earl of Dunraven enlisted the architectural help of James Pain and A W Pugin when creating his mansion in 1832. The enormous entry hall is divided by Gothic stone arches and there's a rococo panelled staircase worth seeing. The house is now an expensive hotel, open for viewing by non-residents, and the grounds by the river make for a pleasant stroll.

Churches

In the village itself there are two churches of interest. The tower and south wall of the **Church of the Most Holy Trinity**, the village's Catholic church, are part of a 13th-century monastery which came to an end when the monks were murdered in 1539, during the dissolution of the monasteries.

The Church of Ireland parish church is the **Augustinian Friary** founded in the 13th century. The tower was added in the 15th century but the original stonework is well preserved.

Places to Stay

The top-notch place is *Adare Manor* (☎ 061-396566), north of the village, charging IR£180 for a single or double in the summer. On Main St the olde-world *Dunraven Arms* (☎ 061-396209) has singles/doubles for IR£63/94. B&Bs abound and accommodation in these is best arranged through the tourist office. Also on Main St, *Village House* (☎ 061-396554) charges from IR£30 for a double and from IR£14 for a single.

Places to Eat

There is nowhere inexpensive to eat. The village pubs are the best bet for lunch. Dinner at the *Dunraven Arms* starts at IR£24; at Adare Manor IR£30. On the main street the *Mustard Seed*, not quite as pricey, has a reputation as one of Ireland's best restaurants.

Getting There & Away

Adare is 16 km (10 miles) southwest of Limerick and the five daily Tralee (County Kerry) to Dublin buses stop at Adare before going on to Limerick.

AROUND ADARE
Matrix Castle

This fine 15th-century Norman tower has been carefully preserved and is full of artefacts and objets d'art. Tours start at 10.30 am and continue at regular intervals until 6.30 pm, seven days a week. Entrance is IR£2.50 (children IR£1.50). The castle is 13 km (7.5

miles) west of Adare on the N21, near the village of Rathkeale.

County Tipperary

County Tipperary occupies a fair chunk of the south midlands of Ireland and is the sort of land farmers dream about owning. Limey, superbly fertile soils put Tipperary at the heart of Irish farming, particularly the south around the area known as the Golden Vale which has some of the country's richest pastures. Most Tipperary farmers earn a good living and that wealth is reflected in the shops, streets and towns of the region.

Tipperary is mostly flat in the centre with hills intruding over the borders from other counties. The River Suir cuts through the heart of the county and every major town lies on the banks of the Suir or one of its tributaries. Some of the towns have very active animal fairs or marts, especially Tipperary Town – which is, incidentally, not the major settlement: prosperous Clonmel, Cahir and Nenagh are far larger.

No WW I movie would be complete without some English private singing:

It's a long way to Tipperary,
It's a long way to go...

The song was written by two Englishmen, Jack Judge and Harry Williams, in 1912 as a marching song, and the word Tipperary was chosen only for its sound.

HISTORY

In common with the rest of the country there is substantial evidence of Stone Age humans in Tipperary, and the Rock of Cashel is likely to have been inhabited from the earliest times in that period. From the 9th century AD, the Vikings sailed up the River Shannon on their way to rich pickings at Clonmacnois in Offaly. There was a local scarcity of helpless monasteries near easily navigable waterways, so Tipperary escaped relatively lightly. The Rock of Cashel probably had plenty of golden goodies by that time, but also had defences well able to keep out the raiders.

In 1185 the Normans arrived in Tipperary with serious intent, quickly took control and set to conquering in their usual fashion, confiscating land and building castles and abbeys. Some of the region was later recovered by the Irish, who built numerous small tower-house castles around the county.

Following a number of plantations and Cromwell's campaign, the Irish in Tipperary were marginalised. The county was split into two, divided into the North and South Ridings. (A similar approach was used in the division of Yorkshire in England.) Famine, land struggle and emigration have all had a major impact on Tipperary, and the population dropped from over 430,000 in 1840 to 135,000 in 1981. Through the 18th and 19th centuries, nationalist feelings ran high, and the Gaelic Athletic Association (GAA) was established in Hayes Hotel, Thurles, in 1884.

NORTH TIPPERARY

Many visitors pass through this area on Shannon cruisers, and make forays into villages like Dromineer and the tiny Terryglass. Dromineer is a popular spot for boating and windsurfing, and has what is described as the third-oldest boat club in the world. Just over the Shannon in County Galway is the attractive country town of **Portumna**. The views across Lough Derg are pleasant, but there is no lakeshore drive along most of the east side. There is a picturesque section between Birdhill and Portroe.

Nenagh & Surrounds

Nenagh is a busy country town serving a large section of northern Tipperary. It's on the main Dublin to Limerick road, and suffers from heavy traffic.

Information There is a tourist office (☎ 067-31610) on Connolly St, open May to September.

Things to See Nenagh Castle was the seat of the first Butler of Ireland, Theobald

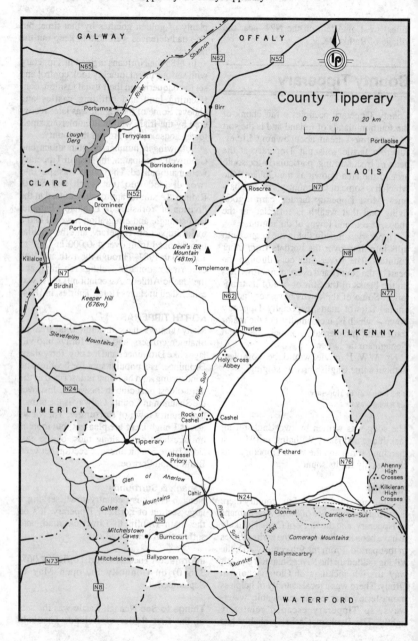

County Tipperary

0   10   20 km

Walter, in the early 13th century and remained in the family's possession for 400 years. The Walters changed their name to Butler and in the late 14th century moved their principal seat of power to Kilkenny Castle (see Kilkenny City and Castle for more details). All that remains of the family castle at Nenagh now is a circular **donjon** or tower dating from 1217. It is over 30 metres (100 feet) tall; the final eight metres were added by the Bishop of Killaloe in 1860.

Across the road is a Doric courthouse and beside it a convent, originally a prison. Some of the buildings are now home to the **Nenagh heritage centre** (☎ 067-32633). The centre is in two parts. The first is the Gatehouse and gaol where criminals were hanged in the last century. The exhibits are related to those events. Up the driveway is the Governor's House, with a display of art and photographs of an old country schoolroom, a kitchen, a forge, a dairy, and an exhibit on Lough Derg.

The centre is open May to September from 10 am to 5 pm on weekdays, closed Saturdays and open from 2.30 to 5 pm on Sundays. Admission is IR£1.50.

Getting There & Away Two Dublin to Limerick trains stop at Nenagh every day. For details ring Thurles railway station (☎ 0504-21733).

The bus stop in Nenagh is on Banba Square in the middle of town although some services stop at Nenagh railway station. There are frequent buses on the Dublin to Limerick express route. A less frequent service runs to Tralee with connections on the northbound bus to Galway, Sligo, Derry, Drogheda, Dundalk and Belfast. There are a couple of buses daily to Roscrea, Killaloe and Limerick (only one on Sundays) and some of these stop at Nenagh railway station only. From late June to early September the Galway to Rosslare Harbour bus stops at Nenagh.

Tuohy's Coaches (☎ 067-312900, a private company, has a daily bus to Dublin, leaving from O'Meara's Hotel at 8.25 am; an extra one on Mondays leaves at 6 am. It also

has services to Scarriff in County Clare and Galway City.

Getting Around J Moynan (☎ 067-31293) on Pearse St is the main bike dealer. In Dromineer, Shannon Sailing Ltd (☎ 067-24295) can provide canoes, yachts, sailing boats or windsurfers to explore the lake. Their two-hour cruise on the *Ku-Ee-Tu* is also available from May to September, costing IR£5 for adults, children IR£3.

Roscrea

On the eastern edge of the county is the medium-sized town of Roscrea, which like Mountrath in Laois can be used as a base for exploring the Slieve Bloom Hills to the north-east. Roscrea would be quite a pleasant country settlement but for the main Limerick to Dublin road which cuts through the town.

Roscrea owes its origin to a 5th-century monk, St Crónán, who set up a way station for the travelling poor. Today, most of the town's historical structures are on or near the main street. As you hit town from the Dublin side, you are faced with a truncated **round tower** built into the wall of a builder's yard, while across the road are the remains of St Crónán's second monastery: the gable end of **St Crónán's Church** with its finely worked stone Romanesque doorway, and a **high cross**, both of which date from the 12th century. The rest of the church was torn down in the early 19th century. The site of St Crónán's first monastery is almost two km east of town and south of the main Dublin road.

A 7th-century illuminated manuscript, 'The Book of Dímma', originated from here and can now be seen in Trinity College, Dublin.

In the centre of town is the recently restored **Norman Castle** from 1280, with substantial remains of a gatehouse, walls and towers. Inside the courtyard of the castle is **Damer House**, the Queen Anne residence of the Damer family, which houses **Roscrea heritage centre** (☎ 0505-21850) with some fine period furniture and a wonderful staircase. The centre also mounts various exhibitions of local interest throughout the year. It is open from June to September, daily from 9.30 am to 6.30 pm, and admission is IR£1, students 70p.

Getting There & Away Two Cork to Limerick trains stop at Roscrea every day. For details ring Thurles train station (☎ 0504-21733).

Frequent Dublin to Limerick express buses stop at Roscrea. There are a couple of buses daily to Nenagh, Killaloe and Limerick, but only one on Sundays. A less frequent service runs from and to Tralee with connections on the northbound bus to Galway, Sligo, Derry, Drogheda, Dundalk and Belfast. Roscrea is also on a daily Cork to Athlone express route which serves Fermoy, Cahir, Cashel, Thurles and Templemore and Birr. For bus details phone Rafferty Travel in Tipperary Town (☎ 062-51555).

CENTRAL TIPPERARY
This part of the country, particularly the area west of Cashel, is known as the Golden Vale, for its flat, easily farmed land and rich soils. An underlying limestone plain produces the soils so suited to raising livestock. It's only from the occasional hill that you get a real sense of the fertility and expanse of the region.

Most visitors to central Tipperary are on their way to Kerry and Cork. But the historic Rock of Cashel is on the way, and this is really worth searching out. Thurles and Tipperary Town have little to offer the tourist, except a diversion to Holy Cross Abbey from Thurles.

Thurles
This large market town 22 km (14 miles) north of Cashel was founded by the Butlers in the 13th century, but little of note has been built since then.

Information There is a tourist information desk (☎ 0504-23579) in the Centrefield building on the Slievenamon road which is north off Liberty Square. It's open May to August from 9.30 am to 5.30 pm. There is a regional museum housed in the same building.

Things to See There are two poor square tower-house ruins left: the 15th-century **Barry's Castle** by the bridge and the other **Black Castle** at the opposite end of Liberty Square behind the shops. There's an incongruous bird sanctuary on an island in the middle of the River Suir. A few hundred metres farther on is the **Catholic cathedral** built in the 1860s in the Italian Romanesque style.

Back in the square is **Hayes Hotel** where, as every Irish schoolchild learns, the Gaelic Athletic Association or GAA was founded in 1884. It was set up to foster the pursuit of Irish sports and pastimes, particularly Gaelic football and hurling, which it continues to oversee. Over the years, the GAA has been the most successful of the Gaelic revivalist groups.

The town square has unfortunately become one big ugly car park.

Getting There & Away Thurles is on the busy Dublin to Limerick and Dublin to Cork rail lines. For details contact Thurles railway station (☎ 0504-21733).

Holy Cross Abbey
Six km (four miles) south-west of Thurles is the picturesque Holy Cross Abbey right beside the River Suir. Until the early 1970s, the abbey was in ruins but a massive restoration project has turned the Cistercian cloisters and chapels into a living church.

Holy Cross was home to a relic of the True Cross, a splinter of wood said to be from Jesus' cross, which attracted pilgrims to the abbey from its foundation in the 1160s. The splinter was said to have been presented by Pope Pascal II to the King of Munster, Murtagh O'Brien, in the early years of the 12th century. It was the only cross relic in the country and was passed on to the nuns of the Ursuline Convent in Cork in the 19th century.

The buildings and cloisters you see today are from the 15th century, when the abbey was largely remodelled. The ground plan is typically Cistercian, with a fine cruciform church with a square tower and cloisters to the east. On top of the 15th-century skeleton is the recent white interior and modern altar. Look out for the small fleurs de lis and other symbols carved on the old stone pillars, the individual trademarks of the stonemasons. There is also a fine medieval fresco showing a hunting scene on one side of the church.

Built into the side of the abbey complex is a nice old pub, which does good food.

Templemore & the Devil's Bit

Templemore, 12 km (eight miles) north of Thurles, is the chief training centre for the Gardaí, the Irish police force and is probably the one place where everyone sticks rigorously to speed limits. The railway station is on the Dublin to Limerick and Dublin to Cork lines.

Six km (four miles) north-west is the Devil's Bit Mountain, a deep cut in the western end of the Slieve Bloom Hills.

The devil is supposed to have taken a bite out of the mountain and flown off. One version says that the devil didn't like the flavour, so he spat it out 34 km (21 miles) away where it became the Rock of Cashel. Another version claims that he was flying over Cashel when he spotted St Patrick preaching and such was the devil's anger that he dropped the rock. Unfortunately, unbelievers have hard evidence against both versions, as the Devil's Bit Mountain is sandstone while the Rock of Cashel is limestone!

The journey here is along lonely country roads and is fine for walkers heading for the Slieve Blooms but is not really worthwhile as a detour.

The Rock of Cashel

The Rock of Cashel (☎ 062-61437) is one of the most spectacular archaeological sites in the country. For 20 or 30 km in every direction there is a grassy plain, but on the outskirts of Cashel is a huge lump of limestone bristling with ancient fortifications. Mighty stone walls encircle a complete round tower, a roofless abbey, the finest 12th-century Romanesque chapel in Ireland,

and numerous smaller buildings and high crosses. For over a thousand years the Rock of Cashel was a symbol of power, the base of kings and churchmen who ruled over the region and large swathes of the country as a whole.

The word Cashel is an anglicised version of the Irish Caiseal meaning 'fortress', and it's easy to imagine that the site developed in territory hostile to the Church. From the Dublin road, the Rock is concealed by smaller hills, until the last minute. The site is busy, especially in summer, so try and go first thing in the morning or in the late afternoon.

In the 4th century, the Rock of Cashel was chosen as a base by the Eóghanachta clan from Wales, who went on to conquer much of Munster and become kings of the region. For some 400 years it rivalled Tara as a centre of power in Ireland.

The clan's links with the church started early; St Patrick converted their leader in the 5th century in a ceremony in which the saint accidentally stabbed the king in the foot with his crozier. The king, thinking this was a painful initiation rite, bore the pain with fortitude. Possibly he was afraid to react, considering the actions taken by St Patrick on previous occasions against unbelievers.

The clan lost possession of the Rock in the 10th century to the O'Brien, or Dál gCais, tribe under the leadership of Brian Boru. In the first year of the 12th century, King Muircheartach O'Brien presented the Rock to the Church, a move designed to curry favour with the powerful bishops and also to stop the Eóghanachta ever regaining the Rock, as they could never ask the Church to return such a present. They certainly couldn't steal it back either from its new owners, so the Eóghanachta, by now the MacCarthys, moved to Cork. As a sign of goodwill Cormac MacCarthy built Cormac's Chapel in 1127 before leaving.

This chapel proved to be too small. A new cathedral was built in 1169 but was replaced in the 13th century.

In 1647, the Rock fell to a Cromwellian army under Lord Inchiquin which sacked and burned its way to the top. Early in the

18th century the Protestant church took it over for 20 years, and this was the last time the rock was officially used as a place of worship. The roof of the abbey only fell in the late 18th or early 19th century.

The Rock of Cashel is open all year round: from mid-September to mid-March, daily from 9.30 am to 4.30 pm, then from March to early June from 9.30 am to 5.30 pm, and from June to mid-September it's open from 9 am to 7.30 pm. Admission is IR£1.75, or IR£1 for students.

The Hall of the Vicars Choral The entrance to the Rock is through this 15th-century house, which now contains the ticket office, a small exhibition centre and the audio-visual presentation room. The presentation runs every half hour for 20 minutes, detailing the Rock's history and attractions as one of the strongholds of the Christian faith. The exhibits downstairs include some rare silverware and **St Patrick's Cross**, a 12th-century crutched cross in poor condition with a crucifixion scene on the west face and interlacing and animals on the opposite side. Tradition held that the kings of Cashel and Munster – including Brian Ború – were inaugurated at the base of the cross.

The Cathedral This 13th-century Gothic structure overshadows the other ruins. Entry is through a small porch across from the Hall of the Vicars Choral, leading into a tiny nave. The west end of the cathedral is formed by the Archbishop's Residence, a 15th-century four-storey castle which had its great hall built over the nave. Soaring above the centre of the cathedral is a huge square tower with a turret tower on the south-west corner.

Scattered throughout are monuments, panels from 16th-century altar-tombs and coats of arms of the Butlers. On the north side of the choir is the recess tomb of Archbishop Hamilton. Opposite this is the tomb of Miler Mac Grath who died in 1621. Miler was Catholic Bishop of Down and Connor until 1569 when he switched to the Protestant faith and ordained himself to the status of Protestant Archbishop of Cashel with the blessing of Elizabeth I. Her forces were busy at the time torturing and executing his rival, the Catholic Archbishop Dermot O'Hurley.

Round Tower On the north-east corner of the cathedral is the sandstone 11th or 12th-century round tower, the earliest building on the rock. It is 28 metres (92 feet) tall and has the doorway 3.5 metres (11 feet) above the ground – perhaps for structural rather than defensive reasons.

Cormac's Chapel This is the Rock of Cashel's pièce de résistance, standing completely intact on the south side of the cathedral. Built from 1127, Cormac's Chapel is a small, solid stone-roofed chapel of cruciform shape with two tall square towers on either side. The chapel is sophisticated in design when compared with most other churches of the same era and displays influences from Britain and continental Europe, including the unusual square towers on either side of the nave.

Outside are impressive Romanesque arches, richly carved. Above the north door (opposite the entrance) in the minute courtyard adjoining the cathedral is a carving of a Norman helmeted figure firing an arrow at a huge lion which has just killed two animals.

The interior of the chapel is dark, its windows either blocked up – perhaps to shield the murals from light – or in the constant shadow of the cathedral. Preservation work is presently being carried out on the remains of paintings in the chancel.

The barrel-vaulted nave is only 12 metres (39 feet) long, with a fine archway into the chancel to the east with many finely carved heads and capitals. The south tower leads to a stone-roofed vault or croft above the nave. Inside the main door to the chapel on the left is the sarcophagus said to house King Cormac, dating from between 1125 and 1150. The deeply cut interlacing design is highly developed, with motifs found more commonly on metalwork from earlier centuries.

Hore Abbey The 13th-century Hore Abbey

is set in farmland less than one km north of the base of the Rock. It was the last daughter house of Mellifont's Cistercians and was a gift from a 13th-century archbishop who

Carved Corbel, Cashel

expelled the Benedictine monks after dreaming that they had plans to murder him. The ruins are fairly extensive and it's a pleasant walk (signposted) from the base of the Rock.

Cashel

Cashel is a prosperous place and thoroughly touristy, with plenty of restaurants, bars, B&Bs and hotels. It's also home to a small folk museum, folk village, Irish-music centre and a library with some rare manuscripts.

The town hall stands in the middle of the main street, and contains Cashel's seasonal tourist office (☎ 062-61333), open from April to September. A small museum is also open here during the same period.

Around town there are a number of ruins which, due to the overpowering presence of the Rock, are sometimes overlooked. The first right-hand turn after leaving the Rock leads onto Dominic St with its small **Dominican Friary** ruin from 1243 which, unlike Hore Abbey, has been engulfed by the town. On this road is the **Folk Village**. The far end of Dominic St leads to the centre of town.

Up a lane directly opposite the Cashel Palace Hotel is the **GPA Bolton Library** (☎ 062-61944) (GPA stands for Guinness Peat Aviation). This small building, which was once a chapter house in the grounds of the Protestant cathedral, is now home to valuable manuscripts and first editions. It's open all year round from 9.30 am to 5.30 pm daily, and from 2.30 pm on Sundays. Admission is IR£1.50, students IR£1.

The **Cashel Palace Hotel** is a lovely Queen Anne residence built by Edward Lovett Pearce (architect of the Bank of Ireland in College Green, Dublin) for Archbishop Bolton in 1730.

One km along the Clonmel Rd is the museum of **Bothán Scóir**, a careful if slightly romanticised reconstruction of a peasant cottage. It is only opened on request; ring ☎ 062-61360.

Places to Stay *Boytonrath IHO Hostel* (☎ 062-72223) is six km (four miles) southwest of Cashel. Turn right off the road to Cahir opposite the Esso petrol station at the edge of town. They charge IR£5 a night and are open April to October.

Across from the Dominican friary on Dominic St is *Abbey House* (☎ 062-61104), a stone's throw from the Rock and Main St, with rooms at IR£13 or IR£15 with own bathroom. *Ros-Guill House* (☎ 062-61507) is one km away on the Kilkenny to Dualla road and has views of the Rock and exceptionally good breakfasts; singles/doubles are IR£19/26 and it's open April to October. *Maryville* (☎ 062-61098) is at Bank Place in Cashel and costs IR£13 B&B sharing or IR£19 single. On Main St *Bailey's* (☎ 062-61937) is a Georgian townhouse with B&B from IR£12.50 to IR£17.50.

The *Cashel Palace Hotel* (☎ 062-61411) on Main St is exquisite, with an unbeatable view of the Rock. A private footpath joins the two. The bad news is that B&B erodes the budget by between IR£64 and IR£135 a night. *Grant's Castle Hotel* (☎ 062-61044) is a 15th-century square tower once known as Quirke's Castle, and now has rooms from as little as IR£14 for a single room without bathroom. Breakfast is extra from around IR£6.

In Dundrum 10 km (six miles) to the north-west are *Dundrum House* (☎ 062-71116) and *Rectory House* (☎ 062-71266). Both are excellent: the former an 18th-century Palladian villa with B&B from IR£40 to IR£50 depending on the season, compared to IR£25 to IR£35 for the latter. They have good restaurants with the Rectory House leaning more to French cuisine. A full dinner costs from IR£20 in either.

Places to Eat Two excellent coffee shop cum restaurants are the *Bakehouse* (☎ 062-61680) on Main St near the traffic lights, and the *Coffee Stop* also on Main St on the corner near the GPA Bolton Library.

There are a few takeaways in Cashel, though none of the fast-food chains have made it out this far. The *Friar St Fryry* on Friar St serves good burgers & chips. The *Spearman's Restaurant* behind the town hall on Main St has middle-of-the-road fare, and next door is *O'Neill's* coffee shop. Beside the Rock of Cashel car park, *Granny's Kitchen* has cheap snacks including desserts flavoured with Guinness. The Cashel Palace Hotel has two restaurants: the *Four Seasons* and the *Buttery*. The first has a good à la carte menu at around IR£30 for dinner. The second is cheaper and more informal.

The best restaurant in the region is *Chez Hans* (☎ 062-61177) just off Main St at the Dublin end of town. It's inside a converted church and the food is terrific. Dinner costs at least IR£20 a head.

Entertainment Down the hill past the Rock's car park is *Brú Ború* (☎ 062-61122), a centre for traditional Irish music which serves it up five nights a week, Tuesdays to Saturdays during the summer season. Starting at 9 pm there is music, song, dance, storytelling and craic (an Irish term for general fun and good times) galore. Admission is IR£5 for the night, and there is an optional pre-show banquet. They also have a genealogy centre here and a coffee shop and restaurant.

For a more authentic Irish-music scene, head for the *Golden Vale* pub on Monday nights; it's in the village of Dundrum, 10 km north-west of Cashel on the R505. For a quiet drink try *Davern's Pub* or *Dowling's*, both on Main St.

Getting There & Away Bus Éireann runs one bus daily each way on the Dublin to Clonmel and Limerick route. There are four daily each way on the Dublin to Cork Expressway service, with three on Sundays. Rafferty's Travel (☎ 062-62121) on Main St handles tickets and enquiries for Bus Éireann.

Kavanagh's (☎ 062-51563) have private buses going daily on a Tipperary Town, Cahir, Cashel, Dublin route leaving Cashel for Dublin at 9 am. Coming back, they leave Dublin at 6 pm and arrive in Cashel at 8.30 pm. They also do a daily run between Cashel and Clonmel, departing from Cashel at noon, and another to Thurles, departing at 3.45 pm. These buses do not run on Sundays.

Athassel Priory

West of Cashel, the N74 brings you to Tipperary Town after 20 km (12 miles). A third of the way over is the village of Golden from which you can detour south for two km to Athassel Priory. This extensive and long-abandoned Norman monastery sits peacefully on the west bank of the River Suir. It was built around 1200 by William de Burgh, who wanted it to be one of the richest and most important in the country. The native Irish, in the guise of the Earl of Desmond and the O'Briens, burned the priory and its accompanying town in 1319 and again in 1329. What's left today are the remains of a gatehouse, gateway, surrounding walls, and the cloisters or arched passageways where monks would walk in prayer, as well as some foundations of various other monastic buildings including the chapter house.

Tipperary Town

Originally an Anglo-Norman settlement, Tipperary Town is a working town which consists essentially of the long Main St with a lively and regular cattle mart on Wednesdays and Fridays, held at the eastern end. In the middle of Main St is a statue to Charles T Kickham (1822-82), a local novelist (author of *Knocknagow*) and a Young Irelander. The tiny **museum** is no more than a large display cabinet in the foyer of the town swimming pool which sits beside the mart. Letters, photographs and artefacts relate to the War of Independence (1919-21) which had its first engagement in a quarry a few km north of the town. It's free but the opening hours are erratic.

There is a **country racetrack** three km out on the Limerick road with regular weekly meetings during the summer. See the local press for details.

The county's only year-round tourist office (☎ 062-51457) is off the west end of Main St on James St. It's on the small side.

Getting There & Away Limerick Junction (☎ 062-51406) is barely three km from Tipperary Town along the Limerick road. It is one of the busiest railway stations in the country, with numerous daily services to Cork, Kerry, Waterford, Rosslare and Dublin. Tipperary itself has a small railway station on the Waterford to Limerick Junction main line, with a couple of daily services to Cahir, Clonmel, Waterford and Rosslare Harbour and multiple connections from Limerick Junction.

Rafferty's Travel (☎ 062-51555) on Main St handles enquiries and bookings for Bus Éireann. Most buses stop near the Brown Trout restaurant on Bridge St, except for the service to Rosslare Harbour which stops outside Rafferty's Travel.

There are regular buses on the Limerick to Waterford express route. There also may be a single daily service from Tipperary Town to Shannon in County Clare

Kavanagh's (☎ 062-51563) have private buses going daily on a Tipperary Town, Cahir, Cashel to Dublin route. These buses do not run on Sundays.

For a taxi call Tony Ryan (☎ 062-52927)

or Eleanor Ryan (☎ 062- 51979). Taxi is a handy way to tour the Glen of Aherlow.

Getting Around Farther up the hill from the tourist office on James St is *O'Carroll's* (☎ 062-51229) which rents out bikes in the summer months at reasonable rates.

Glen of Aherlow & Galtee Mountains

South of Tipperary Town are the Slievenamuck Hills and then the Galtee Mountains, separated by the gently beautiful Glen of Aherlow. Between Tipperary and Cahir is **Bansha** at the eastern end of the glen, which is the start of a 20-km (12-mile) through trip to Galbally, an easy bike ride. It is a nice area for low-key hiking, and there is plenty of country accommodation. Cahir is a good base from which to explore the Galtees.

Places to Stay *Bally David An Óige Hostel* (☎ 062-54148) is an old hunting lodge in the south-east corner of the glen three km off the Tipperary to Cahir road on the north slopes of the Galtees, 10 km from Cahir. A bed costs IR£3.80 in the low season and IR£5.50 from June to September. There are more hostels in and near Cahir.

Ballinacourty House (☎ 062-56230) has B&B for IR£13 and excellent caravan and camping facilities, as well as a fine garden, restaurant, wine bar and tennis court. This oasis is 10 km west-south-west of Bansha on the road to Galbally, but is only open from May to September. The Georgian *Bansha House* (☎ 062-54194) is only 200 metres from Bansha village and does B&B from IR£13 to IR£15.

Close by Bansha House is *Bansha Castle* (☎ 062-54187), a lovely castellated 19th-century house and former residence of some of the Butlers of Ormond. B&B is IR£15 or IR£19 with own bathroom, and dinner from IR£17.

Getting There & Away The express Tipperary Town to Waterford bus stops at Bansha and there are five or six buses daily in both directions. For details contact Rafferty's

Travel (☎ 062-51555) in Tipperary Town. You can also tour the Glen by taxi – see the contact numbers given in the Getting Around section for Tipperary Town.

Cahir

Cahir (pronounced 'Care') is 15 km (nine miles) due south of Cashel, lying at the eastern tip of the Galtees and on the banks of the River Suir. Cahir is a prosperous place on the main Dublin to Cork road, which ensures constant heavy traffic. There is a tourist information point in the reception area of Cahir Castle.

Cahir Castle Cahir's most noteworthy feature is the great 15th-century Butler castle (☎ 052-41011) near the town centre. The Butlers were granted lands in the area in 1192 but didn't get round to building their first castle until the 13th century. The castle is remarkably intact and the one of the largest in Ireland. Its occupants surrendered to Cromwell in 1650 without a struggle – memories were fresh of the battering the place had suffered in 1599 at the hands of the Earl of Essex and his meagre two cannons – and it has been extensively restored. Some of John Boorman's *Excalibur* was filmed in Cahir Castle.

The castle sits on a rocky island in the River Suir, and comprises three wards or yards, surrounded by a thick fortifying curtain wall, with the main structural towers and halls around the innermost ward. Entry to the castle is along the sloping barbican running parallel to the inner-ward wall, and then through to the reception area. This opens out into the small middle ward, overshadowed by the large gatehouse and keep to the right. Go through this gatehouse, under the reconstructed and fully functioning portcullis, and you come to the inner ward. Its buildings are sparsely furnished – it's a pity to have such fine rooms so empty.

Beside the north-east tower is the small **well tower** which offers the best vantage point over the river. The tower spirals down to the river and provided a vital water supply during any extended siege.

The large garden-like outer ward has a 19th-century cottage at the far end, housing an audio-visual show on other sites in the region.

Cahir Castle is open all year round, from April to October, 10 am to 6 pm, with extended hours of 9 am to 7.30 pm from mid June to mid September. The rest of the year it's open from 10 am to 4.30 pm, though closed from 1 to 2 pm. Admission is IR£1, students 70p. During the summer months the castle's reception area (☎ 052-41453) acts also as a regional tourist office.

Swiss Cottage A little over two km south of town in Cahir Park is the Swiss Cottage, a thatched hunting lodge with mature gardens and parkland, and an elevated view of the River Suir. Access to the cottage is only by guided tour. It was designed by John Nash and is slowly recovering from a period of decay; many fine little features remain.

The cottage is open from mid-March to November, with varying hours. Admission is IR£1, students 70p.

Places to Stay & Eat Cahir has two independent hostels nearby. The run-of-the-mill *Lisakyle Hostel* (☎ 052-41963) is two km south of town on a back road to Ardfinnan past the Swiss Cottage, and has inexpensive caravan and camping facilities. In town, Maurice Condon's shop opposite the post office on the Dublin road acts as their office for any enquiries. A bed in a dorm is IR£4.50 or IR£5.50 in a private room while campers are charged IR£2.50 a head.

The excellent *Farmhouse Hostel* (☎ 052-41906) is slightly harder to find. It's six km (four miles) south-west of Cahir, signposted south off the Mitchelstown road at a petrol station. It's on an organic farm, and has free showers, kitchen facilities and a photographic dark room. A bed costs IR£4.50

If you come to Cahir to view a castle, you could well stay the night in one. The 16th-century *Carrigeen Castle* (☎ 052-41370) on the Cork road is often mistaken for Cahir Castle. It's actually a B&B, with four grand rooms at IR£14 to IR£16 sharing or IR£18 single.

One km along the Cashel to Dublin road is *Ashling* (☎ 052-41601) with B&B at IR£13 or IR£16 with own bathroom, or IR£18 single. Also along this road, three km from Cahir, is *Springhill* (☎ 052-41754), with B&B for IR£13.

Right in the centre of town, the *Castle Court Hotel* (☎ 052-41210) on Church St is a pleasant little family-run hotel costing IR£25; it does good food.

The *Kilcornan Lodge Hotel* (☎ 052-41288) is six km (four miles) along the Cork road. This converted Victorian hunting lodge sits on 10 hectares of woodland. Facilities include a pool, health club and solarium. B&B goes from IR£30 to IR£38.

Places to Eat There are a couple of takeaways and cheap places to eat. For substantial meals, the hotels are your best bet. Opposite Cahir Castle car park and above a craft shop is the *Crock of Gold*, a tiny restaurant which serves up light lunches and dinner throughout the day. The *Earl of Glengall* in the square has good solid pub lunches.

Getting There & Away Two trains a day on the Cork to Rosslare Harbour line stop at Cahir. For train information contact Thurles railway station (☎ 0504-21733). Cahir is on the main Waterford to Limerick Junction railway line.

For buses, Cahir is on the main Dublin to Cork express route, the Limerick to Waterford express route, and the Kilkenny to Cork and Cork to Athlone express routes. A less frequent service runs from and to Tralee with connections on the northbound bus to Galway, Sligo, Derry, Drogheda, Dundalk and Belfast. The bus stop is outside the Crock of Gold craft shop and restaurant, across the road from Cahir Castle. For information on bus times, ring ☎ 062-51555.

Kavanagh's (☎ 062-51563) have private buses going daily on a Tipperary Town, Cahir, Cashel to Dublin route. These buses do not run on Sundays.

Mitchelstown Caves

The Galtee Mountains are sandstone, but on the southern side is a narrow band of limestone which is home to the Mitchelstown Caves. They're found near Burncourt, 15 km (nine miles) south-west of Cahir, signposted off the road to Mitchelstown. They are also signposted from the centre of Ballyporeen. These caves are among the most extensive in the country, far superior to the Dunmore Caves of Kilkenny and much less developed for the tourist.

In 1833, Michael Condon was quarrying limestone when he lost his crowbar down a crack in the rock. His efforts to retrieve it opened up the system they called New Caves. There was an earlier known cave system nearby called the Old Caves which were used in prehistoric times and which include the largest chamber of the system. However, it is the New Caves that form the basis of the tour.

It is through Condon's original opening that exploration begins. Internal temperatures are pretty constant at around 54°F (13°C). Underground, there are nearly two km of passages and spectacular chambers full of text-book formations inventively labelled from classical and bibical sources.

The caves (☎ 052-67246) are open all year round from 10 am to 6 pm. Call at the English's farmhouse opposite the car park for tickets and a tour guide. Admission is IR£2, students IR£1.

Places to Stay Five km (three miles) due north of the caves on the slopes of the Galtees is the *Mountain Lodge An Óige Hostel* (☎ 052-67277), north off the main Mitchelstown to Cahir road. It's open from March to September and is a handy base to explore either the Galtees or the Mitchelstown Caves. It costs IR£3.80 low season and IR£5.50 from June to September.

Getting There & Away Buses from Dublin to Cork and back on the express route pass through Mitchelstown. Ring 062-51555 for details.

Clonmel

Clonmel is the largest, liveliest and most cosmopolitan town in Tipperary. It's also the largest inland town in the county. The approach to Clonmel is attractive, particularly from the Kilkenny side, along a good road with well-tended houses and hedges, while the river and mountains give the town a fine backdrop. The town's long prosperity have left it with many fine features.

History After the Norman invasion, Clonmel came under the influence of the de Burgos and the earls of Desmond, which created tension with the Butlers for 250 years. The Butlers were finally victorious in 1583. In 1650, however, Cromwell laid siege to the town for three weeks. The garrison under the command of Hugh Dubh O'Neill exhausted their arsenal in the struggle, and on 17 May they sneaked undetected out of town. The remaining townspeople held out for a fair and honourable surrender. Cromwell had lost 2000 men in this single siege, more than in the whole remainder of his Irish campaign; he fell for the ruse and agreed to the town's request.

Over the centuries the town's wealth has attracted many businesspeople. One of them is now synonymous with Clonmel. Charles Bianconi (1786-1875) arrived in Ireland from northern Italy at the age of 16, sent by his father in an attempt to break a liaison he had formed with a spoken-for young lady. In 1815, Bianconi set up a coach service between Clonmel and Cahir, and the company quickly grew, becoming a nationwide passenger and mail carrier. For putting Clonmel on the map, Bianconi was twice elected mayor. The company's former headquarters is now Hearn's Hotel on Parnell St – Hearn was an assistant to Bianconi.

Orientation The heart of Clonmel lies on the north bank of the River Suir. Set back off the quays and running parallel to the river, the main street from east to west starts off as Parnell St, becoming Mitchel St, O'Connell St, under West Gate and on to Irishtown and Abbey Rd. Running north off this long thoroughfare are Dillon, Gladstone, O'Neill and Cantwell St. Many of the town's narrow streets are one way.

Information There is a seasonal tourist office (☎ 052-22960) in the Chamber of Commerce buildings opposite Hearn's Hotel. It's open from June to early September. The post office is in a courtyard of the one-time county gaol at the north end of Emmet St, which runs north off Mitchel St. The Post House (☎ 052-24955) is a good bookshop on Gladstone St.

Walking Tour A good starting point for a quick tour of the town is **Hearn's Hotel**, which still has material relating to its former incarnation as Bianconi's headquarters.

South off Parnell St is Nelson St with the **County Courthouse** designed by Richard Morrison in 1802. It was here that the Young Irelanders of 1848 including Thomas Francis Meagher were tried and sentenced to the penal colonies of Australia. Back on Parnell St is the **County Museum**, which has the shirt worn by Michael Hogan, captain of the Tipperary Gaelic Football team in Croke Park when they played Dublin on 21 November 1920. In retaliation for the deaths of 14 British Army intelligence officers, the British police auxiliaries known as the Black & Tans opened fire on the crowd and players, killing Hogan and 13 others. This was the first of the Bloody Sundays.

West along Mitchel St, past the town hall and south down Abbey St is the **Franciscan Friary**. Although dating from 1269, much of what is visible is from the late 19th century. The tower is 15th century. Inside, near the door, is a 1533 Butler tomb depicting a knight and his lady. Back up on Mitchel St at the corner of Sarsfield St is the **Main Guard**. It was a Butler courthouse from 1674, based on a design by Christopher Wren, and still bears their coat-of-arms even though it was converted into shops in 1810.

Spanning the far end of O'Connell St is the **West Gate**, an 1831 reconstruction of an old town gate which once arched over the street here. On the east side is a plaque commemorating Laurence Sterne (1713-68), a native of the town and author of *A Sentimental Journey* and *Tristram Shandy*. Just before the arch is Wolfe Tone St which heads north past the old **Wesleyan Chapel** to **Old St Mary's Church**, built in 1204 by William de Burgh. The north and west sides of the site include some of the original medieval town wall.

Through West Gate is Irishtown, named after those native Irish who worked inside the town but were forbidden by law from living within its walls. On the south side of this street is the decorative **St Mary's Church**.

Racing Clonmel is at the heartland of Irish greyhound racing and coursing. At the east end of Parnell St on Davis St is the greyhound track (☎ 052-21118), which has dog racing on Mondays and Thursdays at 8 pm. Powerstown Park Racecourse (☎ 052-22852) is north of the town and has a year-round fixture list, though events may be a few weeks apart. Consult the local press for details.

Places to Stay The independent *Powers the Pot Hostel* (☎ 052-23085) has a Clonmel address even though it lies nine km (six miles) south-east of town on the northern slopes of the Comeragh Mountains, well inside County Waterford. To get there cross south over the river in Clonmel and follow the road to Rathgormack. It has a wine bar and a good little restaurant. It's open May to October, and charges IR£4.50 a night in dorms, IR£5 in private rooms and IR£2.50 per person camping.

Amberville (☎ 052-21470) on Glenconnor Rd, north off Western Rd beside St Luke's Hospital, is well within walking distance of the town centre. B&B costs IR£13, IR£14 with own bathroom or IR£15 single. About the cheapest B&B around is *Cherrymount House* (☎ 052-23129), at 1 Cherrymount, open all year with B&B at around IR£10 to IR£11. Many B&Bs can be found on Marlfield Rd, due west of Irishtown

and Abbey Rd. *Benuala* (☎ 052-22158) and *Hillcourt* (☎ 052-21029) both do B&B at IR£12 to IR£13 sharing. Rooms with bathroom are IR£1 extra. Three km from Clonmel along this road in Marlfield is *New Abbey* (☎ 052-22626) with B&B at IR£16/26 for singles/doubles.

The fine *Clonmel Arms Hotel* (☎ 052-211233) is down from the main street towards the river on Sarsfield St. Spacious, modern rooms with bath/shower cost from IR£30 to IR£40 depending on the season. *Hearn's Hotel* (☎ 052-21611) does B&B for IR£25 to IR£29. Finally there's the *Hotel Minella* (☎ 052-22388), a four-star hotel with gardens south of the River Suir and almost two km east of town on the Coleville road (follow the south quays east). B&B costs from IR£25 to IR£60.

Places to Eat There are plenty of cheap cafés, coffee shops and delis. The Post House bookshop has the excellent and cosy *Featherbed Lane Café* upstairs with good cakes, light meals and excellent coffee available all day. *Niamh's* is a cosy little coffee shop and deli on Mitchel St, while *Nuala's Coffee Shop/Hickey's Bakery* right by the Westgate has fresh home-made snacks and good coffee. Both are open all day until 6 pm.

In the Marystone Centre, *Coyle's Coffee House* is similar, open until 5.30 pm. At 14 Abbey St is the Rainbow Warehouse, with an organic market on Friday and Saturdays and the *Abbey Restaurant* (☎ 052-21457), which serves excellent cheap vegetarian dishes. It's open all day until 5.30 pm.

Bar food is available in *Tierney's Pub* on O'Connell St, *Kinsella's Bar* in Irishtown, the *Market Tavern* on Market St or *Mulcahy's* (☎ 052-22825) pub and restaurant on Gladstone St. The latter also has the more expensive *Mellary Restaurant*. The *Clonmel Arms Hotel* on Sarsfield St is one of the best places in town for a bar lunch and reasonably priced.

The *Emerald Garden* (☎ 052-24270) is a good Chinese restaurant on O'Connell St. The reasonably priced and pleasant *La Scala*

(☎ 052-24147) is on Market St off Gladstone St.

Entertainment Clonmel is lively at night. *Lonergan's* and *Chawke's Bar* on Gladstone St are fine for a pint. Many others bars such as the *Coachman* on Parnell St have local bands and Irish music nights in the summer. There are Irish music and dance sessions in the *Mellery Room* on Gladstone St on Monday evenings in July and August.

Most of the hotels have nightclubs. *Club Nineties* in the Clonmel Arms Hotel is open Thursdays to Sundays, while the Hotel Minella is home to *Streamers* on Saturday nights. *Dan Hearns Night Club* in Hearn's Hotel has discos at weekends.

Clonmel has a three-screen cinema, the *Regal*.

Getting There & Away The railway station (☎ 052-21982) is north of Gladstone St on the Prior Park Rd, walking distance from the town centre. Clonmel is on the Cork to Limerick to Rosslare Harbour line with two trains each way daily, one on Sundays. There is no direct rail link to Dublin, but there are connections from Waterford or Limerick Junction.

Bus Éireann (☎ 051-79000) has two buses daily each way to Dublin and Cork, with a more complicated timetable to Waterford, Limerick and Kilkenny. Contact the Waterford Bus Travel Information Centre, or ask at the Clonmel railway station for details. Rafferty Travel (☎ 052-22622) act as Bus Éireann's ticket agent and the bus stop is at the railway station. Kavanagh's (☎ 062-51563) have private buses going daily between Cashel and Clonmel, leaving Cashel at noon and Clonmel at 3 pm. These buses do not run on Sundays.

Princess Coaches (☎ 052-21389) have a single daily service (Thursdays to Mondays) each way between Clonmel and Dublin.

Around Clonmel
Directly south of Clonmel are the Comeragh Mountains in County Waterford, and there is a fine scenic route south to Ballymacarbry and the Nire Valley. Instead of coming back the same way you can do a circle heading down to Ballymacarbry from the east and heading back up to Clonmel from the west side. For more details about this area see under the Nire Valley section in County Waterford.

The **Munster Way** walking trail passes through Clonmel following the old towpath along the River Suir. At Sir Thomas Bridge the trail cuts south away from the river and into the Comeraghs to Harney's Cross Rds before rejoining the River Suir again at Kilsheelan Bridge from where it follows the river towpath all the way to Carrick-on-Suir. Fron Clonmel you can walk parts of the trail along the towpath as a shorter outing. The main road between Clonmel and Carrick-on-Suir also follows the river through some lovely countryside.

Carrick-on-Suir
This market town is 20 km (12 miles) east of Clonmel. With brewing and wool industries, Carrick-on-Suir grew to considerable importance during the Middle Ages. The seven-arched 15th-century bridge was for a long time the only crossing point of the river for 40 km (25 miles) from the Suir's mouth at Waterford Harbour. In the 18th century the population was 11,000, almost twice what it is today. Old warehouses still crowd the waterfront. Compared to Clonmel, Carrick-on-Suir is quiet and unsophisticated. It's surrounded by rich green farmland and the Comeragh Mountains can be seen in the distance.

Most places only make a fuss of their famous inhabitants long after their demise, but Carrick-on-Suir was quick to honour Sean Kelly, who was one of the world's greatest cyclists in the 1980s. The town square now bears his name.

The Munster Way has one terminus at Carrick-on-Suir, winding its way west to Clonmel before heading south into Waterford. For more on this see County Waterford.

Ormond Castle Carrick-on-Suir was once

the property of the Butlers, the earls of Ormond, who built the 14th-century castle at the east end of Castle St. Anne Boleyn, one of Henry VIII's six wives, is rumoured to have been born here, though many other castles claim this distinction. She was the great-granddaughter of the 7th earl of Ormond. The Elizabethan mansion next to the castle was built by the 10th earl of Ormond, Black Tom Butler, in anticipation of a visit by his cousin, Queen Elizabeth I, who unfortunately never got round to seeing the result of his efforts.

The three-storey mansion is being restored but the parts that have been completed are sparsely furnished. Some rooms have fine 16th-century stuccowork, especially the Long Gallery, with depictions of Elizabeth and the Butler coat of arms. Considering the turmoil of the period it is interesting to note the house's almost complete lack of defences.

The castle (☎ 051-40787) is open from mid-June to September, every day from 9.30 am to 6.30 pm, and admission is IR£1, students 70p.

Tipperary Crystal Only 22 km (13 miles) away from Waterford City and its world-famous glass industry, Carrick-on-Suir is home to one of the many regional crystal enterprises which have sprung up, attempting to rival their neighbour. The factory (☎ 051-41188) is along Clonmel Rd and is open to the public. There is a crystal outlet and coffee shop.

Places to Stay Centrally located on Sean Kelly Square is *Orchard House* (☎ 051-41390), with B&B from IR£13 to IR£14. *Linnaun View* (☎ 051-40663) is three km from town in Three Bridges, and charges a reasonable IR£11 to IR£12 for B&B. The *Grand Inn* (☎ 051-47035) is a 17th-century stone coaching inn, once a stopover on the Bianconi coach line. It's now an unusual B&B costing IR£17/26 for singles/doubles or IR£30 with own bathroom. It's nine km (six miles) north on the main N76 Clonmel

to Kilkenny road at Nine-Mile House, not far from the Ahenny crosses.

The new *Carraig Hotel* (☎ 051-41455) on Main St has rooms with bathroom for around IR£20 for B&B. The 19th-century *Cedarfield House* (☎ 051-40530) one km out on the Waterford Rd costs from IR£25 to IR£35 for B&B.

Places to Eat The *Carraig Hotel* is probably the best place to eat in town. Otherwise the choice of eateries is limited. The *Park Inn Pub* is good for pub food. *Cooney's* attracts the younger crowd for drinks, while *Kehoe's* has an older mixture and the odd music night.

Getting There & Away There are two trains daily on the Cork to Rosslare Harbour line. For information contact Thurles railway station (☎ 0504-21733). Carrick-on-Suir is on the main Waterford to Limerick Junction line with daily services and connections to Dublin, Limerick, Cork, Tralee, Mallow, Cahir, Clonmel, Waterford and Rosslare Harbour.

There are extensive bus services to and from the town. For details ring ☎ 051-79000. On the Limerick to Waterford express route there are up to five buses on weekdays and three on Sundays, serving Tipperary Town, Cahir, Clonmel, and Carrick-on-Suir. Other regular buses serve Clonmel, Dublin, Galway, Rosslare Harbour, Tralee, Cork and Kilkenny.

Ahenny & Kilkieran High Crosses.
Roughly five and eight km (three and five miles) north of Carrick-on-Suir and signposted off the road to Windgap are the two groups of high crosses at Ahenny and Kilkieran. The more easily found are the more distant crosses in the village of Ahenny.

The two Ahenny crosses are impressive, both four metres (12 feet) tall and dating from the 8th century. They are somewhat unusual in that they're almost exclusively covered in an interlacing design in high relief. Only on the base are there any panels depicting the more typical religious scenes.

They are said to represent the transition from the older abstract designs of high crosses to the pictorial 'scenes found on many later crosses. Another odd feature are the removable cap stones, sometimes known as mitres (bishop's hats). Legend has it that these caps can cure migraine headaches if the mitre is placed on the sufferer's head. The victim would have more than migraine to worry about – the stones are on the large side.

On the base of the north cross is a panel depicting seven religious men. The story goes that these were seven bishops who had returned from Rome with a bag of sand each as a memento of their visit. Robbers ambushed them and mistook their bags for purses. The robbers murdered them, convinced that the bishops had turned their gold into sand to save it from being stolen.

There is the base of a third cross still here.

This cross was supposedly the most beautiful of those at Ahenny and rumour has it that it was stolen about 200 years ago. The story goes that the ship which was carrying the cross out of Waterford was lost at sea off Passage East, and that the cross lies somewhere on the sea floor.

About two km nearer Carrick-on-Suir and east off this road are the three Kilkieran crosses in a small graveyard. The west cross is similar to those in Ahenny: four metres tall, richly decorated and with mitre intact. The other is extremely plain. The most interesting is the needle-like Long Shaft Cross, a shape unique in Ireland.

At the far end of the cemetery is a holy well whose waters are said to cure headaches. There must have been a plague of headaches at the time, given the number of cures to be found in the area.

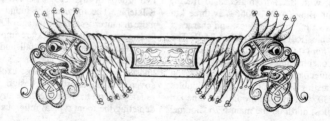

County Kilkenny

A verdant farming county, Kilkenny is pep-pered with solid stone walls, medieval ruins and stands of old trees. The Normans liked this part of Ireland and settled here in numbers, leaving their stamp on Kilkenny City which is a league above most midland towns. The county's most attractive areas are along the rivers Nore and Barrow with charming villages like Inistioge, while nearby Jerpoint Abbey and Kells Priory are two of the finest medieval monastic settle-ments in the country.

In Irish minds, Kilkenny is most closely associated with the ancient game of hurling. Many local shops plaster their windows with the accessories of the game and photos of the great teams of the past.

Since medieval times, Kilkenny's history has been inextricably linked with the for-tunes of one Anglo-Norman family, the Butlers, earls of Ormond. After arriving in 1171, they made the region their own, pro-moting first the Norman cause and then that of the English royal household. They were based in Kilkenny City.

GETTING THERE & AWAY

The express Waterford to Dublin service takes in Mullinavat, Thomastown, Gowran and Carlow en route, and has four buses daily in each direction. Thomastown is also on a summer only express bus route between Galway City, Thurles, Kilkenny and Rosslare Harbour. There is one bus daily in each direction between late June and early September.

Another express route runs between Waterford, Thomastown, Bennettsbridge, Kilkenny, Carlow, Portlaoise, Athlone and Longford, with one bus daily in each direc-tion. On Thursdays only a single bus runs from New Ross through Inistioge, Thomas-town and Bennettsbridge to Kilkenny City.

Kilkenny City

Kilkenny City is perhaps the most attractive large town in the country. It's officially a city, but there are many larger Irish towns, and Kilkenny's status has more to do with its role in the past than in the present.

Cromwell had a bad day when he visited in 1650; he ransacked the place. Kilkenny has managed however to survive as a most impressive medieval town. There's a maze of narrow streets, and Kilkenny Castle is one of the finest in Ireland, overlooking a sweep-ing bend in the river.

In Irish, the city's name is Cill Chainnigh after the monastery of St Cainneach (or Canice or Kenneth), which existed here in the 6th century. The saint's name is also attached to the city's splendid cathedral which has some beautiful Norman tombs.

Kilkenny is sometimes called the 'Marble City' because of the local black limestone which is used to good effect throughout.

HISTORY

Aengus Ossraigh is said to have made Kilkenny his capital around the 1st century BC. He was one of the first kings of Ossory, whose bloodline became the MacGiolla-Phadruig or Fitzpatrick family. They continued to rule in one form or another until

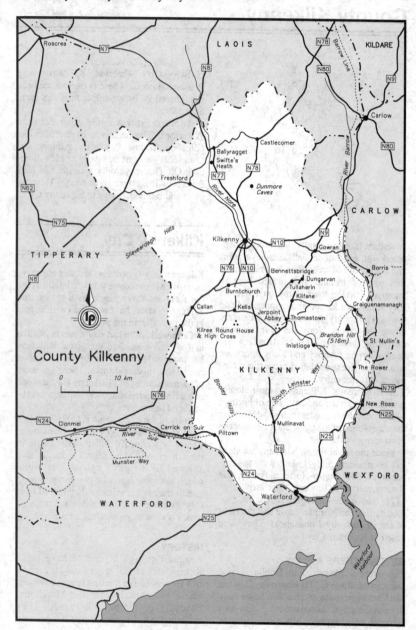

County Kilkenny

the 12th century. In the 5th century, St Kieran is said to have visited Kilkenny City and on the present site of Kilkenny Castle challenged the chieftains of Ossory to accept the Christian faith. St Canice established his monastery in the 6th century.

Kilkenny consolidated its importance in the 13th century, under William Marshall, the Earl of Pembroke and son-in-law of the Norman conqueror Strongbow. Kilkenny Castle was built to secure a crossing point on the Nore. St Canice's Cathedral and a number of abbeys were also constructed around this time.

During the Middle Ages Kilkenny was intermittently the unofficial capital of Ireland, with its own Anglo-Norman parliament. In February 1366 under Lionel Duke of Clarence, second son of King Edward III, the Kilkenny parliament passed a set of laws called the Statutes of Kilkenny, aimed at preventing assimilation of the increasingly assertive Anglo-Normans into Irish society. The Anglo-Normans were thus prohibited from marrying the native Irish, taking part in Irish sports, speaking or dressing like the Irish or playing any of their music. The laws remained theoretically in force for over 200 years although their effects soon dwindled as the Anglo-Normans were enmeshed in native ways, although many remained loyal to the crown.

In 1391 the castle and grounds were bought by James Butler, third Earl of Ormond. Kilkenny Castle became the Butlers' principal seat of power and remained in the family until 1967.

During the 1640s, Kilkenny City was a centre of opposition to the English Protestant parliamentarians, and – under the influence of the earl of Ormond – sided with the royalists in the English Civil War. The Confederation of Kilkenny aimed to bring about the return of land and power to the Catholics. After the execution of Charles I, Cromwell singled out Kilkenny for particular attention. He arrived on 22 March 1650 and laid siege for five days, destroying much of the south wall of the castle before Ormond surrendered.

ORIENTATION

Kilkenny straddles the River Nore, which flows through much of County Kilkenny. From St Canice's Cathedral at the north of the city centre, Kilkenny's main thoroughfare runs south, through St Canice's Place and over the bridge at Irishtown, becoming Parliament St and splitting in two. The eastern fork, St Kieran St, turns left onto St

---

The Butler Family

Kilkenny City and castle are intimately associated with the Butler family, the earls of Ormond. This Anglo-Norman clan were originally known as the Walters but changed their name after Theobald Walter was given the title of Chief Butler of Ireland by Henry II in 1185. The title was nice but what went with it was even better: the butlerage or duty charged on all wine imported into Ireland and England. When a descendant, Walter Butler, was strapped for cash in 1811, he sold the right for nearly £216,000, an extraordinary sum in those days. The three wine glasses on the family shield commemorate this important source of the family wealth.

The Butlers owned vast tracts of land in Tipperary and Kilkenny. During Henry VIII's reign, the family's power extended across much of southern Ireland. The Butlers lost out under Cromwell when the earl was exiled but his wife, Lady Ormond, managed to hang on to the estates. Because her treasonous husband was not in control, Cromwell didn't take away the family's positions or titles.

The Butlers bounced back with the restoration of Charles II in 1660 and picked the victorious side at the Battle of the Boyne in 1690 (although a Catholic cousin controlled the castle for the opposition), only to go down in flames when they backed a planned Spanish invasion of England in 1714. They later managed to reclaim some of their influence but never again reached their earlier heights. Both Tipperary and Kilkenny have numerous castles built by the family, including Carrick-on-Suir Castle, the finest Elizabethan mansion in the country. ∎

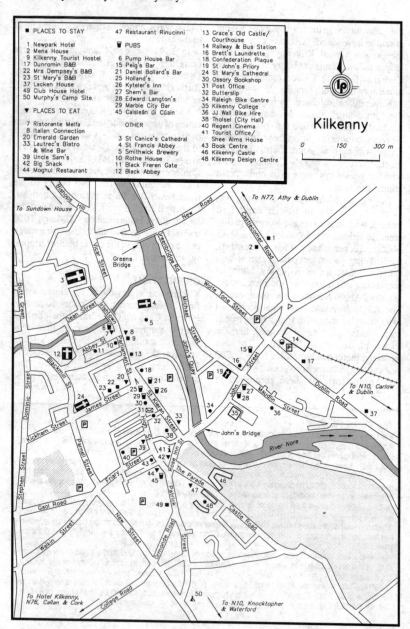

■ PLACES TO STAY
1 Newpark Hotel
2 Mena House
9 Kilkenny Tourist Hostel
17 Dunromin B&B
22 Mrs Dempsey's B&B
23 St Mary's B&B
37 Lacken House
49 Club House Hotel
50 Murphy's Camp Site

▼ PLACES TO EAT
7 Ristorante Melfa
16 Italian Connection
20 Emerald Garden
33 Lautrec's Bistro
   & Wine Bar
39 Uncle Sam's
42 Big Snack
44 Moghul Restaurant

47 Restaurant Rinuccini

▼ PUBS
6 Pump House Bar
15 Peig's Bar
21 Daniel Bollard's Bar
25 Holland's
26 Kyteler's Inn
27 Shem's Bar
28 Edward Langton's
29 Marble City Bar
45 Caisleán úi Cúain

OTHER
3 St Canice's Cathedral
4 St Francis Abbey
5 Smithwick Brewery
10 Rothe House
11 Black Freren Gate
12 Black Abbey

13 Grace's Old Castle/
   Courthouse
14 Railway & Bus Station
16 Brett's Laundrette
18 Confederation Plaque
19 St John's Priory
24 St Mary's Cathedral
31 Ossory Bookshop
31 Post Office
32 Butterslip
34 Raleigh Bike Centre
35 Kilkenny College
36 JJ Wall Bike Hire
38 Tholsel (City Hall)
40 Regent Cinema
41 Tourist Office/
   Shee Alms House
43 Book Centre
46 Kilkenny Castle
48 Kilkenny Design Centre

Kilkenny

0   150   300 m

John's Bridge over the Nore. The western fork, High St, carries on south. Most places of interest can be found on or close to High St/Parliament St, parallel to the river, or John St on the other side of the river across St John's Bridge, which runs north-east. Kilkenny Castle is just south of the city centre.

The castle, long-time centre of Anglo-Norman power, dominates the southern side of the city. At the other end of town off High St/Parliament St, and outside the city walls, the common folk were once concentrated in the area known as Irishtown, below the cathedral. Today only the name remains.

INFORMATION

The tourist office (☎ 056-51500) is in the Shee Alms House of 1581, a lovely stone townhouse on Rose Inn St. From May to August it's open from 9 am to 6 pm Monday to Saturday, and on Sunday from 11 am to 1 pm, then 2 to 5 pm. From September to April, it's open 9 am to 12.45 pm and 2 to 5.15 pm Tuesday to Saturday and is closed on Sunday and Monday. It has excellent maps and guides to the city.

The CityScope Exhibition takes place upstairs every half hour, and comprises a half-hour commentary explaining the sights, which are pinpointed on a model of medieval Kilkenny. Admission is IR£1.

The main post office is on High St. Brett's Laundrette (☎ 056-63200) is on Michael St, west off John St. The Book Centre is at 10 High St while farther down at No 67 the Ossory Bookshop has second-hand books as well as new ones.

KILKENNY CASTLE

The first structure on this strategic site overlooking the River Nore was a wooden tower built in 1172 by the Anglo-Norman conqueror of Ireland, Richard de Clare, better known as Strongbow. Twenty years later, his son-in-law William Marshall erected a stone castle with four towers, three of which survive in the present structure.

The castle was bought by the powerful Butler family in 1391, and their descendants continued to live there until 1935. Maintaining such a structure became an enormous financial strain and most of the furnishings were finally sold at auction. The castle was handed over to the city in 1967 for the princely sum of IR£50.

The Long Gallery (the wing of the castle nearest the river), with its vividly painted ceiling and extensive portrait collection of Butler family members over the centuries, is quite remarkable and the focus of the 40-minute guided tour. It was the most significant part of the work carried out in 1826. At the time of writing only a few other rooms are open, but by the time you read this, all rooms, many of them never previously opened to the public, should be accessible.

The castle is imposingly sited overlooking the River Nore. The 20 hectares of gardens extend to the north-east with a formal rose garden, a fountain to the north end and a well-kept park with a children's playground to the south. Entry to the grounds is free. The castle also has contemporary art exhibits in the Butler Art Gallery, and in the basement the castle kitchen now houses a popular restaurant (see Places to Eat).

Kilkenny Castle (☎ 056-21450) is open 10 am to 7 pm daily between June and September. From October to March, it opens 10.30 am to 12.45 pm and 2 to 5 pm Tuesday to Saturday, while on Sunday it's open 11 am to 12.45 pm and 2 to 5 pm. In April and May it opens 10 am to 5 pm daily. Entry is IR£1 (students and children 40p).

ST CANICE'S CATHEDRAL

St Canice's Cathedral, on the north bank of the River Bregagh, dominates Irishtown at the western end of Parliament St. The approach on foot from Parliament St leads you up St Canice's Steps dating from 1614, and the walls contain fragments of medieval carvings. Around the cathedral are a graveyard, an almost intact round tower and an 18th-century bishop's palace. Although the cathedral in its present form dates from 1251, it has a much longer history and contains some remarkable tombs and monuments.

The *Guide for Visitors* is an excellent investment.

This site may well have had pre-Christian
significance. Legends relate that the first
monastery was built here by St Cainneach,
Canice or Kenneth, Kilkenny's patron saint,
who moved here from Aghaboe, County
Laois, in the 6th century. There are records
of a wooden church on the site which was
burnt down in 1087. The round tower beside
the church is the oldest structure on site and
was built somewhere between 700 and 1000
AD on the site of an earlier Christian cemetery.

St Canice's was built in early English
Gothic style and suffered a history of catastrophe and resurrection. Its first disaster,
when the bell tower collapsed in 1332, is
connected with the story of Kilkenny's legendary witch, Dame Alice Kyteler. In 1650,
Cromwell's forces defaced and damaged the
church, even using it to stable their horses.
Repairs began in 1661, but there was still a
great deal to be done a century later. The
various additions over the centuries have not
been faithful to the church's original design.

Throughout the church, both on the walls
and in the floor, are ancient graveslabs. On
the north wall opposite the entrance is a slab
inscribed in Norman French to Jose de
Keteller, who died in 1280; despite the difference in spelling he was probably the father
of Kilkenny's witch, Alice Kyteler. On the
same wall, read the verse to Mary Stoughton
who died in 1631. The stone chair of St
Kieran embedded in the wall dates from the
13th century.

In 1354 some magnificent stained glass
was made for the church's east window,
depicting the Life, Passion, Resurrection and
Ascension of Jesus. A papal visitor in 1645
was so impressed he offered to buy it for
£700, a huge sum in those days. The offer
was rejected, and only five years later
Cromwell's troops comprehensively
destroyed the 300-year-old masterpiece. The
replacement dates from 1875.

In the south transept is a beautiful white
tomb with effigies of Piers Butler, who died
in 1539, and his wife Margaret Fitzgerald.

Tombs and monuments to a number of other
notable members of the Butler family crowd
this area of the church.

Apart from missing its crown, the 30-
metre-high round tower is in excellent
condition, and you can admire the fine view
from the top for 50p (children 30p). It's only
opened when there are plenty of visitors. It's
a tight squeeze and both hands are needed to
climb the steep ladders.

The Witch of Kilkenny

Dame Alice Kyteler ran through four husbands in suspicious circumstances. She
acquired some powerful enemies along the
way and was charged with witchcraft in 1324.
Witnesses claimed to have seen her sweeping dust to the door of her son, William
Outlawe, while chanting, 'to the house of
William, my son, lie all the wealth of Kilkenny
town'. Worse still, she had supposedly been
seen sacrificing cocks and consorting with
the devil. She was duly convicted, along with
her sister, her son and her maid. Dame Alice
managed to escape to England but the
unfortunate maid, Petronella, was left behind
and burnt at the stake outside the Tholsel.
No-one knows the fate of the sister.

Alice's son escaped from his sentence by
offering to reroof part of the cathedral with
lead tiles. He carried out his side of the
bargain, but the new roof proved too heavy
and collapsed in 1332, bringing the church
tower down with it. Kyteler's Inn at 27 St
Kieran St is Dame Alice's former home, now
a restaurant and bar. ■

BLACK ABBEY

The Dominican Black Abbey on Abbey St,
off Parliament St, was founded in 1225 by
William Marshall and takes its name from
the monks' black habits. After Henry VIII's
dissolution of the monasteries in 1543, it was
turned into a courthouse. After Cromwell's
visit in 1650, it remained a roofless ruin until
restoration in 1866. Much of what survives
dates from the 18th and 19th centuries.

Nearby to the south-east, off James St, is
the small and less interesting Catholic **St
Mary's Cathedral of the Assumption**

(☎ 056-21253). One of the side altars was the work of stonemason James Pearse (father of Patrick, a 1916 Easter Rising leader), and this altar was added to the cathedral during renovations around 1890. The cathedral was founded in 1843, and was named 'the famine church', as its construction provided employment for many local people during lean periods.

ROTHE HOUSE

Rothe House (☎ 056-22893) on Parliament St is a fine old merchant's house dating from 1594. The house, built around a series of courtyards, has a museum with a sparse collection of items from various periods displayed in its old timber-vaulted rooms.

In the 1640s, the wealthy Rothe family played a part in the Confederation of Kilkenny, and Peter Rothe, son of the original builder, had all his property confiscated. His sister was able to reclaim it, but just before the Battle of the Boyne (1690), the family supported James II and this time lost the house permanently. In 1850, a banner from the confederation was discovered in the house and is now in the National Museum, Dublin.

Rothe House is open April to October, 10.30 am to 5 pm from Monday to Saturday, 3 to 5 pm on Sunday. The rest of the year it only opens from 3 to 5 pm on Saturdays and Sundays. Entry is IR£1 (students 60p, children 40p).

SMITHWICK BREWERY

The Smithwick Brewery on Parliament St runs a tour June to September, Monday to Friday at 3 pm. The brewery was founded in 1710 and as well as Smithwick's own brand, Budweiser is brewed here under licence. The Franciscan monks of the restored St Francis Abbey on the brewery site were reputed to be expert brewers. This national monument was founded by William Marshall in 1232, but was desecrated by Cromwell in 1650.

OTHER BUILDINGS & SITES

Various remnants of the old Norman city

walls can still be traced but **Black Freren Gate**, just north of the Black Abbey on Abbey St is the only gate still standing.

The **Shee Alms House** on Rose Inn St was built in 1582 by local benefactor Sir Richard Shee and his wife to provide help to the poor. The house continued in this role as a 12-bed hospital until 1740. It now houses the tourist office. The **Tholsel** or city hall on High St was built in 1761 on the site where Petronella was burnt at the stake in 1324. Just west of the Tholsel is the **Butterslip**, a narrow alleyway, built in 1616 to connect High St with Low Lane (now St Kieran St), once lined with the stalls of butter sellers.

St Kieran St commemorates a church said to have been built here by the saint around 430 AD. The history of Kyteler's Inn is better documented as this was the site of wealthy Dame Alice Kyteler's home. Where St Kieran St meets High St, a plaque on the Bank of Ireland building marks the site of the **Confederate Hall and Parliament** of 1642-49. Next door is **Grace's Old Castle** originally built in 1210 but lost to the family and converted into a prison in 1568 and later into a courthouse (1794), which it remains today. Rebels from the 1798 Rising were executed here.

North of the river stand the ruins of **St John's Priory**, which was founded in 1200 and was noted for its many beautiful windows until Cromwell's visit.

Also north of the river, St John's **Kilkenny College**, on the east end of Lower John St, dates from 1666. Its students included Jonathan Swift and the philosopher George Berkeley. It now houses Kilkenny's county hall.

FESTIVALS

The highlight of the city's year is the Kilkenny Arts Week Festival which takes place in late August, with music, drama and theatrical events all over the city. It's very busy so if you aim to be in town, book ahead. The Confederation of Kilkenny Festival in June also brings the streets to life, with parades, sideshows and historic pageantry.

ORGANISED TOURS

Walking tours are conducted six times daily (four on Sundays) by Tynan Tours (☎ 056-65929) and start from the tourist office. They cost IR£2.50 (students IR£2, children 60p).

PLACES TO STAY

Camping

The nearest officially approved camp site with proper facilities is eight km (five miles) south in Bennettsbridge, but there is an unofficial camp site very near the city centre run by the *Murphys* (☎ 056-62973) at 25 Upper Patrick St. Go south from the junction at the bottom of High St along Patrick St which becomes the Waterford road. The camp site is signposted on the left side. They have room for about 20 tents and charge IR£2.50 per person.

Hostels

The *Kilkenny Tourist Hostel* (☎ 056-63541), at 35 Parliament St, is neat, clean and very central. It has 25 beds at IR£5 a night in dorms or IR£6 in private rooms.

There is an *An Óige Hostel* (☎ 056-67674) in Foulksrath Castle, 13 km (eight miles) north of Kilkenny in Jenkinstown. It occupies a 16th-century Norman castle and costs IR£3.50 to IR£4.50 a night in dorms. During November, December and January, they are open weekends only. During the summer, they serve very reasonably priced meals. At 11.30 am and 5.30 pm from Monday to Saturday a bus with signs for Castlecomer and the hostel departs from near the Kilkenny tourist office. The fare is IR£1.

B&Bs

There are plenty of B&Bs especially south of the city out along Patrick St and beyond. *Mrs Dempsey's* (☎ 056-21954) and *St Mary's* (☎ 056-22091) are two small town houses side by side on quiet James St, very close to the city centre. Each has six rooms and charges IR£14/24 for singles/doubles.

Also very central is *Bregagh* (☎ 056-22315) on Dean St near St Canice's Cathedral, costing IR£13.50 or IR£15 with bathroom. A few doors down is *Kilmore*

(☎ 056-64040), where rooms are IR£16/24 or IR£20/30 with attached bathroom.

Dunromin (☎ 056-61387), near the railway station, has top-notch breakfasts, and costs IR£12 or IR£13 with bathroom. *Mena House* (☎ 056-65362) is on Castlecomer Rd opposite the Newpark Hotel, and costs IR£15 sharing with bathroom or IR£12 per person without bathroom.

Sundown House (☎ 056-21816) is one km out on the Freshford road, and has rooms with bathroom for IR£14 or IR£12 without. To get there, go north through Parliament St, turn right at the traffic lights in Irishtown and head north for one km. Watch out for the sign.

Hotels

The attractive old *Club House Hotel* (☎ 056-21994) on Patrick St has B&B at IR£20 to IR£30 depending on season, plus IR£5 for a room with bathroom, and has good food.

The modern *Newpark Hotel* (☎ 056-22122) has swimming pools, saunas, gym and 20 hectares of parkland. It is north of the railway station just along the Castlecomer Rd. All its rooms have bathrooms. The cost per person is from IR£32 to IR£38 depending on the season. The *Hotel Kilkenny* (☎ 056-62000) has excellent facilities and costs IR£32 to IR£42 per person B&B depending on the season. It's about 10 minutes' walk from the city centre on College Rd.

Guesthouses

If you have a few pounds to spare, *Blanchville House* (☎ 056-27197), Maddoxtown, is a lovely 19th-century Georgian house on its own farm about eight km (five miles) east of the city. B&B is IR£23/40 for singles/doubles, and dinner is IR£15. To get there, go along the main Carlow road and take the first right after the Pike pub, then it's three km to a crossroads and Connolly's pub. Turn left here and it's almost two km down the road on the left.

Lacken House (☎ 056-65611), just out of town on the Carlow Rd, is more expensive, from IR£28/44. This is a highly rated country house with an excellent restaurant.

PLACES TO EAT
Cafés & Takeaways
In summer, the restaurant in the *Kilkenny Castle Kitchen* is a good place for lunch or for delicious home-made scones. It's open 10 am to 7 pm and you don't have to pay the castle admission charge. Right across the road from the castle, the restaurant upstairs in the *Kilkenny Design Centre* (9 am to 5 pm daily) is excellent for snacks or lunch. It attracts coach parties. Always packed and popular is the *Pantry*, a small self-service coffee shop on Kieran St; they have their own bakery and do a set lunch for IR£3.50.

Big Snack on Rose Inn St is a fried chicken and burger place, and *Uncle Sam's* on High St does burgers and cheap pizzas.

Pub Food
On St Kieran St, the 1324 *Kyteler's Inn* has a rustic little restaurant downstairs and a bar upstairs. While the food isn't brilliant, the place is popular. Dishes like chicken kiev or lasagne cost IR£4 to IR£5.

North-east of the river, *Edward Langton's* (☎ 056-21728) at 69 John St is a wonderful pub and restaurant that has won many awards. Lunch will cost a reasonable IR£5, and set dinners, served until 11 pm, cost from IR£12.50 to IR£16.50.

Caisleán uí Cúain is another very popular pub on High St, which turns out good food including a popular buffet in summer, lunch times only. Pasta or Irish stew cost from IR£4 to IR£5.

Restaurants
There's a batch of Italian-Irish restaurants around the city, especially at the cathedral end of Parliament St. The *Italian Connection* at No 38 is good value with pizzas at IR£3 to IR£5 and pasta from IR£4. Near Kyteler's Inn on Kieran St is the late-night *Lautrec's Bistro & Wine Bar*, open until 12.45 am, which serves dishes from IR£4.45 upwards. They also serve lunches.

Kilkenny has some excellent ethnic res-

taurants. On High St, the Chinese *Emerald Garden* (☎ 056-61812) does main courses from IR£6.50. The Indian *Moghul Restaurant* on Pudding Lane (down the alley behind Manning Travel at the south end of High St) is top class, with main courses from IR£7 to IR£11.

A more upmarket Italian place is *Ristorante Rinuccini* (☎ 056-61575), a cellar restaurant on the Parade opposite the castle with delicious pastas, all freshly prepared. Dinner costs from IR£15.

Widely regarded as the best local restaurant is *Lacken House* (☎ 056-61085), just out of town on the Dublin road. Dinner will cost you IR£20 or more.

ENTERTAINMENT
At the castle end of High St, *Caisleán uí Cúain* (the Castle Inn) claims to be the town's music pub. It's a very popular and trendy place, stylishly old-fashioned. The music includes Irish, blues and jazz.

Edward Langton's have discos on Tuesdays and Saturday nights; admission is IR£3. There's often Irish music at *Peig's Bar* on John St, a nice traditional pub. *Holland's*, a bare stone and pine place on High St, won a 'best newcomer pub' award and has a cellar with live rock/pop bands. The *Pump House* on Parliament St is another rock/pop place.

Daniel Bollard's is a nice traditional bar on St Kieran St. *John Cleere* (☎ 056-62573) at 28 Parliament St has regular, year-round productions of plays, poetry readings and anything else that's going. Every Monday night is Traditional Irish Music & Folk night. Spontaneous sessions can happen any time.

The *Regent* is a single-screen cinema in the centre of the city, up a cul-de-sac opposite the Tholsel.

THINGS TO BUY
Opposite the castle on the other side of the Parade are the former Castle Stables (1760) which have been tastefully converted into the famous Kilkenny Design Centre, with an outstanding collection of Irish goods and crafts for sale. Behind the shop through the arched gateway is the Castle Yard and the

studios of various local craftspeople, with gift shops.

GETTING THERE & AWAY
Train
McDonagh Railway Station (☎ 056-22024) is on the Dublin road, north-east of the town centre via John St. There are four trains daily each way on the Dublin (Heuston Station) to Waterford line, three on Sundays. The journey to and from Dublin takes just under two hours. For the full timetable check with the station or phone ☎ 01-730000 for Dublin and Waterford departure times.

Bus
Bus Éireann also operate out of the railway station and provides services to and from Dublin three times daily, twice on Sundays. Kilkenny is on the Dublin to Clonmel route. On the Galway to Rosslare Harbour and Waterford to Longford routes, one bus a day passes through in each direction. There are two buses daily to and from Cork City.

J J Kavanagh & Sons (☎ 056-31106) run private coaches to and from Carlow, Limerick and Cork, largely for college students.

GETTING AROUND
J J Wall (☎ 056-21236) at 88 Maudlin St rents bikes at IR£7 a day, IR£30 a week, plus a deposit of IR£40. There is also the Raleigh Bike Centre (☎ 056-62037) on John St with bikes for IR£7 a day. The countryside around Kilkenny is fine cycling territory and there's a lovely day excursion to Kells, Inistioge, Jerpoint Abbey and Kilfane.

Practical Car Rental (☎ 056-63839) is in Barry Pender Motors on the Dublin road. For taxis contact Michael O'Brien (☎ 056-61333) or Michael Howe (☎ 056-65874).

Around Kilkenny City

BENNETTSBRIDGE
A tiny hamlet on the River Nore, Bennettsbridge has two of Ireland's most renowned potteries. In a big old mill by the river, Nicholas Mosse turns out hand-made spongewear: creamy brown pottery with sponged patterns. The factory shop is on the right on the way down to the mill.

Nicholas's brother Billy continues to mill flour, a trade that has run in the family for centuries. The stone-ground flour makes wonderful brown bread and can be bought plain or as part of Mosse's brown bread mix, which is widely available in good food shops.

Stoneware Jackson, almost two km north of Bennettsbridge on the minor road to Kilkenny City, produces pale-blue pottery with dark blue swirls and pink dots.

Places to Stay & Eat
The only official camp site for a long way in any direction is the *Nore Valley Camping & Caravan Park* (☎ 056-27229). Coming into Bennettsbridge from Kilkenny, turn right just before the bridge and the park is signposted. They charge IR£4.50 per tent or IR£3 if you are hiking or cycling.

The *Nore Tavern* (☎ 056-27275) is a pleasant bar and restaurant right by the bridge. They have snacks during the day and more formal meals in the evening.

DUNMORE CAVES
Dunmore Caves are about 10 km (six miles) north of Kilkenny on the Castlecomer road.

According to some texts, marauding Vikings killed 1000 people at two ring forts near Dunmore Caves in 928 AD. A number of survivors fled and hid in the caverns from where the Vikings tried to smoke them out by lighting fires at the entrance. It is thought that the Vikings found the people who were hiding, dragged off the men for slaves and left the women and children to suffocate.

Excavations in 1973 uncovered the remains of at least 44 people, mostly women and children. They also found a number of coins dating from the 920s but none from any later date. One theory suggests that the coins were dropped by the Vikings (who often carried them in their armpits, secured with wax) while enthusiastically engaged in the slaughter. However, there are few marks of violence on the skeletons, which lends weight to the theory that the people suffocated.

These limestone caves are well lit and spacious. After a steep descent through the large entrance, there are two detours to the left with stalactites, stalagmites and columns, including the six-metre Market Cross stalagmite. The caves are damp and cold, so a sweater or coat is advised. The guided tour is optional but worthwhile.

Entry to the caves (☎ 056-67726) is IR£1 (students and children 40p) and they're open mid-June to September 10 am to 7 pm daily, October to mid-March 10 am to 5 pm Saturdays and Sundays, mid-March to mid-June 10 am to 5 pm Tuesday to Saturday and 2 to 5 pm Sunday.

The caves are almost one km east of the main Kilkenny to Castlecomer road. Buggy's (☎ 056-41264) run a local bus to Castlecomer, which leaves the Kilkenny Tourist Office at 11.30 am and 5.30 pm daily and passes along the main road close to the caves. Bus Éireann buses between Kilkenny and Dublin also run by on the main road; for details check with Kilkenny railway station (☎ 056-22024).

Central Kilkenny

A tour of the county south of Kilkenny City takes in much of the Nore Valley and sections of the Barrow Valley. The most scenic parts are from Graiguenamanagh in the east, down to the Rower and then north on the road to Inistioge, Thomastown, Kells and finally to Callan near the border with Tipperary. There is still a fair chunk of the county below this arc, with pleasant rolling countryside and quiet backroads.

To get to Graiguenamanagh head east on the Carlow road and turn off for Gowran, 12 km (eight miles) east of Kilkenny City, a village famous for its racecourse and 13th-century church with some fine carvings. There is a nice guesthouse here – *Whitethorns* (☎ 056-26102), 300 metres off the main Dublin to Kilkenny road. B&B is IR£12 or IR£13.50 with bathroom.

For bus services to and from Gowran, see the Getting There & Away section at the beginning of this chapter.

KELLS
Only 13 km (eight miles) south of Kilkenny City, Kells is not to be confused with its namesake in County Meath. This is a treat of a little hamlet, nestling beside a fine stone bridge on the King's River – a tributary of the Nore. In Kells Priory, the village has one of Ireland's most impressive monastic sites.

Kells Priory
The earliest remains of the magnificent Kells Priory date from the late 12th century with the bulk of the present ruins from the 15th century. In a sea of rich farmland, a protective wall, largely intact, connects seven dwelling towers. Inside the walls are the bones of an Augustinian abbey and the foundations of some chapels and houses. It's unusually well fortified for a monastery, and the heavy curtain walls hint at a troubled history. Indeed, within a single century from 1250, the abbey was twice fought over and burnt down by squabbling warlords.

Kilree Round Tower & High Cross
Three km (two miles) south at Kilree (signposted from the abbey car park) there's a 29-metre round tower and a simple early high cross, said to be in honour of an Irish high king, Niall Caille. He is supposed to have drowned in the King's River at Callan some time in the 840s while attempting to save a servant. His body was found near Kells. His final resting place and cross are outside the church grounds, as he was not a Christian.

Burntchurch Castle
Five km (three miles) due north of Kells, after turning west at the first crossroad, is Burntchurch Castle, a 15th or 16th-century Fitzgerald castle and adjoining round gate tower. It's possible to climb the square tower.

THOMASTOWN

Thomastown is a little market town, nicely situated by the River Nore. It's also on the main Dublin to Waterford road and would be more attractive but for the constant rumble of heavy traffic. However locals and visitors usually ignore this aspect of the town and concentrate on its drinking establishments, of which it has 11. Some have music and others have reasonable food. There are also some good craft shops; the Grennan Mill Craft School has a craft shop on the edge of town, on the Waterford road.

Named after a Welsh mercenary in 1169, Thomastown has some fragments of a medieval wall, and Mullin's Castle down by the bridge is the sole survivor of 14. There is also the 13th-century church of St Mary, now under restoration. The main point of interest around here is the magnificent Cistercian abbey at Jerpoint 1.5 km to the south-west.

From Inistioge to Thomastown is a gentle eight km (five mile) journey along the Nore, with a number of crossings on old stone bridges, passing people fishing amongst the reeds.

Getting There & Away

Train The town is on the main railway line between Dublin and Waterford with the same service as Kilkenny City.

Bus Bus Éireann (☎ 056-64933) has two connections from Waterford on Thursdays, with a stop at Mullinavat. From Dublin there are regular buses which carry on to Waterford. There are sporadic connections to Galway, Longford and Rosslare Harbour. The bus stop in Thomastown is outside O'Keeffe's Supermarket.

AROUND THOMASTOWN
Jerpoint Abbey

Just south of Thomastown, Jerpoint Abbey (☎ 056-24623) is one of Ireland's finest Cistercian ruins and was established by a king of Ossory in the 12th century. It has been partially restored. The fine tower and cloister are late 14th or early 15th century. Fragments of the monastery's cloister are

particularly interesting with a series of often amusing figures carved on the cloister pillars. There are also stone carvings on the church walls and in the tombs of members of the Butler and Walshe families. Faint traces of a 15th or 16th-century painting remain on the north wall of the church. This chancel area also contains a tomb thought to be that of Felix O'Dullany, Jerpoint's first abbot and bishop of Ossory, who died in 1202.

According to local legend, St Nicholas (or Santa Claus) is buried near the abbey. The Knights of Jerpoint while retreating in the Crusades removed his body from Myra in modern-day Turkey and laid it to rest in the Church of St Nicholas to the west of the abbey. The grave is marked by a broken slab and decorated with a carving of a monk.

Entry to Jerpoint Abbey is IR£1 (students and children 40p). The abbey is open from mid-June to September, 9.30 am to 6.30 pm daily. The rest of the year it's open 10 am to 1 pm and 2 to 5 pm Tuesday to Saturday, and afternoons only on Sunday. Guided tours are available on request.

There is no public transport here, but it's only 1.5 km (one mile) from Thomastown.

Kilfane

Just three km (two miles) north of Thomastown is the village of Kilfane, with a small ruined 15th-century church and Norman tower, well hidden 50 metres off the road but signposted. The church has a remarkable stone carving of the Cantwell Fada or 'long Cantwell', a very tall, thin knight in detailed chainmail armour, brandishing a shield decorated with the coat of arms of the Cantwells. Some of the graves are of Irishmen who perished in WW I.

Tullaherin

Another three km north off the main road at Tullaherin, is a damaged, leaning round tower and ruined church from the 9th century.

INISTIOGE

Inistioge (pronounced 'Inishteeg') is a delightful little village, with a 10-arched stone bridge spanning the Nore and a picturesque tree-lined square. The Protestant church to the north of the new Catholic church sits in part of a medieval priory with some old graveslabs. The village is 10 km (six miles) south-east of Graiguenamanagh on the opposite side of Mt Brandon, and there's a nice journey across through a gap in the mountains. At the bottom of the hill that leads to Woodstock House Demesne is a pottery which produces lovely simple work in light pastel colours.

Walks One km south on Mt Alto is the **Woodstock House Demesne,** and the hike up to it is well worth the effort for the panorama of the valley below and the demesne itself. The 18th-century house was one of the finest in the county, but was destroyed during the Civil War in 1922. The ruin is closed but the elevated garden and forest are now a state park with picnic areas and trails and are open to the public. For another fine walk, follow the river bank and climb any of the surrounding hills.

Getting There & Away
On Thursdays only, a single bus runs between New Ross and Kilkenny, calling at Inistioge en route. It departs from New Ross at 10 am, arriving in Inistioge at 10.40 am before continuing its journey to Kilkenny. In the reverse direction, it leaves from Kilkenny railway station at 1.15 pm and reaches Inistioge at 1.50 pm.

GRAIGUENAMANAGH
Graiguenamanagh (pronounced 'Greg-na-mana') is a small market town on a very attractive stretch of the River Barrow. It lies 23 km (15 miles) south-east of Kilkenny City at the northern foot of Mt Brandon (520 metres).

The area is good for unstrenuous walking up the mountain, along the road to Inistioge or south along the river towards New Ross. Mt Brandon has a megalithic cairn and stone circle on the summit with fine views of the Barrow Valley and Blackstair Mountains to the east. Besides Duiske Abbey, there are

more monastic remains eight km (five miles) down the Barrow towpath at St Mullins in Carlow.

Duiske Abbey
This 13th-century Cistercian abbey is Graiguenamanagh's prime attraction. The name comes from the Irish *Dubh Uisce* or 'Black Water', a tributary of the Barrow. Duiske has been completely restored, and its pleasantly simple interior is now in everyday use.

Inside the abbey to the right of the main entrance is the Knight of Duiske, a 14th-century carving in high relief of a knight in chain mail reaching for his sword. On the floor nearby is a glass panel which reveals some of the original 13th-century floor tiles some way below the present floor level. In the grounds are two very early high crosses, brought here in the last century from the surrounding countryside for protection. The larger, heavier Ballyogan Cross has panels on the east side depicting the Crucifixion, Adam and Eve, Abraham's sacrifice of Isaac and David playing the harp. The west side shows the Massacre of the Innocents.

GOWRAN
The village of Gowran is 12 km (eight miles) east of Kilkenny City, and is famous for its racecourse. It has a 13th-century church with some fine carvings. There is a nice guesthouse here – *Whitethorns* (☎ 056-26102), 300 metres off the main Dublin to Kilkenny road. B&B is IR£12 or IR£13.50 with bathroom.

Southern Kilkenny

Much of southern Kilkenny is sparsely populated. Gentle hills separate the river valleys of the Nore, Barrow and the Suir. Carrick-on-Suir in Tipperary and Waterford City are within easy reach, with a wide choice of accommodation and restaurants. If you want to stay in the area try Mullinavat, 12 km (eight miles) north of Waterford on the Kilkenny road.

Getting There & Away
An express bus service between Dublin and Waterford calls at Mullinavat, with four buses daily in either direction.

THE SOUTH LEINSTER WAY
South Kilkenny is crossed by the South Leinster Way, which runs from Carrick-on-Suir, through Piltown, Mullinavat, Inistioge, Graiguenamanagh and on to Borris in County Carlow. The southerly section of the 95-km (60-mile) trail is not as scenic as the rest but these low hills have their own charm, and on a sunny day they offer fine views south over the Suir Valley and Waterford Harbour. For more information on this trail ask for the Bord Fáilte Information Sheet No 26D.

The Kildare Trails on the Barrow towpath intersects the South Leinster Way at Graiguenamanagh, so trail walkers can head north through Carlow and on into Kildare by the canals. This trail is covered by Bord Fáilte Information Sheet No 26E (Kildare Trails).

Places to Stay & Eat
Around Mullinavat, there is *Tory View* (☎ 051-85513) signposted two km south of the town on the way to Waterford. B&B in smallish rooms is IR£15, and evening meals are available. Alternatively there is the 1644 *Rising Sun* (☎ 051-98173), which is on Mullinavat's Main St. All rooms have bathroom, phone and TV but at IR£22 per person for B&B it's pricey. The upstairs restaurant is good, and bar food is available in the lounge.

North Kilkenny

CASTLECOMER
An attractive town, 18 km (11 miles) north of Kilkenny, Castlecomer is on the River Dinin which flows across the Castlecomer Plateau.

The town became a major mining centre for anthracite after it was discovered nearby in 1636, and the mines only closed for good in the mid 1960s. The anthracite was widely regarded as being the best in Europe with very little sulphur and producing almost no smoke. Castlecomer saw action in the 1798 Rising when the Fenian rebels led by Father John Murphy took the place while en route from Wexford to the midlands. There is little to do here, but the tree-lined square and neat townhouses are pleasant.

Places to Stay
The *Avalon* pub and guesthouse (☎ 056-41302), on the Square near the bridge, are housed in the old mine offices. B&B is IR£14. Alternatively *Wandesforde House* (☎ 056-42441) has six double rooms, all with bathroom; B&B is good value at IR£16. Dinner is IR£13.

Getting There & Away
Castlecomer is on the Kilkenny to Dublin route, serviced by three or four buses daily. Check with Kilkenny railway station (☎ 056-22024) for details. J J Kavanagh's (☎ 056-31106) private bus service also has a daily bus between Clonmel, Kilkenny, Castlecomer, Athy and Dublin; from Castlecomer it takes 75 minutes to Dublin. Buggy's (☎ 056-41644) run a more frequent local service between Carlow, Castlecomer and Kilkenny City.

AROUND CASTLECOMER
Eight km (five miles) west-south-west of Castlecomer is **Ballyragget**, with an almost intact square tower in the 16th-century Butler Castle. Five km (three miles) south on the road to Kilkenny is **Foulksrath Castle** in a similar style. This is now a busy An Óige Hostel (☎ 056-67674) and the setting in a 16th-century square-towered castle is superb. For more details see Places to Stay under Kilkenny City.

Almost two km (one mile) south of

Ballyragget is **Swifte's Heath**, home to Jonathan Swift during his school years in Kilkenny. Eight km (five miles) south-west of here is **Freshford** which has a finely worked Romanesque doorway set into the 18th-century Protestant church. Freshford was the site of a monastery founded in the 6th century by St Lachtain.

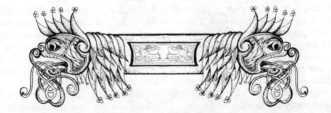

Central South

The four counties of Carlow, Kildare, Laois and Offaly make up a large portion of the Irish midlands. Sites of archaeological interest include the High Cross at Moone in Kildare, Kildare Town's cathedral, the Browne's Hill dolmen just outside Carlow Town, the Rosse Estate and telescope in Birr and, most impressive of all, Clonmacnois on the banks of the Shannon River, which is probably the most important monastic site in the country.

County Kildare

Kildare is mostly rich green farmland in the south, while the fringe of the extensive Bog of Allen peatland lies to the north. Underlying the pasture and bog is a limestone plain.

The main towns are dominated by traffic, but this should soon be much less of a problem since the local councils are busy building bypasses for the worst-affected towns. The county is crossed by nearly all the main arteries to the rest of the country, and by the 18th-century Grand and Royal Canals, now enjoying a new lease of life. The River Barrow marks the county's eastern border while the Curragh is a great sweep of unfenced countryside to the south.

HISTORY

Early archaeological sites of any significance are few and far between, with little remaining of the Bronze Age hill forts on Knockaulin, the Hill of Allen and Lyons Hill in the north-east of the county. Away from Dublin, South Kildare has some fine monastic remains, chiefly at Moone near Castledermot.

From the 12th to the 16th centuries, Kildare and indeed much of Ireland was controlled by the Norman Fitzgerald family, whose principal base was Maynooth Castle. Through clever diplomacy, they managed for a long time to coexist with the crown and sustain their power and influence.

A serious setback to their power and influence occurred in 1536 when the English defeated a rebellion led by Silken Thomas Fitzgerald, after it was rumoured his father had been killed in London by Henry VIII. But the family became Protestant and through some clever diplomacy regained much of its land and titles over the next few decades. From then on the Fitzgeralds were part of the Protestant ascendancy and their power waxed and waned over the ensuing centuries.

Close to Dublin, Kildare was well within the English-controlled Pale, and 18th-century landowners felt secure enough to build some of the grandest mansions in the country. Castletown House near Celbridge is an outstanding example.

HORSES

Kildare has more horseflesh per sq km than any other Irish county, and the racecourses are home to some of the biggest meets of the year. The calcium-rich grass breeds strong-boned horses, while excellent stud facilities and generous tax concessions attract many foreign horseowners.

Travelling through Kildare you will see plenty of studs, most of which are private and

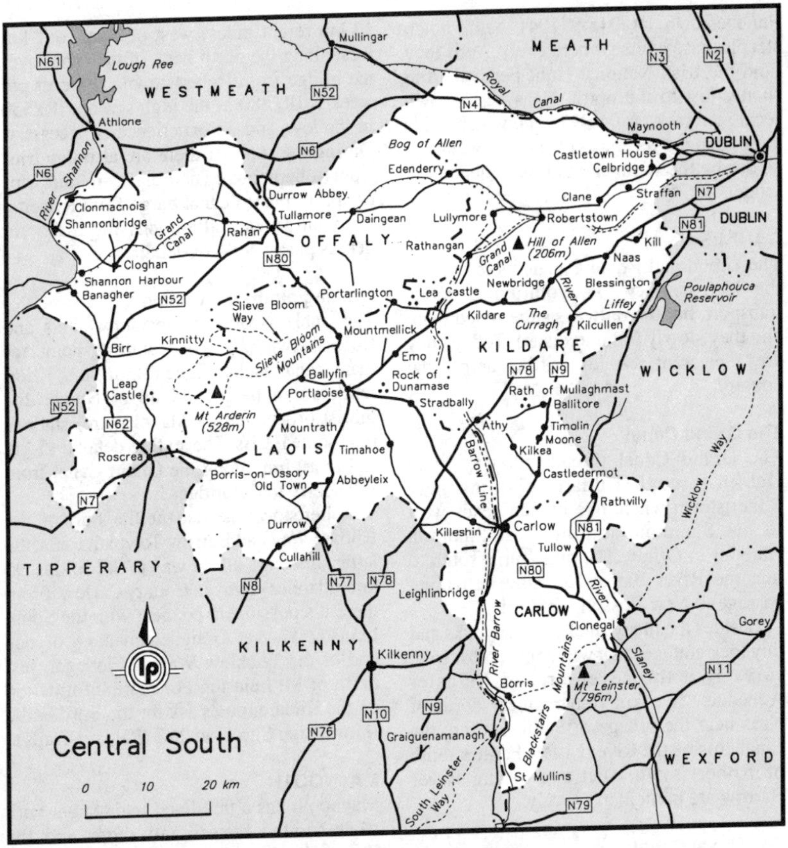

Central South

0   10   20 km

not too keen on visitors. You can, however, visit the state-owned National Stud just outside Kildare Town. You could also check out a thoroughbred auction in Goff's Sales, a huge complex beside the main Dublin road near Kill. Here, you will see spindly thoroughbred foals and yearlings change hands for unbelievable sums.

Everyone goes to the races in Ireland. At race meetings you can see all of Irish society at play: the glitterati in their private boxes swilling champagne, and the ordinary punters oblivious to everything except their bets – and, between races, their drink.

Kildare has three of Ireland's most famous tracks, and there is racing on all year round. The best known is the Curragh, over two km (one mile) west of Newbridge. The racecourse takes its name from the expanse of open countryside surrounding it, which also holds one of the country's biggest army camps. The Curragh Racecourse (☎ 045-41205) has some of the biggest meets of the racing calendar, including the Goff's Irish Thousand Guineas in May and the Irish Derby in June. Their season runs from April to October.

Five km (three miles) south of Naas is

Punchestown (☎ 045-97704), a top-notch steeplechase course where every April they hold the Irish National Hunt Festival. And finally just to the north, Naas has its own local racetrack (☎ 045-97391), which holds well-attended meetings every two weeks or so during the summer and less frequently in winter.

CANALS

The Grand and Royal Canals were built in the 18th century to revolutionise goods transport, but the railways superseded them and they slowly fell into disuse. Today, they are a pleasant way of drifting across the country.

The Grand Canal

The Grand Canal threads its way from Dublin through Kildare, dividing near Robertstown where one branch heads west to the Shannon, joining it at Shannon Harbour in Offaly. The other turns south to join the River Barrow at Athy, providing passage to New Ross in Wexford.

Besides the many finely crafted locks and tiny lock cottages you will come across treasures like the seven-arched Leinster Aqueduct, five km (three miles) north of Naas near the village of Sallins, where the canal crosses the River Liffey. Farther south of Robertstown, sections of the River Barrow are particularly lovely.

The Royal Canal

The Royal Canal follows Kildare's northern border and also wends its way to the Shannon, joining it farther north above Lough Ree, but it is only navigable for a very small part of the way. It was never as profitable as the Grand Canal, and has aged less gracefully than its southerly sister. It's currently under restoration and should be fully navigable within the next 10 years.

Barges & Boats

Boating facilities are only available on the Grand Canal and six-berth Shannon cruiser-style boats with showers and kitchens can be hired in Lowtown Marina (☎ 045-60427),

13 km (eight miles) west of Naas, one km west along the north bank of the canal over the bridge from Robertstown. The cost per week is IR£880 in the high season, IR£550 in the low, and no experience is necessary. During the summer there are also day trips from Robertstown. There are 45-minute trips on a refurbished canal barge from Robertstown on Sunday afternoons for IR£2; for details phone ☎ 045-60808.

Walking along the Canals

The canal towpaths are ideal for walkers, and Robertstown is a good starting-point for many canal walks. Three *Canal Bank Walks* leaflets can be picked up at Newbridge tourist office, certain Maxol petrol stations or at some B&Bs. The leaflets detail a 45-km (28-mile) trail along the Grand Canal from Edenderry to Celbridge.

Robertstown is also at the hub of the Kildare Way and Barrow Towpath trails, the latter stretching all the way to St Mullins, 95 km (60 miles) away in County Carlow. From there it's possible to connect with the South Leinster Way at Graiguenamanagh or one end of the Wicklow Way at Clonegal, just north of Mt Leinster. For more information on the Kildare routes ask for the Bord Fáilte Information Sheet No 26E (Kildare Trails).

MAYNOOTH

Maynooth has a tree-lined main street with stone-fronted houses and shops and the Royal Canal passing by just south of the centre. As it's only 24 km (15 miles) west of Dublin, Maynooth is a dreadful traffic bottleneck, and is best avoided at peak times, especially Friday and Sunday evenings. A proposed bypass should eventually solve this problem.

Carton House

Maynooth's centre was designed to complement the entrance to Carton House, on the Dublin end of the main street. This splendid Georgian mansion was built by the Fitzgeralds, the earls of Kildare, in the mid-18th century and later belonged to the duke and duchess of Leinster. Unfortunately you cannot see the luxurious interior, but you are free to wander around the gardens.

Carton House was designed by Richard Castle, architect of the Fitzgeralds' townhouse, now Leinster House (the Dáil) in Dublin and Russborough House in Wicklow. Castle is buried in St Mary's Church beside the gate of Maynooth College.

St Patrick's College

St Patrick's College & Seminary (☎ 01-628 5499) at the west end of town has been turning out Catholic priests since 1795 and became a college of the National University in 1910. Ironically, the seminary was founded by the English, who were growing alarmed at the prospect of Irish priests studying in France where they might pick up disturbing ideas about revolution and republicanism.

Maynooth Castle

The castle, parts of which date from the 13th century, is by the college entrance. The gatehouse, keep and its great hall survive, and the key can be picked up from the house directly opposite.

The castle was home to the Fitzgeralds. After the rebellion of 1536, led by Silken Thomas Fitzgerald, the English laid siege to the castle. The castle's garrison surrendered after being assured of leniency. In what became known as the 'Pardon of Maynooth', Thomas and his men were summarily executed. The castle was badly damaged in Cromwellian times and ceased to be lived in when the Fitzgeralds moved to Kilkea Castle in the mid-17th century.

Places to Stay

B&Bs *Windgate Lodge* (☎ 01-273415) is three km (two miles) south of Maynooth in Barberstown and costs IR£15 per person. *Breezy Heights* (☎ 0405-41183) is 10 km (seven miles) out, on the Enfield side of Kilcock. Turn right at the sign before Kilcock. B&B is IR£13.

Hotels The attractive old *Leinster Arms Hotel* (☎ 01-6286323) is in the centre of Maynooth, and rooms with bathroom cost IR£10 per person. Breakfast is an extra IR£5. If your trunkload of cash is weighing you down, the lovely Georgian *Moyglare Manor* (☎ 01-6286351) is a couple of km north of Maynooth. It's one of the best country houses in Ireland and costs IR£75 per person including breakfast, plus at least another IR£25 for dinner. The dining room is full of works of art, and lunch here is a special treat.

Places to Eat

The *Elite Coffee Shop & Bakery* in the middle of Main St has freshly baked bread and serves snacks. For a more substantial meal the *Country Restaurant* under the craft shop at the Galway end of Main St serves solid helpings of uninspiring food for around IR£5.

The *Leinster Arms*, in the middle of town, has pub food, a carvery and the more formal *Plough Restaurant*. They are open for food from 12.30 to 9.30 pm and prices are reasonable. Out of town *Moyglare Manor* (☎ 01-6286351) is good although expensive (see Places to Stay).

Entertainment

Brady's and *Caulfield's* are two nice pubs on Main St, while the *Leinster Arms* has bands and ballad sessions on occasion. The *Roost* bar at the west end of Main St has a facade dominated by Greek statuary, since the owner visited Greece.

Getting There & Away

Train Maynooth is linked to Dublin (☎ 01-363333) on the Western Suburban line and is on the main Dublin to Sligo line with three to four trains daily in each direction. Call the Talking Timetable (☎ 01-731111) for details.

Bus Suburban bus Nos 67 and 68 go from Dublin to Celbridge and Maynooth, plus there are numerous long-distance buses passing through en route to Galway and Sligo. For information consult the timetable or ring ☎ 01-366111 or 01-703 2433. The bus terminal in Maynooth is outside Brady's pub on Main St.

AROUND MAYNOOTH
Horse Museum
There is a Horse Museum and Rare Breeds Farm (☎ 01-6287261) in Bridestream near Kilcock. Admission is IR£2.

Canoeing
Leixlip on the River Liffey near Maynooth is an important canoeing centre. It's the starting point of the Irish Sprint Canoe Championships and annual International Liffey Descent Race, when the ESB (Electricity Supply Board) releases 30 million tonnes of water from the Poulaphouca Reservoir into the river to bring it up to flood level. Canoes can be hired here from the Kilcullen Canoe & Outdoor Pursuits Club (☎ 045-81240) in Kilcullen, 10 km (seven miles) south-west of Naas.

CELBRIDGE
Celbridge, a plain little village on the River Liffey, 6.5 km (four miles) south-east of Maynooth, is the home of the magnificent Palladian Castletown House.

Castletown House
This huge Irish mansion, with its tree-lined avenue from the village, is said to be the largest private house in Ireland. It was built between 1722 and 1732 for William Conolly, who started life as the son of a pub owner and rose to become the speaker of the Irish House of Commons. Castletown House was no small undertaking and Conolly financed it from the fortune he made as a land agent in the chaotic aftermath to the Battle of the Boyne.

Castletown was designed by Alessandro Galilei, and continued by Edward Lovett Pearce (creator of the Bank of Ireland building on College Green Dublin), who oversaw the building of the two sweeping columned wings. The house remained in the Conolly family until its 1965 takeover by the Irish Georgian Society; currently it is being run by the voluntary Castletown Foundation.

Many of Castletown's magnificent rooms were decorated well after the building had been finished. Lady Louisa, great-granddaughter of Charles II and wife of William Conolly's grandnephew Tom, took a particular interest in the finer details. The Francini brothers from Italy did the plasterwork in the hall adjacent to the main hall, and their magnificent work continues up the main staircase.

Scattered throughout are paintings from Joshua Reynolds and Nathaniel Hone. Off the upstairs landing is a glass case containing stuffed hedgehogs and stoats which are displayed in an absurd classroom scenario, holding books at their desks.

Castletown has two associated follies, commissioned by William Conolly's wife, Katherine, to provide employment for the poor. The **Obelisk** was designed by Richard Castle and can be seen from the Long Gallery at the back of the house. Built in 1740, it consists of a series of arches, piled one upon another and topped by an obelisk reaching 40 metres (125 feet) in height. The Conolly family used it for picnics.

The other folly, the even more curious **Wonderful Barn**, is off to the north-east on private property just outside Leixlip and dates from 1743. It is made up of four domes mounted one on top of another and scaled by a spiral staircase.

Castletown House (☎ 01-628 8252) is open every day from April to October and on Sundays from November to March. Admission is IR£2.50 (students IR£2). At weekends there is a coffee shop in the basement. You can picnic on the lawn or take a stroll down to the Liffey from the car park. Plans are afoot for the Irish Government to take over the house in 1994 and spend IR£3 million to transform it into a national showpiece.

Coming from Dublin on the N4, turn left just before the Spa Hotel in Lucan. Dublin bus Nos 67 or 67A to Celbridge will drop you off at the gate.

Places to Stay
One km out of Celbridge on the Dublin Rd

Green Acres (☎ 01-6271163) has rooms at IR£13 to IR£15 per person. *Mrs Johnson's* B&B on Hazel Arch Rd costs IR£13. *Setanta House* (☎ 01-6271111) in Celbridge is an elegant, old, family-run hotel; the cost is IR£30 to IR£35 per person.

Places to Eat
Connolly's Restaurant near the church is a pleasant place serving light meals. For good pub food try the *Castletown Inn* which is one km out of town on the Maynooth road. The latter has Irish music nights on Wednesdays and Fridays.

Michelangelo Italian Restaurant (☎ 01-6242086) near the gates to Castletown House is about as upmarket as Italian restaurants go. Dinner will cost from IR£18. It's closed Sundays and Mondays.

Getting There & Away
Bus Nos 67 and 67A go from Dublin to Celbridge, departing every 40 minutes.

BODENSTOWN
In the Bodenstown churchyard is the last resting place of Theobald Wolfe Tone (1763-98), a leader in the 1798 Rising. He committed suicide in prison in Dublin, after he was captured during an attempted French invasion.

To get there take the Naas road out of Clane and turn left after three km (two miles).

OUGHTERARD
One km north of the village of Kill is Oughterard, with the remains of a 10th-century round tower and church. Even those who have no interest in ecclesiastical monuments might like to know that here lies Arthur Guinness, a man who needs no introduction.

RATHANGAN
The sleepy Victorian village of Rathangan, surrounded by the Bog of Allen, is on the Grand Canal 20 km (13 miles) west of Naas but well off the beaten track. There is good

coarse fishing; for information and boat hire contact Mr J Conway (☎ 045-24331).

Peatland World
If you are interested in the finer aspects of bogs, nine km (six miles) north-east of Rathangan in a converted farm in Lullymore is Peatland World (☎ 045-60133), an interpretive centre dealing with every aspect of Ireland's bogs. They have displays covering flora, fauna, fuel and archaeological finds, as well as a video presentation and trails through parts of the bog. It's open on weekdays 9.30 am to 4 pm, and 2 to 6 pm on weekends; admission is IR£2 (students IR£1.50).

Places to Stay
Carasli Caravan & Camping Park (☎ 045-24331) on the outskirts of Rathangan charge IR£4 per tent and 50p per occupant. The entrance is beside the Jet filling station. They rent caravans for IR£98 a week and have free fishing for tench, roach and bream behind the park on the River Barrow.

Milorka (☎ 045-24544) is one km along the Portarlington road in Kilnantogue. The excellent rooms cost IR£14 B&B per person and evening meals are available.

Places to Eat
The *Burrow* with stone, timber and the remains of a Morris Minor inside is probably the most popular of the seven pubs in Rathangan and has Irish music on Wednesdays. It also has the best pub food, although *Dillon's Bar* and the *Village Pump* are worth trying.

Getting There & Away
On Tuesdays and Thursdays only there is a single bus service between Rathangan and Busáras Dublin, via Robertstown, Clane, Sallins and Naas. The bus leaves Rathangan at 9.30 am and leaves Dublin on the return journey at 4.25 pm. For details contact Bus Éireann (☎ 01-366111).

BOG OF ALLEN
The Bog of Allen is Ireland's best known

raised bog, a huge expanse of peat that once covered a large part of the midlands. The bog stretches like a large brown desert through three counties – Offaly, Laois and Kildare – but like other raised bogs it's rapidly being turned into potting compost and fuel.

ROBERTSTOWN

The tiny hamlet of Robertstown might have had all passing traffic diverted for the past 100 years. It's 12 km (eight miles) north-west of Naas, and its old buildings overlook the Grand Canal, which is spanned by a neat stone bridge.

The village has grown and declined in parallel with the canal. On summer Sundays, the refurbished barge sitting out the front of the cheerily red canal hotel offers short cruises (☎ 045-60808). The countryside around, with its rich farmland, narrow lanes and small stone bridges, is delightful in summer.

Getting There & Away

On Tuesdays and Thursdays a single Dublin to Rathangan bus passes through Roberts-town. Contact Bus Éireann (☎ 01-366111) for details.

NAAS

Kildare's county town of Naas (pronounced 'Nace') is about 27 km (17 miles) west of Dublin. The main highway to Cork, Kerry and Limerick now bypasses it to the north. There is a scenic route from Naas to Wicklow, via Blessington, through the Sally Gap and over the Wicklow Mountains.

Jigginstown House

Naas's only ruin of note is Jigginstown House, one km out on the N7 to Kildare Town. It was begun by Thomas Wentworth, Earl of Strafford, and Lord Deputy of Ireland from 1632 to 1641, and it would have been one of the largest brick buildings in Ireland if he hadn't lost his head – literally. It was never finished.

Activities

Horse Racing Punchestown Racecourse (☎ 045-97704) is a famous and beautifully situated steeplechase track, three km (two miles) south of Naas. Their season runs from October to April and the highlight is the National Hunt festival in late April.

During the summer there are meetings every week or two at Naas Racecourse (☎ 045-97391). More a local affair than the Curragh or Punchestown, it's just as enjoyable.

Motor Racing Mondello Park (☎ 045-60200), Ireland's premier racing and rally circuit, is seven km (four miles) to the north-west of Naas, signposted off the N7 motorway. For around IR£70 you can have a lesson in a single-seater Formula Vee racing car with the Racing & Rally School.

Getting There & Away

Naas is well served by buses. There are hourly double-deckers to Dublin, as well as intercity services to Limerick, Kilkenny, Waterford, Clonmel, Portlaoise, Kildare and Newbridge. The bus stop is outside the Pantry at 55 Main St; for bus times, check with them or ring ☎ 01-366111.

THE CURRAGH

The town of Newbridge is the gateway to the Curragh, at around 20 sq km one of the largest pieces of unfenced fertile land in the country and home to the Curragh Racetrack (☎ 045-41205) and a large military training barracks (☎ 045-41301). The racetrack is Ireland's best known and hosts the Irish Derby in June, the Irish 1000 and 2000 Guineas in May, the Irish Oaks in July and the St Leger in September. The Curragh's wide open spaces are used extensively by trainers to exercise their thoroughbred charges. A new highway now runs through the Curragh between Newbridge and Kildare.

THE HILL OF ALLEN

The Hill of Allen rises above the flatlands of Kildare, which as you travel north or west change from green to the desolate brown of the Bog of Allen. Nine km (five miles) north-west of Newbridge and marked today by a folly, the hill has been a strategic spot through the centuries with its commanding views in all directions. The Iron Age fortifications are said to mark the home of Fionn McCumhaill, the leader of the Fianna, a mythical band of warriors who feature in many tales of ancient Ireland.

KILDARE TOWN

Kildare's busy little square is a pleasant change from the county's other nondescript urban centres. The stone building in the centre of the square would be a strong candidate for the title of most attractive public toilet in the country. Kildare is a cathedral and market town and is 24 km (15 miles) south-west of Naas.

Information

The county's main tourist office (☎ 045-22696) is in the Market House in the square. It's open between May and September from 10 am to 6 pm, Monday to Saturday, and closed for lunch from 1 to 2 pm.

St Brigid's Cathedral

St Brigid, one of the country's best loved saints, is remembered by St Brigid's Cross, a simply constructed four-pointed cross woven from reeds and found today in many homes and gift shops. In the 6th century she founded a monastery here, unusual in that it was shared by nuns and monks, who were separated only by screens in church. A fire was kept burning perpetually in a fire temple, looked after by nuns and out of bounds to males, tended only by virgins over the age of 30. It lasted until the 16th-century dissolution of the monasteries. The restored fire pit can be seen in the grounds of the 13th-century Protestant St Brigid's Cathedral, whose solid presence looms over the square.

Round Tower

In the cathedral grounds is a 10th-century round tower, Ireland's second highest, which for IR£1 can be climbed from 10 am to 1 pm Monday to Saturday or between 2 and 5 pm any day. The top has been replaced with an unusual Norman battlement which allows access to the outside roof but has ruined the tower's profile.

The National Stud

More than any other county, Kildare is synonomous with the multimillion-pound bloodstock industry, and Kildare Town is twinned with another famous horse-breeding centre, Lexington-Fayette in Kentucky, USA. The National Stud (☎ 045-21251) is just one km south of the centre and was set up in 1900 by Colonel Hall Walker, then given to the crown in 1915, in return for which he became Lord Wavertree. He must have wanted the title badly. He had been remarkably successful with his horses, although his breeding and training techniques fell somewhere outside the everyday. On the birth of each foal, he devised a horoscope based on the position of the stars and planets and from this decided whether to keep it or not.

The stud remained in the hands of the British until 1943 when they in turn passed it on to the Irish Government. Today its purpose is to breed high-quality stallions who will mate with approved mares from Ireland's private studs. The intention is to improve the overall quality of Irish bloodstocks.

For IR£4 (students IR£3, children IR£2) for entry to both the stud and the Japanese gardens, visitors are free to wander around the impossibly tidy compound, through the various stables, paddocks and meadows, or pop into the foaling unit where you can watch a video of the birth of a foal. The small but interesting horse museum examines the role horses have played in Irish life over the years and includes the skeleton of Arkle. If there was a saint among Irish horses, Arkle was it. He was the object of national adoration and after his death in 1968 the country went into mourning. The stud is open Easter Sunday to 31 October, 10.30 am to 5 pm Monday to Friday, to 6 pm Saturday, 2 to 6 pm Sunday.

Adjacent to the stud, the **Japanese Gardens** (☎ 045-21617) were created for

Lord Wavertree between 1906 and 1910. He went to Japan to bring back two superb gardeners, Tasa Eida and his son Minoru, as overseers and they employed 40 local men for the four years it took to complete the work. They were planted to symbolise the Life of Man, but you need a tour guide or leaflet to follow the cycle. The trees, paths and ponds are all symbolic. There is a large Visitor's Centre with a coffee shop and a selection of expensive bonsai trees for sale.

Places to Stay

In Maddenstown, beyond the entrance to the Japanese Gardens, *Catherine Singleton's B&B* (☎ 045-21964) has three rooms at IR£15/27 for singles/doubles. Alternatively *St Mary's House* (☎ 045-21243) is nearby, charging IR£16/26.

Nearer town, *Freemont* (☎ 045-21604) is just south of the town square on the Tully road and charges IR£16 per person. The *Lord Edward Guesthouse* (☎ 045-22389) is part of the Silken Thomas pub on the square. *Rossa House* (☎ 045-21210) is a good guesthouse just on the Dublin edge of town which charges IR£13 to IR£15 sharing or IR£16 to IR£17 single.

Places to Eat

Silken Thomas (☎ 045-22232), a vast old-world bar, takes up one corner of the square and has a restaurant offering good lunches for IR£5 to IR£6 and dinner for IR£10 or more, as well as sandwiches and pub food. *Boland's Pub* (☎ 045-21263) on the opposite corner has good light snacks. The *Kingsland Chinese Restaurant* (☎ 045-21112), in the centre of town, isn't bad. *Downalong* (☎ 045-22288) is an attractive café and craft shop near the National Stud entrance and offers light meals for around IR£4.

Getting There & Away

Kildare is on the main Dublin to Waterford, Tralee, Galway and Cork lines with many trains daily. For details ring ☎ 01-366222. Just about every main road to the west passes through Kildare and Bus Éireann have plenty of express coaches from the Busáras (☎ 01-366111) in Dublin.

NAAS TO CARLOW

The 48-km stretch of the N9 between Naas and Carlow offers a number of interesting side trips.

Getting There & Away

The Naas to Carlow road is well served by coaches on the Dublin to Carlow, Clonmel and Kilkenny routes. Some of these buses will drop you off at Kilcullen, Ballitore, Moone, Castledermot and Athy, though you should check beforehand because some buses go straight through to Athy or Carlow. On the way to Kilkenny they pass through Leighlinbridge and Castlecomer. Bus Éireann (☎ 01-366111) has two or three buses daily and Kavanagh's (☎ 0503-43081) private bus company offers a similar service.

Kilcullen

The tiny village of Kilcullen is on the River Liffey, 12 km (eight miles) east of Kildare Town. Nearby at **Old Kilcullen**, the scant remains of a high cross and round tower are all that is left of an early Christian settlement.

On the edge of the Curragh, four km (two miles) north-west of Kilcullen on the west side of the L19, **Donnelly's Hollow** was the scene of numerous victories of Dan Donnelly (1788-1820), Ireland's greatest bare-knuckle fighter of the last century. It's said he had a reach so long that he could touch his knees without stooping, and that a fight here attracted 20,000 spectators. An obelisk at the centre of the deep hollow details his glorious career. His 'footprints' lead up the slope from the centre of the hollow.

Back in Kilcullen his mummified arm can be seen in the **Hideout Bar** (☎ 045-81232), a famous and wildly eccentric pub. The arm arrived here after Donnelly's grave was robbed.

Beginners are welcome at **Golden Falls Waterski Centre** in Ballymore Eustace on the Wicklow border not far from Kilcullen, open June to September. Contact Harry

Bridges (☎ 045-64270) for more information.

Ballitore & Timolin

At Ballitore the **Crookstown heritage centre** (☎ 0507-23222) has a functioning water mill and a display covering milling and baking through the centuries (entry IR£2). It also has a coffee shop. Ballitore was originally settled in the 18th century by Quakers, and their influence can be seen throughout the area in the finely built stone courtyards, buildings and graveyards. One of the settlers was an ancestor of Ernest Shackleton, the Antarctic explorer, who was born nearby in Kilkea House.

The **Quaker Museum** (☎ 045-31109) is now open to the public in the old schoolhouse where Edmund Burke, the political philosopher, studied as a pupil. Two km west is the **Rath of Mullaghmast**, an Iron Age hill fort where Daniel O'Connell, champion of Catholic Emancipation, held one of his 'monster meetings' in 1843.

Three km south of Ballitore and just north of Moone, the village of Timolin is home to the the **Irish Pewter Mill & Craft Centre** (☎ 0507-24164).

Moone

The barely noticeable village of Moone is just south of Ballitore and 29 km (18 miles) south-west of Naas. One km west in an early Christian monastic churchyard is the magnificent **Moone High Cross**. This 8th or 9th-century masterpiece is slender and at six metres remarkably tall. The numerous crisply carved panels display biblical scenes including the Loaves & Fishes, the Flight into Egypt and a wonderful representation of the Twelve Apostles. Unfortunately, an ugly wire fence has been erected around the cross to protect it.

Kilkea Castle

This 12th-century castle is five km (three miles) north-west of Castledermot and was once the second home of the Maynooth Fitzgeralds. The castle grounds are supposed to be haunted by the son of Silken Thomas,

Gerald the Wizard Earl, who rises every seven years from the Rath of Mullaghmast to free Ireland from its enemies. This is a neat trick as the Wizard Earl was buried in London. A great deal of reconstruction and restoration was carried out on the castle in the 19th century.

Although the castle is now a very exclusive hotel you can still have a drink in the bar and pick up a booklet on the building's history. Among its oddities is an Evil Eye Stone set high up on the exterior wall at the back of the castle. Thought to date from the 13th or 14th century, this is a depiction of various half-human, animal and birdlike figures engaging in some rather unseemly erotic behaviour. The castle has formal gardens and a forest park.

Castledermot

Castledermot's ruined Franciscan friary is right by the road at the south end of town on Abbey St. The friary dates from the mid-13th century and the key is available from the adjacent cottage.

A little farther north on Main St and back from the road is a churchyard, the site of a monastery founded originally by St Diarmuid in 812 AD. There are two fine 9th or 10th-century high crosses beside the remains of a round tower 20 metres high and a 12th-century Romanesque church doorway. The round tower has a medieval battlement added on top.

Places to Stay & Eat

Woodcourte (☎ 0507-24167) in Timolin has a tennis court, runs arts & crafts weekends and costs IR£12 to IR£14 for B&B. Take the turn beside the Sportsman Inn in Timolin and the house is by the Irish Pewter Mill. The 18th-century *Moone High Cross Inn* (tel-045-24112) is a delightful bar about 100 metres west of the main road, one km south of Moone village. It does plain but hefty pub food including a great Irish stew.

Kilkea Castle (☎ 0503-45156) was completely restored in the 19th century and is now a luxury hotel costing IR£65 to IR£95 B&B. The small and intimate *Doyle's*

Schoolhouse Inn (☎ 0503-44282) in Castledermot has an unusual menu and is consistently rated as one of the best restaurants in the county. Dinner will cost from IR£18 and reservations are essential. The old stone *Kilkea Lodge* (☎ 0503-45112) has big open fires. It's more expensive than most B&Bs at IR£23 a night.

ATHY

Athy (pronounced 'A-thigh'), at the junction of the River Barrow and the Grand Canal, has the feel of a genuine country town, with a nice but somewhat dilapidated old square. A 15th-century tower built by the earls of Kildare is now a private house overlooking the River Barrow.

There is coarse, salmon and trout fishing on the Grand Canal and the Barrow. For information check with Kane's pub (☎ 0507-31434). The Athy Golf Club (☎ 0507-31729) has a nine-hole course. Six km (four miles) north-east on the road to Naas is the 18-metre (55-foot) **Ardscull Motte**, one of the largest of these defensive structures to be built by the Normans.

Places to Stay & Eat

Forest Farm (☎ 0507-31231) is a small country farmhouse five km (three miles) out of Athy on the Dublin road, and *Ballindrum Farm* (☎ 0507-26294) is in Ballindrum. Both charge IR£13 per person.

The *Blackboard* (☎ 0507-38748) is a straightforward restaurant/snack bar just off the square with main courses for IR£4 to IR£5. For cheap and cheerful bar food, try the *Castle Inn* or the *Duke of Leinster* pubs. The *Duck Press Restaurant* (☎ 0507-38952) is good for lunch or dinner.

Tonlegee House (☎ 0507-31473), out of town on the Kilkenny road, is an excellent restaurant but expensive at about IR£20. There are guest rooms upstairs.

Getting There & Away

Buses on the Naas to Carlow road, of which there are a number, stop at Athy, following the Dublin to Carlow, Clonmel and Kilkenny routes. Contact Bus Éireann (☎ 01-366111) for details.

County Carlow

Carlow, the second smallest Irish county, has the scenic Blackstairs Mountains and sections of the rivers Barrow and Slaney, with quietly picturesque villages such as Rathvilly, Leighlinbridge and Borris. The Dublin to Carlow Town route via south-west Wicklow runs through some wild and lightly populated country.

The rest of Carlow is mainly undulating farmland, where you will often see sugarbeet piled by the roadside awaiting collection. Browne's Hill Dolmen is the county's most interesting archaeological feature and is just outside Carlow Town.

HISTORY

Despite its proximity to the Pale, for a long time Carlow remained a hotbed of Irish patriotism, thanks mainly to the fearless MacMurrough Kavanaghs, ancient kings of Leinster. They dominated the region from the 13th century up to Cromwellian times.

One chief in particular, Art Óg, based in Borris, posed such a threat to the Pale that in 1394 King Richard II came over from England to subdue him with a force of 10,000 men. After fierce fighting, Art Óg capitulated, but no sooner had a treaty been agreed and Richard hightailed it back to London, than Art Óg along with the Ulster O'Neills turned on the occupying English army and savaged them. At the pivotal Battle of Kellistown in 1398, Roger Mortimer, next in line to the throne after his cousin King Richard, was killed. In 1399, Richard returned, bent on revenge.

This time Art Óg was ready and gave Richard a miserable time, defeating him again and again. Meanwhile back in London, trouble was brewing for Richard and he was overthrown and killed on his return. The spirit of resistance stayed alive in County Carlow and more than 600 rebels died in

Carlow in the 1798 Rising. The local rebel leader was Father John Murphy, immortalised in the song *Boulavogue*, who was captured and executed in Tullow.

CARLOW TOWN

Carlow was a frontier town for many centuries due to its strategic location on the River Barrow, on the border with the Pale. Today, it's a busy market and industrial centre serving a large rural area. The town itself is unremarkable except for Browne's Hill Dolmen on the outskirts. Carlow was the first town outside Dublin to have electric street lighting, from power generated downstream at Milford. Railway pioneer William Dargan, who founded the National Gallery in Dublin, was born here.

History

After the Normans arrived in Ireland, a motte and bailey fort was erected here in 1180, and shortly afterwards succeeded by Carlow Castle, built by William Marshall, Strongbow's successor in the region. A wall was built to protect Carlow Town in 1361.

During Cromwell's tour of the country, the town surrendered to his son-in-law Ireton in 1650.

In 1798 on Tullow St, over 600 Irish rebels were killed in the bloodiest fighting of the rising. A Celtic high cross marks the Croppie Grave, in Graiguecullen gravel pits just over the river, where most were buried in quicklime.

Information

Dublin St is the city's principal north-south axis, and Tullow St is the main shopping street. The tourist office (☎ 0503-31554), in Traynor House on College St just across from the cathedral, is open on Monday to Friday from 9.30 am to 5.30 pm and on Saturday from 10 am to 6 pm, but closed at lunch times. The post office is just south of the town centre on the corner of Kennedy Ave and Dublin St.

Carlow Castle

Officials at Carlow Castle once had to be paid danger money to live here among the native Irish. The castle survived Cromwell's attentions and would be largely intact if a Dr Middleton had not decided to turn it into an asylum and dynamited it in 1814; the mighty four-walled castle was reduced to a single wall flanked by two towers. Enquire at the Corcoran's Mineral Waters factory on Castle Hill about access to what's left.

Courthouse

It's said that the plans for Carlow and Cork courthouses got mixed up, so this little town ended up with William Morrison's splendid 1830 building, based on the Parthenon in Athens, while Cork had to make do with a less impressive design. The cannons beside the steps are from the Crimean War.

Cathedral of the Assumption

Just down College St from the courthouse, the 1833 cathedral has an elaborately carved pulpit and some fine stained-glass windows. John Hogan's statue of Bishop Doyle, better known as JKL (James of Kildare & Leighin) for his work as a supporter of Catholic Emancipation, includes a woman who represents Ireland, rising up against her oppressors.

County Museum

The small county museum is in the town hall off the Haymarket and is open during the summer from 2.30 to 5.30 pm daily.

Getting There & Away

Train The railway station (☎ 0503-31633) is on Railway St in the north-east of town. Carlow is on the Dublin to Waterford/Kilkenny line with at least three trains daily in each direction and two on Sundays.

Bus Bus Éireann (☎ 01-366111) buses leave from Dean's Newsagency on Barrack St with daily services to Dublin, Waterford, Kilkenny and Clonmel. Kavanagh's (☎ 0503-43081) private bus service, Rapid Express, has four or five buses daily to Dublin and Waterford. You catch them at Inn's Shop (☎ 0503-43081) on Barrack St south of the post office.

Getting Around

A E Coleman (☎ 0503-31273) on Dublin St is a Raleigh dealer with bikes for IR£7 a day or IR£30 a week. Contact Carlow Cab Service (☎ 0503-32404) for taxis. Carlow Rowing Club (☎ 0503-42798) on the quay hire boats for trips on the River Barrow.

AROUND CARLOW TOWN

Browne's Hill Dolmen

This 5000-year-old monster is believed to have the largest capstone in Europe, weighing in at over 100 tonnes. The structure when completed would have been covered with a mound of earth. The dolmen is three km (two miles) east of town on the R726 Hacketstown road; a path leads around the field to the dolmen.

Killeshin Church

Dating from the 11th century, this small building is unremarkable except for a richly carved stone doorway of Hiberno-Romanesque design. Killeshin is just inside County Laois, five km (three miles) west of Carlow on the Abbeyleix road.

Milford

One of the nicer drives to the south is via Milford on the minor road that follows the River Barrow valley. The old mill at Milford was the site of the turbine which first powered Carlow Town's electric street lighting in the 1890s. John Alexander, the present owner, still runs a turbine here and supplies electricity to the ESB – the Electricity Supply Board. There's good fishing here.

LEIGHLINBRIDGE

Leighlinbridge, just off the main Kilkenny road, 13 km (eight miles) south-west of Carlow Town, has one of Ireland's first Norman castles. The rather uninspiring **Black Castle** dates from 1181 and overlooks the first bridge to be built over the River Barrow. This pleasant little village also produced Captain Myles Kehoe, the last of General Custer's men left alive at the Battle of Little Big Horn in Montana, USA.

Three km (two miles) west is **Old**

Leighlin, the site of a 6th-century monastic settlement founded by St Laserian. There is a small cathedral with some finely carved stonework and a Romanesque doorway – nowhere near as good as the one in Killeshin, however.

Places to Stay

Nevin's (☎ 0503-21202) is right next door to the Lord Bagenal Inn. The owner, Martin Nevin, is a teacher with a great interest in local history, and the simple rooms cost IR£12 per person. If they are full try the similarly priced *Brennan's* (☎ 0503-21850), almost two km south of town on the Tullow road.

In Milford, halfway between Carlow Town and Leighlinbridge, *Dermody's Guesthouse* (☎ 0503-46276) is right by the River Barrow and has rooms for IR£11 or IR£12 per person.

Places to Eat

The choice of restaurants outside Carlow Town is limited. The popular *Lord Bagenal Inn* (☎ 0503-21668) on Leighlinbridge's main street has a restaurant and a bar serving pub food. It's an inviting place with a big open fire, excellent steaks and fish and good vegetarian food. Dinner will cost from IR£15. The restaurant is open Tuesday to Saturday, 6 to 10.30 pm and on Sunday until 9 pm.

Getting There & Away

There are plenty of buses passing through daily, on the Dublin to Carlow and Kilkenny route. See the Getting There & Away section under Naas to Carlow for details.

BORRIS

The Georgian village of Borris is 16 km (10 miles) farther south and is overlooked by a disused railway viaduct with 16 arches. **Borris House** is the residence of the MacMurrough Kavanaghs, ancestors of the ancient Kings of Leinster and is still in the family's possession, Andrew MacMurrough Kavanagh being the present occupant.

A most remarkable MacMurrough

Kavanagh was Arthur (1831-89), who was born with only rudimentary limbs yet learned to ride and shoot and later became an MP. The castle is still a private residence and only open to viewing by appointment. The entrance is at the north end of town by Cody's pub.

Borris is a starting point for the Mt Leinster walk or scenic drive and is also on the South Leinster Way. To get to Mt Leinster take the Rahanna road to Kiledmund and head up the mountain. It takes a good two hours on foot or 20 minutes by car. Alternatively, there is a lovely 10-km (six-mile) walk along a towpath beside the River Barrow to Graiguenamanagh, a picturesque little village just inside County Kilkenny.

Places to Stay & Eat

Breen's (☎ 0503-73231) on Church St in Borris has rooms at IR£10 to IR£12 per person. Halfway between Borris and Bagenalstown, the *Lorum Old Rectory* (☎ 0503-75282) is overlooked by the Blackstairs Mountains and charges IR£18, with excellent dinners at IR£15.

The *Green Drake Pub & Restaurant* (☎ 0503-73116) has fairly good pub food and a restaurant where dinner will cost around IR£12.

Entertainment

The popular *Cody's* pub, at the north end of Main St, usually has Irish music on Monday nights and bands at weekends, while the *Green Drake* pub has Irish music on Wednesdays. *O'Shea's* is on Main St too, and is also popular.

Getting There & Away

Kavanagh's (☎ 0503-40351) private bus company includes Borris in their single daily New Ross to Dublin service. Foley's (☎ 0503-24641) private buses stop at Borris on their twice daily route between Graiguenamanagh and Kilkenny. Neither of these services operates on Sunday.

MT LEINSTER

Mt Leinster at 796 metres (2610 ft) has some

of the finest hang-gliding in the country and you will find people there on most weekends during the summer. It's also worth the hike for the panoramic views over Carlow, Wexford and Wicklow. To get there follow the Mt Leinster Scenic Drive signposts 13 km (eight miles) towards Bunclody in Wexford. Just south of Mt Leinster, the Sculleoge Gap is a scenic route between Graiguenamanagh and Kiltealy in Wexford.

ST MULLINS

A quiet village on the River Barrow, St Mullins has numerous ecclesiastical ruins and is 12 km (seven miles) south of Borris. The scant remains of a round tower, various abbeys and chapels were all part of St Moling's original 7th-century monastery. St Moling's Well is by the stream, and a number of people who died during the 1798 Rising were buried in the graveyard, including some who were executed for manufacturing pikes, the rebels' favourite (but unfortunately rather ineffective) weapon. Across the road from the graveyard the grass-covered mound is a good example of a small Anglo-Norman motte.

For somewhere to stay, trythe early Georgian *Sherwood Park House* (☎ 0503-59117) is in Kilbride just off the N80, about halfway between Ballon and Kildavin. B&B costs IR£16 to IR£18; dinner is IR£12.

There is no public transport to St Mullins.

TULLOW

Tullow is a well-known angling town on the River Slaney. Father John Murphy, a local leader of the 1798 Rising, was captured and executed in the Market Square on 2 July 1798. A memorial to him stands in the town centre. Tullow Museum, beside the town bridge, is open on Sunday and Wednesday afternoons.

Five km (three miles) due east of Tullow is the Iron Age ring fort of **Rathgall**. The fort is protected by three outer ring walls, which are overgrown. The final wall is still in good condition, though somewhat lower nowadays. It is said that Rathgall is the burial site of the kings of Leinster.

Tullow is on Bus Éireann's (☎ 01-366111) Dublin to Waterford route, which stops at Tullow, Enniscorthy and New Ross. There are two or three buses daily in each direction.

THE SOUTH LEINSTER WAY

Just south-west of Clonegal, on the north slopes of Mt Leinster is the tiny village of Kildavin, the starting point of the South Leinster Way. This walking trail of 95 km (60 miles) through Carlow and Kilkenny follows remote mountain roads and river towpaths through Borris, Graiguenamanagh, Inistioge, Mullinavat, Piltown and on to the finishing post at Carrick-on-Suir. The route is marked so you should have no difficulty finding your way. For further information ask at a tourist office for the Bord Fáilte Information Sheet No 26D which has all the details on routes and accommodation.

Carlow Town and St Mullins are also on the Kildare Trails on the Barrow Towpath. This trail intersects the South Leinster Way at Graiguenamanagh, so if you're a strict trail-walker you can divert onto this one and head north into Kildare. This trail is covered by Bord Fáilte Information Sheet No 26E (Kildare Trails).

County Laois

Laois, pronounced 'Leash', is 1½ hours drive south-west of Dublin and is as far inland as counties get in Ireland. It's the only inland county surrounded on all sides by neighbours none of whom touch the coast either. For most visitors Laois is simply somewhere you pass through en route to Limerick or Cork. It's a fairly uninteresting landscape of raised bogs and poor farms, but there are some pleasant country towns and the unspoilt Slieve Bloom Mountains.

HISTORY

Most of Laois is underlain by carboniferous limestone deposited some 330 million years ago. The grey rock breaks through the soil and forms low hills in the east of the county.

Some of these, such as Lugacurran and Dunamase, have fortifications dating back to the Iron Age, although the first significant human traces are from the Bronze Age. While no site is of special significance, various burial places and artefacts have been uncovered over the years.

Considering the county's relative proximity to Dublin, Irish families such as the O'Mores, O'Dunnes and Dempseys controlled the county for a remarkable length of time. There were interruptions from the Normans in the 12th and 13th centuries but their influence was only really weakened by the arrival of plantation settlers from England and Scotland in the mid-16th century.

Much of present-day Laois owes its shape to these plantations, the first in Ireland. It was called Queen's County after Queen Mary I, and Portlaoise was given the name Maryborough, while neighbouring Offaly was known as King's County. Many of the towns were developed by Quaker settlers. Laois only really became safe for the settlers when the O'More and Fitzpatrick clans were shifted to Kerry in the 17th century, shortly before Cromwell came along to finish the job. Today Laois has one of the highest Protestant to Catholic ratios in the South.

PORTLAOISE

Although founded by the O'Mores just before the Plantation, Portlaoise is mostly modern, and only the Courthouse by Richard Morrison on the corner of Main and Church Sts is of note. To the west are the Slieve Blooms, while to the east is the only historic site of interest worth a special detour, the Rock of Dunamase on the Stradbally road.

Bristling with wire fencing at the east end of town is the town's 1830 prison. It's the Republic of Ireland's maximum security jail.

The old centre of the town has little charm and been recently bypassed by a loop to the south. The tourist office (☎ 0502-21178) is beside the by-pass on James Fintan Lawlor Ave and is open all year round from 10 am to 6 pm, closed at lunch time.

Getting There & Away

Buses The bus stop in Portlaoise is at Egan's Hostelry on Lower Square at the Dublin end of town. For information on bus times, contact the tourist office.

Portlaoise is on one of the busiest main roads in the country with a large number of daily buses passing between Dublin and Cashel, Cork, Limerick and Kerry. It is also on a Waterford, Kilkenny, Carlow, Athlone and Longford route. Try Bus Éireann, or JJ Kavanagh's private bus company (☎ 056-31106).

Train Portlaoise train station (☎ 0502-21303) is on Railway St, about five minutes' walk from the town centre. Portlaoise is on the main railway line from Dublin to Tipperary, Cork, Limerick and Kerry and is serviced by numerous daily trains.

THE ROCK OF DUNAMASE

Six km (four miles) along the Stradbally road, this fractured limestone hill is covered with the remains of fortifications. It's only 65 metres high, but the surrounding countryside is so flat that the summit gives a fine view in all directions. You can see the round tower at Timahoe to the south and the cooling tower of Portarlington power station to the north-west.

The remains include an Iron Age ring fort and a 12th or 13th-century keep. The slopes of Dunamase can be treacherous, particularly on the north side, and these natural barriers would have complicated any assault on its defenders. First sacked by the Vikings in the 840s, Dunamase was later given away by Dermot MacMurrough, King of Leinster, as part of his daughter Aoife's dowry when she married Strongbow, the Norman invader of Ireland. Dunamase was then reinforced by William Marshall, Strongbow's successor, who built three baileys on the spot.

The local clan, the O'Mores, captured the rock from the English near the end of the 15th century and held it until it was retaken 150 years later in 1641, by Charles Coote. He was a leading Parliamentarian and one of Cromwell's most able leaders in Ireland.

Recaptured five years later by Catholic forces, it was finally taken and wrecked by Cromwell's henchmen Reynolds and Hewson in 1650.

Hewson gave his name to the hill to the south-west, which has the ruined 9th-century church of Dysert, and the earth embankments 500 metres to the east are known as Cromwell's lines, although they are in fact the remains of a much older two-ringed fort.

The main ruins consist of a badly shattered 13th-century castle on the highest point (best seen from the north side) surrounded by an outer wall of which little remains. You enter the complex through the twin-towered gate structure, which leads to the outer bailey and fortified courtyard to the south-east.

J J Kavanagh's bus service (☎ 056-31106) has two daily buses from Portlaoise to Carlow which pass by the rock. It's a good hour's walk from the town centre.

EMO COURT DEMESNE

Emo Court was the county seat of the 1st earl of Portarlington and is 13 km (eight miles) from Portlaoise, signposted off the main road to Dublin. The rather unusual house with its prominent green dome was designed by James Gandon (architect of Dublin's Customs House) and has recently been renovated after serving as a Jesuit novitiate for many years. The estate has long walks winding through forests and by Emo Lake, and is littered with Greek statues.

The house is now a private residence and is only open to the public from 2 to 6 pm on Mondays between April and October. For information ring ☎ 0502-26110; admission is IR£2.50. The gardens are open 10.30 am to 5.30 pm daily all year round and admission is IR£2, payable to a gardener hanging around the car park. From the Emo village gate it is a two-km walk to the house.

South of the village off the main Portlaoise road is **Coolbanagher Church**, also designed by Gandon. This church was built by the 1st earl of Portarlington, to replace a thatched church which was destroyed in 1779, and it's simple Georgian architecture at its best. Inside is a 14th or 15th-century carved font.

Emo is just off the main Portlaoise to Dublin road, and there are daily buses in both directions.

STRADBALLY

The village of Stradbally, 10 km (seven miles) south-east of Portlaoise, was once a seat of the mighty O'More clan. Most of the present buildings date from the 17th century.

The O'Mores were the force behind the Franciscian friary which was established here in 1447. The family were the holders of 'The Book of Leinster', a manuscript compiled between 1151 and 1224 to record all the knowledge of Aéd Crúamthainn, a scribe to the high kings of Ireland. This book contained, among other things, vivid descriptions of the banqueting hall at Tara, the seat of the high kings, and is now to be found in the library at Trinity College, Dublin.

Stradbally Steam Museum

The museum (☎ 0502-252136) has a collection of fire engines, steam tractors and steam rollers, lovingly restored by the Irish Steam Preservation Society. Housed in a tightly packed warehouse the prize exhibits include a Merryweather horse-drawn fire engine from 1880.

The 1895 Guinness Brewery steam locomotive in the village is used for the odd day trip to Dublin. During the three-day Steam Rally in early August the 40 hectares of Cosby Hall are taken over with all types of steam-operated machines and vintage cars. The museum is open Sundays 2 to 6 pm.

Getting There & Away

J J Kavanagh's bus service (☎ 056-31106) has two daily buses from Portlaoise to Carlow via Stradbally. Stradbally is also on a daily Waterford to Longford Bus Éireann (☎ 01-366111) service which passes through Kilkenny, Carlow, Stradbally, Portlaoise and Athlone on its route.

PORTARLINGTON

There are still traces of Portarlington's former prosperity in many of its buildings. It grew under the influence of French Huguenot and German settlers introduced by Lord Arlington, who was granted tracts of land here after the 17th-century Cromwellian wars. Many of the finer 18th-century buildings are a result of the efforts of Henry Dawson, Earl of Portarlington, to improve the town. His family encouraged bankers and upmarket tradespeople like silversmiths to settle here. Unfortunately, many of their houses are now suffering from neglect.

The 1851 **St Paul's Church**, also known as the French Church, was built for the Huguenots, and some of their tombstones stand in one corner of the churchyard. The River Barrow kinks around the town on its journey east; stretches along the border with Kildare and Carlow are lovely.

The large cooling tower of the peat-fuelled **power station** is a landmark. Built in 1936, the power station was the first of its type.

Portarlington is on the main railway lines between Dublin and Galway, Limerick, Kerry and Cork, with numerous daily trains in both directions. For details contact Portlaoise railway station (☎ 0502-21303). There are no buses to Portarlington.

MOUNTMELLICK

Mountmellick is an an attractive if rather faded little market town with many Georgian houses, 10 km (six miles) north of Portlaoise on the Owenass River. Its fortunes rose with Quaker settlers who produced linen which was exported by barge on a branch of the Grand Canal which runs away to the east.

Mountmellick is on a daily Waterford to Longford Bus Éireann service which passes through Kilkenny, Carlow, Stradbally, Portlaoise and Athlone on its route. There is also a daily service to and from Dublin via Naas, Newbridge, Kildare and Portlaoise.

LEA CASTLE

On the banks of the River Barrow four km (two miles) east of Portarlington on the

Monasterevan road, this 13th-century ruin was the stronghold of Maurice Fitzgerald, 2nd baron of Offaly. It consists of a fairly intact towered keep with two outer walls running down to the Barrow and a twin-towered gatehouse. It was burned in 1315 by Edward Bruce, the brother of King Robert Bruce of Scotland. Edward came to Ireland at the invitation of Irish chieftains in 1315 to create trouble for the Anglo-Normans/ English. He hoped this would distract the English and lessen their pressure on his brother in Scotland.

Invited by a number of old Irish Ulster chieftains as part of the Gaelic revival and crowned high king of Ireland, Edward Bruce created a lot of trouble for the forces and colonisers loyal to England, until he was killed in 1318 at the Battle of Faughart near Dundalk. His remains are said to be buried in a churchyard at Faughart four km (2.5 miles) from Castleroche.

The castle was blown up by Cromwell's forces in 1650, fresh from their success at Dunamase. The castle stairways were filled with explosives to maximise the damage.

Much of the remains are now covered in ivy, and at the right time of the day, such as early morning or evening, the place is tranquil and evocative. Access to the castle is through a dilapidated farmyard half a km to the north off the main Dublin road.

MOUNTRATH & AROUND

Like so many other Irish settlements, Mountrath has associations with St Patrick and St Brigid, who are supposed to have established religious houses here, although there are no traces left today. Much of the town and surrounding land belonged to Sir Charles Coote, an ardent Parliamentarian and supporter of Cromwell during and after the Cromwellian wars in the 1640s. Mountrath's halcyon days were in the 17th and 18th centuries when the linen industry generated a fair amount of local wealth.

The town is 13 km (eight miles) south-west of Portlaoise and lies on the Mountrath River, a tributary of the Nore. The Slieve Bloom Mountains are only eight km (five miles) to the north-west.

St Fintan's Tree

Three km (two miles) east on the Portlaoise road, there is little left of Clonenagh, the site of the 6th-century monastery of St Fintan. St Fintan's Tree is a large sycamore with a water-filled groove in one of its lower branches which is said to never dry out. The tree has long been a place of pilgrimage and the many coins embedded in the trunk are offerings by pilgrims who attribute healing powers to the water. The ruined church on the opposite side of the road is unrelated.

Ballyfin House

Eight km (five miles) north of Mountrath off the Mountmellick road is Ballyfin House, built by Sir Charles Henry Coote in 1850 to the designs of Richard Morrison (better known for his courthouses). It has been described as the finest 19th-century house in Ireland, and is pleasantly sited overlooking a small lake in quiet, rolling countryside. Inside, it is well preserved, and some of the ornamentation is completely over the top. The dining room is also known as the 'gold room', and someone ran amok with plaster-work and gold paint. It would look at home in Versailles. Sir Charles reckoned all good houses should have a lake, and the one in front is artificial.

Another and more intriguing piece of aris-tocratic eccentricity at this time was megalithomania, a passion for building imitation Stone Age monuments. Ballyfin has an excellent example on the right of the avenue about 200 metres short of the house. It's a rough stone shelter hidden among the trees on the far side of the fence. These sorts of extravagances were being built just a couple of years after the famine when half the population was starving or leaving the country. The mansion now has a school housed in a rather unattractive modern wing and you can drive up and have a look.

Places to Eat

In Mountrath the choice is fast food or pub

food. *Phelan's* on Main St has burgers and chips.

Entertainment

On the pub front most of the action is in the *Drover's Tavern* which has live bands at the weekends. For music or a quiet drink in a traditional country pub, head out to the *Village Inn* in Coolrain just north-west of Mountrath. They have Irish music at weekends.

Getting There & Away

Mountrath is on the main Bus Éireann Dublin to Limerick route, with up to four buses a day going in each direction.

SLIEVE BLOOM MOUNTAINS

One of the best reasons for visiting Laois is to explore the Slieve Bloom Mountains. Their name means Mountains of Bladhma, after a Celtic warrior who used the mountains as a refuge. Though they cannot compare for spectacle with their cousins in Wicklow and the west, the absence of visitors adds to their appeal. They are well signposted by the county council and you can't miss the brown signs on almost every road that leads to the hills.

The highest point is Arderin Mountain (529 metres, 1735 ft) south of the Glendine Gap on the border with Offaly. On a clear day it's possible to see the highest points of all four of the ancient provinces of Ireland. East is Lugnaquilla in Leinster, west is Nephin in Connacht, north is Slieve Donard in Ulster and south-west is Carrauntuohill in Munster.

Mountrath to the south and the lovely village of Kinnitty to the north of the hills are both good bases to work from. Glenbarrow, south-west of Rosenallis, has a gentle walk up by the River Barrow which has its source just a few km farther up in the hills. There are some waterfalls, a large moraine on the north side of the river and some unusual plants in the area, including orchids, butterwort, and blue fleabane. Other spots worth checking out are Glendine Park near the Glendine Gap, and the Cut mountain pass. The road skirting north of the mountains

from Mountmellick to Birr via Clonaslee and Kinnitty is particularly scenic.

The Slieve Bloom Way

The Slieve Bloom Way is a 50-km (31-mile) signposted trail which does a complete circuit of the mountains taking in almost all the major points of interest. The trail follows tracks, forest firebreaks and old roads, and crosses the Mountrat to Kinnity and Mountrath to Clonaslee roads. The recommended starting point is the car park at Glenbarrow, five km (three miles) from Rosenallis. For more information on the trail collect the Bord Fáilte Information Sheet No 26F from any tourist office or turn up at the car park and follow the signs.

It is forbidden to camp in a state forest, but there is plenty of open space for tents. Otherwise, accommodation en route is almost nonexistent.

There is no public transport to the area, but Dooly's hotel (☎ 0509-20032) in Birr, County Offaly, is organising tours of the Slieve Bloom Mountains for around IR£3 per person.

WEST LAOIS

South of the Slieve Bloom Mountains, **Borris-on-Ossory** was a major coaching stop before the railways developed.

Farther west on the same route, **Ballaghmore** means 'great way or road' and **Ballaghmore Castle** (☎ 0505-21453) controlled the edges of the Fitzpatrick family lands. It is one of several small castles which have recently opened their doors to the public. The square tower fortress dates from 1480 and has recently been restored. If you have good eyesight you may spot the *Sheila-na-gig* in the south wall. These pagan fertility symbols, usually rough carvings of women displaying their genitals, are found all over the country but are usually quite hard to spot. Ballaghmore Castle is open daily, admission IR£2.50.

Borris-on-Ossory is on a Bus Éireann express Dublin to Limerick route, with up to three buses daily in each direction.

ABBEYLEIX

Abbeyleix, 14 km (nine miles) south of Portlaoise, is as well tended a country town as you will find. The town grew around a 12th-century monastery in nearby Old Town. The town centre was moved to its present location in the 18th century by the local landowner, Lord de Vesci, and he supervised the layout of tree-lined streets, neat townhouses and a fountain in the square.

Abbeyleix House, his mansion, was erected in 1773 from a design by William Chambers, and is two km south-west of town on the Rathdowney road, but it is not open to the public.

Getting There & Away

Abbeyleix is on an express Bus Éireann route between Dublin and Cork, with up to three buses daily. On Thursdays only a single bus passes through on a Dublin to Portlaoise, Cahir and Clonmel route. J J Kavanagh's private bus service (☎ 056-31106) has a daily Portlaoise, Abbeyleix, Durrow, Cullahill, Urlingford bus.

TIMAHOE

The tiny village of Timahoe is just a handful of houses around a grassy square, 10 km (seven miles) north-east of Abbeyleix on a minor road. Seven roads converge just south of the village at a fine round tower. The 30-metre tower has a slight tilt and is all that remains of a 12th-century monastery. It now stands in the grounds of a converted Church of Ireland church. The tower has a beautifully worked Romanesque entrance some five metres above the ground which has carved human faces with beards.

The ruins behind are of an associated church which was converted into a castle before falling into decay. The church's 6th-century founder was St Mochúa, who, legend relates, had a wondrous pet fly which would parade on a book, keeping pace with the saint's reading and marking the lines so he would not lose track.

DURROW

Neat rows of houses surround a manicured green, which on the west side has an imposing gateway to Castle Durrow (1716), a large Palladian villa which is now in the hands of private owners. You can only see it from the entrance avenue.

The attractive *Castle Arms Hotel* (☎ 0502-36117) on the square charges IR£20 per person. There is a restaurant and entertainment most weekends.

CULLAHILL

Cullahill is a tiny, well-kept hamlet on the main road eight km (five miles) south of Durrow. The *Sportsman Inn* (☎ 0502-37119) is an excellent place to pause and has the best bar food in the region, served 10.30 am to 7 pm, Monday to Saturday.

Durrow and Cullahill are on the main Dublin to Cork bus route and Durrow is served by up to three Bus Éireann express coaches daily. There is no official stop at Cullahill, so you need to check with the bus driver beforehand if he will drop you off there.

J J Kavanagh's private bus company (☎ 056-31106) has a daily service to Portlaoise, Abbeyleix, Durrow, Cullahill and Urlingford.

KILLESHIN

Killeshin Church is a mere four km (2.5 miles) from Carlow Town. Killeshin used to be one of the biggest settlements in Laois and had one of the finest round towers in the country. It's said the tower was destroyed in the 18th century by a local farmer who was afraid it might collapse and kill his livestock.

The shattered 11th-century church is all that's left of Killeshin's ancient town and monastery. The church has a steeply arched Romanesque doorway bearing fine carvings of patterns and human heads.

County Offaly

Offaly is home to Clonmacnois, one of the most extensive and attractive monastic sites in the country. The county has the typical flat and boggy landscape of central Ireland, including the extensive Bog of Allen and Boora Bog between Ferbane and Kilcormac. The mighty Shannon forms part of Offaly's border with Galway, while the Grand Canal also threads its way through the county. Offaly shares the Slieve Bloom Mountains with County Laois.

HISTORY

County Offaly produced a major archaeological surprise in 1977, when deep in Boora Bog slivers of flint called microliths were discovered. These had been used in the knives and weapons of the middle Stone Age, some 8000 to 9000 years ago. The find showed that nomads were living in the centre of Ireland around this time. After these hunter-gatherers came Ireland's first farmers. Offaly's extensive bogs would not have been attractive to them, the acid bog being unsuitable for agriculture, and few traces of them have been found.

Later on, the glacial ridges or eskers, standing well drained and dry above the surrounding peatlands, were used for ancient highways and settlements such as Clonmacnois. The early Christians liked the isolation and protection afforded by the peatlands but were virtually defenceless against the Vikings, who sailed up the River Shannon and attacked any settlement within reach.

During the Middle Ages, Offaly was a stronghold of the O'Connor, O'Carroll and O'Dempsey families, who used the landscape to their advantage, retreating into the bogs in time of trouble.

The modern shape of the county arose out of the plantations of 1556, when Offaly (King's County) and Laois (Queen's County) were shired or divided among subjects loyal to the crown. Originally, Daingean was the official county capital, named Philipstown after King Philip of Spain, Mary I's husband. But the town never really got going, unlike Tullamore and Birr which became the two main settlements in Offaly.

BIRR

On a small tributary of the Shannon, Birr is Offaly's most attractive town. With formal, tree-lined avenues and Georgian terraces, Birr retains much of its 18th and 19th-century character. Many traditional shopfronts survive along Connaught and Main Sts, and all the main roads converge on Emmet Square, where a statue of the Duke of Cumberland (victor of the Battle of Culloden) stood on the central pillar until 1925. In one corner is Dooly's Hotel dating from 1747, formerly a coaching inn on the busy route west. The buildings around Emmet Square are attractive, but the square itself would benefit from some trees, paved areas and a little creative thinking.

History

After starting life as a 6th-century monastic site founded by St Brendan of Birr, the town acquired an Anglo-Norman castle in 1208. The Gaelic O'Carroll family gained control of the castle and kept it until the 17th century. In the plantations of 1620, the O'Carroll family castle and the 580-hectare estate were handed over to Sir Lawrence Parsons, and Birr became known as Parsonstown. Parsons laid out streets, established a glass factory and issued decrees to the scruffy townspeople that anyone who 'cast dunge rubbidge filth or sweepings in the forestreet' were to be fined four pennies. Any woman who was caught working as a barmaid was to 'be set in the stocks by the constable for three whole market days'.

Later, the Parsons became earls of Rosse. The present earl and his wife still live on the estate, which has remained in the family for 14 generations.

Information

The tourist office (☎ 0509-20110) is directly opposite the castle gates and is open May to September. Out of season, contact Shannon Development (☎ 0509-20440) for information. On Thursdays at 7 pm during the summer there is a guided tour (☎ 0509-20337) of the town, departing from Dooley's

Hotel. The post office is in the north-west corner of Emmet Square near Dooly's Hotel.

Around the Town

There's a comprehensive Tourist Trail leaflet available at the tourist office and **Birr heritage centre** (open April to September) on John's Mall, west of Emmet Square. **John's Mall** has John Henry Foley's 1876 statue to the 3rd Earl of Rosse and a Russian cannon from the Crimean War. Nearby is the **Seffin Stone**, a megalithic stone found in an early Christian monastery and said to have marked the centre of Ireland.

Emmet St, to the north of Emmet Square, joins with **Oxmantown Mall** at St Brendan's Church of Ireland. This mall is the town's prettiest, with a regiment of trees and the castle gates at the western end. The massive stone walls of the Birr Estate form the western limits of the town. South-west of the square are the remains of **Old St Brendan's Church**, reputed to be the site of the first settlement of St Brendan in the 6th century. Some fine Victorian houses built between 1870 and 1878 are on St John's Mall due east of Emmet Square opposite the Birr heritage centre.

There is a fine **riverside walk** along the River Camcor from Oxmantown bridge near the Catholic church, running east out to Elmgrove bridge.

Birr Castle & Demesne

Most visitors to Birr come to see the castle and grounds, which are among the finest in Ireland. Most of the present structure dates from around 1620 when Sir Lawrence Parsons was granted the estate.

A later Lawrence presided over alterations to the castle in the early 19th century, which left it almost exactly as you see it today. In 1820 the castle was fortified again after a local Protestant woman, Mrs Legge, convinced her brethren that the Irish were going to rise up and kill them in their beds.

The demesne, which runs north from the castle, consists of 50 hectares of magnificent gardens set around a large artificial lake. The gardens hold over 1000 species of shrubs and trees from all over the world. Of particular interest is the collection from the Himalayas and China, brought back from the 6th earl's 1935 honeymoon in Peking. You will also find the tallest box hedges in the world, which were planted in the 1780s and now stand some 12 metres (40 feet) high. A catalogue of the plant collection is available at the entrance.

Today the castle is the private home of Lord and Lady Rosse and is not open to casual visitors, although group visits may be possible if arranged well in advance (☎ 01-675 1665 or for the castle ☎ 0509-20056). The gardens are open May to September between 9 am and 6 pm, and for the rest of the year 9 am to 1 pm and 2 to 5 pm. Admission is IR£3.20 May to September, IR£2.60 October to April.

Birr Telescope The castle grounds hold one of the most impressive and extraordinary structures in Ireland. The 3rd earl of Rosse, William Parsons (1800-67), wanted to build the biggest telescope in the world. The resulting 'leviathan of Parsonstown', a 72-inch (183 cm) reflector telescope completed in 1845, remained the largest in existence for 75 years, attracting astronomers and scientists from all over the world. The instrument was used to map the surface of the moon, and made a multitude of discoveries including the spiral galaxies. Amazingly the telescope was built in Birr with local engineering and materials.

The Science Museum in London now has the telescope's huge 72-inch reflector, but the massive walls, 22 metres long and 16 metres high, remain. The telescope's 18-metre wooden tube is 2.5 metres in diameter and was controlled by an impressive mechanism of pulleys and cables, none of which remain in place. A detailed model is on hand. Also within the enclosure is a small exhibition on the history and achievements of the telescope with a five-minute recorded talk by the astronomer Patrick Moore.

This remarkable family (all of whom were educated at home) were not just stargazers. The next Earl of Rosse, Lawrence Parsons, was just as bright as his father, and built a device to measure the heat given off by the moon. Charles Algernon Parsons, Lawrence's brother, invented the steam turbine for the earliest English iron battleships, while their mother, Mary Rosse, the 3rd earl's wife, was a pioneer in 19th-century photography.

Golf
The Birr Golf Club (☎ 0509-21184) has an 18-hole course.

Places to Stay
Hostel The nearest hostel is in Banagher, 13 km (eight miles) to the north.

B&Bs *Roselawn* (☎ 0509-20468) has rooms for IR£13 sharing or IR£15 single, and is three km (two miles) along the Roscrea road. *Ard Na Gréine* (☎ 0509-20256) is in Hillside, one km from Birr along the same road, and charges IR£15/26 for singles/doubles. *A'rd Abhainn* (☎ 0509-21257) is a good place in Riverstown, two km (one mile) along the Borrisokane road, and costs IR£13.

Hotels The friendly *County Arms Hotel* (☎ 0509-20791) is walking distance from the centre on Railway Rd, which becomes the road to Roscrea. The 1810 house has various less-pleasing modern extensions but there is plenty of space, the rooms are well equipped and B&B costs IR£28 to IR£33.

Dooly's (☎ 0509-20032) is another good hotel on Emmet Square. Originally a 1747 hunting lodge, it has 18 comfortable rooms and B&B is IR£29/50 for singles/doubles.

Country Houses The 18th-century *Tullanisk House* (☎ 0509-20572) has delightful rooms on part of the Birr Estate. It's almost two km (one mile) from Birr on the Banagher road up a long avenue on the right. B&B is IR£30.

Whigsborough House (☎ 0509-33025), Five Alley, Birr, is a nicely furnished Georgian house with B&B for IR£23/45 and dinner for IR£15. Take the Tullamore road to

Five Alley for eight km (five miles), turn left opposite the right turn for Kinnitty, and the house is 800 metres on the right.

Places to Eat
The *Cottage Coffee Shop* is a lovely place opposite the castle gates and beside the tourist office. *Dooly's Hotel* (☎ 0509-20032) in the square has an excellent coffee shop (10 am to 10 pm), and lunch is available at the bar (12.30 to 2.30 pm), while the *Emmet Restaurant* in the front of the hotel serves dinner.

North of the square and near the castle walls is the *Stables Restaurant* (☎ 0509-20263), in a converted mews on Oxmantown Mall. They serve dinner Tuesday to Saturday (IR£16) and lunch on Sunday, and the food is straightforward but consistently good. The *County Arms Hotel* (☎ 0509-20791) does a good lunch in the bar and a more than acceptable dinner in the evenings for around IR£14.

Tullanisk House (☎ 0509-20572) blends old English and Far Eastern influences in a IR£18 set dinner (see Places to Stay) but is open to residents only.

Entertainment
Fosters Bar on Connaught St at the back of Dooly's is an old-style pub which gets a good crowd at weekends and usually has music. The *Palace Bar* on O'Connell St often has live bands at weekends, and *Enright's* on the main square is a popular modern place. *Kelly's on the Green* is a locals' haunt, just off the square to the west towards the castle. *Mary Walshe's Bar* has Irish music on Friday and Saturday nights.

The *Anglers Rest*, two km west in Annagh (take the road by Birr Castle and follow the river), has action on Mondays, Wednesdays and Fridays during the summer.

Two km (one mile) along the Roscrea road in Crinkle is the *Thatch*, a tremendous little thatched pub.

Getting There and Away
The Bus Éireann stop is near Harte's shop in Emmet Square. Call the tourist office or Athlone (☎ 0902-72651) for times. There is

a single bus passing through on the Dublin to Portumna route and one daily each way between Cork and Athlone.

Kearns' Coaches (☎ 0509-20776) have a restricted service from Tullamore through Birr to Galway on weekend evenings. The single bus leaves Tullamore at 7 pm and passes through Birr at 7.45 pm. A daily service goes from Portumna to Birr (leaves at 9 am) to Dublin. The bus stop is near the post office in Emmet Square.

Getting Around

P L Dolan & Sons (☎ 0509-20006) on Main St and Wilmer Rd is the Raleigh bicycle dealer, with good bikes for IR£8 a day. Kearn's have a taxi service (☎ 0509-20776), or ring Michael Campbell (☎ 0509-20407).

LEAP CASTLE

Between Kinnitty and Roscrea are the remains of Leap Castle. It lies in one of the few areas of Offaly rich in pre-Christian ring forts and burial mounds, and the site has some good views of the Slieve Bloom Mountains.

The castle was originally an O'Carroll family residence, watching over a crucial route between Munster and Leinster, and was renowned for a 'smelly ghost'. It was said by locals to be one of the most haunted castles in Europe. The castle was destroyed in 1922 during the civil war. The ruins consist of a blocky central tower sitting between two later lower wings.

There is no bus servicing this site.

SLIEVE BLOOM MOUNTAINS

It's a bit of an exaggeration to call them mountains, but the Slieve Bloom Mountains are little visited, and have moorlands, pine forests and hidden river valleys. The hamlet of Kinnitty, a lovely journey from Birr, is the jumping-off point. There's a good trip over the hills to Mountrath in County Laois, and a pleasant drive around the northern flanks of the hills between Kinnitty and Mountmellick. Dooly's hotel (☎ 0509-20032) is set to run tours of the Slieve Bloom

Mountains, taking in most local sites of interest. The cost will be around IR£3 per person.

For more details see the County Laois section.

SHANNON & THE BOGS

The Shannon River forms the border between Offaly and Galway until it veers off west to Lough Derg below Banagher; and it dominates the region geographically and commercially. Towns like Banagher grew up beside the river when it was a busier highway than it is today.

The Grand Canal also threads its way through the county, entering to the east near Edenderry and passing through Tullamore before joining the Shannon at Shannon Harbour, just north of Banagher.

Offaly has two extensive peatlands: the Bog of Allen in the east and Boora Bog in the west. The Bog of Allen is an enormous brown expanse that stretches over into Kildare and which – along with many of Offaly's other bogs – is being mined by the huge machines of the Irish Turf Board (Bord Na Mona), for getting compost and briquettes for fuel. Some of Offaly's bogs, however, most particularly Clara Bog, are remarkably untouched, and these are internationally recognised for their plant and animal life.

Eskers

The flat bog lands in west Offaly have in many areas been prevented from draining off into the Shannon by *eskers*, long glacial ridges which are the fossilised banks of meltwater rivers that ran underneath glaciers. Over time the vegetation built up layers of peat up to 10 metres deep in places. Esker is one of the few Irish words to enter the English language. The best known of these eskers is the Esker Riada which translates as the Kings' Road; this great esker ran across much of the country and was used as the principal highway between Leinster and Connaught. You can still see parts of it today, near the main road to Dublin. Clonmacnois sits on part of this esker in the north-west corner of the Offaly. ∎

BANAGHER

The riverside town of Banagher, 12 km (eight miles) north of Birr, is one of the few crossing points of the Shannon in this area. Going north, the next crossing point is at Athlone. Banagher has the only hostel in the region – the new *Crank House Hostel* (☎ 0509-51458) which charges IR£6 a night – some pleasant pubs and restaurants and a busy marina, but is otherwise quiet.

Anthony Trollope was a post office clerk here in 1841, and wrote his first novels here. Charlotte Brontë spent her honeymoon here, and her husband, the Reverend Arthur Bell Nicholls, spent the rest of his life here after she died in England. Cuba Ave is named in honour of a local boy, George Frazer, who became governor of that island.

On the Galway side of the river is an early 19th-century Martello Tower. Eight km (five miles) south of Banagher on the Galway side is the delightful Meelick Church, one of the oldest in use in Ireland.

There is a tourist information desk (☎ 0509-51458) in the Crank House hostel. The post office is farther up the main street near the Brosna Lodge Hotel, as is the Bank of Ireland.

Getting There & Away

Kearn's Coaches (☎ 0509-20776) include Banagher on their daily Birr to Dublin service and in summer on their daily bus from Birr to Galway. Bus Éireann has a bus to Galway on Tuesdays in July and August.

For taxis contact Brennan's (☎ 0509-51301), Bennett's (☎ 0509-51337) or Sullivan's (☎ 0509-51204).

Getting Around

Kieran Donegan (☎ 0509-51178) has a cycle shop on the main street and rents bikes.

CLOGHAN CASTLE

Cloghan Castle is in Lusmagh near the confluence of the Little Brosna and Shannon rivers, about three km (two miles) south of Banagher and 10 km (seven miles) northwest of Birr. The well-preserved keep has an adjoining 19th-century house and protective walls. The owners keep a fine flock of Jacob's sheep.

Cloghan Castle has been in use for nearly 800 years, starting life as a McCoghlan stronghold, and seeing over the ensuing centuries more than its fair share of bloodshed.

The present owner, Brian Thompson, has brought together an interesting and varied assortment of antiques. Pride of place in the main hall goes to the enormous antlers of an Irish elk. At the end of the 45-minute tour, in the rustic dining room, the visitor can

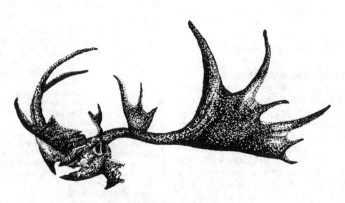

Antlers of Giant Irish Elk

examine some Cromwellian armaments and marvel at just how heavy their breastplates were.

The castle is open Wednesday to Sunday, 2 to 6 pm and admission is IR£3. There is no bus service here, but the owners will collect people from the Banagher tourist desk at the Crank House Hostel by prior arrangement.

CLOGHAN

Seven km north-east of Banagher is Cloghan, where all six roads out of town lead into wide tracts of peat. There is not much here except the *Drift Inn*, a traditional Irish pub, good for lunch and Irish music.

CLONONY CASTLE

Five km from Cloghan, on the road north-west to Shannonbridge, the 16th-century castle's four-storey square tower is enclosed by an overgrown castellated wall. Local tales relate that Anne Boleyn, the second wife of Henry VIII, was born here, but that's unlikely. Her cousins Elizabeth and Mary Boleyn are buried beside the ruined tower.

THE BOG RAILWAY

Just before Shannonbridge, a 45-minute train tour on the Bog Railway (☎ 0905-74114) takes you through a section of the Bog of Allen on the line which used to transport the peat. During the nine-km (six-mile) trip, the bog landscape is explained in detail, with an emphasis on its special flora. The journey begins near the Bord Na Mona Blackwater works. Trips go on the hour from 10 am to 5 pm, April to October, and cost IR£2.85 (students IR£2).

SHANNONBRIDGE

A narrow bridge crosses the river at this point. Shannonbridge is an unremarkable little village except for a 19th-century fort on the west bank just up from the bridge, where heavy artillery was placed to bombard Napoleon, if he was cheeky enough to try and invade via the river. Also nearby is a peat-fired power station which is visible for miles. Part of the road north towards Clonmacnois runs on top of the esker on which Clonmacnois is also built.

CLONMACNOIS

Ireland's most important monastic site is superbly placed, overlooking the Shannon from a ridge. It consists of a walled field containing numerous early churches, high crosses, round towers and graves. Many of the remains are in remarkably good condition and give a real sense of what these monasteries were like in their heyday. The site is surrounded by low marshy ground and fields known as the Shannon Callows. These are home to many wild plants and are one of the last refuges of a seriously endangered bird, the corncrake.

History

Clonmacnois is roughly translated as 'Meadow of the sons of Nós'. The glacial ridge called the Esker Riada on which it stands was once one of the principal cross-country routes between Leinster and Connaught. St Ciarán, the son of a chariotmaker, is said to have founded the site in 545 AD and died only seven months later after building the first church with the personal assistance of Diarmuid, the high king of Tara.

The monastery's beginning was humble, as only eight followers of Ciarán had set out with him, but it became an unrivalled bastion of Irish religion, literature and art. Between the 7th and the 12th centuries monks from all over Europe came to study and pray here. Clonmacnois was one of the reasons Ireland became known as the 'island of saints and scholars' while much of Europe languished in the Dark Ages. Such was Clonmacnois's importance that the high kings of Connaught and Tara were brought here for burial, and many lie in the cathedral, also known as the Church of Kings. The last high king of Tara, Rory O'Connor, who died in 1198, is among them.

Most of the remains date from the 10th to 12th centuries, as the earlier buildings of wood, clay and wattle have long since disappeared. The monks would have lived in small

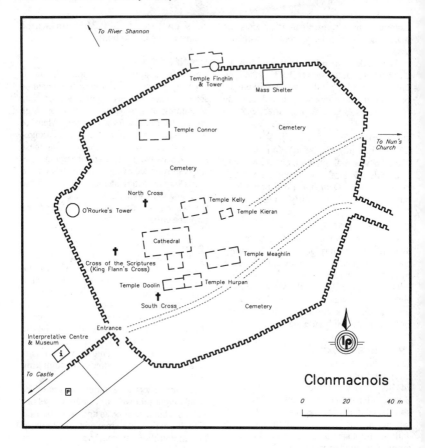

To River Shannon

Temple Finghin & Tower

Mass Shelter

Temple Connor

Cemetery

To Nun's Church

Cemetery

North Cross

O'Rourke's Tower

Temple Kelly

Temple Kieran

Cathedral

Cross of the Scriptures (King Flann's Cross)

Temple Meaghlin

Temple Doolin

Temple Hurpan

South Cross

Cemetery

Entrance

Interpretative Centre & Museum

i

To Castle

P

Clonmacnois

0   20   40 m

huts scattered in and around the monastery, which would probably have been surrounded by a ditch or rampart of earth. It was recorded that there were 106 houses and 13 churches here in 1179 when the site was ravaged by fire. These scattered Irish sites contrast with the strict layout and planning of many monasteries in continental Europe.

The river became a deadly conduit when Viking raiders used it to penetrate right into the heart of Ireland. Clonmacnois was pillaged repeatedly between 830 and 1165 (records suggest on at least eight occasions). It must be said that the Vikings were by no

means the only ones guilty of attacking the place; it was burned down at least 12 times between 720 and 1205 and attacked over 25 times by native Irish forces between 830 and 1165. After the 12th century, it went into decline and by the 15th century it was the home of a bishop of only minor importance. Its final destruction came at the hands of the English in 1552 when it was plundered by the regiment based in Athlone: 'Not a bell, large or small, or an image, or an altar, or a book, or a gem, or even glass in a window, was left which was not carried away'.

Among the treasures which survived this

continuous onslaught are the crozier of the abbots of Clonmacnois in the National Museum and the *Leabhar na hUidhre* ('The Book of the Dun Cow'), now in the Royal Irish Academy in Dublin.

Information

The Office of Public Works has a number of facilities including a museum, an interpretive centre (☎ 0905-74195) and a coffee shop. There is also a tourist office (☎ 0905-74134) in the car park from April through October.

Clonmacnois is open 9 am to 7 pm from June to September, 10 am to 5 pm at other times. Visiting early or late will help you avoid the crowds. Admission is IR£1.50 or 60p for students. A good free guided tour is available on the hour during the summer, which includes an audiovisual show.

High Crosses

In the compound are seven church buildings and three replicas of 9th-century high crosses (the originals are in the museum). The sandstone Cross of the Scriptures is the most richly decorated and has unique upward-tilted arms. Its west face depicts the Crucifixion, soldiers guarding Jesus' tomb and the arrest of Jesus. On the east face are scenes of St Ciarán and King Diarmuid placing the corner stone of the cathedral. It's also known as King Flann's Cross because a rough inscription on the base is said to attribute it to him. He died in 916 AD.

Nearer the river the North Cross dates from around 800 AD, but only the shaft remains, with lions, rich spirals and a single figure, thought to be the Celtic god Cerrunnos or Carnunas, who sits in a Buddha-like position. The two-headed snake is associated with him. The richly decorated South Cross has more carvings including the Crucifixion on the west face.

The Cathedral

The biggest building at Clonmacnois, the cathedral or MacDermot's Church was built in the 12th century, but incorporates part of an earlier 10th-century church. Its most interesting feature is the intricate 15th-century Gothic doorway with carvings of St Francis, St Patrick and St Dominic and a badly worn Latin inscription which, roughly translated, says: 'This doorway was erected for the eternal glory of God'.

The door is also known as the Whispering Door because a whisper carries from one side of it to the other. It is said that lepers would come hear to confess; because of the door's unusual acoustic properties the priest was able to hear the confession from a safe distance.

Around the altar are said to be buried the last high kings of Tara: Turlough Mór O'Connor (died 1156) and his son Ruairí or Rory (died 1198).

The Temples

The small churches are called temples, but the word is in fact a derivation of the Irish word *teampall*, meaning 'church'. Past the scant foundations of the **Temple Kelly** (1167) is the tiny **Temple Kieran**, less than four metres long and 2.5 metres wide. Also known as St Ciarán's Church, it is traditionally thought to be the burial place of St Ciarán, the site's founder; his hand was kept here as a relic until the 16th-century, but is now lost. The remarkable Crozier of the Abbots and a chalice are supposed to have been discovered in here in the 19th century.

The floor level in Temple Kieran is lower than outside because local farmers have for centuries been taking clay from the church to place in the four corners of their fields, where it is said to protect crops against an eelworm parasite and cattle against red water disease. The floor was covered in slabs to stop further digging but the tradition continues in the early spring when handfuls of clay are taken from outside the church.

Near the south-west corner of the temple is a bullaun, or ancient grinding stone, which is reputed to have been used for making medicines for the monastery's hospital. Today the rainwater which collects in it is said to cure warts.

Continuing round the compound there is the 12th-century **Temple Meaghlin**, with its attractive windows, and the twin structures of **Temple Hurpan** and **Temple Doolin**. Doolin is named after Edmund Dowling who repaired this church in 1689 and made it the family crypt, possibly during which he also restored Temple Hurpan, which is also known as Claffey's Church.

The Round Towers

Overlooking the Shannon is the truncated O'Rourke's Tower, a 20-metre tower named after the King of Connaught, Fergal O'Rourke (died 964 AD). The top of the tower is said to have been blown apart by lightning in 1135, but the tower was used up to 1552. The top few levels of masonry are decidedly inferior to the rest.

Round Tower

Temple Finghin and its round tower are on the northern boundary of the site, also overlooking the Shannon. The quaint building, also known as MacCarthy's Church and Tower, appears in most photographs of Clonmacnois and dates from around 1160 to 1170. It has some fine Romanesque carvings and the unusual miniature tower's cone roof has stones set in a herring-bone pattern. This is the only Irish round tower roof that has never been altered. Most round towers were used by monks for protection when their monasteries were attacked, but this one was probably used as a bell tower as the doorway is at ground level.

Other Remains

The **Temple Connor** is a little roofed church still used by Church of Ireland parishioners on the last Sundays of the summer months. Beyond the boundary wall, a half km east through the modern graveyard, is the secluded **Nun's Church** with its fine Romanesque doorways. Above the west doorway is a Sheila-na-gig. West of the church is a cairn said to be the burial place of a servant of St Ciarán who, legend has it, was not allowed to be buried in the monastery graveyard after losing St Ciarán's dun cow.

West of the settlement on the ridge near the car park is a motte with a 13th-century **castle**, now in ruins. It is said to have been built by John de Grey, Bishop of Norwich, to watch over the Shannon.

Museum

The museum near the entrance consists of three beehive-like structures echoing the design of the early monastic dwellings. It contains the originals of the three principal high crosses described and various artefacts uncovered during excavation, including silver pins, beaded glass and an Ogham stone.

The museum and entrance buildings also contain many of Clonmacnois' 8th to 12th-century graveslabs. This is the largest collection of early Christian graveslabs in Europe. Many are in remarkable condition with inscriptions clearly visible, often starting with *oroit do* or *ar* meaning 'a prayer for'.

Places to Eat
The Clonmacnois interpretive centre has a tearoom serving good coffee, sandwiches and snacks.

Getting There & Away
Clonmacnois is seven km (four miles) north of Shannonbridge and about 24 km (15 miles) south of Athlone. There is no public transport service directly to Clonmacnois.

THE CLONFANLOUGH STONE
Almost five km (three miles) east of Clonmacnois, near Clonfanlough Catholic Church, is a curious limestone boulder half buried in the ground. Its surface is engraved with crosses and markings resembling human forms. They are thought to date from the Stone Age and the patterns resemble similar ones found in Spain and France. Some suggest the carvings depict a prehistoric battle. To get there find Clonfanlough Church; a rough path behind leads over fields to the stone.

TULLAMORE
The county town of Tullamore, 80 km (50 miles) due east of Dublin on a nice stretch of the Grand Canal, is pleasant enough. Charleville Castle is the main attraction – there isn't much to the Irish Mist liqueur factory which is nominally another attraction. The market square and some of the old houses are attractive.

Founded in 1750 by the Bury family of Limerick, Tullamore soon superseded Philipstown (now Daingean) as the county capital. In 1785 a hot-air balloon crashed and started a fire that consumed hundreds of homes!

Information
The tourist office (☎ 0506-52617) is open from June to August, and is located on Bury Quay beside the Irish Mist factory. The post office is on O'Connor Square, the main square in the town. Continental Cleaners are 50 metres beyond the car park at the back of the High St Mall.

Charleville Castle
The great Gothic structure of Charleville Castle (☎ 0506-21279) sits in a large estate a km to the west of the town centre. What some call a 'Gothic fantasy castle' with its spires and turrets was the family seat of the Burys, who in 1798 commissioned the design from Francis Johnston, one of Ireland's most famous architects.

From the entrance on Charleville Rd, south of town on the road to Limerick, there is a 1.5 km lane to the castle itself which is popular with joggers. (Tullamore Harriers is one of Ireland's premier running clubs.) The castle's interior has deteriorated although some of the rooms have been maintained and furnished. The Hutton-Burys are the present owners and intend to restore the property and turn it into a classy hotel.

Tours operate haphazardly between 11 am and 5 pm, Wednesday to Sunday, June to September, weekends only in April and May – it's worth checking this with the tourist office first. The 30-minute tour costs IR£2.50 and the castle grounds are also worth exploring.

Irish Mist
The Irish Mist factory is beside the tourist office on Bury Quay. This internationally famous liqueur is a secret combination of herbs and spirits, only blended here. The Irish Mist Visitor's Centre has closed down, so you won't even get a sample tasting these days!

Cruises
Tullamore Celtic Cruisers (☎ 0506-21861) have boats available by the week from IR£234 for two people in the low season up to IR£998 for nine people in the high season. You can cruise west to the Shannon joining it at Shannon Harbour or east to Edenderry, Laytown and down into the Grand Canal and River Barrow systems.

Getting There & Away
There are eight trains daily to Dublin and Galway on weekdays, four at weekends.

The Bus Éireann stop (☎ 0506-21431) is

at the railway station, south of town off the Charleville Rd on the Western Relief Rd. The two buses daily each way on the Dublin to Portumna route, and one daily on the Waterford to Longford route, all pass through Tullamore. Kearn's Coaches (☎ 0509-20776) have a couple of daily buses to Dublin from Tullamore.

RAHAN CHURCHES & CANAL WALK

Eight km (five miles) west of Tullamore are the ruins of two old chapels with fine Romanesque carvings around the doorways. The Protestant church nearby is still used. Rahan is thought to be one of the earliest Christian sites in Ireland, founded by St Camelacus or St Cartage in the 7th century.

There is a lovely eight-km (five-mile) walk from Rahan along the canal to Tullamore. About three km from Rahan you will see the ruined remains of Ballycowan Castle and an aqueduct where the Brosna River flows under the canal.

DURROW ABBEY

St Colmcille founded a monastery at Durrow Abbey in the 6th century, and the monastery's scriptorium later produced 'The Book of Durrow', a Latin gospel now in Trinity College, Dublin. The book was kept here for over 800 years until the 16th-century dissolution of the monasteries, when it fell into the hands of a local farmer. The book's bright illustrations survived being immersed in the farmer's cattle's drinking water to ward off evil spirits. In 1661 the local bishop handed it over to Trinity College.

'The Book of Durrow' fared better than the rest of the monastery. It was damaged in 1186 by Hugh de Lacy, who literally lost his head in the process, a local man taking exception to de Lacy using the monastery stones for a castle. The castle was being built on the fortified mound nearby.

Today, the site's only prominent structures are a Georgian mansion and a derelict 19th-century Protestant church; on a gloomy day, the bedraggled ivy-clad walls and gravestones do have a certain atmosphere. Some High Kings of Tara are said to have been buried here including Donal (died 758) and a grandson of Brian Ború, Murcadh, who died in 1068. The ancient remains include St Colmcille's Well to the north-east of the church and a 10th-century high cross. On the east face of the cross are panels of King David, Abraham's sacrifice of Isaac and the Last Judgement, while the west face includes soldiers guarding Jesus' tomb, and the Crucifixion.

Durrow Abbey is seven km (four miles) from Tullamore down a long lane west off the road.

DAINGEAN

Daingean, once known as Philipstown, is on the Grand Canal 14 km (nine miles) east of Tullamore, and was the administrative centre for the plantatation of Offaly (King's County) until Tullamore took over in 1834. Five km (three miles) due north of Daingean near the hamlet of Croghan is **Croghan Hill**, an extinct volcano, which offers fine views of the surrounding bog, with some burial cairns and Bronze Age earthworks.

EDENDERRY

Edenderry is 16 km (10 miles) beyond Daingean and sprang to life with the arrival of the canal in 1802. Its origins go back to the 14th century and the De Berminghams, whose ruined castle, Carrickoris, is seven km (four miles) north of town. Three km northwest on the Rhode road is the scanty monastic site of **Monasteroris**. It was built for the Franciscans by John De Bermingham in 1325 to quell his conscience over his father's massacre of 32 local chieftains 20 years before in **Carrickoris Castle** on Carrick Hill, north of Edenderry.

The name Edenderry came from the oakwoods that once blanketed the hills around the town. The local O'Connor family used to harry the English and retreat into the bogs that cover the region. There is a nice walk from the town hall along the canal towpath out to the Downshire Bridge.

Places to Eat

The *Eden Inn* on Main St serves reasonable

Left: Jerpoint Abbey, County Kilkenny(TW)
Right: Kilkenny Castle, County Kilkenny (TW)
Bottom: Adare, County Limerick (TW)

Top: Finnavarra Point, County Clare (JM)
Bottom: Turlough (Temporary Lake), The Burren, County Clare (JM)

pub food all day, while *Tiffany's Restaurant* does a plain but dependable dinner in the evenings for around IR£10.

Entertainment
Popular pubs include *Larkins'* on Main St which gets a good young crowd. *Regan's* and the *Huntsman* usually have bands at weekends and discos on Friday and Sunday nights.

Getting There & Away
Bus Éireann has up to four daily buses to Dublin, two on Sundays. A single daily bus goes to and from Tullamore.

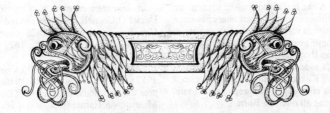

County Clare

County Clare is almost a peninsula, with the Shannon Estuary cutting deep into its southern border and Galway Bay on the northern side. Wedged between Kerry and Galway, Clare's land is mostly poor, with a large sweep of limestone rock in the north of the county forming the famous Burren region.

Clare is in some ways unfortunate. It doesn't get the good press of either Kerry or Galway, although it has special charms of its own. There is some spectacular scenery, particularly around the Cliffs of Moher, and the attraction of the Burren grows with every visit. This limestone landscape has countless monuments, castles and rare flowers, and there are some wonderful walks.

Many of Clare's towns and villages have resisted plastic sign disease as well as the prettification that you see in many more heavily touristed places. Ennis, Clare's county town, retains its charming narrow streets, while villages like Ennistymon have many of their old shops and pubs – the latter often hosting traditional music sessions on long summer evenings. The county has some 250 castles in various stages of preservation: Knappogue near Quin and the famous tower house at Bunratty, which holds 'medieval banquets', are fine examples. There's scuba diving at Kilkee, Doolin and Fanore, excellent rock climbing at Ballyreen near Fanore, and caving all over the Burren.

A couple of villages have become havens for particular breeds of visitor. Doolin attracts music lovers and backpackers, while genteel Ballyvaughan has become a weekend retreat for a wealthier bunch.

The shortest route to Clare if you're travelling up the coast is via the car ferry between Killimer and Tarbert. See the Killimer section for details. Shannon Airport in Clare is Ireland's second-largest airport (see the Shannon Airport section).

Ennis & Around

ENNIS
Ennis, Clare's principal town, is a busy market centre with a population of 16,000. It lies on the banks of the River Fergus which runs south into the Shannon Estuary. The town's medieval origins can be seen in the narrow streets, and there are many old shops and pubs. The abbey, founded in the 13th century, is its most important historic site. Ennis is the cathedral town for the Catholic diocese of Killaloe.

History
The O'Briens, Kings of Thomond, built a castle here in the 13th century and were also the force behind the impressive abbey, the town's principal attraction. Much of the wooden town was destroyed by a great fire in 1249 and again by one of the local O'Briens in 1306.

In the centre of town is a memorial to Daniel O'Connell, who was elected MP for Clare by a massive vote in 1828 – an election result that led directly to the 1829 Act of Catholic Emancipation.

Eamon de Valera was MP for Clare from 1917 to 1959. There is a bronze statue to him near the courthouse and the small De Valera Museum on Harmony Row (no admission

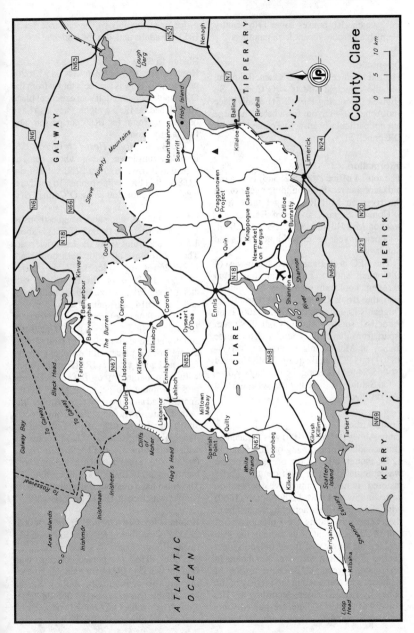

County Clare

fee), which also houses some 17th-century Flemish and more recent Irish paintings.

Orientation

The old town centres on O'Connell Square, and the principal streets – O'Connell St, High St (becoming Parnell St), Bank Place and Abbey St – fan out from here. The large but not particularly attractive cathedral is on O'Connell St.

Information

The tourist office (☎ 065-28366) is in a big old Georgian red-brick building overlooking the river on Mill Rd. To get there from O'Connell Square, go down Bank Place, west on Mill Rd and left at the roundabout. It's open all year but closed lunch times and Sundays.

The GPO is on Bank Place, north-west of O'Connell Square. Ennis Bookstore is an excellent bookshop on Abbey St. There is also the Book Gallery at 68 Parnell St. Duggan's Laundrette (☎ 065-283200) is on Parnell St, south-west of O'Connell Square. Apart from the banks you can also change money at McMahon's Insurances (☎ 065-28307) on O'Connell Square. Ennis Hospital (☎ 065-24464) is along the Galway road.

On Saturdays, there is a market at the Old Market Place.

Ennis Abbey

Ennis Abbey (☎ 065-29100) was founded by Donnchadh O'Brien, King of Thomond, in 1240, though a lot of the present structure was completed in the 14th century. Partly restored, it has an impressive five-section east window and a McMahon tomb (1460) with alabaster panels depicting scenes from the Passion, including the Entombment of Christ. At the height of its fame in the 15th century, the abbey was one of Ireland's great centres of learning, with over 300 monks in residence. Terence O'Brien, a bishop of Killaloe, was murdered in the sacristy of the abbey by Brien O'Brien, according to 'The Annals of Ulster'. There are guided tours June to September; check with the tourist office or at the abbey. The entrance fee is IR£1 for adults and 40p for students.

Places to Stay

Hostels The *Abbey Hostel* (☎ 065-22620) on Harmony Row is a stone's throw from the O'Connell monument. It's an excellent place with 90 beds at IR£5 a night. They also have one double room for IR£6 per person, and two family rooms.

The *Walnut House Hostel* (☎ 065-28956) is older, run-down and nowhere near as spruce as its rival in town. B&B varies from IR£8 to IR£11 in double rooms. To get there, head for the cathedral along O'Connell St.

B&Bs Ennis is not short of guesthouses. *Clare Manor House* (☎ 065-20701) is about 1.5 km (one mile) along the Limerick road. The six rooms, all with bathrooms, are IR£17/26 for singles/doubles. *Laurel Lodge* (☎ 065-21560) is on the right-hand side along Clare Rd. All rooms have bathrooms and cost IR£14 B&B per person.

Two km (one mile) from Ennis is *Newpark House* (☎ 065-21233), a 300-year-old country house in 40 hectares of land. This is a comfortable place with excellent breakfasts, and good value at IR£15 in six rooms with own bathroom or IR£13 B&B per person without. To get there go along the Scarriff road and turn right at the Amber Inn.

In Ennis town, near the Quinnsworth shopping centre just off Francis St, is *Avonlea* (☎ 065-21632). Good rooms all with bathrooms are IR£13. *Ardlea House* (☎ 065-8888) on Clare Rd has rooms with bathroom at IR15/26 for singles/doubles. They also have one room, sleeping up to six people, which costs IR£12 per person.

Hotels The *Old Ground Hotel* (☎ 065-28217) is on Station Rd near the centre of town. Rooms with TVs and phones are IR£35 to IR£45 per person, sharing, with B&B or IR£35 to IR£60 for a single, depending on the season. On Abbey St the comfortable *Queen's Hotel* (☎ 065-28963) is a notch below the Old Ground and a fair bit cheaper, at IR£24 to IR£28 B&B per person

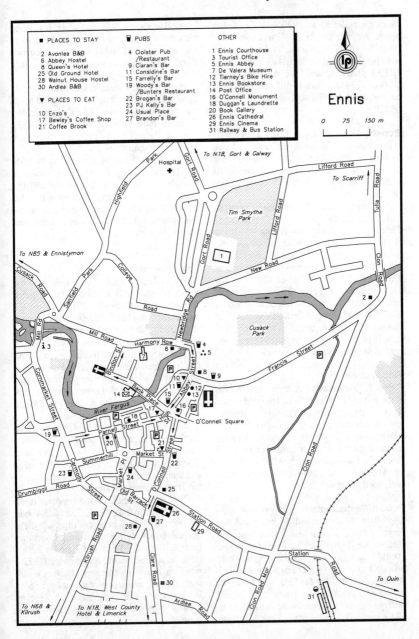

Ennis

PLACES TO STAY
- 2 Avonlea B&B
- 6 Abbey Hostel
- 8 Queen's Hotel
- 25 Old Ground Hotel
- 28 Walnut House Hostel
- 30 Ardlea B&B

PLACES TO EAT
- 10 Enzo's
- 17 Bewley's Coffee Shop
- 21 Coffee Brook

PUBS
- 4 Cloister Pub /Restaurant
- 9 Ciaran's Bar
- 11 Considine's Bar
- 15 Farrelly's Bar
- 19 Woody's Bar /Bunters Restaurant
- 22 Brogan's Bar
- 23 PJ Kelly's Bar
- 24 Usual Place
- 27 Brandon's Bar

OTHER
- 1 Ennis Courthouse
- 3 Tourist Office
- 5 Ennis Abbey
- 7 De Valera Museum
- 12 Tierney's Bike Hire
- 13 Ennis Bookstore
- 14 Post Office
- 16 O'Connell Monument
- 18 Duggan's Laundrette
- 20 Book Gallery
- 26 Ennis Cathedral
- 29 Ennis Cinema
- 31 Railway & Bus Station

0   75   150 m

sharing or IR£30 to IR£35 single. Other hotels are the Grade A *West County Inn* (☎ 065-28421), just south of Ennis on the road to Limerick, which has B&B from IR£39 sharing, and the *Auburn Lodge* (☎ 065-21247), which is just north of Ennis on the road to Galway, with B&B from IR£20.

Country Houses If you fancy a luxurious manor house in the country, *Carnelly House* (☎ 065-28442) is five km (three miles) north of Ennis in Clarecastle. B&B is a mere IR£70 a night and dinner is IR£25 or more per person.

You might also appreciate being a guest of Lord and Lady Inchiquin, O'Briens of Thomond and direct descendants of Brian Ború. They used to live in Dromoland Castle in Quin, which is now a luxury hotel. In the 1960s they built a huge neo-Georgian house, *Thomond House* (☎ 061-368304), in the castle grounds, and now provide very select and expensive accommodation. B&B is IR£75 a head. To get there, head south of Ennis for 11 km (seven miles) and you'll find it, just north of Newmarket-on-Fergus and east of the main road to Limerick.

Places to Eat

Cafés & Takeaways *Bewley's* has a branch at the top of O'Connell St and the coffee and light meals are usually excellent. Another good lunch-time place is the *Coffee Brook* in Market Place. Both are closed in the evenings. *Enzo's* is a good burger place at 32 Abbey St. *Considine's Bar* (☎ 065-29054) at 26 Abbey St has a reasonable coffee shop with food all day.

Pubs & Restaurants *Brogan's* pub (☎ 065-29859) at 24 O'Connell St has good bar food; a three-course lunch will cost you IR£5. Near Brogan's, *Brandon's Bar* (☎ 065-28133) has similar fare, while *Woody's Bar* (☎ 065-28861) has *Bunter's* restaurant, (☎ 065-41152), which serves reasonably priced pizza, pasta, chicken and stirfry with most main courses in the IR£5 to IR£9 range. It's open from 5 pm to 11 pm

every day, except Sundays when it is open between 4 pm and 10 pm. To get there, head out along Mill Road (which becomes Cornmarket St) and turn right at the western end of Parnell St.

Howley's pub-cum-restaurant (☎ 065-29923) on Parnell St serves very good food; dinner will cost you IR£20 or more. *La Fontana* Italian restaurant (☎ 065-41458), also on Parnell St, is the place to go for upmarket Italian cuisine.

The *Cloister Pub & Restaurant* (☎ 065-29521) on Abbey St near the abbey is probably Ennis's best restaurant and the most expensive – from IR£25 per person for dinner. They also do excellent meals in the bar from noon to 10 pm. There is sometimes jazz on Sundays.

Entertainment

As capital of a renowned music county, Ennis is not short of good music pubs. *Brogan's* pub (☎ 065-29859) is one of the best known and has sessions on Tuesdays.

Ciaran's Bar is a small but very cosy place near the Queen's Hotel on Francis St. It's popular with the local football crowd, and has Irish music on Thursdays, Fridays and Saturdays. *Woody's* pub up Parnell St is a little out from the town centre, and has rock music and a trendy crowd. The *Usual Place* pub in the market is an old-style local.

Brandon's Bar (☎ 065-28133) has live music some nights, as does *Farrelly's Bar*, just off the square. *P J Kelly's Bar* at 5 Carmody St has Irish music Friday, Saturday and Sunday nights. *Considine's* on Parnell St has Irish sessions on Thursdays.

One km along the Gort road north of town is a low wooden music hall, *Cois Na hAbhna* (☎ 065-20996), where ceilidhs are held every Wednesday night during the summer from 8.30 to 10.30 pm. On Tuesday nights there is an Irish music stage show (IR£2), while on Thursdays there's an Oiche Ceilidh with dancing and traditional music, and on Wednesday nights they have set dancing classes. They also sell tapes, books and records.

Getting There & Away

Train On Tuesdays, Wednesdays and Thursdays, a special shopping train leaves Ennis Station (☎ 065-40444) on Station Rd for Dublin via Limerick at 7.30 am and returns the same evening. There is also one train to Dublin on Sundays at 5.15 pm; the fare is IR£28.50 single or IR£29.50 return and the journey takes three hours. For regular trains, Limerick (☎ 061-418666) is the nearest station.

Bus The Bus Éireann depot (☎ 065-24177) is at the railway station at the bottom of Station Rd in the south-east corner of town. Buses run from Limerick to Ennis six times a day. There is a direct service to and from Dublin on weekdays, six buses to and from Galway, four a day to and from Cork, and 15 a day to Shannon Airport.

Bill O'Mahoney Coaches (☎ 065-45730) run private buses to Dublin: four on Friday, three on Sunday.

Getting Around

TMT Rentals (☎ 065-24211) at 71 O'Connell St in Ennis can fix you up with anything from a car to a motor home. Michael Tierney (☎ 065-29433) at 17 Abbey St is part of the Raleigh Rent-a-Bike scheme and has well-maintained mountain bikes for IR£7 a day or IR£30 a week plus deposit.

AROUND ENNIS

To the north of Ennis is the early Christian site of Dyseart O'Dea. To the south-east are castles, theme parks and other attractions. East of Ennis, the countryside rolls gently to the Shannon and Lough Derg while west the farms get smaller and the land poorer as you approach the Atlantic. Shannon International Airport is 22 km (14 miles) away to the south-east.

There are local and express buses covering most areas around Ennis but the frequency of service is hugely variable. Many buses run only in summer and on certain days, so you would be best to confirm times and destinations with Ennis bus station (☎ 065-24177).

The express service running between Limerick and Galway can sometimes be picked up in Ennis to get to Clarecastle, Newmarket-on-Fergus and Bunratty. A bus service also operates to Limerick via Clarecastle and Newmarket-on-Fergus.

A summertime weekday service travels north-west to Ennistymon and then south along the coast to Kilkee.

Dyseart O'Dea

Nine km (six miles) north of Ennis on the road to Corofin is the early Christian site of Dyseart O'Dea, where St Tola founded a monastery in the 8th century. The church and High Cross known as the White Cross of Tola date from the 12th or 13th century. The cross depicts Daniel in the Lions' Den on one side and a crucified Christ above a bishop carved in relief. Look for the carvings of animal and human heads on the south doorway of the Romanesque church. There are also the remains of a round tower.

In 1318, the O'Briens and the de Clares of Bunratty fought a pitched battle nearby, which the O'Briens won, thus postponing the Anglo-Norman conquest of Clare. O'Dea Castle (☎ 065-27722) nearby has a museum and interpretive centre and is open May to September 10 am to 6 pm; admission IR£1.50.

Getting There & Away In July and August, there is a daily bus from Monday to Friday coming from Limerick, which leaves Ennis for Corofin and Ennistymon at 2.15 pm, passing by Dyseart O'Dea en route. During the rest of the year, a bus heads out of Ennis on the same route on weekdays only at 3 pm, and at 3.50 pm during school holidays.

Quin

Quin, a tiny village 11 km (seven miles) east of Ennis, was the site of Ireland's greatest find of prehistoric gold, the Great Clare Find of 1854. While working on the Limerick to Ennis railway, labourers uncovered a huge hoard of Celtic gold. Sadly, very few of the several hundred torcs, gorgets and other pieces made it to the National Museum in

Dublin; most were sold and melted down. The source of this and much of ancient Ireland's gold may have been the Wicklow Mountains.

Quin Abbey Surrounded by fresh green countryside, Quin's Franciscan friary was founded in 1433 using part of the walls of an older de Clare castle built in 1280. An elegant belfry rises above the main body of the abbey and you can climb the narrow spiral staircase and look down on the very fine cloister and surrounding countryside.

Despite many periods of persecution, Franciscan monks lived here until the 19th century. In one corner is buried the last friar, Father Hogan, who died in 1820. Another occupant is the impressively named Fireballs McNamara, a notorious duellist and member of the region's ruling family. McNamara castles dot the surrounding countryside. Just beside the friary is a 13th-century Gothic church, St Finghin's.

Knappogue Castle
Knappogue Castle (☎ 061-368103), three km (two miles) south of Quin, was built in 1467 by the McNamaras. They held sway over a large part of Clare from the 5th to mid-15th centuries and built 42 castles in the region. Knappogue's huge walls are intact, and it has a fine collection of period furniture and fireplaces.

When Oliver Cromwell came over from England in 1649 to subdue the Irish, he used Knappogue as a base while he was in this area and this was one of the reasons it was spared destruction. The McNamara family regained the castle after the Restoration in 1660, when many old Irish families had their estates returned to them.

Knappogue Castle is open May to October, 9.30 am to 5.30 pm. Admission is IR£2 (students IR£1.20). It has a small souvenir shop in the courtyard.

Medieval Banquets Knappogue hosts medieval banquets (☎ 061-360788), usually twice in an evening but depending on

demand, from May to October. The times are 5.30 and 8.45 pm and the cost is IR£27.90. See the Bunratty section for more details. Knappogue, unlike Bunratty, lays on knives and forks.

Craggaunowen Project
Six km (four miles) east of Quin, the Craggaunowen Project includes recreated ancient dwelling places such as a crannóg and ring fort, real artefacts like a 2000-year-old oak road, and related items such as Tim Severin's leather boat the *Brendan*, which crossed the Atlantic in 1976-77.

Craggaunowen Castle itself is a small and well-preserved McNamara fortified house. The Craggaunowen Project (☎ 061-367178) is open May to October from 10 am to 6 pm, latest admission 5 pm. The entry fee is IR£3 (students IR£2, children IR£1.30). They have a nice little restaurant for light snacks or lunch. Cullaun Lake nearby is a popular boating and picnic spot with forest trails.

Dromoland Castle
Just north of Newmarket-on-Fergus is Dromoland Castle (☎ 061-368144), a magnificent building and one of Ireland's best hotels. It sits in 220 hectares of vast and beautiful gardens by the River Fergus, and inside oak panels and silken fabrics adorn every wall. The hotel has its own 18-hole golf course. It's way beyond the price range of most people, but you can still venture in for a drink in the bar.

Mooghaun Ring Fort In Dromoland Demesne are the remains of one of Europe's largest Iron Age hill forts: three circular earthen banks enclosing some 13 hectares. The fort's occupants may have been the owners of the huge gold hoard uncovered nearby in Quin in 1854. Access to the fort is through Dromoland Forest which is signposted off the Newmarket to Dromoland road.

East & South-East Clare

Clare's eastern boundary is formed by the River Shannon and Lough Derg, the Republic's largest lake, which stretches some 48 km (30 miles) from Portumna in Galway, to just south of Killaloe. Farther south the road between the two towns swings past the lake through some gentle countryside and picturesque hamlets like Mountshannon. From high ground, there are panoramic views across the lake to the Silvermine Mountains in Tipperary.

East Clare is fishing and shooting country, and the villages on the eastern shores of Lough Derg are favoured by hunting types.

South East Clare is visually unremarkable compared with the county's Atlantic coastline or the lakeside scenery north of Killaloe. Most people pass through quickly, taking in diversions like **Bunratty Castle**, **Quin Abbey** or Cratloe's ancient oakwoods. Twenty-four km (15 miles) west of Limerick City is Shannon Airport, Ireland's second largest airport and the arrival and departure point for many visitors to Ireland.

SHANNON AIRPORT

Shannon, Ireland's second airport, sits in the apparent wilderness of south-east Clare, 22 km (14 miles) from Ennis and almost exactly the same distance from Limerick. Like Gander Airport in Newfoundland, Shannon Airport used to be a vital link in the transatlantic air route, as piston-engined planes barely had enough range to make it across the ocean. If you come through Shannon, the extensive runways and numerous departure gates are reminders of a prosperous past. Irish coffee (a healthy slug of whiskey in a strong coffee) was invented at Shannon for early transatlantic passengers.

Duty-Free

The world's first duty-free when it opened in 1947, Shannon has a huge stock of Irish and international goods. It's worth a browse and is a good place to rid yourself of any leftover cash. However, prices for international goods – jewellery, perfumes etc – are the same as in any duty-free, while Irish tweeds, pottery, clothes and crystal cost the same in any high-street shop.

Information

There is a tourist office (☎ 061-471664, 471665) in the arrivals hall, open 6 am until 6 pm daily. For flight information phone ☎ 061-471444. The Bank of Ireland counter is open from the first flight until 5.30 pm.

Places To Stay

B&Bs The nearest hostels are in Limerick and Ennis. There are plenty of B&Bs five km (three miles) from the airport in Shannon and 11 km (seven miles) away in Bunratty. Only 400 metres from Shannon town centre is *Moloney's B&B* (☎ 061-364185) at 27 Coill Mhara St, down a quiet cul-de-sac, with four rooms at IR£12 B&B. Less than three km (two miles) from the airport, on a hill overlooking the estuary is the stylish modern *Lohan's B&B* (☎ 061-364268) at 35 Tullyglass Crescent, Shannon, which has six rooms for IR£13.50 B&B sharing.

Hotels The comfortable *Great Southern Hotel* (☎ 061-471122) directly in front of the airport terminal costs IR£45.50 to IR£48.50 per person for B&B, but you can book a room for up to three through the airport tourist office for IR£45.

On the road into Shannon town is the *Oak Wood Arms Hotel* (☎ 061-361500), with B&B from IR£35.20 to IR£38. For more accommodation see the sections on Bunratty, Ennis and Newmarket-on-Fergus.

Places to Eat

The airport has the café-style *Courtyard* and the more upmarket *Lindbergh Room* with an all-you-can-eat buffet for IR£11. In Shannon town, *Mr Pickwick's* (☎ 061-364290) is a cheap and cheerful place offering a full Irish breakfast for IR£2.25, a set lunch for IR£3.45 and dinner for IR£10.95, as well as a three-course tourist dinner for IR£6.95. Also in the town centre, the *Terrace Bar* in the Shannon Knights Inn does reasonable bar food. Nearer the airport, the *Olde Lodge* (☎ 061-362789) is a bar and restaurant with regular music sessions.

Getting There & Away

Air Aer Lingus (☎ 061-471666), Ryanair (☎ 061-471444), Delta (☎ 061-471837) and Aeroflot (☎ 061-472299) operate from Shannon.

Bus There are 13 Bus Éireann buses a day to Ennis; nine on Sundays. The ticket office (☎ 061-361311) in the airport opens at 7 am, the first bus leaves at 8 am and the fare is IR£3. There are also numerous services to Limerick (also IR£3 one way), and the journey takes about 40 minutes.

Galway is served by three buses a day, IR£9 single, IR£12 return. And finally there is a single express bus to Dublin, leaving at 8.05 am.

Taxi A taxi locally will cost you about IR£1 a mile plus a pickup charge. A taxi to Limerick costs about IR£15, with possible extra charges for luggage or unsocial hours.

BUNRATTY

Bunratty overlooks the Shannon Estuary. The castle is in excellent condition and well worth a look, but it's a prime tourist attraction and is besieged by coach tours in summer. With an attendant Folk Park and Durty Nelly's pub nearby, the area is starting to resemble a medieval theme park. Go early in the day.

Bunratty Castle

The Vikings built a fortified settlement at this spot, a former island surrounded by a moat. Then came the Normans: Thomas de Clare built the first stone structure on the site in the 1270s. The present castle is the fourth or fifth structure to occupy the location beside the romantically named River Ratty.

The castle was built in the early 1400s by the ubiquitous McNamara family but fell shortly afterwards to the O'Briens, earls of Thomond, in whose possession it remained

until the 17th century. Admiral Penn, father of William Penn, founder of Pennsylvania, resided here for a short while.

In modern times, a complete restoration was carried out, and today the castle's magnificent Great Hall holds a very fine collection of 14th to 18th-century furniture, paintings and wall hangings. Combined admission to the castle (☎ 061-361511) and Folk Park is IR£4 for adults (students IR£1.80), and they are open 9.30 am to 5.30 pm in the winter and 7 pm in the summer.

Bunratty Medieval Banquets

Today, Bunratty Castle's Great Hall hosts 'medieval banquets' (☎ 061-360788, or Freephone 1-800-269811), replete with comely maidens playing the harp, court jesters cracking corny jokes, food à la Middle Ages (a pale imitation) all washed down with mead, a kind of honey wine much favoured by the Irish in times gone by. You eat with your fingers. A seat at the banquet table will set you back a fairly steep IR£27.90 and they are heavily booked with coach parties. The whole thing is stage Irish but taken in spirit can be quite fun.

The banquets at Knappogue and Dunguaire castles are generally smaller, quieter and often more pleasant. All run two banquets a night during the summer at 5.30 pm and 8.45 pm.

Bunratty Folk Park

Bunratty Folk Park is a reconstructed traditional Irish village, with cottages, a forge and working blacksmith, weavers weaving and buttermakers making butter. There is a complete village street with post office, pub and small café, some of them transplanted from the site of Shannon Airport. Agricultural machinery buffs will find a good collection here in Bunratty House overlooking the Folk Park.

Folk Park Ceilidhs Every evening between May and September, 'Shannon Ceilidhs' are held in the Folk Park with music, dancing, Irish stew, apple pie and soda bread. It's meant to show how the peasants passed their time while the gentry gorged themselves in the safety of their castles. The cost is IR£22.90 per person and there are ceilidhs every evening at 5.30 pm and 8.45 pm. For bookings ring the same numbers as for the medieval banquets.

Places to Eat

Durty Nelly's (☎ 065-364861) has fairly good bar food and also houses two restaurants. The *Oyster* downstairs is open from 12 noon to 10 pm and the *Loft* upstairs from 6 to 10 pm. Both are fine, with main courses from IR£10 to IR£14.

In the Folk Park, *Mac's* pub does light meals. A really nice lunch spot is the *Rowanberry Restaurant* in Ballycasey Craft Workshops, a couple of km south of Bunratty on the way to Shannon Airport. *Avoca Cottage Café*, in Avoca Handweavers just down the road from the castle, does excellent lunches.

If you are hungry and looking for quantity at reasonable prices, hotels like the Bunratty Castle do a huge lunch for around IR£7, which will keep you going for the day. *MacCloskey's* (☎ 065-364082) in Bunratty House Mews is the best and most expensive restaurant in the area. Dinner costs IR£25 or more a head, but the food, with mostly Irish ingredients, is top class. *Truffles Restaurant* (☎ 061-36117) in the Fitzpatrick Shannon Shamrock Hotel is a good hotel restaurant, with dinner costing around IR£20.

Entertainment

Durty Nelly's, the gaily coloured pub beside the castle, was built in the early 1600s, and the atmosphere is laid on by the shovel load. A peat fire burns in front of rough wooden chairs and benches. It can be good fun and does attract a local crowd as well as visitors. There is music most evenings.

Mac's pub in the Folk Park has Irish music Wednesday and Friday evenings.

Things to Buy

Avoca Handweavers beyond the Fitzpatrick Shannon Shamrock Hotel do a good selection of tweeds, crafts and woollen suits.

Opposite the same hotel is Sweaters Galore (☎ 061-364299) with every conceivable Irish jumper (sweater). Mike McGlynn Antiques is worth a look, as is Bunratty Cottage Antiques near the castle. Along the Limerick to Shannon road is Ballycasey Craft Workshops, home to weavers, silversmiths, leatherworkers and potters.

Getting There & Away

The bus stop for Bunratty is outside the Fitzpatrick Shannon Shamrock Hotel. Bunratty is on the main Limerick to Galway road so there are plenty of express services in both directions. From Limerick railway station (☎ 061-48666) express buses leave on weekdays at 9 am, and 12.05, 1.20, 3.05 and 5.35 pm. On Sundays, buses leave Limerick at 1, 2.05, 5.30 and 7.05 pm. There's an extra daily service at 11.30 am during July and August.

Buses travelling south through Bunratty leave Ennis railway station (☎ 065-24177) on weekdays at 12.32, 2.07, 4.27 and 7.12 pm and on Sundays at 12.32, 6.02, 7.20 and 9.42 pm. Bunratty is also served by the numerous daily buses on the Shannon Airport to Limerick route.

Getting Around

Bikes can be hired at Hanrahan's (☎ 061-364696), 12 Firgrove, Hurlers Cross, almost four km (two miles) north of Bunratty on the main road to Ennis.

CRATLOE

Three km from Bunratty just north of the main road to Limerick is Cratloe, a picturesque village overlooking the Shannon estuary. Nearby are hills covered in oak forest, a rare sight in Ireland today, although it once blanketed the countryside. The oak roof beams of Westminster Hall in London are supposedly from Cratloe. To reach the woods, go along the Kilmurry road from Cratloe, under a railway bridge and turn right. There are some fine walks in the area and views over the estuary from Woodcock Hill.

Places to Stay

Cratloe has a fair selection of guesthouses. *Cratloe Heights* (☎ 061-87253), Ballymorris, is a smallish house with four rooms. The *Grange* (☎ 061-87389) on the Grange Wood road is two km (one mile) off the main Limerick road; turn north at the Limerick Inn Hotel. Both have B&B at IR£13 per person.

Kilcaskin House (☎ 061-87291), Setrights Cross, has four rooms, two with bathroom. B&B is IR£13 to IR£15. *Sunnybank* (☎ 061-87108) in Ballymorris has four rooms at IR£16/26 for singles/doubles.

Getting There & Away

While there is no bus service directly to Cratloe, there are plenty of buses passing through Bunratty nearby. Visitors can hire a bike in Bunratty (see the Getting Around section for Bunratty) or walk out to Cratloe.

KILLALOE

Killaloe is one of the principal crossings on the River Shannon, and a fine old 13-arched bridge spans the river. On the Tipperary side of the bridge, Killaloe's other half is called Ballina and some of the best pubs and restaurants are on that side. From Killaloe, the Shannon is navigable all the way up to Lough Key in County Sligo, and in summer the town buzzes with weekend sailors.

The town itself has a fine setting, with the Slieve Bearnagh hills rising abruptly to the west, the Arra Mountains to the east and Lough Derg right on its doorstep.

Orientation & Information

The narrow street running from the river on the Killaloe side is Bridge St, which turns right becoming Main St. The tourist office (☎ 0619-376866) is right beside Shannon Bridge.

Killaloe Cathedral

This cathedral, which is also known as St Flannan's Cathedral, dates from the 12th century and was built by the O'Brien family on top of an earlier 6th-century church. Take a look at the carvings around the Romanesque doorway, which dates from an older chapel; these carvings are among the finest in the country.

Near the doorway, the early Christian Thorgrim Stone is unusual in that it bears both the old Scandinavian runic script, and Irish Ogham script. It could be the gravestone of a converted Viking. In the cathedral grounds is St Flannan's Oratory, of 12th-century Romanesque design.

Activities

Shannonside Activity Centre (☎ 061-376622) is an approved sailing centre, offering sailing at IR£10 to IR£20 an hour, windsurfing at IR£8 an hour, canoeing at IR£3 to IR£5 an hour, pony trekking at IR£8 an hour, hillwalking, and biking – road bikes at IR£7.50 a day or IR£35 a week, mountain bikes at IR£12 a day. It's three km out of town on the Scarriff road.

Places to Eat

On the Tipperary side of the bridge in Ballina, *Gooser's Pub & Restaurant* (☎ 0619-376792) has some of the best food in town. The restaurant out back is fine, but expensive at about IR£20 for dinner. *Simply Delicious*, a coffee shop just down from Gooser's, has snacks and lunches.

For fresh seafood, try *Peter's Restaurant* (☎ 061-376162). Just over the bridge in Ballina, down the road that runs beside Irish Molly's pub, the restaurant is open every day for lunch and dinner from 6.30 to 10.30 pm and specialises in seafood. The *Lantern House* (☎ 0619-23034) does simple but wholesome food, including a substantial and reasonable high tea from 6 to 7 pm.

Entertainment

Good pubs are *Irish Molly's*, *Gooser's*, *Crotty's* and *McGrath's*, and most have music at weekends.

Getting There & Away

There are regular buses (☎ 061-42433 for details) from Killaloe to Limerick, Nenagh, Roscrea and Scarriff.

Getting Around

Shannonside Activity Centre (☎ 061-376622), three km (two miles) along the Scarriff road, has bikes for hire.

AROUND KILLALOE

The journey north on either side of Lough Derg to Mountshannon or Portroe is very scenic. One mile north of Killaloe, **Beal Ború** is an earthern mound or fort said to have been Kincora, the palace of the famous Irish King Brian Ború, who defeated the Vikings at the Battle of Clontarf in 1014. Traces of Bronze Age settlement have been found. With its commanding view over Lough Derg, this was obviously a site of strategic importance.

Three km (two miles) north again is Cragliath Hill which has another fort, **Griananlaghna**, named after Brian Ború's great-grandfather King Lachtna.

MOUNTSHANNON

North of Killaloe, on the south-western shores of Lough Derg, Mountshannon is an idyllic 18th-century village. Its stone houses overlook the lake, while anglers pass the evenings in pubs, discussing the day's catch. With luck you will find music in summer.

The small stone harbour is usually busy with fishing boats and is the port for trips to Holy Island, one of Clare's finest early Christian settlements.

Places to Stay

The *Lakeside Watersport Hostel & Campsite* (☎ 0619-27225) has a camp site and charges IR£4 per tent per night and 50p per occupant. Hostel accommodation is in mobile homes or chalets and costs IR£5 to IR£6 per night. There are boats and equipment for hire for windsurfing, rowing and sailing. To get there, go along the Portumna road and take the first turn right.

Oak House (☎ 0619-27185), a country house overlooking the lake, has B&B for IR£16/26 for singles/doubles. *Derg Lodge* (☎ 0619-271800) is also IR£13 a night.

In the village, the delightful *Mount-shannon Hotel* (☎ 0619-27162) has rooms with bathrooms from IR£25 to IR£30.

Getting There & Away

On Saturdays only there is a single bus which leaves Limerick railway station at 2.30 pm and travels to Whitegate via Scarriff and Mountshannon. The journey time to Mountshannon is one hour and 25 minutes. A bus leaves Mountshannon for Limerick each Saturday at 8.50 am.

Getting Around

Guerin's Ivy Stores in the village have bikes for hire at IR£5 a day or IR£20 a week. The Mountshannon Hotel has 10 boats for hire for IR£15 a day.

HOLY ISLAND

From Mountshannon, there are boats to Iniscealtra or Holy Island, the site of a monastic settlement thought to have been founded by St Cáimín in the 7th century. There is a a round tower missing its top storey but still over 27 metres (80 feet) tall, as well as four old chapels, a hermit's cell and some early Christian gravestones dating from the 7th to the 13th century. One of the chapels has an elegant Romanesque arch, and inside an inscription which reads in Irish 'Pray for Tornog who made this cross'.

The Vikings gave this monastery a rough time, but under the subsequent protection of Brian Ború and others it flourished. The Holy Well was once the focus for a lively festival, which was banned in the 1830s because a lot of nonreligious behaviour was creeping in.

NORTH TO GALWAY

North of Mountshannon, the road swerves away from the lake and the views are nondescript. Inland is an area known as the **Clare Lakelands**, based around Feakle. There are numerous lakes with good coarse fishing.

South-West & West Clare

Loop Head at the county's south-western tip is a mighty wedge splitting the Atlantic rollers. North of Kilkee, a popular seaside resort, the road moves inland but there are some worthwhile detours along lonely coast roads and beaches where Spanish Armada ships were wrecked over 400 years ago. The coast between Kilkee and Loop Head has some outstanding cliff scenery. White Strand, Kilkee, Spanish Point and Lahinch have good beaches.

To the north and north-west of Ennis are a number of small villages, such as Corofin and Ennistymon. These are both at the very southern limits of the remarkable Burren region which includes the Hag's Head (a superb walk with excellent views) and the Cliffs of Moher, one of Ireland's most spectacular natural features. From there the road dips downhill towards Doolin, a famous backpacker's rest stop and Irish music centre.

GETTING THERE & AWAY

This region has infrequent local bus services to the coastal towns and villages; some buses run from Limerick and others from Galway, and services are more frequent in summer. Phone Ennis bus station (☎ 065-24177) for exact times and fares.

One express service has its terminus in Ennis or Ennistymon and runs through Lahinch, Lisdoonvarna, Doolin and Kilkee. Another bus goes to Galway, Kinvara, Ballyvaughan, Lisdoonvarna, Ennistymon, Lahinch, Miltown Malbay, Doonbeg, Kilkee and Kilrush. There is also a service to Limerick, Ennis, Ennistymon, Lahinch, Liscannor, the Cliffs of Moher and Doolin, as well as one covering the route between Kilkee, Kilrush, Doonbeg, Quilty, Miltown Malbay, Lahinch, Ennistymon, Ennis and Limerick.

A small bus known as a 'nipper' runs three times daily during the summertime between Lahinch and Lisdoonvarna, passing through Liscannor, the Cliffs of Moher and Doolin en route.

KILLIMER

Killimer is a nondescript village, close to the Shannon estuary and Moneypoint, Ireland's largest power station. At 900 megawatts, Moneypoint is capable of supplying 40% of the country's needs and burns two million tonnes of coal a year. It has a visitors' centre and a guided tour.

The Colleen Bawn, or 'white girl', was a woman called Ellen Hanly who was murdered in 1819 and thrown into the Shannon by her husband, John Scanlon. Her body washed ashore and was buried in Killimer graveyard. Scanlon was hung. The story has inspired novels, plays and operas; unfortunately her tombstone has been dismantled by souvenir hunters.

Getting There & Away

A car ferry runs from Killimer to Tarbert across the Shannon estuary, from April to September, Monday to Saturday 7 am to 9 pm, Sunday 9 am to 9 pm and October to March, Monday to Saturday 7 am to 7 pm, Sunday 10 am to 7 pm. Ferries depart Tarbert on the half hour and from Killimer on the hour. The cost is IR£2 for bikes, IR£6 for cars (IR£8.50 return), and it can be very busy at peak times. If in doubt ring ahead (☎ 065-51060).

KILRUSH

This small town overlooks the Shannon estuary and the hills of Kerry to the south and is not a particularly attractive place. Kilrush has the west coast's newest and biggest marina. If you happen to be interested in stained glass, the Catholic church has some nice examples by well-known craftsman Harry Clarke. East of town is Kilrush Wood, which has some fine old trees and a picnic area. The nearby harbour at Cappa is where you catch the boat to Scattery Island, out in the estuary.

Kilrush has banks, a post office, and a tourist office (☎ 065-51074) on the square which is open through the summer, closed at lunch times. If you want to contact the marina ring ☎ 065-51692.

Bikes can be hired at Gleeson Wholesale (☎ 065-51127) on Henry St, for IR£7 per day or IR£35 per week, with a deposit of IR£40. You can also hire them from the Korner Shop (☎ 065-51037), also on Henry St.

SCATTERY ISLAND

This island is about two km south-west of Cappa pier and is the site of a Christian settlement founded by St Senan in the 6th century. The island is windswept and treeless, and has one of the tallest and best preserved round towers in Ireland. It's over 32 metres (110 feet) high and the entrance is at ground level instead of the usual position high above ground level. There are the remains of five medieval churches.

In order to build his monastery, St Senan had to rid the island of a monster. The Irish name for the island is Inis Cathaigh, Cathach being the legendary sea serpent whose lair was on the island. St Senan banished the monster with the help of the angel Raphael. A local virgin named Cannera wanted to join him, provoking much speculation in rhyme about how he withstood the temptation.

Legend hints that had the maid,
Until morning's light delayed,
And given the saint one rosy smile,
She'd ne'er have left his lonely isle.

Scattery was a beautiful but unfortunate site for a monastery, as it was all too easy for the Vikings to sail up the estuary and raid the place, which they did repeatedly in the 9th and 10th centuries. They occupied the island for 100 years until 970 when they were dislodged by Brian Ború.

During the summer, boats (☎ 061-451327) run from Cappa pier to the island for IR£2.50 return.

KILKEE

During the summer, Kilkee's wide bay is thronged with day trippers and holiday-makers from all over Clare and Limerick.

Kilkee first became popular in Victorian times when rich Limerick families built seaside retreats here. Today, the town is a little too thick with guesthouses, amusement arcades and takeaways.

Visitors come for the fine sheltered beach and the Pollock Holes, natural swimming pools in the Duggerna Rocks to the south of the beach. St George's Head to the north has good cliff walks and scenery, while south of the bay the Duggerna Rocks form an unusual natural amphitheatre. Farther south is a huge sea cave. These sights can be reached by driving to Kilkee's west end and following the coastal path. The west end is also where you will find most of the best B&Bs.

Information

The seasonal tourist office (☎ 065-56112) is on O'Connell St just off the seafront and the staff are very helpful.

Activities

Kilkee is a well-known diving centre. There are shore dives from the Duggerna Rocks fringing the west side of the bay, or boat dives on the Black Rocks farther out. Right at the tip of the Duggerna Rocks is the small inlet of Myles Creek, and there is excellent underwater scenery out from it. A new diving centre has just opened by the harbour with air available and equipment for hire.

Kilkee has plenty of resort diversions like mini-golf, squash and video arcades. There is horse racing on the beach in late August. There are two golf courses; for Kilkee Golf Club ring 065-56048.

Places to Stay

Camping There are plenty of caravan and camp sites. *Cunningham's* (☎ 061-51666) is open May to September and costs IR£4 per tent and IR£1 per person. To get there find the Victoria Hotel on the seafront and turn inland. *Collins' Caravan & Camping* (☎ 065-56140) is also near the town centre, on the Kilrush road. They are open May to September and charge IR£5 per tent.

Hostels *Kilkee Independent Hostel* (☎ 065-

56209) is clean, well-run and open all year round. It's 50 metres from the seafront on O'Curry St, and costs IR£5 a night in a dorm. There are no double rooms. They have a well-equipped kitchen, a laundry room, free shower facilities and a small coffee shop .

B&Bs There are countless guesthouses, usually a little more expensive than other areas. There are some good ones at the west end of Kilkee.

Aran House (☎ 065-56170) is on the seafront overlooking the bay. Nearby is *Dunearn House* (☎ 065-56545). *Harbour Lodge* (☎ 065-56090) is also at the west end near the Victoria Hotel. All three cost IR£14. At busy times, you may have to take whatever the tourist office can get you.

Hotels There are plenty of hotels in Kilkee but for the extra money you don't get much extra luxury. *Halpin's Hotel* (☎ 065-56032) is a pleasant family-run hotel on Erin St. All rooms have bathroom, TV and phone. B&B is IR£20 to IR£29 a night.

Places to Eat
Cafés, Takeaways & Pubs There are plenty of fast-food joints. For good home cooking at reasonable prices try the *Pantry* (☎ 065-56576), halfway up O'Curry St from the seafront on the right. It's open May to September from 9.30 am to 10 pm.

The *Hideout* pub on Erin St has bar food. The *Strand* pub on the seafront is also worth trying.

Restaurants *Krazy Kraut's* (☎ 065-56240) on the Strand does good seafood snacks and lunches during the day and full dinner in the evenings.

Almost two km north of Kilkee is the popular *Manuel's Seafood Restaurant* (☎ 065-56211), only open for dinner, which costs IR£20 or more. Bookings are recommended.

Entertainment
Across from the hostel on O'Curry St is the *Myles Creek* pub, Kilkee's trendiest spot.

The pub is on the band circuit and attracts many of Ireland's best young rock groups. They have Irish sessions on Monday nights. *O'Mara's* on the same street has sessions on Mondays, Wednesdays and Fridays. The popular *Strand* on the seafront has sessions during the week.

Getting Around
Bicycles can be hired at Williams (☎ 065-56041), on Circular Rd near the Catholic church, for IR£7.50 a day or IR£30 a week.

SOUTH OF KILKEE TO LOOP HEAD
The land from Kilkee south to Loop Head is poor and flat but the cliff scenery is spectacular: the coast peppered with sea stacks, arches and wave-sculpted rocks. It's a glorious day's bike ride down to the Head and back. Better still, if you have the energy, is the 24-km (15-mile) cliff walk between Loop Head and Kilkee. The cliffs compare with the more famous Cliffs of Moher to the north and are much less visited.

Intrinsic Bay
Just south of Kilkee is Intrinsic Bay, named after the *Intrinsic*, a ship wrecked here in 1856 en route to America. When the *Edmund* sank nearby in 1850, 100 people drowned.

The summit shadowing the bay is Lookout Hill. To the north are Diamond Rock and **Bishop's Island**, the latter a remarkable pillar of rock with a medieval oratory perched on the summit. The oratory is attributed to the 6th-century St Senan who also built the settlement on Scattery Island in the Shannon estuary. Later a selfish bishop is supposed to have lived here while his people starved in a famine; when the gap to the mainland widened in a storm the bishop himself starved to death.

Kilbaha
On the minor coast road, seven km (four miles) from Loop Head, Kilbaha's tiny church contains an unusual relic of more repressive times. The 'little ark' is a small wooden altar used by Catholics in the 1850s. To hold mass, the altar was wheeled below

the high-tide mark where it was outside the jurisdiction of the local Protestant landlord. A stained-glass window above the church door depicts the ark in use. Father Michael Meehan, the courageous local priest who had the ark built, is buried in the church.

There is a 'submerged forest', a collection of 5000-year-old tree stumps (probably pine) on the shore east of Rinvella Bay, near Kilbaha. They were originally preserved in peat bog, which was washed away as the sea level rose, leaving the stumps visible.

Carrigaholt

On 15 September 1588, seven tattered ships of the Spanish Armada took shelter off Carrigaholt, a tiny village inside the mouth of the Shannon estuary. One, probably the *Annunciada*, was torched and abandoned, sinking somewhere out in the estuary. Today, Carrigaholt has a safe beach and the substantial remains of a McMahon castle overlooking the water.

The *Long Dock* (☎ 065-58106) on West St is a cosy pub-cum-restaurant, with bar food, seafood dinners and Irish music on Friday nights. Also worth trying is *Fennell's* pub (☎ 065-58029) which has music on Wednesday and Saturday nights from June to September.

Loop Head

On a clear day, Loop Head, Clare's southernmost point, has magnificent views south to the Dingle Peninsula crowned by Mt Brandon, and north to the Aran Islands and Galway Bay. There are bracing walks in the area and a long hike running along the cliffs to Kilkee.

NORTH OF KILKEE

North of Kilkee, the real west of Ireland quickly reasserts itself. The road runs inland for some 32 km (20 miles) until it reaches Quilty. Take the odd lane to the west and search out little-visited places like Ballard Bay and White Strand, north of Dunbeg or Doonbeg. Ballard Bay is eight km (five miles) north of Doonbeg, where an old telegraph tower looks over some fine cliffs.

Cúchulainn's Leap

Loop is a corruption of 'leap', and legend has it that the Celtic warrior Cúchulainn was being chased all over Ireland by a hag called Mal. Cornered on this headland, he leapt onto a seastack and when she tried to follow him, Mal fell to her death. The sea turned crimson and her body washed ashore at various points along the coast, giving Hag's Head and Malbay their names. West of the lighthouse, you will find the seastack in question; the gap is known as Cúchulainn's Leap. ■

Doonegal Point has the remains of a promontory fort.

There is good fishing for bass, pollock and mackerel all along the coast, and safe beaches at Seafield, Lough Donnell and Quilty.

Doonbeg

Doonbeg is a tiny fishing village halfway between Kilkee and Miltown Malbay. Near the mouth of the River Doonbeg, another Armada ship, the *San Esteban*, was wrecked on 20 September 1588. The few survivors were later executed at Spanish Point.

White Strand is a quiet beach, two km long and backed by dunes. For campers the side roads around Doonbeg are good places to pitch a tent and watch the sun go down. There are two ruined castles nearby, Doonbeg and Doonmore.

Places to Stay & Eat The Igoe Inn in Doonbeg has the *Olde Kitchen Restaurant* (☎ 065-55039), which does steaks and seafood. *An Tintean* (☎ 065-55036) is a seafood restaurant and guesthouse, with turf fires and good rooms with bathrooms. B&B is IR£15. The *San Esteban* (☎ 065-55105) is one km from Doonbeg in (try and pronounce this) Rhynnagonnaught. They have four rooms, one with bathroom, and B&B is IR£15/26 for singles/doubles.

Entertainment *Morrissey's* pub in Doonbeg often has music as does *Tubridy's* pub

(☎ 065-55041) on Thursdays. The *Ocean View Bar* (☎ 065-55064) has Irish music on Tuesdays, Saturdays and Sundays during the summer.

Quilty

The small village of Quilty lies on a particularly bleak stretch of coast. Quilty is a centre for seaweed production; kelp and other weeds are collected, dried on the stone walls and sent for processing. The resulting alginates are used in toothpaste, beer and agar. Quilty has a good beach and boats are available for deep-sea angling.

One of the most powerful ships of the the Spanish Armada, the *San Marcos,* was wrecked off nearby Mutton Island in September 1588. It had taken a terrible battering in the English Channel and only four of the 1000 sailors on board survived the wreck.

Local guesthouses include *Clonmore Lodge* (☎ 065-87020), *Mullagh* (☎ 065-87179) and *Seafield* (☎ 065-87081), just over one km from the village. B&B in each costs around IR£13.

Miltown Malbay

Like Kilkee, Miltown Malbay was a resort favoured by wealthy Victorians. Having said that, the town isn't actually on the sea: the beach is three km (two miles) away at Spanish Point. Every year Miltown Malbay hosts a Willie Clancy Irish Music Festival as a tribute to one of Ireland's greatest pipers. The festival usually runs in the first week in July, when the town is overrun with wandering minstrels, and drink is consumed by the bucketload. You can also find music in the surrounding villages.

Spanish Point There is an excellent beach at Spanish Point, and when the waves are running there's good surfing.

The beach gets its name from the execution of 60 Armada survivors on Cnoc Na Crocaire (the 'Hill of the Gallows') nearby. They had swum ashore, only to be executed by the local head honcho, Boetius Clancy, Sheriff of Clare, and Turlough O'Brien, the local chief who was loyal to the English crown.

Lahinch

Lahinch is the archetypal seaside resort, full of fast-food joints, amusement arcades and places to stay. The town sits on a protected bay with a fine beach, and the surfing can be good. In 1943, an off-course US bomber landed on the beach and the 12 airmen were repatriated through Northern Ireland. Lahinch is very busy in the summer; you may prefer to move on to Ennistymon, Liscannor or Doolin.

There is a seasonal tourist office (☎ 065-81730) near the post office at the south end of Main St, which is open between 10 am and 7 pm.

Lahinch has two golf courses, one of them a world-famous 18-hole championship links in the dunes to the north of town. In July and August they hold competitions, and it can be difficult to get a round. When you can, green fees are IR£15. Check with Lahinch Golf Club (☎ 065-81408).

Surfboards can be rented on the seafront from the Surf Shop. There is pony trekking (☎ 065-71385) en route to Liscannor.

ENNISTYMON

Ennistymon, a lovely little town just three km (two miles) inland from Lahinch, is on the banks of the River Inagh. The town started out as a settlement around a castle built by Turlough O'Brien in 1588, the year of the Spanish Armada. The town's appearance has scarcely changed in the last 20 or 30 years and its charm derives primarily from the many well-maintained old pubs and shops.

The bridge over the River Inagh is just above the well-known 200-metre rapids known as the Cascades, which are impressive if the river is in flood. There is trout and salmon fishing, and some good Irish music pubs.

Orientation & Information

Kam Knitwear (☎ 065-71387) has some tourist information and is on the Ennis Rd about five minutes' walk south of the town square. Markets are held in the town centre on Tuesdays. Ennistymon is essentially one long main street called Church St.

Things to See

The **River Inagh** runs directly behind and parallel to Church St. The rapids known as the **Cascades** are just down the lane beside the Archway Bar to the south of the Square. It's a pleasant stroll around here in the evenings. When the Inagh is in flood, the waters can rise almost to the houses. Down river, the Falls Hotel is a former residence of the McNamaras and has its own hydropower generator.

Places to Stay

Hostels The *White House Hostel* (☎ 065-26793) is a very basic hostel on a corner in Main St and costs IR£4 per person.

B&Bs *Station House* (☎ 065-71149) is about half a km south of the square on the Ennis road. The six rooms all have bathrooms. In the town centre is *San Antone* (☎ 065-71078), part of McMahon's pub. Both these places cost IR£16/26 for singles/doubles. *Grovemount House* (☎ 065-71431) is a big guesthouse on the Lahinch road. All eight rooms have bathrooms and cost from IR£16 to IR£20.

Hotel The *Falls Hotel* (☎ 065-71004) is a comfortable old country house in 20 hectares of wooded gardens; rooms with bathrooms go from IR£22 to IR£29 B&B.

Places to Eat

Franco's Pizza & Takeaway on Church St is one of the very few decent low-priced eateries in Ennistymon. Otherwise there is really only bar food, apart from *Fitzpatrick's Coffee Shop*, next door to the supermarket on Parliament St, which closes at 6 pm; breakfast is IR£2.20. *Cooley's House* pub on Church St has reasonable bar food and music most evenings during the summer. The *Archway Bar*, just south of the square, serves run-of-the-mill snacks. For something more substantial or upmarket try the *Falls Hotel* where a set lunch is IR£8.50 and set dinner IR£15, or make the journey out to Lahinch.

Entertainment

Daly's pub on Church St (also known as the *Matchmaker's Shack*) is a cosy traditional place and gets a good crowd. It's one of the best places in town for Irish music with sessions most nights in summer. *Phil's Place* across from the Archway Bar has music on Saturday and Sunday nights, while *Nagle's Bar* has music on Wednesdays and weekends. *Cooley's House* pub (☎ 065-71712) has music at weekends.

LISCANNOR

This small fishing village has a fine view over Liscannor Bay and Lahinch as the road winds past on its way to the Cliffs of Moher and Doolin. Liscannor has given its name to a characteristic flagstone with wormlike ripples on the surface. The stone is widely used locally for floors, walls and even roofs.

John P Holland, the inventor of the submarine, was born here. He emigrated to the USA, and he hoped his invention would be used to sink British warships.

The O'Briens

The eccentric O'Briens were one of Clare's most important ruling families. The ruined square castle on the point outside Liscannor was built by the O'Connors, taken later by the O'Briens and at the time of the Spanish Armada was occupied by Turlough O'Brien, who was loyal to the English crown and co-executioner of the Spanish survivors washed up at Spanish Point. Cornelius O'Brien, a rather idiosyncratic descendant, lived in the now ruined manor house north of Liscannor. That O'Brien was MP for Clare in the mid-19th century. To the west is a monument to Cornelius, erected in 1853 by his tenants with some persuasion from the man himself. He also erected the viewing tower at the Cliffs of Moher. ∎

Places to Stay

Hostels *Liscannor Village Hostel* (☎ 065-81385) in the centre of the village is a big, well-run place with 80 beds, all in dorms, at IR£5 a night. The Old Hostel on the road to the Cliffs of Moher is now closed.

B&Bs Coming from Lahinch, just before the village on the right, is *Seahaven B&B* (☎ 065-81385), with four rooms, most with bathrooms, and good hard beds. Five km (three miles) from Liscannor, the closest B&B to the Cliffs of Moher is the friendly *Moher Lodge* (☎ 065-81269). Both places cost IR£13 per person.

Places to Eat

For cheap meals, try the *Village Hostel*, the pubs or the small coffee rooms at the Cliffs of Moher. There is good fresh seafood at the *Captain's Deck Restaurant* (☎ 065-81385) in the middle of the village. It's open 6 to 10 pm with main courses from IR£9 to IR£14. They have a simpler set dinner from 6 to 7.30 pm for IR£10. There is a small seafood restaurant tucked away in a tiny cottage near the Holy Well of St Brigid a few km to the west.

Entertainment

There are a string of pubs in Liscannor, most with music. *Joseph McHugh's* is the best known and is as genuine an old Irish pub as you will find anywhere, down to the groceries and other oddments piled on the shelves. (Ask to see the bull's penis.) For music, try McHugh's on Tuesdays or the comfortable *Egan's* next door on Thursdays. *Vaughan's Bar* has music almost every night during the summer. Alternatively, travel on to Doolin.

AROUND LISCANNOR

On the way to the Cliffs of Moher close to Murphy's and Considine's pubs is the **Holy Well of St Brigid** where people with all sorts of problems come to pray and drink the healing waters. There is usually a collection of crutches and sticks discarded near the well, so it obviously works!

The well's significance probably predates Christian times as its Irish name suggests a connection with a pre-Christian god, Crom Dubh. People from all over Clare and the Aran Islands make the pilgrimage to the well in July, particularly on the last weekend of the month, and there can be from 100 to 400 people there on the Sunday.

Clahane Beach to the west of Liscannor is good and safe. A 'lost city' and church known as Kilstephen are supposed to sit on an underwater reef in Liscannor Bay. On **Slieve Callan** to the south is buried the Celtic hero Conan, who is said to lie with the key to the lost church.

HAG'S HEAD

Hag's Head forms the southern end of the touristy but magnificent Cliffs of Moher. There is a superb walk to Hag's Head (see below) where a signal tower was erected in case Napoleon tried to make a surprise attack on the west coast. The tower is built on the site of an ancient promontory fort called Mothair which has given its name to the famous cliffs to the north.

Hag's Head is named after the formidable Mal, who chased the legendary Celtic hero Cúchulainn all over Ireland. She fell to her death off Loop Head to the south, and her body was reputedly washed ashore here (and in various other places). Some say the headland looks like a seated woman looking out over the Atlantic.

Hag's Head Walk

Hag's Head is an excellent place to view the Cliffs of Moher and the walk out is more than worth the effort. To get there, go just over five km (three miles) out of Liscannor towards the Cliffs of Moher until, just past Moher Lodge B&B, a rough track turns to the left. You can only drive a short distance and then have to walk along the path out towards the point and tower. There is a huge sea arch at the tip and another visible to the north. The hike there and back takes about three hours.

CLIFFS OF MOHER

One of Ireland's most spectacular sights, the Cliffs of Moher rise from Hag's Head to the south and reach their highest point (230 metres, 700 feet) just north of O'Brien's Tower before slowly declining farther north again. On a clear day, the views are tremendous: the Aran Islands stand etched on the waters of Galway Bay and beyond lie the hills and valleys of Connemara in western Galway.

From the cliff edge you can just hear the booming far below as the waves eat into the soft shale and sandstone. Often sections of the cliff give way, and they are generally so unstable that few birds or plants live on them. Sunset is by far the best time to visit and there is a bracing eight-km (five-mile) walk along the cliff edge down to Hag's Head. Part of the walk was walled off with Liscannor stone by the eccentric local landlord Cornelius O'Brien, who built the lookout tower to impress lady visitors.

The seastack covered with seabirds and their guano just below the tower is called Breanan Mor and is itself over 70 metres (200 feet) high.

Information

The visitors' centre (☎ 065-81171) for the Cliffs is open March to October and has tourist information, a shop, a reasonable café and a bureau de change. It must be said that the cliffs are one of the most visited attractions in the country: coaches roll up ceaselessly during the day and stage Irish characters hang about playing tin whistles and looking for money.

A Risky Route

The cliffs just north of Moher are known as Aill Na Searrach or the 'Cliff of the Colts' because some fairy horses are supposed to have leapt into the sea at this point. There is a precipitous and dangerous path to the base of these cliffs, only to be attempted by the fittest walkers, and only in dry weather – be warned. The beginning of the path is about two km (one mile) north of the official Cliffs of Moher entrance.

Where the road comes off the mountain, there is a small bridge and a rough track leading to a galvanised gate. Cross the field

to the dip on the left, where the path begins. At the bottom, massive boulders have been worn smooth and piled high by the Atlantic rollers.

You can also reach this path by following the clifftop path north from O'Brien's Tower, as if you were walking to Doolin. You can clearly see the path which zigzags down to the rocky beach.

Getting There & Away

The bus which runs between Limerick and Lisdoonvarna (more frequently in summer) stops at the Cliffs of Moher as well as the nearby small towns of Ennistymon, Lahinch and Liscannor. Contact Ennis bus station (☎ 065-24177) for exact times and fares. The small bus known locally as the 'nipper' calls at the Cliffs of Moher as well as Liscannor and Doolin en route between Lahinch and Lisdoonvarna, and runs three times daily in the summer months.

The Burren Area

Between Kinvara and Corofin in northern Clare is the Burren region, an extraordinary and unique place. *Boireann* is the Irish for 'rocky place', and when you see the miles of polished limestone stretching in every direction you'll know why one of Cromwell's generals was moved to exclaim that there is 'neither water enough to drown a man, nor a tree to hang him, nor soil enough to bury him' – which shows what was on their minds.

Along the coast are a few settlements including Doolin, a very popular Irish music centre, and Ballyvaughan, an attractive little village on the south coast of Galway Bay.

East of Ballyvaughan the Burren peters out, near Kinvara. This area has a lot of historical sites, notably Corcomroe Abbey and the churches of Oughtmama. The deeply indented coastline has plenty of wildlife and fine walks.

INFORMATION

The nearest tourist information point to the

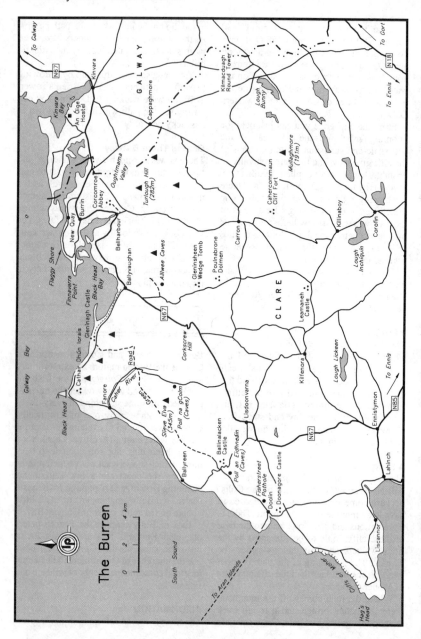

The Burren & the Interpretive Centre
The Office of Public Works (OPW) decided to build an interpretive centre near Mullaghmore Mountain and Lake halfway between Corofin and Gort. This is a particularly beautiful spot and the prospect of a tourist centre, complete with coaches, carparks and toilets, in such a delicate place caused uproar. Construction work commenced in early 1993 and just about every biologist, conservationist and man, woman or child who had a feeling for the Burren objected. Until this time the OPW had not had to go through normal planning procedures and could build almost anything it liked anywhere it liked, with little scope for objectors' views to be expressed or heeded.

The row split the community, as any prospect of providing jobs is not dispensed with lightly, so feelings on both sides were very strong. Many local politicians backed the centre which was being built with the aid of grants from the EC. The opponents of the centre wanted it to be built somewhere else, such as a local village, where it would have caused minimum disruption.

In May 1993, the battle was won – for the time being – by the opponents to the centre who took the OPW to court. The verdict was that the OPW had to go through normal planning procedures for any of its developments and thus the interpretive centres were now illegal. The car park and foundations had already been laid at Mullaghmore but work was immediately abandoned. Even those beginnings have provided an unsightly blot on the landscape. It remains to be seen if the OPW now applies for planning permission and attempts to complete the buildings.

Overall, the OPW does a reasonable job overseeing our national heritage. But it appears recently to have been rushing to package every region or site of interest with interpretive centres, which detract from the very beauty and isolation that people come to these places for. By far the best way to explore the Burren is to get a map and head off on your own. ■

Burren is at the Cliffs of Moher. A must if you intend spending any time here is Tim Robinson's *Burren Map & Guide*. It's available in many shops and shows just about every object and place of interest on the Burren.

GEOLOGY

The Burren is the most extensive limestone region in Britain or Ireland. The craggy limestone landscape is known as 'karst' after a similar area in what used to be Yugoslavia. The Burren is all limestone except for a cap of mud and shale which sits on the higher regions from Lisdoonvarna north to Slieve Elva.

During the Carboniferous period 350 million years ago, this whole area was the bottom of a warm shallow sea. The remains of coral and shells fell to the seabed, and coastal rivers dumped sand and silt on top of these limey deposits. Time and pressure turned the layers to stone: limestone underneath, shale and sandstone above.

Massive rumblings in the earth's crust some 270 million years ago buckled the edges of Europe and forced the seabed above sea level, at the same time bending and fracturing the stone sheets to form long deep cracks. Wind, rain and ice have since removed most of the overlying shale, leaving mountains of limestone.

The difference between the areas of porous limestone and nonporous shale is acute. Shale country is a depressing dull green, covered in acid bogs, marshes and reeds. On limestone the soil is sparse, water disappears and grey rock predominates.

Being slightly acidic, rainwater dissolves the limestone, widening the vertical cracks, which are known as grikes. The horizontal slabs are called clints. The water follows weak points in the rock, carving out underground rivers and caverns. Springs and rivers appear and disappear. Near the surface, the roofs of caves collapse, forming dark swallowholes and squared-off valleys. Rainwater is caught on top of the shale and eventually drains off at the edges into the limestone, which it erodes. A ring of caves appears along the shale/limestone boundary.

The southern boundary of the Burren is roughly where the limestone dips under the shale between Doolin and Lake Inchiquin. Underneath the limestone of the Burren is a huge mass of granite, which surfaces to the north-west in Connemara, County Galway.

During numerous Ice Ages, glaciers have scoured the hills, rounding their edges and sometimes polishing the rock to a mirror finish. They also dumped a skin of rock and soil over the region. Huge boulders were carried by the ice, incongruous aliens on a sea of flat rock. Seen all over the Burren, these 'glacial erratics' are often a visibly different type of rock.

The only surface river in the Burren is the River Caher, which flows down the Khyber Pass before meeting the sea at Fanore. The valley is lined with glacial sediments which stop the water from leaking away.

FLORA & FAUNA

Soil may be scarce here, but the small amount that gathers in the cracks is limey, well-drained and rich in nutrients. This and the soft Atlantic climate support an extraordinary mix of Mediterranean, Arctic and Alpine plants.

The Burren is a stronghold of Ireland's most elusive mammal, the pine marten. They are rarely seen, although there are certainly some living near Gleninagh Castle and up the Caher Valley. Badgers, foxes and even stoats are common throughout the region. Along the shores around Belharbour, New Quay and Finnavarra Point live otters and seals. The estuaries along this northern coast of the Burren are rich in birdlife and frequently have brent geese during the winter. More than 28 of Ireland's 33 species of butterfly are found here, including one endemic species, the Burren green.

Unfortunately, modern farming and EC land improvement grants have had their effect on the Burren. Weedkillers and fertilisers encourage grass and little else. Many ring forts and stone walls have been bulldozed into extinction.

ARCHAEOLOGY

The Burren's bare limestone hills were once covered by soil and light woods. Towards the end of the Stone Age, about 6000 years ago, the first farmers arrived in the area. They began to clear the woodlands and use the upland regions for grazing. Over the centuries, the soil was eroded and the huge mass of limestone we see today began to emerge.

Despite its desolation, the Burren supported quite large numbers of people in ancient times, and has over 2500 historic sites. Chief among them is the 5000-year-old Poulnabrone Dolmen, one of Ireland's finest ancient monuments.

There are at least 65 megalithic tombs erected by the Burren's first settlers. Many of these tombs are wedge-shaped graves, stone boxes tapering both in height and width and about the size of a large double bed. The dead were placed inside and the whole structure was covered in earth and stones. Gleninsheen, east of Aillwee Caves, is a good example.

Ring forts dot the Burren in prodigious numbers. There are almost 500 in all, including Iron Age stone forts like Ballykinvarga and Cahercommaun near Carron.

In later times, many castles were built by the region's ruling families, including Leamenah Castle near Kilfenora, Ballinalacken Castle near Doolin and Gleninagh Castle on the Black Head road.

Green roads are the old highways of the Burren, crossing hills and valleys to some of the remotest corners of the region. Unpaved and possibly dating back thousands of years, they are now used mostly by hikers and the odd farmer. Many are signposted.

CAVING

Serious caving is not for the fainthearted. If you fancy trying it, take a course or at least find an experienced guide.

Tim Robinson's Burren map has many of the cave entrances marked on it and some equipment can be hired at the Bridge Hostel in Fanore. Kilfenora Caving & Outdoor Centre (☎ 065-71422) has walking, caving, pony trekking and climbing. Serious cavers should consult *The Caves of Northwest Clare* by Tratman.

GETTING THERE & AWAY

For precise times and other details of the

buses to the Burren area, ring either Ennis, Limerick or Galway bus stations. Various buses pass through the Burren: a local service runs between Ennis, Ennistymon, Lisdoonvarna, Doolin, Kilrush and Kilkee; another service connects Galway City with Ballyvaughan, Lisdoonvarna, Ennistymon, Lahinch, Kilkee and Tralee, on summer weekdays only; and another runs from Galway City to Kinvara, Ballyvaughan, Lisdoonvarna and Doolin – this service has one bus a day between Monday and Saturday in winter and up to three buses a day in the summer months, from mid-June to the end of September.

From Limerick a bus to Doolin passes through Ennis, Lahinch, the Cliffs of Moher, Ennistymon, and Lisdoonvarna, and this service consists of one bus a day between Monday and Saturday in winter and two every day between mid-June and the end of September.

Buses from Galway City follow the Burren coast via Kinvara, Ballyvaughan, Blackhead, Fanore and Lisdoonvarna to Doolin. There is usually one bus daily in winter, except Sundays, and two in summer, from mid-June to the end of September.

GETTING AROUND
Walking

Walking is by far the best way of seeing the Burren. Particularly good walks are the green road (old highway) from Ballinalackan Castle to Fanore and back through a hidden valley which forms part of the Burren Way, and the climb up Black Head to Cathair Dhun Iorais Iron Age fort. The 40-km (25-mile) Burren Way runs down through the Burren between Ballyvaughan and Ballinalacken Castle near Doolin. From Doolin it travels on south to the Cliffs of Moher and Liscannor. At its northern end, the Burren Way runs from Ballyvaughan along the shore and then turns inland crossing the River Caher before crossing Slieve Elva, the region's highest point. Then it follows green roads inland from Fanore and down to Ballinalacken Castle. The route is clearly marked.

The southern portions of this walk are described in more detail under the section on Fanore and under Doolin. Tim Robinson's Burren map is a must if you are doing the whole route. The best time is late spring or early summer. The route is pretty dry but walking boots are useful as the limestone is sharp. There is an information sheet on the route published by Shannon Development (☎ 061-361555), Shannon Town Centre, County Clare and usually available in tourist offices.

Bicycles

Cycling is second best, and good mountain bikes are available from the Doolin Hostel (☎ 065-74006) or Burkes Garage (☎ 065-74022) on the square in Lisdoonvarna. You can easily ride a bike along the green roads.

DOOLIN

Doolin straggles unattractively for miles along the road, but despite appearances it has some of the best music pubs in the west, two of the best restaurants for miles, and plenty of good cafés, hostels and guesthouses. It's also an excellent base for the Burren, which lies just to the north. There is a ferry to the smallest Aran island of Inisheer, and the Cliffs of Moher are only a few km to the south.

Doolin's popularity among backpackers and music lovers has rocketed over the past few years, and at night the pubs are packed with a cosmopolitan crowd. In high season it can be difficult to get a bed, so book ahead.

Orientation & Information

Doolin, or Fisherstreet on some maps, is made up of three parts. Coming from Lisdoonvarna you first hit the Catholic church, then after less than one km the upper village or Roadford area with shops, restaurants and hostels, and the post office. Then there's a slightly bigger gap before reaching Fisherstreet or the lower village, which has the Doolin Hostel, more shops and O'Connor's pub. It's one more km to the harbour and the ferry to the Aran Islands.

There are no banks, but you can change

money and travellers' cheques in the Doolin Hostel as well as in O'Connor's pub just over the bridge.

Walking Tours

A number of people operate excellent walking tours of the Burren. They come and go, so check hostel and shop windows for details.

Places to Stay

Camping Down by the harbour is the excellent *Doolin Camping & Caravan Park* (☎ 065-74127), with a good kitchen, showers and laundrette. The cost is IR£2 per tent and IR£1 per occupant.

Hostels Budget travellers are well catered for in Doolin. The *Doolin Hostel* (☎ 065-74006) in the lower village is in two parts: a large, modern, obvious building near O'Connor's pub and the original older hostel across the road. The new part houses four to six people per room in bunks and has very good kitchen and bathroom facilities, as well as a small shop, which sells maps and groceries. A bed costs IR£4.50 to IR£5 per night; they are very busy so book ahead. They rent out good mountain bikes for IR£7 a day. The same family runs a good guesthouse 100 metres away.

In the upper village, Roadford, the *Rainbow Hostel* (☎ 065-74415) is near McGann's pub. It is smaller and older than the Doolin Hostel, and its front room has an open turf fire. They have 16 beds, including one double, at IR£4.50 a night. They are open all year.

Off the road on the way down to O'Connor's pub from the upper village is the *Aille River Hostel* (☎ 065-74260), a converted farmhouse with turf fires. The cost is IR£4.50 a night.

B&Bs Formerly a restaurant, *Killilagh House* (☎ 065-74392) in the upper village is on the right going south past the post office. Excellent rooms with bathrooms are IR£13 for B&B. Continuing on past McGann's pub and around the bend on the left is the equally

good *Doolin House* (☎ 065-74259). They have six rooms, all with bathrooms, at IR£16/26 for singles/doubles. *Moloney's* (☎ 065-74006) is near the Doolin Hostel and charges IR£13.

Other good B&Bs include *Island View House* (☎ 065-74346) three km (two miles) from Doolin on the Lisdoonvarna road via Garrahy's Cross and, near the harbour, *Atlantic View* (☎ 065-74189). Both charge IR£13 or IR£14 with bathroom.

Hotel *Aran View* (☎ 065-74061) is a very comfortable country house hotel one km north of town past the Catholic church. Rooms with bathrooms run from IR£20 to IR£25 B&B.

Places to Eat

Both *O'Connor's* in the lower village and *McGann's* in the upper village serve really good bar food. McGann's have Irish stew for around IR£5.

Doolin Craft Gallery (☎ 065-74309), one km along the Lisdoonvarna road, does delicious light meals. The *Doolin Café* ,opposite the post office, and *Ilsa's Kitchen*, by the bridge just up from O'Connor's, do good snacks.

If you feel like splashing out, there are two really nice restaurants, the *Lazy Lobster* (☎ 065-74390) and, next door to McGann's, *Bruach na h'Aille* (☎ 065-74120), both in the upper village. Count on about IR£15 per person including wine.

Entertainment

Doolin is renowned for Irish music which can be heard almost every night during the summer. *O'Connor's* pub is the best known (note the international collection of police department badges behind the bar) but *McGann's* staff can be friendlier. On a good night, the atmosphere in either pubs is hard to beat. *McDermott's*, in Roadford near the post office, is more favoured by locals and quieter. Watch out for sessions in nearby Lisdoonvarna or Kilfenora.

Things to Buy

The Doolin Craft Gallery is past the church on the way to Lisdoonvarna and is excellent, with a huge range of woollen sweaters (jumpers), batik and crafts.

Getting There & Away

Ferry Doolin Harbour is the jumping-off point for the ferry to Inisheer – also spelt Inis Thiar or Inis Oírr – the smallest of the three Aran Islands. In May, June, July and August, there is also a single daily sailing to the biggest Aran island, Inishmór. Otherwise you can get onward connections from Inisheer.

There are two rival companies. Doolin Ferries (☎ 065-74189/77086 or at the pier 065-74455) have the bigger boats, the *Happy Hooker* and the *Tranquility* while Inis Thiar Ferries (☎ 065-74500) operate two smaller boats, the *Dorothy D* and *Saoirse*. There is keen competition for clients, and ugly signs are springing up along the road to the harbour.

It takes around 30 minutes to cross the eight km (five miles) to Inisheer and the return fare is IR£10. Ferries run from April to September, and in June, July and August each company operates around seven sailings a day beginning at 9.30 am and the last returning from Inisheer at around 7 pm. If you intend only to spend the day on Inisheer you should get an early ferry out and book a place on the last one home.

From May through to August, Doolin Ferries operate the single daily sailing to Inishmór, leaving at 10 am and departing Inishmór to come back to Doolin at 4 pm. The trip takes 50 minutes and the fare is IR£10 one way and IR£18 return.

Bus The Bus Éireann stop is outside Moloney's Doolin Hostel (☎ 065-74006) near O'Connor's pub. For fares and times check with the hostel or ring ☎ 065-24177 or ☎ 061-418855. There are Bus Éireann buses between Doolin and Ennis, Galway Bus Station (☎ 091-63555) and Limerick Bus Station (☎ 061-313333). There are connections on to Dublin. For more details, see the

Getting There & Away section under the Burren Area.

Getting Around

Taxi For Doolin's 'safe home' taxi service ring (☎ 065-74557) or try Tim Murphy (☎ 065-81463).

Bicycle Rental The Doolin Hostel (☎ 065-74006) has Raleigh mountain bikes for IR£7 a day or IR£30 a week plus deposit.

AROUND DOOLIN

Caves

Doolin is very popular with cavers. The British seem particularly fond of this pastime and use Doolin as a base, spending their days crawling through dirty holes and their nights drinking pints of Guinness. The Fisherstreet potholes are nearby, and Poll Na gColm, five km (three miles) north-east of Lisdoonvarna, is Ireland's longest with over 12 km (eight miles) of mapped passageways.

A few hundred metres south of Ballinalacken Castle, you will see some low cliffs on the east or inland side across a field. These hide the entrance to Poll an Eidhnain or Ionáin, a cave which, after a difficult and mucky passage, widens to a chamber containing a six-metre (21-foot) stalactite claimed to be the tallest in Western Europe. The cavern is difficult to get to and the farmer is not keen on trespassers, so ask first.

The rocks to the north of Doolin Harbour are honeycombed with an unusual system of undersea caves called the Green Holes of Doolin. They are the longest known undersea caves in temperate waters – one of them has been followed inland underwater for a km. Nondivers can look into 'Hell', a large gash in the rocks, north of the harbour and about 50 metres from the sea. The gash is about six metres (20 feet) deep, and the heaving water at the bottom leads to a maze of submarine passages.

Doonagore Castle

If you follow the coast road for about three km (two miles) south of Doolin you will come to Doonagore Castle, a restored 15th-century tower with its surrounding walled enclosure or *bawn*. There is a lovely view from here over Doolin and the Aran Islands, a perfect sunset spot for photographers.

Ballinalacken Castle

Five km (three miles) north of Doolin en route to Fanore is Ballinalacken Castle. Sitting astride a small cliff, this 15th-century O'Brien tower house is in excellent order. The stairway is intact and there are good views of the Burren from the top. Look out for an original fireplace perched halfway up the interior with the date 1679 carved on it.

In the grounds is a fine old house, *Ballinalacken Castle Hotel* (☎ 065-74025), which caters for guests at IR£20 to IR£25 per person sharing.

Just beside the gateway to Ballinalacken Castle and guesthouse, a minor road leads inland up into the Burren. After about a km, it meets one of the Burren's ancient green roads, and in good weather this route up to Fanore is a lovely walk. It also forms part of the Burren Way. There is a more detailed description of the return part of this route in the section on Fanore.

LISDOONVARNA

Lisdoon, as the town is generally called, is well known for its mineral springs where people have been coming for centuries to drink and bathe. It also used to be home to some serious matchmakers, who for an appropriate fee would fix you up with a soulmate. Most aspiring suitors would hit town in September after the hay was in.

Today, genuine matchmaking is a little thin on the ground, but the Matchmaking Festival, which runs over a couple of weekends in September, is still a great excuse for drinking, merriment and music in the pubs. And with all those singles events, some romances must begin.

Despite all these goings on, Lisdoonvarna is not particularly attractive. The town's halcyon days are long gone and it shows. Only 11 km (seven miles) away on the coast, Doolin is a much more interesting spot.

Orientation & Information

Lisdoonvarna is essentially a one-street town with a square in the middle where you turn west for Doolin and the coast. The town has plenty of shops, pubs, cheap eateries and a post office, but no banks or tourist office.

The Spa Wells Centre

The Centre (☎ 065-74023) is the only working spa in the country. It has the main sulphur spring, a pump house, massage room, sauna and mineral baths, in nice wooded surroundings. The iron, sulphur, magnesium and iodine in the waters are supposed to be good for rheumatic and glandular complaints. So if you have a spot of hyperthyroidism or ankylosing spondylosis, this is the place for you. You can drink the water, but it tastes hideous and the aftertaste can last for ages.

Getting There & Away

For information regarding bus services to Lisdoonvarna, see the Getting There & Away section under the Burren Area.

Getting Around

Burke's Garage (☎ 065-74022) near the Spa Hotel has bikes for hire.

BALLYREEN

Ballyreen or Ballyryan is no more than a deserted stretch of coast about five km (three miles) south of Fanore, but it's a lovely spot and a good place to camp. There's a cliff called Ailladie which has some of Ireland's finest rock climbing. For divers, a barely visible track leads to a small inlet which has some excellent underwater scenery on the left, dropping quickly to a depth of about 20 metres (60 feet), with vertical walls and gullies covered in jewel anemones.

Offshore after heavy rain you may see currents of brown water coming through the clear surface water. These are resurgences: fresh water flooding from an undersea cave. On land, glaciers have polished the limestone to a mirror-like finish. The incongruous stones and boulders are glacial erratics.

Getting There & Away

There is no direct bus to Ballyreen. The coastal bus service which covers the Burren area starts from Galway and goes to Kinvara, Ballyvaughan, Blackhead, Fanore, Lisdoonvarna and Doolin, returning by the same route. There is usually one bus daily from Monday to Saturday in winter and two or three buses a day during the summer months.

FANORE

Fanore could hardly be called a village. It's more like a stretch of coast, with a shop, a pub, and a few houses every now and then along the road. It has a fine sandy beach with an extensive backdrop of dunes: the only safe beach between Lahinch and Ballyvaughan. Behind the dunes is an accompanying caravan and camp site.

The remains of a Stone Age settlement were discovered near the small river that runs down through the dunes. Along the road south of the beach are a scattering of 10th and 11th-century church ruins.

Fanore is five km (three miles) south of Black Head.

Information

Four km (two miles) south of the beach is a small shop and post office with a public phone. O'Donoghue's pub is just down the road and is a friendly place with music on Saturday nights. There are no other shops or bars along the coast. John McNamara at the Admiral's Rest Restaurant (see Places to Stay & Eat) has a diving air compressor at IR£2 a fill.

Things to See & Do

Just behind Fanore Beach, a road goes inland and up the Khyber Pass, or Caher River Valley. This is the only surface river in the Burren. The first few km are very pleasant and there is a village up on the left, deserted since the famine. There are foxes, badgers and pine martens in the area, though you are unlikely to see any.

There are a couple of lovely walks. On the coast road about 400 metres south of the beach, a small road goes inland. After about a km, it meets an old green road which can be followed south to Ballinalackan Castle, part of the Burren Way.

Alternatively, you can park at the Admiral's Rest Restaurant and go straight up through the fields to the green road. On top of this hill are two caves. Poll Dubh is, according to the restaurant's proprietor, an easy cave for amateurs, with delicate stalactites on view. The other, Poll Mor, is home to badgers, foxes, hares and rabbits.

There is a very well-preserved ring fort and souterrain on top of a hill at the south end of Fanore. Heading for Doolin, past the last house, the fort is on top of the hill about one km inland.

There is another good walk south of here. Travelling south, just past the Fanore town sign, the dip before the last hill on the left turns out to be a wonderful hidden valley, which also comes out eventually on the green road to Ballinalackan Castle.

Places to Stay & Eat

Hostels At the north end of Fanore, a few hundred metres inland from where the river crosses the road, is the *Bridge Hostel* (☎ 065-76134). It's a converted police station, with 17 beds at IR£4.50 per night in dorms or IR£5 per person in the two doubles, and they are open March to October. Graham, the owner, will for a fee, take groups on some easy caving.

B&Bs At the south end of Fanore is the *Admiral's Rest B&B & Seafood Restaurant* (☎ 065-76105) run by John McNamara. Clean, tidy rooms cost IR£13 for B&B. John organises a Burren Wildlife Weekend twice a year.

Rocky View Farmhouse (☎ 065-76103) at the north end of Fanore has rooms with bathrooms at IR£13 for B&B.

Getting There & Away

On Tuesdays and Thursdays only, one bus a day runs between Galway and Lisdoonvarna, stopping at Ballyvaughan, Blackhead, Fanore and Ballinalacken Castle en route.

GLENINAGH CASTLE

Down a narrow leafy lane and just off the coast road, about six km (four miles) west of Ballyvaughan, is Gleninagh (Ivy Glen), a 16th-century O'Lochlainn castle. The O'Lochlains were chieftains in this region and people lived here as late as 1840. If the gate is locked, you can with a bit of effort squeeze or climb through and there is a stair to the top. In front of the castle is a holy well still in use, and the ruins of a medieval church. To the east you may find a small horseshoe-shaped mound of earth: a *fulachta fiadh* or Bronze Age cooking place.

BLACK HEAD & THE FORT OF IRGHUS

Black Head, Clare's north-westernmost point, is a bleak but imposing mountain of limestone dropping swiftly into the sea. The head has an unstaffed lighthouse and good shore angling for bass and cod. If you are lucky, you may see dolphins.

There is a great hike up the head to a large Iron Age stone fort: Cathair Dhun Iorais, the 'Fort of Irghus', a legendary builder. The views across Galway Bay and the Aran Islands are exceptional, especially with the steep walls of the fort as a backdrop.

Inland, the hills rise to 318 metres and farther back is Slieve Elva (345 metres) capped with shale. Some of the intervening summits are marked with Bronze Age cairns. On your way up to the fort you cross an old green road.

BALLYVAUGHAN

Ballyvaughan is a small pretty fishing village on a quiet corner of Galway Bay. In the past few years, it has been attracting upmarket visitors, and its nice pubs, restaurants and places to stay make it a good base for visiting the northern part of the Burren.

Just west of the village, past the holiday cottages and the Tea Gardens restaurant, is the quay and Monk's Bar. The harbour was built in 1829 when boats traded with the Aran Islands and Galway, often bringing in turf which was scarce in this area.

Ballyvaughan is a T-junction. Going south and inland brings you to the centre of the

Burren, Aillwee Caves, Poulnabrone Dolmen and Lisdoonvarna. Turning west brings you out on the magnificent coast road to Black Head and down towards Doolin. North-east you reach Kinvara and County Galway.

Information

The Whitethorn Craft & Visitor Centre, east of Ballyvaughan on the way to Kinvara, has tourist information.

The post office is on Main St. There are no banks but you can change money in *Manus Walsh's Craft Shop* on Main St. Opening hours are 10 am to 6 pm. Alternatively try Hyland's Hotel or Monk's Bar.

Places to Stay

Camping You can camp in many of the fields around Ballyvaughan or along the coast just beyond the harbour.

Hostels There are no hostels in Ballyvaughan. The nearest are north on the way to Kinvara at Doorus, or west on the coast in Fanore.

B&Bs Claire Walsh (☎ 065-77029), owner of Claire's Restaurant on Main St, will advise you on many of the B&Bs and self-catering accommodation in the area.

About the cheapest place around is *Lough Rask House* (☎ 065-77026), costing IR£10 to IR£11. Go a few hundred metres along the Kinvara road and turn right at the signpost for the house, up the road and left at the sign.

A particularly good B&B is *Rusheen House* (☎ 065-77092), a little over one km out on the inland road to Lisdoonvarna. It's not cheap at IR£15 to IR£17 a night, but the rooms and breakfast are top class. *Meadowfield* (☎ 065-77083) is 200 metres along the road to Kinvara and costs IR£13. Almost opposite is *Ocean Villa* (☎ 065-77051), with rooms at IR£12. *Stonepark House* (☎ 065-77056) in Bishops Quarter, a km and a bit along the Kinvara road, costs IR£13 a night.

There are many more out around Doorus

and New Quay and they all get busy, so book ahead.

Hotels *Hyland's Hotel* (☎ 065-77037) in the middle of Ballyvaughan is a small, family-run hotel with a cosy atmosphere, costing between IR£22 and IR£27 a night. They serve bar food and the restaurant is good as hotels go.

Five km (three miles) south of Ballyvaughan on the inland road to Lisdoonvarna is *Gregan's Castle Hotel* (☎ 065-77015), a Grade A hotel, costing IR£50 for B&B. The restaurant is excellent though expensive. Dinner is IR£25 or more per person.

Places to Eat
You are spoiled for choice. The *Tea Garden* in an old cottage down towards the harbour, has top-notch soups, salads and home-cooked desserts. They are open till 6 pm. *Monk's Bar*, a popular place on the harbour, has melt-in-your-mouth mussels, seafood and brown bread.

The *T-Junction Café* in the village centre does a good breakfast and serves reasonable snacks all day. Most bars in town serve pub food. The restaurant at the *Aillwee Caves* is great for soups, salads and desserts. The *Whitethorn Craft & Visitor Centre*, north of town en route to Kinvara, has a good coffee-shop-cum-restaurant, open during the day.

Claire's Restaurant (☎ 065-77029) in the village is the best around and the food is top class. Dinner will cost you IR£18 or more a head.

Entertainment
Monk's Bar has music almost every night in summer. *Hyland's Hotel* has music at weekends while *O'Brien's* has music from Thursday to Sunday night. *O'Lochlainn's*, on the left as you head down to the harbour, is a lovely old country pub, much less touristy than Monk's.

Getting There & Away
See the Burren Area's section on Getting There & Away for details of public transport to and from Ballyvaughan.

Getting Around
Monk's Bar (☎ 065-77059) by the harbour has bikes for hire at IR£6 a day, plus deposit.

AROUND BALLYVAUGHAN
Corkscrew Hill
Five km (three miles) south of Ballyvaughan on the Lisdoonvarna road is a series of very severe bends up Corkscrew Hill. The road was built as part of a famine-relief scheme in the 1840s. From the top there are spectacular views of the north Burren and Galway Bay with Aillwee Mountain and Caves on the right and Cappanawalla Hill on the left with the ruins of Newtown Castle at its base. From here, the route to Lisdoonvarna is through boggy and fairly boring countryside.

CENTRAL BURREN
The road through the heart of the Burren runs between Ballyvaughan and Corofin via Leamenah Castle. Travelling south from Ballyvaughan, turn left before Corkscrew Hill at the sign for the Aillwee Caves. The road goes past Gleninsheen Wedge Tomb, Poulnabrone Dolmen and into some really desolate scenery.

To the south of the Burren, it's worth taking a diversion to Kilfenora to take in the Burren Centre and Kilfenora's cathedral and high crosses.

Aillwee Caves
The Aillwee Caves (☎ 065-77036) are a good place to pass a rainy afternoon. The main passage penetrates for 600 metres into the mountain, widening into larger caverns, one with its own waterfall. The caves were carved out by water some two million years ago. Near the entrance are the remains of a brown bear, extinct in Ireland for over 10,000 years.

Aillwee was discovered in 1944 by Jack McCann, a local farmer, and today has a discreetly designed outer building with an excellent café. Behind the cave entrance there is a relatively easy scramble up 300-

metre (1000-foot) Aillwee Mountain. There are fine views from the summit.

You can only go into the cave as part of a guided group and tours are IR£2.50 (children and students IR£1.50). Aillwee is open April to September 10 am to 6 pm. Try and visit early in the day before the crowds.

Gleninsheen Wedge Tomb

This tomb is known in folklore as the 'Druid's Altar' though the druids lived a long time after this was built. The tomb is just beside the road, a little over a km north-west of Poulnabrone Dolmen. It's thought to be from 4000 to 5000 years old and like most of the other tombs in the Burren is up here on high ground.

A magnificent gold collar was found nearby in 1930 by a boy hunting rabbits. The collar was in a crack in the limestone and at first the boy thought it was part of a coffin. It is reckoned to be one of the finest pieces of prehistoric Irish craftwork. Dating from around 700 BC, it's now on display at the National Museum in Dublin.

Poulnabrone Dolmen

Poulnabrone Dolmen is one of Ireland's most photographed ancient monuments, the one you see on all the postcards with the setting sun behind. The dolmen is a three-legged tomb, sitting in a sea of limestone without a house in sight. At quiet times of day, this is a truly lovely place. It is eight km (five miles) inland from Aillwee and signposted from the road.

Poulnabrone was built over 5000 years ago. It was excavated in 1989 and the remains of more than 25 people were found among pieces of pottery and jewellery. Radiocarbon dating suggests they were buried between 3800 and 3200 BC. When the dead were originally buried here, the whole structure was covered in a mound of earth which has since eroded away. Poulnabrone means 'the hole of the quern' and the capstone weighs five tons. Try and visit early in the morning or at sunset for good photographs. Better still, try a moonlit night.

Try to ignore the intrusive iron shed which has been built in the neighbouring field by a local farmer.

Cahercommaun Cliff Fort

Perched on the edge of an inland cliff, three km (two miles) south of the tiny village of Carron, is the great stone fort of Cahercommaun. It was inhabited during the 8th and 9th centuries by a group of people who hunted deer and grew a small amount of grain. There are the remains of a souterrain or underground passage leading from the fort to the outer face of the cliff.

To get there, go south from Carron and take a left turn for Kilinaboy. After 1500 metres, a path on the left leads up to the fort.

East of Carron

If you turn east at Carron, you have two options. The first is to turn north after about two km, which takes you on a magnificent drive through a valley to Cappaghmore in County Galway. If instead you continue directly east you come close to the lovely Mullaghmore Mountain. Later, just over the Galway border on the main road to Gort, is Kilmacduagh, a monastic site with a splendid round tower.

KILFENORA

The tiny, windswept village of Kilfenora lies on the southern fringes of the Burren, eight km (five miles) from Lisdoonvarna. Most visitors come to see the monastic remains, five High Crosses and a tiny 12th-century cathedral. The village itself is a touch forlorn, but has some attractive shopfronts and pubs.

Burren Display Centre

The Burren Display Centre (☎ 065-88030) was built by the local community and has a fair amount of information on the Burren and guidebooks for sale. There is a display, a video presentation and plenty of literature for sale. It's a little expensive at IR£2 (students IR£1.30, children IR£1).

Top: Connemara, County Galway (JM)
ttom: Fishing, Connemara, County Galway (JM)

Top: Inisheer, Aran Islands, County Galway (JM)
Bottom : Aran Islanders, County Galway (JM)

Kilfenora Cathedral

The present pope has the honour of being bishop of Kilfenora and in the past the ruined 12th-century cathedral was an important place of pilgrimage. St Facthna founded the monastery here in the 6th century and it later became capital of Kilfenora diocese, the smallest in the country.

The cathedral is the smallest one you are ever likely to see. Only the ruined structure and nave of the more recent Protestant church are actually part of the cathedral. The chancel has two primitive carved figures on top of two tombs. They are thought to be bishops and it must be said that neither were very handsome gentlemen. The theory goes that after the Black Death in the 14th century there was a general decline in craft skills across the continent, and these poor carvings may be examples of this.

High Crosses

Kilfenora is best known for its high crosses, three in the churchyard and a large 12th-century example in the field about 100 metres to the west.

The most interesting one is the 800-year-old Doorty Cross, standing prominently near the front door of the church. It differs significantly from the standard Irish high cross so beloved of photographers and the Irish Tourist Board, in that it is without the usual pierced disc or wheel on top. It was lying broken in two until the 1950s when it was re-erected. The Doortys are a Tipperary family whose ancestors were bishops here, and you can see the name on many recent headstones.

The east face of the cross is the better preserved. One interpretation of the carvings has Christ on top ordering two figures in the middle to destroy the devil/bird at the bottom which is misbehaving. The west face is much less clear. Christ still appears to be on top, this time surrounded by birds. Directly underneath are delicate designs and a man on horseback holding the ends of the patterns. Some say it is Christ's entry into Jerusalem. One theory suggests the cross may commemorate Kilfenora being made

headquarters of the diocese in the 12th century.

Places to Stay

The *Burren Farmhouse* (☎ 065-71363), two km along the Ennistymon road, is really nice. A km along the Lisdoonvarna road is *Mrs Howley's* (☎ 065-88075), also highly recommended. Both have rooms at IR£13.

Places to Eat & Entertainment

The *Burren Display Centre* has a reasonable tearoom, open 9.30 am to 6 pm. *Vaughan's* pub (☎ 065-88004) on the green has bar food and regular Irish music sessions on Mondays, Wednesdays, Fridays and Saturdays. *Nagle's Bar* (☎ 065-88011) has music at weekends only.

COROFIN

Corofin is a small village on the southern fringes of the Burren. Commonly found in the area are *turloughs*, small lakes which often disappear in dry summers. O'Brien castles abound in this boggy countryside, two of them on the shores of nearby Lake Inchiquin.

Corofin is home to the **Clare heritage centre** (☎ 065-27955) which has a genealogy facility for people with Clare ancestors and a display covering the period around the famine. Over a quarter of a million people lived in Clare before the famine in 1845; a century later there were less than 75,000. Opening hours are 10 am to 6 pm and admission IR£1.75 (children IR£1).

Places to Stay

Hostel *Corofin Village Hostel* (☎ 065-27683) is a fine new hostel with good facilities on Main St in Corofin. A bed in a dorm is IR£5.

B&Bs There are plenty of B&Bs in the area, many of them in Kilinaboy, one to two km along the road north to Lisdoonvarna. Good ones include *Cottage View* (☎ 065-27662), one km from Corofin, which has four rooms, two with bathroom, at IR£12. *Clifden View*

(☎ 065-27779) has three rooms at IR£14/26 for singles/doubles.

Places to Eat

Near the heritage centre is a reasonable coffee shop serving light meals all day. For pub food try the *Anglers Rest* (☎ 065-37203). *Bofey Quinn's* (☎ 065-27627) on Main St is a very popular pub and seafood restaurant serving simple but delicious snacks and meals, open until 10.30 pm but closed in winter.

Getting There & Away

There is an infrequent bus service from Kilkee or Doonbeg to Ennis and Limerick via Corofin. Check with Ennis bus depot (☎ 065-24177), or the Corofin Village Hostel for times.

LEAMENAH CASTLE

Leamenah is a well-preserved castle cum fortified house, five km (three miles) east of Kilfenora and eight km (five miles) north of Corofin. The road north to Ballyvaughan brings you through some of the wildest parts of the Burren and past a number of its highlights such as Poulnabrone Dolmen.

The castle's name is pronounced 'Lay-im-on-ay' and is Irish for 'deer's leap' or 'horse's leap'. If you look carefully, you will see that there are two parts joined together. The five-storey tower house on the right was built around 1480 by the O'Briens and is much more solid and better defended than the main house which Conor O'Brien added in 1640. This has four storeys and its most appealing features are the largely intact stone window frames.

The whole building was originally surrounded by a high wall. Just above the tower house entrance is a vertical shaft or murder hole. If this was the 15th century and you were an uninvited guest, all manner of unspeakable things could be dropped on top of you including boiling oil, tar, arrows and anything else handy. There is a fine view from the top of the tower.

Conor O'Brien, builder of the house, was killed in 1651 fighting for the royalists against Cromwell. His wife, the infamous Maire Rua McMahon, reportedly refused to take his body back into Leamenah Castle. After his death, she offered to marry one of Cromwell's soldiers to ensure her son Donough didn't lose his inheritance. Marry one she did, but they still lost the estate. Despite this setback she and her new husband, John Cooper, stayed together. They regained their property in 1675 but later records suggest she was suspected of murdering Cooper; she was tried for the crime but acquitted. She died in 1686.

NORTH-EAST CLARE

Low farmland stretches south from County Galway until it meets the bluff limestone hills of the Burren. The Burren begins just west of Kinvara and Doorus where the road forks, going inland to Carron or along the coast to Ballyvaughan.

From Oranmore in County Galway all the way down to Ballyvaughan, the coastline wriggles along small inlets and peninsulas, some like Finnavarra and New Quay are worthy of a detour. Just inland near Bellharbour is the largely intact Corcomroe Abbey, and the ancient churches of Oughtmama lie up a quiet side valley.

Galway Bay forms the backdrop to some outstanding scenery: bare stone hills shining in the sun, with small hamlets and rich patches of green wherever there is soil.

Getting There & Away

There is a bus service between Galway City and Cork which passes through Kinvara and Ballyvaughan on summer weekdays only. Another service running between Galway and Doolin also stops in those two places, and offers one bus daily in winter and two or three in summer. Infrequent buses on the Burren coastal route from Galway can drop you in Kinvara or Ballyvaughan; there is usually one bus daily in winter, from Monday to Saturday, and two each day in summer. Details of these services are available from Galway bus station (☎ 091-62000) or Ennis bus station (☎ 065-24177).

New Quay & the Flaggy Shore

New Quay, on the Finnavarra Peninsula, is about two km (one mile) off the main Kinvara to Ballyvaughan road. There are a couple of thatched cottages on the peninsula and the ruins of a 17th-century mansion.

Linnane's pub (☎ 065-78120) in New Quay serves excellent seafood and is right next door to Ireland's biggest oyster farm.

The Flaggy Shore, west of New Quay, is a particularly nice stretch of coastline. Layers of limestone march boldly into the sea, and behind the coastal path swans parade gently on Lough Muirí. There are otters in the area. On the way out to Finnavarra Point is Mt Vernon Lodge, the summer home of Augusta Lady Gregory, playwright and friend of W B Yeats. She was prominent in the Anglo-Irish literary revival.

On Finnavarra Point is one of the west coast's few **Martello towers**, built in the early 1800s to warn Galway in case Napoleon came sailing by and sneaked into Ireland by the back door. The road loops back and joins the main road beside a small lake which is very rich in birdlife including ducks, moorhens and herons.

Bellharbour

Belharbour is no more than a crossroads with some thatched holiday cottages, about eight km (five miles) east of Ballyvaughan. There is an excellent walk along an old green road which begins behind the modern St Patrick's Catholic Church, one km north of Bellharbour, and threads north along Abbey Hill.

Just inland from here is Corcomroe Abbey, the valley and churches of Oughtmama, and the interior road that takes you right through the heart of the Burren.

Wildlife You can almost be guaranteed seals along the coast west of Bellharbour. Go about one km along the Ballyvaughan road until you spot a large dark green farm shed in on the right. Follow the path down to the shore and you may see seals. This inlet is also thick with birds, and winter visitors include brent geese from Arctic Canada.

Corcomroe Abbey

Corcomroe is a Cistercian abbey one km inland from Bellharbour. It lies in its own small valley surrounded by low hills and is a very peaceful place. Another name for it is 'St Mary's of the fertile rock'. It was founded around 1180 by Munsterman Donal Mor O'Brien. His grandson, King Conor O'Brien who died in 1267, occupies the tomb in the north-east wall, and there is a crude carving of him below another effigy of a staring bishop armed with a crozier. Some fine Romanesque carvings are scattered throughout the abbey.

Legend of Corcomroe

In 1317, the Battle of Corcomroe was fought very near the abbey. Two O'Brien clans were fighting for control over Clare. Legend has it that one of the chieftains, Donough, was passing by Lough Rask on his way to battle, when he saw a witch washing a pile of bleeding limbs in the lake. The witch told Donough that her name was Bronach Boirne and that the corpses were of his army, if he insisted on going into battle; and that, to make matters worse, Donough's own head was in the pile.

Donough's men tried to capture her, but she flew up in the air and rained curses on them. To reassure his men, Donough told them Bronach was the lover of his arch rival Dermot and her warnings merely a ploy to frighten them off. Unfortunately for Donough, by that night he and most of his army were lying dead in the abbey.

Incidentally, on Moneen Mountain nearby is a pass called Mam Catha, the 'pass of the battle', which could refer to the route taken by Donough and his army. Dermot, the victor, later defeated de Clare of Bunratty, halting the spread of Norman influence in Clare for some time. ■

Oughtmama Valley

Oughtmama is a lonely and deserted valley hiding some small and very old churches. To get there turn inland at Bellharbour, left at the Y-junction, and up to a clump of trees and a house on the right. A rough track here will bring you east up a blind valley to the churches. St MacDuach, who also built churches on the Aran Islands, founded the monastery here in the 6th century. The three churches were built in the 12th century by monks looking for peace and solitude.

It's a hardy walk up Turlough Hill behind the chapels but the views are tremendous. Near the summit are the remains of an Iron Age hill fort.

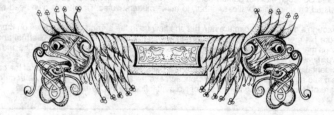

County Galway

County Galway is likely to be one of the highlights of any visit to Ireland. Stretching from Ballinasloe in the midlands through the wilds of Connemara to the craggy Atlantic coastline beyond Clifden, Galway has a huge amount of interest packed into its 5940 sq km. After Cork it is the second largest county in Ireland and Galway City is the west coast's liveliest and most populous settlement.

Galway's neighbour to the south is County Clare, and the Burren limestone region peters out near Kinvara, a picturesque little coastal town just inside the Galway border. However, the limestone surfaces out to sea in a long grey reef which forms Galway's three Aran Islands, famous for their folklore, woollen sweaters, bleak scenery and Irish-speaking population.

Galway's landscape is extremely varied. Lough Corrib cuts off the rugged coastal region from the largely flat interior which makes up the bulk of the county.

Galway City

Galway City is a delight, with its narrow streets, old stone and wooden shopfronts, good restaurants and bustling pubs. It is also the administrative capital of the county, and home to the local government, University

College Galway, and a regional college to the east of town. There is a ferry to the Aran Islands from the docks, although you are better off travelling farther west and taking a boat from near Spiddal or Rossaveal.

In marked contrast to most of the depopulated west coast, Galway was recently classed as Europe's fastest growing city. Northern Telecom, Galway Crystal and Thermo King all have large factories, although the city's prosperity has taken some blows recently with the almost complete shutdown of a huge Digital Computer plant.

Galway City is a gateway for Connemara and the west, as it sits at the southern tip of Lough Corrib which forms a natural border to the region. The city is also a handy base for exploring the Burren, which begins some 30 km to the south in Clare.

Galway City has always attracted a bohemian crowd of musicians, artists, intellectuals and young people. This is partly due to the presence of the university, but the main attraction is the nightlife, and pubs where talk and drink flow by the bucketful. The city is a major Gaelic centre and Irish is widely spoken. The Druid Theatre is one of the best in the country, and the city hosts an annual and hugely popular arts festival in August. The place goes wild during Galway Race Week in the last week in July. If you haven't booked, accommodation is almost impossible to find at these times.

While the city centre deserves its accolades, the approaches and suburbs don't. Coming from the east, you pass by huge modern hotels, barren housing developments and the ugly regional college. The coast road west through the beach resort of Salthill and on to Spiddal is one of the worst examples of ribbon development in the country. Only after Spiddal do the bungalows thin out.

HISTORY

Galway grew from a fishing village in the

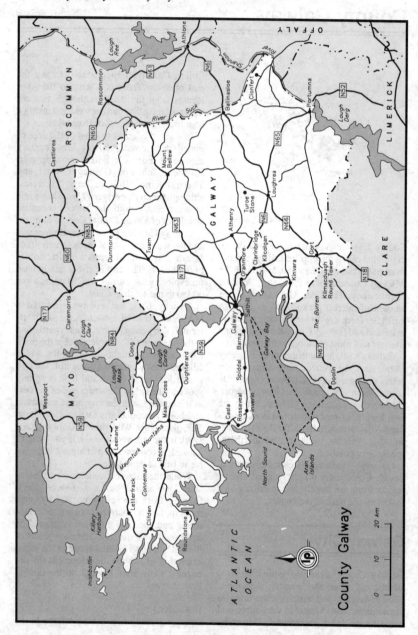

County Galway

Claddagh area at the mouth of the river to become an important walled town when the Anglo-Normans under Richard de Burgo captured territory from the local O'Flahertys in 1234. The Irish for outsider or foreigner is 'gall', which may be the origin of the city's Irish name, Gaillimh. The town walls were built by the Anglo-Normans from around 1270.

Galway City became something of an outpost in the wild west. In 1396, Richard II granted a charter to the city which effectively transferred power from the de Burgos to 14 merchant families or 'tribes'. This led to the name 'City of the Tribes' by which Galway is commonly known. These powerful families were mostly English or Norman in origin. But of course there were tribes outside the walls as well as inside. Clashes with the leading Irish families of Connemara were frequent, and at one time the city's west gate bore the prayer and warning: 'From the fury of the O'Flahertys, good Lord deliver us.' To ensure fury was kept at bay, the city fathers warned that no uninvited 'O' nor 'Mac' should show his face on Galway's fair streets.

English power throughout the region waxed and waned, but the city maintained its independent status, under ruling merchant families who were mostly loyal to the English crown. Galway's relative isolation encouraged a trade in wine, spices, fish and salt with Portugal and Spain. At one point it rivalled Bristol and London in the volume of trade passing through the docks. Many of the ruling families sent their sons to Spain and mainland Europe for education.

For a long while Galway prospered. A huge fire in 1473 destroyed much of the town and created space for a new street layout with many solid stone buildings being erected in the 16th and 17th centuries.

Galway's faithful support of the English crown led to its downfall when Cromwell turned up. The city was besieged in 1651 and fell in April 1652, after nine months' resistance. Cromwell's forces under Charles Coote wreaked their customary havoc and Galway's long period of decline was under

way. In 1691 the city again took the wrong side and King William's forces added to the destruction. The important trade with Spain was almost at an end, and with Dublin and Waterford taking most of the sea traffic, Galway stagnated until its recent revival.

ORIENTATION

Galway's tightly packed town centre lies on both sides of the River Corrib which connects Lough Corrib with the sea. Eyre Square and most of the main shopping areas are east of the river. There are three main bridges; the northernmost, Salmon Weir Bridge, looks over a weir and is overshadowed itself by Galway Cathedral.

Just south of the river mouth is the historic, but now totally redeveloped, Claddagh area, while slightly farther south-west is the beach resort of Salthill, a popular area for accommodation and restaurants. Eyre Square is just north-west of the combined bus and railway station, near the tourist office and is a good central meeting point.

From the north-west corner of Eyre Square, the meandering main shopping street starts as Williamsgate St and becomes William St and then Shop St before splitting into Guard St and High St, which becomes Quay St and crosses the River Corrib on Wolfe Tone Bridge.

INFORMATION

The tourist office (☎ 091-63081) is just south of Eyre Square. At the height of the season it is busy and there can be a delay of an hour or more in making accommodation bookings. There's another branch at the junction of Seapoint Promenade and Upper Salthill Rd at Salthill.

The USIT travel office (☎ 091-24601) is on the university campus.

The Eyre Square Centre is a big shopping centre right off Eyre Square by the tourist office. They've cunningly incorporated a reconstructed stretch of the old city wall in this modern centre. Other shopping centres are Bridge Mills, in an old mill building right by the river, and the Cornstore on Middle St.

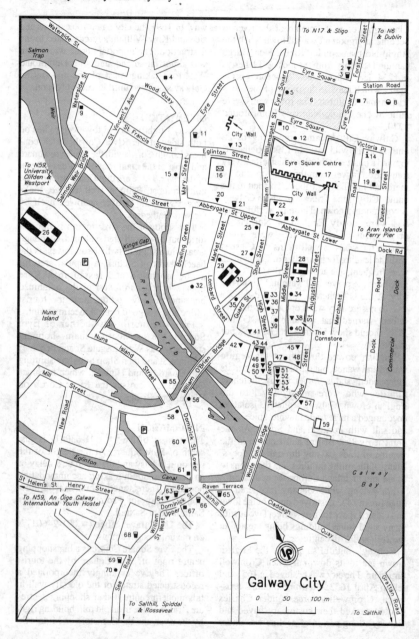

Galway City

0   50   100 m

■ PLACES TO STAY

4	Wood Quay Hostel
7	Great Southern Hotel
9	Corrib Villa Hostel
10	Skeffington Arms Hotel
19	Brennan's Yard Hotel
24	Lydon's B&B
46	Quay Street Hostel
55	St Martin's B&B
61	Galway City Hostel
62	Arch View Hostel
67	Owen's Hostel

▼ PLACES TO EAT

2	Dragon Court
13	Conlon's
17	Sails Café
20	Brannagan's Restaurant
22	House of James
23	Food for Thought Café
31	Brasserie Restaurant
36	Malt House
38	Bewley's Café
41	Toucan Café
42	Country Basket
43	Hungry Grass
44	Neachtain's Bar & Restaurant
45	Pasta Mista
48	Sev'nth Heaven
49	McDonagh's Fish Shop
50	Café Nora Crúb
52	Fat Freddy's Pizzeria
53	Sunflower Vegetarian Restaurant
54	La Mezza Luna
57	Shama Indian Restaurant
60	Left Bank Café
64	Kebab House

☞ PUBS

1	Rabbitt's Bar
3	An Púcán Bar
11	MacSwiggan's Pub
21	Cooke's Wine Bar
33	King's Head Pub
51	Quay's Bar
63	Taylor's Bar
65	Waterfront
66	Monroe's Tavern
68	Galway Shawl Pub
69	Crane's Bar

OTHER

5	Browne's Doorway
6	Kennedy Park
8	Railway & Bus Station
12	Cawley's Rent-a-Bike
14	Tourist Office
15	Laundrette
16	GPO
18	Round the Corner Bike Hire
25	Lynch's Castle
26	St Nicholas' Cathedral
27	Eason's Bookshop
28	Augustinian Church
29	Lynch's Window
30	St Nicholas' Collegiate Church
32	Nora Barnacle's House
34	An Taibhdhearc Theatre
35	Hawkins House Bookshop
37	Kenny's Bookshop & Art Gallery
39	Byrne's Bookshop
40	Sheela Na Gig/Galway Bookshop
47	Druid Theatre
56	Bridge Mills Shopping Centre
58	Police/Garda Station
59	Museum & Spanish Arch
70	Laundrette

Banks

All Irish banks have branches in the city centre. The building societies also have bureaus de change and are open 9.30 am to 5 pm, Monday through Friday.

Post

The GPO is on Eglinton St, north of William St. It's open Monday to Saturday 9 am to 6 pm.

Laundry

There's a laundrette on Sea Rd, just off Upper Dominick St on the west side of the river. Others can be found in the Old Malte Arcade off High St in the centre and at Salthill, near the Stella Maris Hostel.

Books & Bookshops

Hawkins House (☎ 091-67507) is a good bookshop at 14 Churchyard St, right by the Church of St Nicholas. Kenny's Bookshop is on High St above the gallery of the same name. There's also a branch of Easons on Shop St and Byrne's second-hand bookshop across from Bewley's Café on Middle St. Sheila na Gig/The Galway Bookshop is in the Cornstore on Middle St.

A copy of *Medieval Galway – A Rambler's Guide & Map* (Tir Edas) is available in most bookshops.

EYRE SQUARE

This is the focal point for the eastern and most extensive part of Galway City. In spite of Galway's civic pride, the square shows no great imagination in its layout. The train and railway station is at one southern corner, the tourist office just off the other. The south side is almost entirely taken up by the Great Southern Hotel, a great grey limestone building. To the west of the square is Browne's Doorway of 1627, a fragment from the home of one of the city's merchant rulers.

In the centre is the John F Kennedy Memorial Park. Kennedy visited the city in 1963 and a stone tablet in the square commemorates the event. Ronald Reagan also dropped by when the town was celebrating its 500th anniversary in 1984 and the university gave him a doctorate! On the north side of the square is a controversial statue to the Galway-born writer Pádraic O'Conaire (1882-1928), a noted hell-raiser. It's one of the better examples of modern sculpture in the country. Finally there's a curious object behind Browne's Doorway which is supposed to evoke the sails of a traditional Galway hooker. It was designed by Eamon O'Doherty and erected during the city's quincentennial in 1984.

THE COLLEGIATE CHURCH OF ST NICHOLAS OF MYRA

This church on Shop St with its curious pyramidal spire dates from 1320 and is not only Galway's most important monument but also the biggest medieval parish church in Ireland. Although it has been rebuilt and enlarged over the centuries, much of the original form has been retained. After Cromwell's victory, the church suffered the

standard indignity of being used as a stable. Much damage was done but at least it survived; 14 other Galway churches were razed to the ground. Look for the damaged stonework. The church has numerous finely worked stone tombs and memorials. The two bells date from 1590 and 1630.

Parts of the floor are paved with gravestones from the 16th to the 18th centuries and the Lynch Aisle has the tombs of the powerful Lynch family. A large block tomb in one corner is said to be the grave of James Lynch, a former mayor of Galway, who condemned his son to death for killing a young Spanish visitor. None of the townsfolk would act as hangman, and the mayor was so dedicated to upholding justice that he personally acted as hangman, after which he went into seclusion. Or so the story goes – the Lynch Memorial Window, on Market St outside the church, tells the tale and claims to be the spot where he carried out the execution.

At the end of the aisle is the 'empty frame' which is said to have once held a picture of the Virgin Mary which later turned up in Gyor in Hungary.

It's claimed that Christopher Columbus paused in Galway to hear mass and pray at the church. The supposed Galway detour took place either because one of his crew was a Galway man or because Columbus wished to investigate tales of St Brendan's earlier voyage to the Americas.

LYNCH'S CASTLE

On the corner of Shop and Abbeygate Sts, parts of the gargoyled old stone townhouse called Lynch's Castle date back to the 14th century although most of the present building is from around 1600. Reputed to be the finest town castle in Ireland, it now houses a branch of the AIB Bank. The Lynch family were the most powerful of the 14 ruling clans or tribes and members of the family held the position of mayor no less than 80 times between 1480 and 1650 – including the unfortunate James Lynch whose tomb is in St Nicholas' Church.

Lynch's Castle has numerous fine stone features on its facade including the coats of arms of Henry VII and the Earl of Kildare, as well as the gargoyles, unusual in Ireland.

BOWLING GREEN

Across the road from the Lynch Memorial is Bowling Green. No 8 Bowling Green was once the home of Nora Barnacle who married James Joyce. It seems he only visited the house on two occasions, in 1909 and 1912. There is now a small museum dedicated to the couple.

THE SPANISH ARCH

A 1651 pictorial view of Galway clearly shows its extensive city walls, but since the visits of Cromwell in 1652 and King William in 1691, and the subsequent centuries of neglect, the walls have almost completely disappeared. Near the river, the Spanish Arch seems to have been an extension of the walls, through which ships unloaded their goods –

often wine and brandy from Spain. This area used to be the fish market.

The unremarkable Galway City Museum is by the arch. It's open 10 am to 1 pm and 2.15 to 5.15 pm from Monday to Saturday and entry is 50p (children 20p).

ST NICHOLAS' CATHEDRAL

From the Spanish Arch, a pleasant riverside path runs all the way up river and across the Salmon Weir Bridge to the second site in the town dedicated to St Nicholas. Galway Cathedral is a huge and imposing structure, opened in 1965. Tasteful it is not, and critics vie for the most acidic descriptions of this monument to inelegance.

Inside things are a little less grandiose, but it's a mishmash of styles and intentions. Even the cathedral's name is a mouthful; correctly it's the Catholic Cathedral of Our Lady Assumed into Heaven and St Nicholas. The cathedral is just west of the Upper or

---

It Could Happen to a Bishop

Or so goes the Irish saying, and in 1992 it certainly happened to Dr Eamonn Casey, the Bishop of Galway. I happened to be in Galway on the morning the 'shock' announcement was made that the Bishop had zipped off to Rome to tender his resignation. Why? Well no-one was saying, certainly no-one from the church, but there was talk of a woman in the USA whom he once knew. And it was said she had a son. Before you could whisper 'celibacy?' the bishop was on his way to New York, flying 1st class, and then, before you could whisper 'disgraced bishop' he was following that well-trodden route to South America popularised by escaping Nazis and British train robbers.

The bishop wasn't saying and the church certainly wasn't, but his ex-girlfriend and their 18-year-old son soon were, and the damage-control efforts provided high drama for the next weeks. Pages of analysis followed in the papers. My journeys on Irish roads were enlivened by a fascinating series of radio call-in programmes. Some callers tore in to the woman, accusing her of leading the poor man astray. One caller even developed (at length, Irish call-ins tend to be at length) a fascinating theory that it was a KGB plot and she was a highly trained operative, skilled in the seduction of randy bishops. At the end of 20 minutes of this fellow, I was uncertain whether or not this was some kind of skit. The caller who summed it up for me announced that despite all the pontificating, he and his friends found the whole thing hilarious.

Some more serious analysis questioned the whole point of priestly celibacy. The good bishop certainly hadn't. At the same time that he was concealing the existence of his son, he was a conservative on abortion, contraception, celibacy and other sex-related issues. Well, he was a good Catholic, said one of the commentators, since he certainly didn't practise birth control.

The question of Irish double standards also got a wide airing; how much sympathy would have been expressed for a nun who got herself 'in trouble'? What didn't get much questioning was the small matter of IR£70,000 which the good bishop had 'borrowed' from church funds in order to keep things quiet. As the shit hit the fan it was quickly repaid by 'friends of Dr Casey' and the church announced that the financial issue was closed as far as they were concerned. Well – would you trust a bishop who collected speeding tickets in his BMW?

Tony Wheeler

Salmon Weir Bridge with its fine views over the River Corrib.

Until 1992, the cathedral was the base of Bishop Eamonn Casey, one of Ireland's most flamboyant and well-liked clergymen. But in 1992 it emerged that he was the father of a teenage son, and Casey fled Ireland. The story made headlines all over the world.

SALMON WEIR

The Upper or Salmon Weir Bridge crosses the River Corrib in front of the cathedral. Just upstream is the great weir where the waters of the Corrib cascade down one of their final descents before the sea, one km to the south. The weir controls the water levels above it, and when the salmon are running you can often see them waiting in the clear waters before making the rush upstream to spawn. You may see them jumping up the weir, which also has a fish pass allowing them easier passage.

The earliest records of Galway include references to the de Burgo family owning the fisheries on the town's weirs. Today they are owned by the Central Fisheries Board. The salmon and sea trout season is usually from February to September. Most fish pass through the weir during May and June. Fishing licences are obtainable from the Fishery Office (☎ 091-62388), Nuns Island, Galway.

Lough Corrib begins about six km north of the weir and has been world famous for its salmon and trout fishing although it's had a number of poor years recently.

CLADDAGH

Galway's main fishing area used to centre around the Claddagh district. Up to 3000 people and 300 boats were based here at one stage. Many of the boats were traditional Galway vessels with sturdy black hulls and rough rust-coloured sails, known as *púcáns* and *gleótógs*, today collectively called Galway hookers.

Claddagh used to have its own characteristic costume and dialect, and a king. Although the traditional Claddagh is gone, you can still wear a Claddagh ring with a crowned heart nestling between two hands. If the heart points towards the hand then the wearer is taken or married, towards the fingertip means he or she is looking for a mate. The Claddagh ring was the wedding ring used throughout much of Connaught from the mid-18th century.

SALTHILL

Beyond Claddagh, but still within walking distance of the city, is Salthill, a traditional large seaside resort. The beaches are often packed in hot weather but are not particularly good.

ORGANISED TOURS

During the summer months Bus Éireann have a variety of tours from Galway and Salthill including day trips for IR£10 to Connemara or the Burren and shorter trips for IR£7 to Cong or the Knock Shrine. Contact the railway station or the tourist office for details. The *Corrib Princess* does afternoon cruises on the Corrib River from Woodquay, just up river from the Salmon Weir. Bookings can be made at the tourist office.

FESTIVALS

Galway parties with a vengeance at the Galway Arts Festival in late July. The whole town turns out for this two-week extravaganza of theatre, music and art. There's even a parade.

The last week of July is Galway Race Week which is as much an event off the course as on it. The racecourse, six km from the city centre at Ballybrit, hosts a traditional Irish fair and finding a place to stay in Galway at that time can be very, very difficult.

Towards the end of September, the Galway International Oyster Festival takes place, not to be confused with the Clarinbridge Oyster Festival, based as its name implies around Clarinbridge and Kilcolgan to the south.

PLACES TO STAY

Galway has a huge variety of accommodation but you may still have difficulty finding a bed in summer. Watch out for Galway Race Week at the end of July. There is more accommodation in Salthill a couple of km to the south-west.

Camping

The *Salthill Caravan & Camping Park* (☎ 091-22479), *O'Halloran's Caravan Park* and the *Silver Strand Caravan & Camping Park* (☎ 091-92452) are on the coast, just beyond Salthill. *Ballyloughane Caravan & Camping Park* (☎ 091-55338) is on the Dublin Rd. The *Spiddal Caravan & Camping Park* (or Pairc Saoire an Spidéil in Irish) (☎ 091-83372) is 18 km west of Galway on the coast road.

Hostels

There are legions of hostels. The *Quay St Hostel* on Quay St is newly opened and charges IR£6 a night. *Corrib Villa* (☎ 091-62892) is at 4 Waterside north of Eglinton St near the GPO and the town hall. It costs IR£4.90 a night, has good facilities and is open all year round. The glossy new *Woodquay Hostel* (☎ 091-62618) costs IR£6.90 high season, IR£5.90 low season. It's also just north of the city centre, in St Anne's House at 23/24 Woodquay by the old Potato Market. They also have private and family rooms.

The *Arch View Hostel* (☎ 091-66661) is hidden away at the junction of Upper and Lower Dominick Sts, just west of Wolfe Tone Bridge. It costs IR£6.50 high season or IR£5 low season. Next to the Arch View is the *Galway City Hostel* (☎ 091-66367) at IR£5 to IR£6.50 a night and recommended. A few steps away on Upper Dominick St is *Owen's Hostel* costing IR£5. Continue from Upper Dominick St through the name changes to St Mary's Rd, then turn left to find the huge An Óige *Galway International Youth Hostel* (☎ 091-27411). This is a summer hostel in St Mary's College, open only for July and August. It's between central Galway and Salthill. You can take bus No 1 from Eyre Square. It costs IR£8 and also has family rooms.

In Salthill, the *Grand Holiday Hostel* (☎ 091-21150) is right on the promenade and has rooms with two or four beds as well as family rooms, from IR£5 a night. The *Stella Maris Holiday Hostel* (☎ 091-21950) is at 151 Upper Salthill and the rooms all have two or four beds and cost from IR£5 per night in the high season. There's a free bus to the city centre and they hire bicycles. The *Mary Ryan Hostel* (☎ 091-23303) is at 4 Beechmount Ave, Highfield Park, beyond Salthill to the south of the centre. It's about a 20-minute walk from the centre; or you could take bus No 2 from Eyre Square to Taylor Hill Convent. It costs IR£5 including breakfast; ring before heading out there to make sure there are rooms available. The *Galway Tourist Hostel* (☎ 091-25176) is also just beyond Salthill, at Gentian Hill, Knocknacarra. It's just past the golf course and camp site, pleasantly situated near the water and with a camping area.

B&Bs

In summer you may have to travel to remote suburbs. There are not many B&Bs around the city centre but it's worth trying. One central place is *Lydon's* (☎ 091-64914) at 8 Lower Abbeygate St off Shop St, with rooms at IR£13. Also central is *Lynnfield* (☎ 091-67845), at 9 College Rd, which runs east from Eyre Square becoming the Dublin road. They will pick you up from the bus or railway station, and charge IR£20/28 for singles/doubles or more with bathroom. At No 66 College Rd is *Cúchulainn* (☎ 091-65772), charging IR£12. At 134 College Rd, *Lake House* (☎ 091-61519) costs IR£12 to IR£13.

Mrs Sexton's *St Martin's* (☎ 091-68286) at 2 Nuns Island Rd is delightfully situated backing right on to the river. Costs are from IR£12 per person.

There are plenty of places less than 10 minutes' walk away on the Newcastle Rd which is west of the river and runs in a north-south direction, becoming the N59 to Clifden. At 22 Newcastle Rd is *Coolavalla* (☎ 091-22415), which costs IR£15/26. At No 40 is *Villanova* (☎ 091-24849), which charges IR£16/26, or more with bathroom. At No 54 is *De Sota* (☎ 091-65064) with rooms at IR£13 or IR£15 with own bathroom. At 4 Greenfields Rd is *Edelweiss* (☎ 091-24501), which charges IR£16/26.

Salthill and adjacent Renmore are good hunting grounds for B&Bs which typically cost IR£12 to IR£14 per person. Upper and Lower Salthill Rds are packed with places. Particularly good places include *Norman Villa* (☎ 091-21131), at 86 Lower Salthill, for IR£16/26. *Devondell* (☎ 091-23617) is down a cul-de-sac at 47 Devon Park, Lower Salthill. All rooms have their own bathrooms and cost IR£15/26.

In Upper Salthill try *Mandalay* (☎ 091-24177), at 10 Gentian Hill, which costs IR£12 or IR£14 with own bathroom. Also in Gentian Hill is *Bay View House* (☎ 091-22116) in a cul-de-sac, which costs IR£26 for doubles with own bathroom.

Hotels

The *Great Southern Galway Hotel* (☎ 091-64041) takes up one complete side of Eyre Square and does B&B from IR£57 to IR£64 a night. Also on Eyre Square, the *Skeffington Arms* (☎ 091-63173) is an attractive and cheaper place with B&B from IR£25 to IR£35. *Brennan's Yard Hotel* (☎ 091-68166) on Lower Merchants Rd is more intimate than most, an old stone building with B&B from IR£35 to IR£45. A quiet hotel on Taylor's Hill is the *Ardilaun House Hotel* (☎ 091-21433), formerly a fine country mansion. B&B costs from IR£33 to IR£52.

Country Houses

In Creggana, Oranmore, a few km east of the city is *Hazlewood House* (☎ 091-94275), which stands in its own grounds. B&B is IR£13 to IR£15 with own bathroom. The 17th-century *Cregg Castle* (☎ 091-91434) stands on its own grounds in Corrandulla, 14 km (nine miles) north of the city en route to Headford. B&B is IR£18 to IR£20. Nearby is the Georgian *Lisdonagh Manor* (☎ 091-82728) with B&B for IR£25.

PLACES TO EAT
Cafés & Takeaways

There are lots of restaurants, cafés and pubs around the river end of Quay St. *Hungry Grass* on Upper Cross St has good snacks for less than IR£3. A few doors down *Country Basket* (☎ 091-63236) is an equally appealing lunch spot. *Neachtain's* (☎ 091-66172) on Quay St is a pub serving some of the best bar food to be found anywhere, and has a reasonable restaurant upstairs.

Food for Thought does sandwiches and meals, including vegetarian dishes; it has a branch at Lower Abbeygate St, just off Shop St/William St, and another in the tourist office. The *House of James* (☎ 091-67776) is a combined coffee shop, restaurant and craft shop on Castle St, a dead end east off William St, and does excellent home-cooked food. *Conlon's* (☎ 091-62268) on Eglinton St is reasonably priced and the fish is good. There's a *Bewley's Cafe* in the Cornstore on Middle St, while *Sails*, another popular tea-and-coffee specialist, is in the Eyre Square Centre.

The choice isn't so good on the other side of the river. The *Left Bank Café* on Lower Dominick St is a good sandwich place. For late-night eats turn the corner to Upper Dominick St and the *Kebab House*.

Restaurants

Galway's choice of restaurants is positively overkill compared to many Irish towns. *Sev'nth Heaven* (☎ 091-63838) is right beside the Druid Theatre on the corner of Courthouse Lane and Flood St and does excellent pasta (from IR£4) and pizza. *Fat Freddy's* on Quay St is similar. Vegetarians can head for the *Sunflower Vegetarian Restaurant*, near Fat Freddy's on Quay St. Across the road from Fat Freddy's is the *Café Nora Crub* (☎ 091-68376). *La Mezza Luna* nearby is a good Italian place with main courses in the IR£5 to IR£7 range. *McDonagh's Fish Shop* (☎ 091-65001) is at 22 Quay St and the *Quay Wine Bar* (☎ 091-65942). Other interesting choices include the Indian restaurant *Shama* (☎ 091-66696) on Flood St near Spanish Arch, the superb

Dragon Court (☎ 091-65388) Chinese restaurant on Forster St, *Pasta Mista* (☎ 091-65550) at 2 Cross St and the reasonably priced *Brasserie* (☎ 091-61610) on Middle St. Despite the French name, the latter has a lot of US/Mexican food – tacos, steaks and good ice cream.

Cooke's Wine Bar is at 28 Abbeygate Upper and *Brannagan's* is a couple of doors down at No 36. The *Malt House* (☎ 091-67866) in a small courtyard off High St does bar food and has one of the best restaurants in the city out the back.

One of the best restaurants in the country is *Drimcong House* (☎ 091-85115) 14 km (eight miles) along the Clifden road past Moycullen. It cannot be recommended highly enough and has a very reasonable (for its bracket) set menu for IR£16.95.

ENTERTAINMENT
Pubs
There's lots going on in Galway's pubs. On Quay St is the cosy *Neachtain's*, which has a great atmosphere. Back from the river on Shop St, the *King's Head* has music most nights in summer. *MacSwiggan's* on Daly's Place is big and busy. The very popular *Quay's* on Quay St draws a great crowd in summer.

There are some glossier but less atmospheric pubs around Eyre Square including the popular *Skeffington Arms* ('the Skeff') on the square, *An Púcán Bar* just off the square at 11 Forster St (music most nights) and *Rabbitt's Bar* at 23 Forster St.

On the west side of the river there's the busy *Monroe's Tavern* on the corner of Upper Dominick St and Fairhill. *Taylor's Bar* on Upper Dominick St and the *Galway Shawl* and *Crane's Bar*, both round the corner on Sea Rd, all have music, as does *O'Connor's* at Salthill, another popular place.

Theatre
Galway has two good theatres. The *Druid Theatre* (☎ 091-68617) on Chapel Lane is renowned for its new and exciting approach to older plays. *An Taibhdhearc* (☎ 091-

62024) on Middle St regularly puts on plays in Irish.

GETTING THERE & AWAY
Train
Ceannt Railway Station is beside the bus terminus (☎ 091-64222 ext 156). There are four or more trains to and from Dublin, Monday to Saturday, fewer on Sunday.

Bus
The bus station is behind the big grey Great Southern Hotel off Eyre Square in the centre of town, next to the railway station. For travel information ring ☎ 091-62000/63555. There are regular services from Galway to all major cities and points in between. Local bus services go in all directions, though services into Connemara and Mayo are infrequent.

Air
Galway Airport (☎ 091-52874) is in Carnmore, 10 km east of the city. Take the main Dublin road to Oranmore and turn north, then watch out for the signs to the airport. There are two Aer Lingus flights each day to and from Dublin. It's a 45-minute flight and the return fare is IR£75.

GETTING AROUND
You can walk to most points of interest and out to Salthill from the centre, but there are regular buses from Eyre Square. Local Bus Éireann bus No 1 runs from Eyre Square to Salthill and Blackrock, bus No 2 goes from Knocknacarra through Eyre Square to Renmore. Bus No 3 runs between Eyre Square and Castlepark while bus No 4 runs to Newcastle.

Taxi
Galway Taxi (☎ 091-61111) is on Mainguard St, Corrib Cabs (☎ 091-67888) are on Eyre St north off Eyre Square, and there are also a couple of taxi ranks on Eyre Square.

Car Rental
Local operators include Johnson & Perrett

(☎ 091-68888) at Higgin's garage on the Headford road, Budget (☎ 091-66376) and Murray's (☎ 091-62222).

Bicycle Rental
Round the Corner Bicycle Hire (☎ 091-66606) is on Queen St, just round the corner from the Galway tourist office, and at Seapoint, just round the corner from the Salthill tourist office. Other places include Rent-a-Bike (☎ 091-68223) on Dominick St, Europa Cycles (☎ 091-63355) near Galway Cathedral, and Cawley's Rent-a-Bike (☎ 091-66219) behind Eyre Square on Ball Alley Lane.

South of Galway City

Many visitors will pass through the small area of County Galway south of the city, on their way to or from the spectacular limestone Burren in County Clare. The limestone begins in County Galway just south of Kinvara, a picturesque hamlet on a small inlet of Galway Bay. Worth visiting in the area are the tranquil monastic settlement and round tower at Kilmacduagh.

CLARINBRIDGE & KILCOLGAN
Sixteen km south of Galway, Clarinbridge and Kilcolgan are the focus for Galway's famous Clarinbridge Oyster Festival, and *Paddy Burke's Bar & Restaurant* (☎ 091-96107) in Clarinbrudge is a nice old-fashioned place. The food varies in quality. A little farther south, signposted off the road in Kilcolgan, is *Moran's on the Weir* (☎ 091-96113), a wonderful thatched pub and restaurant overlooking the bay where the famous Galway oysters are reared. During the festival, the world oyster-opening championships are held at Moran's. This place is highly recommended and a good stopover on the way to or from Clare.

Getting There & Away
Clarinbridge is on the main Galway to Gort, Ennis and Limerick road and is served by

numerous buses from Galway bus station. Kilcolgan is also on the main road, and Moran's pub is about one mile to the west.

KINVARA
Kinvara is a delightful village tucked away on the south-east corner of Galway Bay. A small stone harbour is home to a number of the Galway 'hookers'. Every August the village hosts 'Cruinniú na mbád', the 'gathering of the boats' festival and celebration of these traditional craft.

For all its quaintness, Kinvara is a relatively quiet spot and doesn't attract anything like the numbers of people that Ballyvaughan 24 km (15 miles) to the west does. A few km west of Kinvara, you come to County Clare and the Burren limestone region.

Dunguaire Castle
Dunguaire Castle is north of Kinvara on the shore and was erected around 1520 by the O'Hynes. It later passed through the hands of Oliver St John Gogarty (1878-1957), a noted writer and wit. The castle is supposedly built on the site of the 6th-century Royal Palace of Guaire, king of Connaught.

Today, it's in superb condition, and each floor of the castle is set up to reflect a particular period in its history, right down to the last mildly eccentric owner who lived here through the 1960s. It has a gift shop, guided tours, and medieval banquets à la Bunratty held during the summer, but on a more intimate scale than Bunratty's. Just south of Dunguaire is a bare stone arch, the only remains of an older castle.

There is an entrance charge of IR£2; for information phone ☎ 091-37108 or to book banquets phone ☎ 061-360788. A bus service (☎ 091-62141) brings banqueteers out from Galway and Salthill.

Places to Stay
Hostels *Johnston's Hostel* (☎ 091-37164) is an independent hostel on Main St, open from June to September. They charge IR£5 a night in dorms and also have a camp site for IR£3 per person.

Six km south and well signposted off the main road to Ballyvaughan is the Burren Hostel also known as *Doorus An Óige Youth Hostel* (☎ 091-37173). Open year round the charge goes from IR£3.50 in winter to IR£5.50 in July and August. The hostel building was once owned by a count called Floribund de Basterot who entertained such notables as W B Yeats, Augusta Lady Gregory, Douglas Hyde and Guy de Maupassant here. Yeats and Lady Gregory are said to have first mooted the idea of the Abbey Theatre while they were here. It's a good base for exploring the Burren.

B&Bs About the cheapest place in town is *Winkle's Hotel* (☎ 091-37137) at a mere IR£11 to IR£12. However it has a new owner and prices and standards may go up. *Windemere* (☎ 091-37151) costs IR£13, and *Kinvara House* (☎ 091-37118) is slightly cheaper at IR£12.

Many local B&Bs are south of town around the Doorus Peninsula. *Teach Caoilte* (☎ 091-37214) and *Burren View Farmhouse* (☎ 091-37142) both charge around IR£12. Farther south near Finnavarra in Clare is *Mrs Nolan's B&B* (☎ 065-78106).

Places to Eat
There is an excellent little coffee shop and wholefood grocers overlooking the harbour with snacks and light meals available all day.

Just up Main St is *Sayre's Restaurant* (☎ 091-37417), a good upmarket restaurant, open summer only and costing at least IR£16 for dinner. *Partners* farther up Main St is cheaper.

Getting There & Away
The bus stop is outside Winkles Hotel just off the main street. One route serves Galway, Kinvara, Ballyvaughan, Lisdoonvarna, Ennistymon, Lahinch, Miltown Malbay, Doonbeg, Kilkee and Kilrush.

Another route serves the Burren coast, running to and from Galway City via Kinvara, Ballyvaughan, Blackhead, Fanore, Lisdoonvarna and Doolin. There is usually one bus daily in winter, Sundays excepted, and two or three in summer.

In winter there is one bus a day from Monday to Saturday only which runs between Galway City, Kinvara, Ballyvaughan, Lisdoonvarna and Doolin. In summer the same service has up to three buses a day, from mid-June to the end of September. Contact Galway City bus station (☎ 091-62000) for details of bus times on all these routes.

KILMACDUAGH
Five km south-west of Gort is the extensive monastic site of Kilmacduagh. Beside a small lake is a well-preserved round tower, the remains of a small cathedral (Teampall Mór MacDuagh), a church of St John the Baptist and various other little chapels. The original monastery is thought to have been founded by St Colman MacDuagh at the beginning of the 7th century, and such was its importance that it became the focus for a new diocese in the 12th century. St MacDuagh founded the monastery under the patronage of King Guaire of Connaught who gave his name to Dunguaire Castle in Kinvara.

The round tower is 33 metres tall and leans some 60 cm from the perpendicular. The doorway is seven metres above ground level. There are fine views over the Burren to the west.

Connemara

Connemara is the wild and barren region west of Galway City and Lough Corrib. It's a stunning patchwork of bogs, lonely valleys, pale grey mountains and small brown lakes. Its devotees – Irish, French, Americans – buy up remote cottages as holiday homes or spend a fortune on a week in a castle hideaway during the salmon fishing season.

Connemara is not a distinct geographical region like the Burren. At its heart are the

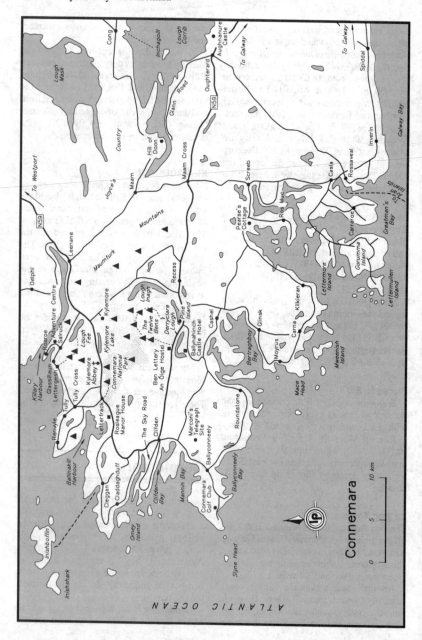

Maumturk Mountains and the grey quartzite peaks of the Twelve Bens, which have tremendous hill walking. They look south over a plain dotted with lakes, melting southwards into the sea around Carna and Roundstone in a maze of rocky islands, tortuous inlets and sparkling white beaches. The coast road west of Spiddal eventually enters this maze, and it is well worth losing yourself for a day, in search of Carraroe, Roundstone, Lettermullen Island and Ballyconneely Bay. Pink Galway granite is the predominant rock in this lower country while the mountains and northern part of the region are made of a mixture of quartzite, gneiss, schist and marble. However, the best scenery is in the middle of the region. The journey from Maam Cross over to Leenane and especially the trip up the Lough Inagh Valley and around by Kylemore Lake would be difficult to surpass anywhere in the country.

County Galway's northern border is marked by Killary Harbour, a long deep gash in the coastline.

One of the most important gaeltachts – Irish-speaking areas – in the country begins just west of Galway City around Barna and stretches west through Spiddal and Inverin, and along much of the coast as far as Carna. Ireland's national Irish-language radio station, Radio Na Gaeltachta, is based out here and does much to sustain the language as a living entity.

Heading west from Galway City you have two options: the coast road through Salthill, Barna and Spiddal, or the inland route through Oughterard which leads directly to the heart of wild and beautiful Connemara.

The Folding Landscapes map company have produced a superb map of Connemara which is a must if you intend any detailed exploration. Their *Connemara, A Hill Walker's Guide* by Tim Robinson and Joss Lynam is also invaluable.

GETTING THERE & AWAY

There are numerous bus services serving most parts of Connemara, many of which originate from Galway bus station (☎ 091-62000), so check there for times and fares.

Services can be very sporadic and many only operate in the summertime.

A service runs between Galway, Oughterard, Maam Cross, Recess, Roundstone, Ballyconneely and on to Clifden; usually one of the summer weekday buses on this service diverts at Maam Cross and travels to Clifden via Leenane. Another less frequent service runs between Westport, Leenane, Kylemore, Letterfrack and Clifden with one bus a day during the summer only.

Galway, Cong, Leenane and Clifden are connected by an infrequent service on weekdays only. Another runs between Galway, Spiddal, Inverin, Rossaveal, Carraroe, Lettermore and Lettermullen Islands. On weekdays only a bus runs between Galway, Oughterard, Maam Cross, Ros Muc, Recess, Glinsk, Carna and Moyrus.

SPIDDAL

Just 17 km (11 miles) from Galway City, Spiddal is a lively little roadside settlement with some good pubs. East of the village is an Irish college which gives summer courses in the Irish language. On the Galway side of Spiddal is Standún's, a massive craft shop which also operates a bureau de change. Nearby, just in front of an extensive craft village, is a good beach which can get crowded during summer. If you are looking for open landscapes and wild coastlines, leave Spiddal behind and head west towards Roundstone.

SPIDDAL TO ROUNDSTONE

West of Spiddal, the scenery gradually improves and at Casla you can turn west off the main road for Carraroe and into a maze of inlets and islands. Before Casla, you will notice the signs for Rossaveal, the main departure point for ferries to the Aran Islands.

It is well worth heading out to Carraroe and back across a series of rugged islands, all connected to the mainland. **Carraroe** is famous for its fine beaches, including the Coral Strand which is composed entirely of shell and fragments of coralline seaweed.

Lettermore, Gorumna and **Lettermullen** islands are low and bleak with a handful of farmers eking out an existence from tiny rocky fields. Fish farming has become big business out here and there are salmon cages floating in some of the bays.

From Screeb you can head up to Maam Cross or continue along the coast down to **Carna**, a small fishing village with a marine biology research station nearby. Carna has cheap accommodation and food at *Mac's Bar & Hostel* (☎ 095-32240). From Carna there are some good walks out to **Mweenish Island** or north to **Moyrus** and out to **Mace Head**. Back on the coast road, it's a lovely journey back up to Cashel and south again to Roundstone.

Places to Stay & Eat

The *Connemara Tourist Hostel* (☎ 091-93104) is west of Spiddal in Inverin and open all year round. They charge IR£4.50 for a bed. There is also an *An Óige Hostel* (☎ 091-93154) in Inverin by the main road. They have 66 beds and charge IR£4.50 a night low season and IR£5.90 high season. They have bikes for hire.

There is camping at Carraroe's *Coilleann Campsite* (☎ 091-95266), open April to September and charging IR£5 per tent.

There are plenty of B&Bs along the road and some exclusive hotels tucked away out here. They are good places to stop for a sandwich, drink or meal if you can rise to their prices. Near Cashel, the *Zetland Hotel* (☎ 095-31111) has B&B for IR£40 to IR£55, while the *Cashel House Hotel* (☎ 095-31001) charges IR£50 to IR£68 B&B.

The lovely *Ballynahinch Castle Hotel* (☎ 095-31006), south of Recess, was formerly the home of Humanity Dick (1754-1834), a local landlord, MP and one of the chief forces behind the Royal Society for the Prevention of Cruelty to Animals (RSPCA). Ballynahinch Castle is well worth a visit even if it's just a for a drink in the bar and a quick scout around the delightful grounds. You can also stay there for IR£38 to IR£56 B&B.

ROUNDSTONE

The small fishing village of Roundstone is 16 km (10 miles) south-west of Recess on a western extension of Bertraghboy Bay. Looming behind the neat stone harbour is Errisbeg at 300 metres (987 feet), the only significant hill along this section of coastline. From the summit there are wonderful views across the bay to the distant humps of the Twelve Bens.

The village itself consists essentially of one main street of tall houses, pubs and shops overlooking the water. The small harbour is home to lobster boats and currachs. At the head of the pier is the home of Tim Robinson, the man behind Folding Landscape Maps – the interesting and detailed maps of the Burren, the Aran Islands and Connemara that you will see for sale everywhere. His house is open to visitors during the summer.

Just south of the village is an IDA (Industrial Development Agency) craft complex with various small factory shops selling everything from teapots to bodhráns, the goatskin drums beloved of traditional Irish musicians. Farther south off the road to Ballyconneely are the magnificent white beaches of Gorteen and Dogs Bay.

Places to Stay

Gorteen Beach Caravan & Camping Park (☎ 095-35882) is two km west of town near Gorteen Beach. It is open March to September and they charge from IR£4.50 to IR£5.50 high season. Hikers and cyclists pay IR£4.50 per tent.

For B&B, *St Joseph's* (☎ 095-35865) on Main St overlooking the harbour, costs IR£12 to IR£13. Out near the turn-off for Gorteen and Dogs Bay are *High Trees* (☎ 095-35881) and *Wood Glen* (☎ 095-35935) at IR£12.

Roundstone House Hotel (☎ 095-35864) is on Main St and has rooms with bathrooms and nice views over the bay to Connemara. B&B costs from IR£22 to IR£24.

Places to Eat

O'Dowd's Pub (☎ 095-35809) in the village has good food in the bar and a restaurant with excellent oysters. There is a nice coffee shop in the IDA Craft Park just outside the village, open all day. *Beola Restaurant* (☎ 095-35871) on Main St serves good seafood, meat and vegetarian dishes, in the IR£10 to IR£14 range. They are open for lunch and dinner between Easter and September.

ROUNDSTONE TO CLIFDEN

Twelve km west of Roundstone is **Ballyconneely**. If you detour south off the Clifden road towards the Connemara Golf Club (☎ 095-32502), you pass the ruins of **Bunowen Castle** before reaching the shore at **Trá Mhóir**, or 'great beach', a superb expanse of pure white sand. The Connemara Golf Club has its good 18-hole golf course behind Trá Mhóir.

Back on the road north to Clifden you pass another fine beach and coral strand in **Mannin Bay**.

OUGHTERARD

The small town of Oughterard, 27 km (17 miles) along the main road from Galway City to Clifden, calls itself 'the Gateway to Connemara'. And sure enough, just west of town, the countryside opens to sweeping panoramas of lakes, mountain and bog that get more spectacular the farther west you travel.

Oughterard itself is a pleasant little town and one of Ireland's principal angling centres. It has a number of good cafés, pubs, and restaurants as well as some fairly exclusive country house establishments hidden in the surrounding countryside. The focus of the anglers' attention is Lough Corrib, just out of sight to the north of town. Nearby attractions include Aughanure Castle to the east and the lovely drive along the Glann Rd by Lough Corrib to a vantage point overlooking the Hill of Doon.

Information

There is a tourist information point in Monahan's (☎ 091-82224) on Main St where they have some literature and guides to the area.

AIB Bank (☎ 091-82366) and the Bank of Ireland (☎ 091-82123) have branches on Main St, and there are bureaus de change in Fuschia Crafts (☎ 091-82644) on Main St and Keogh & Sons (☎ 091-82583) on the square.

Keogh's Laundrette (☎ 091-82542) is on Main St.

Oughterard has a fine 18-hole golf course. For information contact Oughterard Golf Club (☎ 091-82733/82131).

Aughanure Castle

Three km east of Oughterard and off the main Galway road is the 16th-century O'Flaherty fortress, Aughanure Castle, built on the site of earlier structures. The O'Flahertys controlled the region for hundreds of years after they fought off the Normans, and these 'fighting O'Flahertys' were constantly at odds with the forces of Galway City. The six-storey tower house stands on a rocky outcrop overlooking Lough Corrib and has been extensively restored. Surrounding the castle are the remains of an unusual double bawn or perimeter fortification. Underneath the castle, the lake washes through a number of natural caverns and caves.

Aughanure Castle (☎ 091-82214) is open to the public from mid-June to mid-September between 9.30 am and 6.30 pm every day. The entrance fee is 80p or 30p for students.

Places to Stay

Hostels *Lough Corrib Hostel* (☎ 091-82634/80194) is on Camp St. From the centre of town, turn north for the Hill of Doon drive, and it's about 200 metres along on the left. They have bikes for hire, tent sites and boat trips to Inchagoill Island in Lough Corrib. It costs from IR£5 a night.

B&Bs There are legions of B&Bs around Oughterard but they can be expensive. *Woodlawn House* (☎ 091-80198) in Doon, Rosscahill – on the Galway City side of Oughterard – does B&B for IR£13. Also out this way, *Cashelmara Cottage* (☎ 091-80194) costs IR£13 to IR£15.

Further east of Oughterard and travelling

towards Portacarron and the lake, you'll see plenty of signposts.

If you turn north at the main crossroads in Oughterard and travel five km along Glann Rd towards the Hill of Doon, you come to the excellent *Glann House* (☎ 091-82127), which does B&B from IR£13 to IR£15. Another good place on the way along the Glann road is *Pine Grove* (☎ 091-82101).

One km from Oughterard in Claremount is the pleasant *Cloverhill House* (☎ 091-82273) costing from IR£13.

Hotels The *Corrib Hotel* (☎ 091-82329) on Bridge St is a comfortable old hotel with B&B from IR£25 to IR£30.

Country Houses *Sweeney's Oughterard House* (☎ 091-82207) is a delightful old place on the western outskirts of the town. It's opposite a shady weir and river walk, and does good food. It costs between IR£45 and IR£49. *Currarevagh House* (☎ 091-82312) is a 19th-century mansion just outside Oughterard on the shore of Lough Corrib, recommended in just about every good food and accommodation guide. B&B costs from IR£44 to IR£47.

Places to Eat
On Main St, the *Corrib County* (☎ 091-82678) is an excellent low to medium-priced restaurant with good coffee, lunches and dinners. *Fogo's Fast Food* also on Main St does burgers and takeaway. There is another cosy coffee-shop-cum-snack-restaurant, *O'Fatharta's* (☎ 091-82315) farther east on Main St. For good pub food and meals try the *Boat Inn* (☎ 091-82196) on the Square. *Keogh's Bar* on the Square also do reasonable pub food.

On Bridge St, the western extension of Main St, is the upmarket *Water Lily* (☎ 091-82737), right on the river. Also on Bridge St, the *Corrib Hotel* (☎ 091-82329) does a good four-course dinner for around IR£15. For a real treat try *Currarevagh House* (☎ 091-82731) or *Drimcong House* (☎ 091-85115) in Moycullen.

Entertainment
Power's Bar (☎ 091-82712) on Main St often has music in summer. So do *Faherty's* and the *Boat Inn* on the Square.

Getting Around
Ring Sean Conneely (☎ 091-82299) on Main St for a taxi.

Lough Corrib Bike Hire (☎ 091-82634/80194) is opposite the Texaco garage on the Galway City side of Oughterard. Bikes are IR£6 a day. Tuck's (☎ 091-82335) on Main St have bikes and fishing tackle for hire. Bikes are also available from Lough Corrib Hostel.

Boats are available from Michael Healy (☎ 091-82736).

LOUGH CORRIB
The Republic's biggest lake (Lough Neagh in the North is larger), Lough Corrib is over 48 km (30 miles) long and covers some 200 sq km. It virtually cuts off western Galway from the rest of the country and has over 360 islands. The largest one, Inchagoill, has a monastic settlement and can be visited from Oughterard or Cong.

Lough Corrib is world-famous for its salmon, sea trout and brown trout and the area attracts legions of anglers from all over the world. The highlight of the fishing year is the mayfly season when countless billions of these small lacy insects hatch over a few days (usually in May) and drive the fish and fishermen into a feeding frenzy. The hooks are baited with live flies which join their brothers and sisters dancing on the surface of the lake. The main run of salmon does not begin until June.

Many of the guesthouses around Lough Corrib have boats, tacklerooms and other facilities for anglers. These places can be more expensive but there are plenty of ordinary B&Bs too.

Inchagoill Island
The largest island on Lough Corrib, some seven km north-west of Oughterard, Inchagoill is a lonely place hiding many ancient remains. Most fascinating is an

obelisk bearing the carver's name, 'Lia Luguaedon Macc Menueh', the 'stone of luguaedon son of menuah'. It stands some 75 cm tall near the 'Saints' Church', and some people claim the Latin writing on the stone is the oldest Christian inscription in Europe apart from those in the catacombs in Rome. It's certainly the oldest in Ireland in Latin script.

Teampall Padraig or St Patrick's Church is a small oratory of a very early design with some later additions. The prettiest church is the 'Saints Church' of early Romanesque design probably built in the 9th or 10th centuries. It has some carvings around the arched doorway. The name Inchagoill means 'Island of the Foreigner'. The island can be reached by boat from Cong in County Mayo or Oughterard. Look out for details in shop windows or check with the Lough Corrib Hostel (☎ 091-82634) in Oughterard.

MAAM CROSS TO LEENANE

West of Oughterard, Maam Cross is the first settlement along the Clifden Rd. *Peacockes* (☎ 091-82306) is the huge and touristy bar/shop/restaurant/petrol station, with a tacky model donkey and 'traditional' Irish cottage, by the turn-off for Leenane. The trip to Leenane is lovely but if you have only one run through the region it's better to stay on the Clifden road and turn up the Lough Inagh Valley instead. It's also a nice journey south towards Screeb and the coast. An excellent farmhouse B&B near Maam Cross is *Tullaboy House* (☎ 091-82305). To get there, travel five km (three miles) from Maam Cross towards Oughterard on the N59 and you'll see a sign for the house, indicating a side road heading north.

LEENANE

The Irish name, An Lionan, means 'Shallow Sea-Bed', referring to the way the sea edges its way in to Killary harbour. Leenane itself makes a convenient stopover on the way north and the road north-west to Louisburgh is startlingly beautiful. Like nearby Cong the town can boast a film connection, having been the location for *The Field* which was

shot in 1989 and based on a John B Keane story about an argument over the ownership of a field. The dance and pub scenes were filmed in the village and the church scene in Ashleagh church.

Leenane Cultural Centre

The centre focuses on the woollen industry and gives demonstrations of carding, spinning and weaving, with a 15-minute video that sets the historical and social scene. Locally made woollen garments are on sale. Admission is IR£2 and it is open from March to the end of September.

RECESS & AROUND

Recess is nothing more than a few houses on the main road between Clifden and Maam Cross. Turning north here brings you on a minor road through the wonderful Lough Inagh Valley. If, instead, you continue along the main road from Recess towards Clifden, there are some marvellous views over Lough Derryclare and Pine Island, familiar from many postcards. The grassy layby here is an excellent place to camp. About one km west of here off the Clifden road is a dead end road heading north into a great valley enclosed by a ring of six of the Twelve Bens. It's a beautiful drive up this road and there's a challenging circuit hike of the six peaks, beginning or ending near Ben Lettery Hostel.

Back on the main Clifden Rd and another one km west is the An Óige *Ben Lettery Youth Hostel* (☎ 095-34636). This is open all year round and charges IR£3.80 a night low season or IR£5.50 high season. It's an excellent and popular base to explore the Twelve Bens and makes a good starting or finishing point for the walk described above. The hostel is eight km (five miles) from Recess and 13 km (eight miles) from Clifden.

Lough Inagh Valley

The journey north up the Lough Inagh Valley is one of the most scenic in the country. There are two fine approaches up valleys from the south, starting on either side of Recess, and the long sweep of Loughs Derryclare and

Inagh accompanies you for most of the way. On the west side are the brooding Bens, while just out of the valley on the north side is the picturesque drive along Kylemore Lake.

Halfway up the Inagh Valley is the *Inagh Valley Lodge* (☎ 095-34706), an upmarket country house hotel with B&B from IR£38 to IR£56. It's a really nice place to stop for a snack, particularly in good weather. The location is magnificent.

Towards the northern end of the valley, a track leads off the road west up a blind valley, which is also well worth exploring.

Kylemore Abbey & Lake

Just outside the northern end of the beautiful Inagh Valley is the almost equally scenic Kylemore Lake with its accompanying abbey. The road skirts the northern shore of the lake, winding through overhanging trees with magnificent views across the silent lake. South of the lake are the Twelve Bens and Connemara National Park, while the mountains behind the abbey are Dúchruach (530 metres, 1736 feet) and Binn Fhraoigh (545 metres, 1791 feet).

The lake passes under the road and extends to the north, where you will see the castellated towers of the 19th-century Gothic Kylemore Abbey (☎ 095-41146) among trees – and rhododendron bushes, which are slowly choking the oak wood. The abbey was built for a wealthy English businessman, Mitchell Henry, after he had spent his honeymoon in Connemara and fallen in love with the region. During WW I, a group of Benedictine nuns left Ypres in Belgium and eventually set up in Kylemore, turning the place into an abbey.

Today, the nuns run an exclusive convent boarding school with some sections open to the public and a small craft shop and tea room. You can walk up behind the abbey to a statue overlooking Kylemore Lake. The abbey is 17 km (11 miles) from Clifden.

CLIFDEN

Clifden, the capital of Connemara, is some 80 km (50 miles) west of Galway City at the head of Clifden Bay. Astride the Owenglen River, the tightly packed houses and the two needle-sharp spires of the town's churches are shadowed by the steep backdrop of the Twelve Bens to the east. A landlord, John D'Arcy, was the main force behind the establishment of the town around 1812, but the famine ruined the family and their estate along the Sky Rd is now deserted.

Today, the town has around 2000 inhabitants. Unlike many straggling western towns and villages, Clifden has a focus, a definite centre where roads from all directions meet. On the main street, numerous pubs, cafés and restaurants cater to a increasing tide of visitors during the summer.

Information

The seasonal tourist office (☎ 095-21163) is on Lower Market St and open from May to September.

Activities

Errislannan Manor (☎ 095-21134) organises pony trekking. The Irish School of Landscape Painting (☎ 095-21891) is based in Clifden and runs regular courses during the summer. Connemara Golf Club (☎ 095-32502) has a superb 18-hole golf links, 16 km (10 miles) south beyond Ballyconneely. It's beside a magnificent beach. The Connemara Pony Show is held in the third week of August with plenty of these tiny sturdy ponies in action. Heritage Tours on Market St run tours of local sites of archaeological and natural interest with experienced guides.

Places to Stay

Hostels The *Clifden Town Hostel* (☎ 095-21076) is a spanking new hostel on Market St. They charge IR£5.50 in dorms or IR£6.50 in private roooms. *Leo's Hostel* (☎ 095-21429) is right by the square and charges IR£4.50 a night in dorms, IR£5 a night in private rooms, and IR£2 camping. For the An Óige *Ben Lettery Hostel* (☎ 095-34636) see the Around Recess section. There is another hostel in Cleggan to the north-west.

B&Bs In town, *Kingston House* (☎ 095-21470) on Bridge St costs IR£13 or IR£14 with own bathroom. Also on Bridge St is *Ben View House* (☎ 095-21256) at IR£13.50. Just five minutes walk to the west of town on the magnificent Sky Rd is *Dún Aengus* (☎ 095-21069), with splendid views and rooms with own bathroom at IR£18/26 for singles/doubles.

Many B&Bs are to the south in the direction of Ballyconneely. One km from Clifden and signposted off the road is *Mallmore House* (☎ 095-21460), a country house with a Grecian facade on 28 hectares of grounds. B&B is IR£14 in one of six bedrooms with own bathroom. Two km out is *Lough Fadda House* (☎ 095-21165) open March to November and costing IR£13. Also out this way is *Árd Aoibhinn* (☎ 095-21339) at IR£13 and *Winnowing Hill* (☎ 095-21281) at IR£13.

Hotels The *Alcock & Brown* (☎ 095-21086) in the town centre is probably cheapest with B&B from IR£21 to IR£30. The *Clifden Bay Hotel* (☎ 095-21801) is IR£25 to IR£35 B&B. The best place around is probably the *Abbeyglen Castle Hotel* (☎ 095-21201), 500 metres along the Sky Rd. B&B runs from IR£33.50 to IR£50.

Country Houses The *Rock Glen Manor House* (☎ 095-21035) is a lovely old house in Faul two km south of town on the Ballyconneely road, costing IR£37 to IR£44. The mid-19th-century *Kille House* (☎ 095-21849) is open from January to November and costs from IR£15 to IR£20.

Places to Eat

Cafés and Takeaways The *Coffee Shop* on Market St has good cappuccino, espresso and light meals available all day while the *Coffee House* and *My Tea Shop* are similarly reasonable places on Church Hill and Main St. Next door to O'Grady's Restaurant on Market St, the *Salad Shop* (☎ 095-21835) is just what it says and offers excellent packed lunches.

Pub Food For pub food, try *Mitchell's Bar* on the Square. *E. J. Kings* (☎ 095-21215) on the Square serves pub food all year round with a more formal restaurant during the summer. The food is good and reasonably priced with some imaginative vegetarian dishes. On Main St, the *D'Arcy Inn* (☎ 095-21450) does similar fare with some good seafood dishes. They have a restaurant above the bar and often have fish on the menu.

Restaurants *O'Grady's Seafood Restaurant* (☎ 095-21450) is one of the best restaurants in west Galway, open for lunch and dinner. A set lunch is around IR£9, and most main courses at dinner cost IR£10 or more. *Doris's* (☎ 095-21427) on Market St is also worth trying.

High Moors (☎ 095-21342) is a delightful and intimate little restaurant in Dooneen almost two km from Clifden, with a small menu primarily of seafood. It does dinner only and is closed Sunday to Tuesdays.

Getting There & Away

The Bus Éireann stop is outside Cullen's on Market St. For information phone ☎ 091-62000. Buses go between Galway and Clifden via Oughterard and Maam Cross or via Cong and Leenane. For more details, see the Getting There & Away section under Connemara.

In summer there is a daily express bus from Galway to Clifden at 11.15 am, 12.15 and 6 pm. Express buses from Clifden to Galway leave at 8 am, 12.30 and 1.30 pm. In summer a bus leaves from the Island House on Market St at 10.30 am for Cleggan, gateway to Inishboffin Island.

Getting Around

Mannions (☎ 095-21160/21155), Railway View, Clifden, hire out bicycles. For taxis ring M Coyne (☎ 095-21268), Joyce's (☎ 095-21757) or Ben View House (☎ 095-21256).

AROUND CLIFDEN

The road south of Clifden takes you out past the fine beach at **Mannin Bay** to

Ballyconneely, where the road west brings you to the Connemara Golf Club, an 18-hole links overlooking a magnificent pearl-white beach.

Heading directly west from Clifden, the Sky Rd brings you on a loop out to a town-land known as Kingston and back to Clifden through some rugged coastal scenery. The round trip is about 12 km (eight miles) and can easily be walked or cycled. The deeply indented coastline farther north brings you to the tiny village of **Claddaghduff**. Turning west here down by the Catholic church you come out on Omey Strand, and at low tide you can drive or walk across the sand to **Omey Island**, a small low island of rock, grass and sand with a few inhabited houses. During the summer there are horse races held on Omey Strand.

Back on the mainland to the north is **Cleggan**, the kickoff point for ferries to Inishbhoffin island.

Alcock & Brown Memorial

In a bog almost six km (four miles) south west of Clifden en route to Ballyconneely is a memorial to John Alcock and Arthur Brown, the two pilots of the first nonstop transatlantic flight. The flight began in New-foundland and ended when their Vicker Vimy biplane crash-landed in Derrygimlagh Bog on 15 June 1919. They were not injured, and the memorial was erected in 1959.

Appropriately, the building nearby (now ruined) was a wireless station built three years earlier in 1906 by Marconi for his first transatlantic wireless communications.

LETTERFRACK

Letterfrack is barely more than a few pubs and a crossroads some 15 km (nine miles) north-east of Clifden. It lies at the head of Ballinakill Harbour, but the sea is only visible from west of the crossroads and from the entrance to the national park. The head-quarters of the Connemara National Park is here.

Letterfrack was founded by Quakers in the mid-19th century. The large building down from the crossroads was set up as an orphan-age and later became a reform school. Today it's the focus of a community project housing a sports and health clinic and the only wood-work design school in the country.

The Connemara Sea Week is held here, usually during the third week in October, and there are lectures by visiting guests and biol-ogists as well as field trips to the nearby coast. A Connemara Bog Week is usually held in late May.

North from the crossroads you come to Tully Cross, which has a line of neat thatched rent-a-cottages and some nice little pubs. West of here is Tully where *An Teach Ceoil* (☎ 095-43446) has regular music and Irish dancing sessions.

There is a tourist information point (☎ 095-43950) in the Credit Union office in Tully Cross. The nearest banks are in Clifden, but a mobile Bank of Ireland van travels through the area on Mondays and is usually in Letterfrack from 1.30 to 3 pm. Tully Cross has a laundry service (☎ 095-43466).

Diamond's (☎ 095-43431) in Tully and King's (☎ 095-43414) in Lettergesh rent bikes.

CONNEMARA NATIONAL PARK

Connemara National Park – one of the first national parks in Ireland – covers an area of 2000 hectares of bog, mountain and heath in the countryside east of Letterfrack. The headquarters and visitors' centre (☎ 095-41054) are housed in pleasant old buildings just south of the village crossroads.

The park encloses a number of the Twelve Bens including Bencullagh, Benbrack and Benbaun. The heart of the park is Gleann Mór, the 'big glen', through which flows the River Polladirk. There is fine walking up the glen and over the surrounding ountains.

The visitors' centre will give you an insight into the park's flora, fauna and geology as well as showing maps and various trails. Bog biology is interesting so a wander round is not a waste of time. It has an indoor eating area and rudimentary kitchen facilities for hillwalkers.

There are guided nature walks on

Mondays, Wednesdays and Fridays during the summer, leaving the centre at 10.30 am and taking two to three hours. Bring boots and rainwear. If the Bens look too strenuous, you can hike up Diamond Hill nearby.

NORTH OF LETTERFRACK

There is some fine coastal scenery along the coast north of Letterfrack, especially from Tully Cross east to Lettergesh and Salruck, home to the Little Killary Adventure Centre. Continuing past the adventure centre brings you down to Rosroe Pier and the An Óige Killary Harbour Youth Hostel.

Just short of Salruck is Glassillaun Beach, a breathtaking expanse of pure white sand. There are other fine beaches at Gurteen and at Lettergesh, where the beach horseracing sequences for *The Quiet Man* starring John Wayne were filmed. There are fine walks all along the coast and around Renvyle Point to Derryinver Bay. There's an excellent hill-walk, which takes four to five hours each way, from Lettergesh Post Office up Binn Chuanna and Maolchnoc and then down to Lough Fee.

Getting There & Away

There's a bus between Galway and Clifden which calls at Cong, Leenane, Salruck, Lettergesh Post Office, Tully Church, Kylemore, Letterfrack, Cleggan and Claddaghduff en route. One bus a day in either direction travels that route on summer weekdays only.

Activities

Little Killary Adventure Centre (☎ 095-43411) is a well-run place offering accommodation, plus courses in canoeing, sailing, rock climbing, and just about every other adventure sport you can think of. The owners, Jamie and Mary Young, are an adventurous pair; Jamie has canoed around Cape Horn.

On Glassillaun Beach is the new *Scuba-dive West* (☎ 095-43922), offering courses and diving on the surrounding coast and islands. It's a tremendous place to learn, and

the PADI certification is recognised world-wide.

For sea trips or deep-sea angling contact John or Phil Mongan (☎ 095-43473) at Derryinver and for horse trekking contact Joe O'Neill (☎ 095-42269).

Places to Stay & Eat

Camping *Renvyle Beach Caravan & Camping* (☎ 095-43462) is west of Tully and open from Easter to September. They charge IR£4.50 a night for tents or IR£3 for hikers and cyclists. East of Tully Cross near Lettergesh Beach is the *Connemara Caravan & Camping Park* (☎ 095-43406) open May to September. Tents are charged IR£5.50 a night or IR£3 for hikers and cyclists.

Hostels The An Óige *Killary Harbour Hostel* (☎ 095-43417) is 13 km north-east of Tully Cross on Rosroe Pier. Open March to October, they charge IR£3.80 a night low season and IR£5.50 high season. Some food and supplies are available at the hostel, but the nearest shop is five km away in Lettergesh, so stock up in advance. There is a fine hike from the hostel along an old green road by the fjord to Leenane.

Hotels *Renvyle House Hotel* (☎ 095-43511) is a converted country house in Renvyle and was once owned by Oliver St John Gogarty. It's the best place in the area to have a drink or snack or relax after a walk and B&B runs from IR£32 to IR£55.

KILLARY HARBOUR & SURROUNDS

Mussel rafts dot long dark Killary Harbour, which looks like a fjord but may not actually have been glaciated. It's 16 km (10 miles) long and over 45 metres deep in the centre, a superb anchorage, and Mweelrea Mountain (815 metres) towers over its northern shores. From Leenane at the head of the harbour the road runs west for a couple of km along the southern shore before veering inland. However, you can continue walking along the shore to Rosroe on an old green road. Much of the film *The Field* was shot in

Leenane, and the local scenery rivalled Richard Harris for the starring role.

County Mayo begins about two km north of Leenane and there is magnificent scenery around the north side of Killary and up into Delphi and Doolough, one of the most scenic valleys in the country and the stage for a gold mining controversy.

CLEGGAN

Cleggan is a small fishing village 16 km (10 miles) from Clifden and many visitors pass through en route to Inishboffin Island. There are also boats to the much less visited Inishturk (☎ 095-44649).

There are a couple of B&Bs around Cleggan as well as the *Masters House Hostel* (☎ 095-44076) which is open all year round. They charge IR£4.50 a night in dorms and IR£5.50 a night in private rooms. They also have tent sites at IR£2 a night. The hostel has good shower and kitchen facilities.

There is a bus to Cleggan from Clifden every morning at 8 am during the summer, and Cleggan is on an infrequent Galway City, Cong, Leenane, Clifden route. For details contact Bus Éireann (☎ 091-62000).

INISHBOFFIN ISLAND

Inishboffin Island is a haven of peace and tranquillity nine km (six miles) out in the Atlantic from Cleggan. The island is compact, six km long by three km wide. There are no serious hills to speak of and the highest point is a mere 95 metres above sea level. Good sheltered beaches, open grasslands, grassy lanes and a strong sense of offshore isolation are what make Inishboffin special.

The island is made of some of the oldest rocks in Ireland. The birdlife includes corncrakes, choughs, corn bunting and a variety of seabirds.

Just off the north beach is Lough Bó Finne from which the island gets its name. Bó Finne neans 'fair or white cow'. According to legend, the island was once a mysterious and forgotten place, permanently enveloped in a thick blanket of fog. Some fishermen came upon the island, lit a fire near the lake

and immediately the mist began to clear. Coming out of the mist was a woman with a long stick driving a white cow or 'bó finne' in front of her. She hit the white cow with the stick, turning it to stone. Irritated at such behaviour, the fishermen grabbed the stick and struck her, upon which she also turned to stone.

Until the late 19th century, there were two white stones by the lake: the remains of the cow and its owner.

History
Inishboffin's main historical figure of note was a St Colman who at one stage was a bishop in England. He fell out with the English church in 664 over their adoption of a new calendar system, and exiled himself to Inishboffin where he set up a monastery. North-east of the harbour is a small 13th-century church and hollowed stone, or bullaun, which are said to occupy the site of Colman's original monastery.

Grace or Gráinne O'Malley (also known as Gráinnuaile or Granuaile), the famous pirate queen who was based on Clare Island, also used Inishboffin as a base in the 16th century.

Cromwell's forces captured Inishboffin in 1652 and used it as a prison camp for priests and clerics. Many died or were killed, and one bishop was reputedly chained to Bishop's Rock near the harbour and drowned as the tide came in.

Information
Inishboffin has a small post office and a grocery shop but no banks. The bars and the hotels will usually change travellers' cheques and dollar or sterling cash.

Places to Stay & Eat
Camping There is no official camp site but you can camp on most unfenced ground and by the beaches.

Hostels *Inishboffin Hostel* (☎ 095-45855) is a fine hostel 500 metres up from the harbour. It costs IR£5 a night and is open March to September.

Hotels The modern and comfortable *Day's Hotel* (☎ 095-45827/45829) has turf fires and a dining room looking out over the sea. Rooms with bathroom cost from IR£14 to IR£16 in high season and IR£12 to IR£14 low season. The food is creative, with excellent fresh fish. A four-course dinner is around IR£13. *Day's Bar* next door has a good atmosphere. There are bikes for hire.

The *Doonmore Hotel* (☎ 095-45804) has B&B from IR£15 to IR£18. Seafood is their speciality. They also have bikes for hire.

Cottages Traditional Irish cottages can be rented on the island (☎ 095-43473).

Getting There & Away

Boats leave regularly from Cleggan, usually starting around 9.30 am. The fare is around IR£10 return. The different companies doing the crossing don't accept each others' tickets. Ring for details of the *Sundancer* (☎ 095-44649/44690/44761) or the *Dun Aengus* (☎ 095-45806/44642).

The Aran Islands

The same stretch of limestone that created Clare's Burren region surfaces in the middle of Galway Bay to form the three Aran Islands: Inishmór, Inishmaan and Inisheer. The islands are like one long undulating reef, with no significant hills or mountains, although on the western side of Inishmór and Inishmaan the land rises enough to allow for some dramatic cliffs dropping into the Atlantic. As in the Burren, the limestone creates a spectacular moonscape: sheets of grey rock with flowers and grass bursting from the cracks.

The islands have some of the most ancient Christian and pre-Christian remains in Ireland. Farming was once much easier to pursue here than on the densely forested mainland.

The most ancient significant remains on the islands are massive Iron Age stone forts, such as Dún Aengus on Inishmór and Dún Conchuir on Inishmaan. Almost nothing is known about the people who built these structures, partly because their iron implements quickly rusted away. In folklore, the forts are said to have been built by the Fir Bolg, a Celtic tribe who invaded Ireland from Europe in prehistoric times. Christianity reached the islands remarkably quickly and some of the earliest monastic settlements were founded by St Enda or Éanna, in the late 4th and early 5th centuries. Any remains you see today are later, from the 8th century on. Enda appears to have been an Irish chief who converted to Christianity and spent some time studying in Rome before seeking out a suitably bleak spot for his monastery. Many great monks studied under him on Aran, including Colmcille or Columba who went on to found the monastery on Iona in Scotland.

From the 14th century on, control of the islands was disputed by two Gaelic families, the O'Briens and the O'Flahertys. During the reign of Elizabeth I, the English took control and in Cromwell's times a garrison was stationed here. It is widely said (and probably untrue) that the black hair and dark eyes of many natives of Aran today are a legacy of this garrison's stay.

As Galway City's importance waned so too did that of the islands. They became a quiet and windy backwater.

The islands' isolation allowed Irish culture to survive when it had all but disappeared elsewhere. Irish is still the native tongue, and until recently people wore traditional Aran dress: bright red skirts and black shawls for women and baggy woollen trousers and waistcoats with a colourful belt or 'crios' around the waist for men. The classic white Aran sweater knitted in complex patterns was born here. You may still see old people wearing some elements of the traditional dress, particularly on Inishmaan. The other Aran trademark is the 'currach', a featherlight rowing boat of black tar on canvas laid over a wicker frame.

Even the smallest patches of rocky land are bordered by stone walls. Over the centuries, tonnes of seaweed were brought up from the beaches, mixed with sand and laid out on the bare rock to start fields. The walls may be hundreds or even thousands of years old. So have respect for them, and replace any stones you dislodge. On Inishmaan and Inisheer many of the walls are up to eye level, and it's a joy to walk for hours along the sandy lanes between them.

The elemental nature of life on the islands has always attracted writers and artists. John Millington Synge (1871-1909) spent a lot of time on the islands and his play *Riders to the Sea* is set on Inishmaan. His book *The Aran Islands* is the classic account of life out here and is readily available in paperback. The American Robert Flaherty came to the islands in 1934 to shoot *Man of Aran*, a dramatic account of daily life. It became a classic and there are regular screenings of it in Kilronan on Inishmór. The mapmaker Tim Robinson has written a wonderful account of his explorations on Aran, *Stones of Aran*, and his *The Aran Islands – a map & guide* is superb. The islands have produced their own talent, particularly the writer Liam O'Flaherty from Inishmór.

Today, the islands have become major attractions with quick and convenient travel connections to the mainland, a plethora of B&B and hostel accommodation and a veritable armada of mountain bikes waiting to be hired out. Inishmór – the largest – is exceedingly busy during the summer with armies of day trippers and shuttle buses all over the island.

If you have the time try to get to the smaller islands, particularly Inishmaan – the least visited – and allow yourself a few day for exploration. Inisheer is the smallest and closest to land, just eight km (five miles) out from Doolin in Clare.

GETTING THERE & AWAY
Air
If speed is important or seasickness a mortal fear you can fly to the islands with Aer Arann (☎ 091-93034) for IR£33 return, or IR£26 if you are travelling in a group of four or more people. If you book and pay more than two weeks in advance, the standard fare is IR£25

return. For IR£26 you can fly one way and take the ferry the other. Nine-seater planes can be hired privately for IR£185 an hour and they also do regular 20-minute pleasure flights which cost IR£100.

Flights operate to all three islands, and take less than 10 minutes. The mainland departure point is at Minna, near Inverin, 38 km (19 miles) west of Galway. A connecting bus from outside the Galway City tourist office costs IR£3 return.

Ferry
There are several companies and several routes to the islands. The services from Rossaveal, 37 km west of Galway, are popular because the crossing is quick and the services are frequent. The ferry companies compete fiercely with offers of inclusive accommodation and family fares or with claims of impossible speed. Aran Ferries (☎ 091-68903/92447) have a desk in the tourist office in Galway City, while Island Ferries (☎ 091-61767) have a depot opposite the tourist office near the AIB Bank in Eyre Square, Galway City. Bicycles usually travel free.

To/From Galway City There are direct services from Galway between June and September on Aran Ferries' *Galway Bay*. This is a journey of about 46 km (29 miles). It takes 105 minutes, costs IR£18 return and operates twice daily in July and August, once a day in June and September.

O'Brien Shipping (☎ 091-67676) also operate a single daily boat service to all three Aran Islands from June to September, which usually departs from the Galway docks at 10 am.

To/From Rossaveal Also operated by Aran Ferries, the *Aran Flyer* takes 35 minutes to Inishmór. From May to September there are three sailings a day in each direction. Island Ferries' (☎ 091-61767) slightly slower *Aran Seabird* also operates from Rossaveal and takes 45 minutes. During the summer, there are at least five sailings a day from Rossaveal. The regular adult return fare from

Rossaveal is IR£12, but there is almost certain to be some sort of special deal worth taking. Car parking at Rossaveal costs IR£1 or IR£2 a day – ask before you park. Fares inclusive of the Galway-Rossaveal bus, which usually costs IR£3, are also offered. Doolin Ferries (☎ 065-74189/74455) go from Rossaveal to Inishmaan and Inisheer.

To/From Doolin Two ferry companies operate from Doolin in County Clare to Inisheer and Inishmór. It's only eight km to Inisheer, taking about 30 minutes and costing about IR£7 one way or IR£10 return. For more details, see the Doolin section in County Clare.

Inter-island Ferries Inter-island services are irregular but there's usually something connecting with the mainland arrivals. Typical inter-island fares are IR£6 return.

GETTING AROUND

Inisheer and Inishmaan are small enough to explore on foot but on larger Inishmór bikes are the way to go.

INISHMÓR

The island slopes up from its comparatively sheltered northern shores to the southern edge, then plummets sheer into the turmoil of the Atlantic. Once you have climbed the hill west of Kilronan, all you can see is rock, stone walls and boulders, with the odd patch of deep green grass and potato plants. There is a fine beach at Kilmurvey west of Kilronan, and it's nice to stay out here away from the bustle of the island capital. Inishmór has a population of around 900.

Orientation

Inishmór is 13 km long (eight miles) and three km (two miles) wide, running along a north-west to south-east axis. All ferries and boats arrive and depart from Kilronan on Cill Éinne bay on the south-eastern side of the island. The airstrip is two km farther south-east, on the other side of the bay facing Kilronan. One principal road runs the length

of the island with many smaller lanes and paths leading off.

Information

There is a small seasonal tourist office (☎ 099-61263) on the waterfront in Kilronan. There is also a small post office and branch of the Bank of Ireland which opens on Tuesdays and Wednesdays in July and August. Many of the shops and craft shops will change money.

Things to See

Inishmór has three impressive stone forts, probably about 2000 years old. Halfway down the island, **Dún Aengus**, perched on the edge of the sheer southern cliff, is one of the most amazing archaeological sites in the country. It has a remarkable 'chevaux de frise' a defensive forest of sharp stone spikes around the exterior of the fort to stop any would-be attackers. Folklore suggests that Aengus was a king of the Fir Bolgs, a legendary Celtic tribe from Europe who are said to have retreated to Aran and built these forts after falling out with the mainland chiefs. Other sources say that he was a 5th-century Irish chief and pupil of St Enda, the islands' most important saint. Dún Aengus is a magical place and should not be missed. Try and go at a quiet time such as late evening when there are few visitors about.

Halfway between Kilronan and Dún Aengus is the smaller **Dún Eochla** fort, a perfect circular ring fort. Directly south of Kilronan and dramatically perched on a promontory is **Dún Dúchathair**. It's surrounded on three sides by cliffs and is less visited than Dún Aengus.

The ruins of numerous stone churches trace the island's monastic history. The small **St Kieran's** (Teampall Chiaráin), with a high cross in the churchyard, is near Kilronan. Past Kilmurvey are the ruins of various small early Christain remains known rather inaccurately as the **Seven Churches** (Na Seacht Teampaill), consisting of a couple of ruined chapels, monastic houses and some fragments of a High Cross. Near the airstrip are the sunken remains of a church said to be the

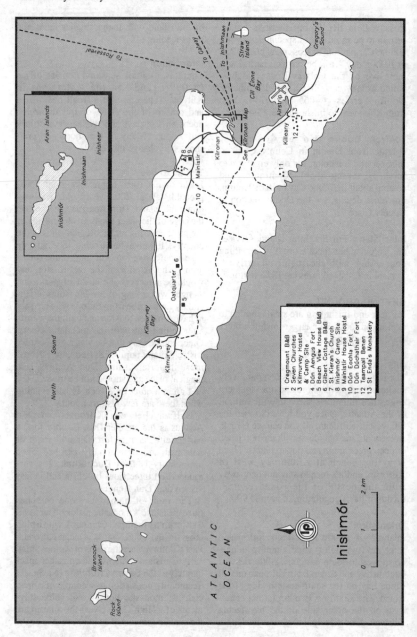

Inishmór

1 Cregmount B&B
2 Seven Churches
3 Kilmurvey Hostel
   & Camp Site
4 Dún Aengus Fort
5 Beach View House B&B
6 Gilbert Cottage B&B
7 St Kieran's Church
8 Inishmór Camp Site
9 Mainistir House Hostel
10 Dún Dúchathair Fort
11 Dún Eochla Fort
12 Teampall Benen
13 St Enda's Monastery

Top: Which Way? Westport, County Mayo (TW)
Bottom: Benbulben, County Sligo (TW)

Top: Beaghmore Stone Circles, County Tyrone (TW)
Bottom: Devenish Island, County Fermanagh (TW)

site of **St Enda's monastery** in the 5th century.

Places to Stay

Camping *Inishmór Camp Site* (☎ 099-61185) has a fine setting near the beach in Mainistir, almost two km north-west of Kilronan and about a 30-minute walk from the pier. Facilities are basic and they charge IR£1 per person. There is also free camping beside Kilmurvey Hostel and you can use the hostel's facilities for a nominal charge.

Hostels *Kilmurvey Hostel* (☎ 099-61318) is near the beach on the west side of Kilmurvey Bay some seven km (4.5 miles) from Kilronan. This is a nice country house with 42 beds, two, three or four to a room. They charge IR£5 a night, have showers and kitchen facilities and a jeep with free rides in and out of Kilronan.

In Kilronan the *Aran Islands Hostel* (☎ 099-61255/61248) is only a short walk from the pier and has dorm beds for IR£6. It's on top of the Joe Mac pub – convenient for a Guinness, not so good for light sleepers. A few km to the north-east is the far superior *Mainistir House Hostel* (☎ 099-61199/61322) at IR£12 for B&B. They have some private rooms, and the dorms only sleep four or six people. The food's very good, and they run a free bus which meets incoming boats.

Aran Ferries offers special discounts with Aran Islands Hostel, Island Ferries with Mainistir House. For example, you can get two nights B&B, one dinner and return fares by bus and ferry from Galway for IR£28.

B&Bs In Kilronan village about 800 metres from the harbour is *An Crugán* (☎ 099-61150) which costs IR£13. *Claí Bán* (☎ 099-61111) is IR£12, or IR£14 with own bathroom. *Cliff House* (☎ 099-61286) overlooks Kilronan Bay, costs IR£14 or IR£16 with own bathroom and does some of the best meals on the island. *Dormer House* (☎ 099-61125) is a good B&B not far from the harbour charging IR£13 to IR£14. Their restaurant is very popular with locals and dinner there costs around IR£12.

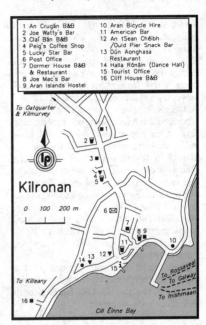

1 An Crugán B&B	10 Aran Bicycle Hire
2 Joe Watty's Bar	11 American Bar
3 Claí Bán B&B	12 An tSean Chéibh
4 Peig's Coffee Shop	/Ould Pier Snack Bar
5 Lucky Star Bar	13 Dún Aonghasa
6 Post Office	Restaurant
7 Dormer House B&B	14 Halla Rónáin (Dance Hall)
& Restaurant	15 Tourist Office
8 Joe Mac's Bar	16 Cliff House B&B
9 Aran Islands Hostel	

Kilronan

Farther away, *Beach View House* (☎ 099-61141) is some five km (3.5 miles) north-west from Kilronan in Oatquarter and charges IR£18/26 for singles/doubles. Also here is the cosy *Gilbert Cottage* (☎ 099-61146) at IR£12 or IR£15 with own bathroom.

At the north-west end of the island, nine km (six miles) from Kilronan in Creggakeerain, is *Cregmount* (☎ 099-61139), which overlooks Galway Bay and costs IR£13.

Places to Eat

Burgers & chips are all too commonly all that's available on the islands.

In Kilronan, about the best place for pub food is *Joe Watty's Bar* (☎ 099-61155) on the way north-west out of Kilronan. There's also the *Ould Pier* snack bar and, a little farther from the centre, *Peig's Coffee Shop* near the Lucky Star bar with good snacks all day. *Dún Aonghasa* (☎ 099-61104) in Kilronan has set meals at IR£8.90 or IR£12.50. They do grills, steaks, chips and good scones and fruitcake. *An tSean Chéibh* (☎ 099-61228), Kilronan serves fairly plain but tasty stews, curries and grills. They have a takeaway next door. *Cliff House B&B* (☎ 099-61286) serves a good dinner for around IR£12.

Mainistir House Hostel (☎ 099-61169) has a reputation for good food: terrific breakfasts with home-made bread and good coffee, and dinner costing IR£5 for residents and IR£6 for non-residents. They offer plenty of choice on their menu of seafood and vegetarian dishes, and the buffet dinner at 8 pm often includes some excellent vegetarian options. Also try *Gilbert Cottage* (☎ 099-61146) which does good evening meals, most costing around IR£10 to IR£12.

Entertainment

There's music in most Kilronan pubs at night. For Irish music, try *Joe Watty's Bar* or *Joe Mac's*. The *American Bar* has rock music and draws a young crowd.

Robert O'Flaherty's classic *Man of Aran* is shown regularly at the Dance Hall (Halla Rónáin) in Kilronan and shows how much life has changed here in the last 60 years. Admission is IR£2.50.

Getting Around

Daily rates for bike hire are around IR£5 but the islands are tough on bikes, so if it's not fairly new, check any bike over carefully before agreeing to rent it.

Aran Bicycle Hire (☎ 099-61132) seems to have pretty good machines. Costelloes (☎ 099-61241) is the other bike hire company, offering similar bikes for similar prices; it's near the American Bar. The rocky back roads are definitely mountain bike territory. You can bring your own bike out on the ferries.

There are plenty of small tour buses which offer speedy trips to some of the island's principal sights for around IR£5. However, walking and cycling will give you more of a sense of the place. Pony traps are used for local transport around Kilronan.

If you can get a group together consider

chartering one of Aer Arann's nine passenger Islander aircraft for an aerial view of the island. Charges are IR£100 to IR£185 an hour. The flights last for about 20 minutes.

INISHMAAN

Inishmaan is the least visited of the three Aran Islands and well worth the effort of getting there.

Inishmaan, or Inis Meáin in Irish, is lozenge-shaped and about five km long by three km wide. The fields are bordered by high stone walls, and it's a delight to wander along these *boreens* and take in some of the tranquillity that attracted the playwright J M Synge and Patrick Pearse, leader of the 1916 Rising.

Most of the houses on Inishmaan are in the centre of the island, while the principal boat landing stage is at An Córa on the east side. There is a reasonable beach just north of the slip. The airstrip is on the north-east corner of the island.

Inishmaan does not seem to be hell bent on attracting tourists. It is the home of a knitwear factory which exports fine woollen garments to some of the world's most exclusive shops. There is a factory shop on the island.

The main archaeological site is **Dún Chonchúir**, a massive stone ring fort. It's similar to Dún Aengus on Inishmór, but it's built inland overlooking a limestone valley. Chonchúir is said to have been a brother of Aengus. Dún Chonchúir's age is a bit of a mystery; it's thought to have been built somewhere between the 1st and the 6th centuries AD. The thatched cottage on the road before you head up to the fort is where J M Synge spent his summers between 1898 and 1902.

Cill Cheannannach is a rough 7th or 8th-century church south of the pier.

Information

The Island Co-operative (☎ 099-73010) is north of the post office, and the manager and his family are very helpful.

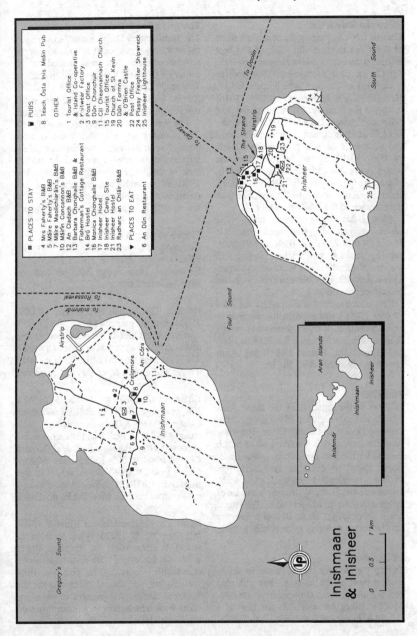

Inishmaan & Inisheer

■ PLACES TO STAY

4   Mrs Faherty's B&B
5   Máire Faherty's B&B
7   Máire Maoilchiaráin's B&B
10 Máirín Concannon's B&B
12 An Cladach B&B
13 Barbara Chonghaile B&B &
    Fisherman's Cottage Restaurant
14 Brú Hostel
16 Monica Chonghaile B&B
17 Inisheer Hotel
18 Inisheer Camp Site
21 Inisheer Hostel
23 Radharc an Chláir B&B

▼ PLACES TO EAT

6   An Dún Restaurant

▼ PUBS

8   Teach Ósta Inis Meáin Pub

OTHER

1   Tourist Office
    & Island Co-operative
2   Knitwear Factory
3   Post Office
9   Dún Chonchúir
11 Cill Cheannannach Church
15 Tourist Office
19 Church of St Kevin
20 Dún Formna
    & O'Brien Castle
22 Post Office
24 Plassy Freighter Shipwreck
25 Inisheer Lighthouse

Gregory's Sound

To Inishmór
To Rossaveal

Airstrip

Creigmore
An Córa

Inishmaan

Foul Sound

To Galway

The Strand
Airstrip

To Doolin

South Sound

Inisheer

Aran Islands

Inishmór
Inishmaan
Inisheer

0   0.5   1 km

Places to Stay & Eat

There is free camping by the beach just north of An Córa landing slip. One of the best B&Bs on the island is *Mrs Faherty's* (☎ 099-73012) in Creigmore about 500 metres north-west of the pier, which costs IR£12. *Mrs Máire Maoilchiaráin's* (☎ 099-73016) is a good B&B on a corner south of the post office and charges IR£8 to IR£9, or a bargain IR£13 including dinner. Another good one in the village is *Máirín Concannon's* B&B (☎ 099-73019), across the road from the island's only pub, and offers B&B for IR£10. *Máire Faherty's* B&B (☎ 099-73027), charging IR£11, is west of the village past the entrance to the Dún Chonchúir.

Most B&Bs serve evening meals. The island has just one pub, *Teach Ósta Inis Meáin* (☎ 099-73003) in Baile an Mhothair, serving snacks, sandwiches, soups and seafood platters between 11.30 am and 6 pm. This is a terrific little bar and hums with life on summer evenings.

The island's only restaurant is *An Dún* (☎ 099-73068), just opposite the entrance to Dún Chonchúir. It offers reasonably priced omelettes, pasta for lunch for IR£5 to IR£6 and dinner for around IR£10 per main course. A set dinner costs IR£16.

INISHEER

Inisheer is the smallest of the three Aran Islands and only eight km (five miles) off the coast of Doolin in County Clare. The view from the ferry is of a sheltered white beach backed by modern bungalows – few traditional thatched cottages and buildings survive – overlooked by a squat stone 15th-century castle. To the south there's a maze of fields without a building in sight. The island has a timelessness about it, and a summer stroll through its sandy lanes is hard to beat.

Information

During the summer there is a tourist information desk at the harbour. You can also contact the Island Co-operative (☎ 099-75008). Bikes are available for hire at a couple of houses near the pier.

Things to See & Do

The 16th-century O'Brien **castle** overlooks the beach and harbour. It is built within the remains of a ring fort from around the 1st century AD. On the beach is the 10th-century **Teampall Chaoimhain** or Church of St Kevin, with some gravestones, and shells from an ancient midden or dumping ground.

The best parts of Inisheer are uninhabited. The eastern road to the lighthouse is more popular but the coast around the west side is wilder. On the eastern shore is the rusting hulk of the *Plassy*, a freighter wrecked in 1960 and thrown high up onto the rocks. The uninhabited lighthouse on the island's southern tip with its neat enclosure is off limits.

Places to Stay & Eat

Camping *Inisheer Camp Site* (☎ 099-75008) by the strand is open from May to September. They charge IR£3 per tent and have basic facilities.

Hostels The largish *Brú Hostel* (☎ 099-75024) near the pier costs IR£5.50 a night. It also does B&B for IR£10 and is open all year round. The small *Inisheer Hostel* (☎ 099-75077) is near the post office, charges IR£5 a night and is open from May to September.

B&Bs *An Cladach* (☎ 099-75033) in West Village charges IR£11 to IR£13. *Radharc an Chláir* (☎ 099-75019) is near the castle, charges IR£11 to IR£12 and is tourist board approved. Other B&Bs include *Mrs Barbara Chonghaile* (☎ 099-75025) and *Monica Chonghaile* (☎ 099-75034), which charge from IR£10 to IR£11 and are in West Village not far from the pier. Most B&Bs do dinner.

Hotel The modern Inisheer Hotel or *Óstán Inis Oirr* (☎ 099-75020) is just up from the strand. It offers B&B for IR£15 or IR£17 with own bathroom. The restaurant serves reasonable seafood. The bar is a little vacuous but you should check out the old *National Geographic* pictures of the island on its walls which show the islanders in their traditional dress.

Places to Eat The *Fisherman's Cottage* restaurant (☎ 099-75073) is not far from the pier in the western part of the village. Lunch is from IR£4 to IR£6 and most main courses for dinner are around IR£10. They offer meat and seafood and there's usually a vegetarian main course for around IR£7.

Eastern Galway

Eastern Galway is markedly different from the wild and bleak landscape of Connemara and west Galway. The two regions are separated naturally by Lough Corrib. Eastern Galway is relatively flat, and its underlying limestone has given it a well-drained, fertile soil. This is the largest section of the county but it lacks any areas of significant interest. Big towns like Ballinasloe, Loughrea and Tuam serve prosperous farming regions.

In the south-east corner of the county, the lakeside town of Portumna is an attractive place and a popular base for boating and fishing on Lough Derg.

CLONFERT CATHEDRAL
Around 15 km south of Ballinasloe is the tiny 12th-century cathedral at Clonfert. The monastery is said to have been founded in the middle of the 6th century by St Brendan the Navigator and was ravaged several times by Vikings between 840 and 1180. The remarkable Romanesque doorway with its human and animal heads dates from the 1160s.

BALLINASLOE
The biggest town in eastern Galway, Ballinasloe was a strategic crossing point over the River Suck. In the early 1100s, Turlough O'Connor, King of Connaught, built a castle to guard the river crossing and this became the nucleus of the town's development. Around eight km (five miles) west of town, Aughrim was the site of a crucial victory by William of Orange over the Catholic forces of James II in 1691. There is a

Turoe Stone

small museum and *Hyne's Hostel* (☎ 0905-73734) nearby charges IR£4.50 a night.

Today, Ballinasloe is on the main Dublin to Galway road with most traffic diverted south around the town centre. The town is pleasant enough but there is no real reason to stay here except possibly over the eight days in October when the Ballinasloe Horse Fair attracts legions of horse buyers, horse sellers and drinkers.

LOUGHREA
Loughrea is a large and busy market town 26 km (17 miles) east of Galway City. It gets its name from the lake at the west end of town. Loughrea has improved a lot in recent years with many plastic signs and garish shopfronts replaced by much more appealing and traditional frontages. **St Brendan's Catholic Cathedral** is renowned for its stained glass.

Seven km (four miles) north of Loughrea near Bullaun is the remarkable **Turoe Stone**, a phallic standing stone covered in delicate La-Tène-style carvings in relief. It dates from between 300 BC and 100 AD. There are similarly carved stones in Brittany, associated with the La Téne Celts. The stone was not found here originally but at an Iron Age fort a few km away.

Counties Mayo & Sligo

County Mayo

Mayo has an identity that distinguishes itself on many different levels: an introspective landscape, a Connaught accent with its own inflexion and a people who seem far removed from cosmopolitan Dublin or touristy Killarney. The recent history of Mayo is one of massive and ongoing emigration, and even before the famine the county was a place of isolation. The relative poverty of the land meant that the invaders left it to last, but what delayed the English is what attracts today's visitors: lakes, mountains, boglands, and a population density among the lowest in Europe.

CONG

Drive straight through and this small town would be just another dot on the map but there's a great deal hidden behind that ordinary main street. In 1951 John Ford and his team came here to film *The Quiet Man* and there are still many reminders of that momentous event.

Information

Tourist information is available during the summer from the old courthouse building opposite the abbey in Abbey St. Get a copy of the Heritage Trail brochure to explore the town and discover the fascinating history of the 1123 Cong Cross, now in the National Museum in Dublin. The local booklets *The Glory of Cong* and *Cong – Walks, Sights, Stories* have more information.

Guided tours focusing on *The Quiet Man* locations depart from the tourist office at 8.45 am each morning and last about 90 minutes.

Cong Abbey

This 12th-century Augustinian abbey, founded by the high king Turlough O'Connor, occupies the site of a 6th-century abbey. It has a carved doorway on the north side and fine windows and decorated stonework in the Chapter House. Just west of the abbey on a small island in the nearby river stands the monks' fishing house, where a bell was rung every time a fish was caught. The modern Catholic church in a corner of the abbey site is a remarkable piece of festering ugliness plonked down with utter disregard for its surroundings. The market cross, at the junction of Main St and Abbey St, is the reconstructed remains of a 14th-century high cross.

Ashford Castle

This Victorian castle, once the home of the Guinness family and now a private hotel, stands on the site of an early Anglo-Norman castle built by the de Burgos family after their defeat of the native O'Connors of Connaught. The interior is strictly for residents and it costs IR£2 (children IR£1) just to enter the grounds and view the fairytale exterior. However, the jetty for cruises on Lough Corrib is beside the castle, and it's also possible to enter the grounds by way of the exit road that comes out in Abbey St, or by crossing the river from the abbey and walking along the other bank.

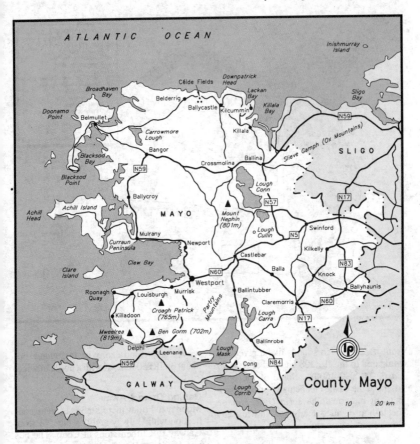

County Mayo

0   10   20 km

Places to Stay

Camping You can camp at the *Hydeout Campsite*, a km out of town towards Clonbur, as well as at the *Cong Hostel* (IR£3 per person) or the *Courtyard Hostel*.

Hostels The *Quiet Man Hostel* (☎ 092-46089) on Abbey St is right in the centre of town. Two km out of town in Lisloughrey, off the road to Galway, is the popular An Óige *Cong Hostel* (☎ 092-46089) with nightly costs of IR£5.50. There's also the *Courtyard Hostel* (☎ 092-46203), five km out in Cross.

B&Bs In and around the town there's a typical collection of B&Bs. Centrally located places include the *White House* (☎ 092-46358) across from the abbey, though *Ryan's Hotel* (☎ 092-46243) has rooms which start from the same price of IR£26 a double. There are a few B&Bs down the street by the side of Connolly's foodstore, the *River Lodge* (☎ 092-46057) being typical. It charges IR£26 for B&B.

Hotels *Danagher's* (☎ 092-46028) is a hotel at the town's main junction with doubles

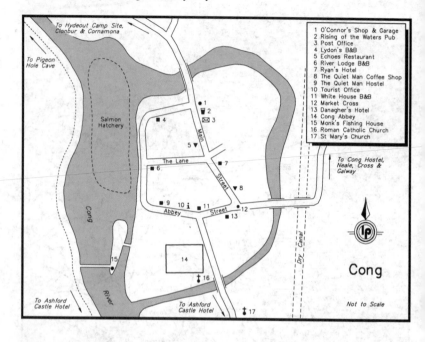

1 O'Connor's Shop & Garage
2 Rising of the Waters Pub
3 Post Office
4 Lydon's B&B
5 Echoes Restaurant
6 River Lodge B&B
7 Ryan's Hotel
8 The Quiet Man Coffee Shop
9 The Quiet Man Hostel
10 Tourist Office
11 White House B&B
12 Market Cross
13 Danagher's Hotel
14 Cong Abbey
15 Monk's Fishing House
16 Roman Catholic Church
17 St Mary's Church

Cong

Not to Scale

from IR£36, which sounds like a giveaway compared to the IR£208 charged at *Ashford Castle* (☎ 092-46003). Some of the boxy rooms at the castle can actually prove disappointing but you do have *The Quiet Man* on the in-house video ready for viewing any time of the day or night.

Places to Eat

The *Rising of the Waters* pub has light meals. At the other end of the street *Danagher's Hotel* has a fine old bar, a straightforward eating area and a fancier restaurant. Vegetarian food is hard to come by though Danagher's will do an omelette for IR£3. Bar food in the IR£7 to IR£10 range is available at *Ryan's Hotel* and dinner between 5 and 7 pm is IR£14.

If your credit card didn't stretch to the Ashford Castle consider unleashing it on *Echoes* on Main St, a restaurant which proves great food can exist in Ireland, but count on IR£50 for two with a bottle of wine.

Getting There & Away

Monday to Friday there's a Bus Éireann connection with Galway and bus No 243 from Galway to Clifden stops at Cong. The bus stop is outside Ryan's Hotel.

If travelling by car or bike farther into Mayo, avoid the main N84 to Castlebar and take the longer but much more attractive route west to Leenane and north to Westport via Delphi.

Getting Around

There are enough interesting sites close to Cong to make a bike worth having. They can be hired from O'Connor's on Main St; it's the combined garage, supermarket, bar and craft shop. The White House B&B next to the tourist office also has bikes for hire by the hour (IR£1.50 for the first hour and 50p

The Quiet Man & Cong

John Ford's cult movie was filmed in and around Cong in 1951 and starred John Wayne, Maureen O'Hara and Barry Fitzgerald. When Sean Thornton (John Wayne) returns to his native Ireland, he succumbs to the beauty of Mary Kate Danagher (Maureen O'Hara). 'It's only a mirage brought on by your terrible thirst', says Mickaleen O'Flynn (Barry Fitzgerald), his friend, drinking partner and go-between.

Thornton marries Mary Kate but falls out with her brother, who withholds the dowry and forces a reluctant Thornton to confront him. This is not an easy matter because back in the USA Thornton had been a champion boxer who quit the ring after killing a man. Mary Kate thinks he is a coward so Thornton does what a man's gotta do, and a Homeric fight between the two men brings a happy ending.

The Quiet Man panders to romantic and patronising views of the Irish, but remains enjoyable and very funny. The Cong location is easy to identify in the film, and for the film buff there are booklets, videos and guided tours of the area. Less easily available in Cong is the original short story written by Maurice Walsh, published in The Quiet Man & Other Stories (Appletree Press, paperback). ■

thereafter) or day (IR£5). The Courtyard hostel also has some bikes.

AROUND CONG

There's a surprising amount to see in the vicinity of Cong including a collection of caves, a canal which never worked, a stone circle and a curious folly. The limestone strata of the Cong area account for the numerous caves, for the failure of the canal and for the local phenomenon known as 'the rising of the waters', where water from Lough Mask percolates through the limestone and emerges from the ground at Cong before flowing down to Lough Corrib.

Caves

The Cong area is riddled with caves, many of them only a short walk from the village. The Pigeon Hole is about 1.5 km west of Cong and can be reached by road or by the walking track from across the river. Stone steps lead down into the cave which at times can be rather wet. There's a local legend about two fairy trout who dwell in the cave.

From the Pigeon Hole take the L101 road towards Clonbur, passing the Giant's Grave turn-off and continuing to a lane turning south about five km (three miles) from Cong. A stream flows into the extensive Ballymaglancy Cave which is off the road to the right. The cave has stalactites and stalagmites and has been explored for about 500 metres.

Two other caves are just to the east of Cong, beside the road to Cross. Captain Webb's Cave is just outside the village, a short distance beyond the dry canal and behind the school grounds. It's actually a deep water-filled hole in the ground where, two centuries ago, a local villain is said to have hurled a succession of local women. A further 200 metres from Cong a wide path leads to Kelly's Cave, which is usually locked up; the key is kept at the Quiet Man Café. Lady's Buttery and Horse Discovery are two other caves, beside a road to the castle.

The Dry Canal

Lough Mask is about 10 metres (30 feet) higher than Lough Corrib, and in the mid-18th century it was decided to cut a canal between the two loughs. The project started in 1848, using labourers who were desperate for work after the deprivations of the famine years. In 1854 the construction was nearing completion, but already the economic basis for the canal was coming into question as railways were rapidly spreading across the country. At this point a much greater problem was discovered – the canal was not watertight. The porous limestone simply soaked up any water that flowed into the canal.

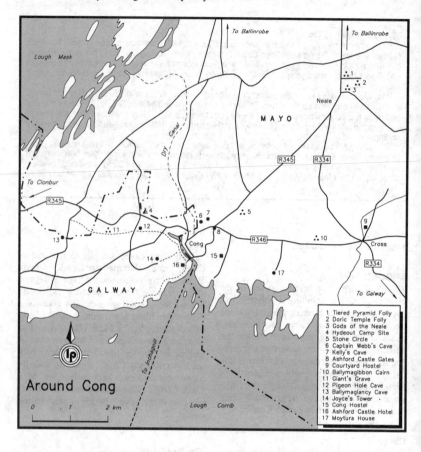

Around Cong

0   1   2 km

1 Tiered Pyramid Folly
2 Doric Temple Folly
3 Gods of the Neale
4 Hydeout Camp Site
5 Stone Circle
6 Captain Webb's Cave
7 Kelly's Cave
8 Ashford Castle Gates
9 Courtyard Hostel
10 Ballymagibbon Cairn
11 Giant's Grave
12 Pigeon Hole Cave
13 Ballymaglancy Cave
14 Joyce's Tower
15 Cong Hostel
16 Ashford Castle Hotel
17 Moytura House

Although various schemes for sealing the canal bed were considered, the whole expensive project was abandoned in 1858. The dry canal, complete with locks for raising and lowering the water level, runs just to the east of Cong.

Circles & Graves

The stone slabs of the megalithic burial chamber known as the Giant's Grave can be conveniently visited between the Pigeon Hole and the Ballymaglancy Cave. A path leads into the forest to the south of the R345

road to Clonbur, about three km (two miles) from Cong. About 100 metres from the road take the turn-off to the left; the grave is off that path to the right.

There are several stone circles in the area including an excellent one just to the east side of the road from Cong to Neale at Nymphsfield, about 1.5 km out of Cong. Just north of the road from Cong to Cross is Ballymagibbon Cairn, supposedly the site of a legendary Celtic battle. Moytura House, near the shores of Lough Corrib, takes its name from this battle and was a childhood home of Oscar Wilde.

Neale

The village of Neale, five km (three miles) north-east of Cong, has several interesting sites. Neale Park is on the east side of the road, and if you take the turn-off at the northern end of the village the curious stone known as the 'Gods of the Neale' is about 200 metres east of the main road, just inside the walls of the park. The slab, originally found in a nearby cave, is carved with figures of a human, an animal and a reptile in low relief.

Inchagoill Island

In the centre of Lough Corrib, the island of Inchagoill in County Galway has the ruins of the 5th-century St Patrick's Church, the later 12th-century Church of the Saint, and an ancient obelisk in the graveyard.

The island can be reached by boat from Cong. For more details see the County Galway chapter.

WESTPORT

Westport, in the south of County Mayo, didn't acquire its postcard prettiness gradually, like so many other small Irish towns. It was designed that way, and the Mall, with the Carrowbeg River running right down the middle of it, is as nice a main street as you could find. The present Westport House was built on the site of an O'Malley castle, which was surrounded by about 60 hovels, the original settlement of Westport. These were moved when the house was planned, and the Brownes, who came here from Sussex in the time of Elizabeth I, even had the course of the river altered to allow the Mall to act as a grand approach to the gates of the house. This wasn't entirely successful, as even today the Mall is subject to occasional flooding.

Information

There's a tourist office (☎ 098-25711) right on the Mall, and a laundrette in High St. Carrais Donn on Bridge St sells crafts and has a postal service.

Westport House

The present house dates from 1730. Commercialisation is taken to the hilt: name a tacky method of pursuing tourist money and they'll do it, from a hokey 'dungeon' to cheap souvenirs. Entry to the house is a pricey IR£4.50 (children IR£2), but if you're planning to visit the zoo, take a boat on the lake and picnic in the park the cost only rises to IR£5 (IR£2.25), and family tickets are available. It's open 10.30 am to 6 pm, six days a week during July and up to 22 August, 2 to 6 pm on Sunday. During May, June, the rest of August and September it opens in the afternoon only.

With a vehicle, head out of town towards Croagh Patrick and Louisburgh and the entry road is on the right. An alternative approach is on foot via the Hotel Westport. Enter through the iron gates to the right of the hotel's entrance near the sign for the Beaches Nightclub and follow the path until you reach the sign for the zoo on the right. Go down to the left here, cross the small red bridge and follow the river to the right.

Heritage Centre

The centre has an interesting selection of local artefacts and documents, including the spinning wheel presented by the people of Ballina to Maud Gonne, the dynamic political rebel who was married briefly to Major John MacBride and was the object of Yeats' adoration. Also housed in this centre are the records of the trial of Patrick Egan, who commandeered Westport House during the 1798 Rising. The centre is open all year from 10 am to 5 pm on weekdays (2 pm in winter), 3 to 6 pm at the weekend.

Fishing

For information about fishing enquire at Hewetson (☎ 098-26018) on Bridge St. A salmon licence and tackle is available. For sea angling contact the Sea Angling Centre (☎ 098-25481/25182) next to the heritage centre by the quay. Boats can be hired, tackle purchased and boat trips to the islands arranged (☎ 098-25283).

Places to Stay

Camping Camping is possible at the *Club Atlantic Hostel* and the *Parkland Caravan & Camping Park* (☎ 098-25141) on the Westport House estate and accessible by the same road that leads to the house. One night's pitch is a stiff IR£13 (IR£8 for cyclists).

Hostels The new and well-equipped *Old Mill Hostel* (☎ 098-27045) is right in the centre on James St and costs IR£5 a night. The equally modern and practical *Club Atlantic* (☎ 098-26644) is on Altamont St near the railway station. This is another hostel which operates both independently and with An Óige affiliation. The cost ranges from IR£5.90 for a dorm bed to IR£7.90 per person in a twin with attached bathroom. If you are heading down to Cong take the opportunity to view *The Quiet Man* free of charge on the hostel's video.

Westport hostels also include the *Granary* (☎ 098-25903) on the Quay, just over a km

from the Octagon and just before the Westport House entrance. The cost is IR£4.50.

B&Bs The tourist office will book rooms in the town's plentiful supply of B&Bs, but if you're arriving late try *Altamont House* (☎ 098-25226) which is within walking distance of the railway on Altamont St. Doubles start at IR£26, singles at IR£18.

Hotels At IR£40 a double, the *Grand Central* (☎ 098-27257) on the Octagon seems good value, but prices may increase when the renovations are done. The *Olde Railway Hotel* (☎ 098-25166) is next to the tourist office. Thackeray chose to stay here on his tour around Ireland in the 19th century. Today it costs IR£55 a double. *Hotel Westport* (☎ 098-25122), on New Rd, is tastelessly functional by comparison.

Places to Eat

Bridge St has a fair selection of cafés. The

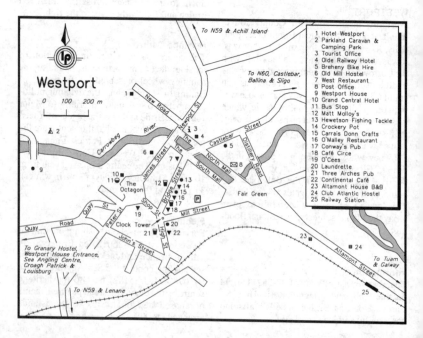

Westport

0   100   200 m

To N59 & Achill Island
To N60, Castlebar, Ballina & Sligo
To Granary Hostel, Westport House Entrance, Sea Angling Centre, Croagh Patrick & Louisburg
To N59 & Lenane
To Tuam & Galway

1 Hotel Westport
2 Parkland Caravan & Camping Park
3 Tourist Office
4 Olde Railway Hotel
5 Breheny Bike Hire
6 Old Mill Hostel
7 West Restaurant
8 Post Office
9 Westport House
10 Grand Central Hotel
11 Bus Stop
12 Matt Molloy's
13 Hewetson Fishing Tackle
14 Crockery Pot
15 Carrais Donn Crafts
16 O'Malley Restaurant
17 Conway's Pub
18 Café Circe
19 O'Cees
20 Laundrette
21 Three Arches Pub
22 Continental Café
23 Altamont House B&B
24 Club Atlantic Hostel
25 Railway Station

Crockery Pot is adorned with photographs of Princess Grace of Monaco who came to Westport in 1961 in search of her roots. For evening meals *Café Circe* and the *West* are at opposite ends of Bridge St. The *O'Malley Restaurant* has the most varied menu to choose from.

Round the corner on High St is the excellent *Continental Café* with good vegetarian food. On the Octagon, *O'Cee's* is a popular soup-and-sandwich place.

Along the coast road on the Quay there are a number of pubs and restaurants mostly specialising in seafood. Near the entrance to Westport House the *Quay Restaurant* (☎ 098-26412) has a nautical theme and lunch specials around IR£4, evening meals IR£12 to IR£15 per head. On the Quay the *Moorings* restaurant is in the house where Major John MacBride, briefly married to Maud Gonne and executed after 1916, was born. Two pubs nearby and next to one another, the *Towers* and the *Ardmore*, serve pub food and dinners for around IR£12.

Entertainment
There are a number of pubs with music throughout the summer. *Matt Molloy's* on Bridge St is owned by Matt Molloy of the Chieftains. The *Three Arches* near the clock tower has regular sessions while *Conway's* on Bridge St is a quieter old-style place.

Getting There & Away
Train The railway station (☎ 098-25253/25329) is up Altamont St from the Club Atlantic Hostel and within walking distance. There are railway connections with Dublin (IR£31.50) via Athlone. During the summer trains leave Westport for Dublin at 7.30 and 10.15 am every day and also at 5 pm on Sunday.

Bus There are bus connections to Achill, Ballina, Belfast, Cork, Galway, Limerick, Shannon, Sligo and Waterford. Buses depart from the Octagon at present, but Bus Éireann is seeking a permanent departure point out of town. A private bus (☎ 095-41043) leaves Clifden at 10 am, arriving in Westport just

before midday and leaving for the return journey at 5 pm from the Octagon. The fare is IR£5 single.

Getting Around
Bicycles can be hired from the Club Atlantic Hostel or from Breheny Bike Hire on Castlebar St just north of the Mall.

AROUND WESTPORT
Croagh Patrick
Croagh Patrick towers to the west of Westport. It was from the top of this mountain that St Patrick performed his snake expulsion act – Ireland has been snake-free ever since. Climbing the 765-metre (2510-foot) peak is a holy feat for thousands of pilgrims on the last Sunday of July. The really enthusiastic make the rocky ascent barefoot. If the weather's clear the two-hour climb (one if you're in a real hurry) gives fine views at any time of year.

Unfortunately the extensive instructions at the bottom of the peak about making a properly pious ascent neglect to add a suggestion that 'thou shalt not litter'. As a result the upper reaches of this holy mountain are richly carpeted with empty soft drink cans.

The trail begins at Campbell's pub in the village of Murrisk, west of Westport. There is a sign between the pub and the car park pointing the way.

Louisburgh
The town gets its name from the fact that it was laid out by the 1st Marquess of Sligo who had a relation who had fought against the French at the Battle of Louisburgh in Canada. The town is home to two museums which will eventually merge into one. The larger of the two is the **Granuaile interpretative centre**, dedicated to the life and times of the most famous of the O'Malley clan – Grace O'Malley (1530-1603). Grace, Granuaile in Irish, achieved notoriety as a pirate queen who harassed the English from her base in Clew Bay and later travelled to London to see Elizabeth I and successfully sue for the release of her brother and a son from prison. The centre also exhibits mate-

Irish Caravan

rial on other matters of local interest. It is open Monday to Friday from 10 am to 6 pm and costs IR£1 (children 50p).

The other museum is a **Famine Centre**, housed in a redundant Protestant church and opened by Archbishop Desmond Tutu in 1991. At the moment there is only a small collection of material relating to the famine but this will be added to and eventually the Granuaile exhibition will be brought here. The Famine Centre is open June to September daily from 10 am to 6 pm (closed 1 to 2 pm) except on Sundays when it opens from 2 to 6 pm. Admission is IR£1.50.

There are some excellent beaches in the vicinity, Old Head Beach and the Silver Strand being particularly sandy and safe.

Doolough Valley

There are two roads connecting Westport and Leenane but the one nearest the coast, via Delphi, travels through the Doolough Valley.

It is wildly beautiful, not least because of the lonely expanse of Doo Lough (the dark lake) with the Mweelrea Mountains behind. At the southern end of the lake Ben Gorm rises to 702 metres (2302 feet). The landscape changes from snooker table green and sparkling wet stone to a forbidding grey as shadows envelop everything when cloudbanks spread in from the Atlantic.

During the famine the valley was the scene of tragedy when some 600 men, women and children walked from Louisburgh to Delphi Lodge in the hope that the landlord would offer them some food. Help was flatly refused, and on the return journey around 400 perished through hunger and exposure. On the road there is a memorial.

Large deposits of gold, worth in excess of IR£400 million, are believed to be in the area. A High Court decision has decided that a mining company can move in and disregard Mayo council's veto on any threat to the natural beauty of the area.

Killadoon

Killadoon is a small village on the coast reached by turning off the main Louisburgh to Leenane road via the Doolough Valley. The main attractions here are the panoramic ocean views and the sandy beaches.

Delphi

The Brownes of Westport were originally a Catholic family but they converted to Protestantism in order to avoid the constraints of the penal laws. This paved the way for one of the family to be ennobled as marquess of Sligo at the time of the Act of the Union in 1800, and the 2nd marquess gave the unlikely name of Delphi to his fishing lodge in Mayo. He was a friend of Byron and travelled in Greece, returning home with the thought that his fishing territory bore an uncanny resemblance to the area around Delphi.

At Delphi Lodge (☎ 095-42213) permits are available for fishing in the local waters, and an adventure centre (☎ 095-42208) has organised sports throughout the summer.

Getting There & Away

There is a daily bus service between Westport and Killadoon via Murrisk for Croagh Patrick and Louisburgh, but there is no bus to Delphi.

CLARE ISLAND

Clare Island (population 200) has the ruins of an abbey and a castle, both associated with Grace O'Malley, the pirate queen. The tower castle was her stronghold, although it was considerably altered when the coastguard service took it over in 1831. Grace is supposed to be buried in the small abbey, which contains a stone with her family motto: 'Invincible on land and sea'.

The island has safe sandy beaches and is perfect for walking and climbing on a clear day. The highest point of Knockmore Mountain is at 463 metres (1520 feet) and it dominates the landscape. The island's only hotel, the Bay View, has tourist information and attracts sea anglers, scuba divers and sailing folk.

Places to Stay & Eat

The *Bay View Hotel* (☎ 098-26307) beside the harbour is the main accommodation centre and a night's bed plus ferry fare and breakfast is IR£17.50. B&B is also available from *Moran's* (☎ 098-26746), 200 metres from the harbour, or *Mary O'Malley* (☎ 098-26216), five km (three miles) from the harbour.

It would be best to bring your own food, although *An Fulacht Fiadh* (☎ 098-25048) serves meals if you ring first for a reservation. Dinner at the Bay View is IR£15.

Getting There & Away

A scheduled ferry service runs from Roonagh Quay, a few km west of Louisburgh, to the island. There are usually two sailings a day, and there is also a daily summer service from Darby's Point on Achill on Tuesday and Friday (☎ 098-26307 for details). The return ferry fare between both places and Clare Island is IR£10.

Historical Safaris (☎ 098-25048) organises day trips to the island for groups of four or more at a cost of IR£25 per person, including transport and packed lunch.

NEWPORT

This small town on the banks of the river Newport is often just passed through on the way to Achill, but it deserves a closer look.

Towards the end of the 19th century the Great Western Railway ran a line from Westport to Achill Sound which continued to operate until 1937. In 1987 the route was pedestrianised and now offers an interesting walk with views of the river and Newport House.

On the road out to Achill there is a mural on the gable end of a house depicting the arrest of Father Manus Sweeney who led the Achill contribution to the 1798 Rising and was later executed.

Tourist information (☎ 098-41116) is available in summer from the portacabin by the side of the road, under the viaduct, that leads to Castlebar.

Places to Eat

Next to the hostel on Main St, *Walsh's Bridge Inn* serves light food for around IR£3, and the café next to DeBille House farther down the street is about the same price. Dinner at Newport House is a stiff IR£28, but the snug little bar is worth a visit any time.

Getting There & Away

In the summer, bus No 124 from Achill to Belfast stops at Newport and goes on through Ballina, Sligo and Enniskillen. Throughout the year, bus No 255 links Achill and Ballina via Newport. The bus stop is outside Chambers' pub.

AROUND NEWPORT
Burrishoole Abbey

The abbey was founded in 1486 by the Dominicans. What remains is a solid tower and the east window of the cloisters. It is beside the river that drains Lough Furnace into the sea. About 2.5 km (1.5 miles) beyond Newport on the Newport-Achill road a sign points the way down to the left.

Rockfleet Castle

Formerly known as Carrigahowley, this castle has a strong association with Grace O'Malley. The story goes that after the death of her first husband she married a second time, on condition that at the end of the first year either party could summarily dissolve the marriage. This duly occurred; she shut herself up in Rockfleet and announced the divorce when her husband tried to enter! Whether the story's true or not, the castle does look impregnable. Grace O'Malley is supposed to have lived out the rest of her years here, and successfully repulsed an English force which besieged the castle. To get there, turn left at the sign about five km (three miles) beyond Newport on the road to Achill.

Mulrany

This small town stands on the isthmus between island-studded Clew Bay and Bellacragher Bay and boasts a lovely big beach. To reach the sand either take the foot-path opposite the now-closed Mulrany Bay Hotel or continue a little way past the hotel and bear left following the Atlantic Drive sign and then left again where the sign points to Mallaranny Strand, another Blue Flag beach.

At some time in the future the Mulrany Bay Hotel may reopen under new management. Hopefully they will retain the Lennon Suite, named after John Lennon when he came here for a visit and ended up purchasing one of the small islands in Clew Bay.

Places to Stay

Achill seems the obvious destination if you're travelling from Newport, but the Curraun Peninsula, joined to Achill Island by bridge, has a couple of B&Bs where you can get away from it all. *Curraun House* (☎ 098-45228) is attached to the George Pub and serves food for lunch and dinner. To get there follow the Atlantic Drive road from Mulrany; the place is on the south-west corner of the peninsula, just before a sign points right up to Achill Sound. Farther up this road, just before the Sound, *Mrs Cannon* (☎ 098-45134) has a bungalow and charges the standard IR£13.

The beach at Mulrany has a field marked out for camping and there are public toilets nearby. A local farmer turns up periodically to collect his dues.

ACHILL ISLAND

Joined to the mainland by a bridge, remote Achill Island combines views, moorland and mountains in one handy package. For most of the 20th century it has remained forgotten by tourists and, many of the islanders would assert, the Dublin government as well. The deserted village of Slievemore is the most dramatic example of a process of decay that continues to this day. The amount of arable land is limited and there are few employment opportunities to keep young people around. As people move away, the small houses are bought up as holiday homes. In recent years, the island has also become a favourite destination for jaded Dubliners in search of solitude and sand.

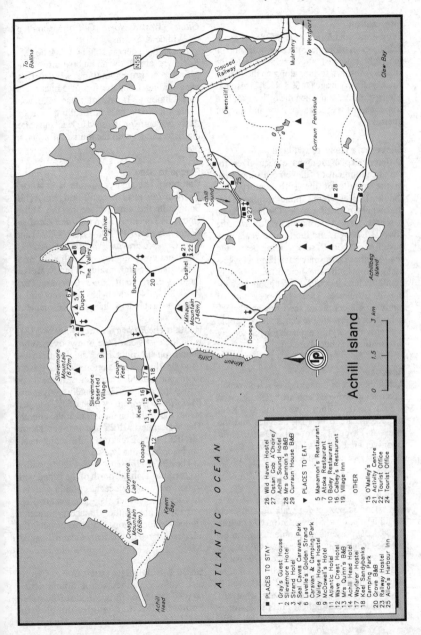

Achill Island

PLACES TO STAY

1 Gray's Guest House
2 Slievemore Hotel
3 Strand Hotel
4 Seal Caves Caravan Park
6 Lavelle's Golden Strand Caravan & Camping Park
8 Valley House Hostel
9 McDowell's Hotel
11 Atlantic Hotel
12 Wave Crest Hotel
13 Mrs Quinn's B&B
14 Achill Head Hotel
16 Wayfarer Hostel
18 Keel Sandybanks Camping Park
20 Grove B&B
23 Railway Hostel
25 Alice's Harbour Inn

26 Wild Haven Hostel
27 Óstán Gob A'Choire/ Achill Sound Hotel
28 Mrs Gannon's B&B
29 Curraun House B&B

▼ PLACES TO EAT

5 Manamon's Restaurant
7 Atoka Restaurant
10 Boley Restaurant
16 Calbey's Restaurant
19 Village Inn

OTHER

15 O'Malley's
21 Activity Centre
22 Tourist Office
24 Tourist Office

ATLANTIC OCEAN

To Ballina
N59
Disused Railway
Owencliff
Mulranny
To Westport
Clew Bay
Curraun Peninsula
Achill Sound
Achillbeg Island
Doniver
The Valley
Dugort
Bunacurry
Cashel
Minaun Mountain (348m)
Dooega
Minaun Cliffs
Slievemore Mountain (672m)
Slievemore Deserted Village
Lough Keel
Keel
Dooagh
Corrymore Lake
Croaghaun Mountain (668m)
Keem Bay
Achill Head

0   1.5   3 km

Information

Tourist information (☎ 098-45384) is available from an office near the souvenir shop on the right side just after crossing onto the island. A few km farther along on the road to Keel, an Esso garage (☎ 098-47242) also has a tourist office, and when the office is closed someone at the garage will try and answer queries.

Slievemore Deserted Village

Different explanations have been given for the abandonment of Slievemore some time in the middle of the 19th century. The 'booley houses' were summer residences for the owners of grazing cattle. The inhabitants, it seems, moved permanently down to the coast at Dooagh, and the famine years may have forced them to seek a living nearer the sea. Another factor may have been a Protestant group which came here in 1834, bought up all the land it could and set about spreading its influence. There has been talk of renovating a couple of the ruins and establishing an interpretative centre; local people will provide varying explanations as to why this venture has not taken off.

Beaches

Achill has some beautiful beaches which never seem crowded and are often deserted even in good weather. Two of them, at Keel and Keem, are Blue Flag beaches and the ones at Dooega, Dooagh, Dugort and Dooniver are equally sandy. Keem Beach is the most westerly and most likely to be empty.

Activities

The island is perfect for walking and even the highest point of Slievemore at 672 metres (2204 feet) presents no problems. It can be climbed from behind the deserted village and from the top there are terrific views of Blacksod Bay. A longer climb would take in Croaghaun (668 metres, 2192 feet), Achill Head and a clifftop walk along what are claimed to be the highest cliffs in Europe. The walk is covered in the *New Irish Walk*

Guides: West & North (Gill & Macmillan) by Whilde & Simms.

Sea angling gear is sold by O'Malley's at Keel, who also know about boat hire.

Other activities include windsurfing, hang-gliding from the top of Minaun and rock climbing. If any of these take your interest it would be worth calling in at the Activity Centre on the road to Keel, just after the Esso garage with the tourist information point.

Places to Stay

Camping The first camp site is at *Alice's Harbour Inn*, just before the bridge to Achill Sound. In the north, close by the Valley House, is *Lavelle's Golden Strand Caravan & Camping Park* (☎ 098-47232/47277) and *Seal Caves Caravan Park* (☎ 098-43262). The latter costs slightly less although Bord Fáilte gives it a higher rating. Finally, at Keel there is *Keel Sandybanks Camping Park* (☎ 098-32054) which has an even higher rating and a standard charge of IR£5 per tent.

Hostels The *Railway Hostel* (☎ 098-45187) is on the east side of the bridge over Achill Sound, on the right hand side of the road opposite the police station. It has private rooms and a laundry, and is close to the shops across the bridge. The equally convenient *Wild Haven Hostel* (☎ 098-45392) is just across the bridge on the left near the church. The basic rate is IR£5 and two-bed rooms cost IR£1 extra. Breakfast and evening meals can be ordered in advance.

The *Valley House* (☎ 098-47204), with a licensed bar, is in the north of the island with some lovely sandy beaches within walking distance. To get there take the road to Keel and turn right at the Bunacurry junction signposted for Dugort. The other hostel is the *Wayfarer* (☎ 098-43266) in the village of Keel.

B&Bs & Hotels The *Ostan Gob A'Choire*, also known as the Achill Sound Hotel (☎ 098-45245), on the west side of the Achill South bridge, has singles/doubles for IR£20/36, increasing to IR£24/44 in July and

August. At the Bunacurry junction where the road to Keel has a turning right for Dugort, the *Grove* (☎ 098-47108) has rooms with shared bathrooms for IR£14/24. In Keel itself, *Mrs Quinn* (☎ 098-43385) charges from IR£14/28 to IR£18/36. The nearby *Achill Head Hotel* (☎ 098-43108) has rooms from IR£14/28 to IR£18/36.

At Dugort the *Slievemore Hotel* (☎ 098-43254) charges IR£17 per person, while the nearby *Strand Hotel* (☎ 098-43241) charges IR£14/32 for rooms with shared bathrooms. *Gray's Guest House* (☎ 098-43244) is dearer than either hotel with rooms for a stiff IR£34/66. *McDowell's* (☎ 098-43148) on Slievemore Rd is more reasonable at IR£17/30 to IR£22/34.

Out at Dooagh, the *Atlantic Hotel* (☎ 098-43239) charges IR14/30 to IR£16/35, depending on the time of year. The other hotel here, the *Wave Crest* (☎ 098-43115) has doubles from IR£34 to IR£40 and singles with shared bathrooms from IR£13 to IR£16.

Self-Catering There are a number of bungalows and cottages available for weekly or weekend hire. The proprietors of the Atoka Restaurant (☎ 098-47229) near the Valley House hostel are agents for a number of properties and enquiries could be made there. Or contact the Bord Fáilte reservation service for the west of Ireland (☎ 091-63081). During July and August expect to pay from IR£125 to IR£250 a week.

Places to Eat

If you are camping or hostelling, it is advisable to buy provisions at either Mulrany or Achill Sound. The only supermarket on the island is at Keel. Nearly all the hotels serve lunch or dinner to non-residents with dinner costing from IR£12.50 at the *Strand* in Dugort to IR£16 at the *Atlantic* in Dooagh.

At Dugort the *Atoka Restaurant* serves seafood lunches from IR£3 to IR£6. Farther along the road, *Manamon's* is worth a try. At Keel the most popular eating place is the *Boley Restaurant* (☎ 098-43147); if this is full try farther down the road at the junction where *Calbey's* is open all day and serves

breakfast. Also close by is the *Village Inn* with pub food and dinner for IR£12 to IR£17.

Entertainment

In summer a number of pubs and hotels have music. The best time of the year for traditional Irish music and dance is the first two weeks of August when Irish culture is promoted through a number of workshops, which end up in the pubs at night.

Getting There & Away

In the summer, from 25 May to 26 September, bus No 124 runs from Dooagh, outside O'Malley's, to Keel, Achill Sound and then on to Westport and eventually Belfast. It leaves Dooagh at 7.30 am and Achill Sound 20 minutes later. Coming from Westport the bus leaves at 5.45 pm.

Throughout the year, bus No 255 runs across the island from Dooagh, taking in Keel, Dugort and Dooega before crossing to Mulrany, Westport and finally Ballina.

Getting Around

Bikes can be hired from the Achill Sound Hotel or O'Malley's in Keel. Some of the hostels and the Grove guesthouse can also make arrangements for bike hire.

BELMULLET PENINSULA

Probably the least visited corner of the whole of Ireland, this strange and remote land, known as the Mullet or the western Barony of Erris, has a population density of only 10 people per sq km. The peninsula is about 30 km (20 miles) in length rarely rising to more than 30 metres (100 feet) above sea level and it is obvious that the boggy land offers a poor livelihood.

Information

There is no tourist information office on the peninsula, the nearest one being at Bangor. The travel agent, McIntyre's Travel (☎ 097-82199), in the main street of Belmullet has local information. The Belmullet Sea Angling Club can be contacted on ☎ 097-81195.

Belmullet

This forlorn-looking place will never win the Tidy Towns competition. Belmullet was founded in 1825 by the local landlord, William Carter, and built on an unimaginative plan, with one main street and side roads at right angles. Carter also designed a canal joining Broadhaven Bay with Blacksod Bay to the south, and a new bridge now crosses the narrow channel.

Blacksod Point

The road south from Belmullet curves around the tip of the peninsula before rejoining itself at Aghleam. Near the point are the remains of an old church, and the view across the bay takes in the spot where *La Rata Santa Maria Encoronada*, part of the 1588 Spanish Armada, came in and was later burned by the captain, who then left to join two other Spanish ships that had found refuge farther north in Elly Bay.

The road south to Blacksod Point goes past sandy Mullaghroe Beach, which is inviting on a warm day. In the early years of this century a whaling station operated at Ardelly Point, just north of the beach. There is also a decent beach at Elly Bay.

Doonamo Point

This typical promontory fort is the main point of interest north of Belmullet and is built on a spit of land and defended by water on three sides. There are other forts farther north near Erris Head but this one is the most accessible.

Places to Stay & Eat

There is the usual run of bungalowed B&Bs on the main road approaching Belmullet, but there are singles/doubles for IR£13/22 at the *Western Strands Hotel* (☎ 097-81096) on Main St. If the 10 rooms here are full, *Mrs Gaughan* (☎ 097-81181) has rooms at Mill House in nearby American St for the same rates.

The nearest hostel is *Owenmore River Lodge* (☎ 097-83497) at Bangor Erris, about 15 km (10 miles) to the east of Belmullet on

the main road, and camping is also possible here.

As for food, the best advice is to bring your own! In Belmullet the hotel serves snacks and dinner for IR£10 and *Katie's Coffee Corner* at the top end of Main St does soup and sandwiches. There is also the *Anchor Bar* and, a couple of km along the road to Bangor, the *Glenside Tavern* does pub food and meals in its restaurant.

Getting There & Away

One bus runs on weekdays from Ballina to Belmullet and then south to Blacksod Point. There are some local private buses that run students to and from Sligo, Castlebar and Galway at weekends. Enquire at the travel agent in Main St.

BALLINA

The largest town in the county is renowned for its fishing, and is a good base for exploring north Mayo. The tourist office has free maps of interesting walks near the town. Ballina itself is a typical Connaught town, with a shabbiness and conservatism rooted in long deprivation and isolation. It was an unlikely environment for the childhood of its most famous inhabitant – Mary Robinson, the liberal feminist president of Ireland.

Information

The tourist office (☎ 096-70848) is on Cathedral Rd overlooking the River Moy and is open from 10 am to 5.45 pm (closed 1 to 2 pm) Monday to Saturday from May to September. There is a laundrette on Tone St and Keohane's bookshop on the other side of the road acts as a bureau de change.

Fishing

The River Moy is one of the most prolific salmon rivers in Europe and a leaflet listing the fisheries and contacts for permits is available from the tourist office or the North Western Regional Fisheries Board (☎ 096-22788) at Ardnaree House in Abbey St.

Nearby, Lough Conn is also an important brown trout fishery and, while a boat is required, there is no shortage of places renting boats and gillies around the lake. A good base for trout fishing in both Lough Conn and Lough Cullen is Pontoon and again there are plenty of places hiring boats and dispensing advice. The daily rate for hiring a boat is around IR£20.

Getting There & Away
Train The Westport to Dublin train stops at Ballina.

Bus Ballina has good connections. Buses go west to Achill, east to Sligo and the North, and south to Limerick, Shannon and Cork. There are also a couple of private bus companies that run scheduled trips at cheaper rates. Treacy's (☎ 096-70968) run a daily service to Sligo departing from outside Dunne's store at the bottom of Pearse St at 7.50 am. The bus leaves the Quay St car park in Sligo at 5.30 pm. Treacy's also run a weekend service to Galway and Athlone, mostly for students. Barton Transport (☎ 01-6286026) run a daily return service between Ballina and Dublin. It leaves the town hall in Ballina at 7.45 am, reaching Dublin at 11.30 am and departs from Wood Quay in Dublin at 6 pm. On Friday it departs from nearby Cook St in Dublin.

Getting Around
Bicycles can be hired from Gerry's Cycle centre on the Crossmolina Rd (☎ 096-70455). The only drawback is that Gerry goes on an annual July holiday and the place closes down for two weeks.

AROUND BALLINA
Rosserk Abbey
Situated close to the Rosserk River, a tributary of the Moy, the Franciscan abbey dates back to the middle of the 15th century. It is remarkably well preserved and there is an interesting carved piscina (a perforated stone basin for carrying away the water used in rinsing the chalices) in the chancel. Like Rathfran Abbey near Killala, Rosserk was burned down by the English governor of Connaught in the 16th century.

Leave Ballina on the R314 for Killala and

after 6.5 km (four miles) turn right at the sign and take the first left at the next crossroads. Beware of the loose sign at this junction which may point in any direction. Continue for another km and turn right at the next sign for the abbey.

Moyne Abbey
This abbey was established around the same time as Rosserk, also by the Franciscans. It too was burned down by Bingham, the Connaught governor, in the 16th century and perhaps he did a better job on this one, as it is in worse condition than its neighbour.

After leaving Rosserk Abbey go back to the main road and continue north for another three km (two miles) until the abbey is seen on the right across a field.

After returning across the field continue north-west for 1.5 km until the main R314 is reached. Turn right for Killala or left for Ballina.

CROSSMOLINA
The town itself is undistinguished but it serves as a quiet retreat for anyone wishing to fish in Lough Conn or explore the lakes and scenery around Mt Nephin. The mountain (807 metres, 2646 feet) takes under two hours to climb and is described, along with other walks in Mayo, in the *New Irish Walk Guides: West & North* (Gill & Macmillan) by Whilde and Simms.

Research & Heritage Centre
If you have a family connection with North Mayo this is the place to contact (☎ 096-31809). An initial assessment will cost about IR£15 and if this looks promising your full family record would be researched for between IR£50 and IR£100.

The heritage centre houses a collection of old farm machinery and domestic implements. It is open from 9 am to 6 pm Monday to Friday and 2 to 6 pm on Saturday during the summer. During the rest of the year the hours are 9 am to 4 pm Monday to Friday. Admission is IR£1.

Errew Abbey

The abbey is the remains of a house of Augustinian canons built around 1250 on the site of an earlier 7th-century church. In common with other abbeys in Mayo, the monks wisely chose to live close to where they could fish, and the location of Errew Abbey is particularly picturesque.

To get there, take the road from Cross-molina that leads to the heritage centre, and one km after the centre turn left at the sign and keep going for another five km (three miles).

Fishing

Arrangements for fishing on Lough Conn can be made through Cloonamoyne Fishery (☎ 096-31112). The nearest access point is Gortnor Abbey pier which is about one km from town off the Lahardane road and boats are often here waiting to be hired.

Places to Eat

The best food in Crossmolina is to be found in *Hiney's* pub in the town centre, though the *Dolphin* is also worth checking out. *Enniscoe House* serves an evening meal for IR£18 but reservations are essential.

Getting There & Away

There are regular bus connections to Ballina and Castlebar. The bus stop is outside Hiney's pub.

KILLALA

It is claimed that St Patrick founded Killala and the 25-metre (84-foot) round tower is evidence of the town's early ecclesiastical history. The tower was struck by lightning in 1800 and the cap is a later reconstruction. The Anglican cathedral in the town is supposed to have been built on the site of the first Christian church where St Patrick installed Muiredach as the town's first bishop.

It's the French connection that really puts this small town on the map. On 22 August 1798 over 1000 troops under the command of General Humbert landed in Killala Bay, the plan being that Irish peasants would rise

in rebellion and help Napoleon in his war against the English. At first there were dramatic successes, with Killala, Ballina and Castlebar falling to the joint enemies of England. On 8 September, however, Humbert was defeated in Longford. The best account of Humbert's arrival in Killala was written by the Protestant Bishop Stock. He was put under house arrest by the French, and his *Narrative* is available in bookshops in Ballina and Castlebar.

Information

Tourist information (☎ 096-32166) is available during the summer from a council building on the left if you're entering Killala on the Ballina road.

Places to Stay & Eat

The well-run *An Óige Hostel* (☎ 096-32172) is easily the best place for accommodation. The only alternatives are B&Bs like the *Tower Bar* (☎ 096-32470) in the town itself or *Rathoma House* (☎ 096-32035) which is four km (2.5 miles) out of town and has five singles at IR£15 and doubles at IR£26. Slightly farther out is *Beach View* (☎ 096-32023), reached by turning right at the sign to the beach.

The hostel serves breakfast for IR£1.75, a packed lunch for IR£2.50 and dinner for IR£5. There are a couple of pubs in town serving food, and while the *Anchor Bar* is best for seafood, the *Tower Bar* also serves food. There is also *Sizzlers*, a fast-food takeaway.

Getting There & Away

The Ballina-Ballycastle bus stops outside the hostel.

Getting Around

The places of interest nearly all require transport and bicycles can be hired from the hostel.

AROUND KILLALA
Rathfran Abbey

The Dominicans came here in 1274 and built their friary of which only the ruins now remain. In 1590 the friary was closed down and burned by the English but the monks remained in the community until the 18th century.

Take the R314 road that heads north out of Killala and after five km (three miles) turn right after crossing the river. After another couple of km turn right at the crossroads.

Breastagh Ogham Stone

The stone is 2.5 metres (eight feet) high but the Ogham writing is not easy to read. It's in a field by the left side of the R314 just past the crossroads which has the turning for Rathfran Abbey. Cross the ditch just where the sign points to the Stone. The verity of the 'Beware of the Bull' notice is something to consider.

Kilcummin

This is the spot where General Humbert and his 1067 men landed in 1798. A right turn off the main R314 is signposted for Kilcummin. It is remarkably undramatic.

The imagination is more easily kindled by the sculpture of the French revolutionary soldier helping a prostrate Irish peasant. It's on the main road just after the turning to Lacken Bay and it records that at this particular place the first French soldier died on Irish soil.

Lackan Bay & Downpatrick Head

Lackan Bay is wonderfully sandy and ideal for young children. Downpatrick Head has a fenced off blowhole which occasionally shoots up plumes of water. The rock stack just off shore is Dun Briste.

Getting There & Away

There is no public transport to these places around Killala, so you need to hire bicycles or some other mode of transport if you don't have your own.

BALLYCASTLE

Ballycastle boasts some of the oldest and most extensive Stone Age archaeological excavations in Europe.

Information

A tourist information point (☎ 096-43256) is open from 10 am to 5 pm (closed 1 to 2 pm) during the summer. If you're entering the town from Killala it is on the right side of the main street at the bottom of town. A video on Céide Fields can be viewed here.

Céide Fields

Over 5000 years ago there was a wheat and barley farming community with domesticated cattle and sheep, just a few km west of Ballycastle. The growth of the bog led to the decline and eventual end of the community and their stone walls and farm buildings disappeared into the bog. Perhaps the farmers, gradually diminishing the soil's fertility, contributed to the growth of the bog or maybe the wet climate made it inevitable. Whatever the cause, the farms lay buried for thousands of years but have now been excavated and opened to the public as the oldest enclosed landscape in Europe and the most extensive Stone Age monument in the world.

The Interpretive Centre incorporates an exhibition court and audiovisual room detailing aspects of the site's architecture, botany and geology. There is also a panoramic viewing platform and tearooms. Admission is currently IR£1.50 (children 60p, a family IR£4) but is likely to increase.

Céide Fields is eight km (five miles) west of Ballycastle on the main R314 road.

Places to Stay & Eat

B&B is available from *Hilltop House* (☎ 096-43089) but the *Céide House* pub (☎ 096-43105) also has rooms. Another possibility (enquire at the tourist point), is *May's*, where apparently Maud Gonne once stayed. Self-catering holiday cottages are also available for rent (☎ 096-43006 & 091-63081).

Beyond Céide Fields at Belderrig, where there is another prehistoric farm site, the *First Fence* (☎ 096-43114) does B&B.

The *Céide House* and the *Castle Lounge* pubs in town serve food. The other possibility is *Doonferry House* which is a few km west of town on the road to Céide Fields and has a restaurant and bar.

Getting There & Away
A bus runs between Ballina and Ballycastle, stopping outside the Castle Lounge pub.

CASTLEBAR
Although this is Mayo's county town it has little appeal compared to Westport or even Ballina. The old shops have been replaced by modern stores and there is little to evoke the history of the place. But Castlebar does have a place in history, for it was here in 1798 that General Humbert and his army of French revolutionary soldiers and dispossessed Irish peasants encountered the numerically stronger English forces under the command of General Lake. The defeat of the English and their ignominious cavalry retreat became known as the Races of Castlebar.

There is a monument in the Mall to the 1798 Rising. The Mall was once the cricket ground of the Lucan family who own a significant amount of property in the area. There is still a Lucan St close by the tourist office, and some tenants in Castlebar are still paying rent to the Lucan estate, or at least they were until the notorious Lord Lucan disappeared after the murder of his children's nanny in London in 1974. The tenants are refusing to pay the rent until he returns and the family want him declared officially dead so that a new Lord Lucan can inherit the estate – including the rents!

Information
The tourist office (☎ 094-21207) is on Linenhall St near the main shopping centre and is open from May to September from 9.30 am to 5.30 pm (closed 1 to 2 pm).

Places to Eat
The *Davitt Restaurant* on Rush St, around the corner from the tourist office, has fish meals for around IR£5. Along Main St the *Singing Kettle* is fine for coffee and snacks and the *Mandalay* for burgers and the like. The best inexpensive place is the *Paradise Grill* on the small lane that leads off Main St

to the market square. A dinner is under IR£5 and pizzas are always available. For more comfort try the *Imperial Hotel* where the bar food is OK and dinner is IR£15.

Getting There & Away
An express bus connecting Westport and Dublin stops outside Flannelly's pub in Main St at 10.30 am with two extra buses in the summer. There is also a direct bus south to Shannon and Cork and east to Sligo and Belfast. The Westport to Dublin train stops at Castlebar; the station is out of town on the road to Galway.

Getting Around
Raleigh bikes can be hired from Robinson's (☎ 094-21355) on Spenser St.

AROUND CASTLEBAR
Turlough Round Tower
The 9th-century tower stands next to a ruined 18th-century church and a graveyard that is still in use.

The tower is a few km out of Castlebar on the main road to Ballina, which branches off to the right at the north end of town just after the Sacred Heart Home. The road to the left goes to Pontoon and Crossmolina.

Michael Davitt Memorial Museum
The museum in Strade is attached to the church and houses a small collection of material relating to the life and times of Michael Davitt (1846-1906), who is buried in the churchyard.

Take the N5 Dublin Rd and turn off onto the N58 to Strade (also spelt Straid). It is 16 km (10 miles) from Castlebar.

Ballintubber Abbey
The only church in Ireland that was founded by an Irish king and is still in daily use, Ballintubber Abbey was over 200 years old when Columbus went to America. It was founded in 1216 next to the site of an earlier church founded by St Patrick after he came down from his vigil on Croagh Patrick. It is one of the most impressive church buildings in Ireland and well worth a visit.

Features of the church include the 15th-century west doorway and 13th-century windows on the right side of the nave. The nave roof was erected in 1965 and is an Irish oak reproduction of the timber one burned down by Cromwell's soldiers in 1653. Inside the church a IR£1 guide leaflet describes the church in detail.

Take the N84 south to Galway and after about 13 km (nine miles) a signposted road on the right leads to the abbey.

KNOCK

This once undistinguished village has been famous for over a century as the site of visions and miracles.

There is a tourist office (☎ 094-88193) near the church that opens from May to September, seven days a week.

Knock Church

On a wet evening in 1879, two women of Knock were struck by the sight of Mary, Joseph and St John standing in light against the south gable end of their church. Others were called to witness the apparition and a church investigation quickly confirmed the miracle. Other miracles followed as the sick and disabled claimed amazing recoveries after visiting the church, and another church commission upheld Knock's status in 1936. Today, the Knock industry continues unabated and crowds of dutiful worshippers are always to be found praying in and outside the basilica of Our Lady, Queen of Ireland, which can accommodate 12,000 people.

Knock Folk Museum

This is one of the better folk museums and also serves as an ideal introduction to the Knock phenomenon. There is plenty of material on the apparition and subsequent church commissions of enquiry, including bizarre photographs of the display of crutches left behind by grateful pilgrims. The museum also houses an extensive collection of craft tools, costumes and various artefacts relating to rural life in the west of Ireland. It is all attractively presented.

The museum is in a separate building near the church and is open from 10 am to 5 pm from May to October. Entry is IR£1.50 (children 75p).

Getting There & Away

Knock Airport (☎ 094-67222) is 15 km (nine miles) north by the N17 and there is a daily flight from Dublin. There are bus connections from Westport, Sligo, Galway, Shannon, Dublin, Cork and the North.

County Sligo

William Butler Yeats (1865-1939) was educated in Dublin and London, but his poetry is inextricably linked with the county of his mother's family. He returned to Sligo many times, becoming a close friend of the Gore-Booth family who lived at Lissadell. There are plentiful reminders of his presence in the county town and in the rolling green hills around it.

SLIGO TOWN

One of the more interesting portrayals of Yeats is a sculpture outside the Ulster Bank in Sligo Town which has his poetry tattooed over every inch of his body. Hard to find are two of his most famous lines, from his poem *Easter 1916*:

All changed, changed utterly:
A terrible beauty is born...

The poem pays homage to the executed rebels of the Easter Rising, including John MacBride who was married to Maud Gonne. Yeats' unrequited love for Maud Gonne underlies many of his greatest love poems. Politics divided them, for while she remained a rebel and a socialist all her life, Yeats ended up alarmingly close to fascism.

Yeats apart, the town's main attractions are a few km outside at Carrowmore and Knocnarea.

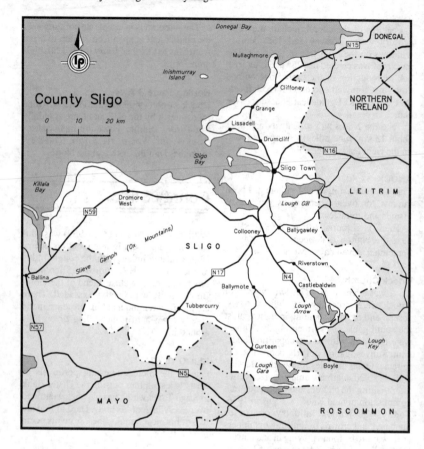

Information

The tourist office (☎ 071-61201) is on Temple St, just south of the centre. There is also a tourist information desk in the Quinsworth shopping arcade which has an entrance on O'Connell St opposite the Ritz. Pam's Laundrette is in Johnston Court, off O'Connell St and the Washeteria is nearby on Harmony Hill.

Museum & Art Gallery

Although there is other material here the main appeal is the Yeats room, chock-a-block with manuscripts, photographs, letters and newspaper cuttings connected with the poet. The room also contains an apron dress worn by Constance Markievicz while interned in Britain after the 1916 Rising. The gallery upstairs has a good selection of paintings by Irish artists like George Russell, Sean Keating and Jack B Yeats, brother of the poet, who said he never did a painting without putting a thought of Sligo into it.

The museum and gallery are open from 10.30 am to 12.30 pm and 2.30 to 4.30 pm, Tuesday to Saturday from June to September. In April, May and October it opens in the morning only. Admission is free.

Sligo Abbey

The town's founder, Maurice FitzGerald, established the abbey around 1250 for the Dominicans but it burnt down in the 15th century and was rebuilt. It was put to the torch once more – and for the last time – in 1641, and ruins are all that remains. The oldest remaining parts of the abbey are the choir, the 15th-century east window and the altar.

If the abbey is locked a key is available from the caretaker, Mr McGuinn, at 6 Charlotte St.

The Courthouse

The Victorian architecture of the courthouse is very unusual for Ireland and it stands out as a reminder of the other power that once ruled the land. The exterior is extravagantly Gothic and modelled on the London Law Courts. Inside, the building still functions as a working courthouse, and on a busy day the foyer takes the overspill from the small public gallery.

Yeats Memorial Building

Near the corner of O'Connell St at the Douglas Hyde Bridge the Yeats Building (☎ 071-42693) is the centre for the Yeats International Summer School, an annual international gathering of scholars. The rest of the year it houses an art gallery and travelling exhibitions, with paintings often up for sale.

Places to Stay

Camping There is a camp site at Strandhill (☎ 071-68120) eight km (five miles) from town and off the road to the airport. The other camp site close to Sligo is the one at Rosses Point (see below).

Hostels On Pearse Rd the excellent An Óige *Eden Hill Hostel* (☎ 071-43204) is about a 10-minute walk south from the centre on the Dublin road and costs IR£5.50. Just north of the town centre on Markievicz Rd the *White House Hostel* (☎ 071-45160) costs IR£5 per night including breakfast. The smaller *Yeats County Hostel* (☎ 071-60241/70120) is just

west of the centre, opposite the railway station at 12 Lord Edward St. It has family rooms and similar rates to the White House Hostel.

B&Bs & Hotels B&Bs can be found all around town and on Pearse Rd that leads out to the N4. *Mrs Leddy's* at 23 Market St (☎ 071-42266) is handy if you want to stay in the town centre; singles/doubles cost IR£14/26. *Bonne Chere* (☎ 071-42014) is also centrally located on High St and charges from IR£12.50, excluding breakfast which will cost you an extra IR£5. *Renate Central House* (☎ 071-62014) on Upper John St is a traditional B&B costing from IR£18/29.

The *Silver Swan* (☎ 071-43231) is a functional hotel close to the centre, costing from IR£60 a double, while the *Clarence* (☎ 071-42211) on Wine St is a small place with doubles for IR£52. Better hotels are out at Rosses Point (see below).

Places to Eat

The *Ritz Restaurant* on O'Connell St is a big place, likely to be crowded but good for lunch or snacks. Also on O'Connell St is *Beezies*, a big old-fashioned place with a very standard Irish menu of almost anything with chips. Round the corner on Grattan St the popular *Gulliver's* has a similar menu, but it also features pizza from IR£3.50 to IR£5.

There are a couple of *4 Lanterns* and an *Abrakebabra* fast-food outlet in the centre.

In the Quinsworth car park area there are a couple of reliable eating places: *Oscar's* is a fast-food joint while the *Rooftop* serves breakfast all day as well as salads and standard meals. The tourist-oriented *Bonne Chere Restaurant* on High St has lunch specials from IR£2 to IR£4 and dinner specials from IR£8 to IR£15.

The bar food at the comfortable *Southern Hotel* near the railway station is reasonable. The restaurant downstairs serves dinner for IR£18 and lunch specials are served in the bar.

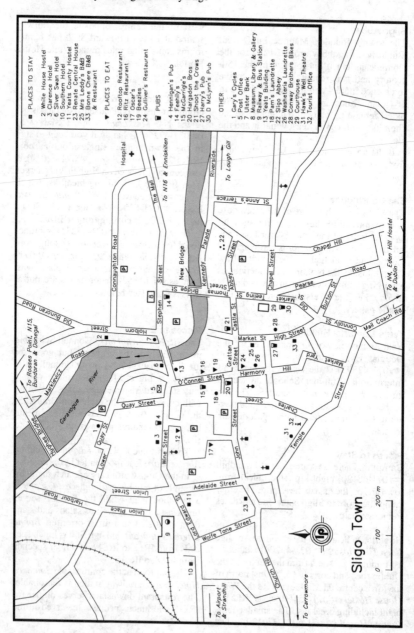

Sligo Town

Entertainment

Sligo has the usual phenomenal number of pubs, many with music at night, particularly the deservedly popular *D McLynn's* on Old Market St just south of the Courthouse. *TD's* on Hughes Bridge St (the Donegal road) has bands most nights of the week.

Hennigan's on Wine St, *Shoot the Crows* on Castle St at Market Square and *Feehily's* on the corner of Bridge and Stephen Sts are other very popular small pubs. The *Silver Swan Hotel*, along from the post office by the river, has jazz sessions on Sunday lunch time and traditional music on Wednesday nights. Jazz on a Wednesday is to be found at *McGarrigle's* on O'Connell St.

Hargadon Bros on O'Connell St doesn't have music but this ancient-looking place is almost a living museum, and you can become part of the display. Serious drinking is best conducted at *Harry's* pub on High St, where there are lots of special offers and it is likely to be busy at 11 in the morning.

The *Hawk's Well Theatre* (☎ 071-61526) is next to the tourist office in Temple St and it is always worth checking to see what is on.

Getting There & Away

Air From Sligo airport (☎ 071-68280) there are two nonstop flights to Dublin daily by Aer Lingus. Flights to other parts of Ireland and Europe are all routed through Dublin.

Bus Bus Éireann (☎ 071-60066) has three services a day to and from Dublin. There's also a Galway-Sligo-Derry service and other connections. Buses operate from the railway station which is just to the west of the centre.

Train The railway station (☎ 071-69888) is close to town for the Dublin service via Mullingar.

Getting Around

There's a bus service from the airport into town or a taxi costs about IR£6. Bike hire is available from Conway Bros (☎ 071-61370), opposite the Dominican Friary on High St, or Gary's Cycles (☎ 071-61370) on Lower Quay St. The Eden Hill Hostel and the White House Hostel also have bikes for hire.

AROUND SLIGO TOWN

Rosses Point

The scene of a battle between two Irish warlords in 1257, Rosses Point is now a picturesque seaside resort easily reached on a town bus, with a lovely Blue Flag beach. Easy to spot is the Metal Man, a brightly coloured buoy that marks the way for boats coming into Sligo.

Carrowmore Megalithic Cemetery

Carrowmore is the site of a megalithic cemetery with over 60 stone circles and passage tombs which make it one of the largest Stone Age cemeteries in Europe. Over the years many of the stones have been removed – a survey in 1839 noted 23 more sites than now exist – and a complicating factor is that some of the best stones are on private land. For various reasons some of the landowners are not encouraging visitors and one farmer has dumped two old cars on either side of stones in his field.

The dolmens were the actual tombs and were probably covered with stones and earth, so it requires an act of imagination to picture what this area, 2.5 km (1.5 miles) wide, might once have looked like when it was dotted with round mounds.

The visitors' centre is open 9.30 am to 6.30 pm in summer and entry is 80p (students & children 30p, family IR£2). Out of season there is nothing to stop you from walking around the site and the tourist office may know about guided tours.

To get there, leave town by Church Hill and carry on for five km (three miles); the site is clearly signposted.

Knocknarea

A couple of km north-west of Carrowmore is the hilltop cairn grave of Knocknarea. About 1000 years younger than Carrowmore, which still makes it quite a venerable age, the huge cairn is popularly supposed to be the grave of the legendary Queen Maeve (Queen Mab in English). The

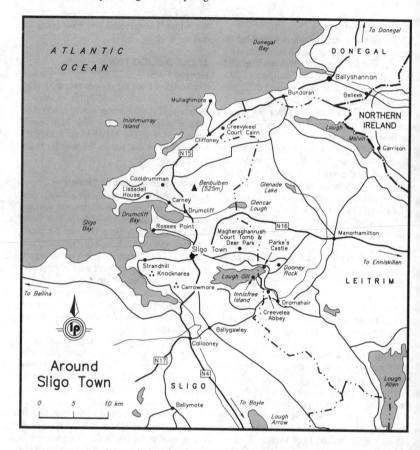

Around Sligo Town

40,000 tons of stone have never been excavated despite speculation that a tomb on the scale of the one at Newgrange in County Meath – the best-preserved passage grave in western Europe – may lie buried underneath.

Leave town as for Carrowmore and a sign shows the way to Knocknarea. If leaving the Carrowmore Centre continue down the road and turn right at the junction with a church. At the next crossroads turn left, signposted Mescan Meadhbha Chambered Cairn, and leave your vehicle at the car park. From here it is only half an hour to the summit and panoramic views.

Magheraghanrush Court Cairn

This impressive court tomb stands on a wooded limestone hill with fine views of Lough Gill. The court area is not outside the front entrance but in the centre of the tomb with two burial chambers opening off at one end and another one at the other end. The site has been dated to around 3000 BC.

Take the N16 out of Sligo and turn off on the R286 for Parke's Castle. Almost immediately after joining this road turn left at the Y-junction on a minor road signposted for Manorhamilton, ignoring the road to the left that is signposted for Parke Castle and

Dromahair. Continue along the minor road for about three km (two miles), park in the Forestry car park and follow the trail through the trees.

Places to Stay

Rosses Point *Greenlands Caravan & Camping Park* (☎ 071-77113/45618) is next to the golf course near the beach. The two hotels at Rosses Point are quite different in character. *Ballincar House Hotel* (☎ 071-45361) is relaxed and peaceful, away from the beach and with an excellent restaurant, while *Yeats Country* (☎ 071-77211) attracts families. A double at Yeats Country is IR£74, while it costs IR£83 a double to stay at the Ballincar House Hotel.

B&Bs are not difficult to find although they can fill up quickly. Try *Mrs Gill* (☎ 071-77202) at Kilvarnet House or, one of the closest to the sea, *Mrs Brady* (☎ 071-77245) at Coral Reef. Both have doubles for IR£28.

Carrowmore The place to stay for a quiet retreat is *Mrs McKiernan* (☎ 071-61449) at Glenwood. It is close to the Carrowmore Centre and has its own stone circle in a nearby field. Singles/doubles cost from IR£17/26 to IR£19/30. Closer to Knocknarea and with similar prices is *Mrs Carter* (☎ 071-62005) at Primrose Grange House, just along the road that leads to the Knocknarea car park.

Places to Eat

A day out to Carrowmore and Knocknarea requires a packed lunch, but there is no shortage of eating places at Rosses Point. The *Bunker* pub on the main road leading to the beach always has pub food, and the *Reveries Restaurant* (☎ 071-77371), close to the Yeats Country Hotel, is open for dinner in the evening. Close by is the *Moorings Restaurant* serving mostly seafood.

Best of all, if your budget stretches to IR£20 a head, is the restaurant at the *Ballincar House Hotel* (☎ 071-45361). A French chef has left a legacy of imaginative cooking which quite sets this place apart but reservations are often necessary.

Getting There & Away

Apart from the town buses which run out to Rosses Point, there is no public transport to the other places of interest in the area. A bicycle hired in Sligo would be the best way of getting around. While it is possible to walk to both Carrowmore and Knocknarea from town, it is a long day's trek on foot there and back.

LOUGH GILL

A round trip of 48 km (30 miles) would take in most of the lough as well as Parke's Castle which, though inside the Leitrim border, is more likely to be visited on a day trip from Sligo. There are legends associated with Lough Gill; one that can be put to the test is the story that a silver bell from the Dominican Abbey in Sligo was thrown into the lough and only those who are free from sin can still hear its pealing.

Information

In the village of Dromahair there is a summer tourist information service operating from the Abbey Hotel, open from 10 am to 2.30 pm Monday to Friday. There is no phone but you could try the hotel (☎ 071-64235).

Dooney Rock

There are good views of the lough and its islands from the top of Dooney Rock. In *The Fiddler of Dooney*, Yeats immortalises the Rock, although his poem about Innisfree has become more famous.

Leave Sligo on the N4 going south and after half a km (a quarter mile) turn left at the sign to Lough Gill. Another left at the T-junction brings you onto the R287/L117 road and the viewpoint of Dooney Rock.

Innisfree

If Yeats hadn't written *The Lake Isle of Innisfree*, this tiny island near the south-east shore would not attract so many visitors and it would probably have kept the air of tranquillity that the poet was moved by:

I will arise and go now, and go to Innisfree,
And a small cabin build there, of clay and wattles
   made;
Nine bean rows will I have there, a hive for the honey
   bee,
And live alone in the bee-loud glade.

From the Dooney Rock car park turn left at the crossroads and after three km (two miles) turn left again for another three km (two miles). A small road leads down to the lake.

A new company (☎ 071-64266) has recently started boat trips on Lough Gill, departing from outside Parke's Castle and taking in Innisfree. The fare is IR£3 (children IR£1); ring first to confirm times.

Creevelea Abbey

This was the last Franciscan friary to be founded in Ireland before they were suppressed in the Reformation. The pillars in the cloister have some interesting carvings of St Francis, one displaying his stigmata and another one showing him in a pulpit with birds perched on a tree. It was burnt in 1590 by Bingham but repaired by the monks before they were again ejected by Cromwellian forces. They returned yet again and thatched the church roof, remaining until the end of the 17th century.

From Innisfree return to the R287/L117 and continue east until the sign for the abbey is seen in the village of Dromhair.

Parke's Castle

The placid setting of the castle, with swans drifting by on the lake, belies the fact that the early Plantation architecture was created out of insecurity and fear by an unwelcome English landlord. The three-storeyed castle, which has been carefully restored, forms part of one of the five sides of the bawn, which also has two rounded turrets at the corners. If possible try to join one of the knowledgeable guided tours after viewing the 20-minute video which gives a general introduction to the antiquities of the area and is likely to whet your appetite for other excursions.

The castle (☎ 071-64149) is open from

9.30 am to 6.30 pm every day between June and September, with shorter hours in October, April and May. Admission is IR£1 (students and children, 40p, family IR£2).

From Creevelea Abbey continue east along the R287/L117. To return to Sligo from Parke's Castle turn west onto the R286/L116. The castle could also be visited on a boat trip from Sligo.

Places to Stay

Along Main St in the village of Dromahair B&B is available at *Stanfords Village Inn* (☎ 071-64140), or the *Breffni Centre* (☎ 071-64199). Both have singles/doubles for IR£17/30. A lot, lot more expensive than either of these is the Georgian *Drumlease Glebe House* (☎ 071-64141) in its own grounds beside the village.

Places to Eat

There are not many eating places on a tour of Lough Gill and a picnic lunch might be best. *Parke's Castle* has a small but friendly café and the *Abbey Hotel* in Dromahair serves instant coffee. A IR£20 dinner can be enjoyed at *Drumlease Glebe House* but ring for a reservation. Dinner at *Stanfords Village Inn* and the *Breffni Centre* costs IR£14.

NORTH OF SLIGO TOWN
Drumcliff & Benbulben

W B Yeats died in 1939 in Roquebrune, France but his wishes were that 'if I die here, bury me up there on the mountain (the mountain cemetery in Roquebrune), and then after a year or so, dig me up and bring me privately to Sligo.' True to his wishes his body was interred in the churchyard at Drumcliff in 1948, where his great-grandfather had been rector, although it was hardly a private affair as the photographs in the Sligo museum make clear. The famous epitaph was his own composition:

Cast a cold eye
On life, on death.
Horseman, pass by!

Nearly 1300 years earlier St Colmcille chose

Top: Guildhall, Derry City (TW)
Left: Derry City, Coat of Arms, Derry (TW)
Right: Mussenden Temple, County Derry (TW)

Top: Carrick-a-rede Rope Bridge, County Antrim (TW)
Bottom: Antrim Coast, County Antrim (JM)

the same location for the foundation of a monastery (see below) and the remains of the round tower, damaged by lightning in 1936, can still be seen. A 10th-century high cross is nearby, depicting Adam and Eve, Cain's murder of Abel, Daniel in the Lions' Den and Christ in Glory. On the west side of the cross the Presentation in the Temple and the Crucifixion can be made out.

Look for the round tower on the N15 road from Sligo.

The Battle of the Book

After Drumcliff the first left turn goes to the village of Carney and just north of the village, in Cooldrumman, is where the Battle of the Book took place in the year 561. At the time St Colmcille borrowed a rare psalter from St Finian and made a pirate edition for his own use. When St Finian found out and demanded the copy the resulting argument found its way to the High King of Ireland who was asked to arbitrate. The delivered judgement was 'To every cow its calf and to every book its copy.' St Colmcille refused to accept the judgement and in the battle that followed over 4000 people were slain. Struck with remorse and shame St Colmcille built a monastery at Drumcliff before departing for ever into voluntary exile on Iona in Scotland.

Lissadell House

This is the ancestral home of the Gore-Booth family, the most famous member of whom was Constance Markievicz (1868-1927), a friend of Yeats and a participant in the 1916 Rising. The death penalty she received for this was later withdrawn and she lived to become the first woman elected to the House of Commons. Like many Irish rebels since, she refused to take her seat, although later while still in prison she became a member of the first Republican Dáil in 1918, and in 1919 she became Europe's first woman minister.

Constance's sister Eva was a poet, and Yeats's poem *In Memory of Eva Gore-Booth and Con Markievicz* is inscribed on a sign at the entrance to the house.

The light of evening, Lissadell,
Great windows, open to the south,
Two girls in silk kimonos....

Yeats was a frequent visitor to Lissadell.

The house is open from June to September, Monday to Saturday, 10 am to 12.15 pm and 2 to 4 pm. The entrance charge is IR£2 and the guided tour takes about 45 minutes. The interior of the house is not especially interesting but the billiard room has a good display of family souvenirs.

To get there, take the N15 road out of Sligo and turn left in Drumcliff.

Mullaghmore

If you turn left at Cliffoney, off the N15, the main road to Mullaghmore first passes **Streedagh Beach**, a grand stretch of sea and sand that was the final resting place for many of the 1300 sailors who perished when three ships from the Spanish Armada were wrecked nearby.

The beach at Mullaghmore is also delightfully wide and safe. It was in this bay however that the IRA assassinated Lord Mountbatten and members of his family in 1979 by blowing up his yacht. On the way to the Mullaghmore headland you pass **Classiebawn Castle** that was built for Lord Palmerston in 1856 and became the home of Lord Mountbatten. The castle is not open to the public.

Inishmurray Island

If access was easier to arrange a visit to Inishmurray would be a must. It contains the remains of three churches, beehive cells and open-air altars. The old monastery is surrounded by a stone wall with five separate entrances to the central area that contains the churches and altars. The monastery was founded in the early 6th century by St Molaise, and a wooden statue of the saint that once stood in the main church is now in the National Museum in Dublin.

The early monks on Inishmurray assembled some fascinating pagan relics. There is a collection of cursing stones; those who wanted to lay a curse did the Stations of the

Cross in reverse, turning over the stones as they went. There were also separate burial grounds for men and women and a strong belief that if a body was placed in the wrong ground it would move itself during the night.

Only six km (four miles) separate Inishmurray from the mainland but there is no regular boat service. Trips can be arranged through Lomax Boats (☎ 071-66124) from Mullaghmore but a group of at least six is necessary to make it worth while. A private trip could also be arranged from Streedagh Point through Joe McGowan (☎ 071-66267). If you were lucky a fishing group might be going out and an arrangement could be made.

Creevykeel Court Cairn

Just past Cliffoney is a court tomb with a wide high front which tapers away to a narrow end. The unroofed court stands outside the front entrance and at some later stage chambers were added to the west side of the cairn. It was constructed around 2500 BC.

Places to Stay

Moneygold Riding & Language Centre (☎ 071-63337) runs a hostel at Grange and is a useful base for the north of Sligo. Horses can be hired for riding on the beaches. B&B is also available here or at *Mrs Waters* (☎ 071-63350) at Shaddan Lodge near Streedagh Beach. Singles/doubles are IR£19/28.

At Drumcliff there are a number of B&Bs including *Mrs Hennigan's* (☎ 071-63211) at Benbulben Farm, Barnaribbon. Singles/doubles are IR£16/29.

At Mullaghmore the *Beach Hotel* (☎ 071-66103, fax 071-66448) has an indoor swimming pool. A double is IR£50 and fishing trips can be arranged.

Places to Eat

Vegetarian food is available at the *Moneygold Riding & Language Centre* at around IR£5 for lunch and IR£12 for dinner. If you're visiting Drumcliff the *Yeats Tavern* is open seven days a week until 10 pm.

Lunch specials are good value. The place is about 100 metres past Yeats' grave on the left of the main road.

Getting There & Away

There are regular bus connections between Sligo, Drumcliff, Grange and Cliffoney as nearly all the buses to Donegal and Derry will take the N15. In Drumcliff the buses stop outside the creamery, in Grange it's outside Rooney's shop and in Cliffoney it's Ena's pub. The first bus stopping at all these places leaves Sligo at 8.45 am.

SOUTH OF SLIGO TOWN
Collooney

The **Teeling Monument** can be found at the northern end of this village. It commemorates the daring of Bartholomew Teeling who was marching with Humbert's French-Irish army when it encountered stiff resistance from an English gunner. Teeling charged up to the gunner and killed him, thus allowing the army to march on to an eventual defeat at the battle of Ballinamuck in Longford. Although the French were treated as prisoners of war, Teeling and 500 other Irishmen were executed.

The other attraction near Collooney is **Markree Castle** (☎ 071-67800) which is signposted off the main road on the left after leaving the village. The castle has remained in the same family since Cromwell's times. When Charles Kingsley stayed here in the 19th century he wrote that he cried over the misery inflicted on the local peasantry while at the same time exalting in the excitement of fishing for salmon in the estate's river. And it is said that Mrs Alexander wrote the hymn *All Things Bright & Beautiful* after her stay there. The castle now functions as a hotel; singles/doubles start at IR£57/94.

B&B at IR£14 is available from *Tess & Des Lang* (☎ 071-67136) at Union Farm just one km outside the village.

Ballymote

This small town, definitely off the tourist trail, has two points of interest. **Ballymote Castle**, on the road from town to

Tubbercurry, looks like a designer ruin but this is the real thing; an early 14th-century castle fought over between Irish chiefs before succumbing to the English in 1577 and now crumbling away in obscurity. It was from here that O'Donnell marched to disaster at the Battle of Kinsale in 1601.

The **Protestant church** is also worth a glance, if only to read the plaque saying that the clock was paid for by the tenants of Ballymote estate as a mark of respect to Sir Robert Gore-Booth of Lissadell. Unlike many of these tributes this one was genuine; Robert Gore-Booth mortgaged Lissadell House during the famine to raise money for food for the starving. Constance Markievicz, his daughter, received a minute-long ovation from the local peasantry here after her release from an English jail in June 1917.

There are a few B&Bs here: *Mrs Mullin's* (☎ 071-83449) at Millhouse and *Mrs McGettrick's* (☎ 071-83398) at Hillcrest both charge IR£13 per person and are signposted from the village. More upmarket is *Temple House* (☎ 071-83329), an old Anglo-Irish home, which gets its name from the Knights Templar. A double room is IR£60.

There are plenty of unpretentious pubs to choose from and *Donald H Tighe* serves reasonable bar food. Near the church the *Picnic Basket* is a fast-food place that opens till the early hours at weekends, but the *Corran* is more comfortable. Under the same management the *Stone Park Restaurant* has meals for between IR£3 and IR£10.

Tubbercurry

Sometime spelt Tobercurry, this is another off-the-beaten-track town. It comes alive around the middle of July when a music summer school takes the place over. On the second Wednesday in August, the town's big Fair Day is celebrated. Nearly all the pubs have musical links, and the first place to call in at is *Killoran's* on the long main street, which functions as a combined pub/restaurant/takeaway/travel agent/off-licence/tourist office. Other pubs with music include the *May Queen* and *Cawley's*.

The *Muckley Hill Hostel* (☎ 071-85880) is signposted off the main N17 some three km (two miles) north of Tubbercurry. Advice and information on local walks are available and bicycle hire can be arranged. A bed is IR£4. In town, B&B at *Cawley's* pub (☎ 071-85025), where singles/doubles start at IR£15/28, is a good bet but if it's full they will direct you elsewhere.

Killoran's is the best place for a snack and has lunch for less than IR£5 and dinner for less than IR£10. *Cawley's*, on the road to Ballymote, offers dinner in its restaurant for IR£12.

Carrowkeel Passage-Tomb Cemetery

Situated on a hilltop in the Bricklieve Mountains overlooking Lough Arrow, this place is uplifting, with panoramic views on a clear day, and also a little spooky given the 14 cairns, various dolmens and scattered remnants of other graves. The place has been dated to the late Stone Age (3000-2000 BC).

The site, off the main N4 road, is closer to Boyle than Sligo. In the village of Castlebaldwin turn right, if coming from Sligo, at the sign, and then left at the fork as indicated. The site is a couple of km uphill from the gateway. You can take bus No 275 from Sligo and ask to be put off at Castlebaldwin.

Coopershill House (☎ 071-65108) is close to the Carrowkeel Passage-Tomb Cemetery, halfway between Sligo and Boyle, and is a handsome retreat for anyone wanting to relax in a Georgian family mansion. Bed & breakfast is IR£48/80 for singles/doubles and you would want to stay two nights to enjoy the boating and fishing that is available.

For a down-to-earth Irish meal with good wine and open log fires, splash out IR£20 for a dinner at *Coopershill House* (☎ 071-65108). Reservations are recommended.

Lough Arrow

Lough Arrow has its own tourist office (☎ 079-66232) open during July and August from 9.30 am to 5.30 pm, seven days a week. It is situated on the main N4 road just north of Boyle, within spitting distance of County Roscommon. The centre is geared towards motoring tourists.

Lough Arrow is of interest to anglers. Mayfly Holidays (☎ 071-65065) of Ballindoon, Riverstown, Sligo, have B&B at IR£12 a night (partial board or self-catering), plus packed lunches and boat hire at IR£10 a day. Inside information on fishing spots is free.

Getting There & Away

The Dublin to Sligo express stops outside Quigley's in Collooney as does the Galway-Derry express which goes on to Tubbercurry. No 248 runs through Collooney, Ballymote and Tubbercurry on the way to Athlone and a local bus runs from Sligo to Collooney.

The Dublin train also stops at Collooney and Ballymote and the fares from Sligo are IR£3 and IR£4 respectively.

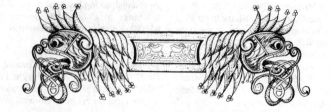

The Central North

Ireland has been described as a dull picture with a wonderful frame, and indeed most visitors do travel around the coast which forms the frame and rarely venture inland to explore the picture. The six counties of the central north – Roscommon, Leitrim, Cavan, Monaghan, Longford and Westmeath – may never attract the tourist hordes but they do have a number of places of great interest. Cavan, Monaghan and Donegal together with the six counties of Northern Ireland make up the province of Ulster.

County Cavan

The low undulating county of Cavan is barely two hours drive from Dublin and just south of the border with Northern Ireland. Cavan is dominated by lakes and drumlins, small round hills deposited and shaped by retreating glaciers during the last Ice Age which ended some 10,000 to 12,000 years ago. In the far west of the county, the wild and barren Cuilcagh Mountains are the source of the Shannon, at over 300 km (220 miles) long the mightiest river in Ireland or Great Britain.

Fishing is a major attraction but the pleasant scenery cannot compare with the wild west coast. Cavan is also famous for its

potholed roads, which are often twisty and badly signposted to boot. The roads seem to go over the drumlins whereas in neighbouring Monaghan they go round them. Cavan was the birthplace of Percy French, the late 19th-century songwriter responsible for *The Mountains of Mourne*.

If you intend travelling into Northern Ireland, the border has official and unofficial crossing points. Although the blocked-off unofficial crossings are sometimes opened by locals travelling to the North, visitors should use the official roads which mostly run between border towns.

FISHING

Anglers from all over Europe converge on Cavan to fish the many lakes along the southern and western border of the county. Cavan has more than its fair share of lakes, some 365 in total according to the locals, one for every day of the year. The fishing is excellent, primarily coarse fishing for pike, bream, perch and roach but also some game angling for trout in Lough Sheelin.

Some of the lakes like Lough Sheelin are recovering after years of serious pollution from the numerous pig farms in the area, and as the fish return so do the fishermen. Most lakes are well signposted, with the types of fish available also marked. Some of the villages and guesthouses depend heavily on anglers, many of whom return year after year.

Lough Sheelin is 24 km (15 miles) south of Cavan Town and on the water's edge the Crover House Hotel (☎ 049-40355) in Mountnugent has fishing boats for hire at IR£22 a day with engine or IR£10 with oars.

HISTORY

Magh Sleacht, a plain near the border village of Ballyconnell, was one of the most important druidic centres in the country around the 5th century, when St Patrick was converting the Irish to Christianity. The principal deity

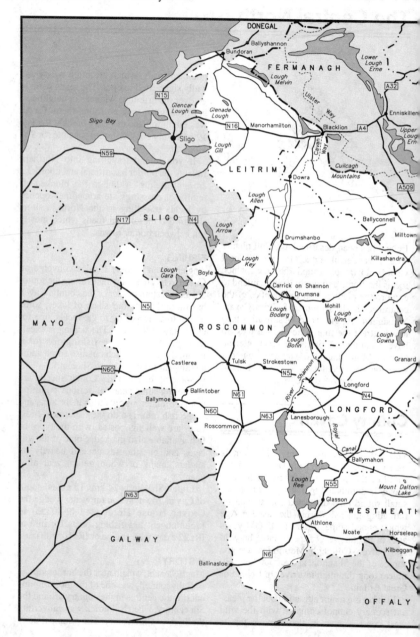

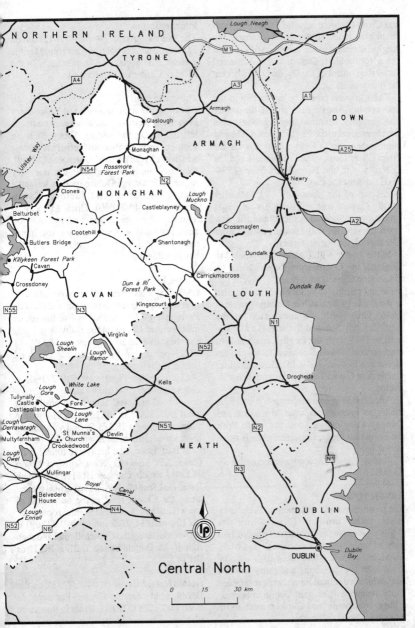

Central North

0   15   30 km

was Crom Cruaich, who didn't last long with Patrick around. In the 12th century, the Anglo-Normans made a concerted effort to get a foothold in Cavan, but it remained under the control of the Gaelic O'Reilly clan for many years.

Their grip on power began to slip in the 16th century. The English 'shired' the county into baronies, dividing these amongst clan members loyal to the English crown. The end came when the O'Reillys joined with the other Ulster lords – the O'Donnells and the O'Neills – in the Nine Years War (1594-1603) against the English.

As part of the plantation of Ulster after 1609, Cavan was divided up amongst English and Scottish settlers, and the new town of Virginia was created, named after Elizabeth I, the Virgin Queen.

In the 1640s, with Charles II in trouble in England, the Confederate Rebellion led by Owen Roe O'Neill took place. This returned exile had one major victory over the English at the Battle of Benburb in County Tyrone in 1646. Only with the conclusion of the English Civil War and the arrival of Cromwell in 1649 were the English again able to take control. Owen Roe died in suspicious circumstances in 1649 in Cloughoughter Castle near Cavan Town; poisoning was suspected.

After the War of Independence in 1922, the Ulster counties of Cavan, Monaghan and Donegal were included with the South. With the border so close, Republicanism is quite strong here.

County Cavan has a population of barely 53,000.

CAVAN TOWN

The most important settlement in the county is the rather ordinary Cavan Town. Its slightly peculiar layout centres around two parallel main streets, Farnham St and Main St. Main St has the feel of an Irish country town with typical shops and pubs on each side, while in contrast Farnham St resembles a city avenue with elegant Georgian houses, a large courthouse and Garda station and a newish Catholic cathedral.

Information
The tourist office (☎ 049-31942) is on Farnham St and is open all year round for the present. The Supaklene laundrette is in the Morgan Centre on Farnham St.

Things to See
Cavan developed around a 13th-century Franciscan friary of which there are no traces left today. On the site in Abbey St is an 18th-century **Protestant church tower** which marks the grave of Owen Roe O'Neill, though it must be said that it's not very impressive. On the Dublin road is Ireland's second-oldest crystal factory, **Cavan Crystal** (☎ 049-31800). Open Monday to Saturday, they have free factory tours by arrangement where you can see the hand-made crystal being blown and cut. They also have a gift shop.

Places to Stay
B&Bs There are some real gems out of town, if you are prepared to push on a little. *Les Pervenche* (☎ 049-38182) is five km (three miles) out of Cavan on the Ballyhaise road, and has five double rooms at IR£12, or IR£21 per person for full board. The food here is really good.

Lisnamandra House (☎ 049-37196) is about eight km (five miles) along the Crossdoney road and well signposted on the left hand side. B&B is IR£13 or IR£14 with a shower, dinner is IR£13.50 and you should book ahead. Breakfast is wonderful.

In Ballyhaise, five km (three miles) from Cavan, is *Slowey's Guesthouse* (☎ 049-38134), which charges IR£11. In Cavan town, *Oakdene* (☎ 049-31698) is 400 metres along the Clones road at the north end of town and has four reasonable rooms for IR£12 to IR£14. *Halcyon* (☎ 049-31809) is 600 metres along the Cootehill road and then right by McDonald's shop. B&B is IR£13 or IR£14.

Hotels *Hotel Kilmore* (☎ 049-32288), on the Dublin road near the Crystal Factory, has B&B for IR£28 to IR£31. Right in the centre of town you could try the very popular

Farnham Arms (☎ 049-32577) with B&B for IR£24 to IR£26.

Places to Eat

The town has fast-food places like *Uncle Sam's* on College St, or *Una's Takeaway* on Main St. *Galligan's Restaurant* (☎ 049-61323), just off Main St on Bridge St, is good for inexpensive lunches and early dinners. Serving a good cup of coffee, *Melburn* is another small restaurant cum coffee shop halfway up Main St. The *Farnham Hotel* has a comfortable lounge with reasonable food.

The best place in town is the *Olde Priory Restaurant* (☎ 049-61898), at the cathedral end of Main St in an old convent basement. The set dinner is a reasonable IR£14.90 and they are closed Mondays.

Entertainment

McGinty's Corner Bar is on the main Dublin road and has won a regional 'pub of the year' title. It has music at weekends. There are heaps of pubs on Cavan's Main St. O'Donoghue's, also known as the *Black Horse Inn*, is popular with locals and has pool tables.

You will occasionally find jazz in *Louis Blessing's* nice rustic bar. *Linus McDonald's* on Ash St is another attractive place.

The cinema is in the centre of town off Farnham St.

Getting There & Away

Bus Bus Éireann (☎ 049-31353) is at the south end of Farnham St, and Cavan is on the Dublin to Donegal and Galway to Belfast routes.

On weekdays there are six daily buses to Dublin. Two buses daily operate to Belfast, three on Fridays. There's a daily service to Galway with an extra one on Friday evening.

Wharton's (☎ 049-37114) have private daily buses between the Lakelands Hotel and Parnell Square, Dublin.

Bus Éireann (☎ 049-31353) have limited services running from Cavan Town through the county to Bawboy, Virginia, Kells and Dunboyne and most other small towns.

Getting Around

Abbey Set Printers (☎ 049-31932) on Farnham St rent bikes for IR£7 a day, IR£30 deposit. 'On Yer Bike Tours' (☎ 049-31932) offer day or week-long leisurely group cycling tours of the area with many excursions, including Corleggy Cheese Farm, well known for its goats' cheese.

AROUND CAVAN TOWN
Kilmore Cathedral

This modest Protestant cathedral is about five km (three miles) west on the Crossdoney road to Killykeen Park. On the west side of this relatively modern building is a fine old doorway brought here from an Augustinian monastery on one of Lough Oughter's many islands. If you look closely you'll notice that some of the stones have not been replaced in the right order. In the churchyard is the grave of Bishop Bedell who commissioned the first translation of the Old Testament into Irish.

Killykeen Forest Park

This forest park is six km (four miles) west of town on the shores of Lough Oughter. Lough Oughter winds a tortuous path around the undulating landscape and the park has some fine walks, nature trails, fishing spots and good chalets for rent amongst its 240 hectares of trees and inlets. Many of the low wooded islands in the lake are likely to have been *crannogs* – a fortified and artificial island.

To the north, within the park, is the inaccessible **Cloughoughter Castle**, built in the 13th century by the O'Reillys on an island in the lake and the place where the rebel leader Owen Roe O'Neill died, reputedly from poisoning. The best way to get near it is from the south-east, along a narrow road running north from the village of Garthrattan. On **Inch Island,** also within the park, there is a ring fort.

Admission to the park is IR£1 for a car. There are self-catering chalets (☎ 049-32541) on the shores of Lough Oughter which sleep six and can be rented for a weekend or longer for IR£140 to IR£320 a week.

Canadian-style canoes can be rented (☎ 049-32842) for a paddle on Lough Oughter or the Erne waterways.

Pighouse Folk Museum

In Crossdoney you'll see signposts for the Pighouse Folk Museum (☎ 049-37248) in Corr House, Cornafean. Its hodgepodge of artefacts are preserved in the original pighouse and barns. If you like rummaging through other people's attics then you'll love this place. It's open whenever Mrs Faris is in – phone ahead just in case. Admission is IR£2.

Drumlane Monastic Site

One km south of Miltown, north of Killeshandra on the road to Belturbet, is Drumlane, a 6th-century monastic site with a small plain church and peculiar round tower just over 11 metres high. The monastery was founded by St Mogue and the site's location between two small lakes – Drumlane and Derrybrick – and the surrounding hills is its most attractive feature.

Belturbet

A small town on the River Erne, Belturbet is an angling centre with cruises available up Lough Erne during the summer. It's 16 km (10 miles) north-west of Cavan Town. On the road back to Cavan town is the pretty little hamlet of Butlersbridge on the River Annalee. Ballyhaise House nearby was designed by Richard Castle (responsible for Dublin's Leinster House) and is worth a quick look for its fine brickwork. It is now an agricultural college.

Turbet Tours (☎ 049-22360) have sailings on the River Erne and Upper Lough Erne in County Fermanagh from June to September at 3 pm with an extra sailing at 6 pm on Sundays. The two-hour tour costs IR£4 per person.

Places to Stay & Eat

B&Bs Just before the river in Butlersbridge is *Ford House* (☎ 049-31427) with six rooms for IR£13 to IR£15 per person B&B. In Belturbet, *Hilltop* (☎ 049-22114) has 10

rooms at IR£16/26 to IR£18/30 for singles/doubles.

Dove Cottage (☎ 049-22654) is six km (three miles) south of Belturbet in Milltown. Rooms are IR£18/26 for singles/doubles, dinner is IR£11 and there are facilities for anglers.

Butlersbridge has the *Derragarra Inn*, a pub by the river which often seems to be the busiest place in the county. The donkey and cart on the roof are hard to miss! The Inn has good bar food, a reasonably priced tourist menu and peat fires.

WEST CAVAN

West Cavan, sometimes known as the Panhandle from its distinctive shape, is dominated by the starkly beautiful but little visited Cuilcagh Mountains. Ballyconnell, 29 km (18 miles) to the north-west of Cavan Town, is the gateway to the region. To the south-west, Magh Sleacht, the area around Kilnavert and Killycluggin, is supposed to have been a druidic centre dedicated to the deity Crom Cruaich. In the far north-west corner of the county, the road travels parallel to the border before forking to Blacklion and Dowra. This is a desolate area with some interesting ancient sites.

There are no buses servicing this remote part of the county. The express Donegal to Dublin buses pass through Swanlinbar which is 16 km (10 miles) from Blacklion.

Dowra & the Black Pig's Dyke

Dowra is on the upper reaches of the River Shannon and between the river and Slievenakilla to the east is a five-km (three-mile) section of the mysterious Black Pig's Race or Dyke, a worm-like earthworks which wriggles across much of the region. It may have been an ancient fortification and frontier of Ulster, perhaps an earlier version of Hadrian's Wall in Scotland.

Blacklion

Five km (three miles) south of Blacklion are the remains of a cashel or ring fort with three large circular embankments. Inside is a sweathouse, a stone beehive hut which served as a type of Turkish bath and was used mostly in the 19th century. Between Dowra and Blacklion there are the remains of quite a number of these curiosities.

The Cavan Way

Blacklion and Dowra are the ends of the 25-km (16-mile) Cavan Way which is covered by Bord Fáilte information sheet No 26I. The Way runs past a number of Stone Age monuments – court cairns, ring forts and tombs. At the midpoint is the Shannon Pot, a pool on the boulder-strewn slopes of the Cuilcagh Mountains and the source of the River Shannon which from here flows into Lough Allen.

Blacklion is also on the Ulster Way which takes you into Northern Ireland. For more details about the Ulster Way see the guidebook *Walking the Ulster Way* (Appletree Press, paperback, IR£6.95) by Alan Warner or contact the Northern Ireland Tourist Board. A new trail will extend the Cavan Way south along the shores of Lough Allen to Drumshanbo, 25 km (15 miles) south of Dowra in County Leitrim. Dowra also joins up with the Leitrim Way which runs between Manorhamilton and Drumshanbo.

Places to Stay & Eat

Hostels The county's only hostel, *Sandville House Hostel* (☎ 049-26297), is just south of Ballyconnell, signposted off the Belturbet road. A bed is IR£4 a night and they have two doubles for the same price per person.

B&Bs *Pinegrove* (☎ 072-53061) is one of the few guesthouses around Blacklion, and costs IR£12 to IR£13 per person. In Ballyconnell, *Snugborough House* (☎ 049-26346) has four rooms at IR£13 to IR£15 per person. Also in Ballyconnell the *Angler's Rest* (☎ 049-26391) is a pub-cum-guesthouse with rooms for IR£12 B&B, or full board for IR£17. You can get snacks and light meals in the pub.

Hotels The huge and brand-new *Slieve Russell Hotel* (☎ 049-26444), two km west

Kingfisher

of Ballyconnell, is already a legend. Built by a local millionaire, it features marble, fountains, restaurants, bars, nightclubs, a swimming pool and a golf course. The latest addition is a 3500-year-old wedge tomb, moved to the front garden of the hotel to prevent its destruction at the original site. B&B is IR£50 to IR£65, but there are frequent weekend and midweek specials.

EAST CAVAN

Heading east, from Cavan Town you move into the heart of drumlin country. The history of foreign settlement has left its mark on the fabric and layout of the main towns.

Getting There & Away

At least four express Bus Éireann (☎ 049-31353) buses on the Donegal to Dublin route pass through Virginia, and there are also three daily passing through on the Cavan Town to Dublin route. Cootehill is on a Dundalk to Cavan Town route with a single bus on Fridays only, while on Tuesdays a Dundalk to Cavan bus travels through Kingscourt.

There are two daily buses on weekdays from Cootehill to Monaghan Town, with just one on Saturdays. There is also a Cootehill-Kingscourt-Dublin service which has three buses on Mondays and Saturdays and two on each of the other weekdays.

Virginia

On the shores of Lough Ramor in the southeast corner of the county, Virginia's origins go back to the Plantation of Ulster in the early 17th century. It was named after Elizabeth I, the Virgin Queen. Six km (four miles) to the north-west is Cuilcagh House, home of the Sheridan family, where Jonathan Swift is said to have come up with the idea for *Gulliver's Travels* while visiting in 1726. There is a nine-hole golf course just outside of town in the grounds of the Park Hotel.

Cootehill

Farther to the north, the small neat market town of Cootehill is named after the Cootes, a planter family who were instrumental in founding the town in the 17th century. This colourful clan had many interesting members including Sir Charles Coote, one of Cromwell's most ruthless and effective leaders, and Richard Coote (1636-1701) who became Governor of New York State, and then New Hampshire and Massachusetts. The Coote mansion, Bellamont Forest (1729), was designed by Edward Lovett Pearce (architect of the Bank of Ireland Building in College Green, Dublin, and supervisor of Castletown House in Kildare) and is described as one of the best Palladian villas anywhere. It's open in the afternoons and for exclusive overnight stays.

Kingscourt

In the far east of the county, Kingscourt is a fairly drab village. St Mary's Catholic Church, has some superb 1940s stained-glass windows by the artist Evie Hone. The church has views of the surrounding region, and just to the north-west is Dun a Rí Forest Park, with wooded walks and picnic spots.

Places to Stay

Camping *Lakelands Caravan & Camping Park* (☎ 042-69488) is about one km west of Shercock on the Cootehill road. Charges are IR£5 per tent or caravan plus IR£0.50p per person, and they are open Easter to September.

Five km (three miles) south of Virginia on the southern tip of Lough Ramor is the somewhat rundown *Lough Ramor Camping & Caravan Park* (☎ 049-47447).

B&Bs One km outside Virginia on the Dublin road, *St Kyran's* (☎ 049-47087) is on the lakeshore. It is open April to September and costs between IR£12 and IR£15. Across the road is *Hillside House* (☎ 049-47125) with three rooms at IR£13 per person. Two km along the Oldcastle road is the *White House* (☎ 049-47515), with three rooms for IR£13 to IR£15 sharing.

In Cootehill, *Knockvilla* (☎ 049-52203) on Station Rd costs IR£11 to IR£12 per person. Also worth trying is the *Beeches* (☎ 049-52307) also on Station Rd, a small cul-de-sac off the Shercock road. One km on the Cavan side of Cootehill is *Riverside House* (☎ 049-52150), an excellent place for IR£13 to IR£15 B&B.

Hotels In Kingscourt, *Mackin's Hotel* (☎ 042-67208) on Church St is an ordinary country hotel with 20 rooms at IR£14 per person. *Cabra Castle* (☎ 042-67030), three km (two miles) out of Kingscourt on the Carrickmacross road, is an imposing structure with its own nine-hole golf course. B&B is IR£30 to IR£55. Just outside Virginia the *Park Hotel* (☎ 049-47235) is an 18th-century building overlooking a small lake, with rooms at IR£39/48 for singles/doubles. They also have a nice little nine-hole golf course.

Places to Eat

Ordinary takeaways are not uncommon but notable eateries certainly are. In Virginia the *Park Hotel* just outside town has good but pricey food. *Sharkey's Hotel* on Main St does teas, coffees and lunches in the bar.

In Cootehill the *Coffee Pot* on Market St has good coffee, sandwiches and lunches during the day. The *White Horse Hotel* at the end of the same street has a good carvery lunch and other dishes. Just outside Kingscourt the *Cabra Castle Hotel* is worth trying for a snack or lunch.

County Monaghan

Few visitors pass through Monaghan's landscape of neat round hills, crisscrossed by unkempt hedgerows and countless scattered farms. The hills are drumlins, dumped by the glaciers of the last Ice Age in a belt stretching from Clew Bay in County Galway across the country to County Down. It's pleasant but never spectacular scenery; walkers and cyclists may enjoy the country lanes if the weather is cooperative. Monaghan has fewer lakes than neighbouring Cavan, though the fishing is still good. Patrick Kavanagh, one of Ireland's most respected poets, was born in this county. *The Great Hunger* which he wrote in 1942, and *Tarry Flynn* written in 1948 evoke the atmosphere and often grim reality of life for the poor farming community.

The barren terrain has restricted the development of large-scale mechanised farming, despite which Monaghan's farming cooperatives are amongst the most active and forward-looking in the country. Monaghan is noted for its lace and the eyestraining tradition of making this extraordinarily fine material continues in Clones and Carrickmacross, the centre of the industry since the early 19th century.

HISTORY

The earliest traces of humans in this region go back to before the Bronze Age. None of these sites measure up to the magnificent monuments of County Meath, though the Tullyrain Ring Fort close to Shantonagh in the south of the county is worth a look, as are Mannor Castle near Carrickmacross and the crannóg in Convent Lake in Monaghan Town. Like Cavan, Monaghan is lacking in religious remains despite its proximity to Armagh, the principal seat of St Patrick. The round tower and high cross in Clones in the west of the county are among the scant remains from this period of Irish history.

The Anglo-Normans were also less influential here than elsewhere. The county was controlled through the early Middle Ages by many Gaelic clans including the O'Carrolls, McKennas and MacMahons. Enemies for a long time of the O'Neills of Armagh, these families united with them on the losing side of the Nine Years War (1594-1603) against the English.

Unlike Cavan and much of Ulster, Monaghan was largely left alone during the plantation of Ulster. The transfer of Monaghan land to English hands came later, after the Cromwellian wars, and much of it was granted to soldiers and adventurers or bought by them from the local chieftains (under pressure and often for a fraction of its worth). These new settlers levelled the forests and built numerous planned towns and villages, each with their own Protestant church. The planning and architecture exemplified their tidy, austere and no-frills approach to life. Disapproving of Irish pastoral farming methods, they introduced arable farming, and the linen industry later became seriously profitable.

Monaghan's historical ties with Ulster were severed by the partition of Ireland in 1922, and although Republicanism is quite strong it is not as visible as you might expect. A number of towns have Sinn Féin Advice Centres.

MONAGHAN TOWN

The county town of Monaghan is 141 km (87 miles) from Dublin and just eight km (five miles) from the border. It's the only town of any size in the county. Its design and buildings reflect the influence of the British newcomers of the time and the money generated by the linen industry in the 18th and 19th centuries. Compared to many midland towns, Monaghan is a pleasant surprise, many of the town's important buildings are elegant limestone edifices built to last more than one lifetime. The locals have produced good maps of the town, provide a heritage tour and have built up an excellent regional museum.

History
Nothing remains of the ruling MacMahons'

1462 friary or their earlier forts, but in Convent Lake, just behind St Louis's Convent, there is a small overgrown crannóg which served as the headquarters for the family around the 14th century. Access to the lake is at the bottom of Dawson St, over the canal.

After the turbulent wars of the 16th and 17th centuries, the town was settled by Scottish Calvinists who built a castle using the rubble of the old friary, some fragments of which can be seen near the Diamond. The 19th-century profits from the linen industry transformed the town and brought many sturdy new buildings.

Orientation & Information

Monaghan's principal streets form a continuous arc, broken up by the town's three main squares or Diamonds. Most of the sights and important buildings can be found on this thoroughfare. There are two small lakes, Peter's Lake to the north of the courthouse and Convent Lake with its crannog at the south-west corner of town.

The tourist office (☎ 047-81122) is at the top of Park St in Market House, which dates from 1792. From June to September, there are Heritage Walks of the town from the County Museum on Hill St. The post office is on Mill St – up Hill St from the museum and take the first right.

Monaghan County Museum

Monaghan County Museum (☎ 047-82928) is behind the tourist office at the junction with Hill St and is one of the best regional museums in Ireland. Taking up two Victorian houses, it ranges from Stone Age to modern times, and has displays on the local lace and linen industries, the abandoned Ulster canal (which runs just to the south of the town and is being renovated) and of course the border with the north.

The museum's prized possession is the Cross of Clogher, a bronze 13th or 14th-century altar cross. Usually local treasures such as this are whisked away to the National Museum. Local and national artists have exhibits in the Art Gallery wing. The museum is open from 11 am to 5 pm Tuesday to Saturday, closed 1 to 2 pm from October to May, and admission is free.

Around Town

At the top of Market St is **Church Square**, the first of the three Diamonds, with an 1857 **obelisk** for a Colonel Dawson who was killed in the Crimean War. Overlooking the square is a fine Doric-style 1830 **Courthouse**, the former Hibernian Bank (1875) and the Gothic St Patrick's Church.

In the centre of town the **Diamond** is the town's original market place, with a Victorian sandstone fountain presented to the town in 1875 in honour of the Baron of Rossmore, a member of the area's former leading family. This spot was once occupied by the **Market Cross**, with its fancy sundial, which was moved to Old Cross Square at the east end of Dublin St to accommodate the Baron's memorial.

Beyond the canal on the Dublin road, **St Macartan's Catholic Cathedral** with its slender spire was designed by J J McCarthy (responsible for the College Chapel in Maynooth, County Kildare), and is said to be his finest building, though some feel it has been marred by the later addition of incongruous Carrara marble statues. It has good views of the surrounding area.

The birthplace of **Charles Gavan Duffy**, one of the leaders of the Young Ireland Movement and a founder of the *Nation* newspaper, is at 10 Dublin St. In the 1840s the *Nation* set out to teach the native Irish about themselves, their history and literature, as well as presenting a non-sectarian view of Irish news. Later Duffy moved to Australia, where he became Premier of Victoria. Nearby, the **Sinn Féin Advice Centre** has a display of Republican literature.

Places to Stay

B&Bs On the Clones road, *Cedars* (☎ 047-82783) has three rooms at IR£12 B&B. *Ashleigh Guesthouse* (☎ 047-81227) on Dublin St has 10 rooms at the same price and facilities for anglers.

Hotels The fine-looking *Westenra Hotel* (☎ 047-82298) at the Diamond in the centre of town has 17 rooms with bathroom at IR£25 per person for B&B. The modern *Four Seasons Hotel* (☎ 047-81888), about two km north on the Derry road in Coolshannagh, is more expensive at IR£32 to IR£36 per person.

Places to Eat
Pizza D'Or (☎ 047-84777) on Market St turns out good, cheap pizzas from 5 pm until late. The *Genoa Restaurant & Ice Cream Parlour* on Dublin St also has pizzas, steaks and good ice cream. The *Coffee Shop Restaurant & Deli* on Church Square has burgers and chips. *Andy's Lounge & Restaurant*, in Market Square across from the tourist office, is one of the better places in town for food or a quiet drink.

Entertainment
Some of the best pubs are on Dublin St, including *McGinn's* and *McKenna's*, and on the Old Cross Square there is *McConnon's Olde Cross Inn*. One of the most popular pubs in town is *Terry's* on Park St. McKenna's have music the odd night. *Jimmy's* on Mill St across from the post office is a quieter locals place.

There is a new three-screen cinema at the Diamond.

Getting There & Away
The Bus Éireann bus station (☎ 047-82377) is on the road to Northern Ireland beside the disused railway station. There are numerous services to Dublin, Letterkenny, Armagh, Belfast, Derry and Portrush. There are also local services to the nearby towns of Ballybay, Castleblayney and Carrickmacross.

McConnon's (☎ 047-82020) private bus company has two daily buses to Dublin serving Carrickmacross and Castleblayney en route, and one daily bus to Clones.

Getting Around
Clerkin's Cycles (☎ 047-81434) on Park St down from the tourist office rent out bikes.

ROSSMORE FOREST PARK
The park, three km (two miles) south-west of Monaghan on the Newbliss road, was originally the home of the Rossmores, but only the buttresses to their castle walls and the entrance stairway remain. Besides forest walks and picnic areas, the park has Californian sequoias, some of the tallest trees in Ireland. Other items include the Rossmores' pet cemetery as well as Iron Age wedge and court tombs. A gold collar or 'lunula' from 1800 BC was found here in the 1930s and removed to the National Museum in Dublin. Admission to the park is free for pedestrians and IR£1 if you bring a car.

GLASLOUGH
Glaslough, nine km (six miles) north-east of Monaghan Town, is a neat little village of cut-stone cottages set beside its namesake, Glaslough (Green Lake), so called because of its curious green colour.

Just outside the village is the 500-hectare demesne of **Castle Leslie** (☎ 047-88109) a magnificent 19th-century Italianate mansion recently opened to the public. Its attractions include a toilet used by Mick Jagger. Greystones Equestrian Centre (☎ 047-88100) have some fine hacks in the demesne.

The castle and gardens are open June to September, 11 am to 8 pm Tuesday to Sunday, and admission is IR£2. They have excellent tearooms in the conservatory, serving hot scones with cream, and plenty of calorific desserts.

CLONES
The border town of Clones, 19 km (12 miles) west of Monaghan, was the site of an important 6th-century monastery which later became an Augustinian abbey. Besides the scant remains of the abbey on Abbey St there is a truncated round tower in the old cemetery south of town and a fine high cross in the town centre.

What is left of the round tower is just 22 metres high and the layout suggests it may be an early example from the 9th century. The Protestant St Tiernach's Church looks out over the square.

In a region renowned for lace, **Clones Lace Gallery** (☎ 047-51051) at the Diamond has a lace collection and teashop. They also run courses in making lace and are open 10 am to 6 pm Tuesday to Saturday. Admission is free.

Places to Stay & Eat

Glynch House (☎ 047-54045) is in Newbliss about seven km (four miles) east of Clones, with six rooms at IR£17/28 for singles/doubles.

Creighton's Hotel (☎ 047-51284) is on Fermanagh St and is popular with anglers. They have 18 simple but comfortable rooms with bathroom at a reasonable IR£15 to IR£18 B&B. This is also a nice place for a snack or lunch. The *Lennard Arms Hotel* (☎ 047-51075), on the Diamond, has 10 rooms with B&B for IR£15 or IR£17 with own bathroom.

For a real treat, *Hilton Park* (☎ 047-56007, fax-56033) is an ideal place to forget the 20th century and blow any spare cash that is weighing you down. Five km (three miles) along the L46 to Scotshouse, this country house has its own estate and serves top-class food in regal surroundings. Many of the ingredients are grown on the estate's organic farm (☎ 047-51023). B&B in splendid rooms is IR£55 and dinner for residents only is IR£19 or more per person.

Getting There & Away

Bus Éireann (☎ 047-82377) has buses from Clones through Monaghan Town and on to Dublin. Ulsterbus (☎ (08) 0365-322633) has a number of daily buses on a route which takes in Monaghan Town, Clones and Enniskillen. McConnon's (☎ 047-82020) has a daily bus between Clones, Monaghan, Carrickmacross and Dublin.

AROUND CLONES

The Ulster Way in Northern Ireland runs through **Newtownbutler**, eight km (five miles) to the north-west of Clones. Just eight km (five miles) away in Fermanagh, north of Newtownbutler, there is a **scenic drive** from Derrawilt to Lisnaskea. South of Clones, the road from Newbliss to Cootehill is quite pretty and takes you to the edge of **Bellamont Forest** which straddles the border with Cavan.

CARRICKMACROSS

An extensive hand-made lace industry helped the early English and Scottish planters develop this pleasant little town. It consists of one wide street boasting some good Georgian houses and an old Protestant church. There used to be a castle on the site of the St Louis Convent, founded by the Earl of Essex, a favourite of Queen Elizabeth I.

The local lace cooperative (☎ 042-62085/62506) runs the remaining small-scale lace industry. They have a display with some of their handiwork for sale in an old toll house on the main street.

Getting There & Away

There are up to eight buses a day to Dublin passing through Carrickmacross, at least three on a Letterkenny to Dublin route, two on a Coleraine to Dublin route and one going between Clones and Dublin. Collins (☎ 042-61631) private bus company has four buses a day to Dublin, three on Sundays. McConnon's (☎ 047-82020) private bus service includes Carrickmacross on its Dublin to Monaghan and Clones route, which also passes through Castleblayney and has two daily buses Monday to Saturday.

The bus stop in Carrickmacross is outside O'Hanlon's shop on Main St.

AROUND CARRICKMACROSS

There's fishing in Loughs Capragh, Spring and Monalty, and in Lough Fea which also has an adjacent mansion and demesne with oak parkland. Five km (three miles) along the Kingscourt road is **Dun a Rí Forest Park** with trails and picnic spots.

Mannan Castle is an enormous and heavily overgrown motte and bailey, five km (three miles) north-west of Carrickmacross in Donaghmoyne. This fortified Norman mound has fragments of a stone castle dating from the 12th century. Both structures were built by the Pipard family, who were given an estate here in 1186 by England's King John.

The village of **Inniskeen**, birthplace of the poet Patrick Kavanagh (1905-67), is 10 km (six miles) north-east of Carrickmacross. Kavanagh is buried in the local graveyard where his cross reads 'And pray for him who walked apart on the hills loving life's miracles'.

In the plain chapel the small local museum is partly in his honour while nearby the forlorn skeletal ruin of a round tower is all that is left of a 6th-century monastery. The museum is only open May to September, 3 to 6 pm on Sunday afternoons.

CASTLEBLAYNEY

Castleblayney is nicely situated near Lough Muckno, Monaghan's most expansive and most scenic lake. This small town takes its name from Sir Edward Blayney and his family who built their castle by the lake in 1622 and who were responsible for the construction of the plain Georgian courthouse, Church of Ireland church and the former Catholic church, an uncommon gesture by a landowner at the time.

Blayney's Castle was sold in the last century to the Hope family and became Hope Castle. In the demesne is the **Lough Muckno Leisure Park** (☎ 042-46356), which has lakeshore and woodland trails as well as golf, cycling and watersports.

Getting There & Away

Castleblayney is on the main Monaghan Town to Dublin route, with up to eight buses daily in each direction. McConnon's (☎ 047-82020) private bus service also has a number of daily buses from Clones and Monaghan through Castleblayney and on to Dublin.

County Roscommon

County Roscommon is more a transit route than a destination in itself, but apart from the lacklustre county town there are places well worth visiting. Strokestown has one of the more interestingly presented mansions in the country as well as a new and unique Famine Museum. Just south of the Sligo boundary, Boyle is also worth a stop.

STROKESTOWN

An unnecessarily wide avenue leads to the arched entrance to Strokestown Park House, built in the 1730s for Thomas Mahon, whose ancestors were granted a 12,000-hectare (30,000-acre) estate by Charles II after the Restoration. The architect was Richard Castle who introduced the Palladian style into Ireland gratifying the desire of the Anglo-Irish gentry for impressive family homes.

Even children will enjoy the tour, which takes in a schoolroom and a child's bedroom, complete with 19th-century toys and funny mirrors.

The fascinating famine period material will soon be moved to the separate **Famine Museum** in the old stables. When the potato crop failed in the 1840s, Major Denis Mahon and his land agent simply evicted the hundreds of starving peasants who could no longer contribute to the estate's coffers and chartered ships to transport them away from Ireland. These overcrowded 'coffin ships' which carried immigrants to America resulted in more suffering and deaths. In 1847 Major Mahon was shot dead just outside the town and one of the documents on display is a newspaper account of how Patrick Hasty and Owen Beirne committed the deed. Their signed confession looks as dubious as the ones which convicted the Birmingham Six of terrorist outrages in Britain in the 1970s.

By 1979, when the family sold up, the estate had dwindled to 120 hectares. *Woodbrook* (see the Books section in the Facts for the Visitor chapter) is the perfect book to read after a visit and is available here. The house (☎ 078-33013) is open from June to mid-September, 12 noon to 5 pm Tuesday to Sunday; a IR£5 lunch is available. The 45-minute tour provides a fascinating glimpse into the whole Anglo-Irish ascendancy and costs IR£2 (children IR£1). The

Famine Museum will have a separate charge of IR£2.50 (children IR£1.75 children) and there are also plans to open a restaurant.

Places to Stay
Mrs Cox (☎ 078-33047) is four km (2.5 miles) out of town with singles/doubles from IR£14/28.

Getting There & Away
If travelling by car, from Roscommon Town or Sligo turn off the N61 at the village of Tulsk to get to Strokestown. The express bus from Roscommon Town to Boyle stops in Strokestown.

BOYLE
Boyle has the fine Boyle Abbey, an impressive dolmen just outside the town and the Lough Key Forest Park.

Information
The tourist office (☎ 079-62145) is open 10 am to 5.30 pm from late May to late September and is located in King House in Military Rd. The friendly tourist officer (☎ 079-62249) may be contacted outside office hours if necessary. There's an arts festival in late July or early August.

Boyle Abbey
Beside the N4, just to the east of Boyle, is one of the finer Cistercian abbeys in Ireland, with remains dating back to its 12th-century foundation by the austere monks from Mellifont in County Louth. In 1659 forces occupied the abbey and turned it into a castle, as shown by the dog kennel built into the left side of the gatehouse entrance. Originally this western side of the abbey was set aside for the monks' sleeping quarters.

The interesting 13th-century nave, in the northern part of the abbey, has Gothic arches on one side which are narrower than the Romanesque arches on the other. The capitals are also distinctively different. On the southern side of the abbey, once the refectory area, there is a fine 16th-century stone chimney built after the monks left and the abbey became a fortified home. Edward

King, whose death by drowning in 1637 inspired the English poet John Milton to compose *Lycidas*, is buried here.

The abbey is open 10 am to 6 pm from June to September, entry is IR£1 (children 30p, family IR£2) and there is a useful brochure for 20p. It is possible to view the abbey at other times by asking for the keys from the neighbouring guesthouse.

Drumanone Dolmen
The superb Drumanone Dolmen measures 4.5 by 3.3 metres. To get there take Patrick St west out of town for two km (one mile), bear left at the junction sign for Lough Gara for another km, passing under a railway arch. A brown sign indicates the path across the railway line.

Lough Key Forest Park
This 320-hectare park was part of the Rockingham estate until it was sold to the Land Commission in 1957. Rockingham House was destroyed by a fire in the same year; all that remains are some stables and other outbuildings. The inexpensive café is open 12.30 to 6 pm and in summer there is a restaurant for lunch and dinner. Lough Key, the northern limit for cruising on the Shannon, has 70-seater waterbuses doing a 45-minute tour for IR£3 (children IR£1.50, family IR£7), and rowing boats at a pricey IR£5 an hour. Entry, from the N4 just south of Boyle, costs IR£1.

Walking Tours
Walking tours on Monday and Thursdays in summer cost IR£2 and take in the Courthouse where Count Plunkett, the first Sinn Féin MP, was elected in a 1917 by-election. There are also archaeological trips (IR£6) on Tuesday and Friday and a ramble up the Curlieu Mountains (IR£3.50) on Wednesday and Saturday. Contact Betty Meyler (☎ 079-62844). The tours start from the Moylurg Inn on the Crescent at 2 pm.

Places to Stay
Camping The *Lough Key Forest Caravan Park* (☎ 079-62212) is in the Forest Park, so

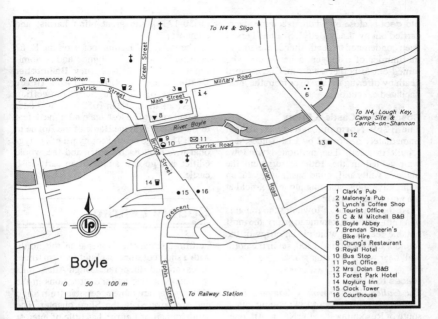

Boyle

0   50   100 m

1 Clark's Pub
2 Maloney's Pub
3 Lynch's Coffee Shop
4 Tourist Office
5 C & M Mitchell B&B
6 Boyle Abbey
7 Brendan Sheerin's
  Bike Hire
8 Chung's Restaurant
9 Royal Hotel
10 Bus Stop
11 Post Office
12 Mrs Dolan B&B
13 Forest Park Hotel
14 Moylurg Inn
15 Clock Tower
16 Courthouse

indicate your intention to camp to avoid the IR£1 entrance charge. Camping costs IR£6.25 for a site or IR£2 per hiker or cyclist.

B&Bs *Mrs Dolan* (☎ 079-62538) on the N4 just outside the town and opposite the Forest Park hotel, and *Mrs Kelly* (☎ 079-62227) three km further south on the N4 both offer B&B. *Lynch's Coffee Shop* is right in town and *C & M Mitchell* (☎ 079-62385) is next to the abbey.

Hotels The *Royal Hotel* (☎ 079-62016) in town, and the *Forest Park* (☎ 079-62229), just outside on the N4, have singles/doubles from IR£32.50/55 and IR£27.50/50 respectively.

Places to Eat
The *Royal* and *Forest Park* hotels do lunch and dinner, while *Lynch's* in Main St does coffee and snacks. Farther along in Patrick St reasonable pub food is available at

Maloney's. Overlooking the river, *Chung's* is a new Chinese restaurant open from 6 pm daily and on Friday for lunch also.

Entertainment
The *Railway Bar* near the station, *Clark's* in Patrick St and the *Moylurg Inn* near the clock tower have music.

Getting There & Away
From Boyle a train goes to Sligo and Dublin via Mullingar. The bus stop is outside the Royal Hotel on Bridge St and there is a regular service to Sligo and Dublin.

Getting Around
Bikes may be hired at Brendan Sheerin's (☎ 079-62010) in Main St.

ROSCOMMON TOWN
Apart from the remains of Roscommon Castle and Priory the town square's Bank of Ireland used to be the old courthouse and the

old gaol is close by where executions were carried out by 'Lady Betty'. She had herself been condemned to death after confessing to the murder of a lodger in her house who turned out to be her own son. She escaped death by offering to take over from the incapacitated executioner.

Roscommon Castle & Priory
The 1269 Norman castle was almost immediately destroyed by Irish forces, and rebuilt in 1280. The mullioned windows were added in the 16th century and the massive walls and round bastions give it an impressive look, standing alone in a field at the north end of town.

At the other end of town are the remains of a 13th-century Dominican priory, the most notable feature of which is an effigy of the founder carved around 1300, set in the north wall near where the altar stood.

Places to Stay
The *Gailey Bay Caravan & Camping Park* (☎ 0903-61058) is about 13 km (eight miles) south of Roscommon on the N61 to Athlone; a sign points left just after the railway and it's a couple of km up the road. A tent is IR£4 plus IR£1 per person; IR£3 for a hiker or cyclist.

The *Royal Hotel* (☎ 0903-26317) in Castle St has doubles for IR£46 and is also the best place for a meal. On the Galway road are B&Bs like *Mrs Campbell's* (☎ 0903-26927) with singles/doubles for IR£12/22 and *Mrs O'Grady's* (☎ 0903-26048) from IR£15/24.

Getting There & Away
Roscommon Town is served by the Dublin-Westport-Ballina railway line. Express buses also stop in the town.

AROUND ROSCOMMON TOWN
To the west of Castlerea, the late 19th-century **Clonalis House** is open to the public during June to September from 11 am to 5.30 pm (2 to 6 pm Sunday) for IR£1.75. The house is rather cold and lacks atmosphere but it does have the harp of Turlough O'Carolan

(1630-1738), the great blind harpist and composer.

The village of Ballintober is on the R367 between Tulsk and Ballymoe and is dominated by the 14th-century **Ballintober Castle**, once the home of the fierce O'Conors of Connaught. Cromwellian forces took the castle in 1652 but it was later restored, only to be lost again after the defeat of the Catholics at the Battle of the Boyne in 1690. The large central courtyard has polygonal towers at each corner and the whole edifice is a good example of an early Irish castle.

County Leitrim

Leitrim stretches to Donegal in the north, with a short coastline of about five km (three miles) around Bundoran. Lough Allen splits the county in two and the attractions in the northern part are more accessible from Sligo and are covered in the Sligo chapter. The southern part of Leitrim has little of interest apart from its lush scenery, and while a cycle tour of the area would be enjoyable most visitors just speed through on their way north.

CARRICK-ON-SHANNON
The main town in the county marks the upper limit of navigation on the river and apart from boating trips there is little to keep the visitor here.

Information
The tourist office (☎ 078-20170) is by the river and is open from May to September, as late as 8 pm in July and August. During the rest of the year tourist information (☎ 078-20857) is available from an office in the old town hall. A signposted walking tour takes in all the buildings and places of local interest.

Costello Chapel
At the top of Bridge St, next to Flynn's bar, is the spooky little Costello Chapel. It mea-

sures only five by 3.6 metres (16 by 12 feet) and was built in 1877 by the distraught Edward Costello after the death of his wife. She is buried on the left side under a heavy slab of glass and her husband was interred on the other side in 1891. Further intimations of mortality come from the fact that the chapel was built on the site of the old courthouse where 19 men were hung in the 19th century.

Boating

Michael Lynch (☎ 078-20034), based across the bridge by the tourist office, has rowing boats for hire at IR£5 an hour, or at IR£7 with a motor. Barges for hire are available through Shannon Barge Lines (☎ 078-20520) while Tara Cruisers (☎ 078-20736), based at the Rosebank Marina on the Dublin road, have more up-market launches. Tom Maher (☎ 078-21124) does river cruises for IR£8 a half-hour or IR£15 an hour.

Places to Stay

The *Town Clock Hostel* (☎ 078-20068), in the town centre at the junction of Main St and Bridge St, is open July to September. Camping is free on the river bank, reached by crossing the bridge near the tourist office. Tokens for the showers at the nearby marina can be purchased from the marina office.

On Station Rd, near the railway station, *Villa Flora* (☎ 078-20338) and *Ariadna* (☎ 078-20205) are both IR£13 per person. The *County Hotel* (☎ 078-20550) has singles/doubles for IR£16/30.

Places to Eat

Opposite the tourist office, *Coffey's* is a busy self-service place. Next door *Cryan's* pub does a IR£3 lunch, while a few doors up there is a pizza takeaway. On Bridge St *Mariner's Reach* has lunch specials for IR£3 to IR£5. The set dinner at IR£8.50 is good value but even better is the three-course bar special until 10 pm for IR£5.50. Just past Gegarty's bike shop on Main St the *Coffee Spot* is another inexpensive place for coffee and light meals.

Getting There & Away

The railway station (☎ 078-20036) is a 15-minute walk from across the bridge near the tourist office. Turn left over the bridge, passing a supermarket on the left.

The bus stop is outside Coffey's self-service restaurant on the corner opposite the tourist office and the main Dublin-Sligo express bus stops here daily. There are buses to Limerick, Cork, Waterford, Galway, Belfast and Derry. Carew's (☎ 071-68138) private bus from Sligo to Dublin stops in Carrick.

Getting Around

Bikes can be hired from Gegarty's (☎ 078-21316) on Main St who also rent out rods and tackle on a daily or weekly basis. The visitor's guidebook from the tourist office includes details of suggested cycling tours.

AROUND CARRICK-on-SHANNON
Turlough O'Carolan

There are two places to visit in Leitrim connected with the famous blind harpist, Turlough O'Carolan (1670-1738). He spent most of his time in Mohill where his patron was based and a sculpture on the main street of the town commemorates the association. To reach Mohill follow the N4 to Dublin and turn left shortly after Drumsna.

O'Carolan is buried in Kilronan church which preserves a 12th-century doorway. To reach the church leave Leitrim by the R280 going north and at the small village of Leitrim turn left on the R284 to Keadue. In Keadue turn left on the R284 to Sligo.

Lough Rynn Estate

Lough Rynn was the home of the Clements family, the earls of Leitrim; and the various buildings put up during the time of the third earl are now open to the public. There's a picnic site, restaurant, and guided tours of the principal buildings. The estate is open May to mid-September from 10 am to 7 pm. Admission to the grounds is IR£3.50 per car, IR£1 per person and the tour is another IR£1 (children 50p).

Drumshanbo

Drumshanbo is mainly a centre for anglers. The visitors' centre has an interesting audio-visual display on the history and culture of the locality, and a non-functioning replica of an ancient Irish sauna. It's open 10 am to 6 pm and costs IR£1 (children 50p).

Mrs Mooney (☎ 078-41013) at 2 Carrick Rd, on the left if entering the town from Carrick, does B&B for IR£22, and provides tourist information.

County Longford

The fishing around Lough Ree and Lanesborough is the main attraction in County Longford. Longford Town is solidly agrarian and very prosperous, to judge by the number of restaurants and hotels, but of little interest to the tourist; you may pass through if you're travelling between Dublin and Mayo or Sligo.

LANESBOROUGH

Also spelt Lanesboro, the town is the site of one of Ireland's first turf-fired generating stations, close to the banks of the Shannon. The station provides a flow of warm water into a channel and when the mayfly appear in May, and later in August and September, this stretch of water becomes prime anglers' territory. Bream and tench are caught early in the morning and at night, while roach are available throughout the day. The water is only just over a metre deep. This is not the only place to fish and enquiries should be made at the Price Wyse tackle shop in the middle of Lanesborough. Boats can be hired from Mark Shields (☎ 043-21510) in Main St.

Places to Stay

The only hotel is the *Sliabh Bán* (☎ 043-21790), also known as the Anchor, with doubles at IR£28. B&B is available at *Dunamase House* (☎ 043-21201), for IR£18/26 singles/doubles, or *Shannon Edge* (☎ 043-21642) by the water's edge. *Marion Herraty* (☎ 043-21651) is a little out of town but boats are made freely available.

Lakebreeze Cottage (☎ 043-25203) is 10 km (six miles) from Lanesborough but sleeps parties of up to eight and a boat is also

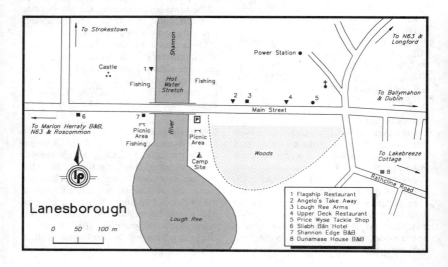

1 Flagship Restaurant
2 Angelo's Take Away
3 Lough Ree Arms
4 Upper Deck Restaurant
5 Price Wyse Tackle Shop
6 Sliabh Bán Hotel
7 Shannon Edge B&B
8 Dunamase House B&B

available free of charge. Self-catering accommodation is available through the *Lough Ree Arms* pub (☎ 043-21145).

Places to Eat

Angelo's Take Away and the *Upper Deck Restaurant* are both on Main St. The *Flagship Restaurant*, near the ruins of the old castle, is a good place, open from 7 am to 10 pm. Lunch is under IR£5 and evening meals start at IR£6.

Getting There & Away

Lanesborough is on the N63, halfway between Longford and Roscommon. The nearest bus and railway stations are at these two towns. Coming from Athlone take the N55 to Longford and turn left at Ballymahon.

County Westmeath

Characterised by lakes and rich pasture land, the county of Westmeath is more noteworthy for its beef than its scenic splendour or historic sites. An exception to the lacklustre landscape is an area north of Athlone, known as Goldsmith Country, while the places of genuine interest in Westmeath – and there are some – are mostly in the vicinity of Mullingar.

MULLINGAR

Mullingar is a prosperous marketing town, with a commuter train service each morning to Dublin, and much of the surrounding area is rather like the rich countryside of England. There are some fine fishing loughs in the vicinity and a preserved bog that delights naturalists. The town itself is one of the few places outside the capital that James Joyce visited. There are also three private museums, each with their own low-key appeal, and Mullingar makes a good base for some interesting local excursions.

The Royal Canal, linking Dublin with the Shannon via Mullingar, was constructed in the 1790s as a rival to the Grand Canal. It never managed to compete successfully with its rival, and by the 1880s passenger business had ceased. There was a slight revival during WW II with a turf trade to Dublin but it finally closed in 1955. Plans to build a motorway to Dublin over the canal course have now been shelved and restoration work west of Mullingar is in progress.

Information

The tourist office (☎ 044-48761) is on the Dublin road on the outskirts of town. It's open June to September 9 am to 1 pm and 2 to 6 pm weekdays, opening at 10 am Saturday. The rest of the year it is open from 9.30 am to 1 pm and 2 to 5.30 pm.

Cathedral & Ecclesiastical Museum

The cathedral was built just before WW II and has large mosaics of St Anne and St Patrick by the Russian artist Boris Arrep. There is a small museum over the sacristy, entered from the side of the church, which has vestments worn by St Oliver Plunkett

---

The Joyce Connection

James Joyce came to Mullingar in his late teens in 1900 and 1901 to visit his father, who had been sent to the town to compile a new electoral register. John Joyce worked in the Courthouse, which is still standing in Mount St, and the Joyces stayed at Levington Park House near Lough Owel.

Parts of *Stephen Hero*, an early novel that would later become *A Portrait of the Artist as a Young Man*, are set in Mullingar. The Greville Arms Hotel is mentioned, as are the Westmeath Examiner Office, the Royal Canal and the Military Barracks (where the military museum is situated). In the lobby of the Greville Arms there is a wax model of Joyce.

In *Ulysses*, Leopold Bloom's daughter is working in Mullingar, employed in a photographer's shop. This is now Fagan's post office and newsagents on Pearse St near the junction with Castle St, but at the time of Joyce's visits it was owned by a photographer, Phil Shaw. Mullingar also makes brief appearances in *Finnegans Wake*. ∎

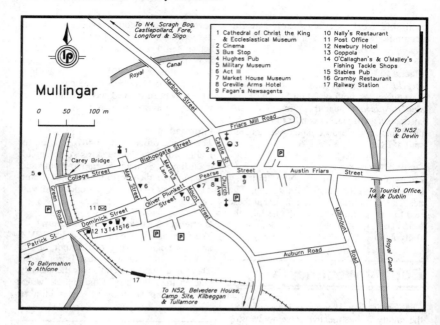

Mullingar

0   50   100 m

To N4, Scragh Bog,
Castlepollard, Fore,
Longford & Sligo

1 Cathedral of Christ the King
   & Ecclesiastical Museum
2 Cinema
3 Bus Stop
4 Hughes Pub
5 Military Museum
6 Act III
7 Market House Museum
8 Greville Arms Hotel
9 Fagan's Newsagents
10 Nally's Restaurant
11 Post Office
12 Newbury Hotel
13 Goppola
14 O'Callaghan's & O'Malley's
   Fishing Tackle Shops
15 Stables Pub
16 Gramby Restaurant
17 Railway Station

(see Drogheda in the Meath & Louth chapter for the whereabouts of his head).

A guided tour operates at 3 pm on Thursday, Saturday and Sunday. Otherwise call at the church house to the right of the cathedral inside the gates or phone ☎ 044-48338.

Military Museum

The Military Museum is reached by taking College St past the cathedral, crossing the canal by the small Carey Bridge and walking across the road to a spire. The military barracks was built by the British in 1813 and the museum is just inside the main entrance on the right, in what were once the punishment cells. The museum is free, and home to a delightful miscellany of artefacts including army chamber pots and a weighing chair for recruits.

Market Hall Museum

The Market Hall museum on Pearse St has an even odder collection including axe-

heads, fossils, a German army helmet, a rubber bullet from the North, a shillelagh, a stone hot water bottle and a grand butter churn. It's open from the last week in June to the end of August, from 2 to 5.30 pm. Entry is 50p (children 20p).

Places to Stay

Camping at the *Lough Ennell Holiday Village* (☎ 044-48101), south of town on the road to Tullamore, costs IR£3.50 per person and it can get busy on sunny weekends. Most of the B&Bs are on the approach roads from Dublin and Sligo; *Mrs McCarthy's* (☎ 044-40905) and *Mrs Healy's* (☎ 044-48905) are both on the Dublin road. The *Greville Arms* (☎ 044-48563) on Pearse St has singles/doubles from IR£30/50, or there's the cheaper *Newbury* (☎ 044-42888) on Dominick St from IR£15/36.

Places to Eat

Both *Nally's* on Oliver Plunkett St and the

more expensive *Gramby Restaurant* on Dominick St have 'tourist menus'. The bar food in the *Greville Arms* on Pearse St is good and they have a *James Joyce Restaurant* with dinner for IR£16. *Act III* in Mary St is a quiet place for coffee and *Goppola* offers takeaways next to the Newbury Hotel.

At the highly regarded *Crookedwood House* (☎ 044-72165), at Crookedwood near the lower end of Lough Derravaragh, lunch is about IR£11, dinner IR£17 and vegetarian meals are available.

Entertainment

Traditional Irish music takes place Wednesday and Thursday at *Hughes'* pub on the corner of Castle and Pearse Sts. The *Stables* in Dominick St attracts blues bands. A visitors' fee of IR£3 opens the doors of the *Squash & Leisure Club* (☎ 044-40949) which offers squash, sauna, snooker and indoor bowls. Swimming is possible in Loughs Lene, Ennel and Owel, but Derravaragh is very deep and has no shallows.

The Mullingar Festival is usually held in the second week of July. It is a low-key affair, the highlight of which is the election of the Queen and the Bachelor of the Festival. Later in the month there is a two-day Agricultural Show

Getting There & Away

The main Dublin to Sligo line runs through town and all the trains stop at Mullingar (☎ 044-48274). There are four trains Monday to Saturday, two on Sunday.

Bus Éireann runs buses daily from Galway to Dundalk, from Westport to Dublin, from Dublin to Ballina and Dublin to Sligo – all stopping at Mullingar. They depart and arrive from opposite the cinema in Castle St but the stop may move to near the railway station.

Getting Around

Bicycles can be rented from Declan & Bernadette Fagan (☎ 0506-35118) in nearby Horseleap.

AROUND MULLINGAR

Belvedere House & Gardens

Belvedere was the scene of a tale which finds its way into Joyce's *Ulysses*. The house was built around 1740 for the recently remarried first Lord Belvedere. He soon accused his young wife of adultery with his younger brother Arthur, and imprisoned her here. She remained under house arrest for 31 years. When Lord Belvedere's death finally released her she was still dressed in the fashion of 30 years earlier. She died still protesting her innocence. Lord Belvedere also sued his brother and had him jailed in London for the rest of his life.

Not far from the house the 'ruined' Jealous Wall was deliberately built that way to block a view of the neighbouring house of a second brother, with whom the lord also fell out. Belvedere House and Gardens is several km south of town on the N52 to Tullamore, just before the camp site. The house itself is closed; entrance to the gardens is IR£1.

Locke's Distillery

South of Mullingar on the road to Tullamore beyond Belvedere House, Locke's distillery (☎ 0506-32134) in the small town of Kilbeggan still has a working mill wheel. Open from 9 am (10 am on Sunday) to 6 pm daily the IR£2 tour (IR£1 children and students) concludes with the customary glass of malt beer. Lunch and snacks are served at the adjoining coffee shop.

Moate Museum

This is a small folk museum with displays of 19th-century farm tools, kitchenware and the like. It is open from June to August, 11 am to 1 pm and 2 to 6 pm Monday to Friday and entry is IR£1 (children 25p). Moate village is halfway between Kilbeggan and Athlone on the N6, about 40 km (25 miles) from Mullingar.

Adolphus Cooke the Eccentric

Mullingar was home not only to the paranoiac Lord Belvedere, but also to the bizarre Adolphus Cooke. This character served under Wellington and survived a shipwreck and a desert island before becoming convinced that his grandfather had been reborn as a turkey. Later he sentenced his dog to death for its loose morals, but when the executioner was attacked by the turkey he realised that the dog was probably related to him also and granted it a reprieve. He wanted his library and favourite chair to be buried with him, and his extraordinary grave is tucked away in a fading Protestant churchyard outside of Mullingar. He thought he might be reborn as a bee.

Take the N52 road to Devlin for 12 km (eight miles) until, after passing a small number of houses, you come to a junction with a sign pointing straight on to Kells. Follow this road for another half km and turn into the fancy arched entrance on the left to the Bee Hive Nite Club. Pass the first sheepgate immediately on the right but cross over the second black gate just after it. Follow the side of the field under the trees and the old church is about 200 metres along. The unmistakeable beehive grave is easily found.

Tullynally Castle & Gardens

The family seat of the Pakenham family and the earldom of Longford is another pretend castle. The original fortress was converted into a house in the first half of the 18th century and various additions were made over the next 150 years. The most notable feature is the extensive Gothic facade which is visually impressive despite the crooked TV aerial and satellite dish. The laundry is wonderfully preserved and there are many workaday items worth examining.

The house is open from mid-July to mid-August with the first tour beginning at 2.30 pm. The charge is IR£3 (IR£1.50 children) and this includes admission to the gardens which are open separately from June to September from 10 am to 6 pm for IR£1 (10p children). It might be worth telephoning (☎ 044-61159) at other times in the possibility of going round with a coach tour. Follow the N4 out of town for Longford and Sligo and the road shortly bears off to the right for

Castlepollard. From there it is clearly signposted.

Scragh Bog

Scragh Bog is home to the rare wintergreen, *Pyrola rotundifolia*, which flowers around willow and beech trees in midsummer. Other, less rare plants are members of the sedge family, orchids and sphagnum species, and there is a profusion of insects. This small bog is seven km (four miles) out of town on the N4 road to Sligo. The Wildlife Service does not recommend unaccompanied visits and waterproof boots are a necessity.

Fishing

Trout fishing is popular in loughs around Mullingar, including Lough Owel, Lough Derravaragh, Lough Glore, White Lake, Lough Lene, Lough Sheelin, Mt Dalton Lake, Pallas Lake and Lough Ennell – where in 1926 a 26-lb trout was landed, still the largest trout ever caught in Ireland. The fishing season is March or May (depending on the lake) to mid-October, and all the lakes except Lough Lene are controlled by the Shannon Regional Fisheries Board, details from Limerick (☎ 061-55171) or Mullingar (☎ 044-48769). For further information contact the tourist office, O'Callaghan's or O'Malley's on Dominick St or Sam's Tackle Shop on Castle St. Sam's can provide boats on Lough Owel or Lough Ennell, ghillies and permits. For Lough Deravarragh contact Mr Newman (☎ 044-71111), for Lough Owel Mrs Doolan (☎ 044-42085) and for Lough Ennell Mrs Hope (☎ 044-40807).

FORE

Just outside the small village of Fore lies a group of early Christian sites that date back to 630 AD when St Fetchin founded a monastery. There are no visible remains of this early settlement, but there are three later buildings still standing in the valley plain, and they are closely associated with a legend that Seven Wonders occurred here.

The Seven Wonders

The oldest of the three buildings is **St**

Fetchin's Church, which may well mark the original monastery. The chancel and baptismal font inside are early 13th century, and over the unusually large entrance there is a huge lintel stone carved with a Greek cross. It was supposed to have been placed through the divine power of St Fetchin's prayers and as such it makes up one of the Seven Wonders of Fore.

A path runs up from the church to the attractive little **Anchorite Cell**, which dates back to the 15th century and is another of the Seven Wonders. The Seven Wonders pub in the village keeps the key to the Cell.

Down on the plain, on the other side of the road, there are extensive remains of a 13th-century **Benedictine priory**, built on what was once bog (another wonder). In the next century it was turned into a fortification; hence the castle-like square towers, each of which formed a separate residence, and loophole windows. The west tower is in a dangerous state – keep clear.

Two other wonders are a mill without a stream and water that flows uphill. The mill site is marked and legend has it that St Fetchin caused water to flow uphill, towards the mill, by throwing his crozier against a rock near Lough Lene, a mile away.

The final two wonders, incidentally, are water that will not boil and a tree which will not burn. Both are associated with St Fetchin's well which is passed on the way to the friary from the road.

Take the N4 for Longford and Sligo out of Mullingar, and at the hospital there is a turning right signposted for Castlepollard. At Castlepollard the road east to Fore is signposted.

AROUND FORE

A trip to Fore could take in two other ecclesiastic sights. On the way to Castlepollard on the N4 a turning right is signposted for **Multyfarnham Franciscan Friary**. In the present church parts of a 15th-century church remain and there are outdoor Stations of the Cross set beside a stream.

On the way back from Fore a left turn at Crookedwood leads up a small road to **St Munna's Church**. It dates from the 15th century, replacing an earlier 7th-century church founded by St Munna. This fortified church has a lovely location and there is a grotesque figure over the north window. Keys to the church are available from the nearby bungalow.

ATHLONE

Despite its historic importance, due mainly to its strategic position on the Shannon opening the way to the west, the county town of Athlone is a fairly drab place; there's more life and interest in Mullingar. You can visit the castle in Athlone and boat trips along the Shannon are worth considering, but there are few other reasons to stay here long except the fishing.

Orientation & Information

The obvious landmark in the town is the castle, prominently located by the river and bridge. The castle contains the tourist office and museum. Cars can be parked behind the castle down by the river without the usual parking discs.

The tourist office (☎ 0902-94630) is open from April to October and is just inside the castle grounds. The office has a Tourist Trail booklet that takes the reader on a three-hour walk, or two 1½-hour walks.

Athlone Castle

The Normans probably had a camp by the ford over the river before they built a castle here in 1210. In 1690 the castle held out for James II but the following year the bridge came under determined Protestant attack and this time the Jacobite city fell to the troops under William of Orange's Dutch commander, Ginkel. The Jacobites retreated to Aughrim and were decisively defeated there by Ginkel. Major alterations took place between the 17th and 19th centuries and the ramp that forms the present entrance is one of these relatively recent additions. The oldest surviving part is the central keep where the museum now is.

Athlone Museum

There are two floors, the upstairs being designated a folk museum, containing a fascinating miscellany of objects. There's an old gramophone which belonged to John McCormack, a native of Athlone and arguably the world's greatest tenor. The gramophone is in working order and there are records of his songs which can be played.

The museum is open from 9.30 to 6 pm, IR£2 (students IR£1.25, children 75p, family IR£5). The price includes a visit to the **interpretative centre** which is an audio-visual presentation of the town's history and flora & fauna.

Fishing

Just below the Church St end of the bridge opposite the castle, the Hooker Tackle Shop is the place to go for information, boats and rods. If the shop is closed ask for Des Dolan in the adjoining pub. A day's hire of boat and guide for mostly pike fishing would cost around IR£50. You can fish for free along the Strand.

River Cruises

Between July and September there is a Wednesday cruise to Clonmacnoise, the ancient monastic site in County Offaly. It costs IR£5 for adults (IR£3.50 children), and departs at 10 am. Every day of the week there are cruises up to Lough Ree, IR£3.50 (IR£2.50 children). The first boat leaves the Strand at 11 am and a timetable is available from the tourist office.

Getting There & Away

From Athlone Station (☎ 0902-72651) there are trains to Westport, Galway (IR£10.50) and Dublin.

Bus Éireann expressway buses also stop at Athlone (☎ 0902-72651) on many routes from the east to the west coast.

Getting Around

Bicycles can be hired from Hardiman's (☎ 0902-78669), opposite the Athlone shopping centre on the road out of town to Dublin.

AROUND ATHLONE

Goldsmith Country

The N55 from Athlone to County Longford runs by the side of Lough Ree and through Goldsmith Country, so called because of the area's associations with the 18th-century poet, playwright and novelist, Oliver Goldsmith.

Cycling Tour

About eight km (five miles) north-west from Athlone is the village of Glasson, and a left turning goes to the Killinure spur on the shore of Lough Ree. The turning is marked by the number eight on the Lough Ree Tourist Trail roadsign (the booklet is available from the tourist office in Athlone) and it is 2.5 km (1.5 miles) to a junction, marked on the road as No 11 on the tourist trail road sign, where another left goes down to a marina at Killinure.

Back at the number 11 junction the road continues for another 2.5 km (1.5 miles) to a junction, No 14 on the tourist trail signs. Turning left leads to Manto's pub by the shore opposite Inchmore Island. Boats can be hired at Manto's. Turning right leads after three km (two miles) to the village of Tubberclair/Tuberclare back on the N55.

Continuing north the road leads into Goldsmith Country proper, with the reminders and remains of:

The never-failing brook, the busy mill,
The decent church that topt the neighbouring hill.

Only the site remains of the schoolhouse where the young Goldsmith and his fellow pupils wondered at the wisdom of their teacher:

And still they gazed, and still the wonder grew
That one small head could carry all he knew.

From the remains of the schoolhouse it's about 15 km (nine miles) back to Athlone on the N55. The whole tour takes a couple of hours.

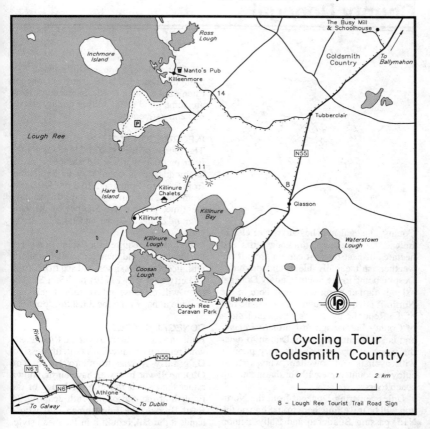

Cycling Tour
Goldsmith Country

0   1   2 km

8 - Lough Ree Tourist Trail Road Sign

Places to Stay

Camping is possible at the *Lough Ree Caravan Park* or at *Manto's* which also does B&B. Self-catering chalets are available at Killinure and at Manto's and enquiries should be made at the tourist office.

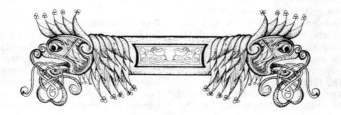

County Donegal

County Donegal matches anywhere else in Ireland for bleakness, dramatic cliffs and hectares of peat bogs; it can be great if the weather isn't equally bleak and dramatic. Despite being in the South, County Donegal extends farther north than anywhere in the North. It is virtually separated from the rest of the Republic by the westward projection of County Fermanagh in Northern Ireland, and is sufficiently far from Dublin to deter the worst of the crowds. It's very popular with cyclists and travellers who want to enjoy the countryside without sharing it with coach tours.

Unless entering Donegal from the North you will be travelling there from Sligo on the N15, passing Bundoran and Ballyshannon on the way to Donegal town.

Donegal Town

The town gets its name from the Vikings, who had a fort here in the 9th century, Dun na nGall being 'the fort of the foreigner'. The town's importance later developed due to its being the main seat of the O'Donnells, the family that controlled this part of Ireland before the 17th century.

Donegal town is principally the jumping off point for the rest of the county, but it's a pleasant and very popular little place. The triangular Diamond is the centre of Donegal, often choked with traffic in summer; there are some good shops selling quality souvenirs and garments.

INFORMATION
The tourist office (☎ 073-21148) is by the river on Ballyshannon Rd and close to the Diamond and is open May to September from 9 am to 1 pm and 2 to 8 pm (10 am to 1 pm and 2 to 6 pm on Sunday). If you have the time, purchase *A Signposted Walking Tour of Donegal Town* and take in all the sights.

Permits are required for fishing in most of the local rivers and these are available, along with licences for salmon and sea trout, from Doherty's (☎ 073-21119) on Main St. The shop will dispense information freely and provide a map of the local fishing spots.

DONEGAL CASTLE
Built on a rocky outcrop over the River Eske, what remains of this castle is still impressive. Originally it was home to Hugh Roe O'Donnell who may well have burnt it down rather than see it fall into the hands of the English at the end of the 16th century. Sir Basil Brooke, the Englishman into whose hands it did fall, rebuilt it in Jacobean style. Notice the floral decoration on the corner turret and the decorated fireplace on the 1st floor. Brooke also built the three-storey manor house adjoining the castle.

The castle is open from June to September and admission is 80p.

THE DIAMOND OBELISK
In 1474 Hugh O'Donnell and his wife Nuala O'Brien founded a Franciscan monastery by the shore in the south of town. It was accidentally blown up in 1601 and very little of it now remains. What makes it famous is that four of its friars chronicled the whole of known Celtic history and mythology from 40

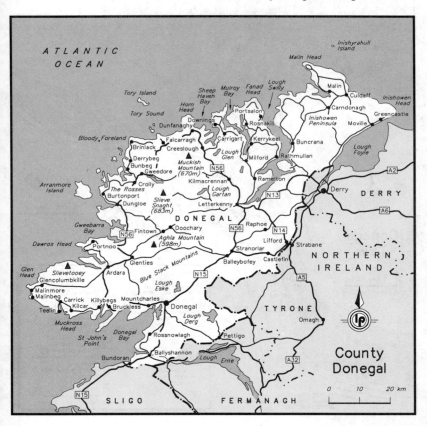

years before the Flood to AD 1618. Known as 'The Annals of the Four Masters' the four researchers and authors were driven by the realisation that the arrival of the English meant the end of Celtic culture.

The obelisk in the Diamond commemorates the prescient Four Masters. The National Library in Dublin displays facsimile pages of their work, which remains an important source for early Irish history.

PLACES TO STAY
Hostels
Peter Feely's (☎ 073-22030) is on the Killybegs Rd just across the river from the centre. He has another place (☎ 073-22805) on the road to Killybegs. The cost is IR£5 in both hostels. For the An Óige *Ball Hill Hostel* (☎ 073-21174) in Ball Hill, keep going in the same direction. It's five km out near the bay, with beds at IR£5.50.

B&Bs
There are plenty of B&Bs within walking distance of the centre. *Drumcliffe House* (☎ 073-21200) on Coast Rd off the Killybegs Rd is a pleasant old place at IR£12. Waterloo Place past the castle has a couple

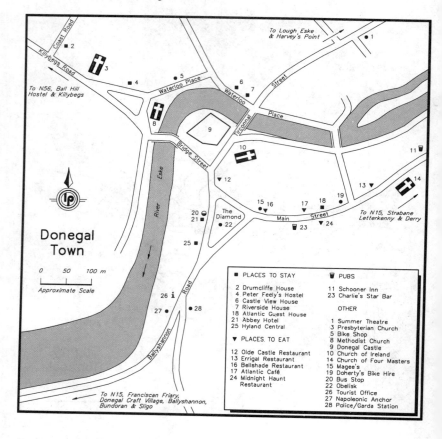

PLACES TO STAY
- 2 Drumcliffe House
- 4 Peter Feely's Hostel
- 6 Castle View House
- 7 Riverside House
- 18 Atlantic Guest House
- 21 Abbey Hotel
- 25 Hyland Central

PLACES TO EAT
- 12 Olde Castle Restaurant
- 13 Errigal Restaurant
- 16 Bellshade Restaurant
- 17 Atlantic Café
- 24 Midnight Haunt Restaurant

PUBS
- 11 Schooner Inn
- 23 Charlie's Star Bar

OTHER
- 1 Summer Theatre
- 3 Presbyterian Church
- 5 Bike Shop
- 8 Methodist Church
- 9 Donegal Castle
- 10 Church of Ireland
- 14 Church of Four Masters
- 15 Magee's
- 19 Doherty's Bike Hire
- 20 Bus Stop
- 22 Obelisk
- 26 Tourist Office
- 27 Napoleonic Anchor
- 28 Police/Garda Station

close by each other: *Riverside House* (☎ 073-21083) and *Castle View House* (☎ 073-22100) both of which have doubles for IR£25; single rooms are available only at Riverside House and cost IR£15. On Main St the *Atlantic Guest House* (☎ 073-21187) has singles/doubles from IR£15/25.

Hotels

The *Abbey Hotel* (☎ 073-21014) and the *Hyland Central* (☎ 073-21027) are both in the Diamond; singles/doubles at the former are from IR£36/62, at the latter from IR£45/70.

For something rural and relaxing try the *Arches Country House* (☎ 073-22029) on the Lough Eske ring road or, more expensive at IR£25 per person, nearby *Ardnamona* (☎ 073-22650), a late 18th-century house with a wonderfully splendid garden. Also overlooking Lough Eske *Harvey's Point Hotel* (☎ 073-22208) has singles/doubles from IR£40/60.

PLACES TO EAT

There are a half dozen places to eat within 100 or so metres of the busy Diamond, quite apart from supermarkets and fast fooderies.

The *Atlantic Café*, the *Abbey Hotel* and the slightly fancier *Olde Castle Restaurant* all feature an absolutely standard menu. The Abbey has a IR£5 menu between 3.30 and 5.30 pm. The Chinese *Midnight Haunt* has surprisingly good Chinese food with main courses at around IR£5 to IR£7.

The *Errigal Restaurant* in Main St does lunch for IR£4 and dinner for IR£6. The *Bellshade Restaurant* on the 2nd floor of Magee's store does a popular lunch for IR£4 which includes vegetarian possibilities but is closed at night.

For something swanky try the Swiss-owned restaurant at *Harvey's Point Country Hotel* (☎ 073-22208), six km (four miles) out of town on the small road to Lough Eske and the Blue Stack Mountains. A nouvelle French dinner is IR£20, reservations and formal attire are expected.

ENTERTAINMENT
Numerous pubs can also be found within a stone's throw of the Diamond. *Charlie's Star Bar* is a bit of a yuppie hangout but often has live music. Also worth checking out for the music is the *Schooner Inn* beyond Main St on the road out to Derry.

The *Summer Theatre* is run by a local theatre group and presents Irish plays in O'Cleary Hall by the junction up past the castle. Posters will be in the shops and tourist office.

THINGS TO BUY
Well worth a browse is Magee's in the Diamond. It has its own garment factory, and its tweed sells by the roll at IR£16 per yard. A mailing service is available. Tweed jackets cost around IR£120, skirts IR£50 and there are lots of Aran sweaters around IR£70. Prices and quality can be compared with the Four Masters store which is almost next door and has two floors of garments and gifts.

Also worth checking out is the Donegal Craft Village, a complex of small art and craft workshops, by the side of the N15 on the way to Bundoran about 1.5 km (one mile) from town. Pottery, crystal, batik, garments and jewellery are all made on the premises

and the automated sculptural pieces from Brian Buckley's shop are fascinating. A coffee shop is open seven days a week.

GETTING THERE & AWAY
There are Bus Éireann connections with Derry, Enniskillen and Belfast in the North, Sligo and Galway to the west and Limerick and Cork in the south. The bus stop is outside the Abbey Hotel and information is available from the hotel shop next to the main entrance. Luggage can be left here, 50p per bag, until 6.30 pm.

Feda O'Donnell (☎ 075-48114) runs a private coach to and from Galway every day, via Bundoran and Sligo. It leaves from the Garda station in Donegal at 9.45 am Monday to Saturday and reaches Galway at 1.15 pm. There are also departures at 4.20 pm on Sunday and at 1.20 and 5.20 pm on Friday. The bus leaves the cathedral in Galway at various times – ring for details (☎ 075-48114 and 091-61656).

It is also worth checking out McGeehan's Coaches (☎ 075-46150) who do a Donegal to Dublin return trip and also depart from outside the Garda station.

GETTING AROUND
The Bike Shop (☎ 073-22515) is a couple of doors from Peter Feely's hostel and rents bicycles for IR£6 a day. There is also Doherty's (☎ 073-21119) on a corner along Main St.

Around Donegal Town

LOUGH DERG
From 1 June to 15 August Lough Derg is alive with pilgrims who leave on boats from Pettigo for three days on a small island in the middle of the lake. Anyone over the age of 14 is welcome, and some 30,000 turn up every year – but be warned: the penitential aspect is taken seriously. Only one meal a day is allowed, it starts with a 24-hour vigil, and everyone is expected to complete the Stations of the Cross in bare feet on the first

day, having fasted from the preceding midnight. Outside the pilgrim season there is no regular boat service to the island.

Places to Stay
There is no need to book accommodation, just turn up at Pettigo and pay in advance for accommodation and the boat fare. In Pettigo *Mrs McVeigh* (☎ 072-61565) on the Donegal Rd and *Mrs McHugh* (☎ 61520) on Lough Derg Rd offer B&B.

Getting There & Away
During the pilgrim season there is a special bus (☎ 01-366111) from Dublin each day as well as bus connections from Sligo and Belfast. The local bus from Sligo stops at Bundoran and Ballyshannon but not Donegal. Cronin's Coaches (☎ 021-509090) in Cork also run a bus. The first boat leaves at 11 am, the last at 3 pm. Further information from the Prior (☎ 072-61518/61550), St Patrick's Purgatory, Lough Derg, Pettigo, County Donegal.

LOUGH ESKE
This is a place for fishing or cycling or walking over the Blue Stack Mountains. If walking consider using the *New Irish Walk Guides: West & North* (Gill & Macmillan), which is available from the bookstores in Donegal's Diamond. It also has an interesting walk around the hills of Lough Derg.

Getting There & Away
Leave Donegal on the N56 to Killybegs and turn right just past the hostel. The ring road eventually joins the N15 to the north-east of Donegal so it makes a convenient cycling trip. If you hire a bike from O'Doherty's in Donegal, they'll give you a photocopied map.

ROSSNOWLAGH
If you want a beach holiday without the amusement arcades then Rossnowlagh is the place to visit. The sandy beach is stunning, extends for nearly five km (three miles) and mostly attracts surfers.

Places to Stay
Camping is available at the *Manor House Caravan & Camping Park* (☎ 072-51477), under the same ownership as the Manor House guesthouse. It costs IR£6.50 to camp per night (IR£3.50 for cyclists), and there's a shop, take away food outlet and restaurant at the camp site.

The *Manor House* (☎ 072-51477) has singles/doubles from IR£16.50/30. *Sand House* (☎ 072-51777) is the beach hotel, charging from IR£35 per person, and the rooms at the front have magnificent sea views.

BALLYSHANNON
This is a busy little town set above the River Erne with a small adjunct of shops and houses south of the river and connected by a bridge. It could be more appealing than Bundoran as a base for exploring the coastline before Donegal. It is also very convenient for trips into the North, and there are regular buses to Belleek and Enniskillen.

Allingham's Grave
The poet William Allingham (1824-89) was born in Ballyshannon and is buried in the graveyard. Take the first left up Main St after the Dorrians Imperial Hotel. The tombstone is on the left side of the churchyard.

Donegal Parian China Visitor Centre
Parian china is lighter and more translucent than bone china. All the pieces available are on display in the centre, which is by the side of the N15 on the way to Bundoran. Prices range from around IR£10 for small pieces to IR£180 for a full tea set. Parian china is also sold at Belleek, just across the border in Fermanagh. Free guided tours, a tea room, a bureau de change and mail order service are all laid on here.

Places to Stay
Duffy's Hostel (☎ 072-51535) is less than one km out of town on the road to Donegal, has 20 beds for IR£4.50 each and is open from March to October.

Macardle House (☎ 072-51846), is at 55

Assaroe Heights and is signposted on the corner opposite the Seán Og pub. Singles/doubles are IR£16/26. The best hotel is the grand *Dorrians Imperial* (☎ 072-51147), with singles/doubles for IR£32.50/53.50.

Places to Eat

Cúchulainn's, on the corner opposite the Seán Og pub, is a pub and takeaway with a restaurant upstairs. Less expensive is an unnamed café next to the unnamed bike shop opposite the bus station. Snacks and lunches are all under IR£5 here. The *Kitchen Bake* where the two main streets meet is a converted 19th-century church and serves cakes and coffee. The bar at *Dorrians Imperial Hotel* serves pub food at lunch time and dinner is IR£14.

A coffee and craft shop has recently opened in the restored mills of a 12th-century Cistercian abbey founded by monks from Boyle. To get there go past the Thatch Pub on the road to Rossnowlagh and turn left into Abbey Lane, or the next left if you need parking space.

Danby House (☎ 072-51138), 1.5 km (one mile) out of town on the coast road, has a restaurant with excellent French-Irish dishes. The meals are served in a large ex-ballroom and an evening meal is IR£18.

Entertainment

Pubs have live music throughout the summer but the perfect time to be entertained in Ballyshannon is during the August bank holiday weekend music festival, the first weekend in August. The pubs to check out are *Seán Og* in Market St, the *Thatch* near Dorrians Imperial Hotel and the *Cellar* which is in the southern part of town across the roundabout on the other side of the river. There is also a cinema in the north of town.

Getting There & Away

The bus station is close to the roundabout and near the distinctive clock tower. There are daily Bus Éireann buses to Bundoran, Derry, Donegal, Glencolumbkille, Sligo and Dublin.

The Feda O'Donnell bus (☎ 075-48114) departs from outside Maggie's Bar for Donegal, Letterkenny, Dunfanaghy and Crolly at 6.35 pm Monday to Thursday and Saturday (also 12.30 pm on Saturday), 8.30 pm on Friday and 11 pm on Sunday. The single fare for anywhere in Donegal is IR£4. It leaves for Sligo (IR£4) and Galway (IR£8) at 10 am Monday to Saturday, also at 1.30 and 5.30 pm on Friday, and 4.30 pm on Sunday.

Getting Around

Bikes can be rented from an unnamed shop (☎ 072-51515) opposite the bus depot. Duffy's Hostel also has bikes for hire.

BUNDORAN

One of the most popular seaside resorts in the whole of Ireland, Bundoran comes alive during the summer and is mostly just driven through for the rest of the year. The main street, made up of East End and West End, is a series of games arcades, including some real antique shove ha'penny games, restaurants of the fish & chips variety, and souvenir shops. Bundoran is used mainly by Catholic Northerners and at nights the traditional music in the pubs veers towards the rebel song rather than the folk song.

Information

The tourist office (☎ 072-41350) is opposite the Holywood Hotel, on the left as you come into town from Sligo. It's open from the end of May to the middle of September from 9 am to 1 pm and 2 to 8 pm (10 am to 1 pm and 2 to 6 pm on Sunday).

Activities

Children enjoy Waterworld where a slide pool, a wave pool and the Jolly Roger burger bar pack them in by the hundred. The noise level in here probably breaks several EC standards. Tickets cost IR£2.50 for the under-sevens and IR£3.50 for everyone else.

An activity that might appeal to children and their parents is horse riding; the Stracomer Riding School (☎ 072-41787) organises hourly sessions as well as residential courses.

Just north of the town centre Tullan Strand is a handsome sandy beach with waves big enough to deter swimmers. The strange cliffside rock formations have whimsical names like the Fairy Bridges and the Puffing Hole.

Places to Eat
There is no shortage of cafés and fast-food places along the main street.

Getting There & Away
Bus Éireann buses stop in the centre of town opposite Pebbles Boutique, and there is a direct daily service to Dublin, Derry, Sligo and Galway. Ulster Buses stop beside the Star of the Sea B&B, just by the turning that leads to the Great Northern Hotel. Ulster Bus has direct services to Belfast and Enniskillen. The Feda O'Donnell bus (☎ 075-48114) from Crolly to Galway stops in Bundoran outside the Hollyrood Hotel. The times of all these buses are available from the tourist office.

Getting Around
There is a bike hire place (☎ 072-47526) at the south end of town. The first day's charge is IR£6, which drops by IR£2 for subsequent days' hire, or IR£24 for the week.

MOUNTCHARLES TO BRUCKLESS
The first town on the coastal road west of Donegal, Mountcharles, has a safe and sandy beach, angling possibilities, and an interesting story-telling festival. Four of the eight pubs have live music at weekends. The road west to Bruckless passes through the village of Inver which has its own small beach. A little farther west at Dunkineely, a minor road runs down the promontory to St John's Point, but there is no sand here.

Storytelling Festival
The event is organised by the Seamus MacManus Society, named after a villager who told stories around the village pump in the 1940s and 1950s. The festival consists of lectures, walks and sessions with modern storytellers, and takes place around the second weekend in July. Telephone for details (☎ 073-35125/35016).

Angling
Michael O'Boyle (☎ 073-35257) has a boat available for deep-sea angling at IR£10 a day and rod and tackle can be hired for another IR£5 a day. He leaves from the Mountcharles pier just past the village.

Places to Stay
Mountcharles *Bosco House Hostel* (☎ 073-35382) is difficult to miss on the main street. It is open all year and a bed is IR£5. Near by is the *Coast Road Guest House* (☎ 073-35018) with beds for IR£12.50, and near the church *Clybawn House* (☎ 073-35076) has singles/doubles for IR£16/26.

Bruckless *Gallagher's Farm Hostel* (☎ 073-37057) is halfway between Dunkineely and Bruckless on the main N56 road. Camping is also possible here at IR£3.50 and there are separate kitchen facilities. *Bruckless House* (☎ 073-37071), just past the hostel, is a cut above the usual B&B and a night in this 18th-century home costs IR£20 to IR£25.

Places to Eat
Apart from the pubs and the hostels there is little choice so stock up before leaving Donegal or Killybegs.

Getting There & Away
The 299 bus leaves Donegal at 9.10 am, 4.15 and 6.15 pm stopping outside Mulhern's in Mountcharles, the Inver post office and McGinley's shop in Dunkineely.

South-Western Donegal

KILLYBEGS
This small town has an important and successful fishing industry. The wild-looking and secluded Fintragh Beach, a couple of km

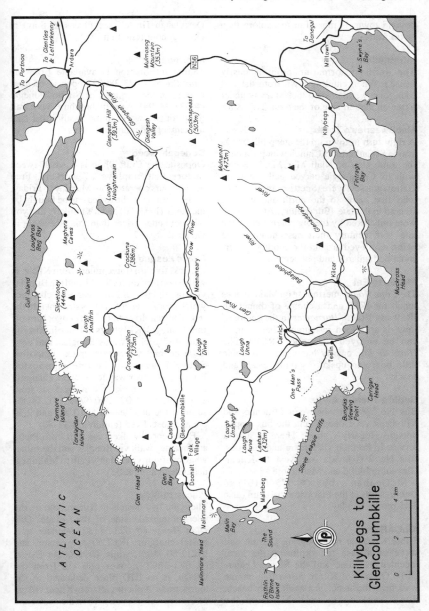

Killybegs to Glencolumbkille

beyond town, is more fun to explore than swim from.

Information

The tourist information point is easily missed. When entering town from the east look for a wooden shed tucked away under a tree on the left side of the road. This is it!

MacSweeney's Tomb

A right turn in town up the steep hill brings you to St Catherine's Church which contains the tomb slab of Niall Mor MacSweeney, with its Celtic-style carved gallowglasses. Gallowglasses were Scottish mercenaries who first came to the north and west of Ireland in the late 13th century. At first they were only hired by the big chiefs but by the late 15th century their descendants were being employed around the country as personal bodyguards and policemen.

Places to Eat

The *Cope House* guesthouse on Main St does lunch for IR£5 and a choice of dinners at IR£9 and IR£13. *Barnacles* in the centre of town is a seafood restaurant where a meal can be enjoyed for under IR£10. The *Harbour Bar* nearby has a claustrophobic little boxroom upstairs serving meals and snacks.

Getting There & Away

Bus No 299 runs between Strabane and Killybegs via Donegal and the bus stop is outside Hegarty's shop. There is also a service to Portnoo via Ardara and Glenties. Bus No 296 heads out west to Kilcar, Glencolumbkille and Malinmore.

McGeehan's bus (☎ 075-46101) to Dublin stops at the Pier bar at 8.10 am (also 3.45 pm on Sunday).

KILCAR

Either Kilcar or neighbouring Carrick will serve as a base for exploring the local indented coastline and the Slieve League cliffs. Outside of Kilcar, just a five-minute walk from the hostel, is a small sandy beach. Pony trekking is available from the

Derrylahan Hostel (see Places to Stay) at IR£8 an hour (children IR£5).

Information

Tourist information is available from the Craft Shop (☎ 073-38002), open seven days a week in the summer, or Studio Donegal (☎ 073-38194). A useful brochure has a trail route for two walks in the locality that take in many of the prehistoric sites.

Donegal Tweed

Opposite the Craft Shop is a small tweed factory that employs 25 workers. Free guided tours operate from Monday to Friday. In the Craft Shop the tweed can be bought by the metre (IR£8.50) and it's unlikely that you will get better prices than this elsewhere in Donegal.

Slieve League

Carrick, five km (three miles) from Kilcar, is where you turn off for Teelin and the Bunglas viewing point of Slieve League, a cliff face which drops over 300 metres straight into the sea. You can drive to the cliff edge; turn off the Donegal-Killybegs-Glencolumbkille road at Carrick towards Bunglas, and continue beyond the narrow track signposted Slieve League to the one signposted Bunglas. Another way to view the changing colours of the rock face is by boat from Teelin Pier (☎ 073-39079/39117). In the summer the boat leaves at 10 am and 2.30 pm and costs IR£5 (children IR£1.50)

Experienced walkers can start from Teelin and in a day walk via Bunglas and the somewhat terrifying One Man's Path to Malinbeg, near Glencolumbkille.

Places to Stay

There are two hostels in Kilcar, both on the Glencolumbkille side of the village. *Dún Ulún House* (☎ 073-38137) operates as a hostel charging IR£7.50 per person and IR£12.50 B&B, while *Derrylahan Hostel* (☎ 073-38079), over one km from the village, is an IHO place dedicated to the tourist trade. A phone call from Kilcar village or Carrick will get you a lift to the hostel and at night there is a bus service to the village pubs. The hostel allows camping for IR£2 and private rooms are also available. For B&B *Mrs Molloy* (☎ 073-38156) in Main St has singles/doubles from IR£16/26.

In Carrick there is a *hostel* (☎ 073-39041) on the corner by the Slieve League pub, with rooms for IR£5.

Places to Eat

The *Piper's Rest* pub serves light food while the *Village Restaurant* in Main St is open during July and August with meals around IR£10 and more. On the road between Kilcar and Killybegs the *Blue Haven* serves lunch and dinner.

Getting There & Away

Buses connect Kilcar and Carrick with Donegal and Glencolumbkille. Enquire at the Craft Shop for full details of the times, which change at weekends and from summer to winter. There is usually a 10 am and 6.15 pm bus leaving Donegal and taking about an hour to reach Kilcar. McGeehan's bus (☎ 075-46101) leaves Kilcar, outside John Joe's, at 7.50 am (also 3.30 pm on Sunday) for Letterkenny (IR£4) and Dublin (IR£12).

GLENCOLUMBKILLE

The village name, the Glen of St Colmcille (also spelt Columbkille or Columcille, which all mean Columba's church in Irish), derives from the fact that St Colmcille lived in the valley, and the remains of his church can still be seen. Every 9 June, his feast day, the locality becomes the focus of a penitential three-hour tour.

Information

The Lace House Centre (☎ 073-30116) will willingly dispense information. They sell a useful archaeological guide to the area, *A Guide to 5000 Years of History in Stone*, as well as a local walking guide.

Every summer the village hosts a number of adult courses in aspects of Irish language and culture, and non-Irish speakers are welcome. Fees range from IR£25 for a weekend language course to IR£50 for a week's course in the design and practice of weaving or archaeology. Accommodation can also be arranged in a hostel, B&B or sharing a self-catering house at IR£35 per person. Details are available from Oideas Gael (☎ 073-30248), Gleann Cholm Cille, Co. Dhun na nGall.

Beaches

The beach opposite the Folk Village can be dangerous due to the undercurrents and it is worth making the short journey west of Glencolumbkille to Doonalt where there are two sandy beaches. Another beach can be found at the end of the road to Malinbeg, where steps descend to a sheltered little cove.

Folk Village

This heritage centre is the most tangible evidence of the work of a priest who played a remarkable role in Glencolumbkille's development. Father James McDyer came here from Tory Island in 1952 and was galvanised into action by a community with a 75% emigration rate. He organised cooperatives and diversified farming practices as well as promoting tourism. By 1964 emigration had dropped to 20% and the village became a symbol of a 'Save the West' consciousness.

The heritage centre was established long before they became trendy – even before there were EC grants to help pay for the expense of setting one up. There are replicas of buildings and artefacts as used by people from the 18th, 19th and 20th centuries. The shebeen house sells local wine for IR£3.50.

The museum is open in summer 10 am to 7 pm Monday to Saturday, noon to 7 pm on Sunday (closing an hour earlier between Easter and the end of May). There's a IR£1 charge (children 50p) for the hourly tour of the site's buildings and entry to the museum. There is a good café in the complex.

Places to Stay

The *Dooey Hostel* (☎ 073-30130) is about 1.5 km beyond the village and offers everything from camping space to private rooms. The road leading to the hostel goes up beside the Folk Village. At Malinmore, about two km past the Folk Village, *Ros Mór* (☎ 073-30083) is a B&B and nearby is the *Glencolumbkille Hotel* (☎ 073-30003) with doubles for IR£45.

Places to Eat

The *Bialanni Restaurant* is near the Folk Village and seafood dishes are available for around IR£5. There is also a restaurant and afternoon teahouse above *Lace House*, open daily until 9.30 pm.

Things to Buy

Between Glencolumbkille village, known as Cashel, and the Folk Village are the Donegal Woollen Centre shops. There is a large selection of Donegal tweed jackets and caps and ties along with lambswool scarves and shawls. Also available are Aran sweaters and handwoven rugs. Most of the shops are open seven days a week.

Rossan is a knitware shop at the Lace House, selling garments, jackets and rugs. Visitors can tour the factory to view the production of sweaters.

Getting There & Away

The Bus Éireann bus leaves for Donegal daily at 8.25 am, with an extra bus on Saturday at 11.50 am. McGeehan's private bus (☎ 075-46101) leaves daily for Donegal and Dublin. From Dublin the bus leaves the Royal Dublin Hotel at 6 pm (extra buses on Friday at 4.30 pm and on Monday at 10 am), arriving Glencolumbkille at 11.30 pm. Departure from Glencolumbkille is at 7.30 am (extra buses on Friday at 5 pm and on Sunday at 3 pm) from outside Biddy's. McGeehan's run to Letterkenny, also leaving at 7.30 am.

Getting Around

Bicycles can be hired from the Glencolumbkille Hotel for IR£6 a day.

ARDARA

The road from Glencolumbkille to Ardara is by way of the scenically stunning Glengesh Pass. The glaciated valley suddenly opens up before you, with long winding bends carry-ing the road down to the river. Before entering Ardara a small road to the left runs down to the tiny village of Maghera and its attractive beach with caves that can be explored. Be careful – some of them flood when the tide comes in. The small peninsula that extends from Ardara and divides Loughros More Bay from Loughros Beg Bay is also well worth walking or cycling.

Places to Stay

Mrs Kennedy (☎ 075-41146) on the corner of the Portnoo Rd does B&B for IR£10.50. The *Nesbitt Arms* (☎ 075-41103) has singles/doubles from IR£14/28.

Places to Eat

The best place for snacks or a meal is *Nancy's* in the *Chas McHugh* pub. The small dark bar has lots of atmosphere and serves burgers, various seafood dishes including garlic oysters (IR£6.50), and a ploughman's lunch for IR£2.60.

Things to Buy

There are a few shops specialising in locally made knitware and prices are competitive. Aran cardigans and sweaters are between IR£30 and IR£70, scarves around IR£12, and tweed jackets from IR£80 to IR£150. Compare prices and styles at Kennedy's, at the top of the main street, Bonner & Son on Front St and John Molloy on the Killybegs road.

Getting There & Away

The Killybegs bus departs at 10 am and 5.05 pm, reaching O'Donnell's in Ardara in about half an hour. At midday and 7 pm buses leave for Killybegs. The Bus Éireann express from Dublin to Donegal is extended to Ardara on Friday and a Sunday bus leaves for Dublin at 4.30 pm.

McGeehan's bus (☎ 075-46150/46101) also runs to Dublin each morning from the post office at 8.30 am (extra Sunday bus at 3.45 pm). The Glencolumbkille-Letterkenny bus, via Glenties, also stops in Ardara.

DAWROS HEAD

The two camping and caravan sites are packed out every summer with holidaymakers from the North and consequently the area is busier than you might expect. The beach at Narin is a big crowd-puller and at low tide you can walk out to Iniskeel Island to the remains of a monastery founded by St Connell, a cousin of St Colmcille.

Places to Stay

Dunmore Caravans (☎ 075-45121) is on the Strand Rd at Portnoo and accepts tents – ring first to check there's still space. The other camp site is the *Tramore Beach Caravan & Camping Park* (☎ 075-51491) at Rosbeg. Take the road from Ardara to Maas and turn off to the left before Narin. There are a few B&Bs at Narin and Portnoo that open for the summer season. *Carnaween House* (☎ 075-45122) and *Mrs Friel* (☎ 075-45151) both charge IR£13.

Getting There & Away

In the summer a bus leaves Killybegs at 10 am and 5.05 pm for Portnoo. The buses leave Portnoo for the return journey at 12.15 and 6.15 pm.

GLENTIES

In this small town there are a number of pubs offering music at night and the place is busy with Northerners. The town was home to Patrick MacGill (1896-1937), the Navvy Poet, and a small festival in his honour takes place during the last week in August.

St Connell's Museum & Heritage Centre

This local history museum is open during the summer from 11 am to 5 pm, Monday to Friday and from 2.30 to 5 pm at weekends. Admission is IR£1 (children 50p).

The museum is opposite the very distinctive St Conal's Church, designed by the Derry architect Liam McCormack.

Places to Stay

Campbell's Hostel (☎ 075-51491) is on the left as you enter from Glencolumbkille. A bed is IR£5 and there is a twin room for IR£13. Two B&Bs are along Glen Rd about one km out of town: *Mrs McCafferty* (☎ 075-51113) and *Avalon* (☎ 075-51292) both with singles/doubles for IR£18/26. *Highlands* (☎ 075-51111) is a hotel with singles/doubles from IR£17.50/31.

Places to Eat

The only place in town is *Rosses Restaurant Bar* which serves light food.

Getting There & Away

On weekdays a bus connects Portnoo and Killybegs, stopping outside the post office in Glenties at 10.45 am and 5.50 pm on the way to Portnoo and at 12.40 and 6.40 pm on the way to Killybegs.

On Friday an express bus leaving Dublin for Donegal at 5.15 pm extends its service to Glenties, arriving at 10.30 pm. On Sunday the bus leaves Glenties at 4.15 pm and reaches Dublin at 9.45 pm.

McGeehan's bus (☎ 075-46161) from Glencolumbkille to Dublin stops outside the Highlands Hotel, 8.15 am from Glencolumbkille (extra bus on Sunday at 3.35 pm), and 10.25 pm from Dublin. There is also a bus to Fintown, and Letterkenny.

INLAND TO THE FINN VALLEY

This is the only part of Donegal that isn't well travelled by visitors – a blessing if you want to get away on your own for some fishing, hillwalking or cycling. The River Finn is a good salmon river, especially if there has been heavy rain before the middle of June. Sea trout are also available and fishing gear is available from Mcelhinys in Ballybofey.

There's good hillwalking on the Blue Stack Mountains and along the Ulster Way, but you need to be prepared with maps and provisions. The Finn Farm Hostel dispenses maps and advice and will even arrange a pick-up at the beginning or end of the trip. A long one-day trek could start from the hostel and end at the Lodge Hostel in Doochary village or Campbell's Hostel in Glenties. A new hostel and activity centre is planned to open at Fintown in mid-1993 (contact either the Finn Farm or Lodge hostel for confirmation) and this will extend the trekking possibilities.

Horse riding is best arranged through the Finn Farm Hostel which organises lessons at IR£7 an hour. Experienced riders can take a horse for the whole day for IR£25. Six-day trips across the border are also arranged at around IR£300, which includes meals, accommodation and horse.

In Ballybofey's Protestant church the grave of Isaac Butt, founder of the Irish Home Rule movement, can be found.

Places to Stay
The *Lodge Hostel* (☎ 075-46151) is in Doochary village and includes private rooms at IR£6; camping is also possible here. Free fishing is possible on the River Gweebarra nearby. The *Finn Farm Hostel* (☎ 074-32261) is two km from Ballybofey and the left turn off the road is signposted on the road to Glenties. When you think you're lost and there can't possibly be a hostel along the green road you've got on to, you'll see it. A bed is IR£6 during July and August, IR£5 the rest of the year. Camping costs IR£3. During the months of April and May seven nights' B&B plus seven hours riding costs IR£90.

An arched bridge connects Ballybofey and Stranorlar and there are B&B possibilities in both market towns. *Finn View House* (☎ 074-31351), Lifford Rd in Ballybofey, has singles/doubles for IR£18/26, and *Mrs Fahey* (☎ 074-31312) on the Letterkenny Rd in Stranorlar charges from IR£15/24. *Kee's Hotel* (☎ 074-31018) in Stranorlar, where the mail horses were changed on the Derry-Sligo run in the 19th century, has singles/doubles for IR£33.50/56 and this includes free use of the leisure club's swimming pool and sauna. *Jackson's Hotel* (☎ 074-31021) is a little cheaper with doubles from IR£52.

Getting There & Away
The Bus Éireann Galway-Derry express stops outside the shopping centre in Ballybofey, connecting the area with Sligo, Donegal and Letterkenny. There are local buses that connect Ballybofey with Killybegs and Letterkenny.

McGeehan (☎ 075-46101) runs a Glencolumbkille-Letterkenny bus that stops in Fintown, at 8.55 am for Letterkenny and 5.45 pm for Glenties, Ardara, Killybegs and Glencolumbkille. There is also a McGeehan bus from Fintown to Ballyfoley at 1 and 5.45 pm.

Getting Around
Bicycles can be rented from Kee's Hotel in Stranorlar.

North-Western Donegal

The various epithets earned by Donegal's scenery – wild, spectacular, dramatic and so on – are nowhere more justified than in the north-west of the county. Despite the absence of large towns you are rarely far from a village or pub, and the area around Gweedore claims to be one of the most densely populated rural regions in western Europe.

The stretch of land between Dungloe in the south and Crolly in the north is a bleak and rocky gaeltacht area known as the Rosses. The main attraction here is the island of Arranmore, reached by ferry from the village of Burtonport.

The other accessible island, the visually distinctive Tory Island further to the north, is even more appealing. The coast around here, between Bunbeg and Dunfanaghy, is absolutely superb and there are wonderful cycling tours to be enjoyed around Bloody Foreland and Horn Head.

DUNGLOE
Information
The tourist office (☎ 075-21297) in Dungloe is open from 10 am to 6 pm (closed 1 to 2 pm) Monday to Saturday. The nearest good beach is just north of Maghery.

Places to Eat

The *Bridge Inn* pub near the tourist office does light snacks but coffee at 70p is a bit much. *Doherty's Cafeteria* is also near the tourist office and is good for inexpensive meals. For a quiet spot seek out *Scrumptious* in the Dungloe Centre shopping arcade.

Annagry is a small village four km (2.4 miles) west of Crolly and 10 km (six miles) north of Dungloe, where you will find the *Danny Minnies Restaurant* which does good seafood (IR£15 in the evening for a meal) or lunch for around IR£6.

Getting There & Away

There is a private bus (☎ 075-21105) that runs to Larne each day in July and August with a 20-minute stopover in Letterkenny. The bus leaves from outside Doherty's at 9 am. McGeehan's bus (☎ 075-46101) leaves from outside Sweeny's Hotel at 7.45 am for Dublin.

There is a small airport at Carrickfinn (☎ 075-48284) near Dungloe, with scheduled services to London and Glasgow by Ryanair and Loganair.

ARRANMORE

This small island, 14 km (nine miles) by five km (three miles), has some spectacular cliff scenery and sandy beaches, as well as pubs and a small festival held each August. The island has been inhabited for thousands of years, and a prehistoric fort can be discerned on the south side. The western and northern parts are wild and rugged with hardly any houses to disturb the sense of isolation.

Places to Stay

The *An Óige Hostel* (no telephone) is open from May to the end of October and there is also the *Glen Hotel* (☎ 075-21505) with 10 beds for IR£14 each. *Mrs Anne Bonner* (☎ 075-21532) does B&B for IR£14 and this can be arranged through Cornelius Bonner, the boatman.

Places to Eat

There are a number of pubs on the island doing food and meals are available at *Bonners Restaurant* at the pier, but if staying over, bring your own. There is a small shop not far from the hostel.

Getting There & Away

The ferry (☎ 075-21532) goes from Burtonport; the 1.5 km trip takes 20 minutes and costs IR£2. In summer there are regular daily crossings, usually starting from 8.30 am.

GWEEDORE, DERRYBEG & BUNBEG
Information

Derrybeg and Bunbeg virtually run into each other and they share an information centre (☎ 075-31510) on the main road which is open from 10 am to 6 pm. It has a bureau de change.

Horseriding (☎ 075-31667) on the beach is available at IR£6 an hour (children IR£5).

Places to Stay

The *Screag An Iolair Hill* hostel (☎ 075-48593) is at Crolly to the south of Gweedore. It charges IR£5 and offers a free pick-up service. In Derrybeg *Mrs Niallais* (☎ 075-31008) has singles/doubles for IR£12/21 while *Mrs McBride* (☎ 075-31258) at Middletown charges IR£14/25. The *Glenveagh* (☎ 075-31767) costs from IR£16/29 and the *Seaview Hotel* (☎ 075-31159) from IR£25/50.

Bunbeg has more B&Bs, with one of the least expensive being *Atlantic View* (☎ 075-31550) on Strand Rd, offering singles/doubles from IR£12.50/22. The most appealing hotel is the *Óstán Gweedore* (☎ 075-31177) which is right by the beach and has a leisure complex as well. B&B for two is IR£70 but for another IR£2 one evening dinner is included.

The nearest hostel is the An Óige one at Errigal (☎ 075-31180), which is three km (1.8 miles) west of the village of Dunlewy and eight km (five miles) west of Gweedore.

Places to Eat

Moonies Restaurant is across the road from the information centre, but only opens during the evening. A meal is around IR£15.

Gweedore has a number of pubs doing bar food. The *Glenveagh* hotel in Derrybeg serves dinner for IR£9, and *Bunbeg House* by the harbour in Bunbeg has dinner for IR£15.

Getting There & Away

Feda O'Donnell Coaches (☎ 075-48114) has buses leaving Gweedore for Letterkenny, Donegal, Sligo and Galway. They depart at 7.10 am Monday to Saturday with extra buses on Friday, from the Bunbeg cross-roads, the Seaview Hotel and Molloy's supermarket. In Galway the bus leaves the Cathedral at 4 pm, 5.30 pm on Friday and 8 pm from Eyre Square on Sunday.

BLOODY FORELAND

The headland gets its name from the colour of the rocks, and the road out is wonderfully remote and ideal for cycling. The tiny village of Brinlack, about one km past the viewing point, has a thatched cottage doing tea and cakes.

Places to Stay

There is a small hotel, the *Foreland Heights* (☎ 075-31785), near the viewing point. Singles/doubles are IR£30/45. At Brinlack, *Ard na Mara* (☎ 075-31364) does B&B from IR£12/14.

TORY ISLAND

Not so long ago a visit to Tory was a precarious venture and visitors could be stranded for days in bad weather. With modern boats, this is no longer a problem and the island is trying to attract as many visitors as possible.

Tory Island has its own indigenous school of painters. The most accomplished of them was James Dixon, who died in 1970 and didn't start painting until he was in his 60s. He was inspired to paint by the English landscape artist Derek Hill who began visiting the island in 1956. Dixon saw him at work, claimed he could do better and was duly presented with paints and paper. Patsy Dan Rogers is now the senior artist working on Tory. The artists' work has been exhibited

around Europe. There is also a permanent exhibition in the island's community hall.

Things to See

St Colmcille is said to have founded a monastery on the island in the 6th century. The only remains of this monastic era are near West Town: the **Tau Cross**, a small undecorated T-shaped cross on the pier, and the **Round Tower**, with a circumference of nearly 16 metres, built of rounded beach-stones and rough granite with a round-headed doorway some way above the ground.

The north-eastern side of the island has cliffs with colonies of puffins. The south-west is quite different, very flat but with dangerous off-shore rocks. It was here that the British gunboat *Wasp* was wrecked in 1884 while on a mission to collect taxes from the inhabitants. There are no sandy beaches and just one pebbly one, but the cliff walks and a visit to the island's one pub at night make a stay here well worth while.

Places to Stay

The accommodation situation has improved dramatically over the last few years. The *co-op* (☎ 074-35502) runs two small hostels with beds for IR£4 and there are a few unregistered B&Bs in the two villages. By the time you read this a new 14-bed hotel, being built by an islander, should also be in operation.

Places to Eat

At the moment the best place to eat is at the café by the pier but when the new hotel opens it will have a restaurant and probably serve pub food.

Getting There & Away

Turasmara Teo is a new boat service operating from Bunbeg (☎ 075-31991) and Magheraroarty (☎ 074-35061). Bunbeg is just west of Gweedore while Magheraroarty is reached by turning off the N56 at the western end of Gortahork near Falcarragh. The road is signposted Coastal Route/ Bloody Foreland. Twice a week there is also a service from Port na Blagh and Downings near Dunfanaghy.

Between June and September the boat leaves Bunbeg at 9 am and returns from Tory at 7 or 9 pm. The cost is IR£12. The boat from Magheraroarty leaves at 11.30 am and returns from Tory at 4.30 pm. The charge is IR£10. On Wednesday from June through September, the boat leaves Port na blagh at 2 pm and returns at 6.30 pm. The charge is IR£12. Each Saturday there is a 2 pm departure from Downings, also IR£12, returning at 6.30 pm. There are several extra services in July and August.

Bicycles are carried free on all the boats.

FALCARRAGH
This village, along with the neighbouring little village of Gortahork, has a significant Irish-speaking community. During the summer the pubs come alive at night, many with live traditional music.

Beach
There is a misleading sign pointing off to the beach at the western end of the village; it takes you down a road for two km and leads to a pier. Instead, at the eastern end of the village, turn down the road by the side of the An Saibleann supermarket, opposite the Bank of Ireland. At the T-junction turn right and follow the road until a sign for Tra (beach) points down to the left. The beach is superb for walking but not for swimming. From the supermarket it is four km (2.5 miles) to the beach.

Places to Stay
The *Shamrock Lodge Hostel* (☎ 074-35859) is in the village pub of the same name and charges IR£5 a bed. *Ballyconnel House* (☎ 074-35363) was once a boarding school, then a teacher training college, and now has hostel accommodation at around IR£5. To get there follow the road to the beach at the Dunfanaghy end of the village. After half a km go through gates with a sign in Irish and English advertising Holiday & Conference Facilities.

Sea View (☎ 074-35552) is one km off the

Puffin

road going to Dunfanaghy and charges IR£11 B&B. Nearer to Falcarragh itself *Chestnut Lodge* (☎ 074-35243) is a little dearer with singles for IR£13 and doubles from IR£23.

Places to Eat
The *Gweedore* pub has a restaurant upstairs and *Ballyconnel House* has coffee and light snacks available during the day.

Getting There & Away
The Feda O'Donnell bus (☎ 075-48114) from Crolly to Galway stops outside the phone box on Main St in Falcarragh at 7.50 am, reaching Letterkenny an hour later and Galway at 1 pm. There are extra buses on Friday and on Sunday it leaves at 2.20 pm.

The Lough Swilly bus (☎ 074-22863) leaves for Derry at 12 noon and 6.40 pm, Monday to Friday. This bus stops on Main St near the hostel.

DUNFANAGHY
This small town is a popular holiday resort in its own small and discreet way; the vast sandy stretches of the beach, when the tide is out, are a big draw, and there are a couple of smart hotels as well as a hostel which is expanding to meet the demand. Compared to

beaches in the south-west of Ireland, the place is idyllically empty, and it makes a good base for trips south to Letterkenny or west to Tory Island.

McAulliffe's craft shop, on the main street, has a selection of Irish tweeds and crystal.

Information

There is no tourist information office but the post office has a bureau de change facility. Only punts can be issued so you will be disappointed if you wanted pounds for a visit to the North.

Horn Head

The towering headland, with quartzite cliffs over 180 metres (600 feet) in height, could be reached by continuing on the from the end of the walk above but the route is perilous at times. Consult the *New Irish Walks Guide: West & North* for details. An alternative is to take the scenic route by bike or car from the Falcarragh end of Dunfanaghy. The road circles the headland with tremendous views on a fine day: the islands of Inishbofin, Inishdooey and Inishbeg to the west, as well as Tory island, Sheep Haven Bay to the east, Malin Head to the north-east, and even, on a good day, the coast of Scotland.

Walking

For an exhilarating walk, take the road west to Falcarragh for about four km and turn right at the first track past the Corcreggan Mill Cottage Hostel. Follow the track down to the sea dunes by first passing a farm and then crossing a field on a clearly indicated pathway. The vast and lovely Tramore Beach opens up below the sand dunes, and you may well be the only person here. Turn to the right and follow the beach to the end where you can find a way up onto a path that leads north to Pollaguill Bay. From the bay you can continue to the cairn at the end of the bay and follow the coastline for a stupendous view of the 20-metre (70-foot) Marble Arch, carved out by the sea.

Places to Stay

Corcreggan Mill Cottage Hostel (☎ 074-36409) is a pleasantly cosy and well-organised place, four km (2.5 miles) from the Esso garage in Dunfanaghy on the road to Falcarragh. Camping is also possible at IR£3 per person.

The biggest hotel is *Arnold's* (☎ 074-36208) with singles/doubles from IR£33/46. The *Carrig Rua* (☎ 074-36133) charges about the same. Both hotels welcome children. *Rosman House* (☎ 074-36273) does B&B from IR£13.50 per person.

Tory View Holiday Homes (☎ 074-35608) is just one of the many self-catering possibilities around Dunfanaghy, and *Arnold's Hotel* has its own chalet for renting at IR£195 a week during July and August.

Places to Eat

The restaurant in *Arnold's Hotel* has good views over the sea and serves hearty dinners from IR£14. The menu at the *Carrig Rua Hotel* is very much the same. The *Danny Collins Restaurant* is also worth a visit and *Danann's* (☎ 074-36150) is popular, with a seafood dinner at IR£7.95 and specials for around IR£6. It's open from 6.30 pm, and reservations will often be necessary. Dunfanaghy also has a couple of fast-food places on the main street.

Getting There & Away

The McGinley bus (☎ 074-35201) for Letterkenny and Dublin leaves Annagry at 6.45 am and reaches Dunfanaghy around 7.20 am. On Friday there are buses leaving for Dublin at 7.20 and 11.45 am, and 3.45 pm. From Dublin the buses leave at 4, 5 and 6 pm.

The Feda O'Donnell bus (☎ 075-48114) to Galway stops in the Square at 8 am, 2.30 pm on Sunday and extra buses on Friday.

The Lough Swilly bus (☎ 074-22863) leaves at 7.30 am and 12.20 and 5.15 pm for Derry, Monday to Friday only, and leaves Derry for Dunfanaghy at 8.50 am and 5 pm.

AROUND DUNFANAGHY
Ards Forest Park

The park has waymarked nature trails, varying in length from a couple of km to 13 km (eight miles). It covers the north shore of the Ards Peninsula which was once an estate of over 800 hectares (2000 acres). In 1930 the southern part was taken over by Franciscans, who still have friary buildings, the grounds of which are open to the public. It costs IR£1 to enter the park (family IR£3).

The park is five km (three miles) north of Creeslough off the N56.

Creeslough

This small village on the N56 near an inlet of Sheep Haven Bay has an interesting church, best viewed against the outline of distant Muckish Mountain.

The mountain is a distinctive landmark, visible after leaving Letterkenny on the N56 and dominating the coast between Dunfanaghy and the Bloody Foreland. The hardest climb is from the Creeslough side; a road turns off to the left two km (1.5 miles) north-west of Creeslough, by a small derelict shop, on the N56. After six km (3.5 miles) along here a rough track begins the ascent. The easier route to the top is by way of Muckish Gap, off the inland road from Falcarragh. Consult *New Irish Walks: West & North* for details of both routes.

Doe Castle

The castle was once the stronghold of the Scottish MacSweeney family, once employed by the O'Donnells. It is picturesquely located on a very low promontory with water on three sides and a moat hewn out of the rock on the land side. The best view is from the road from Carrigart to Cresslough. The castle was built in the early 16th century and was constantly fought over between MacSweeney brothers. Early in the 17th century it passed into English hands and was repaired and lived in until well into the 19th century. The curious tomb slab that rests against the tower near the entrance is thought to belong one of the MacSweeneys.

The castle is five km (three miles) from Creeslough on the Carrigart road and is clearly signposted. There is no charge for visiting the castle, and if the gate is locked a key is available from the nearby house.

Places to Stay

At Port-na-blagh, the nearest town to Dunfanaghy, the *Hotel Port-na-blagh* (☎ 074-36129) has singles/doubles from IR£28.50/57 and that's about it apart from self-catering. *Creeslough Holiday Cottages* (☎ 074-38101) have a number of modern detached cottages that sleep at least half a dozen and cost around IR£180 per week in July and August.

Places to Eat

The best places for a meal are in Dunfanaghy or Letterkenny and not along the N56 that joins them. There is the inexpensive *Red Roof Restaurant* near Creeslough and the town also has a couple of cafés.

If you are hostelling or camping, Creeslough has a supermarket and the next two are at Dunfanaghy and Falcarragh. During the day Lurgyvale Thatched Cottage is open as a teashop.

Letterkenny & Around

There are a number of places of interest near Letterkenny that could also be reached from Dunfanaghy in the north or Dungloe in the west. Letterkenny is the largest town and a good base as most places can be reached from there by bike.

LETTERKENNY

Letterkenny is the county town and is a bustling place which has grown considerably since Derry was effectively cut off from its hinterland by the partition of Ireland.

Information

Main St, said to be the longest main street in Ireland, runs from Dunnes Stores at one end to the Court House at the other end and divides into Main St Upper and Lower. At the top of Main St Upper there is a junction with High Rd leading off to the left and Port Rd going right and down to the bus station and the road out to Derry.

The tourist office (☎ 074-21160) is geared towards the motorist. It's on the main Derry road outside town, but within walking distance of the roundabout where the buses stop. There is a Chamber of Commerce visitor centre (☎ 074-24866) at Crossview House, near the court house and they will gladly help with enquiries. Both offices dispense an inexpensive signposted walking tour of the town and a walking tour should leave the Chamber of Commerce office at 11.15 am and 2 pm, Monday to Friday, for IR£1.50 (children IR£1). If demand is not sufficient, however, the guided walk may only happen on Wednesday and Friday morning, so check beforehand (☎ 074-21768/21160).

The Letterkenny leisure centre is opposite the Tourist Hostel (see Places to Stay) and has swimming for IR£1.50 (children 60p, family IR£4) and sauna for IR£2.

County Museum

This small modern museum has its permanent collection of local archaeological finds upstairs. There are some interesting Iron Age stone heads and early Christian material. The museum is on High Rd, past the Tourist Hostel, and is open from 11 am to 12.30 pm and 1.30 to 4.30 pm, Tuesday to Sunday. Entrance is free.

Fishing

There are a number of salmon and trout rivers in the area surrounding Letterkenny as well as various loughs. The Letterkenny and District Anglers' Association is open to visitors and there are a couple of shops in town where membership and permits are available. At 50 Port Rd there is McGrath's newsagent and there is a tackle shop, Mr O'Neill's, in Main St Upper. Another source is Patsy Cullen (☎ 075-39015) of the Anglers' Haven in Kilmacrennan; boats can be hired here too.

Festival

A four-day international festival of music and dance (☎ 074-21754) is held at the end of August. It features a variety of music from Celtic rock to folk and jazz and includes a busking competition.

Places to Stay

There are two IHO hostels in town. The *Tourist Hostel* (☎ 074-25238) is on High Rd at the top of Main St with beds for IR£4, private rooms for IR£6 and family rooms also available. The *Rosemount Hostel* (☎ 074-26284), with beds at IR£4, is at 3 Rosemount Terrace, just off Rosemount, about halfway up Main St near the Bank of Ireland.

There are plenty of B&Bs.

Places to Eat

Main St has a choice of pizza joints: *Prima Pizza* is past the post office, opposite the shiny white court house, while *Pat's* is about halfway along the street. Pat's sells uncooked pizzas as well as kebabs (IR£2), pitta bread (IR£2) and pasta dishes (IR£3.50). Close to Pat's is the *Central Bar* which does pub food. In Church St *Bakersville* is pleasant enough for coffee and snacks. Also recommended is the *Granary*, off Main St Lower nearly opposite Market Square. It closes at 5.45 pm. The lasagne and quiche at under IR£2 are good value.

The shopping centre by the Derry roundabout has a couple of places serving decent lunches. For dinner *Bushtails* serve a five-course meal for IR£12, while *Gallagher's* in Main St Upper is IR£14. The other town hotel, *Mount Errigal*, does a good dinner for IR£17.

Getting There & Away

The main bus station (☎ 074-22863) is by the big roundabout on the edge of town where the road to Derry begins. Bus Éireann, Lough Swilly and the other private companies all use this area and the Quinsworth supermarket car park.

Bus Éireann (☎ 074-21309) runs an express service from Dublin to Letterkenny via Omagh, and the Derry-Cork express stops at Letterkenny, Sligo, Galway and Limerick. The Derry-Galway bus also stops at Letterkenny before travelling on to Donegal, Bundoran, Sligo and Galway.

Lough Swilly (☎ 074-22400) runs a regular service from Derry to Dungloe, via Letterkenny and Dunfanaghy, as well as a more direct route between Letterkenny and Derry. The single fare to Derry is IR£4.20.

McGinley's (☎ 074-35201) run a bus from Annagry to Dublin through Letterkenny. There's a Feda O'Donnell bus (☎ 075-48114) from Crolly to Galway through Letterkenny. It goes on to Donegal, Bundoran, Sligo and Galway. O'Donnell also runs a coach to Glasgow that leaves each day from the Granary at 10.30 am. The coach from Glasgow (☎ 041-631-3696) leaves from outside the Citizen Theatre in Garbles St at 8 am, arriving in Letterkenny at 4.30 pm.

McGeehan (☎ 075-46101) runs a Letterkenny-Glencolumbkille service from Monday to Saturday. The fare is IR£8.

Getting Around

Bike hire is at Church Street Cycles (☎ 074-25041) in Church St. The street name is not indicated but it's about halfway along the main street and signs point to Conwal Parish Church and St Eunan's College. Bikes can also be hired from the Tourist Hostel.

COLMCILLE HERITAGE CENTRE

Colmcille (St Columba in English) was born in Gartan and the exhibition is devoted to his life and times, with a lavish display on the production of illuminated manuscripts.

Look for the Gartan clay that is associated with the birth of Colmcille. The clay is only found on a townland belonging to the O'Friel family, whose oldest son is the only one allowed to dig it up. The story is that Colmcille's mother, on the run from pagans, haemorrhaged during childbirth and her blood changed the soil's colour from brown to pure white. Ever since, the clay has been regarded as a charm. Ask nicely and the staff may produce some from below the counter.

The centre (☎ 074-21160) is open over Easter and from 12 May to the end of September. Hours are 10.30 am to 6.30 pm, Sunday 1 to 6.30 pm, and the charge is IR£1 (children 50p, students 70p).

Getting There & Away

Leave Letterkenny on the R250 road to Glenties and Ardara and a few km out of town turn right on the R251 to the village of Churchill. Alternatively, from Kilmacrenan on the N56 turn west and follow the signs.

GLEBE HOUSE & GALLERY

The early 19th-century Glebe House was formerly a rectory and then a hotel. It was bought by the artist Derek Hill in 1953. A fascinating guided tour of the house takes about 40 minutes.

Derek Hill was born in England in 1916 and worked in Germany before travelling to Russia and the east. He became interested in Islamic art and things oriental. There is some original William Morris wallpaper in one of the rooms. The kitchen has a wonderfully folksy style and is full of paintings by the Tory artists, including a birdseye view of West End village by James Dixon (see the Tory Island section). Don't miss the weird bathroom.

Glebe House would be worth visiting for the works of art alone. Landseer, Pasmore, Hokusai, Picasso, Gwen John, Jack B Yeats and Kokoschka are all represented.

The house is open from May to September and the Easter period from 11 am to 6.30 pm Monday to Thursday and Saturday, 1 to 6.30 pm on Sunday. The charge is IR£1 (children and students 40p, family IR£4). It's on the shore of Lake Gartan and only a short distance from the Colmcille heritage centre.

DOON WELL & ROCK

During penal times the tradition developed of the well having remarkable curative properties, and some people still believe this to be the case to judge by the bits of cloth left here. There are good views from the top of the rock, which is where the O'Donnell kings were inaugurated.

Getting There & Away

There are a number ways of reaching the well. The most straightforward route is by turning off the N56 just north of Kilmacrenan.

GLENVEAGH NATIONAL PARK

Much of the land making up the park was once farmed by tenants, who were all evicted by John George Adair in 1861. In the 1930s the land was bought by an American who eventually sold it to the State and later donated the castle and gardens.

The visitor centre hosts a useful audiovisual show on the ecology of the park and the infamous landlord. From the centre buses run to the castle.

The Victorian castle is clinical compared to the warmth and colour of Glebe House. A guided tour is the only way to see the various rooms, but it takes in the lifestyle of the American owner, Henry McIlhenny. The drawing room has a splendid 300-year-old Adams-style fireplace bought from the Ards estate by McIlhenny.

The gardens offer a refreshing change to the studied elegance of the house. They were nurtured for decades and include a variety of features: a terrace, an Italian garden, a walled kitchen garden and the Belgian Walk laid by Belgian soldiers who stayed here during WW I.

The park is open all year, and the visitor centre and Castle are open from Easter to October from 10.30 am to 6.30 pm, seven days a week. The charge is IR£1 (children and students 40p, family IR£3) but this does not include the castle which costs another IR£1.

GARTAN OUTDOOR EDUCATION CENTRE

The centre is set on its own 35-hectare (87-acre) estate and conducts a variety of courses throughout the summer: rock climbing, sea canoeing, windsurfing and hill climbing. Courses are run for both adults and children and full details are available from the Gartan Outdoor Education Centre (☎ 074-37032), Churchill, Letterkenny, County Donegal.

Including hostel accommodation, a weekend course for adults costs about IR£40, a five-day course about IR£150.

Places to Eat

The visitor centre at the Glenveagh National Park has a good restaurant serving snacks, and meals from IR£4 to IR£7. In the nearby village of Churchill there are three pubs that do bar food. On the road from Churchill to Letterkenny the *Rock Restaurant* serves dinner from 6 to 10 pm and bar snacks from 10 am.

LURGYVALE THATCHED COTTAGE

During the day the cottage (☎ 074-39216/21160), filled with rural artefacts, is very much aimed at the passing tourist trade, and on Thursday evenings traditional music sessions are held with dancing and a singsong. The entrance charge is IR£1.50. Also during the summer there are demonstrations of traditional crafts on the first Sunday of the month.

Getting There & Away

The cottage is by the side of the road on the N56 in the village of Kilmacrennan, easily spotted because of the large numbers of old farming implements scattered about.

North-Eastern Donegal

ROSGUILL PENINSULA

From Carrigart it is a 15-km (nine-mile) journey around this small peninsula on the road marked Atlantic Drive. Carrigart itself has a lovely beach which is relatively deserted because the camp sites at Downings draw the crowds to the other end of the long strand. The best beach for swimming is Tra na Rossen and the nearby hostel is an added attraction. On no account go swimming in Boveeghter Bay or Mulroy Bay as both have had drownings.

There are no tourist attractions to detract from the landscape. But there is plenty of social life at night in the Downings pubs, packed with holidaymakers from the North staying at the camp site.

Places to Stay

There is an *An Óige Hostel* (☎ 074-55374) at Tra na Rosann which is open all year. It is six km (four miles) from Downings and hitching is the best bet if you're without wheels.

Casey's Caravan Park (☎ 074-55376) has limited camping space so it's best to ring first and check. A family tent is IR£7 a night, and a small tent IR£6.

Singles/doubles at the oddly designed *Hol-Tel Carrigart* (☎ 074-55114) range from IR£26.50/43 and there's an indoor pool. Nearby at Hill House (☎ 074-55221) in Dunmore, B&B is from IR£13/26. There is a little more choice in Downings: *Beach* (☎ 074-55303) is a hotel with over 20 beds costing from IR£14.50/29. *Bay Mount* (☎ 074-55395) and *An Crossóg* (☎ 074-55498) both do B&B for IR£28. All three are easy to find.

Places to Eat

Carrigart itself is the best bet for food. The *North Star* pub has bar food and *Weavers Restaurant & Wine Bar* has meals for around IR£5.

Getting There & Away

There is a local bus between Carrigart and Downings, but that's of limited use for visitors from elsewhere. You really need your own transport for this area.

FANAD HEAD PENINSULA
Western Side

On the western side of the Fanad Peninsula, Kerrykeel has an attractive location overlooking Mulroy Bay and nearby is the 19th-century **Knockalla Fort**, built to warn of any approaching French ships. There is also **Kildooney More portal tomb** to visit, but that's about it. The small villages of Milford and Rosnakill have little to attract visitors and there are no particularly good beaches.

Getting There & Away The Swilly bus leaves Letterkenny at 10 am and 6 pm and reaches Milford an hour later. From Milford it runs on to Kerrykeel in 10 minutes and then on to Portsalon, handy for the camp site.

Ramelton

The eastern side of the Fanad Peninsula is far more interesting. The first town you come to is Ramelton, founded in the early 17th century by William Stewart. It has mainly developed on the eastern side of the river. It has Georgian houses and stone warehouses, and the ruined **Tullyaughnish Church** is worth a visit because of the Romanesque carvings in the east wall which were taken from a far older church on nearby Aughnish Island.

Places to Stay Only B&B is available but there is a choice of half a dozen. Near the town centre the *Manse* (☎ 074-51047) has beds for IR£17, but *Clooney House* (☎ 074-51125) nearby is less expensive at IR£12 and IR£13.

Places to Eat A couple of km out of Letterkenny, before reaching Ramelton, *Carolina House Restaurant* (☎ 074-22480) is a smart establishment that specialises in fish. It only opens during the evenings, Tuesday to Saturday, and dinner is in the IR£20 bracket.

In Ramelton itself *Fish House* is attractively placed in an old stone building by the river and serves tea and snacks. For something more substantial *Mirabeau Steak House* cooks gigantic steaks with homemade sauces.

Getting There & Away The Swilly bus (☎ 074-22400) weaves its way around and across the peninsula, leaving Letterkenny at 10 am and 6 pm and taking 20 minutes to reach Ramelton.

Rathmullan

In 1587, Hugh O'Donnell was only 15 years old but as the heir of this powerful family he was considered fair game for the English. In

Rathmullan he was tricked into boarding a ship and taken to Dublin as a prisoner. He escaped four years later on Christmas Eve and after unsuccessful attempts at revenge died in Spain, aged only 30.

In 1607, the earls of Tyrone and Tyrconnel boarded a ship 'in Rathmullan harbour and left Ireland for good. This decisive act, known as the Flight of the Earls, marked the effective end of Gaelic Ireland. In the aftermath of the earls' flight, large-scale confiscation of their estates took place, preparing for the plantation of Ulster with settlers from Scotland and England.

Heritage Centre The centre focuses on the Flight of the Earls, and will mainly appeal to the historically minded. It's housed in an early 19th-century fort built by the British fearing Napoleon's intentions, and is open from 10 am to 6 pm (12 noon to 6.30 pm on Sunday) from June to September and costs IR£1 (children and students 50p, family IR£3). The sandy area near the pier outside the centre is the only clean part of the town's beach.

Rathmullan Priory This Carmelite friary was founded in the 15th century by the MacSweeneys, and was still in use in 1595 when an English commander named George Bingham raided the place and took off with the church plate and vestments. The fact that it looks so well preserved is due to Bishop Knox's renovation in the early 17th century; he wanted to use it as his own residence. It was from immediately outside the priory that the earls departed in 1607.

Places to Stay The only B&B is just south of town at the *Water's Edge Restaurant* (☎ 074-58182). As the name implies, there are good views from some of the rooms. The nearest hostel is farther north at Bunnaton.

Rathmullan has three hotels, each quite different in style. *Rathmullan House* is a swanky country house with its own indoor heated swimming pool and sauna. Singles/doubles start at IR£22.50/45 but increase to more than double this amount.

The *Pier Hotel* (☎ 074-58178), originally a 19th-century coaching inn, has 10 beds from IR£18 each and is very much a family establishment. *Fort Royal* (☎ 074-58100) has its own private beach and organises sporting activities; singles/doubles are from IR£45/70.

Places to Eat The *Cafe* is a pleasant place for coffee and snacks. It's down the road near the pier that has the White Harte pub on the corner. The *Water's Edge Restaurant*, just south of town, serves a three-course dinner for a reasonable IR£9. The *Pier Hotel* and *Fort Royal* both do bar food, and while all three hotels serve dinner, the Pier charges IR£13 and the other two IR£20.50.

Getting There & Away The Swilly bus arrives in Rathmullan at 10.45 am and 6.45 pm from Letterkenny and departs straightaway for Portsalon via Milford and Kerrykeel.

Portsalon & Fanad Head

Portsalon, once a popular holiday resort with Northerners, has little to offer except a long stretch of golden sand which is safe for swimming. It's another eight km (five miles) to Fanad Head, which also has little to detain the traveller.

INISHOWEN PENINSULA

The Inishowen Peninsula, with Lough Foyle to the east and Lough Swilly to the west, reaches out into the Atlantic and ends with the most northerly point in the whole of Ireland, Malin Head. The landscape is typical of Donegal: rugged, desolate and mountainous. Sites of antique interest abound, but there are also some wonderful beaches and plenty of places where travellers can go off alone. Tourist offices in Donegal, Letterkenny or Derry have free leaflets about walks for the Inishowen area, complete with maps.

The route below follows the road out of Derry up the coast of Lough Foyle to Moville and then north-west to Malin Head before following the western side down to Bun-

ATLANTIC OCEAN

Inishowen Peninsula

0   3   6 km

Malin Head

Tullagh Bay
Pollan Bay
Lag Sand Dunes
Dunaff Head
Carrickbrackey Castle
Malin
Culdaff Bay
Dunmore Head
Trawbreaga Bay
Dunaff
Ballyliffin
Clonmany
Culdaff
Clonca Church & Cross
Tremone Bay
Lenan Head
Mamore Hill (421m)
Carndonagh
Bocan Stone Circle
Kinnagoe Bay
Gap of Mamore
High Cross
Carrowmore High Crosses
Urris Hills
Dunree Head
Dunree
Slieve Snaght (615m)
Inishowen Head
Strove
Dunagree Point
Greencastle
Greencastle Castle
DONEGAL
Cooley
Moville
Magilligan Point
O'Docherty's Keep
Redcastle
Lough Swilly
Buncrana
Carrowkeel
Lough Foyle
Fahan
Cross Slab
NORTHERN IRELAND
Inch Island
Muff
Bridge End
To Letterkenny
N13
Grianan of Aileach
Derry
DERRY
A2
Limavady
To Coleraine

crana. If coming from Donegal the peninsula could be approached from the Lough Swilly side by turning off for Buncrana on the N13 road from Letterkenny to Derry. Leaving from Derry, though, the first village in the Republic is Muff.

Muff to Moville

The tiny village of Muff is only eight km (five miles) from Derry. The bus service across the border is so regular that one could stay here while spending a couple of days around Derry itself. At night the pubs have their fair share of Northerners, and past Muff

along the coast there are larger pubs catering to the same market.

Places to Stay The *Muff Hostel* (☎ 077-84188; from Derry 0003-84188), charging IR£3.50 a night, is in the village at the northern end just before the Burmah petrol station; turn left if you're coming from Derry. The hostel is up this road on the left. Camping is possible there and bikes can be hired. *Mrs Reddin* (☎ 077-84031), next to the post office on Main St, does the only village B&B for IR£12.

Beyond Muff and just before Moville

there is a hotel and a bunch of B&Bs at Redcastle. The *Redcastle Country Hotel* (☎ 077-82073) has all the facilities of a big hotel and singles/doubles from IR£50/70. Next to the village post office, *Fernbank* (☎ 077-83032) does B&B from IR£12.

Places to Eat There are a few pubs serving sandwiches and a village café doing takeaways, but no restaurants. More substantial meals are available at the *Redcastle Country Hotel* farther up the coast before Moville; their tourist menu has three-course meals from IR£6.50 to IR£12, served from 11 am to 6.30 pm. After 7 pm dinner starts at IR£14.50. There are a couple of cafés at Quigley's Point, a few km out of Muff and also on the coast road.

Getting There & Away Lough Swilly buses (☎ 0504-262017 in Derry) run eight buses a day from Derry on the Carndonagh service that stop at Muff, as well as five buses a day to Strove that also go through Muff. There is no Sunday service on either route. Worth considering is their eight-day unlimited-travel ticket for IR£15.

Moville
Now a sleepy seaside town, Moville was once a busy port where emigrants left for a new life in America. The coastal walkway from Moville to Greencastle takes in the stretch of coast where the steamers used to moor.

Cooley Cross & Skull House By the gate of the Cooley graveyard is a slender three-metre (10-foot) high cross made unusual by the ringhole in its head through which the hands of negotiating parties were clasped to seal an agreement. In the graveyard itself there is a small building known as the Skull House still containing some old bones. It may be associated with St Finian, the monk who accused Colmcille of copying a manuscript of his in the 6th century. He lived in a monastery here that was founded by St Patrick and which survived into the 12th century.

Approaching Moville from the south look out for a turning on the left (if you pass a church you've gone too far) which has a sign on the corner for Clarke's furniture store. The graveyard is just over one km up this road on the right.

Places to Stay There are a few B&Bs around Moville. *Baron's Cafe* (☎ 077-82472) in town has beds for IR£12, while on the road out of town *Iona House* (☎ 077-82173) is a small homely place charging IR£11. There are two hotels: *McNamara's* (☎ 077-82010), from IR£22 per person, and *Foyle* (☎ 077-82025) which is less expensive, charging from IR£17/32.

Places to Eat In Moville itself, *Baron's Café* and the two hotels are the best places for food, and *Rosato's*, just outside town after turning left for Carndonagh, serves food until 9 pm. Greencastle is so close that, if you have your own transport, the places there are also worth looking at. Dinner at *McNamara's* is IR£17, at *Foyle* it's IR£12.

Getting There & Away Lough Swilly run a bus between Derry and Strove that stops in Moville. The first bus leaves Derry at 11 am, reaching Moville at 11.50 am. The first bus from Moville to Derry is at 7.50 am, last one at 5.15 pm.

Greencastle
Greencastle Castle was built by Richard de Brugo in 1305. He was known as the Red Earl due to his florid colour. It functioned as a supply base for English armies in Scotland and for this reason was attacked by the Scots under Robert Bruce in the 1320s. In 1555 the castle was demolished, and little is left.

Four Lough Swilly buses travel daily between Derry and Strove but there is no Sunday service.

Inishowen Head
A right turn outside Greencastle leads to Strove from where a sign indicates Inishowen Head is one km to the left. It is possible to drive or cycle part of the way but

it's an easy walk to the headland from where views east take in the Antrim coast as far as the Giant's Causeway. A more demanding walk continues to the sandy beach of Kinnagoe Bay. At Strove, where the road left goes to the headland, a right turn goes to Dunagree Point and back to Greencastle but this loop has little to recommend it.

Carndonagh

At the Buncrana end of Carndonagh, the 8th-century **Carndonagh High Cross** has been re-erected against the wall of an Anglican church. Next to the cross are two small pillars, one said to be showing a man with a sword and shield, who may represent Goliath, next to David and his harp. In the graveyard there is a pillar with a carved marigold on a stem. On the other side of the stone there is a Crucifixion scene.

On the road to Ballyliffin, in a small church by the post office, a collection of local folk items are on display in the **Folk Museum** It only opens in July and August, Monday to Saturday from 2 to 4 pm.

Places to Stay Near the High Cross a sign points the way to *Teirnaleague* (☎ 077-74471) where B&B is IR£12.

Places to Eat The *Moon Fleet* is a restaurant and takeaway in the town square next to the McDonagh store, while *Trawbreaga Bay House* is a better restaurant, also with a takeaway service. If you're off to Malin Head for the day or going on to the camp site at Clonmany, stock up with eatables at Simpson's Supermarket, next to a knitware factory and retail shop.

Getting There & Away A Lough Swilly bus leaves Buncrana for Carndonagh at 8.40 am, 1 and 6.15 pm, returning from Carndonagh at 7.30 and 10 am. They also run a bus between Derry and Carndonagh but neither service runs on Sunday.

Around Carndonagh

There are several neighbouring antiquities that can be visited from the main Moville-Carndonagh road.

Clonca Church & Cross The carved lintel over the door of this 17th-century building is thought to come from an earlier church. In the north-east corner of the church the interesting tombstone was erected by one Magnus MacOrristin and has a sword and hurley stick carved on it. The remains of the cross show the Miracle of the Loaves and Fishes on the east face and geometric designs on the sides.

Look for the turn-off to Culdaff, on the right if coming from Moville, on the left after about six km (four miles) if coming from Carndonagh. The Clonca Church and Cross is 1.5 km (one mile) on the right.

Bocan Stone Circle There are better stone circles in Ireland. This one has only a few of probably over 30 original stones. The surrounding views can help to conjure up the kind of significance the place must have held some 3000 years ago.

From Clonca Church continue along the road until a T-junction is reached. Turn right here and after about half a km turn left. The stone circle is inside the first field gate on the left.

Carrowmore High Crosses Like the Bocan Stone Circle, these high crosses may prove a little disappointing. One is basically a decorated slab showing Christ and a ministering angel while on the other side of the road there is a taller cross with stumpy arms.

From Bocan Stone Circle and Clonca Church retrace the route back to the main Carndonagh-Moville road and turn left and then almost immediately right. The two crosses are just up this road. The sign to the crosses may be pointing in the wrong direction.

Malin Head

At the top of the Inishowen Peninsula is Malin Head, the most northerly point of Ireland, and a familiar name for listeners of radio weather forecasts. The tower on the cliffs was built in 1805 by the British Admiralty and used later as a Lloyds signal station. The huts were used by the Irish army in WW II as lookout posts. Above nearby Ballyhillion Beach the *Cottage* serves tea and food all week from June to September, Sunday only between March and May and in October.

The plantation village of Malin is centred around a triangular green. One of the Inishowen walk leaflets (see above) outlines an interesting circular route from the village green that takes in a local hill with terrific views as well as Lagg Presbyterian Church which is claimed to be the oldest in Ireland. Children will love the massive Lagg sand dunes by the church.

Places to Stay There is one small hotel, the *Malin* (☎ 077-70606), in the village. Singles/doubles are from IR£20/44. B&B is available in the village from *Mrs Gallagher* (☎ 077-70649) for IR£12. At Malin Head there are a few B&Bs, the most northerly in Ireland being *Mrs Hickox* (☎ 077-70249), who charges from IR£13.

Getting There & Away The best way to approach Malin Head is by the R238 from Carndonagh, rather than up the eastern side from Culdaff.

Ballyliffin & Clonmany

This small resort area attracts more Irish than overseas visitors. There's plenty of accommodation in the area.

About one km from Ballyliffin is the lovely expanse of Pollan Bay Beach, which is unfortunately not safe for swimming. A walk to the north brings you to the ruins of Carrickbrackey Castle (also spelt Carrickabraghy), dating back to the 16th century. To reach the beach turn down the road in Ballyliffin by the thatched cottage and the Atlantic ballroom. There is a sign on the road but it's only visible from the Clonmany side.

The other beach is at Tullagh Bay, immediately behind the camp site at Clonmany. It's great for an exhilarating walk but the current can be strong and swimming is not recommended when the tide is going out. There was a drowning here in 1992.

Places to Eat The *Strand Hotel* does lunch for IR£8 as well as bar food, while in the evening dinner costs from IR£10 a head – good value for the generous amount served. Both the Strand and the Ballyliffin do pub food, as does a pub with no name at the junction in Clonmany.

Entertainment Most of the pubs and hotels have music sessions throughout the summer. In Clonmany *McFeeley's* is a very popular pub and *Mackey's Tavern*, near the camp site, has lively music sessions at the weekend.

Getting There & Away A Lough Swilly bus runs between Buncrana and Carndonagh three times daily, Monday to Saturday. It leaves Buncrana at 8.40 am, 1 and 6.15 pm and departs from Carndonagh at 7.30 and 10 am and 4.15 pm, 20 minutes later from Clonmany.

Ballyliffin to Buncrana

There are two routes from Ballyliffin to Buncrana: the scenic coastal road via the Gap of Mamore and Dunree or the speedier, inland road. The Gap of Mamore descends between Mamore Hill and the Urris Hills into a valley where the road follows the River Owenerk most of the way to Dunree.

The only reason for pausing in Dunree would be to visit **Dunree Fort**, now a military museum. Back in 1798 Wolfe Tone, with the help of the French, planned to arrive in Lough Swilly and march on Derry. The British constructed six forts to guard the lough and the museum tells the whole story. It's open from June to September, Monday to Saturday, from 10.30 am to 6 pm, opening at 12.30 pm on Sunday. The charge is IR£1.50 (children 70p).

Buncrana

After Bundoran this must be the most popular resort in Donegal for holidaymakers from Derry and the North. It has a long sandy beach which is safe for swimming, all the pubs you would want, and a couple of places of interest.

Information Coming into town from Clonmany the Roadside Café on the left side of the road serves as a tourist office. A taxi service (☎ 077-61366) is also available from here. At the other end of the long main street there is a laundrette.

Tullyarvan Mill This community-run exhibition, craft shop and café is well worth a visit. The exhibition is devoted to the restoration of the mill, local history, flora & fauna, and is attractively presented. Downstairs the small craft shop has local pottery at prices that are not as outrageous as usual. The place is also worth checking out for its lively traditional music evenings that take place regularly throughout the summer.

The centre is open from 10 am to 6 pm Monday to Friday, afternoons only on Saturday and Sunday. To visit the exhibition costs IR£1.50 (children and students 75p). To find the place take the road out to Dunree and the mill is signposted on the right after the bridge.

Vintage Car & Carriage Museum The vehicles being exhibited are likely to change from time to time as the owner buys and sells but would anyone part with a '29 Rolls or a '57 Chevy? These and many others fill up the large garage space incongruously located behind a bungalow on the seafront. During the summer it is open from 10 am to 8 pm and costs IR£1.50 (children 50p); other times by appointment (☎ 077-61130).

O'Docherty's Keep At the north end of the seafront an early 18th-century six-arched bridge leads to a tower house built by the O'Dochertys, the local chiefs, in the early 15th century. It was burnt by the English and then repaired for their own use. The big house nearby was built in 1718 by John Vaughan, who also built the bridge.

Places to Stay There is no shortage of B&Bs around town but they can fill up

during August. *St Brigid's* (☎ 077-61319) in Cockhill Rd, *Kinvyra* (☎ 077-61461) in St Orans Rd (the road out to Derry) and *Kincora* (☎ 077-61174) in Cahir O'Doherty Ave all charge from around IR£14/24 for singles/doubles.

The *Lake of Shadows Hotel* (☎ 077-61005) has a heated indoor pool and singles/doubles from IR£24/46. The other town hotel is the *White Strand Motor Inn* (☎ 077-61059) with rooms at about the same price.

Places to Eat At the Clonmany end of town the *Roadside Café* lives up to its name, and a takeaway service is also available. The café at the Tullyarvan Mill serves cakes and drinks at sensible prices but the best place for a meal is the *Ubiquitous Chip* which, despite its name, serves a good variety of inexpensive meals, including tasty pizzas. On the opposite side of the road *Wing Tai House* is a Chinese restaurant that does serve chips with everything. On the Derry road going out of town the *Drift Inn* is a strange Gothic-looking pub that serves food.

Entertainment The main form of entertainment is found, unsurprisingly, in the town's many pubs strung out along the main street. The *Atlantic Bar* can be relied on for live music at weekends as can *O'Flaitbeartaiz*. For somewhere quiet and relaxing try *Roddens*.

Getting There & Away From Buncrana, Lough Swilly buses (☎ 077-61340) run a service to Derry seven days a week (IR£2.40 single). There is also a service to Carndonagh.

South of Buncrana
Fahan Cross Slab A monastery was founded in Fahan by St Colmcille in the 6th century and the stone slab in the graveyard beside the Anglican church has been dated to the century after. Each face is decorated with a cross, and the Greek inscription, which is not easily made out, is the only one known from this early Christian period.

Grianan of Aileach This impressive hilltop stone fort has panoramic views of the surrounding countryside. The walls are four metres (13 feet) thick and enclose an area 23 metres (77 feet) in diameter. At least 2000 years old, the site has pagan associations that go back much earlier. Between the 5th and 12th century it was the seat of the O'Neills before being demolished by Murtogh O'Brien, King of Munster. You might be wondering why a fort that was demolished 800 years ago could possibly look so complete. The answer is that in 1870 an amateur archaeologist from Derry set about reconstructing the fort and this is mostly what is seen today.

The design of the attractive church at the bottom of the hill was obviously modelled on that of the fort.

From Fahan travel south on the R238 to Bridge End and then turn right onto the main N13. After three km (two miles) turn left, then right after another km (half a mile) and finally left again after 2.5 km (1.5 miles). The site is easily visited from Derry by taking the main A2 road to Letterkenny and then following the same directions from Bridge End.

Places to Stay Inch Island is not visited that often by tourists but it does have an interesting B&B. *O'Doherty's* (no phone) is on the road to the pier, just past the sign to the strand, and there is usually a US flag flying outside next to an Irish one. If you carry on along the road you will come across the *Meitheal* holistic centre (☎ 077-60323) where a bed and meals is available for around IR£10. People pay to meditate there.

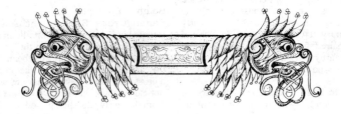

Counties Meath & Louth

Heading north from Dublin along the coast takes you through the counties of Meath and Louth before you cross the border into County Down in Northern Ireland. This low coastal landscape is the opposite of the mountainous country to the south of Dublin, rising only slightly inland to the plain known in folklore as Murtheimne, the stage for many events in the Iron Age saga of the Cattle Raid of Cooley. The climax of the saga took place on Louth's beautiful Cooley Peninsula, and many places there owe their names to the legendary heroes and battles of that time.

The scenery in Meath and Louth is reminiscent of old England: verdant settled farmland with fine old farmhouses throughout. Here are some of the most remarkable legacies of the earliest Irish people: the tombs of Newgrange and Loughcrew and also the fine monasteries at Monasterboice, Mellifont and Kells, built later by Irish Christians.

County Meath

Meath, Dublin's immediate neighbour to the north-west, has long been one of Ireland's premier farming counties, a plain of impossibly rich soil stretching north to the lakelands

of Cavan and Monaghan and west before running into the bleak Bog of Allen. Hidden among the huge fields and old stands of trees, you will glimpse the solid houses of Meath's former settlers and today's wealthy farmers. The isolated hills such as Tara and Slane have immense historical significance.

For a large county, Meath has surprisingly few major settlements. Navan, Trim and Kells are simply medium-sized towns, while places like Ashbourne, Dunshaughlin and Dunboyne on the southern fringe are becoming commuter suburbs to Dublin, and the county's principal attractions are its ancient sites.

HISTORY

Meath's rich soil, laid down during the last Ice Age, attracted settlers as early as 8000 BC, who worked their way up the banks of the River Boyne and began to transform the landscape from forest to farmland. Brugh na Bóinne is an extensive prehistoric necropolis, dating from around 3000 BC, which lies on a meandering section of the Boyne between Drogheda and Slane. There's a group of smaller passage graves at Loughcrew on the Slieve Na Caillighe hills.

The Hill of Tara in Meath was the foremost spiritual and political centre of Ireland, for 1000 years the seat of power for Irish high kings until the coming of St Patrick in the 5th century. Later, Kells became one of the most important and creative monastic settlements in Ireland and lent its name to the famed 'Book of Kells', now displayed in Trinity College, Dublin.

THE COAST

Meath's paltry 10 km of coastline includes a number of small resorts with sand dunes and safe beaches. The Elizabethan **Maiden Watch Tower** in Mornington at the mouth of the Boyne provides a fine view of Drogheda, five km to the west, and the Boyne estuary.

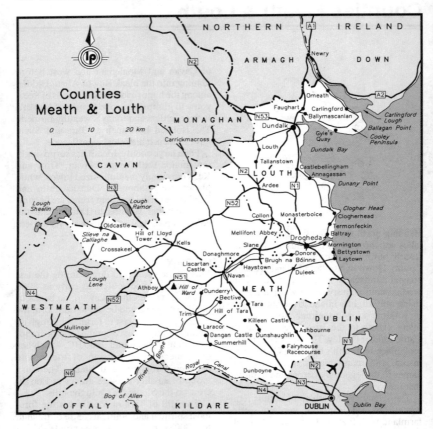

Counties Meath & Louth

Laytown is a busy little place with golf, tennis and good windsurfing. It hosts annual horse races on the beach in mid-August. Barely one km away to the south, **Bettystown**'s claim to fame is that the magnificent Tara Brooch was found here. It is now on display in the National Museum, Dublin.

Places to Stay

Ardilaun (☎ 041-27033) at 41 Beach Park, Laytown, is near the beach, and a single costs IR£12 or IR£14 with bathroom. It's open May to September. The *Neptune* (☎ 041-27107) in Bettystown is an ordinary, medium-priced hotel with B&B at IR£20.

Places to Eat

In Laytown, facing the sea, *Paddy Traynor's* offers chicken & chips and so on.

In Bettystown, *Gary Lynch's* near the beach is similar. Nearby, the *Coastguard Restaurant* (☎ 041-28251) is one of the best in the region. It's right on the shore, and dinner costs from IR£20. It's open Tuesday to Saturday from 6.30 pm and on Sundays for lunch. You'll probably have to book at weekends.

Almost next door is *Tea & Talent*, with coffee, teas and light meals during the day.

Entertainment
In Laytown, the *Cottage Inn* is a nice thatched pub and usually has a good crowd at weekends. The *Lyons Pub* is also popular. In Bettystown, *McDonagh's* is another popular, old-fashioned place.

THE BATTLE OF THE BOYNE
On 1 July 1690, the forces of the Catholic James II were defeated by those of the Protestant William of Orange at the Battle of the Boyne. The victory is still celebrated by Protestants in Northern Ireland as the Glorious Twelfth – the date having been adjusted in 1752 when the Gregorian calendar was adopted.

There is little to see of the battle site except green fields. Nevertheless, a visit may give some understanding of the forces that shaped Ireland then and now, which are examined in the History section of the Facts about the Country chapter.

The battle site is near Oldbridge, four km west of Drogheda, and is is clearly marked with a huge orange billboard. A trail leads to a slight rise overlooking the battlefield. Before the battle, William's army camped just west of Oldbridge in Townley Hall demesne and Forest Park. The Jacobite camp were stretched out along the slopes of Donore Hill, four km south of Oldbridge. James' command post was near the ruined church on the summit.

On 1 July, William's men crossed the river near Slane and Oldbridge, and despite the death of the able Marshal Schomberg (an obelisk at the base of the bridge marks the spot) they outflanked James's forces and in the face of brave resistance routed them. The losers retreated to Donore, then to Duleek, where they spent the night, and then to the Shannon and Dublin.

James himself fled south to Dublin and then to Waterford, from where he crossed back to France and ignominious exile. Remnants of the Catholic forces regrouped and fought on for another year, but symbolically and politically the struggle was over.

DULEEK
Duleek claims to have had Ireland's first stone church, and the town's name comes from 'An Damh Liag' or House of Stones, but no trace of the church remains. The founder was the energetic and omnipresent St Patrick, and it was built by St Cianán somewhere around 450. En route to Armagh, Brian Ború's body lay in state here after his death in 1014 at the Battle of Clontarf, where the Vikings were defeated.

Duleek's abbey and tower ruins date from the 12th century and contain a number of excellent effigies and tombstones, while outside there is a 10th or 11th-century high cross. The town square of Duleek has a wayside cross, erected in 1601 by Lady Jennet Dowdall in memory of her husband William Bathe and herself.

Annesbrook House (☎ 041-23293) is open May to September. This comfortable country house is surrounded by extensive wooded grounds but it's rather expensive at IR£28/46. The house is a 17th-century building with Georgian additions, and George IV paid a visit in 1821.

BRUGH NA BÓINNE
There was extensive settlement along the Boyne Valley in prehistoric times, and the necropolis known as Brugh Na Bóinne (Brugh is pronounced 'broo') was built in the area. This consists of many different sites, the three principal ones being Newgrange, Knowth and Dowth. They were the largest artificial structures in Ireland until the construction of the Anglo-Norman castles.

Over the centuries these tombs decayed, became covered by grass and trees and were plundered by everybody from Vikings to Victorian treasure hunters, whose carved initials can be seen on the great stones of Newgrange. The countryside around them is littered with countless other ancient mounds and standing stones.

Newgrange

Newgrange is a huge, flattened, grass-covered mound about 80 metres in diameter and 13 metres high. The mound covers the finest Stone Age passage tomb in Ireland and one of the most remarkable prehistoric sites in Europe. It dates from around 3200 BC, earlier than either Stonehenge or the Pyramids.

Over the centuries Newgrange, like Dowth and Knowth, deteriorated and was even quarried at one stage. There was a standing stone on the summit until the 17th century. The site was extensively restored in the 1960s and 1970s.

The superbly carved kerbstone with its double and triple spirals stands guarding the tomb's main entrance. The front facade has had a notch left in it during restoration, so that tourists don't have to clamber in over it. Above the entrance is a slit or roof box which lets light in. Another beautifully decorated kerbstone stands at the exact opposite side of the mound. Some experts say that a ring of standing stones encircled the mound forming a Great Circle about 100 metres in diameter, but only 12 of these stones remain, with traces of some others below ground level.

Holding the whole structure together are the 97 boulders of the kerb ring designed to stop the mound from collapsing outwards. Eleven of these are decorated with the motifs similar to the one on the main entrance stone, although only three to any great extent.

The white quartzite was originally brought from Wicklow, 80 km (50 miles) to the south and there is also some granite from the Mountains of Mourne in Northern Ireland. Over 200,000 tonnes of earth and stone went into the mound.

You can walk down the narrow 19-metre passage, lined with 43 stone uprights, which leads into the tomb chamber, about a third of the way into the colossal mound. The chamber has three recesses, and in these are large basin stones which held human bones. Along with the remains would have been funeral offerings of beads and pendants, but these must have been stolen long before the archaeologists arrived.

Above, massive stones, many with intricate engravings, support a six-metre-high corbel-vaulted roof. In 40 centuries the roof has not allowed a drop of water to enter the interior.

At dawn on the winter solstice – the shortest day of the year – the rising sun's rays shine directly through the slit above the entrance, creep slowly down the long passage and illuminate the tomb chamber for about 15 minutes. Places for this annual event are booked up years in advance, and the waiting list is now closed, with over 1000 names on it.

The sun does enter most of the way on the few days either side of the solstice, so you could try and book a place with the site's keepers, the Office of Public Works, either at the site office or at their headquarters in St Stephen's Green, Dublin.

However, for the legions of daily visitors, there is a simulated winter sunrise for every group taken into the mound. Make sure you are near the centre of the chamber floor, otherwise somebody is bound to be in your line of sight.

A couple of things puzzled the archaeologists. The light comes all the way down the passageway a few minutes after sunrise, not at the precise moment, and surprisingly the light stops short of illuminating the centre of the back wall. Recent studies by cosmic physicists have found that the earth's position has shifted; when the mound was built, the sunlight would have illuminated the whole chamber precisely at sunrise.

According to Celtic legend, the god Aengus lived at Newgrange, and the hero Cúchulainn was conceived here.

The site (☎ 041-24488) is open 10 am to 7 pm from June to mid-September. From mid-March to May and mid-September to October, hours are 10 am to 1 pm and 2 to 5 pm. It's open 10 am to 1 pm and 2 to 4.30 pm from November to March but closed on Mondays. Entry is IR£1.50 (children 60p) and access is via a guided tour (you can wander around the exterior afterwards).

In summer, particularly on weekends, Newgrange is crowded (it's the busiest single tourist site in the country), and it's best to come during the week and/or first thing in the morning. The last tours leave about half an hour before closing time. Large groups must be booked in advance.

Across the road is a seasonal tourist office (☎ 041-24274), open April to October. An interpretative centre for the Brugh Na Bóinne is planned for the south bank of the river, probably opening in 1994. Like many other recent projects of the Office of Public Works, it's controversial, and there's a barrage of protest signs on the road leading to Newgrange.

A few hundred metres down the hill from the tomb is Newgrange Farm, a working farm with a wide range of animals on view, a picnic area and a coffee shop. It's a good place to wait for the tour of Newgrange to begin. It's open April to September, and admission is IR£1.75 for adults or children.

Dowth

The circular mound at Dowth is similar in size to Newgrange, about 63 metres in diameter, but at 14 metres high is slightly higher. Dowth has suffered badly at the hands of everyone from roadbuilders to treasure hunters to antiquarians, who scooped out the centre of the tumulus in the last century. For a time Dowth even had a teahouse perched on the summit, erected by a local lord. Relatively untouched by modern archaeologists, Dowth shows what Newgrange and Knowth looked like for most of their history.

There are two entrance passages leading to separate chambers (both barred), and a 24-metre early Christian souterrain with beehive structures at either end which connect up with the west passage. The nine-metre-long west passage leads into a small cruciform chamber, in which a recess acts as an entrance to an additional series of small compartments, a feature unique to Dowth. To the south-west is the entrance to a shorter passage and smaller chamber.

As it's undeveloped, the site is usually uncrowded and there is no admission charge. There are no tour facilities or car park.

North of the tumulus and visible from the summit are the ruins of **Dowth Castle** and **Dowth House**.

A native of the area was one John Boyle O'Reilly (1844-90). For his part in the Irish Republican Brotherhood, O'Reilly was deported to a penal colony in Australia from where he later escaped to the USA. As editor of the *Boston Pilot* newspaper he made an influential contribution to liberal opinion. The people of Boston erected a memorial to him in their city centre while the locals did the same here in the churchyard beside the castle.

Knowth

Knowth, the third principal burial mound of the necropolis, was built around the same time as Newgrange. Knowth seems set to surpass its better-known neighbour, both in the extent and importance of the discoveries here. It has the greatest collection of passage grave art ever uncovered in western Europe. Its complexity is due to the site's having been used over the centuries by many different cultures.

Modern excavations started at Knowth in 1962 and soon cleared a 35-metre passage to the central chamber, much longer than the one at Newgrange. In 1968 a second passage was unearthed on the opposite side of the mound. Although the chambers are separate, they are close enough for archaeologists to hear each other at work. Also in the mound are the remains of six Christian beehive souterrains similar to the one at Dowth. There are 17 'satellite graves' around the main mound. Human activity at Knowth continued for thousands of years after its construction. The Beaker people, so called because they buried their dead with a characteristic beaker, occupied the site in the Bronze Age (circa 1800 BC), as did the Celts in the Iron Age (circa 500 BC). Remnants of bronze and iron workings from these periods have been discovered. Around 800 to 900 AD it was turned into a rath or ring fort, a stronghold of the powerful UiNeill family. In 965, it was the seat of Corgalach McMaelmithic, later a high king of Ireland. The Normans built a motte and bailey here.

In about 1400 the site was abandoned. Excavations continue, and Knowth may reveal far more than Newgrange.

Only part of the site is open. Admission costs IR£1 (children 40p). There is a guided tour and there may be archaeologists at work. It's open 10 am to 5 pm May to October, and stays open for an extra 1½ hours mid-June to mid-September.

Getting There & Away

Newgrange, Knowth and Dowth are all well signposted. Newgrange is 13 km (eight miles) west of Drogheda, just north of the River Boyne. Dowth is between Newgrange and Drogheda while Knowth is about one km north-west of Newgrange or almost four km by road.

There are no buses to any of the sites. But there are a couple of buses between Slane and Drogheda on Mondays, Wednesdays and Fridays which will drop you on the main road about three km (two miles) from Newgrange.

SLANE

Slane is perched on a hillside overlooking the River Boyne, at the junction of the N2 and N51, 15 km (nine miles) west of Drogheda. Built as a manorial village for Slane Castle, it is a charming little place with stone houses, cottages and mature trees. Just to the south of the centre is the massive grey gate to Slane Castle.

A curious quartet of identical houses face each other at the junction of the main roads. A local tale relates that they were built for four sisters who had taken an intense dislike to each other and kept watch on each other from their residences! At the bottom of the hill, the River Boyne glides by under the narrow bridge.

The Hill of Slane

Above the village, one km north, is the Hill of Slane. Tradition holds that St Patrick lit a paschal (Easter) fire here in 433. Such a fire was in direct contravention of a decree issued by Laoghaire, the high king of Ireland, that no flame shall be lit in sight of Tara. Patrick's act thus symbolised Christianity's triumph over paganism. According to legend, Laoghaire was furious but was restrained by his druids who warned that 'the man who had kindled it would surpass kings and princes'. Instead, the king set out to meet with Patrick and question him. The king's attendants were under strict orders to ignore the saint and all but one (named Earc) greeted him scornfully.

During the encounter St Patrick killed one of the cursing men and then summoned an earthquake to subdue the king's guards. The king made peace, and although he refused to be converted he allowed Patrick to continue his work. Earc was converted and became Bishop of Slane. On the eve of Easter Sunday the local parish priest still lights a fire on the hill.

The site originally had a church associated with St Earc and later came a round tower and castle, but nothing remains of either. Later a motte and bailey was constructed and is still visible on the west side of the hill. The church, tower and other buildings come from an early 16th-century Franciscan friary. The tower can be climbed for the fine views of the Boyne Valley, and on a clear day it's said you can see seven counties of Ireland.

St Earc is said to have become a hermit in old age, and a small tumbledown 16th-century church marks the spot where he is thought to have spent his last days around 512 to 514. It's on the north river bank, behind the Protestant church on the Navan road. Its reputation as a hermitage came from two hermits named O'Brien who lived here in the 16th century. The ruins are on the private Conyngham estate and are only open to the public on 15 August.

Modern Ireland still has three hermits officially recognised by the church.

Ledwidge Museum

About one km out of the village on the Drogheda road is the Ledwidge Museum (☎ 041-24285). This labourer's cottage was the birthplace of Francis Ledwidge, a poet who died on the battlefields of Belgium in 1917 at the age of 29. Admission is IR£1, and it is open 10 am to 1 pm and 2 to 6 pm.

Slane Castle

Slane Castle, the private residence of the earl of Mountcharles, is two km along the Navan road and is best known in Ireland as the setting for major outdoor rock concerts. Springsteen and the Stones have appeared here, but the events have dwindled due to local antipathy to hordes of young rock fans.

Built in 1785 in Gothic Revival style by James Wyatt, the building was altered later by Francis Johnson for the visit of George IV to Lady Conyngham. She was allegedly his mistress, and it's said the Dublin to Slane road was built unusually straight and smooth to speed up the randy king's journeys.

Unfortunately much of the castle was destroyed by fire in 1991, and money is now being raised for restoration. The castle had some fine rooms, especially the ballroom, with good portraits and some notable furniture. The castle and grounds are strictly not open to the public.

Places to Stay

Hostel The former *Bridge of the Boyne* An Óige Hostel on the way to Navan is now closed. The nearest hostel is in Kells.

B&Bs *Boyne View* (☎ 041-24121), up the hill towards Slane from the bridge, is friendly and cheap at IR£12. Near the village centre, *Castle Hill House* (☎ 041-24696) at 2 Castle Hill, Slane, costs IR£16/26 for singles/doubles.

Hotels The lovely old *Conyngham Arms* (☎ 041-24155) is near the crossroads in Slane village, and has 16 rooms at IR£24 to IR£26 per person. They have a reasonable restaurant and you can get good snacks in the bar from 10.30 am to 7 pm.

Places to Eat

The *Roadhouse Rest* is attached to a petrol station three km (two miles) south of Slane on the Dublin road, and does generous servings of straightforward food.

The *Craft Shop*, in Slane on the Drogheda road, has a very nice tearoom in summer where you can also get lunches. For a serious meal try the *Conyngham Arms* near the crossroads or *Bartle's Steakhouse* (☎ 041-24664) on the crossroads.

Getting There & Away

Bus From Dublin, Slane is on the Letterkenny and Armagh Bus Éireann routes as well as the less busy routes to Portrush and Derry. There's a service between Slane and Drogheda about three times a day. The stop is at Conlon's shop near the crossroads. For information ring ☎ 01-366111.

Train Only the coast is serviced by the Dublin (Connolly Station) to Belfast line, with the odd stop at Mosney, a holiday camp two km south of Laytown, and Laytown itself, before Drogheda.

SLANE TO NAVAN

The 14-km (eight-mile) journey between Slane and Navan follows the Boyne Valley past a number of great houses, ruined castles, round towers and churches, only of mild interest compared to the fine sites elsewhere in County Meath.

Dunmoe Castle lies down a horrendously bumpy cul-de-sac four km (2.5 miles) from Navan. This D'Arcy castle is a 16th-century ruin with good views of the countryside and of an impressive red-brick manor, Ardmulchan House, on the far side of the River Boyne. Cromwell is supposed to have fired at the castle from the opposite bank in 1649. Local legend holds that a tunnel used to run from the castle vaults under the river. Near Dunmoe Castle is a small overgrown chapel and graveyard, with a crypt containing members of the D'Arcy family. Ardmulchan House, though somewhat dilapidated, is still used as a private residence.

You can't miss the fine 30-metre round tower and 13th-century church of **Donaghmore**, a km nearer Navan. The site has a profusion of modern gravestones, but the tower with its Crucifixion scene above the door is interesting and there are carved faces near the windows.

NAVAN

The county town of Navan at the confluence of the Rivers Boyne and Blackwater is disfigured by a busy road which cuts off the river from the town. Navan was the birthplace of Sir Francis Beaufort of the British Navy, who in 1805 devised the internationally accepted scale for wind strengths. The town has a carpet factory and some big furniture stores. Tara mine, the largest lead and zinc mine in Europe, is three km along the Kells road.

Orientation & Information

The town plan is based around Ludlow, Watergate and Trimgate Sts, which lead from Market Square to the sites of the former town gates. There is a tourist information point in the Leisure Circle newsagent on Trimgate St.

The post office is on Kennedy Rd off Trimgate St, as are the banks and the Garda station. The Bizzy Laundry is beside the Lyric Cinema on Brew's Hill.

Places to Stay

The nearest hostel is in Kells.

B&Bs *Lios Na Greine* (☎ 046-28092), almost two km south of Navan on the R153 Duleek/Ashbourne road, has three rooms at IR£17/26. *Tower View* (☎ 046-23358) is three km (two miles) along the Slane road and costs IR£13 per person.

Balreask House (☎ 046-21155) is three km (two miles) from Navan and has rooms at IR£17/26; go two km along the N3 Dublin road until the Old Bridge Inn, turn right and it's one km along. *Swynnerton Lodge* (☎ 046-21371), one km from Navan on the main road to Slane, is a 19th-century fishing lodge overlooking the Boyne. They cater for fishing and shooting and charge IR£16 to IR£18 per person with a minimum stay of two nights. Dinner is IR£12.

Hotels The *Ardboyne Hotel* (☎ 046-23119) is a first-class hotel on the Dublin road, charging IR£32 to IR£40 per person B&B. The *Beechmount Hotel* (☎ 046-21553), just outside Navan on the Trim road, costs IR£23 to IR£25.

In Kilmessan, 10 km (6.5 miles) south of Navan, the delightful little *Station House Hotel* (☎ 046-25239) costs IR£25 to IR£28. Light meals are available at lunch times and they have a good restaurant open Monday to Saturday 6 to 9.30 pm with an early bird menu before 8 pm.

Places to Eat

Snacks *Susie's Cookhouse* is a good vegetarian place on Market Square. The *Pepper Pot* is a busy little coffee shop handy for lunches, or there's the *Coffee Dock* opposite the church and *Tasty Bites* on Trimgate St.

Pub Food Try the comfortable *O'Flaherty's*, on the corner of Trimgate St and Brew's Hill, *Bernard Reilly's* on Trimgate St or the *Round O* on Flower Hill at the edge of town on the Slane road. The *Flat House Pub* near the roundabout just out on the road to Trim serves good, solid food.

Restaurants On Brew's Hill, the popular *China Gardens* (☎ 046-23938) do excellent Chinese and some European food. On Ludlow St across from Bermingham's Bar is *Jimmy's Cantonese*, although Jimmy has a tendency to disappear windsurfing as a notice in his window often indicates.

Dunderry Lodge (☎ 046-31671) is a sophisticated restaurant in the village of Dunderry, five km (three miles) west, off the Navan to Athboy road. Set dinners are IR£17 to IR£20 and they are open Tuesday to Saturday for dinner and Sunday for lunch.

Entertainment

O'Flaherty's and *Bernard Reilly's* are popular, modern and comfortably furnished pubs on Trimgate St. *Robbie O'Malley's* on Watergate St is similar.

The tiny *Bermingham's Pub* on Ludlow St has an old wooden frontage and faded posters inside. They have music on Thursdays and Sunday mornings. The *Lantern Bar* at the bottom of Watergate St has an Irish music night on Thursdays. There are nightclubs in the Ardboyne and Beechmount hotels.

The Palace Cinema is on Ludlow St and the Lyric on Brew's Hill.

Getting There & Away

Bus Bus Éireann buses stop at McDonagh's Electrical Shop on Market Square. For times check with Walsh & Kealy's pub and shop on the square. There are regular buses to and from Dublin's Busáras.

Sillan Tours (☎ 042-69130), based in Shercock in County Cavan, have a number of coaches going through every morning between 7.20 and 7.30 am, en route to Dublin.

Getting Around

Clarke's Sports Den (☎ 046-21130) on Trimgate St is the local Raleigh dealer, with bikes for IR£7 a day or IR£20 a week, plus a deposit of IR£50.

AROUND NAVAN

There are some nice walks in the area, particularly following the towpath that runs beside the River Boyne towards Slane. On the south bank, you can go out about seven km (four miles) as far as Hayestown and the Bridge o' the Boyne with ease, passing Dunmoe Castle on the opposite bank and Ardmulchan House on the same side as the path. See under Slane to Navan. From the bridge towards Slane is trickier as the path is rough and in some places switches to the opposite side of the bank, with no bridge for you to follow suit.

Just west of town is **Navan Motte**, a scrub-covered mound which tradition holds to be the burial site of Odhbha, the wife of a Celtic prince who had abandoned her for Tea (pronounced Tay-ah), the lady who gave her name to Tara. Odhbha pursued her husband to Navan and died from a broken heart. The mound is thought in reality to have formed naturally; it was then adapted by the Normans as a motte and bailey.

Two km south-east of town are the impressive remains of **Athlumney House**, built by the Dowdall family in the 15th century with 17th-century additions. This relatively intact castle was said to have been set alight in 1690 by its then owner Launcelot Dowdall, after James's defeat at the Battle of the Boyne. Dowdall vowed that the conquering William would never shelter or confiscate his home. He watched the blaze from the opposite bank of the river before leaving for France and Italy. The grounds are now occupied by a convent.

Close to the Kells road, five km (three miles) north-west of Navan, is the large ruin of another castle which once belonged to the Talbot family. **Liscartan Castle** is made up of two 15th-century towers joined by a hall-like room.

TARA

The Hill of Tara has occupied a special place in Irish legend for up to 5000 years, although we don't know exactly when people first settled on this gently sloping hill with its commanding views over the plains of Meath. One of the many mounds on the hill was found to be a Stone Age passage grave from about 2500 BC, and during the Bronze Age important people were certainly being buried here.

Much of Tara's pagan significance seems to have derived from its associations with the goddess Maeve (Medbh) and the mythical powers of the druids or priest-kings who ruled over part of the country from here. By the 2nd and 3rd centuries AD, Tara was the seat of the most powerful rulers in Ireland, a place where the high king and his royal court had their ceremonial residence, feasted and watched over the realm. Whilst Tara's kings may have been more powerful than the others, they would by no means have held sway over the whole country, as there were countless other petty kings and chieftains controlling many smaller areas.

Tara's remains are not visually impressive. Only mounds and depressions in grassy meadows mark where Iron Age hill forts and surrounding ring forts once stood. But on a mellow summer evening, when the shadows lengthen and the sun highlights the hill's earthworks, you can sit back, appreciate the view and get some sense of the commanding power of the place.

As the focus of Irish political influence and a centre of pagan worship, Tara was targeted by the early Christians. A great pagan feis or festival is thought to have been held around what is now Hallowe'en. On Tara St Patrick supposedly used the three-leaved shamrock to illustrate the idea of the Holy Trinity – the Father, the Son and the Holy Ghost acting as one unified force – hence the adoption of the shamrock as a national symbol.

After the 6th century, once Christianity had a widespread hold and Tara's pagan significance waned, Tara's high kings began to desert her. Diarmait McCerrbeoil was the last to stage the great feis here. However, the kings of Leinster continued to be based here.

In August 1843, Tara saw one of the greatest crowds ever to gather in Ireland. Daniel O'Connell, the 'Liberator' and leader of the opposition to union with Great Britain, held one of his 'monster meetings' at Tara, and 750,000 people came to hear him speak. During a recent excavation, traces of O'Connell's wooden platform were uncovered on the Mound of the Hostages.

Entrance to Tara (☎ 046-25903) is IR£1 (40p for students or children). The interpretive centre and tours are open June to September, 9.30 am to 6.30 pm, and in May and October from 10 am to 5 pm. Tara is nine km (six miles) from Navan and 40 km (25 miles) from Dublin, signposted off the Dublin to Navan (N3) road. Entrance to Tara and to the visitor centre costs IR£1.

Visitor Centre

The former Protestant church (with a window by the well-known artist Evie Hone) now houses the Tara visitor centre (☎ 046-25903), and during the summer the tour from here is a must, as the anecdotes really bring the remains to life. The names applied to Tara's various humps and bumps were adopted from ancient texts, and mythology and religion intertwine with the historical facts.

Rath of the Synods

The Protestant church grounds and graveyard spill onto the remains of the Rath of the Synods, a triple-ringed fort supposed to be the location of some of St Patrick's early meetings or synods. Excavations on the Rath suggest it was used between 200 and 400 AD for burials, rituals and living quarters. Originally the ring fort would have contained wooden houses surrounded by timber palisades.

During a digging session in the graveyard in 1810, a boy found a pair of gold torcs, necklaces of twisted gold strips, now in the National Museum in Dublin. During later excavations, there was a surprise when Roman glass, shards of pottery and seals were discovered, showing links with the Roman Empire, which never extended its power to Ireland.

The poor state of the Rath is due in part to a group of British 'Israelites' who in the 1890s dug the place up looking for the Sacred Ark of the Covenant, much to the consternation of the locals. The Israelites' leader claimed to see on the Rath a mysterious pillar, but unfortunately it was invisible to everyone else. After they failed to uncover anything, the invisible pillar moved to the other side of the road, but before the adventurers had time to start work, worried locals chased them away.

The Royal Enclosure

To the south of the church, the Royal Enclosure (Ráth Na Ríogh) is a large oval Iron Age hill fort, 315 metres in diameter, surrounded by a bank and ditch cut through solid rock under the soil. Inside the Royal Enclosure are smaller sites.

Mound of the Hostages This noticeable bump in the north corner of the Rath (Dumha Na nGiall in Irish) is the most ancient known part of Tara and the most visible of the remains. It was supposed to have been a prison cell for hostages of King Cormac, son of Art, in the 3rd century AD. It is in fact a small Stone Age passage grave dating from around 2500 BC and later reused by Bronze

Age people. The passage contains some carved stonework but is closed to the public.

The mound produced a treasure trove of artefacts including some Mediterranean beads of amber and faience from the 16th century BC. Over 35 Bronze Age burials were found in the mound, as well as a mass of cremated remains from the Stone Age.

Cormac's House & Royal Seat Two other earthworks inside the enclosure are Cormac's House (Teach Cormaic) and the Royal Seat (Forradh). They look similar, though the Royal Seat is a ring fort with a house site in the centre, while Cormac's House is a barrow, or burial mound, in the side of the circular bank. Cormac's House commands the best views of the surrounding lowlands of the Boyne and Blackwater valleys.

Inside Cormac's House is the phallic **Stone of Destiny** or Lia Fáil, originally located near the Mound of the Hostages and representing the joining of the gods of the earth and the heavens. It is said to be the inauguration stone of the kings of Tara. The would-be king stood on top of it, and if the stone let out three roars, he was crowned.

Other legends claim the stone is the pillow on which Jacob rested his head and dreamt of an angel descending on a ladder from heaven, with whom he fought. The stone was supposedly later brought to Ireland by Jewish refugees. Others say that it ended up as the Stone of Scone in Westminster Abbey, used during coronations. The mass grave of 37 men who died in a skirmish on Tara during the 1798 Rising is near the stone.

Enclosure of King Laoghaire
South of the Royal Enclosure is the Enclosure of King Laoghaire, a large but worn ring fort where the king is supposedly buried standing upright in his armour to look out for his enemies.

The Banquet Hall
North of the churchyard is Tara's most unusual feature, the Banquet Hall or Teach Miodhchuarta which translates as the 'House of Mead-Circling' (mead, a popular tipple, was fermented from honey). This rectangular earthwork measures 230 metres by 27 metres along a north-south axis. Tradition holds that it was built to cater for thousands of guests during feasts like the feis. Much of this information about the hall comes from the 12th-century 'Book of Leinster' and 'The Yellow Book of Lecan', which even include drawings of it.

Opinion varies as to the site's real purpose. Its orientation suggests that it was a sunken entrance to Tara, leading directly to the Royal Enclosure. More recent research has uncovered graves within the compound and it is possible that the banks are in fact the burial sites of some of the kings of Tara.

Gráinne's Fort
Gráinne's Fort (Ráth Gráinne) and the north and south Sloping Trenches (Claoin Fhearta) off to the north-west are burial mounds. Gráinne's Fort was named after the daughter goddess of King Cormac who was betrothed to Fionn McCumhaill. She eloped with Diarmuid, one of the king's warriors, on her wedding night and started the epic saga of Diarmuid and Gráinne. When the King of Leinster laid siege to Tara around 220 AD, Tara's inhabitants are said to have been slaughtered in the Sloping Trenches.

AROUND TARA
Five km south of Tara on the Kilmessan road is **Dunsany Castle** (☎ 946-25198), the residence of the lords of Dunsany, former owners of the lands around Trim Castle. The Dunsanys are related to the Plunkett family, the most famous Plunkett being St Oliver, who was executed, and whose head is kept in a church in Drogheda.

The present Lord Dunsany opens his house to visitors three months during the summer; it's best to ring ahead and check. Admission is IR£3, and they prefer people to come as part of group tours organised by the Drogheda tourist office and the Irish Georgian Society. There is an impressive private art collection (although paintings by Van Dyck and Jack B Yeats have been stolen) and many other treasures related to important figures in Irish history like Oliver Plunkett and Patrick Sarsfield.

About 1.5 km north-east of Dunsany is the ruined **Killeen Castle**, the seat of another line of the Plunkett family. The 1801 mansion was built around an 1180 Hugh de Lacy original and comprises a neo-Gothic structure between two 12th-century towers.

According to local lore, the surrounding lands were divided at one point amongst the two branches of the family by a race. Starting at the castles, the wives had to run towards each other and a fence was placed where they met. Luckily for the Killeen side, their castle is on higher ground and they made considerable gains, as their woman was running downhill against the uphill struggle faced by Dunsany's representative.

Another five km south-east on the Dublin road is the town of **Dunshaughlin** and **Fairyhouse Racecourse** seven km (four miles) beyond. The Easter holiday races of 1916 attracted a large contingent of English soldiers out of Dublin while the Rising was beginning.

TRIM

Trim is a pleasant, rather sleepy little town on the River Boyne and has several interesting ruins. The name comes from Baile Átha Troim, meaning 'ford of the elder bushes'. At one stage, there were seven monasteries in the immediate area. Few visitors pause to inspect the impressive ruins of Ireland's largest Anglo-Norman structure, Trim Castle, a sprawling construction surmounted by a huge keep.

According to locals, Queen Elizabeth I considered Trim as a possible site for Trinity College, which eventually ended up in Dublin. The Duke of Wellington went to school for a time in St Mary's Abbey/Talbot Castle, which served as a Protestant school in the 18th century. There's an unlikely local tradition that he was born in a stable south of the town, which probably arose from the Duke's observation that being born in a stable didn't make one a horse, and thus his birth in Ireland didn't make him Irish! There

is a Wellington monument at the junction of Patrick and Emmet Sts. After defeating Napoleon at the Battle of Waterloo, the Iron Duke went on to become prime minister of Great Britain and in 1829 passed the Catholic Emancipation Act which repealed the last of the repressive penal laws.

Trim was once home to the county jail, giving rise to the ditty:

Kells for brogues
Navan for rogues
And Trim for hanging people.

Orientation & Information

Once a notorious bottleneck, Trim now has a new by-pass to the east of the centre. The medieval town was a jumble of streets and once had five gates. The summer tourist office (☎ 046-37111) on Mill St sells a handy little *Trim Tourist Trail* walking tour booklet. The post office is at the junction of Emmet St and Market St.

In the same building as the tourist office on Mill St is the Trim interpretive centre and the Meath heritage centre (☎ 046-36633). The former has displays and information on Trim's history and the latter has an extensive genealogical database for people trying to trace Meath ancestors. The heritage centre also runs group tours of Trim and other sites of interest in Meath.

Trim Castle

Hugh de Lacy founded Trim Castle in 1172 but Rory O'Connor, said to have been the last high king of Ireland, destroyed this motte and bailey within a year. De Lacy did not live to see the castle's replacement, and the building you see today was begun around 1200.

King John visited Trim in 1210 to bring the de Lacy family into line, giving the castle its alternative name of King John's Castle. He is supposed never to have actually slept in the castle, as on the eve of his arrival Walter de Lacy locked up the castle and left town, forcing the king to camp in the nearby meadow.

It was de Lacy's grandson-in-law, Geoffrey de Geneville, who was responsible for

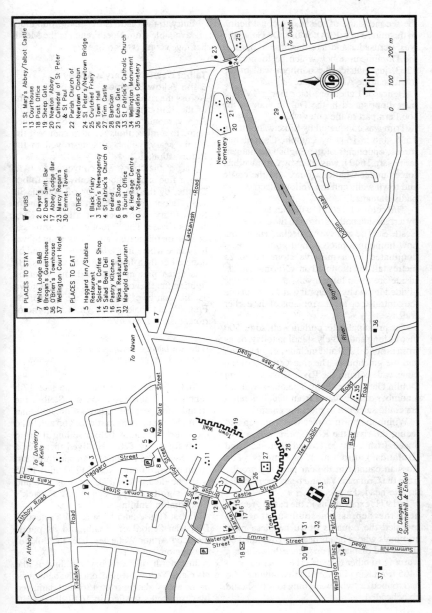

Trim

0   100   200 m

PLACES TO STAY

7   White Lodge B&B
8   Brogan's Guesthouse
36 O'Brien's Townhouse
37 Wellington Court Hotel

PLACES TO EAT

5   Haggard Inn/Stables Restaurant
14 Spicer's Coffee Shop
15 Salad Bowl Deli
16 Wastry Kitchen
31 Woks Restaurant
32 Marigold Restaurant

PUBS

2   Dwyer's
12 Dean Swift Bar
17 Abbey Lodge Bar
23 Marcy Regan's
30 Emmet Tavern

OTHER

1   Black Friary
3   Tobin's Newsagency
4   St Patrick's Church of Ireland
6   Bus Stop
9   Tourist Office & Heritage Centre
10 Yellow Steeple
11 St Mary's Abbey/Talbot Castle
13 Courthouse
18 Post Office
19 Sheep Gate
20 Newton Abbey
21 Cathedral of St Peter & St Paul
22 Parish Church of Newtown Clonbun
24 St Peter's/Newtown Bridge
25 Crutched Friary
26 Town Hall
28 Trim Castle
28 Barbican
29 Echo Gate
33 St Patrick's Catholic Church
34 Wellington Monument
35 Maudlins Cemetery

the second stage of the keep's construction in the mid to late 13th century. De Geneville was a crusader and later became a monk at the Dominican abbey which he founded in 1263, just outside the northern wall of the town near the Athboy Gate.

Henry of Lancaster, later Henry IV, was once imprisoned in the Dublin Gate at the southern part of the outer wall.

Trim was conquered by Silken Thomas in 1536, and in 1647 by Catholic Confederate forces, opponents of the English parliamentarians. In 1649 it was taken by Cromwellian forces under Charles Coote, and the castle and town walls and the Yellow Steeple were badly damaged.

The ruins of Trim Castle can be reached by a riverside path or through the car park on Castle St. The grassy two-hectare enclosure, now home to a pitch & putt golf course, is dominated by a massive stone keep, 25 metres tall and mounted on a Norman motte. Inside are three lofty levels, the lowest one divided in two by a central wall. Just outside the central keep are the remains of the earlier wall.

The principal outer curtain wall, some 500 metres long and largely standing today, dates from around 1250 and includes eight towers and the gatehouse. The finest stretch of the outer wall is from the River Boyne through Dublin Gate to Castle St. The outer wall has a number of sally gates from which defenders could sally out to meet the enemy.

Within the north corner was a church and facing the river the Royal Mint which produced Irish coinage (called 'Patricks' and 'Irelands') into the 15th century. The Russian cannon in the car park is a trophy from the Crimean War and bears the imperial double-headed eagle.

In 1971, excavations in the castle grounds near the depression south of the keep revealed the remains of 10 headless men, criminals whose heads had been mounted on spikes and displayed on the castle walls as a warning to other thieves. The order came in 1465 from King Edward IV that anyone who had robbed or 'who was going to rob' should be beheaded.

Entry to the castle is free and group tours are available from Noel French at the Meath heritage centre (☎ 046-36633).

Talbot Castle/St Mary's Abbey & the Yellow Steeple

Across the river from the castle are the ruins of the 12th-century Augustinian St Mary's Abbey, rebuilt after a fire in 1368 and once home to a miraculous wooden statue of the Virgin Mary, which was destroyed in the Reformation.

Part of the abbey was converted in 1415 into a fine manor house known as **Talbot Castle**, by the then Viceroy of Ireland, Sir John Talbot, later to be created 1st earl of Shrewsbury, who lived for a time in King John's Castle. The Talbot coat of arms can be seen on the north wall. Talbot went to war in France where in 1429 he was defeated by none other than Joan of Arc at Orleans. He was taken prisoner, released and went on fighting the French till 1453. He was known as 'the scourge of France' or 'the whip of the French', and Shakespeare wrote of this notorious man in *Henry VI*:

Is this the Talbot so much feared abroad
That with his name the mothers still their babes?

Talbot Castle was owned in the late 17th century by Esther Johnson or 'Stella', the friend and perhaps mistress of Jonathan Swift. She bought the castle for £65 and lived there for 18 months before selling it on to Swift for a tidy £200. He lived there for a year. Swift was rector of Laracor, three km south of Trim from around 1700 until 1745 when he died. From 1713 he was also and more significantly Dean of St Patrick's Cathedral in Dublin.

Talbot House later became the Protestant Diocesan School of Meath, and its pupils included Arthur Wellesley, later the duke of Wellington.

Just north of the abbey building is the 40-metre Yellow Steeple, once the bell tower of the abbey, dating from 1368 but damaged by Cromwell's soldiers in 1649. It takes its name from the colour of the stonework at dusk.

A part of the 14th-century town wall still stands in the field to the east of the abbey, and includes the **Sheep Gate**, sole survivor of the town's original five gates. It used to be closed from 9 pm to 4 am each night, and a toll was charged for sheep entering to be sold at market.

Newtown Trim

East of town on the Lackanash road, there is an interesting group of ruins in Newtown Cemetery.

The parish church of Newtown Clonbun contains the 16th-century tomb of Sir Luke Dillon, Chief Baron of the Exchequer during the reign of Elizabeth I, and his wife Lady Jane Bathe. The effigies are known locally as 'the jealous man and woman'. It's suggested that the sword which lies between them gave rise to this name. Rainwater which collects between the figures is claimed to cure warts if you place a pin in the puddle and then jab your wart. When the pin becomes covered in rust your warts will vanish. Some say you should leave a pin on the statue as payment for the cure.

The other buildings here are Newtown's **Cathedral of St Peter & St Paul** and the 18th-century **Newtown Abbey**. The cathedral was founded in 1206 and burnt down two centuries later. Parts of the cathedral wall were flattened by the Big Wind in January 1839, which also damaged sections of the Trim Castle wall. Newtown Abbey's full name is the Abbey of the Canons Regular of St Victor of Paris. The abbey wall throws a superb echo back to **Echo Gate** across the river.

East again from these ruins, and just over the river, is the **Crutched Friary**. Built as a hospital after the crusades by the Knights of St John of Jerusalem, there are ruins of a keep and traces of a watchtower and other buildings. **St Peter's Bridge** beside the friary is said to be the second oldest in Ireland, and the green and gold Marcy Regan's pub beside the bridge is claimed to be the second oldest pub, and is now open in the evenings.

Wart Cures

Wart cures are just amusing old folk tales aren't they? Well, in 1991 I paused to have a look at Newtown Cathedral and I daubed some wart-curing rainwater from the statue on my daughter's knee. She'd had an annoying little cluster of warts there for a couple of years, and visits to a skin specialist and a variety of high-tech treatments had failed to shift them. Two weeks later they were all gone and have not returned! I passed through Trim again in 1992 and paused to leave a pin on the statue, payment for a very satisfactory course of treatment.

Tony Wheeler

Other Places in Trim

The site of the Dominican **Black Friary** lies north of the town, near the junction of the Athboy and Kells roads. Only a few mounds remain.

At the other end of town, **Maudlin's Cemetery** has the bronze statue of Our Lady of Trim, linked sentimentally although not in reality with a wooden statue put in St Mary's Abbey after its 1368 restoration. The statue was reputed to have miraculous powers. It survived the abbey's suppression in 1540 and later came into the possession of a powerful local family. After the sack of Drogheda in 1649, Cromwell's commander lodged in the house and the statue was burnt as firewood.

Places to Stay

B&Bs Crannmór (☎ 046-31635) is a converted farmhouse about one km along the road to Dunderry which costs IR£13.50 with bathroom or IR£12 without.

Brogan's Guesthouse (☎ 046-31237) in the centre of Trim on High St has an old-world flavour and charges IR£13. They have an adjoining bar and do lunches. *White Lodge* (☎ 046-36549) is 500 metres out of town at the north end of the Trim by-pass on the road to Navan, overlooking the castle and near the modern Lady of Trim statue. B&B is IR£13 or IR£15 with bathroom. *O'Briens Townhouse* (☎ 046-31745) on the Dublin road costs IR£12.50.

For something a little unusual, try *Knightsbrook House* (☎ 046-31372), an 18th-century Gothic house about six km from Trim. To get there go three km (two miles) along the Summerhill road, turn left at Laracor crossroads and it's about one km along on the left. B&B with bathroom costs IR£20 per person. A good country dinner costs IR£16.

Hotels The fairly ordinary-looking *Wellington Court* (☎ 046-31516) is the town's only hotel, with well-equipped singles/doubles at IR£30/40.

Places to Eat
Emmet St has takeaways and two Chinese restaurants: *Marigolds* (☎ 046-36544) and the nearby *Woks* (☎ 046-36368). *Spicers* is a bakery and coffee shop on Market St, good for a snack. For a more substantial lunch, try the *Salad Bowl Deli* on the same street. The *Dean Swift Bar* on Bridge St and the *Emmet Tavern* on Emmet St are fine for bar food and lunches, as is the *Abbey Lodge Bar* on Market St. The *Pastry Kitchen* on Market St is good for snacks or lunch.

The *Stables Restaurant* (☎ 046-31110) in the Haggard Inn on Haggard St is one of the best places to eat in town and has a three-course tourist menu for around IR£10.

Getting There & Away
Bus The Bus Éireann stop is at Tobin's Newsagency on the corner of Haggard St and Navan Gate St. For information try the shop or ring ☎ 01-366111. Bus Éireann services between Dublin's Busáras and Athboy/Granard pass through Trim five times daily (twice on Sunday) in each direction.

There are daily buses to/from Athlone and Drogheda/Dundalk plus an extra Friday evening service.

AROUND TRIM
Jonathan Swift (1667-1745), author of *Gulliver's Travels*, was the rector of **Laracor** for 15 years before becoming Dean of St Patrick's Cathedral in Dublin in 1713. Laracor is three km from Trim on the road south to Summerhill, but nothing remains of the rectory which stood by the bridge.

Three km farther south, **Dangan Castle**, built by the Wellesley family, was the home of the Duke of Wellington as a boy. The castle is also supposed to have been the birthplace of Don Ambrosio O'Higgins (died 1801), the Spanish viceroy of Peru and Chile at the end of the 18th century. His son Bernardo O'Higgins went on to become the Liberator of Chile, and Santiago's main thoroughfare is named after him. The mansion's current state is the result of the efforts of Roger O'Conor, its last owner, who set it alight on a number of occasions in 1808-09 for the insurance.

On the road you might spot the huge slender mast of **Atlantic 252**, a long-wave radio station which broadcasts to Britain from Ireland.

Summerhill, nine km from Trim, is a pleasant, sleepy little village with a large and tidy green, but there's nothing much to do here except have lunch at *Shaw's*. Swift's connection with the area includes a curious folly in **Castlerichard**, a hamlet 10 km west of Summerhill. By the church over the old bridge is a large pyramid of stone inscribed with the word 'Swifte'.

Near the small town of Athboy is **Rathcarn**, 12 km (eight miles) north-west of Trim, one of the few Irish-speaking or gaeltacht outposts outside the remote western seaboard. Rathcarn's population are descended from a group of Connemara people who were settled on an estate here in the 1930s.

BECTIVE ABBEY
Bective Abbey lies halfway between Trim and Navan, south off the R161 on the Kilmessan road and the west bank of the Boyne.

Founded in 1147, Bective Abbey was the first Cistercian offshoot spawned by Mellifont Abbey in Louth. The remains seen today are 13th and 15th-century additions and consist of the chapter house, church and alleys with fine cloisters. After the dissolution of the monasteries in 1543, it was used as a fortified house, and the tower was built.

In 1186, Hugh de Lacy, Lord of Meath, desecrated the abbey in Durrow, County Offaly, to build a castle, which offended a local man variously known as O'Miadaigh and O'Kearney, who lopped off de Lacy's head and fled. Although de Lacy's body was interred in Bective Abbey, his head went to St Thomas's Abbey, Dublin. A dispute broke out over who should possess all the remains, and it required the intervention of the Pope to decide matters, with St Thomas's Abbey winning out. Their interest was not so much in reuniting the head and torso out of respect for the dead, but in the prestige that went with the complete body of such an important and powerful man.

KELLS

Almost every visitor to Ireland pays homage to 'The Book of Kells' in Dublin's Trinity College; far fewer pause to see where it came from. Little remains of the ancient monastic site in the town of Kells, but there are some fine high crosses in various states of preservation, a 1000-year-old round tower, the even older St Colmcille's House, and an interesting little exhibit in the gallery of the local church. It must be said that present-day Kells is a fairly uninspiring place and doesn't reflect its past glory.

St Colmcille established the monastic settlement here in the 6th century, and in 806 monks arrived from a sister monastery on the remote Scottish island of Iona, retreating from a Viking onslaught in which 68 of their brothers were killed. It is thought that they brought the bones of their revered saint and 'The Book of Kells' with them. The book was stolen in 1007 but the thief was only after its gold case and it was later found buried in a bog. Kells proved to be little safer than Scotland, for Viking raids soon spread to Ireland and Kells was plundered on five occasions between 807 and 1019.

Orientation & Information

The main road to Donegal and Northern Ireland almost bypasses the town. Turning off the main road at the Market High Cross brings you down to a central block and square where you'll find most of the shops and pubs including the Clock, a useful newsagency and grocery which sells disposable mousetraps amongst other remarkable objects. There is no tourist office, but the hostel is helpful with queries.

Detail from the Book of Kells

Round Towers & High Crosses

The comparatively modern and uninteresting Protestant church west of the town centre stands on the grounds of the old monastic settlement. There is an exhibit on the settlement and its famous illuminated book in the church's gallery, with a facsimile on show.

The churchyard has a 30-metre-high, 10th-century round tower on the south side. It's minus its original roof, but it's known to date back to at least 1076, when Muircheartach Maelsechnaill, king of Tara, was murdered in its confined apartments. Access to the grounds are through the main gate, down the hill from the tower and around to the left.

Inside, the churchyard are four 9th-century high crosses in various states of repair. The West Cross at the far end of the compound from the entrance is a stump of a decorated shaft with scenes of the Baptism of Jesus, the Fall of Adam and Eve, and the Judgement of Solomon on the east face, with Noah's Ark on the west face. All that is left of the North Cross is the bowl-like base stone.

Near the tower is the best preserved of the crosses, the Cross of Patrick & Colmcille, with its semilegible inscription 'Patrici et Columbae Crux' on the east side of the base. Above it are scenes of Daniel in the Lions' Den, the Burning Fiery Furnace, the Fall of Adam and Eve and a hunting scene. On the opposite face are the Last Judgement, the Crucifixion, and riders with a chariot and a dog on the base.

The other remaining cross is the East Cross, which is unfinished. On the east side is a carving of the Crucifixion and a group of four figures on the right arm. The three blank, raised panels below these were prepared for carving but the sculptor never got around to them.

Finally, a square church tower dating from the 15th century stands beside the modern church. Above the door is an inscription detailing the addition of the spire in 1783 by the Earl of Bective from a design by Thomas Cooley, architect of Dublin's City Hall. Below this are a number of tombstones and stone heads set into its walls.

St Colmcille's House
From the churchyard exit St Colmcille's House is left up the hill, amongst the row of houses on the right side of the road. Mrs Carpenter, who lives in the brown house near the stop sign on the right, has keys to the monument.

This squat, solid survivor from the old monastic settlement resembles St Flannan's, Killaloe, and St Kevin's Church in Glendalough, County Wicklow, in its construction. The original entrance door to the 1000-year-old building was over two metres above ground level, and inside a ladder leads to a low attic room under the roofline.

Market High Cross
The Market Cross stands in the commercial centre of town on Cross St, marking the boundary of the 10th-century monastery. It is said that it was moved here by Jonathan Swift, and in 1798 the English garrison exe-

cuted rebels by hanging them from the crosspiece, one on each arm so the cross wouldn't fall over. It has suffered some damage over the years: the shaft has had chunks taken out of it and the pinnacle is missing. On the east side are Abraham's sacrifice of Isaac; Cain and Abel; the Fall of Adam and Eve, guards at the tomb of Jesus, and a procession of horsemen. On the west face the Crucifixion is the only discernible image. Finally on the north face is a panel of Jacob wrestling with the angel.

Places to Stay
Kells Independent Youth Hostel (☎ 046-40100) is an excellent place next door to Monaghan's pub on the Cavan road 200 metres from the bus stop. A bed in a dorm costs IR£5 and in a private room IR£6. There's a full kitchen and other facilities. Camping costs IR£3 per person.

The wonderful 200-year-old *Lennoxsbrook House* (☎ 046-45902) is five km (three miles) north of Kells on the road to Cavan. The double rooms cost IR£13 per person B&B. It's open February to November and serves dinner for IR£13.

Outside Kells in Crossakeel, *Deerpark Farm* (☎ 046-43609) costs IR£18/32 for singles/doubles. They serve home-made bread with breakfast and the farm's organic produce often features in the IR£12 dinner.

Places to Eat
In the centre of Kells, *Penny's Place* (☎ 046-41630) is an excellent little café with home-made food and drinks It's open until 6 pm, Monday to Saturday. The *Round Tower* (☎ 046-40844) is a good restaurant near the post office.

O'Shaughnessy's pub is in the centre and does reasonable sandwiches and lunches. *Monaghan's* pub, on the main street, does lunch for around IR£3 and dinner with main courses from IR£4.

Entertainment
In the centre, *O'Shaughnessy's* pleasant pub features lots of rustic timber, while the *Blackwater Pub* has regular Irish music ses-

sions. *Monaghan's* is next door to the hostel so it gets a good young crowd and often has music at weekends.

Getting There & Away

The Bus Éireann stop in Kells is outside the Video Box video rental shop just beside the Market Cross. For fares and times try the shop or phone ☎ 01-366111. Buses run from Dublin to Kells and Cavan and back almost hourly between 7.30 am and 10.30 pm. Two of the buses are express coaches on their way to and from Donegal. There are also regular services to Navan and Bailieboro.

AROUND KELLS
Hill of Lloyd Tower

The 30-metre Hill of Lloyd tower is visible from any high point in town and it's easy to see why it became known as the 'inland lighthouse'. Built in 1791 by the Earl of Bective in memory of his father, it has recently been renovated and if it's open you can climb to the top for IR£1, or picnic in the surrounding park. The tower is two km west of Kells, off the Crossakeel road.

Crosses of Castlekeeran

A little farther down the Crossakeel road, signposted to the right, are the Crosses of Castlekeeran. Access is through a farmyard, from where the farmer's friendly dog may accompany you through the field. Four plainly carved early 9th-century crosses, one in the river, are surrounded by an overgrown cemetery, while at the ruined church in the centre are some early grave slabs and an Ogham stone.

CAIRNS OF LOUGHCREW

The Loughcrew Hills beyond Oldcastle are also known as Slieve na Calliaghe and give marvellous views east and south to the plains of Meath and north into the lake country of Cavan. On the summit of three of the hills are the remains of 30 Stone Age passage graves built around 3000 BC but reused up to the Iron Age. In some cases, a large mound is surrounded by numerous smaller satellite graves. Like Newgrange, larger stones in

some of the graves are decorated with spiral and motif patterns. Archaeologists have unearthed bone fragments and burnt bones, stone balls and beads. Some of the graves look like a large pile of stones, while others are less obvious, the cairn having been removed.

To get there from Kells, head for Oldcastle. About five km from Oldcastle you will see a sign for Sliabh na Calliaghe. Turn right, and at the first house on the right collect the keys to the cairn entrances from Basil Balfe (☎ 049-41256, please telephone in advance).

A deposit of IR£5 (hikers can leave their backpacks as collateral!) is required and a leaflet about the sites is available. A torch (flashlight) is useful on dull days. Coming from the east the first hill is of little interest; the most interesting and intact remains are on the next two, Carnbane East and Carnbane West.

Carnbane East

Carnbane East has a cluster of sites; Cairn T is the biggest at about 35 metres in diameter, and has numerous carved stones. One of its outlying kerbstones is called the 'Hag's Chair' and is covered in gouged holes, circles and other marks. You need the gate key to enter the passageway and a torch to see anything in detail. It takes about half an hour to climb Carnbane East from the car park. From the summit on a reasonably clear day you should be able to see the Hill of Tara to the south-east while the view north is into Cavan with Lough Ramor to the north-east and Lough Sheelin and Oldcastle to the north-west.

Carnbane West

From the same car park, it takes about an hour to the summit of Carnbane West where Cairn D and L are both some 60 metres in diameter. Cairn D has been seriously disturbed in an unsuccessful search for a central chamber. Cairn L, north-east of D, is also in poor condition, although you can enter the passage and chamber, where there are numerous carved stones, and the curved basin stone where human ashes were placed.

County Louth

Although the smallest county in Ireland, Louth is home to the two principal towns of Ireland's north-eastern region. Drogheda makes a good base for exploring the Boyne Valley with its prehistoric sites to the west and the monastic relics to the north. Dundalk is a border town to the north and a gateway to the scenic Cooley Peninsula.

Just west of Dundalk, the lonely moorlands of the Cooley Peninsula are the setting for a large part of Ireland's most famous fable, the Táin Bó Cúailnge or the Cattle Raid of Cooley. The low mountains are really a part of Northern Ireland's Mourne Mountains, but are cut off from them physically by the flooded valley of Carlingford Lough and politically by the border which runs up the centre of the lough. You may see British patrol boats or helicopters parading along the lough. The peninsula is a world of its own and has strong Republican links.

HISTORY

Humans have lived in this region since about 7000 BC, but Louth's Stone Age relics like the Proleek dolmen and passage grave near Dundalk pale in comparison to the Brugh Na Bóinne relics in County Meath. Only with the coming of the Iron Age does Louth rival its neighbour. The north of the county and the Cooley Peninsula are the setting for legends of Cúchulainn, one of the most famous heroes of ancient Ireland, who was born and raised around Faughart, just north of Dundalk. Cúchulainn was the lead player in the story of the Táin Bó Cúailnge (The Cattle Raid of Cooley), one of the great Celtic myths. *The Táin* by Thomas Kinsella (Dolmen Press) is a recent version of this compelling and bloody tale.

St Patrick brought Christianity in the 5th century, and numerous religious communities sprang up in the region. The monastery at Monasterboice and the latei Cistercian abbey at Mellifont, both near Drogheda, are the county's most interesting archaeological sites.

Irish society underwent a huge upheaval with the arrival of the Anglo-Normans in the 12th century. Hugh de Lacy's reward for his Irish conquests was the fertile land of Meath and Louth. Mottes (small fortified artificial hills), such as the one at Millmount in Drogheda, were first built around this time to defend the Anglo-Normans against the hostile Irish.

The Normans' stone castles came later, and smaller satellite castles such as Termonfeckin, north-east of Drogheda, dot the countryside. The Norman invaders were responsible for the development of Dundalk, and for the two towns on opposite banks of the Boyne which united in 1412 to become what is now Drogheda.

These new settlers would become some of the staunchest defenders of Ireland in later centuries, particularly against the English parliamentarians. In 1649 Cromwell's forces massacred the native Irish and old English Catholic defenders of Drogheda for refusing to surrender.

Ireland succumbed to English control in 1690, after the Battle of the Boyne where the Protestant William of Orange defeated his father-in-law, the English Catholic King James II. James had enlisted the help of the Irish in return for greater religious and political freedom, and his defeat resulted in a new influx of Protestant settlers.

DROGHEDA

The historic town of Drogheda hugs a bend on the River Boyne, five km (three miles) from the sea. Drogheda is a compact settlement with a small adjunct to the south of the river around Millmount. The centre retains the feel of an old Norman town with narrow, bustling streets and dark alleyways.

Once fortified, Drogheda still has one town gate in fine condition, together with some interesting old buildings and the curious hump of Millmount south of the river. The embalmed head of the Catholic martyr Oliver Plunkett is housed in St Peter's Roman Catholic Church.

The town's name comes from *Droichead Atha*, the Bridge of the Ford, after the bridge built over the river by the Normans to link the two earlier Viking settlements. Novelist Colleen McCullough featured Drogheda in *The Thornbirds*.

History

There was probably a rough settlement here before the 10th century but Drogheda really began to take shape around 910, when the Danes built defences to guard a strategic crossing point of the River Boyne. In the 12th century, the Normans built a bridge and expanded the two settlements forming on either side of the river. They also built a large defensive motte and bailey castle on the south side at Millmount.

By the 15th century, Drogheda was one of Ireland's four major walled towns. Many Irish parliament sessions were held here, and Poyning's Law, passed in 1494, is the most famous piece of legislation from Irish medieval times. It diminished prospects of home rule or independence for Ireland by granting the English crown the right to veto any measures the Irish proposed to enact.

In 1465 the Irish parliament had conferred on Drogheda the right to a university, but the plan foundered in 1468, when the earl of Desmond was executed in Drogheda for treason. During the period of the Pale, when only a small portion of the country around Dublin was fully controlled by the English, Drogheda was a frontier town. Farther north were the fractious Ulster folk, definitely beyond the Pale.

In 1649, the town was the scene of Cromwell's most notorious Irish slaughter. Marching north from Dublin he met with stiff resistance at Drogheda and when his forces overran the town on the third assault, the defenders were shown no mercy. The order went out to kill every man who had borne arms, and it's estimated that nearly 3000 were massacred, including civilians and children.

The defenders were a combination of native Irish and old English Catholic Royalists led by Sir Arthur Aston, who was beaten to death with his own wooden leg. Some of the survivors were shipped to Barbados. When 100 hid in the steeple of St Peter's Church of Ireland, Cromwell's men simply burnt the church down. 'A righteous judgement of God upon these barbarous wretches', was Cromwell's summation of the butchery. Drogheda also plumped for the wrong side at the Battle of the Boyne in 1690, but surrendered the day after James II was defeated.

It took many years for Drogheda to recover from these events, but in the last century a number of Catholic churches were built. The massive railway viaduct and the string of quayside buildings hint at the town's brief Victorian industrial boom, when it was a centre for cotton and linen manufacture and brewing.

Orientation & Information

Drogheda sits astride the River Boyne with the principal shopping area on the north bank along the main street, called West St and Laurence St. The area south of the river is residential, dull and dominated by the mysterious Millmount mound. The main road to Belfast skirts around the town to the west.

The tourist office (☎ 041-37070) is on the west end of West St and is open June, July and August. The main post office is on the middle of West St, next door to the St Laurence Hotel. Most of the main banks are on West St. The FM Laundrette is on the Quays. Disc parking is in operation throughout the town and discs can be bought in newsagents.

Throughout the summer the Drogheda Historical Society (☎ 041-33946) runs tours of the town at 11 am and 3 pm on weekdays for IR£2. The tours begin at the Drogheda Arts Centre on Stockwell St.

St Peter's Church

On West St, the Gothic-style St Peter's Church dates from 1791 and dominates the centre of town. In a glass case on the left side of the church you can see the head of St Oliver Plunkett (1629-81), executed by the perfidious English.

Plunkett was the Archbishop of Armagh

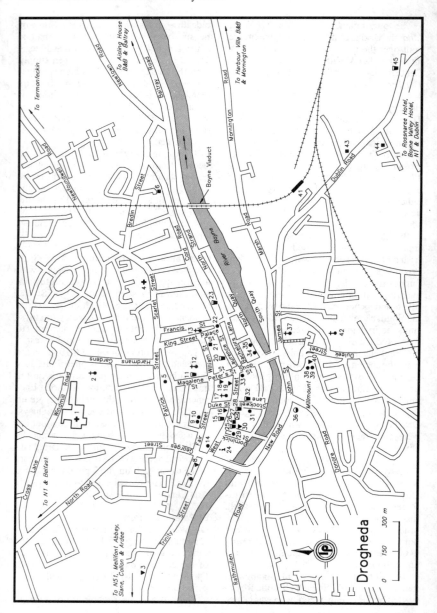

Drogheda

To Termonfeckin

To Aisling House B&B & Balfray

To Harbour Villa B&B & Mornington

To Rossnaree Hotel, Boyne Valley Hotel, N1 & Dublin

To N1 & Belfast

To N51, Mellifont Abbey, Slane, Collon & Ardee

Boyne Viaduct

River Boyne

Newfoundwell Road

Marley's Lane Road

Balfray Road

Mornington Road

Dublin Road

Marsh Road

North Strand

Cord Road

Scarlet Street

Bridin Street

Windmill Road

Cross Lane

North Road

Trinity Street

Georges Street

Patrick Street

Hardmans Gardens

Fair Street

West Street

Dominic Street

New Road

John St

James St

Duleek Street

Millmount

Donore Road

Rathmullen Road

North Quay

South Quay

Francis St

King Street

William St

Peter's St

Magdalene St

Duke St

Shop St

Bachelor's Lane

Stockwell Lane

Palace St

0   150   300 m

■ PLACES TO STAY

6	Caffrey's B&B
21	Harpur House Hostel
26	Walker's Hotel
43	St Gobnait's B&B
44	Orley House B&B

▼ PLACES TO EAT

3	Kings Café
8	Golden House
16	Moorlands Café
18	La Pizzeria
19	Swan House
30	Snackmaster Café
40	Butter Gate Restaurant

🍺 PUBS

11	Branagan's Pub
15	Weavers Pub
20	Matthews Pub (McPhails)
23	Carberry's Pub
25	Gwent Arms
28	Reds Disco Bar
32	Goodfellow's Bar
45	Black Bull Inn

OTHER

1	Our Lady of Lourdes Hospital
2	Our Lady of Lourdes Church
4	Cottage Hospital
5	Magdalene Tower
7	PJ Carolan Bike Hire
9	Courthouse
10	Cornmarket & Market House
12	St Peter's Church of Ireland
13	Presbyterian Church
14	Police/Garda Station
17	St Peter's Catholic Church
22	St Laurence's Gate
24	Tourist Office
27	Post Office
29	Cinema
31	Drogheda Arts Centre
33	Tholsel
34	FM Laundrette
35	Quay Cycles
36	Bus Station
37	St Mary's Catholic Church
38	Butter Gate
39	Millmount & Museum
41	Railway Station
42	St Mary's Church of Ireland

and Primate of all Ireland, and was hauled off to England on the evidence of the perjurer Titus Oates for his alleged role in the 'Popish Plot' to murder King Charles II and re-establish Catholicism in England. He was hung, drawn and quartered at Tyburn (now Marble Arch) in London, but his head was brought back to Ireland in 1721. The rest of Plunkett's body is buried at Downside Abbey near Bath in England. He was raised to sainthood in 1975.

St Laurence's Gate

Astride Laurence St, the eastward extension of the main street through town, is St Laurence's Gate, the finest surviving portion of the city walls and one of only two surviving gates from the original 11.

The 13th-century gate was named after Bishop Laurence O'Toole, mediator in the Anglo-Norman/Irish conflicts in the 12th century. It consists of two lofty towers, a connecting curtain wall and the entrance to the portcullis. This imposing pile of stone is not in fact a gate but a barbican, a fortified structure used to defend the gate, which was farther behind it. When the walls were completed in the 13th century, they ran for three km around the town, enclosing 52 hectares.

Millmount & Museum

Across the river from the town centre, in a sea of dull suburbia, is Millmount, an artificial hill overlooking the town. Millmount may have been a prehistoric burial mound along the lines of nearby Newgrange, but surprisingly it has never been excavated. There's a tale that it was the burial place of a warrior-poet who arrived in Ireland from Spain around 1500 BC. Throughout Irish history poets have held a special place in society and have been both venerated and feared.

The Normans constructed a motte and

bailey on top of this convenient command post overlooking the bridge. It was followed by a castle which in turn was replaced by a Martello tower in 1808. It was at Millmount that the defenders of Drogheda made their last stand before surrendering to Cromwell. Later, an 18th-century English barracks was built around the base, and today this has been converted to craft shops and restaurants, though the courtyard retains the flavour of its former life.

The tower played a dramatic role in the 1922 Civil War and the Millmount Museum has a colourful (and somewhat romanticised) painting of its bombardment. The top of the tower offers a fine view over the centre of Drogheda, on the opposite side of the river.

Millmount Museum A section of the army barracks has been converted into a museum (☎ 041-33097) with interesting displays about the town and its history. They include the last three guild banners in the country from the late 18th century. There's an excellent example of a coracle, a tiny boat used over many centuries from earliest times. The pretty cobbled basement is full of gadgets and kitchen utensils from bygone times. Despite the importance of the Cromwellian massacre of 1649, the museum has no exhibit from this time.

The museum is open 2 to 6 pm, Tuesday to Sunday in summer and entry is 50p (children 20p). During the winter, it's open weekend afternoons. You can drive up to the hilltop or climb Pitcher Hill via the steps from St Mary's Bridge.

Butter Gate The 13th-century Butter Gate, just north-west of the Millmount, is the only genuine town gate to survive. This tower with its arched passageway predates the remains of St Laurence's Gate by about a century. St Mary's Churchyard to the south-east contains some of the original town wall and is reputedly where Cromwell breached the town walls in 1649.

Other Buildings
On the corner of West and Shop Sts is the

Tholsel, an 18th-century limestone town hall now occupied by the Bank of Ireland. Out towards the Termonfeckin road is the more recent and charming **Church of Our Lady of Lourdes**.

North of the centre on William St is **St Peter's Church of Ireland** with the tombstone of Oliver Goldsmith's uncle Isaac and the curious mummified-looking figure on the Edward Golding tombstone on the wall. This is the church whose spire was burnt by Cromwell's men, where 100 people seeking sanctuary died. Today's church (1748) is the second replacement of the original destroyed by Cromwell.

On Fair St is the modest 19th-century **Courthouse** which is home to the sword and mace presented to the town council by William of Orange after the Battle of the Boyne.

Topping the hill behind the main part of town is the **Magdalene Steeple**, dating from the 14th century, the belltower of a Dominican friary which was founded in 1224. England's King Richard II accepted the submission of the Gaelic chiefs here with suitable ceremony in 1395 after arriving with a great army, but peace lasted only a few months and his return to Ireland led to his overthrow in 1399. The Earl of Desmond was beheaded here in 1468 because of his treasonous connections with the Gaelic Irish. The tower is reputed to be haunted by a nun.

Places to Stay
Hostel *Harpur House* (☎ 041-32736) on William St is near the centre of town. A bed costs IR£6 in the dorms or IR£9 in the double rooms. They also do standard B&B for IR£12.

B&Bs It's advisable to book ahead during the summer months. *Harbour Villa* (☎ 041-37441) is two km (one mile) along the river towards the sea on the Mornington road. It overlooks the estuary and has small but pleasant rooms at IR£18/28 for singles/doubles. At the mouth of the estuary near the beach in Baltray is *Aisling House* (☎ 041-

22376) with rooms at IR£13 to IR£14 per person.

Nearer town and south of the river, *Orley House* (☎ 041-36019), 100 metres off the main Dublin road in a housing estate, costs IR£12 per person. Nearby, on the main Dublin road is *St Gobnaits* (☎ 041-37844), costing IR£13 per person.

Hotels The *Boyne Valley Hotel* (☎ 041-37737) is a 19th-century mansion with rooms at IR£32 to IR£38 per person including breakfast. The *Rossnaree Hotel* (☎ 041-37673) is also good and slightly cheaper at IR£22 to IR£25. The excellent restaurant has a set dinner from IR£16. Both hotels are just along the main Dublin road.

Places to Eat

Cafés & Fast Food The *Snackmaster Café* (☎ 041-34760) on Dominic St is run by an Egyptian who serves good and reasonably priced meals. The *Moorlands Cafe & Deli* on West St serves good coffee, snacks and light meals. The busy, Italian-owned *La Pizzeria* (☎ 041-34208) on Peter's St does pizzas from IR£4. The Chinese *Swan House* (☎ 041-35838) is a few doors away, and the *Golden House* on Trinity St also has Chinese food. The *King's Cafe* about one km along the Collon road is a rock-bottom café of the sausage & chips (for IR£3) variety.

Pub Food The popular *Weavers* pub on West St does pub food, or carvery lunches for about IR£5. *Branagan's* (☎ 041-35607) on Magdalene St is also popular, with straightforward lunch and evening meals and main courses in the IR£4 to IR£8 range. About a km along the Dublin road, the *Black Bull Inn* (☎ 041-37139) was once a winner of the 'regional pub of the year' title, but the food is simply dependable. Dinner costs from around IR£10.

Restaurants The cosy *Buttergate Restaurant* (☎ 041-34759) beside the Millmount Museum has excellent food, with meals before 7 pm at IR£7 and others at IR£13 to IR£17. It's open Thursday to Saturday for

dinner and on Sunday for lunch and dinner. The *Forge Gallery Restaurant* (☎ 041-26272) 10 km (seven miles) northwest of town in Collon is one of the best restaurants in the region.

Entertainment

Weavers (☎ 041-32816) on West St always has a youngish crowd and often has music at weekends. *Branagan's* pub (☎ 041-35607) on Magdalene St usually features pop/rock or country & western music.

Reds, a disco bar, and the *Gwent Arms* on West St are lively, with music from jazz to rock & roll on offer, especially at weekends. The *Black Bull Inn*, about one km along the Dublin road, has country music on Thursdays, and rock and pop on Fridays. *Carberry's* pub, on North Strand near Laurence St, have an Irish music session on Tuesdays. *Matthew's* pub on Laurence St, known as McPhails, has Irish music at weekends.

Man Friday's nightclub on Georges St has discos Thursday to Sunday nights. The *Rossnaree* and the *Boyne Valley* hotels on the Dublin Rd both have nightclubs, respectively the *Place* and *Luciano's*. Entry is usually IR£5. There is a modern two-screen cinema at the back of the Abbey shopping centre off West St.

Getting There & Away

Bus Drogheda is only 48 km (30 miles) north of Dublin, on the main N1 route to Belfast. The Bus Éireann station (☎ 041-35023) is on the corner of John St and Donore Rd, just south of the river, and there are hourly connections with Dublin and Dundalk as well as numerous links to Belfast and other centres. There is a handy expressway service from Dundalk to Galway once every morning. You can get off at Athlone for connections to Limerick, Sligo and Donegal. Capital Coaches (☎ 042-40025) have a daily Dundalk to Dublin service through Drogheda.

Train Drogheda Railway Station (☎ 041-38749) is just south of the river and east of the town centre, off the Dublin road. Drogheda is on the main Belfast to Dublin line and there are five or six trains daily each way, three on Sundays.

The train crosses the river just downstream from Drogheda on Sir John McNeill's mid-19th-century Boyne Viaduct, a fine piece of engineering which dominates the seaward view.

Getting Around

You can easily walk around Drogheda Town, and many of the surrounding region's interesting sites are within easy cycling distance. P J Carolan (☎ 041-38242), 77 Trinity St, is part of the Raleigh Rent-a-Bike scheme and has good bikes for IR£7 a day. Quay Cycles (☎ 041-34526) also rent bikes at similar costs.

There are taxi ranks on Laurence St and on Duke St, just off West St, or call 24 Hour Cabs (☎ 041-37663).

AROUND DROGHEDA

Drogheda makes an excellent base for exploring the Boyne Valley sites to the west – see the County Meath section of this chapter for more details. In Louth itself, Mellifont and Monasterboice are two famous and picturesque monastic sites a few km north of Drogheda. Travelling to or from Northern Ireland there's a coast route, the faster and duller N1 main road route and a more circuitous inland route via Collon and Ardee which can include Mellifont and Monasterboice.

Beaulieu House

Five km (three miles) east of Drogheda on the Baltray road is Beaulieu House, built between 1660 and 1666. The land had belonged to the Plunkett family since Anglo-Norman times, and was confiscated under Cromwell. This lovely red-brick mansion is thought to have been designed by Sir Christopher Wren (architect of St Paul's Cathedral in London), and its steep roof and tall chimneys are distinctive.

In 800 years, the estate has been in the possession of only two families, first the Plunketts and then the ancestors of Lord Tichbourne. There's an impressive art collection. Although it's a private residence, there are occasional tours by the Drogheda Historical Society, operating out of the Millmount Museum.

Mellifont Abbey

Mellifont Abbey (☎ 041-26459), eight km (five miles) north-west of Drogheda beside the River Mattock, was Ireland's first Cistercian monastery. In its prime, Mellifont was the Cistercians' most magnificent and important centre in the country. While the remains are well worth seeing, they don't really match the site's former significance.

In 1142 St Malachy, bishop of Down, brought in a new troupe of monks from Clairvaux in France to combat the corruption and lax behaviour of the Irish monastic orders. These straitlaced new monks were deliberately established at this remote location, far from any distracting influences. The French and Irish monks failed to get on, and the visitors soon returned to the continent, but within 10 years nine more Cistercian monasteries followed, and Mellifont was eventually the mother house for more than 30 lesser monasteries.

Mellifont not only brought fresh ideas to the Irish religious scene, it also heralded a new style of architecture. For the first time in Ireland, monasteries were built with the formal layout and structure that was being used on the continent. Only fragments of the original settlement remain, but the plan of the extensive monastery can easily be traced. Like many other Cistercian monasteries, the buildings clustered around an open cloister or courtyard.

To the north side are the remains of a principally 13th-century cross-shaped church. To the south, the chapter house, probably used as a meeting hall by the monks, has been partially floored with medieval glazed tiles, originally found in the church. Here also would have been the refectory or dining area, the kitchen and the warming room, the only place where the austere monks could enjoy the warmth of a fire. The east range would once have had the monks' sleeping quarters.

Mellifont's most recognisable building is the *lavabo*, an octagonal washing house for the monks. It was built in the 13th century and used lead pipe to bring water from the river. It is one of the finest pieces of Cistercian architecture in Ireland. A number of other buildings would have stood around this main part of the abbey.

After the dissolution of the monasteries, a fortified Tudor manor house was built on the site in 1556 by Edward Moore, using materials scavenged from the demolition of many of the buildings. In 1603, this house was the scene of a poignant and crucial turning point in Irish history. After the disastrous Battle of Kinsale, the vanquished Hugh O'Neill, the last of the great Irish chieftains, was given shelter here by Sir Garret Moore until he surrendered to the English Lord Deputy Mountjoy. After his surrender, O'Neill was pardoned, but despairing of his position fled to the continent in 1607 with other old Irish leaders in the 'flight of the earls'.

Entry is 80p (children 30p) and the grounds are open 10 am to 6 pm during the summer months. During the winter, entrance is free. The name comes from the Latin 'Melli-fons' or 'honey fountain'. A back road connects Mellifont with Monasterboice.

Monasterboice

Just off the N1 road to Belfast, about 10 km (six miles) north of Drogheda, is Monasterboice, an intriguing monastic site containing a cemetery, two ancient church ruins, one of the finest and tallest round towers in Ireland and two of the best high crosses.

Down a leafy country lane and set in sweeping farmland, Monasterboice has a special atmosphere, particularly at quiet times. The site can be reached directly from Mellifont via a winding but well signposted route along narrow country lanes.

The original monastic settlement at Monasterboice is said to have been founded by St Buithe in the 4th or 5th century, although the site probably had pre-Christian significance. The saint was a follower of St Patrick. His name somehow got converted to Boyne, and the river is named after him. It's said that he made a direct ascent to heaven via a ladder lowered from above. An invading Viking force took over the settlement in 968, only to be comprehensively expelled by Donal, the Irish high king of Tara, who killed at least 300 of the Vikings in the process.

Entrance to Monasterboice is free and there is a small gift shop outside the compound. To avoid the crowds, come early or late.

High Crosses Monasterboice's high crosses are superb examples of Celtic art with an important didactic use, bringing the gospels alive for the uneducated – cartoons of the scriptures, if you like. Like Greek statues, they were probably brightly painted, but all traces of colour have long disappeared.

Muiredach's Cross, the one nearest to the entrance, dates from the early 10th century. The inscription at the foot reads 'Or do Muiredach Lasndernad i Chros' – 'A prayer for Muiredach for whom the cross was made'. Muiredach was abbot here until 922.

The subjects of the carvings have not been positively identified. On the east face from the bottom up are thought to be: on the first panel the Fall of Adam and Eve and the murder of Abel, on the second David and Goliath, on the third Moses bringing forth water from the rock to the waiting Israelites, and on the fourth the Three Wise Men bearing gifts to Mary and Jesus. The Last Judgement is at the centre of the cross with the risen dead waiting for their verdict, and farther up is St Paul in the desert.

The west face relates more to the New Testament and from the bottom depicts the arrest of Christ, Doubting Thomas, Christ giving a key to St Peter, the Crucifixion in the centre, and Moses praying with Aaron and Hur. The cross is capped by a representation of a gabled-roof church.

The West Cross is near the round tower and stands 6.5 metres high, making it one of the tallest high crosses in Ireland. It is much more weathered, especially at the base, and only a dozen or so of its 50 panels are still legible.

The more distinguishable ones on the east face include David killing a lion and bear, the sacrifice of Isaac, David with Goliath's head and David kneeling before Samuel. The west face has the Resurrection, the crowning with thorns, the Crucifixion, the baptism of Christ, Peter cutting off the servant's ear in the garden of Gethsemane and the kiss of Judas.

A third simpler cross in the north-east corner of the compound is believed to have been smashed by Cromwell's forces and has only a few straightforward carvings. Photographers should note that this cross makes a great evening silhouette picture with the round tower in the background.

The round tower, minus its cap, stands in a corner of the complex. It's still over 30 metres tall but is closed to the public. In 1097, records suggest, the tower interior went up in flames destroying many valuable manuscripts and other treasures. The church ruins are later and of less interest.

COLLON

Collon, a small village 10 km (seven miles) north-west of Drogheda, was planned along English lines in the 18th century. It is now home to the newer Mellifont Cistercian monastery, which is housed in the former landlord's residence north of the village.

On Main St, the *Roundhouse Restaurant* is a medium-priced family restaurant with average food. The expensive and highly recommended *Forge Gallery Restaurant* (☎ 041-26272) features meat, fish, game and some vegetarian dishes with dinner costing from IR£18. It's in an old forge building and exhibits paintings by local artists.

ARDEE

This flower-filled market town on the narrow River Dee is 10 km (seven miles) north of Collon on the N2. Its long tidy main street is dominated by Ardee Castle to the south and Hatch's Castle to the north.

History

For such a small town Ardee has a colourful history. It takes its name from Áth Fhír Diadh, or Fear Diadh's ford, inspired by the well-known tale of the combat between Cúchulainn and Fear Diadh or Ferdia, as recorded by the ancient tale of the Cattle Raid of Cooley.

The duel was a result of the desire of Maeve, the Queen of Connaught, to get her hands on the Brown Bull of Cooley, which belonged to Ulster. All of Ulster's soldiers had fallen mysteriously sick, but at this ford the young Cúchulainn defeated her army one by one as they tried to get across. Maeve finally persuaded a childhood friend and foster brother of Cúchulainn called Ferdia to take him on. Cúchulainn won, and the defeated Ferdia had the ford named after him as was the Celtic custom. A broken tumulus grave to the west of the river is called Ferdia's Grave.

In the 12th century the area was turned into a barony and the town remained in English hands before being taken by the O'Neills in the 17th century. James II had his headquarters here for two months in 1689 prior to the Battle of the Boyne.

Things to See

Ardee Castle, a square tower dating from the 13th century, was an important outpost on the edge of the English Pale, later became a courthouse and is now under restoration to house a museum and gift and coffee shop. Hatch's Castle also dates from this time, and it remained in the hands of the Hatch family from Cromwellian times until 1940. It is still a private residence.

The river bank can be explored around the ford where there is a well-tended riverside walk.

Places to Stay

Carraig Mor (☎ 041-53513), two km south of Ardee on the main Dublin to Donegal road, has rooms at IR£18 single or IR£26 to IR£28 double.

For a real treat, try the lovely Georgian *Red House* (☎ 041-53523), which stands in its own demesne. Take the Dundalk road past Gable's Restaurant and it's about 500 metres along among trees on the left. The elegant rooms cost IR£30 to IR£35 per person including breakfast, and dinner is another IR£18.

There's also accommodation at *Gable's Restaurant* (☎ 041-53789) for IR£14 to IR£18 per person.

Places to Eat

Caffrey's bakery and coffee shop in the centre does light meals. *Larry Tenanty's* on the Square does coffee. *Brian Muldoon's Wine Tavern* on Main St does a good steak.

Gable's Restaurant (☎ 041-53789) costs IR£19 for the set dinner and their desserts are particularly memorable. They're open Tuesday to Saturday and bookings are advisable.

Popular pubs in town include the *Lemon & Clove* and opposite it, down a side street, the *Harp Bar*.

AROUND ARDEE
The Jumping Church of Kildemock

Three km (two miles) south-east of town is the area's oddest landmark, the remains of the Jumping Church of Kildemock. On a thunderous night in February 1715. A storm caused a section of St Catherine's Church to shift from its foundations.

Rather than settle for this rather straightforward explanation, the locals decided the church had miraculously jumped to exclude the remains of an excommunicated member of the flock who had been buried within its walls. Thus was born the jumping church.

In the churchyard is a gravestone to Sara and William Orson, decorated with an unusual skull and crossbones.

Tallanstown

North of Ardee the main road forks to Monaghan and Dundalk. The slightly more interesting route to Dundalk is via Tallanstown, with nearby Louth Hall which belonged to the Plunkett family, the barons of Louth. Oliver Plunkett took shelter here

among his relations in the 1670s. It is not open to the public.

Louth Village

North of Tallanstown the county's namesake is an insignificant little place with some mildly interesting remains. St Mochta's is a small 11th or 12th-century church with enclosure and stone roof. St Mochta was British and a follower of St Patrick; he founded a monastery here in the early 6th century. Nearby is the church of a 15th-century Dominican friary sometimes called Louth Abbey.

Ardpatrick

To the east of Louth is Ardpatrick and Ardpatrick House, the home of Oliver Plunkett. There is a mound here where he is supposed to have illegally ordained priests. It was a good vantage point to spot any advancing English soldiers.

THE COAST ROAD

While the most visually rewarding route to travel between Drogheda and Dundalk is the minor inland road via Mellifont and Collon, the coastal route is also scenic. The latter heads off north under the railway viaduct, passes Baltray with its championship golf course and continues on quiet country roads to Termonfeckin.

Termonfeckin

A 6th-century monastery was founded in Termonfeckin by St Féichín of Cong, County Mayo. All that remains are some gravestones and a 10th-century high cross. Nearby is a well-preserved 15th-century castle or tower house (key from across the road, 10 am to 6 pm) which has two small corbel-vaulted alcoves and an anticlockwise spiral staircase – most go clockwise.

Clogherhead

A couple of km farther north is the busy seaside and fishing centre of Clogherhead, with a good shallow Blue Flag beach. The area around town is pleasant for strolling with good walks along the coast or out to

Port Oriel, an attractive little harbour with views of the Cooley Peninsula and the Mourne Mountains farther north. During the summer, Port Oriel is home to a fleet of trawlers and smaller fishing boats.

On the south side of the headland is the **Red Man's Cave**. At low tide a reddish fungus becomes visible, covering the cave walls. Local stories describe the fate of some people fleeing from Cromwell, whose hiding place was revealed by a barking dog. They were discovered and slaughtered, and their blood splashed on the walls, where it remains to this day. The cave is hard to find so it's sensible to ask a local for directions, but even if you don't find it the walk is satisfying enough.

Annagassan

A minor road with picture-book views continues 12 km (eight miles) north to Annagassan, on the north side of Dunany Point, at the junction of the Dee and Glyde rivers. It's claimed locally that Annagassan is the site of the Vikings' first settlement in Ireland. Records suggest they sacked a monastery here in 842 and may be responsible for the promontory fort, which is now a low mound overlooking the village.

Castlebellingham

North of Annagassan, the coast road joins the busy main N1 at Castlebellingham, only 12 km (eight miles) from Dundalk. The village grew up around its 18th-century mansion, which is something of a disappointment after the imposing castellated entrance. The mansion is on the site of an earlier castle burnt down by James II's troops; the owner, Thomas Bellingham, worked as a guide to William of Orange during his visit to Ireland in 1689-90. The building is now a hotel and restaurant (☎ 042-721176).

The human grandfather of all Irish frogs is buried in the local graveyard. Dr Thomas Guither, a 17th-century physician, is supposed to have reintroduced frogs to Ireland by releasing imported frog spawn in a pond in Trinity College, Dublin. Frogs, along with snakes and toads, had supposedly received their marching orders from St Patrick 1000 years earlier.

Places to Stay

The coast road doesn't have too many places to stay. *Cross Garden* (☎ 041-22675), one km south of Clogherhead on the Termonfeckin road, overlooks the sea and has rooms at IR£13 or IR£14 per person. Nearby is *Tubbertoby* (☎ 041-22124), a friendly place just north of Termonfeckin on the main road, which costs IR£12 per person and is open June to September.

Places to Eat

Triple House Restaurant (☎ 041-22616) at the top of the hill in Termonfeckin serves a lot of fish and some meat. There's a three-course menu prior to 7 pm for IR£10; after that expect to pay IR£15 or more. It's closed Mondays.

The Clogherhead pubs are pretty ordinary but the *Village Inn* is a comfortable bar in Termonfeckin.

DUNDALK

Halfway between Dublin and Belfast, Louth's county town (population 30,000) is only 13 km (eight miles) from the border and is widely regarded as a Republican stronghold.

History

Dundalk's name is derived from Dún Dealgan, a prehistoric fort which was reputedly the home of the hero Cúchulainn. The town grew under the protection of a local estate controlled by the de Verdon family who were granted lands here by King John in 1185. In the Middle Ages, Dundalk was at the northern limits of the English-controlled Pale, strategically located on one of the main highways to the North.

Information & Orientation

Northbound traffic sweeps round to the east of the town centre. The tourist office (☎ 042-35484) is on Market Square near the Maid of Éireann statue. The main post office is on Clanbrassil St.

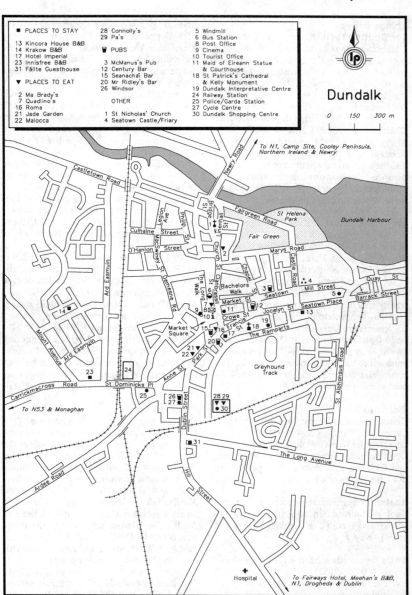

PLACES TO STAY
13 Kincora House B&B
14 Krakow B&B
17 Hotel Imperial
23 Innisfree B&B
31 Fáilte Guesthouse

PLACES TO EAT
2 Ma Brady's
7 Quadlino's
16 Roma
21 Jade Garden
22 Malocca

28 Connolly's
29 Pa's

PUBS
3 McManus's Pub
12 Century Bar
15 Seanachaí Bar
20 Mr Ridley's Bar
26 Windsor

OTHER
1 St Nicholas' Church
4 Seatown Castle/Friary

5 Windmill
6 Bus Station
8 Post Office
9 Cinema
10 Tourist Office
11 Maid of Eireann Statue
11 St Patrick's Cathedral
   & Kelly Monument
18 St Patrick's Cathedral
   & Courthouse
19 Dundalk Interpretative Centre
24 Railway Station
25 Police/Garda Station
27 Cycle Centre
30 Dundalk Shopping Centre

Dundalk

0   150   300 m

Things to See

The **Courthouse** on the corner of Crowe and Clanbrassil Sts is a fine neo-Gothic building with large Doric pillars, which was designed by Richard Morrison who also designed the courthouse in Carlow. In the front square is the stone **Maid of Éireann**, commemorating the Fenian Rising of 1798.

At the top of Church St, **St Nicholas' Church** or the Green Church is the burial site of Agnes Burns, elder sister of Robert, the Scottish poet. She married the local rector, and the monument was erected by the townspeople to honour them both. The 15th-century tower to the right of the church is the oldest structure on the site.

The richly decorated **St Patrick's Cathedral** was modelled on King's College Chapel in Cambridge and in front of it on Jocelyn St is the **Kelly Monument** to a local captain drowned at sea in 1858. Nearby is the newly opened **Dundalk interpretative centre**.

At the east end of Jocelyn St is the Seatown area of Dundalk with its **castle** (really a Franciscan friary tower) and a derelict sail-less **windmill**, the tallest in Ireland. If you arrive in Dundalk by train you pass the 1820 **Garda station** on St Dominicks Place on the way into town. Its first prisoner is believed to have been its architect, who misappropriated funds and was arrested for nonpayment of bills.

Places to Stay

Camping There is camping at Gyles Quay Caravan & Campground (☎ 042-76262) 16 km (10 miles) west, off the road to Greenore. Open April to September, they have excellent facilities and charge IR£6 per tent or IR£4 for hikers or cyclists.

Hostels The nearest hostels are on the Cooley Peninsula in Omeath, 16 km (10 miles) away and Carlingford, 24 km (15 miles) away.

B&Bs An excellent B&B is the *Fáilte Guesthouse* (☎ 042-35152) on the corner of Hill St and The Long Ave, which charges IR£16/28 for singles/doubles. Another which is just as good is *Mrs Meehan's Rosemount* (☎ 042-35878) near the Carroll's cigarette factory about three km (1.8 miles) south of town on the main Dublin road. B&B there is IR£18 single and IR£28 double (IR£32 with own bathroom).

The 18th-century *Kincora House* (☎ 042-38353) is on Seatown Place near the windmill. This is the birthplace of Admiral McClintock, a 19th-century Arctic explorer. The six rooms cost IR£15 to IR£17 single, IR£24 to IR£26 double.

Another nice old house is *Innisfree* (☎ 042-34912) on Carrick Rd close to the railway station with rooms at IR£13 or IR£16 per person. *Krakow* (☎ 042-37535) on Ard Easmuin St, north from the railway station, has rooms for IR£13 to IR£15 per person and dinner is available for IR£11.

Hotels The *Hotel Imperial* (☎ 042-32241) on Park St has a better interior than the outside would suggest. Singles/doubles are IR£40/56 including breakfast. The *Fairways Hotel* (☎ 042-21500) on the Dublin road is modern, plush and costs IR£38/68.

The *Ballymascanlon Hotel* (☎ 042-71124) is a manor hotel with a swimming pool, squash courts, nine-hole golf course and other sporting facilities. It is six km (3.5 miles) north of Dundalk on the way to Carlingford and costs IR£34 to IR£36.50 B&B.

Places to Eat

Dundalk has plenty of cheap eateries. Try *Connolly's*, a small restaurant upstairs in the shopping centre on the ramparts south of the town centre and east of Dublin St. The *Roma* chip shop (☎ 042-34928) on Park St features home-made ice cream, and the *Malocca Restaurant* (☎ 042-34175) is on the same street. *Ma Brady's* is a homely place on Church St where a substantial dinner will cost IR£8 to IR£10. The *Windsor* pub, west of the shopping centre on Dublin St, does light meals all day. *Pa's Restaurant* is a cheap and cheerful place in Dundalk shopping centre.

Better places in town would include *Quadlino's* (☎ 042-38567), an Italian restaurant near the post office where dinner will cost from IR£15. The *Jade Garden* (☎ 042-30378) is an excellent Chinese restaurant on Park St near Dundalk shopping centre. *Cluskey's Restaurant* (☎ 042-74223), 12 km (seven miles) along the Carrickmacross road is small, comfortable and will cost from IR£15 for dinner.

Entertainment

Several good pubs can be found around Park St. *Mr Ridley's* have a back to the '60s session on Monday nights and pop/rock on other nights. *Seanachaí* bar has Irish music on Tuesday night, jazz on Wednesday and whatever is going at weekends. The *Century Bar* at Roden Place and *McManus's* in Seatown are alternatives.

The three-screen Adelphi Cinema is next door to the tourist office.

Getting There & Away

Bus Bus Éireann run an almost hourly service to Dublin and Belfast. The bus station (☎ 042-34075) is behind Clanbrassil St up from the tourist office. There are plenty of local buses and daily connections to centres nationwide. Capital Coaches (☎ 042-40025) operate a daily Dundalk-Drogheda-Dublin service.

Train The railway station (☎ 042-35526/35522) is a few hundred metres west of Park St on Carrickmacross St. Six trains daily (three on Sunday) operate on the Dublin to Belfast line.

Getting Around

The Cycle Centre (☎ 042-37159), opposite the huge shopping centre on Dublin St south of the town centre, has bikes at reasonable rates. The taxi rank is beside the tourist office, or call A-1 Cabs (☎ 042-31444) or Dixon's (☎ 042-30000).

INTO NORTHERN IRELAND

If you are heading for Derry, take the N53 to the west of town, while for Belfast continue north on the main N1 route. If you are hiking or cycling and want to go directly to the Mourne Mountains you can, during the summer, get a ferry from Omeagh to Warrenpoint.

Driving north from Dundalk, you will usually be across the border long before you realise it. Northern Ireland begins about 13 km (eight miles) north of Dundalk, somewhere after the closed Irish customs post and before the first petrol station advertising cheap petrol (by southern standards). Watch the road: the surface improves and there's a concrete kerb once you're in the North.

The British Army checkpoints are well back from the border in more secure and defensible locations. Despite their forbidding appearance, passing through the checkpoint is no hassle: just go slowly and don't advance until you are told to. On the Newry to Belfast road the checkpoint is just south of Newry, and most monitoring of traffic is done by video cameras. The soldiers are usually polite and will ask you for some identification. Don't take people you don't know across the border.

Many roads to the North are 'unapproved' roads and may be patrolled by the British Army or the Royal Ulster Constabulary; you will be stopped, questioned and asked why you are not on one of the approved routes. The official crossings are usually the main roads between towns, and are marked on most maps.

CASTLEROCHE

Five km (three miles) north-west of Dundalk on the Castleblayney road, Baron de Verdon's 1230 Castleroche Castle is impressively sited on a pinnacle of rock. The triangular remnants of the building include a twin-towered entrance house and protective wall. One of the windows on the west side is 'Fuinneóg an Mhurdair' the Murder Window, as the baroness was said to have had the architect thrown from it so no other castle like it would ever be built.

FAUGHART

Faughart, four km (2.5 miles) from Castleroche, has fine views and is reputed to be the birthplace of St Brigid, Ireland's most revered saint after St Patrick. She was the daughter of a local chieftain and settled in Kildare in the 6th century. The grotto and church here mark the spot of a monastery associated with her, and devotions are still carried out on 1 February, her feast day.

In the west corner of the graveyard is the grave of Edward Bruce, a king of Ireland who died in 1318. As part of the Gaelic revival he was invited to Ireland from Scotland and crowned by the Ulster lords, who hoped he would create trouble for the English in Ireland. He accepted the job, hoping this would relieve English pressure at home on his brother, Robert Bruce of Scotland. The hero Cúchulainn is said to have been born near here.

THE COOLEY PENINSULA

Just west of Dundalk, the lonely moorlands of the Cooley Peninsula are the setting for a large part of Ireland's most famous fable, the Táin Bó Cúailnge or the Cattle Raid of Cooley. The low mountains are really a part of Northern Ireland's Mourne Mountains, but are cut off from them physically by the flooded valley of Carlingford Lough and politically by the border which runs up the centre of the lough. You may see British patrol boats or helicopters parading along the lough. The peninsula is a world of its own and has strong Republican links.

The best way to explore the peninsula is by first circum-navigating it on the ring road, perhaps detouring closer to the sea at **Gyles Quay** which has a camp site and safe beach, before arriving in Carlingford and Omeath. Either of these two are ideal bases from which to venture inland over the pensinula's hilltops, soaked in the legends of the Cattle Raid of Cooley, through Windy Gap to the **Long Woman's Grave** and beyond to the picturesque country roads and forests that make the place a haven for walkers.

PROLEEK DOLMEN & GALLERY GRAVE

Heading north from Dundalk, turn right after three km (two miles) towards the Ballymascanlon Hotel, the start of the peninsula ring route. In the grounds of the hotel,

up by the 5th green of the golf course (there is a signposted trail for non-golfers) is the fine Giant's Load Proleek Dolmen and Gallery Grave.

Local legends say it is the grave of Para Buí Mór MhacSeóidín, a Scottish giant who came here to challenge Fionn MacCumhaill, leader of the fabled Fianna warriors. It dates from 3000 BC, and the 47-tonne capstone sits precariously on three uprights. The pebbles on top are recent additions and come from the belief that if you can land a stone on top, any wish will be granted. Single women who achieve this are guaranteed marriage within a year.

CARLINGFORD

Near Carlingford the peninsula's mountains and views really display themselves. This pretty medieval village with its cluster of narrow streets and whitewashed houses nestles on Carlingford Lough, beneath 587-metre (1930-foot) Slieve Foye. Wall murals include the 'Oyster Fisherman', an appropriate subject as Carlingford is Ireland's oyster capital with 20 million of them out in the lough. The Mourne Mountains are just a few km north across the lough. Carlingford is the starting post for the 50-km (30-mile) Táin Trail.

Information

Carlingford heritage centre (☎ 042-73454) is in the Holy Trinity church on Churchyard Rd, Carlingford. It has displays, audiovisual shows and a lot of information on the history and archaeology of the region. The centre also runs tours of the town, taken by local guides.

King John's Castle

Carlingford was first settled by the Vikings, and in the Middle Ages became an English stronghold under the protection of the castle. It was built on a pinnacle in the 11th to 12th centuries to control the entrance to the lough. On the west side, the entrance gateway was constructed to allow only one horse and rider to pass through at a time. King John's name stuck to a remarkable number of places in

Ireland, given that he spent little time in or near any of them. In 1210 he spent a couple of days here en route to a nine-day battle with Hugh de Lacy at Carrickfergus Castle in Antrim. It is suggested that the first few pages of the Magna Carta, the world's first constitutional bill of rights, were drafted while he was here.

Other Sites

Near the disused railway station is **Taafe's Castle**, a 16th-century tower house. The **Mint**, near the square, is of a similar age, but although Edward IV is thought to have granted a charter to a mint in 1467 no coins were produced here. The building has some interesting Celtic carvings around the windows.

Carlingford is the birthplace of Thomas D'Arcy McGee, one of Canada's founding fathers.

Cruises

Carlingford Pleasure Cruises (☎ 042-73239) run one-hour and all-day cruises May to September. The one-hour cruises cost IR£2 per person and departure times depend on the tides. Byrne's fishing boat (☎ 042-71349) does sea trips during the summer.

Places to Stay

Hostels *Carlingford Adventure Centre & Hostel* (☎ 042-73100) is on Tholsel St just off the main street. Dorm beds cost IR£5 to IR£7 in rooms for two to eight people, and bedding costs IR£1 extra. The adventure centre organises rock climbing, orienteering, hill walking or windsurfing.

B&Bs The peninsula B&Bs are of a high standard and it's a better place to stay than Dundalk. In the middle of the village *Carlingford House* (☎ 042-73118) costs IR£14 per person and has a big drawing room with an open turf fire. *Viewpoint* (☎ 042-73149) overlooks the harbour in the village on the Omeath road. The motel-style rooms cost IR£15.50 per person including an excellent breakfast.

Mourneview farmhouse (☎ 042-73551), a

km out of Carlingford in Belmont, costs IR£13 per person. *Shalom* (☎ 042-73151) is a half km along the Greenore road overlooking the village, and has rooms with bathrooms at IR£18/26.

Hotels *McKevitt's Village Hotel* (☎ 042-73116) on Market Square has singles at IR£25 to IR£29, doubles at IR£44 to IR£56, and there's a good bar and restaurant.

Places to Eat

Shane's on the Square does chips and takeaways. The *Carlingford Arms* pub does reasonable pub food as well as hefty Sunday lunches from IR£3. The popular *Oyster Inn* specialises in oysters and light lunches.

The *King John Restaurant* (☎ 042-73223) in Harry Jordan's pub on Newry St is a cosy place overlooking the water with surprisingly sophisticated food. The menu ranges from oysters to unusual Irish dishes like crubeens – pig's trotters. Count on around IR£25 per person with drinks. It's a good idea to make reservations in summer.

Entertainment

Popular pubs include the *Carlingford Arms*, the *Oyster Tavern*, which often has Irish music, and *Jordan's Bar* for food. *PJ's* pub, off the Square on Tholsel St, is a traditional Irish bar with a grocery shop up front.

In mid-August the pubs are packed morning to midnight when the village is overrun by 20,000 visitors to the Oyster Festival, with funfairs, live bands and buskers alongside the official oyster-opening competitions and tastings. Carlingford goes event-crazy with summer schools, medieval festivals and homecoming festivals almost every weekend between June and September.

Getting There & Away

On weekdays, four Bus Éireann buses run from Dundalk to Carlingford and on to Omeath and Newry. Contact Dundalk bus station (☎ 042-34075) for details.

The Táin Bó Cúailnge – The Cattle Raid of Cooley

This remarkable tale of greed and war is one of the oldest stories in any European language and the closest thing Ireland has produced to the Greek epics. Queen Maeve, the powerful ruler of Connaught, was jealous because she could not match the white bull owned by her husband Ailill. She heard tales of the finest bull in Ireland, the brown bull of Cooley, and became determined to rectify the situation.

Maeve gathered her armies and headed for Ulster where she conspired with her druids to place the Ulster armies under a spell. A deep sleep descended on them, leaving the province undefended. The only obstacle remaining was the boy warrior Cúchulainn, and at Ardee in County Louth, Cúchulainn tackled Maeve's soldiers as they tried to ford the river. He killed many of them and halted their advance. Maeve eventually persuaded Cúchulainn's half-brother and close friend, Ferdia, to take him on, but he was defeated after a momentous battle and died in Cúchulainn's arms.

The struggle continued across Louth and on to the Cooley peninsula, where many place names echo the ensuing action. Sex rears its head regularly in the Táin, for Maeve was more interested in her chief warrior Fergus than in her husband Ailill. At various spots in the saga, they sneak off to make love and in one instance Ailill steals the sword of the distracted Fergus, to shame him and show how careless he was.

While Maeve's soldiers were being despatched in all sorts of ways by Cúchulainn, Maeve had managed to capture the brown bull and spirit him away to Connaught. The wounded Cúchulainn defeated her armies but the bull was gone. In the end the brown bull killed Ailill's white bull and thundered around Ireland leaving bits of his victim all over the place. Finally, spent with rage, he died near Ulster at a place called Druim Tarb, the ridge of the bull. Cúchulainn and Ulster then made peace with Maeve and thus the saga ended. ■

AROUND CARLINGFORD

The best way to explore the peninsula is by first circumnavigating it on the ring road, perhaps detouring closer to the sea at **Gyles Quay** which has a fine Blue Flag beach. The well-equipped *Gyles Quay Caravan & Camping Park* (☎ 042-76262) is open April to September and costs IR£6 for tents or IR£4 if you are hiking or cycling. The site has a cheap snack bar and licensed club.

The once pretty village of Greenore has been scarred by the development of a major container port.

Carlingford and Omeath are ideal bases from which to venture inland over the pensinula's hilltops, soaked in the legends of the Cattle Raid of Cooley. For the best views on the peninsula, head for the **Carlingford/Slieve Foye Forest Park** three km (two miles) north-west of Carlingford off the road to Omeath. A corkscrew road ascends the mountain to a viewing point near the summit, with a picnic area and nature trails.

Five km (three miles) farther north-west is the village of **Omeath**, a vantage point across the lough to Rostrevor and Warren-point at the base of the Mourne Mountains. Omeath was once a stronghold of the Irish language, but since the village's Irish college moved to Donegal, everyday use of language has all but died. There is a simple *An Óige Hostel* (☎ 042-75142), some two km south of Omeath on the road inland to the peninsula. Beds cost IR£3.50 to IR£4.50.

The road between Carlingford and Omeath passes over the mountains and through the **Windy Gap**, a basin-shaped area surrounded by mountains on all sides. This is reputedly Bernas Bó Cúailnge from the Cattle Raid of Cooley where Ailill stole Fergus's sword.

The **Long Woman's Grave** in Windy Gap is a stone cairn reputedly the burial site of a Spanish princess. She was brought here by her lover, a local Irish chieftain, with the promise that vast tracts of land would be hers if she married him. Upon seeing the desolate and limited landscape she died of shock and was buried in the cairn.

The Táin Trail

Carlingford is the start and finish of the

30-km (19-mile) Táin Trail, which covers most of the wildest paths and best scenery on the peninsula. The trail is covered in detail by Bord Fáilte Information Sheet No 26H. You could cover the trail in a long day, but people often camp en route or spend a night at a B&B or at the hostel in Omeath. The trail follows forest tracks and moorland trails, so strong boots are a good idea. There are markers along the route so you are unlikely to get lost.

Getting There & Away

For hikers and cyclists, a ferry to Warrenpoint operates from Omeath over weekends from Easter, and daily during July and August, saving a trip into Newry, 13 km (eight miles) north-west. The cost is IR£1 return. From Warrenpoint you can explore the Mourne Mountains, but if you wish to stay in the south the return trip leading over the hills and back to Dundalk is worth the effort.

Northern
Ireland

Northern Ireland

Two decades of bad publicity have resulted in Northern Ireland being far less visited than the Republic of Ireland. However, despite the sometimes oppressive military presence, drunken and erratic Irish drivers are probably the biggest danger to tourists in Ireland, North or South. The accent is distinctly different in the North, but otherwise the changes across the border are insignificant. The Northern Irish are certainly no less friendly than their compatriots in the South.

The rewards of a foray to the North, however, are well worthwhile – the Antrim Coast Road is a truly stunning stretch of coastline, there are some fascinating early Christian remains around Lough Erne, and Derry has one of the best preserved old city walls in Europe. Nor should the Troubles be ignored: the wall murals in Belfast and Derry, the black taxis and the military roadblocks are as much a part of Ireland these days as green fields and noisy pubs.

HISTORY

With the industrial revolution, Belfast and the surrounding counties became the major industrial centre on the island. The wealth of Belfast's industrial expansion went primarily to the Protestant community. In the late 19th and early 20th centuries, when Home Rule for Ireland became a possibility, the Protestant citizens of Belfast joined the Ulster Volunteer Force in large numbers to resist any such move. The Catholic minority felt increasingly alienated, and while violence was nothing like as frequent as today there was the odd sectarian attack.

Northern Ireland's relationship with the Republic of Ireland was tenuous from the moment of partition. In the Government of Ireland Act of 1920 Lloyd George split Ireland into two and allowed for parliaments both north and south. The division of the island was a rough and ready one. The Unionist leaders demanded only the six of Ulster's nine counties where they were sup-

ported by half or more of the population. While the South was overwhelmingly Catholic with a very small Protestant minority (5%), the balance was very different in the North, with a substantial Catholic minority (over 30%) and many areas where Catholics were actually in the majority. The Anglo-Irish Treaty which partitioned the country and granted Ireland its independence was less than completely clear on the future of the North. A Boundary Commission was supposed to reconsider the borders and make adjustments as necessary; it never did.

On 22 June 1921 the Northern Ireland Parliament came into being; the first prime minister was James Craig. In 1923 the Civil War in the South ground to an exhausted halt with reluctant acceptance of Ireland's division.

In the North, Catholic nationalists elected to the new Northern Ireland parliament took up their seats with equal reluctance, but only in 1925, after the Boundary Commission had collapsed. The politics of the North became increasingly divided on religious grounds, with one prime minister declaring that the government of Northern Ireland was 'a Protestant Parliament and a Protestant state' and another proudly proclaiming that he did not employ a single Catholic.

The Northern Ireland Parliament sat from 1920 until 1972. The Protestant majority made sure their rule was absolute by systematically excluding Catholics from power. There was widespread and ongoing discrimination against Catholics in housing, employment and social welfare.

The Protestant reluctance to share the country with Catholics was exacerbated by the shortage of things to share out. The effects of the 1930s depression were even more severe in Northern Ireland than elsewhere in the UK and unemployment averaged 25% in that decade. Per capita income was only about 60% of the level in Britain, and statistics in every area from

Edward Carson

It was Edward Carson (1854-1935), a Protestant lawyer from Dublin, who spearheaded the Ulster opposition to Home Rule and led the movement which eventually resulted in Ireland's partition. Carson's career in law included numerous successful prosecutions of Irish tenants on behalf of English absentee landlords, and he played a leading role in the conviction of Oscar Wilde for homosexuality in 1895.

Carson was elected to the British House of Commons in 1892 and was the solicitor general for Britain from 1900 to 1905. He was in line for the leadership of the Conservative Party until, in 1910, his fervent distaste for Home Rule and Irish independence led him to take the leadership of the Irish Unionists. Carson believed that without Belfast's heavy industries an independent Ireland would be economically unviable, and that he could frustrate Irish independence simply by keeping the north separate. The British Liberal government's determination to enact Home Rule was frustrated by Carson's parliamentary maneouvres in 1912, and a year later he actually established a provisional government for the North in Belfast.

Carson threatened an armed struggle for a separate Northern Ireland if independence was granted to Ireland. In 1913 he had established a private Ulster army, and weapons were landed from Germany at Larne in 1914, shortly before the outbreak of WW I. The British began to bend before this Ulster opposition, and in July 1914 Carson agreed that Home Rule could go through for Ireland, so long as Ulster was kept separate. The events of WW I and the Easter Rising in Dublin in 1916 shifted the whole question from Home Rule to complete independence. By 1921 however, the Ulster opposition which Carson had nurtured was so strong that the country was carved up.

A statue of Carson defiantly fronts Stormont, the now unused parliament building which remains a symbol of Northern opposition to a united Ireland. Carson himself is buried in St Anne's Cathedral in central Belfast. ■

housing to public health were considerably worse than elsewhere in Britain. The government at every level from local councils to the Stormont parliament was Protestant-dominated and consistently followed a 'jobs for the boys' mentality – Protestant boys, of course. In the early 1970s Belfast's population was 25% Catholic but only 2.5% of Belfast Corporation jobs were held by Catholics.

In spite of all this, Northern Ireland remained a relatively peaceful place for many years after partition, in spite of serious rioting in Belfast in 1922, a spilling over the border of the bitter struggle going on in the South, and 11 deaths in riots in Belfast in 1935.

In WW II, Belfast was heavily bombed. There were many deaths and large areas were flattened. The first US Army forces to land in Europe passed through Belfast on 26 January 1942, and a stone column outside the city hall commemorates their arrival. This strong support for Britain's war effort further entrenched British backing for Northern

Ireland's continued existence and independence.

In 1949 the creation of the Republic of Ireland cut the South's final links, via the British Commonwealth, with the North, but even though the new republic's constitution enshrined its eventual goal of regaining the North, this caused little stir. It was not until the 1960s that Northern Ireland's basic instability began to reveal itself. The government, under Prime Minister Terence O'Neill, took the first very tentative steps towards dealing with the problems of the North's Catholics. A meeting with the South's prime minister and a visit to a Catholic girls' school were hardly earth-shattering moves, but the reaction to these symbolic initiatives propelled the Reverend Ian Paisley to the front of the stage as the ranting personifcation of Protestant extremism. The next innocent addition to what was soon to become a very messy stew was the creation of the Northern Ireland Civil Rights Association in 1967, to campaign for fairer representation for the North's Catholics.

It was in Londonderry that Protestant political domination was at its most outrageous, and in Londonderry that 50 years of Catholic anger at the rigging of council elections finally boiled over in the late 1960s. Londonderry's population was split approximately 60% Catholic to 40% Protestant yet the city's council was consistently elected with exactly the reverse ratio. This was accomplished not only by a long-running gerrymander of the electoral boundaries, but also by handing out more votes to the Protestants via residency and home ownership requirements.

In October 1968 a civil rights march in Derry was violently broken up by the Royal Ulster Constabulary and the Troubles were under way. In January 1969 People's Democracy, another civil rights movement, organised a Belfast to Derry march to demand a fairer division of jobs and housing and an end to unfair voting practices. Just outside Derry a Protestant mob attacked the marchers. The police stood to one side and then compounded the problem with a sweep through the predominantly Catholic Bogside area of Derry. Further marches and protests followed, but increasingly exasperation on one side was met with violence from the other, and far from keeping the two sides apart the police were becoming part of the mob. Finally in August 1969 British troops were sent into Derry and, two days later, Belfast, to maintain law and order.

Though the British army was initially welcomed by the Catholics, it soon came to be seen as a tool of the Protestant majority. The peaceful civil rights movement lost ground, and the hibernating IRA found itself with new and willing recruits from among the beleaguered Catholic minority. Socialists like Bernadette Devlin provided a brief flash of leadership, but it was 'the men with the guns' who soon called the play.

For over 20 years the story of the Troubles, as they are euphemistically known in Northern Ireland, has been one of lost opportunities, intransigence on both sides and fleeting moments of hope. Suspected IRA sympathisers were interned without trial, and on 'Bloody Sunday' 1972 in Derry 13 civilians were killed by troops. Northern Ireland's increasingly ineffective parliament was abolished in 1972, although substantial progress had been made to meet the original civil rights demands. A new power-sharing agreement was worked out in the 1973 Sunningdale agreement, but it was first rejected by the Protestants and then killed stone dead by the massive and overwhelmingly Protestant Ulster Workers' Strike of 1974. Northern Ireland has been ruled from London ever since.

Whilst continuing to target people in Northern Ireland, the IRA also moved their campaign of violence and terror to mainland Britain, bombing pubs and shops and killing many civilians. Their activities were increasingly criticised by citizens on all sides of the political spectrum, and today the IRA are roundly condemned by all mainstream political parties in Britain and the Republic. Meanwhile Loyalist paramilitaries were running a sectarian murder campaign against Catholics.

The Troubles rolled back and forth throughout the 1970s, and although they slowed during the 1980s an answer to the Irish problem seems nowhere nearer. Passions reached fever pitch in 1981 when Republican prisoners in the North went on a hunger strike protest and 12 fasted to death. The best known was an elected MP, Bobby Sands.

An Anglo-Irish Agreement was signed in 1986 which gave the Dublin government an official consultative role in Northern Ireland affairs for the first time. The idea was to make northern nationalists feel that someone was looking out for their interests. However the Unionist politicians were outraged by what they saw as meddling by the Republic and have protested against and boycotted anything to do with the agreement.

The waters have been further muddied by an incredible variety of parties, groups, splinter groups and even splinters of splinter groups, each with its own agenda. The Royal Ulster Constabulary (RUC) has been reorganised and retrained, while the IRA has

---

A Tropical Ireland?

There are intriguing parallels between Ireland and another small island with a north-south religious divide, sectarian violence, paramilitary extremists, car bombs and no immediate solution in sight. The country? Sri Lanka. Ireland has five million people and 84,000 sq km. Sri Lanka has 17 million people and 66,000 sq km. Ireland is about 20% Protestant and 80% Catholic. Sri Lanka has a small minority of Muslims but the rest of the population is about 20% Hindu and 80% Buddhist. Ireland's Protestant minority is concentrated in the North; so is Sri Lanka's Hindu minority. The British army went into Northern Ireland in 1969 to try to keep the peace; the Indian army went into northern Sri Lanka in 1987 to try to keep the peace.

The Tamils, the Hindu minority, have other things in commons with the Northern Irish Protestants. They have a reputation of being canny and hard-working, as if they had been infected with a tropical version of the Protestant work ethic.

The big difference is that Sri Lanka is one country which the Tamil 'Tigers' want to make into two while Ireland is two countries which the IRA want to make into one. The IRA have been enthusiastic about expressing solidarity with other liberation organisations but it's unlikely they'd be too keen on the Tamil Tigers, struggling to achieve the precise opposite of the IRA's aim. ∎

---

been split between official and provisional wings and supplemented with even more extreme republican organisations. Protestant loyalist paramilitary organisations have sprung up in opposition to the IRA, and violence is frequently met with violence, indiscriminate outrage with indiscriminate outrage.

In 1991, the various factions got together for talks under Peter Brooke, the British government's representative in Northern Ireland and while this may lead to further developments, not much has come out of them to date.

It's easy to line up the 'if onlys' when it comes to the problems of Ireland. If only the Home Rule movement had not been so violently opposed to Irish independence in the early part of this century. Ireland might be one country today and the problem would simply not exist. Northern fears might have been reduced if only the Republic had not pandered to them by allowing the Catholic church's prejudices on sex, marriage, censorship and the position of the church to insinuate themselves into so many corners of the country. Northern Catholics' antipathy to Northern Protestants might have been much less if only they had been treated with a modicum of fairness between the 1920s and 1970s. Northern fears of Southern impoverishment might be lower if only the republic's

government had not pursued its vision of a rural arcadia for far longer than was sensible. The British army's unpopularity might be far less if only there had not been over-reactions to IRA provocation. And the North's unwillingness to countenance any agreement with the South might be less if only the IRA had not so frequently been so callously indiscriminate in their violence or, equally frequently, so callously inept.

The British home secretary in 1970, the hapless Reginald Maudling, was castigated for observing that the best hope for Northern Ireland was to achieve 'an acceptable level of violence'. Twenty-four years later that was precisely what had been achieved. The average Northern Irish civilian is 10 times more likely to be killed in a car accident than from a bomb or a bullet. San Francisco in 1987 was over three times more dangerous (18 violent deaths per 100,000 population) than Northern Ireland (five deaths per 100,000).

London talks to Dublin but Belfast cannot be persuaded to join the discussion. The British government has said that they will not go against the will of the Northern Ireland majority – but if the growing Catholic percentage of the population eventually reaches 51% (and all 51% want to reunite the island, by no means a certainty), does that mean the problem will be automatically solved? That could still leave 49% bitterly opposed to reunification and an equally intractable problem.

On the bright side the European Community has reduced the differences between North and South, while economic progress in Ireland has shrunk the disparity between Northern and Southern standards of living. The role of the Catholic church in the South has also diminished, but for all the forward progress and glimmers of new understanding the Northern Ireland problem looks set to continue into the next century.

During 1993 Sinn Féin, the political wing of the IRA, showed a willingness to be more flexible about the terms needed for a ceasefire, but the difficulties of securing a settlement are still formidable. Not least of the problems is the rise of loyalist paramilitary groups who are now carrying out more political killings than the IRA. The governments of the UK and the Republic of Ireland are now putting heavy pressure on the IRA to lay down their arms and on the Unionists to agree to negotiate in the future with an unarmed IRA.

GOVERNMENT

Northern Ireland is part of the United Kingdom of Great Britain and Northern Ireland, and is now governed from London. The main Protestant parties in the North are the Ulster Unionist Party, currently led by Jim Molyneux, and the Democratic Unionist Party, led by the controversial Reverend Ian Paisley. Trying to occupy the middle-of-the-road Catholic and nationalist ground is the Social Democratic & Labour Party (SDLP), led by John Hume, while Sinn Féin ('Ourselves Alone') is the political wing of the IRA and attracts the hard-line nationalist voters. Their current leader is Gerry Adams.

Sinn Féin are banned from speaking on TV or radio both in the UK and the Republic.

ECONOMY

Northern Ireland's shipbuilding and other industries have declined dramatically, but new industries have developed and, of course, the region is heavily supported from Britain. The North has traditionally been regarded as an economic black hole for Britain and much of the spending is on defence and security.

Northern Ireland suffers from unemployment of around 16 to 17%, which while very significant is not as high as the Republic's. It is much worse than the British average but is largely a result of the de-industrialisation of the region and would arguably be much worse without the attention and money which has poured into Northern Ireland in the last 20 years. Half of the working population in the North are employed in one way or another by the government and there are many departments doing work for mainland Britain. Agriculture employs around 8% of the labour force and manufacturing and construction around 24%.

Unemployment in Northern Ireland used to be far greater amongst the Catholic community, but this imbalance has declined in recent years. Huge expenditure on public housing has turned the region's appalling housing conditions around. Someone dubbed Northern Ireland the 'independent Keynesian republic' in the 1980s, as it seemed to be the one area of Thatcher's Britain exempt from public expenditure cuts. Northern Ireland also boasts hospital standards better than the British average, and educational test results that consistently outpace the rest of Britain.

Belfast

Without the Troubles, the capital of Northern Ireland would simply be a big industrial city – nicely situated and with some imposing and impressive Victorian architecture but past its prime. The strife which has torn Belfast since the late 1960s gives it quite another edge. If your only view of the city has been through the media's lens, you may be surprised to find it's actually quite a busy, bustling and prosperous place with more glossy shopping centres and shiny new cars than Dublin. However, a 'black taxi' ride through the strictly divided working-class areas of the Falls and Shankill Rds in West Belfast will show you the flip side of the coin.

Much of the city centre is pedestrianised for security reasons, and the most obvious signs of the Troubles are the armoured Land-Rovers straight out of *Mad Max*, the ever-cautious police and the flak-jacketed soldiers. The faint smell of tension gives a bite to the Belfast air. You may be reassured to know that there have been no tourists killed or injured since the Troubles got going in the early 1970s. In fact statistically Belfast is a much safer city for a visitor than even the most touristically inclined US metropolis. Another feature of Belfast is its size; the centre is compact and most points of interest are within easy walking distance of each other.

The rocks and green slopes of Cave Hill loom over the city to the west, while the sweep of Belfast Lough cuts right into the city centre from the north-east.

HISTORY

Belfast's name comes from Beál Feirste, or 'mouth of the sandy ford'. In 1177, the Norman John de Courcy built a castle by the River Lagan, and a small settlement grew up around it. Both were destroyed 20 years later, and the region was controlled for a long time afterwards by the Irish O'Neill family. In the early years of the 17th century, land in the area was granted to the Chichester family from Devon. However, even during the late 17th century Belfast was hardly more than a village. The population was a mere 550 in 1657.

The first significant wave of foreign settlers were Huguenots: French Protestants, fleeing from persecution in France, and they laid the foundations for a thriving linen industry. More Scottish and English settlers arrived, and other industries such as rope-making, tobacco, engineering and shipbuilding were also developed.

A strong antagonism between Protestants and Catholics only really developed during the 19th century. Prior to this, Belfast had produced many Protestant supporters of an independent Ireland and a fairer society. The United Irishmen, who pushed for increasing independence from England, were actually founded in Belfast in 1791, and the struggle for fairer trading terms enjoyed Protestant and Catholic support. The 1798 rebellion, for example, was not purely religious. In Belfast a number of Protestant ministers who supported the revolt were hanged.

Belfast during the 18th and 19th centuries was the one city in Ireland which really experienced the industrial revolution. Sturdy rows of brick terraced houses were built for the factory and shipyard workers. From around 20,000 people in 1800 Belfast grew to around 400,000 at the start of WW I, by which time it had nearly overtaken Dublin in size. Some suspected that the frequent adjustments to the Dublin city boundaries were made partly in order to ensure the city's population remained a step ahead of the northern upstart.

Queen Victoria visited Belfast in 1849 and her brief foray through the city has been immortalised by a large number of streets, corners and monuments named after her. Belfast was granted city status by Victoria in 1888.

The division of Ireland after WW I and independence in the South gave Belfast a new role as the capital of Northern Ireland. It also marked the end of the city's industrial growth although the decline did not really set in until after WW II.

For nearly 50 years from 1922 until the late 1960s, Northern Ireland was a comparatively quiet place and as a result it was studiously ignored by the British government. The Protestant-dominated Unionist government was left to run things as it saw fit, and since Catholic complaints were relatively subdued, and were generally suppressed when they did get too loud, the underlying instability of the region was not noticed.

Since the initial outbreak of violence in 1969, Belfast has seen more than its fair share of violence and bloodshed and shocking pictures of extremist bombings and killings, often matched by security force brutality, have made the city a household name around the world.

The mayhem reached its peak in the 1970s, and through the 1980s and into the 1990s Belfast seems to have simmered down to an 'acceptable level' of violence. Greater Belfast's population of around 500,000 is about one-third of all of Northern Ireland. While unemployment is relatively high, there is a burgeoning middle class which benefits from the reasonable tax rates and relative cheapness of everyday living. Belfast has plenty of new cars and pin-neat suburban houses, the city restaurants always seem to be full, and huge expenditure on

public housing has brightened even the bleak areas of West Belfast. The city is a much brighter and more cheerful place than its gloomy reputation leads visitors to expect.

ORIENTATION

The city centre is a compact area with the imposing City Hall in Donegall Square as a convenient central landmark. North of the square is Donegall Place/Royal Ave which leads to Donegall St and Belfast Cathedral. This is Belfast's principal shopping district. Reminders of the Victorian era can be found in the narrow alleys known as the Entries off Ann and High Sts, in the wonderful old Grand Opera House and in the museum-like Crown Liquor Saloon on Great Victoria St.

If you are looking for restaurants or accommodation head south from the square down Great Victoria St to University Rd, where you will find Queen's University, the Botanic Gardens and the Ulster Museum. This stretch is called the Golden Mile, and at night it's the most energetic and cheerful area of a generally hard-working city.

To the east of Donegall Square is Chichester St which runs down to the Royal Courts of Justice, the bus station and the River Lagan. East of the river are Samson and Goliath, the giant cranes dominating the Harland & Wolff shipyards. The Shorts aircraft factory is beside the Belfast City Airport.

West of the centre the Westlink Motorway divides the city from West Belfast, 'the wrong side of the tracks'. The (Protestant) Shankill Rd and the (Catholic) Falls Rd run west into West Belfast but there's a real no-man's land separating the two roads and it's not possible to travel directly from one enclave to another. This 'Peace Line' is a straightforward safety measure to discourage extremists of either ilk from creating mayhem then scuttling quickly back to their side of the tracks.

It's worth remembering that Belfast was a product of the industrial revolution and, like many cities in England's depressed midlands, has fallen on hard times, particularly in areas like West Belfast. Nevertheless a

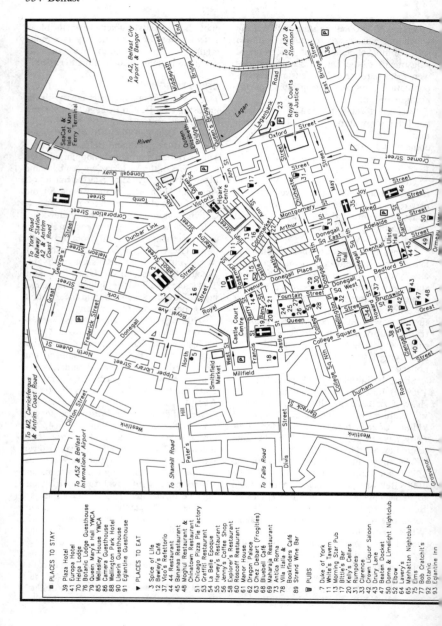

■ PLACES TO STAY
39 Plaza Hotel
41 Europa Hotel
70 Helga Lodge
76 Botanic Lodge Guesthouse
79 Queen Mary's Hall YWCA
85 Wellesley House YWCA
86 Camera Guesthouse
88 Wellington Park Hotel
90 Liserin Guesthouse
91 Eglantine Guesthouse

▼ PLACES TO EAT
3   Spice of Life
12 Bewley's Café
37 Vico's Refettorio
44 44 Restaurant
45 Bananas Restaurant
48 Moghul Restaurant &
    Chinatown Restaurant
51 Chicago Pizza Pie Factory
53 Graffiti Restaurant
54 La Belle Epoque
56 Jenny's Coffee Shop
58 Harvey's Restaurant
60 Explorer's Restaurant
61 Roscoff Restaurant
62 Manor House
63 Dragon Palace
63 Chez Delbart (Frogities)
68 Bluebell Café
69 Maharaja Restaurant
73 Antica Roma
78 Villa Italia &
    Bookfinders Café
89 Strand Wine Bar

▦ PUBS
7   Duke of York
11 White's Tavern
13 Morning Star Pub
17 Bittle's Bar
20 Kelly's Cellars
31 Rumpoles
33 Clarence
42 Crown Liquor Saloon
43 Drury Lane
47 Beaten Docket
50 Dome & Limelight Nightclub
52 Elbow
64 Lavery's
65 Manhattan Nightclub
75 Elms
77 Bob Cratchit's
92 Botanic
93 Eglantine Inn

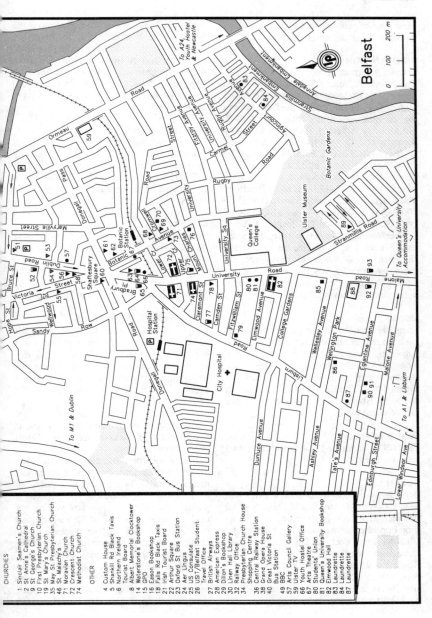

Belfast

0   100   200 m

CHURCHES

1   Sinclair Seamen's Church
2   St Anne's Cathedral
9   St George's Church
10 First Presbyterian Church
19 St Mary's Church
35 May St Presbyterian Church
46 St Malachy's
71 Moravian Church
72 Crescent Church
74 Methodist Church

OTHER

4   Custom House
5   Shankill Rd Black Taxis
6   Northern Ireland
    Tourist Board
8   Albert Memorial Clocktower
14 Waterstone's Bookshop
15 GPO
16 Eason Bookshop
18 Falls Rd Black Taxis
21 Irish Tourist Board
22 Arthur Square
23 Oxford St Bus Station
24 Aer Lingus
25 US Consulate
26 USIT/Belfast Student
    Travel Office
27 British Airways
28 American Express
29 Dillon's Bookshop
30 Linen Hall Library
32 Railway Office
34 Presbyterian Church House
36 Shopping Centre
    Central Railway Station
38 Grand Opera House
40 Great Victoria St
    Bus Station
49 BBC
57 Arts Council Gallery
59 Ulster TV
66 Youth Hostel Office
67 Arts Theatre
80 Students' Union
81 Queen's University Bookshop
82 Elmwood Hall
83 Laundrette
84 Laundrette
87 Laundrette

great deal of renovation and reconstruction is, belatedly, going on in the area.

INFORMATION
Tourist Information
The Northern Ireland Tourist Board tourist office (☎ 0232-246609) is at St Annes Court, 59 North St. In July and August, the peak of the summer season, it's open 9 am to 7.30 pm Monday to Friday, 9 am to 5.15 pm on Saturday and 12 noon to 4 pm on Sunday.

The Irish Tourist Board, Bord Fáilte (☎ 0232-327888) is at 53 Castle St. The Youth Hostel Association of Northern Ireland (☎ 0232-324733) is at 56 Bradbury Place, near the university. The AA (☎ 0345-500600) is at 108 Great Victoria St, the RAC (☎ 0232-240261) is at 79 Chichester St.

The Northern Buzz is a recently established 'what's on' magazine for Belfast and Northern Ireland, but since it only comes out every two months it's not very good for rapidly changing events and doesn't even try to list cinema showings.

Money
There are branches of the major British and Irish banks in the centre of Belfast and numerous cash machines which dispense money to Visa and MasterCard (Access) customers. American Express are at Hamilton Travel (☎ 0232-322455) at 10 College St, opposite British Airways. They do not handle client mail.

Post & Telephone
The GPO is on Castle Place, between the two tourist offices.

Bookshops
Bookshops include Waterstone's at 8 Royal Ave, Eason at 16 Ann St and Dillon's at 42 Fountain St. Queen's University has a bookshop opposite the main university building.

Roma Ryan's at 73 Dublin Rd stocks prints and rare books. Nearby is Prospect House Books at 93 Dublin Rd, another rare book specialist. Bookfinders at 47 University Rd is a straightforward secondhand bookshop with a popular café upstairs.

See the Books & Bookshops section in the Facts for the Visitor chapter for books on Northern Ireland's turbulent history, visitors' accounts and fiction by Northern Irish writers. *Belfast – The Making of the City* (Appletree Press paperback, Belfast, 1983) covers Belfast during its prime years from 1800 to 1914.

Medical Services
The Royal Victoria Hospital (☎ 0232-240503) is on the Falls Rd west of the city centre. Belfast City Hospital (☎ 0232-329241) is on the Lisburn Rd. If you need an ambulance or an emergency service phone ☎ 999.

Laundry
In the university area there are laundrettes at 46 and 120 Agincourt Ave and at 160 Lisburn Rd.

Shops
Shops are open until 9 pm on Thursday.

DANGERS & ANNOYANCES
Despite Belfast's front-line reputation it's actually not a dangerous place to visit – this is not Miami or New York! The callous violence between the IRA (and its various offspring) and the equivalent Protestant paramilitaries is usually aimed at specific people.

Nevertheless there are some rules to obey. Bomb scares usually include warnings; if you're told to get out of the area, do so. Don't hang around to gawk.

Be careful where you park your car. Cars illegally (or suspiciously) parked can expect rough treatment. In practice this is not quite as fearsome as it sounds; if you overstay a parking meter by 10 minutes you're not likely to come back to find the bomb squad in action! Most attractive places for car bombs are simply unparkable; the street may be blocked off or cars may be excluded. Parking is not allowed at all in the prominently marked Control Zones. When you park in regular commercial parking lots, your car will be subjected to a quick overall inspection before you leave it – mirrors allow them to look underneath, and the luggage and engine compartments will both be inspected.

Left luggage can get a similar treatment to left cars and it's worth noting that there are no luggage storage facilities at bus or train stations. Bags and cases may also be subjected to inspection when you enter shopping centres or even walk along busy shopping streets.

You should also be prepared for military or police checkpoints and document inspections. Always carry some form of identification on you; your passport is particularly good as it proves you're a real visitor. Don't attempt to photograph military personnel or their equipment or military posts. If you do you will quickly find out just how observant they are.

You're unlikely to get into furious political or religious arguments in Belfast pubs because both topics are studiously avoided with outsiders. In staunchly single-minded pubs of either persuasion, outsiders are also studiously avoided!

AROUND THE CENTRE

Donegall Place runs north from Donegall Square then changes name to Royal Ave. The city's busy and mainly pedestrianised shopping centre spreads out either side of this important avenue. The pedestrianisation of the centre is in part a by-product of the Troubles. At their height in the 1970s, terrorist activities turned the whole centre into a heavily militarised zone, but the security presence is much lower profile today, and modern city planning would probably have got around to excluding cars in any case.

The **Cornmarket**, just east of Donegall Place, takes its name from an older agricultural Belfast but is still a popular meeting place. Two modern shopping centres, Hipark to the east and Castle Court to the west, are symbols of the vibrant Belfast that has grown up in spite of the Troubles.

Belfast City Hall

The industrial revolution transformed

Illegal Parking

The one incident with an illegally parked car which I witnessed in Belfast didn't go quite the way I'd expected. The car blocked in an unfortunate plumber behind my B&B and he eventually called the police to complain that he couldn't get his van out. The police came round, kicked the tyres and told the plumber that if he wanted to smash a window to get in they'd turn their back, and help him push it out of the way afterwards. They did, he did and, of course, the owner finally turned up 10 minutes later.

Tony Wheeler

Belfast, and that rapid rise to muck-and-brass prosperity shows to this day. The Portland stone City Hall in Donegall Square was completed in 1906. Built in the Classical Renaissance style, it has some fine marble inside and a great deal of pomp and splendour outside. The first meeting of the Northern Ireland Parliament was held here in 1921, but it subsequently met at the Union Theological College until Stormont was completed in 1932.

The most noticeable feature of the exterior used to be the huge 'Belfast Says No' banner displayed along the top of the building. This was placed here by the Unionist city fathers to show their objections to the Anglo-Irish Agreement, which was signed in 1985 and formed the basis of ongoing consultations between Britain and the Republic over the North. Most Unionist city councillors have also refused to take part in council affairs while the agreement is in force.

The banner's days would appear to be numbered, as the Unionists are expected to lose their council majority soon. In 1993 the building was covered over for a major cleaning and it will be interesting to see if the banner is still there when the wraps come off.

The hall is fronted by a statue of a rather dour Queen Vic; hubby Prince Albert has a leaning clocktower in the city. Statues of city mayors also guard the building on the Donegall Square North side.

At the north-east corner of the City Hall

grounds is a statue of Sir Edward Harland, the Yorkshire-born marine engineer who founded the Harland & Wolff shipyards. In its prime the shipyard was one of Belfast's biggest businesses and it still survives, in much quieter form. The yard's most famous construction was the ill-fated *Titanic* which sank in 1912, after colliding with an iceberg on its maiden voyage to America. A memorial to the disaster and its victims stands on the east side of the building.

The Marquess of Dufferin (1826-1902), whose career included postings as ambassador to Constantinople in Ottoman Turkey, St Petersburg in Tsarist Russia, Paris and Rome, and as governor-general to Canada and viceroy to India, has an extremely ornate temple-like memorial on the west side of the City Hall. He was responsible for adding Burma to the British Empire in 1886.

Tours of the City Hall are available but must be booked in advance by phoning ☎ 0232-320202 ext 2227; they usually take place on Wednesday mornings at 10.30 am. There is no charge.

Linen Hall Library

At 17 Donegall Square North, looking across the square to the City Hall, the Linen Hall Library (☎ 0232-321707) was established in 1788, although not in this building, and has a major Irish collection. It includes the most complete collection of early Belfast and Ulster printing and key research collections in Irish and local studies.

Thomas Russell was the first librarian; he was a founder member of the United Irishmen and a close friend of Wolfe Tone – a reminder that this movement for independence from Britain had its origins in Belfast. Russell was hanged in 1803 after Robert Emmet's abortive rebellion.

For over a century the library was in the White Linen Hall, which was built from 1784 but demolished to make way for the City Hall. The entrance doorway to the present library is draped with stone linen and topped by the red hand of Ulster.

The library is open to its members from 9.30 am Monday to Saturday, to 4 pm on

Theobald Wolfe Tone

Saturday, 8.30 pm on Thursday and 5.30 pm on the other days.

Other Donegall Square Buildings

Donegall Square, with the City Hall squarely in the middle, is undoubtedly the centre of Belfast. If you come into town by local bus you're likely to be dropped there as most local bus services arrive and depart from around the square.

There are a number of interesting buildings around the square but easily the most magnificent is the wonderfully ornate **Scottish Provident Building** built from 1899 to 1902, overlooking the City Hall from Donegall Square West. It's decorated with a veritable riot of statuary, including several allusions to the industries that assured Victorian Belfast's prosperity as well as sphinxes, dolphins and a variety of lions' heads.

The building was the work of the architectural partnership of Young & MacKenzie who counterbalanced it in the same year with the **Pearl Assurance Building** on the Donegall Square East corner. Between these two examples of turn-of-the-century extravagance is the equally fine **Robinson & Cleaver Building**, once Belfast's finest department store.

The Entries

The area immediately north of High St was the oldest part of Belfast but it suffered considerable damage during WW II bombing. The narrow alleyways known as the **Entries** run off High St and Ann St in the pedestrianised shopping centre. At one time they were bustling commercial and residential centres, Pottinger's Entry had 34 houses in 1822. Today pubs are just about all that survives down these reclusive hideaways.

The **Morning Star** on Pottinger's Entry is one of the most attractive of these wonderful old Belfast bars. **Joy's Entry** commemorates the Joy family. In 1737 Francis Joy founded the *Belfast News Letter*, the first daily newspaper in Britain. It's still in business today. One of his grandsons, Henry Joy McCracken, was executed for supporting the 1798 United Irishmen's revolt.

The United Irishmen were founded in 1791 by Wolfe Tone in Peggy Barclay's tavern in **Crown Entry**. They used to meet in **Kelly's Cellars** on Bank St off Royal Ave. **White's Tavern** on Wine Cellar Entry is the oldest pub in the city and is still a popular lunch-time meeting spot to this day.

Albert Memorial Clocktower

W J Barre's 1867 Albert Memorial Clocktower in Queen's Square at the junction of High St and Victoria St is not so dramatically out of kilter as the famous tower in Pisa, Italy, but it is, nevertheless, a leaning tower. Although Queen Victoria paid a visit to Belfast, hubby Albert never dropped by, so his grandiose memorial is a bit of a mystery.

Around the Clocktower

Looking across the River Lagan from the clocktower, east Belfast is dominated by the huge cranes of the Harland & Wolff shipyards. Many of the buildings around the clocktower are the work of Sir Charles Lanyon, the pre-eminent architect of Belfast in its prime. The modern Queen Elizabeth Bridge crosses the Lagan just to the south, but immediately south again is **Queen's Bridge** with its ornate lamps. Completed in

1843, this was Lanyon's first important Belfast construction.

Immediately to the north of the clocktower is a white stone building occupied by the TSB but originally completed in 1852 by Lanyon as the head office of the Northern Bank. East towards the river is the **Custom House**, built by Lanyon in Italianate style in 1854-57. It's not open to the public, but on the waterfront side you can admire the pediment with its sculptured portrayals of Britannia, Neptune and Mercury. Follow the waterfront round to the SeaCat and Isle of Man ferry terminal beside the **Harbour Office**. The office has exhibits relating to the city's maritime history but is only rarely open to the public. The churches section describes the intriguing Sinclair Seamen's Church which is right next door.

The Crown Liquor Saloon

Across from the Europa Hotel on Great Victoria St, the Crown Liquor Saloon was built by Patrick Flanagan in 1885 and displays Victorian architectural flamboyance at its most extravagant. Owned by the National Trust, who have removed some newer embellishments, and operated by Bass Ireland, this pub is on every visitor's itinerary. The exterior is decorated with a myriad different coloured and shaped tiles, while the interior has a mass of stained and cut glass, marble, mosaics and mahogany furniture. A lengthy and highly decorated bar dominates one side of the pub while on the other is a row of ornate wooden snugs topped by stirring mottoes. Private drinkers can call for further refreshments from within their snugs by signalling to the bell board behind the bar.

The Grand Opera House

One of Belfast's great landmarks is the Grand Opera House (☎ 0232-240411), just north of the Europa Hotel and across the road from the Crown Liquor Saloon on Great Victoria St. Opened in 1895, the Opera House was closed for a considerable part of the 1970s before a restoration project completely refurbished both the interior and the red-brick exterior. Inside it's over-the-top

---

Van Morrison

James Joyce claimed that Dublin could be recreated using his books as the plan. Belfast, on the other hand, could probably be sketched out from Van Morrison's songs. The Belfast Cowboy fronted the Northern Ireland band Them to fleeting success in the swinging '60s with songs like *Here Comes the Night* and the classic *Gloria*, but in 1966 Them fell apart, and their short, intense and utterly uncharismatic lead singer moved to the USA where he managed one top 10 hit and a quickly forgotten solo LP. Morrison might have become just another '60s rock & roll victim, his 15 minutes run its course, when he drifted back to Ireland. But in 1968 he was back in the US and in just two days recorded *Astral Weeks*, an LP which to this day critics hail as one of the seminal records of the era. Over 20 records later, every one of them a solid success, 'Van the Man's' unique blend of folk, jazz, blues, gospel and a healthy slug of Celtic mysticism has given him one of the most loyal followings in rock music.

Even in *Astral Weeks* those Belfast clues started to appear. One track is named *Cyprus Avenue*, after a street in east Belfast, while *Madame George*, the record's most enigmatic and intriguing song, wanders 'up and down the Sandy Row', a staunchly Protestant street just south of the city centre. More recently the 1991 *Hymns to the Silence* conjures up Belfast in the late 1950s and early 1960s in the track titled *On Hyndford St*. The 1990 record *Enlightenment* also journeys backs to a forgotten Belfast of the 1950s *In the Days before Rock 'n' Roll*.

The 1989 *Avalon Sunset* has a track titled *Orangefield*, after the unmemorable Belfast suburb of that name, but *Coney Island* on the same record is a positive delight. It's a real wander around Northern Ireland, taking you from Downpatrick to St John's Point for a spot of birdwatching and good crack! Then it's on to Strangford Lough, Shrigly, Killyleagh, the Lecale District, Ardglass and finally Coney Island, all with a flavour so golden you wish you could be there too.

Views of Belfast also appear on his record sleeves, most notably on the 1984 *Live at the Grand Opera House Belfast*, while two different views of Hyndford St pop up on the sleeve and sleeve notes for *Hymns to the Silence*. It's a reminder that for all his mellow music Morrison is a notably prickly character, visibly uncomfortable on stage and famously difficult with journalists. When the Belfast Blues Society tried to put a commemorative plaque on his former home on Hyndford St in the east Belfast suburb of Bloomfield he set the lawyers on them. They must have failed: the plaque's there at No 125. ■

Victoriana, with purple satin in abundance and swirling wood and plasterwork.

The Opera House is constantly busy with music shows, operas and plays but has suffered grievously at the hands of the IRA in recent years. A 1000 lb truck bomb was their 1991 Christmas gift to Belfast culture, and a multi-million-pound reconstruction had barely been completed before they parked another well-loaded truck outside on 20 May 1993. Repairs are once more under way.

SOUTH OF THE CENTRE
Sandy Row

Just a block west of Great Victoria St, the road which leads from the city centre to the university, is the curving Sandy Row. This used to be the main road south out of the city, and it's still a working-class and Protestant enclave, wedged in beside the wealthier

Golden Mile area. Here you'll find red, white and blue kerbstones and unionist murals, just like on the Shankill Rd in West Belfast. Van Morrison fans may remember that he wandered 'up and down the Sandy Row' in his 1968 album *Astral Weeks*.

Ulster Museum

The Ulster Museum (☎ 0232-381251) is beside the Botanic Gardens near the university. There are good displays on Irish art, wildlife, dinosaurs, steam and industrial machines, minerals and fossils, and it can take several hours to do the circuit properly.

Items from the 1588 Spanish Armada wreck of the *Girona* (see Dunluce Castle in County Antrim) are a highlight, especially the gold jewellery which includes a ruby-encrusted salamander and an inscribed gold ring. Many of the Armada ships were wrecked along the west coast of Ireland, but the *Girona* came to grief on the north-east coast, off the Giant's Causeway. The wreck was investigated by the Belgian marine archaeologist Robert Stenuit in 1968, 380 years later.

The museum was designed in 1911 but not completed until late in the 1920s. An extension was added to the museum in 1971, and the complex includes a shop and a café overlooking the Botanic Gardens. Entry to the museum is free and it's open 10 am to 5 pm Monday to Friday, from 1 pm Saturday and from 2 pm Sunday. Bus No 69 or 71 will get you there.

Botanic Gardens

The somewhat tatty Botanic Gardens are a restful oasis away from the busy main road and worth a wander about. The gardens date from 1827 and their centrepiece is the fine Palm House with its cast-iron and curvilinear glass construction, built between 1839 and 1852 and housing palms and other hot house flora. Although Belfast's pre-eminent architect Charles Lanyon played a part in its creation, the Palm House was essentially the work of Richard Turner of Dublin. He also built glasshouses in the Dublin Botanic Gardens and at Kew Gardens in London and worked on the 1851 Crystal Palace in London. Just inside the gardens at the Stranmillis Rd gate is a statue to Belfast-born Lord Kelvin who invented the Kelvin Scale which measures temperatures from absolute zero (-273°C or 0°K).

Belfast has a number of other parks and gardens, and the Parks Department produces a booklet titled *On Foot in Belfast* detailing good walks in and around the city.

Queen's University

One km south of Donegall Square and City Hall is the muted red and yellow brick Queen's College building of Queen's University. Queen's is Northern Ireland's most prestigious university; it caters to around 8000 students and has a particularly strong reputation in the sciences. Although the plan of the college building is based on Magdalen College in Oxford, it was, once again,

Charles Lanyon who was responsible for the design. Queen Victoria was present for the laying of the foundation stone in 1845, and the building was completed in 1849.

The lofty entrance hall leads into the quadrangle. On the south side a chimney has brickwork spelling out VR 1848 (Victoria Regina). Beyond the college building is Old Library, designed by Lanyon's assistant W H Lynn and built in 1864, then extended in 1913. Surrounding the university are quiet tree-lined streets with small cafés full of students. University Square, on the north side of the campus, dates from 1848-53 and is one of the finest terraced streets in Ireland. It was once known as the Harley St of Belfast, and is now owned by the university.

Behind the Queen's College building, across Botanic Ave, is the colonnaded Union Theological College, originally the Presbyterian College. It opened in 1853 and, yes, it too was a Lanyon design. From the partition of Ireland until 1932 it served as the Northern Ireland Parliament, but the Stormont building took over for the next 40 years.

BELFAST CHURCHES

Although Belfast has numerous churches none are of very great interest. Most of the Protestant churches are only open for very limited hours, in many cases only on Sundays and even then only around the times of services.

St Anne's Anglican Cathedral was built between 1899 and 1904 and stands just north of the city centre. Edward Carson, whose opposition to Home Rule was a principal cause of the separation of Ireland and Northern Ireland, is buried here. A slab simply announcing 'Carson', can be found about half way along the right wall of the nave.

In the pedestrianised central shopping area, the **First Presbyterian Church** on Rosemary St dates from 1783 and has an interesting oval-shaped interior with enclosed pews, each entered by a door. It's open on Sundays, and also on Wednesdays from 10 am to 4 pm. On High St at the corner with Victoria St, right across from the Albert Memorial Clocktower, is the 1816 Anglican

St George's. The superb classical portico is the most noticeable feature of the church but it didn't start life here. It was originally the front of Ballyscullion House in Bellaghy, between Belfast and Derry. The colourful earl of Bristol (who also happened to be the bishop of Derry) abandoned the house before it was completed and the facade was dismantled and rebuilt here. See the section on the Mussenden Temple near Derry for more on this unusual character.

Further north of the centre, on Corporation Square beside the Harbour Office and the Isle of Man and SeaCat ferry terminal, the 1857 **Sinclair Seamen's Church** is one of Belfast's most interesting churches. The church was designed by that busiest of Belfast architects, Charles Lanyon, and features a pulpit designed to look like a ship's bow. It contains enough nautical memorabilia to qualify as a marine museum!

The Catholic **St Malachy's** on Alfred St, just south of the centre, was built in 1844 and has an ornate fan-vaulted ceiling and a pulpit frosted like a wedding cake, while outside there are interesting pink-trimmed turrets. Nearby is the 1829 **May St Presbyterian Church**, a classical-style building also known as the Cooke Memorial Church after the pedantic Dr Henry Cooke. The Reverend Cooke dedicated his religious life to arcane arguments about Biblical interpretations, and his memorial notes 'his eminent and successful labour for the truth against the prevailing errors of the time.' He also laboured in the Protestant cause and served as a foretaste of the modern 'Orangeman'.

At the northern end of University Rd, in the Golden Mile area south of the centre, there's a cluster of Victorian churches. The 1887 **Crescent Church** was built of Scrabo stone in a style modelled on French church designs of the 13th century. The pierced tower, looking like an open framework, is an instantly recognisable landmark. Across the road the **Moravian Church** also dates from 1887 and was also built of Scrabo stone. Completing this University Rd trio is the 1865 **Methodist Church**, just a few steps further along the road. There are elements of

Italian design in this church which was the work of W J Barre, best known for the leaning Albert Clocktower in the docks area.

Built in 1862 in a exotic interpretation of Italian architectural styles **Elmwood Hall** also started life as a church but is now used as a university concert hall. It's further along University Rd, opposite the Queen's College building.

The **Knockbreda Parish Church**, the oldest church in Belfast, dates from 1737 and is on the A24 south of the centre and just before the ring road, very close to the Belfast Youth Hostel. Perched on a hill, it was designed by Richard Castle, who was also responsible for many buildings in Dublin including Leinster House.

ART GALLERIES
The Ulster Museum has a collection of Irish art, but Belfast's principal modern art gallery is the **Arts Council Gallery** (☎ 0232-321402) at 56 Dublin Rd near Shaftesbury Square. This is a temporary home after it was bombed out of its Bedford St location in 1992 so it may be on the move again.

Malone House (☎ 0232-681246) has exhibitions on Belfast parks and an art gallery. It's well to the south of the centre in Barnett Park on Upper Malone Rd and is open Monday to Saturday from 10 am to 4.30 pm.

Private galleries in Belfast include the Tom Caldwell Gallery (☎ 0232-323226) at 40 Bradbury Place, the Crescent Arts Centre (☎ 0232-242338) at 2 University Rd, the Bell Gallery (☎ 0232-662998) at 13 Adelaide Park, the Fenderesky Gallery (☎ 0232-235245) at 5 Upper Crescent and the Eakin Gallery (☎ 0232-668522) at 237 Lisburn Rd.

WALK 1 – PRINCE ALBERT TO QUEEN VICTORIA
This walking tour takes you from a memorial to Prince Albert, Queen Victoria's husband, to another to Queen Victoria herself, and the walk explores the city's Victorian heartland.

The leaning (1) Albert Memorial Clocktower on Queen's Square makes an

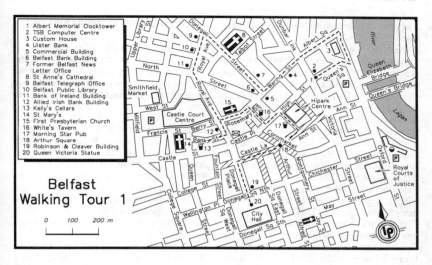

1 Albert Memorial Clocktower
2 TSB Computer Centre
3 Custom House
4 Ulster Bank
5 Commercial Building
6 Belfast Bank Building
7 Former Belfast News
  Letter Office
8 St Anne's Cathedral
9 Belfast Telegraph Office
10 Belfast Public Library
11 Bank of Ireland Building
12 Allied Irish Bank Building
13 Kelly's Cellars
14 St Mary's
15 First Presbyterian Church
16 White's Tavern
17 Morning Star Pub
18 Arthur Square
19 Robinson & Cleaver Building
20 Queen Victoria Statue

**Belfast
Walking Tour 1**

0   100   200 m

easily located start for the walk. Immediately north of the clocktower is the (2) TSB Computer Centre in the 1852 building Sir Charles Lanyon built for the Northern Bank. This walk passes by several other Lanyon buildings including the 1857 (3) Custom House. From the waterfront side you can see the sculptured pediment at the front of the building. Across the road is the now disused Calder Fountain, erected in memory of a naval commander who installed cattle troughs in Belfast in the 1840s and founded the local Society for the Prevention of Cruelty to Animals.

Turn down Albert Square and cross Victoria St to Waring St where the grandiose 1860 (4) Ulster Bank survived wartime bombing that obliterated much of this area. The imposing building has iron railings decorated with the red hand of Ulster, cast-iron lamp standards, soaring columns and sculptured figures of Britannia, Justice and Commerce. The rooftop figures were by Thomas Fitzpatrick who was also responsible for the carvings on the nearby Custom House.

At the junction of Waring St with Donegall St is the 1822 (5) Commercial

Building, easily identified by the prominent name of the Northern Whig Printing Company. Opposite is the (6) Belfast Bank Building, now occupied by the Northern Bank. This is the oldest public building in the city although it bears little relationship to its original design. The building started life as a single-storey market house in 1769, became the Assembly Rooms, with the addition of an upper storey, in 1777 and in 1845 was remodelled by Charles Lanyon to become the bank buildings.

Turn up Donegall St, looking for Commercial Court, a narrow laneway hiding the Duke of York pub. The former home of the (7) *Belfast News Letter* at No 59 is an 1873 building decorated with bas-relief portraits of literary figures – we'll meet a similar decorative style on Walk 2. The imposing (8) *St Anne's Cathedral* was built from 1899 but is of little interest inside apart from the grave of Edward Carson. At Royal Ave turn left, noting the modern offices of the (9) *Belfast Telegraph* and then the red sandstone (10) Belfast Public Library. Continue along Royal Avenue as it bends to the left, but look back to the (11) Bank of Ireland Building, a fine example of 1920s art deco and elegantly placed at the junction of North St and Royal Ave.

Past the Castle Court Centre and the Virgin Megastore is the 1868 (12) building designed by W J Barre who was also responsible for the Albert Clocktower at the start of this walk. The building is now occupied by the Allied Irish Bank. Turn right by the bank into Bank Place and (13) Kelly's Cellars, a whitewashed 18th-century pub where the United Irishmen once met. Just beyond the pub is the decorative grotto of (14) St Mary's, the first Catholic church in Belfast, which opened in 1784.

Return to Royal Ave and backtrack to the Virgin Megastore then turn right into Rosemary St, past the 1783 (15) First Presbyterian Church with its curious elliptical interior. A few steps further, a right turn leads into Wine Cellar Entry where Belfast's oldest pub, (16) White's Tavern, lurks. It's been here since 1630 although it was rebuilt in 1790. A left turn takes you into High St with its narrow 'entries'. Turn right down Pottinger's Entry past the (17) Morning Star Pub. Pottinger's Entry emerges on to pedestrianised Ann St: note the arm holding up an umbrella which emerges from the building opposite the entry.

Turn right down Ann St to (18) Arthur Square, where five pedestrianised streets meet with a bandstand, newstands, buskers, preachers, hawkers and all sorts of other activity. This was once the central traffic junction in the city but the traffic has long been diverted. It was also the site of the Abercorn, a popular café before the Troubles, until one crowded Saturday lunchtime in 1972 a terrorist bomb was set off. Redevelopment has removed all trace of the place. Continue along Castle Lane and turn left down Donegall Place with the City Hall towering in front of you.

At the corner of Donegall Place and Donegall Square North is the ornate carved stone facade of the (19) Robinson & Cleaver Building. Resolutely guarding the front of the City Hall the (20) statue of Queen Victoria in time-honoured 'not amused' pose marks the end of this walk.

WALK 2 – QUEEN VICTORIA TO LORD KELVIN

The (1) statue of Queen Victoria in front of the City Hall marked the end of Walk 1 and marks the beginning of this walk south of the city centre to the university area, botanic gardens and the restaurant-studded 'Golden Mile'.

See the City Hall section for information about this symbol of Belfast at the height of the industrial revolution. Standing in front of the Victoria statue and looking, like her, down Donegall Place, you can see the (2) Robinson & Cleaver Building on the corner of the square and Donegall Place. To the right on the corner of the square is the magnificent (3) Pearl Assurance Building. To the left is the even more magnificent (4) Scottish Provident Building.

Bid Victoria farewell and turn left along Donegall Square North noting the (5) Linen Hall Library whose history, though not all at this site, dates back to 1788. Continue down Wellington Place towards the (6) statue of Dr Henry Cooke (1788-1868). It's typical that this prickly character should stand not beside the road but right in the middle of it. We'll be meeting him again shortly.

Behind his statue is the (7) Technical Institute of 1907 and (8) Royal Belfast Academical Institution or 'Inst' of 1814. The Inst is a story of frustrated plans – it stands on College Square which is actually only half a square because the west and south sides were never built. The building itself was not completed to its original plans due to shortage of funds and the Technical Institute was plonked in front of it due to another college cash shortage.

Turn left down College Square past the bulk of the (9) Presbyterian Church House which dates from 1905 and is decorated with angels, eagles and dragons and now houses shops and a café. Turn left on to Howard St, which shortly becomes Donegall Square South and takes you along the back of the City Hall. The White Linen Hall once occupied the City Hall site and as a result the surrounding area was crowded with linen warehouses, most of them long gone. On the

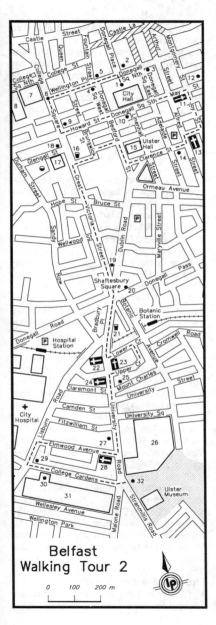

1   Queen Victoria Statue
2   Robinson & Cleaver Building
3   Pearl Assurance Building
4   Scottish Provident Building
5   Linen Hall Library
6   Dr Henry Cooke Statue
7   Technical Institute
8   Royal Belfast Academical Institution
9   Presbyterian Church House
10 Yorkshire House
11 May St Presbyterian Church
12 Dunlop Plaque
13 St Malachy's Church
14 Robinson Patterson Office
15 Ulster Hall
16 Crown Liquor Saloon
17 Europa Hotel
18 Grand Opera House
19 Ulster Bank Statues
20 RUC Guardpost
21 Lavery's Gin Palace
22 Moravian Church
23 Crescent Church
24 Methodist Church
25 Mount Charles Villas
26 Queen's College
27 Student's Union
28 Elmwood Hall
29 Gate Lodge
30 McArthur's Hall
31 Methodist College
32 Lord Kelvin Statue

corner with Linenhall St is (10) Yorkshire
House, with 16 sculptured heads of various
personages, real and imaginary. Donegall
Square South changes names to become May
St and passes the (11) May St Presbyterian
Church, built in 1829 and also known as the
Cooke Memorial Church. Yes, it's named
after the same Dr Henry Cooke who stands
resolutely in the middle of the street on
College Square.

Continue along May St to Joy St. Across
the road is an empty car parking lot, of zero
interest except for the (12) plaque on the east
wall. This was the former site of John Boyd
Dunlop's workshop, where he developed the
first pneumatic tyre in the 1880s.

Turn down Joy St and then right on to
Russell St and left past (13) St Malachy's
Church. Another right takes you on to Clar-

ence St and past the (14) Robinson Patterson architectural office, an intriguing redevelopment of a 19th-century warehouse which sliced the end off the building and glassed it over to produce a building which won a 'Building of the Year' architectural award.

Turn right into Bedford St, past the (15) Ulster Hall and then left into Franklin St to Brunswick St, passing Surf Mountain, a reminder to surfing enthusiasts that Northern Ireland has some good waves. A left and right takes you past the Drury Lane pub and the wonderful (16) Crown Liquor Saloon.

Across the road are the (17) Europa Hotel and the (18) Grand Opera House, which unfortunately is also in danger of collecting the 'much bombed' accolade. Turn south down Great Victoria St, noting the memorial statue to working women just south of the Europa Hotel. The occasional interesting building can't make up for the fact that this is a stretch due for redevelopment.

Shaftesbury Square marks the start of the university area, but look back at the junction to the (19) statuary tacked onto the front of the Ulster Bank Building. The figures are known locally as Draft and Overdraft.

Continue across Shaftesbury Square, more a road junction than a square in the conventional sense, noting Donegall Pass which runs off the junction to the left (east). This is the only remaining 'pass' into Belfast, a reminder that the city was once bounded on this side by private land belonging to Lord Donegall, and the passes through Cromac Woods were the only access to the city. Today Donegall Pass is guarded at the Shaftesbury Square end by a typically forbidding (20) RUC guardpost.

Bradbury Place runs south from the junction, but a narrow alley disappears down the back of the buildings, and this was once used as a discreet back entry to (21) Lavery's Gin Palace. Today it's just a popular student pub, but Lavery's has a long bohemian and literary tradition in Belfast. Bradbury Place becomes University Rd and on the right side of the road is the 1887 (22) Moravian Church. A left turn takes you into Lower Crescent, beside the 1887 (23) Crescent Church, with its instantly recognisable skeleton-like bell tower.

The green behind the church is enclosed by Lower Crescent, Crescent Gardens and Upper Crescent. Walking round the green takes you past mid-19th-century, neo-classical-style terraces reminiscent of Bath in England. They were built by Robert Corry, a local entrepreneur, and may have been designed by Charles Lanyon. Across University Rd, W J Barre's (24) Methodist Church of 1865 completes the trio of University Rd churches.

Continuing along University Rd the next street left is Mt Charles with an attractive group of (25) villas dating from 1842. University Square, also to the left from University Rd, has another group of fine terrace houses. Queen Victoria herself laid the foundation stone for (26) Queen's College in 1845. It's the principal building of Queen's University and was yet another Charles Lanyon design.

Across University Rd from the college building is the modern (27) Student's Union, a great contrast to the exotic (28) Elmwood Hall. Built by John Corry, the architect son of Robert Corry whose Bath-style crescents were seen earlier on this walk, the Italian-inspired church building is now used as a university concert hall. Walk along Elmwood Ave beside Elmwood Hall, then left on to Lisburn Rd and left again, beside a toy-like (29) gate lodge into College Gardens. The road takes you past (30) McArthur's Hall and the grandiose (31) Methodist College, built in High Victorian style in 1865-68.

Cross University Rd to enter the Stranmillis Rd gate of the Botanic Gardens. Just inside the gate is a (32) statue of Lord Kelvin (1824-1907) who invented the Kelvin Scale and patented inventions for underwater submarine cables. This eminent Victorian scientist makes a fitting end to this walk.

THE FALLS & THE SHANKILL

The Catholic Falls Rd and the Protestant Shankill Rd have been battlefronts for the

Troubles, and apart from the occasional bright flash of a wall mural they're grey and rather dismal. For visitors they're quite safe, and more modern (and enlightened) public housing is not only replacing the old Victorian slums but also the 1960s tower blocks. These areas are worth venturing into, if only to see the large murals expressing local political and religious passions. King Billy on his white steed and hooded IRA gunmen are two of the more memorable images. Less noticeable to first-time visitors are the red, white and blue-painted pavement kerbs which adorn staunch Protestant loyalist areas, and the green, white and orange kerbs in the Catholic areas.

West Belfast grew up around the linen mills which propelled the city into its industrial revolution prosperity. It was an area of low-cost working-class housing, and even in the Victorian era it was becoming rigidly divided on religious lines. The advent of the Troubles in 1968 solidified that sectarian division, and the construction of the Westlink Motorway neatly divided the area, and its problems, from central Belfast. Since the start of the Troubles, working-class religious segregation has been steadily growing and West Belfast is becoming almost wholly Catholic. Although the Shankill Rd is the Protestant flip side of the Catholic Falls Rd, it's actually in retreat, and were it not for its strong symbolic importance the shrinking proportion of Protestants in West Belfast would undoubtedly be even smaller. There are other Protestant working-class enclaves around the city, such as along the Newtownards Rd to the east of the centre, where you'll also find the brightly painted sectarian murals.

The ideologically sound way to visit the sectarian zones of the Falls and Shankill Rd is by black taxi. These recycled London cabs run a bus-like service up and down their respective roads from terminuses in the city. Shankill Rd taxis go from North St, Falls Rd taxis from Castle St, both sites close to the modern Castle Court Centre. The Falls Rd taxis are the first line at the Castle St taxi park. They're quite used to doing tourist

circuits of the Falls and typically charge £10 for a one-hour visit which takes in the main points of interest from republican murals to British army bases.

If you simply want to share a black taxi down the Falls Rd the fare is 55p to 75p depending on the distance, and your fellow passengers are likely to be women and children returning from a city shopping trip or men coming back from the pubs. Fares are similar on the Shankill Rd taxis. Alternatively bus No 12, 13, 14 or 15 will take you down the Falls Rd; bus No 39, 55, 63 or 73 goes down the Shankill.

The Falls Rd

The Falls Rd taxis start from the taxi park beside the Smithfield Market, a pale reflection of the bustling market which used to operate here. Separated from the city centre by the Westlink Motorway, but actually a very short distance west of the centre, the ugly and infamous Divis Flats take their name from Divis Mountain, the highest summit in the hills which surround Belfast. They were constructed in the late 1960s during the world-wide mania for high-rise public housing, and as elsewhere in the world they quickly became 'vertical slums'. During their planning and construction they were actually welcomed by local residents as both an alternative to sub-standard housing and as a way of retaining the local community. The Catholic churches in the vicinity, fearful of losing their congregations, were particularly enthusiastic backers.

Predictably the Divis Flats were a disaster in Belfast, like their equivalents elsewhere in the world, and the Troubles quickly turned them into the scene of many confrontations between residents and the army. Today they're a particularly depressing scene since the medium-rise flats have been abandoned, bricked up and boarded over, and are in the process of being demolished.

The single block of high-rise flats overlooks the other buildings and the motorway but the top storeys are occupied by the British Army who come and go by helicopter. No photography is permitted of army personnel, vehicles, equipment or bases in Belfast, and if you want to check just how alert they are, try taking a photograph here. Your taxi is most probably being scrutinised through binoculars, you and your camera will be noted and before you get much further down the road you may well find yourself pulled over to answer some searching enquiries.

From the flats Divis St runs west, shortly becoming the Falls Rd which runs in a south-westerly direction through the area known as the Lower Falls. On the right is a swimming pool and the heavily protected Sinn Féin offices; the massive boulders are to deter car bombs. If you turn right (north) off the Falls Rd into the side streets you'll quickly come up against the 'Peace Line', a rough corrugated iron wall separating Catholics from their Protestant neighbours. In places you could almost lean out of a back window and touch the wall.

On the other side of the Falls Rd in the Lower Falls, the old slums which stood here before the Troubles are now being replaced with newer public housing. It's a reminder of the huge expenditure on public housing in the 1970s and 1980s. Even at the height of the Thatcher era, Northern Ireland remained relatively immune to public spending cutbacks. The Falls Rd passes the Royal Victoria Hospital, which developed a well-earned reputation for dealing with medical emergencies at the height of the Troubles in the 1970s.

The area's famous murals are found along the Falls and in adjacent streets. It's a constantly changing art show with new murals appearing over old and demolition and reconstruction removing and replacing the canvases. Beyond the Lower Falls the road is of less interest until it reaches the Milltown Cemetery, the main site for republican burials with the graves of numerous noted republicans who have died in shoot-outs, hunger strikes and other events of the Troubles. The junction of Glen Rd and Andersonstown Rd marks the end of the Falls Rd with a strongly fortified army base looking down the Falls from its position in

the fork. It's one of four 'forts' in West Belfast.

Andersonstown (Andytown) is about three km (two miles) from the centre and beyond here is Twinbrook, another staunchly republican suburb and the former home of Bobby Sands, the first hunger striker to die. In the surprisingly neat, tidy and modern development where he lived, one end of a block has been turned into a memorial. More murals, slogans and graffiti can be found in the Ballymurphy area by taking Whiterock Rd or Springfield Rd, north of the Falls.

The Shankill Rd
The Shankill Rd begins not far west of Belfast Cathedral and runs north-west towards the Crumlin Rd. Although the Shankill has been given less media and tourist attention than the Falls it's also of interest. The street's name comes from *sean chill*, the old church, and once again the brightly painted murals are the central attraction. Here the villains and heroes have switched roles, and the hooded and menacing paramilitaries are members of the UDA and other Protestant groups, not the IRA or INLA.

NORTH & EAST OF THE CENTRE
Harland & Wolff Shipyards
Although you cannot easily arrange to visit the Harland & Wolff shipyards, they certainly dominate East Belfast, separated from the city centre by the River Lagan. The giant cranes known as Samson and Goliath, one of them over 100 metres high and 140 metres long, straddle a 550-metre-long shipbuilding dock. The good ship *Titanic* was built here and more recent constructions have included oil tankers and passenger vessels, including the *Canberra* in 1960. The Harland & Wolff dry dock is one of the biggest in the world, capable of handling ships of up to 200,000 tons.

With substantial British government support the shipyard managed to continue in existence through the 1970s and 1980s, when most European shipbuilding crumbled

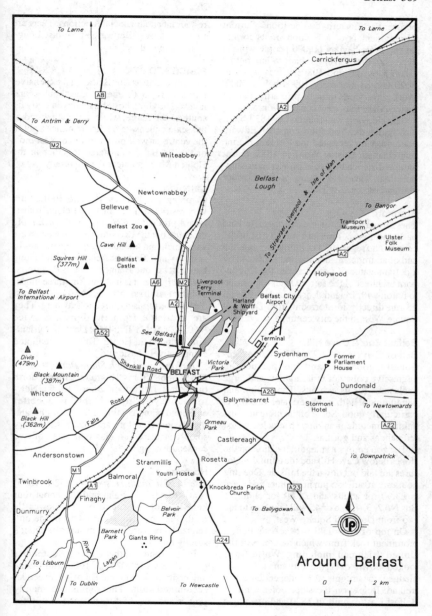

Around Belfast

0   1   2 km

before Far Eastern competition. Current employment is at a fraction of its former levels. In its heyday 60,000 people worked here; by the 1970s it had fallen below 10,000; by the mid-1980s it was down to 5000 and by the early 1990s below 2000. Work at the yards today is primarily maintenance rather than new construction.

The shipyard was founded in 1833 but it was under the Yorkshire engineer Edward Harland, who recruited the German marine draughtsman Gustav Wolff in 1858, that it assumed its leading role in Victorian shipbuilding. There's a statue of Sir Edward Harland by the City Hall.

Stormont

The former home of the Northern Ireland parliament is six km (four miles) east of the centre. The regal 1932 building stands at the end of an imposing avenue and is fronted by a defiant statue of Lord Carson, the Dublin-born architect of the fierce Ulster opposition to union with Ireland. Local bus Nos 22 and 23 run directly to Stormont from Donegall Square West in the city centre.

Belfast Zoo & Cave Hill

Belfast Zoo (☎ 0232-776277) is an exceptionally good one and has pursued an aggressive policy of building new and large enclosures for its exhibits. The sealion and penguin pool with its underwater viewing is particularly good. Some of the more unusual animals include tamarins, spectacled bears, red pandas and gorillas.

The zoo enjoys a splendid location on the slopes below Cave Hill and the animal enclosures are laid out down the hillside. Opening hours are 10 am to 5 pm in summer and entry is £3.90 for adults and £1.80 for children. Bus No 2, 3, 4, 5, 6 or 45 will take you to the zoo from Donegall Square West.

On top of Cave Hill is MacArt's Fort, a prominent rock from which members of the United Irishmen including Wolfe Tone looked down over the city in 1795 and pledged to struggle for independence for Ireland. Below on the slopes of the hill is Belfast Castle, built in 1870 and open as a

restaurant and for social functions. There are fine views over Belfast and Belfast Lough from Cave Hill.

PLACES TO STAY

Accommodation in Belfast is expensive, particularly in the better guesthouses and hotels. The youth hostel is inconveniently far south of the centre, while at the other end of the scale expensive hotels are either right in the centre or well out of it. In contrast most of the B&Bs are clustered together in the Golden Mile area near the university.

Camping

Camping possibilities close to Belfast are very restricted. The Northern Ireland Tourist Board produce a *Camping & Caravanning* brochure but the two sites close to Belfast are very small and intended only for caravans or campervans. Tent sites can be found along the coast beyond Bangor towards Portaferry.

Belvoir Forest is just five km (three miles) south of Belfast off the A504. A Forest Service permit is required to stay here. They are available from the Forest Service (☎ 0232-650111 Ext 456), Dept of Agriculture, Dundonald House. This is a small and comparatively basic site.

Jordanstown Lough Shore Park (☎ 0232-863133/868751) is 10 km (six miles) north of central Belfast on Shore Rd in Newtownabbey. Although this is a better equipped site, costing £6 per night and mainly intended for caravans, it's still very small and there is a maximum stay of two consecutive nights.

Hostels

The *Belfast Youth Hostel* (☎ 0232-647865) is at Ardmore, 11 Saintfield Rd, about four km south of the centre on the Newcastle road. Take bus No 38 or 84 from the city centre. It costs around £8 in summer and it's strictly run.

From June to the end of September *Queen's Elms* (☎ 0232-381608) run by the university at 78 Malone Rd offers excellent accommodation. The rooms are mainly singles and cost £7 for students, £11.16 for nonstudents. They often have a take-your-chances price of about £5; you make up your own bed and the room may not have been cleaned. There are cooking and laundry facilities and on weekdays breakfast is available for £1.50. Rooms may also be available during the one-month vacations at Christmas and Easter.

There are two YWCAs close to the university, for both men and women. *Queen Mary's Hall* (☎ 0232-240439) is at 70 Fitzwilliam St and has single and double rooms at £13 per person including breakfast. The other YWCA is *Wellesley House* (☎ 0232-668347) at 3 Malone Rd and costs £14 a night or £12.50 sharing, again including breakfast. At 30 Adelaide Park is the *Ulster People's College* (☎ 0232-665161) which has B&B for £12.50 per person.

B&Bs

The tourist office will make bookings at B&Bs. There are many in the university area with prices around £15. This area is close to the centre, safe and well stocked with restaurants and pubs. Botanic Ave, Malone Rd, Wellington Park and Eglantine Ave are good hunting grounds.

Botanic Ave near Queen's University is a pleasant residential street. The comfortable *Helga Lodge* (☎ 0232-324820) at 7 Cromwell Rd, just off Botanic Ave, costs £17/30 for singles/doubles. Note the colourful pink frontage and the flowers. All rooms have their own bathrooms with TV and phones. Nearby is the handsome *Botanic Lodge Guest House* (☎ 0232-327682/247439) at 87 Botanic Ave, where the rooms all have TV and cost £18/32. Bus No 83, 85 or 86 will get you to these two.

Also in this popular university area, the *Queen's University Common Room* (☎ 0232-665938) offers B&B for £32/47 at 1 College Gardens.

Eglantine Ave, 1.5 km (one mile) south of the city centre, is reasonably quiet and packed with guesthouses and B&Bs. The *Eglantine Guesthouse* (☎ 0232-667585) at No 21 has B&B for £15/28. At No 17 is *Liserin Guesthouse* (☎ 0232-660769),

costing £18/36. At No 30 is *Marine House* (☎ 0232-662828) at £15/26. The *George* (☎ 0232-683212) at No 9 is £15/30.

At 11 Malone Rd *Pearl Court House* (☎ 0232-666145) has B&B for £16 per person. More expensive places include the well-equipped Edwardian *Camera House* (☎ 0232-660026) at 44 Wellington Park with B&B for £25/35.

Beaumont House (☎ 0232-667965) at 237 Stranmillis Rd has seven bedrooms with B&B for £15 per person. Along the Antrim Rd, there are a number of good places including *Drumragh House* (☎ 0232-773063) at No 647. It's three km from the city centre and close to the zoo and costs £16/28. Also out here is *Aisling House* (☎ 0232-771529) at 7 Taunton Ave off the Antrim road, in a quiet residential area with B&B at £15/28.

Hotels

Although there is no longer a shortage of hotel beds in Belfast, prices are still comparatively high. It's worth phoning to check if there are any cheap deals available, particularly at weekends.

The much-bombed *Europa Hotel* (☎ 0232-327000) is a Belfast landmark – many city directions begin with, 'do you know the Europa?' It's one of the city's best hotels and costs from £110 for a double.

The modern *Plaza Hotel* (☎ 0232-333555) is at 15 Brunswick St, behind the Crown Liquor Saloon and only a short stroll from the Europa. Rooms cost £65/75 including breakfast, and as this is a business hotel cheaper weekend rates are often available. The *Wellington Park Hotel* (☎ 0232-381111) is another smaller hotel at 21 Malone Rd, close to the Ulster Museum and Queen's University. Doubles here cost £88 including breakfast. The *Malone Lodge* (☎ 0232-382409) at 60 Eglantine Ave has rooms including breakfast at £50/70 dropping to £30/44 at weekends.

Belfast's glossiest hotel (there's even an external glass lift) is the modern *Stormont Hotel* (☎ 0232-6758621), directly across from the Stormont parliament building on Upper Newtownards Rd. It's some distance

---

Europa Hotel

A mid-1993 article on war zone hotels in *The Guardian* gave the Europa the blue riband as 'the world's most bombed hotel', ahead of such strong contenders as the Holiday Inn, Sarajevo, and the Commodore, Beirut. When the Europa opened in the late 1960s it was several stars better than anything Belfast had previously seen, but with the start of the Troubles it quickly took on a new role as the nerve centre for a nervous city as well as the most visible target for bomb-happy terrorists.

During the 1970s the Europa was bombed no less than 29 times, but every single time the broken glass was swept up, new drinks appeared on the bar and life continued. The Europa was where journalists from around the world gathered to interview paramilitary spokespeople from both religious extremes, who often left by the back door just as military personnel entered by the front to conduct yet another press briefing.

However, two big blasts – the latter in May 1993 – almost brought the Europa to its knees. The British government once again picked up the repair bill, new owners have taken over, and the Europa should be open again by the time you read this. ■

---

out from the centre and costs around £100 for a double room, but you even get a rubber duck to float in the bathtub. At Belfast International Airport at Aldergrove, the brand-new *Novotel* (☎ 08484-22888) is part of the international chain, with excellent rooms and facilities at around £60 per person.

Country Houses

The lovingly restored *Cottage* (☎ 0247-878189) at 377 Comber Rd, Dundonald, about 16 km (10 miles) south-east of the city has two bedrooms with B&B for £16/31. The Georgian *Holestone House* (☎ 09603-52306) is in wooded grounds at 23 Deer Park, Doagh, Ballyclare, 21 km (13 miles) north-west of the city, and B&B runs from £15.

Off the main road to Carrickfergus is the pleasant *Glenavna House Hotel* (☎ 0232-864461) at 588 Shore Rd, Newtownabbey, standing in quiet parkland, with rooms at £60/75.

PLACES TO EAT

Belfast has a surprising number and variety of restaurants including one of the very best restaurants in all of Ireland. More than one journalist has noted that the Troubles seem to have given the citizens of Belfast a positive passion for eating out! Although there are plenty of pubs, cafés and fast-food places

around the centre, Belfast's best eating is found south of the city centre along the 'Golden Mile' towards the university.

Cafés & Fast Food

There's a food centre in the *Hipark Centre* on High St, offering a variety of food possibilities from fish & chips to Chinese. International fast-food chains including *McDonalds, Pizza Hut, Burger King* and *Kentucky Fried* are well represented both in the city centre and along the Golden Mile. Belfast is famous for its excellent bread and you'll find innumerable bakeries around the city centre and along Botanic Ave near the university.

In the centre there's a branch of the popular *Bewley's Oriental Café* (☎ 0232-234955) chain in an arcade on Rosemary St. Also centrally located is the *Spice of Life* (☎ 0232-332744) at 62 Lower Donegall St, right across from St Anne's Cathedral. This relaxed little wholefood and vegetarian café is open Monday to Saturday from 9.30 am to 5 pm, to 11 pm on Thursday and Friday. On the corner of College Square and Howard St, near the Opera House, the imposing Presbyterian Church House is now a modern shopping centre where you'll find *Spices*, another pleasant and centrally located café

South of the centre in the Golden Mile area *Jenny's Coffee Shop* is a pleasant little café cum sandwich bar at 81 Dublin Rd. Also in the university area is the friendly *Bluebell's*, at 50 Botanic Ave near the Botanic Rail Station, which has good ice cream, makes an excellent capuccino and (a Belfast rarity) is open for breakfast on Sunday morning. At 47 University Rd, *Bookfinder's Café* (☎ 0232-328269) is an excellent place for a quick lunch, located upstairs above a bookshop.

Finally the *Student Union Cafeteria* is on the 2nd and 3rd floors of the Student Union building, on University Rd directly opposite Queen's College.

Pub Food

At the *Crown Liquor Saloon* (☎ 0232-249476) on Great Victoria St in the centre you can get oysters and beef stews, and at the same time take in the magnificent decor. They have food from 11 am to 3 pm.

Even more centrally located is the *Clarence* (☎ 0232-238862) on Donegall Square East beside the City Hall. They offer good although somewhat more expensive bar lunches as well as more sophisticated main courses from around £7. At 81 Chichester St, on the corner of Victoria St near the Royal Courts of Justice, *Rumpole's* (☎ 0232-232840) is good for lunch.

A block further north at 103 Victoria St *Bittle's Bar* (☎ 0232-311088) can also be entered from 70 Upper Church Lane. They specialise in local dishes like *champ*, an Ulster speciality consisting of sausages, spring onions and mashed potates. *White's Tavern* (☎ 0232-243080) at Winecellar Entry between Rosemary and High Sts is one of Belfast's most historic taverns and a popular lunch-time meeting spot. The *Duke of York* (☎ 0232-241062) is one of Belfast's oldest bars and serves excellent solid pub lunches for less than £5. It's hidden away down narrow Commercial Court, an alleyway leading off Donegall St just south of St Anne's Cathedral.

Cheaper Restaurants

In the centre *Vico's Refettorio* (☎ 0232-321447) at 10 Brunswick St turns out excellent pizzas and other Italian dishes. Also centrally located, near the Crown Liquor Saloon and the Opera House, the *Moghul Restaurant* (☎ 0232-243727) at 60 Great Victoria St offers a standard Indian menu. *Chinatown* (☎ 0232-230115) is a Chinese restaurant at the same address.

There are numerous cheaper restaurants south of the centre in the Golden Mile area and around the university. Deep pan pizzas and other American food can be found at the *Chicago Pizza Pie Factory* at the back of the MGM cinema complex on Dublin Rd. *Harvey's* (☎ 0232-233433) at 95 Great Victoria St is good for anything from tacos to pizzas or spare ribs.

Italian restaurants are popular in Belfast, *Graffiti* (☎ 0232-249269) is a good example at 50 Dublin Rd while *Villa Italia* (☎ 0232-328356 is a pleasant Italian restaurant and pizzeria at 39 University Rd.

Chez Delbart (0232-238020) (also known as *Frogities)* is a cheap and cheerful French restaurant at 10 Bradbury Place. *Explorer's* (☎ 0232-245550) at 89 Dublin Rd is a restaurant and wine bar with a travel and exploration-related menu – this is the place to try Chicken Tutankhamun!

Indian and Chinese restaurants can also be found in the university area. The *Balti House* on Shaftesbury Square next to the expensive Roscoff's offers that local variety of Indian food which starting in Birmingham has swept the British midlands. It's basically a takeaway but they do have a few tables.

The *Maharaja* (☎ 0232-234200), upstairs at 62 Botanic Ave, is a more traditional Indian restaurant in the heart of the university area. In the same area, the *Dragon Palace* (☎ 0232-323869) at 16 Botanic Ave offers Chinese food, or you can turn the corner past the forbidding checkpost to *Manor House* (☎ 0232-238755) at 47 Donegall Pass which has excellent Cantonese food.

There are many other Indian and Chinese restaurants around Belfast, many of them further from the centre along Lisburn Rd and Ormeau Rd.

More Expensive Restaurants

Close to the centre the tropical ambience at

Bananas (☎ 0232-339999) at 4 Clarence St may feel a trifle odd, but the adventurous international mix of dishes (kebabs, thalis, tapas, crostini) is well done and reasonably priced. It's open Monday to Friday for lunch, Monday to Saturday for dinner. Bananas shares a kitchen with the more formal *44 Restaurant* (☎ 0232-244844), which is next door but in Bedford St at No 44.

The *Strand Wine Bar & Restaurant* (☎ 0232-682266) at 12 Stranmillis Rd, right behind the Ulster Museum, is highly recommended. This staunchly old-fashioned restaurant offers traditional dishes and a popular Sunday brunch. Pricier French cuisine can be sampled in *La Belle Epoque* (☎ 0232-223244) at 61 Dublin Rd, Belfast's most authentic French restaurant. It's closed on Sundays. The stylish *Antica Roma* (☎ 0232-311121) is at 67 Botanic Ave near the university.

Behind an anonymous frosted glass facade *Roscoff* (☎ 0232-331532) at 7 Lesley House, Shaftesbury Square, serves superb food in very modern surroundings. Paul Rankin has a tremendous reputation and this is one of only two restaurants in Ireland with a Michelin star; the other is in Dublin. A complete dinner could set you back £40 per person but lunch is cheaper and on some night there's a a set dinner for £18.

ENTERTAINMENT
Pubs
Belfast has some pubs which are as much museums as drinking places, particularly the wonderful old *Crown Liquor Saloon* opposite the Opera House, which even teetotal Belfast visitors should have a look at.

The narrow alleys known as the Entries shelter a plethora of older pubs. Good ones to sample include the rough-edged *Morning Star* on Pottinger's Entry, the historic *White's Tavern* on Winecellar Entry and the *Globe Tavern* on Joy's Entry. Other older pubs in the centre include *Kelly's Tavern* on Bank St, the *Clarence* on Donegall Square East beside the City Hall or the *Duke of York*, hidden away down Commercial Court near St Anne's Cathedral.

Belfast also has modern pubs like the very popular *Drury Lane* at 2 Amelia St, looking out on to the modern square behind the Crown Liquor Saloon. At the opposite side the same square is the equally modern *George C McClatchy's* in the Plaza Hotel. On Great Victoria St, just a few steps south from the Crown Liquor Saloon, is the *Beaten Docket*.

In the university area *Bob Cratchit's* on Lisburn Rd is a trendy, modern pickup joint. Somewhat less trendy *Lavery's* on Bradbury Place is popular amongst students and has a long and colourful history as Lavery's Gin Palace. The *Elbow* on the corner of Dublin Rd and Ventry St is worth trying, while the *Elms* is another popular student pub at 36 University Rd. Farther south the *Eglantine Inn* and the *Botanic* are institutions, packed at weekends with crowds of students. Known as the Egg and Bott, they face each other across Malone Rd.

Music & Nightclubs
Music, either disco or live, features in many of Belfast's pubs including the *Eglantine Inn* (☎ 0232-381994), the *Botanic* (☎ 0232-660460), the *Elbow* (☎ 0232-326423) and *Bob Cratchit's* (☎ 0232-332526). The *Elms* (☎ 0232-322106) and the *Chicago Pizza Pie Factory* also have live music. Further out from the centre the *Rosetta Bar* (☎ 0232-649297) at 75 Rosetta Rd is a rock venue and the *Errigle Inn* (☎ 0232-641410) at 320 Ormeau Rd, south of the centre, is also popular.

Nightclub style discos can be found at the *Dome & Limelight* (☎ 0232-325968) at 17 Ormeau Ave and at the *Manhattan* (☎ 0232-233131) at Bradbury Place close to the university. When there's music on most of these places make entry charges, typically between £1 and £4 depending on the night and the venue.

Music & Theatre
The Belfast *Grand Opera House* (☎ 0232-241919) on Great Victoria St is host to a mixture of good theatre, opera and music shows. On Botanic Ave in the university area

the *Arts Theatre* (☎ 0232-224936) chiefly puts on popular plays or comedies. Further out from the centre on Ridgeway St, the *Lyric Theatre* (☎ 0232-381081) has a more serious bent and includes Irish plays in its repertory. Performances also take place at *Whitla Hall* in Queen's University.

Northern Ireland's excellent Ulster Orchestra often plays in the *Ulster Hall* (☎ 0232-323900) on Linenhall St , and this is also the venue for larger rock music events. The *Group Theatre* (☎ 0232-329685) next door stages plays by local playwrights. *King's Hall* (☎ 0232-665225) at Balmoral is another centre for big rock events.

Performances also take place at *Elmwood Hall*, the church building now used as a concert hall at the university. It's on University Rd directly opposite Queen's College. The *Crescent Arts Centre* (☎ 0232-242338), at 2 University Rd, is another smaller music venue.

Cinema

Belfast's biggest cinema complex, the 10-screen MGM Centre (☎ 0232-245700), opened in mid-93 at the north end of Dublin Rd, just south of the city centre. The older four-screen Cannon (☎ 0232-222484) is on Great Victoria St, near the Grand Opera House. The Yorkgate (☎ 0232-741746) is another new cinema centre, it has five screens and is north of the centre near the York Rd Railway Station. The Queen's Film Theatre at the university is the nearest Belfast has to an art house cinema.

THINGS TO BUY

The Craftworks Gallery (☎ 0232-236334) at 13 Linenhall St specialises in Northern Irish crafts with work from craftspeople all over Ulster.

For camping gas cylinders, other camping equipment or for surfing gear, Surf Mountain (☎ 0232-248877) at 12 Brunswick St in the centre is excellent.

GETTING THERE & AWAY

The USIT/Belfast Student Travel office (☎ 0232-324073) is at 136 Fountain Centre, College St. See the introductory Getting There & Away chapter for international flights and ferries to Belfast.

Air

There are flights from some regional airports in Britain to the convenient Belfast City Airport (☎ 0232-457745), and everything else goes to Belfast International Airport (☎ 08494-22888), 30 km (20 miles) north of the city by the M2. For more details see the introductory Getting There & Away chapter.

Road

The principal motorways out of Belfast are the M1 heading south-east towards Fermanagh, the M2 past Aldergrove Airport and on to Derry, and the M5 north-east towards Carrickfergus. If you're heading for Dublin take the M1 and then branch off on the A1, which becomes the N1 south of the border.

Bus

Bus connections to Counties Antrim, Down and Derry (the eastern side) operate from the centrally located Oxford St Bus Station.

For everywhere else in Northern Ireland, the Republic, the international airport and the Larne ferries, the equally central Great Victoria St Bus Station is used. It's right behind the big Europa Hotel. Phone ☎ 0232-320111 for Ulsterbus information or ☎ 0232-333000 for timetable information. Ulsterbus produce an excellent free *Exploring Ulster* booklet with information on bus services and fares to major attractions all over Northern Ireland.

There are three Belfast-Dublin services daily taking about four hours and costing £10 one-way. There are also three express coaches daily (two on Sunday) and these take three hours. For connections to Derry and Donegal contact the Lough Swilly Bus Company (☎ 080504-262017) in Derry.

Due to security concerns there are no left-luggage facilities at Belfast train and bus stations. On weekdays it may be possible for backpackers to leave their bags at the YMCA at 12 Wellington Place. Phone ☎ 0232-327231 for details.

Train

For tickets and information, Northern Ireland Railways Travel (☎ 0232-230671/230310) is at 17 Wellington Place close to the City Hall. Trains to and from Larne operate from the York Rd Station, directly north of the centre.

For all other destinations including Derry, Dublin, Newry, Portadown and Bangor, trains arrive and depart from the Central Railway Station (☎ 0232-438220) on East Bridge St east of the city centre. There's a free (to train passengers) connecting bus every 10 minutes from one station to the other via the city centre. Dublin-Belfast trains run up to six times a day (three on Sunday) and take about two hours at a cost of £12.50 one-way. Some of the trains make stops at Lisburn, Newry and Portadown while others are nonstop express services.

Ferry

Ferries to and from Northern Ireland come into one of three terminals. Closest to the centre is the SeaCat and Isle of Man terminal on Donegall Quay, a little further out is the Liverpool terminal, while the Larne terminal is 30 km (18 miles) north along the coast. There are trains from Larne to Belfast's York Rd Station. Ulsterbus services, to and from Belfast's Great Victoria St Bus Station, also connect with the Larne ferries.

Norse Irish Ferries (☎ 051-944 1010) have a service between Belfast and Heysham to the south of Liverpool and operate from the Liverpool terminal. Isle of Man Steam Packet (☎ 0232-351009) operates between the Isle of Man and Belfast from the centrally located SeaCat terminal. SeaCat (☎ 0232-310910) operate huge Australian catamaran car ferries that make a 1½-hour crossing between Belfast City and Stranraer.

The conventional ferries to and from Scotland, dock at Larne, 30 km north of Belfast where both Sealink Stena and P&O have their offices. Sealink Stena Line (☎ 0232-327525) operate between Stranraer and Larne, the trip takes two to three hours. P&O (☎ 0574-274321) operate between Cairnryan and Larne.

GETTING AROUND
To/From the Airports

Belfast International Airport (☎ 08494-22888) is 30 km (20 miles) from the city. Buses connect it with Great Victoria St Bus Station behind the Europa Hotel for £3.50. A taxi would cost £20 to £25.

The very convenient Belfast City Airport (☎ 0232-457745) is only six km from the centre, and you can cross the road from the terminal to the Sydenham Halt train station.

Bus

Very short trips in the centre are just 40p, but in general around the city the standard bus fare is 65p. The fare increases by zones as you travel farther, but 65p will get you all the way to Cave Hill or the youth hostel. A multitrip ticket costs £4.50 and gives you eight rides at slightly lower cost and much greater convenience. A Day Ticket gives you unlimited travel within the City Zone from 9.30 am on weekdays or all day on weekends for £2. Most local bus services depart from Donegall Square, near the City Hall. Timetables are available from the kiosk on Donegall Square West, or you can phone for information to ☎ 0232-246485.

Taxis

Black taxis operate bus-like services down the Shankill Rd from North St and down the Falls Rd from Castle St. Fares are 55 to 75p. Regular taxis are pricey with £2 flagfall.

Car

If you're driving be fastidious about where you park. Do not park within the well-marked control zones, you could get far more than a parking ticket. Tales of foolish tourists coming back to find their car about to be blown up by a bomb demolition squad are however essentially urban myths. There are plenty of car parks in Belfast; use them, even though they tend to be rather expensive. Because of the same fear of car bombs, cars

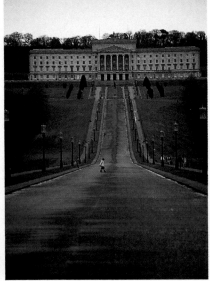

Top: St George's Church, Belfast (TW)
Left: Robinson & Cleaver Building, Belfast (TW)
Right: Stormont (Former Parliament House), Belfast (TW)

Murals, Northern Ireland

illegally parked elsewhere can also expect rough treatment.

Avis (☎ 0232-240404) have desks at both the Belfast airports and their city office is at 69 Great Victoria St. Dan Dooley Rent-a-Car (☎ 08494-52522) is at Aldergrove Airport. Belfast Rent-a-Car (☎ 0232-401344) is at 188a Saintfield Rd. Godfrey Davis Europcar (☎ 0232-757401) is at 58 Antrim Rd. CC Economy Car Hire (☎ 0232-840366) is at 2 Ballyduff Rd.

Bicycle

Try McConvey Cycles (☎ 0232-491163) at 467 Ormeau Rd for bicycle hire. Bikeit (☎ 0232-471141) at 4 Belmont Rd and Mobile Activities (☎ 0232-330218) are Raleigh Rent-A-Bike dealers. Coates (☎ 0232-471912) at 108 Grand Parade and Wilfit Bike & Auto (☎ 0232-323832) at 21 High St are other possibilities. Prices are £6 to £7 a day and a deposit of around £30 is required. Coate's and McConvey's hire rates are usually cheaper than the others.

Tours

There is a 3½-hour, £4.50 (children £2.50) Citybus tour (☎ 0232-246485) taking in all the city sights including Stormont, the shipyards and Belfast Castle. It begins at Castle Place at 2 pm Tuesday, Wednesday and Thursday during the summer months.

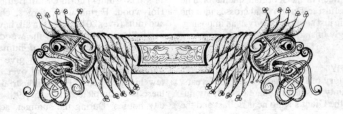

Counties Down & Armagh

County Down

County Down is Northern Ireland's sunny south-east, being relatively dry. Neighbouring Belfast delivers hordes of day trippers to the many seaside resorts on the coast from Bangor to Newcastle and beyond. The shoreline runs from the flat finger-like Ards Peninsula encompassing the drowned drumlins and nature reserves of Strangford Lough, to the Mourne Mountains which coax the traveller farther south. In the famous lyrics by Percy French, the Mournes 'sweep down to the sea': they are the highlight of Down. Besides tourists, more permanent visitors reside in the numerous retirement homes in the seaside towns – look out for elderly pedestrians!

The interior of the county is well past its Industrial Revolution heyday. Hillsborough retains much of its Georgian splendour. The main Belfast to Dublin road crosses into the Republic just south of Newry at an imposing, seemingly unstaffed security checkpoint.

HISTORY

The history of Down goes back 7000 years. The county has its fair share of early monuments; the Giant's Ring near Belfast and the Legananny Dolmen near Ballynahinch are two of the best examples.

St Patrick landed in Strangford Lough in 432, and died in the area in 461. The whereabouts of his remains is disputed, though Downpatrick Cathedral is the favourite site. By the time of his death Ireland was Christian, a crusade which he had started in Ulster, which made him one of the few genuinely national heroes.

After his death, Irish monasteries flourished and multiplied, surviving repeated Viking attacks. They were finally to lose out to the Normans in the 12th century, who ousted the Irish monks and built Grey Abbey on the Ards Peninsula and Inch Abbey near Downpatrick. Castles were their main priority, however, and many along the coast survive today.

The Scottish and English settlers who arrived with the Plantation of Ulster in the 17th century were given large tracts of land previously occupied by the native Irish. They built towns and roads, and were responsible for the development of the linen industry in the 17th and 18th centuries.

BELFAST TO BANGOR

Belfast creeps east along the south shores of Belfast Lough towards the Irish Sea. The A2 road out of Belfast follows the railway line and is a pleasant route to the Ards Peninsula.

Ulster Folk & Transport Museum

This is one of the finest museums in Ireland, 11 km (six miles) north-east of Belfast, near Holywood. Farmhouses, forges, churches and mills (over 20 buildings in all) have been carefully reconstructed on the wooded 60-hectare site, with plenty of human and animal extras combining to give strong impressions of life in Ireland over the last few hundred years. From industrial times, there is a complete terrace of 19th-century city houses. During the summer, activities

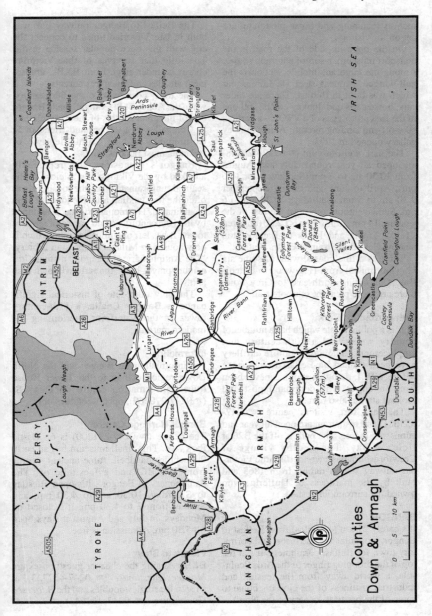

Counties
Down & Armagh

such as thatching and horse ploughing are put on for visitors.

On the opposite side of the road is the transport museum, a sort of automotive zoo. Among the large automobile section is the gull-winged stainless steel De Lorean car which was built in Belfast. There are older cars, horse carts and donkey creels, and one of the first prototypes of a VTOL – a vertical take-off and landing aircraft. A new railway gallery opened in 1993.

The park and museum (☎ 0232-428428) are open all year round: July and August from 10.30 am to 6 pm (Sundays noon to 6 pm); April to June and during September 9.30 am to 5 pm (Saturdays 10.30 am to 6 pm, Sundays noon to 6 pm); the rest of the year until 4 pm. Admission is £2.60 (children £1.30). Trains and buses to Bangor stop nearby. Get off the train at Cultra Station.

There is a fine coastal walk of some six km (four miles) from Holywood to Helen's Bay. Continuing north-east to Grey Point there are more pleasant seashore trails.

Crawfordsburn Park

This is a public estate which has a number of country walks and a 20th-century gun emplacement. The large-calibre artillery have been trained on Belfast Lough since before WW I, though a shot has never been fired in anger. The command post and lookout station also remain.

The park, fort, visitors' centre (☎ 0247-853621) and restaurant are open all year and admission is free. The park is off the B20 at Helen's Bay. The nearby village of Crawfordsburn has a wonderful little Victorian railway station dating from 1865 and built by the marquess of Dufferin, who owned the surrounding estate.

BANGOR

It's barely 21 km (13 miles) from Belfast to Bangor, a popular seaside resort and dormitory town for Belfast commuters. It's at the top of the drooping finger of the Ards Peninsula, a world away from the tension and industrial grittiness of the city. It's home to some of the prettiest scenery in the North.

The Belfast to Bangor railway line was built in late Victorian times to connect the city with this once popular seaside resort. The little that survives of that Victorian charm is under siege from B&Bs, amusement arcades and cheap restaurants.

The town goes back to the 6th century, when the Abbey of St Comgall made Bangor one of the great centres of the early church. St Comgall was a teacher and friend of St Columbanus and St Colmcille, two of Ireland's most famous saints.

Bangor's monastery was repeatedly attacked by the Vikings. It was close to the sea and, unfortunately for the locals, it was often the first landfall after the journey from Scandinavia. The monastery was abandoned by the 10th century and no trace of it remains today. It has left one priceless relic which is now housed in Milan's Ambrosian Library: 'The Antiphonary of Bangor', a small 7th-century prayer-book, the earliest known Irish text.

The only other site of historical significance is **Bangor Castle**, a 17th-century tower on the waterfront overlooking the modern marina.

Information

For information on Bangor and the North Down region call in to the Tower House tourist information centre on Quay St (☎ 0247-270069), open weekdays only.

Bangor Heritage Centre

The centre (☎ 0247-271200) is on Castle Park Ave. This small museum has an early 9th-century handbell, some ancient swords from 500 BC, and a facsimile of 'The Antiphonary of Bangor'. It's open Tuesday to Saturday, 10.30 am to 4.30 pm, and Sunday from 2 to 4.30 pm; it's closed on Mondays. In July and August it stays open till 5.30 pm. Admission is free.

Places to Stay

B&Bs Among the cheaper guesthouses are *Mardee Guesthouse* (☎ 0247-457733), at £13/26 for singles/doubles and the *Battersea Guesthouse* (☎ 0247-461643) at £13/26.

De Lorean

Cocaine, financial scandals and a stainless-steel time machine: Belfast had them all with the gullwing door De Lorean sports car. The formula was simple. Former American General Motors whiz kid John De Lorean dreamed of a car bearing his own name, and the British government dreamed of something, anything, to reduce the horrific level of Northern Ireland's unemployment. In 1978 De Lorean and £80 million of government money got together and in 1980 the first of his cars (any colour as long as it was stainless steel and with doors that swung up from the roof, like a gull's wings) hit the road. Unfortunately the world was in recession, buyers of expensive sports car weren't buying and the firm was soon heading towards bankruptcy, speeded on its way by De Lorean's arrest in the US for his part in a cocaine-smuggling scam, ostensibly to provide working capital for the foundering business.

But where had the Industrial Development Board for Northern Ireland's £80 million gone? Not all, it soon turned out, on building sports cars, or even on whisking Mr De Lorean back and forth on Concorde. Some of it had simply followed the time-honoured path to numbered Swiss bank accounts. Colin Chapman, the brilliant engineer who founded Lotus cars, had done much of the development work on the De Lorean and for his pains had quietly salted away over £4 million on the side. He died of a heart attack before he could be charged, but the chairman of Group Lotus ended up with a three-year jail sentence. Surprisingly the government did get some of its money back – £5 million of the Lotus money was recovered from Switzerland and nearly US$18 million was dragged back from De Lorean himself. The liquidators even managed to make him sell his Park Ave penthouse in New York.

And the time machine? Well the De Lorean car's one real starring role was as the high-speed time machine in the hit movie *Back to the Future*. Most of the De Loreans made ended up in the US, although there is one in the Belfast Transport Museum. John De Lorean is unlikely to come back to have a look at it, as a warrant remains out for his arrest. ■

Both are on Queen's Parade overlooking the marina. *Emmaus* (☎ 0247-456887) on Holborn Ave has rooms for as little as £11/20.

Hotels The *Tedworth Hotel* (☎ 0247-463928) on Princetown Rd does B&B at around £35/55 for singles/doubles. On Seacliff Rd is the *Sands Hotel* (☎ 0247-270696) with B&B for £49/66, or less at weekends.

Country House Almost five km west of Bangor and south-west of Groomsport is the modern *Sandeel Lodge* (☎ 0247-883139), at 18 Sandeel Lane off the Groomsport to Donaghadee road. It has a heated swimming pool, sea views and well-furnished bedrooms, at £25-plus for B&B. It's near the National Trust reserve of Ballymacormick Point and Orlock.

Places to Eat

There are plenty of takeaways and cheap restaurants on Main St. *Wolsey's* on High St are a local setup worth trying for lasagne and pizza. At 94 Main St, the *Heatherlea Tea Rooms* (☎ 0247-453157) have terrific light meals all day. The *Schooner* on Quay St is good for fish and steaks, and *Jenny Watt's* on High St for inexpensive ribs and stirfry. The *Dragon Palace* (☎ 0247-457817) on Crosby St does Chinese meals at £8 to £10 for dinner, and *Simas* (☎ 0247-2717220) on Crosby St does good Indian food, costing £12.50 for dinner. The best places for more expensive meals are the *Sands Hotel* (☎ 0247- 270696) on Queen's Parade, and particularly *O'Hara's Royal Hotel* (☎ 0247-271866) on Quay St, where dinner costs £12.50.

Just outside Groomsport on the Donaghadee road is the excellent *Abelboden Lodge* (☎ 0247-464288). Dinner costs £16 or more, and there are always good vegetarian dishes. They are open from 5 pm to 11.30 pm and closed Sundays. They also do high teas.

Getting There & Away

Bus Ulsterbus Nos 1 and 2 from Belfast

depart from Oxford St Bus Station (☎ 0232-320011) for Bangor's Abbey St Bus Station (☎ 0247-271143). There is a bus each way every 20 minutes or so on weekdays (and every half hour or hour at the weekends) and the one-way fare is around £1.75.

From Bangor bus Nos 3 and 6 travel regularly around the north of the Ards Peninsula as far as Millisle and Newtownards.

Train There is a regular half-hourly service to Bangor (and the Folk & Transport Museum) from Belfast's central railway station (☎ 0232-230310). Bangor Station (☎ 0247-474143) is on Abbey St.

Road There are two or three routes south from Bangor, of which the most scenic is the road from Newtownards to Portaferry along the shores of Strangford Lough.

Getting Around
Anderson's Car Rental (☎ 0247-464447) on Dufferin Ave have a small fleet on offer.

STORMONT
The A20 due east from Belfast to Newtownards is uneventful except for Stormont Castle (☎ 0093-666999), eight km (five miles) from the city centre. Stormont is where Northern Ireland's parliament sat until 1972, when power was transferred to London. Stormont is a very large neoclassical building, enhanced by its position at the far end of a long dipping avenue. Visits must be arranged in advance.

NEWTOWNARDS
The planned town of Newtownards is another six km (four miles) farther east; like Bangor it was founded as a 6th-century ecclesiastical centre. There's a 6th-century **Dominican friary** on Court St, and the scant remains of **Movilla Abbey** and its 13th-century church are 1.5 km (one mile) to the east. There is some fine 17th and 18th-century architecture in town, especially the **Market Cross** building on High St – formerly the town's prison.

Information
The Ards Borough Council have a tourist office (☎ 0247-812215) on Church St for information on Newtownards and the Ards Peninsula. It's closed at weekends.

Scrabo Hill Country Park
The park was once the site of extensive prehistoric earthworks, but these were largely removed during the construction of the 1857 Memorial Tower in honour of the marquess of Dufferin. The summit (after 122 steps) of the 41-metre (135-foot) tower offers some expansive views of Strangford Lough. The park (☎ 0247-811491) is two km south-west of town. It is open all year round, while the tower is open from 2 pm to 5.30 pm daily, June to September except Mondays. Admission to both is free.

Places to Stay
B&Bs The attractive modern *Cuan Chalet* (☎ 0247-812302) is on Milecross Rd west of town. B&B is £12.50 single or sharing, and it's open all year round. Right beside the Scrabo Park is the comfortable *Maynard* (☎ 0247-812069) which costs £15/25 for singles/doubles. The pleasant *Greenacres* (☎ 0247-816193) on Manse Rd near the Ards Centre costs £18 a night with bathroom.

Hotels The neat, three-star *Strangford Arms Hotel* (☎ 0247-814141) on Church St does B&B from £38 to £58 a night.

Places to Eat
For light meals, try *Knott's Coffee Shop* at 45 High St, open all day (but closed Thursday) until 5 pm. The excellent *Ming Court* (☎ 0247-815073) on Court St is reasonably priced and open until 11.30 pm every night except Sunday when it closes half an hour early. The nearby Indian *Ganges* (☎ 0247-811426) is also good. For Italian food try *Roma's* (☎ 0247-812841) at 4 Regent St or *Giuseppe's Ristorante* (☎ 0247-812244) at 31 Francis St.

The *Gaslamp* (☎ 0247-811225), also on Court St in the heart of Newtownards, is famous for opening on Christmas Day if the demand is there. The food is good, expensive (£18-20) and French, from an older age when helpings were bigger and sauces heavier.

The *Strangford Arms Hotel* (see Places to Stay) has a good restaurant, which does a set dinner, including wine, for £12.50.

Getting Around

Bikes & Models (☎ 0247-818505) on Mill St have bike for £5 a day, £22 a week, plus deposit. The Strangford Arms (see Places to Stay) also rents bikes for £5 a day.

ARDS PENINSULA

The Ards Peninsula encloses the eastern side of Strangford Lough. There's a pleasant journey down the western, seaward side of the peninsula through Grey Abbey to Portaferry.

Relatively flat, the peninsula is about six km (four miles) wide and 35 km (22 miles) long, with some good beaches. In Donaghadee it's possible to get a boat out to the Copeland Islands, which were abandoned at the turn of the century and left to the birds. Back in the village is Grace Neill's Bar down by the harbour, dating from 1611. Among its 17th-century guests was Peter the Great, tsar and later emperor of Russia, who popped by for lunch in 1697 on his grand tour of Europe.

South from Donaghadee is the **Ballycopeland Windmill** (☎ 0247-861413) just north-west of Millisle. This 18th-century tower mill was in commercial use until 1915. It's been restored to working order, and has an adjacent visitors' centre. During April to September it's open from 10 am to 7 pm Tuesday to Saturday, and 2 to 7 pm on Sundays. It closes at 4 pm during the other months. It's closed Mondays, and lunch times 1 to 1.30 pm. Admission is 75p.

Places to Stay

Caravan & Camping The Ards seashore is awash with caravan parks, although few take tents. *Donaghadee Park* (☎ 0247-882369) on the Millisle Rd has tent sites for £4 a night. *Ballywhiskin Park* (☎ 0247-862304) in Millisle has pitches for only £2.50. In Cloughey, *Kirkstown Park* (☎ 02477-71183) at 55 Main Rd have pitches for £5 a night.

B&Bs The *Deans* (☎ 0247-882204) at 52 Northfield Rd, Donaghadee, and *Bridge House* (☎ 02477-883348) on 93 Windmill Rd, three km from Donaghadee, both do B&B at £14/28 for singles/doubles. One of the cheapest B&Bs around Donaghadee is *Woodside* (☎ 02477-883653) at 7 Newtownards Rd, with B&B at £12/24.

In Millisle, *Crossdoney* (☎ 02477-861526) at 216 Abbey Rd does B&B for £12.50/25 and *Millbrook* (☎ 02477-861788) at 2 Mill Rd charges £11.50/21.

In Ballywalter, *Rockdene* (☎ 0247-758205) at 4 Springvale Rd on the coast does B&B for £12/24. *Greenlea Farm* (☎ 02477-58218) is a modernised farmhouse and charges £12.50/25. *Brimar* (☎ 02477-8881) at 4 Cardy Rd is about the cheapest at £10.50/21.

In Ballyhalbert try *Glastry House* (☎ 0247-738555), an old country house almost two km out at 18 Victoria Rd, which costs £12/24.

Places to Eat

Eating establishments on the coast road are mostly pubs, grills and takeaways. Donaghadee is about the only place you'll find anything else. In the Market House on New St is *Coffee Plus* for light meals and coffee breaks in daytime. For pub food or lunch try *Grace Neill's* pub at 33 High St; they have a beer garden open at the rear in good weather. The *Moat Inn* on Moat St is fine for spaghetti or steaks though not at budget prices. *Copeland's Hotel* is adequate.

In Ballywalter try the *Pink Geranium* at 1 Harbour Rd for straightforward grills, snacks and teas. *Greenlea Farm* (☎ 02477-58218) does prebookable evening meals.

STRANGFORD LOUGH

Cut off from the sea by the Ards Peninsula, except for a one-km wide strait at Portaferry, Strangford Lough is almost a lake. It is 25 km (16 miles long, about six km (four miles) wide on average and up to 45 metres deep. Large colonies of grey seals live in and around the lough, particularly at the southern tip of the peninsula where the exit channel widens out into the sea. Birds abound on the shores and mudflats, including brent geese wintering from Arctic Canada. Underwater the muddy lough has a very diverse marine biology, which can be seen at closer quarters in the aquarium in Portaferry. Killer whales have occasionally come into the lough and spent a few days there, causing a sensation.

There is a pleasant 20-km (12-mile) waterside journey up the lough from Grey Abbey to Portaferry. The shorelines en route are rich in birdlife and often have brent and Greenland white-fronted geese during the winter.

The lough is a great leisure resource, with boats and yachts plying their way up and down its sheltered waters. At Portaferry, however, 400,000 tonnes of tidal water surge pass through the strait four times a day; you can get some idea of the current's strength by watching the Portaferry/Strangford ferry being whipped sideways by the riptide.

The western side of Strangford Lough is nothing like as scenic or interesting as the east, although it's the route followed by the Ulster Way walking trail. The main roads between Killyleagh and Comber or Downpatrick and Belfast are remarkably straight, considering the number of drumlins locally.

Getting There & Away

Bus Ulsterbus Nos 9 & 10 go to Portaferry and Grey Abbey from Belfast every hour or so.

Ferry The ferry (☎ 0396-86637) sails every half hour from Portaferry to Strangford and back between 7.45 am and 10.45 pm Mondays to Fridays, 8.15 am to 11.15 pm on Saturdays, and 9.45 am to 10.45 pm on Sundays. The journey time is only around five minutes. The fare is £2.10 for a car and driver, 50p for passengers and those on foot.

Mount Stewart House & Gardens

Eight km (five miles) south of Newtownards on the A20 is Mount Stewart (☎ 02477-88387). The magnificent 18th-century house and gardens were the home of the marquess of Londonderry, though much of the landscaping was carried out early this century by Lady Edith, wife of the 7th marquess, for the benefit of her children. The 35 hectares form one of the finest gardens in Ireland or Britain and are now in the charge of the National Trust.

The gardens are a cosmopolitan affair, with gardens, woodlands and lakes, elegantly populated by a vast collection of plants and statues. Unusual creatures from history (dinosaurs and dodos) and myth (griffins and mermaids) join forces with curious giant frogs and duck-billed platypuses, a world of adventure for children. The 18th-century owners constructed the Temple of the Winds, a folly in the classical Greek style built on a high point above the lough.

The classical house still has lavish plasterwork, marble nudes and valuable paintings (including works by George Stubbs, the painter of animals). Kings have stayed here in bedrooms dedicated to the great European cities.

Viscount Castlereagh was born here; he went on to become British Foreign Secretary and was responsible for the passing of the Act of Union in 1801, the dissolving of the Dublin Parliament, making Ireland legally a part of Britain. Another member of the family was a general under the Duke of Wellington.

The opening hours are unusually complicated. The garden is open daily from April to September from 10.30 am to 6 pm and at the weekends during October. The house (☎ 02477-88387) is only open at the weekends during April and October and daily (except Tuesdays) May to September. The hours are from 1 to 6 pm. The temple is open the same days as the house but only from 2 to 5 pm. £3.30 provides access to the gardens, house and temple, or for £2.70 you can bypass the house. There is a shop and tearoom on the grounds.

Places to Stay Along the A20 Mount

Stewart road from Newtownards is *Ballycastle House* (☎ 02477-88357) an 18th-century farmhouse near the Mount Stewart gardens. B&B is £15 with top-class breakfasts.

Grey Abbey

In the village of Grey Abbey three km southeast of Mount Stewart are the fine ruins of a Cistercian abbey founded in 1193 by Affreca, wife of the Norman John de Courcy. The abbey was a daughter house of Holm Cultram Abbey in Wales and was used for worship as late as the 18th century.

What remains is a characteristic 12th-century Cistercian ground plan, consisting of a large cruciform church, two chapels and parts of a refectory, chapter house and rest rooms. Much of the more detailed work, like the west doorway, date from the height of the Irish Romanesque period. At the far end of the church is a carved tomb possibly depicting Affreca; her husband may be represented by the effigy in the north transept. The grounds are awash with trees, flowers and lawns, making it an ideal picnic spot.

During April to September the grounds are open from 10 am to 7 pm, Tuesday to Saturday, and Sundays 2 to 7 pm. The rest of the year closing time is 4 pm. They are closed Mondays and lunch times 1 to 1.30 pm. Admission is 50p.

Places to Stay *Abbey Farm* (☎ 02477-88207) is two km from Grey Abbey on the road to Ballywalter. B&B costs £15/26 for single/doubles. *Gordonall Farmhouse* (☎ 02477-88325) at 93 Newtownards Rd is handy for Mount Stewart and Grey Abbey and B&B costs £15/26. *Mervue* (☎ 02477-88619) at 28 Portaferry Rd has B&B at £15/30 in the low season and £17.50/35 in summer; all rooms have their own bathroom.

Portaferry

Portaferry is the most substantial settlement on the Ards Peninsula. A neat little huddle of streets, Portaferry was originally called Ballyphilip; its new, duller name relates to its position as the terminus for the short ferry ride across the lough to Strangford. There is a renowned marine biology station on the waterfront, which uses the lough as an outdoor laboratory.

The town itself is a sleepy place that feels like the end of the road, which of course it is. In good weather, you can sit outside the pubs on the waterfront and watch the lough and the ferry go by.

There is a small 15th-century castle on Castle Lane and Northern Ireland's only **aquarium** (☎ 02477-28062) on Castle St, concentrating on the marine life from Strangford Lough. The latter is open all year round, daily from April to August, from 10 am to 6 pm, opening at 1 pm on Sundays. The rest of the year it's open from 10.30 am to 5 pm daily (closed Mondays), Sundays 1 to 5 pm. Admission is £1.25. They also have a tearoom.

Places to Stay The *Square* (☎ 02477-28412) is a modest guesthouse in the centre of the village, with B&B at £11. It's open all year round. At 15 High St, *White's* (☎ 02477-28580) charges £12.50/25 for singles/doubles. Five km (three miles) along the Cloughey road from Portaferry is *Ballyfindra House* (☎ 02477-28341), a handsome farmhouse with B&B at £10 – the cheapest you'll find anywhere. *Lough Cowey Lodge* (☎ 02477-28263) is a few minutes out of Portaferry at 9 Lough Cowey Rd. B&B is £12.50/25. The upmarket *Portaferry Hotel* (☎ 0247-28231) does B&B for £75/90.

Places to Eat For pub food, try the *Coach Inn* on Ann St or *Cleary's Bar* on High St.

The three-star *Portaferry Hotel* (☎ 02477-28231) is just across from the ferry landing. The tiny dining room serves very good seafood, and they also serve bar food, the emphasis again on seafood, with snacks available from 12.30 to 2.30 pm and 5.30 to 7 pm.

Western Shore

Castle Espie Centre Two km south-east of Comber is a haven for fledgling ornithologists, and for a large gathering of geese, ducks and swans in the hands of the Wildfowl & Wetlands Trust. The centre (☎ 0247-874146) is open 10.30 am to 5 pm daily, Sundays 11.30 to 5 pm. There's a small restaurant. Admission is £2.20.

Trench Farm (☎ 0247-872558) is almost four km from Comber on the Ringcreevy Rd, with B&B at £12.50/25 for singles/doubles.

Comber's *Old Schoolhouse* (☎ 0238-541182) just south of town is the area's best-known restaurant, though it is expensive. It concentrates on seafood and has a set dinner for £13. Six km (four miles) south of Comber on the A22 in the hamlet of Lisbane is *Lisbarnet House* for good, inexpensive and familiar food like garlic steaks.

Nendrum Abbey The abbey is on Mahee Island, which is connected to the western shore of the lough by a causeway. Nendrum is earlier than Grey Abbey on the opposite shore; it was built in the 5th century under the guidance of St Mochaoi (St Mahee). The scant remains provide a surprisingly clear outline of its early plan. Foundations exist from a number of churches, round towers, beehive cells and other buildings, as well as three concentric stone ramparts and a monks' cemetery, all in a wonderful country setting. One interesting relic is the vertical stone sundial, which has been reconstructed with some of the original pieces.

The ruins were only uncovered in 1844, even though the island has long been inhabited. There are the remains of a 15th-century castle down by the causeway. Access to the site is free.

Tides Reach (☎ 0238-541347) in White-rock Bay, Killinchy, is south-west of Mahee Island on the lough shore. There is a boat at guests' disposal. B&B is £18.50/34 for singles/doubles in rooms with TV and bathroom. *Barnageeha* (☎ 0238-541011) at 90 Ardmillan Rd, Killinchy, does B&B at £20/40.

Killyleagh The A22 continues south to Killyleagh, an old fishing village dominated by the impressive hilltop **castle** of the Hamilton family. Built originally by the Norman John de Courcy in the 12th century, this partly 14th and 17th-century structure sits on the original motte and bailey and was heavily restored in 1850 into the romantic version we see today. It's in private hands but you can walk up from the village to the gatehouse for a closer look. Outside the gatehouse is a commemorative stone to Sir Hans Sloane, a naturalist whose collection was the basis for the founding of the British Museum and who gave his name to Sloane Square in London. The parish church has the tombs of members of the Dufferin family, some of whom lost their lives in the battles of Trafalgar and Waterloo.

The *Dufferin Arms* on High St is good value for meat and fish dishes.

LECALE PENINSULA

The knob of land protruding east from Downpatrick underneath Strangford Lough is known as the Lecale Peninsula. If you follow the coastline, you'll probably end up in Strangford, with the option of taking the ferry across to Portaferry and the Ards Peninsula. St John's Point, the southern tip of the Lecale Peninsula, is surmounted by an automatic lighthouse.

It's a wonder that St John managed to get a mention around this part of the world, because the Lecale Peninsula is unequivocally St Patrick's territory.

St Patrick (as you'll probably know by now) was originally kidnapped from Britain by Irish pirates and spent six years tending sheep on Slemish Mountain in County Antrim before escaping back to Britain. He then felt the urge to return to Ireland and preach the faith. After religious training he did return in 432 and is said to have made landfall near the mouth of the Slaney Burn river.

Patrick's first church was in a sheep shelter near Saul, to the north-east of Downpatrick. He made Saul his base from which he made forays out into the country. After some 30 years of evangelising he returned to Saul to die and is buried in the vicinity, or so the locals believe.

Strangford This is a small and very quaint

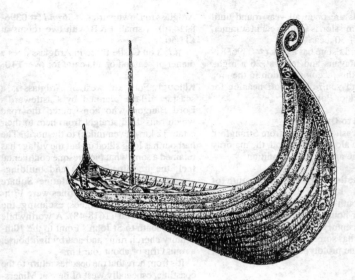

The Osebery, Viking Long Ship

fishing village 16 km (10 miles) north-east of Downpatrick. The Vikings sailed into the lough and noted the strong tidal currents through the strait – hence 'strong fjord'.

There is a good 16th-century tower house. There are 90-minute tours around the lough on the *Islander Marine* (☎ 039686-303) from the slip, operating from April to October on Wednesdays, Saturdays and Sundays at 3 pm. The fare is £5.

The excellent *Lobster Pot Bar* (☎ 0396881-288) on the Square does seafood and is open for lunch and dinner. The *Cuan Bar & Restaurant* (☎ 0396881-222) also on the Square does hot and cold buffet lunches.

Castleward This huge estate stretches away from the inlet to the west. The house is two km off the Downpatrick road. It was built in the 1760s by Lord and Lady Bangor – Bernard Ward and his wife Anne. They were quite a pair. Their tastes were poles apart, and diverging all the time. The result was

Castleward House (and a subsequent divorce). Bernard favoured the neoclassical Palladian approach, and was victorious in the design of the front facade and the classical staircase. Anne had leanings towards the Strawberry Hill Gothic style, which she implemented on the back facade and in her Gothic boudoir with its incredible fan vaulting. The rest of this great house is a mixture of their different aesthetic views.

Around the grounds are some decent walks with vistas of the lough, a Greek folly, a fine 16th-century Plantation tower house, Castle Audley by the lough, a Victorian laundry museum, and tearooms (open the same hours as the house) which also do light lunches. The garden lakes have plenty of birds.

Castleward Estate (☎ 0396881-204) is in the hands of the National Trust. The house is open daily (except Thursdays) 1 to 6 pm from May to August and at the same time at weekends during April, September and October. Admission to the house is £2.50.

The grounds are open all year round until dusk and admission is £3 for a car in summer, otherwise £1.50 a car.

Castleward Estate has a park (☎ 0396881-680) for caravans and tents at £6 a night. Other than this, accommodation in the area is scarce and you're better off heading for Downpatrick or Portaferry.

Strangford to Dundrum

A string of castles stretches from Strangford to Dundrum along the A2 road, the majority of them large and in good condition.

Kilclief Castle Only four km south of Strangford, Kilclief Castle guards the seaward mouth of the strait. This is the the oldest tower-house castle in the county, built in the 15th century by the adulterous bishop of Down. It has some elaborate details and is viewed as the prototype for other castles in the region.

Ardglass The next stop is 13 km (eight miles) south of Strangford, a fishing village with no less than seven castles or fortified houses from the 14th and 16th centuries. Ardglass Castle (now the clubhouse for the local golf club) and Gowd Castle adjoining it, have Horn and Margaret Castle towers nearby, while King's and Queen's Castles reside on a hilltop above the village. The only one open to the public is **Jordan's Castle** on Low Rd, a four-storey tower near the harbour. Like the others this was built by wealthy merchants at the dawn of economic development in Ulster. The castle now houses a local museum and a collection of antiques gathered together by its last owner. It's open June to September from 10 am to 7 pm Tuesdays to Saturdays, and from 2 to 7 pm on Sundays. It's closed Mondays and lunch times 1 to 1.30 pm. Admission is 50p.

On the hill north of the village is a 19th-century folly built by Aubrey de Vere Beauclerc as a gazebo for his disabled daughter.

In Ardglass on the Killough Rd is *Coney Island Park* (☎ 0396-841448) with tent spaces at £3 a night. On the B1 road from Ardglass to Downpatrick is *Strand* (☎ 0396-841446), a small B&B with two rooms at £11.50.

Aldo's on Castle Place in Ardglass does a dinner of seafood or à la carte for over £10.

Killough Four km west of Ardglass is a seaside village planned by Castleward's Lord Bangor, who constructed the road which runs dead straight from here to their estate 12 km (seven miles) to the north. The harbour has long silted up but the village has retained a somewhat picturesque continental feel, the tree-lined streets and buildings around Palatine St and Palatine Square exemplifying this. The Palatines were 17th-century German refugees escaping the Thirty Years War (1618-48). A worthwhile walk is south to St John's Point to the 10th-century church ruins and nearby lighthouse, a round trip of about four km.

It's from here that the beaches return to the coastline, especially west of here at Minerstown and Tyrella Strand, a seven-km stretch of firm sand.

Clough This small town lies at the northern end of a long and narrow inlet which is almost landlocked by a spit formed by Tyrella Strand. It's at the crossroads of east and south Down and is home to yet another castle. Clough Castle at the junction of the A24 and A25 is a good example of a Norman motte-and-bailey with a small stone keep.

The beautiful *Tyrella House* (☎ 0396-85422) has its own stretch of sandy beach at Tyrella. B&B costs £35 for a single. The excellent dinner is £18 a head.

Dundrum The final castle on this trip is four km south of Clough on the shore of the bay. Dundrum Castle was built in 1177 by de Courcy on the site of an earlier Irish fortification. The ruins dominate the village, a rugged fortress on a rocky outcrop amidst the trees. De Courcy's castle was made of wood, and his successor, de Lacy, was probably responsible for most of the walls in the first years of the 13th century. King John confiscated the castle in 1210 and added the donjon at the highest point, its thick walls still containing the accessible stairway to the top. After a few changes in ownership it was captured from the Magennises by Cromwell, who blew it up in 1652.

Access to the castle is on foot from the village centre, and it's open all year round. From April to September opening hours are from 10 am to 7 pm, Tuesday to Saturday, and 2 to 7 pm on Sundays. It closes at 4 pm during the rest of the year. It's closed Mondays and lunch times 1 to 1.30 pm. Admission is 50p.

The *Bay Inn* (☎ 039675-209) on Main St has rooms for only £10. There's pub food available in places like the *Murlough Tavern* or the *Marina Bar*. The *Bucks Head Restaurant* (☎ 0396-75868) does good seafood lunches and dinners.

DOWNPATRICK

Downpatrick's name comes from Ireland's patron saint who is associated with numerous places in this corner of Down. From Saul and Downpatrick Cathedral, he built the island into what was to become the 'land of saints and scholars'. St Patrick had tried to land in Wicklow but was blown ashore at Strangford Lough near Saul.

Downpatrick is the county's administrative centre and capital, 32 km (20 miles) south of Belfast. It was settled long before the saint's arrival, his first church here being constructed inside the Dún or fort of Rath Celtchair, an earthwork still visible to the south-west of the cathedral. The place later became known as Dún Padraic, anglicised to Downpatrick in the 17th century. In the 11th century St Malachy moved the diocesan seat to Bangor, but the transfer was shortlived. The Norman John de Courcy claimed in 1176 to have brought the relics of St Colmcille and St Brigid to Downpatrick to rest with the remains of St Patrick. This may have been a ploy to protect the churches of the town from the native Irish, who were disgruntled because the Irish clergy had been removed and replaced with Benedictines and Cistercians.

Later the town declined along with the cathedral until the the 17th and 18th centuries, when the Southwell family developed the town into more like what we see today. Much of the Georgian work is centred around English, Irish and Scotch Sts, which radiate from the town centre. The street names derive from the ethnic insularity of Downpatrick in the 17th century.

Information

The tourist office (☎ 0396-613426) here is in the Down leisure centre on Market St. It's closed at lunch times and weekends.

Down Cathedral

Sixteen hundred years have created a cathedral that is a conglomerate of reconstructions. Repeated Viking attacks wiped away all trace of the earliest churches and monasteries here, while the Irish Augustinians produced little before being evicted by the Norman Benedictines. Their cathedral and settlements were destroyed by Edward Bruce in 1315. The rubble of those times was used in the 15th-century construction, which was finished in 1512 and lasted until 1538; after the dissolution of the monasteries it fell into ruins. Today's structure is a 17th and 18th-century reconstruction with a few additions.

In the grounds are a 9th-century high cross in poor condition and, to the south, a turn-of-the-century monolith with the inscription 'Patric'. It has been believed since de Courcy's time that the saint is buried somewhere nearby. The legend goes that Patrick died in Saul, where his followers were told by angels to place his body on an ox-cart and that the angels would guide the cart to the spot where the saint was to be buried. They supposedly halted at the church on the hill of Down, now the site of the cathedral.

The interior (open daily from 9 am to 5 pm) reveals a bygone era of churchgoing. The private pews are the last of their kind still in use in Ireland. Note the pillar capitals, the east window representing the Apostles, and the fine 18th-century church organ. There is a memorial to an Oliver Cromwell, though not 'the' Cromwell. All the treasured relics of St Patrick wouldn't save a church in Ireland from destruction if it housed this man's namesake.

Inch Abbey

Visible across the river from the cathedral is this abbey, built by de Courcy for the Cistercians in 1180 over an earlier Irish monastic site. The Cistercians arrived from Lancashire in England with a strict policy of nondmittance to Irishmen and managed this for nearly 400 years before closing in 1542. Much of the remains consist of foundations and low walls only; the groomed setting in the marshes of the River Quoile is its most memorable feature.

The grounds are open all year round. From April to September the abbey's open daily (except Mondays, and lunch times 1 to 1.30 pm) 10 am to 7 pm, Sundays 2 to 7 pm. The rest of the year it closes at 4 pm. Admission is 50p. To get here head out of town for one km on the Belfast road and turn left just before the Abbey Lodge Hotel.

Down County Museum

Down the Mall from the cathedral is the county museum (☎ 0396-615218), housed in an extensive 18th-century gaol complex. You could say the biggest exhibit is out back, for a short signposted trail from here leads to the **Mound of Down**, a good example of a Norman motte and bailey.

The museum is open all year round: on Tuesdays to Fridays from 11 am to 5 pm, and on Saturdays from 2 to 5 pm. During July to September it's also open on Mondays from 11 am to 5 pm and Sundays 2 to 5 pm. Admission is free.

Places to Stay

B&Bs *Rathtulla* (☎ 0396- 612068) is on Rathkeltair Rd, with rooms for £12 (one with bathroom). *Hillcrest* (☎ 0396-612583) on Strangford Rd charges £12.50. Further afield is the 200-year-old *Havine Farm* (☎ 0396-85242), about seven km (four miles) south-west of Downpatrick and three km north of Tyrella in Ballykilbeg. It has four bedrooms and B&B is £14 in a truly rural environment.

Hotels The two-star *Abbey Lodge Hotel* (☎ 0396-614511) has rooms at £45/70 for singles/doubles.

Places to Eat

Eating cheaply is easy. *Portofino* on Irish St has the usual pizzas and lasagne until late, the *Golden Dragon* on Scotch St combines Chinese and European menus, while *Russell's* on Church St have good light lunches. Finally, *Rea's* on Market St is a moderately priced place with open fires; the menu specialises in seafood (including squid) as well as the more familiar chicken and beef, and dinner costs from about £10.

The *Abbey Lodge Hotel* has a good seafood-orientated restaurant with a set dinner at £12.50.

Getting There & Away

From Belfast Ulsterbus No 15 departs from Belfast's Victoria St Bus Station (☎ 0232-320011) for Downpatrick Station (☎ 0396-612384) on Market St every half hour or so.

AROUND DOWNPATRICK
Saul

Saul is three km outside Downpatrick off the Strangford road to the north-east. Upon landing near here in 432, St Patrick made his first convert, Díchú, the local chieftain, who gave St Patrick a sheep barn ('sabhal' meaning barn in Irish) from which to preach. This was the saint's favourite spot; he returned here regularly and came here to die.

Just west of the village is the supposed site of the barn, marked now by a mock 10th-century church and round tower built in 1932 to mark the 1500th anniversary of his arrival. There is a surviving wall of a medieval abbey beside this church. At the same time a massive 10-metre (33-foot) statue was erected on the nearby Slieve Patrick, with Stations of the Cross along its ascent to occupy any climbing pilgrims.

Streull Wells

Two km east of Downpatrick, on a back road behind the hospital, is the final pilgrimage site associated with the saint. Since the Middle Ages the waters from these wells have been popular cures of all ills, with one well specially set aside for eye ailments. The site's popularity was at its peak in the 17th century, and the men's and women's bath houses date from this time.

CENTRAL COUNTY DOWN

South of Belfast is pastoral countryside, with towns like Saintfield, Ballynahinch, Hillsborough and Banbridge servicing the region. Hillsborough is a particularly attractive little town. Only Slieve Croob south-west of Ballynahinch breaks the flatness of the terrain. Down's greatest megalithic artefacts are in this region, including the Giant's Ring and the Legananny Dolmen.

The Giant's Ring

This earthwork is within easy reach of Belfast, only eight km (five miles) south of the city centre, west of the A24 in Ballynahatty. The ring is a huge prehistoric enclosure nearly 200 metres (660 feet) in diameter, enclosing nearly three hectares. In the centre is the Druid's Altar, a dolmen from around 4000 BC. Prehistoric rings were commonly believed to be the home of fairies, and consequently treated with respect, but this one was commandeered in the last century as a racetrack. The four-metre (13-foot) embankment was a natural grandstand and course barrier.

Legananny Dolmen

This is perhaps Ulster's most famous Stone Age monument, and features extensively in tourist literature. Situated on the south-eastern slopes of Slieve Croob, the tripod dolmen is less bulky than most, and its elevated position offers a great backdrop of the Mournes to the south. On Slieve Croob (528 metres, 1755 feet) is the source of Belfast's River Lagan, and the mountain is crowned with the remains of a court cairn. The summit also presents a much wider panorama of the county. To reach the mountain, head west from Ballynahinch to Dromara; from here are roads leading south-east across the slopes.

Ballynahinch

Ballynahinch, 20 km (12 miles) south of Belfast, was once a spa town and is now a plain market and agricultural centre. It has a tourist office of sorts (☎ 0238-561950) in the Ballynahinch Centre on Windmill St which can offer some advice to tourists about the area.

Hillsborough

The very elegant town of Hillsborough is 15 km (nine miles) south-west out of Belfast. It was founded in the 1640s by a Colonel Hill who built a fort here to quell Irish insurgents. There is some fine Georgian architecture in the town square and along Arthur St. The most notable building is **Hillsborough House**, built in the 1780s; it's the official royal residence in Northern Ireland, and the official residence of the Secretary of State for Northern Ireland, the British government's main man. It still hosts official receptions and is not open to the public. The most notable exterior feature is the elaborate wrought-iron gates dating from 1745.

Elsewhere around town are the Georgian **Market House** and **Court House** and **St Malachy's Parish Church**, which has two of the finest 18th-century organs in Ireland. Nearby just off the town square is **Hillsborough Fort**, a small fort on Colonel Hill's original site but dating mostly from the 18th century. Only the ramparts date from Hill's day. The fort (☎ 0846-683285) is open daily for tours all year round from 10 am to 7 pm, except Mondays and lunch times 1 to 1.30 pm, Sundays from 2 to 7 pm. During the winter months it closes earlier at 4 pm. Admission is 50p.

Hillsborough has a surprising number of antique shops, for which the town is widely known.

Places to Stay *Growell House* (☎ 0238-

532271) is on the Dromore road with two rooms at £14.

Places to Eat The *Hillside Bar* (☎ 0846-682765) on Main St is handy; it serves good bar food until 7.30 pm (8 pm on Fridays) and nouvelle cuisine and seafood in its more formal restaurant until 9 pm. Dinner is expensive, from around £19. *Ritchies* on Ballynahinch St is similar, with a good bar and a restaurant with an old-fashioned feel. It serves up less fancy fare of steaks, pastas and lasagne.

Out on the Dromore road is the *White Gables Hotel* (☎ 0846-682755), with a nice little restaurant which relies on the best of local produce for its à la carte menu. Dinner costs between £12 and £15. It also serves food in the bar and has tea rooms for the less hungry.

Getting There & Away Bus Nos 38 and 238 run regularly from Belfast's Glengall St Station.

Banbridge
Fifteen km (nine miles) south-west of Hillsborough is Banbridge, another Industrial Revolution town.

Near the centre is the **statue to Captain Francis Crozier**, complete with polar bears. A native of Banbridge, he was commander of HMS *Terror* in the 1840s, and explored the uncharted Antarctic continent. Later he went with Sir John Franklin in search of the elusive North-West Passage. Franklin died on that voyage in 1847, and Crozier and his crew starved to death a year later, their bodies remaining lost in the Arctic for 10 years.

The main street of Banbridge has an unusual Victorian **underpass** in the middle, to enable coaches to manage the steep hill.

Banbridge is the start of **Brontë Homeland Drive** which travels the River Bann valley to Rathfriland 12 km to the south. Patrick Brontë, father of Charlotte, Emily and Anne, was born here and taught in a local school. The locals like to think that her

father's tales of the Mournes inspired the bleak setting for Emily's *Wuthering Heights*.

Places to Stay *Lisdrum* (☎ 08206-22663) is on the main road to Newry, in well over 10 hectares of nicely tended gardens. Its flatlets, each with a small lounge, cost £14 for B&B. It's open all year round.

Places to Eat There is cheap food, from takeaways to pub grub, on offer, especially along Newry and Bridge Sts.

Getting There & Away
Bus Nos 38 and 238 run regularly from Belfast's Glengall St Station.

SOUTH DOWN & MOUNTAINS OF MOURNE
The relatively compact yet impressive Mountains of Mourne have long resisted human settlement. Today they are surrounded on all sides by towns and villages, but they are crossed only by the B27 road between Kilkeel and Hilltown. The reservoirs of the Silent Valley and Spelga are among the few intrusions on nature. The steep and craggy granite peaks have suffered less than other similar ranges from glaciation. There are no low polished hills to be found here.

The highest peak, and indeed the most accessible, is **Slieve Donard** (848 metres, 2796 feet). In its shadow, the town of Newcastle is the best base for exploring this or other peaks, as the Mourne Countryside Centre here provides detailed information. The less adventurous can visit the numerous forest parks around Newcastle. For walkers, J S Doran's *Hill Walks in the Mournes* is worth getting.

The **Silent Valley Park** plunges into the range's heart, surrounded by most of the peaks. **Ben Crom**, **Slieve Muck** and **Slievelamagan** are good for strenuous hiking. Westwards is the B27 road which passes **Spelga Reservoir**, a picturesque drive in the evening, when the sun goes down behind **Eagle Mountain** and **Pigeon Rock**

Mountain. There's good rock climbing in this area.

As in Connemara, the farmers here have produced the characteristic patchwork of small fields with dry stone walls out of the boulder-strewn landscape .

The biggest of the walls, the **Mourne Wall**, is a different kettle of fish; it was built early this century to provide employment and to enclose the catchment area of the Silent Valley reservoir; it stretches for 35 km (22 miles) over numerous peaks.

Newcastle

All along the coast from the north of the county the Mournes beckon. If you stick to the coastline you'll eventually end up in Newcastle, 46 km (29 miles) away from Belfast. It has a marvellous setting: the backdrop is the huge Slieve Donard stretching up behind the town. Newcastle is the Bangor of south Down, with plenty of accommodation and food, the usual seaside assortment of entertainment and five km of beaches.

Information There is a tourist office (☎ 03967-22222) in the Newcastle Centre & Tropicana Complex on Central Promenade. It's open seven days a week, all year round.

For more details on the Mournes, drop into the Mourne Countryside Centre (☎ 03967-24059) just south of the Newcastle Centre. During the summer months (9 am to 6 pm weekdays, 12 to 6 pm weekends) it provides more information on history and scenery in the form of exhibitions, brochures and maps of suggested walks. On Mondays and Saturdays at 10 am they provide free guided walks of varying distances (four to 14 km) into the mountains from the centre.

Places to Stay *Newcastle Youth Hostel* (☎ 03967-22133)) is near the promenade at 30 Downs Rd. It charges £5.95 a night including bed linen, and is open from March to December.

For value for money there are few B&Bs better than *Glenside Farmhouse* (☎ 03967-22628) one km from Tollymore Forest Park on Tullybrannigan Rd with simple rooms

available for only £8. The *Briars* (☎ 03967-24347) is a delightful old farmhouse almost one km from Newcastle at 39 Middle Tollymore Rd; B&B is £16. The huge modern *Golf Links House* (☎ 03967-22054) is at 109 Dundrum Rd, adjacent to the Royal County Down Golf Club, hence the name. B&B is good value at £12 and evening meals are reasonably priced. Finally there's *Fitzpatrick's* (☎ 03967-24947) on Marguerite Ave at £11 a night.

At £28, the *Donard Hotel* (☎ 03967-22203) on Main St is the cheapest hotel. It's not to be confused with the dominating *Slieve Donard Hotel* (☎ 03967-23681) on Downs Rd, which offers rooms for a minimum of £65 but has all the perks. Bryansford Rd has some good-value hotels like the *Brook Cottage Hotel* (☎ 03967-22204), with pleasant rooms at £20 a night for a single. Finally there's the *Burrendale Hotel & Country Club* (☎ 03967-22599), a three-star establishment with spacious rooms for £52/80 for singles/doubles and the best restaurant in Newcastle.

Places to Eat Main St abounds with every kind of fast food.

On the seafront is the *Strand Palace Café*, more upmarket but with main courses from £3 to £6. It has a light and inexpensive à la carte menu and also does sandwiches. It is open until 11 pm in summer and 6 pm in winter. The popular *Mario's* on Central Promenade tends towards Italian as well as à la carte dishes in comfortable surroundings. The *Pavilion* on Downs Rd opposite the entrance to the Slieve Donard Hotel is more seafood-orientated, and has an à la carte selection; a set dinner costs £13.

The *Burrendale Hotel* (☎ 03967-22599) has a high-quality restaurant with dinner at £15 or more. Snacks are available on the premises in the *Cottage Bar*. The *Slieve Donard Hotel* restaurant (☎ 03967-23681) isn't bad either and booking is essential for a table.

Getting There & Away The bus station (☎ 03967-22296) is on Railway St and there is an hourly service from Belfast on Ulsterbus Nos 18 and 20 through Ballynahinch. Alternatively go from Belfast to Downpatrick and connect with Ulsterbus No 17 between Newcastle and Downpatrick.

Getting Around During July and August Ulsterbus No 34A tours from Newcastle (☎ 03967-22296) to the Silent Valley and the Spelga Dam, with three buses on weekdays, two on Saturdays.

Wiki Wiki Wheels on Donard Corner rents bikes for £7 a day, £27 a week. In nearby Castlewellan on Clarkhill Rd is Ross Cycles (☎ 03967-78029), the region's main Raleigh dealer. Bikes are £5 a day or £22 a week, with a £30 deposit required.

Around Newcastle

Newcastle is an ideal base from which to explore the Mournes, and there are three forest parks close by, for walks, hikes and pony treks. **Donard Park** at the south edge of town is the best place from which to ascend Slieve Donard. On a good day the three-hour effort is well rewarded, with Down's patchwork of fields, Scotland, Wales and the Isle of Man all on show at varying splendid perspectives. Two cairns can be found near the summit and were long believed to have been cells of St Donard, who retreated here to pray in early Christian times.

Tollymore Forest Park is three km (two miles) north-east of town. Its 500 hectares offer lengthy walks along the Shimno River and the north slopes of the Mournes. The park and visitor centre (☎ 03967-22428) are open every day, 10 am to sunset and admission is £2.20 for a car, or 80p for a pedestrian. Tollymore Outdoor Centre (☎ 0232-381222) runs courses on hill walking, rock climbing and canoeing.

Further north-east is the finest but slightly smaller park, **Castlewellan Forest Park** (☎ 03967-78664), and its lovely lake. Trout fishing is allowed (daily permit £7) and there is also boat hire. The Arboretum here is well established, dating from 1760, and is internationally known, with a wide variety of fine shrubs and trees. Opening hours and admission are identical to those of Tollymore. Just outside the park is the **Mount Pleasant Horse Trekking Centre** (☎ 03967-78651), which caters both to the experienced rider and to the beginner, with various treks into the park.

Places to Stay There are plenty of camp sites on offer though they can fill up at the height of summer. Both *Castlewellan* (☎ 03967-78664) and *Tollymore* (☎ 03967-22428) have spaces for tents from £4 to £7 depending on the season. Nearer the town is *Lazy BJ Park* (☎ 03967-23533) on the Dundrum road, which is similarly priced.

Mournes Coast Road

The coastal drive along the A2 south and around the sweeping Mourne slopes is the most memorable journey in Down. Annalong, Kilkeel, Rostrevor and Warrenpoint offer convenient stopping points, from which you can detour into the mountains. If you take the Head Rd, following the sign for the Silent Valley one km north of Annalong, you come into the beautiful stone-wall countryside, past the Silent Valley, and back to Kilkeel.

Annalong This busy little tourist spot with its shingle beach is 12 km (seven miles) south of Newcastle. Overlooking the harbour is the **Annalong Corn Mill** (☎ 0693-67226) an 1830 watermill, nicely preserved, which still mills flour. The café and antique shop are open sporadically, while the mill is open from June to September in the afternoons from 2 to 6 pm; admission is £1.20.

For B&B in the £14 to £15 range there are *Dairy Farm* (☎ 03967-68433) and the neighbouring *Sycamores* (☎ 03967-68279), both on Major Hill.

Annalong's *Glassdrumman Lodge* (☎ 03967- 68451) is a very expensive guesthouse (£65/85 for singles/doubles) which also serves up French cuisine from £20 a go. It has the *Kitchen Garden* for more moderately priced meals. Back down to earth is the *Harbour Inn* (☎ 03967-68678) down by

Annalong's waterfront, serving up fish, steaks and pub food daily.

Kilkeel Kilkeel, nine km (six miles) farther south, is larger than Annalong, with a quayside fish market. From here the B27 ventures north into the mountains.

Chestnut Park camp site (☎ 06937-62653) is good, with pitches at £6 a night.

B&Bs within the £14 to £15 range are *Mourne Abbey Guesthouse* (☎ 06937-62426) just south of town on Greencastle Rd, and *Ashcroft Farmhouse* (☎ 03967-62736) five km north-west on the A2 in Ballymartin. Both of these are only open from March to September. Out of season, *Hill View* (☎ 06937-64269), six km (four miles) north of Kilkeel, just off the B27 is open all year round and does B&B at £11 to £13.

The homely *Kilmorey Arms Hotel* (☎ 06937-62220) is on Greencastle St and costs £24/38. It does a medium-priced menu of familiar à la carte dishes.

The Silent Valley Just east of Kilkeel is the Head Rd, which leads to the beautiful Silent Valley six km (four miles) north of here. In the valley the Kilkeel River has been dammed to provide water to Belfast.

The dry-stone **Mourne Wall** surrounds the valley and climbs over the summits of 15 of the nearby peaks. Two metres high and over 35 km (22 miles) long, it was built in 1910-22 and outlines the watershed of the springs which feed the two lakes.

At the south end of the valley is the Silent Valley information centre (☎ 0232-746581). From the car park (admission £2) there is a bus up the valley to the top of Ben Crom. This operates during July to September and costs 80p return. Otherwise it's a fine walk. The centre and coffee shop are open from 10 am to 6 pm from April to September and until 4.30 pm during the rest of the year.

Green Castle Six km (four miles) southwest of Kilkeel on the tip of a promontory across Carlingford Lough is Green Castle. The first castle was built in 1261 as a companion to Carlingford Castle on the opposite side of the lough in County Louth. However, the square, turreted remains date from the 14th century. Once the property of the earls of Kildare, it was seized by the crown and given to the Bagenal family of Newry in the 1550s. They maintained it as a royal garrison until it was destroyed by Cromwell's forces in 1652. The rooftop provides a good vantage point west up the lough.

The interior is open sporadically during the year, every day except Mondays from April to September, 10 am to 7 pm, Sundays 2 to 7 pm. During winter it's open weekends, Saturdays 10 am to 4 pm, Sundays 2 to 4 pm. It's closed lunch times 1 to 1.30 pm. Admission is 50p.

Cranfield Point to the south-east is the most southerly tip of Northern Ireland.

Rostrevor From Kilkeel the journey is westward along Carlingford Lough. Rostrevor is 13 km (eight miles) to the west, a very picturesque Victorian seaside resort at the base of Slievemartin.

Just before entering the town from the north, the road passes a large **obelisk** to Major General Ross, an English commander in the American War of 1812. His achievement was the capturing of Washington DC and the burning of the White House. Up until this point the presidential residence was stone gray, but it had to be painted white to cover the smoke and scorch marks left behind by Ross's men.

From **Kilbroney Forest Park** to the west of the town, there's a forest drive and then a footpath to the top of Slievemartin, or a strenuous trek up the steepest side of the mountain. The Kilbroney Forest Park *camp site* (☎ 06937-38134) on Shore Rd costs only £3.75 a tent.

Near Rostrevor, two km inland by the Fairy Glen, is the early 18th-century *Forestbrook House* (☎ 06937-38105) on Forestbrook Rd. It charges £13 for B&B. In Rostrevor itself try the *Cloughmor Inn* on Bridge St for burgers or meat pies, or the *Fisherman's Restaurant* for a more relaxed dinner.

Warrenpoint At the head of the lough, on the way to Newry, is Warrenpoint, another spacious and picturesque resort. It's one of the livelier towns around, with an active nightlife in the pubs and halls.

Garden House (☎ 06937-73723) sits in gardens surrounding Narrow Water Castle, east of Warrenpoint, and used to house one of the estate gardeners. Singles/doubles go for £12/24.

For pub food, try *Bennett's* on Church St, or the *Duke of Mourne* on Duke St, with the *Tai-Pan* above it for good Chinese food.

There is a ferry from Warrenpoint to Omeath in County Louth from June to September. It is more like a tour, as the *Red Star Ferry* (☎ 06937-73776) only takes passengers. It operates every 20 minutes between 1 and 6 pm from the beach or Marine Parade and costs £1.50 return. For lengthy cruises around the lough there is the *Maid of Mourne* (☎ 6937-72950). The fare is £3 for a 90-minute tour.

For sailing timetables and tickets you could also call in on the tourist information kiosk (☎ 06937-72950) at Warrenpoint marina.

Newry

Newry has long been a frontier town, guardian of the Gap of the North which lies between the Mournes to the east and Slieve Gullion to the south-west. Its name derives from a yew tree which was planted here by St Patrick in an early monastery, of which nothing remains. A stone castle was first built in the town in 1180 by de Courcy, but it was repeatedly attacked. Cistercian monks came to shelter near the castle, until their abbey was taken over by Nicholas Bagenal in the 1570s. As Grand Marshal of all English forces in Ireland, he had great power, and attracted the attention of some of the local rulers. One, Sean 'the Proud' O'Neill, completely destroyed the castle and house in 1566. In 1575 Nicholas Bagenal used the rubble to construct the first Protestant church in Ireland. He is buried in the grounds of St Patrick's Church of Ireland on Stream St.

The Newry canal, built in 1740, was a forerunner of the English network which led England into the Industrial Revolution. It brought trade, and later its decline led to the decline of the town.

Today Newry is again prosperous, lying on the main Dublin to Belfast road. The shopping area bustles with Southerners, especially around Christmas, who come for the cheaper products. The turbulence of the currency market in the 1990s has lessened their numbers, however.

Information The Arts Centre & Museum beside the town hall has a few shelves in the lobby stacked with brochures and free booklets. Try the Newry District Council (☎ 0693-67226) on Warrenpoint Rd for any queries.

The Newry Bookshop (☎ 0693-64999), just off Monaghan St opposite Dunnes Stores, has a fairly good selection on offer.

Newry Museum The small Newry Museum (☎ 0693-66232) in the Arts Centre on Bank Parade presents a detailed historical account of the town, and has some intriguing exhibits, including Admiral Nelson's cabin table from the HMS *Victory*. This piece sits near the base of the entrance stairs, its glass case bearing only a small plaque naming the benefactor.

The museum is open daily from 11 am to 5 pm weekdays, 10 am to 1 pm on Saturdays, closed Sundays. Admission is free.

Places to Stay *Ashton House* (☎ 0693-62120) is on Fathom Line on the Omeath Rd, close to town. It does B&B for £14, and all rooms have their own bathroom. The modern *Hillside* (☎ 0693-65484) is eight km (five miles) north off the Belfast road and charges £14 for B&B in a single room. Finally for somewhere central, *Castle View* (☎ 0693-68786) is on Chapel St, and charges £13 for B&B in a single room.

The large modern *Mourne Country Hotel* (☎ 0693-67922) was bombed in 1993 and was closed at the time of writing.

Places to Eat There are numerous places to

stop for a bite. The *Friar Tuck* fast-food outlets on Monaghan St and Sugar Island are good of their kind. Pub food can be had in *McLogan's* on Canal St. The *Ambassador* on Hill St is good for familiar set fare at reasonable prices. For good steaks the *Brass Monkey* on Trevor Hill is the usual grill and is relatively cheap. Chinese dishes are best in the *Rose Garden Restaurant & Take-away* on Sugar Island, with dinner at around £10.

Getting There & Away From Belfast's Europa Bus Station (☎ 0232-320011) on Glengall St comes a very regular service to Newry Station (☎ 0693-63531) on Edward St. From the Mall in Newry, Ulsterbus No 39 leaves once or twice an hour for Kilkeel through Rostrevor and Warrenpoint.

Getting Around Central Taxis (☎ 0693-69988) are one of the many companies in the town.

County Armagh

County Armagh could be – should be – a major tourist attraction. Quite apart from the venerable town of Armagh, there are some wonderful prehistoric sites, and sights, in the surrounding countryside and a week or more could easily be spent here.

Unfortunately, modern history is close to rendering the county a no-go area. Apart from small Protestant outposts like Bessbrook, County Armagh is strongly Catholic and its nationalist identity is keenly felt. The resolve of its people to refuse incorporation into the UK is steadfastly maintained; nowhere else is there so strong a sense of Ireland being occupied by a foreign force. In south Armagh the British military and the IRA are locked in combat, and going there can be an unsettling experience.

But Armagh is also very beautiful and deserves more visitors than circling helicopters and British soldiers.

ARMAGH TOWN

Armagh, one of the towns most worth visiting in the North, has suffered badly from the social and political unrest. Even now, as in other hot spots in the North, an event such as a minor traffic accident calls dozens of armed men wearing flak jackets into the streets, stopping cars and dodging behind bins. Typically, everyone else ignores them, and children and old people chat idly beside crouching and scared armed men.

History

This compact little city lays claim to being one of the oldest settlements in Ireland. Legend has it that the hill now home to the Church of Ireland cathedral once was the power base of Queen Macha, wife of Nevry, some time during the first millennium BC. She gave her name to the city, whose Irish form, Ard Macha, means 'Macha's height'. St Patrick set up the first Christian church in Ireland here, on a site at the base of the hill. Later the local chieftain, a convert to the new religion, gave Patrick the hilltop, and a church of some kind has stood on that spot for over 15 centuries, predating Canterbury as a Christian religious site.

By the 8th century Armagh was one of Europe's best known centres of religion, learning and craftwork. Its fame was its undoing, as the Vikings raided the city 10 times between 831 and 1013, taking slaves and valuables, and leaving many dead in their wake. Brian Ború, who died in 1014 near Dublin during the last great battle to defeat the Vikings, was buried on the north side of the cathedral.

With the Vikings gone, the Irish clans fought each other for the city, and the Norman settlement in the 12th and 13th centuries saw more attacks. But the religious life continued, with the conversion from Celtic Christianity to Catholic customs in the 12th century and the establishment of a Franciscan friary in 1263.

What the Vikings and Normans hadn't managed, the Reformation did. The monasteries and educational establishments were destroyed by either English or Irish forces

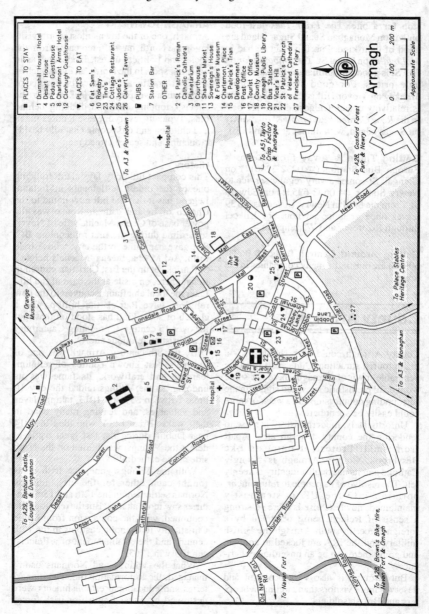

Armagh

PLACES TO STAY
1 Drumshill House Hotel
4 Desart House
5 Padua Guesthouse
8 Charlemont Arms Hotel
12 Clonhugh Guesthouse

PLACES TO EAT
6 Fat Sam's
10 Rokeby
23 Tino's
24 Cottage Restaurant
25 Jodie's
26 Calvert's Tavern

PUBS
7 Station Bar

OTHER
2 St Patrick's Roman Catholic Cathedral
3 Planetarium
9 Courthouse
11 Shambles Market
13 Sovereign's House & Fusiliers' Museum
14 Charlemont Place
15 St Patrick's Trian Development
16 Post Office
17 Tourist Office
18 County Museum
19 Armagh Public Library
20 Bus Station
21 Vicar's Hill
22 St Patrick's Church of Ireland Cathedral
27 Franciscan Friary

0   100   200 m

Approximate Scale

fighting yet again for control of the city. By the 17th century little was left of a once flourishing city. During the Plantation, Irish landowners were thrown off their lands, and settlers from England and Scotland took their place.

Today's Armagh City is a Georgian construct and owes its distinctive architecture to Richard Robinson, a Church of Ireland primate. By the time of his arrival in 1765 Armagh had recovered, economically at least, from the many invasions and had a flourishing linen industry.

Information

The tourist office (☎ 0861-527808) is in English St, within the restricted zone, but there is parking farther up English St. It is open 9 am to 6 pm, Monday to Saturday, all year round. It can provide information on the limited places to stay, restaurants and music bars. It also has maps of a good walking tour of the city, taking in most of the interesting architecture.

If you are intending to spend just one day in Armagh don't do it on Sunday when, like the rest of Northern Ireland, Armagh more or less closes down.

St Patrick's Church of Ireland Cathedral

The core of the building dates back to medieval times while the rather dull sandstone-clad exterior is the result of a 19th-century restoration by Primate Beresford. Around the exterior are a series of carved heads, and inside, along with the chilly wooden pews of established religion, are some interesting plaques and an 11th-century Celtic cross.

The chapter house has assorted paraphernalia from the ancient city. Every time anyone has knocked down a house or rebuilt a wall and found some ancient object, it has been deposited here, unexamined and unexplained. There is usually someone around who can tell you what's known about the collection. On the west wall of the north transept is a plaque commemorating the burial of Brian Ború.

Near the cathedral, **Vicar's Hill** is one of the oldest terraces in Ireland, built in the 18th century by Richard Castle in the Palladian style. The ghost of a green lady is said to haunt the area.

On the corner of this road and Abbey St is the **Public Library** (☎ 0861-523142), which has several ancient manuscripts, a set of 1838 Ordnance Survey maps and a first edition of *Gulliver's Travels*, annotated by Swift himself. The library is open from 10 am to 12.30 pm and 2 to 4 pm, Monday to Friday.

St Patrick's Roman Catholic Cathedral

From the Church of Ireland cathedral you can walk down Dawson St and Edward St to the other St Patrick's Cathedral, built between 1840 and 1873. The famine interrupted building for a while. It is built in the Gothic Revival style, with huge twin towers dominating the approach up flight after flight of steps. Inside it seems almost Byzantine, with every piece of wall and ceiling covered in brilliantly coloured mosaics.

The sanctuary was modernised in 1981 by Liam McCormick and has a distinctive tabernacle holder and crucifix which seem out of place among the mosaics and statues of the rest of the church.

The place has an amazing sense of calm, and the visitor can spend hours just gazing around its walls.

The Mall

Back along English St (stopping to admire the Shambles at the corner of English St and Cathedral Rd) and Russell St, you come to the Mall: not a collection of supermarkets and dress shops, but a pleasantly laid out park which once held horse races, cock fighting and bull baiting sessions, until Richard Robinson decided it was a bit low-class for a city of learning.

At the top of the Mall behind wire mesh fences, barbed wire and video cameras is the **Courthouse**, built in 1809 by Armagh man Francis Johnston, who later became one of Ireland's most famous architects. On the opposite corner is the **Sovereign's House**, built for the Armagh equivalent of mayor. It now houses the Fusiliers Museum.

Further along the Mall East, away from the courthouse, is a series of Georgian terraces. Charlemont Place is a creation of Francis Johnston, and so is the County Museum's portico, fronting a more workaday building originally built as a school.

County Museum

Armagh has one of the nicer small museums (☎ 0861-523070) in Ireland. Its showcases are pleasantly filled with prehistoric axeheads, items found in bogs, old clothes, corn dollies and strawboy outfits, plus some very dead stuffed wildlife, as well as military costumes and equipment.

The museum is on the Mall East, and is open from 10 am to 1 pm and 2 to 5 pm, Monday to Saturday. It sometimes closes on bank holidays. Admission is free.

The Royal Irish Fusiliers Museum

The Fusiliers Museum (☎ 0861-522911) is in the old Sovereign's House, near the Courthouse. It is full of the paraphernalia of war: polished silver and brass abound, and medals drip from the walls. More interesting are the little personal items that survive from the many battles the Fusiliers have fought. The museum is open 10 to 12.30 am and 2 to 4 pm. Admission is free; knock to get in.

Planetarium

A healthy walk up College Hill from the Mall brings you to the Observatory & Planetarium. The Observatory is not open to the public but the Planetarium (☎ 0861-52389) is. Both buildings are set in gardens which are open to the public during office hours. The Observatory is over 200 years old but still contributes to astronomical research. The Planetarium has shows at 2 and 3 pm, Monday to Saturday. Admission to the one-hour show is £2.50 (children £1.50). The exhibition downstairs is free and quite interesting, with lots of hands-on stuff and a shop.

Palace Stables Heritage Centre

The heritage centre is slightly out of town off Friary Rd but walking distance from the town centre. Amazingly, it is open on Sunday afternoons. It stands in the grounds of the Palace Demesne, built by Archbishop Robinson when he was appointed primate of Ireland in 1769. The palace now houses council offices but the ground floor lobby still retains some of the grandeur of earlier days.

Next door to the centre is the Primate's Chapel, now deconsecrated. It was designed by Thomas Cooley but Francis Johnston had a hand in it. Inside are fine oak carvings, an elaborate coffered ceiling and stained-glass windows. Still under redevelopment are the old passageways used by the servants (no-one wanted to have servants on view, so they built underground passageways for them to get from one part of the estate to another) and the ice house. Also in the grounds, just as you turn into the demesne, are the ruins of the Franciscan friary dating back to the 13th century. Much of its stonework was taken to build the demesne walls.

The Palace Stables house a set of tableaux of Richard Robinson and his contemporaries, with information from the records of the time. A little video room shows the story of the area in truly patronising style. Downstairs however is good fun. It recreates the life of the bishop's coachman, with period furniture and a 19th-century coach on display in the cobbled yard. There is also a nice coffee shop and craft shop and a children's play room. The Palace Stables are open Monday to Saturday 10 am to 7 pm and Sunday 1 to 7 pm.

St Patrick's Trian Development

This development, in the old second Presbyterian church behind the tourist office, had not yet opened at the time of writing. It will probably be yet another heritage centre job, with the theme of Lilliput, since Jonathan Swift was kind enough to spend some time in the area.

Places to Stay

Camping There are no budget places to stay. The cheapest place if you have a tent is at

Gosford Forest Park (☎ 0861-551277) south of town on the A28 near Markethill. It has a good camp site with lots of facilities and you don't need to get an advance permit. Camping is £3 a night.

B&Bs Armagh's B&Bs have tiny signs if any. The tourist office will give you a current list. Beyond the cathedral in Cathedral Rd are *Padua Guest House* (☎ 0861-523584/522039) at No 63, with rooms at £10 for a single, and the posher *Desart House* (☎ 0861-522387) at No 99 with rooms at £15. On College Hill a few doors up from the Fusiliers Museum is *Clonhugh Guest House* (☎ 0861-522693), with rooms at £12 per person.

Hotels The *Charlemont Arms Hotel* (☎ 0861-522009) in English St has wire mesh on the windows and a locked front door. Singles/doubles with bathroom are £22/40.

On Moy Rd is *Drumshill House Hotel* (☎ 0861-522009/522006). It is small, and offers B&B at £35/55 for singles/doubles. It also has a nightclub at weekends.

Places to Eat
In town there are lots of places to get lunch but evening meals are harder to find. *Tino's* on Thomas St does fairly inexpensive food in heated trays, so early is best – but there's no offensive muzak and the tables are quite private. *Fat Sam's* in Lower English St does nice jacket potatoes with assorted fillings for between £1.20 and £2.20. In Gazette Arcade off Scotch St is the *Cottage Restaurant* – all muzak, soft lighting and single flowers in vases on the table, but it has a good selection of lunches at around £2.50 or less.

For evening meals at reasonable prices there is *Jodie's* in Scotch St, which also does lunch specials for £3 or less and afternoon coffee. Other than that, the two hotels offer evening meals at around £10 to £15. The Charlemont does children's meals while both do inexpensive lunches. Two new restaurants are *Calvert's Tavern* at the corner of Scotch and Barrack Sts, and *Rokeby* on College St near the Courthouse.

Entertainment
Rafferty's bar, beside Wellworth's in town, has traditional music on Saturday nights, while the *Station* bar in Lower English St has live music of some kind on Tuesdays and Thursdays. Out of town, *McAleavey's* in Keady has traditional music, set dancing and singing on Wednesdays. The excellent *Stray Leaf Folk Club* (☎ 0693-888284) at Forkhill meets on the second and last Saturday of each month.

Getting There & Away
The bus station (☎ 0861-522266) is in the Mall West. There are connections with Belfast, Cookstown and Enniskillen. There is also a service to Dublin that involves a change of bus at Monaghan. The Belfast-Galway bus also stops in Armagh.

Getting Around
Bikes can be hired at Brown's Bikes (☎ 0861-522782) for £5 per day. Brown's is in Killylea, about eight km (five miles) out of Armagh to the west on the A28.

AROUND ARMAGH TOWN
Navan Fort
Two miles west of Armagh is Navan Fort or Eamhain Macha, the principal archaeological site in Ulster. The Egyptian geographer Ptolemy marked this site on his map of the known world in the 2nd century AD, naming it Isamnion. Legend has it that a pregnant woman called Macha was forced to race the king's horses here; at the end of the race she died giving birth to twins, and the name Eamhain Macha means 'twins of Macha'. Another legend says that it was the great Queen Macha who began this place, marking out the area with her brooch.

Whatever its origins, the place was the site for homes and a huge temple during both the Iron and Bronze Ages. At one stage an enormous temple was filled with lime and deliberately burnt, suggesting that it was sent on its way to heaven rather than sacked by its enemies. Close by is a Bronze Age pond now called the King's Stables where remains of bronze castings have been found. With a history like this the fort ought to be awe-inspiring, but these days it's just a grassy mound with some pretty views back to Armagh. The new interpretive centre may bring back the legends and history of Eamhain Macha to a population which badly needs some sense of a common heritage.

Orange Museum

This Orange Order museum is 10 km (six miles) from Armagh at Loughgall and was created in 1961 on the premises of what was then a pub. It is open during office hours; enquire in the building next door. It contains sashes and banners, and weapons from the Battle of the Diamond in 1795 between Protestant 'Peep o' Day Boys' and Catholic 'Defenders'. This took place at Diamond Hill five km (three miles) north-east of the village and led to the founding of the Orange Order.

Ardress House

The 17th-century Ardress House (☎ 0762-851236) started life as a farmhouse and was upgraded to a manor house in 1760. Much of the original interior remains and the farmyard still functions, with a piggery and smithy. There are pleasant walks around the wooded grounds.

The house has complex opening dates and times, and it's best to enquire before visiting. Entry fees also vary according to what combination of adult, child, farmyard or building you are or want to see.

Ardress House is reached by taking the road to Loughgall, which is on the right shortly after the beginning of the A29 to Dungannon. It's 14 km (nine miles) from Armagh.

Tayto Crisp Factory

The crisps (potato chips to North Americans) factory at Tandragee on the A51 can be inspected. The factory is inside a castle which was destroyed and rebuilt on many occasions, the last rebuilding, by Lord Man-

deville, taking place in 1836. Every stage of the potatoes' mutation from living vegetable to addictive snack can be seen, and you get to sample the freshly made delicacies. Great crack except for the two weeks in mid-July when the factory closes. Phone ☎ 0762-840249 to arrange a tour or see if there is one you can tack on to. Tours usually operate between 10 am and 3 pm, Tuesday to Thursday.

Benburb Castle & Museum

The castle was founded by Shane O'Neill, who had a stronghold here long before the English arrived; not a trace of this now remains. In 1611 Sir Richard Wingfield added a bawn which does still stand. In the 19th century floors were raised and a private house was incorporated into the building. During WW II American troops used the place as a hospital and the towers were altered to allow access to the roofs. Benburb Castle is now entering its fifth life as a tourist attraction restored along 17th-century lines. At the moment the key to the building can be collected from the Benburb Centre at the Servite Priory nearby, but when the restoration is complete it will open at regular hours.

The **O'Neill Historical Society Museum** is in the basement of the Benburb Centre in the Priory. It contains a mixture of military memorabilia and folk crafts. Entrance is free, but there are no regular hours. Ask for the key from the Centre, which keeps office hours of 9 am to 5 pm.

Planned developments include the restoration of a linen mill and canal lock in the area and a walkway from the Centre to the Castle. Enquire either at the tourist office in Armagh or at the Centre.

The village of Benburb in County Tyrone is 11 km (seven miles) north-west of Armagh; take the A29 and then turn left onto the B128. The Centre is on the left and clearly marked, and the Castle is a short distance farther along the road.

Gosford Forest Park

At this relaxing picnic spot children will enjoy the weird and wonderful poultry on display. Nature trails work their way around the park and through the trees and in the middle of it all is a vast mock-Norman castle that is not open to the public. Admission to the park is 50p (cars £1, children 25p).

The park is by the side of the A28, south-east of town near Markethill. Town buses to Markethill stop outside.

SOUTH ARMAGH

The notoriety of south Armagh has earned it the forbidding epithet of Bandit Country, which is hardly likely to attract visitors. The intensity of the armed conflict between the IRA and the British Army is nowhere more evident or dramatic. Many small towns are effectively sealed off by the British military, and army helicopters buzz overhead. Wreaths by the roadside bear silent homage to the many victims of the fighting, and around Crossmaglen, IRA posters nailed to the telephone posts carry an ominous warning that they should not be removed.

The area is heavily Catholic with small Protestant communities living a beleaguered existence that seems to depends on the army for protection. It is very likely that as a visitor to the area you will be questioned by the army and some form of identification will be required. There will be no restrictions on your travel unless an incident has occurred in the locality.

The military situation should not deter the visitor from seeing south Armagh. It is a lovely part of Ireland and there are some interesting archaeological and ecclesiastical places to see. You should, however, exercise caution. If you have an English accent, it may not be advisable to spend an evening drinking in a pub. No tourist, to our knowledge, has ever been attacked in south Armagh, but feelings can run high, especially if you happen to be there at a difficult time.

Most places worth seeing could be taken in on a half-day trip by car. On a bicycle give yourself the whole day. The following itinerary starts from Armagh or Newry.

Bessbrook

This small town was founded in the mid-19th century by a Quaker industrialist, and the layout of the houses and shops later gave the Cadbury family the idea of building Bournville near Birmingham in England. Most of the buildings are made from local granite and arranged around two squares. Originally everyone here worked in the manufacturing of linen, and because of the Quaker influence no pubs were built. There is still not even a café in the town and due to an army base here the place is heavily guarded.

From Newry take the A25 west and turn right onto the B133 to Bessbrook. From Armagh take the B31 south to Newtownhamilton and turn left onto the A25 and then, before Newry, left again onto the B133.

Camlough

Camlough is only a short distance from Bessbrook but quite different in character and political allegiance, as the flying tricolours make plain. There is a fish and chip shop here and a couple of pubs serving bar food.

To get to Camlough, do not return to the B133, but leave Bessbrook from the other end that you came in and turn left immediately after the army control box. Continue down to the main road and turn right back onto the A25. Camlough is a short distance along this road.

Killevy Churches

Surrounded by beech trees, these Siamese-twin churches were built on the site of a 5th-century nunnery founded by St Monenna and plundered by the Vikings in 923. During the Middle Ages a convent of Augustinian nuns was founded, but it was dissolved in 1542; the last abbess was Alicia O'Hanlon.

The eastern church is 15th-century, while the western one is 12th-century and the massive lintel on the western door with the granite jambs may be 200 years older still. Originally the two churches were nearly a metre apart but became joined at an unknown date. To the north, the traditional site of St Monenna's grave is marked by a granite slab, and a signed walkway leads to a holy well.

Heading west out of Camlough, turn left at the crossroads, keeping the lough on the right. A junction on the road points right to the churches and left to Bernish Rock Viewpoint. The churches are five km (three miles) from Camlough.

Clonlum South Cairn

From the Killevy churches, travel south, passing after one km a sign on the left side of the road to the tomb.

Mainly of specialist interest, this tomb is on the way to the Slieve Gullion Forest Park. The stones enclose a single chamber with the big stone slabs bearing a now broken capstone.

Slieve Gullion Forest Park

From the Clonlum South Cairn continue along the road for about 1.5 km (one mile) and turn right into the B113 for the Forest Park. The coniferous forest covers the lower slopes of Slieve Gullion and a 13-km (eight-mile) drive takes in a walk to a lake. The drive emerges from the trees to picturesque views of the Ring of Gullion, a circle of small hills around Slieve Gullion.

Slieve Gullion can be climbed from the south or north. The south approach has a forest road for the first part of the journey, while the north approach is made a little easier because of a rough path all the way. On the summit there are two cairns from the early Bronze Age.

The park has an interpretive centre which is only open on Sundays from 1 to 7 pm and houses a small collection of old tools. The park itself is open from Easter to September from 10 am. Admission is £1.50 per car.

Ballymacdermot Cairn

From the Slieve Gullion Forest Park turn right at the exit, down to a crossroads and left for the road back to the churches. Turn right at the junction where the churches are, in order to return to the crossroads where the sign for Bernish Viewpoint was seen earlier. Go straight across and carry on for a couple

of km. At a junction a sign points left for the cairn.

The cairn is in an attractive position on the slopes of Ballymacdermot Mountain overlooking a plain. There are two burial chambers with sections of the roofs still intact. When the site was excavated some 30 years ago, Neolithic artefacts were found.

At the cairn the road continues three km (two miles) into Newry.

Kilnasaggart Stone & Moyry Castle

From Ballymacdermot Cairn, retrace the three km (two miles) back to the crossroads, and this time turn left for Jonesborough. At the next junction, by a post office and corner shop, turn right (signposted for Forkhill) for 1.5 km (one mile) and then left for Jonesborough at the sign. After one km turn left at the T-junction signposted for Crossmaglen and Jonesborough, and after a couple of hundred metres turn right as indicated by the sign. From here it is a short distance to another T-junction where you should leave your bicycle or car. Follow the footpath across two fields and stiles to the stone.

The 8th-century granite pillar marks the site of an early Christian cemetery on the great Slighe Miodhluachra road from Drogheda to Dunseverick on the Causeway Coast in County Antrim. The Irish inscription records a dedication by Ternohc, son of Ceran Bic. On the other side are a number of carefully inscribed crosses inside circles.

At the T-junction it is a short walk to the right and Moyry Castle, built in 1601 by Lord Mountjoy to secure the Moyry Pass (the Gap of the North). All that remains is a tower with gun- loops.

Crossmaglen

From the T-junction nearest to the Kilnasaggart Stone, retrace the 1.5 km (one mile) back to the crossroads and turn left. After a couple of hundred metres turn right, signposted for Newry. The B113 is straight ahead; take a left for Forkhill. Turn left in the village of Forkhill and carry on for about two km (1.3 miles) until an unmarked T-junction is reached. Turn right for Crossmaglen.

This small town has a fierce reputation, with more than 20 soldiers having been killed in the square alone; the 3001st victim of the Troubles was another soldier killed here in mid-1992. The town is dominated by an ugly army post. Notwithstanding, people go about their daily business as if oblivious to the helicopters and the listening devices; a visit here is educational, to say the least.

About seven km (4.5 miles) from Crossmaglen on the road to Newry there is a small **folk museum** containing a miscellany of mostly local items. It is easily missed because the sign is only visible when coming from Newry. The opening hours are irregular.

Places to Stay

In Crossmaglen there's a small B&B at 6 Newry St (☎ 0693-861630). This is the road you would have entered the town on and a double here is £19; there's no evening meal available.

On the B136 road halfway between Crossmaglen and Newtownhamilton, B&B is available at *Glenside House* (☎ 0693-861075), 22a Tullynavall Rd, Cullyhanna, for £20. On the B30 back to Newry, just after the junction with the A29, *Lima* (☎ 0693-861944) at 16 Drumalt Rd, Silverbridge, is the same price. Both these places do an evening meal for about £6 extra.

Places to Eat

In Forkhill the *Welcome Inn* on the main street, near a small antique shop, does soup and sandwiches most of the time. In Crossmaglen the *Glen* in the square is a pleasant café doing light meals like burgers and curried chips. There are also a few pubs in the square doing bar food. *Chums* is close to the Glen while *McConvillie's* is a larger place on the other side.

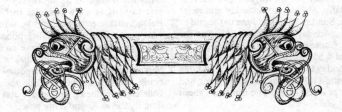

Counties Derry & Antrim

Ireland is not short of fine stretches of coast, but the Causeway Coast from Portstewart in County Derry to Ballycastle in County Antrim, and the Antrim Coast from Bally-castle to Belfast, are as magnificent as you could ask for. Most spectacular of all is the surreal landscape of the Giant's Causeway, familiar from many a postcard and calendar, and looking like some weird image from a Magritte painting.

In winter it's difficult to explore the Causeway and Antrim Coasts using public transport, but in summer there are two regular bus services.

The Antrim Coaster – No 252 – operates between Belfast and Coleraine twice daily, Monday to Saturday from early June to late September. It leaves Belfast at 9.10 am and 2 pm, and Coleraine at 9.50 am and 4.10 pm. The trip takes about four hours.

The Open-Topper runs an open-top double-decker bus (weather permitting) from the Giant's Causeway to Coleraine four times daily, Monday to Saturday and twice daily on Sunday from late June to the end of August. Monday to Saturday it leaves the Giant's Causeway at 10.15 am and 12.30, 3.05 and 4.55 pm, and Sunday at 3 and 4.55 pm. Monday to Saturday it leaves Coleraine at 9.20 and 11.30 am and 2.10 and 4 pm, and Sunday at 2 and 4 pm. The trip takes about an hour.

County Derry

The chief attraction of the county is the town of Derry itself, nestled poetically by the wide sweep of the River Foyle. There is a terribly sad contrast between the cosy feel of the town itself and the wider political and social context that speaks of injustice and bitterness. Inland from Derry the towns are dour and staunchly Protestant, evoking and living out the history of apartheid they represent. After the defeat of Hugh O'Neill in 1603, this part of the county was systematically planted with English and Scottish settlers and there is little here to attract the tourist. Back on the coast, though, the atmosphere perks up in Portstewart.

DERRY CITY

Merely saying the name of the second largest town of Northern Ireland can be a political statement. It's Derry if you're following signs from the Republic, Londonderry if you're coming from Britain or from elsewhere in Northern Ireland. Doire, the original Irish name, means 'grove of oaks', the 'London' having been appended in the 17th century after large areas of land in the area were granted to London livery companies. Most people simply refer to the town as Derry, and when it's called Londonderry there is often a conscious political affiliation.

Derry is now more peaceful than at any time since the 1960s, but there is still a razor-sharp edge to its atmosphere. It is as safe to visit as anywhere else in Northern Ireland, although it wouldn't be sensible to visit some of the nationalist pubs in the Bogside or Creggan if you have an English accent. The walled city area has a schizophrenic quality, with the Shipquay St end being lively and relaxed while the Bishop Gate end is rendered oppressive and forbidding by the RUC and army post.

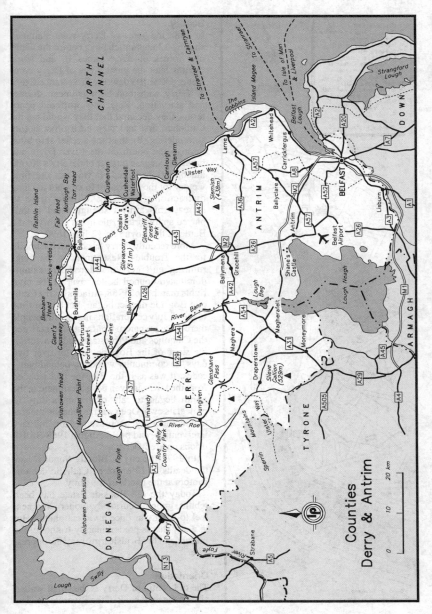

Counties
Derry & Antrim

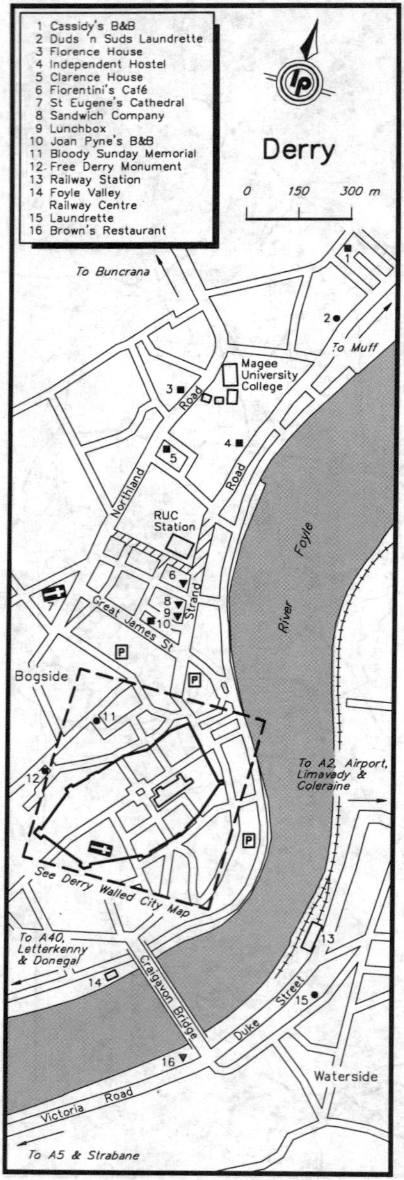

```
 1  Cassidy's B&B
 2  Duds 'n Suds Laundrette
 3  Florence House
 4  Independent Hostel
 5  Clarence House
 6  Fiorentini's Café
 7  St Eugene's Cathedral
 8  Sandwich Company
 9  Lunchbox
10  Joan Pyne's B&B
11  Bloody Sunday Memorial
12  Free Derry Monument
13  Railway Station
14  Foyle Valley
    Railway Centre
15  Laundrette
16  Brown's Restaurant
```

Derry

0   150   300 m

To Buncrana

To Muff

Magee University College

Northland Road

Strand Road

RUC Station

Great James St

Bogside

River Foyle

P

P

P

See Derry Walled City Map

To A2, Airport, Limavady & Coleraine

To A40, Letterkenny & Donegal

Craigavon Bridge

Duke Street

Waterside

To A5 & Strabane

Victoria Road

History

In 1688 the gates of Derry were slammed shut by 13 apprentice boys before the Catholic forces of King James II, and some months later the great Siege of Derry commenced. For 105 days the Protestant citizens of Derry withstood bombardment, disease and starvation. Rejecting proffered peace terms, they declared that they would eat the Catholics first and then each other before surrendering. By the time a relief ship burst through the boom on the River Foyle and broke the siege, a quarter of the city's 30,000 inhabitants had died. It was not the final victory for the Protestant forces, but the long distraction gave King William time to increase his army's strength, and it thus played an important role in his victory at the Battle of the Boyne on 12 July 1690.

More recently Derry has been a flashpoint for the Troubles. Resentment at the long-running and gerrymandered Protestant-dominated council boiled over in the civil rights marches of 1968. Attacks on the Catholic Bogside district began, but by the time of the 12 July celebrations in 1969 the people there were prepared. Confrontation between the Catholics and Protestants led to a veritable siege of the Bogside, and for over two days the community withdrew behind barricades. It was as if the Bogside had seceded from the UK, and even the government in the South began to talk of Ireland's duty to protect its own. Open warfare and disintegration could only be prevented by military intervention, and on 14 August 1968 British troops entered Derry.

In 1972 the city's 'Bloody Sunday' saw the deaths of 13 unarmed Catholic demonstrators at the hands of the army.

Today the old Bogside estate has been rebuilt, giving a curiously modern and neat feel to what was once a violent ghetto. But in a city that is predominantly Catholic, the presence of the British army remains oppressive.

Orientation

The old centre of Derry is the small walled city on the west bank of the River Foyle. The

Top: Inch Abbey, County Down (TW)
Left: St Patrick's Grave, Downpatrick, County Down (TW)
Right: Legananny Dolmen, County Down (TW)

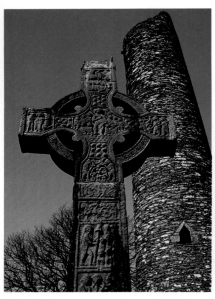

High Crosses

Catholic Bogside area is below the walls to the west while to the south is a Protestant estate known as the Fountain. Catholic and Protestant areas of Derry are clearly delineated. There's a convenient car park on Butcher St but it closes around 6 pm.

Information

There's a modern tourist office at 8 Bishop St in the old city. It houses both the Northern Ireland Tourist Board (☎ 0504-267284) and the Bord Fáilte (☎ 0504-369501). A number of new developments are planned, including a new hostel, an exhibition centre and the reopening of O'Doherty's Tower – a modern tower within the city walls that will house a history museum.

Next to the tourist office a genealogy centre (☎ 0504-269792) is open from Monday to Friday for anyone wishing to trace their ancestors. All the banks will change punts into pounds and vice versa. Outside banking hours go to the top floor of the Richmond Centre, where a bureau de change is open until 5.30 pm from Monday to Wednesday and Saturday, and until 9.30 pm on Thursday and Friday.

Bookshops

The Bookworm is a good local bookshop at 16-18 Bishop St. It stocks general books as well as material on the Troubles, including a useful little *Political Guide to Derry* for about £2. The guide has a street map of places associated with the city's political life, past and present. The Shipquay Bookshop is a smaller place on Shipquay St.

Laundry

There's a laundrette at 147 Spencer Rd near the railway station on the east bank of the river. Or on the west side visit Duds 'n' Suds at 141 Strand Rd, positively the most glamorous laundrette you'll meet anywhere in Europe – it has a pool table, electronic games and a snack bar!

City Walls

Derry may have the finest city walls in Europe, but stretches of them are run down and neglected while other parts are closed because the army uses them. Gunner's Bastion, Coward's Bastion and Water Bastion have all been demolished and the four original gates (Shipquay, Ferryquay, Bishop's and Butcher) have all been rebuilt, while three new gates (New, Ferry and Castle) have been added. The walls were built between 1613 and 1618 making Derry the last walled city to be built in Ireland. They're about eight metres (25 feet) high, nine metres (30 feet) thick, and go around the old city for a length of 1.5 km (one mile). Derry's sobriquet, the Maiden City, derives from the fact that the city walls have never been breached.

The south-west end, overlooking the cathedral on the inside and the Bogside to the north-west, is wired up and provides an army lookout point for the Bogside. Behind the walls that run beside the cathedral is the Fountain estate, a fenced and battered area that suggests the Protestants there have a lot in common with their Catholic neighbours.

An excellent overview of the Bogside and its defiant murals can be had by going up on to the city walls between Butcher Gate and the army post. There you will also see behind you in Society St the paint-spattered and well-defended Apprentice Boys' Hall. Cannons, relics of the siege of 1689, still point out over the Bogside.

St Columb's Cathedral

St Columb's Cathedral dates from 1628 and stands within the walls of the old city. It has the austerity of many of the other Church of Ireland cathedrals, with dark carved wood pews, an open timbered roof resting on the carved heads of past bishops, and some gruesome skull-and-crossbone wall tablets on the north aisle. Behind the altar is a cross of nails donated by Coventry Cathedral. The Bishop's throne is unusually placed in the nave; its style of beautifully carved 18th-century mahogany is known as Chinese Chippendale.

In the porch of the cathedral is a mortar

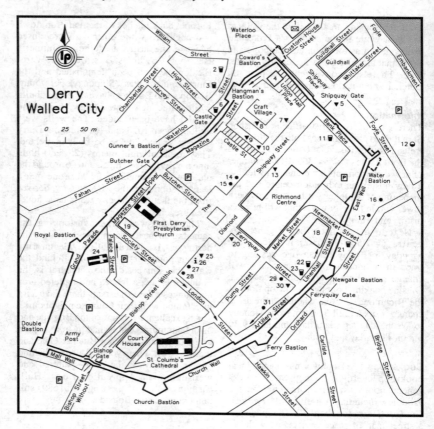

Derry Walled City

shell lobbed into the city during the siege by the Jacobites, which carried the terms of surrender. In the Chapter House, now designated a museum, are some bits of flag, silverware and other paraphernalia hardly worth the 50p you are supposed to put into the honesty box outside as an entrance fee.

Built in Perpendicular style with an embattled exterior, the cathedral now sits rather forlornly surrounded by the barbed wire and surveillance cameras of a more recent siege. Walk around the building to admire the architecture and watch the video cameras watching you.

Guildhall

The fine Guildhall was originally built in 1890 and rebuilt after a fire in 1908. As the seat of the old Londonderry Corporation, which institutionalised discrimination against Catholics in the areas of housing and employment, it incurred the wrath of nationalists and the building was bombed by the IRA in 1972. One of the convicted bombers was elected to the new council in 1985!

It's just outside the city walls and is noted for its wonderful stained-glass windows. Those on the stairs commemorate the various London livery companies that played so divisive a role in the city's development. It is open from 9 am to 5 pm, Monday to Friday.

St Eugene's Cathedral
This Catholic cathedral was dedicated to St Eugene in 1873 by Bishop Keely, and the handsome east window is a memorial to the bishop. It may serve as a focal point for a walk through the Bogside.

Bogside & the Free Derry Monument
As you step out of Butcher's Gate, the Bogside comes into view, and down on the left is the famous 'You Are Now Entering Free Derry' monument. This was once the end wall of a row of old houses; the area has been rebuilt with modern low-level flats, and is now traversed by a dual carriageway. During the early 1970s, until Operation Motorman by the army in July 1972 smashed the barricades, this was a no-go area as far as the military authorities were concerned. It took 5000 soldiers with Chieftain tanks to bring down the barriers. The monument, with its much repainted slogan, remains as a defiant response to the army watchtowers that continue to look down on the Bogside.

Bloody Sunday Memorial
On Sunday, 30 January 1972, some 20,000 civilians marched through Derry in protest at the policy of internment without trial. It now seems clear that the 1st Batallion of the Parachute Regiment opened fire on the unarmed marchers. By the end of the day 13 unarmed people were dead, some shot through the back, and a 14th subsequently died of his injuries. None of those who fired the 108 bullets, or those who gave the order to fire, were ever brought to trial or even disciplined. The subsequent enquiry was a whitewash.

To reach the monument leave the walled city by Butcher Gate; it's a little to the right down near the roadside.

Foyle Valley Railway Centre
This is just outside the walled city by the bridge and is open from April to September, Tuesday to Saturday from 10 am to 5 pm, Sunday 2 to 6 pm. Admission is £1.25 (children 75p). The centre was once the junction of four railway lines and as well as telling the story of the railways there is a 20-minute excursion train driven by a diesel engine (not included in the admission charge).

Organised Tours
Between June and September a walking tour departs from the tourist office at 10.30 am and 2.30 pm, Monday to Friday. It costs £1.50 (children & students 75p) and lasts

about one hour. Every Wednesday during July and August there is also a bus tour of the city, departing from the tourist office at 2 pm, lasting over two hours and costing £2.50 (children £1.50).

Places to Stay

Hostels YHANI may have temporary *youth hostel* accommodation at 17 Crawford Square for £5.95 but this needs confirmation (☎ 0504-267829 or the Belfast office 0232-324733). There is a small *independent hostel* (☎ 0504-370011) at 29 Aberfoyle Terrace, Strand Rd, just north of the centre and past the RUC headquarters, with beds at £6.50. It's marked with a discreet 'H' over the door.

The *Muff Hostel* (☎ 077-84188) costs IR£5 a night and is eight km (five miles) from Derry, across the border in Muff, County Donegal. Lough Swilly buses run there regularly for £1.10.

In summer you may be able to stay at *Magee University* (☎ 0504-265621) on Northland Rd, at £13.75/19.25 for singles/doubles.

B&Bs *Joan Pyne* (☎ 0504-269691) at 36 Great James St is within walking distance of the bus station. Farther north, at 15 Northland St, there is the slightly officious (but very well run) *Clarence House* (☎ 0504-265342). Farther along at No 16, *Florence House* (☎ 0504-26 8093) is slightly less expensive at £11 per person. Farther north again at 86 Duncreggan Rd, *Mrs Cassidy* (☎ 0504-268943) charges £10.

Farmhouse accommodation costs about the same as B&B and there are quite a few places out at Eglinton on the A2 to Limavady. *Mrs Boggs* (☎ 0504-810239) and *Mrs Montgomery* (☎ 0504-810422) are both £20 for a double. On the other side of town the cosy *Tully Farm* (☎ 0504-42832) at 109 Victoria Rd, New Buildings, is about eight km (five miles) along the A5 road and is excellent value at £22 for a double. The tourist office has a complete list and will make bookings.

Hotels Two top hotels, at around £80 a double, can be found south of the city and on the east side of the river. The *Beech Hill Country House Hotel* (☎ 0504-49279) is at 32 Ardmore Rd, Ardmore, while the *Everglades Hotel* (☎ 0504-46722) is closer in on Prehen Rd, just off the A5 (Victoria Rd).

Three other hotels are also on the east side of the river but north of the city. The *Broomhill* (☎ 0504-47995) is £68 and is easy to find on the Limavady Rd. A little farther out the *White Horse Inn* (☎ 0504-860606) is at 86 Clooney Rd and costs £40 a room. Nearby and beside the Caw Roundabout at 14 Cloney Rd, the circular *Waterfoot Hotel* (☎ 0504-45500) has doubles including breakfast for £60.

Places to Eat

Cafés & Fast Food In the walled city there is plenty of choice around Shipquay St. The *Beehive Restaurant* in the Richmond shopping centre is open until midnight Wednesday to Saturday, and serves inexpensive meals throughout the day for around £3. Across the road the *Galley Restaurant* is similar. A little farther down Shipquay St, *Wheeler's* is a fast-food specialist. There are a couple of *Open Oven* sandwich places, one just outside the city walls across from the Guildhall, the other just inside Ferryquay Gate.

More upmarket is the *Boston Tea Party* in the Čraft Village off Shipquay St, but it is only open until 5.30 pm. *Austin's* Department Store on the Diamond has a coffee shop with a good selection of cakes and sandwiches and fine views over the city centre. Towards Bishop Gate, *Malibu* does interesting lunch specials.

Outside the city walls on Strand St, inexpensive places include *Fiorentini's* and the *Sandwich Company* while the *Lunchbox* serves breakfast for just 99p and a three-course lunch for just £2.

Pub Food & Restaurants Pub food is available at the *Anchor Inn* and the *Linen Hall* by Ferryquay Gate, just down from the Diamond. The *Dungloe* on Waterloo St is a pleasant place with photographs of the old Bogside on the walls.

Thran Maggie's in the Craft Village off Shipquay St is one of the few places to dine in the walled city. On Victoria Rd, just across the bridge from the centre, *Brown's* is pleasantly trendy with reasonable food at only moderately expensive prices. Continue on Victoria Rd – it's the A5 – four km to the big and expensive *Bell's Restaurant*. Underneath it is *Johnny B's* where good, pub-style food is great value from £4 for main courses.

More expensive meals can be enjoyed at the *Seminole* restaurant at the Everglades Hotel (dinner for £11.50) or at the *Beech Hill Country House* (dinner for £30).

Entertainment

The liveliest pubs are those along Waterloo St, like the *Gweedore*, which hosts regular music and quiz functions, the *Dungloe* and the *Castle Bar*. Be careful if you're out drinking at night; many of these are strong nationalist pubs. The *Metro Bar* on Bank St, just inside the walls, is very popular. Others include the *Anchor Inn* and the *Linen Hall* by Ferryquay Gate and *Badger's Place* on the corner of on Newmarket and Orchard Sts just outside the walls. *Bridie's Cottage* in the Craft Village holds music and dance sessions.

Classical music shows are often scheduled during the summer months for performance at *Magee University* or the *Guildhall*. The tourist office will have the details. The *Orchard Gallery* (☎ 0504-262567/260516) in Orchard St has regular exhibitions, concerts and drama. Theatrical events take place regularly in summer at the *Playhouse* in Artillery St, the *Rialto Entertainment Centre* nearby in Linenhall St and *St Columb's Hall* in Orchard St.

Things to Buy

Derry Craft Village is tucked away in one of the corner blocks of the walled city. It contains a number of craft shops selling Derry crystal (with a mail service), handwoven cloth and other items crafted by local people. Most of the shops are open Monday to Saturday from 9.30 am to 5.30 pm and some open on Sunday during the summer.

Close to the Diamond in Shipquay St, the Donegal Shop sells garments, tweeds and souvenirs. Austin's on the corner in the Diamond is also worth a look.

Getting There & Away

There's a USIT travel office on Ferryquay St.

Air Eglington Airport (☎ 0504-810784) has daily flights with Loganair (☎ 0504-810784), Scotland's airline, direct to Glasgow (£102 return) and Manchester (£109 return).

Train Northern Ireland Railways have a half dozen daily Belfast-Derry services (only two on Sundays) taking about three hours. The earliest train for Portrush departs at 6.20 am (11.05 on Sunday), the last one at 7 pm. The railway station (☎ 0504-42228) is on the east side of the River Foyle.

Bus Ulsterbus services between Belfast and Derry operate with similar frequency. Bus No 212, the Maiden City Flyer, is the fastest, followed by bus No 272 that goes via Omagh.

A bus to Portstewart and Portrush leaves at 2.15 pm on Thursday and Sunday for most of June, and on Thursday, Friday and Saturday in most of July and August.

Each day at 8.20 am a bus leaves Derry for Cork, arriving at 7.15 pm. The Cork bus leaves at 9.15 am and arrives in Derry at 8.30 pm. Bus Éireann operates a Derry-Galway service three times daily, via Donegal and Sligo.

Lough Swilly buses (☎ 0504-262017) connect with County Donegal, across the border. During the summer a bus leaves for Buncrana at 7.05 and 8 pm, and for Malin Head at 11 am and 4.15 pm Monday to Friday. On Sunday the Derry-Buncrana bus leaves at 1 and 6.15 pm. There is also a very useful Derry to Dungloe service, via Letterkenny and Dunfanaghy.

Feda O'Donnell's private buses (☎ 075-48114 & 091-61656) include a service from

Linen

The manufacture of linen, probably the earliest textile made from plants, was once of vital significance to the Ulster economy. Linen was made in ancient Egypt and introduced into Britain by the Romans. The real boost to linen-making in Ulster, though, came with the arrival of Huguenot weavers seeking sanctuary in the late 17th century.

The flax plant was sown in the north of Ireland from March to May and harvested in mid-August. The first stage in the harvesting was the pulling of the flax plants and bundling them into stacks for open-air drying. The seeds were removed and crushed for linseed oil or kept for the following year's planting. The second stage was a messy and smelly one, entailing the soaking of the bundles of flax in freshwater ponds, or 'lint holes', for up to two weeks. This process of 'retting' softened the outer stem and the 'scutching' could begin.

Scutching separated the dried flax stem; with the introduction of water wheels in the 18th century, large wooden blades pounded and loosened the flax. The fibres were then ready for spinning on a wheel before being woven into lengths of cloth.

The next stage was the bleaching, carried out in the open air after the cloth had been soaked in water for hours. Huge lengths of the cloth were stretched out across fields and left in the sunlight. The moisture in the material reacted with the sunlight to produce hydrogen peroxide which bleached the cloth. The final stage involved the hammering of the cloth by wooden hammers, or beetles, which smoothed out the material and made it ready for selling to the public. A beetling mill can be visited outside of Cookstown in County Tyrone.

Flax growing died out in the North towards the end of the 19th century but was reborn during WW I with the demand for parachute material. There was a similar resurgence during WW II, but most of the linen now purchased is made in Scandinavia with the aid of chemicals. In recent years there has been an attempt to reintroduce flax growing in Ulster, and the occasional field of blue flax flowers may be spotted. ■

Letterkenny to Glasgow via Derry. It leaves from the bus station at 11 am, reaches Larne at 1 pm and Glasgow around 8 pm. The coach from Glasgow leaves at 8 am from the Citizen Theatre in Garbles St (☎ 041-631 3696) and reaches Derry around 4 pm.

The bus station (☎ 0504-262261) is just outside the city walls, on Foyle St near the Guildhall.

Getting Around

Auto Cabs (☎ 0504-45100), Central Taxis (☎ 0504-261911) and Quick Cabs (☎ 0504-260515) operate from the city centre, and will go to all areas.

COLERAINE

Coleraine is not a particularly attractive place, and the town centre is depressingly un-Irish; you could be in any English pedestrianised shopping area. But Coleraine is on the main bus and railway lines and you could well find yourself here waiting for a connection. There are plenty of shops catering to the largely Protestant population, who first arrived in 1613 when the land was given by James I to loyal Londoners. Just north of town, the University of Ulster was established in 1968.

Information

The tourist office (☎ 0265-44723) is near the railway station on Railway Rd and next to the leisure centre. It's open 10 am to 1 pm and 1.30 to 5 pm Monday to Friday, closing at 4 pm on Saturday.

Mountsandel Mount

The age and purpose of this large oval mound is something of a mystery. It may have been an early Christian stronghold or a later Anglo-Norman fortification. Just to the north-east of the mound, a Mesolithic site dating back to the 7th millennium BC has been excavated; post-holes, hearths and pits bear testimony to the early inhabitants of the area.

The site is signposted from the Lodge Rd roundabout. At the T-junction after the roundabout turn right. There's parking at the heavily fortified courthouse on the right; from there cross over the road where a sign points the way. From here it is a 15-minute walk through the forest. Bicycles are not allowed.

Places to Stay
In the *Lodge Hotel* (☎ 0265-44848), on Lodge Rd which joins Railway Rd, doubles are £48. You can get a bed for £10 at the *University* (☎ 0265-44141) but it's often full and cannot be relied on. B&Bs are out of town. *Alan Badger* (☎ 02657-31816) is off the B17 to Bushmills and charges £25 for a double. *Mrs King* (☎ 0265-42982) is off the A54, five km (three miles) south of town; the house is 17th-century and is worth the £15 per person.

Grandest of all is *Blackheath House* (☎ 0265-868433), built as the home of an eccentric 18th-century bishop of Derry, who would surely have approved of the indoor swimming pool. The house is 13 km (eight miles) south of Coleraine at 112 Killeague Rd, Blackhill, and costs £60 for two.

Places to Eat
There are plenty of eating places around the pedestrianised precinct. *Twenty Two* is opposite Woolworths and has hearty lunches for around £3. *Brook's Wine Bar*, near the car park at the back of Dunne's store just off the main shopping area, has burgers and steaks. *Blackheath House* is open to nonresidents for dinner, which costs £18. It's closed on Sunday and Monday.

Getting There & Away
The Belfast-Derry trains stop at Coleraine and there is a branch line to Portrush. The Ulsterbus Atlantic Express bus No 218 travels between Portrush, Portstewart and Belfast via Coleraine and Antrim. In summer, the Antrim Coaster travels between Coleraine and Belfast. Bus No 234 runs to Derry.

LIMAVADY
The town's claim to fame is 51 Main St where a plaque records that Jane Ross (1810-

79) lived. Jane Ross heard a travelling fiddler playing a song which she noted down – *Danny Boy*, probably the most famous Irish song of all.

Information
The tourist office (☎ 05047-22226) is in the council offices in Connell St and open 9 am to 12.30 pm and 1.30 to 5 pm.

Roe Valley Country Park
The park stretches for five km (three miles) either side of the River Roe, just south of Limavady. The area is associated with the O'Cahans, who ruled the valley until the Plantations. The 17th-century settlers saw the flax-growing potential of the damp river valley and the area became an important linen manufacturing centre. In the visitors' centre there are some excellent old photographs of the flax industry and around the park are relics of that time. The weaving shed now houses a small museum near the main entrance. The scutch mill, where the flax was pounded, is a 45-minute walk away, along the river, past two watch towers that were built to guard the linen when it was spread out in the fields for bleaching.

Flax Plant

The park also contains Ulster's first domestic hydro-electric power station, opened in 1896. The plant is open to visitors, as are all the industrial relics, free of charge between 9 am and 4 pm. The park itself is always accessible and the visitors' centre and café stay open till 9 pm during July and August.

The park is clearly marked off the B68 road between Limavady and Dungiven. Bus No 146 from Limavady to Dungiven will drop you on the main road, but there is no weekend service.

Places to Stay

Camping is at the *Roe Valley Country Park* (☎ 05047-22074), just off the B68 to Dungiven.

The only hotel is the *Gorteen House Hotel* (☎ 05047-22333 on Roe Mill Rd, £40 a double. If you're coming in from Derry on the A2 turn right just after crossing the bridge and follow Roe Mill Rd down until it turns to the left past a cemetery and the hotel is off to the right.

The *Alexander Arms* (☎ 05047-63443) on Main St, just up from Connell St and the tourist office, offers B&B for £16/27.

Places to Eat

The *Alexander Arms* on Main St is OK for bar food and there's a three-course lunch for £4. *Gentry's*, on the same street, has an Indian lunch for the same price and pizzas are also available.

Getting There & Away

Two buses travel between Coleraine and Limavady, Nos 134 and 234. Bus No 143 runs to Derry almost hourly. There is no direct bus to Belfast but connections can be made at Coleraine or Dungiven.

DUNGIVEN

Dungiven's only attractions are nearby ecclesiastical sites and one of the North's very few independent hostels. This could make it a better base than Limavady if you're travelling between Belfast and Derry.

Dungiven Priory

The remains of this Augustinian priory date back to the 12th century, when they replaced a pre-Norman monastery. The church contains the ornate tomb of Cooey-na-Gal, a chieftain of the O'Cahans who died in 1385. On the front of the tomb are figures of six kilted gallowglasses, mercenaries from Scotland hired by Cooey O'Cahan as minders and earning him the nickname na-Gal (of the foreigners). In the 17th century another foreigner, Sir Edward Doddington, who built the walls of Derry, remodelled the priory and an adjacent small castle built by the O'Cahans. He constructed a private dwelling of which only the foundations remain.

Nearby is a bullaun, a hollowed stone originally used by the monks for grinding grain but now collecting rainwater and used by people seeking cures for illnesses. The priory is signposted off the A6 road to Antrim.

Maghera Old Church

The church site goes back to a 6th-century monastery that was plundered by the Vikings in 832. The nave of the present ruins is 10th-century while the Romanesque door on the west side is two centuries younger. There are interesting motifs on the door jambs, and the lintel carries a fine Crucifixion scene that is every bit as good as the carvings on the celebrated high crosses. In the churchyard there is an unmistakable pillar stone, carved with a ringed cross, which is said to mark the grave of the 6th-century founder, St Lurach.

The town of Maghera is on the A6 Derry to Belfast road, and the best approach to the town is from Dungiven via the Glenshane Pass. Rising to 555 metres (1818 feet) the road through the Sperrin Mountains offers dramatic views. In town turn right at the north end of the main street into Bank Square and then left to the car park.

Places to Stay

The *Flax Mill Hostel*, Mill Lane, Derrylane, Dungiven, has no electricity and, as yet, no telephone. It costs £4.50 a night or £2 to camp. The hostel is five km (three miles) from Dungiven: take the A6 to Derry and after crossing the river take the first road on the right, signposted for Limavady and the Roe Valley Country Park. Then take the third road on the left, Altmover Rd, and the hostel is on the first lane on the left. The German-run hostel is sometimes full with groups from Germany but every effort is made to accommodate other travellers.

Mrs McMaken (☎ 05047-41346), 132 Main St, does B&B for £18 a double.

Places to Eat

The *Cosy Inn* and *Castle Inn* both do pub food, but only the latter serves food on Sunday. *Carraig Rua* at 40 Main St serves evening meals in the £10 to £15 range. If you're travelling to Maghera on the A6, *Ponderosa* at the top of the Glenshane Pass does steaks and seafood.

Getting There & Away

Express bus No 212 between Derry and Belfast operates nine times daily (three times on Sunday) and stops on Main St in Dungiven. Ulsterbus No 146 travels between Limavady and Dungiven.

PLANTATION TOWNS

The rest of inland Derry, to the south of Dungiven, is strong Protestant territory made up of towns planned and created thanks to the London companies with gracious thanks to King William of Orange for the grants of land. In Draperstown, Magherafelt and Móneymore the kerbstones are often painted red, white and blue, and for weeks after 12 July, celebrating the victory of King Billy over the Catholics, flags and banners proclaim the diehard patriotism of the locals.

Springhill

An interesting example of early Plantation architecture is to be found at Springhill, 1.5 km south of Moneymore on the B18. The original house was built about 1695 by the Conynghams who came here from Scotland after acquiring the 120-hectare (300-acre) Springhill estate. It was built at the same time

as Hezlett House near Portstewart, but has little in common with that more humble abode. The central block has a high pitched roof, enlarged by the addition of the wings in the 18th century which give a more solid air of Baroque assurance to the house. The barn is also late 17th-century and was built to accommodate a warning bell. The Williamite war was over but then, as now, a certain siege mentality remained.

Inside the house is some old oak furniture, a library, a collection of weapons and many costumes. The house (☎ 06487-48210) is open 2 to 6 pm on weekend from April to September and daily during July and August. Admission is £1.80 (children 90p).

PORTSTEWART

When the English novelist Thackeray visited Portstewart in 1842, he noted the 'air of comfort and neatness'; 150 years later this still rings true and the place has an air of superiority that distinguishes it from the more proletarian Portrush, only six km (four miles) farther down the coast in County Antrim.

A day could easily be passed visiting the excellent beaches in the vicinity, and the town makes a convenient base for the Giant's Causeway and other attractions along this stretch of coastline.

Orientation & Information

Portstewart consists of one long promenade. To the east it heads along the coast to Ballycastle, and to the west it leads to a fine beach. If you're coming from Derry the place is wonderfully relaxed; there is no control zone and cars can be left unattended anywhere. The attractions that lie farther west can only be reached in a roundabout manner by going inland to Coleraine and then north again up the other side of a narrow inlet.

In May the North-West 200 motorcycle race is run on a road circuit between Portrush, Portstewart and Coleraine. This classic race is one of the last to be run on closed public roads anywhere in Europe; most such events are now considered too dangerous. It attracts up to 70,000 spectators.

The tourist office (☎ 0265-832286) is in the town hall at the western end of town and is open 10 am to 4 pm, Monday to Saturday in July and August.

Portstewart Strand

The beach is west of town, easily reached by turning right at the roundabout past the Edgewater Hotel. The firm sand can accommodate over 1000 cars and despite the fact that the Strand is a National Trust site, vehicles are allowed to use it. If someone is on duty there's a £2 charge to take cars on the beach.

Places to Stay

Hostel The *Causeway Coast Hostel* (☎ 0265-833789) is at the western end of town at 4 Victoria Terrace, Atlantic Circle, and costs £5 in dorms, £6 in private rooms.

Camping Camp sites are plentiful along the coast road. *Carrick Dhu Caravan Park* (☎ 0265-823712) is on Ballyreagh Rd, while the *Golf Links Hotel Caravan Park* (☎ 0265-823539) and *Margoth Caravan Park* (☎ 0265-822531) are both on Dunluce Rd. Pitching a tent for one night is around £6 at all three. There is also the *Portrush Caravan Park* (☎ 0265-823537). The *Benone Tourist Complex* (☎ 05047-50555) and the larger *Golden Sands Caravan Park* (☎ 05047-50324) are both at Benone Beach.

B&Bs B&Bs are easy to find around Atlantic Circle at the eastern end of town. *Bendigo* (☎ 0265-833697) at No 11 costs £24 for a double, while at No 5 *Salem* (☎ 0265-834584) costs £20 and also does dinner for £5. At 23 The Promenade, *Craigmore* (☎ 0265- 832120) costs £25 for a double plus £6 each for dinner. *Marie's* at No 75 (☎ 0265-832067) is the same price.

Hotels The *Edgewater* (☎ 0265-833314) at the end of Strand Rd is a pleasant hotel with doubles for £80. The *Windsor* (☎ 0265-832523) on the Promenade and the *Sea Splash* (☎ 0265-832688) on Kinora Terrace are both £38 for a double.

Self-Catering The cottages at *Rock Castle* (☎ 0265-832277) overlook Portstewart Strand and vary from £120 a week for a one-bedroom unit in the low season to £400 for a two-bedroom unit in the high season.

Places to Eat

Compared to Portrush, there is a dearth of eating places in Portstewart. *Morelli's* on the Promenade is popular, often full, and usually has a vegetarian special for around £4. Their ice-cream parlour is one of the best in the North.

A takeaway place a few doors down does surprisingly tasty and inexpensive pizzas. Dinner costs around £7 in the *Windsor Hotel* restaurant on the Promenade. The *Edgewater Hotel* is only a little more expensive, but the bar and restaurant have good views of the broad beach. The *York Bar* in Station Rd serves decent food. The *Peppercorn* on the Promenade has a mixed menu of Indian and European dishes and is open daily for lunch but only on Friday and Saturday for dinner.

Heading out of town *Some Plaice Else* (☎ 0265-824945) is a large seafood restaurant on the sea side of the coast road between Portstewart and Portrush.

Getting There & Away

Bus See the introduction to this chapter for information on the summertime Antrim Coaster and Open Topper bus services along the coast. Departures are from the Promenade bus stop in Portstewart.

Ulsterbus No 218 leaves Portstewart for Belfast eight times daily on weekdays, four times on Saturday, twice on Sunday. Stops include Coleraine, Ballymoney and Antrim.

Bus No 243 leaves for Derry at 8.25 am, arriving at 9.25 am Thursday and Sunday fror most of June. For most of July and August it leaves on Thursday, Friday, Saturday and Sunday. It leaves Derry at 2.15 pm.

Train The nearest station is at Portrush, which connects with the Derry-Belfast train at Coleraine. See the Portrush section for details.

AROUND PORTSTEWART

To reach the attractions west of Portstewart take the A2 from Coleraine and head west.

Hezlett House, Castlerock

The house was built in the late 17th century, a single-storey thatched cottage noted for its cruck truss roof gables of stone and turf strengthened with wooden crucks or crutches. The interior decoration is Victorian. The house is owned by the National Trust and open daily (except Tuesday) at Easter and during July and August, from 1 to 5 pm. From April to June and September it's open the same hours Saturday and Sunday only. Admission is £1.20 (children 60p) and there is a car park across the road.

The house is eight km (five miles) west of Coleraine at Liffock on the A2.

Mussenden Temple & Downhill

An eccentric and very rich bishop of Derry was also the earl of Bristol, and his fine home at Downhill was built in 1722. It was burnt down in 1851, rebuilt in 1870 and abandoned after WW II. The roof was taken down for its scrap value and the remains of the small castellated building now stand forlornly in a field.

The major attraction, a short walk from the house, is the curious little Mussenden Temple, perched right on the cliff edge and built by the energetic bishop either to house his library or his mistress – opinions differ! He conducted an affair with the mistress of Frederick William II of Prussia well into his old age.

It is a pleasant walk to the temple and the reward is fine views of the sand at Portstewart and Magilligan, the railway line below disappearing into a tunnel, and the hills of Donegal across the water. The beach immediately below is where the bishop set his own clergy to race on horseback, rewarding the winners by appointing them to the more lucrative parishes. In the distance shadowy outlines of the Scottish mountains are usually visible. The bishop inscribed a quotation from Lucretius on a frieze:

It is pleasant to see from the safe shore
The pitching of ships and hear the storm's roar.

– and it's thoroughly appropriate on a windy day.

The site is about 20 km (13 miles) west of Portstewart by road, much closer as the crow flies. It is now owned by the National Trust but there is no admission charge. The temple is open April, May, June and September on Saturday and Sunday from 12 noon to 6 pm. July, August and Easter it is open daily the same hours.

Bar food is available at the nearby *Downhill Inn* which opens its restaurant at 6 pm. Immediately past the Downhill Inn, Bishop's Rd forks up to the left, leading over the mountains to Limavady, with terrific views from Gortmore picnic area.

Benone/Magilligan Beach

Some 10 km (six miles) in length and hundreds of metres wide at low tide, this Blue Flag beach – called both Benone and Magilligan – is worth a visit. It sweeps out to Magilligan Point where a Martello tower stands and from where sailplanes and hanggliders can be seen riding the wind. Look for the sign to the Benone Tourist Complex on the A2 and phone ☎ 05047-62105 for information.

County Antrim

Just east of Ballycastle the distinctive cliffs of Fair Head mark the point where the coast turns southwards and the Antrim coast makes its way down to Larne before turning inland for Carrickfergus and Belfast Lough. This coastal strip is known as the Glens of Antrim after the series of valleys which cut across the range of hills between Ballycastle and Larne.

The A2 road runs along the coast for most of the way and it's an exciting route for cyclists. The short run between Waterfoot and Carnlough is particularly fine.

Inland Antrim is perhaps the least interesting part of Northern Ireland, and Antrim Town has little to recommend it.

To the south of nearby Lisburn the infamous Long Kesh prison was the scene of the hunger strikes in 1981 which led to the deaths of 10 men who were campaigning for the right to be recognised as political prisoners. The Thatcher government refused to negotiate and allowed them to die one by one.

Most visitors pass along Antrim's coast and there is little here to remind one of the Troubles. The scenery is delightful all the way and everyone is drawn towards a coastline that bears the name of the distinguished Giant's Causeway.

PORTRUSH

This is a busy little resort that only comes alive in the summer. It attracts few foreign tourists, being orientated to families from other parts of the North.

Information

The tourist office (☎ 0265-823333) in the town hall opens from Easter to September from 9 am to 8 pm, Monday to Saturday, and 12 noon to 5 pm on Sunday. The office is due to move to the Gateway Centre next to the bus station.

Activities

Boat trips (☎ 0267-823369 or contact the tourist office) depart regularly in the summer for cruising or fishing and cost about £10 including the hire of rods. Waterworld (☎ 0265-822001) at the harbour is a major draw for children, while Traks (☎ 0265-822112) disco is equally popular with adults.

For pony trekking contact the Ballywillan Riding Centre (☎ 0265-823372), half a mile from the town centre on Ballywillan Rd, or Maddybenny Farm (☎ 0265-823603 after 6 pm).

Places to Stay

There is no hostel and the camp sites close to Portrush are listed under Portstewart. Double rooms at *Magherabuoy House* (☎ 0265-823507) are £65 while at the *Eglinton Hotel* (☎ 0265-822371) they are £50. The *Langholm Hotel* (☎ 0265-822293) is good value at £38.

B&Bs can easily fill up during the summer months and it's advisable to book in advance through the tourist office. Guesthouses with sea views on Landsdowne Crescent include *Clarement* (☎ 0265-822397) and *Belvedere* (☎ 0265-822771) with doubles at £36 in the high season. The *Clarence* (☎ 0265-823575) at 7 Bath Terrace also overlooks the sea and is less expensive.

Places to Eat

Rowland's at 92 Main St, the end away from the town hall, does reasonable Italian-style dishes for around £5. Around the corner from here *Skerries Pantry* is OK for snacks. Cafés and fast-food places jostle with amusement arcades along Main St, and the hotels are reliable places for a more substantial repast. *Magherabuoy House* does a three-course lunch from £5, and generous helpings make the Sunday lunch good value at £7.50.

Ramore (☎ 0265-823444) is a pricey wine bar and restaurant with a good reputation. The wine bar opens for two hours at lunch time and then from 5 pm; the restaurant doesn't open until 7 pm. *Dionysus* on Eglinton St is open daily and serves Greek and European dishes from £10.

Getting There & Away

Bus See the introduction to this chapter for information on the summertime Antrim Coaster and Open Topper bus services along the coast.

Ulsterbus No 218 leaves daily from Portrush for Belfast, travelling inland via Portstewart, Coleraine, Ballymoney, Ballymena and Antrim.

The bus station is on Dunluce Ave near the railway station.

Train Portrush is served by train from Coleraine roughly every hour for the 13-minute journey. The earliest train leaves Coleraine at 7 am, the latest at 10.14 pm; from Portrush the times are 6.45 am and 10.30 pm respectively. At Coleraine connections can be made

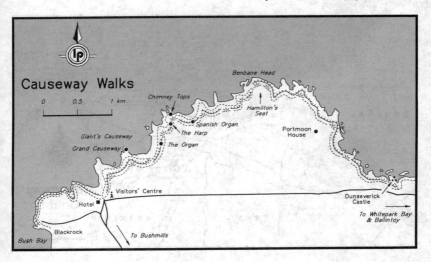

for Belfast or Derry. Travelling to Dublin and changing at Coleraine and Belfast would take nearly five hours. Contact Portrush Station (☎ 0265-822395) for more details.

Getting Around

Bikes can be hired from Causeway Coast Cycles (☎ 0265-824334) at 6 Bath St. For taxis call J O'Neil (☎ 0265-823421) at 3 Coleraine Rd.

THE GIANT'S CAUSEWAY

The chances are you've seen pictures of the North's No 1 tourist attraction long before getting here. A bishop of Derry, who became interested in geology after seeing Vesuvius erupt, commissioned the paintings of the site that led to its fame. Today, school geography books still regard its inclusion as mandatory. The hexagonal basalt columns are impressive, and do look as if a giant might have playfully tipped out all 37,000 of them, if you count the ones under the water. According to legend the giant in question, Finn McCool, fancied some stepping stones to the Scottish island of Staffa where, indeed, similar rock formations are to be found.

The modern story is that red-hot lava erupted from an underground fissure and crystallised some 60 million years ago into the shapes that we see today.

The phenomenon is clearly explained in the visitors' centre, including the surprising fact that the Causeway only came to general notice as late as 1740. The audiovisual section, however, is more of an animated tourist brochure, and is hardly worth the charge of £1.10 (children 60p). The static exhibition can be seen for 50p.

It costs nothing to make the pleasant 1.5-km (one-mile) pilgrimage to the actual site. Minibuses with wheelchair access ply the route regularly. Different areas of the rock formations have their own names but these seem to have been invented by the many Victorian guides who made a summer living by escorting the tourists who came on an electric tram from Coleraine.

Past the main spill of columns, the pathway brings into view a formation that does deserve its own name. Chimney Tops was identified by ships of the Spanish Armada in 1588 as part of Dunluce Castle, and consequently fired upon.

Two well-established footpaths at different levels start from just outside the visitors'

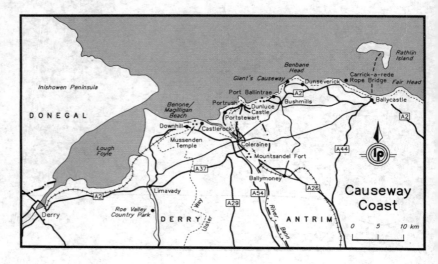

centre, allowing a circular walk to Benbane Head and back. From the clifftop at Hamilton's Seat, there is one of the best views of the causeway and headlands to the west, including Malin Head and Inishowen. The complete circular walk is eight km (five miles) and takes about two hours.

If you want to go farther, the path continues around Benbane Head, and the sandy beach of Whitepark Bay comes into view. On the right is Portmoon House. The headlands become lower and lower until the path reaches the main road near Dunseverick Castle. The walk from the visitors' centre to the castle and back is around 15 km (nine miles).

From below the remains of the castle there is a path that goes up and round to the east, ending at Ballintoy. It crosses a number of small wooden bridges before reaching the beach of White Park. There is a YHANI hostel at Ballintoy, so the whole 16-km (10-mile) journey from the Giant's Causeway could be done in one day.

These walks follow the North Antrim Cliff Path, which actually begins west of the visitors' centre at Blackrock, a short walk of about 2.5 km (1.5 miles).

A useful 40p map from the visitors' centre sets out the walks, including the various rock formations that can be seen along the way.

The Giant's Causeway can be visited free of charge any time but the car park costs £1.50. The visitors' centre includes a café – with hexagonal chairs! It is open seven days a week from 15 March to the end of October. From May it's open from 11 am to 5 pm, and in June half an hour later. In July and August it's open 10 am to 7 pm, and September and October 11 am to 5 pm Monday to Friday, 10.30 am to 5.30 Saturday and Sunday.

Next to the visitors' centre, and mainly of interest to children, the Causeway School Museum opens July and August from 10 am to 4 pm, 75p (children 50p, family £2).

Getting There & Away

The B146 Causeway to Dunseverick road runs parallel to the A2 but closer to the coast and can be joined east of Bushmills or west of Ballycastle and the Carrick-a-rede rope bridge.

See the introduction to this chapter for information on the summertime Antrim Coaster and Open Topper bus services along the coast.

AROUND THE CAUSEWAY
Dunluce Castle

The site was used for defensive purposes long before a stone castle was constructed, as shown by the existence of a 1000-year-old souterrain. Parts of the castle are dated as 14th century, but some time in the 16th century it came into the hands of the Scottish Sorley Boy MacDonnell family, who extended the buildings and tried to strengthen its walls after a serious artillery attack by the English. The south wall, facing the mainland, has two openings cut into it which were made to hold cannons that were salvaged from the wreck of the *Gerona*, a ship from the Spanish Armada that foundered nearby.

The military value of a castle perched 30 metres (100 feet) above the sea is obvious, and the extensive remains inside the walls give a good idea of life here. The palatial hall needed two fireplaces, while the kitchen area has ovens, storage space and a drainage system all built into the stone. The lower yard retains the original cobbling and was surrounded by service rooms, some of which collapsed into the sea in 1639; servants and a night's dinner were lost.

The castle is open from 10 am to 7 pm Monday to Saturday and 2 to 7 pm on Sunday from April to the end of September. The rest of the year it's 10 am to 4 pm Monday to Saturday and 2 to 4 pm on Sunday. Entry is 70p (children 35p). The castle is beside the A2 coast road, midway between Portrush and Bushmills.

Bushmills Distillery

Whiskey was first officially distilled here in 1608, but records indicate that the activity was going on for hundreds of years before that. Bushmills whiskey is distilled nowhere else in the world. After the tour of the industrial process, you are rewarded with a tot of the hard stuff in the Postill Bar, where an exhibition area has been created in what were once malt kilns.

The distillery is open all year, Monday to Thursday, 9 am to 12 noon and 1.30 to 3.30 pm and on Friday, 9 to 11.45 am. During

July, August and September it opens from 12 noon to 3 pm on Friday and from 10 am to 3 pm on Saturday as well. There is no admission charge. The distillery is signposted from the town of Bushmills on the A2 coast road.

Dunseverick Castle

This is an older castle than Dunluce, but unfortunately very little remains. It was once the home of Conal Cearnac, a famous wrestler and swordsman said to have been present at the Crucifixion; he reputedly moved the stone at Christ's sepulchre. St Patrick is also said to have visited the castle, and a road was laid from here to Tara, the headquarters of the pagan high kings of Ireland. The castle remains are by the side of the B146 which is reached off the A2 coast road.

Carrick-a-rede Rope Bridge
It's a scary traipse across the Carrick-a-rede rope bridge to a small island with a salmon fishery. The 20-metre (66-foot) bridge sways some 25 metres (80 feet) above the rock-strewn water. It's especially frightening if it's windy, but there are secure handrails to help steady your nerves and your balance. The bridge is put up every spring by fishermen who work the fishery. Once on the island there are good views of Rathlin Island and Fair Head to the east.

You can cross the bridge free, but the National Trust car park costs £1.50. There is a small information centre open at weekends from Easter to June and daily from 11 am to 6 pm from July to mid-September.

Places to Stay
All the sites and attractions along the Causeway Coast could be visited from a base in Portstewart, Portrush or Ballycastle, the three main accommodation centres in the area. There are also hotels and guesthouses in Bushmills and Portballintrae, the closest towns to the Giant's Causeway itself.

Hostel *Whitepark Bay Youth Hostel* (☎ 02657-31745) is six km (four miles) east of Bushmills on the A2 coast road. This YHANI hostel overlooks the bay.

Camping The *Portballintrae Caravan Park* (☎ 02657-31478) is on Ballaghmore Rd in Portballintrae and has space for only six tents at £4 a night.

B&Bs *Keeve-Na* (☎ 02657-32184) at 62 Ballaghmore Rd, Portballintrae, next to the camp site, costs £12. *Pineview* (☎ 02657-41527) is a farmhouse five km (three miles) from Bushmills on the B66 and charges £26 a double. *Mrs Ramage* (☎ 02657-31385) is

on the coast road, 107 Causeway Rd, just 1.5 km (one mile) from the Causeway and charges £24 for two.

At 23 Causeway Rd, *Carnside* (☎ 02657-31337) charges £32 and at No 71 *Burnbrae* (☎ 02657-31673) charges £30.

Hotels If you want to stay as close to the Giant's Causeway as possible, the *Causeway Hotel* (☎ 0265-31226) is within spitting distance at £46 for a double. In Portballintrae the *Bayview Hotel* (☎ 02657-31453) has an indoor heated swimming pool and costs £56 while the *Beach House Hotel* (☎ 02657-31214) costs £62. The *Bushmills Inn* (☎ 02657-32339), Main St, Bushmills, costs £68 a double.

Places to Eat
The *Causeway visitors' centre café* is OK. More substantial meals can be enjoyed at one of the hotels in Portballintrae or Bushmills. There is also the *Ballintrae Inn* in Portballintrae, open seven days a week, at around £10 to £15, or *Sweeney's Wine Bar* on Seaport Ave serving steaks.

Bushmills has the *Coffee Shop* at the Diamond serving snacks and sandwiches. At the other end of the price range, *Auberge de Seneirl* (☎ 02657-41536) at 28 Ballyclough Rd, signposted off the road to Coleraine, is a French restaurant in the £50-for-two bracket.

Getting There & Away
See the introduction to this chapter for information on the summertime Antrim Coaster and Open Topper bus services along the coast. It's only five minutes by bus from the Giant's Causeway to the Diamond in Bushmills and another five minutes to Portballintrae.

Getting Around
Near the Causeway bikes can be hired, at a costly £10 per day, from Mitch's Mountain Bikes (☎ 02657-31497) at 10 Runkerry Rd, the road that runs from the A2 to the Causeway. A pick-up and delivery service can be arranged. The next nearest bike hire is in Portrush at Causeway Coast Cycles

(☎ 0265-824334) on Bath St. The YHANI hostel has its own bikes for hire.

BALLYCASTLE

Ballycastle, where the Atlantic Ocean meets the Irish Sea, also marks the end of the Causeway Coast. The town's location makes it a natural base and although there is nothing outstanding about the place it is pleasant enough for a short stay while exploring the coasts to the west or south. The Giant's Causeway, Bushmills distillery and the rope bridge are all less than 16 km (10 miles) away and the Glens of Antrim are due south.

There are some large caravan parks just outside town and there's a seaside feel to the harbour area. The beach itself is nothing special.

Information

The tourist office (☎ 02657-62024) is in the council offices on Mary St. To charter a boat for fishing trips contact Mr McCaughan (☎ 02657-62074).

There is a three-day music and dance festival in June and a bigger Ould Lammas Fair held on the last Monday and Tuesday of August. This is one of the oldest established

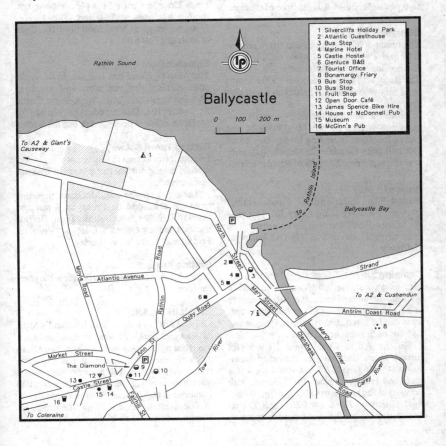

1 Silvercliffs Holiday Park
2 Atlantic Guesthouse
3 Bus Stop
4 Marine Hotel
5 Castle Hostel
6 Glenluce B&B
7 Tourist Office
8 Bonamargy Friary
9 Bus Stop
10 Bus Stop
11 Fruit Shop
12 Open Door Café
13 James Spence Bike Hire
14 House of McDonnell Pub
15 Museum
16 McGinn's Pub

Ballycastle

Rathlin Sound

0   100   200 m

To A2 & Giant's Causeway

To Rathlin Island

Ballycastle Bay

North Street

Atlantic Avenue

Moyle Road

Rathlin Road

Quay Road

Mary Street

Strand

To A2 & Cushendun

Antrim Coast Road

Tow River

Glenshesk River

Margy River

Carey River

Market Street

The Diamond

Castle Street

Ann St

Fairhill St

Road

To Coleraine

fairs in Ireland, dating back to 1606, and is associated with the sale of two traditional foods. *Yellowman* is a soft toffee while *dulse* is a dried seaweed that is sold heavily salted and ready to eat, although some people toast it. Always available during the Ould Lammas Fair, dulse is on sale generally from June to September while yellowman is available throughout the year. The Fruit Shop at the Diamond stocks both delicacies.

Museum
There is a tiny museum in the town's 18th-century courthouse on Castle St that opens 2 to 6 pm in July and August, free of charge.

Bonamargy Friary
The remains of this Franciscan friary are one km (half a mile) east of town on the A2 to Cushendun, on the Ballycastle golf course. The friary was founded around 1500 and was used for two centuries. There is no admission charge.

From the south of the friary a vault contains the bodies of the MacDonnells, the earls of Antrim, including Sorley Boy Mac-Donnell from Dunluce Castle, whose family was thrown from the cliffs of Rathlin Island.

Places to Stay
Hostel The independent *Castle Hostel* (☎ 02657-62337) is on Quay Rd, just past the Marine Hotel and charges £5 a night. The next nearest one is the YHANI hostel at Ballintoy.

Camping *Silver Cliffs* (☎ 02657-62550) is a big, noisy caravan and camp site within walking distance of town. It is also expensive at £8 per tent. Large and comfortable caravans can be hired, £35 for the first night and £15 for each subsequent night.

On the A2 to Cushendun, 10 km (six miles) from Ballycastle, *Watertop Open Farm* (☎ 02657-62576) has space for a few tents and is a good place for children, with pony trekking and farm tours on offer. *Whitehall Caravan Park* (☎ 02657-62077) on Whitepark Rd has limited camping space.

B&Bs If you want to be close to the sea, the *Atlantic Guest House* (☎ 02657-62412) overlooks the harbour. A double here is £30, while *Glenluce* (☎ 02657-62914) at 42 Quay Rd is £18. There are other places to check out along this road.

Hotels The *Marine Hotel* (☎ 02657-62222) is central and costs £55 a double. The smaller *Antrim Arms Hotel* (☎ 02657-62284) is on Castle St and costs £35 a double.

Places to Eat
There are the usual small cafés around and *Open Door* in Castle St is pleasant enough, though it closes at 5.30 pm. The *Marine Hotel* serves good hotel food until 10.30 pm at around £7 to £10.

Entertainment
The *Marine Hotel* has live music at weekends during the summer, and so does *McGinn's* pub on Castle St. Also on Castle St, near the Diamond, the *House of McDonnell* has a beer garden out the back.

Getting There & Away
See the introduction to this chapter for information on the summertime Antrim Coaster bus services.

There is a private bus, McGinns, that runs from the Diamond on Friday at 4 pm and Sunday at 7.30 pm to Belfast. From Belfast the bus leaves Queen's Gate at 6 pm on Friday and 9.30 pm on Sunday.

Getting Around
James Spence on Castle St has a few bicycles for hire.

RATHLIN ISLAND
Only 22 km (14 miles) from Scotland's Mull of Kintyre, Rathlin Island is itself only six km (four miles) long and nowhere more than 1.5 km (one mile) across. It has a pub, a restaurant, two shops, a camp site and a guesthouse, along with approximately 100 inhabitants and thousands of seabirds.

The island, which Pliny mentions as Ricnia, was raided by Vikings in AD 795 and suffered again in 1595 when Sorley Boy MacDonnell sent his family here for safety only to have them massacred by the English along with all the inhabitants. Its most illustrious visitor was Robert the Bruce who spent some time in 1306 in a small cave on the north-east point learning a lesson about fortitude. Watching a spider's resoluteness in repeatedly trying to spin a web gave him the courage to have another go at the English, whom he subsequently defeated at Bannockburn.

Another claim to fame is the fact that Rathlin was the first place to have a wireless. Marconi's assistant contacted Rathlin by radio in 1898 to prove to Lloyd's of London that the idea worked.

A bird sanctuary at the western end of the island is a chief attraction. During the summer a minibus waits at the quayside and will take you out for £2 return (children £1). The service does not run to a timetable so check your return time. Kittiwakes, razorbills and puffins can be seen around West Lighthouse, but by late summer they are no longer nesting or rearing their young and are difficult to spot from the land.

Places to Stay
The *Rathlin Guesthouse* (☎ 02657-63916/7) is by the harbour and does B&B for £20 for two. Camping space is provided by the owner of the one pub, just a short distance east of the harbour.

Getting There & Away
The mailboat leaves Ballycastle harbour each Monday, Wednesday and Friday morning at 10.30, returning from Rathlin at 4 pm. A private boat (☎ 02657-62024) goes at 12 noon and returns at 5 pm. The cost is £5 return. Before Easter and after September the service is restricted and enquiries should be made at the tourist office.

MURLOUGH BAY
The coast between Ballycastle and Cushendun is best covered not by the main A2 but by a more scenic coastal road that takes in Murlough Bay. This is the most stupendous part of the Antrim coastline. Leave your transport at the first car park – there are three altogether – where a map display sets out the walking possibilities. Walk No 1 is from the first car park to Coolanlough, and is a 3.5 km (two miles) return trip. The views from Fair Head are magnificent. From a vantage point 186 metres (600 feet) above the sea, Rathlin Island is to the left, while out to sea the peaks of the Isle of Arran can be seen on a clear day behind the Mull of Kintyre. The walk also takes in Lough na Cranagh with an ancient crannóg in the middle.

The second walk begins from the second car park farther down the road; follow the clear pathway to the west. It leads to some abandoned coal mines, indicated only by arches in the rock, which are probably not safe to explore.

By following the main road down past the second car park you come to a third parking area on the right. From here the road down becomes a green track and ends in a cul-de-sac by a small house.

Between the first and second car parks, the remains of a cross can be seen, a memorial to Roger Casement whose family came from this area. Casement, who was hanged in London in 1916 for enlisting the aid of Germany in the nationalist struggle, made a last request to his cousin: 'take my body back with you and let it lie in the old churchyard in Murlough Bay.' It was 50 years before the British consented to release the body.

Places to Stay
Murlough House (☎ 02657-69696) is a B&B halfway down the road to Murlough Bay. It is quite isolated and with lovely views it makes for a perfect night's retreat, especially if you're walking the Ulster Way, which comes through Murlough Bay.

Getting There & Away
From Ballycastle take the sign pointing to Torr Head and Cushendun Scenic Route, as opposed to the A2 that goes to Cushendun. From Cushendun take the Scenic Route to Torr Head.

The A2 goes inland between Cushendun and Ballycastle and cannot compete with the grandeur of the coastal route. The only reason for travelling on this part of the A2, apart from speed, is to visit the Watertop Open Farm or Ballypatrick Forest, an over-organised forest park.

CUSHENDUN

The distinctive houses at the southern end are National Trust property, the work of Clough Williams-Ellis, designer of Portmeirion in North Wales, who came here to work for Lord Cushendun. The village is on the Ulster Way and part of the walk could be undertaken from Cushendun. Going north the walk goes inland before heading down to Murlough Bay and then along the coast to Ballycastle. Going south the walk goes inland nearly all of the way to Cushendall.

Information

The National Trust tourist office (☎ 026674-506) is open daily 12 noon to 6 pm in July and August. From Easter to June and in September it opens the same hours on Saturday and Sunday only.

Permits for fishing on the River Dun that runs into Cushendun Bay are available from McFetridge's Garage, 116 Tromara Rd, Castle Green.

Places to Stay

There is only one hotel, the *Bay Hotel* (☎ 026674-267), with rooms at £28 for a double. A few doors away, the largish *Cushendun* (☎ 026674-266) calls itself a guesthouse, perhaps because it's only open during July and August. A double here is £30. The *Villa* (☎ 026674-252) at 185 Torr Rd does B&B for £24.

Camping is possible at *Cushendun Caravan Park* (☎ 026674-254), 14 Glendun Rd, run by the local council.

Self-catering houses and flats around Cushendun go for around £100 to £150 a week. Try *Ash Cottage* (☎ 0247-463249) or *Tybann House Apartments* (☎ 026674-289).

Places to Eat

The *tearoom* at the tourist office serves snacks and salads. Bar food is available at the *Bay Hotel* and the *Cushendun*, and both places serve evening meals. If you phone beforehand, the *Villa* does home-made meals until 7.30 pm for around £8.

On the opposite side of the road to the tourist office a drink can be enjoyed, if you can squeeze in, at *McBride's* pub. *Pubs of the North* by J J Tohill reckons that MacBride's is the smallest pub in Ireland at 1.5 by 2.8 metres (five by 9.5 feet). No children are allowed in, but maybe that's because they take up valuable space.

Getting There & Away

Ulsterbus No 150 connects Cushendun with Ballymena, from where a connection to Belfast can be made. Bus No 162 travels to Larne five times daily, three times on Saturday and once on Sunday and it's a short hop from Larne to Belfast. See the introduction to this chapter for information on the summertime Antrim Coaster bus services along the coast.

CUSHENDALL

This picturesque little village has a red sandstone tower at the crossroads which was built in the early 19th century by Francis Turnly. From the village the B14 road runs inland to the Glenariff Forest Park, in the loveliest of Antrim's nine glens, from where the A43 returns to the south of Cushendall and the A2 at Glenariff, also known as Waterfoot.

Information

The tourist office (☎ 02667-71180) is easy to miss; it's in a portacabin in a car park off the road at the Cushendun end of the village. It's open all year Tuesday to Saturday 10 am to 1 pm, with afternoon opening May to September.

Boats and tackle can be hired for sea fishing from Red Bay Boats (☎ 02667-71331/71373) on the main road.

Layde Old Church

This ruined church and churchyard stand

beside a fast-flowing stream that heads straight down to the sea. The church was founded by Franciscans but was used as a parish church from the early 14th century until 1790. The tombstones in the graveyard include MacDonnell memorials, and there's a very pagan-looking one immediately on the left after entering the grounds. The church is over one km up a steep coast road which goes north to Cushendun, not the A2, and passes the YHANI hostel. There is a car park outside.

Ossian's Grave

Romantically, but inaccurately, named after the legendary warrior-poet of the 3rd century AD, this Neolithic court tomb consists of a two-chambered burial ground once enclosed by an oval cairn. The site is signposted off the A2 outside of Cushendall on the Cushendun side. Another sign closer to the site is only seen if coming from the opposite direction so it's easy to miss. Park at the farm and walk up.

Glenariff Forest Park

Over 800 hectares (2000 acres) of woodland make up the park, and the main attraction is a waterfall, about half an hour's walk from the visitors' centre. Views of the valley led the English novelist Thackeray to exclaim that it was a 'Switzerland in miniature'. There are various walks, not all of them clearly marked; the longest is a three-hour circular mountain trail.

There is a £2.20 charge for cars (£1 for motorcycles) or there's parking at the Manor Lodge Restaurant, on the road to the park.

Places to Stay

Hostel & Camping The *YHANI Hostel* (☎ 02667-71344) costs £5.95 and is on the Layde road that leads from Cushendall village up to the Layde Old Church. Camping is possible at the *Glenariff Forest Park* (☎ 026673-232), while the *Cushendall Caravan Park* (☎ 02667-71699) on the coast road has a small camping area. So too does *Glenville Caravan Park* (☎ 02667-71520) on the Layde road.

Hotels & B&Bs The *Thornlea Hotel* (☎ 02667-71223) has doubles for £38.50. Next door *Trosben Villa* (☎ 02667-71130) does B&B for £22. Farther up the road, at 1 Kilnadore Rd, *Mountain View* (☎ 02667-71246) is a couple of pounds cheaper.

Near Glenariff, B&B places include *Glen Vista* (☎ 02667-71439) at 245 Garron Rd at £18 for a double, and *Mr & Mrs Montgomery* (☎ 026673-362) at 105 Glenariff Rd where a double goes for £20 and an evening meal is good value at £5.

Places to Eat

The *Moyle Inn Café* is open from 12 noon to 7.30 pm. Pub food is available from the *Central Bar* and *Trosben Villa* serves afternoon tea and a high tea for £5. The *Thornlea Hotel* has a pricey but substantial dinner for £13.50. More expensive still is a country house dinner at *McAuley's* (☎ 02667-71733) at 63 Ballyeamon Rd.

Glenariff Forest Park has its own *Waterfall Restaurant* with meals from £4 to £8. On the road to the park the *Manor Lodge* does steaks and in Waterfoot pub food is available from the *Mariners' Bar* or the *Glenariff Inn*.

Getting There & Away

The three buses serving Cushendall are the same as the ones for Cushendun: No 150 to Ballymena, No 162 to Larne and No 252 to Belfast. No 252 leaves at 11.33 am and 6.01 pm.

CARNLOUGH

The good beach attracts holidaymakers and many of the buildings distinguish themselves due to the abundance of local limestone used when the building work was commissioned by the Marquess of Londonderry in 1854. The limestone quarries were used until 30 years ago, and the white stone bridge across the village carried the trains bringing the stone down to the harbour for transport abroad.

Information

The tourist office is in the post office, just by the Londonderry Arms Hotel.

Places to Stay

Camping Both *Bay View Caravan Park* (☎ 0574-885685) and *Whitehill Caravan Park* (☎ 0574-885233) have some limited camping space.

Hotels & B&Bs The prosperous and solid *Londonderry Arms Hotel* (☎ 0574-885255) was built as a coaching inn by the Marchioness of Londonderry in the mid-19th century. It was eventually inherited by a distant relation of hers, William Churchill, who sold it to the present owners. A standard double is £52, but there are various specials worth enquiring about if staying more than one night, such as B&B with high tea for three nights at £64 each in a double. Also on Harbour Rd, *Ocean House* (☎ 0574-885279) does B&B for £20.

Places to Eat

For sandwiches and hamburgers try *Black's Bar* on Harbour Rd or the *Bridge Inn* on Bridge St which serves a set lunch. The *Londonderry Arms Hotel* serves up locally caught fish, and a wild salmon steak for £8 is difficult to resist. At night the bar has live music throughout the summer and dances are regularly held. The *Arkle Bar* in the hotel, named by loyal followers of the Irish horse that won 27 of its 35 races before being put down in 1970, is decorated with photographs of the famous horse.

Getting There & Away

Bus No 128 travels to and from Ballymena five times a day on Monday to Saturday and once on Sunday, with connections to Belfast. Bus No 162 between Cushendun and Larne stops at Carnlough. See the introduction to this chapter for information on the summertime Antrim Coaster bus services.

GLENARM

This is the oldest village in the glens and the first one you come to if travelling up from Belfast or Larne. Many of the buildings are coated white from the limestone dust of the local quarries. In the glen stands Glenarm Castle which dates back to the early 17th century; it was remodelled in the 19th century and is privately owned.

Places to Stay & Eat

Drumnagreagh Hotel (☎ 0574-841651) has doubles for £55, and *Dunluce* (☎ 0574-841279), 5 The Cloney, charges £20 for B&B. The hotel is the best place for a meal, though the *Heather Dew Tavern* is OK for grills and salad and there is often live music here at weekends. If you're coming from Carnlough, turn right at the crossroads for *Margaret's Guest House*, which has a café and does B&B.

Getting There & Away

The buses that serve Carnlough stop at Glenarm as well.

LARNE

If you arrive here from Scotland, Larne is a poor introduction to the spectacular Antrim coast and the rest of Northern Ireland. Conversely, if you travel down the coast, you can easily forget the troubles of the North; the sectarian graffiti around Larne brings it all rudely back. In 1914 Edward Carson's Ulster Volunteers imported 20,000 rifles through Larne, in case of Home Rule for the whole of Ireland.

Information & Orientation

The tourist office (☎ 0574-260088) is open Monday to Saturday, 9 am to 7.30 pm in July and August, 9 am to 5.30 pm the rest of the year. It is geared to the visitor just off the ferry and can deal with more than just local information. It is close to the centre beside the Murrayfield shopping centre, and is signposted at the roundabouts approaching town.

Olderfleet Castle

Don't let the name deceive you. This is just a ruined four-storey tower dated to some time in the 16th century. It is crumbling away at the end of a row of houses not far from the harbour and is signposted from the roundabout that leads to the harbour.

Places to Stay

Camping One of Ireland's better little camp sites is at *Carnfunnock Country Park* (☎ 0574-70541), a few km north of town off the A2. It's a modest little place but well run and very pleasantly situated. A tent costs £3 a night. The most convenient, if you're just off a ferry or about to catch one, is *Curran Caravan Park* (☎ 0574-73797), five minutes from the harbour, on the left of the road reached by following the sign to the town centre. It costs £6 a night. There is also *Brown's Bay Caravan Park* (☎ 0574-72313) on Islandmagee, at £5.

Hostel The nearest hostel is the YHANI *Ballygally Youth Hostel* (☎ 0574-583377) which costs £5.95 and is six km (four miles) north of Larne on the A2 coast road, just before the village of Ballygally.

B&Bs Within walking distance of the harbour, *Moneydara* (☎ 0574-272912) at 149 Curran Rd costs £22 for a double, while the *Seaview Guest House* (☎ 0574-272438), across the road at No 157, is £24. There are other B&Bs along the main road from the harbour to the first roundabout.

Hotels *Magheramorne House Hotel* (☎ 0574-279444), 59 Shore Rd, is a classy Victorian establishment on the A2 south of Larne, at £69.50 for a double. On Donaghy's Lane, a mile from town, the *Highways Hotel* (☎ 0574-272272) has doubles for £42. Both *Curran Court Hotel* (☎ 0574-275505), 84 Curran Rd near the harbour and just past the camp site, and *Kilwaughter House* (☎ 0574-272591), 61 Shanes Hill Rd, are £30.

Places to Eat

There is one long main street running through town and the inexpensive places are to be found at the harbour end. *Carriages* does reasonable pizzas and steaks for £5 to £10. It is open for lunch six days a week and dinner every day, opening at 5 pm. Next door *Le Pandoro* is a little pricier with a similar menu. A Chinese takeaway, popular with taxi drivers, is next door.

More typically Irish meals – meat-dependent and substantial – are available at any of the four hotels. *Kiln* (☎ 0574-260924) is on the Old Glenarm Rd and has a good reputation; it's in the £10 to £15 bracket.

Getting There & Away

Ferry P&O handle the route from Larne to Cairnryan in Scotland. The standard return is £34 (cycles free) for foot passengers, £30 for drivers and car passengers, with car rates varying from £120 to £180 depending on the season and departure time. For full details of the eight daily sailings contact the P&O office, Larne Harbour, Larne, County Antrim BT40 1AQ (☎ 0574-274321) or Cairnyan, Stranraer, Wigtownshire DG9 8RF, Scotland (☎ 05812-276). The journey time is just over two hours.

Sealink do the Larne to Stranraer route and the prices are basically the same. Contact the Sealink Travel Centre, Passenger Terminal, Larne Harbour BT40 1AW (☎ 0574-273616) or Sealink Travel Centre, Sea Terminal, Stranraer DG9 8EL (☎ 0776-2262) for reservations. The crossing time is two hours and 20 minutes.

Bus See the introduction to this chapter for information on the summertime Monday to Saturday Antrim Coaster bus services along the coast.

Bus No 156 is the regular service to and from Belfast. The earliest bus leaves the bus station, without calling at the harbour, at 7.15 am and the last one goes at 7.20 pm. It takes just over an hour and there are only three buses on a Sunday.

Bus No 162 runs up and down the coast, calling at Glenarm, Carnlough, Waterfoot, Cushendall and Cushendun. It operates from the bus station and not the harbour.

ISLANDMAGEE

A day trip to Islandmagee (also known as Island Magee) makes a pleasant excursion. The name is deceptive in that this is a peninsula 11 by three km (seven by two miles) and not an island, but you get there by ferry. Close to the ferry landing point the

Ballylumford Dolmen is domestically situated in the front garden of a private home. Also at this north end of the peninsula is Brown's Bay, which has a sandy beach.

Taking the more picturesque east coast road brings you to the Gobbins: over a mile of basalt cliffs with a path cut into the rock. During the 1641 rebellion, the garrison at Carrickfergus, seeking to revenge their fellow Protestants, massacred the Catholic inhabitants of the peninsula, throwing live and dead bodies over the cliffs.

Getting There & Away

The first ferries leave Larne at 7.30, 8 and 8.30 am, then hourly on the hour until 3 pm, and then every half hour until 5.30 pm.

CARRICKFERGUS

Carrickfergus is a commuter suburb just north of Belfast, noted for its wonderfully situated castle.

Information

Tourist information (☎ 09603-63604) is available from the town hall but the castle is on the main road, bypassing the town centre.

Carrickfergus Castle

Theatrically sited on a rocky promontory, commanding the entrance to Belfast Lough, this fine castle was built by John de Courcy soon after his 1177 invasion of Ulster. Besieged by King John in 1210, Edward Bruce in 1315 and briefly captured by the French in 1760, the castle also witnessed the attack on a British vessel in 1778 by the American John Paul Jones in the *Ranger*.

The oldest part of the castle, going back to its Anglo-Norman origins, is the inner ward which is enclosed by a high wall. The keep houses a museum telling the castle's history and life-size figures on the battlements add colour to what is undoubtedly the best Norman castle in Ireland.

The castle is open 10 am to 6 pm Monday to Saturday and 2 to 6 pm Sunday. Entry is £1.50.

St Nicholas' Church

The pillars in the nave are 12th-century, going back to the establishment of the church after the Anglo-Norman invasion of Ulster by de Courcy. Most of the rest dates to 17th-century restoration work, and a particularly fine example of such an addition is the Chichester memorial in the transept known as the Donegal aisle. It is probably the work of an English master mason who was clearly influenced by the Renaissance style of northern Europe. Stained glass in the south side and the nave's west end is 16th-century Irish work. Access to the church is via the pedestrianised street, passing the large tombstones in the grounds.

Andrew Jackson Centre

The parents of the US president left Carrickfergus in the second half of the 18th century, and so we have the Andrew Jackson Centre, a reconstructed dwelling of that era complete with fireside crane and earthen floor. The actual site of the ancestral home is indicated by a blue plaque just down the road from the centre. The centre is open from 10 am to 1 pm and 2 to 6 pm Monday to Friday, 2 to 6 pm Saturday and Sunday. Entry is 60p.

The centre is just over three km (two miles) north of Carrickfergus where there is a signposted right turn into Donaldson's Ave.

Places to Stay

Dobbins Inn Hotel (☎ 09603-51905), which has been around for over three centuries, is just across the road from the castle in the town centre, costing £65 for two. The least expensive B&B at £20 a double is *Marathon House* (☎ 0232-862475) at 3 Upper Station Rd.

Places to Eat

The restaurant at the *Dobbins Inn Hotel* serves steak and bar meals as well as a set lunch. An evening meal is £10 at least. For just snacks and coffee, *Number 10* along the pedestrianised West St is OK, or try *Home Bakery & Restaurant* farther up from the Dobbins Inn.

The *Windrose* is a fancy restaurant at the

Marina, just a short distance past the castle in the direction of Belfast. Nearby and less expensive is the huge *Fergus Inn* with bar food and an à la carte menu. And if all else fails there's a *Kentucky Fried Chicken* on the Belfast Rd.

Getting There & Away

Ulsterbus No 165 takes 15 minutes to hop to Belfast, and bus No 163 takes 45 minutes.

ANTRIM TOWN

Antrim Town is no more interesting than the rest of inland County Antrim. In 1649 the town was burnt by General Monro, and in 1798 it resisted an attack by the United Irishmen.

Information

The tourist office (☎ 08494-63113) is at Pogue's Entry in Church St. Belfast Airport is only six km (four miles) to the south.

Round Tower

This 10th-century tower, 27 metres (90 feet) high, is all that remains of a monastery that once stood on the site. The walls are over a metre (four feet) thick and the 10th-century dating is strong evidence for linking these towers with the Viking raids. The Antrim tower is in Steeple Park, about one mile out of town.

Pogue's Entry

In a narrow alley at the end of the main street a blue plaque marks the home of Alexander Irvine (1863-1941), missionary and writer. His *My Lady of the Chimney Corner* tells the story of his mother's brave struggle against poverty.

Places to Stay

It is best to avoid having to stay a night in Antrim if possible. There is only one hotel, *Deerpark Hotel* (☎ 08494-62480), on Dublin Rd, with doubles for £45. The camp site, *Sixmilewater Caravan Park*, is near the Antrim Forum just to the south-west of town. Washing facilities are a long walk away at the Forum but will be locked outside office

hours. The camp site itself is only an open field and there is no attempt at any kind of security. B&Bs don't seem to exist.

Getting There & Away

Ulsterbus No 20 from Ballymena to Belfast makes a stop in Antrim. There is also bus No 109 between Antrim and Belfast via Lisburn.

AROUND ANTRIM TOWN

Lough Neagh

The largest lake in Britain and Ireland covers 400 sq km (153 sq miles), and legend has it that the giant Finn McCool created it by scooping out a lump of earth and throwing it into the Irish Sea, thus also creating the Isle of Man (which does bear a resemblance in shape and size to the lough).

The *Maid of Antrim* cruises the lough but the schedule varies according to demand and it is best to check with the tourist office about the times. Usually there is a choice of a one-hour trip for £2 (children £1), which often leaves at 12 noon, and a 3½-hour trip for £4 (children £2) at 2.30 pm. The boat leaves from the marina just past the Antrim Forum.

Shane's Castle & Railway

A narrow-gauge (one metre/three feet) steam railway runs along the shore of Lough Neagh for 2.5 km (1.5 miles). It ends at the ruins of Shane's Castle, the seat of the O'Neill family since the early 17th century. There are nine trains a day, the first is at 12.30 pm and the last at 5.40 pm. The fare is £3 (children 1.50) and it's open from Easter to the end of September but closed Monday and Friday.

An alternative route to the castle ruins is by way of a nature trail that starts at the main entrance. Along the way there's a hide from which the birds on Lough Neagh may be observed. The castle entrance is 400 metres west of Antrim on the A6.

Ballymena

This is the home town of Ian Paisley, founder leader of the Free Presbyterian Church and the stridently anti-Catholic Democratic Unionist Party. The town council was the first in the North to fall under control of the

Democratic Unionist Party in 1977. The council unanimously voted to remove all mention of Darwin's theory of evolution from religious education in Ballymena's schools, for, as the mayor explained, 'if you believe you come from a monkey you'll act like a monkey'.

To get there, take the A26, a journey of 18 km (11 miles).

Gracehill

In the mid-18th century the Moravians fled from Bohemia to escape religious persecution and some of them settled in Gracehill where they became part of the larger Protestant community persecuting the Catholics. The Georgian architecture of their elegant village square includes a church, on the right as you enter the square, with separate entrances for men and women worshippers. Even the graveyard at the back of the church is laid out for men on the left and women on the right, with the numbered tombstones laying flat either side of the walkway!

To get to Gracehill from Ballymena, 18 km (11 miles) away, take the A42, which is the road that passes the bus and rail station in Ballymena. Look for a brown sign with a church marked on it and take the turning to the left.

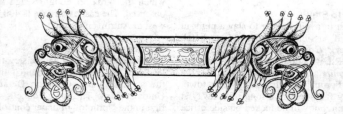

Counties Tyrone & Fermanagh

County Tyrone

The attractions of County Tyrone are disparate ones – historical and forest parks, prehistoric sites, the lonely Sperrin Mountains – spread out between less than interesting towns in a way that makes if difficult for the visitor to get a feel for the county as a whole. But it's worth the effort of trying to get to know the place, for Tyrone has an illustrious history and its unspoiled countryside is perfect for anyone wanting to 'get away from it all'.

For centuries County Tyrone was the territory of the O'Neills, until the day when Hugh O'Neill, Earl of Tyrone, finally submitted to the English at Mellifont in 1603. This marked the end of Gaelic Ireland. The planters moved in, introducing linen in the 18th century. Many local people subsequently migrated to America, and there are still links with the USA today. The huge Ulster-American Folk Park, sufficient reason in itself for visiting Tyrone, tells the story.

OMAGH
The county town of Tyrone is pleasantly situated at the confluence of the Rivers Camowen and Drumragh, which join to form the Strule. From the river the main street heads up to the classical 19th-century courthouse and divides in front of it. Although there are no special attractions in the town itself, it serves as a useful base for the surrounding area, and there are plenty of restaurants and shops. It's also a useful start or finish to a trip to the Sperrin Mountains or a local 16-km (10-mile) section of the Ulster Way. Decent places to eat are few and far between outside Omagh.

Information
The centrally located tourist office (☎ 0662-247831) on the corner of Market St is open 9 am to 1 pm and 2 to 5 pm Monday to Friday, and also on Saturday during July and August.

There is fishing along stretches of the three rivers around Omagh, mainly brown and sea trout, and salmon during the season from 1 April to 10 October. Permits, advice and information are available from Tyrone Angling Supplies in Bridge St, or contact the Omagh Anglers' Association (☎ 0266-3151) at 13 High St.

Places to Stay
The *Gortin Glen Caravan Park* (☎ 06626-48108) is 10 km (six miles) north of town on the B48 Omagh to Gortin road. Bus Nos 92 and 213 (summer only) will stop nearby. The camp site is a few minutes from the Ulster Way, and campers get a discount at the Omagh Leisure Complex. The same distance to the north-east of Omagh is *Mountfield Caravan Park* (☎ 0662-247831), but there is only room for half a dozen pitches and only one night's stay is allowed. Both charge IR£4 a night.

A standard B&B, charging £24 for two, is *Ardmore* (☎ 0662-243381). Go up High St from the tourist office, heading for the Courthouse, and take the left turn in front of the church up to James St. The house is at 12 Tamlaght Rd. *Mrs Devine* (☎ 0662-241719)

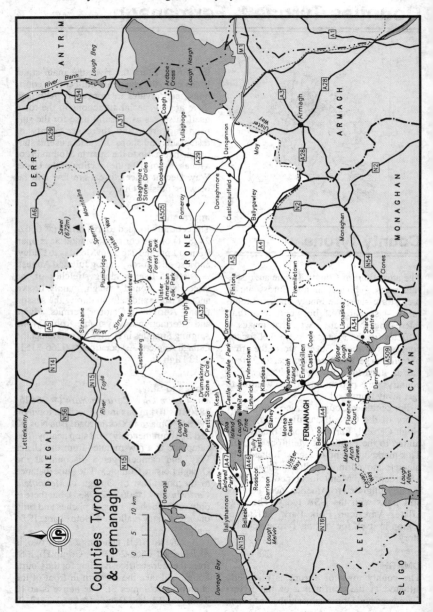

Counties Tyrone
& Fermanagh

at 1 Arleston Park has two rooms at £10 per person.

The oldest hotel in Omagh is the *Royal Arms Hotel* (☎ 0662-243262) on High St, just up from the tourist office, where doubles are £55. *Knock-Na-Moe Castle* (☎ 0662-243131) at 59 Old Mountfield Rd is £36.

Places to Eat

The *Memory Lane Lounge* in the Royal Arms Hotel has pub lunches for around £3, a couple of pounds more for dinner. The *Hunting Lodge*, also in the hotel, is a coffee lounge with tempting home-made snacks and sandwiches. Finally, there's the *Village Gossip Restaurant* in the hotel at which dinner for two costs around £20.

Opposite the hotel the *Shoppers' Restaurant* does lunches and salads, while the *Pink Elephant*, back on the hotel side, serves breakfast and lunches for under £3. Next to the town hall, *Dragon Castle* is a Chinese restaurant also serving European food and with a lunch special for £3 between 12 noon and 2 pm. *Mister G*, down an alleyway opposite the tourist office, does pizzas and snacks.

Down Bridge St towards the bus station is another bunch of inexpensive restaurants. *Caesar's* is open till midnight with the *Bridge* upstairs, and *Old MacDonald's* next door is suitable for fast-food fans.

Out of town, on the A5 road to Newtownstewart, the *Mellon Country Inn* is handily opposite the Ulster-American Folk Park. Lunch and dinner ranges from £5 at the bar to £20 à la carte on Sunday only.

Getting There & Away

Ulsterbus services connect Omagh with a number of towns in the North and the Republic. The main Belfast-Derry bus No 273 stops at Omagh. The earliest one leaves for Derry at 9.15 am and for Belfast at 8.13 am. A number of other buses from Belfast stop at Omagh before going on to Derry and Enniskillen, with connections for Donegal, Killybegs and Glenties. Bus No 296 between Derry and Cork leaves Omagh for Derry at 7.58 pm and for Cork at 10 pm, with connec-

tions to Athlone, Galway, Limerick and Waterford.

The bus station (☎ 0662-242711) is a short walk from the town centre, down Bridge St in Mountjoy Rd.

Getting Around

Bicycles can be hired from CAM (☎ 0662-243887) at 27 Market St or Conway Cycles (☎ 06627-61258) at 157 Loughmacrory Rd. There are no hire places nearer to the Sperrin Mountains.

AROUND OMAGH
Ulster-American Folk Park

This is one of the best museums in Ireland and well worth a visit. Thousands of Ulster people left their country to forge a new life across the Atlantic: 200,000 in the 18th century alone. The American Declaration of Independence was signed by five Ulster men, and the Exhibition Hall is able to offer many more instances of this transatlantic link.

The real appeal of the Folk Park, though, is the outdoor museum. The number of life-size exhibits is impressive: a forge, weaver's cottage, Presbyterian meeting house, school-house, log cabins, a 19th-century Ulster street, an early American street, and a ship and dockside gallery with reconstructed parts of an emigration ship. Costumed guides and craftspeople are on hand to chat and explain the art of cooking, spinning, weaving, candle making and so on. There is almost too much to take in on one visit and it needs at least half a day to do it justice.

Admission is £3 (children and students £1.50, family £9). From Easter to early September it is open Monday to Saturday from 11 am to 6.30 pm, Sunday to 7 pm. The rest of the year it's open Monday to Friday from 10.30 am to 5 pm.

The park is eight km (five miles) north of Omagh on the A5 to Newtownstewart. Bus No 97 stops outside and there is a regular service to and from Omagh. On Tuesday and Thursday, in July and August only, bus No 213, the Sperrin Sprinter, leaves Omagh at

1.45 pm and passes the park, but you'd need to catch bus No 97 back.

Ulster History Park

The theme of this park is the story of settlements in Ireland from the Stone Age to the Plantation. Full-scale models are on show of a Mesolithic encampment, Neolithic houses, a late Bronze Age crannóg, a 12th-century church settlement complete with stone round tower, and a Norman motte and bailey. There is also a new reception building with a cafeteria, shop and audio-visual theatre and a model Plantation settlement.

The park is over-reliant on models and reconstructions, giving it a rather phoney feel. A reconstructed early Christian stone tower just cannot work on the imagination in the way even the ruins of a real one do.

It's open from April to September, from 11 am to 6 pm, Monday to Friday, Saturday to 7 pm and Sunday from 1 to 7 pm. From October to March the hours are 11 am to 5 pm. Admission is £1.50 (children and students £1).

The park is off the B48 road to Gortin, north of Omagh. Bus No 92 between Omagh and Gortin stops nearby (no Sunday service).

Gortin Glen Forest Park

Over 400 hectares (1000 acres) of the Gortin Glen Forest form the Forest Park, mostly planted with conifers. It's a car-oriented park, an eight-km (five-mile) tarmac drive being the main way to get around. Near the main car park there are some wildlife enclosures, an indoor exhibit, a small nature trail and a café. If the ranger is on duty it costs £1.50 for a car (£1 for motorbikes).

There's a manageable day's walk from Gortin Forest Park to the Ulster-American Folk Park, along a section of the Ulster Way. The 16-km (10-mile) trip is mostly over small roads, forest roads and tracks, and from the Folk Park bus No 97 could be caught back to Omagh. The last bus leaves the Folk Park at 7.30 pm. A £1 leaflet, entitled *The Ulster Way, North-West Section*, covers this section with a map and should be available from the Omagh tourist office or by post from the Sports Council for Northern Ireland, House of Sports, Upper Malone Rd, Belfast BT9 5LA (☎ 0232-381222).

Beaghmore Stone Circles

On the fringe of the Sperrin Mountains set on desolate moorland, this series of Bronze Age (2000-1200 BC) circles, cairns and stone alignments pose a mystery for archaeologists and visitors alike. Especially intriguing is the 'Dragon's Teeth', one of the larger of the seven circles. It is filled with closely-set stones that jut out of the ground in an apparently random manner. Various explanations have been suggested for these monuments – religious, astronomical and social – but the plain fact is that no-one knows for sure.

The circles are signposted off the A505 Omagh-Cookstown road, 14 km (nine miles) north-west of Cookstown.

Sperrin Heritage Centre

The gentle contours of the Sperrin Mountains, 64 km (40 miles) from east to west, reach their highest point at Mt Sawel, 672 metres (2240 feet), just behind the Sperrin heritage centre. Computer presentations and other displays are devoted to the historical, social and ecological aspects of the region.

Gold has been found in the mountains and part of the exhibition is devoted to it. Barry McGuigan, the Irish world champion boxer, had his first gold medal made from the local gold, and a mining company is exploring the commercial possibilities. Not surprisingly, there are difficulties obtaining the necessary explosives in this part of Ireland!

If you are thinking of climbing Mt Sawel, enquire at the Centre as to the best route to take. The climb is easy, but some farmers are more accommodating than others. The Ulster Way comes in this direction, and it could be joined at Leagh's Bridge six km (four miles) away. This point is roughly halfway along the Dungiven to Gortin section of the Ulster Way, 55 km (34 miles) in all. Another outdoor trip through the Sperrins would be on horseback. The Edergole Riding Centre (see under Places to Stay for

Cookstown) organises three-day trekking trips through the mountains.

The Centre (☎ 026626-48142) has a café and is open June to September, 11 am to 6 pm Monday to Friday, 11.30 am to 6 pm Saturday and 2 to 7 pm Sunday. Admission is £1.65 (children 65p). For 65p extra (children 35p) you can try your luck at prospecting for gold in a nearby stream.

The centre is on the B47; from Omagh you go through Gortin to Plumbridge on the B48 and then east. It can also be reached from the Dungiven or Cookstown side.

Places to Stay

If you wanted to make a day of it visiting the two museums, *Camphill Farm* (☎ 0662-245400) is very close to the Ulster-American Folk Park at 5 Mellon Rd, Mountjoy, and costs £25. Another, less expensive place close to the Folk Park is *Daleview* (☎ 0662-241182) at 96 Beltany Rd on the A5 just past the Folk Park, with rooms for £22.

COOKSTOWN

Cookstown is Northern Ireland at its most forbidding. The town was founded in 1609 by one Alan Cooke and has one long, wide street, with Catholics living at one end and Protestants at the other. There's an army base next to the Catholic school, and children will tell you how often they have hours off school due to bomb scares. Both approaches to the 2.5 km (1.5 mile) main street are heavily guarded by army posts, with signs saying 'We apologise for the inconvenience caused. Blame the terrorists.' – small comfort when an Armalite rifle is being pointed at your head by a very young and very nervous soldier. In 1992 a vanload of Protestant building workers were blown up outside Cookstown, on their way home after working for the security forces.

Information

The tourist office (☎ 06487-66727) at 48 Molesworth St is open April to September, 9 am to 5 pm Monday to Friday. Molesworth St is the beginning of the B73 road to Coagh, to the west off the main street.

Bernadette Devlin

In 1947 Bernadette Devlin was born at the Catholic end of Cookstown. As a student she became involved in the Civil Rights movement, and was elected to Westminster in 1969 as the youngest-ever MP.

She was imprisoned for her part in the 1969 Bogside battle in Derry, and after Bloody Sunday in 1972 her notoriety reached its height when she physically attacked the British Home Secretary in the House of Commons. After withdrawing from parliamentary politics, she was lucky to survive a Protestant assassination squad that attacked her home and family in 1981 and left her badly wounded. ■

Places to Stay

The least expensive B&B is the *Central Inn* (☎ 06487-62255), 27 William St, at £22 a double. *Edergole* (☎ 06487-62924), 70 Moneymore Rd, is £31 and has a riding school with three-day Sperrin trails, or hourly hire at £6.

Hotels in town are *Glenavon House* (☎ 08687-64949) on Drum Rd, the road to Omagh, at £60 a double, *Greenvale Hotel* (☎ 06487-62243), on the same road at £40, and on Coagh St the *Royal Hotel* (☎ 06487-62224), also at £40.

Places to Eat

For takeaways and café cuisine, *Joe Mac's* is on the same street as the tourist office. *Al Capone's* on the long main street is open till midnight and later at weekends, serving baked potatoes and burgers to eat there or take away. Inexpensive Chinese and European food is available at *Dragon Palace*, by the army checkpoint at the southern approach into town. Also nearby is *Le Curé Wine Bar* with kebabs and steaks for under £5.

Lunches and dinner are available at the three hotels; the *Greenvale* is the most expensive at £12 for dinner. *Glenavon House* charges £8.

Getting There & Away

Bus No 80 shuttles regularly between

Dungannon and Cookstown, connecting with bus No 273 to Belfast and Derry. Bus No 110 also goes to Belfast, changing to bus No 120 at Antrim. Bus No 210 goes direct to Belfast. Bus No 273 is the fastest bus to and from Omagh.

AROUND COOKSTOWN
Wellbrook Beetling Mill

Beetling is a stage in the making of linen where the cloth is beaten with wooden hammers, or beetles, to give it a smooth sheen. There were once six mills at Wellbrook. The hammers were driven by water; one of them has been well maintained by the National Trust, and can be seen at work – it was literally deafening for those employed in these mills.

In July and August and over Easter, the mill is open 2 to 6 pm daily except Tuesday. From April to June and in September it is only open on Saturday, Sunday and bank holidays from 2 to 6 pm. Admission is £1.20 (children 60p). To get there take the A505 west and after five km (three miles) turn right for another three km (two miles).

Cregganconroe Chambered Cairn

This cairn, like most, is ancient but not spectacular. The lintel stone has collapsed onto the two portal stones that led into the burial gallery, and the huge capstone has also slipped. The site has not been excavated.

To get there, take the A505 west from Cookstown and after a few km look for the signpost on the left. From here it is 10 km (six miles) to the site.

Tullaghoge Fort

Unusually, something is known about the inhabitants of this hill fort. It was the burial ground of the O'Hagans and the inauguration place of the O'Neills in the 11th century. A 1601 map marks the spot, on the hillside to the south-east, where the stone inauguration chair stood. The following year the chair was destroyed by the English.

To get there leave town on the A29 south to Dungannon and turn left onto the B162 Cookstown to Stewartstown road. Four km

(2.5 miles) on, turn left at a sharp corner into a car park from where a path leads to the site.

Ardboe High Cross

A 10th-century high cross stands in front of a 6th-century monastery site, now housing the ruins of a 17th-century church – and with Lough Neagh in the background it ought to be more dramatic than it is. However, the cross is one of the best preserved in Ulster, with the east side showing Old Testament scenes and the west side New Testament ones. On the east side try making out Adam and Eve, the sacrifice of Isaac, Daniel and the Lions, the Burning Fiery Furnace, a bishop with people around, and Christ in glory. The New Testament side has the Magi, the Miracle at Cana, the Miracle of the Loaves and Fishes, the entry into Jerusalem, the arrest of Christ and the Crucifixion. Easier to decipher are some of the 18th-century tombstones in the churchyard. To get there take the B73 from Cookstown, signposted for Coagh, for 16 km (10 miles).

Places to Stay

The *Drum Manor Forest Park* (☎ 06487-62774 or 08687-58256), six km (four miles) west of Cookstown on the A505 road to Omagh, has a small camping area costing £5 a night. It's a pleasant enough park, with a butterfly farm and arboretum, but there is no hot water or showers. You're likely to have the place to yourself, and a small barbecue could easily be set up. If you have a car be sure to arrive before 4 pm when a barrier goes down, and collect a key if you're intending to leave early in the morning.

DUNGANNON

Until 1602, when the castle and town were burnt to prevent them falling into the hands of the English, Dungannon was one of the chief seats of the O'Neill family. In 1969 the town once again entered the history books when the Civil Rights Association, formed a year earlier to protest at the rampant social and political inequalities suffered by Catholics, organised its first march from Coalisland to Dungannon. The crowd of

4000 was met by a police cordon outside the town, and although there was no serious violence it was the beginning of a new era.

Information

Tourist information is available from the council offices (☎ 08687-25311) in Circular Rd, from 9 am to 1 pm and 2 to 5 pm, Monday to Friday.

The control zone in the town centre is enforced, which is why parked cars have at least one person inside, so use the car park close to the square, which will cost a lot less than the £15 fine for leaving a vehicle unattended. Or park for free in the car park behind the Tree Tops restaurant on the way into town from Armagh.

Tyrone Crystal

Once threatened with closure, Tyrone Crystal managed to survive and moved into new premises just outside of town. Tours of the factory cover the different stages in the production of the crystal, starting with a visit to the furnace where the molten glass is prepared and then hand-blown. The glass pieces are then checked for faults, bevelled, marked, cut and polished.

The showroom contains examples of all the crystal, including slightly imperfect pieces that do not bear the Tyrone Crystal insignia but cost about 25% less. Tyrone Crystal may not have the illustrious reputation of Waterford glass but it makes a splendid gift or souvenir. Prices range from £13 for a tumbler to £100 and more for vases and bowls.

The tour is free. The factory is open 9.30 am to 3.30 pm Monday to Saturday, mornings only on Friday. To get there take the A45 north-east from town; it is clearly signposted.

Places to Stay

Parkanaur Forest Park (☎ 08687-58256), 6.4 km (four miles) west of Dungannon on the A4, doesn't have hot water or showers. Camping costs £3 a night but there may be a minimum two-night stay and a deposit is required for the barrier key. The local

council's *Killymaddy Centre* (☎ 08687-67259/25311) on Ballygawley Rd, the A4, has better facilities and only costs £2.

Mrs McCaul (☎ 08687-23037) at 65 Coalisland Rd runs the least expensive B&B at £9 per person. Dungannon's two hotels both charge £55 a double. The *Inn on the Park* (☎ 08687-25151) is on Moy Rd, while the *Glengannon Hotel* (☎ 08687-27311) is at Drumgormal on the A4 Ballygawley Rd.

Places to Eat

Tree Tops, on the left entering Dungannon from Armagh, is an inexpensive self-service restaurant open till 5.50 pm Monday to Thursday, to 10 on Friday and Saturday. In the town square the *Dunowen Inn* serves pub food and set meals. The restaurant at the *Inn on the Park* serves decent steaks and fish for around £10.

For something fancy in the £20 a head range, try the *Grange Lodge* (☎ 08687-84212) near Moy. This award-winning restaurant specialises in locally reared duckling. To get there take the A29 south towards Armagh for 2.5 km (1.5 miles) and turn left at the signpost.

Getting There & Away

The 50-minute journey between Dungannon and Belfast is possible on a number of very regular services (£3.70 single). There are buses, many direct, to just about every big town in Ulster, as well as routes to Donegal and the rest of the Republic.

AROUND DUNGANNON
Peatlands Park

To get to this park, which is at the Birches east of Dungannon, take Exit 13 off the M1. The visitor centre here has an informative display about peat, aimed at a young audience. The bog garden is worth a visit if only to familiarise yourself with the sundew, one of Ireland's two carnivorous plants. It is a tiny plant, easily missed. There are also pitcher plants thriving in the garden, but these were introduced into Ireland a century ago from Canada.

The open-top railway does a 15-minute

circuit of the park for children. From Easter to the end of September the trains run on Saturday and Sunday from 2 to 6 pm, daily during July and August, for 70p (children 30p). The visitor centre has the same hours.

Donaghmore High Cross

The cross is a hybrid, being made of the base and shaft of one cross and the head and part shaft of another with the join clearly visible. The decorated biblical scenes are similar to those on the Arboe Cross. On the east side the Angel and the Shepherds, the Adoration of the Magi, the Miracle at Cana, the Miracle of the Loaves and Fishes and the arrest of Christ and the Crucifixion. On the west side are Adam and Eve, Cain and Abel and Abraham and Isaac.

The cross is four km (2.5 miles) north-west of Dungannon on the B43 road to Pomeroy, easily spotted at a road junction.

Castlecaulfield

Not a castle as such, but the remains of what was once a substantial Jacobean house, Castlecaulfield was built in the early 17th century by Sir Toby Caulfield on the site of an earlier Gaelic fort belonging to the O'Donnellys. Over the gatehouse the Caulfield coat of arms can be made out, and this survived the Donnellys' act of revenge in 1641 when the house was burned down. It was rebuilt; and hosted a church service by John Wesley, the founder of Methodism, in 1767.

To get there take the A4 out of Dungannon and after about six km (four miles) a small road is signposted to the right.

Parkanaur Forest Park

An oak forest is being developed on what was once the Burgess estate, the Victorian dwelling now being a centre for the disabled. The old farm buildings display farm and forest machinery and there is a short nature trail. The deer in the park are descended from the oldest deer herd in Ireland, going back to 1595 when a doe and hart, a gift from Elizabeth I to her goddaughter, were raised at Mallow Castle. Parkanaur Park brought five deer from Mallow in 1978 and there are now about 30.

There is an entry charge of £1 for cars (50p for motorcycles) if a ranger is on duty. The park entrance is 11 km (seven miles) west of Dungannon on the A4.

Ulysses S Grant Ancestral Homestead

Ulysses S Grant led Union forces to victory in the American Civil War and later became the 18th US president. The home of his mother's family has been restored in the style of a typical 19th-century Irish small farm. The furniture is not authentic, but the original field plan of this 10-acre farm is still there, together with various old farming implements.

The visitor centre has an exhibition and café and is open May to September, from 10 am to 6 pm Monday to Thursday, an hour later on Friday, Saturday and Sunday. The rest of the year it's open from 10.30 am to 4.30 pm Monday to Friday. Admission is 80p (children 30p) The site is 18 km (11 miles) from Dungannon. Take the A4 west from Dungannon and look for the sign on the left before the village of Ballygawley.

The Argory

This neo-classical house dates from 1824 and the National Trust advertise it as a 'time capsule' due to its complete turn-of-the-century furnishings. There is no electricity; the central stove and the oxyacetylene gas plant help to define the late-Victorian and Edwardian character of the house.

Tours of the building and grounds take in the drawing room, with its rosewood Steinway piano, the study and billiard room and dining room. The courtyards house further displays as well as a shop and tearoom.

The Argory is open April to June and September, on Saturday and Sunday from 2 to 6 pm. During July and August, and the Easter period, it is open daily except Thursday from 2 to 6 pm. Admission is £1.80 (children 90p) plus 50p for the car park. From Dungannon it is 10 km (six miles) to the south-east by the B34. From the M1 it is five km (three miles) from exit 14.

County Fermanagh

The River Erne wanders through County Fermanagh – one of the smallest counties in Ireland – into a lake which is 80 km (50 miles) long. Where Lough Erne constricts in the middle sits the town of Enniskillen, the obvious base for any exploration of the county. The town's tourist office serves the whole county and its literature includes a useful free booklet that gives comprehensive details of all types of accommodation in Fermanagh.

Lower Lough Erne attracts people for different reasons: the fishing is superb, there are good facilities for water sports outside Enniskillen, and the islands of Devenish and White have remarkable ecclesiastical remains. A third island, Boa, has a cemetery with a unique stone statue dating back around 2000 years.

In was not until after 1600, when Enniskillen finally fell to the English, that foreigners moved in and quickly established a series of castles around Lough Erne. The town of Enniskillen was transformed into a centre of colonial power and its strategic importance to the British led to its unparalleled boast of possessing two royal regiments. At the time of Partition, Fermanagh was reluctantly drawn into Northern Ireland but there is little evidence of its nationalist spirit diminishing. The British Parliament does not like to be reminded that one of its members was allowed to starve himself to death in an effort to establish political recognition for IRA prisoners. Bobby Sands was elected as MP for Fermanagh and South Tyrone in the spring of 1981, and he died 66 days after beginning his fast, without ever taking up his seat in Westminster.

ENNISKILLEN
The small town of Enniskillen is a handy centre for activities on Upper and Lower Lough Erne and the antiquities around them. Oscar Wilde and Samuel Beckett were both pupils at the Portora Royal School. The town is Catholic, close to the border, and lacks the dourness of some of the North's towns.

In 1987 an IRA bomb exploded at a Remembrance Day service in Enniskillen and 13 innocent people lost their lives.

Information
The well-run Fermanagh tourist information centre (☎ 0365-323110/325050), near the Lakeland Forum, just south of the town centre, dispenses tourist information. From April to June and September it is open 9 am to 5 pm (5.30 in June and September) Monday to Friday, 10 am to 5 pm Saturday. In July and August it is open 9 am to 6.30 pm Monday to Friday, 10 am to 5 pm on Saturday and 10 am to 3 pm on Sunday. The rest of the year it is open from 9 am to 5 pm Monday to Friday, closed between 1 and 2 pm each day.

The town centre is on an island in the waterway connecting the upper and lower loughs. Vehicles should not be left unattended in the town centre, but there are plenty of nearby car parks. The main street changes name every few steps, but the clocktower marks the centre. There's a laundrette on the East Bridge St section of the main street. Apart from at the banks and the post office, you can also change money at the Crow's Nest pub and restaurant in High St.

The Coles Monument
The monument was named after the son of the first earl of Enniskillen. The 108 steps inside this Doric column can be climbed for rewarding views of the surrounding area. From mid-May to mid-September it is open 11 am to 1 pm and 2 to 5 pm Monday to Friday. At weekends it is open from 2 to 6 pm. Entry is 30p. It is in Forthill Park at the eastern end of town.

Castle & Museums
The county museum and the Regimental

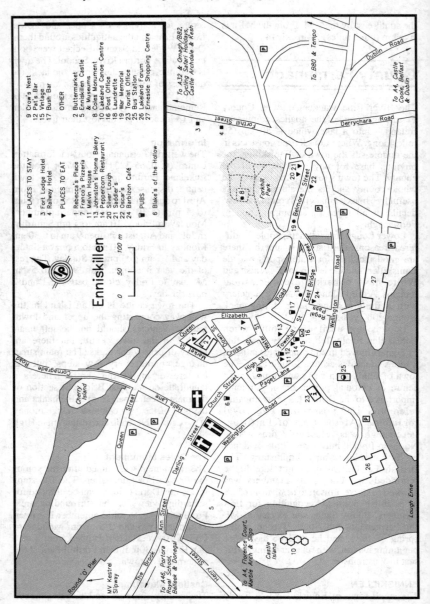

Enniskillen

0 50 100 m

PLACES TO STAY
- 3 Fort Lodge Hotel
- 4 Railway Hotel

PLACES TO EAT
- 1 Rebecca's Place
- 7 Franco's Pizzeria
- 11 Melvin House
- 13 Johnston's Home Bakery
- 14 Peppercorn Restaurant
- 20 Silver Lough
- 21 Saddler's
- 22 Oscar's
- 24 Barbizon Café

PUBS
- 6 Blake's of the Hollow
- 9 Crow's Nest
- 12 Pat's Bar
- 15 Vintage
- 17 Bush Bar

OTHER
- 2 Buttermarket
- 5 Enniskillen Castle & Museums
- 8 Coles Monument
- 10 Lakeland Canoe Centre
- 16 Post Office
- 18 Laundrette
- 19 War Memorial
- 23 Tourist Office
- 25 Bus Station
- 26 Lakeland Forum
- 27 Erneside Shopping Centre

Museum of the Royal Inniskilling Fusiliers are both inside the castle. From land the castle looks unimpressive, but the turreted building known as **Watergate** looks good from the water.

The museum occupies the central keep but it is not particularly interesting. The Regimental Museum is crammed full of medals, guns and uniforms. Both are open from 10 am to 5 pm Tuesday to Friday and 2 to 5 pm Saturday to Monday. The cost is £1 (75p students, 50p children).

Water Sports
The best place for hiring equipment for water sports is at the Lakeland Canoe Centre (☎ 0365-32450) on Castle Island in Enniskillen. Free ferries depart from the Lakeland Forum just behind the Fermanagh tourist information centre. Canoes, sailboards, sailing boats and jet skis are all available for hire.

Places to Stay
Camping & Hostel There is hostel-style accommodation and a camp site at the *Lakeland Canoe Centre* (☎ 0365-324250/322411) on Castle Island, which is reached by ferry from the Lakeland Forum. It costs £8 per person and there is no charge for the ferry.

B&Bs B&Bs can be found on the outskirts of town along the A4 Sligo road. *Carraig Aonrai* (☎ 0365-324889) at No 19 is the least expensive at £17 for a double. *Rossole House* (☎ 0365-323462) at No 85 is £26. *Willoughby Guest House* (☎ 0365-325275) at No 24 costs £14/26 and is neat and tidy, but only has baths, not showers.

At the other side of town, B&Bs like *Lackaboy Farm House* (☎ 0365-322488) can be found along the B80 road to Tempo. *Drumcoo House* (☎ 0365-326672) is at 32 Cherryville, Cornagrade Rd, by the roundabout on the road north to Castle Archdale and Omagh. Rooms are £13/23.

Hotels The *Railway Hotel* (☎ 0365-322084) is at 34 Forthill St, at the eastern side of town

on the road out to Omagh. Just a little past it is the *Fort Lodge Hotel* (☎ 0365-323275). Both charge £50 for a double. More expensive, at £70 for a double, the *Killyhevlin* (☎ 0365-323481) is on the Dublin road.

Self-Catering The *Belmore Court Motel* (☎ 0365-326633), on the B80 road to Tempo, is good value, with double rooms at £120 a week. Other places average around £200 a week.

Places to Eat
For snacks and coffee try *Rebecca's Place* in the Buttermarket. *Franco's Pizzeria* on Queen Elizabeth Rd on the north side of town is adventurous: what other restaurant in Ireland dares to announce on the menu: 'we serve no chips'? Pizzas are £2.80 to £4.25, pasta dishes £4.25, and there's much more on offer, including a seafood bar, in this very popular restaurant. It's closed on Sunday.

Johnston's Home Bakery on Townhall St, just east of the clock tower in the centre, has good sandwiches and pies. Along the main East Bridge St the *Barbizon Café* is OK for snacks and a set lunch but closes at 6 pm. Farther along in Townhall St the *Peppercorn Restaurant* is pleasant, serving breakfast and meals for under £5. The *Crow's Nest* in High St is aimed at the tourist, with menus in French and German. The *Ardhowen Theatre* off the A4 road to Dublin has a restaurant serving lunch and snacks.

For steaks, *Melvin House*, just a few doors away, closes at 6 pm Monday to Thursday, and at 9.30 pm Friday and Saturday. On the roundabout at the end of Belmore St, *Saddler's* is another steakhouse, but it's open daily and is a little less expensive. Exotic fare is on offer nearby at *Oscar's*, with vindaloo curry for £7; and the *Silver Lough* across the road has Chinese and English menus and is open until midnight seven days a week.

The multiple-named main street through town has a number of popular pubs including the resolutely Victorian *William Blake's* (Blake's of the Hollow) on Church St, the *Crow's Nest* on the High St, the *Vintage* on Townhall St, the *Bush Bar* on East Bridge St and *Pat's Bar*, next to Melvin House, which occasionally has music at night.

Things to Buy

Small shops along Enniskillen's long main street sell Belleek pottery, but the showroom at Belleek has the complete range. In town itself the best place for shopping is the Buttermarket, off Queen Elizabeth Rd. The refurbished buildings of the old market place now house a variety of craft shops making and selling their wares – at US-tour-group prices. Ceramics and jewellery are the best buys. More mundane shopping is available at the Erneside Centre, a modern complex of shops, cafés and supermarket on the Shore Rd near the visitor centre.

Getting There & Away

Ulsterbus No 261 runs more than half a dozen daily services to Belfast Monday to Saturday, less on Sunday, for £5.20. It's £2.30 to Omagh, where you change for Derry. Express buses also connect with Dublin. There is also a service from Enniskillen to Bundoran via Belleek. The bus station (☎ 0365-322633) is conveniently located across from the visitor centre on Shore Rd.

Getting Around

Bicycles can be hired at the Lakeland Canoe Centre (☎ 0365-32450) on Castle Island or from Erne Tours (☎ 0365-322882), who run the Kestrel cruises from the Round 'O' pier at Brookside. Cycling Safari Holidays (☎ 0365 323597, fax 327996) hire on a daily basis at £7.50 as well as organising day trips and longer cycling packages. Their address is 31 Chanterhill Park, Enniskillen, County Fermanagh BT74 4BG.

AROUND ENNISKILLEN
Castle Coole

Towards the end of the 18th century, designers influenced by Greek and Roman models promoted the neoclassical style, and Castle Coole ranks as probably the purest expression of this school of architecture in Ireland. The house was completed in 1798. Over the following two centuries the Portland stone exterior absorbed water to the point at which the walls started to crumble. The National Trust embarked on an expensive rebuilding of the outside walls and an extensive redecoration of the interior. (The present earl still lives on the 500-hectare estate.) The result is that now the house displays the pristine elegance of its original conception. The austerity of the design borders on sterility; the obsession with symmetry is almost neurotic; and the guided tour takes in many examples of form triumphing over substance: fake doors balancing real ones, hollow columns painted to resemble marble ones, a lavish state bedroom that was never used, keyhole covers on doors which have no keyholes.

The tour first visits the male sanctuary of the library where, as the guide points out, the doors once locked could only be opened from the inside, so who knows what they got up to. Most of the furniture is original, and the curtain rail is typical of the extravagance of the second earl of Belmore, who decorated the house. The first earl spent so much money having the place built that he had nothing left for decorations.

Outside the house are grilles which let some light into the servants' basement. Their quarters may soon be opened up.

The castle is open June to August, 2 to 6 pm Friday to Wednesday. From April to May and September it opens Saturday, Sunday and bank holidays from 2 to 6 pm. Over Easter it also opens daily. Admission is £2.20 (children £1.10). Castle Coole is on the main Belfast to Enniskillen A4 road, 2.5 km (1.5 miles) from Enniskillen.

Florence Court

This Palladian mansion is named after the wife of John Cole who settled in the area in the early 18th century. His son built the present central block and the wings were added by *his* son, although the architect is unknown. The house was acquired by the National Trust in the 1950s and partly rebuilt after a fire in 1955. It is said that every Irish yew tree has its origin from one in the garden of Florence Court!

Unlike Castle Coole, Florence Court has a lived-in character, and despite the fire much of the original rococo plasterwork remains – the staircase is the best place for appreciating it.

The house is 13 km (eight miles) from Enniskillen. Take the A4 road to Sligo and turn on to the A32 Swanlinbar road. During July and August a private bus (☎ 0365-322555) runs from the Enniskillen visitor centre to Florence Court, from Thursday to Sunday, departing at 11.30 am, 2 pm and 4 pm and returning at 12.10, 2.40 and 4.20 pm. The return fare is £2.50.

Marble Arch Caves & Forest

The extensive Marble Arch Caves are south of Enniskillen near the border. They're very commercialised and very popular; it's wise to phone ahead (☎ 036582-8855) and book on a tour. During July and August the caves are open seven days a week from 11 am with the last tour at 5 pm. The cost is £4 (students £3, children £2, family £12) and starts with a boat trip on the river which runs through the caves. During the summer there are occasional free guided walks through the surrounding limestone hills conducted by the Department of the Environment. Enquire at the visitor centre in Enniskillen or contact the Nature Reserve Office (☎ 0365-621588) at the Castle Archdale Country Park.

The caves are 16 km (10 miles) south-west of Enniskillen by the A4 and A32. The private bus that runs to Florence Court continues on to the caves and returns at 2.30 and 4.30 pm.

LOUGH ERNE
Fishing

The lakes of Fermanagh are renowned for coarse fishing, but trout are found in the northern part of Lough Erne, close to Boa Island and Kesh Bay. Lough Melvin, near the town of Garrison, is home to the Gillaroo trout.

The Lough Erne trout fishing season is from the beginning of March to the end of September. Salmon fishing begins in June and also continues to the end of September. The mayfly season usually lasts a month from the second week in May. There is no closed season for pike, perch, rudd or bream.

A coarse fishing licence or permit is required for Lough Erne and a game permit or licence for fishing in Lower Lough Erne other than from the shore. These can be purchased from Castle Marine (☎ 03656-28118) at Castle Archdale County Park, which also hires day boats. A 15-day joint licence and permit is £10.65 for coarse and £29.20 for game fishing. Most of the rivers in Fermanagh are privately owned, and information on those rivers where permission need not be sought is available from the visitor centre.

Cruising Lough Erne

The MV *Kestrel* (☎ 0365-322882) is a 63-seater waterbus that cruises the lough for nearly two hours, calling at Devenish Island along the way. It departs from the Round 'O' pier at Brook Park, a short distance out of Enniskillen on the A46 to Beleek. During May and June it departs at 2.30 pm daily, in July and August at 10.30 am, 2.15 and 4.15 pm, and in September at 2.30 pm on Tuesday, Saturday and Sunday. The cost is £3 (£1.50 for children).

There is also a Viking Cruise (☎ 03657-22122) from the Share Centre at Lisnaskea. The longboat does 90-minute cruises on Upper Lough Erne on Monday, Wednesday, Thursday and Friday at 3 pm, Saturday at 11 am and 3 pm, Sunday at 3 pm. The cost is £3 (£1.50 children, £8 family ticket).

There are half a dozen companies around Fermanagh that hire out cruisers on a weekly basis. The rates vary from £300 for a four berth in the low season to nearly £900 for an eight-berth in the high season. Full details are available from the Lakeland visitor centre, or contact the companies direct (☎ 0365-324368, 28100, 31414).

Erne Boat Services (☎ 0365-82328), at the Moorings in Bellanaleck, hire out electric boats at £30 per half-day or £45 for the whole day. They also have diesel boats for day hire, which are less expensive. Bellanaleck is on the A509 road to Derrylin.

AROUND LOUGH ERNE

There are a number of ancient religious sites and other antiquities around Lough Erne. In early Christian times the lough was an important highway providing a route from the Donegal coast to inland Leitrim. Churches and monasteries acted as staging posts and in medieval times there was an important pilgrim route to Station Island in Donegal that went via the lough.

The small town of Belleek, famous for its china, is just inside the border and easily reached from either side of the lough.

The places below are set out in an anti-clockwise tour from Enniskillen.

Devenish Island

The most extensive of the ancient sites is Devenish Island. This monastery was sacked by Vikings in 837 AD in just one incident in its colourful history. There are church and abbey ruins, some fascinating old gravestones, an unusual high cross, an excellent small museum and one of the best round towers in Ireland. The 25-metre high tower is in perfect condition and you can climb to the top.

A ferry runs across to the site from Trory Point landing, about six km (about four miles) north of Enniskillen. To get there take the A32 to Omagh out of town and after five km (three miles) look for the sign on the left. It is just after a Burmah garage and before the junction where the road forks left to Kesh and right to Omagh. The ferry runs about once an hour from 10 am to 7 pm Tuesday to Saturday, from 2 pm Sunday. Return fare is £2 (children £1) and the crossing takes 10 minutes.

Killadeas Churchyard

Tucked away in a small graveyard stands the Bishop's Stone, a remarkable stone carving that encapsulates the transition from Celtic paganism to Christianity. The face that stares out from the front seems quite at odds with

the side engraving of a bishop with bell and crozier.

Just after the turn off for Devenish Island on the A32 take the B82 for Kesh and look for the sign to the Manor House Hotel. Continue past this sign for 1.1 km (0.7 mile) and look for the small church on the left side of the road, opposite a house and Killadeas post office.

White Island

White Island, close to the eastern shore of the lough, has the remains of a small 12th-century church containing a line of eight statues thought to date from around the 6th century. Nothing remains of the earlier monastic settlement except the boundary bank which may still be discerned on the far side of the church. The most impressive surviving part of the church is the Romanesque door.

The eight stone figures are intriguing. The first bears much resemblance to a Sheila-na-gig, while the next is of someone reading a book or holding some object. Number three is obviously ecclesiastical, and while the next one has been identified as the Boy David, the meaning of his hand pointing to

Stone Figure, White Island

Sheila Na Gig

The term sheila na gig is probably an anglicisation of *Síle na gcíoch* (Sheila of the paps). It refers to carvings of women displaying exaggerated genitalia. One theory traces their origin back to male and female exhibitionist figures found in French Romanesque churches. These were used to illustrate the ungodly powers which threaten men, and may well reflect the fear of women among a male clergy.

Another theory is that they are representations of Celtic war goddesses. Early Irish sagas like the epic Táin Bó Cúailnge refer to women using overt genital display as a weapon to subdue Cúchulainn. This may have encouraged the belief that the 'sheilas' could ward off evil and hence explain their incorporation into the architecture of early Christian churches. According to this interpretation, the figure on White Island would be related to the stone figure in the chapter house of Armagh Cathedral. The weakness of this theory is that female exhibitionist figures are not found in Ireland before the 9th or 10th centuries. ■

his mouth has been lost. Number five is a curly-haired figure holding the necks of two gryphon-like birds. Number six has a military appearance, number seven is unfinished and the last one is a single frowning face that resembles a death mask.

During the summer a ferry runs across to the island from the Castle Archdale Marina. It operates the same hours and for the same fare as the Devenish Island ferry.

Places to Stay There's a good hostel at the *Castle Archdale Country Park* (☎ 03656-28118). A bed is £6, and like all the YHANI hostels family rooms are available. The park also has a camp site (☎ 0365-21333), which is huge and dominated by site caravans, but has good facilities. Ulsterbus No 194 from Enniskillen to Pettigo will stop outside the park, from where the hostel is a 15-minute walk.

Getting Around Bikes can be hired from Castle Marine (☎ 03656-28118) at Castle Archdale Country Park.

Drumskinny Stone Circle & Alignment

This circle is made up of 39 stones with a small cairn and an alignment of 24 stones and has been dated to the Bronze Age. The circle is seven km (4.5 miles) north of Kesh and signposted just beyond the junction where the road goes to Boa.

Boa Island

At the north end of the lough is Boa Island where the Janus figure in Caldragh graveyard could be 2000 years old, one of the oldest stone statues in Ireland and quite unparalleled. There's just a small sign to the cemetery, about a km (less than a mile) from the bridge at the west end of the island, six km (almost four miles) from the east end bridge. It is well worth the trip to see the figure, which exudes a kind of pagan strength.

Castle Caldwell Forest Park

At the entrance to the park the Fiddler's Stone is a memorial to a fiddler who in 1770 fell off a boat in a drunken stupor and drowned. The castle itself was built in 1612, but all that now remains is a ruin that is not safe to explore. It is a few minutes walk from the café and small exhibition room. The park area is now the main breeding ground of the common scoter duck.

Belleek

The only reason for stopping here is to visit the world-famous Belleek pottery works. The production of this pottery has provided work for the village since 1857. There are regular tours from Monday to Friday from 9 am, the last tour beginning at 4.15 pm (closed for lunch 12.15 to 2.15 pm). The small museum, showroom and café are open seven days a week, from 9 am to 6 pm Monday to Saturday and 2 to 6 pm on

Sunday. A lot of the china is marked with a design of shamrocks, disconcertingly similar to the cheap souvenirs found in tourist shops. Looking at the exhibition of photographs of old Belleek designs, I felt like suggesting that they dump the clover leaves and reintroduce some of the old stuff.

Tully Castle

A signposted left turn 16 km (10 miles) beyond Belleek leads to Tully Castle. The castle was built in the early 17th century as a fortified home for a planter's family from Scotland, but it was captured, burned and abandoned in 1641. The bawn has four corner towers and retains a lot of the original paving. The vaulted ground floor has a large fireplace with an equally large staircase leading to the 2nd floor and attics above that.

The castle is open from April to September, 10 am to 7 pm Monday to Saturday, 2 to 6 pm Sunday. Entrance is £1.

Monea Castle

Continuing south on the A46 to Enniskillen there is a signposted turn to the right for Monea Castle. This was built as the best of Fermanagh's Plantation castles around the same time as Tully Castle. It too was captured in the 1641 Rising but remained in use until the mid-18th century when it was gutted by fire. The main entrance has two imposing circular towers topped with built-out squares in a style that can be found in contemporary Scottish castles. There is no charge for viewing the remains.

Places to Stay

Camping There is a camp site at Blaney (☎ 0365-64634), 13 km (eight miles) from town on the A46 to Belleek, behind the Blaney service station. On the other side of the lough at Kesh, the *Lakeland Caravan Park* (☎ 03656-31578) also has camping. Near Lisnaskea, south of Enniskillen near Upper Lough Erne, camping is possible at the *Lisnaskea Caravan Park* (☎ 03657-21040) and the *Share Centre Caravan Park* (☎ 03657-22122).

B&Bs There are plenty of B&Bs along the roads that skirt either side of Lough Erne. The *Lakeview Farm* (☎ 0365-64263) is on the A46 at Blaney, 16 km (10 miles) from town, and on the other side of the lough at Killadeas, the *Beeches* (☎ 03656-21557) has boats for hire. *Manville House* (☎ 03656-31668) is at Letter, 13 km (eight miles) from Kesh on the road to Belleek, and is well situated for the angler, with boat hire available.

Hotels The grandly situated *Manor House Hotel* (☎ 03656-21561) is about eight km (five miles) from Enniskillen on the B82 to Kesh. At Irvinestown, *Mahon's Hotel* (☎ 03656-21656) is in the town centre and the bar is packed with locals at weekends. Lisnaskea has the *Ortine Hotel* (☎ 03657-21206) and on the other side of Upper Lough Erne the *Mountview Hotel* (☎ 0365-74226) is close to the Marble Arch Caves.

Places to Eat

The restaurant at the *Manor House Hotel*, on the B82 to Kesh, overlooks Lough Erne and has a set dinner as well as à la carte at around £10 to £15 per person. Music, traditional and country, is always organised at weekends in summer. It is open seven days a week, and Sunday is a bit of a family day with a four-course lunch for £8. Farther along this road, the *Cedars* restaurant is popular but closes on Monday and Tuesday.

Irvinestown is 13 km (eight miles) north of Enniskillen and has the *Hollander Restaurant* (☎ 03656-21231) in the main street. This family-run restaurant and pub has a deserved reputation for good food at reasonable prices. Reservations are recommended, vegetarian meals are always featured and you should count on £10 to £15 per person. Bar food is also available and the pub has some interesting photographs of the Catalina and Sunderland flying boats that operated from the nearby base at Castle Archduke. There is even a model of the plane that left here and spotted the *Bismarck*. Across the road from the Hollander, the *Central Bar* was a popular drinking hole for US pilots, and only the TV sets detract from the 1940s style of the place.

Beyond Kesh on Boa Island, reservations are recommended for *Drumrush Lodge* (☎ 03656-31578) or *Mullynaval Lodge* (☎ 03656-31995). Pub food is available at the *May Fly* on the main street of Kesh or *Cleary's Corner Bar* in Belleek. The *Carlton* *Inn* in Belleek serves meals seven days a week for £5 to £10.

Getting Around

Cycle-Ops in Kesh (☎ 03656-31850) will deliver and collect bikes for £6, including tandems and child seats.

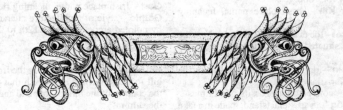

Glossary

An Óige – Irish Youth Hostel Association

Anglo-Norman – Norman, English and Welsh peoples who invaded Ireland in the 12th century

Ard – Irish place name, meaning *high*

Bailey – the space enclosed by castle walls

Bawn – enclosure surrounded by walls outside the main castle, acting as a defense as well as a place to keep cattle in time of trouble

Beehive hut – circular stone building, fashioned after the shape of an old-fashioned beehive

Black & Tans – British recruits to the Royal Irish Constabulary shortly after WW I, noted for their brutality

Bodhrán – (pronounced *bore-run*) handheld goatskin drum

Bord Fáilte – Irish Tourist Board

Boreen – small lane

Bronze Age – the earliest metal-using period, around 2000 BC to 500 BC in Ireland, after the *Stone Age* and before the *Iron Age*

B-specials – Northern Irish auxiliary police force, disbanded in 1971

Bullauns – stone with a depression which was probably used as a mortar

Cairn – a mound of stones heaped over a prehistoric grave

Cashel – stone-walled circular fort, see *rath*

Cath – Irish place name, meaning battle

Celts – Iron Age warrior tribes which arrived in Ireland around 300 BC and controlled the country for 1000 years

Cill or Kill – Irish place name, meaning church

Chancel – the east end of a church where the altar is situated, reserved for the clergy and choir

Clochan – dry-stone beehive hut from the early Christian period.

Crack – conversation, gossip, good times

Crannóg – an artificial island, made in a lake to provide habitation in a good defensive position

Creel – basket

Currach – rowing boat made of framework of laths covered with tarred canvas

Dáil – lower house of the Irish parliament

Demesne – landed property close to a house or castle

Dolmen – tomb chamber or portal tomb made of vertical stones topped by a huge capstone. From around 2000 BC

Drumlin – rounded hill formed by retreating glacier

DUP – Democratic Unionist Party, hard-line Northern Irish Protestant loyalist party founded by Ian Paisley

Dun – a fort, usually constructed of stone

Eire – Irish name for the Republic of Ireland

Fianna Fáil – Major political party in the Republic of Ireland, originating from the Sinn Fein faction opposed to the 1921 treaty with Britain

Fine Gael – The other major political party, originating from the Sinn Fein faction which favoured the 1921 treaty with Britain. Formed the first government of independent Ireland but has subsequently only gained power as part of a coalition

Fir – man, sign on men's toilets

Gaeltacht – Irish-speaking area

Gardaí – Irish Republic police

Gort – Irish place name, meaning field

Gothic – style of architecture characterised by pointed arches, from the 12th to the 16th centuries AD

Hill fort – Usually dating from the Iron Age, hill forts are formed by a ditch that follows the contour of the hill to surround and fortify the summit

INLA – Irish National Liberation Army, extremist IRA splinter group

IRA – Irish Republican Army, dedicated to the removal of British troops from the North and the reunification of Ireland

Iron Age – In Ireland the Iron Age lasted from around the end of the Bronze Age in 500 BC to the arrival of Christianity in the 5th century

Keep – the main tower of a castle

Lambeg drum – a very large drum associated with Protestant loyalist marches

Loyalist – person, usually a Northern Irish Protestant, insisting on the continuation of Northern Ireland's links with Britain

Mesolithic – Middle Stone Age, the time of the first human settlers in Ireland

Mná – women, sign on women's toilets

Motte (or mott) – early Norman fortification consisting of a raised, flattened mound with a keep on top. When attached to a bailey it is known as a motte-and-bailey, many of which were built in Ireland until the early 13th century

Naomh – saint

Nationalists – proponents of a united Ireland

Neolithic – Also known as the new stone age, a period characterised by a settled agriculture and lasting until around 2000 BC in Ireland

The North – the term refers to Northern Ireland, not the northernmost part of Ireland (not Donegal, for example)

Ogham Stones – earliest forms of writing in Ireland, using a variety of notched strokes placed above, below or across a keyline, usually on stone

Orange Order – loyalist Protestant organisation in Northern Ireland which takes its name from William of Orange, the Protestant victor of the Battle of the Boyne. Members of the Orange Order are known as Orangemen and they meet in Orange Lodges

OUP – Official Unionist Party, the principal Northern Irish Protestant political party

Partition – the division of Ireland in 1921

Passage grave – Celtic tomb with tomb chamber reached by a narrow passage, typically buried in a mound

Penal laws – laws passed in the 18th century forbidding Catholics to buy land, hold public office etc

Plantation – the settlement of Protestant migrants in Ireland in the 17th century

Poteen – (pronounced *potcheen*), illegally brewed potato-based firewater

Prod – slang for Northern Irish Protestant

Provisionals – the Provisional IRA, formed after a break with the Official IRA who are now largely inconsequential. The Provisionals, named after the provisional government declared in 1916, are the main force combatting the British army in the North.

Rath – ring fort with earth banks around a circular timber wall, see *cashel*.

Ring fort – used from the Bronze Age right through to the Middle Ages, particularly in the early Christian period. Basically a circular habitation area surrounded by banks and ditches.

Romanesque – A style of architecture which dominated Europe until the arrival of Gothic in the 12th century. Characterised by rounded arches and vaulting.

Round tower – tall circular tower from around the 9th to 11th century, built as a lookout and as a sanctuary during the period when monasteries were frequently subject to Viking raids.

RUC – Royal Ulster Constabulary, armed Northern Irish police force.

SDLP – Social Democratic Labour Party of Northern Ireland. The party represents predominantly liberal, middle-class opinion opposed to violence. Mostly Catholic.

Shebeens – drinking places.

Sheila-na-gig – A female figure with exaggerated genitalia, carved in stone on the exteriors of some churches and castles. Various explanations have been offered for the iconography, ranging from male clerics warning against the perils of sex to an early feminist cult that was stamped out by the Church

Sinn Féin – 'We ourselves', political wing of the IRA

Six Counties – the six out of nine counties of the old province of Ulster which form Northern Ireland

Snug – partioned-off drinking area in a pub

Standing stone – Upright stone set in the ground. Such stones are common across Ireland and date from a variety of periods. Usually the purpose is obscure though some are burial markers.

Souterrain – an underground chamber usually associated with ring forts and hill forts. The purpose may have been to provide a hiding place or an escape route in times of trouble and/or a storage place for goods.

Taoiseach – Irish prime minister.

TD – teachta Dála, member of the Irish parliament.

Tinkers – gypsies.

Treaty – the Anglo-Irish Treaty of 1921, which divided Ireland and gave relative independence to the South. Cause of the civil war of 1922-3

Tricolour – green, white and orange Irish flag. It was designed to symbolise the hoped for union of the green Catholic southern Irish with the orange Protestant northern Irish.

Twenty-Six Counties – the Republic of Ireland, the South.

UDA – Ulster Defence Organisation, legal Northern Irish paramilitary organisation.

UDF – Ulster Defence Force, illegal Northern Irish paramilitary organisation.

UFF – Ulster Freedom Fighters, another illegal Northern Irish paramilitary organisation.

Unionists – Northern Irish who want to retain the links with Britain.

United Irishmen – organisation founded in 1791 aiming to reduce British power in Ireland, which led a series of unsuccessful risings and invasions

UVF – Ulster Volunteer Force, and yet another illegal Northern Irish paramilitary organisation.

Index

TEXT

Map references are in **bold** type.

Keep in touch!

We love hearing from you and think you'd like to hear from us.

The Lonely Planet Newsletter covers the when, where, how and what of travel. (AND it's free!)

When...is the right time to see reindeer in Finland?
Where...can you hear the best palm-wine music in Ghana?
How...do you get from Asunción to Areguá by steam train?
What...should you leave behind to avoid hassles with customs in Iran?

To join our mailing list just contact us at any of our offices. (details below)

Every issue includes:

- *a letter from Lonely Planet founders Tony and Maureen Wheeler*
- *travel diary from a Lonely Planet author - find out what it's really like out on the road*
- *feature article on an important and topical travel issue*
- *a selection of recent letters from our readers*
- *the latest travel news from all over the world*
- *details on Lonely Planet's new and forthcoming releases*

Also available Lonely Planet T-shirts. 100% heavyweight cotton (S, M, L, XL)

LONELY PLANET PUBLICATIONS

Australia: PO Box 617, Hawthorn 3122, Victoria (tel: 03-819 1877)
USA: Embarcadero West, 155 Filbert Street, Suite 251, Oakland, CA 94607 (tel: 510-893 8555)
UK: Devonshire House, 12 Barley Mow Passage, Chiswick, London W4 4PH (tel: 081-742 3161)

Lonely Planet guides to Europe

Eastern Europe on a shoestring
This guide has opened up a whole new world for travellers – Albania, Bulgaria, Czechoslovakia, eastern Germany, Hungary, Poland, Romania and former republics of Yugoslavia.

'...a thorough, well-researched book. Only a fool would go East without it.' – *Great Expeditions*

Mediterranean Europe on a shoestring
Details on hundreds of galleries, museums and architectural masterpieces and information on outdoor activities including hiking, sailing and skiing. Information on travelling in Albania, Andorra, Cyprus, France, Greece, Italy, Malta, Morocco, Portugal, Spain, Tunisia, Turkey and former republics of Yugoslavia.

Scandinavian & Baltic Europe on a shoestring
A comprehensive guide to travelling in this region including details on galleries, festivals and museums, as well as outdoor activities, national parks and wildlife. Countries featured are Denmark, Estonia, the Faroe Islands, Finland, Iceland, Latvia, Lithuania, Norway and Sweden.

Western Europe on a shoestring
This long-awaited guide covers all of Western Europe's well-loved sights and provides routes for cycling and driving tours, plus details on hiking, climbing and skiing. All the travel facts on Andorra, Austria, Belgium, Britain, France, Germany, Ireland, Italy, Liechtenstein, Luxembourg, Netherlands, Portugal, Spain and Switzerland.

Dublin – city guide
Where to enjoy a pint of Guinness and a plate of Irish stew, where to see spectacular Georgian architecture or experience Irish hospitality – Dublin city guide will ensure you won't miss out on anything.

Finland – travel survival kit
Finland is an intriguing blend of Swedish and Russian influences. With its medieval stone castles, picturesque wooden houses, vast forest and lake district, and interesting wildlife, it is a wonderland to delight any traveller.

Hungary – travel survival kit
Formerly seen as the gateway to eastern Europe, Hungary is a romantic country of music, wine and folklore. This guide contains detailed background information on Hungary's cultural and historical past as well as practical advice on the many activities available to travellers.

Iceland, Greenland & the Faroe Islands – travel survival kit
Iceland, Greenland & the Faroe Islands contain some of the most beautiful wilderness areas in the world. This practical guidebook will help travellers discover the dramatic beauty of this region, no matter what their budget.

Italy – travel survival kit
Italy is art – not just in the galleries and museums. You'll discover it's charm on the streets and in the markets, in rustic hill-top villages and in the glamorous city boutiques. A thorough guide to the thousands of attractions of this ever-popular destination.

Poland – travel survival kit
With the collapse of communism, Poland has opened up to travellers,

revealing a rich cultural heritage and unspoiled beauty. This guide will help you make the most of this safe and friendly country.

Switzerland – travel survival kit
Ski enthusiasts and chocolate addicts know two excellent reasons for heading to Switzerland. This travel survival kit gives travellers many more; jazz, cafés, boating trips...and the Alps of course!

Turkey – a travel survival kit
This acclaimed guide takes you from Istanbul bazaars to Mediterranean beaches, from historic battlegrounds to the stamping grounds of St Paul, Alexander the Great, the Emperor Constantine, King Croesus and Omar Khayyam.

USSR – travel survival kit
Invaluable advice on getting around and beating red tape for individual and group travellers alike. This comprehensive guide includes an unsanitised historical background and complete information on art and culture. Over 130 reliable maps, and all place names are given in Cyrillic script. (includes the independent states)

Trekking in Greece
Mountainous landscape, the solitude of ancient pathways and secluded beaches await those who dare to extend their horizons beyond Athens and the antiquities. Covers the main trekking regions and includes contoured maps of trekking routes.

Trekking in Spain
Aimed at both overnight trekkers and day hikers, this guidebook includes useful maps and full details on hikes in some of Spain's most beautiful wilderness areas.

Trekking in Turkey
Few people are aware that Turkey boasts mountains with walks to rival those found in Nepal. This book gives details on treks that are destined to become as popular as those further east.

Also available:
Eastern Europe phrasebook
Discover the most enjoyable way to get around and make friends in Bulgarian, Czech, Hungarian, Polish, Romanian and Slovak.

Mediterranean Europe phrasebook
Ask for directions to the galleries and museums in Albanian, Greek, Italian, Macedonian, Maltese, Serbian & Croatian and Slovene.

Scandinavian Europe phrasebook
Find your way around the ski trails and enjoy the local festivals in Danish, Finnish, Icelandic, Norwegian and Swedish.

Western Europe phrasebook
Show your appreciation for the great masters in Basque, Catalan, Dutch, French, German, Irish, Portuguese and Spanish (Castilian).

Also:
Look out for **Lonely Planet travel survival kits** to the Baltic states, France and Greece.

Lonely Planet Guidebooks

Lonely Planet guidebooks cover every accessible part of Asia as well as Australia, the Pacific, South America, Africa, the Middle East, Europe and parts of North America. There are five series: *travel survival kits*, covering a country for a range of budgets; *shoestring guides* with compact information for low-budget travel in a major region; *walking guides*; *city guides* and *phrasebooks*.

Australia & the Pacific
Australia
Bushwalking in Australia
Islands of Australia's Great Barrier Reef
Fiji
Melbourne city guide
Micronesia
New Caledonia
New Zealand
Tramping in New Zealand
Papua New Guinea
Bushwalking in Papua New Guinea
Papua New Guinea phrasebook
Rarotonga & the Cook Islands
Samoa
Solomon Islands
Sydney city guide
Tahiti & French Polynesia
Tonga
Vanuatu
Victoria

South-East Asia
Bali & Lombok
Bangkok city guide
Cambodia
Indonesia
Indonesia phrasebook
Laos
Malaysia, Singapore & Brunei
Myanmar (Burma)
Burmese phrasebook
Philippines
Pilipino phrasebook
Singapore city guide
South-East Asia on a shoestring
Thailand
Thai phrasebook
Vietnam
Vietnamese phrasebook

North-East Asia
China
Beijing city guide
Mandarin Chinese phrasebook
Hong Kong, Macau & Canton
Japan
Japanese phrasebook
Korea
Korean phrasebook
Mongolia
North-East Asia on a shoestring
Seoul city guide
Taiwan
Tibet
Tibet phrasebook
Tokyo city guide

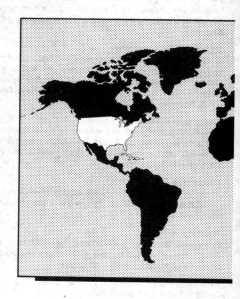

West Asia
Trekking in Turkey
Turkey
Turkish phrasebook
West Asia on a shoestring

Middle East
Arab Gulf States
Egypt & the Sudan
Arabic (Egyptian) phrasebook
Iran
Israel
Jordan & Syria
Yemen

Indian Ocean
Madagascar & Comoros
Maldives & Islands of the East Indian Ocean
Mauritius, Réunion & Seychelles

Mail Order

Lonely Planet guidebooks are distributed worldwide. They are also available by mail order from Lonely Planet, so if you have difficulty finding a title please write to us. US and Canadian residents should write to Embarcadero West, 155 Filbert St, Suite 251, Oakland CA 94607, USA ; European residents should write to Devonshire House, 12 Barley Mow Passage, Chiswick, London W4 4PH; and residents of other countries to PO Box 617, Hawthorn, Victoria 3122, Australia.

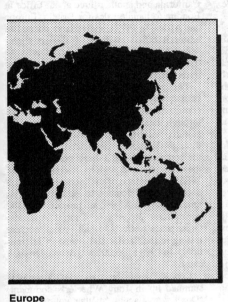

Indian Subcontinent
Bangladesh
India
Hindi/Urdu phrasebook
Trekking in the Indian Himalaya
Karakoram Highway
Kashmir, Ladakh & Zanskar
Nepal
Trekking in the Nepal Himalaya
Nepali phrasebook
Pakistan
Sri Lanka
Sri Lanka phrasebook

Africa
Africa on a shoestring
Central Africa
East Africa
Trekking in East Africa
Kenya
Swahili phrasebook
Morocco, Algeria & Tunisia
Arabic (Moroccan) phrasebook
South Africa, Lesotho & Swaziland
Zimbabwe, Botswana & Namibia
West Africa

Central America
Baja California
Central America on a shoestring
Costa Rica
La Ruta Maya
Mexico

North America
Alaska
Canada
Hawaii

South America
Argentina, Uruguay & Paraguay
Bolivia
Brazil
Brazilian phrasebook
Chile & Easter Island
Colombia
Ecuador & the Galápagos Islands
Latin American Spanish phrasebook
Peru
Quechua phrasebook
South America on a shoestring
Trekking in the Patagonian Andes

Europe
Dublin city guide
Eastern Europe on a shoestring
Eastern Europe phrasebook
Finland
Hungary
Iceland, Greenland & the Faroe Islands
Ireland
Italy
Mediterranean Europe on a shoestring
Mediterranean Europe phrasebook
Poland
Scandinavian & Baltic Europe on a shoestring
Scandinavian Europe phrasebook
Switzerland
Trekking in Spain
Trekking in Greece
USSR
Russian phrasebook
Western Europe on a shoestring
Western Europe phrasebook

The Lonely Planet Story

Lonely Planet published its first book in 1973 in response to the numerous 'How did you do it?' questions Maureen and Tony Wheeler were asked after driving, bussing, hitching, sailing and railing their way from England to Australia.

Written at a kitchen table and hand collated, trimmed and stapled, *Across Asia on the Cheap* became an instant local bestseller, inspiring thoughts of another book.

Eighteen months in South-East Asia resulted in their second guide, *South-East Asia on a shoestring*, which they put together in a backstreet Chinese hotel in Singapore in 1975. The 'yellow bible' as it quickly became known to backpackers around the world, soon became *the* guide to the region. It has sold well over half a million copies and is now in its 7th edition, still retaining its familiar yellow cover.

Today there are over 120 Lonely Planet titles in print – books that have that same adventurous approach to travel as those early guides; books that 'assume you know how to get your luggage off the carousel' as one reviewer put it.

Although Lonely Planet initially specialised in guides to Asia, they now cover most regions of the world, including the Pacific, South America, Africa, the Middle East and Europe. The list of *walking guides* and *phrasebooks* (for 'unusual' languages such as Quechua, Swahili, Nepalese and Egyptian Arabic) is also growing rapidly.

The emphasis continues to be on travel for independent travellers. Tony and Maureen still travel for several months of each year and play an active part in the writing, updating and quality control of Lonely Planet's guides.

They have been joined by over 50 authors, 54 staff – mainly editors, cartographers, & designers – at our office in Melbourne, Australia, 10 at our US office in Oakland, California and another three at our office in London to handle sales for Britain, Europe and Africa. In 1992 Lonely Planet opened an editorial office in Paris. Travellers themselves also make a valuable contribution to the guides through the feedback we receive in thousands of letters each year.

The people at Lonely Planet strongly believe that travellers can make a positive contribution to the countries they visit, both through their appreciation of the countries' culture, wildlife and natural features, and through the money they spend. In addition, the company makes a direct contribution to the countries and regions it covers. Since 1986 a percentage of the income from each book has been donated to ventures such as famine relief in Africa; aid projects in India; agricultural projects in Central America; Greenpeace's efforts to halt French nuclear testing in the Pacific and Amnesty International. In 1993 $100,000 was donated to such causes.

Lonely Planet's basic travel philosophy is summed up in Tony Wheeler's comment, 'Don't worry about whether your trip will work out. Just go!'